Cook on C
2021

[redacted]

Simon Middleton is a District Judge and Regional Costs Judge. He has sat on both the Midland and Western regions. Prior to judicial appointment he was a solicitor in private practice for 17 years and had higher court rights of advocacy (civil).

Simon was a member of the Judicial College Civil tutor team for 7 years. He was also one of the Judicial College Course Directors for 4 years. His primary educational responsibilities in both these roles were the design, delivery and teaching of courses on the subjects of costs and costs/case management.

Simon has been interested in costs throughout his career and has lectured and written on the topic of costs extensively over the years. He would say that he never had a chance as he was an articled clerk at Messrs Ward Bowie when the senior partner of that firm was none other than Michael Cook. He is delighted to have the opportunity to maintain the 'Ward Bowie' link with this text.

Jason Rowley is a Costs Judge, or Taxing Master, at the Senior Courts Costs Office, having previously been a Deputy Master since 2006. He has been involved in costs matters since 1993 when he attended a conference chaired by Michael Cook and which left him with a desire to know far more about the world of costs.

Jason was the Forum of Insurance Lawyers' inaugural Chair of its Special Interest Group on costs and intervened on FOIL's behalf in cases such as *Callery v Gray* before running test cases on behalf of clients involving Claims Direct and The Accident Group. This led to stints on the Law Society's Civil Litigation Committee, including drafting the 2005 model CFA, as well as participation in the 'Big Tents' convened to broker industry agreements on success fees.

Jason started as a solicitor in an insurance practice dealing mainly with personal injury claims. He was a partner for 11 years, the last 5 of which were as Managing Partner. Thereafter he was the CEO of a barristers' chambers in the Inner Temple and a senior underwriting manager at a legal expenses insurance company.

Cook on Costs 2021

A guide to legal remuneration in civil contentious and non-contentious business

Simon Middleton

Jason Rowley

LexisNexis®

LexisNexis® UK & Worldwide

United Kingdom	RELX (UK) Limited trading as LexisNexis®, 1–3 Strand, London WC2N 5JR and 9–10 St Andrew Square, Edinburgh EH2 2AF
LNUK Global Partners	LexisNexis® encompasses authoritative legal publishing brands dating back to the 19th century including: Butterworths® in the United Kingdom, Canada and the Asia-Pacific region; Les Editions du Juris Classeur in France; and Matthew Bender® worldwide. Details of LexisNexis® locations worldwide can be found at www.lexisnexis.com

Published by LexisNexis
This is a Tolley title

A CIP Catalogue record for this book is available from the British Library.

ISBN for this volume: 9781474314527

Printed and bound by CPI Group (UK) Ltd, Croydon, CR0 4YY

Visit LexisNexis UK at www.lexisnexis.co.uk

Preface

It has proved to be irresistible not to use the phrase 2020 hindsight when looking back over the past year. It has been, we can only hope, a year like no other. Yet, in amongst the difficulties we have all faced, necessity has once more proved to be the mother of invention. For the last four or five years I have been asked by receiving parties who use electronic case management systems whether they can provide electronic copies of their documents to support the bill rather than felling more trees to print out paper copies. Pre-pandemic, we had got as far as accepting a laptop with such documents upon it. But memory sticks, file sharing platforms (and similar) all proved to be too racy for use in court hearings.

However, as soon as we were all required to stay at home, there seemed to be no technology that the courts were not prepared to countenance in order to keep cases running. Whilst much of that felt foreign at first, the use of electronic documents has been hastened by probably a factor of 5 years. It has proved, as emails did in the 1990s, that if the technology is useful it will quickly be adopted. Ultimately, I think 2020 may well be remembered as the year that assessment of costs truly moved into the 21st century. To celebrate this, Chapter 28 regarding detailed assessments has been expanded to cover these developments in the use of electronic documents and remote hearings so that you are bang up to date.

Stepping away from the 'electronification' of costs issues, the impact of the virus on courts being open seemed likely to limit the number of noteworthy cases and to prevent the Rules Committee from producing amendments. But, to the contrary, there have been numerous important cases considered throughout this edition. To take but one example, the removal of the 'Arkin' cap by the Court of Appeal in *Chapelgate Credit Opportunity Master Fund Ltd v Money and others* looks set to have serious ramifications in the ever increasing world of cases funded commercially by third parties. Similarly, the revisions to the budgeting rules, especially regarding the vexed question of variation are extensively analysed.

We like to think that Cook on Costs is a must read on costs matters. So too are the Costs Law Reports and it is very sad to report that this year has seen the passing of the last of the original editors, Michael Bacon. The twinkle in his eye will be sorely missed by all those who were lucky enough to know him.

He would certainly appreciate the irony of my final comment for this year's edition. Shortly after the lockdown occurred I received a letter from a receiving party's solicitors seeking an adjournment on the basis that 'if the court remains open, the court's resources could be better used at this current time on matters other than costs'. Not really the best argument when writing to the SCCO, but as I have recently spotted the letter was dated 1 April so it may have been more knowing than it first appeared!

The law is stated as at 30 October 2020.

Jason Rowley

Preface to the 2014 edition

I remember a letter from a client being circulated amongst the staff during my articles praising the work of a particular fee earner (not me I hasten to add). On it one of the partners had written 'I taught her all she knows'. Below that the senior partner had written 'And I taught you all you know and somebody else taught me all I know'. Those words have remained with me and the more experienced (older) I become the more I realise that knowledge is something to be shared and not hoarded in the hope that one knows something more than the next person. A text such as this offers the opportunity to do so.

For the record the senior partner in question was Michael Cook. In his preface to the first edition of this text he was at pains to attribute his 'understanding of, and enthusiasm for, costs' to his late partner Lionel Cranfield. Whilst Michael's understanding and enthusiasm remain as acute as ever, he has chosen to move on to pastures new. It would be wrong if I did not mark the occasion by thanking him both for the assistance that the previous editions has provided to me and, more importantly, for instilling in me 30 years ago that same enthusiasm for costs. It is a privilege to have the opportunity to follow in his footsteps. However, acknowledging that, despite his best efforts, my understanding does not match Michael's, it is an enormous relief and a great pleasure to be joined by Jason Rowley, who for many years has sat as an assessor on costs hearings and is now, of course, a master of the Senior Courts Costs Office. Together we take on responsibility for editing the text.

Our timing may leave something to be desired. We take over the text in a year that has seen the most radical overhaul of costs since the introduction of the CPR in 1999. As a result some of the views we express are speculative. We await with interest decisions of the Higher Courts that enable more authoritative comment on key concepts such as costs management and the new proportionality test. In the meantime, though, as lawyers seek to persuade the court to define and refine the April amendments to the CPR, Lionel Cranfield's description of costs as 'the interesting part' resonates as clearly as it did all those years ago.

Some of you may note that the actual text is a slimmed down version from that of recent vintages with the relevant parts of the CPR as appendices. Our response is that it is deliberately so and that this, inevitably, is our acknowledgement of the primacy of proportionality.

The law is stated as at 1 October 2013.

Simon Middleton

Preface to the First Edition

When the publishers asked me to write a preface I cavilled on the two grounds that no-one reads prefaces and they serve no useful purpose. I was told that the purpose is to explain the aims and intention of the work; in other words, why I have written the book and why you should read it. Fair enough. My late partner, Lionel Cranfield, at the end of some heavy litigation used to say, 'Now we come to the interesting part – the costs!'. In the quarter of a century since Lionel was killed in the hunting field, the profession has become increasingly aware that money is the life-blood of a solicitor's practice, but I continue to be perplexed that, in spite of this realisation, most solicitors and their clients lose out financially because of the profession's basic lack of understanding and interest in all aspects of costs. In a College of Law survey of the areas of skills on which solicitors wished the Law Society's new Legal Practice course to be based, costs did not even appear in the list.

And that is why I have written this book. It does not contain any facts and figures you cannot find elsewhere – apart from it being illustrated from my collection of unreported cases – but I have tried to write about costs in an interesting, coherent and digestible way. My aim in writing the book is therefore to impart to you the understanding of, and enthusiasm for, costs that Lionel Cranfield aroused in me all those years ago.

I much appreciate the kindness of Philip Ely in writing a foreword to the book in his year as President of the Law Society. I am seriously indebted to my old friend Master Michael Devonshire of the Supreme Court Taxing Office for reading the manuscript of the book and making many useful suggestions on the condition that I did not mention his name.

The law is stated as at 1 October 1991.

Michael Cook

Limpsfield
October 1991

Contents

PART II FUNDING

Table of Statutes

References in the right-hand column are to paragraph numbers. Paragraph references printed in **bold** type indicate where the statute is set out in part or in full.

Table of Statutory Instruments

References in the right-hand column are to paragraph numbers. Paragraph references printed in **bold** type indicate where the statutory instrument is set out in part or in full.

Table of Civil Procedure Rules

References in the right-hand column are to paragraph numbers. Paragraph references printed in **bold** type indicate where the CPR is set out in part or in full.

Table of Non-Statutory Provisions

References in the right-hand column are to paragraph numbers. Paragraph references printed in **bold** type indicate where the Provisions are set out in part or in full.

Table of Cases

C

E

F

G

H

I

J

K

M

O

P

Q

R

S

T

U

V

W

X

Y

Z

Decisions of the European Court of Justice are listed below numerically. These decisions are also included in the preceding alphabetical list.

Part I

Solicitor and client

CHAPTER 1

THE RETAINER

INTRODUCTION TO THE RETAINER

[1.1]

The relationship between the client and his solicitor is at the heart of the law of costs. The giving of instructions by a client to a solicitor constitutes the solicitor's retainer by the client. It is a contract. It creates the solicitor's right to be paid. The rights and liabilities of the parties are governed by the ordinary law of contract, but the relationship is also subject to the special provisions which govern contracts between a solicitor and his client. These come in two forms – the statutory kind, such as the provisions of the Solicitors Act 1974: and the regulatory kind, in particular, the Codes of Conduct introduced by the Law Society and then the Solicitors Regulation Authority. The statutory provisions affecting the retainer are dealt with throughout the book. They are particularly prominent in this Part and Part II in relation to funding agreements. The regulatory provisions are dealt with in this chapter, after we have looked at the general contractual provisions and before we reach the termination issues.

'Solicitor' and 'client' etc

[1.2]

It will not have escaped your attention that the lawyer representing a client can no longer simply be described as a solicitor. This book has always been written directly to the legal representative and that provides an immediacy that is often helpful, particularly when dealing with the solicitor and client aspects of civil remuneration. The word 'you' refers to the legal representative and 'we' refers to the writers of this work. Some of that immediacy would be lost if we were to use some all embracing nomenclature such as 'legal representative' or 'fee earner'. Rather than do this, we have used the word solicitor as shorthand for the party's lawyer with due apology to the various other kinds of legal representative who may read this book.

As well as using the words 'we' and 'you' throughout this book, you will also find many instances of 'he' and 'his' but not very many 'she' or 'her' (or 'their'). We would be quite happy for all the generic he's to become she's – perhaps on a revolving annual basis – but neither of us wishes to go gender neutral. It doesn't sound right to our ears, but in the end it's a matter for our editor. She will decide.

Also for readability, we have used the word client rather than 'party chargeable' when considering Solicitors Act 1974 assessments. Hopefully we have made it clear where a third party interest applies rather than a client in the strict sense, but that is a fairly rare occurrence and the word client hugely aids readability. If you want to read a detailed discussion of who is and is not a party chargeable, please see HHJ Russen's decision in *Richard Slade & Co v Abbhi* [2019] EWHC 355 (Comm).

Finally, a number of judges, whose decisions have been referred to here, have risen through the ranks. We have decided to refrain from endless 'as he (she) then was' to show that they went on to greater things and simply recorded the title held by the judge at the time. No discourtesy is intended.

THE CONTRACT

[1.3]

It is an implied term of the contract that the client will pay the solicitor's charges and disbursements. Other than for certain contingency based arrangements, the retainer need not be in writing. In *Abbhi v Slade (trading as Richard Slade and Co)* [2019] EWCA Civ 2175, [2019] Costs LR 2039, the client's son in law agreed to meet the solicitors' bills. The Court of Appeal held that it was a funding agreement rather than a guarantee because it was clear from the outset that the client could not pay the bills. However, if the true construction of an arrangement is that the solicitor's costs are guaranteed by a third party, then the requirement that a guarantee must be in writing applies to the arrangement between the solicitor and the third party: see *Manches LLP v Freer* [2006] EWHC 991 (QB) where the work done for a company was guaranteed by the defendant as a director. The defendant accepted that he had signed the engagement letter but said it was on behalf of the company and not so as to make him personally liable. The court agreed with the defendant and held that for the defendant to be personally liable as a guarantor he had to have signed the letter both as a director and in his personal capacity, or preferably he should have signed two letters. The director put pen to paper in *Udondem v Wallace LLP* (QBD 16/05/18 Walker J) and was found personally liable notwithstanding the agreement that the company was the client.

Where there is a dispute between a solicitor and his client about the terms of an oral retainer, the word of the client is to be preferred to the word of the solicitor, or, at least, more weight is to be given to it. The reason is plain. It is because the client is ignorant and the solicitor is, or should be, learned in the law. If the solicitor does not take the precaution of getting a written retainer, he has only himself to blame for being at variance with his client over it and must take the consequences. The onus is on the solicitor to establish the terms of the retainer and in the absence of persuasive evidence the court should prefer the client's version. 'It is up to the solicitor to take the appropriate steps to clarify precisely the extent of his retainer' (*Gray v Buss Merton (a firm)* [1999] PNLR 882 & 892) 'because the client, through ignorance of the correct terminology, may not be able to express his instructions clearly' (*Sibley & Co v Reachbyte Ltd and Kris Motor Spares Ltd* [2008] EWHC 2665 (Ch)). The position is not entirely hopeless for the solicitor. For example, in the *Abbhi* case, the court preferred the solicitor's evidence as to the terms of the oral agreement: but it is much harder work than if it had been recorded in writing at the time.

Where the client is a consumer within the meaning of the Consumer Rights Act 2015, the court will also need to consider the fairness of any disputed term, even if neither party has raised the issue, as long as there is sufficient material before the court to do so (s 71).

An entire contract

[1.4]

A retainer is normally a contract under which the solicitor is to do certain work for the client and cannot seek any remuneration until that work has been completed or the retainer has been terminated in some other way. This is described by the law of contract as an 'entire contract.' The solicitor is not entitled to any payment on account of his costs other than disbursements.

The only circumstances in which the retainer is not an entire contract is if the parties have agreed to interim payments; there is a request from the client for a final bill; or it is contentious business and s 65(2) of the Solicitors Act 1974 applies.

If the solicitor wrongfully terminates the retainer he is not entitled to any payment at all for the work he has done, either on a quantum meruit or any other basis. In *Gill v Heer Manak Solicitors* [2018] EWHC 2881 (QB), the solicitors closed down as a result of failing to secure professional indemnity insurance. They gave no notice to Mr Gill of this prior to terminating the retainer. As such, the entire obligations under the contract had not been completed and Walker J concluded that, absent reasonable notice, the solicitors were not entitled to any remuneration for the work done on Mr Gill's behalf.

The previous paragraphs are worth re-reading as they set out a reality that is often not grasped by solicitors. The subject of interim bills is dealt with in detail in the next chapter but time and again solicitors consider withdrawing their labour as a result of tardy or non-payment of interim bills by the client.

As will be seen from the two following cases, the Court of Appeal at least, has started to soften the strict contractual approach. But bills of costs are regularly thrown out in full for the solicitor repudiating the contract and the message to take away is twofold. First, if this situation happens to you, alarm bells should ring and you should look very carefully at the steps you take to encourage your client to pay up. Secondly, time spent by solicitors on their terms of business is seldom wasted.

In *Wong v Vizards (a firm)* [1997] 2 Costs LR 46, QBD, solicitors declined to represent their client at a hearing unless he made a substantial payment on account of a disputed bill. The judge held that because the amount claimed by the solicitors was unreasonable they had wrongfully terminated the retainer on the grounds of non-payment and were therefore not entitled to any payment at all for the work they had done in preparation for the hearing.

In *Minkin v Cawdery Kaye Fireman and Taylor (a firm)* [2011] EWHC 177 (QB), the solicitors had to go up to the Court of Appeal to recover their costs. The costs judge had held that the solicitors were in repudiatory breach when they delivered an interim bill substantially in excess of their estimate and refused to continue to act until it was paid and therefore they were not entitled to any payment at all. The solicitors' appeal to a High Court judge was dismissed.

The solicitors obtained permission to go to the Court of Appeal which held that the complaint that the bill exceeded the estimate could not stand in the face of the fact that the letter enclosing the terms of business made plain that estimates were not intended to be fixed or binding and that other factors might have meant that the estimate would be varied from time to time. The terms of business further informed the client that estimates were given 'as a guide' only. There was no guarantee that the final charge would not exceed the estimate because there were many factors outside the solicitors' control which might affect the level of costs. Refusal to pay could not be justified on that ground. Moreover, the client was fully informed of his right to challenge in court any bill which he felt was excessive. The reality was that the client was short of money and could not readily pay for his solicitors' services in coping with a new and unexpected turn of events. The comparatively simple case had become more complicated and as a result more expensive. The unexpected complication did not justify a refusal to pay a bill which became payable on presentation. The client was obliged by the payment terms set out in the terms of business to pay bills on presentation. He did not do so and that put him in breach.

The client had no reasonable justification for not meeting the bill presented to him. It was the client who repudiated the contract, not the firm. Not being prepared to act until money was paid showed a willingness to act when there was money on account.

The retainer came to an end when the client communicated to the solicitors that he had lost confidence in them. The client's termination of the retainer absolved the solicitor from any further performance of the contract but it did not absolve the client from the payment of the costs properly incurred to that date. The costs judge was therefore wrong not to order the payment of the costs as they were assessed and he was also wrong to order the solicitors to make repayment to the client.

In delivering judgment Lord Justice Ward said 'The client was short of money and could not pay for his solicitors in coping with a new and unexpected turn of events that complicated the case. Every solicitor will encounter, in one way or another, the kind of problem which gives rise to this appeal'. Lord Justice Elias added: 'Any other view would compel a solicitor to carry on working for a client even though there may be little realistic prospect of payment'.

Increases in the hourly rate

[1.5]

For charging rates to be increased the solicitor must have reserved the contractual right to do so in the retainer. It has nothing to do with the Code of Conduct even though successive versions have required the client to be kept informed of any increases as a matter of professional conduct. In any event, a favourite paying party challenge on assessment is the question of whether the client was aware of any increases in the hourly rate during the course of the case. So, you must make sure that the client care letter provides for a periodic review and increase where appropriate and that you have a system which remembers to notify your client of the increase promptly when that periodic review has taken place.

Client's instructions

[1.6]

Where instructions are received not from a client but from a third party purporting to represent that client, it is prudent for the solicitor to obtain written instructions from the client that he or she wishes him or her to act. Similarly where instructions are given by only one client on behalf of others in a joint matter, it is unwise to proceed without checking that all clients agree with the instructions given.

It is a wise solicitor who knows his own client. Is the client the trade union or its member? The driver of the car or his insurers? The employer or his insurers? The insured or the legal expenses insurers? The limited company or its director personally? A husband and wife or just one of them? The solicitor who does not ascertain clearly at the outset who his client is may repent at leisure if it transpires he has taken instructions from the wrong person or finds his bill rejected by the person to whom he renders it.

Cancellable Agreements

[1.7]

From 13 June 2014, the Consumer Contracts (Information, Cancellation and Additional Charges) Regulations 2013 apply to agreements made at a solicitors' offices (an 'on-premises' contract). They also apply to agreements made elsewhere where the client is personally attended ('off-premises') or purely at the end of a telephone or internet connection ('distance' contract). All three forms of contract require information to be provided to the client. Unless it is an on-premises contract, that information includes how to cancel the contract without liability. The usual period is 14 days. As with all consumer litigation there is a wealth of detail in the Regulations.

Prior to June 2014 the Cancellation of Contracts made in a Consumer's Home or Place of Work etc, Regulations 2008, SI 2008/1816 applied where the contract was made on or after 1 October 2008. Before then, the equally snappily entitled 'Consumer Protection (Cancellation of Contracts Concluded away from Business Premises) Regulations 1987' applied. The 2008 Regulations extended the seven day cooling-off period for contracts made at a consumer's home or place of work to legal services. The 1987 Regulations applied in similar circumstances except where a meeting had been solicited by the client. The prospect of an unsolicited visit by a solicitor (presumably therefore an 'unsolicitor') to a potential client is sufficiently rare for it to be excluded for the purposes of this book.

Although the regulations' applicability to solicitors' retainers was originally doubted (a matter of wishful thinking) that has been put beyond doubt (see *Cox v Woodlands Manor Care Home* [2015] EWCA Civ 415 (see [**4.14**]). The regulations can apply even where the retainer is entered into at the solicitor's office following a visit to the client's home or place of work. In *Howes Percival LLP v Page* [2013] EWHC 4104 (Ch) the judge found that one attendance at home was merely 'happenstance' and no offer was made at that visit, nor was there any concluded contract. As such, the judge concluded that the 2008 Regulations were not engaged in these particular circumstances.

Where the regulations apply, the client (unless it is an on-premises contract) needs to be notified in writing of the right to cancel. Model wording is provided in Sch 3 to the Regulations which, if followed, provides the information required. In the 2008 Regulations, reg 7(5) required the notice to be set out in a separate box in the same document, although that was widened somewhat by case law to a linked document.

As with the Consumer Credit Act 1974 itself, a failure to get the documentation and procedure correct can lead to the entire agreement becoming unenforceable. This is a regular source of enquiry in between the parties' assessments. In particular, where a claimant has used a CFA for which the explanation and signature process has been at least partially dealt with at the client's house (or place of work). In *Howes Percival* no cancellation period was contained in the agreement and so it would have been unenforceable if the Regulations had been engaged.

In *Kupeli v Cyprus Turkish Airlines* [2017] EWCA Civ 1037, the solicitors arranged to meet potential claimants at a community centre with a view to signing CFAs and taking initial instructions. That meeting between solicitor and client was held to have occurred during a 'visit' rather than an 'excursion' under the 2008 Regulations. Consequently, the CFAs did not need to contain cancellation notices to be valid agreements.

Where the client decides to cancel the agreement, then unlike termination of the retainer by the client generally (see **[1.27]** below), cancellation has the effect of the retainer being treated as if it had never existed. Consequently, no fees would be payable and this may well be a deterrent to a solicitor carrying out any work or making any disbursement during the cooling off period. However, in a case of urgency the client care letter may include a provision that the client accepts liability for any costs or disbursements incurred during the cooling off period.

QUOTATIONS AND ESTIMATES

[1.8]

As we shall see, the 2011 Code of Conduct looks for, amongst other things, a clear explanation by the solicitor of the fees to be charged. There is no specific reference to quotations and estimates, which are, of course, governed by the law of contract. We will start by looking at how the solicitor should describe his 'fee indications' so as not to fall foul of the law before going on to see how they should be phrased so that the Regulatory Gods are equally pleased.

Quotations

[1.9]

Do you really know the difference between a quotation and an estimate in respect of solicitors' costs? A quotation is a fixed price for doing the work which cannot be exceeded in any circumstances except with the freely given consent of the client. Common examples are the buying and selling of houses and the drawing of wills.

Estimates

[1.10]

Estimates have a chameleon quality. They have a tendency to turn into quotations when you are not looking. An unqualified estimate, for example, is for all practical purposes a fixed price quotation. On 20 February 2003, the Law Society Gazette recorded a case where a firm of solicitors had informed the client at the outset of his matrimonial proceedings that he could expect a bill in the region of £2,500. The firm regularly rendered interim bills, the penultimate one leaving the total cost just a little short of the original estimate. Nine months later, after the fee earner who had dealt with the client had left the firm, the solicitors sent the client an additional bill that took his costs £750 above the estimate he had been given originally. The Regulator ordered the firm to refund to the client the costs in excess of the estimate.

Successive Codes of Conduct have required solicitors to give the best possible information to their clients at the outset of the likely costs to be incurred. That inevitably means estimating the likely future cost (and for this purpose it matters not whether it is described as an estimate or a budget or anything else.)

When doing so, you should make it clear that the estimate is not intended to be fixed. This makes the fee indication into a qualified estimate. Solicitors should inform the client that if there are unforeseen developments and/or complications the estimate may need to be revised and updated and the client will be advised of this as the matter progresses. In protracted matters such as litigation, it may be advisable for solicitors to give staged estimates, with an overall estimate at a later stage once all the issues have been identified.

In *Mastercigars Direct Ltd v Withers LLP* [2007] EWHC 2733 (Ch), the relevant wording of Withers' qualified estimate is worth noting: 'When you instruct us we will do our best to tell you the likely level of our fees. Unless we tell you otherwise, this will be an estimate only, not a fixed quotation. If you ask for a fixed quotation we will try to provide one. However it may not be possible to predict the amount of time we will need to deal with the matter. You may set an upper limit on our costs. We will not do any work that will take our fees over this limit without your permission . . . ' The SCCO Master had held that in the circumstances Withers had failed to update their estimate and were bound by it but Withers' appeal was allowed. Morgan J held that their estimate was not a fixed quotation, nor was it an upper limit on costs, nor did it define the work to be done. The retainer was subject to the Supply of Goods and Services Act 1982, s 15 and it was therefore an implied term that the solicitors would be paid reasonable remuneration for their services. Although the solicitors had given a contractual promise to update the costs estimate, that was not a condition precedent to them recovering any sum in addition to the sums set out in the estimate. He held that where a costs estimate is given but the costs subsequently claimed exceeded the estimate, it does not follow that the solicitor would be restricted to recovering the sum in the estimate. The question was 'What, in all the circumstances, is it reasonable for the client to be expected to pay?' And the estimate was one, but only one, of those circumstances. As explained in *Leigh v Michelin Tyre plc* [2003] EWCA Civ 1766, the court could have regard to the estimate and it was a factor to be taken into consideration as a yardstick in determining what was reasonable. The greater the difference between an estimate and the final bill, the greater the explanation called for. However, if there is a satisfactory explanation of the difference an estimate may cease to be a useful yardstick. Reliance on the estimate by the client is another factor. It was not necessary to imply into the contract of retainer a term that the solicitors had to comply with the Solicitors Costs Information and Client Care Code in respect of updating costs information.

The case went back to the SCCO Master for consideration of whether the client relied on the estimate (this is dealt with in more detail below.) The Master's decision on this point was also appealed. Morgan J overturned this decision and the claimant sought to appeal his judgment. When refusing permission to appeal ([2009] EWCA Civ 1526) the Court of Appeal endorsed paragraph 54 of the second judgment of Morgan J which included the sentence 'it is not the proper function of the court to punish the solicitor for providing a wrong estimate or for failing to keep it up to date as events unfolded'.

[The case of *Minkin v Cawdery Kaye Fireman and Taylor* referred to above is also an example of an effective qualification of an estimate.]

In *Howard Kennedy LLP v Spartafield Ltd* [2019] EWHC 1218 (Ch), the Deputy High Court judge upheld the senior costs judge's use of the solicitor's estimate as a yardstick when considering the reasonableness of certain costs claimed. There was no need for the client to have demonstrated reliance on that estimate when using it in this fashion.

Quotations that used to be estimates

[1.11]

Even a qualified estimate is not carte blanche to charge whatever sum is justified by the time recorded. A qualified estimate is an indication of price which is qualified by a statement that the solicitor may have to charge more if the matter involves more work than he expects. There are circumstances in which what started out in life as a qualified estimate can finish up as binding on the solicitor as a quotation.

In particular, the final amount payable should not vary substantially from the estimate unless there has been a change in circumstances of which the client has been informed. The qualified estimate should have stated the circumstances which might give rise to an increase and the client should have been informed when any of those circumstances arose. The fact that the solicitor has seriously underestimated the work or disbursements involved will not necessarily be a changed circumstance – indeed it could be a strong indication of negligence on the part of the solicitor in preparing the original estimate. A factor in considering whether any upward revision of an estimate is reasonable is whether the client instructed the solicitor after shopping around and taking the lowest estimate he had been given.

In *Reynolds v Stone Rowe Brewer (a firm)* [2008] EWHC 497 (QB), the claimant instructed the defendant solicitors to represent her in a dispute with a building contractor and they informed her that the estimated cost of taking the matter forward and through to trial would be in the region of £10,000–£18,000 plus VAT. Throughout the course of the litigation, the defendants rendered a number of invoices and they then wrote to the claimant saying that their estimate of the likely cost of the case had to be revised to around £30,000 plus VAT. The court upheld the finding of the costs judge that the revised estimate had been an attempt to correct an 'earlier under-estimate' and was not attributable to any change in the facts. The solicitors were not saved by the provision in their client care letter that 'This is only of course an estimate which could be increased depending on how strenuously the matter is defended'. There had been no significantly unusual developments before the revised estimate such as to explain the difference between the £18,000 estimate and the £30,000 revised estimate.

Increasing the estimate

[1.12]

The best time to rectify an errant estimate is obviously before things get out of hand. While the client is relying on you in respect of the case, he will be much more receptive to revising the likely cost than once the case has come to an end. The best approach is always to address the issue before the costs are incurred which will cause the earlier estimate to be exceeded. Indeed, previous Law Society guidance stated that 'clients should be informed immediately if it appears that the estimate will be, or is likely to be, exceeded. In most cases this should happen before undertaking the work that exceeds the estimate'.

This guidance was in place long before the concept of budgets in the manner that we have now came to light. But it remains good advice. Clients, as much as opponents and the court, want to be appraised of increases in the cost of the litigation before it occurs and not afterwards. It means that some alternatives to the current plan might be considered – fewer or different experts; alternative cases abandoned and so forth. Almost as importantly, it gives the client the impression that you are on top of the financial aspects of the case and not simply the legal aspects. Solicitors may think that it is acceptable to dismiss overspends with generic comments about the behaviour of the opponent, but clients are often less than impressed that they have incurred costs unknowingly that will cause problems in settlement or assessment in due course.

Exceeding the estimate

[1.13]

In *Wong* v *Vizards* (a firm) [1997] 2 Costs LR 46, the solicitors in a letter to their client allowed for profit costs of £9,955 stating 'the fee proposal hopefully sets out the fullest extent of your liability to this firm for costs likely to be incurred in the future'. Although this did not amount to a binding agreement that in no circumstances would the solicitors' fees exceed their fee proposal, it was a clear and considered indication of the maximum, upon which the client was likely to rely and did rely. The solicitors in fact delivered bills exceeding £45,000. In considering whether a reasonable amount for the work done should exceed what the fee-payer had been led to believe was a worst case assessment, regard should be had to any explanation of the divergence. It had not been suggested there was any unexpected development between the date of the solicitors' letter and the date of trial, and no satisfactory explanation had been given why the solicitors should be entitled to profit costs exceeding the amount put forward as their worst case assessment. The judge limited the solicitors' costs to £9,955.

But, that was not the end of the story. The trial had taken two days less than estimated by the solicitors at a charge of £660 a day. The client argued that the estimate should therefore be reduced by the resultant saving of £1,320. This was about 15% of the total estimate and the judge thought it not unreasonable to give the solicitors the benefit of this margin and therefore allowed them to recover the full amount of their estimate. And it is from this that the myth has arisen that *Wong* v *Vizards* is authority for the proposition that solicitors may exceed their estimates by a margin of 15%.

The judge in *Mastercigars*, while allowing the solicitors to exceed their estimate, confirmed there is no 15% margin. The judge in *Reynolds*, while not allowing any increase, said it was not possible to say that the sum he would have allowed represented any particular margin over the estimates. However, in at least two SCCO cases costs judges have found it helpful to apply it, and this was one of the matters on which the assessors disagreed with the judge in *Mastercigars*. On appeal from the costs judge, who had applied a 20% margin, the High Court judge addressed margins in these terms: 'The adoption of an approach which involves adding a margin, usually expressed as a percentage, to the estimate as the conventional approach and the majority of cases would pay scant, if any, regard to that legal process. While there are advantages to the margin approach, it should not be systematically endorsed. The adoption of a margin approach greatly simplifies the steps which a costs judge needs to take when carrying out a detailed assessment of the bill which has been preceded by a lower estimate. If the margin approach became the permissible conventional approach, then the costs of the detailed assessment could be reduced and the outcome would be more predictable. But even where a court had followed the proper assessment process, it can never be right for costs to be expressed by reference to a margin.'

The client's reliance on estimates

[1.14]

The longer an estimate is left unrevised, the more risk there is that the client will come to rely heavily on the estimate. After all, why shouldn't the client believe that your estimate holds good if you do not revisit it?

In *Mastercigars*, the judge said the following in respect of how the court should look at the client's apparent reliance on an estimate. He said:

> 'In my judgment, the legal process involved in a case where a client contends that its reliance on an estimate should be taken into account in determining the figure which it is reasonable for the client to pay is as follows. The court should determine whether the client did rely on the estimate. The court should determine how the client relied on the estimate. The court should try to determine the above without conducting an elaborate and detailed investigation. The court should decide whether the costs claimed should be reduced by reason of its findings as to reliance and, if so, in what way and by how much. Whether there should be a reduction, and if so to what extent, is a matter of judgment. Specific deductions can be made from the costs otherwise recoverable to reflect the impact which an erroneous and uncorrected estimate had on the conduct of the client. Such an approach requires the court to form an assessment of the impact of the estimate on the conduct of the client. The court should consider the deductions which are needed in order to do justice between the parties. It is not the proper function of the court to punish the solicitor for providing a wrong estimate or for failing to keep it up to date as events unfolded. In terms of the sequence of the decisions to be made by the court, it has been suggested that the court should determine whether, and if so how, it will reflect the estimate in the detailed assessment before carrying out the detailed assessment. The suggestion as to the sequence of decision making may not always be appropriate.

> The suggestion is put forward as practical guidance rather than as a legal imperative. The ultimate question is as to the sum which it is reasonable for the client to pay, having regard to the estimate and any other relevant matter.'

If you don't want to leave it to the judgment of a judge, make sure that the estimate (and the client) is kept up to date. But even that sage piece of advice requires some qualification. An updated estimate which is in line with the costs ultimately incurred will not always save the day where an earlier estimate (or estimates) prove to be manifestly too low. In *Harrison v Eversheds LLP* [2017] EWHC 2594 (QB) the costs judge took the view that the second of four estimates was the one on which the client had placed reliance. The subsequent events did not justify the increases in the later estimates, the last of which exceeded the costs actually incurred. Accordingly, the *Mastercigars* test of what was reasonable for the client to pay was invoked. Slade J took the view that the costs judge was overly generous to the solicitors in the amount above the second estimate that could be allowed. In considering estimates, quotations and reliance, she said the following:

> 'An estimate is to be distinguished from a quotation of fees: an offer which is accepted. An estimate is what it says. It gives an idea, which from a professional firm can be taken as reasonably and carefully made taking into account all relevant considerations, of what the future costs of work on a case is likely to be. A solicitor cannot be held to be restricted to recovering the exact sum set out in an estimate. However a client is entitled to place some reliance on the estimate. The nature, degree and reasonableness of that reliance will no doubt be one factor in the view taken on an assessment under Section 70 of the Solicitors Act 1974 of how much more than the estimate it is reasonable for the client to pay.'

Not giving an estimate

[1.15]

Garbutt v Edwards [2005] EWCA Civ 1206, held that, between the parties, failure to give an estimate was merely a matter for the costs judge, who should consider whether this has in any way increased the costs over what they would have been if an estimate had been given.

Between solicitor and client, the position appears to be that if a solicitor gives a costs estimate he is bound by it, but there is still no effective sanction for failing to do so. If so, we reach the bizarre position that solicitors who provide estimates which prove to be inaccurate are in a worse position than those who provide no estimates at all. The regulatory sanctions for such a failure ought to be significant.

The effect of budgets on estimates

[1.16]

The great majority of cases which appear to be multi-track in value are going to require a costs budget to be prepared once proceedings are commenced (see Chapter 16 for detailed commentary on this). The recoverable fee for creating a budget is limited to 1% of the budget or £1,000, whichever is the greater. If the solicitor has to start from scratch, such sum is not going to be adequate to cover the costs of completing the precedent form in a sizeable case.

It was said, when the requirements for budgeting were being unveiled, that the fee was based on an assumption that most of the work had already been carried out in providing the client with a costs estimate at the outset. As such, those figures (and their assumptions) could simply be transposed on to the Precedent H spreadsheet.

The costs estimates provided to clients in client care letters to date have been broad figures – or brackets of broad figures – with generally no explanation of how they have been reached. Explanatory comments have tended to be no more than 'in our experience' fees up to, for example the issue of proceedings or disclosure, 'for this type of work' are in the order of £X,000, or between £X,000 and £Y,000. Often there is a comment that 'hopefully' the other side will see sense and the case will be settled earlier, just in case the client takes fright at the figures that have been set out.

Although budgets have become common, there does not appear to have been any general change in practice when providing an estimate to the client. As such the court estimate continues to be produced from scratch.

The wording of PD 44, paragraph 3 continues the relevance of estimates in the form of budgets where no Case Management Order has been made. In such cases, there is no need to show a good reason to depart from the last agreed or approved budget because there has been no approved budget. The paying party may argue that the budget was agreed but, for whatever reason the court did not make a CMO, and as such CPR Part 3 is engaged but that would look to be an uphill battle in the absence of a CMO. The pre-April 2013 case law on what was ss 6.5A and 6.6 of the Costs Practice Direction will continue to be relevant in such cases. In particular, the decision of Master Gordon-Saker in *Tribe v Southdown Gliding Club Ltd* [2007] EWHC 90080 (Costs) repays reading where the paying party alleges reliance on the erroneous estimate.

The effect of recoverable fixed costs on estimates

[1.17]

Section 74(3) of the Solicitors Act 1974 states that a solicitor may only recover from his client on assessment the costs which are recoverable on a between the parties' assessment. This statement is made with the proviso that it only relates to the County Court and not the High Court. Furthermore, it can be displaced by rules of court. CPR 46.9(2) disapplies s 74(3) if there is a written agreement between the solicitor and his client.

Why is this important? The implementation of fixed costs on the small claims track and, sooner or later, the fast track means that solicitors will be limited to these fixed figures unless they have set out in writing that s 74(3) is not to apply to their agreement. Indeed, it is prudent for the solicitor at the outset of litigation to identify the probability of a shortfall to the client as the result of fixed costs (or the proportionality test), and to obtain the client's signature to an agreement that the solicitor and client costs may exceed those recoverable between the parties.

CLIENT CARE

[1.18]

Last year's edition was published just as the Solicitors Regulation Authority brought in a completely new system of regulation. The 'current' regulatory position was consequently described in two periods, pre- and post-25 November 2019.

As is described more fully below, the prescriptive approach to solicitor regulation has gradually become looser or more 'high level' during the last ten years. No longer could the completion of a list of items guarantee compliance with the regulatory requirements. More recently, much more abstract concepts and principles have had to be considered with the outcome for the client becoming the cornerstone of client care.

As from November 2019, that signpost to good client care is no longer present. What is now the current code is very high level indeed. Consequently, a look back to the outcomes and indicative behaviours for the previous code may assist. The more prescriptive approach of earlier regulation may also help in setting up systems. Earlier editions of this book set out the information in detail that was required under older regulations (see **[1.20]**). For this year's edition, we split the regimes chronologically into 'old', 'previous' and 'current'.

[1.19]

The key client care issue for this book is the provision of information about costs to the client and the subsequent updating of that information from time to time. We therefore concentrate on this aspect in our review of the regulatory provision. The information at the outset must include the various forms of funding set out in this part of the book, even if they are not all options that you provide. The case law on this issue comes from the 'costs wars' since defendants viewed some options available to claimants as cheaper than others and so challenged the adequacy of the advice given to claimant's solicitors. You can find commentary on this at **[6.18]**.

If it were needed, confirmation of a solicitors' continuing duty to advise clients was given in *Andrews v Messrs Beg Ltd (formerly RWP solicitors) and David Lowe QC* [2019] EWHC 911 (Ch). It contrasted with (leading) counsel who, although he gave discrete advice on funding matters, had no such duty.

Old Regulatory Position

[1.20]

The Solicitors Practice Rules came into effect as far back as 1936. The last version of the SPR was produced in 1990 and included Practice Rule 15 (costs information and client care). It was revised periodically until it was replaced by the Solicitors' Code of Conduct 2007. During the 17 years up to 2007 solicitors gradually became used to the concept of providing their clients with prospective costs estimates as well as information on how their case was to be run. The phrase 'Rule 15 letter' is still regularly heard as a synonym for a client care letter: not least because since 2007 there have been several further revisions of the Code so that the relevant rule number has not stayed long enough with practitioners for the number 15 to have been displaced.

[1.21]

In 2011, a further Code of Conduct was introduced with its focus being on the outcome for the client of the service provided rather than whether prescriptive regulations had been met (a so-called 'tick-box' approach). The latest regulations are considered in detail below. Therefore, compared with the 2007 Code, there is a lack of prescription as to what is required to provide appropriate information on costs.

Previous Regulatory Position

[1.22]

The SRA Code of Conduct 2011 forms part of the SRA Handbook which came into effect on 6 October 2011. In addition to the Code are the ten mandatory SRA Principles which are at the heart of the new regime. These apply to all solicitors and to all firms that are regulated by the SRA and everybody who works in them – including owners in an Alternative Business Structure who are not lawyers.

The principles state that 'you must:

(1) uphold the rule of law and the proper administration of justice,
(2) act with integrity,
(3) not allow your independence to be compromised,
(4) act in the best interests of each client,
(5) provide a proper standard of service to your clients,
(6) behave in a way that maintains the trust the public places in you and in the provision of legal services,
(7) comply with your legal and regulatory obligations and deal with your regulators and ombudsmen in an open, timely and co-operative manner,
(8) run your business or carry out your role in the business effectively and in accordance with proper governance and sound financial and risk management principles,
(9) run your business or carry out your role in the business in a way that encourages equality of opportunity and respect for diversity, and
(10) protect client money and assets.'

The Handbook gives the following guidance on the Principles: 'They define the fundamental ethical and professional standards that we expect of all firms and individuals (including owners who may not be lawyers) when providing legal services. You should always have regard to the Principles and use them as your starting point when faced with an ethical dilemma. Where two or more Principles come into conflict, the Principle which takes precedence is the one which best serves the public interest in the particular circumstances, especially the public interest in the proper administration of justice.'

Client care moved up the batting order from Rule 15 in 1990 to Rule 2 in 2007. In the latest Code it has reached Chapter 1 which is a testament to the continuing complaints received by clients of the care they receive – generally in respect of service rather than advice – as much as anything else. Chapter 1 concerns providing a proper standard of service, which takes into account the individual needs and circumstances of each client. This includes providing clients with the information they need to make informed decisions about the services they need, how these will be delivered and how much they will cost. It confirms solicitors are generally free to decide whether or not to accept instructions in any matter, provided they do not discriminate unlawfully.

Outcomes Focused Regulation

[1.23]

The introductory text of Chapter 1 is short (as with the other chapters). Most of the text relates to 'Outcomes' which must be achieved and by 'Indicative behaviours' which 'may' tend to show that the outcomes have been achieved and as such you have complied with the Principles set out above.

This approach is a veritable sea change to the regulation of legal services. Previously, a conscientious solicitor could be assured of complying with his professional obligations if he read through the Rules and noted any with which he did not seem to be complying and took steps to address them. An exhaustive list could be produced and each one ticked off as they were completed.

The variation in solicitors' practices from multinational firms with thousands of partners to sole practitioners, not to mention Alternative Business Structures, meant, at least as far as the SRA were concerned, that one set of prescriptive Rules, even with Guidance, could not fit all circumstances. Consequently, the 2011 Code looks from the other end of the telescope to see how things turned out, particularly for the client. If your client has a good outcome (not necessarily the same as having been successful) then you have adhered to the Principles. How do you know whether your client has had a good outcome? A good question. The indicative behaviours are meant to show how good practice might achieve the right outcome but they are no more than examples and may not be relevant in your situation. They are, in practice, likely to be something that is only looked at when trying to demonstrate that the outcomes were achieved following a complaint by the client.

In *Solicitors Regulation Authority v Anderson Solicitors* [2013] EWHC 4021 (Admin), the Divisional Court drew a contrast between r 10 of the 2007 Rules and Outcome O (1.1) in the 2011 version. The former had a subjective element unlike the objective Outcome. Consequently, the solicitors were acquitted of misleading their clients because they had not deliberately used their position to take unfair advantage of their clients. It was not enough to look at the end result: a very stark contrast to the 2011 Regulations.

Outcomes Focused Regulation and costs

[1.24]

This is a book about costs not regulatory compliance. You need to be aware that non-compliance may affect your remuneration but it is beyond the scope of this book in our view to set out all of the Outcomes and Indicative behaviours with commentary. There are other books where that can be obtained and the Handbook itself can be obtained from the SRA website (www.sra.org.uk).

Outcomes

The Outcomes particularly relevant to the issue of costs are as follows:

> **'The Outcomes**
>
> The outcomes in this chapter show how the Principles apply in the context of client care. They are mandatory.
>
> You must achieve these outcomes:
>
> **O(1.6)** you only enter into fee agreements with your clients that are legal, and which you consider are suitable for the client's needs and take account of the client's best interests;'

Entering into an agreement which is legal (O(1.6)) sounds as if it is so obvious that it does not need saying. Nevertheless, there is an indicative behaviour (IB(1.27)) to show what would not demonstrate achieving a good outcome namely 'entering into unlawful fee arrangements such as an unlawful contingency fee' so it must have been concluded by the SRA that this was not obvious. However, there is certainly case law to suggest that a solicitor foolish enough to enter into an agreement that is unenforceable because it is unlawful unintentionally provides the client with free legal services which may well be a very good outcome for the client.

> **'O(1.12)** clients are in a position to make informed decisions about the services they need, how their matter will be handled and the options available to them;'

O(1.12), and its compatriot indicative behaviour IB(1.1) (below), presage a change in working practice which is quite new. Traditionally, solicitors have provided the same level of service to all their clients, at least in theory. This Outcome, however, provides the solicitor with the opportunity to agree different service levels with different clients which may, or may not, simply reflect the ability of the client to pay for the solicitors' full service. It is but a short step to see the so-called 'unbundling' of the solicitor's assistance to his client so that certain stages or elements are dealt with by the client himself, or by using the assistance of a third party, and the solicitor is only involved in those parts that really require his expertise. The effect of such arrangements on time-hallowed concepts such as being 'on the court record' will have to be worked out in due course. A Practice Note on unbundling civil legal services was reissued on 19 March 2015 to assist practitioners.

An early example of this issue can be found in *Minkin v Lesley Landsberg (practising as Barnet Family Law)* [2015] EWCA Civ 1152 where the Court of Appeal upheld the defendant's contention that her retainer was limited to the putting of a Consent Order agreed by the parties into a form acceptable to the court and not to advise the claimant on whether it represented a suitable settlement for her.

The Court of Appeal however did not accept the purported limitation of the retainer by the solicitor in *Hughmans (a firm) v Dunhill (Suing on her own behalf and as litigation friend on behalf of W (a young person))* [2017] EWCA Civ 97. This decision relates to overturning summary judgment given to the solicitors. As such, it only speaks of the client's prospects of disputing the alleged extent of the retainer. Nevertheless, it is instructive in the issues a court may consider as to the reasonableness of limiting the work to be done by the solicitor.

> **'O(1.13)** clients receive the best possible information, both at the time of engagement and when appropriate as their matter progresses, about the likely overall cost of their matter;
>
> **O(1.14)** clients are informed of their right to challenge or complain about your

bill and the circumstances in which they may be liable to pay interest on an unpaid bill;'

Providing the client with the best possible information at the outset (O(1.13)) and information on how to challenge bills (O(1.14)) follow on from previous Codes and highlight the client's statutory entitlement (see [3.13]ff) to such information.

Indicative Behaviours

[1.25]

The most relevant Indicative behaviours are set out below. As you will see there is an entire section headed 'fee arrangements with your client' in addition to the more general indicative behaviours. They are all worth studying.

'Dealing with the client's matter

IB(1.1) agreeing an appropriate level of service with your client, for example the type and frequency of communications;
IB(1.4) explaining any arrangements, such as fee sharing or referral arrangements, which are relevant to the client's instructions;
IB(1.5) explaining any limitations or conditions on what you can do for the client, for example, because of the way the client's matter is funded;

Fee arrangements with your client

IB(1.13) discussing whether the potential outcomes of the client's matter are likely to justify the expense or risk involved, including any risk of having to pay someone else's legal fees;
IB(1.14) clearly explaining your fees and if and when they are likely to change;
IB(1.15) warning about any other payments for which the client may be responsible;
IB(1.16) discussing how the client will pay, including whether public funding may be available, whether the client has insurance that might cover the fees, and whether the fees may be paid by someone else such as a trade union;
IB(1.17) where you are acting for a client under a fee arrangement governed by statute, such as a conditional fee agreement, giving the client all relevant information relating to that arrangement;
IB(1.18) where you are acting for a publicly funded client, explaining how their publicly funded status affects the costs;
IB(1.19) providing the information in a clear and accessible form which is appropriate to the needs and circumstances of the client;
IB(1.20) where you receive a financial benefit as a result of acting for a client, either:

- paying it to the client;
- offsetting it against your fees; or
- keeping it only where you can justify keeping it, you have told the client the amount of the benefit (or an approximation if you do not know the exact amount) and the client has agreed that you can keep it;

IB(1.21) ensuring that disbursements included in your bill reflect the actual amount spent or to be spent on behalf of the client;'

Current Regulatory Position (after 25 November 2019)

[1.26]

In 2016, the SRA consulted upon a comprehensive rewrite of the Code in a consultation exercise entitled 'Looking to the future – flexibility and public protection'. The new 'Standards and Regulations' are the end product of the SRA's consultation.

Separately, a qualitative report entitled 'Research into client care letters' was produced in October 2016, having been commissioned jointly by the various legal regulators. The Consumer Panel chair commented on the report that client-care letters were mostly ineffective at conveying the information consumers prioritised, such as information on cost, timescales and basic client-relation contact details. Worryingly, the research also showed that client-care letters did not meet the needs of vulnerable consumers. It might seem strange therefore that the SRA, in its response to its own consultation, stated that:

> 'Our view is that solicitors and firms do not need pages and pages of detailed, prescriptive rules to do the right thing'.

This is particularly odd given the ever increasing prescription up to the 2007 Code was a reflection of the belief that solicitors needed exactly the opposite. Nevertheless, we should give full marks to the SRA for being consistent in that view based on the new Standards and Regulations.

Standards and Regulations

[1.27]

The new terminology of Standards and Regulations appears to have replaced the less formal 'handbook'. As with the 2011 provisions, the new regime begins with a set of core principles. These are said to be the 'fundamental tenets of ethical behaviour' which the individuals and firms regulated by the SRA are expected to uphold. As would be expected, they cover much the same ground as those in the 2011 Code as follows:

> 'The principles are as follows:
>
> You act:
>
> 1. in a way that upholds the constitutional principle of the rule of law, and the proper administration of justice.
> 2. in a way that upholds public trust and confidence in the solicitors' profession and in legal services provided by authorised persons.
> 3. with independence.
> 4. with honesty.
> 5. with integrity.
> 6. in a way that encourages equality, diversity and inclusion.
> 7. in the best interests of each client.'

Codes of Conduct

[1.28]

There are then two separate codes of conduct – one for individuals and one for firms. In the code for individuals, under the heading 'Client information and publicity' it reads:

> '8.6 You give clients information in a way they can understand. You ensure they are in a position to make informed decisions about the services they need, how their matter will be handled and the options available to them.
> 8.7 You ensure that clients receive the best possible information about how their matter will be priced and, both at the time of engagement and when appropriate as their matter progresses, about the likely overall cost of the matter and any costs incurred.'

And that's it. There is nothing else in the individual's code. The only reference in the firm's code is at 7.1 where it imports a number of provisions, including 8.6 and 8.7 above, from the individual's code. You would be forgiven for thinking that everything is sunny in the garden of client care. Far from 'pages and pages' of prescription, there is barely a reference to costs information whatsoever. Guidance given to solicitors on client care letters by the SRA acknowledges that 'a lack of clarity around costs' is a major source of complaint by clients but simply refers to the above entries in the code of conduct.

[1.29]

There is rather more in the introduction to the individual's code about the SRA's expectations:

> 'You must exercise your judgement in applying these standards to the situations you are in and deciding on a course of action, bearing in mind your role and responsibilities, areas of practice, and the nature of your clients (which in an in house context will generally include your employer and may include other persons or groups within or outside your employer organisation).
>
> You are personally accountable for compliance with this Code - and our other regulatory requirements that apply to you - and must always be prepared to justify your decisions and actions.
>
> A serious failure to meet our standards or a serious breach of our regulatory requirements may result in our taking regulatory action against you. A failure or breach may be serious either in isolation or because it comprises a persistent or concerning pattern of behaviour.'

Drawing this together, it would appear that in order for a solicitor to act 'in the best interests of each client' (principle 7), he must ensure that they receive the best possible information at the outset and where appropriate thereafter in a manner in which they can understand it. That sounds perfectly fine. How are solicitors to ensure this happens? By exercising their judgement and being prepared to explain themselves if held accountable for any shortcomings. This approach certainly puts the responsibility on the solicitor to think about how they operate.

In *Darby v Law Society* [2003] EWHC 2270 (Admin), the Administrative Court upheld the Solicitors Disciplinary Tribunal's decision against Mr Darby. The entire judgment repays reading if you are looking at making sure you comply with your costs information responsibilities in the light of the new regime. Mr Darby did not produce his Rule 15 (as it was then) letter until 14 months after instruction. Until that point he considered he had been firefighting since his client had a default judgment against him. There then appeared to be a period of negotiation and it was only when his client confirmed that he wished Mr Darby to take the case to trial, that he considered his retainer to be a full one and so send his terms and conditions to the client. The court (as did the Tribunal) accepted that the client was a businessman experienced in instructing solicitors. Nevertheless, as Auld LJ said, giving the judgment of the court:

> 'Careful attention to the need for such advice, both at the beginning of the solicitor/client relationship and thereafter periodically as the matter progresses, is highly important in the interest of the client and the solicitor and in the integrity and efficacy, regardless of outcome, of the litigation process on which they are both embarked. There is, it seems to us, a heavy onus on a solicitor to establish that his client is so sophisticated in matters of litigation, and so attentive to the cost implications of the litigation in question, that Rule 15 may be disregarded.'

[1.30]

One notable exception to the increasingly less prescriptive approach to costs regulation by the SRA is the SRA Transparency Rules. They relate to conveyancing, probate and employment claims as well as the simpler end of debt recovery and magistrates' court work. The fees payable, or at least an easy to understand formula for calculating those fees, needs to be advertised so that they can be read before the client contacts you.

COMPLAINTS

[1.31]

Whether under the previous regime or the current one, solicitors need to inform their clients at the outset of how they may complain about them if needed. The number of complaints dealt with by the Legal Ombudsman (in respect of service) and the SRA (in respect of a breach of the SRA Principles) each year suggests that there is a very real need for clients to understand their rights in this area.

Clients are encouraged to contact their solicitor directly initially but if that proves unsuccessful, the client can then contact the Legal Ombudsman. Clients' complaints need to be dealt with promptly, fairly, openly and effectively. Such an approach does not sit naturally with most professionals and needs to be worked at constantly.

In *Brien v Irwin Mitchell LLP* [2017] EWHC 742 (Ch), the solicitors provided no explanation in response to the client's complaint regarding a failure to transfer monies following a property transaction. In fact, they refused to speak to him and consequently he issued Part 8 proceedings. During those proceedings it became clear that the lack of communication was at the insistence of the Metropolitan Police regarding a suspected Proceeds of Crime matter. Mr Brien did not consider this to be a good excuse and sought his costs of the proceedings. The court decided that no order as to costs was the appropriate outcome up to the point when the solicitors produced a letter from the police. Thereafter Mr Brien should have ceased his claim (rather than go to two further hearings) and so he was required to make a contribution to Irwin Mitchell's costs.

The Legal Ombudsman

[1.32]

That complaints to the Legal Ombudsman include enquiring into overcharging or wrongful charging was confirmed by Phillips J in *Layard Horsfall Ltd v The Legal Ombudsman* [2013] EWHC 4137 (Admin). In order to consider the quality and levels of service, the ombudsman had to be able to consider the correct contractual starting point for the charges. When the defendant went bankrupt before trial, the solicitor's advice to the claimant regarding discontinuance fell short of the required standard. Notwithstanding the use of a CFA, the claimant was asked to pay £5,000 by way of fees. The ombudsman reduced this to £1,500 plus VAT; a decision considered entirely fair and reasonable by the judge.

Similarly, in *Leonard Ejiofor (t/a Mitchell & Co Solicitors) v the Legal Ombudsman* [2016] EWHC 1933 (Admin), Wyn Williams J upheld the Ombudsman's decision to reduce the fees claimed by the solicitor. The client was one of three children whose parents had died intestate leaving a property as the main asset. The other two children took out a grant of probate and instructed solicitors to sell the property. The client paid her solicitor's initial invoice but then indicated she had no money to meet any payment on account though she was keen to pursue her claim. The solicitor offered a contingency fee agreement of 20% plus VAT to avoid the client having to pay anything upfront. Time was of the essence because the property was about to be sold. Nevertheless, the court considered that a contingency fee agreement should have been drafted and put before the client in order for her to consider its reasonableness, a proposition that might seem difficult to achieve, particularly where there is urgency. The court was understandably influenced by the strength of the claim and that, by the time the agreement was made, the executors' solicitors had agreed to hold the sale proceeds until the client's claim had been dealt with. The solicitors claimed a contingency fee of £37,806.88 inclusive of VAT. The Ombudsman reduced that figure by £34,000 leaving the balance to reflect the work actually done. Whilst the justice of the case appears to be entirely with the client, the expectations raised by this authority are potentially wide-reaching. They are also a salutary warning to those who think that a referral to the Ombudsman is something to take lightly.

Status of personnel

[1.33]

One of the other general indicative behaviours is to ensure that the client is told in writing the name and status of the people dealing with the case and whoever is responsible for its supervision (IB(1.3)). A similar provision in the 1990 Code enabled the Court of Appeal to uphold the client's refusal to pay his solicitor's bill on the grounds that he had asked for an appointment with a solicitor but it transpired that the person to whom he was referred by the receptionist was neither a solicitor nor a qualified legal executive. In *Pilbrow v Pearless De Rougemont & Co (a firm)* [1999] 3 All ER 355, [1999] 2 FLR 139, CA, the work had been done to the standard of a competent solicitor. Nevertheless, the contract was one to provide legal services by a solicitor and therefore the firm had not performed that contract at all. The firm should have trained its receptionist when faced with a request to see a solicitor to do one of the following:

(i) refer the client to a solicitor;

(ii) refer the client to someone who was not a solicitor but inform the client that that person was not a solicitor; or

(iii) refer the client to someone who the receptionist knew was not a solicitor, refrain from telling the client that fact and alert the referee to the fact that the client had asked for a solicitor.

If the last course were adopted then it would be the duty of the referee straight away to make clear to the client that he was not a solicitor.

The indicative behaviour talks of setting out the name and status in writing rather than on meeting. Compliance with this behaviour is usually achieved in the client care letter and arguably therefore the situation in *Pilbrow* would be rectified by that subsequent letter even if the client was still under a misapprehension when he left the building after his consultation with his 'solicitor'.

In *Gooding v North Tees & Hartlepool NHS Trust (Middlesbrough Employment Tribunal 3 April 2017)*, a struck-off solicitor acted as a legal advisor to the claimant in an unsuccessful tribunal claim. The client sought wasted costs against her 'solicitor'. She had understood him to be her solicitor and he had not corrected that impression. It was only a comment from the Tribunal judge which revealed the true position. The judge found that the client was entitled to a wasted costs order and disallowed the balance of the amount that he had charged her for representation (£4,459.75) net of interim payments of £1,250.

ENDING THE AGREEMENT

By the client

[1.34]

The client may terminate a retainer at any time for any reason.

The retainer may also be terminated by the effluxion of time if it was for a fixed period, or by the death, bankruptcy or insanity of the solicitor or the client, or if its continuance becomes unlawful. In *Higgins & Co Lawyers Ltd v Evans* [2019] EWHC 2809 (QB) the client in an asbestosis personal injury case died having instructed his solicitors under a CFA. It used the Law Society standard terms in respect of termination and these provided for a liability on the part of the client for the basic costs. The deputy costs judge held those terms to be unusual and onerous and as such were unenforceable. Having heard rather more detailed submissions, Saini J overturned that decision. The clause struck a balance of risk run by the parties and could not properly be described as either unusual or onerous under the common law nor could it be held unenforceable under the Consumer Rights Act 2015.

The client may have the right to cancel under the Consumer Contracts (Information, Cancellation and Additional Charges) Regulations 2013 or earlier Regulations made in 1987 and 2008 (see [1.7] above).

But a client who seeks to end the retainer in order to deprive his solicitor of fees by claiming them directly from the opponent will be prevented by the solicitor's lien if the money is in the solicitor's client account. If it goes directly to the client, the Court of Appeal's decision in *Khans Solicitors (a firm) v Chifuntwe* [2013] EWCA Civ 481, makes clear that the paying party makes payment to your client at his own risk if he is on notice of your interest in the money (or is colluding with the client to deprive you of your fees). If the paying party is unsure as to whom he should pay the costs, he can apply to the court for guidance or to enable him to pay the money into court to discharge his debt.

In *Gavin Edmondson Solicitors Ltd v Haven Insurance Co Ltd* [2018] UKSC 21, the Supreme Court decided that the client had a contractual relationship with his solicitor which gave rise to an equitable lien in the solicitor's favour over the settlement sums. A paying party who sought to engineer the payment of damages to the client without paying costs in addition to his solicitors was unconscionable and so was ineffective against that equitable lien. However, in *Bott & Co Solicitors Ltd v Ryanair DAC* [2018] EWHC 534 (Ch), the court held that the solicitors had not done anything more than negotiation (and often little of that) prior to litigation and such was insufficient to raise an equitable lien.

By the solicitor

(i) Under the Solicitors Act 1974, s 65(2)

[1.35]

In respect of contentious business only, a solicitor can request a client to pay a reasonable sum of money on account of costs incurred and to be incurred. If the client fails to make that payment within a reasonable time, this would entitle the solicitor to terminate the retainer (having given reasonable notice to the client).

(ii) For good cause

[1.36]

There is an implied term that the solicitor may terminate the retainer upon reasonable notice for good cause, such as a failure to provide funds for disbursements or give adequate instructions; the client requiring the solicitor to behave unlawfully or unethically; obstructing the solicitor, or preventing him from dealing with the matter, and where there is a serious breakdown in confidence between them.

The main issue in *Richard Buxton (a firm) v Mills-Owens* [2010] EWCA Civ 122, was whether a solicitor had 'good reason' for terminating the retainer if the client insisted on his putting forward a case and instructing counsel to argue a case that was 'doomed to disaster' or which the solicitor believed was 'bound to fail'.

The Court decided that there was no comprehensive definition of what amounts to a 'good reason' to terminate because it is a fact-sensitive question. It was wrong to restrict the circumstances in which a solicitor could lawfully terminate his retainer to those in which he was instructed to do something improper. Solicitors should not lightly be able lawfully to terminate their retainers, but the desirability of protecting a client from an arbitrary and unreasonable termination was not a sufficient justification for a narrow interpretation of the phrase 'good reason'.

It would be improper in a statutory planning appeal to advance an argument based on the merits of the decision by the planning inspector, which was hopeless and not genuinely arguable. As the client had insisted that such arguments be advanced, the solicitors had good reason for terminating the retainer. The retainer was an entire contract that had not been completed, but as it had been terminated for good reason, the solicitors were entitled to their proper costs and disbursements for work done prior to the termination.

(iii) Where the client loses capacity

[1.37]

What should you do if your client loses capacity to enter into a contract or (more likely) continue to give instructions?

Guidance to the Solicitors Code of Conduct 2007 gave this helpful advice: 'If your client loses mental capacity after you have started to act, the law will automatically end the contractual relationship. However, it is important that the client, who is in a very vulnerable situation, is not left without legal representation. Consequently, you should notify an appropriate person (eg the Court of Protection), or you may look for someone legally entitled to provide you with instructions, such as an attorney under an enduring power of attorney, or take the appropriate steps for such a person to be appointed, such as a receiver or a litigation friend. This is a particularly complex legal issue and you should satisfy yourself as to the law before deciding on your course of action.'

What if your client only loses capacity temporarily? You may not be aware of this happening unless it happens over a relatively lengthy period or happens repeatedly. In *Blankley v Central Manchester and Manchester Children's University Hospitals NHS Trust* [2014] EWHC 168 (QB), the opponent became aware of the temporary lack of capacity. It alleged that the result was the retainer was frustrated or ended in some similar way so that there was no liability for the defendant to pay the claimant's costs under the indemnity principle. Phillips J reached the conclusion that any intervening incapacity does not frustrate or otherwise terminate a solicitor's retainer. It did have the effect of removing the solicitor's authority to act for the client during the incapacity. But that authority can be restored when either a deputy is appointed or if and when the client regains capacity.

CONTINGENCY AGREEMENT ISSUES

[1.38]

A private paying client who decides to terminate the retainer with his solicitor can do so for any reason and simply needs to pay whatever sum is outstanding in respect of the solicitors' charges. To the extent they are in dispute, they can be assessed by the court (see Chapter 3) and any lien the solicitor has will be resolved, or an undertaking given by subsequent solicitors instructed by the claimant. This was the position for hundreds of years.

However, when conditional fee agreements became available in 1995 and now damages-based agreements can be used in contentious matters, the position becomes more complicated. At the time the retainer comes to an end, the determination of whether the case has been successful or not will be a matter of conjecture if the case is still proceeding. Is a success fee or slice of the damages going to be paid? Or is there in fact no liability to the solicitor at all?

The Law Society has published a model CFA whenever significant changes have been made to the regime. Each set of Law Society Conditions sets out what happens if the agreement ends before the claims for damages ends. These cover most, if not all, eventualities in respect of the outcome of the case. But these have not dealt with issues such as the firm of solicitors becoming insolvent or merging with another firm or being intervened by the SRA etc. This seems to excite paying parties to argue that there is a flaw in the receiving party's retainer for some or all of the time covered by the case on regular occasions. To avoid this, if you decide to draft your own CFA, you should take considerable care to make sure that every eventuality that you can conceive is dealt with in the termination provision.

There is no Law Society DBA and so you are on your own in drafting suitable provisions, although the CFA terms are the obvious starting point.

WRITING OFF/WAIVING COSTS

[1.39]

In *Slatter v Ronaldsons (a firm)* [2002] 2 Costs LR 267 the defendant solicitors had acted for the claimant in matrimonial proceedings for which they had outstanding costs. When the claimant became unemployed they concluded that it would be uneconomic to pursue him for the balance of their costs and accordingly 'wrote them off', obtaining the appropriate VAT refund. Subsequently the client instructed other solicitors who wrote to the defendants requesting delivery up of all relevant papers which the defendants refused to do, contending that they had a lien over the papers until their bills were discharged in full. The judge, on appeal, upheld the lien (see **[3.29]** below for more on liens). The contractual liability to pay the balance of the bills survived their 'writing off' and there was no evidence that the claimant acted to his detriment entitling him to promissory estoppel, on the basis that the balance of the bills had been written off.

Similarly, where solicitors had agreed not to charge for work done after judgment was handed down they were not precluded from claiming costs for work done after that date because there was no consideration for their waiver (*Ashia Centur Ltd v Barker Gillette LLP* [2011] EWHC 148 (QB)).

CHAPTER 2

BILLING THE CLIENT

INTRODUCTION TO BILLING THE CLIENT

[2.1]

This Chapter is split into three sections. The first covers the surprisingly complex area of interim bills. The second deals with the final bill rendered to the client and is the introduction to the next Chapter regarding suing the client where necessary for payment. The final section concerns VAT which is something which catches people out all too often and, like most things, is much easier to get right first time than to have to remedy errors that have been made.

Before getting on to these sections we should say a few words about two subjects which impact on this Chapter and indeed the next – terminology which is particularly important here and the fundamental question of to whom can you render your bill?

TERMINOLOGY WHEN BILLING THE CLIENT

[2.2]

When communicating with clients, solicitors are apt to call their bill by a plethora of different names – an invoice, an account, a fee note, 'a note of my charges' etc. In each case, the solicitor is referring to a document on which is set out the sums payable to his firm for the firm's efforts together with those of other people engaged or payments made to third parties. As will soon be seen, there is more than one kind of interim bill that can be rendered. There is more than one kind of final bill as well. An interim bill may in fact only be a request for a payment on account, rather than a formal bill, anyway. We use the word 'bill' in this Chapter to cover most if not all of these documents. You need to be clear about the concepts behind the distinctions (and their effect) rather than slavishly following the correct terminology. In our experience, even the most skilled advocates trip over the correct terminology from time to time.

WHO CAN YOU BILL?

[2.3]

Save for those with a contract with the Legal Aid Agency, there is only one source from which a solicitor can be remunerated and that is the client. It is fundamental to an understanding of the law of costs to appreciate this but it is regularly said by solicitors that they are seeking an order from a court for 'their costs' and not the client's. This is completely wrong, even where the client has been told that the solicitor will take whatever can be recovered from the other side and render no additional bill to the client.

It may well be that the client has rights against other persons or funds, which will ultimately pay the solicitor's fees. The trustee looks to a trust fund for reimbursement; a successful party in litigation can expect an order for costs against the loser; the landlord may provide in the lease that his legal costs be paid by the tenant, but none of this affects the solicitor and client relationship between the trustee, the successful litigant or the landlord and their respective solicitors. The solicitor on behalf of his client seeks to recover money due to the client from the trust fund, the unsuccessful litigant or the tenant, but he does not have any personal relationship with them. The solicitor looks to his client for payment of the costs whether or not the client is reimbursed by a third party. The solicitor must therefore deliver a bill to his client for the whole of his costs and give credit for any sum that has been received. This is the strict legal position and has been since at least 1908. In *Cobbett v Wood* [1908] 2 KB 420, 77 LJKB 878, CA, the Court of Appeal held that a bill of costs which excluded the between the parties' items and simply referred to the excess chargeable as between solicitor and own client was not a proper bill. Whether a court would take such a strict line now may be open to question. But the fact that the costs are the client's rather than the solicitor's is beyond doubt.

Misunderstandings about this arise frequently when a third party who is paying the client's costs wishes to have an invoice on which he can recover the VAT. For example, leases regularly contain clauses where the landlord has obtained an undertaking from the tenant to pay his costs. Such a clause also regularly provides that the landlord should be 'compensated fully' or 'indemnified' for costs and expenses incurred as a result of the tenant's breach of the lease. Similar clauses appear in most mortgage deeds. The solicitor is providing legal services to his client, not the third party tenant (for example), and so that tenant cannot obtain a VAT invoice even though he has ultimately funded payment of the client's bill. For more on costs in contractual situations, please see Chapter 36.

INTERIM BILLS

[2.4]

Solicitors have always been free to agree the terms of their retainer with their clients in respect of both non-contentious and contentious business. It is only in recent years that solicitors have realised what has long been appreciated in every other walk of life: that without stage payments by the client the entire burden of financing the work falls upon he who is doing it. 'Cash is King' as every managing partner, chief executive and their bank manager can tell you without hesitation. Without cash flow, any business is in difficulties.

Litigation in particular can be protracted, complicated and lingering, as indeed can some non-contentious work. An agreement with a client that the firm will render interim bills at monthly, three-monthly or six-monthly intervals will transform a firm's cash flow. Any basic system of time recording and costing will enable simple interim bills to be produced based on time spent and hourly rates. If done correctly (see below) any anomalies or inequities can be rectified in the final bill. The clients will be grateful. Solicitors live in fear of offending their clients with requests for payments on account of costs and disbursements, but it is nothing compared with the fear of the clients of the ever-growing size of an unknown bill which they know they will inevitably receive. (This is true now even of most CFA clients who used to have the luxury of being told that they would receive all their compensation and not have to pay any costs to their solicitor or their opponent, whatever the circumstances.) Clients welcome knowing the amount of costs they have incurred to date, even if it may mean them crying 'Halt!' before any more costs are incurred; they will (generally) also welcome the opportunity of making stage payments. Furthermore, clients appreciate that a solicitor who is efficient in the conduct of his own affairs is likely to be no less efficient in looking after theirs.

There are two kinds of interim bill, and the difference between them is crucial. When deciding what sort of interim bills you want to send out, you need to consider in particular whether you think you might need:

- to sue the client on such bills (and not simply on a final bill); and/or
- to seek a different amount from your client at the end of the case for the period the interim bill covers

Keep these questions in mind as we now look at interim bills on account and interim statute bills.

(a) Interim bills on account

[2.5]

A bill on account is really nothing more than a request for payment on account in fancy dress. Not being a statute bill it cannot be sued on by the solicitor, the client cannot apply for a detailed assessment of it and, therefore, the time limits for applying for a detailed assessment do not run.

In *Turner & Co v O Palomo SA* [1999] 4 All ER 353, [2000] 1 WLR 37, CA, five bills rendered during the course of litigation had been headed 'on account of charges and disbursements incurred or to be incurred'. It was held these could not be construed as final or statute bills in respect of the work covered by them, and accordingly the time limits for applying for a detailed assessment under the Solicitors Act had not started to run. In contentious business, if the client does not pay a bill on account the solicitor should give him 'reasonable notice' according to s 65(2), that unless payment is made within a stipulated (reasonable) time, the solicitor will withdraw from the retainer. But you should note that if the client regards the amount requested on account as excessive he can invite the solicitor to render a statute bill which he may then have assessed. If the solicitor then fails to render a statute bill the client can obtain an order from the court that he should do so, pursuant to the Solicitors Act 1974, s 68.

One advantage to the solicitor of rendering a bill on account is that it need not be the final quantification of all the work included in it, but is merely the minimum amount of his charges to date. It also avoids the risk of limiting any between the parties' costs recoverable in respect of this period to the amount of the bill on account under the indemnity principle. Furthermore, unless the sum charged is based on the unsuccessful rate set out in a CFA, there is a risk of appearing to charge by results without the benefit of a statutorily compliant

CFA. For this reason it is important to make it clear to the client that the bill on account is simply a request for payment on account of the final (statute) bill which will be delivered later.

A bill on account constitutes a written intimation to the client of the amount of costs incurred to date and therefore entitles a solicitor to transfer from his client account into his office account money received from the client in accordance with the SRA Accounts Rules. Such a transfer is restricted to the amount of costs already incurred and must not cover anticipated future costs. A bill on account must therefore be restricted to costs incurred. Any request for money on account of future costs must, in respect of contentious business, comply with the requirements of the Solicitors Act 1974, s 65(2) and in respect of non-contentious costs must be pursuant to an agreement with the client.

Therefore if you are looking to improve cash flow and leave flexibility as to the final bill, a bill on account is the interim bill for you. It does mean that you cannot pursue your client on such bills but a separate final bill can be delivered and pursued where necessary. You need to be careful that the payment on account does not turn into a statute bill by mistake (see [2.7]) and which inadvertence may cause you problems, such as being limited to the sums you can claim.

(b) Interim statute bills

[2.6]

These are called statute bills because they comply with all the requirements of the Solicitors Act 1974 and result in all the consequences which flow from such compliance – the solicitor can enforce payment by suing the client, the client can obtain an order for a Solicitors Act 1974 assessment and the various time limits relating to the client's rights to an assessment run from the date of their delivery. Although they are interim bills they are also final bills in respect of the work covered by them. There can be no subsequent adjustment in the light of the outcome of the business. They are complete, self-contained bills of costs to date.

How complete and self-contained do such bills have to be? In *Richard Slade & Co v Boodia and Boodia* [2018] EWCA Civ 2667, the Court of Appeal considered this phrase of long standing. It overturned the view of the costs judge and appeal judge that it required such bills to include profit costs and disbursements for the particular period. Newey LJ concluded a review of the provisions of the Solicitors Act and case law by stating:

> 'I do not think it can be inferred that a statute bill must always, or even usually, include both profit costs and disbursements. Separate billing for profit costs and disbursements is common with modern, digital billing, and I do not accept that that need give rise to problems.'

In *Sprey v Rawlison Butler LLP* [2018] EWHC 354 (QB), the court had to consider a retainer which the drafters of the Solicitors Act 1974 could not possibly have contemplated. The claimant's case was run on a CFA where a fee based on a lower hourly rate was to be paid if the case was not successful. That fee was paid via regular invoices during the life of the case in response to invoices being rendered. The claimant was in fact successful in his case and so the solicitors were entitled to their full hourly rate and a success fee. Those two elements were claimed via two invoices. It was common ground that the invoice relating to the success fee should be assessed given the speed with which the claimant brought Solicitors Act 1974 proceedings. The parties disagreed as to whether the periodic invoices could be interim statute bills (and largely outside the 12-month period for seeking assessment if they were) given the second invoice which claimed the remaining fees based on the balance of the hourly rate multiplied by all of the time claimed in the case. The costs judge at first instance sided with the solicitors but Nicklin J overturned that decision on the basis that the periodic invoices had been adjusted by the 'balancing' invoice and so they could only have been payments on account and all invoices could be assessed.

Interim statute bills during the currency of the retainer can arise in only two ways: by natural break or agreement. These days it is rare for a client care letter not to cater for the making of interim payments.

By Agreement

[2.7]

'Before a solicitor is entitled to require a bill to be treated as a complete self-contained bill of costs to date, he must make it plain to the client expressly or by implication that that is the purpose of his sending in that bill for that amount at that time. Then of course one looks to see what the client's reaction is. If the client's reaction is to pay the bill in its entirety without demur, it is not difficult to infer an agreement that the bill is to be treated as a self-contained bill of costs to date.'

That was how Roskill LJ put it in *Davidsons v Jones-Fenleigh* (1980) 124 Sol Jo 204, (1980) Times, 11 March, CA. In that case the court found that each of four bills delivered was complete and final in its own right and that the time for challenging three of them had expired. In *Abedi v Penningtons (a firm)* [2000] NLJR 465, CA, the solicitors had not agreed with their client that they could deliver interim bills and there were no natural breaks in the litigation, but the solicitors did in fact deliver bills on a monthly basis, each purporting to be a final bill for the period in question. The client at first paid regularly, but then stopped, leaving five bills unpaid and four bills partially paid. The client then alleged that she had been overcharged and sought a detailed assessment under the Solicitors Act. She was so long out of time in making her application that if each of the bills was treated as a final (statute) bill she was not entitled to have any of them assessed under the Act. The Court of Appeal upheld the award of summary judgment to the solicitors on the grounds that the possibility of interim bills being statute bills could arise by virtue of an inferred as well as an express agreement. The client, far from disputing the bills, had paid them regularly and had promised to pay the outstanding bills. The case was distinguished from *Re Romer and Haslam* [1893] 2 QB 286, 62 LJQB 610, CA, because in that case the solicitors had never asked for payment of any of their bills, but merely sought and obtained payment on account.

In *Adams v Mackinnes* SCCO Case No 13 of 2001 the retainer commenced in 1990 with a client care letter, no copy of which survived. In August 1994 the solicitors sent a further client care letter, which was available, stating they would apply an uplift for care and conduct but probably not until the end of the action, when they could decide what mark-up was merited. However, they did not change the format of their bills until May 1996, when they bore a prominent message that the bill was an interim bill. Prior to then the bills were drawn in a way which made them look like final bills. They set out exactly what work had been done, the rate being charged and the period covered by the bill, and each carried a notice informing the client of his rights to detailed assessment under the Solicitors Act. In these circumstances the solicitors were not entitled to any uplift for care and conduct prior to their client care letter of August 1994. It was not mentioned in this short report, but on the face of it, it would be arguable that the format of the bills until May 1996 resulted in them being final bills on which no mark-up could subsequently be claimed.

Natural break

[2.8]

If there is no agreement in the client care letter or other document regarding the delivery of interim bills, the solicitor has to rely on the concept of a natural break in protracted litigation. There is authority for the rendering of an interim statute bill at such points but unfortunately, there is little authority to help to identify what is a natural break. In *Chamberlain v Boodle and King (a firm)* [1982] 3 All ER 188, [1982] 1 WLR 1443, CA, Lord Denning said: 'It is a question of fact whether there are natural breaks in the work done by a solicitor so that each portion of it can and should be treated as a separate and distinct part in itself, capable of and rightly being charged separately and taxed separately'. In that case the Court of Appeal held that there had been no natural breaks justifying treating a series of accounts rendered during litigation as final accounts and that they should accordingly be treated as one bill all of which could be assessed.

In *Wilson v William Sturges & Co* [2006] EWHC 792 (QB), a bill delivered at the end of the first stage of proceedings was held to be a statute bill. Even though the court held it to be 20% in excess of the proper amount, the solicitors' insistence on it being paid before proceeding further did not terminate the retainer and disentitle the solicitors to their reasonable costs. The Law Society's advice is not to rely on the 'natural break' principle as a ground for delivering an interim statute bill except in the clearest circumstances.

So if you take the view that your clients may need suing and/or are likely to challenge your bill, you should consider rendering formal interim statute bills rather than a bill on account. The all-important time limits for challenging the bill (see **[3.16]**) start running from when the statute bill is delivered. The limitation period may well have run out on at least some bills if the litigation carries on for a long period of time. Bills that were paid quite happily by the client originally have a nasty habit of appearing far less reasonable to them at a later stage, particularly if the litigation has not gone so well in the meantime.

FINAL BILLS

Form and content

[2.9]

The formalities governing the delivery of a bill are surprisingly few. The Solicitors Act 1974 is silent as to the form of a bill for non-contentious work and in respect of contentious business s 64 merely prescribes that the bill of costs may, at the option of the solicitor, be either a bill containing detailed items or a gross sum bill. Since the Solicitors Act does not set out what needs to be done, regard is to be had to case law where the requirements are discussed. Ward LJ described this exercise in *Ralph Hume Garry (a firm) v Gwillim* [2002] EWCA Civ 1500 in the following, slightly world weary, fashion:

> 'There is no other hint or help in the Act to determine what is or is not bona fide compliance with the Act. To discover the answer one may have to trawl through statute and case law stretching back over 273 years. It has been an interesting, if not entirely satisfactory exercise.'

It must be such as to be regarded as a demand for payment. Where an invoice was produced for negotiation with a third party and, according to the covering email, it had been 'pitched high', it was not a bill of costs in accordance with s 69 of the Solicitors Act 1974: *Kingstons Solicitors v Reiss Solicitors* [2014] EWCA Civ 172. Nor was an invoice lying on the solicitors file which was disclosed to the client but had never been sent: *Parvez v Mooney Everett Solicitors Ltd* [2018] EWHC 62 (QB).

A bill of costs must contain sufficient particulars to enable the client to judge the fairness of the charges. Furthermore, it needs to be sufficiently particularised for (another) solicitor to advise on it and a court to judge the propriety of the various items of which it is composed. Unsurprisingly, in *Re Kingsley* (1978) 122 Sol Jo 457 a bill merely stating 'for professional services' (and without any informative documents in support) was held to be void as inadequate.

This problem has been superseded in the main by two practical answers arising from s 64 of the Solicitors Act 1974. First, in respect of contentious business, the client can require the solicitor to replace the uninformative gross sum bill with a detailed one (for more on this see Chapter 3 at **[3.14]**). The client has to be within various time limits to do so. Sometimes clients ask for some clarification which may (or may not) amount to a request for a fully detailed bill in substitution for the gross sum bill. It is prudent when receiving such a request to write to the client and ascertain precisely what the client wants. At the same time, you can point out that s 64(2) (which gives the client the right to request the detailed bill), entitles you to submit a replacement detailed bill that exceeds the amount of the gross sum bill, if the work done justifies it. In *Parissis v Matthian Gentle Page Hassan LLP (2017)* [2017] EWHC 761 (QB) the solicitor did not answer the client's request and paid the costs of Solicitors Act proceedings notwithstanding that the client paid the bill in full having received a breakdown following a court direction to do so.

Second, the solicitor is required to 'furnish the costs officer with such details of any of the costs covered by the bill as the costs officer may require.' This is translated by the court rules which require, at rule 46.10(2) the solicitor to provide a breakdown of the costs claimed so that the client and the court can see what is being claimed in more detail.

In non-contentious business, a client used to be able to request a Remuneration Certificate to check that the fee charged was fair and reasonable but that route was removed when the relevant Order was repealed (see **[8.15]**).

The law in this area was reviewed by the Court of Appeal in *Ralph Hume Garry (a firm) v Gwillim* [2002] EWCA Civ 1500. A balance must be struck between protection of the client's right to seek a Solicitors Act assessment and the solicitor's right to payment not being defeated by 'opportunistic resort to technicality'. To establish that a bill was not in 'bona fide compliance' with the Act, a client must establish (i) it contained no sufficient narrative to identify what he was being charged for; and (ii) he did not have sufficient knowledge from documents in his possession, or from what he had been told, to take advice about challenging the bill. The more the client knows, the less the need for the bill to spell it out.

In these days of computerised time recording and standard documents generated via case management systems, it is tempting simply to create a bill which merely sets out a mathematical calculation of the time spent because it can be done virtually automatically. But, in the absence of at least a sufficient summary of the work done, such a bill might well be treated by the court as not being a properly delivered bill. Nevertheless, a computer print out can help to provide clients with additional information to a suitable summary as Ward LJ's cri de coeur at the end of *Ralph Hume Garry* makes clear:

> 'I add this postscript for the profession's consideration so that an unseemly dispute of this kind does not happen again. Surely in 2002 every second of time spent, certainly on contentious business, is recorded on the Account Department's computer with a description of the fee-earner, the rate of charging and some description of the work done. A copy of the print-out, adjusted as may be necessary to remove items recorded for administrative purposes but not chargeable to the client, could so easily be rendered and all the problems that have arisen here would be avoided. In these days where there seems to be a need for transparency in all things, is a print-out not the least a client is entitled to expect?'

A full narrative could include details embarrassing to the client who wishes to use the bill as a VAT invoice and there are various methods of preserving this confidentiality, the most usual being to set out the narrative either on a separate sheet or on a tear-off portion at the end of the bill.

Taking account of interim bills

[2.10]

Where interim bills on account have been rendered pursuant to s 65(2) of the Solicitors Act 1974 these should be ignored for the purposes of the final bill and treated as requests for payment of money on account. The final bill should therefore be for the total amount of the solicitor's charges and disbursements with any additional mark-up (or mark-down) on the interim bills and give credit for all payments received as a result of bills on account.

If pursuant to an agreement with your client (or where there have been natural breaks) you have been rendering interim statute bills, each bill is a self-contained account for the work done during the period which it covers. Therefore the final bill will only be for the fees incurred since the period covered by the last interim statute bill.

Unpaid disbursements

[2.11]

The bill may include unpaid disbursements, as well as those that have been paid, but only if they are described in the bill as not yet paid. The defect is fatal to these items if they are challenged on a subsequent assessment (Solicitors Act 1974, s 67). The only remedy would be to ask the costs judge for an adjournment, apply to the court for leave to withdraw the entire bill, re-deliver it and then start again. Even if you were not ordered to pay all the costs thrown away by the client, the economics of starting again will often be questionable.

In *Tearle & Co v Sherring* (29 October 1993, unreported), QBD, Wright J held that where a solicitor has acted in good faith but by inadvertence has omitted to describe disbursements as unpaid, the court not only had power to give him leave to withdraw his bill and deliver another one, to save costs it could in an appropriate case give leave to amend his bill by adding the words 'unpaid'. He tentatively expressed the view that a costs officer might have the same powers.

Section 67 says that, if the bill is assessed, the unpaid disbursement 'shall not be allowed' unless it is paid before the assessment is completed. If the assessment is lengthy, one practical answer would of course be simply for the solicitor to pay the disbursement before the assessment is completed.

Cash account

[2.12]

The first question most solicitors ask in reference to a cash account is 'what is it?' It is defined at sub-paragraph 6.6 in the Practice Direction to Part 46 as an account 'showing money received by the solicitor to the credit of the client and sums paid out of that money on behalf of the client but not payments out which were made in satisfaction of the bill or of any items which are claimed in the bill.'

The breakdown required by CPR 46.10(2) (see **[2.9]**) includes a cash account so that the court can see the whole picture between the solicitor and client. In effect the cash account deals with money expended by the solicitor on behalf of the client for anything which is not in the bill (or which ought to be there).

Items which the solicitor is not bound by law or custom to make, such as purchase money, interest, sums paid into court, or damages, costs paid to an opponent, estate duty and Land Registry fees, are properly charged in the cash account.

Items which should have been included in the bill as disbursements are, for example, court fees, counsel's fees, expenses of witnesses, agents and stationers.

It is important to know what disbursements should appear in the bill itself and what should be charged in the cash account because, perhaps obviously, only those items in the bill can be recovered from the client. Many solicitors lose money on assessments of costs by regarding as cash account entries which should have been disbursements.

Matters are not helped by the fact that definitions of disbursements are only to be found in Victorian cases such as *Re Remnant* (1849) 11 Beav 603. They are said to be 'such payments as the solicitor in the due discharge of his duty is bound to make whether his client furnishes him with money for the purpose, with money on account, or not'. Rather more recent cases such as *Flatman v Germany* [2013] EWCA Civ 278, have skirted round whether there is any worthwhile distinction to be drawn between disbursements and expenses when many of the examples given above are financed by the solicitor rather than paid from money received from the client.

The exception to prove the rule in the previous paragraph is the case of *Herbert v HH Law Ltd* [2019] EWCA Civ 527. The Court of Appeal reviewed the authorities and described the test for deciding which disbursements need to be in the bill of costs as being:

> 'The test is not what is agreed between an individual solicitor and the client but what every solicitor, as such, is obliged to pay irrespective of funding by the client or what is properly included in a bill of costs on assessment as a matter of general custom of the profession.'

The court had no doubt that the ATE premium purchased by the claimant was not a solicitor's disbursement and so should not have been included in the bill. Instead, it should have been in the cash account. This meant that the client could not challenge it via a Solicitors Act assessment. Whilst this makes it less convenient, it does, in our view follow the point reiterated by the court that the ATE policy is a contract between the client and the insurer, not the solicitor.

VALUE ADDED TAX

Does VAT have to be charged at all?

[2.13]

A solicitor's services to his client are subject to VAT at the standard rate unless the solicitor is not registered for VAT or the services are zero-rated. In previous editions we have reproduced a VAT chargeability chart originally produced by Michael Cook in the first edition. It has kept up to date with HM Revenue and Customs published guidance but we have come to the conclusion that the issue it covered – do you have to charge VAT on your services depending upon where your client is based – is becoming progressively more difficult to precis. There is really nothing for it if you are faced with a VAT question but to persevere with HMRC Form 700 and its subordinate documents armed with a cold towel wrapped around your head.

The difficulty is encapsulated by the fact that PD 44, para 2.6 indicates that in case of a dispute about whether VAT is zero-rated or the costs are exempt from VAT, the advice of HMRC is to be obtained, rather than there simply being a certificate from the receiving party's legal representatives or auditors PD 44, para 2.5). In our experience, a case-specific answer is never forthcoming from HMRC.

What rate to charge?

[2.14]

The standard rate of VAT since 4 January 2011 has been 20%. It changed regularly between 2008 and 2011 (between 15% and 17.5%) and it was at the latter rate prior to 1 December 2008.

A VAT invoice is normally raised when the service is completed. However, in circumstances where work is yet to be completed, the rate of VAT to be charged will depend on the date at which the supply of service, the tax point, occurs.

Where the client could claim the VAT as input tax, the difference in rates mattered only modestly to the client. The rate changes did not make much difference to the solicitor either. But if the client was not VAT registered and was liable to pay all the costs at the end, for example, as in a CFA, the difference could be significant. When parties seek to recover costs against their opponents in such circumstances, the bill should be split to reflect the work done in different VAT periods. To do otherwise means the paying party is being asked to pay more than would have been the case if the receiving party had been billed as the case progressed. The Practice Direction to Part 44 assumes that the client will have elected to receive bills at the lower rate and puts the receiving party to the burden of justifying his course of action where this has not been done.

The Tax Point

[2.15]

The basic rule is that the tax point for services is the date on which their performance is completed. VAT becomes payable on that date irrespective of when the bill is delivered.

For solicitors there is a minor exception. If a tax invoice is issued within three months of the basic tax point, the date of the invoice becomes the actual tax point. VAT is therefore payable by a solicitor when the work is completed or when his bill is delivered provided that this is within three months of the completion of the work (HMRC Notice 700.)

Disbursements

[2.16]

In respect of which litigation disbursements should a client be charged VAT? The simple answer is 'none'. Unfortunately this gives rise to the much more complicated question 'what is a disbursement?' The detailed answer is to be found in the VAT Guide (HMRC Notice 700) on the HMRC website, which sets out eight criteria. The test is whether the goods or services are supplied to the solicitor to enable him to render his service to the client, in which event they are not a disbursement and VAT is chargeable. For example, postage, telephone calls, travelling and hotel expenses are not disbursements and VAT must be charged on them. A disbursement is a payment which relates to goods or services supplied to the client, even if it is, in the first place, paid for by the solicitor. Examples are oath and court fees. A method of avoiding VAT on a payment which would otherwise attract VAT, such as an air fare, is for the client to pay for it direct. The solicitor need not then include it in his account.

VAT on medical reports?

[2.17]

In *Barratt v HMRC and The Law Society* [2011] Costs LR 409 the First-tier Tribunal judge accepted the proposition that although the use of medical reports and records is part of the legal services provided and upon which VAT was already charged as part of the tax payable on the lawyer's fees, the 'obtaining' of the reports was a separate service carried out, as an agent, on behalf of the injured party, and any expense incurred was merely a disbursement and so not subject to VAT.

The Court of Appeal, in *British Airways plc v Prosser* [2019] EWCA Civ 547, [2019] 1 WLR 4513, [2019] SWTI 956, considered *Barratt* might be correctly decided where the solicitor instructed the medical expert directly. Where a Medical Reporting Organisation was involved, it would usually be the case that it should charge VAT on both its own efforts and those of the expert. The court made it clear that the 'economic and commercial reality' needed to be considered with reference to who did what work in any particular case.

Counsel's fees

[2.18]

The fees of counsel are part of the service rendered by the solicitor and should therefore be included in the solicitor's bill and attract VAT even if the barrister is not registered for VAT. However, there is a long-standing concession under which HMRC permit solicitors to re-address counsel's fee notes to the lay client, who then makes payment direct (or is requested by the solicitor to return the fee note to him with a separate cheque payable to counsel) so that counsel's fees do not pass through the solicitor's books at all. Where this is done the fees of the unregistered barrister do not attract VAT, and the solicitor avoids incurring VAT liability on counsel's fees because he need not include them in his VAT quarterly return.

VAT on fixed costs recovered

[2.19]

Fixed costs recovered under CPR Rule 45 Part I contain no element of VAT. The solicitor may either divide the fixed costs into profit costs and VAT and simply charge the client an amount equal to the fixed costs recovered; or he may charge the client VAT on top of the fixed costs as if the opponent had specifically paid the VAT exclusive sum: in both cases giving credit for the sum recovered. VAT is recoverable from the opponent in the normal way under the remainder of CPR Rule 45, for example on fast track trial fixed costs, provided the client is not registered for VAT.

Insurance claims

(a) Policy holder can recover VAT

[2.20]

If the insurance relates to the client's business and it is VAT registered the client will be able to take a full input tax credit for the VAT on the solicitor's bill. In these circumstances the insurers will only be responsible to their policy holder for the amount of the solicitor's bill exclusive of VAT.

Where the policy holder does not pay the VAT element, the insurer will generally meet this part of the solicitor's fee as well because the only alternative, the solicitor writing off the VAT output tax, disadvantages the solicitor and so is not really an alternative.

(b) Policy holder cannot recover VAT

[2.21]

Where the client is partly exempt, or the insurance does not relate to his business, or he is not VAT registered, the solicitor's bill must still be addressed to the client and include VAT. In the circumstances there is no objection to the client sending the entire bill to the insurers for payment, as previously. If, for internal accounting purposes, the insurers wish solicitors to issue invoices directly to them, this may be done but the invoice so delivered will not be a VAT invoice.

Solicitors Act claims

[2.22]

It may seem obvious but it still escapes many that a solicitor whose bills are being assessed is representing himself in Solicitors Act proceedings. As such his work in those proceedings is not a taxable supply for the purposes of VAT and so no VAT is chargeable and therefore payable on any costs that are awarded. If he instructs another firm of solicitors, costs lawyers or counsel to represent him, their VAT is also not recoverable from the opponent. It is recoverable by the solicitor as input tax as with any other VAT registered client.

CHAPTER 3

RECOVERY OF COSTS FROM CLIENTS

INTRODUCTION TO THE RECOVERY OF COSTS FROM CLIENTS

[3.1]

Litigation is meant to be the last resort and never a truer statement was made in the context of solicitors and their clients. Things have normally gone badly wrong if you are contemplating the issuing of proceedings or taking other forceful steps to recover your fees from your client. The irrecoverable cost of pursuing the client – in terms of lost fee earning and management time – should make you stop and consider whether a deal, any deal, with this client might be better in the long run. Learning lessons on what to do (or not do) next time will be more palatable if a large amount of the costs of pursuing the client are not thrown away in addition. In particular, is your client going to be able to pay the sum assessed by the court or is his non-payment of bills to date a clue that he cannot pay you even if he wanted to do so? Many a complaint about negligent work has been made to cover up a lack of cash.

In this Chapter we look at what needs to be done before commencing proceedings as well as during them; what rights the client has to request further and better information as well as an assessment itself; and what steps you might take outside assessment proceedings, including enforcement options to recoup your fees.

BEFORE ISSUING

Credit Checks

[3.2]

Unless you know your client's finances very well, now is the time to make some enquiries. Many accounts departments have direct access to online checks as part of the Know Your Client procedures.

Final bill

[3.3]

It is essential that a final bill in the form and content described in Chapter 2 has been delivered. Where there has been a series of interim bills on account no proceedings may be commenced until the delivery of a final statute bill. This bill should be for the entirety of the work done and disbursements incurred throughout, either at the agreed charging rate or the direct cost with an appropriate mark-up in light of all the factors including the outcome of the matter, giving credit for payments received.

The foregoing paragraph represents the position as it should be. However, it is not uncommon for there to be a challenge as to whether any of the bills before the court are actually statute bills capable of being assessed under the Solicitors Act. If the client can establish that the bills said to be rendered by the solicitor as statute bills are only payments on account, then the client's rights to assessment are preserved because the time for challenging the fees has not begun to run. An example of this is *Vlamaki v Sookias & Sookias* [2015] EWHC 3334 (QB), where Walker J upheld Master Campbell's view that the bills rendered were plagued with ambiguity and so found in favour of the client. (The final invoice was clearly insufficient to found a 'Chamberlain' arrangement (see next paragraph).)

Alternatively, courts have been prepared to conclude that the disputed bills, when taken as a series, amount to statutorily compliant bills, particularly when the retainer has clearly ended and there would be no benefit in the solicitor having to serve a variation upon his previously rendered bill to comply with a statutory requirement. Such bills are sometimes called 'Chamberlain' bills following the decision in *Chamberlain v Boodle and King (a firm)* [1982] 3 All ER 188, [1982] 1 WLR 1443, CA.

Signature

[3.4]

Although not essential to the validity of the bill, a solicitor may not sue for his costs unless he has complied with the requirements of the Solicitors Act 1974, s 69 as to signature.

Until 7 March 2008, s 69 of the Solicitors Act 1974 provided that a solicitor's bill of costs to the client must be signed by the solicitor or one of his partners, either in his own name, or in the name of the firm (or be accompanied by a letter which is so signed and refers to the bill). For bills delivered after 7 March 2008, the Legal Services Act 2007 amended s 69 to enable a bill to be signed on the solicitor's behalf by an employee authorised by the solicitor to sign.

The practical difference between a bill which is valid but unenforceable by court proceedings because it is not signed and an invalid bill, is that the former entitles a solicitor to appropriate money paid on account in settlement of the bill or to exercise a lien until the bill is paid, while the latter is of no effect for any purpose. However, if an action on a defective bill gets before the court, the judge has the discretion in appropriate circumstances to give leave for the bill to be withdrawn and replaced without commencing fresh proceedings (*Zuliani v Veira* [1994] 1 WLR 1149, PC).

Delivery of bill

[3.5]

The Solicitors Act 1974, s 69(2)(b) also provides that the bill must be delivered to the client either personally or by being sent to him by post to, or left for him at, his place of business, dwelling house or last known place of abode.

In *Parvez v Mooney Everett Solicitors Ltd* [2018] EWHC 62 (QB), the client obtained a copy of the solicitors' file and upon it lay an invoice which had not been sent to her. In response to the client's request for a statute bill to be delivered to her, a different document was served by the solicitors. The client nevertheless brought proceedings in which she sought to have assessed the invoice in the solicitors' papers. The district judge found that she was not entitled to an assessment because the document was not a statute bill. On appeal, Soole J upheld the district judge and, as part of further arguments regarding the de facto delivery of the bill, made it clear that it had not been delivered. Section 68 required the delivery of a bill and not a specified document. It was a matter for the solicitors as to the form of the bill they decided to deliver to their client.

In *Richard Slade & Co v Abbhi* [2019] EWHC 355 (Comm), the defendant funded his father in law's case by giving him money to forward to the solicitors. Although he had previously been found to be a party with a primary liability and not simply a guarantor (see [**1.3**]), the specific arrangements were not sufficient to support his argument that he should have been served with the bills (and that as such his time for challenging them had not begun to run).

Elapse of one month

[3.6]

One month must have elapsed since the delivery of the bill unless the client is about to: quit England and Wales; become bankrupt or to compound with his creditors or do any other act which tends to prevent or delay the solicitor obtaining payment. In these circumstances the solicitor can seek leave to issue proceedings within a month (Solicitors Act 1974, s 69(1)).

No application or order for a detailed assessment

[3.7]

The client must not have either made an application to the court for a detailed assessment of the costs within one month of delivery of the bill or obtained an order for the bill to be assessed, in either of which events no action may be commenced on the bill or proceeded with until the assessment is completed: Solicitors Act 1974, s 70(1), (2).

Client information

[3.8]

All of the SRA Codes (see Chapter 1) require clients to be informed of their right to challenge or complain about a solicitor's bill. The requisite information nowadays is generally printed on the paper used for creating the firm's bills (or embedded in templates) so that it is there without having to remember it. A lack of such information is a pointer that the bill is not a statute bill at all.

Limitation Act 1980

[3.9]

As with any contract, proceedings must be commenced within six years from the day after the cause of action arose, otherwise the claim would be statute barred by the Limitation Act 1980 (*Marren v Dawson Bentley & Co Ltd* [1961] 2 QB 135, [1961] 2 All ER 270). This is when the solicitor becomes entitled to his fees under the retainer whether or not they have been quantified and irrespective of the requirement that one month must have expired since the bill was delivered before proceedings may be commenced. The Act provides for an extension of the six-year period where the client acknowledges or part pays the debt during the initial six years.

The recoverable costs trap

[3.10]

Unless the solicitor and client have entered into a written agreement pursuant to CPR Rule 46.9(2) expressly permitting payment to a solicitor of an amount of costs greater than that which the client could have recovered from another party in the proceedings, the Solicitors Act 1974, s 74(3), limits the solicitor's entitlement to that amount (in county court proceedings).

In other words, there is no point pursuing a client for bills of costs which exceed the sums recovered from the other side if you do not have an express written agreement with your client allowing you to do so.

Reference to this point was made by the Regional Costs Judge sitting in the County Court at Birmingham in *A and M (by their father and litigation friend MS) v Royal Mail Group* (18 September 2015). The success fee and ATE premium were being sought from the child claimants' damages since they were no longer recoverable from the defendant. The solicitors' retainer made no reference to disapplying s 74(3). Consequently, if the solicitors were to seek further costs from the litigation friend on a solicitor and client assessment, they might well be limited to the recoverable costs obtained at the approval hearing.

APPLICATIONS BY THE SOLICITOR

Where to start

[3.11]

A solicitor can sue for his fees in the High Court using a Part 7 Claim Form. But if the client disputes only the amount of the bill, usually on an application for summary judgment, the order will direct that the bill be referred to a costs judge and that the solicitor be entitled to sign judgment for the costs as assessed, together with the costs of the action. The client can also obtain such an order by making an application in an existing action under CPR Part 23.

More usually a solicitor brings proceedings to have his costs assessed under the Solicitors Act 1974 by using CPR Part 8 (as modified by CPR 67.3) if it is an originating application (as is usually the case) or CPR Part 23 in existing proceedings.

The application is normally made in the Senior Courts Costs Office. But, where a solicitor's bill of costs relates wholly or partly to contentious business done in the County Court and the amount of the bill does not exceed £5,000, then the powers of the court relating to assessment of the solicitor's bill under the Solicitors Act 1974, ss 70 and 71 may be exercised and performed by the County Court (s 69(3)).

The Claim Form is accompanied by the bill (or bills) to be assessed. There are model precedents in the Schedule of Costs Precedents to the CPR to assist. Precedent J is the model Claim Form. If the costs relate to a CFA, a copy of that agreement also needs to accompany the Claim Form.

Default judgments and interim payments

[3.12]

There is no mechanism for a default judgment or default costs certificate in solicitor and client assessment because CPR 47.11 is disapplied. But there is no similar disapplication of CPR 44.2(8) and so the court ought to consider making an interim payment order unless there is good reason not to do so. If such an order is not made, the solicitor can seek an interim payment on account of costs using the procedure set out in Part 25. Where the client has commenced proceedings within one month of receiving the bill, an interim payment cannot be ordered, at least when giving directions as part of the initial order for an assessment of the solicitor's bill to take place (s 70(1)).

APPLICATIONS BY THE CLIENT

Application for delivery of a bill

[3.13]

Section 68 of the Solicitors Act 1974 empowers the court on an application by the client to order the solicitor to deliver a bill. The jurisdiction in the High Court extends to all cases, including those in which no business has been done by the solicitor in the High Court, while the County Court has similar jurisdiction where the bill of costs relates wholly or partly to contentious business done by the solicitor in that court. There are two common circumstances which may give rise to such an application. The first is where the solicitor attempts to retain money paid on account without having delivered an adequate bill. The second is where the solicitor makes what the client regards as an excessive demand for an interim payment on account.

In respect of the first of these situations, a spate of applications under s 68 were heard by the SCCO and in a number of courts around the country. In one of those cases, *Hanley v JC&A Solicitors Ltd*, the costs judge gave permission to appeal and Soole J delivered judgment in favour of the solicitors ([2018] EWHC 2592 (QB)). He decided that there was no inherent jurisdiction to order the solicitors to provide copies of documents which were their own property, nor did s 68 provide the jurisdiction to do so. He did not expressly comment on whether solicitors should provide copies of documents previously sent to clients who had then lost them (a seemingly common occurrence). But he did suggest that solicitors might not 'press their rights to the legal limit' where a document such as a CFA was needed by the client to consider whether to bring proceedings under s 70.

This has not been a killer blow to the applications being made under s 68 and it may be because the documents sought are not necessarily required to contemplate the bringing of proceedings under s 70. It would be a difficult argument for the solicitors to run that they have never rendered a formal bill to their client but should not have to produce a bill in response to the application. As such a simple application for a bill under s 68 ought not to be controversial. The disputed aspect has been the requesting of all of the solicitors' papers. Since the costs have been paid, there is no question of a lien. It is simply a matter of which documents the client is entitled to see and what fees, if any, the solicitors are entitled to charge for producing them. Unfortunately, Soole J was not asked to provide an answer to these questions.

Application for further information

[3.14]

Section 64(2) provides that the client may, before he is served with proceedings and within three months of the date on which the bill was delivered to him (whichever is the earlier), require the solicitor to deliver a bill containing detailed items in lieu of the original bill. This has the dramatic consequence that the gross sum bill is of no effect. Accordingly, the solicitor is no longer bound by the amount of the gross sum bill and he is free to deliver a detailed bill for a higher amount if his new calculations justify this (*Polak v Marchioness of Winchester* [1956] 2 All ER 660, [1956] 1 WLR 818, CA). The court's invariable practice of requiring a breakdown to be provided – now enshrined in the Practice Direction to Part 46 (see 'Directions' below) – means that applications under s 64(2) are perhaps less important than when *Polak* was decided. Nevertheless, it is an important right for a client to use for the understandable wish to resolve matters outside any formal court proceedings.

Application to set aside a Contentious or Non-Contentious Business Agreement

[3.15]

Contentious and Non-Contentious Business Agreements are considered in Chapter 8. Their aim is to make all of the terms of the agreement clear and definite. The attraction for the solicitor is that the agreement reached as to fees within the (N)CBA is then enforceable without the rigmarole of a detailed assessment. The (N)CBA can only be set aside if the client can show that it is unfair or unreasonable as a whole. It is intended to be a difficult test to achieve. But, the result is that in practice they are set aside for a lack of certainty in their terms more often than because they are inherently unfair. In order to create room for argument, an application to set aside a CBA needs to be made when the solicitor applies for leave to enforce the agreement. If it is a (N)CBA, then the application can be made in the response to the Part 8 proceedings or as a free standing application by the client.

Application for detailed assessment

[3.16]

The Solicitors Act 1974 tries to reward those clients who actively deal with their solicitors' costs and puts to the test those who sit on their hands. The solicitor has to wait for one month from the delivery of his bill before commencing proceedings (see **[3.6]** above). If the client applies to the court within this time for the costs to be assessed, the court will automatically grant such application. Furthermore there will be no requirement for the client to pay any money into court and no other proceedings can be commenced by the solicitor until the bill has been assessed.

If the client makes the application between one and twelve months from delivery of the bill, the court may order the assessment on such terms as it thinks fit and order a stay on any proceedings that the solicitor has commenced in the meantime.

If the client waits until after 12 months have expired, the court will only make an order if 'special circumstances' can be shown (see below).

These time limits apply if there has been no payment of the bill and suggest that there is a dispute between the solicitor and client. Where the client has paid the bill and then seeks to have the court assess it, the requirements are more strict after the first month. If the request is made between 1 and 12 months of payment of the bill, the client will need to show 'special circumstances' for the court to order an assessment. If the request is made after 12 months then the court has no power to make such an order. These provisions of the Solicitors Act s 70 may be presented in the following table.

Bill not paid	Bill paid	The Court . . .
Application made within 1 month of receiving the bill.	Application made within 1 month of paying the bill.	. . . will automatically make an order for assessment.
Application made more than 1 month and less than 12 months of receiving the bill.	–	. . . may make an order for assessment on such terms as it sees fit.
Application made after 12 months of receiving the bill.	Application made after 1 month but within 12 months of paying the bill.	. . . will only make an order for assessment if 'special circumstances' are demonstrated.
–	Application made more than 12 months after paying the bill.	. . . has no power to make an order for assessment.

What if the client has partly paid the bill? Part payment is insufficient to treat the client as having paid and so the 'Bill not paid' column above will apply (see eg *Rippon Patel and French LLP v Mowlam* [2020] EWHC 1079 (QB)).

The client may well be a litigant in person and the court will be more concerned with substance than form where the client has made the application. In *Szekeres v Alan Smeath & Co* [2005] EWHC 1733 (Ch), defects in the client's claim form seeking the detailed assessment of eight bills of costs did not prevent the proceedings having been validly commenced within one month. Accordingly the costs judge had been in error by refusing to make an order for detailed assessment of the bills because of the formal deficiencies.

What are special circumstances?

[3.17]

Where 12 months have expired from the delivery of the bill or after a judgment has been obtained or where the bill has been paid within 12 months of the application, no order shall be made except in 'special circumstances' (s 70(3)).

The cases are inevitably fact specific and as such previous case law simply provides examples of what was considered to be a special circumstance in that particular case. In *Falmouth House Freehold Co Ltd v Morgan Walker LLP* [2010] EWHC 3092 (Ch), Lewinson J reviewed a number of older cases when considering how the Costs Judge had dealt with the issue in 2010. He stated that whether special circumstances exist is essentially a value judgment. It depended on comparing the particular case with the run-of-the-mill case, in order to decide whether a detailed assessment was justified despite the restrictions contained in s 70(3). The Court of Appeal had said previously (in *Re Cheesman* (1891) 2 Ch 289 CA) that it would not interfere with the decision of the first-instance judge on whether special circumstances existed except in a strong case. That was especially so, according to Lewinson J, where the value judgment had been made by a specialist costs judge.

In *Falmouth House* the costs judge had taken into account the fact that an invoice called for an explanation. It was also for a large sum which was something that could be taken into account.

In *Kralj v Birkbeck Montague* (18 February 1988, unreported), CA the Court of Appeal found special circumstances where the solicitors had dissuaded their client from having their costs assessed and had charged her substantially more than was recovered between the parties, including such items as time spent with law reporters. In *A v BCD (a firm)* (5 June 1997, unreported), QBD, the court observed that the word used was 'special' and not 'exceptional'. The court also dismissed the practice of a client paying a bill in full while unilaterally 'reserving the right' to have the bill assessed. Although the solicitor could, by agreement in return for payment, waive the right to resist an order for assessment out of time, the most the client could do was to pay under protest and deploy the protest as a special circumstance if possible. In *Arrowfield Services v BP Collins* SCCO Case No 15 of 2003 the Court held that it was difficult to conceive of a more powerful special circumstance for assessing a bill out of time than where the solicitor has agreed to such an assessment, because by his agreement that the assessment should take place, he had apparently agreed that the protection given to him by the time limits should not apply.

Interestingly, in *Re Metal Distributors (UK) Ltd* [2004] EWHC 2535 (Ch), it was held that the refusal of solicitors to provide a breakdown of their costs, whether or not it was good client management, did not amount to special circumstances justifying an application being made after the expiration of the 12-month period.

No power after 12 months following payment

[3.18]

Even where there are special circumstances, the court has no power to order an assessment on an application by the client after the expiration of 12 months from the payment of the bill. It is important to remember that this provision also affects third parties liable to meet the solicitor's bill to his client, such as mortgagors and lessors. This cannot be circumvented by resorting to the inherent jurisdiction of the court: *Harrison v Tew* [1990] 2 AC 523, [1990] 1 All ER 321, HL.

A third party should be aware of the risk of losing their right to an assessment as the result of this provision. If a mortgagee has paid his solicitor's costs in respect of possession proceedings which resulted in a suspended order, and added those costs to the mortgage debt, the mortgagor may not discover this until long after the 12-month period has expired. It would therefore be prudent for the mortgagor after any such litigation to ascertain the amount of the mortgagee's solicitor's costs so that an application for an assessment may be made within the requisite time.

Payment means full payment of the invoice and not only part of it. For example, see *Rippon Patel and French LLP v Mowlam* [2020] EWHC 1079 (QB) where, at most, the client had paid only the VAT exclusive sum and was entitled to bring proceedings several years after the bill had been rendered (having also been able to demonstrate that special circumstances existed).

Challenging the level of costs only

[3.19]

However, all is not lost if you are acting for the client. While the right to a detailed assessment has been lost, the common law right to make a claimant (here, the solicitor) prove the quantum of an unspecified claim remains. Accordingly, if a solicitor sues on its invoices, the client can defend quantum on the basis that, like other forms of damages, the claimant has to prove its loss. The obvious judges to ascertain the loss are costs judges and so the case can be put before them for a judicial assessment. This may be more along the lines of a quantum meruit trial than a detailed assessment but it prevents a solicitor claimant from obtaining a default judgment for whatever sum the solicitor saw fit to bill. This line of authority comes from the Court of Appeal decision in *Watts (Thomas) & Co (a firm) v Smith* [1998] 2 Costs LR 59, CA). The Court of Appeal heard a further case the following year (*Turner & Co v O Palomo SA* [1999] 4 All ER 353, [2000] 1 WLR 37, CA) which followed *Watts*. The bill was ordered to be sent for assessment (but not for detailed assessment) by a costs judge. The one-fifth rule does not apply to a common law assessment and so the client will be liable for the assessment costs unless he makes a Part 36 offer since otherwise the solicitor will be the 'winner' and entitled to its costs (see *Ahmud & Co Solicitors v Macpherson* [2015] EWHC 2240 (QB)).

A further option for an individual client is to bring a claim in accordance with the Consumer Rights Act 2015. Sections 54–56 entitle a client to a price reduction by an appropriate amount in certain circumstances. The right to a price reduction is dependent upon giving the solicitor the opportunity to repeat the service provided within a reasonable time and without any significant inconvenience (presumably including cost) to the client. If a repeat performance proves to be impossible, the client can go straight for a price reduction (or refund). Even if repeating the work is possible, it is unlikely to be attractive to either the client or solicitor. The threat of repeating the work may make you decide to negotiate with a client rather than having to do so, even if the client's time for challenging a bill they have paid has already expired.

Directions

[3.20]

Upon receipt of the court file the judge will usually list a directions hearing at which he will give directions for a breakdown of the bill to be served by the solicitor. The breakdown includes both 'details of the work done' and a cash account (see **[2.12]** above). Breakdowns are usually drafted in a very similar way to a bill of costs. But there is no requirement for the breakdown to be signed and nor for it to be produced as an electronic bill even if the work was done after 6 April 2018.

Thereafter the directions will deal with service of Points of Dispute (often including an entitlement to inspect the solicitor's files by the client or his representative beforehand) and any Replies. Standard directions also include a stay on any proceedings for the bills in question and a resolution of the solicitors' lien on papers once the bills have been assessed.

Depending upon the circumstances of the case, the judge may also give directions as to evidence to deal with disputes of fact or to have a 'special circumstances' (see [**3.17**]) hearing before requiring any other directions to be followed.

Once the directions have been complied with the parties may then request a hearing date if no settlement has been reached. There is a specific Notice to be used (N258C) and the appropriate fee for a detailed assessment has to be paid. The court will then fix a date for the hearing. In practice at the SCCO a date will often have been provisionally fixed as part of the directions being given.

In *Eurasian Natural Resources Corpn Ltd v Dechert LLP* [2016] EWCA Civ 375, the Court of Appeal agreed with Roth J that an application by the claimant for the detailed assessment to be heard in private should be allowed. There was no particular public interest on the facts of that case for holding the hearing in public and the subject matter underlying the claim for costs involved confidential information.

ENRC subsequently began separate proceedings alleging professional negligence against Dechert LLP. In accordance with long standing convention, the detailed assessment proceedings were stayed. In *Stephenson Harwood LL v Geneva Trust Co SA* (QBD) (Comm) (24/05/19), the parties disagreed upon the appropriate forum for the dispute. Teare J decided that the Commercial Court was the better place for disputed allegations of negligence etc to be determined (which is exactly why the SCCO convention came about).

Basis of assessment

[3.21]

This is the indemnity basis used for some between the parties' assessments. It is sometimes described as being a 'modified indemnity basis' because CPR 46.9(3) says that costs are to be presumed to be reasonably incurred and/or reasonable in amount if they have been expressly or impliedly approved by the client. However, they will be presumed to be unreasonably incurred if they are unusual in nature or amount and the solicitor did not tell the client they might not be recovered from the opponent on assessment.

You might question what is left of the indemnity basis after these significant presumptions have been imposed. The answer in a nutshell is that there is no proportionality test to be imposed, as there would be if the costs were assessed on the standard basis. The other distinction between standard and indemnity basis costs is the reversal of the benefit of the doubt (so that it is in favour of the solicitor as the receiving party). But 'where there's no doubt, there's no difference' and the presumptions in CPR 46.9(3) go a long way to dispelling any doubt the court might have on most items in the bill.

Where an item of costs is considered unusual in nature or amount, the question will often be whether the client was properly informed of its unusual nature. The client needs to give 'informed consent' (see *MacDougall v Boote Edgar Esterkin* [2001] 1 Costs LR 118) and so the fact that the issue has been covered in, for example, the client care letter is not necessarily going to be sufficient to maintain the presumption of reasonableness. The Court of Appeal in *Herbert v HH Law Ltd* [2019] EWCA Civ 527 revisited this area and confirmed that the fact the written material was not misleading was conclusive proof that the client was bound by its terms. Nevertheless, the client could still seek to prove that the information was insufficient to allow an informed consent. The court considered how this question should be evidenced. At para 38 it said:

> 'We consider that where, as here, the client brings proceedings under the Solicitors Act 1974 s.70(1), it is for the client to state the point of dispute and the grounds for it. If the solicitor wishes to rebut the challenge by relying on the presumption in CPR 46.9(3)(a) or (b), the burden lies on the solicitor to show that the pre-condition of the presumption, informed approval, is satisfied. Once the solicitor has adduced evidence to show that the client gave informed consent, the evidential burden will move to the client to show why, as a result of having been given insufficiently clear or accurate or comprehensive information by the solicitor or for some other reason, there was no consent or it was not informed consent. The overall burden of showing that informed consent was given remains on the solicitor.'

In *Herbert*, Soole J had upheld the district judge's decision that a 100% success fee for a rear end shunt was unusual and should have been discussed with the client. The solicitors' argument was that, in a post-LASPO environment, the best way to run a business of low value personal injury claims was to seek 100% success fees from each client subject to the statutory limit of 25% of some of the damages (see **[4.9]** for details). This approach filled the hole left by success fees no longer being recoverable and was more equitable than other options considered such as higher hourly rates. There was no point, in such circumstances, in completing individual risk assessments or, by implication, discussing the matter with the client specifically. Such arguments cut no ice with the Court of Appeal who determined that claiming a 100% success fee in every case was an unusual approach and so the client's informed consent should have been obtained.

The fact that costs might not be recovered from the other party needs to be treated with some caution. Too literal an approach regarding non-recoverability making an item unusual leads down a path to the costs allowed between solicitor and client being no more than essentially on a standard basis. Where, as in *Herbert*, the item of cost is not recoverable from the opponent (there the ATE premium) there can be no presumption that its irrecoverability makes it unusual.

Costs of the assessment

[3.22]

The award of costs of the proceedings is not left to the discretion of the judge in the way of between the parties' assessments. Section 70(9) expects the order made to be based on the outcome. If one-fifth of the amount of the bill or more is disallowed, the solicitor pays the costs, if not, the client pays. There is some discretion left to the assessing judge by s 70(10) but he has to certify that there are 'special circumstances' relating to the bill, or the assessment of it, to vary the one-fifth rule. Where some of the costs claimed are outside the scope of the solicitor's retainer, they will be disallowed on assessment for want of retainer. But when it comes to considering the extent of the sums disallowed – and therefore who should pay the costs under the one-fifth rule – such costs will be taken into account: *Bentine and Bentine v The Official Solicitor and Wilsons Solicitors LLP* [2015] EWCA Civ 1168.

In *Stone Rowe Brewer v Just Costs Ltd*, heard by the Court of Appeal at the same time as *Bentine*, the parties reached agreement prior to the hearing on the costs payable based on 15 bills rendered by the defendant. But the parties could not agree on who should pay the costs of the proceedings. The agreed sum represented a reduction of 29% on the aggregate of the bills. As such the costs of the proceedings would be the claimant's, absent any special circumstances. Master O'Hare considered that there were such circumstances. Most of the costs were comprised in five bills and of those five, four had been recovered in their entirety by the defendant. Master O'Hare awarded costs to the defendant but reduced them to reflect the one bill of the five large bills which had been reduced and the other ten smaller bills which had also been reduced by agreement. He awarded the defendant 70% of its costs. The Court of Appeal accepted that Master O'Hare was entitled to conclude that special circumstances existed. The majority upheld the resulting order albeit Sir Bernard Rix considered that the costs judge should have taken the starting point (costs to the claimant) into consideration when deciding what order to make. The court confirmed that 'special circumstances' under s 70(10) involves the same test as 'special circumstances' under s 70(3) (see **[3.17]**).

A client may seek an order for detailed assessment (see **[3.16]**). Where he does so, and with this provision in mind, the client may think it prudent to limit the order to the profit costs only if there are substantial disbursements which he does not wish to challenge or, conversely, limited to counsel's or expert's fees if these are all that he wishes to challenge (s 70(6)).

It is important to appreciate that any breakdown ordered by the court is for the purposes of the assessment only and it is still the original bill delivered to the client that at the end of the assessment will be either upheld or reduced. Accordingly, although the detailed breakdown may quite properly justify a figure considerably higher than the amount of the bill, it is of no relevance to the question of whether or not the bill has been reduced by one-fifth.

One slightly peculiar aspect to s 70(9) is that if the client does not attend the detailed assessment (and the proceedings had been started by the solicitor rather than the client) the one-fifth rule does not apply. It may be that no costs are payable but it is more likely that the court will consider the imposition of a costs order based on special circumstances where the client has not settled the costs prior to a hearing and then not turned up for it.

THIRD PARTIES

[3.23]

Section 71(1) of the Solicitors Act 1974 provides that a person, other than the client, who is liable to pay a bill either to the solicitor or to the client may apply to the High Court for an order for the assessment of the bill as if he were the client, and the court may make the same order (if any) as it might have made if the application had been made by the client.

Although the assessment must be conducted as between the solicitor and his client, a third party does not, by obtaining an order to assess, increase his liability to the solicitor's client. For example, if a mortgagor has the costs of the mortgagee's solicitor assessed, items which the mortgagor would not be liable to pay as between himself and the mortgagee will be disallowed even if the solicitor is entitled to charge them against his client, the mortgagee (*Re Longbotham & Sons* [1904] 2 Ch 152, 73 LJ Ch 681, CA).

Mortgagee's costs (and similar)

[3.24]

What is the position where one party is contractually obliged to meet the costs of the other party? For example, a bank takes steps to enforce a mortgage against its borrower, using solicitors in the process. It claims to be entitled to recover all of its costs from the borrower, including those for which it is liable to the solicitor. It can do so directly or sometimes, more easily, by deduction from the proceeds of the sale of the mortgaged property. It may have no particular incentive to query the amount of the solicitor's bill of costs. It agrees those costs and pays them. The borrower wishes to challenge the amount recoverable from it by way of the solicitor's costs.

At first sight, this looks to be the sort of situation for which s 71 was drafted. The borrower is the party liable to pay the costs rather than the solicitor's client, namely the bank. If the client has not yet paid anything in respect of the bill (or only sums on account which are less than the amount properly allowable) then the s 71 assessment may be useful to the third party, because he should not be liable to pay more than the amount so certified.

But the situation is not so straightforward where the bank (in this case) has already paid the solicitors' charges from the sale proceeds. Any reductions on assessment will not actually reduce the solicitors' fees because they have been paid. Indeed, they have been paid by the borrower from the sale proceeds which would otherwise go to the borrower. To the extent that there is any repayment to be made (because a particular item is not recoverable as against the borrower) the shortfall would need to be paid by the bank as the client.

In these circumstances, the case of *Tim Martin Interiors Ltd v Akin Gump LLP* [2011] EWCA Civ 1574 suggests that the third party ought to bring proceedings against the client to establish how much was due from him to the client. In a mortgage case such as in *Tim Martin Interiors*, the proceedings would be conventional proceedings for an account of what was due under the mortgage. Such proceedings would enable the court to determine the correct issue as between the correct parties, and if appropriate to order repayment by the mortgagee to the mortgagor. In such proceedings it would be possible for the court to do what cannot be done under a s 71 assessment, namely to disallow part of an amount claimed on the basis that something was due, but not as much as is claimed – for example by substituting a lower hourly rate.

Instead of seeking an assessment under s 71, therefore, in almost all cases a mortgagor or other party seeking to challenge the costs claimed and received by a mortgagee, the mortgagor should, according to the Court of Appeal, bring a claim for an account of the sums due under the mortgage.

Lloyd LJ concluded his judgment in *Tim Martin Interiors* by saying:

> 'In the light of this judgment it may be anticipated that third party assessments will become rare, whereas claims for an account, and like proceedings in other types of case, where the real issue is as to the reasonableness of legal costs, best resolved by those experienced in the assessment of costs, may become much more frequent. With that in mind, it seems to me that it might be sensible for a dispute which is only, or mainly, about legal costs to be able to be commenced as an application for an account directly in the SCCO, rather than having to go via the Chancery Division.'

One situation in which a third party cannot bring Solicitors Act proceedings is where liquidators of a company wish to challenge solicitors' fees agreed by the administrators whilst in office. The remedy, if any, is in misfeasance proceedings against the administrators: *Hosking (as joint liquidators of Hellas Telecommunications (Luxembourg) II SCA) v Slaughter and May* [2016] EWCA Civ 474.

Residuary beneficiaries

[3.25]

Such beneficiaries are able to complain and to expect the solicitor to respond to the matter under the solicitors' complaints handling procedure. This is in line with a residuary beneficiary's ability to seek third party assessment of costs under s 71(1) of the Solicitors Act 1974, whether or not the solicitor is an executor of the estate.

It is obviously good practice for solicitors to provide relevant client care information to residuary beneficiaries for reference at the outset, together with costs estimates and any later revisions. If a residuary beneficiary complains to the firm at any point in the administration, then this should be dealt with in the same manner as you would handle a complaint from a client.

A claim for an account as per the *Tim Martin* guidance might be thought an option in the case of a trust or the administration of an estate. But in *Richenda Chopping v Cowan and Dewey (17 April 2013)*, Master Marsh in the Chancery Division decided that an inquiry of the sort contemplated by Lloyd LJ was not made out. Whilst the master was careful to limit his comments to the case before him, it seems clear from the decision that he thought this would be so in any other case brought against a professional who has incurred fees in administering an estate. The indication given was that *Tim Martin* proceedings were more likely to be appropriate in mortgagee cases.

In *Mussell & Williams v Patience & Patience* [2018] EWHC 430 (Ch), HHJ Mathews, a former colleague of Master Marsh, took a similar view of the effectiveness of beneficiaries challenging the legal costs incurred by an executor of an estate. In essence, the executor did not have to provide sufficient information for the beneficiaries to decide whether to bring proceedings under s 71. All that had to be shown was that work had been done in the 'fair execution' of administering the estate. A receipt coupled with an invoice was all that was required (see also **[38.6]**).

RECOVERY WITHOUT PROCEEDINGS

[3.26]

There are two strands to this part of the Chapter. The first is to look at the use of Statutory Demands and Insolvency Petitions as an aggressive manoeuvre outside the general civil court approach. The second is to consider the use of the solicitors' lien as a method by which a client may be forced to compromise with his solicitor over fees in order to deal with his case.

STATUTORY DEMAND

[3.27]

Service of a statutory demand for payment of a solicitor's costs does not constitute the bringing of an action for the purposes of the Solicitors Act 1974, s 69(1) which prohibits solicitors from bringing any action to recover costs within one month of delivery of their bill without special leave of the court. The consequence, to which a statutory demand leads if not complied with, is a presumption that the debtor is unable to pay the debt in question. This, in turn, enables the creditor to present a bankruptcy or winding up petition. In general the court should exercise its discretion to set aside the statutory demand if, but only if, it would not be just for those consequences to apply in the circumstances. Arguments based on s 69 do not amount to sufficient grounds for setting aside the demand. Accordingly, a solicitor may serve a statutory demand for payment of his costs before the expiration of a month from the date of delivery of his bill of costs (*Re A Debtor (No 88 of 1991)* [1993] Ch 286, [1992] 4 All ER 301).

The Law Society has recommended that solicitors should be wary of following this course of action because of the power to set aside a statutory demand on the grounds of injustice (*Re A Debtor* (No 88 of 1991). Another reason for caution is that the decision in *Turner & Co v O Palomo SA* [1999] 4 All ER 353, [2000] 1 WLR 37, CA could be interpreted as precluding statutory demands based on a solicitor's bill because the amount of the bill is always open to challenge in proceedings brought to recover it even after the time limit for a detailed assessment has expired and therefore it is not a liquidated demand. In such circumstances, the decision of Warner J in *Re Cannon Screen Entertainment Ltd* [1989] BCLC 660, 5 BCC 207 indicates that an alleged creditor who chooses to short circuit court proceedings by using a statutory demand instead will pay the costs of finding out that there is effectively a defence.

BANKRUPTCY PETITION

[3.28]

In *Truex v Toll* [2009] EWHC 396 (Ch) the defendant client presented a list of perceived complaints about the solicitor's services in respect of her matrimonial proceedings. The solicitor served a statutory demand for his outstanding fees and followed it up with a bankruptcy petition. It was held on appeal that as the costs did not form the subject of a judgment, assessment or agreement, they were not a liquidated sum for the purpose of founding a bankruptcy petition; the bill as a whole was capable of challenge as to quantum and was thus for an unliquidated sum. It was not possible to say that any part of the work done by the solicitor had been quantified, or was quantifiable by the bankruptcy court as a mere matter of arithmetic. The sum claimed only became a liquidated sum once the fees had been assessed by a costs judge, determined in an action, or agreed. Whether a sum is liquidated and whether there is a defence to the claim are separate issues, and the first must be determined before the second is addressed.

If the statutory demand is not complied with within 21 days of service the solicitor may present a bankruptcy petition, but because this is an action within the meaning of s 69 (unlike the Statutory Demand), a petition may not be issued within a month without leave (*Re A Debtor (No 88 of 1991)*).

The considerations regarding a winding up petition in respect of a corporate client are, for the purposes of this commentary at least, exactly the same as for an individual client.

Where a former client had been made bankrupt, a solicitor was entitled to take part in a Creditors' meeting since it was clear that he had done work under a CFA. But as the work was so poorly set out that the extent of the debt was unascertained, the debt was estimated at £1 solely so that the solicitor could vote: *Rowbury v Official Receiver, sub nom Re Mark Forstater (Keystone Law LLP)* [2015] EWHC 2951 (Ch).

SOLICITOR'S LIEN

General Lien

[3.29]

A solicitor has, at common law, a general lien to retain any money, papers or other property belonging to his client which properly come into his possession until payment of his costs, whether or not the property was acquired in connection with the matter for which the costs were incurred. The solicitor may retain, until payment of his costs, property other than money to any value even if it greatly exceeds the amount due, but he cannot hold money in excess of the amount due. A solicitor is not entitled to sell property held under a lien or to transfer it into his ownership without an order from the court.

Particular Lien

[3.30]

A solicitor also has at common law a particular lien on property recovered or preserved by him in litigation which extends to all costs incurred, both billed and unbilled. Unlike the general lien, a particular lien covers property not in the solicitor's possession and gives him an equitable right to have the property transferred into his possession. The costs are incurred when work is done under the retainer entitling the solicitor to exercise a general or a particular lien until the costs are paid. Recent cases involving defendants seeking to avoid the costs of solicitors incurred by claimants have involved the higher courts considering the boundaries of an equitable lien: see **[1.34]**.

If some of the costs are unbilled the client's remedy is to request a bill for any outstanding costs. If the solicitor does not comply with the request the client may apply to the court under section 68 of the Solicitors Act 1974 for an order that he does so (see [**3.13**]).

Solicitors Act Charging Order

[3.31]

The lien on property recovered is in effect extended by the Solicitors Act 1974, s 73, which provides that any court in which a solicitor has been employed to prosecute or defend any suit, matter or proceeding may at any time 'declare the solicitor entitled to a charge on any property recovered or preserved . . . ; and make such orders for the assessment of those costs and for raising money to pay or for paying them out of the property recovered or preserved as the court thinks fit'. Note that the property needs to be the subject matter of the retainer between the client and the solicitor. It is not enough that your client owns other property on which a charging order might attach. If that is the case, you would require a charging order to enforce a judgment against the client in the ordinary way via Part 73.

A Solicitors Act Charging Order differs from a general lien in two particular ways. First, it applies to real as well as personal property and, second, it does not apply where the claim for costs is statute barred (a solicitor's lien on the other hand cannot become statute barred.)

The heading to s 73 is 'charging orders' but what is actually obtained is a declaration rather than a formal charging order. As such, if the property concerns real property, ie land, the s 73 order will not prevent the purchase of the land that has been charged (unlike a standard charging order) so long as the purchaser is 'Equity's darling' in other words, a bona fide purchaser who pays full value for the property and does not know there is a charge upon it. Any other transaction will be void as against the solicitor.

Charging orders obtained via Part 73 in accordance with the Charging Orders Act 1979 are obtained in two stages, an interim order obtained without notice to the debtor and a final order obtained following a hearing where the debtor has an opportunity to present any contrary arguments. Both the interim order and the final order can be registered at the Land Registry if the property being charged is real property. By contrast, a s 73 Order cannot be registered at the Land Registry. It is therefore advisable to consider seeking an interim declaration under Part 25 so that the debtor and his legal representatives' room for manoeuvre can be limited pending a final hearing of the application.

The application is made by a Part 8 Claim where the property has arisen from proceedings that have concluded. If there are still proceedings afoot, it would appear from rule 67.2 that a Part 23 application can be made by one of the parties' solicitors against that party. The granting of a declaration/charging order is not automatic but there is a presumption that it will be made to protect the solicitor's position – 'there is a constant repetition in the authorities of the justice of a solicitor being given such an order': *Clifford Harris and Co v Solland International Ltd* [2005] EWHC 141 (Ch).

A more exotic agreement regarding international litigation was secured by way of a floating charge against the company client. Unfortunately, the company went into liquidation shortly afterwards and the agreed fixed fee was overturned by the Court of Appeal and the value of the fees had to be determined: see the case of *Crumpler v Candey Ltd* [2018] EWCA Civ 2256 at [8.8].

Loss of lien

[3.32]

CPR 25.1(1)(m) provides that where the defendant to a claim for the recovery of personal property does not dispute the title of the party making the claim but claims to be entitled to retain the property by virtue of a lien, the court may make an order permitting the claimant to pay money into court pending the outcome of the proceedings and directing that if he does so, the property shall be given up to him.

If at any stage the solicitor takes alternative security from a client with the intention of satisfying his claim for fees by this alternative may mean his lien has been waived. This is because the taking of security for costs generally is inconsistent with the lien and the solicitor who does not expressly preserve his lien when taking the security will be taken to have abandoned it. For a detailed consideration of equitable liens and the effect of taking of security via a deed, see the judgment of Rose LJ in *Candey Ltd v Crumpler and Farmer (as joint liquidators of Peak Hotels & Resorts Ltd (in liq))* [2020] EWCA Civ 26. Amongst the many points made is that simply advising a client to seek independent legal advice on the alternative security does not absolve you from the need to give the client information about the situation, in particular, whether you intend to reserve the lien in addition to taking security.

In *FPH Law v Martyn Robert Brown (t/a Integrum Law)* [2016] EWHC 1681 (QB) the lien was lost because the defendant, who had left the partnership of the claimant when taking a client with him, then breached his undertaking to preserve the claimant's lien. The breached prevented the claimant from a loss of chance of fees when the former client's case was compromised. This was so, notwithstanding that the CFA which had been used was subsequently ruled to be unenforceable.

Who ended the retainer?

[3.33]

If the retainer is terminated by the client other than for misconduct by the solicitor, the solicitor's lien is virtually absolute. He cannot be required to hand over or produce for inspection any papers in his possession and he is entitled to keep them until his costs have been paid. In *French v Carter Lemon*

Camerons LLP [2012] EWCA Civ 1180, the claimant instructed the defendant solicitors to act for her in litigation against an insurance company but complained about their conduct of the litigation. Ultimately she stated that she was left with no choice but to represent herself in the insurance litigation and requested a copy of her file. The defendant exercised its purported right to a lien in respect of its unpaid fees. The claimant issued proceedings seeking recovery of those files. The application was dismissed in the lower courts and the claimant appealed to the Court of Appeal who upheld the decision. The retainer spelled out the rights of each party to terminate the retainer and the solicitors' entitlement to be paid their fees in the event of termination.

But the court went on to say that if the solicitor terminates the retainer, he may be ordered to hand over the papers to the new solicitor on the new solicitor's undertaking to hold them without prejudice to his lien, to return them intact after the action is over and to allow the former solicitor access to them in the meantime and if necessary to prosecute the proceedings in an active manner. The case of *Gamlen Chemical Co (UK) Ltd v Rochem Ltd* [1980] 1 All ER 1049, [1980] 1 WLR 614, CA is the authority for the extent of the undertakings which a solicitor can expect from a client's new solicitors.

Substituting the lien for an undertaking is not automatic and the court needs to exercise its discretion. In approaching the matter, the overriding principle is that the order made should be that which would best serve, or at least not frustrate, the interests of justice. The principle that a litigant should not be deprived of material relevant to the conduct of his case and so driven from the judgment seat is to be weighed against the principle that litigation should be conducted with due regard to the interests of the court's own officers, who should not be left without payment for what was justly due to them. Where the solicitors have behaved impeccably and of whose conduct there has been no criticism, while their clients, without any excuse, have not paid the costs and there is a default judgment against them, the balance of hardship would be far greater on the solicitors if the lien were not enforced, because they would then probably recover nothing, whereas it was open to the clients to preserve their position by paying the solicitor's costs.

Where the retainer is discharged by the solicitor, he has only a qualified lien over the papers. Unless there are exceptional circumstances, the fact that the solicitor had reasonable cause to end the retainer would not justify modifying the overriding principle that a solicitor discharging himself should not be allowed to exert his lien so as to interfere with the course of justice. He would be entitled to the appropriate undertakings from the new solicitors. A review of the authorities in this area can be found in the case of *Evelyn Donaghy v JJ Haughey Solicitors Ltd* [2019] NICh 1.

State funding

[3.34]

A solicitor's lien arises in respect of costs due for work done on the instructions of the client, for which the client has undertaken personal liability. Pre-certificate costs and disbursements will fall within this category. However, once a legal aid certificate has been issued the situation is altered, since the assisted person's solicitor has a statutory right to be paid out of the fund, and may not take any payment other than from the fund (Civil Legal Aid (General) Regulations 1989, reg 64).

When a certificate is amended to enable a new solicitor to have the conduct of a legally aided person's case, it does not appear logical that a common law lien can arise in respect of costs and disbursements payable under the statutory certificate. Indeed, the Law Society has taken the view that a solicitor's costs are secured by an order for assessment or certificate and as such it would be inappropriate even to call for a professional undertaking from the successor solicitor to pay the costs except in respect of any outstanding pre-certificate costs.

A solicitor should not part with the papers on a legally aided matter until the certificate is transferred to the successor solicitor, although they should be made available for inspection in the meantime or copies provided.

In order to make sure the solicitor is not prejudiced in claiming costs due from the fund it is quite proper to ask for an undertaking requiring the successor solicitor to:

(i) return the papers promptly on completion to enable a bill of costs to be drawn up; or
(ii) have the first solicitor's costs included in the successor solicitor's bill, collect those costs and pay them to the first solicitor.

Accordingly, where, under a certificate, a change of solicitor is authorised, subject to (a) there being no lien in respect of pre-certificate costs and disbursements, and (b) an undertaking being given by the new solicitor as to the eventual assessment of costs, there is no reason why the papers should not be expeditiously transferred to the new solicitor.

Documents to be handed over

[3.35]

What papers should be handed over by a solicitor on the termination of his retainer and lien? A full answer is complicated and outside the scope of this book. Suffice to say, the client is not strictly speaking entitled to the whole file but as records become more heavily computerised, the ability to store documents without hardship means that it is often easier to give the client/successor solicitor the entire paper files rather than spend unproductive time weeding things out. Furthermore, an incomplete file is likely to result in further correspondence with the client/new solicitor which is time wasted by all concerned.

Client's remedy

[3.36]

Where there is a valid and enforceable lien, the only practical remedy for the client who wishes to obtain without delay documents on which his previous solicitor is claiming a lien is to pay his costs. Sometimes the solicitor is willing to agree to the money being paid into a joint account to await the outcome of a Solicitors Act assessment. If not, the client should obtain either the original solicitor's consent to a Solicitors Act assessment or an order from the court before making the payment, as otherwise the court might not order an assessment. This course not only has the advantage of securing the immediate release of the papers, but it also enables the new solicitors to inspect and consider them at their leisure in order to advise whether the costs should be challenged – and, if so, on what grounds – before proceeding with the assessment.

Part II

Funding

INTRODUCTION TO FUNDING

[4.1]

The old businessman's adage drummed into managing partners is that 'turnover is vanity, profit is sanity, but cash flow is king.' The amount of revenue your firm makes is of very little value unless it outstrips your expenditure. Moreover, if you cannot afford to keep the business running while the revenue is generated you simply cannot trade.

This part of the book concerns the funding of cases, but not in the manner that any businessman would recognise. The solicitor actually funds the case in the sense of providing the cash flow. The 'funding' agreement with the client is really only a mechanism to establish how much the client will eventually pay for the solicitor's services. The concept of an 'entire contract' (see **[1.4]** above) demonstrates the idea that the solicitor will only be paid once the job has been completed. Primary legislation and the development of case law eventually allowed for interim payments to be made as the case progressed. But essentially, the solicitor funded his client's case and was paid at the conclusion. That payment then funded future clients' cases.

The importance of funding can be seen from cases which regularly occur in the High Court concerning a party's wish to use funds for legal representation which have previously been frozen by the court. If those funds are ostensibly the party's own, the court will look at limiting the costs to an amount which will allow representation but not dissipate funds which an earlier court has concluded should be restrained. If the frozen monies are the subject of the dispute, then the party seeking to use them may in fact end up spending their opponent's money. In such cases, there may be no money allowed to be used. A recent example of these issues can be found at *Kea Investments Ltd v Watson* [2020] EWHC 472 (Ch).

The agreements that we consider in this Part are consistent in that they try to make clients more comfortable with embarking on the expensive business that is involved in using a lawyer to create, enforce or defend rights. These agreements try to spell out the client's potential liability – either to a specific sum or to a percentage or similar calculation – if things go badly. The client's liability in the event of a successful outcome is sometimes, but not always, less explicitly described because the assumption is that the opponent will be liable for the majority if not all of the costs. If the Woolf and Jackson Reforms tell us anything about clients' wishes, it is that they would prefer as much certainty as possible as to costs, win or lose. The fixing of fees in the small and fast tracks and prospective budget setting in the multi-track all point towards a drive for certainty for the client. The risk of under reward for the work done is transferred squarely to the lawyers. Consequently, it is not just managing partners who need to keep a close eye on whether the work is profitable and capable of being turned into cash sufficiently quickly to keep the practice viable – you do too.

4.1 *Introduction to funding*

The enactment of LASPO 2012 and its subordinate legislation changed the landscape more in the area of funding than almost anywhere else. This part of the book is largely written on the basis of agreements entered into after 1 April 2013. Readers concerned with agreements before that date – in particular CFAs – will need to look at Chapter 6 as well.

We have taken the view that state funding via the Legal Aid Agency and its predecessors is no longer an area that this book should cover directly. It has become so specialised that those who practice with it, will know the regulations inside out and will not gain benefit from a further chapter here. Most readers will have no dealings with legal aid any longer and so will not be interested in such a chapter. We have covered eligibility etc sufficiently to make sure that professional obligations on funding advice are satisfied. We also still deal with situations that arise where the opponent is legally aided in Chapter 10.

We start with Conditional Fee Agreements because they are the most prevalent of the funding agreements currently. We then deal with Damages-Based Agreements which may become more popular over time, followed by Contentious and Non-Contentious Business Agreements which, in an age of increasing certainty may have a comeback in popularity. Then we look at insurance, both before and after the event. Traditionally such insurance has been used with a particular funding agreement, most obviously ATE with CFAs. But the need to be more client specific with funding arrangements may well mean that the boundaries are blurred and that insurance is used in different ways with different arrangements: so we deal with the insurance options on their own. At the end of the insurance chapter (Chapter 9), we look at the position where the solicitor decides to take on the responsibility for funding adverse outcomes rather than insuring them. Finally in this part we look at litigation funding arrangements by commercial third parties.

CHAPTER 4

CREATING CONDITIONAL FEE AGREEMENTS

[4.2]

On 1 April 2013 the landscape changed considerably for those who wanted to use CFAs to fund their cases. In order to keep this book clear and concise, the law and practice in relation to CFAs is split into 3 chapters. This Chapter deals with the setting up of the CFA and concentrates on drafting requirements and risk assessment. The next (Chapter 5) deals with issues during the life of the CFA and in particular when the outcome of the case is known. These two chapters deal with CFAs taken out on or after April 1 2013, although much of what is said is relevant to all CFAs, whenever they have been taken out. Pre-April 2013 agreements can still be found, even though they were obviously entered into a considerable time ago. Issues which relate to those agreements, particularly in respect of the recoverability of success fees is dealt with in the third chapter (Chapter 6).

THE GOLDEN RULE

[4.3]

Traditionally the idea that a solicitor would be financially interested in the outcome of his client's case was seen as an undesirable state of affairs. The lawyer should be disinterested in order to give impartial and proper advice. He would therefore need to be paid the same whether the case was won or lost. An agreement which depended upon the outcome of events would run counter to this requirement. Consequently, agreements which did so were considered to be 'maintaining' the action and if they included a sharing of the spoils of the litigation they were said to be 'champertous'. Maintenance and champerty were crimes up to the middle of the last century. Even when abolished as crimes, they remained as torts and still rendered solicitors' agreements unenforceable when CFAs came to be considered at the end of the 1980s.

(None of this applied to non-contentious business such as conveyancing where agreements which were dependent on say, completion taking place, were seen as quite proper. The prohibition on contingency agreements related solely to contentious business. (See Chapter 8 regarding the definitions of contentious and non-contentious business in more detail.))

The Courts and Legal Services Act 1990 ('CLSA') created CFAs. The wording of s 58 is not the simplest to understand because it recognises that agreements contingent on the outcome of events are generally unenforceable. So, it carved out an area of contingency fee agreements which would be enforceable, but did not otherwise alter the general position. As Ian Burnett QC (now Burnett LCJ) poetically put it in *Hollins v Russell* [2003] EWCA Civ 718, CFAs are 'islands of legality in a sea of illegality.' They have now been joined in this situation by Damages-Based Agreements as of April 2013.

So the Golden Rule to remember in respect of CFAs is that they need to comply with the Courts and Legal Services Act 1990 and any subordinate legislation. If they do not, they become unenforceable contingency fee agreements. They are then unenforceable against the client and, by operation of the indemnity principle, fees generated under such an agreement cannot be recovered from the opponent.

This effect is the root cause of the so-called 'Costs Wars' in the early part of this century. Non-compliance was comparatively easy to demonstrate based on the original regulations. Much of those have been swept away but new Regulations and a new CFA Order came into being on 1 April 2013 and attempts by paying parties continue to use them to render successful parties' agreements unenforceable. Similarly, the use of consumer legislation relating to cancellable agreements affords the opportunity for challenges to be brought: see for example *Kupeli v Cyprus Turkish Airlines* [2017] EWCA Civ 1037 and [**1.7**] generally.

REQUIREMENTS OF CONDITIONAL FEE AGREEMENTS

[4.4]

The requirements for creating a valid CFA are now quite limited. A CFA needs to:

- be in writing;
- not be in relation to family or criminal proceedings.

Any success fee:

- must be no more than 100% of the base fees; and
- may need to be limited to a percentage of the client's damages.

Let us look at each one of these in turn.

In writing

[4.5]

All of the terms need to be in writing. There have been various decisions at first instance to the effect that other documents, such as the client care letter, can be looked at in addition to the CFA itself to ascertain the terms. But agreements which are partly in writing and partly oral do not comply with the requirements and such agreements are unenforceable (see eg *Radford v Frade* [2018] EWCA Civ 119).

The terms can be varied in due course but such variations also need to be in writing. A general retainer which was varied in respect of a discrete hearing to create a CFA for that hearing was held to remain valid when the unenforceable CFA element was severed: *Garnat Trading & Shipping (Singapore) PTE Ltd v Thomas Cooper (a firm)* [2016] EWHC 18 (Ch).

Not in relation to family or criminal proceedings

[4.6]

The precise wording of the requirement is that the CFA 'must not relate to proceedings which cannot be the subject of an enforceable conditional fee agreement' (s 58(3)(b)). The provisions of s 58A(1) of the CLSA 1990 describes those proceedings as 'criminal proceedings, apart from proceedings under s 82 of the Environmental Protection Act 1990' or 'family proceedings.' There then follow 11 sub-sections defining the relevant statutes which are considered to be family proceedings. The impact in a nutshell is that, for public policy reasons, it is inappropriate for a solicitor advising his client in criminal or family matters to be paid depending upon the outcome.

Any success fee must be no more than 100% of the base fees

[4.7]

A CFA does not need to have any success fee but if there is one, it must not be more than a doubling of the base fees.

So in *Oyston v Royal Bank of Scotland* [2006] EWHC 90053 (Costs) an agreement for the solicitors to receive a £50,000 bonus if the damages recovered were over £1m rendered the CFA invalid where the solicitor was already entitled to a 100% success fee.

This case came hard on the heels of *Jones v Caradon Catnic Ltd* [2007] EWCA Civ 1821 where the Court of Appeal held that a success fee set at 120% rendered the agreement unenforceable even though on assessment the claim was limited to 100%. The Court of Appeal was clear that claiming a success fee over and above the maximum allowed by the CFA Order 2000 (now replaced by the CFA Order 2013) was contrary to the administration of justice even if not so obviously contrary to the interest of the client (who would never pay it).

Any success fee may be limited to a percentage of the client's damages

[4.8]

When the subordinate legislation bringing the CLSA 1990 into effect was originally introduced in 1995, the success fee in a CFA was not recoverable from the opponent and there was no limit on the extent to which the client's damages could be depleted to pay for that success fee by the client. The Law Society gave professional conduct guidance that the limit should be 25% of the client's damages but there was nothing in the legislation to require this. When recoverability of success fees was introduced in April 2000 the need to seek payment of any fees by the client dissipated. The 'market' in personal injury and debt recovery work (the main areas for using CFAs) was very much the need to offer the client a 100% recovery of damages with the solicitor taking whatever fees could be recovered. Some firms did still seek payments from their clients but that was relatively rare and the sums sought limited.

With the ending of recoverability from the opponent by LASPO 2012, the issue of payment of the success fee has reappeared. This time, the secondary legislation has prescribed limits to the amount that can be claimed from the client in personal injury and clinical negligence cases, albeit not in any other case.

Personal injury and clinical negligence cases

[4.9]

A new provision (s 58(4B)) has been added to CLSA 1990 by LASPO 2012 with which the CFA needs to comply:

> '(4B) The additional conditions are that—
>
> (a) the agreement must provide that the success fee is subject to a maximum limit,
> (b) the maximum limit must be expressed as a percentage of the descriptions of damages awarded in the proceedings that are specified in the agreement,
> (c) that percentage must not exceed the percentage specified by order made by the Lord Chancellor in relation to the proceedings or calculated in a manner so specified, and
> (d) those descriptions of damages may only include descriptions of damages specified by order made by the Lord Chancellor in relation to the proceedings.'

As with all Parliamentary drafting, it is done in a style which needs to be read more than once. The 'maximum limit' is a reference to how much of the client's damages can be taken in fees by the solicitor. The limit has to be expressed as a percentage of the damages. Since many people see personal injury damages as sacrosanct, some of the heads of damage claimed cannot be reduced by the agreement, particularly future losses.

The order of the Lord Chancellor referred to in (4B)(c) above is the CFA Order 2013 and the description of damages in that order from which a percentage can be deducted is set out at Article 5(2) of the Order as follows
(a) general damages for pain, suffering, and loss of amenity; and
(b) damages for pecuniary loss, other than future pecuniary loss
So, future losses are untouchable which makes the largest personal injury and clinical negligence claims less attractive from this stand point than they would be otherwise. Where the Compensation Recovery Unit is entitled to recover sums for benefits paid or treatment rendered, those sums are also removed from the pot before a percentage can be taken.

What is the maximum percentage that can be deducted? Article 5(1) says:
(a) in proceedings at first instance, 25%; and
(b) in all other proceedings, 100%.
The 25% figure is not a surprise given the previous limit expected by the Law Society. This figure is also reflected in the Damages-Based Agreements Regulations considered later in this part of the book. The increase to 100% in relation to appeals is perhaps more surprising. The widely used model Law Society CFA expects an appeal by the opponent to be covered under that agreement. As a result the step change in the potential liability to the client has to be explained and which almost inevitably will reduce the simplicity of the explanation to the client and with it the client's understanding of his liability.

The Law Society model does not cover appeals by the client so that the solicitor can take stock before deciding whether to continue under a CFA and without any risk of breaching the entire contract. If it is the opponent who is appealing the theory is that the client must have had a good result at first instance and is in a strong position to defend the opponent's appeal. It may be better to remove the automatic right for the client to be covered on an appeal by any other party and enter into a new agreement in the future. That way, the

25% cap can be explained at the outset. If the case reaches an appeal, a second CFA might be used so that a case-specific cap of up to 100% can be put on the extent of the damages that might be risked by the appeal.

DRAFTING CONSIDERATIONS

General approach

[4.10]

The sting in the tail to the amendment to s 58 of the CLSA 1990 is not that the client will now start to pay some of his solicitor's fees with his damages. It is the risk that a badly drafted CFA will be found to be unenforceable. S 58(3)(c) requires the CFA to comply with such requirements as are prescribed by the Lord Chancellor. This must therefore include the CFA Order 2013. If the wording does not comply with that set out above, the defendant will be seeking to avoid any liability for costs under the 'Golden Rule' described earlier in this Chapter.

It is not surprising therefore that the statutory requirements, such as those of the CFA Order 2013 are written into the Law Society model agreement more or less verbatim. It may not help the client to understand the terms of the agreement – when compared with the use of plainer English – but it has the undoubted value of making the agreement more robust to challenges. If you decide to draft your own CFA, it is something to which you must give some thought. One option that superficially is attractive is to draft the agreement in the language of the legislation and provide an explanatory note or leaflet to go with it. Be careful. That way leads to inconsistencies ripe for exploitation by paying parties seeking to allege uncertainty and non-compliance. Even copious phrases explaining that the wording of the CFA is to take precedence over such a leaflet if there is any inconsistency can be grist to the challenger's mill. 'What is the purpose of a leaflet which concedes it is (or may be) inconsistent with the document it is explaining? There must be more to it, probably an oral explanation which creates terms (and thereby a partly oral CFA which is inevitably unenforceable.)'

Given that a CFA is fundamentally an agreement between a solicitor and his client, it has always seemed odd to go to counsel to get that agreement right. But if you are looking to use a CFA in standard terms on many cases (or perhaps a few cases but of potentially significant value), there may be some comfort in using another professional's professional indemnity insurance as a potential backstop.

One area of drafting in which problems have regularly occurred is the definition of the proceedings and more particularly, the identity of the opponent. The recent case of *Malone v Birmingham Community NHS Trust* [2018] EWCA Civ 1376 gives hope to the lax drafter after a number of cases held that a more restricted approach was appropriate (see **[6.12]** for a more detailed analysis). This chapter is aimed at best practice and that cannot be achieved by requiring a court to consider the context to save a CFA. As long as the general nature of the proceedings is identified, it is a much better approach to avoid specifically naming the opponent (or to use some catch all phrase) so as to avoid challenges. After all, private paying retainers are not required to specify the proposed opponent or, if an opponent is identified, to suffer any penalty if that opponent turns out to be incorrect.

The rest of this Chapter is based on the assumption that the success fee is based on the risks to the client and/or solicitor in running the case. If, as a general consideration, you take the view that you will charge the maximum success fee on every case, there is no need to consider the risk in the same way. There are still management reasons for doing so, but obviously not for deciding to run the case as such. If you take this view, beware that the court is likely to consider it an unusual approach, even if the success fee is limited in personal injury cases to 25% of the relevant damages. Consequently, you will need to consider how you give your client the necessary information for informed consent. Drafting a clear document is not sufficient according to the Court of Appeal (see [**3.21**]).

Relationship with DBAs

[4.11]

As we will see in Chapter 7 on Damages-Based Agreements, the aim is to make the agreement simpler. The current regime may not do that, but it may well be in time that CFAs can use some DBA terminology to create a shorter, simpler agreement. Furthermore, where the fees are fixed if the case is won (because the recoverable fixed fees are all that will be taken by the solicitor) and no fees will be charged if unsuccessful, the agreement ought to be capable of being expressed in many fewer words. The Law Society model seeks to give options and cover various situations. Your CFA may not need to do so, depending upon the case on which you are instructed.

Speculative agreements

[4.12]

Arguably the simplest agreement is one where the client is told that you will accept whatever is received from the other side, but nothing otherwise. This used to be called 'speccing' because the case was brought entirely speculatively by the solicitor, at least insofar as his own costs were concerned. Such agreements offended the indemnity principle and impecunious clients who retained solicitors to pursue claims were often seen as being parties to a speccing agreement as in the case of *British Waterways Board v Norman* (1993) 26 HLR 232, [1993] NPC 143.

Once CFAs became lawful, the need for speccing agreements reduced. Those who drafted CFAs which altered the definition of a 'win' to the recovery of costs rather than simply the award of costs found themselves met with indemnity principle arguments as to the client's liability. These CFAs were called CFA Lite(s) because they reduced the client's liability for costs to whatever sum was recovered from the opponent. If the case failed, the client was not liable for his solicitor's costs and essentially the client had achieved a costs free environment. The CFA (Miscellaneous Amendments) Regulations 2003) established that such agreements do not offend the indemnity principle.

It is not just impecunious clients who wish to benefit from a CFA Lite. Businesses which pursue debt collection claims and Insolvency Practitioners seeking to make sure funds are not dissipated in legal fees are amongst those who are keen to agree no recovery, no fee arrangements.

Termination provisions

[4.13]

These are fundamental to all contracts. Where payment depends upon the outcome of the case, as in CFAs, particular care needs to be taken on how to deal with the ending of the retainer before that outcome is known. We deal with these situations in more detail in the next Chapter but you should be aware of the issues when drafting the agreement. The Law Society model has always covered problems of the client's making such as a lack of co-operation or wishing to continue against the lawyer's advice. It also covers the death of the client and those specific provisions were considered by Saini J in *Higgins & Co Lawyers Ltd v Evans* [2019] EWHC 2809 (QB) (see [**1.34**]).

It did not originally deal with any issues affecting the law firm's existence. The change of many firms to LLP status called into question the effectiveness of the original CFA thereafter and various ways were tried by firms to get around perceived problems. The latest Law Society model includes the following provision.

> '**Cessation of Business**
>
> If we stop carrying on business then you must pay us or any successor to our business (or that part of our business which takes over conduct of your claim) our basic charges and our expenses and disbursements including barristers' fees and success fees if you go on to win your claim for damages.'

On the face of it, this provision is wide enough to cover most situations that can be contemplated. How it fits together with the specific provisions about success fees may be tested. Interventions, for example, have a nasty habit of happening more or less overnight. There may be a very limited (or no) opportunity for the law firm to elect whether to risk waiting for payment of all fees including success fees at the end of the case or to require payment of the base fees upon termination. An example of the effect of terminating without reasonable notice can be seen in the case of *Gill v Heer Manak Solicitors* at [**1.4**].

Cancellable agreements

[4.14]

You will also need to consider at the outset the requirements of the Consumer Contracts (Information, Cancellation and Additional Charges) Regulations 2013 if you intend to use CFAs with 'consumers' ie natural persons (see [**1.7**]). This is particularly so if you see them outside of your offices at any stage during the signing up process (or sign them up entirely at a distance via the telephone or internet). Whilst the Regulations, and their predecessors, may be aimed at doorstep salesmen and cold callers, they undoubtedly cover solicitors as well and Cancellation Notices ought to be used if there is any doubt at all.

The cooling off period of 14 days enables the client to terminate the agreement during that period without incurring any costs, unless there has been a specific agreement that work done during this period will still be payable in the event of cancellation.

In *Cox v Woodlands Manor Care Home* [2015] EWCA Civ 415, [2015] 3 Costs LO 327 the Court of Appeal concluded that the claimant and her solicitor became legally committed under the terms of the CFA when it was signed at her house, notwithstanding a condition regarding the possibility of using BTE insurance. Underhill LJ giving the leading judgment concluded:

> 'I reach this decision with regret. It means that Wards [the solicitors] will not recover at all for the legal services which they rendered to the Appellant and which procured her very substantial damages. It is clear that she was entirely satisfied with their services and is dismayed at the fact that they will go unrewarded. District Judge Britton, who had occasion to review the file, also spoke highly of the service which the Appellant had received from Wards generally and Mrs Underhill in particular. The outcome is all the harder because Mrs Underhill only attended at the Appellant's home because her injuries meant that it was difficult for her to come to Wards' offices. It is difficult to think that a case like this falls within the mischief of the Regulations. Indeed we are told that they have now been replaced by regulations which are somewhat less inflexible. But the fact is that the relevant provisions are clear, and on a strict, albeit unsympathetic, view Wards should have been aware of them and complied with their obligations under them.'

You have been warned. Doing a good job will not help you recover your fees from the other side. Having failed to do so, it will be virtually impossible from a professional conduct standpoint to do so from your client instead. *Cox* was decided under the 2008 Regulations (see [**1.7**]) and the newer Regulations are the ones referred to above. Unless you are extremely familiar with their nuances you would be well advised to assume that they are just as unsympathetic.

DIFFERENTIAL RATES

[4.15]

The definition of a CFA in s 58 refers to an agreement 'which provides for his fees and expenses, or any part of them, to be payable only in specified circumstances.' There are three points to make about this part of the definition.

Fees <u>and</u> expenses

[4.16]

The agreement can deal with expenses and not just fees in different ways depending upon the outcome. This is an important consideration in respect of drafting agreements. It is dealt with later in this part of the book at Chapter 9 regarding solicitors taking more of the funding risk.

Specifying circumstances

[4.17]

The specification of circumstances can be as simple or as complicated as the solicitor and his client wish. The great majority of CFAs have been used in personal injury cases where an hourly rate and success fee would be payable if the case won and no payment at all if the case lost. Initially, the success fee would be a single figure whenever the case settled. But with judicial encouragement from the Court of Appeal in landmark cases such as *Callery v Gray* [2001] EWCA Civ 1117, and the industry agreements under the auspices of the Civil Justice Council, a number of success fees were potentially payable depending upon the exact circumstances of settlement. ('Staged' success fees were enshrined in Part 45 for personal injury cases arising out of road traffic accidents and claims against employers (see **[6.38]** in Chapter 6).

In commercial cases, different base fees and not just the success fee have been specified to be applicable in certain circumstances. In other cases a fixed sum for a successful outcome has been agreed in addition to a percentage uplift. This has not always ended happily – see for example the case of *Oyston v Royal Bank of Scotland* [2006] EWHC 90053 (Costs) – but the theory is sound, the client and his solicitor are able to specify the circumstances in infinite variety should they wish to do so.

Fees where unsuccessful

[4.18]

The market in personal injury and to some extent clinical negligence claims prior to 1 April 2013, was that of 'no win, no fee'. While inaccurate in some respects, this description did clearly represent the position that there would be no fee if the claimant lost his case. That outcome was not attractive in other areas where the prospect of an unsuccessful outcome was much more likely.

So, defendants' solicitors in personal injury cases (who usually do not achieve 'success' in obtaining an order for costs from the claimant), have agreed collective CFAs with insurance companies which have higher (usually court guideline) rates where successful and lower rates where unsuccessful. The lower rates reflect the general agreements reached between the law firm and insurer. Such agreement for unsuccessful cases might be a fixed figure rather than a lower hourly rate. In commercial cases, the unsuccessful fee would generally be a lower hourly rate with figures in the region of 50% of the successful rate not uncommon.

These agreements are described in myriad ways. They are differential fee agreements, or hybrid agreements or 'No win, low(er) fee' agreements. Those which have no fee where unsuccessful are sometimes called 'pure CFAs' but perhaps fortunately those where there is a lower rate have not been called 'impure CFAs' or any other antonym to pure.

ASSESSING THE RISK

The limits of risk assessment

[4.19]

'We do not consider that it can ever be said that a case is without risk' said Lord Woolf in *Callery v Gray* [2001] EWCA Civ 1117. All litigators know of cases that seemed to be stone cold certainties that failed to succeed when they went to court. Equally, most can point to cases which they ran as much in hope as in expectation but which triumphed at trial. Where the case was paid for privately, the outcome did not matter to the lawyer financially. As such, if the client wished to risk triumph or disaster on an obviously risky case, it was very much their choice. Those twin imposters would have been considered by the client's lawyers at the outset when advice on prospects was rendered. Those prospects would have been reconsidered as the case progressed, and reviewed prior to preparing for trial. No matter how many times the risks were assessed, however, the essential prospects of the case would be unlikely to alter significantly. A risky case remains a risky case however often those risks are assessed. Parties and their lawyers may strive to find evidence and arguments to improve the case's prospects but a case that starts as a risky one rarely becomes a very strong case by the time it gets to trial.

The benefits of risk assessment

[4.20]

Consequently, there is a school of thought that says that there are only three kinds of case – good ones; bad ones; all the ones in the middle. The first category are the ones you would always wish to run, whether on a CFA or otherwise. The second category contains those that you should jettison unless the client wishes to pay you irrespective of the result. The third category has those cases where you need to consider the risk and decide whether you wish to take it on or not. If you do decide to do so, you must remember that the risks have not disappeared simply because you have assessed those risks and decided to accept them. It is surprising how many litigators treat a case with an accepted risk as being as good as a strong case and pursue it as if all the time and effort invested is almost certainly going to be recouped at the end of the case.

There is another school of thought that says the risks can be weighed in a much more sophisticated and scientific manner. There have been many books written on the assessment of risk generally. There have even been some solely on assessing risk in relation to conditional fee agreements. Risk assessment is ultimately, like faith, very much a personal thing. You either think the risks can be gone through with the fine tooth comb or just the broad brush, or perhaps some implement in between.

Wherever you stand on this issue, there are sound management reasons for assessing the risk to see if the rewards are commensurate to the risks that your firm is running. Therefore even if you think assessing the prospects of success is just a gut reaction, you should consider a more formal risk assessment to consider whether taking on the case stacks up generally. For example, will it involve a huge amount of resource or tie up unpaid fees for an inordinate amount of time? Furthermore, your firm will only benefit properly from the risk assessments if you record information centrally to be able to build up a picture of your success and profitability in any given area.

The other reason for creating a risk assessment regardless of your belief in its relevance has ended with the change in regime. While success fees were recoverable, a contemporaneous risk assessment was a key document to support the risks as seen by the litigator when the CFA was created. It was a nervous litigator's charter because every risk that could be imagined was put down since there was no reason not to do so. Even if the risks suggested that a success fee well over 100% could be justified, they were still worth setting down because they might just persuade the assessing judge that the success fee actually claimed was a very reasonable one given the risks. (A tension recognised by the Court of Appeal in *Drake v Fripp* (see **[6.21]**)). This is no longer required but the risk assessments are still valuable in older cases going through the courts and which are considered in Chapter 6.

Forms of risk assessment

[4.21]

The Risk Assessment forms perused by the courts have often been described as unhelpful or designed to establish a high success fee in every case. There is no Law Society model risk assessment to go with the model CFA. The model CFA simply takes the 'assessment of the risks in your case' as being one of the factors to justify the success fee claimed in Schedule 1 to the agreement.

Most risk assessments are variations on a table which sets out all the risks the solicitor can think of down one side and levels of risk along the other axis. So, the solicitor may consider 'expert evidence' to be a risk and have the options of low, medium or high to categorise that risk. Variations include many more options to each risk so that expert evidence might be broken down into risks regarding the client's expert as distinct from the opponent's; or from the risk of single joint expert. Instead of low, medium and high, there might be several categories to distinguish the level of risk. There may be a method of using figures rather than words so that risks might be 1 to 9 to give more refinement to the perceived level. Whatever amount of detail is used, the resulting figures (or impression if ticks are used against the level of risk) produce a risk percentage which shows the prospects of success or failure.

This percentage is then used, conventionally, in a purely arithmetical way to be converted to a percentage success fee by using a ready reckoner first made widely known by the Law Society book on Conditional Fees written by Michael Napier and Fiona Bawdon when CFAs were first introduced. The ready reckoner's simplicity has found favour with the judiciary on many occasions.

The Ready Reckoner

[4.22]

The simplest way of explaining its use is by an example. Supposing that your risk assessment suggested that you considered that there was a 75% prospect of success (or 25% prospect of failure.) The ready reckoner below would give you a 33% success fee to be claimed on your base costs.

The logic for the ready reckoner is this. A 75% prospect of success is the same as saying that if several cloned cases of this one were run to trial, 3 out of every 4 would succeed. Therefore there is a risk that this particular case is the other 1 of the 4. In order to guard against that risk, a success fee is claimed. Mathematically the calculation is to divide the prospects of failure (25%) by the prospect of success (75%) and multiply by 100. This calculation has been done for each prospect of success or 'chance of winning' of 50% or more as follows

Chance of winning	Success Fee	Chance of winning	Success Fee
50	100%	75	33%
51	96%	76	32%
52	92%	77	30%
53	89%	78	28%
54	85%	79	27%
55	82%	80	25%
56	79%	81	23%
57	75%	82	22%
58	72%	83	20%
59	69%	84	19%
60	67%	85	18%
61	64%	86	16%
62	61%	87	15%
63	59%	88	14%
64	56%	89	12%
65	54%	90	11%
66	52%	91	10%
67	49%	92	9%
68	47%	93	8%
69	45%	94	6%
70	43%	95	5%
71	41%	96	4%
72	39%	97	3%
73	37%	98	2%
74	35%	99	1%

It will not take you long to realise that there is a certain amount of artificiality in this approach. It assumes in particular that the costs of each case, whether won or lost, are the same (which is why we have described them as 'cloned'). Nevertheless it is relatively easy to explain to clients and, since it is mathematical, is seen to be objective rather than a subjective figure plucked from the air. What most clients do not appreciate is that the success fee depends upon the original risk assessment and so the gloomier the risk assessment, the higher the success fee is bound to be. The level of gloom is entirely in the hands of the assessor of the risk.

RISK AND THE COST OF FUNDING

[4.23]

The payment of fees (and, in some cases, disbursements) will be postponed until the outcome of the case. The fact that the cost of this delay is effectively carried by the solicitor is discussed at **[4.1]**.

Regulation 3(1)(b) of the CFA Regulations 2000 raised the concept of the cost of funding being reflected in the success fee. The original Law Society model drafted in 1995 made no reference to such a concept. The success fee was simply a reflection of the risk as calculated by the ready reckoner.

Having seen reg 3(1(b), the revised Law Society model contained a schedule for calculating the success fee and the first two factors to be considered were:

> '(a) the fact that if you win we will not be paid our basic charges until the end of the claim;
> (b) our arrangements with you about paying disbursements'

The schedule went on to say that 'the matters set out at paragraphs (a) and (b) above together make up [ ]% of the increase on basic charges.'

With minor amendments and a demotion in the batting order to (d) and (e) these two factors continue in the latest model agreement.

An unnecessary complication

[4.24]

The main difference between then and now is that in 2000 the funding factors were considered to justify a separate success fee from the risk factors. This made the schedule more complicated and resulted in a number of solicitors seeking a composite success fee above 100%. In particular, a 100% risk success fee became invariable for cases going to trial (with a lower fee for earlier settlement). In addition a further 5% or 10% was claimed for the cost of funding resulting in a total success fee claimed of 105% or 110% which was starkly in breach of the CFA Order 2000 maximum of 100% and rendered the agreement unenforceable.

Why make this system more complicated? It is a good question. There was never any explanation why a percentage applied to the base costs was a good method of seeking compensation for funding the case. It would have been much more obvious to seek a sum based on interest charged on the base fees and disbursements that were outstanding. The need for separation from the risk factor success fee was precisely because the risk factor element was recoverable from the losing party but the cost of the funding element was not. This was provided for by the CPR in response to reg 3(1)(b). But those solicitors who kept the success fee purely for the risk made completion of the CFA, and explanations to the client, much simpler. Now, while the schedule reflects the fact of a delay in payment until the end of the case, it is included within the single success fee claimed in the CFA. Since it is the client who is now paying the success fee, there is no need to make any distinction between the two elements.

What to do now

[4.25]

If you intend to charge your client for the delay in payment, you need to consider how this is to be charged. If the Law Society model wording is used, it is included in the success fee. If you decide to make a separate calculation paragraphs (d) and (e) need to be removed from the standard schedule. In either event, the charge will need to be included in the 25% cap if you are dealing with a personal injury case.

Funding disbursements

[4.26]

As mentioned above, and dealt with in detail in Chapter 9 below, the client's expenses can be part of the CFA, and not just the solicitor's fees. Accordingly, they will be paid by the opponent if the client succeeds, and paid by the solicitor if unsuccessful. If you are considering taking this approach, you should consider what if any charge you propose to make for funding those disbursements in the interim. Presumably, such a charge would usually only be made in the event of success.

COST OF SETTING UP A FUNDING ARRANGEMENT

[4.27]

The cost of setting up the client retainer is a matter between the solicitor and his client. Where there is a funding arrangement included in that retainer the time spent in setting everything up may take rather longer. For example, in commercial litigation there may be discussions with (third party) litigation funders (see Chapter 10) and after the event insurers (Chapter 9) as well as a conditional fee agreement to sort out. In group litigation there may be these factors and more.

It is perhaps surprising therefore that it was not until 2011 that we had a decision concerning the recovery of the cost of explaining CFAs to clients and of putting in place ATE insurance. In *Motto v Trafigura Ltd* SCCO (2011) 15 February 2011 the Senior Costs Judge answered the following question 'yes': 'Is the work undertaken by solicitors, counsel, costs draftsmen and insurers in establishing and setting up (1) the conditional fee arrangements and (2) the insurance policy recoverable in principle?' On appeal, the Court of Appeal overturned that decision ([2011] EWCA Civ 1150). Claimants cannot recover the cost of preparing and advising on CFAs nor can they recover costs incurred in discussing litigation with or taking instructions from ATE insurers.

The court's reasoning was that the expertise and effort devoted by solicitors to identifying a potential claimant, and negotiating the terms on which they were to be engaged by the claimant, in connection with litigation, could not be properly described as an item incurred by the client for the purposes of the litigation. Until the CFA was signed, the potential claimant was not a client let alone a claimant. Liaising with ATE insurers after the insurance was in place was collateral to the action and liaising with insurers was designed to ensure the claimant was protected against costs.

CHAPTER 5

RUNNING CASES WITH CONDITIONAL FEE AGREEMENTS

DURING THE CASE

Payments on account

[5.1]

Where you have agreed a CFA with your client that is not a 'No win, no fee' agreement, you are bound to receive some fees regardless of the outcome. In many commercial cases, the unsuccessful hourly rate is in the region of 50% of the successful rate. As such, half of your fees ought to be paid by your client as the case progresses. Your client will be reimbursed in the event of a win from the recovered costs.

If you had been instructed on a traditional private paying arrangement, you would expect to render regular bills. You should also do so using a CFA wherever possible. The client is never going to be delirious about paying your fees, but unless he really cannot do so, it will help your cash flow and make your client understand the costs involved if he pays a proportion of them as they are incurred. It is usually the case that clients are more positive about paying your fees while the case is proceeding since they believe they will win and therefore recover them anyway.

In order to be able to do this, you need to have express wording agreed with your client otherwise you have to rely on natural breaks etc discussed at **[2.9]**. There is no need for this. You should have it in your client care letter anyway. But if you do not, make sure it is in your CFA.

The interim bill could be either a payment on account or an interim statute bill. The differences are discussed in more detail at **[2.4]**. For the purposes of this chapter, it is simply worth considering the risk of an interim statute bill providing an argument to your opponent that the amount billed to your client is the full extent of your client's liability for the period covered by each individual statute bill. If you are billing say 50% of the successful fees as the amount you will receive win or lose, you are risking the other 50% if your opponent establishes the effect of your statute bills is to limit your client's liability to the statute bills. You need to be very careful about the wording of your interim bills and unless there is a benefit to the certainty created by an interim statute bill there is plenty to be said for the flexibility of an interim payment on account.

There are two further reasons why the choice of interim payments on account may be the better option. They both relate to the difficulty of persuading courts that interim statute bills are appropriate during the course of litigation. The need for the client to issue Solicitors Act proceedings on a monthly basis to retain rights to pursue a challenge to such bills against their current solicitors is obviously unattractive. It will invariably found a 'special circumstance' to enable a client to pursue a challenge after the initial month has passed. The second reason is the restrictive nature of what constitutes a compliant statute bill based on the case of *Sprey* where a case is being run on a differential CFA (see [**2.6**]).

NO NOTICE OF FUNDING

[5.2]

One of the main matters which solicitors needed to keep in mind prior to 1 April 2013 was the notification of the CFA to the opponent. This might be in the letter before action or subsequently by a Notice of Funding in form N251. There is more detail on this requirement in the next chapter. Such notification was required wherever a CFA had a success fee and so the opponent needed to be told of the 'additional liability' that was being incurred over and above base costs. Where a CFA did not have a success fee, but merely different hourly rates depending upon the outcome, there was no need to serve a notice. So differential CFAs, as were often used by defendants in personal injury cases, did not have to be alerted to the opponent. Now that success fees are no longer recoverable (save for certain discrete areas discussed below) there is no longer any need to notify the opponent of the existence of the CFA.

Traditionally, and save for Legally Aided cases, each party's financing of the case was a matter for the client and not discussed between the parties. The use of Notices of Funding in some forms of litigation has become so widespread that parties appear to believe that they are entitled to know their opponent's arrangements. It will be interesting to see whether this prurience dies down or whether a more open approach will become the norm.

NOTICE OF FUNDING

[5.3]

Cases where the CFA was entered into prior to 1 April 2013 still need to follow the old rules in accordance with CPR 48.1 and 48.2. This includes the need for notification.

Furthermore those cases where recoverability of additional liabilities has not been withdrawn for the time being – mesothelioma claims; those involving Insolvency Practitioners (up to April 2016); or against the media for publication and privacy actions (up to April 2019) – will also need to be notified by virtue of the same provisions.

ESTIMATES OF COSTS

[5.4]

CFA clients are just as entitled to be kept up to date in respect of the costs their solicitors have incurred as any other client. That would seem obvious, particularly where the client is simply paying a different hourly rate depending upon the outcome. But where the client was on a 'pure' CFA and so nothing would be paid if the case was unsuccessful, there have been many who took the view that the client simply would not be interested in the costs involved and keeping mum would save unnecessary conversations and correspondence with the client (which may well not be recoverable from the opponent.) This was a particularly prevalent view in personal injury work when the success fee was recoverable and the client was guaranteed to receive his full damages.

The removal of recoverability has meant that many clients will now end up parting with some of their damages to pay for their lawyer's fees and it becomes obvious once more that they ought to be kept informed. The eventual introduction of fixed fees in the fast track along with budgeting in the multi-track will make estimating costs easier. Such figures are of course only those that are recoverable from the opponent. To the extent that the solicitor's fees will not be fully met from such sums, the client will still be liable to his solicitor in the event of success.

COUNSEL

Replacing traditional arrangements

[5.5]

For hundreds of years, solicitors instructed counsel in contentious matters based on the 'honorarium' approach. In other words, the solicitor would send instructions to the barrister who would advise in writing or in conference or attend court on the client's behalf. The fee for each piece of work would be agreed, usually in advance of the work being done, and the solicitor would pay for the work in due course. If the client did not put the solicitor in funds to pay counsel, the solicitor was still required as a matter of professional conduct to pay counsel's fees. Counsel could not sue on the agreement and if there was a disagreement between the solicitor and barrister regarding the fee a Joint Tribunal would be convened consisting of solicitors and barristers to adjudicate. Whatever fee was deemed payable by the Tribunal then had to be paid by the solicitor, again as a matter of professional conduct.

However, from 2007 the solicitor stopped having a professional obligation to meet counsel's fees if his client did not put him in funds to do so. This change took some time to be widely noticed and there are many solicitors who still believe they are professionally obligated. But, a solicitor's continued use of the chambers in which counsel is based was unlikely in such circumstances and that had been of sufficient concern to many solicitors to encourage them to pay counsel even if they had to do so themselves.

[5.6]

The Joint Tribunal arrangements and counsel's inability to sue created an unsatisfactory situation for the Bar. The Bar Council and the Law Society spent several years trying to agree terms but were unable to do so. Consequently, the Bar introduced default contractual terms as from January 2013 to replace the honorarium arrangement. The parties are free to vary these terms and many chambers have varied the standard provisions to a greater or lesser extent. But the variation must be agreed in writing and that should prevent most disputes as to the agreed variation.

Now if a solicitor does not pay, he and/or his client, can be sued in the courts in the ordinary way. Interestingly, the Joint Tribunal can be used as an alternative and which presumably is seen as a slightly more gentlemanly form of fighting over fees.

A solicitor who did not pay up following a Joint Tribunal would find himself unable to instruct any barrister on the usual credit terms but would have to send money with the brief. A list of such solicitors was kept by the Bar Council and regularly circulated amongst chambers to make sure that no services on credit were being provided. The contractual terms were seen by the Bar Council as sufficiently robust for this additional sanction to be otiose. So a solicitor who finds himself on the List of Defaulting solicitors (previously the Withdrawal of Credit list) is able to go to other counsel on the same case and seek credit with that counsel/chambers. This has been an unnecessary shot straight through the metatarsal by the Bar Council in the view of many chambers whose practical methods of enforcement are limited.

These changes have not really altered the way in which solicitors and counsel interact during the life of a case. Counsel is still usually paid win or lose and so is prepared to draft pleadings, advise on merits etc and 'do his best' in court regardless of the merits. It is only if, for example, counsel is asked to plead fraud without evidence or otherwise argue a point so hopeless that he will incur the wrath of the court or the censure of the Bar Standards Board, that he will decline instructions.

The use of CFAs by counsel

[5.7]

The use of conditional fee agreements (and potentially Damages-Based Agreements since 1 April 2013) has altered the relationship between solicitors and counsel. It is surprising that it has not altered more in fact but, ironically, some changes that should have taken place have not done so because seemingly neither the solicitor nor the barrister have read the CFA closely enough and acted upon it.

Instructions to advise using a CFA

[5.8]

The first time many counsel see a CFA backed case is when they are asked to advise on the merits. If this is requested in writing, counsel can take the view that the case does not have sufficient merits for him to take it on under a CFA. But if the advice is in conference with the papers arriving relatively shortly beforehand, counsel and his instructing solicitor can be embarrassed if counsel has to decline the instructions at the last minute because he does not have confidence in the case. In practice, counsel have often taken the view that the better course is to conduct the conference and see if any merits emerge. If they do not, the preparation and conference time will have to be written off.

Brief to appear

[5.9]

Similarly, if counsel attends at a trial having only received the papers shortly beforehand, he either has to return the papers and cause professional embarrassment all round or prepare and appear in the expectation that he will not be paid for so doing. The choice is often governed by the value placed on the relationship with the instructing solicitor.

Since counsel is being paid on the outcome of the case, he cannot be compelled to take the brief and the 'cab rank' rule specifically does not apply to CFA cases for this reason.

Counsel can also decline the brief on a CFA if he thinks that he is too senior to deal with it on the basis that he is unlikely to be able to recover the sort of fee he usually commands on that hearing.

Being kept informed

[5.10]

The biggest change ought to be in relation to informing counsel of the progress of the case. The agreements drafted by the Personal Injury Bar Association (with APIL), the Chancery Bar Association and the Bar Council all contain numerous requirements during the life of the case which are honoured in the breach by many solicitors. The requirements are not simply updates regarding progress in the court timetable. They also expect papers to be sent to counsel for advice at specific stages and before certain decisions are taken. Nevertheless, it is a common complaint that cases on which counsel have outstanding fees, for example, for an early advice on the merits, are abandoned by the solicitor without counsel knowing, let along having any input on the decision.

Post-April 2013 agreements

[5.11]

The restrictions on the recoverability of success fees and the deductions from the client's damages applied equally to counsel as they did to solicitors. Therefore, all of the solicitor and counsel agreements needed to be rewritten. The venerable APIL/PIBA agreement for personal injury and clinical negligence cases was updated to version 9. It lost the tick box success fee calculator and acquired a section with options regarding any fees not recovered on settlement or assessment. Both alterations reflected the end of recoverability for success fees and the issue of who will now pay counsel's fees. The other regularly seen agreement, the Chancery Bar Association's CFA was also updated, although it requires rather more effort on the part of the drafter in using its precedent.

The central question is on what basis will counsel be instructed? Anecdotally, it appears that many counsel have attempted to return to a disbursement basis to avoid taking some of the client's damages for a success fee.

Counsel's fees where the solicitor and client CFA is unenforceable

[5.12]

The solicitor's CFA with his client has been challenged as to its validity ever since the advent of recoverability of additional liabilities for the reasons described as the Golden Rule at [**4.3**]. But it has never been clear as to the basis on which the client is liable for the fees of counsel instructed by his solicitor where the solicitor's entitlement to seek payment from his client (via a CFA) has been found to be unenforceable. There is no direct link between the client and counsel in a traditional relationship. It is not obvious that a solicitor's professional obligation to meet counsel's fees would be sufficient to found recovery from the opponent. In any event, as discussed above, that professional obligation ended in 2007.

It is perhaps surprising in these circumstances to find that there has been no authoritative ruling on this issue. The nearest pronouncement is contained in Warby J's decision in the case of *Radford v Frade* [2016] EWHC 1600 (QB). Whilst the decision relies heavily on the wording and scope of the various CFAs involved, it is clear that the client's obligation to pay his solicitor is a pre-requisite for the client to have any liability for the payment of counsel's fees. In the Court of Appeal ([2018] EWCA Civ 119), the Court found that the work done outside the terms of the CFA was carried out under an implied CFA which was ineffective for not being reduced to writing. The argument that the fees reverted to the original retainer letter or to some form of quantum meruit was rejected as it had been for the solicitors.

INTERIM APPLICATIONS

[5.13]

The drafting of most CFAs seeks to cater for the situation where an order for costs is made on the way to a successfully concluded case. The definition of a win is generally based on an award of damages and it is sometimes argued by defendants that until such time as an award for damages has been made, the claimant has not been successful as defined in the CFA. That means that the claimant does not have to pay his solicitor any fees and so the defendant should not have to do so either.

The Law Society model CFA seeks to get round the problem in this way:

> 'If on the way to winning or losing you are awarded any costs, by agreement or court order, then we are entitled to payment of those costs, together with a success fee on those charges if you win overall.'

What does 'if you win overall' mean in this sentence? It seems clear that it is intended to refer solely to the success fee. The entitlement to payment of the base costs is meant to be crystallised when the client is awarded costs. However it can quite plausibly be argued that the base costs, together with the success fee, only become an entitlement if and when the case is won overall. For example, in *Plevin v DAS Legal Expense Insurance Co Ltd* [2019] EWHC 1339 (Comm), HHJ Pearce, sitting as a High Court judge, described the concept of a client being liable to pay her solicitors because of an interim award en route to losing the claim overall was 'unlikely' and 'contrary to the whole concept of a "no win no fee agreement"'.

Most courts in fact seem to consider this to be a satisfactory form of words. They take the view that the ultimate outcome does not matter, other than for the success fee. With the end of recoverability of the success fee, it may well be that the general argument outlined above, is not pursued by paying parties since courts are not going to be very keen to deprive a party of his base costs following an application unless there is a clear problem with the wording of the agreement.

CHANGING ARRANGEMENTS

Dating of CFAs

[5.14]

In order to begin work under a CFA it is normally prepared and dated as soon as possible. The work done is usually described as being from 'now' until the agreement ends. But in some litigation, it is not always possible to sign up the client to a CFA at the outset because the prospects are too uncertain. In other situations, a new CFA is required because the original party needs to be substituted, through death, insolvency, incapacity etc.

The question therefore was always going to crop up of 'can I make my CFA cover work done before the CFA was signed?' The first judicial pronouncement on this was from the then Senior Costs Judge, Master Hurst in *King v Telegraph Group Ltd* [2005] EWHC 90015 (Costs) where he approved the concept as a matter of contract in relation to the base fees but not in respect of the success fees.

Master Hurst described the process as 'back dating' but this was disapproved by Stanley Burnton J in *Holmes v Alfred McAlpine Homes (Yorkshire) Ltd* [2006] EWHC 110 (QB). The correct approach was for the agreement to be dated on the date it was signed but for the wording to be revised to make clear that it had retrospective effect. The judge put it like this:

> 'Mr Wilkinson submitted that the agreement was on its face, retrospective. That is incorrect. It was not retrospective: it was back-dated, which is a very different thing. A properly drafted agreement would have borne the date on which it was executed, but would have expressly provided for its application to work done from the prior date agreed by the parties. The written agreement in this case was misleading.'

The claimant was lucky in *Holmes* because he succeeded on other grounds to show the CFA was enforceable. He, or perhaps more accurately his solicitors, got the essential point wrong regarding back dating rather than making agreements properly retrospective. Parties sometimes also refer to the case of *Forde v Birmingham City Council* [2009] EWHC 12 (QB), where the position described in *Holmes* was confirmed.

How should you make your CFA retrospective? The standard amendment to the Law Society wording is made under the heading 'Basic Charges' where the original wording is 'These are for work done from now until this agreement ends.' Amendments are usually either to remove the word 'now' in order to say 'These are for work done from xx/yy/zzzz . . . ' (being the date on which the client was first seen) or 'These are for work done from when you first instructed us . . . .' Wording along these lines was used in *King* and has been widely used thereafter.

Creating an unintended CFA

[5.15]

The use of solicitors to deal with part of a case while the client deals with other parts is said to be the inevitable future of solicitor client relationships in many areas given the inherent cost of legal representation. Whether that is true for you, the case of *Rees v Gateley Wareing (a firm)* [2014] EWCA Civ 1351, demonstrates the danger of providing limited services without considering properly the nature of the retainer being created. The defendants acted for the claimants in respect of some negotiations prior to the commencement of proceedings and as shadow solicitors to another firm who were on the court record. The parties understood that the arrangement was a conditional fee agreement, but since it was for a percentage of any damages recovered it was more properly described as a contingency fee agreement (or even a DBA). The statutory requirements under s 58 were not followed and the defendants sought to argue that they were not providing litigation services and so were not caught by s 58. Lewinson LJ, giving the lead judgment, accepted the claimants' argument that it was not a question of whether the solicitors were on the record or not, but whether the work was of the sort which would ordinarily be done by solicitors on the record who were conducting litigation. Otherwise solicitors could easily side-step the strict regulatory controls in litigation as to working for a percentage of the sums recovered.

In *Radford* the parties' CFA was limited to certain steps in the litigation. When the case continued the additional work done was held to have been carried out under an implied CFA even though neither the solicitor nor clients ever appeared to consider it. The first instance and appeal courts were all clear that the parties' expectations were that the work was being carried out under a CFA. Since the one they had signed did not cover the additional work, the parties must have created an unintended CFA which was unenforceable as it was not in writing.

Assignment of CFAs

[5.16]

In *Jenkins v Young Brothers Transport Ltd* [2006] EWHC 151 (QB), the claimant instituted proceedings funded by a CFA. When the solicitor acting for him changed firms, the CFA was assigned from the first firm to the second. The solicitor changed firms again and once again the CFA was assigned. The case was settled on terms of damages of £445,000 with costs to be agreed. The defendant challenged the lawfulness of the CFA on the basis that it could not be assigned as a matter of general contract law.

The court held that it would be a novel approach to the administration of justice if the court were to seek to interfere with a professional relationship whose propriety and worth had never been challenged. In these circumstances the benefit and burden of the CFA could be assigned as an exception to the general rule.

Whilst the decision in *Jenkins* had a number of detractors, it remained essentially the only case on the subject until LASPO created a temporal cliff edge between CFAs with recoverable success fees and CFAs without them. If a paying party could demonstrate that a change in circumstance meant that a new, post-April 2013 agreement had been created, the success fees would no longer be recoverable. This financial benefit was worth spending time consulting the text books regarding the assignment of choses in action etc.

In *Budana v The Leeds Teaching Hospitals NHS Trust* (4 February 2016), a regional costs judge found against the claimant's arrangements. He decided that the CFA had been terminated with the first firm and a novated agreement entered into with the second. If he were wrong about that, he would have accepted that the agreement had been assigned in accordance with *Jenkins*. The Court of Appeal took the view that the first CFA had not in fact been terminated. When the solicitors informed the client that they were ending their personal injury work and had sold their cases to the second firm, this was a repudiatory breach of the CFA by the solicitors. But that did not mean that the agreement was necessarily ended. The client had the option of either treating the CFA as terminated or could instead affirm the CFA. The court found she had done the latter by her conduct in signing the deed of assignment and also a back-up CFA in case the first was considered not to have been validly signed.

The court went further in deciding that the success fee was still recoverable as part of the benefits and burdens transferred between the parties by the deed of assignment. This was so notwithstanding that the claimant signed the various documents after 1 April 2013 – they were to take effect from 22 March 2013 when the claimant's first solicitors told her that they were ceasing to act.

Cancellation of CFAs

[5.17]

If the client terminates a CFA through his cancellation rights under the Consumer Contracts (Information, Cancellation and Additional Charges) Regulations 2013 that is the end of the CFA and the client has no other liability to the solicitor.

However, if the CFA is cancelled otherwise, for example, under the provisions requiring the client not to mislead the solicitor, residual fees may be payable under an underlying retainer. In *Kris Motor Spares Ltd v Fox Williams LLP* [2009] EWHC 2813 (QB), the client misled the solicitors as to the independence of an expert witness whose evidence was crucial. The solicitors terminated the CFA on terms that they would continue to provide services to conclude the case on ordinary fee terms, the opponents having offered a 'drop hands' outcome. The CFA provided for full fees to be paid in the event of such termination. Had the solicitors not terminated at that stage the case would have concluded as a loss under the CFA and the solicitors would have only recovered 70% of their fees. It was held that the CFA had been validly terminated, the retainer remained and therefore the client was not left unrepresented but had a liability for costs. It should be kept in mind that termination of a retainer at common law requires a good reason to terminate the retainer and also reasonable notice to cease acting.

SECURITY FOR COSTS

[5.18]

We deal with security for costs applications in detail in Chapter 19. But where the client is using a CFA, there are some considerations which do not apply to other forms of funding. In particular, it is sometimes possible to purchase ATE insurance, essentially in the form of a bond, in order to persuade the court that the opponent's concerns about the client being good for the money are exaggerated.

On many occasions an opponent will accept the existence of an ATE policy as being sufficient not to proceed with a security for costs application. But to do so, in our view, suggests that they have not really considered the relationship between the client and the ATE insurer sufficiently closely. All ATE policies have their policy terms requiring the client to comply with various matters regarding the conduct of the litigation. If the client fails to do so, the insurer will be at liberty to cancel the policy. This may mean that adverse costs incurred after the date of cancellation will not be met. In a more serious case, the policy might be avoided ab initio and as such the opponent will not be able to take any benefit of the ATE policy indemnity unless the client is made insolvent and the opponent successfully sues the ATE insurer in the client's shoes (which would involve demonstrating that the policy should not have been cancelled or avoided as the case may be.)

The opponent ought to have been notified of the cancellation of the policy when Notices of Funding were obligatory, but that did not always happen. Now that such Notices are no longer required there is very little prospect of such notification taking place.

The potential inadequacy of ATE policies in security for costs applications was considered in *Al-Koronky v Time-Life Entertainment Group Ltd* [2005] EWHC 1688 (QB). The court held that the existence of a satisfactory ATE policy could help in resisting an application. But since the policy did not pay out if the claimant had been untruthful, and as this was a libel claim where the only real issue was the truthfulness of the claimant, the policy was in effect worthless.

In *Michael Phillips Architects Ltd v Riklin* [2010] EWHC 834 (TCC), Akenhead J set out the following common sense guide to ATE in security for costs cases:

(a) There is no reason in principle why an ATE insurance policy could not provide some or some element of security.
(b) It will be a rare case where the ATE insurance policy can provide as good security as a payment into court or a bank bond or guarantee.
(c) A claimant must demonstrate that the policy actually does provide some security: there must not be terms pursuant to which or circumstances in which the insurers can readily but legitimately and contractually avoid liability to pay out for the defendant's costs.
(d) There is no reason in principle why the amount fixed by a security for costs order could not be somewhat reduced to take into account any realistic probability that the ATE insurance would cover the costs of the defendant.

As can be seen from Chapter 9, some claimants take a belt and braces approach to security but it is still not enough for some defendants (see **[9.30]**).

The question that arose in *Mengi v Hermitage* [2012] EWHC 2045 (QB), was whether an order for security ought to take into account a defendant's potential success fee. Tugendhat J included an allowance for a 100% success fee without seeing the CFA, reasoning that to take into account that costs would involve an uplift for the CFA did not involve any illegitimate speculation. Obviously this is a case that is only relevant where the case is sufficiently old for the defendant to have entered into a CFA or CCFA prior to 1 April 2013 and therefore to have a recoverable success fee. (Or involve one of the discrete areas where additional liabilities have remained recoverable.)

ENDING THE RETAINER BEFORE THE CASE CONCLUDES

[5.19]

As is always said, a client can end a retainer at any time, a solicitor only for good reason and with reasonable notice. The position changes with a funding arrangement in respect of terminating that arrangement. A client can still effectively end it at any time because he is free to instruct the solicitor of his choice. If he decides to move his case to another firm, that is the end of the funding arrangement as well as the retainer. The client may have to pay costs to retrieve his papers but is not limited otherwise. The difference comes with the solicitor's entitlement to end the CFA. As we have seen in *Kris Motor Spares Ltd v Fox Williams LLP* above, the CFA funding arrangement can be ended without the underlying retainer of the solicitor bringing proceedings on the instruction of the client concluding.

Why would you want to end the CFA? The usual reasons for ending a CFA before the end of a case are:

(a) a different form of funding is more appropriate
(b) the prospects of success are not sufficient to continue
(c) the client is not co-operating

Let us take these in turn

Other funding

[5.20]

Alternative funding enquiries are meant to have been carried out at the beginning of the case so a decision that another option is more appropriate during the case ought to be rare. It is likely to be the case that BTE insurance has come to light either through more diligent searching or a belated response from a potential insurer. It could possibly be – though this is now extremely rare – that the client is now eligible for legal aid funding but was not previously. Even if this is so, it is not necessarily the case that to continue with a CFA would be an unreasonable choice and the decision would be very much case specific. The same is true if a different form of funding, such as union backing, became available part way through a case.

It was not the case that the use of CFAs and ATE insurance was always to be the last resort purely because they would be more expensive for the opponent. Nevertheless, that was generally the approach taken on assessment by the courts where the party could have used Legal Aid or BTE insurance (or had started off doing so but changed to a CFA and ATE insurance during the case): see, for example, the case of *Surrey* at **[6.21]**. Now that these additional liabilities are no longer recoverable from the opponent the concept of a CFA being a last resort has presumably ended. It may still have been an unreasonable choice on its facts, but that would be a matter for the client to take up, not the opponent.

Lack of Prospects

[5.21]

Much CFA litigation is conducted with ATE insurance firmly in tow. If the prospects drop below the insurer's minimum threshold, the diminution in prospects has to be reported and the likelihood is that the ATE insurance will be cancelled from that point. The consequence for the solicitor is that any further disbursements will not be recoverable from the ATE insurer if they are not recovered from the opponent. This is a sizeable hurdle to surmount even if the solicitor is prepared to spend more time and effort in trying to improve the prospects, difficult though that almost always is.

Where the prospects have deteriorated slowly, particularly in ways about which the opponent is not yet aware, the solicitor will be expected to try to bring a resolution to the claim so that the policy does not have to be formally cancelled and potentially notification given to the opponent. Acceptance of a nuisance offer, even out of time, or a drop hands settlement has been preferable to a discontinuance from the ATE insurer's point of view and they are likely to allow the solicitor a little time in which to try to bring this about. The arrival of Qualified One Way Costs shifting will affect some of the assumptions made to date since the ATE insurer will not have a liability in respect of a discontinuance unless there is some suggestion of fraud, but the ATE insurer will not want to be backing cases with slim prospects of success in any event.

Since payment is based on the outcome of the case, all CFAs contain a clause allowing the solicitor to bail out if the prospects have reduced. To do otherwise would be to lock in the legal team to a case that could not win but would involve the lawyers in (potentially considerable) irrecoverable costs. The existence of this bail out clause has been used by paying parties to argue that the risk assessment of a case is skewed in the solicitor's favour because the case will not always reach the end of the litigation, ie a trial. Accordingly, the prospects are improved in the solicitor's favour. See **[6.31]** for a discussion of the case of *McCarthy v Essex Rivers Healthcare NHS Trust* [2010] 1 Costs LR 59 on this point.

Lack of capacity

[5.22]

Where a party loses the capacity to pursue or defend his case, a litigation friend needs to be appointed (see Chapter 34). A new retainer will be required and if the party was using a CFA, it is very often the case that the litigation friend will enter into a CFA on similar or identical terms. But what happens if the client only loses capacity temporarily? Is the retainer frustrated so that it automatically comes to an end? Can a successful party seeks costs based on that CFA even for periods when he was incapable of giving instructions? The answer, according to Phillips J in *Blankley v Central Manchester and Manchester Children's University Hospitals NHS Trust* [2014] EWHC 168 (QB), is that the retainer continues:

> 'I have reached the . . . conclusion . . . that the intervening incapacity of a party does not frustrate or otherwise terminate a solicitor's retainer. While such incapacity does have the effect of removing the authority of the solicitor to act on behalf of the party lacking capacity for the duration of that incapacity, such authority can be restored when a deputy is appointed and provides instructions to the solicitors in that capacity, or otherwise if and when the claimant regains capacity. There is no reason, as a matter of authority or legal principle, why an inability to instruct solicitors in the intervening period (which may be quite short) should be taken to have the effect of immediately ending a solicitor's retainer.'

Where the litigation friend has to cease acting, an agreement with the replacement litigation friend can easily be agreed with the continuing solicitors. But what happens where a litigation friend enters into a CFA pre-April 2013 but has to be replaced after April 2013? Can the CFA be assigned or is it a new agreement (and as such cannot involve recoverable success fees (generally))? Master Brown took the view in *Mole v Parkdean Holiday Parks Ltd* [2017] EWHC B10 (Costs) that a change of litigation friend did not affect the continuing agreement between the claimant and his solicitor and so the CFA could be ratified and affirmed by the new litigation friend.

Non-cooperation

[5.23]

Some forms of non-cooperation are not always the client's fault eg, death or insolvency but they still impact on the solicitor's ability to run the case. See **[1.34]** for a discussion of the case of *Higgins & Co Lawyers Ltd v Evans* where the client died and challenges were made to the CFA's termination provisions.

The provision of inadequate instructions is problematic whether looked at through the prism of the CFA or the retainer as a whole. If the situation is bad enough to end the CFA through it, the relationship with the client is likely to be at end in any event.

In *Butler v Bankside Commercial Ltd* [2020] EWCA Civ 203, [2020] 4 All ER 340, [2020] Costs LR 309, the Court of Appeal upheld Turner J's decision on the situation where a client rejected advice about making a settlement. The client sought to argue that the phrase had a narrow meaning regarding essentially an offer made by the opponent which would lead to settlement. The judiciary, however, accepted the solicitors' argument that it had a rather broader meaning regarding negotiations more generally.

It is not always the case that the solicitor can rely on advice being rejected to bring a CFA to an end. In *Karis Developments Ltd v EMW Law LLP* (13 January 2020), Master Brown concluded that the solicitors' advice was unreasonable and so reliance could not be placed upon it by them and they had terminated the agreement contrary to the requirement to complete the entire contract. As such, they were not entitled to any fees for the work done.

Which rate?

[5.24]

If the CFA comes to an end at a point where it can be said that the client may still win, the solicitor should be entitled to seek his costs at the successful rate. The usual provisions allow for such base costs to be paid out upon termination. Alternatively the base costs and any success fee will be paid if and when the client has been successful.

If the CFA comes to an end because the case is unlikely to win, then the unsuccessful rates will apply. In a personal injury case, this rate may well be nothing. But in a commercial matter, there is likely to be a lower rate payable and which should be charged, if it has not already been charged as the case progressed. The drafting of the CFA is much more complicated in relation to the termination provisions if there is a lower fee when unsuccessful than where it is a no win, no fee agreement.

AFTER THE CASE ENDS

Payment on account following a hearing

[5.25]

We deal with payments on account in detail in Chapter 25. The following comments are made in the context of unlocking the Work in Progress on your file which is inevitable when using an agreement whose terms are contingent on the outcome of the case.

Where your client has succeeded at a final hearing, you have succeeded within the terms of your CFA. If you have not yet satisfied the definition of success at that point, then let us hope that it is because your client has only won on liability, to use that term in a relatively loose sense for some forms of litigation. As such, you still need to agree the damages and/or have a hearing to determine how much. You may have obtained an order for costs of the liability trial already. If it is a forthwith order then you could have the costs assessed, but not otherwise (CPR 47.1). So if your opponent can easily establish that you have not really 'won' yet according to your CFA then better to wait. In that case you can come back to this chapter later.

If you have agreed a form of CFA Lite so that recovery is a requirement and not just an award of costs, you should still be in a position to seek an interim payment because logically that is only hastening the payment that your client has agreed with you anyway. Furthermore, the recovery is usually based on a recovery of damages rather than costs which is the purpose of the interim payment here.

If there is some other reason why the definition has not been triggered you may be in some difficulties in recovering anything under that agreement.

CPR 44.2(8) states that 'where the court orders a party to pay costs subject to detailed assessment, it will order that party to pay a reasonable amount on account of costs, unless there is good reason not to do so.'

This rule came into force on 1 April 2013. Before then, the court might make an order for an interim payment. Now, as with much of the Jackson inspired legislation the court is exhorted to make a positive order. The theory is that if a sizeable interim payment is made by the loser to the winner, the remaining sum will be more easily agreed because the overall playing field for the parties has been reduced. Make sure that you or your advocate have worked out how much you will be seeking on an interim payment application at the end of the hearing. You will need an estimate or your latest approved budget for this purpose. While it will take time to be sure how judges will react, our assumption is that trial judges will be willing to make an award of a larger percentage of the overall costs where there is a budget than if there is only an estimate before the court.

This legislative encouragement has persuaded courts to award interim payments as to costs where liability has been determined but not quantum. The liability costs can be assessed (a forthwith order being helpful) and that has always been so. Newly, quantum costs have been allowed even though the level of quantum has not been finalised. See Master Cook's case management decision in *RXK (A child proceeding by her mother and litigation friend GXK) v Hampshire Hospitals NHS Foundation Trust* [2019] EWHC 2751 (QB) for a discussion of this point.

What should a court do when faced with a sizeable success fee claimed as part of the interim payment? The practical answer is that the judge will undoubtedly take a view about how risky he thought the case was and will factor that into his decision. Whether he will pronounce this publicly is a different matter. Some judges are quite willing to assess the success fee at the time of the trial and record it rather than leaving it for the judge on assessment. In *Crema v Cenkos Securities plc* [2011] EWCA Civ 10, the Court of Appeal considered this issue in the light of a 100% success fee amounting to £250,000. Neither side could point to any previous case law on whether a large uplift should be taken into account when ordering an interim payment. On the basis that the court should order what will almost certainly be recovered the figure arrived at was £300,000. As such Crema would almost certainly get some uplift.

Payment on account following an agreement

[5.26]

Where agreement has been reached by acceptance of a Part 36 offer, the opportunity to be before the court to seek an interim payment of costs obviously does not occur. Instead a deemed order has been made by virtue of Part 36. There are good policy reasons for requiring parties to get on with the detailed assessment proceedings in accordance with Part 47 and so an application for an interim costs certificate is the usual mechanism for obtaining a payment on account of costs. Once a detailed assessment hearing has been requested (so that an application for an interim certificate can be made) there can be no argument regarding jurisdiction. Consequently, these circumstances should prove a powerful incentive for you to get your breakdown or bill drafted and submitted to the other side as soon as possible. If, however, you wish to make an application before requesting a hearing date, we would refer you to Chapter 25 regarding applications for interim payments, particularly given the Court of Appeal's decision in *Global Assets Advisory Services Ltd v Grandlane Developments Ltd* [2019] EWCA Civ 1764.

Where there has been a mediation or other form of negotiation which requires a consent order to be prepared for the court's approval, there is scope for you to include an order for an interim payment. Given the wording of CPR 44.2(8) it will be difficult for your opponent to justify any outright opposition to an interim payment.

The laudable aim of provisional assessments is that they will be completed within six weeks of the request for detailed assessment. It is unlikely that courts will entertain interim costs certificate applications if the delay in getting a provisionally assessed bill is well under two months. If the courts do not manage to hold the six week target, they are likely to be sufficiently overwhelmed with work that they are not necessarily going to be dealing with interim costs applications speedily in any event. So if your costs are under £75,000 in total you definitely need to make sure that you seek an interim payment when the case concludes and do not leave it until later.

CALCULATION OF THE CAP

Personal injury cases

[5.27]

The requirements of s 58(4B) of the Courts and Legal Services Act 1990 added by LASPO 2012 were discussed in Chapter 4. In essence, a personal injury client's damages cannot be reduced by more than 25% of his PSLA award and past losses. This cap only applies to personal injury cases and does not apply in respect of an appeal where the limit is 100% of these damages.

By defining the percentage as being based on various heads of damage, the effect of any finding of contributory negligence will be to reduce the damages and therefore the success fee available to the solicitor. Deductions to the damages also have to be made for any recoupable CRU benefits with the same shrinking effect to the potential pot.

The evil of delay

[5.28]

Clients have often complained about the lack of speed with which their claims have been brought. These complaints may well have more weight to them in the future. The longer the case takes to get to trial, the more that future losses will become past losses and thereby become susceptible to deduction. Meticulous records of who caused what delay could well prove to be very valuable if a claim of dilatoriness is made by the client at the end of the case.

The need for communication

[5.29]

A superficial glance at this structure is enough to see that communication with the client prior to settlement is paramount. The more the client understands the likely damages he may receive before the defendant makes a Part 36 offer or round table proposal (or the case gets to trial), the more that his expectations can be managed. Defendants are not going to make life easy for the claimants and offers are unlikely to be broken down so that easy calculations can be made of the costs consequences to the client of acceptance. Court judgments will hopefully be clear on how a damages figure is calculated but if it is not, it will be very difficult to get further clarification from the court. A client who knows in round terms what his past pecuniary losses and PSLA awards are can make an informed choice. A client who comes upon the options for the first time when the offer is made will almost certainly feel pressured into settlement to some degree however balanced and objective the advice may be.

QOCS

[5.30]

The issue of QOCS is dealt with in Chapter 11 but it is easy to see how it may impact in the situations being discussed here. If the claimant does not beat the defendant's Part 36 offer, a proportion of his damages will be kept by the defendant to meet his own costs. If the damages are extinguished by such costs then at least there is no need to discuss this point further with your client because 25% of nothing needs no discussion. But if the expected damages are halved by QOCS, for example, the profitability of the case may be called into question. (Cases involving fundamental dishonesty or struck out for lack of progress are not going to be problematic in the same way because there will not be any damages in the first place.)

Which costs have to fit into the cap? The legislation is clear that success fees are subject to the maximum limit. But any disbursements, including any ATE premium fall outside that limit and can be sought separately. If counsel is being paid by an ordinary retainer, his fees will be dealt with separately as well. But if he is using a CFA as well as the solicitor, there is a further success fee which needs to fit within the maximum limit.

Will there be room? It must be doubtful. Even a success fee of 12.5% of the costs may well be a significant proportion of the damages and since the standard figures for success fees in personal injury cases have been removed from the rules for new cases, there is no reason to expect continued adherence to those figures.

If there is not enough room, will counsel be prepared to continue to act on a no win, no fee basis but without a success fee? Or will the solicitor or client be prepared to pay a smaller fee – but still some fee – in the event of a loss? A number of counsel would wish to go back to being a disbursement paid win or lose and therefore without any success fee. Some have suggested increasing their hourly rate so that they build in the success fee into that rate. Why that increased rate is going to seem reasonable on either a between the parties or solicitor and client assessment is not immediately obvious. Perhaps the agreement of the client at the outset is thought to change an unreasonable rate into a reasonable one. The need for informed consent of unusual items may go well beyond simply recording matters in the client care letter: see *Herbert v HH Law Ltd* [2019] EWCA Civ 527 discussed at **[3.21]**.

NOTIFICATION TO INSURERS

[5.31]

Where the case is backed by any form of legal expenses insurance, you should make sure that the insurers are notified of the outcome. In many cases this is now possible online. It is far easier to remember to do this straightaway than to be chased for information months or years later when the files have been archived.

If you make sure you do this regularly, it also affords an opportunity to make any claims for unrecovered disbursements that can be paid under the policy but will not be paid very willingly if claimed a long time after the case has ended.

INTEREST ON COSTS

[5.32]

As with payments on account (see [**5.25**]) this subject has its own Chapter later in this book (Chapter 32). The comments made here are simply to round off the economics of running cases on CFAs and that includes claiming interest on costs which, given the applicable rates, may prove quite lucrative.

There are two aspects to interest on costs that need to be considered. The first is the court admonishing the defendant for failing to accept the offer your claimant client made which your client subsequently beat at the hearing. The second is the question of interest on costs which have been 'fructifying in the wrong pocket' to quote one of the old authorities.

Punitive interest

[5.33]

The decisions in this area are very much fact sensitive. In *Crema v Cenkos Securities* the Court of Appeal considered that the winning claimant had taken a number of time consuming, bad points and so only allowed the claimant 75% of his costs. Nevertheless, since the claimant beat his own Part 36 offer, the costs were not only to be assessed on the indemnity basis but also would attract interest at the rate of 5% above base rate.

By contrast, the fee arrangements in *Pankhurst v White* [2010] EWCA Civ 1445, came in for severe criticism from Jackson LJ who was moved to describe them as 'grotesque'. The chronology of the facts is sufficiently complicated for both parties to have been able to claim that their opponent would have been better off taking their offer than continuing. The judge at first instance declined to give the claimant indemnity costs or interest on the costs. The Court of Appeal took the view that the level of the success fee claimed where liability was admitted, the fact that the client still paid the solicitor in the event of not beating a Part 36 offer, and that there was ATE insurance against Part 36 adverse costs meant that the decision not to award interest on the costs was fully justified.

Out of pocket interest

[5.34]

A number of first instance decisions took the view that a CFA funded client should not get interest on his costs until they had been assessed because the client had not paid them. This assumed that the claimant had not been billed once the case had been successful and had settled the solicitor's fees pending the detailed assessment. But this assumption certainly followed the general practice of not asking clients to pay out for anything if at all possible. The best known of these cases is called *Gray v Toner* (11 November 2010, Liverpool County Court).

The Court of Appeal found an opportunity to consider this issue in *Simcoe v Jacuzzi UK Group plc* [2012] EWCA Civ 137. The Court held that the starting point under CPR 40.8 is the same as the rule under the County Courts (Interest on Judgment Debts) Order 1991, namely that interest runs from the date ordered not the date assessed or agreed. This is often referred to as the 'incipitur' rule rather than the 'allocatur' rule. The Court then considered whether the existence of a CFA was relevant in deciding whether to make an order on cases to which CPR 40.8 applied. It was held that the existence of a CFA was not relevant and so the usual order would be that interest runs from the date costs are ordered.

In *Re Southern Counties Fresh Foods Ltd, Cobden Investments Ltd v Romford Wholesale Meats Ltd* [2011] EWHC 1370 (Ch), the client had paid substantial interim costs before entering into a CFA. The judge held that he had a discretion to allow interest on the costs incurred prior to the date of the costs order in order to compensate the claimant for being out of pocket.

WHERE UNSUCCESSFUL

[5.35]

If you have been operating under a pure no win, no fee agreement, your fees are unfortunately written off since there is no-one to pay them. The same will be the case for expenses if you have agreed with your client that both fees and expenses will be conditional upon the outcome. Alternatively, you or your client may have insured the case using either BTE or ATE insurance and in which case it will be important to get your claim form in before any claim for adverse costs comes in from your opponent. If it is a case to which costs protection under QOCS applies, that risk is obviously lower.

If, on the other hand, your client has agreed to a CFA with differential fee rates, you will need to render a final bill. You will need to check whether you have sought and obtained money on account through interim bills. If they are not statute bills, you need to look at whether there was any additional work carried out during the case that has not been charged for and include it in the final invoice. Similar considerations apply if you have agreed a fixed figure in the event of an unsuccessful outcome. If you have had payments on account they will need to be offset against the fixed sum. Hopefully, this will not mean a reimbursement to the client but if it does it will no doubt inform your estimation of the fee (or the appropriate interim bills) next time.

WHERE NEITHER SUCCESSFUL NOR UNSUCCESSFUL

[5.36]

As a footnote to the perils of running cases whose payment is contingent upon the outcome it seems fitting to end with the case of *Marley v Rawlings* [2014] UKSC 51, which related to contentious probate proceedings following a mix up in the signing of spouses' mirror wills. Counsel for the successful appellants were instructed under CFAs in the Supreme Court, but not for the unsuccessful appeals below. When it came to concluding whether the other parties or the estate ought to meet the costs, the Supreme Court took an interventionist approach and suggested that counsel might wish to forgo their success fees in order for an appropriate order as to costs to be made. It would have been a brave member of the Bar who declined such an invitation and the successful barristers walked away with only their base fees.

CHAPTER 6

'OLD' CONDITIONAL FEE AGREEMENTS AND ATE INSURANCE

INTRODUCTION TO 'OLD' CONDITIONAL FEE AGREEMENTS AND ATE INSURANCE

[6.1]

In this chapter we look at the issues that arise specifically in respect of CFAs and ATE insurance taken out prior to 1 April 2013 and which, as a result, generally involve 'additional liabilities' being paid by the losing opponent. More than seven years after 'J' Day, there are still such cases coming to a detailed assessment. For simplicity, this chapter assumes that 'pre-commencement' means any date prior to the implementation of the Legal Aid Sentencing and Punishment of Offenders Act 2012 ('LASPO 2012') on 1 April 2013 although the comments in this chapter also apply to those discrete areas where claims could still be brought with a recoverable success fee or insurance policy. In other words, claims concerning mesothelioma, privacy and publication (up to April 2019 for success fees), or (some) insolvency (up to April 2016). This also includes, to a certain extent, ATE policies in clinical negligence claims. More information regarding the transitional provisions can be found at the end of this chapter.

Prior to April 2000, additional liabilities were not recoverable from the opponent and the changes in April 2013 essentially returned litigators to that position. For the intervening dozen or so years the parties played on a differently laid out playing field and this resulted in different tactics being employed on all sides. Most of the following issues raised are woven together by the desire of the paying party – very often a defendant liability insurer in a personal injury case – to persuade a court that, for one reason or another, the additional liability should not be recoverable. Some of the arguments raised have the effect of making all fees irrecoverable because of the indemnity principle (see the Golden Rule at [4.3]) and this has meant that the consequences of losing a generic point have driven a number of firms out of business.

For some time now we have taken the view that it is unnecessary to cover the regime in place prior to April 2000. As from the 2018 edition, we have taken essentially the same view regarding CFAs which pre-date 30 November 2005 (the next significant milestone) since they have dwindled to the point of negligibility. Commentary on the complex regulations from that period can be found in earlier editions of Cook should you find yourself dealing with an ancient case.

Throughout the period during which additional liabilities have been recoverable in defamation claims, the media defendants have brought various challenges. Some have been on the level of recoverability and some have challenged the very entitlement to additional costs given the 'chilling effect' it may have on the freedom of the press under article 10 ECHR. In April 2017, the Supreme Court handed down its judgment in *Times Newspapers Ltd v Flood* [2017] UKSC 33. Whilst accepting that the defendants' article 10 rights in the three conjoined cases were engaged, they were much weaker in 'phone hacking' cases than in *MGN v UK* (2011) 53 EHRR 5 on which the defendants had built their case. The end of obtaining information which was of interest to the public (but not actually in the public interest) had not come close to justifying the means. As such, additional liabilities remain recoverable in defamation cases.

The issues in this chapter revolve around:

(a) the various legislative provisions that have applied during the period from 1 April 2000 to 31 March 2013
(b) compliance with those requirements, as considered by the courts
(c) professional conduct compliance
(d) the level of the success fees claimed as dealt with by the courts and by the CPR
(e) challenges to the level of ATE premiums
(f) the giving of notice of the existence of the CFA or ATE policy.

The issues are dealt with in this order below.

THE PRIMARY LEGISLATION

[6.2]

The relevant primary legislation is the Courts and Legal Services Act ('CLSA') 1990 as amended by the Access to Justice Act ('AJA') 1999.

Advocacy or Litigation Services

[6.3]

Section 58(1) applies to the provision of litigation services which are defined in s 119(1) as 'any services which it would be reasonable to expect a person who is exercising, or is contemplating exercising, a right to conduct litigation in relation to any proceedings, or any contemplated proceedings, to provide'. In *Gaynor v Central West London Buses Ltd* [2006] EWCA Civ 1120, the retainer letter included the provision: 'If your claim is disputed by your opponent and you decide not to pursue your claim then we will not make a charge for the work we have done to date'. The claim was pursued and the client awarded her costs. Did this provision make the agreement a CFA and thus unenforceable because it did not comply with the CFA legislation? 'No' said the Court of Appeal. The work done before a decision was made not to pursue the claim was pre-litigation work which did not constitute the provision of litigation services under section 119(1). The solicitors were not exercising their right to conduct litigation and could not be said to be contemplating exercising that right until the potential defendant disputed the claim. Advising on the merits and writing a letter before action did not amount to litigation services. Therefore the agreement was not a CFA and the costs were recoverable.

It is possible to make either too much or too little of this decision. Clearly the use of the disputed provision does not render a retainer unenforceable. Although pre-proceedings work is by definition non-contentious business this does not prevent the parties entering into a CFA in respect of it at the outset. Most CFAs are entered into at the non-contentious business stage and many of them relate to claims which are settled without the issuing of proceedings (and which would retrospectively convert the work into contentious business (see Chapter 8)). The curiosity of this decision is that although the work in question was subsequently converted into contentious business by the commencement of proceedings it was not litigation services for the purposes of s 119(1). The Court of Appeal appears to have identified the new category of 'pre-litigation contentious business'.

Gaynor was considered and applied by the Court of Appeal in *Rees v Gateley Wareing (a firm)* [2014] EWCA Civ 1351, but not in a way that benefitted the solicitor defendants. They were instructed to try to resolve a dispute on a commercial basis and without commencing proceedings. When other parties took the claimants to court, they (the claimants) instructed a different firm to go on the record and the defendants were used to 'shadow' the work of those other solicitors. The Court of Appeal considered this to fall within the definition of litigation services under s 119(1) because the work they did could only be done by those entitled to conduct litigation. On the facts the CFA was unenforceable and the defendant could not recover any costs from the claimants. If the defendants had not been providing litigation services (as the judge at first instance had found) then solicitors could sidestep the regulatory regime and its safeguards by assisting the solicitors actually on the record and that could not be right according to the Court of Appeal.

Section 58 also applies to the exercise of a right of audience and in *Fosberry v Revenue & Customs Comrs* [2006] EWHC 90061 (Costs) the parties conceded that the VAT Tribunal was a Court for the purposes of this section. It was held that the tribunal had granted a non-legal professional advisor a right of audience and the right to conduct litigation. Accordingly his fee arrangement was governed by s 58, and was, unhappily, an invalid CFA, a decision upheld on appeal to the High Court.

Happier news for solicitors occurred in *Pentecost v John* [2015] EWHC 1970 (QB), Turner J overturned the Senior Costs Judge's decision that a CCFA did not comply with s 58. A CCFA between the solicitors and the GMB union was in place when the claimant had his accident in 2008. A risk assessment setting out the success fee for the particular case was produced in accordance with that agreement. A new CCFA was entered into in 2009 which widened the scope of the cases to be covered by it but otherwise was in essentially the same terms as its predecessor. It was said to supersede the 2008 agreement and to act retrospectively to cover all pre-existing cases. No risk assessment was carried out under that agreement and so, it was said, the new agreement did not comply with s 58 because the agreement was required to state the percentage claimed in the particular case. Chief Master Gordon-Saker was persuaded by this argument and that the new agreement was a novation of the old agreement rather than a variation of it. Turner J agreed with the costs judge about the novation but decided that the original risk assessment document was sufficient to bring the second CCFA within s 58 because it set out the percentage increase in writing.

Environmental Protection Act 1990, s 82

[6.4]

For the purposes of CLSA 1990, s 58(4) provides that a success may be claimed in all enforceable conditional fee agreements except in proceedings under s 82 of the Environmental Protection Act 1990. This is a halfway house provision since it is the only form of arguably 'criminal' proceedings where a CFA can be used at all. Someone must have thought that allowing a success fee would be one step too far.

COMPLIANCE WITH THE SECONDARY LEGISLATION

[6.5]

The advent of the recoverability era came via the CFA Order 2000, the CFA Regulations 2000 and the Access to Justice (Membership Organisations) Regulations 2000. Three months later they were joined by the CCFA Regulations 2000 dealing with collective CFAs and which appeared to be drafted as an afterthought.

As will be seen below, amendments to the CFA and CCFA Regulations were made in 2003 before being revoked in 2005. The Membership Organisations were altered in 2005 but remained in existence until 2013. The CFA Order was neither amended nor revoked in 2005 but remained in existence until 2013 and so applies to all CFAs during this period.

2000

[6.6]

The CFA Regulations 2000 were the most important of the secondary legislation. In particular, reg 2 required a CFA to specify the proceedings to which it related. Regulation 3 contained extra requirements for CFAs which provided for a success fee including brief reasons for setting the success fee. Regulation 4 caused the most difficulties for compliance. It set out the information to be given to clients before they entered into a CFA – some of which had to be given orally and some had to be both orally and in writing. The scope for inconsistency between the two – often solely to make the explanation simpler – seemed endless. Regulation 5 required the agreement to be signed by both parties unless it was between the solicitor and another legal representative (usually counsel) and reg 6 required information, such as that in reg 4, to be repeated to clients before an amendment occurred.

[6.7]

The Collective Conditional Fee Agreements Regulations 2000 were a response to concerns expressed during the passage of the AJA 1999 that the individual CFA regime was not administratively suitable for the bulk purchase of legal services. On the whole these regulations did not excite as much litigation as the CFA Regulations 2000.

These regulations made provision for all CCFAs irrespective of the context in which they were to be used. The regulations applied to bulk purchasers of legal services, such as the legal department of a multi-national company, and to bulk providers of legal services such as the legal representatives retained by a trade union to act for its members. There is a crucial difference between these two categories in that the bulk purchaser was also the client, whereas the bulk provider's CCFA would involve numerous clients who were not funding the litigation. The regulations, however, applied consumer protection provisions to all CCFAs, including those where the client was also the funder.

There never were any provisions in the CPR for CCFAs and no changes have been made following the commencement of s 31 of the AJA 1999 to disapply the indemnity principle. There was therefore a question as to the validity of CCFAs where the party to the proceedings was not also the funder. In *Thornley v Lang* [2003] EWCA Civ 1484, the Court of Appeal reviewed the line of authorities dealing with trade union funding and held that the member here was liable on the basis of the CCFA. It reached that result by alternative routes. Either the union agreed with the authority of its member or the member ratified the union's agreement. On either footing there was a contract under which the member was liable and that contract was a CCFA. The court expressly rejected the argument that the member had entered into a CFA on an individual basis which would be subject to the CFA Regulations.

[6.8]

The Access to Justice (Membership Organisations) Regulations 2000 defined the bodies which were prescribed for the purpose of AJA 1999, s 30. They were able to recover a sum as part of legal costs from unsuccessful opponents to reflect the provision of legal help for members and their families. The sum was prescribed to be no greater than the equivalent of the cost to a member of taking out an ATE insurance policy covering adverse costs only.

2003

[6.9]

The onslaught from the word go of challenges from paying parties; the seeming inability for compliance with the regulations by receiving parties; and the courts' willingness to disallow the entirety of the solicitors' costs for non-compliance caused the Government to intervene. Consequently, from 2 June 2003 the CFA (Miscellaneous Amendments) Regulations 2003 amended the CFA Regulations 2000 in two ways.

First, by inserting reg 3A into them to provide that a CFA was still enforceable even though the client was only liable to pay his legal representative's fees and expenses if, and to the extent that, he recovered damages or costs in the proceedings. These were colloquially known as a 'CFA Lite'. Amendments made to the CPR provided that costs payable under such a CFA were recoverable under the old Parts 44 to 48. The indemnity principle was in effect abrogated in relation to this type of CFA.

Simplification was achieved because regs 2, 3 and 4 of the CFA Regulations 2000 did not apply to these simplified CFAs, although they still had to state the circumstances in which fees and expenses were payable – ie they had to define a 'win' and brief reasons for the percentage success fee still had to be given. As a safeguard against the runaway client operating in a costs-free environment, reg 3A(5) permitted the solicitor to include a provision imposing liability on the client for fees and expenses in specified circumstances of non-cooperation or misbehaviour by him or by his death or insolvency.

The CFA (Miscellaneous Amendments) Regulations 2003 also introduced a simplified version of a CCFA which restricted own costs liabilities to any sums recovered. Where a CCFA was being used by a membership organisation it is probable that the member was intended to retain all his damages even under a standard CCFA. The difference is that this regulation means the agreement could actually say so, but it is subject to the same wording as the simplified individual agreement 'sums are recovered . . . whether by way of costs or otherwise'.

2005

[6.10]

The sole purpose of the CFA (Revocation) Regulations 2005 was to remove the 2000 and 2003 Regulations for both individual and collective CFAs. The client care aspects of the earlier regulations – which had caused most of the problems – were left to the Solicitors Regulation Authority whose code contained similar provisions anyway.

The revocation of the Regulations from 1 November 2005 means that a CCFA made after 1 November 2005 need only comply with s 58 of the CLSA 1990 and the CFA Order 2000. As can be seen from Chapter 4, the requirements are limited.

The Access to Justice (Membership Organisations) Regulations 2005 replaced the 2000 Regulations from 1 November 2005. They simplified the requirements but still left the organisation responsible for the administration of the litigation and for ensuring that an agreement with the member existed which could give rise to the recoupment of the costs.

Maximum success fee of 100%

[6.11]

The CFA Order 2000 (Article 4) stated that the maximum success fee that could be claimed in a CFA was 100%. The Order was made in accordance with s 58(4)(c) of the CLSA 1990 and so a CFA which sought more than 100% breached the provisions of both the primary and secondary legislation.

In *Jones v Caradon Catnic Ltd* [2005] EWCA Civ 1821, the Court of Appeal held that a statement in a CFA's risk assessment of a 120% success fee was such a stark departure from the 100% maximum that the CFA could not be saved by a 100% cap elsewhere in the agreement even though neither party would be the loser. If this breach were held to be immaterial, all breaches would be held to be immaterial and the administration of justice would suffer. The robust language of the judgment was quoted with approval in *Garrett* (see below).

Following swiftly on from *Jones* was the case of *Oyston v Royal Bank of Scotland* [2006] EWHC 90053 (Costs) where the CFA provided for a 100% success fee and a £50,000 bonus if more than £1m was recovered. A deed of variation that removed the reference to the bonus payment was then made to try to avoid invalidity. The Senior Costs Judge held against the claimant. No retrospective rectification could be made once the substantive proceedings had concluded (a point also made by the Privy Council in *Kellar v Williams* [2004] UKPC 30). The breach would inescapably have a materially adverse effect on the proper administration of justice and there should be no severance of the offending term from the remainder of the agreement. The persuasiveness of the Privy Council's decision in these circumstances was confirmed by McCombe LJ when giving the lead judgment in *Radford v Frade* [2018] EWCA Civ 119.

In *Gloucestershire County Council v Evans* [2008] EWCA Civ 21, the local authority had a collective CFA providing for an hourly rate of £95 payable irrespective of outcome and a rate of £145 for a win. A success fee of 100% was to apply to the higher rate in the event of a win. It might be assumed that the percentage increase is an increase on base costs – model CFAs take that approach. But the statute talks not of the base costs you are charging in the CFA but a fee that you would have charged had there been no CFA at all – of course no one ever states what that fee would have been. The CFA in question referred to 'basic charges' (£145) and 'discounted charges' (£95) and applied the success fee only to the former.

It was argued that the success fee sought by the local authority really amounted to 290% based on the fact that the costs at risk were only £50 per hour. (Clearly even referring to the £95 rate would have left a success fee in excess of 100% anyway but that was not the argument run.) The court held that the success fee applied to the basic charges and did not offend the statute. The agreement provided for basic charges of £145 per hour. That was the amount of the fees that would be payable if the agreement was not a CFA and so no more than a 100% success fee had been claimed in the CFA.

A similar result was reached in the SCCO case of *Morris v Dennis* [2008] EWHC 90112 (Costs) where the CFA defined the base charges to which a 100% success fee was applied plus an administration charge of £150. It was held that the charge (although only payable on success) was not part of the uplift which accordingly did not exceed the 100% maximum.

Commissioners for HMRC v Blue Sphere Global Ltd [2011] EWHC 90217 (Costs) provides a useful example of an assessment of the reasonableness of a success fee where only part of the solicitor's fees are at risk. The CFA provided for a discounted fee arrangement of two hourly fee levels, one payable in any event and a higher one if an appeal by the opponent failed. There was in addition a success fee of 80% based on the higher hourly rate. Applying *Gloucestershire County Council v Evans* the solicitors were only at risk for the difference between the discounted fee rate (£300) and the higher fee rate (£500). On the facts it was held that the risk was 50/50 which would of course justify a 100% success fee if all of the base costs were at risk. Master Gordon-Saker held that to reflect the real risk of only £200 per hour the correct calculation was to divide the hourly rate at risk by the basic rate and multiply that figure by the prospects of success. In other words 200 ÷ 500 x 50%. That produced a success fee of 20% to apply to the higher hourly rate.

Defining the opponent

[6.12]

In *Brierley v Prescott* 2006 (SCCO Ref: 0504718) the CFA referred to a claim against an insurer. In the proceedings the driver's name was later substituted for that of the insurer. On assessment it was argued that there was no liability under the CFA in respect of the claim against the driver and that therefore the driver could not be liable to indemnify those costs. It was held that the CFA covered a claim arising out of the accident and costs were therefore payable by the client and recoverable. A similar decision was reached in *Scott v Transport for London* (December 2009 unreported) (Hastings County Court) where the CFA named a local authority and not the defendant. No harm was done because the CFA Regulations did not require the defendant to be named in the CFA.

However, in *Law v Liverpool City Council* [2005] EWHC 90020 (Costs), the court found that a definition in the following terms 'Your claim against Liverpool City Council for damages for personal injury' did not include the costs incurred in also pursuing the Housing Association which had taken over responsibility for the premises shortly before the accident occurred. Similar approaches were taken in *Brookes v DC Leisure Management Ltd* (HHJ Cotter QC Exeter CC 17/9/13) and in *Engeham v London & Quadrant Housing Trust* [2015] EWCA Civ 1530. (Albeit that in the latter case the wording of the disputed Tomlin Order scuppered the second defendant's attempt to avoid being liable for costs in any event.)

The case of *Law* was relied upon by the defendant in *Malone v Birmingham Community NHS Trust* [2018] EWCA Civ 1376 but that decision was distinguished on its facts by the court. In *Malone*, the CFA referred only to a claim against the 'Home Office' but proceedings were brought against the Ministry of Justice as well as two Health bodies given that the claim related to negligent medical treatment in prison. The named defendant settled the case without proceedings having to be served on the other two defendants. The court accepted both that the correct defendant was unclear and that in any event it could not be the Home Office. The poor drafting of the agreement led the court to take the contextual approach out of its contract construing tool bag and considered the factual matrix surrounding the claim. Using that approach, the uncertainty of the defendant meant that the wording in the CFA was no more than a description of the nature of the claim rather than any limiting or defining of the opponent. Although the court said that it also reached the same conclusion in favour of the claimant by a textual analysis (another tool available to the court) it seems clear that the court leant heavily on the context for its decision.

Defining a win

[6.13]

In *Milne v David Price Solicitors 2005* (SCCO) 04/P8/340) the client agreed a settlement with his opponent that did not amount to a win which was defined in the CFA as settlement at a specified sum. His acceptance of the settlement was held to be a termination of the CFA with the result that he had to pay solely his base costs.

The definition of 'win' given in the Law Society model CFA is as follows: 'Your claim for damages is finally decided in your favour whether by a court decision or an agreement to pay your damages.' In *Fortune v Roe* [2011] EWHC 2953 (QB), the CFA in model form had been entered into after judgment had been entered with damages to be assessed. It was argued that the definition of win had therefore already been satisfied. It was held that the defining words required an agreement to have been reached as to the amount of damages and not merely that some damages will be paid.

The same wording was significant also in *Manning v King's College Hospital NHS Trust* [2011] EWHC 2954 (QB). An original claim for clinical negligence brought by the widower of the patient of the defendant trust was taken over by the widower's executors upon his death. The widower had been represented by solicitors and leading counsel under a CFA which provided for the lawyers to take the risk on Part 36. New CFAs were entered into with the executors but the wording did not put the lawyers at risk on Part 36. The executor CFAs were made after trial but before judgment. Spencer J held that although the executor CFAs had in strict terms not put the Part 36 risk onto the lawyers, unlike the original CFAs, it was clearly the intention of the executors and the lawyers to have done so. Accordingly the CFAs did place the Part 36 risk onto the lawyers, and until judgment was given that risk remained. Given that the trial had already taken place and the trial judge had yet to make up his mind at the time of the widower's death, the risk was 50/50. You may think it quite a step for the court to have interpreted the new CFAs to have the same effect as the originals, even though the necessary words were not there at all.

In *Hanley v Smith and MIB* [2009] EWHC 90144 (Costs) the CFA was made two years after a standard retainer and by then the first defendant had admitted liability albeit not its extent. It was argued that the definition of win in the Law Society model had already been satisfied. That argument failed with the court holding that the claim against the MIB was an essential ingredient of the claim, a reasonable person would have understood that the central purpose of the litigation would not be satisfied merely by obtaining a worthless (but necessary) judgment against the driver. The Deputy Master decided therefore that a win (however defined) was not enough. What if none, or only part of, the damages awarded and between the parties' costs are recovered because, for example, the defendant is, or becomes, insolvent? Unless the formula is 'no recovery, no pay' the empty-handed client will have nothing to pay with. The lawyers will be entitled to their costs and success fee, so the client will, in fact, be substantially worse off than if he had lost the action. This decision does not sit easily with the general view expressed by courts that a 'win' merely involves getting an order from the court (or the agreement of the opponent). Recovery of the agreed damages and costs is only relevant where a 'no recovery, no fee' agreement is created.

What effect does a successful counterclaim, perhaps arising out of an allegation of contributory negligence, have on the specified circumstances? The result in *Horth v Thompson* [2010] EWHC 1674 (QB), is not for the faint-hearted. The defendant pursued a counter-claim in respect of a collision. The defendant was found to be 65% responsible. His own damage was far greater than that of the claimant but he was still over £300 down after apportioning the blame. The judge ordered each party to pay the other's costs of the entire claim and counterclaim combined. The defendant was represented under a CFA so his costs were significantly greater than those of the claimant. So, the defendant, who was far more to blame and had received more damage than he had himself caused the claimant, ended up receiving costs from the claimant.

The Law Society's Model CFA defines a win in terms only of a final decision on the claim in the client's favour. A win might be defined in terms of actual recovery and the Senior Costs Judge expressed the view in *Sharratt v London*

Central Bus Co and other cases (No 2), The Accident Group Test Cases [2003] NLJR 790, 147 Sol Jo LB 657 that a standard CFA could in any event define win in terms of recovery. The issue was put beyond doubt at the time by the 2003 Regulations.

In *Ultimate Products Ltd and Henleys Clothing Ltd v Nigel Woolley & Timesource Ltd* [2014] EWHC 1919 (Ch) Mr Christopher Pymont QC found that the standard Law Society definition of 'payment of damages' was sufficient to defeat an argument that only some parts of the claimant's claim had succeeded when the bespoke wording of the CFA required all aspects to do so to qualify as a success.

Pre-action applications

[6.14]

The standard Law Society wording in its model CFA is as follows:

> 'If on the way to winning or losing you are awarded any costs by agreement or Court order, then we are entitled to payment of those costs together with a success fee on those charges if you win overall.'

Does the client have a liability to pay the costs of a pre-action application for disclosure based on this provision? 'Yes' said Master Haworth in *Connaughton v Imperial College Healthcare NHS Trust* [2010] EWHC 90173 (Costs) and there was therefore no breach of the indemnity principle in ordering the opponent to pay the costs of a pre-action application. A lay person's reasonable expectation would be that non-compliance with a pre-action protocol which was part of the pre-litigation process and necessitated an application to the court would be covered under the terms of this CFA.

A twist in this case was that the claimant was not now proceeding against the defendant, but against another party – the defendant's cleaner. Did that mean the PAD application could not be 'within the claim' by virtue of the fact that proceedings had now been brought against another party? No. The fact that proceedings had not been issued against the defendant, did not mean that the claimant was not claiming against the defendant in accordance with the definition of 'claim' within the CFA.

Similar arguments concerning pre-action work failed again in *Rogers v Mouchel* (unreported – 2010 Case No OMY01382, HHJ Birtles). It was held that the words 'your claim' contained in the Law Society Model CFA were to be given a broad and purposive intention so as to include pre-action conduct even if no proceedings were ever issued.

CCFAs, ATE and Membership Organisations

[6.15]

A CCFA can be used to transfer the own costs risk to a client or funder's lawyers who can seek to cover that risk by success fees in successful cases. A membership organisation can also make use of an ATE policy as an alternative to going along the s 30 of the AJA 1999 route. Alternatively, on the basis of *Thornley v Lang* (above) the individual has a costs liability for his own costs as well as his opponent's costs and could therefore insure by use of an individual ATE policy and seek then to recover the premium under s 29. Such a route deals with own disbursements where the case loses, s 30 does not. It is possible that a membership organisation may fund the ATE premium or negotiate deferred premiums. If the organisation were to take out its own insurance the premium would be the 'provision' made by the organisation but that would lead to seemingly insurmountable problems in apportioning any part of such provision to an individual case. Nevertheless, increasingly s 30 was abandoned in practice in favour of a CFA with ATE insurance.

COURT APPROACH TO LEGISLATIVE COMPLIANCE

'Technical challenges'

[6.16]

In view of the Golden Rule (see **[4.3]**) paying parties wasted no time in challenging CFAs as soon as success fees became recoverable in April 2000. The two Court of Appeal decisions in *Callery v Gray* in 2001 together with *Sarwar v Alam* (see below) later the same year gave the higher courts a taste of the warfare being conducted in courts of first instance. Seemingly endless allegations of non-compliance with the legislation came in 2002. In *Burstein v Times Newspapers Ltd* [2002] EWCA Civ 1739, Latham LJ ended the judgment of the court with these words:

> '. . . The deputy costs judge is to be commended for ensuring that the detailed assessment did not become an excuse for further expensive litigation at the behest of a disappointed but persistent litigant. Satellite litigation about costs has become a growth industry, and one that is a blot on the civil justice system. Costs Judges should be astute to prevent such proceedings from being protracted by allegations that are without substance. In future district judges and costs judges must be equally astute to prevent satellite litigation about costs from being protracted by allegations about breaches of the CFA Regulations where the breaches do not matter. They should remember that the law does not care about the very little things, and that they should only declare a CFA unenforceable if the breach does matter and if the client could have relied on it successfully against his solicitor.'

So by the time the case of *Hollins v Russell* [2003] EWCA Civ 718 reached the Court of Appeal, the judiciary were fully aware that a war was being conducted, particularly in the personal injury field. The court in *Hollins* (and several conjoined cases) considered several alleged breaches of the secondary legislation. The defendants' arguments were described by the court as being 'as unattractive as they were unmeritorious' and held that a departure from the regulations did not affect the validity or enforceability of a CFA unless the departure was both material and adversely affected the client or the administration of justice. None of the challenges considered by the Court of Appeal were successful and, optimistically, the profession interpreted *Hollins* as heralding the end of these so-called 'technical' challenges unless the client had suffered some material detriment. The court summarised its 228-paragraph judgment as: 'The court should be watchful when it considers allegations that there have been breaches of the regulations. The parliamentary purpose is to enhance access to justice, not to impede it, and to create better ways of delivering litigation services, not worse ones. These purposes will be thwarted if those who render good service to their clients under CFAs are at risk of going unremunerated at the culmination of the bitter trench warfare which has been such an unhappy feature of the recent litigation scene.'

In *Crook v Birmingham City Council* [2007] EWHC 1415 (Admin), the solicitor agreed with a number of clients of modest means in housing litigation that if they recovered damages of £3,000 or less but no costs they would be charged at the solicitors' usual hourly rate with a cap of £1,000. The defendants contended that the reduced level of fees represented what the market would bear and therefore the increment amounted to a success fee. It was held that there was no success fee but simply a discount from the 'normal fee'. If the defendant's analysis were right it could be argued in every case and would obliterate the distinction in conditional fee agreements between the 'base fee' and the 'success fee'.

Disclosure

[6.17]

The Court in *Hollins* said that it should become normal practice for a CFA to be disclosed for the purpose of costs proceedings in which a success fee is claimed, subject to the provision in paragraph 40.14 of the Costs Practice Direction that the judge may ask the receiving party to elect whether to disclose the CFA to the paying party in order to rely on it or whether to decline disclosure and instead rely on other evidence (see **[28.63]**). If the CFA contains confidential information relating to other proceedings, it may be suitably redacted before disclosure takes place. A party given that option who then refuses to provide the CFA or sufficient other evidence of compliance will suffer the consequences of failing to recover costs, the exact outcome in *David Smith v Countrywide Farmers plc* (11 February 2010, unreported), QBD, Cardiff District Registry).

Attendance notes and other correspondence should not ordinarily be disclosed, but the judge conducting the assessment may require the disclosure of material of this kind if it is to be a relied upon where a genuine issue is raised. A genuine issue is one in which there is a real chance that the CFA is unenforceable as a result of failure to satisfy the applicable conditions (*Pratt v Bull, Worth v McKenna* [2003] EWCA Civ 718.

Since the revocation of the 2000 Regulations from 1 November 2005, a CFA needs only to be in writing (seemingly it need not be signed) but that did not stop an application for disclosure in *Ashley Cole v News Group* (2006) October 18 SCCO. That application failed simply because no points of dispute had been served hence CPR 47.14 and CPD 40.14 did not apply. The applicability of *Hollins* to post-1 November 2005 CFAs was considered in *Findlay v Cantor Index Ltd* [2008] EWHC 90116 (Costs) where disclosure was sought of the CFA, the reasons for the success fee and counsel's opinion. Master Campbell held that Costs Practice Direction 32.5 could have no application to post 1 November 2005 CFAs (where there was no requirement to state reasons for the success fee) and thus the paying party has no right to information concerning the setting of the success fee, and presumably no proof other than the solicitor's assertion as to what it was. Nonetheless, arguing for a success fee without showing how it was set is likely to be a fraught endeavour. As to the CFA, *Hollins* still required it to be disclosed at the costs stage although counsel's opinion was privileged despite being referred to in a disclosed risk assessment. This gap was closed by amendments to the Costs Practice Direction in 2009 so that a statement of reasons for the success fee (unless the percentage is fixed by the CPR) together with either the CFA or at least certain parts of the CFA (regarding the definition of a 'win'; the payments provisions following a Part 36 Offer etc) has to be disclosed when setting the case down for a detailed assessment hearing.

Alternative forms of funding

[6.18]

The Court of Appeal heard *Sarwar v Alam* [2001] EWCA Civ 1401, on September 11, 2001. It was mentioned by the court at the end of *Callery v Gray (No 2)* as being a case which was in the process of being fast tracked to the Court of Appeal. Whilst it was reconsidered in detail by the case of *Myatt* five years later, it is still of importance in considering whether the use of an ATE policy could be seen as reasonable rather than an existing BTE policy.

Lord Justice Brooke provided the following helpful summary:

> 'This is another appeal concerned with the new arrangements for financing the costs of personal injury litigation which came into effect last year. Legal Aid is now no longer available for most litigation of this type. In *Callery v Gray*, the Court of Appeal was concerned two months ago with issues relating to the appropriate size of a success fee in a conditional fee agreement made in connection with a small claim for personal injuries suffered in a road traffic accident which was settled quite quickly without any need to bring court proceedings. In that case a passenger in a car had made a claim against the driver of the car involved in an accident. The court was also concerned with the appropriateness of taking out "after the event" ("ATE") insurance in connection with such a claim, and the reasonableness of the ATE premium claimed in that case.
>
> The present appeal is concerned with a similar claim brought by a passenger against the driver of the car in which he was travelling. The court below had disallowed the recovery of an ATE premium on the grounds that the claimant ought to have enquired into the availability of "before the event" ("BTE") legal expenses insurance which formed part of the cover provided by the driver's insurance policy, and then made use of that cover. This policy covered the costs and expenses of both sides in a claim brought by a passenger in the car against the insured driver himself up to a limit of £50,000.'

The Court of Appeal allowed the appeal on the grounds that the policy did not provide the claimant with appropriate cover in the circumstances of this case. Representation arranged by the insurer of the opposing party, to which the claimant had never been a party, and of which he had no knowledge of the time it was entered into and where the opposing insurer through its chosen representative reserved to itself the full conduct and control of the claim, was not a reasonable alternative to representation by a lawyer of the claimant's own choice, backed by an ATE policy.

The court suggested that the position might be different if BTE insurers financed some transparently independent organisation to handle such claims, and made it clear in the policy that this is what they were doing.

The court said, however, that if a claimant making a relatively small (ie less than about £5,000) claim in a road traffic accident had access to pre-existing BTE cover which appeared to be satisfactory for a claim of that size, that in the ordinary course of things he/she should be referred to the relevant BTE insurer.

The court gave guidance as to the nature of the enquiries a solicitor should make in this class of case into the availability of BTE cover and the insurance policies and other documents the solicitor should ask the client to produce. A solicitor should normally invite a client, by means of a standard form letter, to bring to the first interview any relevant motor and household insurance policy, as well as any stand-alone LEI policy belonging to the client and/or spouse or partner. However, regard has always to be had to the amount at stake, and a solicitor was not obliged to embark upon a treasure hunt. The court emphasised that this guidance should not be treated as an inflexible code, and that the overriding principle was that the claimant, assisted by his/her solicitor, should act in a manner that was reasonable. Now that this sort of claim would go into the Portal, it must be arguable that the extent of the 'treasure hunt' is now limited by the fixed recoverable costs involved.

In *Samonini v London General Transport Services Ltd* [2005] EWHC 90001 (Costs) the client said he had no existing legal expenses cover and the solicitor took his word for it without further enquiry. The client was correct — he had no BTE and however diligently the solicitor had searched he would have found nothing because there was nothing to find. Nevertheless, the Senior Costs Judge held that the solicitor's failure to comply with reg 4(2)(d) (which required him to 'consider' the availability of legal expenses insurance) was a material breach invalidating the CFA.

In *Garrett v Halton Borough Council; Myatt v National Coal Board* [2006] EWCA Civ 1017, the Court of Appeal gave what it described as 'guidance' on CFAs concerning a solicitor's duty to consider existing legal expenses insurance under CFA reg 4(2)(c). However, as the regulation had been revoked on 1 November 2005, the decisions were not so much guidance but more of a checklist for those wishing to embark on satellite litigation in respect of CFAs that had been created prior to that date. The Court held that enforceability of a CFA was to be determined as at the date of its commencement and not in the light of its consequences. It was not necessary for there to be any actual material detriment to the client or to the administration of justice to constitute a breach. The language of s 58 CLSA 1990 was clear and uncompromising. The statutory scheme provided that if any of the conditions were not satisfied, the CFA would not be enforceable and the solicitor would not be paid. That was clear and stark. Such a policy was tough but not irrational: it was designed to protect clients and to encourage solicitors to comply with the statutory requirements. *Hollins* had done no more than deal a fatal blow to challenges which were based on literal but trivial grounds and immaterial departures from the statutory requirements.

In *Myatt* the solicitor asked the wrong question in her attempt to comply with reg 4(2)(c). She should not simply have asked unsophisticated clients whether they had credit cards, household or motor insurance policies or trade union membership which would entitle them to legal expenses insurance in respect of the contemplated claim. The solicitor was required to take reasonable steps to ascertain whether the client's risk for costs was already insured and those steps would depend on a variety of circumstances such as the nature of the client, the circumstances in which the solicitor was instructed and the nature of the claim. The cost of the ATE premium might be a relevant factor and so too was whether a referring body has already investigated the availability of BTE. The requirement in *Sarwar v Alam* that the client should be invited to bring all relevant policy and other documents to the first interview should be treated with considerable caution in high-volume low-value litigation – in which the solicitor might never have a first interview. In any event, *Sarwar* related not to reg 4 but to the reasonableness of entering into a CFA or ATE insurance.

Disclosing an interest

[6.19]

In *Garrett* the solicitors were members of a panel which referred work to them provided they recommended a particular policy of insurance. This was clearly an interest disclosable under reg 4(2)(e) and it was not sufficient merely to inform the client of membership of the panel without explaining its implications. Further consideration was given to reg 4(2)(e) in the context of the Accident Line Protect (ALP) insurance scheme. In *Tankard v John Fredricks Plastics Ltd* [2008] EWCA Civ 1375, the court said a solicitor has an interest if a reasonable person with knowledge of the relevant facts would think that the existence of the interest might affect the advice given by the solicitor to his client. The ALP scheme did not involve such an interest. The court went on to consider, albeit obiter, what level of disclosure would be required where a solicitor did have an interest. The client should have been told what the nature of the interest is – it was not enough just to say that there was an interest. The regulation says the solicitor must when recommending insurance inform the client 'whether he has an interest in doing so'. Once the solicitor has an interest, using the test set out above, he must explain the nature of that interest to the client. The court in *Garrett* did not dissent from its decision in *Hollins* that it is not necessary to state that a solicitor has no interest in the insurance he is recommending – it is only necessary to state when he has.

Challenges after *Garrett* and *Myatt*

[6.20]

In the light of the Court of Appeal's guidance, it seemed inevitable that the spate of satellite costs litigation would continue unabated for so long as the indemnity principle survived. It did survive and there was no abatement for some time. A robust approach was taken in *David Smith v Countrywide Farmers plc* (11 February 2010, unreported), QBD Judge Seys-Llewellyn QC sitting as a deputy judge of the High Court declaring that it was in principle and in practice wrong for a judge to trawl through a CFA to check compliance. Here is a sample of the cases on breach of the regulations. In *Bevan v Power Panels Electrical Systems Ltd* [2007] EWHC 90073 (Costs) both Garrett and Myatt points were taken. Myatt also tripped up solicitors in *Andrews v Dawkes* (2006) (QBD Birmingham) where the solicitors did not check that their client was unlikely to have access to before the event insurance (BTE). In *Berry v Spousals* (2007) Birmingham CC BM 309007 solicitors did not at any time check claims management company arrangement to see if it would cover costs rather than use a CFA. Myatt featured in *Choudhury v Kingston Hospital Trust* [2006] EWHC 90057 (Costs) but there the client consultant anaesthetist wrote to the solicitors confirming she had no BTE – a sophisticated client answering the Myatt ultimate question. The same result occurred in *Kashmiri v Ejaz* [2007] EWHC 90074 (Costs) with a commercial client able to provide all the *Myatt* answers himself.

BTE has caused particular difficulties in cases involving buses with no consistency in the lower courts as to whether a solicitor before 2005 could have been expected to check the bus company's insurance to see if it covered injured passengers. Paying parties should consult *Tranter v Hansons* [2009] EWHC 90145 (Costs), receiving parties *Dole v ECT* (17 September 2007, unreported). More recently, the client successfully challenged their own solicitors' costs in *Langsam v Beachcroft LLP* [2011] EWHC 1451 (Ch). The replacement CFA did not contain the cap on total fees that the original CFA had contained. The failure to explain the change was a breach of Regulation 4(3) and the CFA was unenforceable. In *McDaniel & Co v Clarke* [2014] EWHC 3826 (QB) the failure was to explore the possibility of free trades union representation. Hickinbottom J upheld the costs judge's conclusion that proper advice would have led to such representation having been used in the circumstances of the case.

Membership of Accident Line was the basis of a *Garrett* challenge in *Myers v Bonnington* [2007] EWHC 90077 (Costs). The firm had received 24 referrals over six years – a de minimis factor and not enough to amount to an interest. Finally, in *O'Driscoll v Liverpool City Council* (2007) (Liverpool County Court) there had been no 'positive averment' that solicitors would lose TAG panel membership if their client had not taken a policy with TAG, and therefore no basis for an inference to be drawn as that in *Myatt* that the solicitors had an interest in recommending an insurance policy.

Challenges arising from LASPO 2012

[6.21]

As discussed at the beginning of Chapter 4, the funding landscape changed hugely on 1 April 2013 with the coming into force of the relevant sections of LASPO 2012. You will find comments on the post-LASPO 2012 clinical negligence ATE policy in Chapter 9 **[9.16]**. Here we refer you to two cases regarding alternative funding challenges. They both arise from the use of Legal Aid until shortly before April 2013 and then a change of funding arrangement to a CFA and ATE policy.

In *Milton Keynes Hospital NHS Foundation Trust v Hyde* [2017] EWCA Civ 399, the Court of Appeal upheld the judgment of Soole J which found that the decision to change was a reasonable one. The solicitors had reached the costs limitation under the certificate and the judge accepted the claimant's argument that the certificate was 'spent'. As such no formal notice of discharge was required before taking up the CFA in the same manner previously allowed where the assisted party had become a litigant in person or the step authorised by the limited certificate had been reached.

The Court of Appeal in *Surrey v Barnet & Chase Farm Hospitals NHS Trust* [2018] EWCA Civ 451 and two conjoined cases reinstated the various first instance decisions concerning the adequacy of the advice given. The failure to advise the client about the loss of an extra 10% damages (via *Simmons v Castle*) when changing funding was material in two of the cases: the erroneous calculations regarding the amount spent was prominent in the other one. In each case, the advice was flawed and, since the advice was accepted by the claimants, the advice constituted the reasons for the switch. The defendants were entitled to ask why the change in funding had occurred given the extra costs involved as a result. The flawed advice rendered the claimants' decision to change funding unreasonable and so the additional liabilities were not recoverable.

Following the Court of Appeal's decision in *Surrey*, there have been several High Court decisions (and one Court of Appeal decision – *XDE v North Middlesex University Hospital NHS Trust* [2020] EWCA Civ 543) implementing its approach to cases where funding changed from legal aid to a CFA and ATE insurance shortly before April 2013. Most cases have upheld costs judge decisions which found the change to be unreasonable. One case where the change was found to be reasonable by a regional costs judge was upheld by Dingemans J on appeal (*AB (a protected party by his mother and litigation friend YZ) v Mid Cheshire Hospitals NHS Foundation Trust* [2019] EWHC 1889 (QB)). Dingemans J emphasised the Court of Appeal's insistence that fact specific issues rather than high level criticisms of the legal aid arrangements were required.

PROFESSIONAL CONDUCT COMPLIANCE

[6.22]

The transferring of regulation to the SRA from the secondary legislation managed to put an end to costs satellite litigation between the parties. The paying party briefly sought to argue that a breach of the code of conduct, since it has statutory force, meant that the client could still contend that the retainer was unenforceable (or at least that the solicitor's costs entitlement is reduced). Consequently, the paying party ought to be able to rely on the indemnity principle to avoid liability for payment. These arguments were addressed in *Garbutt v Edwards* [2005] EWCA Civ 1206, where the Court of Appeal confirmed that the practice rules and client care code did have statutory effect, but held that the particular breach in this case did not make the agreement unenforceable. In terms of providing costs information such as an estimate, the word 'shall' in Rule 15 was not mandatory. The sanctions for non-compliance were disciplinary and a client could not be penalised for not initiating disciplinary proceedings against his own solicitor. Between the parties, the costs judge should consider whether and if so, to what extent, the costs claimed would have been significantly lower had an estimate been given. The judgment contains clear comments that the court did not want to see paying parties seeking to take advantage of any such 'technical' points based on the SRA code of conduct.

ASSESSING THE LEVEL OF SUCCESS FEE – COURT DECISIONS

[6.23]

In *Callery v Gray* [2001] EWCA Civ 1117, the court dealt with the defendant's argument that a CFA should not be entered into until a risk assessment could be carried out by the claimant in possession of (at least most of) the facts by turning the argument on its head. Instead of there being little or no success fee recoverable until the risk assessment could be carried out, the court took the view that a higher success fee should be set with the facility for that fee to be reduced if the case settled early, or at least the risk reduced (which generally would mean the admission of liability.) The court gave no guidance as to how the two figures should be calculated but it envisaged both figures being set at the outset. If the case settled in the Protocol period the lower fee would apply to the whole case; if the case did not settle, the higher figure would apply to the whole case. The court gave an example of a 100% fee rebated to 5% if the claim settled within the Protocol period.

The defendant took *Callery* to the House of Lords ([2002] 3 All ER 417). The House largely washed its hands of the problem by asserting that the appropriate forum to monitor the new funding regime and resolve its teething problems was the Court of Appeal. Their Lordships did comment, however, that a 20% success fee for simple cases (as the Court of Appeal had allowed 'as a maximum' in *Callery*) looked too high and that two-stage success fees might indeed be the way ahead.

In *Halloran v Delaney* [2002] EWCA Civ 1258, Brooke LJ stunned the costs industry when he said:

> 'After taking advice from our assessor, and after considering the arguments in the present case, we consider that judges concerned with questions relating to the recoverability of a success fee in claims as simple as this which are settled without the need to commence proceedings should now ordinarily decide to allow an uplift of 5% on the claimant's lawyers' costs (including the costs of any costs only proceedings which are awarded to them) pursuant to their powers contained in CPD 11.8(2) unless persuaded that a higher uplift is appropriate in the particular circumstances of the case. This policy should be adopted in relation to all CFAs, however they are structured, which are entered into on and after 1st August 2001, when both *Callery* judgments had been published and the main uncertainties about costs recovery had been removed.'

So, no sooner had the ink dried on the House of Lords decision not to interfere in *Callery*, than the Court of Appeal had not only replaced the 20% success fee benchmark with 5%, but also backdated its effect to 1 August 2001. All was not, however, as it seemed. Brooke LJ in the *Claims Direct Test Cases* [2003] EWCA Civ 136 provided the following 'clarification' of his judgment in *Halloran*:

> 'Subsequent events have shown that I should have expressed myself with greater clarity. The type of case to which I was referring was a case similar to *Callery v Gray* and *Halloran v Delaney* in which, to adopt the 'ready reckoner' in *Cook on Costs* (2003), p 545, the prospects of success are virtually 100%. The two-step fee advocated by the court in *Callery v Gray (No 1)* is apt to allow a solicitor in such a case to cater for the wholly unexpected risk lurking below the limpid waters of the simplest of claims. It did not require any research evidence or submissions from other parties in the industry to persuade the court that in this type of extremely simple claim a success fee of over 5% was no longer tenable in all the circumstances. The guidance given in that judgment was not intended to have any wider application.'

Yet more clarification and further encouragement for two-stage success fees was provided in *Atack v Lee* [2004] EWCA Civ 1712. In *Atack* the Court upheld the reduction of a success fee from 100% to 50% in a case which went to trial and then settled for £30,000 after a finding of liability. In the conjoined case of *Ellerton* the court reduced the success fee from 30% to 20% on the basis that it was a straight forward case and therefore 20% was the maximum to be awarded. The only significant risk was the possibility of the claimant accepting her solicitor's advice and then not beating a payment-in, which was just one of the rare risks which justified a success fee set as high as 20% in the simplest of claims.

Brooke LJ, who to this point had been in all of the landmark decisions, provided this summary:

> 'Because there seems to be some lingering uncertainty about the combined effect of *Callery v Gray* and *Halloran v Delaney* we feel that we ought to restate for the benefit of district judges and costs judges the principles in cases governed by the old regime. The reasonableness of the success fee has to be assessed as at the time the CFA was agreed. It is permissible for any CFA to include a two-stage success fee, and this is to be encouraged. In other words the success fee may be a higher percentage (up to 100% in an appropriate case) in the event that a claim does not settle within the protocol period, and a lower success fee (down to 5% in the very simplest of cases) in claims which do settle within that period. Further statistical evidence is now available to which it will be legitimate for parties to refer in relation to success fees agreed in an old regime case after the date of this judgment.'

The reference to the 'old regime' was to cases which did not fall into the fixed success fee rules that by now had started to come into Part 45 (see below.)

The case of *U v Liverpool City Council* [2005] EWCA Civ 475, considered the reasonableness of a single stage success fee of 100% set in October 2001 in a personal injury claim involving a four year old child who had stepped into a hole in a grass verge. The Court allowed 50% as a single stage success fee but set out the reasoning behind the use of two stage fees:

> '[21] When deciding upon a success fee [the claimant's solicitor] had two choices. He could have taken the view that this claim would probably settle without fuss at a reasonably early stage, but he wished to protect himself against the risk that the claim might go the full distance and might eventually fail. In those circumstances he could select the two-stage success fee discussed by this court in *Callery v Gray* [2001] EWCA 1117 at [106]–[112]. In this situation he would be willing to restrict himself to a low success fee if the case settled within the protocol period – or within such other period, perhaps until the service of the defence, as he might choose – and to have the benefit of a high success fee for the cases that did not settle early. As things turned out, he would have benefited on the facts of this case if he had adopted this course: a high two-stage success fee would have been more readily defensible in a case which did not settle until proceedings were quite far advanced.
>
> [22] Alternatively, he could have selected, as he did in fact, a single-stage success fee, being a fee which he would seek to recover at the same level however quickly or slowly the claim was resolved. In those circumstances it would not be possible to justify so high a success fee.'

The judgment endorsed Lord Woolf's encouragement to lawyers in *Callery v Gray* to take seriously the possibility of agreeing an initial success fee of, say 100%, on the basis that if the claim settled within the protocol period (or some other period identified by the parties to the CFA) a lower success fee would be recoverable under the CFA. At the assessment of costs attention would then be paid to the reasonableness of the success fee which was recoverable as things turned out, and this type of arrangement would lead to a greater chance of establishing the reasonableness of a higher success fee where the claim did not settle within the agreed period.

The message from the Court of Appeal was that where the CFA was entered into before the *Callery* judgment on 1 August 2001 the guidance given in *Callery* applies so that even a simple road traffic case would attract a single step success fee of 20%. Where the CFA was made after 1 August 2001 and a two stage fee was provided, then, again in simple cases, the lower figure should be 5%. There had been repeated encouragement to use a two-stage fee and the carrot of the award of a substantially higher second stage fee had been dangled.

But, even the Court of Appeal has not always fully embraced these messages. In *C v W* [2008] EWCA Civ 1459, the court decided that a 20% success fee in a road traffic passenger claim where liability had been admitted was about right. (No two stage fee in this case). The court did say that if a solicitor agrees to forgo all fees post Part 36 if the offer is not beaten then the success fee could be reviewed during the life of the CFA – quite how that is to be achieved was not explained. The statute requires the percentage to be stated. That in practice means putting the stages in the agreement at the time that it is signed. A two stage fee states the percentage for each stage – how a reviewable fee would fit the statutory requirement must be in some doubt.

The most recent re-iteration of its preference for staged success fees by the Court of Appeal was in *Motto v Trafigura* [2008] EWCA Civ 1150. A single stage success fee of 100% was reduced to 58% with the court again stressing that a more sympathetic view might be taken of relatively high success fees where the level is 'reviewable as the case progresses'. Again the Court of Appeal seems to have in mind a success fee that changes in response to changes in prospects once the case is up and running. It is hard to see how such a provision in a CFA could satisfy the statutory requirement to state the success fee at the time the CFA is made. The concept of a staged success fee is that different percentages are fixed at the outset to reflect the progress of the case. (This is the approach taken by the fixed figures set out in the old Part 45).

We do at least have recognition that the mere fact that a success fee is staged does not remove the need for it also to be reasonable. In *Fortune v Roe* [2011] EWHC 2953 (QB), the CFA was entered into after an admission of liability and judgment entered on liability in a catastrophic injury case. The staged success fee was 100% payable if the case settled within three months of the trial date and 25% for any earlier settlement. The case settled less than a month before trial. The risk assessment identified Part 36 as the major risk. The claimant pointed to the fact that if the case had been within the Part 45 scheme a 100% success fee would be recoverable as the fixed success fee at a trial. On appeal it was held that the mere fact that a success fee is staged does not mean it is reasonable. The question still remains as to what the level of risk was and what success fee was justified. There was an admission on liability and no risk of any substance until any Part 36 offer was made. Such an offer was likely to be made only close to the trial in this particular case. The Claimant's solicitors' costs up to that time, which would have been substantial, were secured. A success fee of 100% in such circumstances was unreasonable. A reasonable success fee, whether single or second stage, in the circumstances which pertained when the CFA was entered into, was 20%. In the more recent case of *Bright v Motor Insurers' Bureau* [2014] EWHC 1557 (QB) Slade J came to similar conclusions on a two stage success fee in the CFA set out in virtually identical terms to the one used in *Roe*.

For an example of a staged success fee in a defamation case: see *Peacock (Matthew) v MGN Ltd* [2010] EWHC 90174 (Costs). The success fee was in three stages: 100% of the basic charges, where the claim proceeded past 28 days after service of the defence; 50% if the case settled after proceedings were issued but before 28 days after the defence is served; or 25% if the case settled before proceedings were issued. Given MGN continued with a reasoned defence to stage three Master Campbell allowed the 100% success fee claimed.

Routine or straight forward cases

[6.24]

In *Bensusan v Freedman* [2001] All ER (D) 212 (Oct), SCCO the Senior Costs Judge equated a simple clinical negligence case, which involved a dental tool being dropped in the claimant's mouth who then swallowed it, with a personal injury action arising out of a rear-end shunt. While the costs judge accepted that the risk of failure in a clinical negligence action could be greater than in a personal injury case, this particular case was 'simple and straightforward'. In *Callery v Gray* the Court of Appeal indicated that in a routine road traffic accident action the success fee should not exceed 20% and the Senior Costs Judge took the same view in this case, reducing a success fee of 50% to 20%. Using *Callery* as 'no more than a starting point', he said the effect of the Costs Practice Direction was to prevent excessive claims for success fees in cases which settle without the need for proceedings when it was clear, or ought to have been clear, from the outset that the risk of having to commence proceedings was minimal.

In *Edwards v Smiths Dock Ltd* [2004] EWHC 1116 (QB), the court, in approving an 87% success fee, distinguished a complicated assessment of quantum from a simple claim as in *Callery*. These early cases can be contrasted with the decision in *C v W* where a 20% success fee was allowed in a road traffic claim where liability had been admitted.

Nonetheless, similar sentiments to those expressed in *Bensusan* appeared in the field of construction adjudications in *Redwing Construction Ltd v Wishart* [2011] EWHC 19 (TCC), where Akenhead J held that CFAs and ATE could be used in enforcement proceedings provided there was no exemption in the CPR from the usual rules relating to funding arrangements. It needed to be borne in mind however that the large majority of reported cases on adjudication enforcements are successful and are usually pursued (as here) via an application for summary judgment because there is no realistic defence. It was important that claimants did not use CFAs and ATE insurance primarily as a commercial threat to defendants. It was legitimate for the Court to ask itself whether, in any particular case, a CFA or ATE insurance was a reasonable and proportionate arrangement to make.

CFAs taken out at an early stage

[6.25]

The essence of *Callery v Gray* was that a client could be offered a CFA at the outset of a case. The question then arises as to how the success fee is to be calculated when at such an early stage little is known about the risks of the case. According to the judgment, *McCarthy v Essex Rivers Healthcare NHS Trust (Case No HQ06X03686)* [2010] 1 Costs LR 59 was the fourth case in which the same clinical negligence firm's CFA had been reviewed by a court. This time the point taken was that the CFA (as do most) provided that it could be terminated ' . . . if we believe that you are unlikely to win'. That, said Mackay J, was relevant to the level of a single stage success fee (claimed at 100%). Also relevant was the fact that this was not a two stage success fee. The success fee had been reduced to 80% by the Costs Judge and this appeal against that decision failed. It was accepted that the case was, at the time taken on, a 50:50 risk. Mackay J took the view that the termination clause meant that at a fairly early stage cases below a 50% chance can be removed leaving claims falling into the range of 50% to 80% prospects. In *Oliver (executor of the estate of Oliver) v Whipps Cross University Hospital NHS* [2009] EWHC 1104 (QB), John Frederick Oliver had died of septicaemia in a hospital run by the defendants. The same solicitors agreed to act under the same conditional fee agreement as in *McCarthy* with a success fee of 100%, which represented a notional 50% prospect of success in the action. The agreement noted that the solicitors had not yet had the opportunity to test the credibility of the evidence or assess the relevant facts of expert witnesses. Accordingly the prospects of success were uncertain and it was impossible to assess the percentage chance of success with any mathematical precision. The proceedings were settled. The costs judge reduced the success fee to 67% which represented a 60% chance of success on the grounds that the solicitors must have thought there was more than a 50% chance of success, otherwise the claim would not have been accepted. On appeal, the judge held that the claim was of a kind that faced difficulties and had uncertain prospects, and based on what the solicitors knew when the conditional fee agreement was made, it was one that could easily have been assessed as having chances of success lower than 50%. Accordingly, the costs judge was wrong to take the view that he did. The judge also rejected the view that there had to be a two stage fee if a 100% figure was ever to be approved. The result was he approved a single stage 100% fee.

Liability admitted cases

[6.26]

C v W considered the success fee that could be set where liability had been admitted prior to the CFA being made. The figure arrived at was 20%. The Court of Appeal's consideration of solicitors' success fees in this situation has proved definitive in the sense that no other case tends to be quoted on assessment.

In *NJL v PTE* [2018] EWHC 3570 (QB), Martin Spencer J took a forensic approach to the level of the success fee. He looked at both the likely timing of a Part 36 offer in a significant personal injury case and (separately) the prospect of it being wrongly rejected. Drawing on his own experience of personal injury work at the Bar, he considered that even 20% was generous. He allowed that figure knowing that it would be reduced to 12.5% by the operation of the old CPR 45.18 and CPR 45.19.

In the unusual circumstances of *Thornley (by his litigation friend Lavinia Thornley) v Ministry of Defence* [2010] EWHC 2584 (QB), counsel entered into a CFA with a 100% success fee at a time when liability and causation had been admitted. Counsel's CFA provided for fees to be paid even if counsel advised rejection of a Part 36 offer which was subsequently not beaten. In all of those circumstances there was no realistic possibility that counsel would not get her fees. No success fee was allowed. See also Jackson LJ's trenchant observations as to the fee arrangements in *Pankhurst v White* [2010] EWCA Civ 1445.

High value

[6.27]

In *Cox v MGN* [2006] EWHC 1235 (QB), a media privacy action, the solicitor claimed a 95% success fee and the paying party offered 5%. Unfortunately for the solicitor, leading counsel's pre-CFA opinion was 'bullish' and the success fee was reduced on assessment to 40%, a figure held on appeal to be within the range of reasonable assessments. The CFA was entered into in 2002 at a time when the law on privacy was not as clear as it is now. Today the success fee allowed would probably be lower.

In *C v W* Moore-Bick LJ queried the assumption that a higher value case made the risks greater rather than simply requiring more work. He said (at paragraph 15):

> 'It is probably true in general that high value claims tend to be more complex and to involve a greater amount of work than claims of lower value, but that does not of itself increase the risk of losing.'

However, he did accept that there might be a larger number of potential pitfalls in a bigger case and in which case this could be reflected in the risk assessment and from there into the success fee. It was not correct simply to add, as in that case, a further 20% to the success fee solely to reflect the size of the claim. As is often argued on assessment, a larger value case will encourage the potential paying party to look under more stones for possible defences than he would in a smaller value case.

The approach set out in *C v W* contrasts with the provisions in the old Part 45 (rule 45.18) where the escape clause is triggered by value rather than anything else.

Retrospective success fees

[6.28]

Forde v Birmingham City Council [2009] EWHC 12 (QB), was an appeal from the decision of Master Campbell that a CFA can be retrospective but the success fee, following the decision of the Senior Costs Judge in *King v Telegraph Group Ltd* [2005] EWHC 90015 (Costs), could not. On appeal Christopher Clarke J took a different view. Retrospective success fees are permitted. There were at least three situations where such fees might arise: an ordinary retainer later turned into a CFA with a success fee; a CFA which took some time to conclude terms and which included a success fee; a CFA with a success fee at x% initially and later changed, retrospectively to y%. The only limit to validity (even if not reasonableness) appears to be that, following *Harrington v Wakeling* [2007] EWHC 1184 (Ch), the CFA must be made before the close of the case – otherwise there is no element of futurity.

In *O'Brien (a protected party suing by his father and litigation friend O'Brien) v Shorrock* [2015] EWHC 1630 (QB), Edis J grappled with the amount of a success fee to be allowed for the retrospective period. The first instance judge had allowed a success fee of 40% which was not challenged. The Notice of Funding was dated 24 March 2010. It related to a CFA which had been signed on 21 October 2009 and had retrospective effect from 6 November 2008. The Notice of Funding recorded the CFA as being dated 6 November 2008. Edis J held this to be misleading and that it should have stated 21 October 2009. If it had done so, the nature of the success fee claimed from November 2008 would have been clear. The delay in notification required an application for relief from sanctions. Edis J considered the breach significant and that there was no good reason for the breach. Looking at all the circumstances overall he allowed a 20% success fee to be recoverable, ie half of the amount that would otherwise have been received for the retrospective period.

Multiple claims and global success fees

[6.29]

In *Bray Walker Solicitors (a firm) v Silvera* [2010] EWCA Civ 332, one CFA covered two claims. The first claim was for the costs of litigation negligently pursued by solicitors. The prospects there were 70% to 80%. The second claim was for loss of chance of success in that negligently pursued litigation. There the prospects were rather lower. The CFA provided for a single success fee of 70% triggered if any recovery at all was made. Wilson LJ took the view (obiter) that the global success fee had to reflect the split on risk and that 70% was too high. The level of the success fee did not fall to be determined but these observations leave the very difficult question of how to set a success fee where different heads of claim carry different risks.

Disbursement liability

[6.30]

Section 11.8(1)(b) of the Costs Practice Direction expressly stated that the legal representative's liability for any disbursements is a factor to be taken into account in assessing the reasonableness of the success fee. The success fee is applied to the fees charged and not to the disbursements.

Nervous litigator's charter

[6.31]

Immediately after *Trafigura*, the then Master of the Rolls, Lord Neuberger, was concerned with the setting of unreasonably high success fees in *Drake v Fripp* [2011] EWCA Civ 1282. This was an unsuccessful appeal in a boundary dispute which had lasted less than a day. Junior and leading counsel for the respondent had 100% success fees. The 100% success fee was reduced to 50%. Lord Neuberger expressed himself in these terms:

> 'I believe that there may be a regrettable, if understandable, tendency to charge the maximum success fee of 100% in every case. The client with whom the fee is negotiated by the lawyer has no interest in the level of success fee (at least in a case such as this, where he has to pay no more than he is entitled to recover from the paying party), and the lawyer has an obvious and strong interest in the success fee being as high as possible. In many cases, it is easy for a lawyer, acting in complete

> good faith, to persuade himself that the prospects of his client's case succeeding are no better than 50% when it is in his interest to do so, and when he has no negotiations with the party who will or may have to pay the success fee. The court has a particular duty, therefore, to be vigilant in considering the reasonableness of the level of success fee agreed, but, as I have said, this does not mean that the court can invoke the wisdom of hindsight or should adopt an unduly harsh approach.'

It has always been thus. The more risks the solicitor can reasonably recite, the lower the prospects of success and therefore the higher the success fee that can be justified.

ASSESSING THE LEVEL OF SUCCESS FEE – CPR PART 45

Statistics

[6.32]

Lying behind the fixed success fee regime in the old Part 45 Sections III, IV and V is a set of statistics produced for the Civil Justice Council and which used to be available on the costs debate page of its website. The Court of Appeal made it clear in *Atack v Lee* that the fixed success fees themselves cannot be used for cases that do not fall under that regime but the underlying statistics can be used as guidance.

Fixed success fees

[6.33]

It should be kept in mind that costs belong to the client. The old Part 45 fixes the success fee which can be ordered against a paying party. The CFA will govern the level of fees payable to the solicitor and thought must be given to drafting the CFA to reflect the fixed fee steps. These multiple variations are not easy to explain to the client but if they are not included then the client will keep the difference between the costs allowed and those specified in the CFA. The Law Society Model CFA sets out the success fee in steps for fixed success fee cases.

For ease of reference the following table summarises the recoverable success fees in personal injury claims arising from road traffic accidents, EL/PL accidents or EL disease claims. It assumes a degree of knowledge of the working of the system and is provided as a reference point. Otherwise, you will need to consult the rules fully.

There have been three cases which have clarified certain aspects of the following table. In *Broni v Ministry of Defence* [2015] EWHC 66 (QB) Supperstone J determined that members of the armed forces were not employees and so did not come within the fixed-EL accident or disease figures. Previously, in *Patterson v Ministry of Defence* [2012] EWHC 2767 (QB) non-freezing cold injury (or 'trenchfoot') was held not to be a disease but an injury by Males J. However, the subsequent decision in Broni means that Patterson makes little difference since the success fee is at large in any event. In *Dalton v British Telecommunications plc* [2015] EWHC 616 (QB) Phillips J confirmed that Noise Induced Hearing Loss (or 'deafness') claims were disease claims and not accident cases. Given that the CRU statistics on which the figures were originally agreed specifically highlighted NIHL within the Type C diseases, it is no surprise that Phillips J had some critical words for the defendants who decided to run the appeal.

Type of Case	Standard Percentage (solicitor or barrister)	Settlement near to trial (barrister only)*	Percentage at trial (solicitor or barrister)
RTA	12.5	50/75	100
EL Accident	25**	50/75	100
Type A Disease	27.5**	50/75	100
Type B Disease	100	100	100
Type C Disease	62.5***	62.5/75	100

* If a fast track case settles within 14 days of the trial, the standard percentage is increased to the first figure. If the case is in the multi-track, the trigger point is 21 days of trial and the increase is to the second figure.

** A further 2.5% may be claimed if an AJA 1999, s 30 undertaking is involved

*** A further 7.5% may be claimed if an AJA 1999, s 30 undertaking is involved

Escape

[6.34]

The figures in the table can be varied where the damages arising from the accident are over £500,000 or from the disease are over £250,000. The escape mechanism is set out at old CPR 45.18, CPR 45.22 and CPR 45.26 and was considered by HHJ Wood QC sitting as a High Court judge in *William Dronsfield (a protected party who proceeds by his litigation friend Alison Millington) v Benjamin Street* (Manchester District Registry 25 June 2013).

How is the case to be valued? It is usually simple where the parties have agreed damages but if issues of liability were unresolved the situation can be more complex. Each provision of the CPR allows an application where the parties have agreed a lower figure for damages but 'it is reasonable to expect that if the court had made an award of damages', it would have done so above the relevant threshold, 'disregarding any reduction the court may have made in respect of contributory negligence'. In *Hussain v Chartis Insurance UK Ltd* [2013] EWHC 4740 (QB) Simler J considered the approach to be taken to this task. She concluded that issues of primary liability were to be taken as having been established so that only issues of contributory negligence/causation should be considered by the assessing judge.

Where the court accepts that a case escapes in accordance with CPR 45.18, the success fee is said to be 'at large'. The court will consider a reasonable success fee based on the circumstances of the case. The relevance of the fact that the case is, by definition, a large personal injury claim is usually challenged by reference to *C v W* (see **[6.33]**).

Note should be taken of the costs provisions relating to applications under CPR 45.18, 45.22 or 45.26. The applicant party has to persuade the court that the reasonable success fee is sufficiently different from the standard figure or else the standard figure will be applied and the applicant will pay the costs. So, in RTA cases, the success fee needs to be increased beyond 20% or reduced below 7.5% (depending upon which party is applying to escape the standard figure). If the success fee is adjudged to be at any point within the range of 7.5%–20% the sum to be allowed will be 12.5% as if the application had never been made.

Challenges

[6.35]

The practical effect of the fixed success fees has, perhaps inevitably, been tested by the parties. The courts have clearly been determined to make the arrangements work, even to the extent of some surprising outcomes. Certainty has arguably trumped everything else, particularly in the case of *Lamont v Burton* [2007] EWCA Civ 429, where the claimant (or perhaps that should be his solicitors) still achieved a 100% success fee because the case went to trial, even though the claimant failed to beat the defendant's Part 36 offer. The base costs were divided between pre- and post- offer in the usual way: but the success fee was unaffected. This led to a number of commentators with handy examples demonstrating that in some instances it was better for the solicitor to tell the client to take his chance at court regardless of the offer because the solicitor's increased success fee of 100% over, say 12.5%, made up for the potential loss in base costs.

In *Kilby v Gawith* [2008] EWCA Civ 812, the court decided that the defendant's admission of liability before the claimant had entered into a CFA had no effect on the recoverable success fee as the court had no discretion to vary it. Challenges brought on questions of potential alternative funding (*Wetzel v KBC Fidea* [2007] EWHC 90079 (Costs) and the validity of the CFA itself (*Nizami v Butt* [2006] EWHC 159 (QB), Simon J) were given similarly short shrift by the courts.

Concluding at trial

[6.36]

The defendants' challenges to the meaning of 'concludes at trial' in CPR 45.16 have been more successful. A number of judges have concluded that the phrase can only be interpreted as meaning that the trial must have started and not simply settled on the day of the hearing. A helpful discussion of the factors to be considered is set out in *James v Ireland* [2015] EWHC 1259 (QB), where a number of interactions between counsel and the judge were not sufficient to say that a trial had started within the terms of CPR 45.16.

If you are looking to argue that settlement on the day of the trial is sufficient you may find some succour in Coulson J's decision in *Mendes v Hochtief (UK) Construction Ltd* [2016] EWHC 976 (QB). He distinguished the wording of the new rule 45.29C from the old rule 45.16 but another judge may perhaps be persuaded by the rationale of this more recent decision.

ATE INSURANCE

Challenging the contents of the premium

[6.37]

The level of premium may be challenged on the basis that not all of the sum paid was in fact premium. This type of challenge featured early before the courts. In *Callery v Gray (No 2)* [2001] EWCA Civ 1246 the court considered the make up of an ATE policy based on submissions received from intervenors and which were largely encompassed in the report of Master O'Hare who was also sitting as an assessor. The Court of Appeal reconsidered the peripheral benefits that might come within a premium the following year in *Re Claims Direct Test Cases* [2002] All ER (D) 76 (Sep) and in challenges to the scheme known as The Accident Group, see *The Accident Group (TAG) test cases* 2003 SCCO Case No: PTH 0204771 15 May. Since then there have been few if any challenges to the level of the premium based upon its contents and whether they all comprise insurance recoverable within the terms of AJA 1999, s 29.

Challenging the level of the premium

[6.38]

The provisions of the old CPR 44.4(1) and (2) and 44.5(3) (the seven pillars of wisdom) and paras 11.1, 11.5, 11.7 and 11.10 of the Costs Practice Direction are especially relevant to the assessment of premiums.

In the *RSA Pursuit Test Cases* [2005] EWHC 90003 (Costs) the Senior Costs Judge set out the test:

> ' . . . the court should look both at the costs risks and at the size of the claim when considering the premium' [261]

On the basis that no other ATE policy had been obtainable, exceptionally high premiums were allowed once the insurer's flawed method of calculation had been corrected. Master Hurst concluded that the method was flawed because it was based on estimates of costs with no provision for reflecting true costs. A formula based on the opponent's actual costs was accepted. That same formula was used in arriving at the £9m premium in *Motto v Trafigura* [2011] EWCA Civ 1150, with a prospects of success figure of 65% being used by the insurer. The premium rate thus arrived at (62% including administration and profit) was applied to the totality of the defendant's costs, irrespective of the risk level at the time those costs were incurred.

General guidance has also been provided by the Court of Appeal as to how a costs assessor can hope to approach the question of the level of premium. Brooke LJ had this to say in *Rogers v Merthyr Tydfil County Borough Council* [2006] EWCA Civ 1134:

> 'District Judges and Costs Judges do not as Lord Hoffmann observed in *Callery v Gray (Nos 1 and 2)* have the expertise to judge the reasonableness of a premium except in very broad brush terms and the viability of the ATE market will be in peril if they regard themselves (without the assistance of expert advice) as better qualified than the underwriter to rate the financial risk the insurer faces. Although the Claimant very often does not have to pay the premium himself this does not mean

> that there are no competitive or other pressures at all in the market. The evidence before this court shows it is not in an insurer's interest to fix a premium at a level which will attract frequent challenges.'

That passage is often cited in decisions on recovery of premium, for example, by Martin Spencer J in the case of *Percy v Anderson-Young* [2017] EWHC 2712 (QB). It was also the focus of the judgment of Simon J in *Kris Motor Spares Ltd v Fox Williams* [2010] EWHC 1008 (QB), who made it clear that, without reversing the burden of proof, the paying party must produce some evidence that the premium is unreasonable, remembering that doubt must be resolved in its favour. He provided the following guidance:

> ' . . . challenges must be resolved on the basis of evidence and analysis, rather than by assertion and counter-assertion. The issue should be identified promptly and, where necessary, there should be directions for the proper determination of specific issues. This may involve the Costs Judge looking at the proposal; and in the receiving party providing a note for a one-off ATE premium and not just for a staged premium.' [46]

The requirement for 'a note' is a reference to the decision in *Rogers* (see below). Simon J also dismissed the argument that taking ATE insurance late in the proceedings was unreasonable. The solicitor defendants had insured their increasing down side only days before a hearing.

There have been several decisions where the judge has decided that he is able to re-assess the level of the premium. This tends to be where the judge has taken the view that the level of indemnity is unreasonably high (a distinction referred to by Martin Spencer J in *Percy*). Only in two well-publicised cases has the judge felt able to enter into the sphere of the underwriter, notwithstanding the absence of any underwriting evidence. In *Kelly v Black Horse Ltd* (27/9/2013) Senior Costs Judge Hurst concluded that the information given to the underwriter must have been wildly inaccurate and as such the level of the premium was far too high at £15,000. He allowed £3,677 having also reduced the level of indemnity required. In *Redwing Construction Ltd v Wishart* [2011] EWHC 19 (TCC), Akenhead J took aim at all of the additional liabilities and reduced them on a broad brush basis to reflect the lack of risk to the claimant of the litigation.

Staged premiums

[6.39]

In *Rogers v Merthyr Tydfil County Borough Council* the court considered the stepped premium model offered by the DAS 80e policy. The court allowed the premium in full, even though it was twice the amount of the damages in a simple tripping claim. There was no objection to staged premiums in principle. The evidence showed that it was necessary for solicitors to sign up to provide products from particular insurers. DAS imposed such an obligation. The solicitor explained why he chose DAS as a provider, and his reasons were legitimate. Since the premium appeared disproportionate according to the *Lownds* test, the premium needed to be necessary and not simply reasonable. However, the need for the solicitor to subscribe to DAS in all of his cases meant that it was necessary to incur the premium in the present claim and so the *Lownds* test was satisfied. 'Necessity . . . may be demonstrated by the application of strategic considerations which travel beyond the dictates of the particular case. Thus it may include the unavoidable characteristics of the market in insurance of this kind. It does so because this very market is integral to the means of providing access to justice in civil disputes in what may be called the post-legal aid world.' It was wrong to consider proportionality only with reference to the size of the damages. The court had to take 'all the circumstances' into account (CPR 44.5(1)), and this included the risk to which the insurer was exposed. Here the costs exposure of about £6,500 justified the premium claimed in any event, even though the damages claimed did not exceed half this amount.

The court gave the following guidance:

(a) A party who has an ATE insurance policy incorporating two or more staged premiums should inform his opponent that the policy is staged, and should set out accurately the trigger moments at which the second or later stages will be reached. If this is done, the opponent has been given fair notice of the staging, and unless there are features of the case that are out of the ordinary, his liability to pay at the second or third stage a higher premium than he would have had to pay if the claim had been settled at the first stage should not prove to be a contentious issue.

(b) If an issue arises about the size of a second or third stage premium, it will ordinarily be sufficient for a claimant's solicitor to write a brief note for the purposes of the costs assessment explaining how he came to choose the particular ATE product for his client, and the basis on which the premium is rated – whether block rated or individually rated.

In practice, a bald statement that, for example, 'this premium is individually rated' does little to quell the paying party's desire for further information. As the case law stands, the receiving party is well within his rights to refuse to provide any further information until such time as the paying party produces some credible, alternative insurance which the receiving party would have taken out instead. This has been an irritant to paying parties from the moment that the judgment in *Rogers* was handed down. What exactly would be credible evidence? If it has to be evidence from another ATE underwriter, it is not hard to see how difficult that might be to obtain. This is all the more so since the evidence would now be historical. The Court of Appeal considered this point in the conjoined appeals of *West* and *Demouilpied v Stockport NHS Foundation Trust* in the context of post-LASPO policies (see **[9.17]**). If anything, the need for expert evidence, particularly in relation to block rated policies, has become all the more fundamental to any sustainable challenge.

If the description of the stages is not clear from the policy wording, the level of premium recoverable may be affected. In *Mushtaq v Empire Transport Ltd* (2/10/2013) (HHJ Platts) the wording had been altered to take into account the RTA Portal. But some descriptions, such as 'liability denied within protocol period' did not actually describe a stage and as such had to be ignored.

ATE and appeals

[6.40]

In *Hawksford Trustees Jersey Ltd v Stella Global UK Ltd* [2012] EWCA Civ 987, the Court of Appeal was divided on the answer to the question of whether an appeal was to be regarded as the same proceedings as the trial when considering the costs order to be made following an appeal. The majority held that the appeal was separate from the trial:

(1) The word 'proceedings' in s 29 of the Access to Justice Act 1999 should be given its traditional meaning which distinguishes between proceedings at trial and on appeal.
(2) The risk that the incidence of costs at trial might be changed by the costs order of the appeal court may be a new risk of the appeal, but the costs liability and costs order in question remain those of the trial: the risk insured against is a risk of incurring a liability in the trial proceedings not in the appeal proceedings.
(3) The costs liability in respect of which the premium has been taken out remains a costs liability in the trial proceedings, not in the appeal proceedings.

It followed that an ATE policy taken out to defend the appeal, but which gave cover for trial costs (which were at risk had the appeal succeeded), gave rise to a recoverable premium only in respect of the cover for the appeal and not for the trial costs element of the premium. The court made it clear that where a claimant takes out ATE insurance before trial and loses at trial but wins on appeal that premium would be allowed as costs of the trial. In the current case the policy had only been taken out after the trial and therefore at trial there was no premium.

NOTIFICATION OF ADDITIONAL LIABILITIES

The need to notify

[6.41]

Traditionally, a party's funding of his case was a private matter between the client and his solicitor. If the client had to take out a loan or incur some other loss in order to fund the case, he would not be able to claim that additional interest or other sum from his opponent even if he was successful. As such the opponent had no entitlement to know about any such arrangement.

This position was breached with the introduction of Legal Aid. The granting of a certificate, and the likelihood that the opponent would not be able to recover any costs from the legally aided party, was of sufficient moment that the opponent was entitled to be made aware of it so that he could consider whether to continue to pursue or defend the claim as the case may be.

When additional liabilities became recoverable in April 2000, the opponent's potential exposure to costs more or less doubled. The prospect of a 100% success fee and an ATE premium were sufficient to persuade the rule makers that the opponent should be notified in a similar way to a legally aided party. Indeed some argued that the extent of the additional liabilities needed to be notified since otherwise there was a potential breach of ECHR rights. But the argument that such information might prejudice a party's strategy or give away the strength of belief in the case held sway. Consequently only the existence, and not the amount, was to be notified. This means that a party who changes solicitor needs to notify his opponent of the CFA with each solicitor if that is to be the case. This will confirm to the opponent whether he remains at risk of an additional liability, albeit not whether the percentage uplift has gone up or down as a result of the change. If a party's solicitor decides to replace his CFA with a new one for any of a number of reasons, he will need to make sure that the opponent is notified of the existence of the new CFA and, strictly speaking, the ending of the old CFA (there is scope on the N251 to provide both pieces of information at the same time). What the opponent is meant to make of such notification is not clear but it will provide him with some ammunition for the detailed assessment proceedings in all probability. Neither of these situations necessarily leads to an increase in the opponent's liability. There are several situations where that liability will be increased but no notice needs to be given (see below).

Notice of Funding

[6.42]

In order to ensure that parties provided the requisite information in CPD Section 19.4, a notice of funding (N251) was produced. Section 19.4, and therefore the form, changed to allow for more information to be provided from 1 October 2009 in the light of experience but it is rare for any serious point to be taken on the information on the form (unless it is an error as to dates): issues invariably arise from a failure to serve the notice at all.

Where the information changes so that the notice of funding is no longer accurate, notice of the change must be filed and served on the opponent. The practice direction confirms that the notice of change is in fact a further N251 rather than any other form of notice. The fact that more information had to be provided in notices of funding served after 1 October 2009 does not render notices served before that date inaccurate since the provision is not retrospective.

The Court of Appeal in *Bexbes LLP v Beer* [2009] EWCA Civ 628, was required to consider whether notice of the CFA had been given in relation to the appeal. Bexbes had given notice before trial of a CFA which provided for a success fee, and the Court of Appeal concluded, having consulted with the Senior Costs Judge, that there was no separate requirement to give notice of a CFA in an appeal and opponents and advisers should know that a standard Law Society model CFA would continue if the opponent brought an appeal.

Service of the Notice

[6.43]

(a) Pre-proceedings – until October 2009, the pre-action protocols only said that notice of funding, in whatever format, 'should' be given. This was interpreted in several decisions to mean that no sanction would apply if notice was not given until the commencement of proceedings. From 1 October 2009, the provision was changed so that notice 'must' be given and that change has brought pre-proceedings notification into line with the post-commencement provisions ie requiring notification to be given 'as soon as possible': see *Springer* below.

(b) At the beginning of proceedings – The claimant needs to serve his N251 when commencing proceedings. This may be by providing sufficient copies with the proceedings when they are issued and served by the court or by adding a copy to the other documents when serving if this is to be done by the solicitors. The defendant needs to serve his N251 with the unimaginatively entitled 'first document.' What this document is depends upon the circumstances of the case. It may be an acknowledgment of service. It may be a defence. If a default judgment has been obtained it may be the application to set judgment aside. The rationale is clear. It needs to be served at the earliest opportunity by each party.

(c) At any other time – If the funding arrangement is not entered into until part way through proceedings, for example because a new solicitor has been instructed or a top up ATE policy from a different insurer has been purchased, the N251 clearly cannot be served with the proceedings or with the first document. The rationale of notifying the opponent as soon as possible still applies and the party has seven days within which to file and serve the requisite notice.

(d) Notice of change of funding arrangement – As with notification 'at any other time' a party has seven days within which to file and serve the N251 showing the altered information.

In *Springer v University of Leicester NHS Trust* [2018] EWCA Civ 436, the court clarified that 'as soon as possible' (see (a) and (c) above) meant what it said. Accordingly, even though the practice direction went on to say that notification was to be given 'in any event' within seven days of entering into the CFA or in the letter before action if that had not yet been sent, these two options did not provide an alternative time frame. Whilst applying the Court of Appeal's decision in *Springer*, a Deputy High Court judge took a seemingly more lenient approach in *Anglia Autoflow North America LLC v Anglia Autoflow Ltd* (QB (Merc) Julia Dyas QC 28/06/19). In that case, the N251 information was given in the letter of claim five years after the CFA had been made. The judge described the breach as being 'quite trivial' though not 'entirely trivial'.

In *Solicitors Regulation Authority v Malins* [2018] EWCA Civ 366, a solicitor was struck off the roll following a delay in serving a notice of funding. Before you get too concerned, you would hopefully make an application for relief from sanctions rather than create and serve a backdated notice as Mr Malins chose to do. Not surprisingly, he was found to lack integrity and honesty.

No need to notify

[6.44]

In the following situations there is no need to notify the opponent of the existence of, or any change to, a party's arrangements:

(1) If the CFA has no success fee – but simply different hourly rates payable depending upon the outcome – there is no need to give the other party any notice of the existence of the CFA. The rationale is simple. The opponent does not face any additional liability if he loses than if the party with the CFA was instructing his solicitor on a private paying basis.

(2) If the CFA is between a solicitor and 'an additional legal representative' – this will usually be counsel but could be a solicitor agent or solicitor advocate. CPD 19.3(2)(a) is clear that no notice needs to be given though why that should be so is hard to fathom since counsel's fees may be significant and therefore so too may be his success fee. The wording of the practice direction does suggest that notice of the solicitors own CFA with his client has to have been given already for counsel's CFA

not to be notified. It would be a rare case where counsel used a CFA but the solicitor did not do so. In any event, there would still be little logic in counsel's CFA being notified in one circumstance but not another.

(3) If an ATE policy has been 'topped up' – if the limit of indemnity has been increased from the original policy limit the level of premium is likely to have increased as well thereby increasing the opponent's potential liability. Nevertheless, CPD 19.3(2)(b) indicates that where notice of 'some insurance cover' has been notified already, there is no need to notify the opponent of any change in that cover unless it is that the policy has been cancelled. If further insurance cover is obtained by taking out a policy with another insurer, notification of that new policy does need to be notified.

Failure to notify

[6.45]

The contents of the old CPR 44.3B are stark. With the usual proviso that the court may order otherwise, a party who fails to notify his opponent of a pre-LASPO success fee or ATE premium in accordance with court rule, practice direction or order cannot recover any additional liability for the period of default: CPR 44.3B (1)(c).

Where there has been no notification, the opponent is by definition unaware of the existence of the additional liability. Accordingly, he will not usually be in any position to take a point about this failure until he serves his points of dispute (or raises it in correspondence where a schedule of costs has been put forward by the receiving party for negotiation.) Equally, a party who has overlooked serving notice usually remains oblivious to the failure until the paying party raises it. Why this does not become apparent when the bill of costs is being drafted is not clear. Perhaps receiving parties take the view that they will see whether the paying party will take the point. If so, that is optimistic to say the least since the bill will be considerably higher than would otherwise be the case and is one of the first points that any drafter of points of dispute is likely to take.

Applications for relief from sanctions

[6.46]

Applications for relief from the sanction imposed by CPR 44.3B have generally been made in the detailed assessment proceedings. Indeed, there is a specific provision in the costs practice direction (10.1) in relation to such applications. Consequently, most of the reported decisions are those of costs judges at the SCCO and appeals from those decisions prior to April 2013. The cases divide in general terms between those where no notification was given and those where the paying party knew something but not everything he was entitled to know. Where there has been no notice, prejudice to the paying party almost goes without saying and so applications face an uphill task in front of most of the judiciary. If the paying party was aware that, for example, the receiving party was using a CFA, but not exactly when that started, it will be more difficult for the paying party to demonstrate any prejudice, not least with CFAs potentially being retrospective. Nevertheless, a delay in notification may still be too steep an uphill task for the claimant to overcome. In *Springer* (see above), notification was given in the letter before claim but that was two years after the claimant's first solicitors were instructed (and six months after the second solicitors' CFA was made). The court noted the absence of any good reason for the breach and took the view that there was prejudice to the defendant in the lost opportunity to take an alternative course of action. Even though the defendant did not adduce any evidence in support of this, it could not have harmed its case that it settled the case very quickly after proceedings were served.

The change in emphasis in applications for relief from sanctions under CPR 3.9 from April 2013 is covered fully in Part 3 of this book. That change in emphasis means that the reported decisions before then are of only limited guidance for the future. We offer *Supperstone v Hurst* [2008] EWHC 735 (Ch) as an example of pre-April 2013 decisions just in case you need to refer to the historic cases. It is one where no notification at all had been given. Floyd J said that relief from sanctions should not be granted lightly (albeit that he decided to do so there) and a party who failed to comply with the CPR ran a significant risk that he would be refused relief. If a party did not have a very good explanation, or the other side was prejudiced by his failure, relief from sanctions would usually be refused.

The CPD Section 32.5 sets out the information that needs to be included with the notice of commencement in respect of additional liabilities. If you are serving a notice of commencement, it is worth checking this lengthy provision in the practice direction because a failure to comply with its terms brings CPR rule 44.3B into play. Rules 44.3B(1)(d) and 44.3B(1)(e) relate specifically to failures to provide the required information in detailed assessment proceedings for CFAs and ATE policies respectively. They suggest that a failure to notify will render the entire additional liability irrecoverable. As such, it makes a failure to comply with these provisions worse than a failure to notify the opponent of the existence of the additional liabilities in the first place. Notwithstanding the apparent application of rules 44.3B(1)(d) and (e) to detailed assessment proceedings, Barling J in *Long v Value Properties Ltd and Ocean Trade Ltd* [2014] EWHC 2981 (Ch) concluded that 44.3B(1)(c) was the relevant provision in these circumstances. Consequently, the extent of the sanction was only for the period during which the information had not been provided. He also concluded that the failure was a 'trivial' or non-significant / serious one and so would grant relief if that were required to escape the consequences of rule 44.3B(1)(d).

Some paying parties will invite receiving parties to make a formal application for relief from sanctions to rectify this default. If this is not done, or not done promptly, applications made at detailed assessment hearings have been known to result in the additional liability being disallowed notwithstanding the fact that it was notified within the substantive proceedings themselves. This practice has reduced given the comments in *Denton* regarding the taking of opportunistic points (a comment specifically supported in *Long* in these circumstances). Nevertheless, if you are invited to make an application, it is generally better to be safe and a little poorer in terms of a modest adverse costs order than sorry with no success fee or an awkward conversation with your ATE provider.

Disclosure

[6.47]

In relation to CFAs, disclosure of a copy of the CFA will ensure that there are no difficulties under this section. If you do not wish to serve even a redacted version of the CFA, you will need to serve a statement setting out certain provisions in any event (CPD 32.5(1)(d). This requirement is in addition to the risk assessment or statement of reasons regarding the level of the success fee (unless it is one prescribed by Part 45).

For the ATE policy, the key document is the 'insurance certificate' (CPD 32.5(2)). Many ATE providers do not produce a document with the word 'certificate' upon it. The closest document is the schedule to the policy and which will generally be accepted by the paying party albeit that it does not always cover all of the information required by CPD 32.5(2). The only sure way to cover this aspect is to disclose the full wording of the policy but that is something that may need the prior agreement of the ATE insurer.

TRANSITIONAL PROVISIONS

[6.48]

The transitional provisions are contained in Part 48 and are relatively brief. The old costs rules and practice directions are preserved, as if in aspic, by rule 48.1 for 'pre-commencement' CFAs, CCFAs, ATE policies and Membership Organisation undertakings. So if you have a pre-commencement additional liability, you can continue to rely on the provisions set out in this chapter regardless of when the costs come to be assessed.

'Pre-commencement'

[6.49]

The phrase 'pre-commencement' applies to all CFAs and ATE policies entered into before 1 April 2013. It also applies to CFAs and ATE policies in the three discrete areas of mesothelioma claims; privacy and publication claims; and insolvency related claims. The precise wording of these three areas can be found at rule 48.2 and PD 48. The primary and secondary legislation used to carve out these three areas always suggested a lack of permanence in any of them. This has proved to be the case in respect of both insolvency-related and privacy and publication claims. As of April 2016, additional liabilities ceased to be recoverable in insolvency claims. From April 2019, only ATE premiums (not success fees) remain recoverable in privacy and publication claims. Elsewhere, some form of Portalesque fixed fee regime is proposed for mesothelioma claims.

The precise wording of the scope of insolvency proceedings which were originally 'saved' from the effects of LASPO 2012 has produced little case law and since it ended in 2016, that is likely to continue to be the case. Nevertheless, there remain cases which relate to the three-year window of recoverability and one of those is *Candey Ltd v Crumpler (as joint liquidators of Peak Hotels and Resorts Ltd (in liq))* [2020] EWCA Civ 26, [2020] Bus LR

1452, [2020] Costs LR 131. The need for the proceedings to be brought by a liquidator was found not to include BVI liquidators whose liquidation of the company had been recognised by the High Court and proceedings had then been brought in London against the company's former solicitors, Candey Ltd. The interesting point is the court's acceptance that a success fee could be claimed in principle by the defendants of such claims and not solely by the liquidators (for whom the saving appeared to have been made.)

Clinical negligence claims

[6.50]

Section 46(1) of LASPO 2012 carved out one seemingly permanent exception to the ending of recoverability of ATE premiums. As fleshed out by the Recovery of Costs Insurance Premiums in Clinical Negligence Proceedings (No 2) Regulations 2013 (SI 2013/79), it enables ATE policies which insure the costs of certain expert's reports to be recoverable. The limitations on the policies are considerable. They can only relate to experts dealing with breach of duty or causation rather than quantum. They only relate to the reports and not to the costs of any attendance upon either counsel or the judge at trial (or even possibly the opposing witness for the purpose of a joint statement). Section 46 allowed for the regulations to deal with the cost of such premiums but the Government decided to leave that to the courts to determine. Further commentary, particularly in relation to the Court of Appeal's decision in *West and Demouilpied v Stockport NHS Foundation Trust* [2019] EWCA Civ 1220, can be found at **[9.17]**.

Additional liabilities and proportionality

[6.51]

Under the CPR prior to April 2013, the proportionality of success fees and ATE premiums as 'additional liabilities' under the *Lownds* test were assessed separately from the base costs of the solicitors and counsel if either or both were acting under the terms of a CFA. The *Lownds* proportionality test has now usually given way to the proportionality test set out in Rule 44.3(5) (see **[28.70]**) on detailed assessments. The question arises as to whether the recoverable success fees and ATE premiums should continue to be assessed separately or should now form part of the overall figure on which the new proportionality test should apply. The Court of Appeal confirmed in *BNM v MGN* [2017] EWCA Civ 1767 that additional liabilities should be considered separately from base costs. It did not deal with the potentially bizarre result of dealing with the two elements using different tests. The extent of the success fees are of course dependent upon the level of base costs allowed as being reasonable and proportionate. But as things stand, the judge needs to consider the additional liabilities at the outset under the *Lownds* test and the base costs at the end under CPR 44.3(5). How is the judge to consider the proportionality of the additional liabilities before he knows how much they are?

Using both pre- and post-commencement arrangements?

[6.52]

One of the many imponderables prior to 1 April 2013 was whether it would be possible to jettison a CFA and ATE arrangement entered into whilst additional liabilities were recoverable in order to take advantage of QOCS protection post-1 April 2013. It seemed logical that if the CFA was torn up as if it had never existed (so claiming no base costs or success fee under that CFA if successful), there would be no impediment to using a post-April 2013 CFA with no recoverable success fee and be protected by QOCS. Where base costs were still claimed under a pre-commencement CFA, the logic faltered since there was clearly still a pre-commencement CFA in existence which would prevent the use of QOCS.

However, as the Court of Appeal decided in *Catalano v Esply-Tyas Development Group Ltd* [2017] EWCA Civ 1132, the very existence of a pre-commencement CFA prevented the use of QOCS whether or not it was subsequently torn up. To do otherwise would enable a claimant with a pre-commencement CFA to have 'the best of both worlds'. If, near to trial the case looked strong, the CFA would continue with the prospect of a success fee to be recovered. If the prospects looked doubtful, the CFA could be replaced with a post-commencement version and the cloak of QOCS protection could be donned before the final reckoning. That, the Court of Appeal concluded, could not be what the legislative draftsman had intended.

CHAPTER 7

DAMAGES-BASED AGREEMENTS

INTRODUCTION TO DAMAGES-BASED AGREEMENTS

[7.1]

As we have discussed at the outset of this part of the book, there is more than one kind of agreement where the entitlement to fees depends upon the outcome of the case. In other words, the extent of the fees is 'contingent' upon the outcome. All of these agreements can therefore be described as contingency fee agreements. However, the law of costs tends to treat the phrase contingency fee agreement as meaning a particular type of agreement, namely one where the lawyer agrees to act for the client on the basis of receiving a share of the subject matter as his payment. While these are not uncommon in non-contentious business, such agreements are unenforceable at common law as being champertous where they relate to contentious business. It is only an agreement that complies with a statutory exception which can legitimately depend upon the outcome. So, conditional fee agreements are lawful contingency fee agreements. So too, are retainers which comply with the Legal Aid Agency requirements (because the hourly rates recoverable if the client wins are far higher than those recoverable from the Agency if the client loses.) But the purest form of contingency fee agreement is a damages-based agreement and these only became available in contentious business in 2013.

There have been many who have championed the use of contingency fees in litigation for some considerable time. The simplicity of the concept of the client agreeing to pay over a share of his damages for his representation has seemed very desirable when compared with some of the tortuous descriptions required to be given by those using conditional fee agreements. But there is only room for one use of the acronym CFA and since conditional fees arrived on the Statute Books first, contingency fee agreements have had to be branded damages-based agreements so that they are DBAs rather than a further form of CFA.

Simplicity of concept is no guarantee of simple implementation (as anyone who has read the 'Portal' protocols and practice direction will confirm). DBAs have had a number of teething problems since their introduction and a thorough review took place not long afterwards. The recommendations for reform waited for implementation (or at least a Government response) for longer than the regime was in place originally. Those recommendations have led to proposed having now been drafted which have some fundamental differences to the 2013 version and are discussed at the end of this Chapter.

Finally, by way of introduction, DBAs are for lawyers, not claims management companies. They have their own litigation funding agreements which are not caught by the regulatory requirements strewn throughout this chapter: *UK Trucks Claim Ltd v Fiat Chrysler Autos NV* [2019] CAT 26.

THE ONTARIO MODEL

[7.2]

Since the Statute of Gloucester in the thirteenth century, the basic rule has been that costs follow the event. In other words, the winning party will have at least a contribution towards his costs paid by the losing party. This basic tenet causes a difficulty with the concept of a DBA where the client pays his lawyer out of his share of the damages – what does the client/solicitor do with the order for costs payable by the other side? To ignore it would be to give a windfall to opponents at the expense of the client. But to capitalise upon it would be to destroy the inherent simplicity of the model by importing rules regarding the taking into account of the opponent's contribution to the client's costs.

As we shall see, these rules do not just cause headaches as to whether the agreement is in the client's best interest (though that is a significant concern). They also require the agreement to deal with matters such as hourly rates which would not be required under a pure contingency fee agreement and which inevitably turn the agreement into something resembling a CFA.

Now that recoverability of success fees has largely ended, a CFA might be described as an agreement based on hourly rates which are recoverable from the opponent in the event of success with the client meeting any shortfall from his damages, up to a capped limit. The form of DBA now available can be described as an agreement based on a share of the damages up to a capped limit but which is reduced by such sums as are recoverable from the opponent in the event of success calculated using hourly rates. Confused? Some figures may help to explain the last two sentences but at this point you should simply be aware that to a large extent a DBA and a CFA have similar mechanisms even if in certain cases, the outcome can be very different. We will look at some figures later in the chapter but first we shall look at the statutory requirements of a DBA and which is very much based on a Canadian arrangement described by Sir Rupert Jackson as the 'Ontario model'.

STATUTORY FRAMEWORK

[7.3]

The wording of s 58AA of the Courts and Legal Services Act 1990 (brought in by LASPO 2012) is very similar to s 58 in respect of CFAs. An agreement created under s 58AA is not unenforceable simply because it is a DBA. This double negative definition nods at the common law position that a DBA is unenforceable at common law. Consequently, as with CFAs, the Act creates an island of legality in the sea of illegality that is the common law. In order to comply with s 58AA a DBA must be:

- entered into on or after 1 April 2013;
- in writing;
- in accordance with the Damages-Based Agreements Regulations 2013.

Regulation 3 of the DBA Regulations requires the DBA to:

- specify the claim or proceedings to which it relates;
- the circumstances in which the solicitors fees are payable;
- the reasons for setting the level of the percentage.

Let us look at these in turn.

Entered into on or after 1 April 2013

[7.4]

Proceedings brought in the employment tribunal have always been considered to be non-contentious business which just goes to show that you cannot always rely on the ordinary meaning of words. The effect of this is that contingency fees have always been available in employment cases and indeed are widely used by solicitors. Counsel, for professional conduct reasons, were not allowed to use a contingency fee agreement. They were able to use a CFA and, since there is no costs recovery generally in the employment tribunal, the fees were almost always paid out of the client's damages which made the prohibition a distinction without a difference. Such contingency fee agreements between solicitors and clients were regulated by the Damages-Based Agreements Regulations 2010. These regulations continue to apply to agreements entered into before April 2013 but are otherwise revoked.

In non-employment matters, however, a DBA pre April 2013 cannot comply with s 58AA and is unenforceable. While it is probable that the same ability to make retrospective agreements will apply to DBAs as it does to CFAs, the contractual abilities of the parties will not overcome the fact that the statute is not retrospective in effect.

In writing

[7.5]

A degree of formality is required to make sure that everyone knows the bargain they have struck. It may well be that the client understands the cap on DBAs more easily than on CFAs but, for the reasons set out below on tactical and professional considerations, it is imperative that the terms of the bargain, and the explanation of it, are clearly set out in writing. The fact that it is a statutory requirement, as with CFAs, ought to be irrelevant. However, agreements reached in a rush, because circumstances have changed or limitation is imminent, can easily be reduced only partly in writing. Such agreements will be vulnerable to challenge if the paying party gets wind of the oral elements, particularly if they tend to disadvantage the claimant.

In Regulation 1 'costs' are defined as 'the total of the representative's time reasonably spent, in respect of the claim or proceedings, multiplied by the reasonable hourly rate of remuneration of the representative.' In order to be able to quantify the costs recoverable from the opponent, it is very important that the hourly rates are set out. Provisions for revising the hourly rates on a periodical basis ought to be included. A simple alternative to bespoke rates might be to refer to the hourly rates set from time to time for your local court by virtue of the Guideline Rates for Summary Assessment.

Where to put the hourly rate information? If the DBA is going to include client care type information anyway, then the obvious answer is 'in the DBA itself.' But many firms send a separate client care letter which sets out hourly rates amongst many other pieces of information. It is easy for the wording of the client care letter and the DBA to get out of synchronisation, including the hourly rates, if they are not regularly reviewed.

There is another issue regarding a separate client care letter which sets up a retainer with the client in addition to the DBA. The law of costs is ambivalent about the idea of there being concurrent retainers. But it would seem to be the only method which potentially will allow a DBA to be used and still be able to charge some fees if the case does not succeed. This is set out in detail below but mention is made here so that you can consider what you wish to include in your client care letter when also using a DBA.

In employment matters, reg 5 sets out the information that needs to be given in writing to the client. There is nothing which says that such information must be given prior to the commencement of the DBA. But the wording is very similar to the CFA Regulations 2000 and which required the information to be given at the outset. From a client care point of view, the information is the sort that ought to be provided at the beginning of the matter anyway. The information to be provided is set out as follows:

- The circumstances in which the client may seek a review of the representative's costs and expenses and the procedure for doing so;
- The dispute resolution service provided by ACAS regarding actual and potential claims (presumably in relation to the underlying proceedings rather than a putative problem between the solicitor and client);
- Other methods of funding that may be available such as Legal aid, legal expenses insurance, trade union funding or pro bono advice. If any are available, information on how they apply to the particular case;
- The point at which expenses become payable and a reasonable estimate of the amount likely to be spent on expenses (including VAT).

If the client asks for further explanation, advice or information, the *representative* needs to provide it. Civil litigators could do worse than use these categories as part of their template for providing clients with costs information.

Specifying the proceedings

[7.6]

The need to specify the proceedings, or parts of them, to which the agreement relates has unfortunate echoes of reg 2 of the CFA Regulations 2000. Cases such as *Blair v Danesh* [2009] EWCA Civ 516 were brought by the paying party in an attempt to show non-compliance with the regulations and therefore a lack of enforceability of the agreement against either the claimant or the defendant.

Problems have tended to crop up where there is more than one defendant. If there is only a single defendant, then a general description of a claim against that defendant, even if it changes its name or entity through merger etc, will usually be adequate. Where, however a defendant brings a Part 20 claim against a third party and the claimant joins that party as second defendant, it is easy to overlook amending the agreement with the client to include the second defendant in the specification of the proceedings in the DBA. There are an infinite variety of such possibilities. One option is to make the definition of the proceedings wide enough to encompass 'any additional defendants brought into the claim' or similar but you should be careful not to make it so vague that the reverse argument of the description being so wide as to lack any contract certainty becomes available.

In employment matters, reg 6 requires any amendment to a DBA to cover additional causes of action must be in writing and signed by the client and the representative. There is no mention of amendment to a non-employment DBA in the Regulations.

The circumstances in which fees and expenses are payable

[7.7]

This is another concept brought in from the CFA Regulations and to which old cases may be relevant. Generally the idea of payment in the event of success but not otherwise has been relatively easy to define. However, the meaning of payment in the DBA Regulations is rather more complicated than in the CFA Regulations.

A DBA cannot require the client to pay any more than the agreed 'payment'. This is the percentage of damages that has been agreed can be deducted and which is subject to statutory limits (see below). The payment is the shortfall after any costs and expenses have been recovered from the opponent. In civil cases, it includes both solicitors' costs and counsel's fees but excludes expenses, and which would include After the Event insurance if that was used in conjunction with a DBA. In employment matters, counsel's fees are treated as an expense and so are not part of the payment itself.

What happens if the agreement ends before the case concludes? There is no 'payment' to share. According to HHJ Parfitt QC in *Lexlaw Ltd* (see **[7.18]**) termination provisions can, in effect, include payment from other sources.

'Hybrid' Damages-Based Agreements

[7.8]

The definition of payment is in reg 1 of the DBA Regulations and starts off with the phrase 'that part of the sum recovered in respect of the claim or damages awarded the client agrees to pay . . . ' From this it is clear that the client can only be someone who is recovering damages, ie the claimant and not a defendant (unless there is a counterclaim).

It precludes any form of differential or 'no win, low fee' fee agreement because the absence of success will mean there is nothing recovered from which the lawyers could be paid. It is said by those who want to use such agreements that this provision prevents a good deal of litigation being carried on under DBAs. If it were altered so that a lower hourly rate or fixed fee was payable in the event of failure, it would be more attractive as an option but it would also mean that the distinctions between a DBA and a CFA would continue to be more and more blurred.

The prospect of failure can evolve during a case. Based upon the decision in *Lexlaw Ltd* (see **[7.18]**), if the case starts going south, you would be better to terminate an agreement (if the client has behaved unreasonably) or get your client to end it, for any reason, so that you are paid for your time up to that date and for which sum payment does not need to be made from any recovery from the opponent. Whilst the judge's reasoning in this case is powerful, it does leave the parties in a rather odd position. The client might be well advised to settle or discontinue in order to limit his opponent's costs but in doing so runs the risk of finding himself liable for his own solicitor's costs if the retainer is determined to have been terminated before the case concluded.

The only method for making a hybrid DBA work so far has been achieved where the claimant has involved a commercial funder of the sort referred to in Chapter 10. Such funders enter into a separate litigation funding agreement directly with the solicitor which enables the solicitor to receive a payment based on hourly rates (or a fixed fee) without involving the client and so has nothing to do with the DBA itself. You may ask why the solicitor is not entitled to enter into an agreement which still makes some payment in the event of failure. For solicitors this is seen as a necessary financial safeguard to undertake work that would otherwise be unattractive. But for the Government such agreements are seen as being ones where the solicitor takes no real risk and simply profits on the successful cases.

At the time of writing this edition, the Government was consulting on the implementation of LASPO etc after five years. Loud calls for hybrid DBAs were to be heard at consultation meetings and it may be that the Government will alter its position on this point by the time the 2020 edition is published. By contrast, the Scottish Parliament recently enacted the Civil Litigation (Expenses and Group Proceedings) (Scotland) Act 2018 which enables a DBA, known as a 'success fee agreement', to provide for payment to a solicitor at one figure where successful and either no payment or one of a lower amount where unsuccessful.

Reasons for setting the level of the percentage

[7.9]

The attraction to clients of DBAs is the certainty with which they are provided. Whatever the outcome they know that they are not going to be liable to pay out more than X% of their damages for their legal fees. (This figure might well be increased to pay expenses and it does not deal with adverse costs but they can be dealt with separately.) On the other side of this coin is the realisation on the part of the solicitor that there is a finite sum that can be recovered in payment of your fees. The ability to recover costs from the opponent based on an hourly rate at first sight seems to guarantee that a reasonable sum will be recovered for a reasonable amount of work. But, as we shall see below, the workings of the Ontario Model often militate against this. It will be the naïve solicitor who does not consider the sum likely to be achieved via a percentage of the client's damages before starting any work.

Ideally, you should have some idea at the outset of:

(a) the overall value of the claim (or the relevant heads of claim if it is a personal injury case (see below);
(b) the overall cost of reaching a trial and proving the case there;
(c) the prospects of the case settling successfully earlier than at trial;
(d) the likely recoverable costs on assessment or by agreement;
(e) the firm's appetite for taking on such work and any guidelines in place which affect the cost of doing so.

These factors can all be summed up by the phrase 'risk reward.' If the case is not very valuable in terms of damages, but is likely to take a good deal of time to prepare and is unlikely to settle short of trial, it does not present a very attractive picture. Even if the case is successful, the amount of money recovered in fees may be nowhere near the sort of return expected based on a calculation of time spent multiplied by your hourly rate.

Conversely a strong case on liability with an easily calculated quantum, such as is set out on invoices, may well suggest that the case will settle quickly and without a great deal of work. In such cases, the prospects of taking a percentage of the costs for limited effort sounds promising.

Then of course there are all the cases in the middle. Some, such as those involving personal injury or negligence, are unlikely to crystallise early in terms of quantum even if liability or breach of duty is clear cut. Others, such as commercial disputes will often suffer from a lack of any objective third party evidence (such as is often available in personal injury cases) to be able to be confident on liability for some time even if the quantum is clear from the beginning.

How much will it cost to get the case 'home' at trial?

[7.10]

Factor (b) above is perhaps more important than any other. It is certainly the one that is most in danger of being overlooked. It is true that very few cases get to trial, but if you start from the assumption that it will usually settle early, you will almost certainly take a bath on a number of occasions. You will also be prone to feeling that you are going to be under rewarded during the life of the case. If you have a long track record in the area in which you are considering using DBAs you may be able to take a more bullish approach. But even so, there are uncertainties as to opponent's tactics once they are aware of the fact that you are using a DBA. This will become clear to them relatively soon if you are involved in repeat litigation with regular opponents, notwithstanding the fact that there is no need to serve any form of notice of funding. The need to keep statistics; to take heed of judicial dicta such as that of HHJ Alton in *Stevens v Watts* (cited anonymously but with approval by Lord Woolf in both *Jefferson v NFC* and *Home Office v Lownds*); as well as to budget carefully has never been greater, nor as likely to provide significant advantages to your calculation of profitability.

Likely recoverable costs on assessment

[7.11]

Factor (d) is relevant if you charge an hourly rate for your work which does not generally find favour with the court on a between the parties' assessment. This may be perfectly proper. For example, in *Jones v Wrexham Borough Council* [2007] EWCA Civ 1356, the rates claimed by a Reading firm were based on City of London rates because many of the lawyers had come from City firms to do similar work but in a different environment. The firm was successful in that case in charging higher rates. You might consider your expertise to justify something similar but have not yet persuaded the local judiciary that this is so. There is nothing to prevent you charging such rates to your client in ordinary retainer cases. If you do this using a DBA, you will know that there is very likely to be a shortfall on assessment as a result and such sum is limited to what can be claimed from the client as the payment in addition to the costs recovered from the opponent. Similar considerations would apply if you use specialist counsel in your area of work and their fees are also considered to be vulnerable to challenge on assessment.

If you are instructed in relation to an employment matter, the reasons for setting the level of the percentage have to have regard (where appropriate) to whether the claim or proceedings is one of several similar claims or proceedings. Perhaps peculiarly if you are instructed on a group action in civil proceedings, that does not seem to be a relevant consideration when setting the percentage level.

MAXIMUM LEVEL OF THE RECOVERABLE PERCENTAGE

[7.12]

You need to make sure that your agreement does not inadvertently exceed the maximum level of recoverable fees from your client. Similar provisions in CFA legislation rendered a number of agreements unenforceable even though the parties to the agreement were perfectly content with the terms of the bargain struck. Once the opponent was able to demonstrate that the maximum level had been exceeded, it was but a short step for the Court of Appeal to consider that the administration of justice was affected, even if the client could not really be said to be prejudiced. In *Jones v Caradon Catnic Ltd* [2005] EWCA Civ 1821, Lord Justice Laws was particularly vehement in his condemnation of agreements which flouted the statutory requirements. They went 'flat against the grain' of the will of Parliament, amongst other comments.

The headline maximum levels are as follows. Each needs some explanation of the finer detail:

- Personal injury 25%
- Employment 35%
- All other civil cases 50%
- Appeals 100%

Personal injury

[7.13]

In personal injury cases the 25% deduction can only come from the damages for pain, suffering and loss of amenity and past pecuniary losses (net of the recoupment of any CRU benefits). This is the same arrangement as for the deductible element in CFAs.

The 25% includes VAT on the solicitors' charges as well as counsel's fees (including VAT if any). It does not include expenses (reg 4(1) of the DBA Regulations 2013).

These provisions are bound to cause problems. By limiting the heads of damage from which sums can be deducted, a solicitor and his client will always have divergent interests in allocating offers to those heads of claim where a global offer is made by the defendant. There is little prospect of a defendant offering to breakdown a Part 36 offer or similar. Discussions between the solicitor, counsel and the client will need to be carried out while the lawyers walk a professional tightrope in providing appropriate advice while keeping their commercial interests at bay.

Employment

[7.14]

The figure of 35% in employment cases continues from the DBA Regulations 2010. Unlike personal injury and civil cases, counsel's fees are treated as being expenses and so are not included within the 35%. The client is therefore liable to hand over a rather higher percentage of his damages than the headline figure suggests. Many solicitors, particularly since their own remuneration is capped by the percentage, will use counsel for advocacy rather than do it themselves.

Other civil cases including appeals

[7.15]

The limit of 50% was a surprise to many people. The rationale for finally allowing contingency fees to be used in contentious work was largely based on allowing parties the freedom to contract on whatever terms they wished. As such, the parties' options were increased from the existing methods of funding. By restricting parties to a 50/50 split between the solicitor and client, the freedom of contract argument has rather been sidelined. Presumably the idea of the lawyers taking the majority of the spoils of litigation was a newspaper headline the Ministry of Justice did not wish to see. But that does not sit very happily with reg 4(4) which states that the limitation to 50% only relates to cases at first instance. If it is accepted that there may be sufficient risk for a party justifiably to give most of his damages away if successful on appeal, there does not appear to be much logic in preventing this from happening earlier. Not all clients are consumers needing protection. Many are sophisticated and large businesses, often with their own in-house legal department well able to agree terms with external solicitors.

REDUCTION IN DAMAGES OR COSTS

[7.16]

The hinge on which DBAs work is the sum recovered by way of damages and costs. Anything which reduces either element of this sum will have the effect of reducing the pot from which the solicitor can claim his fees.

Accordingly, consideration of the risk reward potential needs to include the possibility that the damages or costs may be reduced by court findings. There are a number of possibilities here. Findings of contributory negligence will obviously reduce the claim itself. Counterclaims or other forms of set off may have exactly the same effect (see below). In personal injury cases, the operation of the Compensation Recovery Unit recoupment provisions will also need to be 'netted off.' The one consoling factor is that the spectre of a reduction in the damages in any of these ways should be relatively obvious from an early stage. The extent of the reduction will not be clear in most situations but the possibility will be.

By comparison, the likelihood of an issues based costs order or a percentage order will not become clear (other than a theoretical possibility in any case) until later. It is unusual for issues to be run without any real expectation that they will be successful. Properly alternative cases do not necessarily result in only a percentage of costs being allowed. The conduct of the parties often seems to be the catalyst for orders which are less than a full order for costs. Such conduct invariably occurs during the currency of the case and so can only be considered by a regular and objective monitoring of the conduct of the litigation.

RECOVERABILITY

[7.17]

Further consideration also needs to be given to whether the sums will be physically recovered from the opponent. If there is no insurance, or the opponent is not of any obvious substance, this may well be a concern. Does the word 'recovered' denote a settlement short of a court hearing or does it in fact require money to be received by the client before he is liable to discharge his solicitor's fees?

Regulation 4, when defining 'payment', refers to amounts 'that have been paid or are payable by another party to the proceedings by agreement or order.' So at first blush that suggests that it is only the award of costs that is required. But in fact it is the opposite because the clause is written in a negative fashion. A DBA must not require a payment by the client to his lawyer other than one that has taken into account the sums that have been paid or are payable by the opponent. If the opponent has not paid the between the parties element, the lawyer will only be able to claim from his client the additional sum. To put this into some very simple figures – the client damages are £12,000 and he has agreed to pay 25% to his solicitor net of any recovery from the opponent. The between the parties costs are assessed at £2,000. The client is liable to pay his solicitor £3,000 as the 25% share. He can offset the £2,000 and pay his solicitor the £1,000 balance. If the opponent is not good for the £2,000 it appears that the risk is on the solicitor.

Legal Aid practitioners of any vintage appreciate that the statutory charge bites on any property 'recovered (or preserved)'. In the absence of anything physically recovered, whether in cash or property, there would be nothing on which the statutory charge could bite. The wording of the relevant regulations certainly appears to suggest that recovered means actually received in that context.

However, in the commercial context, the decision in *Arkin v Borchard Lines Ltd* [2001] CP Rep 108 considered the meaning of the word 'recover' in relation to a CFA. Colman J decided that there was a distinction between 'recover' and 'paid'. He decided that counsel had entered into a CFA because the client was unable to pay under an ordinary retainer. The idea that counsel would make payment of their fees also contingent upon the defendant's means was one he found to be 'completely inconceivable.'

It is dangerous to assume that parties and their lawyers will always do what would seem to be logical. The idea of solicitors buying in work for which they would use a 'pure' CFA with no success fee would also have seemed unlikely at the time Colman J was hearing the *Arkin* case. However, that is what solicitors running the Accident Group cases agreed to do, in great and small numbers, before the scheme fell apart in 2003. There is likely to be further argument on this point even if the solicitors are able to take enforcement proceedings in the client's name as of right.

Given that, as things stand, lawyers can only be paid out of the damages recovered, there is certainly something to be said for looking to secure the damages under s 73 of the Solicitors Act 1974 (see **[3.31]**).

TERMINATION

[7.18]

Regulation 8 of the DBA Regulations deals with the question of early termination of the agreement in an employment matter. The general law of contract is preserved but two particular issues of concern in respect of a DBA are addressed. First, a solicitor may only charge fees on a time basis for his fees and expenses if the agreement ends early. In other words, he cannot seek a sum equivalent to a percentage of the likely damages. Secondly, the client cannot validly terminate the agreement after a settlement has been agreed or within a week of the tribunal hearing. No doubt some unscrupulous clients will seek to use their lawyers for as long as possible and then try to sack them just before the damages become available. These provisions help to prevent that from occurring.

It is perhaps disappointing therefore that there are no parallel provisions in relation to non-employment matters. On the face of it, the client could seek to remove his obligations to his solicitor in exactly the same way in a civil case as for an employment matter. There will also be cases where either the solicitor or client decides that a case ought not to be pursued further, whether on a lack of prospects or on a risk reward basis. Why the use of a quantum meruit approach is not equally good for civil cases in these circumstances is hard to fathom. There was a storm of protest when the original (overly detailed) DBA Regulations were unveiled. It may be that which made the Government's draftsman decide to put the bare minimum into the Regulations instead, thereby allowing the parties to contract on any further aspects. If that is so, civil litigation lawyers would be well advised to consider following the employment matter provisions when drafting their DBA.

One firm who took this approach was the claimant in *Lexlaw Ltd v Mrs Shaista Zuberi* [2020] EWHC 1855 (Ch). The defendant sought to terminate her agreement with the claimant in May 2015 and reached an agreement with her opponent in July 2015. The claimant, seemingly in accordance with the agreement, provided an invoice based on 12% of the damages recovered. The defendant argued that the provision for payment on termination was contrary to reg 4 (see **[7.8]**) and as such rendered the entire agreement unenforceable based on jurisprudence from CFAs which had contravened secondary legislation (see **[6.16]**–**[6.18]**). In such circumstances, the defendant had no liability to the claimant. HHJ Parfitt QC, sitting as a High Court judge rejected this argument and accepted that the termination provisions were separate from the limitation in reg 4 regarding payment from the sums recovered. Regulation 4 was there to deal with the division of the spoils so that the DBA did not fall foul of the common law. This decision has been given permission to appeal to the Court of Appeal so it may not be the last word. It was a judgment on a preliminary issue and without some facts having been finally determined – so it cannot be said for certain – but the timing of the termination does suggest that the defendant was seeking to achieve the objective set out in the first paragraph under this heading and which has usually not ended well before the Court of Appeal in similar circumstances (see **[1.34]**).

OPERATION OF THE INDEMNITY PRINCIPLE

[7.19]

When CFAs were first introduced in 1995, they had no impact on the opponent in the sense that they did not make it more expensive for a losing opponent than was already the case (based on a traditional retainer.) When recoverability was introduced, the success fee made cases potentially almost twice as expensive and consequently paying parties' interest was engaged in attacking the validity of such arrangements. Knowledge of the impact of the indemnity principle became widespread for the reasons described as the Golden Rule and discussed at **[4.3]**. Removal of recoverability may mean that the paying parties' interest will wane. It is likely to lead courts to consider any inadequacy of drafting to be a matter between the solicitor and his own client.

The introduction of DBAs has no detrimental impact on the opponent. CPR 44.18(1) specifically says that the fact of the DBA 'will not affect the making of any order for costs which otherwise would be made in favour of the [successful] party'. Rule 44.18(2) confirms that the assessment of costs under that order will be carried out in accordance with rule 44.3 (as would any other order for costs). Furthermore, whatever is the extent of the DBA client's liability to his solicitor (in other words, the percentage share of damages) is the most that the opponent can be required to pay when calculated on a time spent basis. In some situations the opponent's liabilities will be decreased by the operation of the indemnity principle. The comments in this paragraph can be demonstrated with a simple example.

A commercial client successfully sues for damages in the sum of £50,000. His agreement with his solicitor is for the lawyer to take 30% of the damages (ie £15,000) as payment. The costs based on the time spent are £10,000. The opponent has to pay this £10,000 and the client pays the remaining £5,000 in order to make up the 30% share.

But if the time costs had amounted to £20,000 instead, the opponent's liability would still only be £15,000 since that is the client's maximum liability. The opponent would therefore only hand over £15,000. Notably, there would be no shortfall for the client to pay and so the client pays nothing from the damages to his solicitor and the solicitor will have to write off the extra £5,000 of fees that he has incurred in the case. This in a nutshell, is why the risk of a case becoming protracted is entirely the solicitor's. Once his fees have reached the value of the percentage share, the solicitor is effectively providing his client with free representation and the opponent is also at no further costs risk. Hence the need to consider the risk reward very carefully at the outset and keep it in mind thereafter (see **[7.8]**). This exacerbates the potential for solicitor and client conflicts as to whether a case should be settled or not.

In the case of *Dial Partners LLP v Eastern Airways International Ltd* [2018] EWHC B1 (Costs), the claimants agreed with their solicitors to move from a DBA to a CFA shortly before the trial. The case then settled on the eve of trial and the defendants' costs liability increased markedly from the position under the DBA which they understood to be still in effect. Nevertheless, the costs judge was persuaded that the change was not tactical in itself and was justified in the circumstances as simply removing a cap which represented a windfall to the defendants but did not actually increase the work that had been done or would be done. Whether all clients would have been prepared to go through with this must be in some doubt; at least if they were told that there was almost certainly going to be a challenge to the switch. It may be that the fact it was a CFA Lite and therefore the client was at no real costs risk was persuasive.

DBAS, CFAS AND (N)CBAS

[7.20]

In *Bolt Burdon Kemp v Tariq* [2016] EWHC 811 (QB) the claimant solicitors entered into a 'Contingency Fee Arrangement' with their client. The fee was 50% of the damages recovered together with VAT and disbursements. It was expressly described not to relate to contentious business and was accepted by all to be a Non-Contentious Business Agreement. Spencer J decided its terms were fair and reasonable and as such the client was unable to challenge the level of the fee via a Solicitors Act assessment.

Whilst dicta on DBAs remains scarce, the conclusions of Spencer J are well worth reading, in particular his distinguishing of contingency fee agreements from CFAs (see para 163ff). There is nothing in principle to distinguish the terms agreed as a non-contentious business agreement from a DBA and indeed the solicitors' advocate drew a comparison with the percentages allowed under DBAs.

CONFLICT OF INTEREST

[7.21]

It is obvious that if there is a finite amount of money as the potential reward, the longer the case takes to bring to a conclusion, the less remunerative it is for the solicitor. The reverse is true for the client. Giving the solicitor 25% of the claim may be a good deal if the litigation is likely to be hard fought. But if not much more than a stiff letter before action is required, it does not look to be such a bargain.

The client care provisions discussed in Chapter 1, and the natural wish to look after a client's best interests, can easily lead to muddled thinking and a tying of your professional soul in knots. No client will expect you to offer a choice of agreements at the beginning of a case and then to select whichever is least advantageous to you at the end of it as some manifestation of professional ethics. As long as the pros and cons of agreements are spelled out to clients at the beginning of the case, they will be content to follow the chosen agreement regardless of the outcome. Moreover, the Legal Ombudsman is unlikely to criticise any agreement which ostensibly dealt reasonably with the client's circumstances. You may well decide not to offer all of the options that could be used to run a case. That is a matter for you. As long as the client is aware that there are other options, but that you do not offer them, he cannot validly criticise you later if, in the eventual circumstances, one of those other options might have suited him better.

By way of illustration, there are many practitioners who are currently unwilling to offer DBAs to clients because of the 'hybrid' issue. There is no reason for them to offer an agreement that either does not suit their practice (because there are no fees at all if unsuccessful) or risks being found unenforceable (if a 'low fee' based on an hourly rate is agreed). There is no suggestion that this unwillingness is unprofessional. It is a perfectly rational choice and if you do not want to run cases on any form of contingent agreement you are entitled to do so.

The case of *Dial Partners LLP* above shows that clients may be prepared to agree to their solicitors moving to a more advantageous arrangement towards the end of a case. If the client is not obviously prejudiced by that change, there appears to be no conflict of interest in suggesting it.

CHALLENGES BY THE CLIENT

[7.22]

Embarking on a practice using DBAs is not for the faint-hearted, though some traps can be avoided by looking at the evolution of CFAs and the challenges to them. One final concern to bear in mind is one which did not occur with CFAs with recoverable success fees. It applied before the age of recoverability but was not a point that was taken at the time. It may occur now and applies equally to DBAs. It goes back to the beginning of this chapter and the concept that all contingency fees are unenforceable unless they comply with the statutory provisions that created them. A shrewd client will appreciate that if his lawyer is using a DBA (or CFA) and that agreement is unenforceable, there will be no deduction from his damages because the solicitors' fees will be irrecoverable. Therefore, such a client would seek to find some non-compliance with the legislation once the case has concluded and take the solicitor to an assessment under Part III of the Solicitors Act 1974 to determine the point.

In *Lexlaw Ltd v Mrs Shaista Zuberi* [2017] EWHC 1350 (Ch), in amongst allegations of undue influence and misrepresentation, the client alleged that the DBA was unenforceable as a result of non-compliance with section 58AA of the CSLA 1990. Master Clark in the Chancery Division accepted the client's application for a preliminary issue on this point. HHJ Parfitt QC ruled against the defendant and the case is now going to the Court of Appeal (see **[7.18]**).

REFORM?

[7.23]

As early as December 2014, ie little more than 18 months after their implementation, the Government minister in charge of such matters requested the Civil Justice Council to look at improving the regulatory regime for DBAs, albeit without doing so in a way that would encourage litigation. This was clearly a recognition that the 2013 Regulations did not fit their purpose. The CJC set up a working party under the chairmanship of Professor Rachael Mulheron with the title of the Damages-Based Agreements Reform Project. In September 2015 the working party produced a comprehensive report spanning 156 pages. It consisted of two parts – the first related to technical issues concerning the wording of the 2013 Regulations and draft 2015 Regulations which were provided by the Government as something of an Aunt Sally to enable the working party to focus on specific drafting issues. The working party identified 20 specific areas of concern. The second part dealt with policy issues but steered clear of the thorny issue of hybrid DBAs given the Government's steer in the meantime that it did not propose to deal with matters as lawyers would like and as discussed at [7.8] above.

In February 2019, roughly four years after the Reform Project's report was produced, the Government responded as part of a wide ranging review of the implementation of the Civil Procedure Reforms in LASPO 2012. With some masterly understatement, the Government identified that 'the DBA regulations would benefit from additional clarity and certainty'. As such it would 'give careful consideration to the way forward' in the light of 'the independent review of the drafting of the regulations which is being undertaken by Professor Rachael Mulheron and Nicholas Bacon QC'. They produced draft regulations for consultation in October 2019 which build on the concepts set out in the 2015 report.

- The Ontario model would be abandoned in favour of an alternative 'success fee' model where the lawyers would take recoverable costs in addition to a percentage of the damages.
- The parties and their solicitors would be allowed to define the meaning of 'financial benefit' in their individual case so that it may encompass real property or shares or other objects which would immediately translate into money (ie 'money's worth').
- Hybrid arrangements would be allowed to an extent so that the lawyers would be paid a percentage of their costs if the case was unsuccessful.
- The new regulations would only deal with civil cases. Employment claims would be dealt with under the existing regulations.

The devil is always in the detail and the draft regulations are simply an attempt to move the conversation forward. The abandonment of the Ontario model has the blessing of Sir Rupert Jackson (on the basis that the indemnity principle has not been done away with as he had recommended.) The initiative also has support from the Government in principle. The publicly stated intention, at the time of writing, is for a supplementary report analysing the responses to the draft regulations to be provided to the government in the later part of 2020. Although we like to think that this long overdue reform is finally nearing fruition, the earliest on which we can set out the detail will be in the 2022 edition.

CHAPTER 8

CONTENTIOUS AND NON-CONTENTIOUS BUSINESS AGREEMENTS

INTRODUCTION TO CONTENTIOUS AND NON-CONTENTIOUS BUSINESS AGREEMENTS

[8.1]

The difference between contentious and non-contentious business has been said to be fundamental to the remuneration of solicitors for decades if not centuries. But there are more similarities than differences in the two forms of business. Furthermore, events over the last few years have reduced the relevance of the distinction to the point where there is little practical difference between the two in most circumstances. Consequently, this Chapter, having discussed the meaning of contentious and non-contentious work, deals with the two together in considering the benefit and detriment to solicitors and their clients of formal business agreements to which provisions of the Solicitors Act 1974 apply.

DEFINING CONTENTIOUS AND NON-CONTENTIOUS BUSINESS

[8.2]

There is a drafting convention of defining something by saying that it is everything other than something else. That is the approach used to describe non-contentious business (it is everything other than contentious business) in s 87 of the Solicitors Act 1974. It is off-putting to the extent that contentious business is not a phrase that is necessarily obvious in its meaning. But this approach does make sure that nothing falls between the cracks. It is either one thing or the other. Matters are not helped by the definition of contentious business (which also appears at s 87) concluding with the phrase 'not being business which falls within the definition of non-contentious or common form probate business'. It is easy to have sympathy with Ward LJ in *Ralph Hume Garry (a firm) v Gwillim* ([2002] EWCA Civ 1500) where he described s 87 as 'a fairly useless circular definition of contentious and non-contentious costs'.

The distinguishing part of the definition of contentious business is that it 'means business done, whether as solicitor or advocate, in or for the purposes of proceedings begun before a court or before an arbitrator'. Consequently, all proceedings before a court, once litigated are contentious business. Work done in anticipation of court proceedings is non-contentious unless and until court proceedings are actually commenced. When that happens, the work converts to becoming contentious business retrospectively. The only exception to this may be where the work has already been billed with a statute bill and as such has crystallised the work done. The point will be an academic one in most circumstances.

Non-contentious business usually covers work that is transactional rather than litigious in nature. Private client work such as conveyancing and wills and probate (other than contentious probate naturally) is non-contentious. So too is commercial work in mergers and acquisitions, construction projects and contracts generally. Often the words transactional and non-contentious are used as synonyms in these areas. Less obviously, the bringing of claims in tribunals has been considered to be non-contentious work, even if tribunal proceedings are commenced. As such, employment matters are non-contentious business. However, that position is likely to change in our view with the reorganisation of the Tribunals structure. There are now two 'tiers' for the majority of tribunals. There are seven 'chambers' in the first tier and four chambers in the upper tier. The upper tier includes the Upper Tribunal (Lands Chamber) (formerly the Lands Tribunal). The Employment Appeals Tribunal is not within this structure. These two tribunals were previously considered to be courts of record and so proceedings before them would be considered to be contentious business. It appears that all of the tribunals are starting to become costs (and court fee) bearing, and it will be odd if they are not considered to be contentious business in the relatively near future.

BUSINESS AGREEMENTS

[8.3]

Section 57 of the Solicitors Act 1974 deals with non-contentious business agreements. Sections 59 to 63 deal with contentious business agreements. While using different terms in places, there is a great deal of overlap in these sections. So, to avoid the reader searching for differences that do not exist simply because of some of the language, we have dealt with them together under the following headings. Obviously where there are differences, these are pointed out.

Representative Party

[8.4]

The agreement will of course usually be between the solicitor and the client. But there are some circumstances where the person contracting with the solicitor is in fact representing the ultimate client. In such circumstances, apart from any drafting issues, the representative party needs to be aware of the provisions of s 62. Such representative capacity would occur if the 'client' signs the agreement as guardian; trustee under a deed or will; Court of Protection deputy or other person authorised under that Act.

The crucial point is that the agreement needs to be put before a costs officer before any payment is made. If the representative party pays the solicitor's fee without doing this, he runs the risk of being held to account for any shortfall that the ultimate client would have achieved if the agreement had gone before the court.

Timing

[8.5]

A solicitor may make an agreement with his client as to his remuneration before, during or after doing the work. It is therefore explicit that such agreements can have retrospective effect.

In writing

[8.6]

The business agreement must be in writing. A non-contentious business agreement must also be signed by the client or his agent. According to Lord Denning in *Chamberlain v Boodle and King (a firm)* ([1982] 3 All ER 188, [1982] 1 WLR 1443, CA) a contentious business agreement can be created by an exchange of letters which would mean it was in writing but not signed by the client as if it were a single document. Given that the benefit of these agreements is very largely in the solicitor's favour and therefore to the detriment of the client, it is imperative that you obtain a signature from your client to a document setting out the agreed terms. It may be that your business agreement is essentially a client care letter. If so, the client should be supplied with an extra copy of the letter with a request to countersign it and return it.

In passing, there is another advantage from the solicitor's point of view in getting the letter (or equivalent) signed. The letter will constitute express authority from the client in respect of the matters contained in it and these agreed terms are therefore, pursuant to CPR 46.9, presumed to be reasonable (see the end of this Chapter). Therefore, whatever view the judge takes as to the enforceability of the agreement, on any subsequent Solicitors Act assessment of costs the client is bound by the agreed terms.

Methods of Charging

[8.7]

A business agreement may provide for remuneration by:

- reference to an hourly rate

  Until s 98 of the Courts and Legal Services Act 1990 was enacted, a business agreement could not be made based on hourly rates. The use of hourly rates brings a risk of uncertainty to the agreement and, as can be seen below, the trade-off for limiting the client's rights to assessment is based on the certainty as to fees which a business agreement gives them.

  Where an hourly rate is agreed, the client is bound by that agreement. Only the number of hours spent can be challenged subsequently (see [8.12]).

  A contentious business agreement using an hourly rate is expressly permitted to be 'at a higher or lower rate than that at which he would otherwise have been entitled to be remunerated' (s 59(1)). There is no reason in principle why the same should not apply to a non-contentious business agreement.
- a gross sum

These days we tend to talk of a fixed fee rather than a gross sum. It is the perfect type of fee arrangement to encompass within a business agreement because it is the most certain of all the possibilities. Even if there are in fact a number of fixed fees depending upon the circumstances, this remains the case. So a building block approach or a menu of fees as a case progresses would fit the bill. So too, would an agreement that set out different figures depending upon the stage at which the case concluded. One which set out different figures depending upon success or failure however would fall foul of s 59(2) and would probably also be difficult to convert into a CFA (see 'a percentage' below).

- a commission

  In Chapter 31 we look at the concept of value billing as an alternative to charging based solely on the time spent. The case of *Jemma Trust Co Ltd v Liptrott* [2003] EWCA Civ 1476, remains the most recent exposition of the appropriateness of this idea. In essence the solicitor charges on an hourly rate and then additionally claims a percentage of the estate or property involved. The idea is to reflect the value and therefore skill of the solicitor. The hourly rate is often suppressed to acknowledge the separate value element. This is an approach used in non-contentious work, generally property or probate based. It is not strictly contingent upon the outcome because there is no success or failure as such. In any event, it has always been acceptable to carry out non-contentious work on a results basis.
- a percentage

  Section 59(2) expressly forbids a contentious business agreement to found a contingency fee agreement, particularly a champertous one. So the agreement must not give the solicitor any interest in the proceedings, nor depend upon success for payment.

  There are now two ways around the statutory prohibition. The first is that a conditional fee agreement can be entered into in accordance with s 58 of the CLSA 1990 stipulating for payment only in the event of success and which will make it legal. The agreement may also be capable of fulfilling the terms of a contentious business agreement (the Court of Appeal found this to be so in *Hollins v Russell* [2003] EWCA Civ 718). But if the agreement does not comply with the requirements of s 58 of the CLSA it will be unenforceable against the client by virtue of s 59(2) and therefore irrecoverable against the opponent by s 60(3) (a statutory version of the indemnity principle.)

  Secondly, as discussed in Chapter 7, DBAs became lawful in April 2013 for use in court work ie contentious business.
- a salary

  There is nothing wrong in principle with your client employing you to carry out work on his behalf. There are a whole host of regulatory issues to consider and economically it might not make sense in many situations, but it is an option for you to look at. If, at the end of the case, your client has a costs order in his favour, your fees would be assessed at an hourly rate in the usual way without the need for any calculations about the actual cost of your employment. In *Re Eastwood, Lloyds Bank Ltd v Eastwood* [1975] Ch 112, [1973] 3 All ER

1079, CA the Court of Appeal made it clear that the costs of an employed lawyer should be assessed in the same way as for an independent solicitor in private practice.

- or otherwise
  An example of an alternative to the named options is payment by shares in new companies which proved popular during the 'dot.com' era. This approach is sometimes the only way a start-up company can realistically pay for legal services.

Achieving Certainty

[8.8]

This is the fundamental point of a business agreement. If the terms as to payment cannot be set out with certainty there is very little point attempting to create a business agreement, whether contentious or non-contentious.

In order to be a binding contract, it must show all the terms of the bargain. The leading case on this point remains *Chamberlain v Boodle and King (a firm)* [1982] 3 All ER 188, [1982] 1 WLR 1443, CA) which is an indication that such agreements have fallen out of favour. When solicitors were used to receiving a fixed sum for their work, such agreements were much more attractive than when hourly rates took hold of the legal profession. As clients demand more certainty and the rules of court require prospective budgets where fees are not actually fixed, it may be that the idea of certainty is one which will encourage the use of business agreements once more.

The following extract from Lord Denning's judgment in *Chamberlain* shows how much certainty is required. In effect any purely hourly rate based agreement is going to have difficulty coming within the requirements.

> 'Further, the agreement must be sufficiently specific – so as to tell the client what he is letting himself in for by way of costs. It seems to me that the letters in this case did not give the client the least idea of what he is letting himself in for . . . .Take for instance the rate . . . It is £60 to £80 an hour. What rate is to be charged? And for what partner? Of what standard? [etc.] . . .
>
> I only make those observations because it seems to me that this is not an agreement as to remuneration at all. It is simply an indication of the rate of charging on which the solicitors propose to make up the bill. It is by no means an agreement in writing as to the remuneration.'

More recent cases have tended to fall down on the basis of brackets of hourly rates for a particular grade of fee earner (as it did in *Chamberlain*.) Even an open ended right to review the hourly rates annually has created a degree of uncertainty for the courts. If hourly rates are to be used they need to be specified figures, preferably linked to the main fee earners. Any review needs to reflect a specified percentage increase or a link to an objective figure such as the Retail Prices Index.

The courts' attitude is perhaps not surprising. The Solicitors Act gives solicitors an opportunity to make a contract with their client which, if done correctly, prevents the court from having virtually any say in the reasonableness of the remuneration sought thereafter. If, on the other hand, the client's liability is not certain, the court is going to want to protect the lay client from the professional adviser. If the agreement is certain, it may be a bad bargain, but that is a matter for the client and would cut across the client's freedom to contract if the court could interfere.

The important case of *Bolt Burdon Kemp v Ariq* is discussed at [**8.11**]. In order to reach his conclusions, Spencer J had to make various findings of fact as to what the terms of the agreement were because they were disputed by the parties. Having done so he was able to consider whether it was fair and reasonable. The fact that there was a dispute as to the terms of the agreement did not make the terms themselves uncertain. Otherwise it would always be open to one party or the other to allege a dispute in order to extricate itself from an agreement. The *Chamberlain* case demonstrates an uncertainty as to the amount the client had to pay under the agreement on any reading of its terms.

Occasionally, there are situations where even a fixed fee cannot make the terms of an agreement 'fair and reasonable'. In *Crumpler (as liquidators of Peak Hotels and Resorts Ltd) v Candey Ltd* [2019] EWCA Civ 345, the defendant had agreed a fixed fee for conducting several pieces of litigation with the company which was on the cusp of insolvency. The solicitors were granted a floating charge over the company's assets as security for the fee. At first instance, the judge accepted the expert witness's evidence that the fee charged was fair and reasonable and within the terms of s 61 of the Solicitors Act 1974. The Court of Appeal, however, concluded that the relevant provision of the Insolvency Act 1985 (s 245) required the goods or services to be valued, essentially as a quantum meruit, to establish the level of the secured costs. The fixed fee was irrelevant in such circumstances and therefore so too was the evidence regarding the fairness and reasonableness of that sum.

The case of *Crumpler* was remitted to the original trial judge, HHJ Davis-White QC, sitting as a High Court Judge for the purposes of valuing the work done. To the extent that it was 'new' work it could be secured by the floating charge, the remainder would be an unsecured debt. The difference between the original fixed fee agreement (£3.8m) and the time costs based on ledger entries (£1.2m) explains why the liquidators took the point. The judge decided to assess the value of the work rather than, for example, send it to a costs judge to assess. The result is a curious cross between a summary and detailed assessment and there is an interesting discussion regarding hourly rates (see [**31.24**]). For the purposes of this part of the book, the issue to bear in mind is the failure of the solicitors to get to grips with demonstrating the time actually spent on the case where there had been an expectation that a fixed fee would be charged. Evidence that not all work had been recorded which would need a costs draftsman to gather up and include in a detailed breakdown of costs did not find favour with the judge. Putting a specific figure on this unrecorded time might have improved the chances of obtaining relief from sanctions and being able to rely upon late evidence. But the impression given by the judge is that he was determined to bring the proceedings to an end before any further monies were dissipated from the insolvent company's coffers ([2019] EWHC 3558 (Ch)). The lesson is that time recording should be dispensed with only after careful reflection since its uses are not always obvious.

Early Termination

[8.9]

Where some work has been carried out under a contentious business agreement, but before completing it, the client decides to change solicitor (or indeed if the solicitor dies or becomes incapacitated), s 63 comes into play. Unlike the usual position (see next heading), the court may order an assessment of the fees even if it considers the terms of the agreement to be fair and reasonable.

Where the client has decided to change solicitor, the court will look to see if there has been any default, negligence, improper delay or other conduct such as to justify allowing less than the full amount of the remuneration agreed. If there are none of these aggravating factors, then the fee ought to be allowed in full. This provision does not apply where the solicitor is not able to keep to his side of the bargain.

RESTRICTING CHALLENGES TO FEES

Invalid Business Agreements

[8.10]

Where the business agreement has been found wanting in its construction, the solicitors' costs will be assessed via a solicitor and client assessment as described in Chapter 3.

If the work was contentious the costs will be assessed in accordance with the rules of court and in particular the factors set out at CPR 44.4. If the work is non-contentious then obviously there has been no litigation, save for the Part 8 proceedings bringing the question of costs before the court. The various Remuneration Orders produced under the powers in s 56 of the Solicitors Act 1974 set out the factors that the court should take into account when assessing non-contentious work. Article 3 of the Solicitors' Remuneration (Non-Contentious Business) Order 2009 sets them out as follows:

> 'A solicitor's costs must be fair and reasonable having regard to all the circumstances of the case and in particular to-
>
> (a) the complexity of the matter or the difficulty or novelty of the questions raised;
> (b) the skill, labour, specialised knowledge and responsibility involved;
> (c) the time spent on the business;
> (d) the number and importance of the documents prepared or considered, without regard to length;
> (e) the place where and the circumstances in which the business or any part of the business is transacted;
> (f) the amount or value of any money or property involved;
> (g) whether any land involved is registered land within the meaning of the Land Registration Act 2002;
> (h) the importance of the matter to the client; and
> (i) the approval (express or implied) of the entitled person or the express approval of the testator to-
> (i) the solicitor undertaking all or any part of the work giving rise to the costs; or
> (ii) the amount of the costs.'

Apart from the specific property and probate factors, this list essentially sets out the same 'seven pillars of wisdom' as are seen in the court rules. It is noteworthy that the time spent on the matter is a factor even if the bill is rendered as a result of a fixed fee, salary, commission etc and not solely when by reference to an hourly rate.

Valid Business Agreements

[8.11]

Where the agreement is a valid one, however, then the fees ought to be payable without difficulty by the client. If the client changes his mind about the reasonableness of the bargain he originally struck he will have to persuade a court that the fee he is being asked to pay is not a 'fair and reasonable' one. Only if he can do this, will the agreement be overturned so that a detailed assessment can take place. The test is the same whether or not the business agreement relates to contentious or non-contentious work.

How does the court come to consider whether the fees are fair and reasonable? It is not a precise science. According to Donaldson J in *Property and Reversionary Investment Corpn Ltd v Secretary of State for the Environment* [1975] 2 All ER 436, [1975] 1 WLR 1504, 119 Sol Jo 274:

> 'It is an exercise in assessment, an exercise in balanced judgment – not an arithmetical calculation. It follows that different people may reach different conclusions as to what sum is fair and reasonable, although all should fall within a bracket which, in the vast majority of cases, will be narrow.'

Later in the judgment he described it as a 'value judgment based on discretion and experience'. As such, 'it might not be the right figure, and indeed such a figure probably does not exist, but we hope that it will be a right figure'.

You would be forgiven for thinking that the bulwark against the opening of the agreement is therefore less than certain. That would be ironic given the need for certainty in the original agreement. In order to give any effect to the provisions of the Solicitors Act, the bar has to be set fairly high. In practice, it is often clear that either the solicitor or the client is on the moral high ground and it is the other party who is trying to set aside (or uphold) the agreement purely on tactical grounds.

In *Bolt Burdon Kemp v Ariq* [2016] EWHC 811 (QB) Spencer J considered whether a non-contentious business agreement was fair and reasonable under s 57(5) of the Solicitors Act 1974. The solicitors had agreed to represent the defendant in a claim for compensation against the defendant's former bankers who had sold him an 'interest rate swap' just before the financial crash. The defendant pursued his claim with the assistance of a financial advisor initially. By the time the claimant was approached, it appeared that a claim through the courts was statute barred and an appeal against the original review of the bank's selling of the swap was uncertain in its prospects. The defendant was not prepared to risk his money on the case and the claimant was not prepared to offer a CFA. The judge found that it was the defendant who proposed that the solicitors should take 50% of any recovery made to encourage the solicitors to take on the case. This figure was agreed although whether it had been agreed that VAT and disbursements should be added was in dispute. Spencer J commented that there was little authority on the approach to be adopted under s 57(5) notwithstanding it had been in existence since at least 1893. He drew some assistance from the judgment of Lord Esher MR in *Re Stuart, ex p Cathcart* [1893] 2 QB 201. Spencer J said that:

> 'I find the analysis in that case helpful to the extent of identifying that the issues of fairness and reasonableness must be considered separately. Fairness relates principally to the manner in which the agreement came to be made. Reasonableness relates principally to the terms of the agreement.'

The experience of the defendant as a businessman, the prospects of success, the defendant's reticence to wager any of his own money, and his awareness of the potential size of the fee were among the factors taken into account by the judge in concluding that the defendant knew exactly what he was entering into and that the agreement was not unfair. The judge also concluded that the fee claimed was reasonable. He accepted the argument that reasonableness needed to be considered in the light of what was known at the time of entering into the agreement and not by the outcome. According to the judge:

> 'In truth the Agreement represented a speculative joint business venture in which the solicitors were taking all the risk and the client was exposed to no risk at all.'

Whilst the fee was considerably more than the time recorded against the case it was entirely possible that the recorded time would have had to be written off in the absence of any recovery made.

Although the court requires only prima facie evidence of unfairness or unreasonableness in order to intervene, in the opinion of Mustill J in *Walton v Egan* [1982] QB 1232, [1982] 3 All ER 849, [1982] 3 WLR 352 'from a practical point of view the agreement of the client is the strongest evidence that the fee is reasonable'.

Hourly rates

[8.12]

If the client does not allege that the business agreement is unfair or unreasonable, he can still challenge the amount of hours spent on his case if the agreement is based on hourly rates rather than, for example, a fixed fee. The amount of the hourly rate will be binding on the client, but the costs officer may inquire into (a) the number of hours worked by the solicitor, and (b) whether the number of hours worked by him or her was excessive.

PROCEDURE

Non-contentious business

[8.13]

Where a solicitor seeks payment of fees due under a non-contentious business agreement, he will begin proceedings under Part III of the Solicitors Act 1974 as described in Chapter 3. If the proceedings are contested, the solicitor can rely upon the terms of the agreement to defeat arguments raised about the fees (other than the number of hours spent if it is an hourly rates based agreement) that are challenged.

If the terms are challenged, the costs officer will enquire into the facts surrounding the agreement and certify whether the fees are fair and reasonable or not. If they are, then they are payable under the terms of the agreement. If they are not, then the court will give consequential directions for a detailed assessment.

One reason for a solicitor to consider the use of a non-contentious business agreement was that the provisions of the Solicitors' Remuneration (Non-Contentious Business) Order 1994 did not apply to it and therefore the client was precluded from applying for a remuneration certificate. That reason no longer applies unless the work done was before August 2009 when the new Order came into force. This procedure is described in more detail at **[8.15]**.

Contentious business

[8.14]

The effect of a contentious business agreement is to preclude a Solicitors Act assessment of the costs as between the solicitor and the client except in respect of agreements by reference to hourly rates. The agreement itself does not give a cause of action and before a solicitor can rely on it, he must apply to the court for leave to enforce the agreement. Equally, the client may apply to the court to set it aside. Both applications are made under CPR Part 8. The outcome will depend on whether or not the court is of the opinion that the agreement is fair and reasonable. Applications in respect of bills less than £25,000 must be made in the County Court (CLSA 1990, s 3). An application may be made at any time before the bill is paid or before the work has been done. An application can still be made after the bill has been paid for the court to re-open the agreement and assess the costs. The court will need to find that there are special circumstances in order to do so. Such applications are to be made within 12 months of payment although the court may allow further time if it appears to be reasonable to do so.

NON-CONTENTIOUS WORK PRIOR TO 2009

[8.15]

On 11 August 2009, the Solicitors' Remuneration (Non-Contentious Business) Order 2009 replaced the 1994 version. However, the earlier Order still applies to any work carried out prior to 11 August 2009. The 1994 Order provides for a procedure whereby the client can challenge the costs charged by his solicitors without having the costs assessed by the court. Instead the client can request a Remuneration Certificate to be provided by the Law Society as to what sum is a fair and reasonable one to pay. The client has to have paid at least half of the value of the bill(s) he is seeking to challenge before he can use the procedure. Having done so, a solicitor in another practice will, on behalf of the Law Society, look at the file and determine whether the work done was fair and reasonable. If it was not reasonable, a different figure will be substituted.

If the client does not like the decision, he could still require the costs to be assessed through the court. But, as mentioned earlier, this procedure is not available, even for pre-2009 work, if there is a valid non-contentious business agreement in existence.

SOLICITOR MORTGAGEE'S COSTS

[8.16]

Section 58 of the Solicitors Act 1974 contains specific provisions to deal with the circumstance of where a solicitor is a mortgagee, or is one of a number of mortgagees. In such circumstances the solicitor is entitled to charge as if he were the solicitor to the mortgagee and employed by him to investigate title, negotiate the loan etc.

CHAPTER 9

INSURANCE ARRANGEMENTS

INTRODUCTION TO INSURANCE ARRANGEMENTS

[9.1]

We began this part of the book by pointing out that the word 'funding' used in the context of lawyers was not one which necessarily accorded with accepted wisdom in other spheres. Much of the so-called funding is really no more than a fee arrangement with the client, particularly where it limits the client's liability in the event of failure, and typically avoids the need for a client to pay fees in the meantime (the very antithesis of funding as most people would see it.) The use of legal expenses insurance ('LEI') to cover the risk of litigation is a prime example of a concept misdescribed as a funding option but which is undoubtedly something which you need to consider with your client as part of providing the best information as to costs generally.

Much of the effort of rule makers, judges, parties and their lawyers in respect of insurance has concentrated on the vexed question of 'recoverability.' That subject, together with the related provisions concerning solicitors' success fees, can be found in detail at Chapter 6. This chapter only deals with recoverability to the extent that LASPO 2012 and its subordinate legislation has allowed certain niche areas to remain, at least for the time being.

It is conventional to deal with Before the Event ('BTE') insurance and After the Event ('ATE') insurance separately as if the twain would never meet. While there are separate headings in this chapter, you will soon realise that custom and practice has meant that they are more intertwined than is often realised. The virtual end to recoverability of ATE premiums is in our view likely to enhance this situation rather than reduce it.

One of the questions arising from LASPO 2012 is whether or not a solicitor should in fact advise his client not to trouble to use any insurance at all. This might be because the risks have diminished following the implementation of Qualified One way Costs Shifting (QOCS). It might be because the lawyer is prepared to take on some of the adverse risk himself. Possibilities here include that the solicitor wants to charge for 'funding' and make some money on doing so; the client cannot afford to pay for insurance but the solicitor is keen to run the case; or the client is sufficiently important to the solicitor that he can require the latter to take the risk anyway. Whatever is the situation, the role of the solicitor as a quasi-insurer is considered at the end of this chapter.

BEFORE THE EVENT INSURANCE

[9.2]

Chronologically, if not alphabetically, BTE insurance comes before ATE insurance. As the name implies it pre-dates the cause of action at the centre of the litigation. Like motor or property insurance it is bought in the hope that it will never be required and statistically, it will not be required in the great majority of cases. Consequently the BTE insurer does not pay out very often and the cost is limited because the premiums of 'the many pay for the few' as the insurance maxim has it.

Funding via BTE insurance

[9.3]

There will be some who read the introduction and who frowned at the idea that BTE insurance does not fund litigation. In theory fees and disbursements have been payable as the case progressed. But in practice fees in particular and disbursements to a lesser extent have not been paid by BTE insurers as part of the panel arrangements. Indeed some agreements have had the expectation, if not necessarily the explicit wording, that disbursements would not be paid, win or lose. As with much of insurance arrangements, they differ from one insurer to the next.

There are a number of motor and household insurance policies which have included BTE cover for free. That practice has reduced for two reasons. The first is that its inclusion was, for some insurers, simply a tactic at the height of the 'costs wars', to cause claimants some difficulty in recovering the cost of ATE premiums (and success fees). That imperative appears to have waned. More recently, the comparison websites have obliged insurers to place a nominal cost against add-ons such as BTE insurance so that the policies can be compared against other providers. Anecdotally, this has caused the take up of BTE insurance to drop considerably where potential policyholders look to minimise the cost of their insurance.

This development would suggest that the encouragement given by Sir Rupert Jackson in his Final Report to the BTE industry as a way to underwrite litigation at a proportionate cost has fallen on stony ground.

BTE USAGE

[9.4]

Prior to the advent of recoverability, BTE insurance tended to be used by claimants via firms of solicitors with whom the insurer had panel arrangements. The ferocity with which potential claimants are now courted by various organisations to sign up with them did not exist in the 1990s and clients would generally be content to use the insurer's recommendation if they did not have their own solicitor already. In the latter event, the existence of the BTE insurance was largely ignored.

Once recoverability of ATE premiums from defendants arrived in April 2000, BTE insurance became a considerably cheaper option from the defendant liability insurers' point of view and had to be considered by all solicitors as an alternative form of funding to using a CFA (see Chapter 6). As a result, BTE insurers found themselves being asked to indemnify non-panel firms against costs, many of whom were unknown to them. While approaches varied, most BTE insurers initially took a hard line and refused to cover these firms and required the case to be transferred to panel solicitors if the client wanted the benefit of the BTE cover. Most BTE insurers gradually softened this line but some still relied on the Ombudsman's decision that the Insurance Companies (Legal Expenses Insurance) Regulations 1990 did not give the client freedom of choice of solicitor until proceedings had been commenced.

In April 2013, the world turned again. Many solicitors had spent a decade trying to justify not using a client's BTE cover in order to recover success fees and ATE premiums. Suddenly, a client's pre-paid insurance was a valuable commodity when compared with the cost of ATE insurance that the client would have to pay. It became difficult to justify not using BTE cover unless it was clearly insufficient for the case or was otherwise unsuitable and if the BTE insurer continued to refuse to indemnify a particular solicitor as to costs prior to issue, that may no longer be a reason not to use it. That was particularly so in lower value personal injury work (where most of the BTE insurance exists) since the introduction of the Portals which significantly limit the costs risks to the claimant even if proceedings are commenced (see Chapter 26).

BTE COVERAGE

[9.5]

BTE insurance traditionally covers all sides' costs. Therefore it is unlike (most) ATE insurance which does not cover the own solicitor's costs, but merely disbursements and the other sides' costs. This can result in the level of indemnity in a BTE policy being exhausted relatively quickly because all sides are burning the indemnity at the same time.

The fact that the claimant's solicitor's fees were underwritten scuppered any arguments that panel firms had in using a collective CFA on cases sent via the BTE insurer. In particular they could not claim a success fee to offset the cost of the losers when they were paid even if the client lost. Consequently, at their panel firms' urging, some BTE insurers reduced the level of coverage so that they no longer covered the claimant's solicitor's costs but just the disbursements. As such the policy mirrored an ATE policy. The BTE insurers were content with this as it reduced their potential exposure and the solicitors were free to pursue claims using a CFA but without the need for any ATE cover. Some BTE insurers extended this arrangement to non-panel firms who sought to use the BTE cover on behalf of their clients. Some were prepared to reduce their level of cover on an ad hoc basis when requested to do so by non-panel firms in order to be able to use the cover. This approach tended to mean that the BTE insurer's objection to using a non-panel firm – that they might run a poor case at great expense – largely disappeared.

With the recoverability of ATE premiums having ended, BTE insurers received more requests to use the insurance to fund cases. Some agreed to do so based on the terms of the existing policy. Others were prepared to do so only if it was altered to mirror ATE insurance. Some would do neither. It became a question of asking the BTE insurer what, if anything, it was prepared to do in any particular case.

Top up cover

[9.6]

In the infancy of ATE insurance, a request for a policy which provided additional cover to a client who had BTE insurance was met with grave suspicion. The whole ethos of insurance is to insure a large basket of cases so that the odd loser is paid for by the premiums from the much larger number of winners. A one-off proposal for insurance was therefore a clear example of 'adverse selection' ie that the solicitor was only seeking to insure his riskiest cases without insuring the basket of less risky cases. A one-off proposal where the case was sufficiently advanced to have exhausted the BTE cover was an aggravated form of adverse selection. Not surprisingly such proposals were invariably rejected.

As time passed, the concept of taking out an ATE policy to increase the amount of insurance cover (usually known as a 'top up' policy) became understood by insurers as one which often resulted in sizeable premium income rather than huge losses. The need for additional cover did not always mean that the case was a difficult one. Often, the defendant would fight hard and expensively, even though his battle was very much uphill. This knowledge enabled many ATE insurers to start providing additional cover on cases initially being run with the benefit of BTE insurance. Providing an excess layer of cover was if anything less risky than cover from the ground up. Any modest adverse costs order would probably be met by the underlying BTE cover. The same applied where one ATE insurer was giving additional cover to an ATE policy provided by a different ATE insurer.

The client's indemnity

[9.7]

Sometimes the BTE insurer will agree to you running the case with the benefit of the BTE insurance, but upon reading the insurer's protocol agreement, you decide that it is not workable. What do you do?

If the stumbling block relates to reporting provisions, level of indemnity etc it will probably require a discussion with your client about the pros and cons of using the insurance. The cover is ultimately no more than an indemnity against expense and if your client would rather instruct you than use the insurance cover, that is a perfectly proper decision to make as long as the potential repercussions have been clearly explained and understood beforehand. As with all such matters, obtaining the client's agreement in writing is a must.

Hourly rates

[9.8]

The most awkward stumbling block – and it is a regular one – is the question of your fees and in particular your hourly rate. BTE insurer panel agreements generally limit the hourly rates payable based on the volume of work being provided to the firm. There is often also a non-panel agreement containing rates which the insurer considers to be reasonable to pay on individual cases. The differential can be catered for by using a CFA where your client is a claimant. Your usual hourly rate is the successful rate. The insurer's lower rate is the unsuccessful rate.

If you do not use a CFA and yet you still wish to claim a higher rate than the one payable by the insurer, you need to ensure that the wording of any BTE agreement is appropriate. If there is no written agreement the standard position that the BTE insurer is providing an indemnity against your client's costs should prevail. Given the issue of your hourly rates, that indemnity will be partial and your client will still be liable for the remainder. But if there is an agreement and it limits the costs sought from the client to those agreed with the insurer, you may well run into indemnity principle arguments.

If your client is not the claimant (and so is less likely to obtain an order for costs), or is in a regime, such as the employment tribunal, where costs are generally not recoverable, a CFA is not a solution anyway.

In *Brown-Quinn v Equity Syndicate Management Ltd* [2011] EWHC 2661 (Comm), the clients (there were three conjoined cases) had been involved in employment tribunal matters. The defendant had a non-panel costs rate that was below the rate the solicitors would ordinarily charge. It argued originally that it was not liable to meet any costs if it did not agree to the insured's choice of solicitor. By the time of the hearing before Burton J the defendant had revised its position (rightly in the judge's view). The defendant no longer contended that it could prevent the choice of solicitor: merely that the rate it was liable to pay should be based on the non-panel rate where there had been no agreement as to the applicable rate to charge. The judge however decided that any Solicitors Act assessment of costs due should use the insurer's non-panel costs rate, not as a starting point, but as a comparator. It would thus be necessary and right for the court assessing the costs to take into account the availability of any other suitable firms on lesser rates negotiated with the insurers.

This case has been held up by some commentators as a great victory for non-panel firms. The same it has to be said was true of the case of *Eschig v UNIQA Sachversicherung AG: C-199/08* [2009] ECR I-08295, [2010] 1 All ER (Comm) 576, ECJ. However that case opened no floodgates and this one also appears to be quite dependent upon its facts. One, for example, was the agreement to the non-panel solicitors being the 'appointed representative' to the claimant under the terms of the policy. Having agreed that, but not having agreed fee rates, the insurer put itself in a difficult position. If this case gains any traction it will be a simple matter for insurers to make sure they do not agree one part without the other. Furthermore, there is a considerable difference between civil cases where the solicitor is likely to recover his costs and an employment case where he is unlikely to do so. Finally, if solicitors do manage to charge higher rates to the BTE insurer (and which cannot be passed on to the opponent) the premiums will inevitably increase, or the sales will reduce, or quite possibly both.

AFTER THE EVENT INSURANCE

The price isn't right

[9.9]

ATE insurance has had a curious existence. At its inception as an adjunct to the Law Society Model CFA it provided the answer to the question of paying for the defendant's costs and subsequently the client's disbursements. But the price of £85 for £100,000 of cover soon resulted in the underwriters leaving the market licking their wounds. With the advent of recoverability, the ATE insurers became 'entrepreneurs doing the Government's business' when providing the statutory objective of new and better legal services according to CLSA 1990, s 17. Almost immediately the premiums charged were said to be too high and were only ever to be seen on cases that couldn't lose. The underwriting of this oft-called 'fragile market' was a mystery to all but the underwriters and the courts were told by the higher courts that they should not try to second guess that underwriting. However, when Master Hurst did 'deconstruct' the policies sold by Claims Direct and the Accident Group he found policies in which non-recoverable aspects were embedded so the premiums had to be reduced. Moreover, the cases told a tale of underwriters' fingers being burned by claims management companies and seeking to take an ever larger share of the premium to offset their mounting losses. At the time the premium levels could quite properly be described as being both too low and too high.

The size of the policy premiums, particularly in cases where the damages were not high, remained an issue ever after. When Sir Rupert Jackson proposed removing recoverability, he was pushing at an open door with the judiciary and many parts of the civil litigation world. He was vehemently opposed by the ATE insurers and those who used their products, particularly claimant personal injury and clinical negligence practitioners, but to no avail.

The end of recoverability was a coming of age moment for ATE insurers. Some fell by the wayside following the reduction in premium income overall but a smaller number appear to have carved out niches in the post-LASPO world. For the ATE insurers, the silver lining in the LASPO cloud is the fact that they no longer have to justify their premiums to third parties whose only interest is to reduce the figure in front of them. Instead the policyholders will pay for their insurance because they value the transfer of risk that it represents.

RISKS COVERED

[9.10]

Initially, ATE insurance solely covered adverse costs risks. In other words the opponents' costs if the client lost his case, whether at trial or by earlier discontinuance. This left a gap in the funding arrangements on unsuccessful cases. The opponents' costs were covered by the ATE policy. The solicitor's own fees were not payable by virtue of the CFA. But the client's disbursements still had to be met by the client and in some cases, particularly clinical negligence, that could amount to a considerable sum.

ATE insurance quickly evolved to cover 'own disbursements'. Often this did not include counsel's fees because counsel was expected to share in the risk with a CFA as the solicitor had already done. But some ATE insurers did cover counsel's fees, albeit that then made it difficult for counsel to recover success fees if they positively did wish to act under a CFA.

In the early days of ATE insurance, there was a dichotomy of view between the insurers as to the appropriate shape of policies. A number of insurers offered a policy which, like BTE insurance, covered both sides' costs and disbursements. The selling point of such policies was that the solicitor did not need to use a CFA because he would be paid win or lose. That was understandably attractive to a profession which did not generally wish to move to a position of gambling its fees on the outcome of the case. The difficulty with it however, was that solicitors who used it did not necessarily alter their previous practice and so continued to take cases whose prospects were comparatively modest because their fees did not depend upon the result. Consequently the claims experience of insurers offering both side's cover tended to be poor and the premium levels were high.

Claims Direct was the main exponent of running cases on this model and its influence at the time was such that a provision in the Costs Practice Direction at the commencement of the CPR was directly aimed at making sure that the cost of such policies did not greatly exceed the use of a CFA and the more standard ATE insurance (see Section 11.10(1) CPD).

Personal injury cases

[9.11]

Trades Unions, and other Membership Organisations, did not cover own disbursements, but rather left this to their panel firms. Consequently, the statutory provisions making the cost of their undertakings recoverable (in the same way as if they had provided a formal insurance policy) did not make the cost of covering own disbursements recoverable (see Chapter 6 for more detail).

When Sir Rupert Jackson recommended the ending of recoverability of ATE premiums, he proposed Qualified One Way Costs Shifting as a method of removing the adverse costs risk from the client who might otherwise have to pay for ATE insurance himself. QOCS does not deal with the problem of the client's own disbursements. Sir Rupert's view was that this was a matter for the claimant and his solicitor. According to his Final Report, it would be 'perverse' for a vindicated defendant to have to pay for them (via other cases where claimants were successful) and defendants were making a sufficient contribution to the system by having to bear their own costs as a result of QOCS.

So the risks covered in personal injury cases by ATE policies are the own disbursement risk and the adverse costs risk in the event that QOCS protection is removed. That would occur without limit in relation to a claim found to be 'fundamentally dishonest' but is of little significance to ATE policies because they would not respond if the insured was found to have been fraudulent in this fashion. Where the claim had been struck out, then depending upon the consequences, the policy may provide cover. The opponents' claim in such circumstances is again unlimited. Where the claimant has failed to beat a

Part 36 offer, the adverse costs risk is limited to the extent of the damages that were awarded. This gives the appearance of ATE insurance protecting the client's damages rather than covering the opponents' costs in some circumstances.

It is unquestionably the case that the risk to ATE insurers has significantly decreased where QOCS applies and premium levels have reduced as a result. The introduction of fixed costs for cases that 'escape' the Portals is likely to reduce the levels further. In personal injury cases, more than any other area of litigation, the question for each client is whether there is sufficient benefit in the protection afforded to justify the irrecoverable cost of the ATE premium.

Clinical negligence cases

[9.12]

Much of what is said in respect of personal injury cases applies equally to clinical negligence cases. As discussed below, part of the premium remains recoverable, but a significant part does not. The advent of QOCS reduces the risk to the insurer because a loss or discontinuance is no longer likely to trigger any payment for adverse risks under the policy.

But the parties in clinical negligence cases are heavily dependent upon their expert evidence. The risk of the expert changing his view, or simply not being accepted by the court, is ever present. The fees for an expert attending conferences with counsel and at any hearing are not covered by the recoverable insurance policy and it is a rare client who will be prepared to risk being liable for such fees without insurance. As such, ATE insurance is likely to continue to be taken up by most clinical negligence claimants, whether individually or by some firm-wide scheme.

All other cases

[9.13]

Arguably the financial imperative for taking out ATE insurance in civil and commercial cases has not altered a great deal by the implementation of LASPO 2012. Most cases were compromised anyway and they would often be settled via a global deal which left a single pot for damages, costs and disbursements including the premium. For all practical purposes, the premium was therefore already payable by the client in many cases.

Outside the emotive area of damages for personal injury, civil cases are really about money and the costs risk as to obtaining/denying that claim for money. The transfer of the costs risk to an insurer for the payment of a premium is a classic insurance arrangement and many clients see a benefit in transferring that risk. The risks remain those of own disbursements and adverse costs. There are no QOCS issues (although QOCS may well spread to other civil cases) to consider. The place for ATE insurance in such disputes is likely to remain. It may or may not be in conjunction with CFAs since there is no actual need for a CFA to be in place to operate an ATE policy. It is simply that most ATE insurers like the solicitors to be taking some risk even if the CFA is of the 'hybrid' variety where lower fees are still payable if the case loses.

PREMIUMS STILL RECOVERABLE

[9.14]

The general position on recoverability after 1 April 2013 is that, in principle:

- Policies taken out before 1 April 2013 are recoverable from a losing opponent: but policies taken out thereafter are not;
- Policies in respect of certain experts' reports in clinical negligence claims are recoverable;
- Policies in respect of publication and privacy proceedings and mesothelioma claims are recoverable for the time being;
- Policies in respect of certain insolvency proceedings are recoverable if they were taken out before 1 April 2016.

Let us look at these in turn.

Policies taken out prior to 1 April 2013

[9.15]

These are described as being 'pre-commencement' policies because they were taken out before the effect of LASPO 2012 commenced on 1 April 2013. They continue to be recoverable even though the order for costs obtained by the client post-dates April 2013. The issue of recoverability generally is dealt with in detail in Chapter 6. There remain at least a couple of areas where judicial input is very likely to be required on how the transitional provisions relate to ATE premiums.

One issue that has proved to be more illusory than real is whether a staged premium policy is affected by the change of regime. Some commentators suggested that the increased levels in the later stages contravened the legislation by seeking additional sums post April 2013. That was an argument we found difficult to follow. The agreement was taken out 'pre-commencement' and specified the premium that would be payable depending upon the point at which the case successfully settled. Once the case settled, there seemed to us to be no reason in principle why the level agreed by the client at the outset could not be claimed from the opponent. If the premiums decreased rather than increased as the case progressed there would presumably have been no argument from a paying party about a later stage being claimed.

An issue which was always likely to be more contentious was whether a pre-commencement policy which was 'topped up' to provide additional cover became wholly or partly a post-commencement policy as a result of the varied terms. Had the agreement been novated in some way rather than simply varied by consent? The issue was settled by the Supreme Court in *Plevin v Paragon Personal Finance* [2017] UKSC 23. The decision came by the unusual route of an appeal against the costs allowed in proceedings already in the Supreme Court. The decision was therefore on appeal from a decision of the costs officers of the Supreme Court, rather than a first instance decision which had been appealed at least once already. Sumption JSC gave the lead judgment and decided that the toppings up had been no more than variations of the policy which covered the underlying matters in dispute. Whilst the definition of 'proceedings' depended upon the context, the successful party below ought to be entitled to defend the appeals against the original judgment on the same funding basis as had been put in place at the outset.

Policies in Clinical Negligence proceedings

[9.16]

Section 58C was added to the CLSA 1990 by LASPO 2012. It deals solely with ATE insurance recovery and starts by ending recoverability generally. It then goes on to carve out a specific exception in relation to clinical negligence proceedings. This is contrary to the methods used to continue recoverability in other areas discussed below. It would appear that the clinical negligence arrangement is intended to be permanent.

Section 58C allows for the costs of a 'costs insurance policy' ie an ATE policy, to be included in a successful party's order for costs. The risk covered by the policy is in respect of 'incurring a liability to pay for one or more expert reports in respect of clinical negligence.' The fact that the cover only relates to the report of the expert(s) is significant. Much of the costs of expert evidence in clinical negligence cases relates to further work done by the expert in conferences with counsel and attending at court. On the face of it, such work is not covered. Also, it is not clear that a joint report following a meeting of the experts – a pre-requisite in most proceedings – is necessarily covered by this description.

In order to flesh out the detail of this section, it allows for the use of subordinate regulations. These took two goes to be passed by Parliament and so the relevant ones are called 'The Recovery of Costs Insurance Premiums in Clinical Negligence Proceedings (No 2) Regulations 2013'. The prescribed description of eligible policies is that:

(a) the underlying damages claim must exceed £1,000;
(b) the expert report or reports must relate to 'liability or causation'.

Presumably the minimum figure in (a) will go up if the small claims limit for such cases is increased beyond £1,000. The limitation in (b) shows the rationale of the Government behind this exception to the ending of recoverability. Invariably, the questions of breach of duty (rather than 'liability') and causation are investigated first in potential clinical negligence claims. If they can be established then issues regarding quantum can be pursued. The idea of being able to insure the early reports is intended to assist parties to investigate claims without having to expose themselves to a costs risk of unsupportive medical evidence. The theory therefore is that everyone can take out insurance, investigate their claim and then either pay for the medical evidence from the insurance if it cannot be pursued or claim the cost of the insurance from the defendant in due course if it is pursued.

The regulations might have prescribed a maximum amount for the costs of this premium either as a monetary figure or as some form of percentage of the wider policy premium, but the Government decided after consultation not to do this. Instead, the assessment of the premium level has been left to the courts. This might just have been a postponement of the problem. ATE insurers have not generally underwritten clinical negligence in the way described above. They have tended to want some evidence from a claimant before insuring the case. This has usually meant the claimant has had to risk paying for the cost of an unsupportive report. The new scheme expects insurance to be in place before the report is commissioned. Faced with this prospect, the ATE insurers may only make such insurance available to firms with a good track record. For everyone else, the likelihood is that policies will still only be incepted once some form of (perhaps informal) report has been obtained. Nevertheless, if an insurer is content to insure as per the Government's intended approach, the Court of Appeal has confirmed that the taking out of the policy at the outset of the case as originally confirmed by *Callery v Gray (No 1)* [2002] UKHL 28 has survived the recasting of the rules by LASPO and the Jackson reforms in April 2013 (see *Peterborough & Stamford Hospitals NHS Trust v McMenemy* [2017] EWCA Civ 1941).

The cover provided by the recoverable element of the insurance, however, is going to be insufficient for most claimants since they cannot guarantee that their case will win without incurring additional expert fees in the manner outlined above. It is just enough cover to get the claimant into serious difficulties. Almost inevitably, claimants are going to have to pay for additional insurance themselves. Since the Government's approach might be considered to be either too much or too little (but not 'just right') you might wonder why clinical negligence schemes should be treated differently from any other case.

Challenges to the recoverability of clinical negligence premiums

[9.17]

The size of the recoverable premium compared with the irrecoverable element was always bound to mean that defendant organisations would put the reasonableness of the recoverable premium to the test before the courts. Step forward, Master Leonard. In *Nokes v Heart of England Foundation NHS Trust* [2015] EWHC B6 (Costs), he considered various arguments based on previous case law in respect of a post-LASPO policy. He also concluded that the use of block rated policies continued to be an acceptable practice post-LASPO in *Mitchell v Gilling-Smith* [2017] EWHC B18 (Costs).

Master Leonard was then one of two assessors (with Kerr J) who were taxed by the Court of Appeal to produce a report to assist the court in the conjoined cases of *West* and *Demouilpied v Stockport NHS Foundation Trust* [2019] EWCA Civ 1220. Their 70-page report dealt with specific questions set by the court regarding the working of the ATE market and the detailed assessment of ATE premiums in practice. In particular, the thorny question of what evidence was required to challenge a premium was considered in the light of both sides giving evidence of what was required or possible.

The Court of Appeal's conclusions must have come as a bitter blow to the defendant. The decision in *Rogers v Merthyr Tydfil County Borough Council* (see **[6.38]**ff) in 2006 had put the lid on the coffin regarding challenges to ATE premiums being disproportionate since they were necessary and the only issue was whether they were reasonable. Subsequent High Court cases such as *Kris Motor Spares* required the paying party to produce evidence rather than assertion in respect of the reasonable level of the premium. According to the court in *West*, the practice of paying parties had evolved into offering a minimal amount for the premium, often backed up with schedules from other policies said to be comparable, thereby putting the claimant to the task of seeking to justify the level of the premium.

The court clearly deprecated this approach and banged several more nails into the challenges' coffin when coming to the following conclusions in respect of block rated policies:

> '65. As regards a block-rated policy, such as the policies in the present appeals, the ability of the paying party to mount a sustainable challenge will be much more restricted. The majority of challenges to block-rated premiums must relate back to

> the market in one way or another, and would therefore require expert evidence to resolve. In particular, it will not usually be enough for the paying party simply to give evidence that another policy was cheaper. It is not for district judges or costs judges to have to plough through the detail of allegedly comparable policies, still less to be required to assess the effect of any differences in content. An expert's report would be required to the effect that the other policy was directly comparable to the policy under review.
> 66. Moreover, by reason of the contract terms commonly agreed between insurers and solicitors, an alternative block-rated policy may not in fact have been available to the receiving party in any event. That may not of itself rule out consideration of that policy as a comparable, but the challenge would involve difficult issues as to reasonableness to be resolved on the facts of the particular case.
> 67. Finally, a simple comparison between the value of the claim (either the claim made or the settlement sum) and the amount of the premium paid is not a reliable measure of the reasonableness of the ATE insurance premium. That would ignore the way in which the premium payable for a block-rated policy is fixed taking into account a basket of a wide range of cases.'

As per the beginning of paragraph 65 above, the court indicated that challenges to bespoke, ie one-off, policies may be wider because the individual underwriting might be attacked if the risks were wrongly assessed. But our understanding is that the clinical negligence market is now largely a block-rated world and so this small amount of succour may not be relevant. It would not be surprising if any bespoke arrangements were converted into block-rated schemes as far as possible in the light of this decision in any event.

The Court concluded by making it clear that if and when any further challenges were to be brought because circumstances were said to have changed, then test cases would need to be grouped together and brought before the Court. A not very subtle indicator that such cases should not be brought unless there were very good grounds to do so.

The Court of Appeal has declared the issue 'settled' for the foreseeable future. It is clear from the assessors' report that the defendant did not produce any expert evidence for the Court from insurers. This, in our view, highlights the difficulty in obtaining such evidence and so substantial future challenges to premiums are likely to be few and far between.

Policies in respect of publication and privacy proceedings and mesothelioma claims

[9.18]

The fifth commencement order under LASPO 2012 brought the end-of-recoverability provisions into force. It 'saved', ie prevented, this occurring in relation to certain types of proceedings in accordance with written answers previously provided by Government Ministers. As can be seen from the next heading, it only takes a further commencement order to lift the brake on these proceedings and end recoverability thereafter. As such, there does not appear to be a great deal of permanence about this mechanism. It reflects the intention of dealing with these different types of claim in new ways in the near future. The definition of each set of proceedings is as follows:

- Publication and privacy – proceedings for defamation, malicious falsehood, breach of confidence involving publication to the general public, misuse of private information or harassment where the defendant is a news publisher.

- Mesothelioma – a claim for damages in respect of diffuse mesothelioma (within the meaning of the Pneumoconiosis etc (Workers' Compensation) Act 1979)).

The rules of court to back up the Commencement Order can be found in CPR 48.2.

The exception for publication and privacy proceedings was a late change and followed the views expressed by Leveson LJ in his report at the end of his inquiry into press ethics. He favoured the use of QOCS but at the end of 2018, the government announced that it would end the recoverability of success fees but allow ATE premiums to be claimed. This change took place with effect from 1 April 2019. Consequently, the carve-out from s 44 may be more permanent than it first appeared.

Mesothelioma claims have benefited from a bespoke procedure which has meant that claims are dealt with very quickly in the hope of concluding before the claimant dies. It is not at all obvious why this category of personal injury claim should benefit from the saving on recoverability but a specific provision (LASPO 2012, s 48) was included well before the end of the Parliamentary process. Other options, such as an online process, are being considered as an alternative to the current proceedings. If a different option is available that reduces or eliminates the claimant's adverse costs risk, presumably ATE premiums will cease to be recoverable.

Policies in respect of insolvency proceedings

[9.19]

Additional liabilities in insolvency proceedings brought by a liquidator of a company or an administrator under the Insolvency Act 1986 were 'saved' (as per the previous heading) when the general cessation of recoverability occurred on 1 April 2013. These proceedings also include ones brought by a company being wound up or which had entered administration under that Act.

The singling out of insolvency-related proceedings for retention of success fees and ATE premiums was queried from the off because the justification for its saving was not clear. Cynics suggested that HM Revenue & Customs wished to benefit from recoverable premiums in proceedings it brought. But in the absence of any clear justification, it was always open to doubt as to how long that position could remain. The Government committed itself to the ending of this exemption as of 1 April 2015 according to the written statement of the Minister then responsible. But the coup de grâce was only administered almost exactly a year later (6 April 2016) by virtue of the Legal Aid, Sentencing and Punishment of Offenders Act 2012 (Commencement No 12) Order 2016.

CAN THE CLIENT CHALLENGE THE PREMIUM LEVEL?

[9.20]

The premium, as with all of the other policy terms, is a matter of contract between the insurer and insured and the law does not prevent a party from entering into a bad bargain. So, in the absence of misrepresentation or any other breach of contract point, the premium agreed is the premium payable. Proceedings for a breach of contract claim would be required in these circumstances.

What of the solicitor's involvement in the taking out of insurance? In *Herbert v HH Law Ltd* [2019] EWCA Civ 527, the Court of Appeal was asked to consider whether the ATE premium should be included in a solicitor's bill as a professional disbursement, or whether it ought to be recorded as an ordinary disbursement in the cash account. The issue is discussed at **[2.12]**. The court decided that the premium should not be in the bill and consequently, its level cannot be challenged via the Solicitors Act 1974.

CONTENTS OF AN ATE POLICY

[9.21]

Notwithstanding the following comments on some specific matters, the wording of ATE policies did not change greatly with the arrival of LASPO 2012. Furthermore, each insurer has its own wording and a detailed discussion of the different options is outside the scope of this book.

Collateral benefits

[9.22]

The Court of Appeal in *Callery v Gray (No 2)* [2001] EWCA Civ 1246 originally clarified the limits of insurance premiums made recoverable by s 29 of the Access to Justice Act 1999. At the time there was some concern by defendants that items outside those contemplated by the Parliamentary draftsman would be included and their cost would be reflected in the ATE premium sought. They were described as 'collateral benefits'. Perhaps the defendant's shot across the ATE insurers' bows prevented this from occurring. In any event the contents of ATE policies were largely uniform amongst the major players.

The ending of recoverability means that the policy contents are no longer of any interest to the defendant. If a claimant wishes to have a bells and whistles policy then he can pay for the additional items. It is only the recoverable policies – particularly the new clinical negligence policy – where the defendant will be keen to make sure additional benefits have not been loaded into the wording and additional premium charged as a result. Otherwise a party is free to contract with his insurer on whatever terms he wishes.

Counsel's fees

[9.23]

Some insurers have always covered these fees but many have not. The capping of success fees against the client's damages has caused some barristers to propose returning to a 'disbursement' basis so that the success fee can be foregone. This allows the solicitor more room to agree his own success fee with the client. If counsel is insured under an ATE policy, the client does not need to worry about payment of counsel's fees if the case does not go well.

Retrospective cover

[9.24]

Coverage under some policies is retrospective. This allows for cases to be worked up at no original risk to the insurer in terms of disbursements. If the case appears to have good prospects, it can then be insured and any disbursements already incurred can be covered in case the proceedings do not turn out as well as was hoped. However, this is a world away from the situation in *Hawksford Trustees Jersey Ltd v Stella Global UK Ltd* [2012] EWCA Civ 987, where a retrospective policy completely altered the balance of the costs claimed. In *Hawksford*, the respondent, a party who had not taken out insurance in the first instance proceedings, sought to buy cover during the appeal that covered not just the appeal but also the costs of the first instance proceedings. The result was that a premium of £394,638 was claimed by the respondent even though the appellant's estimate for the appeal was only £68,502. The Court accepted that if the appellant had won, the respondent was likely to be liable to pay both the cost of the appeal and of first instance. Nevertheless, by a majority decision the Court concluded that they were separate proceedings and that the proper construction of s 29 was that it related to the proceedings in which the policy was taken out and that other proceedings were separate and therefore not covered.

PAYING ADVERSE COSTS

[9.25]

There is no requirement upon a solicitor to advise his client that he must obtain ATE insurance. Whilst the premium for such insurance was recoverable, it was a relatively easy task to persuade a client to take out ATE insurance. Now that the client has to pay for it if he wins, the task is rather harder. Consequently, it is likely to be the case that more clients will have no adverse costs protection in the future. In such circumstances, the winning party will regularly look to see if someone else can meet those costs. Where the solicitor is self insuring (see **[9.31]** below) the position is relatively clear. But what if the solicitor has advised the client to obtain ATE insurance but has failed in some way to bring this about? In *Heron v TNT (UK) Ltd* [2013] EWCA Civ 469 the solicitor had not sought any ATE insurance; a fact of which the opponent was aware. The solicitor's client failed to beat Part 36 offers at trial and so had adverse costs orders made against it. The opponent was unable to show 'conscious impropriety' in the failure to obtain insurance. As such, he was obliged to seek to show that the solicitor was the 'real party' in accordance with *Dymocks Franchise Systems (NSW) Pty v Todd (Costs)* [2004] UKPC 39. The Court of Appeal considered that a solicitor was entitled to act on a CFA for an impecunious client without becoming the real party. There may be a professional negligence claim between the client and his solicitor regarding costs the client was liable to pay absent insurance. That would be the appropriate forum to test any such claim, not an application for a non-party costs order.

Where an insured party loses, the opponent has no direct right against the insured party's insurers. If the insurer refuses to indemnify the insured and the insured cannot meet his liability to the opponent, the opponent has two choices if he wishes to take matters further.

Proceedings against the insurer

[9.26]

If the opponent believes the insurer has been actively involved in conducting the litigation, he can seek a non-party costs order against the insurer under s 51 of the Senior Courts Act 1981. Otherwise, he needs to step into the shoes of the insured to exercise the insured's rights against the insurer in accordance with The Third Parties (Rights against Insurers) Act 2010. The 2010 Act has ended any lingering doubt under the previous statute as to whether voluntarily purchased insurance, such as LEI, comes within the provisions of the legislation. It will also allow a claim to be brought before the amount of the claim has been crystallised. The previous 1930 Act had required the amount of costs to be assessed (unless agreed) before proceedings could be brought. Now the quantification exercise can be brought as part of the claim against the insurer so that expense does not have to be incurred before it is known whether a recovery from the insurer may be made in principle.

In order to pursue the insurer, the insured has to be made insolvent and so these are proceedings not to be taken lightly. Furthermore, the opponent has no better right to make a claim than the insured. Therefore, if the insurer has avoided the policy in accordance with its terms, the opponent will not be able to seek payment any more than the insured could. In order to see how this works in practice, two good examples under the 1930 Act are *Persimmon Homes Ltd v Great Lakes Reinsurance (UK) plc* [2010] EWHC 1705 (Comm) and *Denso Manufacturing UK Ltd v Great Lakes Reinsurance (UK) plc* [2017] EWHC 391 (Comm).

It is worth noting that the 2010 Act only came into effect on 1 August 2016 and it is not retrospective in effect: *Redman v (1) Zurich Insurance plc (2) ESJS1 Ltd* [2017] EWHC 1919 (QB).

Avoidance of a policy

[9.27]

The fact that the ATE insurance is based on a contract has been regularly overlooked by successful opponents, particularly in personal injury cases. It may be that the compulsory nature of motor and employer's liability insurance leads to the belief that all insurance will pay claims even if the insured has acted in contravention of the policy terms. But this is clearly not the case. If a claimant is found to be fundamentally dishonest in a personal injury claim, and therefore he loses his QOCS protection, it should be no surprise to the opponent (who must have been alleging and proving the deception) if the ATE insurer avoids the policy for material misrepresentations as to the underlying facts of the case on which the proposal for insurance was founded.

The difficulties faced by a party in seeking a payment from its unsuccessful opponent's ATE insurers are clearly set out by HHJ Seymour sitting as a High Court Judge in *IHC (a firm) v Amtrust Europe Ltd* [2015] EWHC 257 (QB). The defendant's claim is described as pure Alice in Wonderland. The successful party, standing in the insured's shoes via the 1930 Act, had to accept that there had been fraudulent misrepresentations but argued that the insurer was estopped from relying on them by conduct which amounted to a waiver. This equitable relief was described as being to help 'a crook to the disadvantage of an innocent party defrauded by the crook'. The hurdle is a high one indeed and has not been lowered by the arrival of the 2010 Act. Nevertheless, the comparative simplicity of the procedure under the 2010 Act will no doubt tempt some defendants to try their luck with applications.

Order of payment?

[9.28]

Not all policies specify the order in which payments under the indemnity need to be made by the insurer. If it is not clear to you that there is any ranking, you should make sure you make a claim for unrecovered disbursements promptly if there is any prospect of adverse costs having to be paid and thereby reducing the indemnity available.

ATE AND PROSPECTIVE COSTS CONTROL

Costs Budgeting

[9.29]

If there ever was a need to include in a party's budget any additional liabilities – success fee or ATE premium – that effectively ceased when recoverability ended because the budget only deals with recoverable costs. There are of course many cases where proceedings have commenced after 1 April 2013 (and so need to be budgeted) where there is a pre-commencement CFA and/or ATE policy. As such there are a number of situations where the existence of the ATE premium needs to be alerted to the court and the opponent in order to make sure that it is recoverable in principle at the end of the case. The method of doing so continues to be the Notice of Funding in form N251. As described earlier in this chapter, all publication, privacy and mesothelioma cases continue to be 'pre-commencement' in the sense that the premium remains recoverable.

Security for Costs

[9.30]

We deal with security for costs applications in detail in Chapter 19. ATE insurance is essentially an unsatisfactory substitute for a bond or guarantee because of the insurer's contractual rights to deny coverage where the insured has not kept to the policy conditions. Nevertheless some parties do agree to the use of ATE as security for costs. But where that happens, the court has no power to vary the coverage of that policy: *Harlequin Property (SVG) Ltd v Wilkins Kennedy (a firm)* [2015] EWHC 3050 (TCC). On the other hand, the terms of an indemnity offered by an ATE insurer, rather than an ATE policy or a guarantee, were considered in detail by O'Farrell J in *Lewis Thermal v Cleveland Cable* [2018] EWHC 3033 (TCC). She made a number of amendments to the draft deed in the light of the opponent's concerns.

Some parties appear never to be satisfied. In *Mayr v CMS Cameron McKenna LLP* (QBD (Comm) Andrew Baker J 21/11/2017), the claimants had ATE insurance which they backed up with a deed of indemnity from a 'first class insurer' to the same level of indemnity as the ATE in case the ATE insurer avoided its liability. The indemnity was to be provided in three stages to avoid having to pay for it all if the case settled early. The first premium had been paid and the remainder was held by the claimants' solicitors who offered undertakings as to payment. This was not sufficient for the defendants but the court considered the arrangement likely to be effective and demonstrated satisfactory security for costs.

It is also worth noting in passing that the proceeds of a policy taken out by an insolvent party to meet a security for costs application was considered not to fall into the general funds of the administration in *GSM Export (UK) Ltd (in administration) v Revenue and Customs Comrs* [2014] UKUT 457 (TCC).

Costs Capping

[9.31]

In *Barr v Biffa Waste Services Ltd* [2009] EWHC 2444 (TCC), Coulson J thought it entirely random to link the amount at which a claimant's costs could be capped to the amount that a defendant could recover against the claimants under an ATE policy, particularly where the latter figure was outside the control of the defendant and, at least directly, outside the control of the court. What mattered were the criteria in CPR 44.18(5) namely:

(1) Is there a risk that costs will be disproportionately incurred?
(2) If so, can that risk be adequately controlled by case management and/or detailed assessment of costs?
(3) In all the circumstances, is it in the interests of justice to make a costs capping order?

No costs capping order was made. The case is also a good example of the point made at the end of the section headed 'paying adverse costs.' The court seems to consider that the limit of indemnity is always available to meet the opponent's costs and does not take any note of the client's own disbursements. This can often be a significant sum.

SOLICITOR SELF INSURANCE

Client's Disbursements

[9.32]

A solicitor can carry the liability for disbursements in the event that the case fails without taking himself outside the normal practice of a solicitor and turning himself into a funder. This is fortunate since, if it were not so, solicitors could find themselves not only left out of pocket in respect of disbursements in an unsuccessful case, but also having to pay some or all of the opponent's costs. This would be up to the value of twice the disbursements that the solicitor agreed to meet based on the decision in *Arkin v Borchard Lines*, or more given the recent decision of *Davey v Money* (see **[10.10]**).

This position on liability was confirmed by the Court of Appeal in *Flatman v Germany* [2013] EWCA Civ 278. The decision overturned the judgment of Eady J which had said that a solicitor who agreed to fund disbursements as the case progressed and not to seek them from the client if they could not be obtained from the opponent at the end had put himself into the position of a commercial funder. The subsequent High Court decision in *Tinseltime Ltd v Roberts* [2012] EWHC 2628 (TCC), doubted Eady J and held that the funding of disbursements by a solicitor was insufficient reason to make a third party costs order. The Court of Appeal in *Flatman* agreed with the judge in *Tinseltime*. The Court of Appeal had the benefit of an intervention from the Law Society who pointed out that CLSA 1990, s 58, the starting point for CFAs, referred to agreements regarding 'fees and expenses' being paid dependent upon the outcome of the case. Notwithstanding a spirited argument from the defendant that there was a material difference between expenses and disbursements, the Court of Appeal (and the judge in *Tinseltime* who had seen the Law Society's skeleton argument) considered the solicitor was simply providing legal services in accordance with the statute.

There are postscripts to both *Flatman* and *Tinseltime* that are worth noting. In *Flatman* the appeal overall failed. It was an appeal against an order for disclosure of information in the detailed assessment proceedings. The Court of Appeal concluded that, although Eady J had fallen into error, there were other circumstances revealed on the appeal that justified the orders that Eady J had made. In *Tinseltime*, the solicitor thought that the disbursements would be modest and that, together with the fact that the company was on its uppers, persuaded him to act on the company's behalf. He also thought that the prospects were good but that was proved wrong when the claims were struck out. The solicitor was left with £22,000 to pay in disbursements: not a modest sum at all. This case is well worth reading if you are contemplating taking on any liability for your client to see just how easy it is to be led into difficulty.

Opponent's Costs

[9.33]

Offering to indemnify the client against the opponent's costs is a much more fraught undertaking than offering to meet disbursements. For a start you have much less say in the extent of the liability being incurred. Furthermore, the bargain of indemnifying the client in order to get the claim going, tends to have the appearance of champerty about it. There is also the question of whether you are acting as a quasi insurer without the necessary, regulatory approval.

Although Deputy Master Williams in *Dix v Townend* [2008] EWHC 90117 (Costs) found that a solicitor undertaking to indemnify the client against adverse costs gave rise to a champertous agreement, this was not followed in the decisions of MacDuff J in *Morris v London Borough of Southwark* [2010] EWHC 901 or of Master O' Hare in *Murray Lewis v Tennants Distribution Ltd* [2010] EWHC 90161 (Costs). In the former the risk to the solicitor in having to pay opponent's costs under the arrangement made with their client was small and far outweighed by the advantages of the arrangements as a whole. In the latter it was simply not accepted that an agreement to shoulder the risk of adverse costs orders ought to be regarded as threatening the integrity of any solicitor.

The decision of MacDuff J in *Morris* was the subject of a conjoined appeal in *Sibthorpe v Southwark London Borough Council* [2011] EWCA Civ 25 and in which the Law Society intervened. The claimants' solicitors did not have a legal aid contract for housing work and the claimants could not afford the premium for after-the-event insurance, even if a policy could be found. The solicitors therefore offered to provide costs protection for their two housing disrepair claims to enable the tenants to proceed. In return the clients agreed to use CFAs which provided for success fees of 10%, limited in respect of the solicitors' costs to costs recovered. The defendants contended that the indemnity against the liability to pay the opponent's costs was tainted by champerty or maintenance because it gave the solicitors a financial interest, and therefore the whole CFA became unenforceable. The Court of Appeal held that although CLSA 1990, s 58 permitted some previously champertous agreements to be entered into, the arrangements in the present case were not covered by the Act. However, in no case cited to a court had it been held to be champertous for a person to agree to run the risk of a loss should the action fail without enjoying any gain should the action succeed. To hold the indemnity in such a case to be champertous would involve extending the law of champerty at a time when its scope was being curtailed rather than extended. The indemnity was accordingly not champertous.

As a side note, the defendant also sought to argue that the arrangement was a provision of insurance within the terms of the Financial Services and Markets Act 2000 (Regulated Activities) Order 2001. Such insurance could only be provided by an entity authorised by the FSMA 2000 and since the solicitors were not so authorised the CFA was void in accordance with s 26(1) of that Act. This ground of appeal was not given leave to appeal but it was dealt with in any event at the end of the Court of Appeal judgment. The CFA was for the provision of legal services. While it provided an indemnity, it could not be categorised as a contract of insurance because its principal object was to provide legal services, not insurance.

Practical considerations

[9.34]

It is tempting with the fixing of recoverable costs in various areas and the introduction of QOCS to consider this option rather than take out insurance. If nothing else it avoids a conversation about some (more) of your client's damages being taken as a result of the litigation process. It may be that, in the course of time, LEI insurers will be prepared to provide some form of excess layer or catastrophe insurance to allow solicitors to underwrite themselves up to a certain limit. If there is no insurance in place and an indemnity given to the client, your liability is only limited by what can be agreed or is assessed by the court.

Given that *Dix* is the only decision in which the solicitor has been held to fall foul of the Financial Services and Markets Act 2000 in providing quasi-insurance it appears that this is a theoretical risk rather than a practical one. So you may only be struck off for being bankrupted, not for failing to comply with the Prudential Regulation Authority's code.

CHAPTER 10

STATE AND COMMERCIAL FUNDING

INTRODUCTION TO STATE AND COMMERCIAL FUNDING

[10.1]

In this Chapter we look at funding via the Legal Aid Agency and by Third Party Funders (aka Litigation Funders). We have said at the beginning of this part of the book that the use of Legal Aid is now so specialised that there is little point in dealing with it in detail. Those who might find such a chapter useful already know the detail: most people have no need for a detailed exposition. Similarly, those who regularly use commercial funding will be au fait with the mechanics involved. Anecdotally, the commercial funders' evidence to Sir Rupert Jackson was that fewer than 100 cases had been backed by such funding at the time. It appears that the take up has increased significantly since then. But even if that is not so, do not let that stop you reading this brief chapter. There are three very good reasons why you should do so.

The first is that litigation funding is likely to continue to increase over time and therefore it will become more relevant to more people. The second is that you need to be able to consider whether your potential client is eligible for Legal Aid or might benefit from commercial funding, when giving the best information possible to him at the outset of the case (and thereafter). This is so, even if you do not work with either form of funding. The correct advice to your client might be to go elsewhere so that the client can benefit from such funding. That sort of advice is at the core of being a professional advisor and is easy to forget in the ever more commercialised world in which the law is practised. In the case of *David Truex (a firm) v Kitchin* [2007] EWCA Civ 618, the Court of Appeal dismissed a solicitor's claim for costs against a client who was eligible for public funding on the grounds that solicitors are bound at the outset to consider whether a client might be eligible for public funding, rather than continue to take instructions and run up costs while they gathered information before considering public funding eligibility.

The third reason is that at paras **[10.8]–[10.9]** we look at the procedure for pursuing a costs order against a legally aided party. This is the one part of this chapter which potentially applies to many litigators. Finally, if you are looking for commentary on the issue of transferring from state funding to other methods of funding, particularly CFAs, please go to **[6.28]**.

STATE FUNDING

[10.2]

In April 2013 the Legal Services Commission was replaced by the Legal Aid Agency, an Executive Agency of the Ministry of Justice, and its powers and functions were transferred to the Lord Chancellor. It does not appear to have made much practical difference but at least it means that everyone could go back to using the phrase 'legally aided' rather than attempting various less attractive phrases based on the Legal Services Commission.

Not for everyone

[10.3]

In February 1999 the Legal Services Commission (as it then was) started to contract with legal service providers to the exclusion of any lawyers who did not have such a contract. It was the beginning of the end of any solicitor who wished to act for a client with the benefit of state funding being able to do so. The restriction started in clinical negligence cases, but in 2000 it extended to the giving of any initial help in any civil matter or provide any level of service (ie including full blown representation) in family and immigration cases. In the same year most personal injury cases (except clinical negligence) were excluded from public funding. On 1 April 2001, the civil contracting scheme was extended to cover all levels of service for all types of case, which can now only be supplied under a contract (the latest version being the 2018 civil contract). Further amendments have continued to be made since 2001, particularly with the enactment of LASPO 2012 to limit further the use of public funds in clinical negligence matters.

In short, unless you have a contract with the Legal Aid Agency (as it now is), you cannot act for your client with the benefit of public funds. Even if you do have such a contract, there are many types of claim which are no longer eligible for assistance. For example, Schedule 2 to LASPO 2012 provides that excluded from funding are civil legal services provided in relation to:

(a) personal injury or death;
(b) conveyancing;
(c) damage to property;
(d) the making of wills;
(e) matters of trust law;
(f) defamation or malicious falsehood;
(g) matters of company or partnership law;
(h) other matters arising out of the carrying on of a business;
(i) claims in tort in respect of negligence, assault, battery or false imprisonment, trespass to goods or to land;
(j) claims in tort in respect of breach of statutory duty.

Criteria

[10.4]

So, depending upon the nature of your client (for example, a company) or the type of case, you may well be able to advise your client at this point that they are not eligible for public funding. But if they are still potentially eligible, there are three aspects of the case and the client to consider.

- The merits of the case
- The costs benefit analysis
- The client's financial eligibility

In practice, you may want to start with the third aspect first since it will determine (negatively) the prospects more quickly than the other two. But let us consider them in order.

Merits

[10.5]

This is covered in regs 42 and 43 of the Civil Legal Aid (Merits Criteria) Regulations 2013 as amended. In a nutshell the merits have to be high and not the borderline prospects that might still justify a CFA or modest prospects which would be pursued under an ordinary pay as you go retainer. While there are several classifications – very good (80% or more); good (60%–80%); moderate (50%–60%); marginal (45%–50%); poor (less than 45%) – the cost benefit analysis will mean in most cases that only those with very good prospects are going to be funded sufficiently to get to trial if needs be. The percentages in the brackets above are in reg 5 rather than regs 42 and 43. The classification of borderline cases (those whose prospects are uncertain), marginal and poor cases are adjusted on roughly an annual basis by secondary legislation. It is clear that the Legal Aid Agency is attempting to keep a tight rein on funding whilst at the same time putting into effect the Government's legal obligations.

Costs benefit analysis

[10.6]

One man's costs benefit might be described, somewhat contentiously perhaps, as another man's justice at proportionate cost. Regulation 42 of the Civil Legal Aid (Merits Criteria) Regulations 2013 sets outs the test for establishing whether the merits of the case justify its likely costs. The better the prospects of success (as set out above), the more costs in proportion to those prospects will be sanctioned. In itself it is not a bad approach and it might benefit you in considering your firm's approach generally to the investment in the case relative to its prospects. Of course if your payment is not dependent upon the outcome you can continue to consider prospects with a certain amount of equanimity.

Where the prospects of success are:

- Very Good – the anticipated damages must exceed the costs.
- Good – the estimated damages must exceed the costs by a ratio of two to one.
- Moderate – the estimated damages must exceed the costs by a ratio of four to one.
- Borderline cases and those with prospects less than 50% only qualify for funding if they are of significant wider public interest or are of 'overwhelming' importance to the individual (or for public law claims which affect an individual's convention rights).

Financial eligibility

[10.7]

The acronym MINELAS (Middle Income Not Eligible for Legal Aid Support) was coined many years ago to highlight the many people who were not sufficiently wealthy to litigate without financial concern but who could not obtain Legal Aid. That position has steadily increased as the qualifying means have decreased. The criteria defy any brief description which would be of benefit to the practitioner. But it is safe to say that if you have a client who has a good case which can be taken to trial within the costs benefit analysis, they will have to be extremely lacking in income and capital to be able to take up Legal Aid funding in most circumstances. You may need to develop a relationship with a firm which has a contract if you regularly come across such clients so that they can assess the client's financial eligibility. If you need to look at something for yourself you can go to the website www.gov.uk/legal-aid/eligibility.

Claims for costs against legally aided parties

[10.8]

A party who defends a claim brought by a legally aided individual and who seeks recovery of costs under an order for costs against that legally aided party needs to proceed under s 26 of LASPO 2012 and the Civil Legal Aid (Costs) Regulations 2013. (An order made before 1 April 2013 would need to be dealt with by s 11 of the Access to Justice Act 1999.) The 2012 Act and Regulations are detailed and require study if a claim is to be made. There are certain crucial points to note:

- The costs are most likely to be payable by the Lord Chancellor (in the guise of the Legal Aid Agency). As such it is fundamental to note that there is a time limit of three months for an application under s 26 to be made (reg 10). Whilst there is a provision for extending that time limit for good reason, ignorance of the time limit is not going to be such a reason and the Agency will undoubtedly take the point.
- The financial resources of all the parties are taken into account. The applicant needs to demonstrate that he will sustain financial hardship if an order is not made. That will be a very high hurdle for a well-resourced or insured applicant. There is no need to demonstrate such hardship where the costs relate to an appeal, although the court will still consider the resources of all the parties.
- A claiming party has to have his costs assessed before the court will consider how much, if any of it, ought to be paid by the legally aided party. There is no mechanism for ascertaining how much the legally aided party may be ordered to pay before incurring the costs of preparing a bill etc.

[10.9]

The Regulations provide for the judge who makes the order for costs to deal with some or all of (a) the amount of costs to be allowed and (b) how much, if any, is to be paid by the legally aided party. In practice, the judge tends simply to make an order and leaves the assessment to the costs judge to deal with the detail.

Applications to the SCCO generally receive a standard order setting out directions for the provision of evidence as to resources before a hearing date which is usually fixed from the outset. The exception to this procedure is where it appears that the application has been made more than three months after the order for costs has been made. In such cases, a directions hearing or similar is likely to be listed in order to deal with this issue before the parties are put to any other expense.

COMMERCIAL FUNDING

[10.10]

Many cases are commercially funded by banks providing their solicitor clients with loans and overdrafts. Variations on this approach are many and varied with lending institutions offering loans to individuals (usually in respect of disbursements) and often backed by a guarantee from the solicitor. This chapter does not deal with such arrangements since they are too disparate to describe in any detail. Moreover they are easily understood albeit that they can still lead to difficulties; see for example *Sutherland Professional Funding Ltd v Bakewells* [2013] EWHC 2685 (QB) where the solicitor's 'guarantee' was in fact found to be a primary obligation owed to the funder by the solicitor. This chapter concentrates on the novel, sharing, arrangements which are now available.

In order to deal with the current arrangements for litigation funding it is necessary to look briefly at the history of attempts by third parties to become involved in the disputes of others. There are many cases on this subject but we will look at just a few to give you the flavour of the issues involved. The common law restrictions on maintenance and champerty still remain, and the courts therefore still have to decide on the facts of each litigation funding agreement whether the contract is unenforceable on the grounds of public policy.

Maintenance and Champerty

[10.11]

These two concepts are at the heart of why funding by third parties has proved problematic over the years.

Maintenance is said to be 'the procurement, by direct or indirect financial assistance, of another person to institute, or carry on or defend civil proceedings without lawful justification' (The Law Commission 1966). More flamboyantly, the definition in the case law comes from *British Cash and Parcel Conveyors Ltd v Lamson Store Service Co Ltd* [1908] 1 KB 1006, 77 LJKB 649, CA: 'Maintenance is the wanton and officious intermeddling with the disputes of others in which the maintainer has no interest whatever, and where the assistance he renders to the one or other party is without justification or excuse'.

Champerty, as described by the House of Lords judges in the case of *Giles v Thompson* [1994] 1 AC 142, [1993] 3 All ER 321, HL is (a) 'an aggravated form of maintenance. The distinguishing feature of champerty is the support of litigation by a stranger in return for a share of the proceeds' or (b) 'Champerty is maintenance with the addition of a division of the spoils of the litigation'.

On the face of it therefore, an agreement for a third party to fund the cost of a case in return for (say) a third of the damages is both champertous and maintenance.

The extent of a funder's liability

[10.12]

In *Arkin v Borchard Lines Ltd (No 5)* [2003] EWHC 2844 (Comm), the Part 20 defendant (MPC), a professional funding company, entered into a funding agreement with the claimant. MPC agreed to fund the employment of expert witnesses, the preparation of their evidence and the organisation of the enormous quantities of documents which it became necessary to investigate before the trial.

When the claimant lost, the defendants applied for a costs order against MPC. The defendants laid stress on the very substantial proportion of any recoverable damages or settlement payments (25% of the first £5 million and 23% of any excess) which MPC was to receive under its funding agreement. The amount of the claim, including exemplary damages, eventually reached $160 million. That would have meant a payment of some $40 million to the funders. The defendants also drew attention to the absence of any undertaking by MPC to pay the defendants' recoverable costs or to take out after-the-event (ATE) insurance cover in respect of such costs. They submitted that, in principle, professional funders, as distinct from pure funders (such as friends or family who back a case without expecting any reward), and who are maintaining litigation for their profit, should be liable for the costs of the defendants if their claim fails, which in this case it did.

MPC argued that funding agreements with professional funders which have the purpose of enabling impecunious claimants to pursue claims of real substance which, but for such funding, they could not have done, should not be visited with costs orders against the funders if the claim fails.

The High Court favoured MPC's public policy arguments and refused to make an order for costs against the Part 20 defendant. On appeal the Court of Appeal held that a professional funder, who finances part of a claimant's costs of litigation, should be potentially liable for the costs of the opposing party *to the extent of the funding provided*. In its judgment the court said:

> 'The effect of this will, of course, be that, if the funding is provided on a contingency basis of recovery, the funder will require, as the price of the funding, a greater share of the recovery should the claim succeed. In the individual case, the net recovery of a successful claimant will be diminished. While this is unfortunate, it seems to us that it is a cost that the impecunious claimant can reasonably be expected to bear. Overall justice will be better served than leaving defendants in a position where they have no right to recover any costs from a professional funder whose intervention has permitted the continuation of a claim which has ultimately proved to be without merit.'

The decision is very much policy driven – but unfortunately the Court clearly did not think that either policy objective completely outweighed the other. As such, the result is something of a half-way house. A professional funder who finances litigation to the cost of £500,000 will, if the client loses, expect to pay up to a further £500,000 in costs to the opponent. If the access to justice arguments had won, the funder would have paid nothing to the opponent. If the causation arguments had won (ie the case was only run because of the funding) the funder would have had to pay all of the opponent's costs.

In the chapter of his report on litigation funding by a third party, Sir Rupert Jackson suggested that this rule should be revisited by judges asked to consider awards of costs against funders – his steer suggesting that they should consider whether *Arkin* should be varied to make the funder liable for the whole amount. An example of that steer being exercised may be seen in the case of *Merchantbridge & Co Ltd v Safron General Partner 1 Ltd* [2011] EWHC 1524 (Comm). In that case the defendant was funded by third party investment banks who had an interest in the proceedings while not being a party to it. The Claimant succeeded and the judge determined that the investment banks should be liable to the full extent of the claimants' costs, in a departure from *Arkin*.

Similarly, in *Davey v Money* [2019] EWHC 997 (Ch), Snowden J decided to depart from the *Arkin* cap. Having analysed the authorities, he said the Court of Appeal's comments in Arkin were intended to be 'considered for application in cases involving a commercial funder as a means of achieving a just result in all the circumstances of the particular case. But I do not think that it is a rule to be applied automatically in all cases involving commercial funders, whatever the facts, and however unjust the result of doing so might be'.

The funder of the unsuccessful claimant had accepted that it should be subject to a non-party costs order on the indemnity (as was the claimant and in accordance with the decision in *Excalibur* (see below)) but contended that the limit of its liability was a sum equivalent to the amount of funding given to the claimant (£1.275m) as per *Arkin*. Snowden J rejected this position for a multiplicity of reasons. Chief amongst them appears to be the aggressive nature of the commercial agreement struck with the claimant – the multiple of the sum invested; the order of priority of payment if (partially) successful etc. In addition, the support of a case with serious but unfounded allegations against the defendants resulting in an indemnity basis order and the fact that the lender funded the entire case rather than part of it (as in *Arkin*) added to the reasons why an order under s 51 of the Senior Courts Act 1981 was appropriate.

By contrast, the first instance judge and the Court of Appeal maintained the *Arkin* approach in *Excalibur Ventures LLC v Texas Keystone Inc* [2016] EWCA Civ 1144. The commercial funders sought to argue that the costs orders should not 'follow the fortunes' of the case – which involved the Claimant's case losing badly. However, Christopher Clarke LJ (as he was by the time he gave judgment at first instance) took the view that the claimant's case was so bad that he should award indemnity costs against the funders. This approach was upheld by the Court of Appeal. There was no suggestion by the receiving parties that the extent of the various funders' liability should be any more than sums equivalent to their respective investments in the case ie the *Arkin* approach.

The weakening of the rigidity of the *Arkin* cap, as demonstrated by some of the above cases and Sir Rupert's criticisms was completed by the Court of Appeal's decision in *Money v Chapelgate Credit Opportunity Master Fund Ltd* [2020] EWCA Civ 246, [2020] 1 WLR 1751, [2020] 2 BCLC 170 which consigns the cap to an earlier time and emphasises the need for the court simply to exercise its discretion justly in the circumstances of the case. This judicial exercise is considered at [40.8]. The result of that exercise may logically be that the same figure as would have been allowed in *Arkin* is the correct figure in any event. This was the conclusion of Zacaroli J in *Burnden Holdings (UK) Ltd (in liq) v Fielding* [2019] EWHC 2995 (Ch), 169 NLJ 7866, [2019] Costs LR 2061 (a decision which actually preceded *Chapelgate*).

These decisions are usually made at the end of the case, not surprisingly given the outcome needs to be known before deciding whether the funder has any liability. But in *Bailey v Glaxosmithkline UK Ltd* [2017] EWHC 3195 (QB), [2018] 4 WLR 7, [2017] 6 Costs LR 1209, Foskett J was asked to look at the funder's potential liability as part of a security for costs application. He decided that he was not bound by the cap because that would only be considered at the end of the case and may or may not be imposed in any event. He took the view that he should allow security based on half of the costs he considered likely to be allowed (which was 2/3 of the sums claimed). He deducted the ATE policy (having discounted it for the possibility of it being avoided) and ordered the litigation funder to pay the balance. The effect was an order for £1.75m as against the £1.2m of funding which the funder had provided.

Funding of expert evidence

[10.13]

In *R (on the application of Factortame) v Secretary of State for Transport, Environments and the Regions (No 2)* [2002] EWCA Civ 932 impecunious Spanish trawler owners had obtained judgment against the British Government for damages for breaches of their fishing rights. Unfortunately, they could not afford to proceed with the assessment of damages. Accountants agreed to provide litigation support in the form of handling documents and programming services, as well as undertaking to pay the fees of expert witnesses, in exchange for 8% of any amount recovered. The Court of Appeal held that the agreement was not champertous, saying:

> 'Where the law expressly restricts the circumstances in which agreements in support of litigation are lawful, this provides a powerful indication of the limits of public policy in analogous situations. Where this is not the case, then we believe one must today look at the facts of the particular case and consider whether those facts suggest that the agreement in question might tempt the allegedly champertous maintainer for his personal gain to inflame the damages, to suppress evidence, to suborn witnesses or otherwise to undermine the ends of justice.'

The Court bore in mind the fact that the share of the damages taken by Grant Thornton was only 8%. They were a firm of accountants and so were members of a respectable and regulated profession. While they played an important role in the preparation of the computer model on which the damages claims were based, this was subject to checking by the other side and was transparent. The claimants were in any event represented by highly experienced solicitors and counsel, and the solicitors had very properly insisted on remaining in control of the conduct of the litigation. In these circumstances, there was no realistic prospect of there being any undermining of justice by the 8% agreement. It was also clear to the Court that there was no other realistic way of the accountants being paid for work they had already done, other than to support the litigation in the manner they had chosen to do.

Current position

[10.14]

In *London and Regional (St George's Court) Ltd v Ministry of Defence* [2008] EWHC 526 (TCC), Coulson J summarised the present state of the authorities as:

- the mere fact that litigation services have been provided in return for a promise in the share of the proceeds is not by itself sufficient to justify that promise being held to be unenforceable;
- in considering whether an agreement is unlawful on grounds of maintenance or champerty, the question is whether the agreement has *a tendency to corrupt public justice*, and such a question requires the closest attention to the nature and surrounding circumstance of a particular agreement;
- the modern authorities demonstrate a flexible approach where courts have generally declined to hold that an agreement under which a party provided assistance with litigation in return for a share of the proceeds was unenforceable;
- the rules against champerty, so far as they have survived, are primarily concerned with the protection of the integrity of the litigation process by the limitation of control of the conduct of the action by a third party.

THE FUNDING AGREEMENT

[10.15]

A litigation funder covers all the costs (or such costs as the funded party seeks to have covered by the funder) of the litigation in return for a share of the proceeds of the action, including its own legal costs, expert's and court fees and any adverse costs orders.

There is no need for a CFA (though funders will no doubt look more favourably on cases where the solicitor is prepared to act on at least a partial conditional fee agreement as a demonstration of their belief in the merits of the case in question). It is also said that there is no need for ATE insurance although this is usually sought to limit the funder's risk of an *Arkin* payment having to be made. The price is typically 20%–50% of the amount recovered, depending on how long this takes to achieve. This form of funding is not champertous provided the funder does not (and is not entitled to) control the conduct of the action by the client.

Agreements must be structured so that the client retains full control over the way in which they conduct their action. This includes the funder not being permitted to set minimum settlement levels when signing up a case, or interfering in the day to day conduct of the matter. Withdrawal of funding if the claim's merits plummet does not amount to interference.

Once the case is signed up, the client is then left to run his litigation in the usual way. The funding agreement sets out the responsibilities and liabilities of the parties. If at any stage the claim's merits suffer a 'material adverse decline' (which will include the ability of any successful judgment to be enforced against the defendant, the position on liability or claim value, or the conduct of the claimant, amongst other things), the funder has the right to terminate the funding, while retaining the liability for all own side and adverse costs up to that date.

Litigation funders will say that the fact that they are only interested in funding good claims sends a powerful message to the opponent that a dispassionate and commercially focused third party also thinks the claim is good. Where the involvement of funders in accelerating settlement discussions has occurred, this has inevitably been a welcome development for third party funded claimants. ATE insurers used to say very much the same thing about the signal given to the opponent by their independent backing of the claim. To the extent that this was so, it lessened in importance over time as the use of ATE funding became more common. It will be interesting to see whether there is any impact in the announcement of the existence of third party funding (which is not something required by the CPR) and if so, whether its influence dissipates if it becomes more common place.

The courts have become more willing to require parties to disclose their backers in recent times. In the *XYZ v Travelers* group litigation, several applications were made to establish the size of the defendants' pockets. It was not until the case reached the Supreme Court that the traditional position was essentially re-established. We deal with the detail of the court's conclusions at **[40.11]** and its effect on group litigation at **[37.14]**. Here, we simply mention the specific point made in the lead judgment of Lord Briggs that the defendant and its insurers were entitled to keep the extent of the cover to themselves.

Given some of the later events, this was a perfectly understandable approach (see Chapter 37). In the endless litigation involving JSC BTA Bank, Mukhtar Ablyazov and a host of others on a rolling basis, Patricia Robertson QC ordered disclosure of the funding of Ilyas Khrapunov, the second defendant where it appeared that he might be funding his litigation in a manner inconsistent with the worldwide freezing order against him: [2018] EWHC 1368 (Comm).

PROFILE OF FUNDED CASES

[10.16]

Litigation funding by a third party is not currently available to everyone, although new entrants continue to expand availability. There need to be sufficient damages available to make the time and effort invested in considering and setting up the claim worthwhile. In addition to value, the minimum eligibility criteria for considering funding a claim are:

- a defendant who can pay the amount claimed;
- good legal merits ie both in relation to liability and with a demonstrable (not aspirational) minimum claim value;
- where the costs of pursuing the matter are proportionate to the size of the claim; and
- the lawyer who it is proposed will run the claim is demonstrably experienced in the area to which the claim relates.

If you cannot afford to litigate otherwise, foregoing a percentage of the damages on success under a litigation funding agreement is of course a lot better than nothing. The alternatives of CFAs and ATE tend to have more value for the lower value claims. But now that success fees and premiums have ceased to be recoverable, litigation funding by a third party may be a more attractive option in some cases. It is certainly the case that in all substantial litigation, whatever the financial position of the client, the solicitor now has a duty to advise on this new method of finance.

THE ASSOCIATION OF LITIGATION FUNDERS

[10.17]

In November 2011 the Association of Litigation Funders (ALF) was formed (www.associationoflitigationfunders.com) as a forum for funders and non-funders alike to discuss matters relating to funding and provide a contact point for those using funding. At the same time a Code of Conduct was launched and the ALF is responsible for future developments of the Code.

The Code sets out the standards of best practice and behaviour for litigation funders in the UK. It provides transparency to claimants and their solicitors and requires litigation funders to provide satisfactory answers to certain key questions before entering into relationships with claimants.

Under the Code, litigation funders are required to give assurances to claimants that, among other things, the litigation funder will not try to take control of the litigation, the litigation funder has the money to pay for the costs of the funded litigation and the litigation funder will not terminate funding absent a material adverse development.

The Code was originally encouraged and ultimately approved by Sir Rupert Jackson and commended by Lord Neuberger. A copy of the Code can be found on the ALF website.

At present the bulk of funding occurs in commercial litigation. If there are new entrants who operate solely in consumer based litigation, there may well need to be a separate code and association to deal with the issues arising there. In the meantime of course, the consumer has the protection of the Consumer Credit Act 1974 and Consumer Rights Act 2015.

FEE SHARING IN PERSONAL INJURY CASES

[10.18]

Up to, and including, the SRA Code 2007, it was contrary to the solicitor's code of conduct for a solicitor to share any fees with a third party funder (or indeed anyone else other than another lawyer) in personal injury cases. The final incarnation of the relevant rule was Rule 9 but that was not replicated in the 2011 version. The change in emphasis from prescriptive regulation to a concentration on the outcome means that a direct successor to Rule 9 would have been problematic. Furthermore, the ending of recoverability in CFAs and the introduction of DBAs all point towards the idea of the claimant parting with a share of his damages in order to secure representation. Although a commercial funder is not strictly part of the legal team, the same considerations apply.

As set out in the *London and Regional* decision, the modern view is that an agreement of this sort is not, without more, inimical to the client's best interests or those of the administration of justice. Consequently, an unhappy client who subsequently complains about the solicitor's conduct in using a third party funder, is unlikely to succeed unless the outcome of his litigation was prejudiced in some way as a result.

FUNDING IN FAMILY CASES

[10.19]

It has always been the case that contingency fee agreements such as CFAs were not available in matrimonial and other family proceedings (see **[4.6]**). The prospect of either the wife or the husband's solicitors walking off with money from the family's pot is inherently unattractive, even if the parties have as much money as the wife in *Akhmedova v Akhmedov* [2020] EWHC 1526 Fam. The plethora of defendants in this case results from the fact the decision relates to proceedings seeking to recover assets sought to be put beyond the reach of the wife: not that there were ten in the marriage and that made it a bit crowded etc.

In answer to the proceedings brought to recover nearly £500 million, the 10th respondent (the claimant's son) argued that the wife's use of a litigation funding agreement was akin to using a CFA. It was champertous and involved the funder controlling litigation in which it had played no earlier part. Knowles J rejected this argument. Funding was not the same as a CFA and had been approved in litigation generally as promoting access to justice. Use of funding where the funder followed the ALF's code of conduct did not allow for any intermeddling. Some specific prejudice would be required to make this argument more than simply that litigation funding should not be available in family cases. There was no prejudice shown.

This judgment seems to us fully to follow the Superior Courts' dicta regarding the use of funding in litigation so long as the parties and their solicitors control the litigation rather than the funders. It is not surprising given earlier court pronouncements in family cases about the difficulties in funding (see Chapter 39) and the long-standing use of 'Sears Tooth' agreements for parties whose ability to pay depends upon a recovery of assets from the other party (see **[39.39]**).

FUNDING OF CLAIMS MANAGEMENT SERVICES

[10.20]

Ever since claims management companies appeared at the turn of the century, they have offered to assist would be claimants via the use of contingency fee agreements where they receive a percentage of the sums recovered in recompense for their assistance. For the avoidance of doubt, such litigation funding agreements, as they are generally known, do not amount to Damages Based Agreements, notwithstanding certain similarities, and as such are not caught by the primary and secondary legislation's requirements regarding DBAs: *UK Trucks Claim Ltd v Fiat Chrysler Autos NV* [2019] CAT 26.

Part III

Between the parties

CHAPTER 11

AN OVERVIEW OF SIGNIFICANT COSTS DEVELOPMENTS IN THE LAST YEAR AND A SUMMARY OF THE KEY COSTS PROVISIONS IN THE CIVIL PROCEDURE RULES

INTRODUCTION

[11.1]

In his May 2015 'Confronting Costs Management' lecture, Sir Rupert Jackson ended with the prediction that within ten years costs management will be accepted as an entirely normal discipline. We have not quite reached that anniversary, but, almost eight years from the 2013 reforms, the time has surely come to see them not as 'the brave new world', but, in costs parlance, as 'the norm'. In addition, not all of the changes to the costs landscape since 2013 result from the reforms of that year. This is not to downplay the continuing effect of those reforms, nor to ignore the fact that some of Sir Rupert Jackson's recommendations are still subject to further review (Damages Based Agreements) or remain to be implemented (Fixed Costs for all fast track cases). The result is, that whilst the previous seven versions of this chapter have seen a charting of the changes, year on year, in this edition, we have restricted comment to significant changes, either as a result of case law or of procedural revision, from the last year and a brief summary of the core costs provisions of the Civil Procedure Rules. Anyone wishing to chart the progress of reform will find this in the 2020 edition.

2020/2021

[11.2]

This year had been a relatively quiet one, no doubt in part due to the forced focus of the Civil Rules Procedure Committee ('CPRC') on emergency amendments necessitated by the Covid-19 pandemic. However, almost unnoticed was the establishment in March of a sub-committee of the Civil Justice Council to review and report back to the Deputy Head of Civil Justice with recommendations in respect of guideline hourly rates. These rates have not been increased since 2010. The outcome will post-date this edition, but the mere fact that formal consideration of the rates is under review is a significant step.

We say 'had been a relatively quiet one', but in July, the CPRC published the outcome of its re-visit to the costs management provisions – particularly in respect of retrospective budgeting on variation, but also making changes between the rule and its PD and the withdrawal of the Guidance Note. That this was necessary, was highlighted in the previous edition. The result is considered in more detail in Chapter 15.

Costs aficionados will have their own favourite cases of the last 12 months. However, it is hard to look beyond the erosion of the 'Arkin cap' on non-party funding in *Chapelgate Credit Opportunity Master Fund Ltd v Money* [2020] EWCA Civ 246 (considered in detail in Chapter 40) as that giving rise to the most significant change. Elsewhere, *Ho v Adelekun* [2020] EWCA Civ 517 signposted an area to watch in respect of the ability of a defendant in a qualified one-way costs case to off-set a costs award in its favour against any costs awarded against it in favour of the claimant (see Chapter 22).

[11.3]

Although the significant costs provisions are considered in more detail elsewhere in this text, what follows in this chapter will be a brief introduction to them. This is not intended to be an exhaustive look at where all the costs provisions can be found. The first two are not costs specific, but are fundamental to the control of costs.

THE OVERRIDING OBJECTIVE

[11.4]

As we shall see later (see Chapter 14 – Control of Costs – Proportionality), proportionality of cost is the guiding principle underlying the control of costs in the civil courts. It is no surprise, then, to find that it appears in the 'Holy Grail' that is the overriding objective. The rules are designed to enable the court to deal with cases justly *and at proportionate cost*. Justice is qualified and this qualification resonates at every procedural stage. Given the definition of proportionality in CPR 44.3(5) it is clear that rather than neatly sidestepping costs issues in most claims, leaving them to be resolved with, if necessary, in the words of Brooke LJ, an axe on assessment, the court is charged with placing costs at centre stage throughout the claim. Every procedural decision must be made against a consideration of the cost implications.

The overriding objective at CPR 1.1(2)(f) reflects the second non-costs specific provision of key importance – relief from sanction.

RELIEF FROM SANCTION

[11.5]

What has relief from sanction to do with costs? The answer is everything. CPR 3.9 places emphasis on the need for the efficient and proportionate conduct of litigation, while enforcing compliance with orders, rules and practice directions. This makes it clear that dilatory conduct, whether deliberate or by mere oversight, which inevitably increases the costs, will not be tolerated. Failure to comply with orders or rules drives a coach and horses through carefully constructed case management, which will have been informed in the multi-track by agreed and/or approved budgets and in the fast track by reference to the overriding objective – in other words by consideration of the reasonable and proportionate costs for the litigation. As the Court of Appeal has made plain, it is not enough to suggest that the consequences of breach on the 'innocent party' can be compensated for by an order for costs.

PART 36

[11.6]

The MoJ website introducing the current CPR 36 commented as follows:

> 'Part 36 of the CPR set outs the procedure to be followed where a party makes an offer to settle a matter, or part of a matter, and the consequences of making such offers. Since the rules were substantially amended in 2007 there has been a large amount of case law in respect of the application of the rules to various aspects of settlement including fraudulent claims and offers in respect of a split trial. The changes reflect the case law and aim to simplify the rules as far as possible to make them more accessible to court users, particularly litigants in person.'

While it is correct that much of the change codified the guidance given on the previous version of CPR 36 by the courts, there were some fundamental changes that had nothing to do with the CPR 36 jurisprudence. The current CPR 36 contains additional specific provisions dealing with withdrawal of offers, the effect of such offers where the offeror has fallen foul of CPR 3.14 (and is limited in future budget to court fees only) and the treatment of CPR 36 offers after a preliminary trial. However, seemingly inevitably, the revised Part 36 is already accumulating its own body of jurisprudence. Detailed consideration of all the Part 36 provisions can be found in Chapter 20.

PART 44

[11.7]

While sections of Part 44 remained familiar, many were subject to a numbering change in 2013. CPR 44 contains general rules about costs, including the definitions sub-rule and the core provisions relating to the award, and quantification, of costs.

Albeit having gone through a renumbering exercise in 2013, most of these provisions have long been etched in the rules. Two major additions in 2013, that have still to bed in properly, and respectively are generating jurisprudence and critical reconsideration are those relating to QOCS and to Damages Based Agreements.

Qualified one-way costs shifting

[11.8]

During Sir Rupert Jackson's preliminary investigations it was suggested to him by an unnamed insurance company that the cost recovered by the insurance industry in those personal injury/fatal accident cases that it successfully defended was less than the amount it paid out in after the event insurance premiums on those claims it lost. A suggestion was made that if the insurance industry waived its right to costs in those claims it defended successfully, then there would be no risk to claimants of adverse costs orders and therefore no need to insure against that risk (justifying the simultaneous abolition of the recoverability of insurance premiums between the parties).

This suggestion found its way into the CPR in respect of proceedings which include claims for damages for personal injury, under the Fatal Accidents Act 1976 or which arise out of death or personal injury and survive for the benefit of an estate under the Law Reform (Miscellaneous Provisions) Act 1934. This definition was considered by the court in *Siddiqui v University of Oxford* [2018] EWHC 536 (QB), in which the court concluded that even though there was an overlap in the evidence presented in support of claims for personal injury and non-personal injury, this did not alter the fact that the claims were separate and so the latter claim was not within the QOCS regime. Even for those claims falling to be considered within the regime there are four qualifications, two requiring permission of the court and two not:

(i) An adverse costs order may be enforced against the claimant *without court permission* BUT only up to the level of any damages and interest that the claimant has recovered (ie as an offset). This provision is intended to ensure that there is some sanction in respect of any interim applications upon which the defendant is the successful party and some risk to a claimant in respect of CPR Part 36.

(ii) An adverse costs order may be enforced in full against the claimant *without court permission* if the claim has been struck out on the basis that it discloses no reasonable grounds, if it is an abuse of court or if the conduct of the claimant or a person acting on the claimant's behalf, and of whose conduct the claimant has knowledge, is likely to obstruct the just disposal of proceedings. Without this exception there would be no risk to deter a claim that is so flawed or conduct that is so culpable that the claim merits being struck out.

(iii) An adverse costs order may be enforced in full *with court permission* where the claim is found on the balance of probabilities to be fundamentally dishonest. This should prove to be an interesting battleground, raising many a question. What is fundamentally dishonest? The rule refers to the claim, suggesting the entirety of the claim. What of those cases where there is an injury for which compensation is recovered, but there has been substantial exaggeration, the claimant has not beaten a Part 36 offer, but the defendants costs dwarf the amount they can offset against the damages under i) above? Given that most claims where there is exaggeration seem to settle soon after service of surveillance evidence, and the practice direction supporting the rules suggests that issues relating to allegations that a claim is fundamentally dishonest will normally be determined at trial and only in exceptional circumstances will the court order that the issues are determined when the claim has settled, does this exception have any real teeth? No doubt costs judges breathed a sigh of relief that determination of 'fundamentally dishonest' will not fall at their door in the course of a detailed assessment. The approach to determining fundamental dishonesty was considered by the Court of Appeal in *Howlett v Davies* [2017] EWCA Civ 1696, in which the court refers to the early decision on this issue by HHJ Moloney QC with approval:

'As noted above, one-way costs shifting can be displaced if a claim is found to be "fundamentally dishonest". The meaning of this expression was considered by His Honour Judge Moloney QC, sitting in the County Court at Cambridge, in *Gosling v Hailo* (29 April 2014). He said this in his judgment:

"44. It appears to me that this phrase in the rules has to be interpreted purposively and contextually in the light of the context. This is, of course, the determination of whether the claimant is 'deserving', as Jackson LJ put it, of the protection (from the costs liability that would otherwise fall on him) extended, for reasons of social policy, by the QOCS rules. It appears to me that when one looks at the matter in that way, one sees that what the rules are doing is distinguishing between two levels of dishonesty: dishonesty in relation to the claim which is not fundamental so as to expose such a claimant to costs liability, and dishonesty which is fundamental, so as to give rise to costs liability.

45. The corollary term to 'fundamental' would be a word with some such meaning as 'incidental' or 'collateral'. Thus, a claimant should not be exposed to costs liability merely because he is shown to have been dishonest as to some collateral matter or perhaps as to some minor, self-contained head of damage. If, on the other hand, the dishonesty went to the root of either the whole of his claim or a substantial part of his claim, then it appears to me that it would be a fundamentally dishonest claim: a claim which depended as to a substantial or important part of itself upon dishonesty."

17. In the present case, neither counsel sought to challenge Judge Moloney QC's approach. Mr Bartlett spoke of it being common sense. I agree.'

(iv) An adverse costs order may be enforced in full *with court permission*:

(a) where the claim is made for the financial benefit of someone other than the claimant or a dependant under the Fatal Accidents Act 1976. This does NOT include claims for gratuitous care, for medical expenses or for an employer; and

(b) where the claim is made for the benefit of the claimant other than a claim to which this section applies. This provision under CPR 44.16(2)(b) was considered in detail by the High Court in *Jeffreys v Metropolitan Police Comr* [2017] EWHC 1505 (QB); *Saddiqui v The Chancellor, Masters and Scholars of the University of Oxford* [2018] EWHC 536 (QB) and *Metropolitan Police Comr v Brown* [2018] EWHC 2046 (Admin). Definitive authority and guidance on application was given by the by the Court of Appeal in the last of these cases, *Brown v Metropolitan Police Comr* [2019] EWCA Civ 1724, in which where the court concluded that:

' . . . the exception at r.44.16(2)(b) was designed to deal with the situation where a claim for damages for personal injury was only one of the claims being made in the proceedings. In those circumstances, the automatic nature of the QOCS protection falls away. But of course, that is not the end of the matter: it then becomes a question of the judge's discretion . . . ' (para.33)

> The court then tendered guidance on practical application, at paras 54–58, identifying those proceedings where a loss is consequent upon the incurrence of a physical injury (eg medical treatment, loss of earnings etc.) and those cases where the loss is not consequent upon the physical injury (eg repairs to a vehicle or hire of a substitute vehicle) and then, in respect of the latter type of case. Offering some general views on the exercise of the residual discretion in CPR 44.16(2)(b).

Even in cases where QOCS may/will apply, the court ought still to determine the award of costs and the basis of assessment and, where appropriate, summarily assess the costs. It is only the enforcement of payment that is affected by the provisions set out above.

CPR 44.13–CPR 44.17 are not retrospective. The transitional arrangements provide that QOCS does not apply to claims under funding arrangements entered in to before 1 April 2013. *Catalano v Espley-Tyas Development Group Ltd* [2017] EWCA Civ 1132 adopted a broad interpretation of a pre-1 April 2013 funding arrangement to include such arrangements that had subsequently been terminated. A funding arrangement refers to:

- agreements for advocacy or litigation services which provide for payment of a success fee or under which work has already been done; or
- where an insurance policy was taken out prior to 1 April 2013; or
- where an agreement has been entered in to with a membership organisation to meet costs prior to 1 April 2013.

In *Wickes Building Supplies Ltd v Blair (No 2) (Costs)* [2020] EWCA Civ 17, the court confirmed that 'proceedings' in CPR 44.13(1) included both first instance proceedings and any subsequent appeal 'which concerns the outcome of the claim for damages for personal injuries, or the procedure by which such a claim is to be determined', rejecting the submission that an appeal is separate and distinct from the appeal process.

There is a sting in the tail with a trap for the unwary as this provision does *not* apply to applications for pre-action disclosure. This is not at all surprising as, of course, a claim for pre-action disclosure is a free standing claim and is not a claim for personal injury, a claim under the Fatal Accidents Act 1976 or a claim under the Law Reform (Miscellaneous Provisions) Act 1934 (although the decision in *Sharp v Leeds City Council* [2017] EWCA Civ 33 challenges this proposition, albeit in the context of the fixed costs regime at CPR 45 Section IIIA, determining such an application to be an interim one under CPR 45.29H).

Damages Based Agreements

[11.9]

CPR 44.18 provides the procedural support for the statutory introduction of this method of funding (see Chapter 7 – Funding for more detail on Damages Based Agreements). While the wording of the regulations offers little financial incentive (indeed it offers an enormous disincentive) to enter into these agreements, they have been used in low value personal injury claims and have caused some concern for the judiciary when dealing with children approvals (see Chapter 34 for further consideration of this). The drafting of the regulations received sustained criticism as part of the Government's review of the effects of the LASPO 2012 reforms, including from Sir Rupert Jackson.

PART 45

[11.10]

Part 45 is headed 'fixed costs'. Whilst it is correct that CPR 45 is home to the fixed cost provisions, it is not quite so restricted. Section IV covers the provisions for scale costs in the Intellectual Property Enterprise Court and Section VI deals with the costs limits in Aarhus Convention claims.

PART 46

[11.11]

Part 46 is what had been Part 48 prior to April 2013, save that the former Part 48.3 – 'Amount of costs where costs are payable pursuant to a contract' – moved to Part 44 and by way of a trade the provisions relating to pro bono costs, costs only proceedings and reallocation moved in the opposite direction. This part now contains provisions for both costs capping orders and for costs against interveners in judicial review proceedings (at CPR 46.16–46.19 and 46.15 respectively).

PART 47

[11.12]

Part 47 is concerned with assessments. This includes changes of significance introduced in 2013 to introduce i) the procedure for provisional assessment of between the parties bills where costs are £75,000 or less (CPR 47.15) and ii) the sanctions of Part 36 to a receiving party's costs offer (CPR 47.20). In respect of the former CPR PD 47, para 14.1 simply gives a total figure and so, at first blush, fewer bills than expected appear to fall within the provisional scheme. However, CPR 47.15 and CPR PD 47, para 14.1 refer to the £75,000 limit as being on the 'costs claimed'. The definition of costs in CPR 44.1 does not include VAT. Accordingly the court should be undertaking provisional assessments of all bills where the net of VAT figure is £75,000 or less. The decision in *BNM v MGN Ltd* [2017] EWCA Civ 1767, in which the Court of Appeal concluded that recoverable pre-1 April 2013 additional liabilities do not fall within the definition of costs under the current CPR 44.1, has the, perhaps unintended, consequence, that these should not be considered when determining whether a bill falls within the provisional assessment scheme.

PART 48

[11.13]

It is almost time to throw out all the old rules as increasingly fewer cases remain that are still subject, in part, to the pre-2013 regime. Part 48 contains the transitional provisions. These provide that the pre-1 April 2013 rules apply to funding arrangements in place before that date. CPR 48.2 defines such a funding arrangement. It should come with an ice pack and a darkened room. It must come with the old rules as CPR 43.2(1)(k) is essential if the provision is to be understood. However, in broad terms, if there was a pre-1 April 2013 funding agreement, as defined in CPR 43.2(1)(k) or, in respect of a collective conditional fee agreement, services were provided to the party under that agreement, then the old rules apply. (See *Catalano v Espley-Tyas Development Group Ltd* [2017] EWCA Civ 1132 above in respect of the definition of a pre-1 April 2013 funding arrangement.)

Beware, though, for Part 48 only deals with transitional provisions in respect of funding arrangements in place before 1 April 2013. Other transitional provisions crop up in different locations.

OTHER TRANSITIONAL PROVISIONS

Proportionality

[11.14]

The proportionality test (CPR 44.3(5) and 44.4(1)) and 'proportionality trumping necessity' (CPR 44.3(2)(a)) (see Chapter 14 Control of Costs – Proportionality) do not apply to cases commenced before 1 April 2013 or, if the case had not been issued by that date, but work had been done on it, then to the cost of the work undertaken prior to that date (see CPR 44.3(7)). However, experience suggests that the transitional provision, or the current provisions, are still not as well understood as they might be – with parties still raising proportionality under the old *Lownds* test at the outset of the assessment when, in fact, a particular case falls within CPR 44.3(2)(a).

The transitional provision does mean that for a period the court is still having to apply two different proportionality tests to separate parts of work done on the same case at assessment. The continuing stream of cases concerned with funding arrangements suggests that there are still cases where the previous regime remains relevant. An amendment to CPR PD 47, para 5.8(7) from 6 April 2016 ensures that where the transitional proportionality provisions do apply, any bill prepared for detailed assessment must be divided in such a way that distinguishes between costs incurred before 1 April 2013 and after 31 March 2013. There is no similar provision in respect of summary assessments (even in the pilot Forms N260A and, more particularly, N260B). However, practitioners should be facilitating this by providing, where appropriate, separate Forms N260 on summary assessment (one for the work under the 'old' test and one for work under the new). If this is not done for summary assessment then expect the court to apply some sanction, with the upshot that the summary assessment will either be put off until another day when there are separate Forms N260, to order that there will be a detailed assessment with, in both cases, the defaulting receiving party paying the costs of the further court process required, or a more robust approach which concludes that an adjournment of any sort is disproportionate when applying the overriding objective and that it will proceed 'doing the best it can on the available evidence', which involves treating all costs under the 'new regime' where no effort has been made to separate them.

In *BNM v MGN Ltd* [2017] EWCA Civ 1767, the Court of Appeal made it clear that the post-31 March 2013 definition of costs in CPR 44.1(1) does not include additional liabilities. Accordingly, pre-1 April 2013 recoverable additional liabilities fall under the 'old' costs rules and so fall to be considered under the *Lownds* proportionality test.

QOCS

[11.15]

Part 44.17 makes it clear that QOCS only applies where the claim is one where no funding arrangement was in place before 1 April 2013. In *Corstorphine (a child by his mother and litigation friend Laura Ellis) v Liverpool City Council* [2018] EWCA Civ 270, the court considered a pre-commencement funding arrangement ('PCFA') under CPR 48.2 in the context of a claim issued against the first defendant before 1 April 2013, but where additional claims, not contemplated at the time of the PCFA, were added after that date and the additional parties were also added as second and third defendants. All the claims failed. The trial judge had ordered the claimant to pay the costs of all three defendants in the primary claim and that the first defendant's costs should include the costs it had been ordered to pay the second and third defendants in the additional claim. The trial judge found that QOCS protection did not extend to any costs the claimant had been ordered to pay. The Court of Appeal allowed the appeal, determining that for the purposes of the CPR 48.2(1)(a)(i)(aa) the 'matter' was the claim for damages for personal injury against the first defendant and that claim was the 'subject of the proceedings' for which the claimant had entered into the PCFA. As a result, any potential costs liability as between the claimant and the second and third defendants (including in respect of the costs incurred by the first defendant pursuing the additional claims) fell within the scope of QOCS protection. Accordingly, the claimant was protected by QOCS in respect of the order to pay the second and third defendants' costs of the primary claim and the order to pay the first defendant those costs it had to pay to the second and third defendants in the additional claim was discharged as it made the claimant indirectly liable for costs that could not be enforced directly against him.

THE COSTS PRACTICE DIRECTION

[11.16]

It would be wrong not to mention the costs practice directions. Instead of one practice direction, from April 2013 there are specific practice directions that relate to the individual costs parts of the CPR.

CHAPTER 12

THE INDEMNITY PRINCIPLE

[12.1]

From the new, all the reforms from the April 2013 CPR amendments onwards, where else can any consideration of costs between the parties go than to the old and the indemnity principle? In England and Wales it is usual for the loser of litigation (whether that is at a discrete interim hearing or a trial or an appeal) to be ordered to pay the winner's costs. Costs are awarded to indemnify the winning party for the costs and expenses incurred. Although this is called an indemnity it is rarely, if ever, a full indemnity for a variety of reasons: the costs that the client has agreed to pay to the solicitor, the barrister or for disbursements are unreasonably incurred or are reasonably incurred but unreasonable in amount or are reasonably incurred and reasonable in amount but are disproportionate. All of these reflect situations over which the loser has no control and it would be wrong for the winner to be indemnified for them.

NO PROFIT

[12.2]

Although it is extremely unusual for the costs ordered between the parties to be as much as the receiving party's solicitor and client costs (although client pressure following a costs management order may make this less unlikely or reduce the difference between the two), what is certain as a general rule is that costs between the parties can never exceed the solicitor and client costs. Every general rule is qualified and the indemnity principle is no different. The obvious exceptions arise as a result of the application of one of the fixed recoverable cost schemes (although given the concerns over the economic viability of undertaking work under such schemes it is hard to conceive of a situation where the fixed cost would now exceed the solicitor and client cost) and where the receiving party has made an effective offer under CPR 36 or CPR 47.20 and is entitled to an extra percentage on the costs assessed (although it is unlikely that this percentage is strictly 'costs' anyway, as it seems to be a free-standing 'additional amount'). Apart from any permitted exceptions the receiving party is entitled only to be indemnified for the actual liability to the solicitor and cannot make a profit out of the costs recovered from the other party. The first record of this principle being expounded was in *Harold v Smith* (1860) 5 H & N 381:

> 'Costs as between party and party are given by the law as an indemnity to the person entitled to them: they are not imposed as a punishment on the party who pays them, nor given as a bonus to the party who receives them. Therefore, if the extent of the indemnification can be found out, the extent to which costs ought to be allowed is also ascertained.'

POSSIBLE PITFALLS AND SOME EXCEPTIONS

(a) Agreements to charge no fee and impecunious clients

[12.3]

If a solicitor agrees to work for nothing then the client has no liability for costs and, therefore, has no need for, nor entitlement to, an indemnity from the other party even if successful in the litigation. The seminal case on this is *Gundry v Sainsbury* [1910] 1 KB 645, 79 LJKB 713, CA in which the Court of Appeal held that to award costs to a client whose solicitor had agreed not to charge costs would have been giving a bonus to the party receiving them. This is a simple application of the law as laid down in *Harold v Smith*.

However, it is, perhaps, more understandable that a solicitor may agree to act on the basis that there will be no charge unless the claim succeeds. If a potential client has no money, but a good claim, the solicitor will wish to obtain the instruction. The client cannot afford to pay unless the claim is successful and so a creative retainer is required. Sadly what may seem creative may also fall foul of the law. In *Gundry v Sainsbury* itself, the successful client had said in cross examination 'I could not pay costs and I had arranged with my solicitor not to pay the costs of the action'. While the solicitor disagreed, he was precluded by the Attorneys and Solicitors Act 1870, s 4 from giving evidence and stating his version of the retainer. As a result there was no recovery of costs between the parties.

In *British Waterways Board v Norman* (1993) 26 HLR 232, [1993] NPC 143, the court held that where solicitors agreed to act for a client whose financial circumstances were such that there was no prospect of the client paying the solicitors' costs unless the claim succeeded, in the absence of a specific agreement to the contrary, there must have been an understanding between the solicitors and the client that they would not look to her for any costs if she lost.

This case is often referred to as having been overruled by *Thai Trading Co (a firm) v Taylor* [1998] QB 781, [1998] 3 All ER 65, CA. However, *Thai Trading* was concerned about the lawfulness of a 'no win, no fee' agreement and it was only this aspect of the judgment in *British Waterways Board v Norman* that was overruled by *Thai Trading*. The basic tenet remains that, if a solicitor expressly or impliedly agrees that there will not in any circumstances be a charge to the client, no costs are recoverable from the other party.

The effect of impecuniosity of the client arose in *Burstein v Times Newspapers Ltd (No 2)* [2002] EWCA Civ 1739, where the claimant was awarded the costs of a successful libel action against the defendants. The defendants contended that when the claimant's solicitors became aware that their client was no longer able to pay their costs, the agreement to pay their costs in the retainer became a sham and unenforceable. Accordingly, the defendants contended that the claimant had no liability to the solicitors for costs. The judge and the Court of Appeal rejected that argument. The defendants' proposition that a retainer was, or became, champertous and therefore unlawful and unenforceable if solicitors became aware at any time that their client could not afford to pay the costs, was a proposition which could not on the authorities be supported.

The problems with the impecunious client have subsequently reappeared, albeit in a different context. In *Heron v TNT (UK) Ltd* [2013] EWCA Civ 469, it was suggested, amongst other submissions, that the failure of the paying party's solicitors to seek after the event insurance demonstrated that the firm had become a party to the action and, as such, a non-party costs order under s 51 of the Senior Courts Act 1981 and CPR 46.2 should be made. In *Flatman v Germany* [2013] EWCA Civ 278, the successful defendants argued that where a claimant pursued a claim under a CFA, with no after the event insurance, was impecunious and where disbursements might have been paid by the solicitors on behalf of the client, then this, too, might form the basis for a non-party costs order. In both cases the receiving party was unsuccessful. Neither the failure to obtain after the event insurance, nor the funding of disbursements rendered a solicitor a 'real party' to the claim (see Chapter 40 Costs against Non-Parties at **[40.18]**).

(b) Pro bono

[12.4]

A topical example of working for no fee, whatever the outcome of the litigation, is that of the professional pro bono groups. However, the increasing number of court users unable to obtain paid representation and having to resort to pro bono assistance resulted in a further, but limited, exception to the indemnity principle. In its consultation paper, '*Costs Recovery in Pro Bono Assisted Cases*', the Department for Constitutional Affairs (now the Ministry of Justice) said:

> 'Pro bono work is an important adjunct to the main strands of the provision of legal services. However, there is an injustice caused by the fact that costs cannot be recovered from the losing party if the successful party is represented pro bono, even though a pro bono assisted party would be liable for his opponent's costs if his opponent won. In such cases, the opponent is aware that if he loses, he will not be asked to pay the other party's costs because that party is represented pro bono. It is intended that the sums recovered will go, not to those providing the representation but, to a prescribed charitable body that will administer and distribute monies received to voluntary organisations that provide free legal support to the community.'

The result was s 194 of the Legal Services Act 2007 and the abrogation of the indemnity principle in pro bono assisted cases. Section 61 of the Legal Aid, Sentencing and Punishment of Offenders Act 2012 extends the provision by permitting the Supreme Court to make pro bono costs awards. The procedure is set out at CPR 46.7 and the prescribed charity is the 'Access to Justice Foundation'. The consensus appears to be that the possibility of pro bono orders being made in the Supreme Court may serve to publicise the possibility of such orders and lead to an increase in their number.

(c) Payment by a third party

[12.5]

Litigation is increasingly being funded under arrangements whereby the solicitor's costs are to be paid by a third party, perhaps a before the event insurer, a trade union, an insurance company or a pure litigation funder. In order to recover costs from another party in such a situation it must be shown that the client had a primary, or dual, liability for the solicitor's costs, as the client was able to do in *R v Miller (Raymond)* [1983] 3 All ER 186, [1983] 1 WLR 1056, DC. It is therefore important expressly to incorporate in the client care letter the right to look to the client for payment of the solicitor and client costs if the case is won, and, indeed, if it is lost, unless there is a valid conditional fee or damages based agreement. Otherwise, on the basis of *British Waterways Board v Norman*, it may be argued that there is an implication to the contrary and that the client has no liability to the solicitor for which there is an entitlement to be indemnified between the parties.

In *Ilangaratne v British Medical Association* [2007] EWHC 920 (Ch), the insurers of the BMA, who were successful in the action, had instructed the solicitors and the claimant alleged there was therefore no retainer between the defendant and the solicitors. However, there was a standing arrangement between the insurers and the solicitors as to costs, evidenced by a letter between them. Although the letter itself was not a written contract or retainer, it was evidence of a standing arrangement that any instructions to the solicitors on behalf of the insurer's customers would give rise to a retainer between the customer and the solicitor on terms already advised and agreed, including the charging rate previously agreed with the insurers. There was therefore a retainer.

A useful summary of the principles applicable to the making of a costs order in favour of parties who benefit from an undertaking that someone else will meet their costs liability to their own solicitors can be found in *Revenue and Customs Comrs v Gardiner* [2018] EWHC 1716 (QB) in which the court concluded that the indemnity principle would not be breached if:

> '1. The putative receiving party establishes a contract with solicitors or representatives to act on their behalf;
>
> 2. The contract derives from a retainer or agreement which may be express or implied;
>
> 3. The receiving party may have sole liability for costs or dual liability with a solicitor or other representative or by reason of the solicitor or representative acting as their agent;
>
> 4. Absent an express term to that effect it is likely to be an implied term of such a contract that the client will be liable for costs incurred on his behalf;
>
> 5. If the receiving party establishes a contractual liability to pay the costs at issue, it matters not that it is highly or vanishingly unlikely that the receiving party will in fact be called upon to pay those costs. It is liability to pay rather than who makes payment which is material.
>
> 6. The presumption that a client instructing a solicitor or representative to represent them will be liable for costs incurred for such representation may be rebutted by the paying party proving that there was a bargain between the client and the representative that under no circumstances was the client to be liable for costs.' (para 30)

(d) Fixed fee

[12.6]

Where a solicitor agrees to work for a fixed fee, then that is the maximum amount that can be recovered from another party. As will become apparent when considering 'item by item' at (f) below and 'Costs Control', this may present some interesting challenges when a case is costs managed.

(e) Interim bill

[12.7]

If, during the course of litigation, the solicitor delivers a bill to the client for work done to date – a stage payment – that bill is a statute bill and not merely a request for payment on account and the solicitor has fixed costs at that amount for the work done during the period covered by the bill and cannot recover a higher amount from another party for that period (see Chapter 2 Billing the client at [2.4]–[2.8]).

(f) Item-by-item

[12.8]

A dramatic development in the application of the indemnity principle was the decision of the Court of Appeal in *General of Berne Insurance Co v Jardine Reinsurance Management Ltd* [1998] 2 All ER 301, [1998] 1 WLR 1231, CA. This followed conflicting decisions on whether the application of the indemnity principle should be on an item-by-item basis, or whether it only provides a global cap, so that the receiving party may recover on assessment uplifted hourly expense rates which are judged to be reasonable, even if they exceed the rates that the solicitors were entitled to receive from their client under a contentious business agreement, provided that the total amount allowed between the parties did not exceed the total amount the solicitors were entitled to recover from their client. There were arguments both ways and, in the words of the Court of Appeal, 'each of the parties' cases has its problems'. The court came down in favour of the item-by-item approach, even though it accepted that examples could arise where complicated and painstaking reductions might be required, commenting 'taxation [assessment] of costs can be a laborious procedure in any event, and can be expensive in taxing [assessing] fees'. No one would quarrel with that. *Nederlandse Reassurantie Groep Holding NV v Bacon & Woodrow* ([1998] 2 Costs LR 32, QBD), a review of a taxation [*detailed assessment*] by Tucker J, confirmed that the General of *Berne v Jardine* interpretation of the indemnity principle applied to all retainers, whether or not a formal contentious business agreement was in place.

This problem becomes more pronounced when the claim in which the solicitor is representing the client on a global fixed fee comes within the costs management provisions of CPR 3.12–CPR 3.18. Precedent H is broken down into phases with the budget set by reference to a sum for each phase (CPR PD 3E, para 7.3). How is a global fixed fee to be split between the phases? Will solicitors undertaking fixed fee work have to agree how the overall sum is to be split between the phases with the client at the time of creating the retainer? If not how will the solicitors complete Precedent H?

The change to the statement of truth on Precedent H makes completion of the form easier, in the sense that the solicitor is not signing to a budget that breaches the indemnity principle. This is because the incurred costs are no longer limited to those actually incurred, but instead to what it would have been reasonable and proportionate to incur. However, as the budgeted costs remain set by phases then, unless there is 'good reason' to depart from the budgeted costs, any bill on a standard basis assessment 'between the parties' will be assessed by phases and the sum allowed will be the sum approved/agreed as budgeted costs for those phases. It is clear that there remains a significant practical problem. The change to the statement of truth is one of form. It does not lead to a permitted breach of the indemnity principle. Accordingly, it must be a 'good reason' to depart from the budgeted costs on assessment, if failure to do so would lead to a breach of the indemnity principle. When preparing the bill of costs, if not before, the solicitor will be compelled to compare the fixed fee with the component phases of the budget.

In addition, merely being within the overall fixed fee which is higher than the budgeted costs does not satisfy the requirement to be within the budgeted costs per phase. With an increase in the number of clients demanding fixed fee work and certain umbrella organisations demanding that member firms of solicitors move to fixed fee pricing only, this is not merely an academic point. Will creative fixed fee retainer writing provide the solution? eg 'The fixed fee for this work will be £x. How this sum is divided between the various phases of the budget for the purpose of any costs management order made and assessment by the court is a matter for the solicitors in their absolute discretion.'

(g) Disclosure

[12.9]

A matter which has bedevilled assessments of costs for some years is how is the paying party to discover the terms of the retainer to ascertain the level of the indemnity to which the receiving party is entitled? Almost invariably the first challenge in the Points of Dispute relates to whether or not there is a valid retainer. There can be no doubt that the onus should be on the receiving party to satisfy the court that the terms of the retainer provide an entitlement to the indemnity for costs sought. This view received support in *Bailey v IBC Vehicles Ltd* [1998] 3 All ER 570, 142 Sol Jo LB 126, CA, in which the court held that in future, any client care letter setting out the terms of the client's financial obligations to the solicitors should be attached to the bill of costs together with any contentious business agreement or other relevant documents.

However, Henry LJ suggested that the signing of the 'between the parties' bill of costs by the solicitor as an officer of the court was effectively a certificate that the receiving party's solicitors were not seeking to recover, in relation to any item, more than they had agreed to charge their client and was, usually, sufficient confirmation that there had been no breach of the indemnity principle. There was a presumption of trust and any breach of that trust should be treated as a most serious disciplinary offence.

This suggestion was rejected by the Court of Appeal in *Hollins v Russell* [2003] EWCA Civ 718, in respect of challenges to conditional fee agreements, which it distinguished from conventional challenges, as in *Bailey*. In *Bailey* the paying party was not saying that there was no liability at all to pay any costs to the receiving party, but was challenging the hourly rate and mark-up being applied to it.

This *Hollins* type challenge to retainer and the principle of paying anything at all increased the stakes significantly from a mere challenge to the figures produced. The conditional fee agreement (CFA) regulations introduced a new level of complexity. The solicitor's certificate as to accuracy might not be sufficient evidence of there being no breach of the indemnity principle where the quality and quantity of the information served on the paying party about the success fee was less than would be made available in respect of the other aspects of the bill in the case of an assessment where there was no additional liability claimed. The question of whether a CFA complies with the Courts and Legal Services Act 1990 is principally a matter of law, while challenges to conventional bills are generally questions of fact.

In practice post *Hollins* there tends to have been voluntary disclosure of CFAs in detailed assessment proceedings. If that does not happen then the court ought not to take it upon itself to examine the CFA to determine the dispute without disclosure to the paying party unless the parties are happy for this to be the approach. In *Dickinson (t/a Dickinson Equipment Finance) v Rushmer (t/a FJ Associates)* [2002] NLJR 58, ChD, there was an appeal from a detailed assessment by a costs judge to Rimer J sitting with assessors. On the detailed assessment the paying party (the defendant) invoked the indemnity principle, asserting that the receiving party (the claimant) could not have assumed a personal responsibility to pay costs of the amount claimed in the solicitor's bills. The claimant's solicitors produced to the costs judge documents to prove the terms of the retainer and demonstrate there was no breach of the indemnity principle. The costs judge refused to allow the defendant to see the documents on the grounds they were privileged. It was held that the costs judge was wrong. It is one of the most basic principles of natural justice that each side is entitled to know what the other side's case is and to see the documentary material on which reliance is placed. The receiving party, without producing any documents, could ask the costs judge to direct whether the paying party had raised a genuine issue which needed to be met by evidence, or if the signature certification on the bill of costs resulted in an acceptance that the indemnity principle had not been offended. If the receiving party pre-empts any such decision by the costs judge by producing the documents, the paying party is entitled to see them, even though they are privileged.

In *South Coast Shipping Co Ltd v Havant Borough Council* [2002] 3 All ER 779, [2002] NLJR 59 the costs judge had been shown documents which the paying party had not been allowed to see on the grounds that they were privileged. The appeal raised human rights issues, in particular the conflict between the right to privilege and the right to a fair trial. If the costs judge, having seen the documents in question, required the receiving party to elect between giving secondary evidence of the retainer and waiving the privilege, there was no incompatibility with the principles articulated by the European Convention for Human Rights. That was not intended to suggest that a costs judge should put the receiving party to its election in respect of every document relied on, regardless of its degree of relevance. In the great majority of cases the paying party should be (and is) content to agree that the costs judge alone should see privileged documents. Only where it is necessary and proportionate should the receiving party be put to the election. Otherwise the redaction and production of privileged documents, or the adducing of further evidence, will lead to additional delay and increase costs. In practice, frequently the parties are content for the retainer issue to be resolved by the court examining the relevant documentation (which must be filed where there is a dispute pursuant to CPR PD 47, para 13.2 (i)) and indicating whether or not it is satisfied there is a valid retainer.

The issue of whether there has been a breach of the indemnity principle should have become less common following the abolition of recoverable additional liabilities, but still seems to appear as a routine challenge in Points of Dispute. Where it is raised when the court is undertaking a provisional assessment on paper without the parties present, experience suggests that the court is giving the challenge short shrift if it is a 'routine' challenge to retainer that amounts to no more than a fishing expedition. If it does raise a genuine line of enquiry then there have already been cases where the court has determined that this is a valid reason to depart from the provisional assessment scheme and list for an attended detailed assessment pursuant to CPR 47.15(6). Parties raising indemnity principle may want to consider the possible costs consequence of so doing. If an attended assessment is convened simply to explore indemnity and the challenge is unsuccessful then the increased costs exposure, once the protection afforded by the cap on provisional assessment is lost, is likely to be substantial.

(h) Unlawful retainer

[12.10]

If a solicitor enters into an invalid retainer with the client it is unenforceable against the client and the client can therefore recover nothing from the other party. This has been the case where the court has found CFAs to be unenforceable. With CFA funding still available and still subject to some statutory regulation and with the jury still out on Damages Based Agreements this remains a genuine risk to solicitors undertaking work on these types of retainer.

(i) Fixed costs

[12.11]

In *Butt v Nizami* [2006] EWHC 159 (QB), sometimes reported as *Nizami v Butt*, the claimants both suffered whiplash injuries when the car they were travelling in was hit by the defendant's car. Their claims were settled, but costs could not be agreed. They commenced costs-only proceedings under CPR Part 8 claiming fixed recoverable costs under CPR 45.9 (now CPR 45.11), disbursements under CPR 45.10 (now CPR 45.12) and a fixed success fee under CPR 45.11 (now not recoverable). The defendant alleged that the claimants' solicitors had failed to make appropriate enquiries about the availability of before-the-event insurance and sought a direction for the solicitors to certify compliance with the Conditional Fee Agreement Regulations 2000. The costs judge held that the claimants' entitlement to costs depended not on the existence of a valid and enforceable conditional fee agreement, but on their entitlement under the fixed recoverable costs rule. This was upheld on appeal.

The intention underlying CPR 45.7–CPR 45.14 (now CPR 45.9–CPR 45.15) is to provide an agreed scheme of recovery that is certain and easily calculated by providing fixed levels of remuneration, which might over-reward in some cases and under-reward in others, but which are regarded as fair when taken as a whole. The amendment to s 51(2) of the Senior Courts Act 1981 significantly modified the indemnity principle and permitted changes in the rules to give this effect.

The court concluded that it was clear that the indemnity principle should not apply to the figures that were recoverable, and accordingly there was little reason why the principle should have any application to CPR 45.9 (now CPR 45.11) and CPR 45.11(no longer relevant), and good reasons why it should not. The CPR had successfully disapplied the indemnity principle in relation to the fixed recoverable costs scheme.

CPR Part 45 now encompasses all the fixed recoverable costs regimes. The decision in *Nizami* illustrates that whatever type of fee retainer solicitors are acting under it is implicit in all fixed costs regimes that the indemnity principle is disapplied. In Section 1, Table I gives the fixed costs on commencement, Table II costs on entry of judgment, Table III the fixed costs on commencement of a claim for the recovery of land or a demotion claim, Table IV miscellaneous fixed costs, which are concerned mainly with service of documents and Table V fixed enforcement costs. The prescribed amounts are payable without any enquiry into the terms of the retainer between the receiving party and their solicitor. Section II is concerned with fixed recoverable costs in road traffic accident claims. Section III applies to pre-action protocol low value personal injury claims and Section IIIA applies to claims no longer continuing in the low value injury protocols. A further form of fixed costs is the fixed trial costs on the fast track, which, as seen in the preceding chapter, are now at Section VI, which prescribe that the court shall not award less than the amount shown in the table (unless CPR 45.39 applies). Again, this clearly precludes an investigation into the terms of the successful party's retainer and, for example, it is accepted that the amount of counsel's brief fee or the solicitor advocate's time costs are of no relevance, even if they are substantially less than the prescribed amount of the fixed costs. The attraction of the certainty and consistency of fixed, or predictable costs, would be undermined if they were subject to the indemnity principle. Fixed costs are an incentive to efficiency and a sanction against inefficiency. They are also designed to keep both the substantive claim and the costs determination proportionate.

(j) BTE insurance

[12.12]

In *Ghadami v Lyon Cole Insurance Group Ltd* [2010] EWCA Civ 767, the claimant pursued a claim against the defendant who had a before-the-event indemnity insurance policy covering the costs of the proceedings subject to an excess of £1,000. The defendant paid its solicitors the excess and the insurers paid the balance of their costs. The claimant lost and was ordered to pay the defendant's cost. The claimant contended that as the defendant's liability for costs was limited to the excess of £1,000, the indemnity principle prevented the defendant recovering more than the excess from the claimant. On appeal it was held that there was an implicit agreement that the solicitors would act for the defendant in relation to the claim without any express terms as to costs. There was therefore no agreement whereby the liability of the defendant for its solicitor's fees and disbursements was expressly limited to £1,000 and it was entitled to recover the full 'between the parties' costs.

(k) In-House solicitors

[12.13]

In *R (on the application of Kuznetsov) v London Borough of Camden* [2019] EWHC 3910 (Admin), the court had cause to visit the hourly rate in the context of employed solicitors. In so doing, the court confirmed that the case of *Re Eastwood (deceased)* [1975] Ch 112 survived the advent of the Civil Procedure Rules. In that case, Russell J stated:

> 'There might be special cases in which it appears reasonably plain that the principle [the indemnity principle] will be infringed if the method of taxation appropriate to an independent solicitor's bill is entirely applied. But it would be impracticable and wrong in all cases of an employed solicitor to require a total exposition and breakdown of the activities and expenses of the Department with a view to ensuring that the principle is not infringed, and it is doubtful to say the least whether by any methods, certainty on the point could be reached.'

In conclusion in *R (on the application of Kuznetsov)*, Mostyn J, in applying the guideline hourly rate contended for by the London Borough of Camden, declined to treat the case as a special one, concurring with Russell J that to investigate this matter would be unworkable in practice and to push abstract principle to the point where it ceases to give results consistent with justice.

THE FUTURE OF THE INDEMNITY PRINCIPLE

[12.14]

For years there has been a clamour for abolition of the indemnity principle. Sir Rupert Jackson described in his final report how he had received forceful submissions from both pro and anti-abolitionists. He concluded that the principle should be abrogated. It was thought that the introduction of damages based agreements ('DBAs'), which are no more than contingency agreements by another name, might sound the final death knell. However, the indemnity principle has survived the latest reforms and, indeed, as a consequence, rendered damages based agreements unattractive for nearly all cases (see reg 4 of the Damages Based Agreements Regulations 2013). This seems curious when:

- there are the numerous permitted exceptions to which reference has already been made, further fixed recoverable costs schemes are on the horizon, following Sir Rupert Jackson's supplemental report on this in July 2017, and DBAs were intended to render permissible pure contingency funding;
- costs management removes the risk of utterly unchecked costs; and

- the statutory framework already exists – s 31 of the Access to Justice Act 1999, which has not been implemented, amends s 51 of the Senior Courts Act 1981 to provide that the amount recovered by way of costs may not be limited to 'what would have been payable by him (the client) to them (the solicitors) if he had not been awarded costs.'

For the time being, though, the indemnity principle survives, albeit with an ever-increasing number of permitted exceptions. It has survived the Government's Legal Aid, Sentencing and Punishment of Offenders Act 2012 Post-Implementation Review published in February 2019 despite the review noting, when considering Damages Based Agreements, that:

> 'Almost all respondents, across the spectrum, agreed that DBAs are rarely used and that the current DBA regulations are not effective . . . Where respondents and stakeholders elaborated on specific concerns they cited issues including: the lack of payment of a reasonable sum for work done on termination; uncertainty around early termination and the indemnity principle; . . . ' (para 116)

The further work anticipated in the review has now been concluded. It puts the indemnity principle in this context back in the spotlight by suggesting that the DBA payment is separate from, and in addition to, the recoverable costs. Developments are still awaited.

CHAPTER 13

PROSPECTIVE COSTS CONTROL – INTRODUCTION

[13.1]

It had long been acknowledged that the major failure of the Woolf reforms, introduced as the CPR in 1999, was the failure to control costs. In part, this may be an unfair criticism as the introduction of recoverable 'additional liabilities' in 2000, which led to the beginning of over a decade of 'costs wars', and the failure of the government to implement a fixed costs scheme in the fast track, had exacerbated the situation. Certainly the focus on costs had not been in the direction that Lord Woolf intended when stating in his Final Report:

> 'I recognise that my reforms involve learning new skills. These will have to be learned not only by judges but by members of the profession generally. The profession as well as the judiciary must pay more attention to and be better informed about costs than they are at present. My objective is to require greater attention to be focused on costs throughout the process of resolving disputes by everyone involved: judges, litigants and lawyers.'

Instead the emphasis, by dint of restrictive rules on costs capping, a lack of policing of the then existing powers under the CPR to require costs estimates (and limited use of those estimates that were filed) and a reliance on ex post facto cost assessment, had served only to shift the gaze very much to the end of the court process. As a result, as courts at all levels had repeatedly said, by the time many claims reached trial the case was no longer about the original dispute, but instead was all about the costs because neither party could afford to lose. The other inevitable consequence of that approach was that prospective litigants were deterred from pursuing legitimate claims because of their inability to fund the costs.

It was in recognition of this failing that Sir Rupert Jackson focussed much of his attention on prospective costs control by the court, not only to curb expenditure, but also to ensure that litigants are able to make informed decisions knowing the cost consequences of pursuing or defending claims and to enable the court to allocate increasingly restricted resources proportionately between cases.

As a result, formal costs management was introduced in April 2013. The scheme has undergone both review and change (in 2014, 2016, 2017, 2019 and, again, in 2020). The proposals advanced in Sir Rupert Jackson's review of fixed recoverable costs in July 2017, in terms of the scope of the recommended extensions to existing schemes, and his comments as to the increasing acceptance of the budgeting regime, suggests that costs management is here to stay. We have repeatedly advocated that costs management renders costs capping redundant. However, despite indications to the contrary throughout the deliberations of the Civil Procedure Rules Committee in 2015, it, too, remains an option, as does an entirely separate costs capping regime that was introduced in August 2016 in judicial review proceedings and 2019 has seen the commencement of a voluntary two-year capped costs pilot in the London Circuit Commercial Court and the Business and Property Courts

District Registries in Leeds and Manchester. In addition, an increasing emphasis on ADR and amendments to CPR Part 36 are designed to offer parties greater incentives to settle claims, and these changes were extended to the detailed assessment process at CPR 47.20 to try to discourage retrospective arguments on costs.

The architect of the reforms in Part 2 of the Legal Aid, Sentencing and Punishment of Offenders Act 2012 ('LASPO 2012'), Sir Rupert Jackson, took stock on his retirement from the Court of Appeal in March 2018. In a lecture entitled 'Was it all worth it', he considered the various reforms, and whilst accepting that there was still work to be done, answered his own question in the affirmative. The Government's five-year review of Part 2 of LASPO 2012 concluded that the reforms had largely been successful in meeting the original objectives, with further consideration to be given to both Damages Based Agreements and extension of the QOCS regime.

At the heart of Sir Rupert Jackson's 2013 reforms, consequential rule amendments, subsequent costs capping regimes and the prospect of extensions to fixed costs regimes, all designed to control costs, is the concept of proportionality – long familiar in name to those conducting civil litigation, but with centre stage comes an increased importance.

CHAPTER 14

PROSPECTIVE COSTS CONTROL – PROPORTIONALITY

INTRODUCTION TO PROSPECTIVE COSTS CONTROL – PROPORTIONALITY

[14.1]

The concept of proportionality permeates throughout the CPR, from the overriding objective, through case and costs management, to costs assessment at the conclusion of a claim. In theory this is nothing new. Prior to April 2013, CPR 1.1(2)(c) included in its definition of 'dealing with a case justly', the requirement to deal 'with the case in ways which are proportionate'. Case managers, with an eye to the overriding objective, ought to have been giving directions that were proportionate. In addition, the case of *Lownds v Home Office* [2002] EWCA Civ 365, introduced the test of proportionality to the assessments of costs – if the global costs claimed by the receiving party were disproportionate then individual items would only be recoverable if *necessarily* incurred and reasonable in amount. The need to keep control over costs, linked to proportionality, was reinforced in *Leigh v Michelin Tyre plc* [2003] EWCA Civ 1766, and subsequently codified in Section 6 of the Costs Practice Direction. So why has proportionality taken on such importance following April 2013 and why has it attracted so much comment over the last eight years – much of which is highly critical? Is the criticism justified?

THE CASE FOR REFORM

[14.2]

While Lord Woolf went on to qualify his definition of proportionality in *Lownds*, his earlier comments in that case set out the purists' position:

> 'If, because of lack of planning or due to other causes, the global costs are disproportionately high, then the requirement that the costs should be proportionate means that no more should be payable than would have been payable if the litigation had been conducted in a proportionate manner.'

However, it became accepted wisdom that applying the two – fold test of *Lownds* did not necessarily achieve this desired outcome. Even after preliminary findings that the global costs of cases were not proportionate in amount, there was a perception that assessments could, and frequently did, still lead to assessed costs, on an item by item basis, that remained disproportionate (See for example the comments of May LJ set out at Chapter 3, para 4.7 of the '*Review of Civil Litigation Costs: Final Report*').

This was a theme picked up Sir Rupert Jackson in his Final Report. His remit was, as he described, 'to promote access to justice at proportionate cost'. He devoted an entire chapter to consideration of proportionality and returned to what he saw as the causes of disproportionate costs at various points in his analysis and conclusions. His clear verdict was that:

> 'Access to justice is only practicable if the costs of litigation are proportionate.'

It was with this desire to preserve access to justice in mind that Sir Rupert Jackson set out the proposals that have become enshrined in the Civil Procedure Rules from 1 April 2013.

THE REFORM

The proportionality test

[14.3]

As we have already seen, in order to leave no one in any doubt as to the prominence of proportionality after April 2013, the overriding objective, was amended to provide at CPR 1.1(1) that:

> 'These Rules are a new procedural code with the overriding objective of enabling the court to deal with cases justly and at proportionate cost.'

In simple terms this means that when making procedural decisions on any case the court must ensure that the outcome enables the claim to be determined at proportionate cost. This led to concern from across the legal community that pursuit of justice had been qualified – that claims would no longer be investigated fully. In some quarters, the concern still remains that the court is compelled to dispense a lesser, cost constrained, version of justice. This debate will be considered in more detail below.

Proportionality is expressly defined within the rules. CPR 44.3(5) provides as follows:

> 'Costs incurred are proportionate if they bear a reasonable relationship to—
> (a) the sums in issue in the proceedings;
> (b) the value of any non-monetary relief in issue in the proceedings;
> (c) the complexity of the litigation;
> (d) any additional work generated by the conduct of the paying party; and
> (e) any wider factors involved in the proceedings, such as reputation or public importance.'

However, in *West v Stockport NHS Foundation Trust* [2019] EWCA Civ 1220, the Court of Appeal concluded that the definition in CPR 44.3(5) was not an exclusive one. Whilst costs will be proportionate if they are determined to be so when judged against these criteria, the fact that they are not does not necessarily lead to a finding of disproportionality. This is because, amongst other things, CPR 44.3(5) does not say 'if, and only if'. The court found that under the rules 'questions of proportionality are to be considered by reference to the specific matters noted in 44.3(5) and, if relevant, any wider circumstances identified under r.44.4(1)'. Accordingly, the test of proportionality is broader than some of us thought, although by how much is a matter of conjecture, for as we have repeatedly advocated, CPR 44.3(5) is, itself, suitably crafted to cover almost every relevant circumstance. Accordingly, even expressly adding in 'all the circumstances' to the consideration of proportionality, still begs the question, what does this all mean? Like many statutory and procedural checklists and considerations of 'all the circumstances', this does not lead to a clear and precise specific outcome. Indeed the additional consideration of 'all the circumstances', arguably, just broadens the exercise of discretion. One person's view of proportionality may still differ from that of another. The answer is that, ultimately, the outcome will be whatever an individual judge, in the context of the particular case before the court, decides is proportionate within the parameters of a reasonable exercise of judicial discretion. Unsurprisingly, this, too, has come in for sustained criticism. Different judges considering the same case might come to different views. The easy answer is that this is nothing new! Up and down the country every day this happens – not just on a procedural level, but also in terms of the final decisions made. Exercises of discretion and particular factual findings, inevitably lead to different conclusions.

The clarification that CPR 44.3(5) is not the only route to a determination of proportionality, raises the clear possibility of a two-stage approach to determinations of proportionality. This is because it is only if the consideration of the CPR 44.3(5) criteria leads to the conclusion that the costs are not proportionate, that the court will need to consider 'all the circumstances' to see if those add anything that renders the costs proportionate. As an exercise in keeping proportionate the determination of proportionality itself, we would expect the court to consider CPR 44.3(5) first and only proceed to submissions and judgment under 'all the circumstances' if it needs so to do.

The application of the test – Introduction

[14.4]

Many commentators spent nearly seven years waiting eagerly for the Court of Appeal to give guidance on the proportionality test. We have consistently said that such guidance could only ever, at best, be general, as proportionality in pure monetary terms will, in the absence of the absolute certainty of a full 'fixed recoverable costs' regime, always be case specific. Whilst the Court of Appeal spoke in *West*, the guidance given was, inevitably, in general terms. We wonder if those who urged Court of Appeal intervention think that the breath holding exercise was justified. Certainly, the guidance provided some clarification, but, as we shall explore in **[14.5]** below, in so doing it is arguable that this is off-set by the creation of fresh fields of uncertainty and, despite an express statement to the contrary, a nod in the direction of *Lownds* and necessary costs.

The application of the test – Court of Appeal Guidance

[14.5]

In *West* the Court of Appeal also took the opportunity to make some general observations about the practice and process for determining proportionality.

As we shall see below, the guidance given introduces some practical challenges for budgeting and assessing judges, some new costs battles on fields of uncertainty and possibly a move away from proportionality. The guidance provides that:

- whilst the assessing judge should first go through the bill on an item-by-item basis assessing reasonableness, where appropriate there is no reason why the court cannot undertake the assessment of the proportionality of an item at the same time. However, the court acknowledged that these are separate exercises that are 'conceptually distinct'. Our difficulty with this, as set out in the 2019 edition, is that there is a danger of eliding the rules and drawing no clear distinction between the separate functions with which the assessing judge is charged. This remains a real concern (particularly on a summary assessment where reasons for decisions are correctly brief). Another concern is that when the court steps back at the end of the item-by-item assessment to consider overall proportionality there is a genuine risk of an element of double deduction, if the court is not astute to those findings on proportionality it has already made;
- once the court has concluded the item-by-item assessment, it must assess the proportionality of that total figure (guarding against the double deduction to which reference is made above). If that total figure is found to be proportionate, then no further assessment is required. However, if the court regards the overall figure as disproportionate, then a further assessment is required. The Court of Appeal was clear that this should not be line-by-line, but should instead be by consideration of various categories of cost, such as disclosure or experts' reports, or specific periods where particular costs were incurred, or particular parts of the profit costs. Whilst this is more targeted than one overall proportionality determination, it should still be a relatively short and straightforward process as the court will be familiar with the case at this stage and ideally placed to determine where further deductions should be made.
- when the court considers proportionality those items of cost which are fixed and unavoidable, or which have an irreducible minimum, without which the litigation could not have been progressed 'are to be left out of account' (paras 81 and 82). The first of these exceptions presents no problem. A classic illustration is court fees. It matters not whether one simply makes the assumption that they are proportionate or leaves them out of the account altogether, the reality is that they must be approved (for budgeting) or allowed (on assessment) as they are mandatory and fixed in prescribed sums. However, we struggle to reconcile the second exception with CPR 44.3(2)(a). Whilst the court was keen to stress that it should be apparent that the decision does not resurrect *Lownds*, the reality is that, at first blush, taking out of the proportionality account those items reasonably incurred which have irreducible minimums, regardless of amount, resonates uncomfortably with the recovery of costs necessarily incurred. They are still part of the 'global costs' to which Sir Rupert referred. The exercise becomes one of semantics, not financial reality. The fact that it may be only certain items, still has the potential to undermine overall proportionality. We say 'potential' because of matters considered in the bullet point below.

- As there is a financial incentive to exclude items from the constraints of proportionality, it seems inevitable that arguments will abound as to whether certain expenditure is an irreducible minimum and should be excluded (eg in the context of expert fees).
- the exclusion of some items from the proportionality considerations should not undermine overall proportionality. However, this is easier to state than to comprehend and/or apply, in particular the clear tension between para 84, which states:

> 'This [the exclusion of costs which are fixed and unavoidable, or which have an irreducible minimum] ought not to disadvantage the paying party. Take as an example a claim that was settled for £10,000 but where the costs were £50,000, of which £5,000 was made up of the recoverable element of the ATE insurance premium. In those circumstances, when working through the various categories of cost to assess proportionality, the judge may have some overall figure in mind that would be proportionate. That figure will remain unchanged: the reductions to achieve it will simply be by reference to other elements of cost, not the ATE insurance premium.'

and the explanation of the proportionality cross-check at the end of the assessment as set out in para 92, which states:

> 'The judge will undertake the proportionality assessment by looking at the different categories of costs (excluding the unavoidable items noted above) and considering, in. respect of each such category, whether the costs incurred were disproportionate. If yes, then the judge will make such reduction as is appropriate. In that way, reductions for proportionality will be clear and transparent for both sides.'

The tension arises if, on undertaking the proportionality assessment, the costs of the different categories of costs are deemed to be proportionate but the addition of the costs excluded renders the overall figure the judge has in mind disproportionate. Paragraph 84 suggests that, in order to ensure that the paying party is not disadvantaged, the court will have to make reductions to the elements of costs not excluded to achieve the overall figure. How can the court do that fairly, when the cross-check of the non-excluded categories of costs under para 92 leads to the conclusion that they are proportionate?

The application of the test – some general points

[14.6]

There are some things that seem to be established and clear:

1. Consideration of proportionality under CPR 44.3(5), involves all five factors, as the Senior Costs Judge succinctly stated in *Wave 1 of the Mirror Newspapers Hacking Litigation v MGN Ltd* [2018] EWHC B13 (Costs):

> 'Rule 44.3(5) does not identify any of the five factors as being more important than the others.'

That certain factors do not arise in a particular case is as important to the determination of proportionality as those that do.

2. Proportionality is central to the costs management regime. CPR PD 3E, para 12 sets out the way in which the court will determine the budget. It provides:

> 'When reviewing budgeted costs, the court will not undertake a detailed assessment in advance, but rather will consider whether the budgeted costs fall within the range of reasonable and proportionate costs.'

In other words, the court will consider the CPR 44.4(3) and CPR 44.3(5) factors and 'all the circumstances' and will then determine the reasonable and proportionate costs for each phase of the proceedings. As the budget figure for each phase will be set as a total sum under CPR 3.15(8), and as under CPR 44.3(2)(a) considerations of proportionality prevail over determinations of reasonableness, it is the consideration of proportionality that ultimately will usually be determinative of that amount (see below for consideration of CPR 44.3(2)(a)) and, in synthesis, the appropriate case management decision.

At first blush, it seems curious that one of the five factors seemingly cannot inform that decision. At the time of setting the budget, the identity of the paying party will not be known. Does this mean that the court must assume, for the purposes of setting a particular party's budget, that it will be the receiving party? This was the approach adopted by the court in *Group Seven Ltd v Nasir* [2016] EWHC 629 (Ch), albeit that the court accepted this to be hypothetical. However, there is nothing expressly in CPR 3.12–CPR 3.18 or CPR PD 3E that supports this broad interpretation. Accordingly, it is arguable that even if the conduct of one party has already increased the costs of the other, this cannot be taken in to account at this stage as that party may not ultimately be the paying party.

There is certainly an argument to be made for ignoring conduct at the costs management stage. This is because unless the parties have agreed all the incurred costs or those on any specific phase (CPR 3.15(2)(c)), the court is not able to make a costs management order in respect of costs already incurred. It is also not, at this stage, undertaking an assessment of those costs. Accordingly, any arguments on conduct increasing incurred costs can be taken when considering the reasonableness of costs and the overall proportionality at any subsequent assessment.

However, this argument overlooks the fact that when setting the budget for a phase the court is required to take into account the incurred expenditure under CPR 3.17(3)(b). There may well be situations where the party whose budget is being set has incurred costs of a significantly higher level than might be expected because of the conduct of the other party. If that is the case, then this should be taken into account by the costs managing court as otherwise the budgeted costs under CPR 3.15(2) may be too low, because the court has taken account of the incurred costs without accepting that, whilst high, part of this is due to the other party's conduct.

As an aside there has been some concern that the conduct of the receiving party is omitted from the proportionality checklist. This can be readily explained – it would be superfluous. In respect of those costs not budgeted, then any conduct issues will be dealt with, as appropriate, on the award of costs (CPR 44.2(5)), whether in respect of free standing applications or the overall claim, and at any subsequent assessment of the reasonable costs under such orders (CPR 44.4(3)). Both these provisions contain clear obligations on the court to consider conduct. In respect of budgeted costs, as has already been stated, these are set by reference to reasonableness as well as proportionality. Accordingly, there is already provision for the consideration of conduct in the 'reasonableness' part of the determination – indeed the Guidance Notes on Precedent H expressly refer to CPR 44.4(3).

3. Despite the concerns expressed above about the effect of excluding from the proportionality determination items of work with an irreducible minimum cost as per West, the final proportionality procedural change in 2013 was intended to be the most pervasive and seismic. It resulted in the demise of the *Lownds* test and its replacement by something altogether more consequential. *Lownds* had received sustained criticism from the Court of Appeal and it was no surprise to find that Sir Rupert Jackson recommended its reversal in the final report:

> 'In other words, I propose that in an assessment of costs on the standard basis, proportionality should prevail over reasonableness and the proportionality test should be applied on a global basis. The court should first make an assessment of reasonable costs, having regard to the individual items in the bill, the time reasonably spent on those items and the other factors listed in CPR rule 44.5(3). The court should then stand back and consider whether the total figure is proportionate. If the total figure is not proportionate, the court should make an appropriate reduction.'

This recommendation found its way in to the CPR at CPR 44.3(2)(a):

> 'Where the amount of costs is to be assessed on the standard basis, the court will—
>
> (a) only allow costs which are proportionate to the matters in issue. Costs which are disproportionate in amount may be disallowed or reduced even if they were reasonably or necessarily incurred;'

Whilst stating clearly that the exclusion from the proportionality determination costs that are subject to an irreducible minimum did not reintroduce the *Lownds* test by making the point that under that test, necessity always trumped proportionality and that was not the effect of their decision, it is arguable that it has done precisely that. However, it is undeniable that a consequence of *West* is to water down the effect of CPR 44.3(2)(a). By how much will become clearer as the court grapples to identify those costs subject to an irreducible minimum.

TRANSITIONAL PROVISIONS

[14.7]

As some cases remain extant that are subject to the transitional provisions, they still merit consideration. They are found in CPR 44.3(7), which provides that the provisions of CPR 44.3(2)(a) and CPR 44.3(5) do not apply to cases commenced before 1 April 2013 and, in cases issued after that date, to the costs incurred before that date. The Court of Appeal decision in *BNM v MGN Ltd* [2017] EWCA Civ 1767 clarified that the pre-April 2013 '*Lownds*' proportionality test applies to recoverable additional liabilities. The court reached this conclusion by the following route:

- The definition of costs in CPR 44.1 no longer includes additional liabilities, so they cannot be governed by the proportionality provisions at CPR 44.3(2)(a) and CPR 44.3(5) as these provisions relate only to costs as defined under CPR 44.1.

- In contrast the 'old' definition of costs included reference to additional liabilities and this rule is mentioned in CPR PD 48, para 3.1. As the 'Lownds' proportionality test applies to costs falling within the pre-April 2013 definition of costs, then this test is the one that relates to funding arrangements (even though it is not expressly mentioned in CPR PD 48).

Albeit as an aside, we pause to note that the conclusion that additional liabilities are not 'costs' under CPR 44.1 extends beyond the determination of BNM. There are still many bills for detailed assessment that include recoverable additional liabilities. We suspect that in calculating whether the costs exceed the £75,000 limit for provisional assessment under CPR 47.15, most practitioners and courts have been including the additional liabilities. However, as the limit is expressly in respect of costs claimed, and as additional liabilities are not 'costs', then they should be excluded from the calculation. If this is correct, then, for the run-off period of recoverable additional liabilities, it may be that more cases fall within the provisional assessment regime than was previously thought.

PROPORTIONALITY AND BUDGETED COSTS

[14.8]

The prospect of a proportionality cross-check at the conclusion of an assessment of costs, ought to be enough to persuade parties to sign up willingly to prospective costs management! The combination of Sir Rupert Jackson's comments and the rule itself suggest that the court will undertake an assessment of the non-budgeted costs on a reasonableness test, stand back at the end and, if the overall costs are not proportionate (budgeted plus non-budgeted), reduce the overall amount to the figure that the court determines to be proportionate by application of the CPR 44.3(5) factors. The irreducible minimum will be the budgeted costs as, of course, unless there is a 'good reason' to depart from the budget, CPR 3.18 protects the budgeted costs (see analysis in Chapter 15).

We say that the provisions of CPR 3.18 protect the budgeted costs because they have already been subjected to a proportionality (and indeed reasonableness) analysis under CPR PD 3E, para 12 when the budget was set. However, it may be that this certainty has to be tempered slightly as a result of comments made by Davis LJ in giving judgment (with which the MR and Black LJ agreed) in *Harrison* (above). At para 52, he commented:

> 'I add that where, as here, a costs judge on detailed assessment will be assessing incurred costs in the usual way and also will be considering budgeted costs (and not departing from such budgeted costs in the absence of "good reason") the costs judge ordinarily will still, as I see it, ultimately have to look at matters in the round and consider whether the resulting aggregate figure is proportionate having regard to CPR 44.3(2)(a) and (5) . . . '

Some have taken the comments in para 52 to suggest that under CPR 44.3(2)(a), the court may, at the end of the assessment, determine an overall proportionality figure below the budgeted costs (see for example *Reynolds v One Stop Stores Ltd* (21 September 2018, unreported, CC). This argument relies on there being no qualification in para 52 limiting any reduction to the sum of the budgeted costs, as opposed to a positive affirmation that CPR 44.3(2)(a) permits the court to revisit the proportionality of budgeted costs. The contrary view is supported by a reading of the judgment as a whole. It is patently apparent that the court was astute to the fact that budgeted costs have already been subjected to a determination of proportionality – see paras 31–33, in particular the comment at para 32 that:

> 'In this regard, it is also in my view particularly important overall to bear in mind that a judge who is being asked to approve a budget at a costs management hearing must take into account, in assessing each budgeted phase, considerations both of reasonableness and of proportionality.'

We remain firmly of the view that revisiting reasonableness and proportionality of budgeted costs on assessment will be extremely rare and can only be done within an argument that there is 'good reason' to depart from the budget – eg where decisions on the reasonableness and proportionality of a claimant's costs have been made by the costs managing judge on the basis of a high value claim that transpires to have been exaggerated. In other words, the application of CPR 44.3(2)(a) on the assessed non-budgeted costs and the budgeted costs cannot, in the absence of 'good reason', result in a lower figure than the total of the budgeted costs. Whether anyone has the appetite to try to take this argument back to the Court of Appeal remains to be seen.

In any event the wording of CPR 44.3(2)(a) has consequences that extend far further than merely to an assessment of costs. It is simply here that it becomes glaringly apparent that proportionality trumps necessity. It is the practical consequences of this provision at a far earlier stage on case and costs management that support the argument of those who believe justice has been compromised.

PROPORTIONALITY AND JUSTICE

[14.9]

The concerns expressed by the legal community, which became more vocal as 1 April 2013 approached, and which still have far from subsided, have been referred to above – cut price justice not being justice at all, unpredictability as one court may take a different view of proportionality from another (even one sitting in the court/room next door) and a victory of process over outcome. Seven and a half years on the debate about 'justice' and the pleas for more guidance on the practical application of proportionality have not disappeared. Some have taken the approach to proportionality in the frequently cited case of *Kazakhstan Kagazy v Zhunus* [2015] EWHC 404 (Comm) as watering down the primacy of proportionality. In that case the court purported to define proportionality as ' . . . the lowest amount (of costs) which it (a party) could reasonably have been expected to spend in order to have its case conducted and presented proficiently, having regard to all the circumstances'. However, this definition should be treated with extreme caution as it sits unhappily with CPR 44.3(2)(a), which is not mentioned in the judgment, and which unequivocally states that costs may be disproportionate even if they were reasonably or necessarily incurred. It should also be remembered that the decision was one about the amount of a payment on account of costs and was not an assessment of costs.

Even the staunchest supporters of the reforms accept that in some cases proportionate costs management (which inevitably involves robust case management) will result in less just outcomes than had there been a lesser form of costs control. The analysis set out in Chapter 15 – Prospective Costs Control – Costs and Case Management below, of how directions may have to be tailored out of the cloth available, renders this an inevitability.

However, those supporters are keen to stress that in the majority of cases there will be no discernible difference in outcome. In the large part the 2013 reforms were aimed to take waste out of the justice system. To target statements to essential material by limiting the number of witnesses and the length of their statements, to limit disclosure to fewer, key documents (that this is so is confirmed by the acceptance that disclosure has become unmanageable and disproportionate in its current guise, with a two-year pilot introducing reduced disclosure obligations having commenced on 1 January 2019 in the Business and Property Courts), to avoid waste of valuable resources by ensuring that parties comply with court orders and rules and to reduce the length of the trial, will avoid prolix and unfocused hearings where the judge is referred to only a few pages of the plethora of paper paginated in many lever arch files and hears a number of witnesses saying the same thing and will ensure that cases are pursued efficiently or run the risk of being struck out.

Those advocates of proportionality of process advance the case that without change justice had become the right of all, but the privilege of only the few – those with sufficient financial resources or those under a funding scheme that gave them total immunity from risk (and therefore no interest in controlling cost). This view was adopted by Briggs LJ at para 5.23 of his December 2015 Civil Courts Structure Review: Interim Report and repeated by Sir Rupert Jackson at para 1.9 of Chapter 1 of his July 2017 Review of Civil Litigation Costs: Supplemental Report Fixed Recoverable Costs. As such, an imperfect system that re-opens the court doors to a greater number, results in better justice than where many cannot afford the entry fee to ring the doorbell, which is no system at all. At a time when 'exorbitant' and 'very disturbing costs' have troubled even the Supreme Court in the context of Human Rights, this argument carries weight (see *Coventry v Lawrence* [2015] UKSC 50).

Whatever the force of the competing views, the proportionality reforms have been in place for almost seven years. Proportionality, in its new guise, is centre stage and practitioners and judges have moved from theory to practice. The final word goes to Jacob LJ in *Nichia Corpn v Argos Ltd* [2007] EWCA Civ 741, who, perhaps, best expresses the inevitable compromise necessary:

> ' "Perfect justice" in one sense involves a tribunal examining every conceivable aspect of a dispute . . . No stone, however small, should remain unturned . . . But a system which sought . . . "perfect justice" in every case would actually defeat justice. The cost and time involved would make it impossible to decide all but the most vastly funded cases. The cost of nearly every case would be greater than what it is about. Life is too short to investigate everything in that way. So a compromise is made: one makes do with a lesser procedure even though it may

result in the justice being rougher. Putting it another way, better justice is achieved by risking a little bit of injustice.'

CHAPTER 15

PROSPECTIVE COSTS CONTROL – COSTS AND CASE MANAGEMENT

INTRODUCTION TO PROSPECTIVE COSTS CONTROL – COSTS AND CASE MANAGEMENT

[15.1]

Sir Rupert Jackson's Final Report identified that, in conjunction with the requirement for the court to case manage proceedings, there was also need for costs management to become part of that process. His view was that case and costs management are inextricably linked – that no claim should be case managed without consideration of the costs implications of any given step in those proceedings. This view became central to the costs management scheme introduced in CPR Part 3. Indeed CPR 3.12(2) could not make this any clearer:

> 'The purpose of costs management is that the court should manage both the steps to be taken and the costs to be incurred by the parties to any proceedings so as to further the overriding objective.'

However, the link between the two exists even if we take a broader view of costs management than that within the formal scheme at CPR 3.12–CPR 3.18. This is because the overriding objective makes it plain that proportionality of costs lies at the heart of every case – whatever track it may be on and in whatever division it may be issued. This is reinforced in multi-track cases by CPR 3.17 which leaves no room for doubt that even in non-budgeted cases every case management decision comes with a price tag.

WHAT IS COSTS MANAGEMENT?

[15.2]

A costs management order ('CMO') enables the court to control the parties' expenditure throughout the proceedings. Strictly this is qualified to the extent that all that the court does by a CMO is set the amount that, in the absence of a 'good reason' to depart from the prescribed budget, will be recoverable between the parties on an assessment on the standard basis in respect of the budgeted costs of those phases budgeted (an oddity is that whilst the court may now make a costs management order in respect of any agreed incurred costs, CPR 3.18 only prescribes the effect of a costs management order in respect of budgeted costs. The rules do not make any provision for the effect of a costs management order made under CPR 3.15(2)(c) – see **[15.11]** below). In any event, as we shall see when looking at some specific examples of routine case management decisions, the inextricable tie between case and costs management means that the effect of a CMO may trespass into, and influence, solicitor and client costs. This is because the requirement for the parties to provide information as to their estimated costs, as well as costs already incurred, will enable the court to consider the estimates alongside the directions to be given for the case management of the proceedings. Where a court considers the estimated costs to be disproportionate, taking account of the incurred costs, it will tailor the directions to bring the costs down to a reasonable and proportionate level; this is particularly likely to affect those phases of the litigation where costs have traditionally been disproportionate such as disclosure, experts' reports and trial.

CMOs may take one of the following three forms:

- A record of the extent to which budgeted costs (to be incurred costs) are agreed between the parties (CPR 3.15(2)(a)) – it is clear from the reference to the extent of any agreement, that a party may agree some, but not all, phases of another party's budget.
- Where no agreement has been reached a record of the court's approval of budgeted costs (to be incurred costs) after the court has made appropriate revisions (CPR 3.15(2)(b)). Where some phases are agreed and others not, then the CMO will be a mix of recording agreement and approval.
- A record of the extent, if any, to which incurred costs are agreed (CPR 3.15(2)(c)).

As is clear from the third type of CMO above, the court may only costs manage incurred costs if there is agreement about these. In the absence of any agreement, both CPR 3.12(2) and CPR 3.15(1) are clear that the court may only manage costs 'to be incurred' (these are defined as 'the budgeted costs'). When agreeing costs for the first costs management order, parties must be clear whether that agreement extends to incurred costs, enabling an order under CPR 3.15(2)(c) to be made.

The court may also set a timetable, give directions for future reviews of budgets or make provision for parties to notify it of any agreed changes to the budget. In addition, the court may consider holding further costs management conferences (eg where it only budgets to a certain stage in the proceedings).

THE COSTS MANAGEMENT EXPERIENCE TO DATE

[15.3]

Although costs management has now been part of the civil litigation landscape for almost eight years (if one does not include the two limited pilot schemes) its application has been the subject of perceived inconsistency; it has already been subject to a number of procedural revisions and this year has proved no exception with a significant amendment to the provisions for variation of budgets and the elevation of certain provisions from the accompanying Practice Direction (PD 3E) to the rules themselves. This combination of rule change and some welcome clarification by the Court of Appeal has provided necessary (but, dare we say it, fairly obvious) certainty in most areas of contention. The looming presence of extensions to the fixed recoverable costs schemes also has seen a warming of attitudes to the costs management regime, in part because many of those who previously 'protested too much' about costs management are less attracted to the offered alternative. Perhaps

Sir Rupert Jackson's conclusion in his May 2015 'Confronting Costs Management' lecture that 'I predict that within ten years costs management will be accepted as an entirely normal discipline and people will wonder what all the fuss was about' was more prescient that many perceived it to be at the time. Amongst other matters raised in that lecture, Sir Rupert identified the 'iterative process' to budget setting, which we have advocated in previous editions and which is set out in **[15.33]** below and which we believe remains the most efficient and effective form of budgeting even after the rule and PD revisions of this year.

Sir Rupert's Supplemental Report on Fixed Recoverable Costs, published at the end of July 2017, proposed a more limited extension to the existing fixed costs schemes than had been predicted at the outset of the review. The Ministry of Justice consultation on implementation has long closed and yet the outcome is still awaited. Even if the recommendations are implemented, it is clear that, for the moment anyway, costs management remains a large part of daily multi-track life.

In addition, as we anticipated in previous editions and as indicated above, higher court authorities, clarifying certain areas of contention have emerged, although it is right to acknowledge that they also reveal some differing practices (see for example below at **[15.35]**).

Accordingly, almost eight years in, the introduction period for costs management is definitely over. The discipline is well-established. Case law and procedural revisions have smoothed, and continue to polish, some of the rougher edges. This is not to say that there are no remaining areas of uncertainty. However, those identified are becoming fewer and, as is apparent from the further CPR amendments in the last year, the Civil Procedure Rules Committee ('CPRC') is prepared to revisit the provisions to provide clarity. We hope that there will be some further intervention (whether by the CPRC or by the higher courts) to provide assistance on the effect on budgets where claims resolve mid-phase/s. Beyond that, we anticipate only case specific decisions about proportionality and 'good reason' to depart.

THE SCOPE OF THE COSTS MANAGEMENT REGIME UNDER CPR 3.12–CPR 3.18 AND CPR PD 3E

[15.4]

The formal costs management scheme applies to most multi-track cases commenced on or after 1 April 2013. There have been some revisions to the provisions, but the upshot is that the current rule found at CPR 3.12 provides that the costs management regime applies to all multi-track Part 7 claims except those:

- where the claim commenced after 21 April 2014 and the amount of money claimed on the claim form is £10m or more;
- where the claim commenced after 21 April 2014 and which are monetary claims which are not quantified (at all or in part), but where the claim form contains a statement of value of £10m or more;
- where in proceedings commenced after 6 April 2016 a claim is made by or on behalf of a child (and this exemption continues upon a child reaching majority unless the court otherwise orders);

- subject to fixed or scale costs regimes;
- where the court itself orders that costs budgeting will not apply. (There remains no assistance within the rules as to why the court might make such an order – although CPR 3.15(2) provides guidance on the limited circumstances in which the court may decide not to costs manage once budgets have been filed – and therefore it will be interesting to see the extent to which such orders are made.) There is a school of thought that costs management may be unnecessary for defendants in those claims subject to the QOCS provisions. Why put the defendant to the expenditure of budget production when, in the majority of cases, the maximum recovery will be limited to the level of damages (excluding any consideration of costs set off under CPR 44.12 – see CHAPTER **22** at **[22.34]**)? There are many answers. Two obvious ones are that if there is a valid offer under CPR Part 36 in a high value case the defendant might still be able to recover all the costs by way of set off (under CPR 44.14). Another is that the court needs the costs information to fulfil its function to case manage proportionately. Sir Rupert Jackson considered this in his May 2015 lecture and concluded that defendants' costs in QOCS cases should be budgeted and this appears to be the view of the CPRC.

In addition, CPR PD 3E, para 1 provides that the court will ordinarily disapply the costs management regime in cases where the claimant has a limited or severely impaired life expectation (five years or less remaining).

However, there is a sting in the tail as CPR 3.12(1A) permits the court to apply the costs management provisions to any other proceedings. This was considered in *CIP Properties (AIPT) Ltd v Galliford Try Infrastructure Ltd* [2014] EWHC 3546 (TCC), where the court was unequivocal that it has an unfettered discretion to bring claims within the costs management regime. The court should weigh up all the particular circumstances of the claim in exercising that discretion. In *Simpkin v The Berkeley Group Holdings plc* [2016] EWHC 1619 (QB) the court exercised its discretion to costs manage a claim that might have a value of over £10m because there was an enormous disparity of resource between the parties and costs management might level the playing field and would certainly inform the claimant and any funders of the extent of the potential costs liability.

CPR PD 3E provides more guidance on other types of case that may be particularly appropriate for costs management at CPR PD 3E, para 2. Some courts are using this judicial 'opt in' provision in personal injury claims where it is not clear at the first CCMC whether the claim will be in the multi-track and so allocation does not take place (because the diagnosis and prognosis remains unclear) or where the value of the claim for proportionality consideration purposes is not clear (and so any budgeting would be on an entirely speculative view of 'sums in issue' under CPR 44.3(5)(a)), where further medical evidence is required to determine these issues, but where the court wishes to budget that step. The approach adopted seems to be to apply CPR 3.12(1A) and budget the immediate expert evidence steps to be taken and the restored allocation hearing/CCMC that will follow. To ensure that further costs are not incurred pending the ultimate allocation, no further steps are permitted pending the restored hearing. This way the court retains as much control as possible over the future expenditure.

THE PROCEDURAL CODE

Filing and service of the budget

[15.5]

Apart from litigants in person who are excluded from the requirement to prepare costs budgets (CPR 3.13(6)), all parties in cases falling within the regime must file and exchange budgets. In general terms where the value of the claim stated on the claim form is less than £50,000 these should be filed and served with the directions questionnaire. In all other claims the budgets must be filed and exchanged not less than 21 days before the first case management conference. In respect of those cases where the court exercises its power under CPR 3.12(1A), either of its own initiative or on the application of a party, to order budgets in cases not otherwise within the scheme, the court will make provision for when these are to be filed and exchanged.

The consequence of not filing and serving the budget

[15.6]

The timing of the trigger for filing and exchange of costs budgets is not a matter of idle academic speculation. Failure to comply with the rules has a draconian consequence. CPR 3.14 provides that a party failing to file the budget in accordance with the rule will be treated as though having filed a budget limited to court fees only! Whilst the court has the discretion to order otherwise, it is clear that CPR 3.14 is a sanction and so CPR 3.9 is engaged. Although each case is fact-specific, parties may well find that the court is unsympathetic. In the case of *Mitchell v News Group Newspapers Ltd* [2013] EWHC 2179 (QB), the court limited the claimant's budget to court fees only as the claimant had failed to file and serve his costs budget in accordance with the Defamation Pilot at CPR PD 51D. The master subsequently also refused relief from this sanction (*Mitchell v News Group Newspapers Ltd* [2013] EWHC 2355 (QB)). The Court of Appeal famously or infamously (depending upon your point of view) dismissed the appeal (*Mitchell v News Group Newspapers Ltd* [2013] EWCA Civ 1537). While the Court of Appeal revisited 'triviality' in *Denton v T H White Ltd* [2014] EWCA Civ 906 (see below at [15.30]), the reality is that the case specific decision in Mitchell stands and those relying on a less robust approach do so at their peril. That this is so was confirmed by the Court of Appeal in *Jamadar v Bradford Teaching Hospitals NHS Foundation Trust* [2016] EWCA Civ 1001. *Lakhani v Ibrahim Sheikh Abadullah Mahmub* [2017] EWHC 1713 (Ch) is a salutary reminder that, depending upon context, even being only a day late with a budget may not lead to relief being granted. It is a brave representative who is prepared to rely upon the uncertainty of a court exercise of discretion. Even in the last year, by way of example, in *Heathfield International LLC v Axiom Stone (London) Ltd* [2020] EWHC 1075 (Ch), one court refused to disapply the sanction in CPR 3.14 when a budget was six days late and another, in *Manchester Shipping Ltd v Balfour Shipping Ltd* [2020] EWHC 164 (Comm) granted relief where a budget was 13 days late. Of course, the simple solution is to comply with the requirements for filing and exchanging budgets in the first place. If that is not done, then, as was made abundantly plain in *BMCE Bank v Phoenix Commodities* [2018] EWHC 3380 (Comm), a prompt application for relief from the sanction of CPR 3.14 is essential.

Curiously the failure to exchange budgets under CPR 3.13 merits no mention in the rules – even where one party has indicated it is ready to do so and the failure to exchange falls expressly at the door of another party.

CPR 36 offers a partial salvation at CPR 36.23. This provides that in certain limited circumstances a party restricted to future court fees as a result of breach of CPR 3.13 may still recover 50% of costs assessed without reference to the budget limitation imposed by CPR 3.14. However, see [**15.12**] below.

The combined effect of CPR 3.14 and CPR 36.23 in this context was considered in *Ali v Channel 5 Broadcast Ltd* [2018] EWHC 840 (Ch), [2018] 2 Costs LR 373, in which the court had to decide whether the limitation of recovery to 50% applies to all recoverable costs after the date of breach of CPR 3.13 or only of those costs after the costs management hearing. The court concluded that once there was a breach of CPR 3.14 then the restriction applies to all recoverable costs after the breach. This decision has potential implications beyond the discrete provision of CPR 36.23. If it is the fact of breach itself and not when the effect of the sanction imposed for the breach bites, namely the time when the court costs manages based on a restricted budget, then, by extension, arguably, even the date of the breach is irrelevant, as CPR 3.14 refers to the entire budget (both incurred and estimated costs) being treated as containing applicable court fees only. This would mean that all incurred costs are also subject to the sanction. This is a challenging interpretation as the budget is filed to enable the court to manage costs 'to be incurred' and the effect of a costs management order under CPR 3.18 only applies to costs so managed under CPR 3.15(2)(a) and (b). It seems curious that under a provision stated in CPR 3.12 to have as its purpose the management of 'costs to be incurred', the court cannot make a costs management order (other than by recording an agreement) in respect of incurred costs, but can, as part of the costs management provisions, retrospectively restrict their recovery. It was said in the case that it would undermine the purpose of CPR 3.14 if it had no effect on costs between the date of breach and the date of costs management. Those having to manage a case where the effect is only on the budgeted costs may consider that sanction alone sufficiently underpins CPR 3.14.

Approval/agreement of the budget and the costs management order

[15.7]

The effect of CPR 3.15(2) is that costs management will take place in the vast majority of those cases where a budget has been filed and exchanged. Where costs budgets have been filed and exchanged the court 'will' make a costs management order unless it is satisfied that the litigation can be justly conducted at proportionate cost in accordance with the overriding objective. This is a clear fetter on the court's discretion not to costs manage.

Previously we have said that it is hard to think of many (any) cases where the exception should apply. Experience suggests that there is a situation where the court may wish not to make a costs management order. This is where the parties agree budgets that the court regards as disproportionate, but those budgets are predicated on proportionate directions (and so the court cannot use the imposition of proportionate directions to revisit the budgets). While there is a compelling argument that even a costs management order recording an agreed budget on this basis is better than leaving costs at large, another approach, and one that one of us has adopted, is to record that the court is not making a costs management order because, whilst it accepts the directions are proportionate, the sums agreed by way of budgets are not, record what the court thinks is the proportionate overall sum and reserve any subsequent 'between the parties' assessment to the case managing judge (ie to the one making these recitals) and recite a reminder to the parties of the terms of CPR 44.3(2)(a) – namely that proportionality trumps reasonableness. The clear message is that the court does not want to be limited to the 'incurred costs' only at a subsequent assessment (assuming that these, too, are not agreed), so that, instead, the CPR 44.3(2)(a) proportionality cross check applies to all costs. The hope is that this will compel the legal representatives to discuss with the clients the implications so that those clients can make an informed decision about proceeding, knowing that the court is likely to disallow significant expenditure later. This is not ideal, but from a client perspective surely is still better than either a costs management order recording the agreement of 'to be incurred' costs at a disproportionate level or only finding out at the end that the court has allowed the recovery of a fraction of the costs by the application of CPR 44.3(2)(a), leaving the client with an unexpected shortfall. Of course, this does require the case managing judge to be the one undertaking the assessment and so is primarily an approach for the District Bench.

If the court has made a costs management order, whether by recording the agreed costs or, if not agreed, by recording the court's approval after making appropriate revisions, each party must re-file and re-serve the budget in the form approved annexed to the order approving it or recording the agreement (CPR 3.15(7)). For reasons considered later concerning clarity about what work has been included within an agreed or approved budget, our view is that if the directions accompanying the budget revisions do not make clear what assumptions the claim proceeds under, then the obligation to file the amended budget in the form approved extends to revising the assumptions section. Even if there is no such obligation a prudent party may wish to do this to avoid later uncertainty – see **Completing Precedent H** below. In most cases, this should be unnecessary as the assumptions behind the approved budget ought to be clear from the case management directions that have been ordered and these documents should be viewed together.

An increasing number of courts are budgeting by use of the Precedent H in electronic version. The judge budgets by using the totals column for each phase budgeted on page one of the budget identifying those phases budgeted (eg by putting them in bold typeface), with the budgeted sum being the total sum per phase budgeted less the incurred sum per phase budgeted. This has the advantage that the Precedent H automatically recalculates and the court and the parties can be clear as to what has been budgeted at the hearing. If budgeting is undertaken in this fashion, then a quick run through at the end of the hearing enables everyone to be able to agree what has been done and obviates the need for the parties to recalculate and refile the final budget as the court can print off the page one of each party's budget and attach it to the case management order which includes a costs management order as follows:

> 'The court makes a costs management order in respect of the costs of [insert those parties in respect of whose budgets a costs management order has been made]. The budgeted sum is as per the attached page 1 of the Precedents H, with the budgeted

> phases being those where the total is in **bold** typeface and the budgeted sum for those phases being the total sum for the phase less the incurred sum for the phase.'

This should be accompanied by a specific order relieving the parties of the obligation to comply with CPR 3.15(7). Adopting this approach has a number of benefits, namely it:

- provides absolute clarity of outcome (there is no scope for disagreement after the hearing as to what was budgeted);
- enables the court and the parties to see the total expenditure (both budgeted and non-budgeted) so that they can step back and determine if that is proportionate or if directions and budgets need to be revisited in pursuit of overall proportionality;
- reduces the amount of work after the hearing and so is a proportionate exercise;
- enables any judge subsequently dealing with the file to have one directions order that also neatly sets out which phases have been budgeted and in what amount (reducing the risks if judicial continuity is not feasible); and
- enables an easy understanding of the assumptions upon which the court has budgeted as the budget is attached to the directions given.

There is nothing to prevent the court adopting this approach even when budgeting manually, provided amendments are done legibly and a method of identifying the budgeted phases is readily apparent. An example of such an order would be:

> 'The court makes a costs management order in respect of the costs of [insert those parties in respect of whose budgets a costs management order has been made]. The budgeted sum is as per the attached page 1 of the Precedents H, with the budgeted phases being those where the total is marked with an * and the budgeted sum for those phases being the total sum for the phase less the incurred sum for the phase.'

The wording of either form of order will require amendment where, under CPR 3.15(2)(c), there is some agreement of incurred costs. A composite order that can be used by deletion of those parts inappropriate is:

> 'The court has made costs management orders as per the attached pages 1 of the parties' precedents H as follows:
>
> i) in respect of budgeted costs (under CPR 3.15(2)(a) and (b) The phases budgeted by court approval are those where the figure in the total column is in bold typeface (if doing electronically)/marked with an * (if doing manually) The budgeted costs for each such phase, whether by approval or agreement, are the total less the incurred costs for that phase
>
> ii) In respect of incurred costs (under CPR 3.15(2)(c) The court records agreement of the incurred costs in those phases where the title of the phase on the left hand side of page 1 is followed by +++ (whether budgeting electronically or manually).'

If costs management is not done in this way, then, for the sake of certainty of outcome, it is imperative that the parties comply with CPR 3.15(7). This was highlighted in *Broom v Archer* (28 March 2018, unreported) QBD (TCC), in which the parties had failed to comply with this provision and so failed to note a mathematical error, rectification of which necessitated a hearing. Orders that simply record a total for the budgets of each party are unhelpful to any judges charged with either an application to vary or an assessment of the costs as they do not readily enable identification of the phases budgeted, nor the amount budgeted for those phases.

Retrospection and revision of the budget

[15.8]

It is in respect of this topic that the amendments to CPR 3 Section II and PD 3E made under the Civil Procedure (Amendment No 3) Rules 2020 (SI 2020/747) have introduced real change. Both CPR 3.12 and CPR 3.15 previously referred to budgeting costs 'to be incurred', suggesting that there could be no retrospective budgeting. As a result, we have previously suggested that this meant that there could be:

- No costs budgeting of the case/costs management conference because it would, by definition, have started if the court is case and costs managing and further preparation for the hearing will have taken place after the filing of the budget. Accordingly, it is not a 'to be incurred' cost. However, anecdotally we had understood that some courts were costs managing the CMC, other than by agreement of the phase costs. An amendment to CPR PD 3E, para 7.4, from 1 October 2019 in CPR Update 109, seemed to be aimed at clarifying the first point, making it clear that the court could not costs manage the CMC, other than under CPR 3.15(2)(c). This remains the position under the amended CPR as CPR 3.17(3) provides that:

  > 'Subject to rule 3.15A, the court –
  >
  > (a) may not approve costs incurred before the date of any costs management hearing ...'

  This brings us neatly to a consideration of the new CPR 3.15A on variation of budget.
- No retrospective element to variation of any budget. This was notwithstanding that in *Sharp v Blank* [2017] EWHC 3390 (Ch), Chief Master Marsh concluded that 'future' in this context in the then CPR PD 3E, para 7.6 meant after the last approved or agreed budget and, as such, in respect of variation to a budget the court could costs manage by approval both incurred and 'to be incurred' costs in respect of the development. We shall not trouble with the arguments we advanced against this interpretation of the then wording of the provisions as the CPRC has spoken in a new language, removing scope for debate and permitting some retrospection. This is in the new CPR 3.15A.

Under this new provision, parties must promptly upon what they perceive as a significant development necessitating variation of a budget, submit a revision to the other party/ies and the court. This must be in Form T (see CPR PD 3E, para 3(b)), which contains a certificate that, if the variation is upwards, the additional costs were not included in any previous budgeted costs or permitted variation. The submission to the court must be accompanied by a copy of the last approved or agreed budget and an explanation of the points of difference if the variation has not been agreed.

On receipt, the court may either approve, vary or disallow the proposed variations, considering any significant developments which have occurred since the last approval or agreement of the budget or may list a further costs management conference (CPR 3.15A(5)).

The real change is at CPR 3.15A(6), which permits the court, as part of the process, to vary the budget for costs relating to that variation that have been incurred before the order for variation, but after the costs management order. No guidance is given on this, but we must assume that the extent of the retrospective variation will be limited by the court's interpretation of when the obligation to serve and submit details of the obligation promptly arose. In other words, tardiness in following the procedure may limit the extent to which the court will permit retrospective variation.

This provision also raises the interesting issues of whether the court simply permits a total variation to the budget for the particular phase under consideration, which accords with the costs management process under CPR 3.15(8) or whether it has to identify those costs of the variation to which retrospection applies and those that are to be incurred. Either way, if the court accepts that there is a significant development that merits variation, but budgets that variation at less than is sought on the basis of reasonableness and proportionality, it seems that the court may, in effect, be undertaking some form of very broad brush, retrospective assessment.

Our residual concern with the procedural endorsement of retrospection is that it reduces the ability of the parties to make informed decisions based on their known costs exposure (for 'costs between the parties' and/or for any unrecovered 'solicitor/client' costs). In allowing retrospective revision to a budget, the rules deprive the other party/ies of the opportunity of deciding whether to maintain the claim or the defence of it before those particular costs are incurred and become subject to the recovery provisions of CPR 3.18. That said, the jurisdiction of the court to deal with all the costs of significant development under CPR 3.15A sits more happily with its obligation under CPR 3.15(3) to control the parties budgets in respect of recoverable costs after a costs management order has been made, than if it was not able to deal with the incurred element of the variation costs.

The revised procedure, which necessarily involves the court under CPR 3.15A(5), removes previous concerns that an approved budget may be varied by agreement without the court knowing, which always sat unhappily with the obligation of the court under CPR 3.15(3).

It is worth making the point that CPR 3.15A(1) maintains the previous mandatory requirement to vary downwards, as well as upwards, if a significant development so requires. This is not surprising as there may be significant developments in the litigation that narrow issues (for example the discontinuance of part of the claim). There is a clear obligation on parties to recognise this and reduce the set budget.

There is no strict definition of 'significant development'. Decisions on whether something constitutes a 'significant development' in the litigation, warranting revision, are inevitably case specific. What seems clear from the emerging authorities is, unsurprisingly, if the alleged development should always have been seen as part and parcel of a case or compliance with a specific direction, then no variation will be permitted (see, for example both *Chalfont St Peter Parish Council v Holy Sisters Trustees Inc* unreported 29 January 2019 (QBD) and *Churchill v Boot* [2016] EWHC 1322 (QB)). Endorsing the case specific nature of any decision, in *Churchill v Boot*, the court concluded that whilst it did not do so in that case, an adjournment of a trial could amount to a significant development.

The court has confirmed, again unsurprisingly, that if there is a significant development leading to increased costs in a claim where one party has fallen foul of CPR 3.14 and has had a budget set at future costs only, that party will be able to seek an upward variation for the additional work linked to the significant variation (see *Asgar v Bhatti* [2017] EWHC 1702 (QB)).

Costs outside the scope of the budget

[15.9]

CPR 3.17(4), states that if there are interim applications during the claim that were not provided for in the budget, then any costs that arise from them are treated as additional to the budget. In other words, the court should assess what order for costs to make on any such applications and then, as appropriate, undertake a summary assessment of those costs in the usual way. A classic example would be in respect of an application to enforce compliance with the directions timetable. Obviously, some applications may have been sufficiently likely at the time of approving the budget that they fall within already allowed contingent costs.

The costs of costs management

[15.10]

Inevitably the costs management process adds an additional expense to litigation. Rather than allow for protracted argument about how much, the rules prescribe the sums that will be recoverable. There was some uncertainty in respect of the relevant provision previously at CPR PD 3E, para 7.2. Amendments were made to provide clarity in November 2017. The current version of the provision is found at CPR 3.15(5) as follows:

> '(5) Save in exceptional circumstances –
> (a) the recoverable costs of initially completing Precedent H (the form to be used for a costs budget) shall not exceed the higher of –
> (i) £1,000; or
> (ii) 1% of the total of the incurred costs (as agreed or allowed on assessment) and the budgeted costs (agreed or approved); and
> (b) all other recoverable costs of the budgeting and costs management process shall not exceed 2% of the total of the incurred costs (as agreed or allowed on assessment) and the budgeted (agreed or approved) costs.'

It follows from this that the percentages will apply to incurred costs (whether agreed or not) as well as to the budgeted costs. As a result of the inclusion of the incurred costs in the calculation, expect the court to remind parties that:

- the mechanisms in CPR 3.15(5) only provide caps;
- it is inappropriate for the final fees to be calculated until after any subsequent agreement or assessment of the incurred costs (which explains why CPR PD 3E, para 8 corrects the folly of its predecessor provision in Guidance Notes on Precedent H and states that 'The maximum figures permitted under rule 3.15(5) should be inserted once the costs budget has been approved by the court' (our emphasis). 'Maximum figures', because obviously, unless incurred costs have been agreed at this stage, the actual figure cannot be calculated at that stage.

CPR PD 3E, para 8 also provides that parties must not include time spent on budget preparation and associated materials in any phase of the budget, as it is a freestanding amount to be calculated separately after the budget has been set (see also the table in CPR PD 3E, para 10 in the CMC phase). This is obvious as otherwise there would be an element of double recovery. Accordingly, it is strange to note that the revised rule and PD maintains in the assumptions table the previous guidance requiring inclusion of work 'reviewing opponent's budget' and 'correspondence with opponent to agree . . . budgets' to be inserted in the CMC phase. Surely, this may see the same work that is remunerated under the mechanism in CPR 3.15(5)(b) also contained within the incurred CMC costs with a clear risk of double recovery at some stage. This was considered in *Woodburn v Thomas* [2017] EWHC B16 (Costs), in which the court concluded that a change in the rules to make it clear that no costs of preparing Precedent H or other recoverable costs of the budgeting and costs management process should appear in the phases, would provide the requisite clarity. This must be correct and a change to the guidance would be welcomed. However, it is pleasing to note that the previous reference to budgets in the PTR phase has been removed, recognising that budget revision only takes place under CPR 3.15A and not, as a matter of routine, at the PTR stage.

The relevance of the budget set to ultimate costs recovery under a standard basis assessment

[15.11]

The importance of the budget on recoverable costs on standard basis assessments is profound. Unless there is *'good reason'* to do so the court will not depart from the last approved or agreed budget – CPR 3.18. The rule always seemed clear and unequivocal to us. However, it took intervention from both the High Court and Court of Appeal to see off a concerted attack on this simplicity. Indeed, the attack was successful at first instance in *Merrix v Heart of England NHS Foundation Trust* [2016] EWHC B28 (QB), where the Regional Costs Judge concluded 'that the powers and discretion of a costs judge on detailed assessment are not fettered by the costs budgeting regime save that the budgeted figures should not be exceeded unless good reason can be shown'. In allowing the appeal (*Merrix v Heart of England NHS Foundation Trust* [2017] EWHC 346 (QB), [2017] 1 Costs LR 91), this conclusion was roundly rejected by Carr J who stated:

> 'The words are clear. The court will not – the words are mandatory - depart from the budget, absent good reason. On a detailed assessment on a standard basis, the costs judge is bound by the agreed or approved costs budget, unless there is good reason to depart from it. No distinction is made between the situation where it is claimed that budgeted figures are or are not to be exceeded. It is not possible to square the words of CPR 3.18 with the suggestion that the assessing costs judge may nevertheless depart from the budget without good reason and carry out a line by line assessment, merely using the budget as a guide or factor to be taken into account in the subsequent detailed assessment exercise.'

Recognising that her decision was unlikely to be the final word on the topic, and to avoid the piecemeal emergence of jurisprudence, Carr J suggested, presciently, that the matter was ripe for early consideration by the Court of Appeal '*raising, as it does, an important point of principle or practice*'. On cue, the final 'say' duly came from the Court of Appeal in *Harrison v University Hospitals Coventry and Warwickshire NHS Trust* [2017] EWCA Civ 792. That 'say' was that the wording of CPR 3.18 is unambiguous and means precisely what we had thought it to mean, namely any departure from the last approved or agreed budgeted costs, whether upwards or downwards, can only be on the basis of there being a 'good reason' to depart from the last approved or agreed budget. In other words, the court does not undertake a 'traditional' item by item assessment of the budgeted costs on detailed assessment. Instead, it assesses those costs as they were budgeted unless there is good reason to depart.

On a separate note, there have been suggestions that the comments at para 52 of *Harrison* identify another area of contention. Commenting on the proportionality cross check under CPR 44.3(2)(a), Davis LJ said:

> 'I add that where, as here, a costs judge on detailed assessment will be assessing incurred costs in the usual way and also will be considering budgeted costs (and not departing from such budgeted costs in the absence of 'good reason') the costs judge ordinarily will still, as I see it, ultimately have to look at matters in the round and consider whether the resulting aggregate figure is proportionate ...'

That CPR 44.3(2)(a) requires the court at the end of an assessment to step back and undertake a cross check of the sum assessed to ensure that the sum is proportionate (taking account of any individual proportionality decisions it may have chosen to take during the course of the assessment of reasonableness – see paras 88–93 of *West v Stockport NHS Foundation Trust: Demouilpied v Stockport NHS Foundation Trust* [2019] EWCA Civ 1220) is uncontroversial. However, where part of the assessed sum represents budgeted costs, then as those have already been subjected to a proportionality determination at the time of setting the budget (under CPR PD 3E, para 12), prevailing wisdom was that if the CPR 44.3(2)(a) cross check revealed the sum assessed to be disproportionate, the court could not reduce the costs to a level below that which the court had already concluded was proportionate at costs management (ie the total of the budgeted costs). Does paragraph 52 alter this and mean that under CPR 44.3(2)(a), the court may, at the end of the assessment, determine an overall proportionality figure below the budgeted costs? Our view is that it does not.

The argument that the court can re-determine the proportionality of budgeted costs relies on there being no qualification in para 52 limiting any reduction to the level of those costs, as opposed to a positive affirmation that CPR 44.3(2)(a) permits the court to revisit the proportionality of budgeted costs. The contrary (and our) view is supported by a reading of the judgment as a whole. It is patently apparent that the court was astute to the fact that budgeted costs have already been subjected to a determination of proportionality – see paras 31–33, and, in particular, the comment at para 32 that:

> 'In this regard, it is also in my view particularly important overall to bear in mind that a judge who is being asked to approve a budget at a costs management hearing must take into account, in assessing each budgeted phase, considerations both of reasonableness and of proportionality.'

As mentioned at **[15.2]** a residual curiosity, though, is that CPR 3.18 does not prescribe the effect at assessment of a costs management order under the recently introduced CPR 3.15(2)(c). This is because CPR 3.18(a) and (b) only refer to the receiving party's last approved or agreed budgeted costs. Budgeted costs are defined in CPR 3.15(1) as the costs to be incurred. In other words, agreed incurred costs are not budgeted costs. As such, they are not caught by

CPR 3.18(a) and (b). They are not caught by CPR 3.18(c) as they are not the subject of comment, but rather are the subject of a costs management order. If this is a deliberate omission from CPR 3.18, it seems an odd one, as it begs the questions what is the point of a costs management order under CPR 3.15(2)(c) and how are assessing judges meant to approach such orders at subsequent assessment?

(See **[15.13]** below for further consideration of 'good reason'.)

The relevance of the budget set to ultimate costs recovery under an indemnity basis assessment

[15.12]

An inevitable consequence of the wording of CPR 3.18 would appear to be that the budget has no part to play in an assessment ordered on the indemnity basis. CPR 3.18 is expressly limited to standard basis assessments for an entirely logical reason. Budgets are set by reference to reasonable and proportionate costs. CPR 44.3(3) makes it plain that costs on an indemnity basis are set by reference to reasonableness only. Proportionality is not mentioned. Accordingly, to extend the relevance of a budget to an indemnity basis assessment appears to import a proportionality test that is not relevant to the assessment.

We have always urged caution in placing any reliance on the case of *Elvanite Full Circle Ltd v AMEC Earth and Environmental (UK) Ltd* [2013] EWHC 1643 (TCC) which did suggest some link between indemnity costs and budgeted costs. Our caution was well placed. In *Denton v T H White Ltd* [2014] EWCA Civ 906 (see below at **[15.30]**), when dealing with potential costs penalties against those who play tactical games with the rules the Master of the Rolls said this:

> 'If the offending party ultimately loses, then its conduct may be a good reason to order it to pay indemnity costs. Such an order would free the winning party from the operation of CPR rule 3.18 in relation to its costs budget.'

If there remained any doubt, this was dispelled by the unequivocal view of the Court of Appeal in *Lejonvarn v Burgess* [2020] EWCA Civ 114. Giving the judgment, Coulson LJ referred to earlier decisions he had given at first instance and concluded that:

> 'In principle, the assessment of costs on an indemnity basis is not constrained by the approved costs budget, and to the extent that my obiter comments in *Elvanite or Bank of Ireland v Watts* suggested the contrary, they should be disregarded'

This is an unambiguous statement that an indemnity costs order severs the link between claimed costs and the budget set by the court on assessment.

In the light of the above, the reference to CPR 36.17(4)(b) in CPR 36.23 is a curious one, as the limitation in CPR 3.14 is only of relevance when the court is assessing costs on the standard basis under CPR 3.18 and by definition CPR 36.17(4)(b) relates to a party assessing under an indemnity costs order (see **[20.21]** for further consideration of this).

Good reason

[15.13]

What the courts consider to constitute a good reason remains to be seen, although authorities are starting to emerge. What is clear is that decisions will be entirely contextual based on the specific facts of a particular case and are likely to be rare. This was confirmed by the Court of Appeal in *Harrison v University Hospitals Coventry and Warwickshire NHS Trust* [2017] EWCA Civ 792 (above):

> 'As to what will constitute "good reason" in any given case I think it much better not to seek to proffer any further, necessarily generalised, guidance or examples. The matter can safely be left to the individual appraisal and evaluation of costs judges by reference to the circumstances of each individual case.' (Davis LJ, para 44).

However, the court was at pains to stress that 'good reason' was 'a significant fetter' on the court having an unrestricted discretion and cautioned judges not to adopt a lax or over-indulgent approach to the need to find 'good reason'.

Having predicted that instances of 'good reason' will be few and far between, some seem reasonably obvious, eg where not to depart from the budget would see a breach of the indemnity principle as the receiving party has not incurred the full amount of the budgeted costs for a specific phase. This was precisely the conclusion reached in *Barts Health NHS Trust v Salmon* unreported 17 January 2019 County Court at Central London HHJ Dight, with the court determining that:

> 'In my judgment, having regard to what was said by Lord Justice Davis in the Harrison judgment, the fact that the sum claimed is lower than the budgeted figure, because of the indemnity principle, is itself capable of being a good reason. Awarding the lower figure would be, in my judgment, a departure from the budget, which requires a good reason to be established: in this case, once that had been done it was open to the paying party to challenge the figure which was then being claimed by the receiving party, and they did not have to assert a further good reason to enable the court to do so.' (para 22)

The court went on to consider the consequences flowing from a finding of 'good reason', concluding, amongst other things, that:

- establishing a good reason means that the court may depart from the budget for a phase when assessing costs on the standard basis;
- once a good reason has been established, and the court is given the right to depart from the budget, it will assess the costs of that phase in the usual way, and, in that respect, it is left to the good sense and expertise of the costs judge to undertake that assessment in an appropriate and insofar as possible practical way, whether line-by-line or in a more broad-brush way;
- once the court has a right to depart from the budget, neither the receiving party nor the paying party needs to establish a further good reason within CPR 3.18 if they wish to persuade the costs judge to make a further or different adjustment to the bill for the phase in which 'good reason' has arisen. In other words, if the initial 'good reason' would lead to a specific reduction (eg in the example of a limit on recovery imposed by the indemnity principle, down to the level of the

costs actually incurred), that is not the end of the matter, as once a 'good reason' is established, the court is not constrained in the extent of the departure from the budgeted costs.

It remains to be seen the extent to, and the way in, which this decision on approach is adopted. Certainly, a line-by-line assessment in the conventional way, risks robbing the costs management regime of its costs saving impact on detailed assessments. We have also seen some suggestions that this may produce inconsistency between phases of the budget if the hourly rate is reduced for a phase after a finding of 'good reason'. We do not understand this, as budgeted costs are not set by an exercise of rate x time. Accordingly, there is no inconsistency because budgeted costs are not set by rate for any phase and so there is no rate within the budgeted costs with which any subsequent determination of rate after a finding of 'good reason' can conflict (see *Yirenki v Ministry of Justice* [2018] EWHC 3102 (QB) and **[15.34]** below and CPR 3.15(8) confirming that it is not the role of the court in undertaking costs management to fix or approve hourly rates). For our part, in the interests of proportionality, we would prefer the determination of amount after departure for 'good reason' to be undertaken in the same broad-brush, but principled way, as the setting of the budgeted costs – namely by the consideration of CPR 44.3(5), 44.4(3) and any wider circumstances resulting in a single figure for those costs no longer assessed in accordance with the last approved or agreed sum for that phase.

Whilst the decisions in *Capital for Enterprise Fund A LP v Bibby Financial Services Ltd* (18 November 2015, unreported), Ch and *Car Giant Ltd v The Mayor and Burgesses of the London Borough of Hammersmith* [2017] EWHC 464 (TCC) suggest that even if there is a jurisdiction, which the court doubted in the former case, but accepted in the latter case, for the trial judge to indicate for the benefit of the assessing judge that there should be a departure from the budget, the court should be slow to do so, we are unconvinced. There seem to be three compelling reasons why the trial judge should assist the assessing judge:

- The trial judge may have information that will not be available to the assessing judge unless it is expressly conveyed.
- Were the trial judge to undertake a summary assessment of the costs, then the information would form part of the assessment process. Why should that be different simply because the assessment is a detailed one by a different judge? If the information is relevant, then it is relevant regardless, otherwise there is immediately the risk of inconsistency of outcome.
- There is established authority that trial judges should assist assessing judges by providing relevant information and doing so on 'good reason' does no more than that (see *Northstar Systems Ltd v Fielding* [2006] EWCA Civ 1660 and *Drew v Whitbread* [2010] EWCA Civ 53 and Chapter 22 at **[22.24]**).

Anecdotally it appears that many parties are either overlooking the need to apply to vary the budget or are taking a view that they would prefer to rely upon 'good reason' later under CPR 3.18. If this is correct we can expect further guidance to emerge. However, for costs management to work to ensure costs are proportionate, and given that the court will have made a proportionality assessment under CPR 44.3(5) and 44.4(1) and a reasonableness determination under CPR 44.4(3) when first case and costs managing, and failure to comply with CPR 3.15A (which is mandatory – 'a party must revise') or simply spending more than budgeted where there is no significant development will undermine that, we expect the court to be robust when considering 'good reason'. Certainly in *Re Tradeouts Ltd* (9 March 2018, unreported), Ch D (Companies Court) the court reminded parties of the need to apply prospectively to increase costs budgets.

One of the aims of costs budgeting is to avoid costly and time consuming detailed assessments – a process more likely to be avoided if costs budgeting is used correctly, the court interprets CPR 3.18(b) as a sanction, the trial judge offers assistance to the assessing judge, and later argument on 'good reason' is discouraged.

Litigants in person

[15.14]

While litigants in person are excluded from the obligation to prepare costs budgets they must be provided with a copy of the budget of any represented party (CPR 3.13(6)). However, what of the situation where a party is unrepresented at the time of the first case management conference, but subsequently instructs solicitors? On the face of it the rules make no provision for that party's costs to be budgeted. It may be that in such a situation the other side may make an application for the court to fix a costs management hearing pursuant to CPR 3.16. Alternatively, it may be that some judges instigate internal practices that in any claims where notices of acting are filed where previously a party was unrepresented, the file is referred to the judge to consider convening a costs management conference. There is also an argument that this is a significant development in the litigation (for example representation may reduce the trial time estimate) and as such the newly represented party should follow the procedure in CPR 3.15A and submit a budget to the other party for agreement and in default of agreement apply to the court. Indeed, the budgeted party may take the view that representation alone represents a significant development and wish to vary the budget adopting the same procedure, which may put the matter before the court anyway. Our view is that the purpose of costs management is such that, whether there is a specific provision or not, the prudent solicitor in such a situation ought, at the very least, to try to agree a budget with the other party and, in default, apply to the court for a costs management hearing. As a slight aside, courts are likely to be wary of applications in the context of a change of solicitor, that do not constitute 'a significant development', but are no more than an attempt at budget repair (because the 2nd set of solicitors does not think the 1st set of solicitors has budgeted sufficient for a specific phase, although does not challenge the direction/assumption upon which the sum was set).

PRECEDENT H

[15.15]

The costs budget must be in the form of Precedent H, unless the court orders otherwise, although there is no requirement for a specific font or font size; the requirement is simply for an easily legible typeface in landscape format (see CPR PD 3E, para 4). The court may, in substantial cases, direct budgets limited initially to certain parts of the proceedings (CPR 3.13(4)). However, this is for the court to direct: it is not for the parties to make assumptions that this will happen. For example, if one party believes that there should be a preliminary trial on limitation they must still file a budget for the entire proceedings. If they wish not to do this, then, at the very least, before the date for filing and exchanging of budgets they should make an application to the court to extend the time for compliance and seek directions that budgets are limited to the preliminary trial costs. If they fail to make such an application and simply file and exchange a budget limited to the preliminary trial costs, then strictly they have not filed a budget in Precedent H that covers the whole proceedings and may find themselves caught by CPR 3.14 (see *Page v RGC Restaurants* [2018] EWHC 2688 (QB), in which the court concluded that the claimant, who had filed a materially incomplete budget – in that he had considered a 2nd case/costs management conference was necessary before listing and budgeting for a trial and so had not provided figures for all the phases – had failed to file a budget as required by the rules and so suffered the consequences of CPR 3.14).

The content of Precedent H still generates discussion. For our part we would prefer it to be simply the first page (but with the assumptions re-inserted on that page, rather than at the bottom of each phase). As CPR 3.15(8) requires the court to set budgets for phases as lump sums and not by determination of hourly rate, amount of time and specific disbursements, why is the rest of the form, that simply provides a breakdown to that detail, required? All this does is compel the parties, when preparing the budgets, to focus on the traditional way of approaching costs rather than considering the proportionate overall sums. The form of costs management that we suggest is undertaken solely by reference to the first page – and now the assumptions at the bottom of each phase page – (see **[15.7]** above) and immediately avoids the risk of the process becoming a prospective assessment of costs (which CPR PD 3E, para 12 expressly cautions against). Whilst changes in April 2016 mean that only page 1 needs to be completed where either the budgeted costs do not exceed £25,000 (see **[15.17]** below for consideration of what this means as this is something of a Catch-22 as budgeted costs are not ascertained until after the costs management conference) or the statement of value on the claim form is less than £50,000 (CPR PD 3E, para 4(b) – see **[15.17]** below) a more detailed consideration of Precedent H is required.

COMPLETING THE PRECEDENT H

[15.16]

Precedent H provides the other party/ies and the court with a detailed breakdown of both the costs a party has incurred to date and the costs that party estimates will be incurred from the time of the budget onwards. The form is divided in to a summary page, costs incurred and estimated for 10 specific phases of litigation, with an expert fee summary breakdown for the expert phase, and a contingency section. There is no longer a guide to completion of the Precedent H. This is incorporated into the amended CPR PD 3E in force from 1 October 2020 (see CPR PD 3E, para 6 and the table after para 10). While the table has been updated a number of times, there remain a few oddities (such as why pre-action settlement work is included within the pre-action phase despite any work incurred pre-action in relation to any other phase in the budget, such as ADR/Settlement, expressly being excluded from the pre-action phase). One remaining problem is where does one put interim applications that have been issued by the time the budget is prepared, so they are neither anticipated nor free standing applications under CPR 3.17(4)? Even if one chooses to put them as contingencies – as they are more likely than not to happen and do not fall anywhere else in the form – it is impossible to provide the detail required to budget them as the contingency phases no longer have incurred costs columns. At least if the detail is included in Precedent H, the issue is before the court, which can determine whether it wants to budget an application and how to do so, or determine unequivocally that the application will fall within CPR 3.17(4).

Page 1 – The summary and the assumptions for each phase

[15.17]

Apart from making sure that the correct form is used, it is vital that the form contains accurate details of the costs, both incurred and estimated for the future, which it would be reasonable and proportionate to incur and that the phases set out clearly the assumptions upon which the budget has been based. We cannot stress enough the importance that should be attached to ensuring that the assumptions underlying the sums in each phase of the budget are specifically identified. This is important for a number of reasons:

- The assumptions are, in effect, a case plan. They should illustrate to the court that thought has been given to how to progress the claim. If they do not, then the impression that is conveyed is that the case has not been adequately planned. This is bound to have an adverse effect on the view that the court takes of the costs.
- The assumptions justify the costs. If, for example, the expenditure on witness statements is high, but for a valid reason, eg there are a number of witnesses and they are hard to trace adding complexity, then say so and use the assumptions as an opportunity to inform the court of the reasons for the expenditure, linking them to the proportionality factors at CPR 44.3(5) and any wider circumstances. The figures in isolation mean nothing. It is only when they are viewed with the assumptions of how the claim will progress and why that is a proportionate approach, that they have any purpose.
- As the court will be linking proportionate case management to the budget it will need to understand the basis upon which the costs have been calculated to assist in the determination of what is reasonable and proportionate.
- As any subsequent revision of the budget can only be where there has been a significant development in the litigation, the court may look back to the original assumptions upon which a budget was agreed or approved to check that the claim has indeed taken a different course from that originally costed if the directions order itself does not make this clear.

However, while the assumptions underlying each phase should illustrate a clear case plan, beware of descending to the minutiae of detail. CPR PD 3E, para 10(a) precludes lodging any documents (other than Precedent R later – see below) relating to the budget, save in exceptional circumstances. Accordingly, those in the habit of filing separate disbursement schedules and/or more detailed breakdowns of the form do so at their peril. Not only is this not permitted, turning the exercise into something similar to a bill for detailed assessment, but it suggests a disproportionate approach to the exercise (and maybe the case generally). Recently we have noticed increasing use of an 'addendum' attached to Precedents H. Beware, as the court may decide that this will not be viewed. If it contains the assumptions, then these may have to be articulated, lengthening the hearing and at the risk of a costs sanction.

Remember that the Precedent H will be considered in conjunction with the directions questionnaire, the proposed directions and the disclosure report, (in all but personal injury multi-track claims – where the disclosure report N263 is not required). These documents add to the assumptions as they should reveal a clear case plan. However, if these documents are contradictory (eg the estimate of costs for the expert evidence in the directions questionnaire differs from that in the budget) that will immediately raise concerns about the amount of control being exercised over costs. Linked to this is the position where a party provides insufficient information in the directions questionnaire. We have all seen questionnaires that answer key questions, such as what witness are to be called and on what issues, with unhelpful answers. If in doubt 'TBA/TBC' (to be advised/to be confirmed) seems to be the stock answer. Not only is the court unlikely to accept directions questionnaires filled in with incomplete information, but it will also highlight serious issues with the proposed budget. How can a party who can neither name witnesses, nor identify the issues that those witnesses will address, have possibly drafted detailed assumptions about the evidence to be called and included anything other than a speculative figure for the witness statement phase of the Precedent H? This situation is compounded if by the time of the costs case management hearing, that party can still not provide the requisite detail of experts/witnesses.

As stated above, if the budgeted costs do not exceed £25,000 or the stated value of the claim on the claim form is less than £50,000 the only requirement is to complete page 1 of the costs budget. It seems logical that as contingencies are included in the Precedent H, then if the amount of any budgeted contingencies takes the overall budget over £25,000 the entire Precedent H must be completed. The wording 'budgeted costs' is defined in CPR 3.15(1) as the 'to be incurred' costs. Does this mean that it is only if these costs in Precedent H exceed £25,000 that the entire form must be completed? We suspect not, because the Practice Direction already referred to 'budgeted costs' before CPR 3.15(1) was amended to define these words and so previously referred to the total of incurred and estimated costs. Having said this, the October 2020 amendments to CPR 3 Section II and PD 3E represent something of an overhaul rather than fine tuning, and we must assume that the wording is deliberate. As such if a party only produces page 1 where the to be incurred costs do not exceed £25,000, but the overall Precedent H total exceeds £25,000, strictly there can be no criticism of this.

The removal of the assumptions from page 1 to appear, instead, under each phase page, creates an obvious difficulty where only page 1 is to be completed – the court and the other party/ies do not see the assumptions upon which the budget is predicated. Indeed CPR PD 3E, para 10(b) confirms that the court will not normally require written assumptions in these cases. This makes the proper completion of directions questionnaires and draft directions even more important, as these will be viewed as the case plan justifying the budget.

The phases

[15.18]

There are ten phases: Pre-action costs, issue/statements of case, CMC, disclosure, witness statements, expert reports, PTR, trial preparation, trial and settlement/ADR and a summary page for experts' fees. These are followed by 'contingent cost A' and 'contingent cost B'.

There are valid concerns over completion of the form. Sometimes work done is hard to categorise. An example often given is work on valuing a personal injury claim. Legitimately this may fall within both 'statements of case' and 'trial preparation' if it involves preparing or revising a schedule of loss. It might also happily sit in the 'settlement' phase if it is part of preparation for a round table meeting even though it is still a statement of case. Where should this work feature in the budget? Unless the guidance becomes more specific the answer seems straightforward to us. Use the assumptions column to explain what has been included within each phase. Any later analysis of the agreed or approved budget is then clearly measurable against specific tasks allocated to, and undertaken within, a particular phase. This also gives the court the opportunity to move that expenditure to another phase if it approves it, but believes the work to have been categorised wrongly.

Further problems arise in ensuring that the time spent by fee earners is recorded against the correct phase. This occurs where work done on a particular occasion is in part on one phase and in part on another – eg consideration of documents as part of the process of preparing witness statements. Is the time to be recorded against disclosure or witness statements? Is there a temptation to record against one of the phases to ensure the work stays within the budget? In reality we suspect that it will be clear to the fee earner involved what the purpose was of the task being undertaken at any given time. In the example given, we suspect that the fee earner should record that time against the witness statement phase.

As the tabular guidance in CPR PD 3E directs parties to include work done pre-action which meets the definition of other phases as incurred work in those phases (save in respect of settlement work – see **[15.16]** above) as incurred work in those phases, the pre-action phase is always likely to be relatively small as most work will be incurred work on disclosure, witness statements, experts and preparing statements of case for issue. If there is what seems a large pre-action phase total in the context of the claim, expect the court to ask for a breakdown of how this has been calculated as it will wish to ensure that the work has been correctly allocated. This is particularly so where the 'incurred costs' on phases where the court would have expected work to have been undertaken already (eg disclosure, witness statements, experts) are low, suggesting the costs have been incorrectly allocated between phases – sadly nearly eight years on this problem still arises. If this happens and no breakdown has been ordered, then there is a real risk that the court will simply make bold assumptions as to how much of that is 'incurred expenditure' within certain other phases of the budget.

The importance of correct allocation of 'incurred costs' serves a legitimate purpose, for, as we have said, the court needs to use the already incurred figure for a phase to inform its decision about what further expenditure on that phase is reasonable and proportionate (see CPR 3.17(3)(b)).

Contingencies

[15.19]

We mentioned above the uncertainty caused by contingencies. In *Yeo v Times Newspapers Ltd* [2015] EWHC 209 (QB), [2015] 1 WLR 3031, [2015] 2 Costs LO 243 this point was specifically considered by Warby J who concluded:

> 'In my judgment work should be included as a contingency only if it is foreseen as more likely than not to be required. This seems to me a clear criterion that provides a practical solution, consistent with PD3E 7.4 and 7.9. If work that falls outside one of the main categories is not thought probable, it can reasonably and should be excluded from the budget. The time and costs involved in estimating how much work would cost are not easily justified if the work is no more than a possibility or is unlikely. If work identified as a contingency is included in a budget but not considered probable by the court no budget for it should be approved. If the improbable occurs, in the form of an unexpected interim application, the costs will be added to the budget pursuant to PD3E 7.9, unless the matter involves a 'significant development' within para 7.4 in which case, if time permits, a revised budget should be prepared and agreed or approved.'

This approach met with general approval and CPR PD 3E, para 9 adopts this 'balance of probabilities' test, which provides welcome consistency.

The comments also give a simple explanation of the relationship between contingencies and CPR 3.15A and 3.17(4). We would have preferred the reference to CPR PD 3E, para 7.9 (as it was, now CPR 3.17(4)) to refer to these costs being 'over and above the budget' rather than to be 'added to the budget' as the provision itself regards them as separate from the budgeted sum. However, the effect is the same – they are additional to the sum originally budgeted.

Note that CPR PD 3E, para 9 is clear that parties should not include 'costs which are disputed' as a contingency, but in the appropriate phase of the budget. An example is given of the need for a particular expert. The wording might have been clearer. It is the underlying case management direction sought (which generates the costs), which is disputed, rather than, necessarily, the costs, as a party may object to a particular direction, but agree the costs that would be associated with it.

Counsel

[15.20]

This is a pithy point. Do not forget to allow for counsel's fees. It is as well to obtain an early estimate of these so that it does not become hard to retain counsel later because the budgeted fees are too low or counsel is constrained to do the work for a low fee out of a sense of commercial loyalty or necessity or the client has a large portion of counsel's fees that are irrecoverable win or lose the claim. Anecdotally, many chambers report that they are still not consulted at the time of preparation of the budget and are then presented with a 'fait accompli' after the costs management order has been made.

Specifically excluded costs

[15.21]

Precedent H also stipulates that certain costs are specifically excluded from the budget. These are set out on page 1 of Precedent H and are VAT (if applicable), success fees and ATE insurance premiums (if applicable), costs of detailed assessment, costs of any appeals and the costs of enforcing any judgment. As such we find the decision of the Senior Costs Judge referred to in *BP v Cardiff and Vale University Local Health Board* [2015] EWHC B13 (Costs), which refers to his earlier decision in that case, that recoverable additional liabilities are included when calculating the budget preparation fees, challenging. Not only are additional liabilities not part of any approved or agreed budget, but they are specifically excluded from inclusion in Precedent H itself and so it is hard to see how preparation costs could possibly arise. The position has not been made any clearer by the amendment to what is now CPR 3.15(5). A strict interpretation of this might suggest that the percentage applies to incurred costs (as the amount agreed or allowed on assessment would include the success fee), but does not apply to the budgeted costs (as the agreed or approved budgeted costs do not include the success fee).

The decision in *Various Claimants v MGN Ltd* [2016] EWHC 1894 (Ch) that success fees and ATE insurance premiums formed no part of the budgeting process is wholly unremarkable, but supports the view set out above as to the effect of CPR 3.15(5) in respect of budgeted costs.

Statement of truth

[15.22]

The costs budget must contain a statement of truth (CPR 3.13(5)). This must be signed by a senior legal representative of the party. The wording for this verifies the budget. The statement of truth required is at CPR PD 22, para 2.2A:

> **'Statement of truth**
>
> This budget is a fair and accurate statement of incurred and estimated costs which it would be reasonable and proportionate for my client to incur in this litigation.'

The statement of truth is included in the text of the Precedent H. This is because there has been litigation concerning the lack of a statement of truth on the Precedent H. In *Bank of Ireland v Philip Pank Partnership* [2014] EWHC 284 (TCC) a budget had been signed by the solicitor but it contained no formal statement of truth. Stuart-Smith J concluded that this did not render the budget a nullity and therefore CPR 3.14 was not engaged. In the event that he was incorrect he indicated that were CPR 3.14 engaged then he would grant relief as the omission was one of form and not substance.

Points have also been taken about the definition of 'a senior legal representative' – a term used in CPR 3.13(5), but not defined by the rules. Indeed, this was specifically considered in *Americhem Europe Ltd v Rakem Ltd* [2014] EWHC 1881 (TCC). Head them off at the pass by making sure that someone who is unarguably 'senior' signs the budget. As a party considering making this challenge, think twice. The courts are increasingly making noises about the conduct of parties in taking unreasonable technical challenges and the continuing need for parties to co-operate to further the overriding objective still enshrined in CPR 1.3 (see for example the comments of Leggatt J in *Summit Navigation Ltd v Generali Romania Asigurare Reasigurare SA* [2014] EWHC 398 (Comm) and the clear statement of principle upon this from the Court of Appeal in *Denton v T H White* – see below at [**15.30**]).

In *Americhem* the court held that the signature by someone not a 'senior legal representative', similarly did not render the budget a nullity and was a minor irregularity only. The proportionate route may be to ask the party to reserve the budget with a different signature and only if that is not forthcoming to contemplate an application.

There is no provision in the costs budget for any statement by the client that the costs budget has been discussed with them and it has been approved; notwithstanding that it is the client who will be liable to pay the costs. From a practical perspective, discussions must be undertaken with the client prior to completion of the budget. The client may well have a very different idea as to what budget is required to pursue, or defend a case and this must be addressed at the outset. An explanation should be provided as to the costs that will need to be incurred; incurred costs should already have been discussed. The client should understand that what costs the solicitor thinks are reasonable and necessary may not accord with what the court thinks are proportionate costs (see CPR 44.3(2)(a)) and should understand why it may be that the court sets a lower figure than that in the budget. It is also essential to explain that the costs budget will provide the basis for determining the recoverable costs at the end of the proceedings. This is particularly so in the County Court where s 74(3) of the Solicitors Act 1974 applies (see also CPR 46.9(2)). At the end of the day the client may decide to spend more than what the court determines to be a reasonable and proportionate budget and there is nothing to prevent the client from doing so (other than court case management limiting disclosure, witness evidence, number of experts etc which is considered at [**15.24**] below). The client should also be aware of the assumptions on which the budget is based to understand the practical effect of the financial constraint.

One consequence of the silence in the rules on the need to serve the Precedent H on the client is that judges may decide to hold some CCMCs with the parties actually present. This way the court may be sure that the client knows the costs that are being bandied around and the court's concerns about proportionality. The thinking is that this may lead to earlier compromise. The sorts of cases suitable might be low value monetary claims, boundary and right of way disputes, Inheritance Act claims and Trusts of Land and Appointment of Trustees Act claims – where often the case management conference represents the last chance for settlement before the costs escalate to such an extent that the claim becomes about the costs rather than the original dispute. However, it is essential that the client understands that the costs the court is budgeting are those between the parties. Any solicitor client amount on top will be irrecoverable. This is not to say that courts are not undertaking costs management by telephone. Proportionality often demands that a telephone hearing is convened rather than an actual attendance, eg in personal injury cases where the representatives may be based miles from the court hearing centre in which the claim proceeds or where the claim is not one that benefits from having the parties present at the extra cost an attended hearing engenders. As an alternative to insisting upon the presence of the parties the court could insist that they are present on a telephone CCMC. There is also nothing to prevent the court including recitals on the overall proportionality assessment, recording comments on incurred costs, recording general observations on the proportionality implications of the claim and, in appropriate cases, ordering that a copy of the order is served on the clients. The necessary adaptation by the judiciary to the constraints on 'face-to-face' hearings caused by the Covid-19 pandemic has seen CCMCs become almost exclusively 'remote hearings'.

As a final thought, it remains interesting to see how comfortable solicitors are when signing a statement of truth that the costs stated in the budget are a fair and accurate estimate of proportionate costs. It will be even more interesting, when budgets have been agreed, to see how willing to stick to such a certification solicitors will be once the court has declined to make the case management directions upon which the agreed budget was based. This control that the court is still able to exert by robust case management, and the ways in which this may arise, requires more detailed consideration.

PRECEDENT R – BUDGET DISCUSSION REPORTS

[15.23]

CPR 3.13(2) provides that in all cases where a party files and exchanges a budget, other party/ies, except for any litigants in person, must file an agreed budget discussion report no later than seven days before the first CCMC. The format of the report is provided at Precedent R. In essence, this should identify which phases are agreed and which are not (and if not agreed, why not). The court will have to be astute to ensure that these reports do not become points of dispute in another guise, as that will defeat the drive to ensure that the process is a proportionate one. At its most useful, the fact that the report has to be filed will a) encourage discussion between the parties and facilitate agreement and b) highlight to the court those areas in issue for the CCMC and enable informed preparation.

Completion of Precedent R should not be undertaken lightly. In *Findcharm Ltd v Churchill Group Ltd* [2017] EWHC 1108 (TCC), the court regarded the defendant's completion of Precedent R as 'completely unrealistic' and of 'no utility'. As a result, it was disregarded and the claimant's costs budget was found to be both proportionate and reasonable. In *Red and White Services Ltd v Phil Anslow Ltd* [2018] EWHC 1699 (Ch), the court was 'not at all attracted' to the defendant's Precedent R, that largely sought to limit the budgets of the other parties to its own proposed budget, which was 'too low' and 'not a good guide'.

The fact that Precedent R requires the parties to divide claimed and offered sums between time costs and disbursements respectively, seems curious, as CPR 3.13(8) requires that the court's approval relates only to total figures for the phases of the budgets and Precedent R, itself, acknowledges this by having only one column for the judge's total per phase.

A cautionary final note comes from the case of *Gray v Metropolitan Police Comr* [2019] EWHC 1780 (QB) in which the court confirmed that a judge may set the budget for a phase below the sum offered by the other party, if that offer has not been accepted. We say confirmed, because this is no more than simple contract law and Lambert J dismissed a suggestion that the offer created a 'bottom line' with brevity in these terms:

> ' . . . I find that the Judge was not required to spell out why the figure which she allowed for witness statements was less than the figure offered by the defendant. The reason is obvious: the figure offered by the defendant was not the proportionate figure. It goes without saying that, if a defendant (or any other party) makes an offer, that offer does not become the benchmark below which the costs cannot be budgeted.'

THE INTERACTION BETWEEN CASE AND COSTS MANAGEMENT

[15.24]

Let there be no doubt that the judiciary sees robust and effective case management as the vital ingredient essential to the effective control of costs. This is plain from:

- The comments of Sir Rupert Jackson in the executive summary to his final report:

  > 'One of the points that was impressed upon me during the Costs Review was that judges should take a more robust approach to case management, to ensure that (realistic) timetables are observed and that costs are kept proportionate. Case management can and should be an effective tool for costs control.'

  and in his eagerness to highlight the experience of Singapore when implementing its own procedural reforms in the 1990s. The impact of the case management reforms there was 'electric'. There, as here, there was deep discontent about the reforms within the legal profession. However, as the profession came to terms with the new provisions 'it was generally recognised that the long-term effect of these reforms was highly beneficial.'
- The clear indications that were given to the judiciary in 2013, that it could expect the support of the Court of Appeal where robust, but proportionate, case management decisions have been reached. This was reinforced by the announcement at the time by the then Master of the Rolls, Lord Dyson, of a small cadre of Lord Justices designated to hear costs and case management appeals. These were the Master of the Rolls himself, the then Deputy Head of Civil Justice, Lord Justice Stephen Richards and Lord Justices Jackson, Davis and Lewison. Although nothing has been said expressly, we presume that the new Master of the

Rolls and Deputy Head of Civil Justice assume the roles of their predecessors in this respect. Of course, the architect of the reforms, Sir Rupert Jackson has also now retired from the judiciary.

- The comments made by Sir Rupert Jackson in his May 2015 lecture 'Confronting costs management' that case and costs management should be an iterative process at a single hearing and that 'the amended case management rules enable the court to steer the case, so that it proceeds within the bounds of proportionate costs' (para 7.2).
- The wording of CPR 3.17 linking any case management decision with the costs involved in each procedural step.

While some may see the decision in *Denton v T H White Ltd* (see above and below in more detail at **[15.30]** as suggesting a weakening of this resolve, they should pause and consider. The Court of Appeal was at pains to stress in both *Mitchell* (see above) and *Chartwell Estate Agents Ltd v Fergies Properties SA* [2014] EWCA Civ 506 that robust case management decisions will not be interfered with lightly. Even in Denton the Court of Appeal referred to the 'culture of compliance that the new rules are intended to promote'. Indeed, in his preface to the 2015 White Book Sir Rupert Jackson cautioned 'that in the euphoria with which some have greeted Denton, we do not slip back into the "old culture" of non-compliance'. The robust case management rules extend far beyond CPR 3.9. How does this approach to case management sit with costs management? The procedural issues raised below illustrate clearly the impact of costs management on case management decisions.

(i) Allocation

[15.25]

The primacy of proportionality has seen the reduction in the allocation to multi-track of those fast track value claims that makes their way in to the multi-track solely due to the time estimate based on the number of witnesses. Increasingly, case management orders limit the number of witnesses (see below) and, where necessary, are prescriptive about the trial timetable to ensure that the claim is disposed of within five hours. In addition, the deletion of CPR 26.7(3) in respect of claims issued after 31 March 2013, which had prevented the court allocating a claim to a track with a financial limit lower than the value of the claim without the consent of the parties, means that the court may decide that a claim over £10,000 should still be allocated to the small claims track as a proportionate case management decision (see Chapter 22 Costs Awards Between the Parties – Small Claims Track Costs, below).

(ii) Use of standard direction templates

[15.26]

Although this may seem like small beer in the overall drive to proportionality, there is no doubt that the introduction of standard directions (CPR 29.1(2)) and the mandatory filing requirement with directions questionnaires in multi-track, should have assisted by forcing parties to address case management at an earlier stage and avoid the expense for both parties and the court in preparing bespoke orders. Anecdotal evidence suggests that the professions (and some courts) have not embraced the standard directions. Some courts still prefer their own directions and are not using the CPR 29.1(2) model and standard directions as their starting point either. If in doubt, use the 29.1(2) directions as no court could legitimately criticise compliance with the CPR.

(iii) Witnesses and witness statements

[15.27]

While the court has always had powers under the CPR to control evidence, CPR 32.2(3) take this further. As stated above, the judiciary is increasingly using these powers. Directions questionnaires are being scrutinised to see upon what witness evidence the parties propose to rely. In multi-track claims this is cross-referenced to the proposed budget for that phase. If the budget is not reasonable and proportionate then parties may have to select their best evidence. In other cases, the court is looking to limit the witness evidence to that which will enable the trial to be completed within a proportionate time estimate. Parties must expect orders limiting the number of witnesses, the issues that are to be addressed by those witnesses, the length of the statements, the paper and font size and, either at this stage or at pre-trial checklist/pre-trial review stage, an order timetabling witness evidence at trial (which may involve parties having to select their best cross-examination points) to ensure that the trial can be completed within a proportionate time estimate.

(iv) Disclosure

[15.28]

Sir Rupert Jackson made no secret of his view that disclosure is one of the main drivers of cost in litigation. The proliferation of e-disclosure has only served to heighten the difficulties and increase this cost, as can be seen from a cursory glance at *West African Gas Pipeline Co Ltd v Willbros Global Holdings Inc* [2012] EWHC 396 (TCC), at paragraph 65 and *Wyche v Careforce Group plc* QBD (Comm) 25 July 2013. CPR 31.5(7) offers a menu of disclosure options, with, in multi-track non personal injury claims, standard disclosure being the last, and least attractive, of these. This, combined with the requirement to file and serve disclosure reports 14 days before the first case management conference and for discussion between the parties about the method of disclosure seven days before the first case management conference, is meant to ensure that the court is far better informed to make a proportionate disclosure order from the menu. In multi-track cases this consideration goes hand in hand with a comparison with the phase budget proposed in Precedent H.

Notwithstanding the above, it is apparent that 'standard disclosure' remains the default option for parties in non-personal injury cases (a concern raised by Sir Rupert Jackson in his October 2016 'Disclosure' lecture to the Law Society's Commercial Litigation Conference and referred to again in his Fixed Recoverable Costs review report). We have suggested previously that this may be because standard disclosure remains the default order in the CPR 29.1(2) templates and that the focus of the parties when completing the Form N263 (Disclosure Report) is on the cost of standard disclosure as the form requires this information.

Sir Rupert Jackson conceded in his farewell lecture, 'Was it all worth it?' in March 2018, that CPR 32.5(7) was not working well, largely because 'people have taken little notice of it'. Even prior to this a working party had been established, chaired by Gloster LJ, to tackle the problem. The result is a two-year pilot, under CPR PD 51U, which commenced on 1 January 2019 in the Business and Property Courts in London, Birmingham, Bristol, Cardiff, Leeds, Liverpool, Manchester and Newcastle. This sees initial disclosure with a party's statement of case and, then, various forms of extended disclosure related to the identified Issues for Disclosure. There are five models of extended disclosure. The intent is that this will reduce the burden and cost of the disclosure process in business and commercial litigation. However, although CPR PD 51U, para 6.6 states that the disclosure models should not be used to increase costs, the court has already had to warn against this. In *McParland & Partners Ltd v Whitehead* [2020] EWHC 298 (Ch), the Chancellor of the High Court felt compelled to make this general statement:

> 'It is clear that some parties to litigation in all areas of the Business and Property Courts have sought to use the Disclosure Pilot as a stick with which to beat their opponents. Such conduct is entirely unacceptable, and parties can expect to be met with immediately payable adverse costs orders if that is what has happened. No advantage can be gained by being difficult about the agreement of issues for Disclosure or of a DRD, and I would expect judges at all levels to be astute to call out any parties that fail properly to cooperate as the Disclosure Pilot requires.'

(v) Experts

[15.29]

Another battleground between necessary work and proportionality is that of expert evidence. The judiciary is more astute to the increased reliance upon single joint experts and to tighter prescription by the court of the specific issues upon which an expert is to report (shorter, focused reports will be the order of the day) and budgeting effectively operates to impose limits on experts' recoverable fees. CPR 35.4(2) and (3) require up front estimates of an expert's fee (which will be necessary if the Precedent H is to be accurately completed in any event) and identification of the issues to be addressed by that expert. Practitioners who do not follow pre-action protocols for expert nomination are finding increased difficulty in obtaining permission to rely upon the expert evidence then obtained (and for which the client has already incurred a cost liability). The overriding objective of dealing with a case justly and at proportionate cost is very much to the fore when determining requirements for expert evidence.

There was a pilot run on concurrent expert evidence in the Manchester 'Technology and Construction' and 'Mercantile' Courts. The feedback from that was limited, inevitably due to the small number of cases involved prior to the pilot report. Subsequently, the Civil Justice Council published a report in August 2016, which, at page 10, illustrates the breadth of case type in which concurrent expert evidence had been used. Interestingly, one area where the report recommended further work was in respect of the costs savings achieved by concurrent expert evidence, as, of those providing evidence to the Council, a relatively low percentage were of the view that there was necessarily any saving, although the same evidence revealed that time at trial was saved by adopting this process. The report made recommendations for amendment to CPR PD 35, para 11. Jackson LJ in a lecture in June 2016 concluded with the hope that the use of concurrent expert evidence will increase as the benefits become more widely appreciated. Some amendments to the CPR duly followed, but not all the recommendations were implemented. The PD currently provides that the judge will initiate discussion if concurrent expert evidence is to be given and sets out in more detail how that process may proceed in practice (PD 35.11(4)). The PD (at 11.2) also provides guidance for the court on control of oral expert evidence when it is not taken concurrently (eg experts sequentially on an issue-by-issue basis). The PD also stresses the importance of consideration of an agenda for the taking of expert evidence and that if ordered it should, understandably, be based on the areas of disagreement identified in the experts' joint statement.

By way of aside it is worth noting that the court has had some ability to restrict the recoverability of experts' fees under the CPR prior to the introduction of costs management. CPR 35.4 has long provided for the court to limit the amount of an expert's fees and expenses that are recoverable between the parties and CPR 35.6 provides that where an expert fails to answer a question posed by a party other than the one which instructed him, the court may order that the expert's fees are irrecoverable.

(vi) Relief from sanctions

[15.30]

We have already considered CPR 3.9 in Chapter 11 – An Overview of the Key Costs Amendments to the Civil Procedural Rules. Failure to comply with orders, the CPR and practice directions is a drain on the resources of the court and parties alike; the court because non-compliance may result in an increase in the number of interim hearings or paper case management or, at worst, adjournment of a trial leaving a valuable slot of court time that cannot be filled: parties because efforts to compel compliance inevitably cost money. Rapidly the best laid plans for a claim to be resolved proportionately can be left in tatters. Not so since the advent of the current form of CPR 3.9 in April 2013. As we have said the court is quicker to make 'unless orders' to compel compliance and keep claims on the rails and slower to grant relief from sanction for those who fail to comply. Conversely the court does not tolerate 'point scoring' applications where parties seek to take opportunistic advantage of mistakes made by another party where it is plain that relief will be granted. What emerged from *Denton v T H White Ltd* (above) is that the court will penalise this type of opportunism. This may well impact on costs management, either in operating as a 'good reason to depart from a budget' or by the award of indemnity costs depending upon whether the 'opportunistic party' ultimately is entitled to a costs order or not. At paragraph 43 of the majority judgment the Court of Appeal said this:

> '. . . Heavy costs sanctions should, therefore, be imposed on parties who behave unreasonably in refusing to agree extensions of time or unreasonably oppose applications for relief from sanctions. An order to pay the costs of the application under rule 3.9 may not always be sufficient. The court can, in an appropriate case, also record in its order that the opposition to the relief application was unreasonable conduct to be taken into account under CPR rule 44.11 when costs are dealt with at the end of the case. If the offending party ultimately wins, the court may make a substantial reduction in its costs recovery on grounds of conduct under rule 44.11. If the offending party ultimately loses, then its conduct may be a good reason to order it to pay indemnity costs. Such an order would free the offending party from the operation of CPR rule 3.18 in relation to its costs budget.'

Precisely this occurred in *Viridor Waste Management v Veolia Environmental Services* [2015] EWHC 2321 (Comm), a case where the particulars of claim were served five days late, but a copy had been received by the defendant only one day late. The defendant opposed the granting of relief from sanction. Popplewell J concluded that this was an attempt to take an opportunistic and unreasonable advantage of a mistake in the hope of a windfall and one that had taken half a day of court time with an impact on other court users. As a result, the defendant was subjected to an indemnity costs order. Whilst stressing the importance of compliance with the CPR, but with the expressed intent 'pour encourager les autres', Coulson J in *Freeborn v Marcal (t/a Marcal Architects)* [2017] EWHC 3046 (TCC) issued a stark reminder to parties to be reasonable:

> 'It is, of course, extremely important, post-*Mitchell* and post-*Denton*, for the parties to civil litigation to ensure that they comply with the CPR. Courts will be far less forgiving of non-compliance than they ever used to be. But that tougher approach must not be abused in the way that occurred here. Parties need to consider carefully whether the alleged breach of the rules is, on analysis, any such thing and, even if it is, whether it is proportionate and appropriate to require or oppose an application for relief from sanctions in all the circumstances of the case.'

In any event the grant of relief or refusal to grant relief from sanction may well be a significant development in the case and necessitate a variation of the budget (whether of one's own budget or that of another party). Rather than leave this to an argument on 'good reason' at any subsequent assessment, this is something better raised as soon as the decision on relief is known. An illustration of this would be a case where one party fails to serve expert evidence in accordance with a court order and the sanction was that unless so served that party could not rely upon the evidence. The budgets were originally set on the basis of an expert for each party, a joint meeting and attendance at trial. In those circumstances the fact that one party no longer has expert evidence is a significant development that impacts on the budget of all parties.

(vii) Trial

[15.31]

The court has always had the power to set the trial timetable and control the way in which evidence is presented. However, the court now has, as part of the overriding objective, the obligation to keep the trial proportionate. With civil court time at a premium the judiciary is increasingly invoking this power, particularly as the trial phase is one of, if not, the most expensive.

The increase in the small claim track limit to £10,000 has seen more substantial claims being conducted by litigants in person. Many have had no previous experience of the court process. Litigants in person often arrive at court having no idea what to expect. To ensure that this extended jurisdiction does not lead to the court allocating a disproportionate amount of a finite resource, then judges are imposing strict timetables for evidence in chief and cross examination, to ensure these hearings are proportionately constrained. Of course, the proposed online court is being designed to provide far greater clarity of issues and a streamlined process to resolution in most of those claims that currently proceed through the small claims track.

This is as true of the fast track – particularly, as already suggested, as claims that might previously have been allocated to the multi-track solely on time estimate are being kept within the fast track. Again, it is worth noting that the proposals for the online court see many cases currently allocated to the fast track destined for the new court, with a recommendation of only limited 'between the parties' costs recovery.

(viii) Assessments of costs

[15.32]

The effect on the outcome of assessments of costs with proportionality overreaching all else at CPR 44.3(2)(a) has already been highlighted (and it is worth noting that even though the first instance decision in *May v Wavell Group plc* [2016] EWHC B16 (Costs) was overturned, the costs assessed by the Costs Judge as reasonable were still reduced on appeal ((22 December 2017, unreported), CC) by dint of the proportionality cross check (see Chapter 14 at [**14.5**]). However, on a more rudimentary note, parties should find the court eager to undertake more assessments on a summary basis. Why? Well, the decision of whether to undertake a summary or detailed assessment is a case management one. All case management decisions are taken with consideration of cost and proportionality. Detailed assessment costs more than summary assessment (even with the costs limit on provisional assessments) and results in more court time being allotted to a case. Accordingly, summary assessment must be the preferred option whenever possible. The pilot under CPR PD 51X and, in particular, the introduction of Form N260B enables comparison between budget and costs claimed, removing an impediment to summary assessment in costs managed claims.

Where detailed assessment is ordered, the provisional assessment procedure under CPR 47.15, which limits the recoverable costs within the assessment and is designed to reduce the use of court time on the assessment, operates to ensure that the process itself is proportionate. The high threshold required for a successful challenge to the provisional assessment set out at CPR 47.15(10) will deter most unsatisfied parties.

The introduction of CPR 47.6(1)(c) and PD 47, para 5.8(8) in respect of bills prepared for a standard basis assessment, requiring a breakdown to accompany the bill and, within the bill itself, separate parts for each phase budgeted and, within each separate part, a breakdown of those costs shown as incurred and those estimated in the last agreed or approved budget, and the introduction of the electronic bill should make comparison between bill and budget less onerous. A model form for the breakdown can be found in CPR PD 47 as Precedent Q. The 'new bill' is at Precedent S attached to CPR PD 47.

SETTING THE BUDGET

Introduction

[15.33]

We know that proportionality is the key to the budget, that every direction has a price tag and that the court will use robust case management to assist in the budget setting process. This all seems quite clear. What is less certain is how this translates in to actual figures. The pilot schemes, the various implementation lectures, the Civil Procedure Rules and Sir Rupert Jackson's *'Confronting costs management'* lecture in May 2015 give some pointers – but not always in the same direction.

One of the first, if not the first, decisions emerging from the defamation pilot is informative in that it illustrates the learning curve involved for the judiciary. In that case, *Morrison v Buckinghamshire County Council* [2011] EWHC 3444 (QB) the case managing judge set the directions and convened another appointment when a budget would be set by the SCCO for the claim based on those directions. The difficulties with this approach are obvious:

- The directions have been set before the cost implications of them are considered and as such the directions determine the budget
- In consequence it will be a matter of chance whether the budgeting of these directions leads to a proportionate expenditure rather than this being a considered and tailored exercise
- If a robust approach were subsequently taken to the costing exercise to set a proportionate budget, that would still leave the parties to comply with the directions with inadequate funds to do so

In fact, this case is extremely helpful as a learning tool. It reinforces what we have stressed throughout this chapter and what Sir Rupert Jackson concluded in his lecture *'Confronting costs management'* – namely that case and costs management should go hand in hand. If case and costs management are to go hand in hand how does that translate in to practice?

Many of us thought that what Sir Rupert Jackson sought was overall proportionality: in other words that he was not concerned with micro management of particular aspects of expenditure provided that a party's overall costs were within a global budget set. Of course, from the outset, the pilots required completion of a budget in broadly the same format as the Precedent H, giving a steer that something more was required and that the court would be interested in the costs associated with the various procedural steps to be undertaken. So it proved. CPR 3.15(8) is plain that the court is required to budget by the phases of the proceedings. This is reinforced in the same part by the fact that the parties can plainly agree parts of the budget, even if they cannot agree the entire budget. CPR 3.18 completes this approach by providing that on an assessment on the standard basis the court will have regard to the last approved or agreed budget 'for each phase of the proceedings' and not depart from that budget unless there is good reason.

The budget is set by phases. However, our view is that this cannot be undertaken without a clear idea of overall proportionality to enable the court to case and costs manage in a context. It would surely defeat the object of the exercise if the court budgeted a claim by reference to the phases in isolation, added the total up, concluded that the overall cost was disproportionate when judged against the criteria at CPR 44.3(5) and the wider circumstances and could do nothing about it. This would involve the court approving a budget that permitted the litigation to be undertaken disproportionately.

The answer is surely that the court should begin by taking an overall view of reasonableness and proportionality (in general terms), then budget and set directions for the individual phases to bring the claim to trial within the overall proportionate figure, with the ability to tweak the overall view of proportionality slightly in the light of the information that emerges when setting the spend on the phases. If the end result is that the budget exceeds the preliminary view, then the court may have to revisit some of the directions to see if a more proportionate option is available (eg further restricting witnesses, disclosure obligations etc) so that the budget for certain phases can be reduced to ensure the claim is kept within the overall proportionality figure. In his May 2015 lecture *'Confronting costs management'* referred to this approach as an iterative one and suggested it was a good illustration of how to apply the April 2013 package of reforms (at para 7.6)

This approach involves the court hearing brief initial submissions on overall reasonableness and proportionality, if the budgets are not agreed (even if certain phases are agreed), articulating the relevant reasonableness and proportionality factors by reference to CPR 44.4(3), CPR 44.3(5) and any wider circumstances under CPR 44.4(1), and forming an initial view of overall reasonableness and proportionality (probably by reference to a range of figures). Good practice is for the court to record these figures as a recital. If the budgets are agreed this presents a more challenging approach. It will be for the court to raise its concerns on proportionality and confront parties who are united in opposition to court intervention (usually by challenging the case management directions upon which the agreement of budgets has been predicated)! Even in these cases the court may want to record its view of overall proportionality as this may impact on the subsequent assessment of incurred costs, if those are 'live', and on any subsequent applications to vary the budget.

Undertaking this overall proportionality exercise at the outset also helps in identifying particular phases where the relevance of a/some relevant CPR 44.3(5) factor/s means a larger budget than might have been expected (eg in a clinical negligence case with complex issues on breach and causation the overview will result in an expectation that the proportionate costs for the expert evidence phase will be significant). This was a point made in *Various Claimants v Scott Fowler Solicitors (a firm)* [2018] EWHC 1891 (Ch).

More problematic is where the incurred costs prevent proportionality even with robust case and costs management (either because they exceed the sum the court thinks is proportionate for conduct of the case through to trial or because, when added to phases where there are no incurred costs to take into account under CPR 3.17(3), eg trial preparation and trial, the figure exceeds that which is proportionate for the entire claim). We have considered this above in [**15.8**] and consider it in more detail in [**15.35**] below.

Our view is that if the incurred costs are such that even taking them into account within the specific phases when the budget is set and proportionate directions are given, results in an overall sum (incurred plus budgeted costs) that is in excess of the preliminary view given on overall proportionality, the court cannot do anything other than record this, including recording its view of overall proportionality of the claim and its view of what the overall proportionate figure is per phase. This serves two functions as follows:

- It may persuade the receiving party, if it is that budget that exceeds overall proportionality, to recognise the inevitable difficulties to be encountered on a subsequent detailed assessment of the incurred costs and adopt a realistic approach to negotiation. Warby J adopted the approach of making comments for precisely this purpose in *Yeo v Times Newspapers Ltd* [2015] EWHC 209 (QB), at para 61. If, as may well be the case in the County Court and District Registries, the costs managing judge is also going to be the assessing judge it will be a brave or foolhardy receiving party who does not compromise.

- If the costs are not compromised, it will give a clear steer to any assessing judge who is not the case/costs managing judge, what view the costs managing judge took of the incurred costs.

The relevance of hourly rates

[15.34]

So far this discussion has been in general terms, but once the court starts to set a budget this will involve specific sums. Two clear camps formed on how it would do so. On the one hand were those who saw it as inevitable that the court would set the budget by reference to hourly rates. After all, Precedent H, which must be completed, makes provision for hourly rates and time to be inserted and, by dint of the self-calculating nature of the form, this produces the resultant figures per phase. In the opposite encampment were those who believed that hourly rate has no, or at best a limited, role in budgeting. We have always been firmly in this latter camp. We took (and take) this view on the bases that:

- Hourly rate is only of relevance if it is multiplied by an amount of time. Consideration of time chimes of 'need' and, as we have seen, proportionality trumps need. If the court does become sucked in to rate setting, then it must consider time (for rate alone is purposeless). What does the court do if the figure that emerges from this multiplication is disproportionate? Revisit rate? Revisit time? The only certainty is that the budget setting exercise itself will then take a disproportionate amount of court time with no guarantee of reaching a proportionate end sum.
- CPR 3.15(8) specifically states that 'A costs management order concerns the totals allowed for each phase of the budget . . . it is not the role of the court in the costs management hearing to fix or approve the hourly rates claimed'. In other words, the court is not charged with approving (setting) rates.
- CPR PD 3E, para 12 also steers the court away from undertaking a prospective detailed assessment. What could be more akin to a detailed assessment than lengthy arguments on appropriate hourly rate? To do so also occupies a significant amount of court time, making the costs management process itself utterly disproportionate. This is another reason for avoiding assumptions that are, in fact, no more than a breakdown of costs akin to a bill for detailed assessment.
- CPR PD 3E, para 12 defines the task of the court when setting the phase budget to consider ' . . . whether the budgeted costs fall within the range of reasonable and proportionate costs'. This is not language that resonates with descending to the detail that is required to determine hourly rates
- Setting a budget by hourly rates creates later uncertainty. Who is to say that the work will then be undertaken by a fee earner commanding that hourly rate, as the mere setting of the budget cannot compel that? As the budgeted sum is what will be recovered on a standard basis assessment unless there is a good reason to the contrary, this raises the

spectre of either a possible breach of the indemnity principle or an increase in detailed assessments with paying parties seeking to ascertain who has actually done the work. This immediately undermines one of the aims of budgeting, which is to reduce the number of assessments.

- Setting hourly rate opens the door to forum shopping in those cases that are not geographically constrained to be issued in a specific court. If word emerges that in Court A budgets are set by reference to hourly rate and the rate currently allowed for a grade A fee earner is £100 per hour more than Court B, which also sets budgets by reference to hourly rate, allows, before too long Court A will be inundated with claims while Court B sits empty.
- Setting rates permits the uncertainty that arose in *MXX (By her litigation friend and husband RXX) v United Lincolnshire NHS Trust* [2019]1624 EWHC (QB), in which the claimant's solicitors had stated an hourly rate in the budget for a fee earner in excess of the rate payable by the client. The costs managing judge had set the budget by an exercise of rate multiplied by hours. The paying party sought remedies in relation to misconduct under CPR 44.11. On appeal the court found that the Master had erred in making certain assumptions as to how the costs managing judge had reached a conclusion on the rate adopted. Had the budget been set by determination of the reasonable and proportionate sums by the method we advocate in **[15.36]** below, ignoring hourly rates and time, then the Master could have been confident that the overstatement of rate in Precedent H had affected the outcome by the difference between what the incurred costs were stated to be for each phase budgeted at the time of the costs management exercise and what they actually were for each phase budgeted. This is because the process of setting figures we advocate is that the court determines an overall proportionate figure for a phase, deducts what has already been incurred and approves what, if anything, remains. Undertaking the costs management exercise in this fashion means an overstatement of rates in the estimated costs phases causes no prejudice as the court does not consider rate and hours going forward. However, as the incurred costs are relevant to approving the budgeted costs under CPR 3.17(3)(b), an overstatement of them directly impacts on the approved budgeted costs. Adopting our approach, the budgeted costs would have been more if the incurred costs had been less. Perhaps that, and the loss of the costs of the costs management process, are sufficient sanctions under CPR 44.11 (see below for a similar conclusion when considering the relationship between reductions in hourly rate and 'good reason' at assessments).
- Setting hourly rate holds out a hostage to fortune at the subsequent assessment. What happens if the assessing judge sets an hourly rate for non-budgeted costs and it transpires this is a different rate from that set within the budget? Does that lead to an argument about 'good reason' to depart from the budget? If so, it means that the aim of curtailing assessments is utterly defeated (see the analysis of *RNB v London Borough of Newham* [2017] EWHC B15 (Costs) below, where precisely this mischief arose).

The view that hourly rate has no role in budget setting is surely correct. In his May 2015 'Confronting costs management' lecture Sir Rupert Jackson said:

'The courts should not specify rates or number of hours. That adds to the length of CCMCs and is unnecessary micro-management'. (para 3.4(ii))

The CPRC moved swiftly to confirm this (although our view was that CPR PD 3E, para 7.3 said it all already), by introducing an additional paragraph 7.10 to the Practice Direction 3E. This is now found at CPR 3.15(8) and leaves no scope for debate, stating unequivocally:

' . . . It is not the role of the court in the costs management hearing to fix or approve the hourly rates claimed in the budget'

It is to reinforce that the budgeting exercise is not a question of rate multiplied by time and to focus the attention of the parties on the CPR 44.3(5) factors and wider circumstances under CPR 44.4(1), that we would prefer a Precedent H that moves away from rates and time and ensures that the focus is on one figure per phase that is reasonable and proportionate and that the party is then free to spend as it sees fit as that is the effect of the budget setting exercise undertaken by the court. Interestingly the form will work without such information, simply with totals being inserted for each phase. It is simply a matter of formatting. The change to the scope of those cases where only page 1 of the Precedent H is required is certainly a step in the right direction.

Cases emerging from the SCCO, such as *RNB v London Borough of Newham* [2017] EWHC B15 (Costs), *Nash v Ministry of Defence* [2018] EWHC B4 (Costs) 2017 and *Jallow v Ministry of Defence* [2018] EWHC B7 (Costs), considering whether a reduction in hourly rate in respect of incurred costs is a 'good reason' to depart from the budgeted costs, attracted much interest. Our view remains that as hourly rate is utterly irrelevant to the budget approval process prescribed at CPR 3.15(8) and PD 3E, para 12, which expressly require the budget to be set by a figure that is reasonable and proportionate and not by reference to hourly rates multiplied by time, a reduction in the hourly rate for incurred costs does not mean there is a good reason to depart downwards from the approved budget costs, as those costs were not approved by reference to an hourly rate, but instead as a figure based on consideration of the CPR 44.4(3) and CPR 44.3(5) factors and any relevant wider circumstances. A better argument would be that a reduction in non-costs managed incurred costs by reason of a reduction in hourly rate, might present a good reason to increase the approved budgeted costs. This is because the approved budgeted costs will have been set taking into account incurred costs under CPR 3.17(3)(b). A reduction in those incurred costs to reflect a lower hourly rate, may mean that the court had 'under budgeted' future costs by deducting incurred costs as set out in Precedent H from what it regarded as the overall reasonable and proportionate sum for each phase when calculating the budgeted costs to be approved. Accordingly, any difficulty is not with hourly rates, but with the challenging issue of the treatment of incurred costs.

Incurred costs

[15.35]

In what is an interesting decision, Coulson J in *CIP Properties (AIPT) Ltd v Galliford Try Infrastructure Ltd* [2015] EWHC 481 (TCC), 158 ConLR 229, [2015] BLR 285, adopted a broad approach to incurred costs, which resulted in him, in effect, budgeting the entire costs. He was confronted by 'incurred expenditure' at a 'very high level of costs'. Having undertaken an overall proportionality view of the claimant's costs that 'both incurred and estimated are disproportionate' he considered the options available to him, recognising that if incurred costs were used under what is now CPR 3.17(3)(b) to inform the estimated costs budgeted, that opened the door to potential unfairness if the assessing judge then reduced the incurred costs at any subsequent assessment. His solution was to limit the recoverable incurred costs per phase, but to introduce a mechanism by which any amount allowed over that sum at subsequent assessment, would result in an equivalent amount being deducted from the budgeted costs. In other words, regardless of how ultimately the costs were divided between those incurred and those budgeted, the claimant would be limited to the overall sum permitted by this off-setting mechanism. This approach raises a number of challenging issues, which explains the use of the word 'interesting'. The issues are:

- The extent to which the budgeting judge may limit recoverable 'incurred costs' by a prospective assessment of costs (and the jurisdictional basis for this) – albeit that this was qualified to allow additional incurred costs on assessment but at the expense of budgeted costs. Paragraph 98 plainly refers to 'assessed costs'.
- If the budgeting judge can adopt the approach above, the extent to which incurred costs in one phase can be offset against budgeted costs in another phase (see para 97(a) where additional incurred costs on the pre-action phase were to be set off against future costs generally). CPR 3.17(3)(b) does not expressly limit the consideration of incurred costs on a phase-by-phase basis, but, as stated above, CPR 3.15(8) and PD 3E, para 12 require the court to set a reasonable and proportionate sum by phase. A general offset of incurred costs on one phase against budgeted costs on another may result in the budgeted phase sum eventually being less than that which is reasonable and proportionate for that phase.
- If the budgeting judge can adopt the approach above, the extent to which the court can effectively set a budget for a phase to include both incurred and estimated costs by adopting the set off mechanism. This seems hard to reconcile with the terms of CPR 3.12 and 3.15 which talk of budgets being in respect of 'costs to be incurred'. By adopting the set off approach and applying it to the amount considered recoverable on assessment, the effect is a sum for all the costs of a phase (both incurred and estimated). Indeed, when talking of the defendant's overall costs (incurred and those approved estimated costs) the court talked of 'the approved costs budget' whereas CPR 3.15 uses the word 'approval' in the context of a costs management order which only 'manages the costs to be incurred'. When adopting the CIP approach in *GSK Project Management Ltd (in liq) v QPR Holdings Ltd* [2015] EWHC 2274 (TCC), Stuart-Smith J expressly approved in the spreadsheet at para 52, only one sum per phase. In other words, he approved incurred and estimated costs and approved the costs of the pre-action phase, although having done so he then adopted the Coulson J approach of off-setting and his total figure of £425,000 was then phrased as being 'incurred costs/approved budget'.

- The extent to which the budgeting judge can/should 'approve the prospective costs in the maximum sum of £150,000' as part of a costs management order. 'Maximum' resonates more with a costs capping regime and not with the more specific budgeting of an actual sum required under the costs management regime. It also provides scope for the paying party later to argue the amount on assessment without needing to raise 'good reason', as the amount up to the maximum is still a live issue. This encourages more detailed assessments and not fewer.
- Whether the effect of setting a total sum (para 98) precludes arguments under 'good reason' for the estimated sums to be increased on assessment.
- Whether the budgeting judge has the jurisdiction to bind the assessing judge on 'good reason' to depart downwards from the budget where the assessed 'incurred costs' are higher than the budgeting judge considered recoverable when setting the budget going forward and that judge prospectively orders a departure from the budget by way of £ for £ offset.

Even if the CIP approach is not adopted, front loading work exposes a greater level of costs to the retrospective overall proportionality cross check on a detailed assessment under CPR 44.3(2)(a). The continued criticism that the proportionality cross-check at the end of an assessment is an opaque and unpredictable process suggest to us that it is better to have the certainty of knowing in advance what the recoverable costs expenditure will be, rather than finding out once the money has been spent that this sum is disproportionate and that a significant proportion is irrecoverable (see **[15.33]** above). In addition, the costs already incurred still have a significant role to play in setting the budgeted costs. The court can record its comments on those incurred costs and these costs will be considered when determining whether the budgeted costs going forward are reasonable and proportionate, eg if the reasonable and proportionate costs of the disclosure phase are, say, £20,000 and £20,000 has already been spent, the court will approve no further expenditure on that phase going forward. Suggestions that it is unfair to make a proportionate case management decision that requires future work to be undertaken, but approve no budgeted costs for that work, overlook the point that the court has determined, by the required process under CPR 3.15(8) and 3.17(3)(b), that there is a proportionate expenditure to match the direction, but that a party has chosen to have spent that sum already.

Setting the figure

[15.36]

Having turned our backs on the traditional costs calculation of hourly rate multiplied by an amount of time we still have to establish how the precise budget figures will be calculated.

Our view is that the court should adopt a far broader approach. It is required to set the budget for each phase by total figure. The approach we advance is that the court will identify the salient features of reasonableness under CPR 44.4(3) and proportionality under the CPR 44.3(5) checklist and any identified wider circumstances under CPR 44.4(1). It will then apply those features to each phase and determine an appropriate total sum linked to proportionate directions relevant to that phase. In practice this will involve the court giving a brief judgment identifying which of the CPR 44.3(5) and 44.4(3) factors and any wider circumstances that are relevant, and in what way, to a particular case, setting out its range of overall reasonable and proportionate figures (so that it can then case and costs manage a case within an overall context) and then, adopting the wording of CPR 3.15(8) and CPR PD 3E, para 12, and using a formula of words for each phase along the lines of 'Having identified the relevant considerations on reasonableness and proportionality of costs in this claim, the appropriate case management order is [y] and the reasonable and proportionate budget for this phase is [£x]', it will set the budgeted costs sum. Critics of this approach may see this as too opaque a process. However, it seems to be precisely what the rules require, linking costs and case management by reference to reasonableness and proportionality. Anything more complicated can only be trespassing in to the territory of a detailed assessment and risks failure to address the requirements of proportionality, both in terms of the costs budgeted and the time and costs spent on the costs management process itself. Those courts adopting this approach seem to be reducing the time spent at the CCMC.

CONCLUSION TO PROSPECTIVE COSTS CONTROL – COSTS AND CASES MANAGEMENT

[15.37]

For the last few years we have predicted that the focus on case and costs management would shift to the 'nuts and bolts' of costs management and that this would prove interesting. We were right on both fronts. The Civil Procedure Rules Committee continues to make amendments, the most recent being to elevate much of the important detail of PD 3E into Part 3 Section II, to amend the rules on budget variation by the introduction of CPR 3.15A and to reduce the sources of assistance by the incorporation of the former guidance note into PD 3E. Anecdotal evidence is that as the judiciary and practitioners become more familiar with the process, hearing times are reducing and the incidence of agreed budgets is on the rise. Whilst there remains scope for further amendments to CPR 3, Section II and PD 3E, to clarify certain residual ambiguities and oddities, much has been resolved this year. It has taken almost eight years but, and say it very quietly, the bedding-in period seems, finally, to be over.

CHAPTER 16

PROSPECTIVE CONTROL OF COSTS – THE RELEVANCE OF COSTS BUDGETS IN CASES NOT COSTS MANAGED

[16.1]

In the 16th Costs implementation lecture in May 2012, Mr Justice Ramsey noted that:

> 'As costs management is a necessary adjunct to proper case management and to the furtherance of the overriding objective there will, in most cases, be a presumption in favour of making a costs management order.'

This is reinforced by CPR 3.12, CPR PD 3E and, particularly, CPR 3.15, which significantly limit judicial discretion not to costs manage.

It is clear, then, that CPR Part 7 multi-track cases and CPR Part 8 cases of a type prescribed in CPR PD 3E, para 2 where a costs management order is not made after the filing of a Precedent H should be few and far between. However, even in these cases where any budget has been filed and served pursuant to CPR 3.13, it will remain relevant for reasons known to those familiar with the previous Costs Practice Direction Section 6.

Section 6 required parties to provide the court with estimates of the base costs already incurred and those to be incurred with allocation questionnaires and pre-trial checklists. It had as its genesis the Court of Appeal decision in *Leigh v Michelin Tyre plc* [2003] EWCA Civ 1766. In that case, the court had deprecated the circuit judge's description of costs estimates as being 'damp squibs', had stressed the importance of costs estimates and had given the guidance about the use to which those estimates would be put. Section 6 effectively codified the views expressed in Leigh. It provided that where there was a 20% or more difference between an estimate and the costs claimed, that required an explanation. The paying party then had the opportunity to argue reliance upon the estimate. At detailed assessment the court could have regard to the estimate when assessing reasonableness and proportionality of the costs. If the difference was 20% or more and either the receiving party had not provided a satisfactory explanation for this or the paying party showed reliance, then the court could regard the difference as evidence that the costs claimed were unreasonable or disproportionate.

These provisions were largely imported into CPR PD 44, subsection 3, but with some important changes.

Subsection 3.1 provides that the section only relates to budgets filed under CPR PD 3E and only where the court has not made a costs management order. CPR 3.12 expressly limits CPR PD 3E to most Part 7 multi-track claims (with the exceptions already considered). In other words, subsection 3 only covers certain claims in the multi-track. This may seem obvious as there is no longer an obligation to file an estimate in the fast track. However, this restriction seems to overlook three other situations where there may be a budget. These are

(i) Cases where the notice of provisional allocation under CPR 26.3 allocates to the multi-track. As such, then in cases where the value of the claim stated on the claim form is less than £50,000, parties must file and exchange Precedent H at the time of filing the directions questionnaire. The case managing judge may subsequently decide that the provisional allocation was incorrect and formally allocate to fast track. Do the provisions of subsection 3 then apply? The logical answer is that the claim is not in the multi-track and is therefore excluded. However, it is hard to imagine that the court on assessment will ignore the budget altogether if there are significant departures from it.

(ii) Where the court has exercised its case management power under the curiously titled CPR 3.1(2)(II) to order a party to file and exchange a costs budget. As CPR 3.1(1) makes it clear this power is in addition to any powers given by any other rule, then by definition this cannot be a budget under CPR PD 3E and so CPR PD 44, para 3 cannot apply. Again, what is the relevance of this budget at assessment?

(iii) Cases where the parties have complied with the requirement set out in the preamble to Form N170 (Pre-trial checklist) requiring them, in cases where there has been no costs management order, to attach estimates of costs incurred and likely overall costs. There is nothing in the CPR that supports this requirement, other than by circularity, as CPR PD 29, para 8.1(1) specifies that the pre-trial checklist must be in Form 170 and CPR PD 28, para 6.1(2) also refers to Form N170. The provision becomes even more curious when one notes that for 'substantial cases' (undefined) the estimate (no form of this is suggested) should be provided 'in accordance with CPR' (with no specified provision). Our view is that the reference in Form N170 fails to take account of the 2013 CPR amendments. This view is supported by the fact that CPR PD 28, para 6.1 still refers to Section 6 of the previous Costs Practice Direction. Two things seem clear:

    (1) any estimate filed in compliance with the wording on Form N170 is not a costs budget under CPR PD 3E and so CPR 44 PD 44, para 3 cannot apply to it; and

    (2) nearly eight years on from the relevant CPR amendments, Form N170 is long overdue for revision.

It is odd that fast track claims are excluded entirely from the estimating process (with the possible exception referred to under CPR 28 PD, para 6.1(2) above). We accept that to have full blown costs management in the fast track will, in the most part, itself be a disproportionate process, but the absence of any requirement to provide even an estimate in non-fixed costs cases (in a specified form and with a consequence) seems unfortunate. Experience shows that it is often fast track claims that are the epitome of disproportionality. We suspect the exclusion was because the expectation was that all fast track claims would be dealt with under fixed fee schemes. Fast track personal injury claims arising out of road traffic, employer liability and public liability claims became subject to such a regime from 31 July 2013. Whilst, Jackson LJ's Fixed Recoverable Costs Review, with the subsequent Ministry of Justice consultation on this, and the Government's desire to introduce a scheme for clinical negligence disputes, suggest the wider introduction of fixed fee schemes, nothing has, to date, been implemented, other than the inclusion within the fixed costs regime of claims under the Pre-Action Protocol for Resolution of Package Travel

Claims from 7 May 2018. Accordingly, in the meantime, there is the curious situation that in non-fixed fee fast track claims the court has only prospective case management and retrospective costs assessment tools in its armoury, unless the court, of its own volition, decides to take the bold step of using the proviso at CPR 3.12(1A) to costs manage a fast track claim. Whilst we can see the attraction of that, case selection is paramount to ensure that the costs management exercise is not, itself, disproportionate. Otherwise, for those conducting fast track claims, the sting is very much in the tail. Remember the provisions of CPR 44.3(2)(a) and (5). The last thing that the court will do on an assessment is the proportionality cross-check. It is at this point, when the court, having assessed the reasonable amount of costs, considers those further by reference to the proportionality factors, that the certainty of prospective budgeting may seem more attractive.

The major amendment in Section 3 is to add a clearer sanction in the situation where the paying party can show reliance on the budget and there is a difference of 20% or more between the costs claimed and those shown in the budget. Instead of this simply enabling the court to treat this as evidence that the costs claimed are unreasonable or disproportionate (which remains the position where the receiving party has not provided a satisfactory explanation for the difference), the court may now restrict the recovery to the amount it is reasonable for the paying party to pay in the light of the reliance *even* if that is a lesser amount than the reasonably and proportionately incurred costs of the receiving party. A genuine sanction, a much clearer steer for the assessing judge and a greater degree of certainty for the parties as to the likely outcome of a finding of reliance.

If there is a difference of less than 20% then subsection 3.4 provides that at the assessment the court will assess the reasonableness and proportionality of the costs claimed and in doing so may consider the budgets filed by any of the parties. However, because of the wording of CPR PD 44, para 3.1 the reference to 'any other budget' can only be to 'any other budget' filed under CPR PD 3E. Why 3.4 refers to the last approved or agreed budget is also a mystery as, under 3.1, this section (CPR PD 44, para 3) does not apply where a costs management order has been made, and by definition one must have been to have an approved or agreed budget. Removal of this reference to agreed or approved budgets in 3.4 would provide welcome consistency with 3.1. This has been pointed out to the Civil Procedure Rules Committee, but to date no amendment has been forthcoming.

Another curiosity is that CPR PD 44, para 3.2 only requires a statement from the receiving party if there is a 20% or more difference between the costs claimed by a party at detailed assessment and the costs shown in a budget filed by that party. It may be that the logic is that at the time parties prepare a Form N260 or N260B in anticipation of a summary assessment, the court has yet to determine who is to be the receiving party. However, how does the court then deal with CPR PD 44, para 3.7, which is not limited to detailed assessment? The answer, presumably, is by hearing an oral explanation giving the reasons for the difference. In direct contrast, the requirement on a paying party claiming reliance on the budget to serve a statement under CPR PD 44, para 3.3 is not limited to detailed assessment. It seems that parties must anticipate that they may be the paying party before the court has determined this if they wish to rely on the provisions of CPR PD 44, para 3.6 at a summary assessment. In practice this is likely to lead to requests for a detailed assessment, which flies in the face of proportionality.

CHAPTER 17

PROSPECTIVE COSTS CONTROL – COSTS CAPPING

A BRIEF SUMMARY OF PROSPECTIVE COSTS CONTROL – COSTS CAPPING

[17.1]

Costs capping now comes in different shapes and sizes, with some versions adopting pseudonyms eg costs limits, scale costs and protective costs orders. Scale costs under Section IV of CPR 45 are considered in Chapter 26 and costs limits under Section VII of CPR 45 are considered in Chapter 18. Whilst costs capping in judicial review proceedings is touched upon at [17.7] below, it is examined in more detail in Chapter 18, as the regime draws heavily from its origins in protective costs orders. This chapter is limited to commentary on Section III of CPR 3 and consideration of the costs capping pilot under CPR PD 51W.

COSTS CAPPING UNDER PART 3, SECTION III

[17.2]

Since the introduction of costs management we have consistently said that we see no case for the retention of the costs capping discipline in Section III of CPR 3. At one stage, this view appeared prescient. In response to a question at the end of his lecture *'Confronting Costs Management'* (13 May 2015), when asked whether there remained a place for costs capping Sir Rupert Jackson responded:

> 'No, in my view the costs capping rules should be repealed.'

This was followed by clear indications from the minutes of the Civil Procedure Rules Committee ('CPRC') throughout 2015 that the costs capping jurisdiction was to be removed. However, at the 11th hour the CPRC granted a reprieve on the basis that it appears that in some lower value pension and trust fund cases in the Chancery Division, the threat, rather than the reality, of a costs capping order is deemed a useful tool in prompting an agreement. Accordingly the jurisdiction remains, but seemingly by way of brooding presence in the background of very few cases. This is borne out by the fact that the only significant costs capping cases to emerge after March 2013 have been *Tidal Energy Ltd v Bank of Scotland plc* [2014] EWCA Civ 847 and *Hegglin v Person(s) Unknown* [2014] EWHC 3793 (QB), [2015] 1 Costs LO 65. In the first of these the Court of Appeal declined to make a costs capping order that would have prevented the respondent using leading counsel, being satisfied that this was a risk of costs being disproportionately incurred that could be controlled by detailed assessment. The court was keen to stress that 'adequate control' did not equate to elimination of the risk. In the second Edis J refused a late application to cap costs, but made a costs management order instead, stating this about CPR 3.19(5)(c):

> '. . . I am not able to derive any general principle which would define when detailed assessment may not be an adequate control on the risk of disproportionate expenditure. I think that cases where that part of the test is satisfied must be rare, but to define it too narrowly would deprive the Rule of any content. The risk in question, which is to be controlled, is that costs will be disproportionately incurred, not that they will be disproportionately awarded.'

The limited use of Section III of CPR 3 justifies merely a brief commentary on the current position.

THE PROCEDURAL CODE UNDER PART 3, SECTION III

[17.3]

The rules, which were first introduced into the Civil Procedure Rules by the Civil Procedure (Amendment No 3) Rules 2008 on 6 April 2009, are now found, almost unchanged, at CPR 3.19–CPR 3.21 and at CPR PD 3F.

In summary the rules provide that:

- The court will make a costs capping order only in exceptional circumstances (CPR PD 3F, para 1.1) and may do so if it is in the interests of justice to do so, there is a substantial risk that without such an order costs will be disproportionately incurred and this risk cannot be managed by case management decisions and detailed assessment of costs (CPR 3.19(5)).
- The application should be made as soon as possible – preferably before or at the first case management conference (CPR PD 3F, para 1.2).
- Costs capping cannot be retrospective (CPR 3.19).
- The court does not have to cap the costs of all parties (CPR 3.19(5) – 'all or any parties').

The rules explain why costs capping is so rarely used. Costs capping orders may be made only in exceptional cases where (i) it is in the interests of justice to do so, (ii) there is a substantial risk that without the imposition of a cap, disproportionate costs will be incurred and (iii) where conventional case management and a detailed assessment are not sufficient to control costs adequately.

That these are virtually insuperable hurdles was demonstrated by Coulson J in *Barr v Biffa Waste Services Ltd* [2009] EWHC 2444 (TCC), and Eady J in *Peacock v MGN Ltd* [2009] EWHC 769 (QB). In the words of Coulson J:

> 'It would be a very unusual case in which a High Court judge did not feel able to utilise one or both of [the tools of case management and detailed assessment] to control disproportionate costs. That is, after all, what they are there for.'

The addition to Coulson J's list of costs management orders, militates further against the making of costs capping orders, as exemplified by *Hegglin* above.

At what stage in the proceedings should the court exercise it jurisdiction?

[17.4]

In *Henry v BBC* [2005] EWHC 2503 (QB), the judge refused a costs capping order on the ground that the application was made too late. This reinforced the view expressed by HHJ Kirkham when refusing an application for a costs capping order in *Petursson v Hutchison 3G UK Ltd* [2004] EWHC 2609 (TCC) The appropriate time to consider a costs cap is at an early stage of an action when the parties and the court could together plan the steps needed to bring the matter to trial, the costs implications of those steps and whether a cap was appropriate.

COSTS CAPPING IN JUDICIAL REVIEW PROCEEDINGS

[17.5]

The relevant rules appear in CPR 46 at 46.16–46.19. They permit costs capping in judicial review proceedings and replace protective costs orders traditionally made in such litigation. In summary the rules provide that an 'on notice' application is made under CPR 23 and this must be supported by evidence providing:

- reasons why an order should be made (by reference to the matters raised in ss 88 and 89 of the Criminal Justice and Courts Act 2015 – see the appendix);
- a summary of the applicant's resources;
- details of the future costs the applicant considers are likely to be incurred by the parties and, if the applicant is a body corporate, whether it is able to demonstrate that it is likely to have the financial resources available to meet liabilities arising from the proceedings (and if the answer is it cannot demonstrate this, the court must consider obtaining evidence about the applicant's members and their ability to provide financial support for the proceedings).

CPR 46.19 sets out a procedure for applications to vary an order made.

(See Chapter 18 for further and more detailed consideration of these provisions).

THE CAPPED COSTS LIST PILOT SCHEME

[17.6]

In his Supplemental Report, Sir Rupert Jackson concluded that because of the 'vast and inhomogeneous mass' of lower value business and property claims (under £250,000) a capped stage costs scheme would operate more successfully than a 'pure' fixed costs' regime (see Chapter 9 of the report). He recommended that this should be tested by a voluntary pilot in a small number of the Business and Property Courts. The result of this recommendation is the two-year pilot that commenced on 14 January 2019 in the London Circuit Commercial Court and the Circuit Commercial Courts, the Technology and Construction Courts and the Chancery Division in Leeds and Manchester.

The pilot has been implemented under CPR PD 51W, largely adopting the proposed rule set out in the supplemental report. Acknowledging Sir Rupert's view 'that if recoverable costs are capped . . . the work to be done must also be controlled . . . That requires a streamlined procedure and robust case management', the pilot contains its own discrete provisions for the key stages of a claim, namely pre-issue conduct, statements of case, disclosure, witness statements, expert evidence and trial. The emphasis is on proportionality eg limiting the extent of disclosure, the number of witnesses, the use of expert evidence and controlling the trial by adherence to a strict timetable.

The costs provisions are contained in CPR PD 51W, para 3. In summary these are that:

- costs budgeting does not apply;
- there will be a summary assessment of costs under any order for 'between the parties' costs, with each party filing and exchanging schedules of their costs not later than 21 days after the conclusion of the trial;
- the assessment will be in accordance with prescribed amounts for each stage of the claim, with a maximum overall total for costs of £80,000 (this sum is after any set-off of costs under CPR 44.12), unless there is a relevant CPR 36 offer;
- the cap does not include court fees, costs of enforcement of any court order, any wasted costs ordered, VAT and the costs of an interim application if the paying party has behaved unreasonably; and
- CPR 36 applies, but with the costs limited under a valid CPR 36.17(3) offer to the capped costs and under a valid CPR 36.17(4) offer to costs on the indemnity basis, with the maximum costs allowed increased by 25% per stage, but subject to an increased overall cap of £100,000.

The capped costs per stage (subject to the overall cap) are as follows:

Work done in respect of—	**Maximum amount of costs**
Pre-action	£10,000.00
Particulars of claim	£7,000.00
Defence and counterclaim	£7,000.00
Reply and defence to counterclaim	£6,000.00
Case management conference	£6,000.00
Disclosure	£6,000.00
Witness statements	£8,000.00
Experts' reports	£10,000.00
Trial and judgment	£20,000.00
Settlement/negotiations/mediation	£10,000.00
Making or responding to an application	£3,000.00
Work done post-issue which is not otherwise covered by any of the stages above	£5,000.00

CONCLUSION TO PROSPECTIVE COSTS CONTROL – COSTS CAPPING

[17.7]

Whilst costs capping under Section III of CPR 3 may be obsolete (no doubt tempting fate and leading to a resurgence in such orders), Section VI of CPR 46 in judicial review proceedings and the capped costs pilot ensure that, in some form, the jurisdiction remains alive. It will be interesting to see what follows the pilot after its conclusion in January 2021.

In the meantime, should the court have to consider an order under Section III of CPR 3, it may come as a surprise to all involved that the level of the cap is to be set, pursuant to CPR PD 3F, para 4, by taking account of the factors at CPR 44.5 (the seven pillars under the old rules). CPR 44.5 has, for the last seven and a half years dealt with cases determining the amount of costs payable under a contract. This is a serious point, as the fact that this has gone unaltered for so long suggests that the court has never had to engage the principle. However, as the jurisdiction survives, the PD is long overdue for correction.

CHAPTER 18

PROSPECTIVE CONTROL OF COSTS – PROTECTIVE COSTS ORDERS

INTRODUCTION TO PROSPECTIVE CONTROL OF COSTS – PROTECTIVE COSTS ORDERS

[18.1]

It is important to define our terminology at the outset of this chapter. Many of the procedures that we have considered in previous chapters under the umbrella heading of *'Prospective costs control'* lead, to a greater or lesser extent, to the provision of some form of costs protection. At the end of this chapter we shall consider *Beddoe orders* – although strictly these are better described as pre-emptive costs orders. That leaves something else as *protective costs orders*. That something is an advance order that if a party, usually claimants, but, as we shall see below, it can be defendants, are unsuccessful either they will not be ordered to pay the costs of the successful party/ies or that their liability under any such costs orders is limited or capped to a specific amount.

Section VI of CPR 46 applies to applications for judicial review made after 7 August 2016. Section VI prescribes the procedure for applications for costs capping made under ss 88 and 89 of the Criminal Justice and Courts Act 2015 ('the statute') (the full text of these sections appears in the appendix). The provisions of Section VI replace protective costs orders in judicial review applications (except certain environmental cases – see **[18.13]** below). However, as these sections have their origins in the general 'protective costs orders' jurisprudence and some of the guidance given may remain informative, a brief summary of the case law and principles is merited (**[18.2]** and **[18.3]** below). That this is so is confirmed by consideration of this jurisprudence in applications made in non-judicial review proceedings eg *Maugham v Uber London Ltd* [2019] EWHC 391(Ch), and under the statute eg *Hawking v Secretary of State for Health and Social Care* (22 February 2018, unreported), QBD (Admin) Cheema-Grubb J.

Notwithstanding that the Court of Appeal has been clear that 'protective costs orders cannot be made in private litigation' (*Eweida v British Airways plc* [2009] EWCA Civ 1025, para 38, an interpretation tested, but confirmed as an essential part of the court's reasoning in that case in *Maugham* paras 35–47 and stated to be 'a binding authority that the policy and practice of the courts is that a protective costs order should not be made in private litigation' in *Swift v Carpenter* [2020] EWCA Civ 165, para 44), there are other discrete regimes which provide costs protection (other than pure costs capping governed by CPR 3 – see Chapter 17) and these are considered at the end of the chapter at **[18.11]** onwards. There are also some statutory appeals where the judicial review costs capping provisions do not apply and an application for a protective costs order continues to engage the principles set out at **[18.2]** below (see for example the decision in *Revenue and Customs Comrs v TGH Commercial Ltd* [2016] UKUT 519 (TCC), confirming that these principles governed applications for protective costs orders in appeals to the Upper Tribunal).

CASE LAW – GENERAL PRINCIPLES AND PROCEDURE THAT EMERGED

[18.2]

One of the first cases where guidance was given in respect of protective costs orders was in *R v Lord Chancellor, ex p Child Poverty Action Group* [1998] 2 All ER 755, [1999] 1 WLR 347. Dyson J suggested that such orders should only be made in exceptional circumstances and gave the following guidance:

(i) The court must be satisfied that the issues raised are truly ones of general public importance;
(ii) The court must be satisfied, following short argument, that it has a sufficient appreciation of the merits of the claim that it can be concluded that it is in the public interest to make the order;
(iii) The court must have regard to the financial resources of the applicant and respondent, and the amount of costs likely to be in issue;
(iv) The court will be more likely to make an order where the respondent clearly has a superior capacity to bear the costs of the proceedings than the applicant, and where it is satisfied that, unless the order is made, the applicant will probably discontinue the proceedings, and will be acting reasonably in so doing.

The authorities and philosophy of protective costs orders were considered in *R (on the application of Corner House Research) v Secretary of State for Trade and Industry* [2005] EWCA Civ 192. The Court of Appeal, having considered the statutory framework for awarding costs and the historical perspective on protective costs orders offered clear guidelines as follows:

- Such orders will only be made in exceptional circumstances.
- The governing principles are:
  - A protective costs order may be made at any stage of the proceedings, on such conditions as the court thinks fit, provided that the court is satisfied that:
    - the issues raised are of general public importance;
    - the public interest requires that those issues should be resolved;
    - the applicant has no private interest in the outcome of the case;
    - having regard to the financial resources of the applicant and the respondent and to the amount of costs that are likely to be involved it is fair and just to make the order;
    - if the order were not made the applicant would probably discontinue the proceedings and would be acting reasonably in so doing.
- If those acting for the applicant were doing so *pro bono* that would be likely to enhance the merits of the application for a protective costs order.

- It is for the court, in its discretion, to decide whether it is fair and just to make the order in the light of the above considerations.
- A protective costs order can take a number of different forms and the choice of form is an important aspect of the judge's discretion. Where an applicant is seeking an order for costs if it is successful, the court should prescribe by way of a capping order a total amount of the recoverable costs, which allows for modest legal representation.
- A claimant should apply for a protective costs order in his claim form, which should include a schedule of the claimant's future costs, of and incidental to, the full judicial review application. A defendant should set out any reasons for resisting an order in its acknowledgment of service. The judge should consider making an order on paper with any actual hearing being brief and, recognising the costs of the process itself, proportionate.

In *R (on the application of Buglife, The Invertebrate Conservation Trust) v Thurrock Thames Gateway Development Corpn* [2008] EWCA Civ 1209, the applicant Conservation Trust applied for a protective costs order capping its liability in costs in a dispute with the respondent local planning authority, which in turn applied for an order capping its own liability in costs to the applicant. The Court of Appeal stressed that courts should do their utmost to dissuade the parties from engaging in expensive satellite litigation on the question of whether protective costs orders and cost capping orders should be made. In *Buglife* the guidelines had not been followed. The local authority's written reasons were not put before the court on paper before the application for permission to appeal and for a protective costs order were considered by the judge. It was of great importance that issues relating to permission to appeal and to a protective costs order and a consequent cost capping order should all be considered at the same time and on paper. In the present case, because the claimant had been granted permission to appeal, it should have some protection but it would be unfair for it to have total protection, especially given the fact that there was a significant risk that it would lose. The just order was to limit the claimant's costs exposure in the Court of Appeal to a further £10,000 making its potential total liability £20,000. It was right to cap the authority's liability to the claimant in an appropriate sum, which was also £10,000.

The Master of the Rolls said:

> 'In the rare case in which it is necessary to have an oral hearing, it should last a short time as contemplated in Corner House and it should take place in good time before the hearing of the substantive application for judicial review, so that the parties may know the position as to their potential liabilities for costs in advance of incurring the costs.'

CASE LAW – PUBLIC INTEREST

[18.3]

A number of cases have demonstrated the difficulty in satisfying the dual requirements of there being a public interest but there being no private interest (for as already stated protective costs orders may not be made in private law cases – see *Eweida v British Airways plc* at **[18.1]** above). This tension between public and private interest in the proceedings was revisited by the Court of Appeal in *IS v Director Legal Aid Casework* [2014] EWCA Civ 886, where the court concluded that there was a need to allow flexibility in applying the test. The mere fact that there was some private interest in the outcome should not preclude a protective costs order. The real question was the nature and extent of the interest. In this case, while there was a private interest, the issues raised were of sufficient public interest that the balance was heavily in favour of public interest and a protective order was made. As we shall see below, s 88 of the statute descends to some detail in attempting to define public interest. It seems that flexibility has not been completely removed by the decision in *Swift v Carpenter* [2020] EWCA Civ 165 (above), but is more clearly defined by the court:

> 'The binding nature of *Corner House* and *Eweida* as precedents must be qualified to the following extent. As we have emphasised, those decisions are about how the wide discretion of the court as to costs should be exercised. They are not decisions on law but on policy and practice. Like any other policy or practice, they may be subject to adjustment in the light of circumstances that did not exist or were not anticipated at the time they were set.' (para 50)

THE STATUTORY FRAMEWORK – WHO MAY APPLY AND WHOSE COSTS LIABILITY MAY BE LIMITED?

[18.4]

Section 88(4) of the statute provides that the court may only make a costs capping order on the application of the applicant for judicial review and only if permission to apply for judicial review has been given. If a costs capping order is made that limits or removes the liability of the applicant to pay costs if the review is unsuccessful, then the order must also limit or remove the liability of the other party to pay the applicant's costs if the review is successful (s 89(2)).

THE STATUTORY FRAMEWORK – BY WHOM CAN AN ORDER BE MADE?

[18.5]

CPR 46.16(1)(a) provides that a judicial review costs capping order may be made by both the High Court and the Court of Appeal. This mirrors s 88(1) of the statute, albeit that the latter provision is an exclusive one, confirming that costs capping orders in judicial review may only be made by these courts under the statutory provision.

THE STATUTORY FRAMEWORK – WHEN SHOULD THE APPLICATION BE MADE AND WHAT INFORMATION IS REQUIRED?

[18.6]

CPR PD 46, para 10.2 sets out that an application for a judicial review costs capping order must normally be made within or accompanying the claim form. However, CPR 46.17(1) is clear that the application must be on notice adopting the CPR 23 procedure. Any potential tension is resolved by CPR 23.3(2)(b) which allows an application without a notice (eg in a claim form) when permitted by a rule or practice direction. Oddly no specific provision is made for when the application must be made on any appeal. In the case of *R (on the application of Compton) v Wiltshire Primary Care Trust* [2008] EWCA Civ 749, which predated the implementation of the statutory regime, the Court of Appeal stated that if the recipient of the protective costs order in the court below wished to appeal, an application for an order should be lodged with an application for permission to appeal. Preservation of this approach seems logically to follow the provision at CPR PD 46, para 10.2.

CPR 46.17 provides that an application must be supported by evidence (whether made in the claim form or in a freestanding application notice). The evidence must set out why an order should be made, a summary of the applicant's financial resources, the costs (and disbursements) which the applicant believes the parties are likely to incur in the future conduct of the proceedings and, if the applicant is a body corporate, whether it is likely to have the resources to meet liabilities arising from the proceedings. (Note the inconsistency of the application of rules within the CPR as CPR 44.1 defines costs as including disbursements anyway.)

In *R (on the application of Victoria Harvey) v Leighton Linslade Town Council* [2019] EWHC 760 (Admin), the court found that 'financial resources' in ss 88 and 89 of the statute included a prospective inheritance under the applicant's father's will, albeit one hard to value. As a result, an earlier costs cap of £4,000 was set aside and a fresh one of five times the original sum was imposed.

Evidence of why an order should be made specifically includes consideration of the factors set out at ss 88(6) and 89(1) of the statute. These factors bear a striking resemblance to the *Child Poverty Action Group* and *Corner House* guidelines at **[18.2]** above and are:

- that the proceedings are of public interest;
- that the applicant would withdraw or cease to participate in the proceedings without an order and this approach would be reasonable;
- the financial resources of the parties and anyone who may provide financial support to them (CPR PD 46, para 10.1(a) and (b) provides more information of the detail required);
- the extent to which the applicant will benefit if relief is granted in the proceedings;
- the extent to which any financial supporter of the applicant will benefit if relief is granted in the proceedings;
- whether any legal representatives acting for the applicant are acting free of charge;
- whether the applicant is an appropriate person to represent the interests of others or the public interest generally.

RECONSIDERATION OF ANY 'PAPER' DISPOSAL OF THE APPLICATION

[18.7]

Where the court has considered the application and disposed of it on paper, there is no requirement of exceptionality as a condition of the court reconsidering that decision (*Hawking v Secretary of State for Health and Social Care* (above)).

THE STATUTORY FRAMEWORK – PUBLIC INTEREST

[18.8]

As indicated in **[18.3]** above the statute endeavours to codify an approach to the determination of whether proceedings are in the public interest. The criteria are set out at s 88(7) and (8). The former provides that proceedings are public interest proceedings only if:

- the proceedings raise an issue of general public importance;
- the public interest requires the issue to be resolved; and
- the proceedings are likely to provide an appropriate means of resolving that issue,

and the latter sets out a non-exhaustive list of the matters the court must have regard to when determining this issue. These matters are:

- the number of people likely to be directly affected if relief is granted;
- how significant is the effect likely to be on these people;
- whether the proceedings involve consideration of a point of law of general public importance.

The criteria have already been considered in *R (on the application of Hannah Beety) v Nursing Midwifery Council & Independent Midwives UK and Lucina Ltd (both interested parties)* (14 June 2017, unreported), Admin Ouseley J, in which the court concluded that although the number of midwives affected by a decision of the defendant represented a small proportion of all midwives, the effect upon them would be significant. Although determining that (1) the potential clients and the families of those clients could not be categorised as directly affected and (2) there was no point of law of general public interest, the court concluded that judicial review was an appropriate way of resolving the issue and decided that the proceedings satisfied the public interest test (narrowly).

THE STATUTORY FRAMEWORK – TERMS OF ANY ORDER

[18.9]

Under s 88(2) a judicial review costs capping order limits or removes the liability of a party to judicial review proceedings to pay another party's costs in connection with any stage of the proceedings. Remember, also, the requirement at s 89(2), that if the court makes an order limiting or removing the liability of the applicant for judicial review if unsuccessful, the court must limit or remove the liability of the other party to pay the costs if the proceedings are successful. In *R (on the application of Beety & ors)* (above) the court capped the claimants' liability for costs at £25,000 and the defendant's liability at £65,000 and in *Hawking v Secretary of State for Health and Social Care* (above) at £160,000 and £115,000 respectively.

THE STATUTORY FRAMEWORK – VARIATION OF ORDERS

[18.10]

CPR 46.19 sets out the procedure for variation. As s 89(2) provides that any costs capping order must apply to all parties, it seems that any party may apply to vary. What is not clear is if this preserves the court's previous ability to vary to the extent of removal of costs protection. In *Howard v Wigan City Council* [2015] EWHC 3643 (Admin) a protective costs order was made in claim one. A second claim was subsequently made and later an additional ground was added to the second claim. The protective costs order was extended to the second claim. The additional ground was found to be without any foundation and accordingly the protective costs order was varied to permit the defendant to recover its costs in respect of that ground. The rationale was that if the second ground had been advanced at the appropriate time, a protective costs order would not have been made in respect of it. It should be noted that the judge, when allowing the new ground, had expressly preserved the right of the defendants to apply later to vary the protective costs order if that ground was found to be without foundation. It should also be noted that the application was phrased as one to 'vary' the protective costs order.

PROTECTIVE COSTS ORDER OUTSIDE THE STATUTORY REGIME – NO PUBLIC INTEREST

[18.11]

The case of *Begg v HM Treasury* [2015] EWHC 1851 (Admin), raises the possibility of a qualified protective costs order in non-judicial review proceedings where the public interest requirement is not only not met, but, instead, where the case has to be of real benefit to the applicant. The issue arose in the context of an application to declare a designation under the Terrorist Asset-Freezing etc Act 2010 void. It was made against a backdrop of reliance upon closed material. The Court of Appeal allowed an appeal against the decision to defer determination of whether or not to make such an order until after disclosure had taken place (*Begg v HM Treasury* [2016] EWCA Civ 568). However, it accepted the conclusions of the lower court that:

- as a matter of principle, it may be appropriate to make protective costs orders where individuals are accused of terrorism, but cannot assess the merits of the case as disclosure of closed material is withheld;
- protective orders should only be made in such cases if four conditions are met.

The case was remitted to determine whether all the conditions were met. These four conditions are:

- the case must be of real benefit to the individual bringing it;
- that individual must not be able to assess the prospects in the usual way because of reliance on closed material, but the open material must suggest that it is reasonable to litigate;
- having regard to the resources of the individual and the likely costs exposure involved it is just to make the order; and
- if a protective costs order is not made the applicant is likely to make a reasonable decision to discontinue.

The lower court also concluded that individuals should not benefit from such an order if their conduct is later adjudged unreasonable or abusive – hence the reference above to a 'qualified protective costs order' as subsequent determination may remove the protection.

PROTECTIVE COSTS ORDER OUTSIDE THE STATUTORY REGIME – CPR 52.19

[18.12]

CPR 52.19 affords any appellate court the power to limit recoverable costs on an appeal where costs recovery is either normally limited or excluded at first instance. The exercise is one of judicial discretion with CPR 52.19(2) and (3) setting out the basis upon which that discretion should be exercised. The appellate court must consider the means of both parties, all the circumstances of the case, the need to facilitate access to justice and whether the appeal raises an issue of principle or practice upon which substantial sums may turn (in which case it may not be appropriate to limit the costs). CPR 52.19(4) is clear that any application must be made as soon as possible.

This provision was considered in *JE (Jamaica) v Secretary of State for the Home Department* [2014] EWCA Civ 192 in which the appellant sought orders that certain disbursements inevitably incurred would be paid by the respondent in any event, that there would not be any liability for the respondent's costs if the claim was lost, but that if it was successful in full or in part the usual costs orders would apply. The Court of Appeal rejected the application stressing that this provision was not a form of one-way costs shifting and did not contemplate orders in favour of one party and not the other. It referred to the heading of the provision which restricts its application to 'the recoverable costs of an appeal'. In other words, the rule does not simply contemplate an order in favour of one party, but the costs recoverable by the winning party on the appeal, whoever the winner may turn out to be (see *Swift* above at **[18.1]** and **[18.4]**. The Court of Appeal also took the opportunity to stress the need to apply promptly.

A more robust provision applies under CPR 52.19A in respect of appeals in Aarhus Convention claims, which are considered below at **[18.13]**. In such appeals, the court must i) consider whether the costs of the proceedings will be prohibitively expensive for any party who was a claimant and, ii) if it considers they will be, make an order limiting the costs to the extent necessary to prevent this.

PROTECTIVE COSTS ORDER OUTSIDE THE STATUTORY REGIME – AARHUS CONVENTION AND OTHER ENVIRONMENTAL CASES

[18.13]

Although arguably something that falls within either the later comments on various fixed costs regimes or costs capping, the addition to the CPR in the April 2013 amendments to include recoverable costs limits in Aarhus convention claims is founded on the need to prevent the risk of prohibitive costs acting as a bar on such proceedings. As such, while not a pure protective costs order, the purpose is that of providing prospective costs protection. The rules are set out at CPR 45.41–45.45. These were subject to unexpected amendment in April 2017 and consequential amendments in December 2017 and April 2018. Amongst other changes, there is now no accompanying practice direction (or more accurately, reference is made in CPR PD 45, para 5 to Aarhus claims, but the relevant provisions have been omitted). It is important to stress that the regime is limited to judicial review proceedings within the scope of the convention. This is strictly defined by CPR 45.41(1).

Under CPR 45.42(2) a claimant may opt out of the provisions and does so by stating this in the claim form. If there are multiple claimants, then individual claimants may opt out (CPR 45.42(3)).

Assuming that the claim falls within the regime and subject to the power of the court to vary or remove the limits altogether under CPR 45.44, if the claimant is the paying party the limit is £5,000 where the claimant is an individual and not acting as or on behalf of a business or other legal person or £10,000 in all other cases. If the paying party is the defendant the limit is £35,000. If there are multiple claimants and/or defendants, then the limits apply in relation to each claimant/defendant. In *Campaign for Rural England – Kent Branch v Secretary of State for Communities and Local Government* [2019] EWCA Civ 1230, the court concluded that:

- the caps are the total liability, regardless of the number of defendants and interested parties (CPR 45.43(4) is clear that the cap is irrespective of the number of receiving parties);
- the costs of interested parties fall within the cap ('receiving parties' in CPR 45.43(4) makes no distinction between defendants and interested parties);
- the caps are global. They are applied to the reasonable and proportionate costs that have been incurred by the successful party/ies, at whatever stage the costs assessment is being done. The caps are arbitrary ones and do not reflect the cost of a claim that is only concluded after a substantial hearing. There are no lower caps for claims that fail at the permission stage. If costs are reasonable and proportionate, then the only limit on recovery is the relevant cap, regardless of the stage at which the claim is determined. Similarly, the fact that the costs fall below the relevant cap does not mean that they are automatically recoverable. They must still be reasonable and proportionate.

The cap resulted in a sizeable reduction to the interested party's costs and not those of the defendants. The court rationalised this on the basis that as an interested party and not a defendant there was a greater freedom to choose the extent of involvement in the challenge at the permission stage.

The court appears to be keen to apply the Aarhus Convention in an inclusive fashion. In *Austin v Miller Argent (South Wales) Ltd* [2014] EWCA Civ 1012, it was held that private nuisance claims where there was a significant public interest (by way of significant public environmental benefit) could come within the Aarhus Convention and afford costs protection to the individual claimant.

In *R (on the application of Edwards) v Environment Agency (No 2)* [2013] UKSC 78, the court had to consider the European Union principle that environmental proceedings should not be 'prohibitively expensive', having made a reference to the European Court of Justice. It concluded that:

- the test was not a purely subjective one;
- there was no definitive guidance on what was objectively reasonable;
- the court could take into account the merits of the claim, itemising these as the reasonable prospects, the importance of what was at stake for the claimant and in respect of the protection of the environment, the complexity of the law involved and the frivolous nature of the claim at various stages;
- the fact that the claimant had continued undeterred pending the outcome of this consideration was not determinative; and
- the same criteria would apply at first instance and on appeal.

In this case the Supreme Court concluded that the £25,000 previously the subject of a security for costs order was neither subjectively nor objectively unreasonable.

In the case of *R (on the application of HS2 Action Alliance Ltd) v Secretary of State for Transport* [2015] EWCA Civ 203, the Court of Appeal concluded that once it was determined that a case fell within the definition of an 'Aarhus Convention claim' under CPR 45.41(2), then an application would be dealt with under the relevant provisions of CPR 45 and not by further reference to the convention and it would be wrong to exclude local authorities from the costs protection set out in CPR PD 45, para 5.1(b) as was (the costs protection is now set out in CPR 45.43).

We stated that the rules were subject to unexpected amendment. They were, themselves, then challenged by judicial review. In *Royal Society for the Protection of Birds v Secretary of State for Justice* [2017] EWHC 2309 (Admin), the court considered challenges to the lawfulness of the amendments on three grounds as follows:

- that there is scope within the rules to vary the costs cap removing the certainty of potential costs liability at the outset, preventing informed decisions about the pursuit of proceedings and deterring claims;
- that there is a requirement for a claimant and any third-party funder to provide financial information on any application to vary the cap and this information may become public, again acting as a deterrent to claims.
- that the claimant's own costs should be included in the determination of whether a variation in or removal of the cap would either make proceedings prohibitively expensive under CPR 45.44(2)(a) or would render proceedings that would otherwise be prohibitively expensive possible to pursue under CPR 45.44(2)(b).

The court concluded that:

- Read as a whole, and with the overriding objective, any contention by a defendant that the cap should be varied must be identified in the acknowledgement of service and this results in the issue being determined at an appropriately early stage of the proceedings. In so far as the rules permit variation of the cap at any stage of the litigation, if the application is subsequently made because the defendant has failed to consider this at the permission stage, then it will be too late to do so, absent good reason – material change in the claimant's financial circumstances or false or misleading information in the schedule of financial information would be circumstances where variation would be reasonably predictable.
- Confidential information is provided in a variation hearing, engaging CPR 39.2(3)(c). CPR PD 39A, para 1.5 should be amended to include an application to vary a cap, so that the hearing should be, in the first instance, in private. This applies equally where the financial information is from individual claimants, claimants who are other legal persons and third-party funders. (Note that since this decision CPR PD 39 has been omitted from the rules. However, CPR 39.2(3)(c) remains.)
- The concession made by the defendants in this case that the claimant's costs may be a material matter for the court to consider was properly made. It would be a matter of discretion for the court in each case.

As a result of this decision, CPR 45.44 was amended in April 2018 to add provisions at CPR 45.44(5)–(7) to reflect the conclusions reached by the court in *Royal Society for the Protection of Birds v Secretary of State for Justice* under the first bullet point above. It is also worth noting that there is a specific cross-reference at the end of CPR 45.44 to the provisions of CPR 39.2(3)(c).

Whilst on the topic of variation, the Court of Appeal concluded in *Campaign to Protect Rural England – Kent Branch v The Secretary of State for Communities and Local Government* [2019] EWCA Civ 1230, that the Aarhus cap applies in respect of the costs of an interested party. This was taken a stage further in *R (on the application of Bertoncini) v London Borough of Hammersmith and Fulham* unreported 2 June 2020 (HHJ Bird), in which the court determined that an interested party does have the right to apply for a variation of the Aarhus cap.

(See **[18.12]** above for consideration of the position on appeal.)

Costs are also relevant in Aarhus claims when the court is considering whether to impose, and the extent of, any cross-undertaking in damages on a claimant when it makes an interim injunction (see CPR PD 25, para 5.3).

BEDDOE ORDERS

[18.14]

Until the advent of the type of prospective cost orders considered above, the only form of pre-emptive costs orders were to be found in the Chancery Division. There they remain an option and if the wording in the practice direction to CPR Part 64 is to be adopted we must call these prospective costs orders as well.

If trustees or personal representative are concerned that in commencing or defending a claim it might subsequently be suggested that they have acted unreasonably, they may apply to the court prospectively for an order that, win or lose, the costs that they incur will come out of the fund or the estate. As this applies as much to defending a claim as pursuing one, it is not unusual to see a claim stayed while trustees or personal representatives make this application in the Chancery Division. For more than a hundred years these applications and the ensuing orders have been known as *'Beddoe applications'* and *'Beddoe orders'* after the case of *Re Beddoe, Downes v Cottam* [1893] 1 Ch 547, 62 LJ Ch 233, CA.

The procedure is set out at CPR PD 64B, which comes very loosely from the general provision at CPR 64.2(a) that enables the court to determine any question arising in the administration of an estate or the execution of a trust. In summary:

- The application should be made under CPR Part 8.
- The application must be supported by evidence and, to ensure that the trustees or personal representatives are properly protected, that evidence must give full disclosure of all relevant matters.
- The evidence in support of the application must cover the advice of a lawyer as to the prospects of success, the value to the fund of the dispute, details of the likely costs the trustees or personal representative and other parties.
- The evidence must provide any known information about the means of the other parties.
- The evidence must identify any other relevant factors that may influence the court's decision.
- The evidence must indicate the extent and outcome of discussion with beneficiaries.
- In respect of any litigation, information about whether any relevant pre-action protocols have been complied with and whether ADR has been proposed or will be (and if not, why not).
- If a beneficiary opposes the application he should be a defendant to the Part 8 claim

Ordinarily the court will dispose of the application on paper. If either the claimant or the defendant believes a court hearing is required then they must expressly state this and give reasons. The court is not obliged to hold a hearing, but where it makes an order without one then it will give the parties an opportunity to apply to vary or discharge the order at an oral hearing. Any order sanctioning proceedings or the defence of proceedings can be limited to a particular stage and be subject to review on the material then available. See Chapter 38 –Trustees for further consideration of this.

CHAPTER 19

PROSPECTIVE COSTS ORDERS – SECURITY FOR COSTS

INTRODUCTION TO PROSPECTIVE COSTS ORDERS – SECURITY FOR COSTS

[19.1]

One party to litigation may be ordered to provide security for the costs of the other party in the very limited circumstances prescribed by CPR 25.12–25.15 and the Arbitration Act 1996, s 38. In addition there is a limited discretion under CPR 3.1(3) and (5) to order a payment in to court which CPR 3.1(6A) refers to as security for any sum payable by that party (which would include costs). Beyond that there is no inherent jurisdiction to order parties to provide security for costs (*WU v Hellard* (2013) Ch D 25/11/2013). There was also provision to apply for security under the Companies Act 1985, s 726(1). That provision was repealed (October 2009), but much of the case law that emerged from it, and the principles established by it, have a resonance with the provisions in CPR Part 25, particularly under CPR 25.13(2)(c).

UNDER THE CIVIL PROCEDURE RULES, RULES 25.12–25.14

Who may make an application?

[19.2]

The procedural code sets out at CPR 25.12 that only a defendant may apply for security. However, although there can be no order for security for costs against a defendant who is solely exercising the right to defend, even though resident out of the jurisdiction, there may be such an order in respect of a counterclaim. This is because under CPR 20.3 an additional claim (the definition of which includes a counterclaim) is treated as a claim and CPR 2.3(1) defines a defendant as 'a person against whom a claim is made'.

As a general rule, where a counterclaim can properly be relied upon as a set-off and where it arises out of the same subject matter as the claim, the counter-claiming defendant ought not to be required to give security for the costs of that counterclaim unless there are exceptional circumstances (*Ashworth v Berkeley-Walbrood Ltd* (1989) Independent, 9 October, CA). It is important to note that component parts of a counterclaim can be separated and those that are genuinely independent of the claim are susceptible to security (see *Ultimate Utilities Ltd v McNicholas Construction* QBD (TCC) 9/4/14 where Ramsey J found that one third of the litigation dealt solely with the counterclaim and security could be ordered in respect of that third. Contrast this to the situations in both *Re F1 Call Ltd sub nom Apex Global*

Management Ltd v F1 Call Ltd [2014] EWHC 779 (Ch), where the issues of the claim and counterclaim could not be satisfactorily separated and *Plymouth (Notte Street) Ltd v Mears Ltd* (12 July 2019, unreported (TCC)), in which the counterclaim formed the mainstay of the proceedings). In both cases, the court concluded that to order the claimants to give security would, effectively, give the defendants security in respect of the pursuit of their own claims.

A counterclaim is more than a mere defence to a claim: it is a claim which has a 'vitality of its own' (*Jones v Environcom Ltd* [2009] EWHC 16 (Comm)) or 'independent vitality' (*TC Developments (South East) Ltd v Investin Quay House Ltd* [2019] EWHC 1432 (TCC)). The inference that the defendant has a claim which has a vitality of its own can be drawn where (i) the defendant would have issued proceedings and it was a matter of chance which party issued proceedings first and (ii) the defendant would continue with the proceedings pursuing the counterclaim even if the claimant discontinued its claim.

The marked discrepancy in size between the amount claimed in the action and the very much greater amount claimed by the counterclaim is relevant to the consideration of whether a counterclaim is a mere defence or a cross-claim with 'vitality of its own', which might well stand alone and be pursued even if the original claim were abandoned (*Hutchison Telephone (UK) Ltd v Ultimate Response Ltd* [1993] BCLC 307, CA). The court in *TC Developments* (above), in deciding to grant security to the claimant, put it in these terms:

> 'However, when one looks at the substance of this action and asks the question whether the Defendant in this case is simply defending itself or is going beyond mere self-defence and launching a cross-claim with an independent vitality of its own, the combination of the factual scope of the Counterclaim and the asserted very substantial overtopping of the Claimants' claims lead me to the conclusion that the Defendant has gone well beyond mere defence.'

Interestingly, in *Petromin SA v Secnav Marine Ltd* [1995] 1 Lloyd's Rep 603, QBD where both parties were making substantial claims based on the same set of facts, the order for security for costs of the counterclaim was for the full amount of those costs and not merely for the amount by which the claimant's costs were increased in defending the counterclaim. The claimant was entitled to be secured in respect of costs no less fully than if it were merely a defendant to the claim advanced in the counterclaim, notwithstanding that it was also claimant in the action.

There are two exceptions to the general rule that the court will not exercise its discretion under CPR 25.12 to order security for costs if the same issues arise on the claim and the counterclaim and the costs incurred in defending the claim would also be incurred in prosecuting the counterclaim. These are:

(1) Where the claim raises substantial factual enquiries which are not the subject of the counterclaim, an order for security might be appropriate notwithstanding the fact that the claim provided a defence to the counterclaim. However, in such a situation the security may be limited to the costs of the additional issues raised by the claim (see *Re F1*, above);

(2) Where the claim and counterclaim both raise additional issues it might also be relevant to consider whether the quantum of the claim in respect of which security is sought is substantially greater than the counterclaim (*Dumrul v Standard Chartered Bank* [2010] EWHC 2625 (Comm)).

The fact that some form of protection may be held as a result of other proceedings does not necessarily preclude an application for security. In *Flender Werft AG v Aegean Maritime Ltd* [1990] 2 Lloyd's Rep 27, QBD it was held that obtaining a freezing injunction against the claimant in an arbitration as security for a counterclaim did not prevent the defendant obtaining an order for security for costs of the claim. The freezing of the funds relating to the counterclaim was not relevant to the issue of security for costs in the main action, in respect of which the defendant was entitled to a separate security. Similarly in *Peak Hotels and Resorts Ltd v Tarek Investments Ltd* [2015] EWHC 386 (Ch), [2015] 2 Costs LR 277, funds in court as security for cross-undertakings given were not available for costs.

In *Autoweld Systems Ltd v Kito Enterprises LLC* [2010] EWCA Civ 1469 the court rejected the notion that an equitable set-off of sums due under the claim could provide security in the case where there was a counterclaim, as those sums would be set off against the amount due under the counterclaim.

However, there is no jurisdiction to order a defendant seeking an enquiry as to damages arising out the claimant's interim injunction to provide security for the claimant's costs arising from the defendant's application (*Bowring (CT) & Co (Insurance) Ltd v Corsi & Partners Ltd* [1994] 2 Lloyd's Rep 567).

Security for costs other than from the claimant

[19.3]

CPR 25.14 provides that an order may be sought against someone who has assigned a claim to the claimant with a view to avoiding an adverse order for costs or who has contributed or agreed to contribute to the claimant's costs in exchange for a share of any money or property the claimant may recover. Given the increase in 'litigation funding' agreements this may prove to be a more frequently relied upon provision. That the court has the power to order security under CPR 25.14 from a litigation funder is clear (see, for example *Re Ingenious Litigation* [2020] EWHC 235 (Ch)). The very fact that a claimant has sought external funding in exchange for a financial interest in the claim may be an indication that the claimant does not have the means to meet an adverse costs order. In *Re Hellas Communications (Luxembourg)* (20 July 2017, unreported), Ch D, Snowden J concluded that there was an inherent or implied power following CPR 25.14, to make it purposeful, to order disclosure, properly controlled, of the identity of a funder and the terms of any such funding. The court accepted that it could undertake a two-stage approach, ordering initially only disclosure of the terms of the funding and then, subsequently, if an application was made for security, consider on its merits whether an order for security was appropriate. However, such an approach involved considerations of proportionality, but in this case knowledge of the identity of the funders might determine if an application was made at all and, if so, in what terms. This point was also considered in *RBS Rights Issue Litigation* [2017] EWHC 1217 (Ch), where the court ordered disclosure of the identity of the third party funders, but not the ATE Insurer (see [**37.14**]).

Under CPR 20.3, this provision applies equally to a counterclaiming defendant where the criteria in CPR 25.14 are met.

General conditions to be satisfied for applications under Part 25.12

[19.4]

These are set out at CPR 25.13. In effect there is a twofold test. The court has to be satisfied, having regard to all the circumstances of the case, that it is just to make an order AND at least one of the conditions set out at CPR 25.13(2) must be met or some other statutory provision permits such an order. In practice the tests tend to be taken the other way around, for if the defendant cannot satisfy the court under CPR 25.13(2), then the court does not need to exercise its discretion under CPR 25.13(1)(a). In *Dass v Beggs* [2014] EWHC 164 (Ch) the court suggested that save where 'it takes the view that in any event the evaluation of all the circumstances would lead it to refuse the order as a matter of discretion' it is usual to consider the specific gateway/s under CPR 25.13(2) as the first stage of the process. There are six conditions in CPR 25.13(2).

THE CONDITIONS UNDER CPR 25.13(2)

(1) Residence outside the jurisdiction but not resident in a Brussels Convention state, a Hague Convention state or a state bound by the Lugano Convention

[19.5]

CPR 25.13(2)(a) provides that an individual claimant or company ordinarily resident out of the jurisdiction in a country which is not a party to the Brussels, Hague or Lugano Conventions, may be ordered to give security. The test of whether or not a corporation is ordinarily resident outside the jurisdiction requires the court to locate its central management and control (*Re Little Olympian Each Ways Ltd* [1994] 4 All ER 561, [1995] 1 WLR 560). This provision covers claimants resident in the Isle of Man and the Channel Islands.

Although residence abroad is a condition precedent to the application, this alone is not sufficient to justify an order for security (*Berkeley Administration Inc v McClelland* [1990] 2 QB 407, [1990] 1 All ER 958, CA). Such an approach would be discriminatory and contrary to art 14 of the European Convention for the Protection of Human Rights. The court has now moved to a more flexible approach and the discretion should be exercised on objectively justified grounds relating to obstacles to, or the burden of, enforcement in the context of the particular country concerned. In *Nasser v United Bank of Kuwait* [2001] EWCA Civ 556, the Court of Appeal limited the security to the additional costs that would arise as a result of enforcement abroad. It is important to note that the additional costs arise in the country where the claimant's assets are held, which may not be the same as the country of residence. The Court of Appeal revisited this provision in *Bestfort Development LLP v Ras Al Khaimah Investment Authority* [2016] EWCA Civ 1099 and concluded that:

- CPR 25.13(2)(a) is prima facie discriminatory;

- the discrimination is on the basis of residence and not nationality (distinguishing Nasser);
- there is a rational justification for the provision, but the discretion afforded to the court in exercising its powers must not be used in a discriminatory fashion, but on objectively rational grounds (eg the difficulties of enforcement); and
- the correct test to apply is whether, on the evidence adduced, on objectively justified grounds relating to obstacles to, or the burden of, enforcement, there is a real risk that the defendant will not be in a position to enforce an order for costs against the claimant and that, in all the circumstances, it is just to make an order for security. Whether the evidence is sufficient to satisfy the court in any particular case that there is a real risk of serious obstacles to enforcement, will depend on the circumstances of the case. In other words, the appropriate test is not one of likelihood. A test of real risk of enforceability provides rational and objective justification for discrimination against non-Convention state residents (Gloster LJ, para 77).

There is no basis upon which an order can be made against an individual claimant who resides in the EC on the grounds of residence abroad. In *De Beer v Kanaar & Co (a firm)* [2001] EWCA Civ 1318, the fact that the claimant, a Dutch national residing in Florida, had assets in Holland and Switzerland did not protect him from an order for security for costs under CPR 25.13(2)(a)(ii) as being 'a person against whom a claim [could] be enforced under the Brussels Conventions or the Lugano Convention'. The rule is aimed at the juridical characteristics of the claimant, regardless of the assets that are owned or where those assets might be situated. A claimant who was not ordinarily resident in the UK or a Convention state could not escape liability to give security for costs merely by placing an asset in a Convention state. However, *Mustafa Ontulmus v Sir Ian Collett* [2014] EWHC 294 (QB) determined that while there is a burden on a party not resident in the UK to satisfy the court of residence in a contracting, convention or regulation state under CPR 25.13(2)(a), this obligation does not extend as far as proving residence at a particular address.

There is also no settled rule of practice that no order will be made against a foreign claimant if there are co-claimants resident in England (*Slazengers Ltd v Seaspeed Ferries International Ltd, The Seaspeed Dora* [1987] 3 All ER 967, [1988] 1 WLR 221, CA).

Whilst the amount of security is considered at **[19.23]** below, the case *Chernukhin v Danilina* [2018] EWCA Civ 1802, involved consideration of a point of principle relating to this condition – namely as the starting point for determination of the amount of security, whether, once it is found that there is a real risk of non-enforcement of a judgment against a claimant resident in a non-Convention jurisdiction, it is appropriate to grade that risk and to discount the costs to be secured accordingly. It concluded that the risk should not be graded on a sliding scale, instead determining that:

> ' . . . once it has been established that there are "substantial obstacles" sufficient to create a real risk of non-enforcement, the starting point is that the defendant should have security for the entirety of the costs and there is no room for discounting the security figure by grading the risk using a sliding scale approach. That is the starting point but it by no means follows that security for all or indeed any of those

costs will be ordered. The quantum of security is a matter of discretion and discretionary factors such as, for example, delay or stifling, may affect the amount of security to be ordered, if any.'

(2) The claimant is a company or other body (whether incorporated inside or outside Great Britain) and there is reason to believe that it will be unable to pay the defendant's costs if so ordered

[19.6]

CPR 25.13(2)(c) covers the impecunious company, whether within the jurisdiction or not. It is important to note that there has to be reason to believe that the claimant 'will', as opposed to 'may' not be able to pay the defendant's costs.

Inability to pay

[19.7]

The fact that a company is in liquidation is, on the face of it, evidence that it is unable to pay the defendant's costs unless evidence to the contrary is given (*Northampton Coal, Iron and Waggon Co v Midland Waggon Co* (1878) 7 Ch D 500, CA). Otherwise, an application for security must be supported by a statement which credibly and reasonably shows the inability of the company to pay the costs if the defendant is successful. The mere issuing of a debenture charging all the company's assets is not a sufficient reason to order security. Where a company's accountant deposed to there being sufficient cash-flow to meet an order for costs, despite a shortage of assets, the court accepted this in the absence of expert evidence to the contrary (*Kim Barker Ltd v Aegon Insurance Co (UK) Ltd* (1989) Times, 9 October, CA).

In *Automotive Latch Systems Ltd v Honeywell International Inc* [2006] EWHC 2340 (Comm), the court rejected the claimant's submission that in respect of orders for security for costs, CPR 25.13(2)(c) looked to the ability to pay costs at the time an order to pay was made and that as a matter of jurisdiction, the defendant could not show that in two years' time or so, when any litigation would be likely to be the subject of a judgment and a costs order, that the claimant's finances would not be such as to enable it to pay the defendant's costs. The court also rejected the claimant's submission that the defendant had caused its financial difficulties because to do so would be to pre-judge one of the major issues in dispute in the proceedings.

(3) The claimant has changed address since the litigation was commenced with a view to evading the consequences of litigation

[19.8]

Although it seems obvious in a rule that relates to the provision of security for costs, one of the 'consequences of litigation' is the possibility of being ordered to give security (*Aoun v Bahri* [2002] EWHC 29 (Comm)). Accordingly if a change of address can be linked to the evasion of any consequence of litigation then this ground is satisfied – Moore-Bick J stated that once a change of address was established then 'the only question is whether' a party 'has done so with a view to evading the consequences of the litigation.'

(4) The claimant failed to give his address in the claim form, or gave an incorrect address on that form

[19.9]

This situation arose in *Auon v Bahri* (above). Of course, the rationale behind the provision is obvious. If no address or an incorrect address is given then that may make enforcement of any costs order harder and more expensive.

(5) The claimant is acting as a nominal claimant, other than as a representative claimant under Part 19, and there is reason to believe he will be unable to pay the defendant's costs

[19.10]

CPR 2.3 defines a claimant as 'a person who brings a claim'. It does not offer any definition of a nominal claimant. Further consideration suggests that this condition will be of limited, if any, application. CPR Part 19 representative claimants are specifically excluded. A defendant bringing a counterclaim is not a nominal claimant, but is clearly a claimant in the counterclaim for the reasons already considered. A trustee in bankruptcy bringing a claim in that capacity is also clearly a claimant. We have already considered the provisions of CPR 25.14 in respect of assigned debts and litigation funders. This leaves only limited scope for a claimant to be nominal only, eg, a trustee in bankruptcy continuing a claim brought by the bankrupt. However, even then there is already a separate provision for security under s 49 of the County Courts Act 1984, which provides:

> '49(1) The bankruptcy of the plaintiff (claimant) in any action in a county court which the trustee might maintain for the benefit of the creditors shall not cause the action to abate if, within such reasonable time as the court orders, the trustee elects to continue the action and to give security for the costs of the action.'

There remains the rather unattractive possibility that a litigation friend under CPR Part 21 may be treated as a 'nominal claimant'. The N235 'Certificate of suitability' already provides for the litigation friend of a claimant to undertake to pay costs, but this is subject to a right to recover these from the claimant. Strictly in such claims the claimant is the child or protected party anyway.

In *Envis v Thakkar* (1995) Times, 2 May, [1997] BPIR 189, CA the court concluded that before a person could be labelled a 'nominal claimant' there had to be some element of deliberate duplicity or window-dressing operating to the detriment of the defendant eg a claimant who has assigned the benefit of a claim to a non-party and has retained no interest in it (*Semler v Murphy* [1968] Ch 183) or, possibly, even where a relatively small interest is retained by the claimant, as otherwise the 'nominal claimant' provision could be too easily circumvented (*Farmer v Mosely (Holdings) Ltd* [2001] 2 BCLC 572) This conclusion was confirmed in *Chuku v Chuku* [2017] EWHC 541 (Ch), in which the court reviewed the authorities on 'nominal claimant'.

(6) The claimant has taken steps in relation to assets that would make it difficult to enforce an order for costs

[19.11]

This provision does not require the defendant to show the claimant's intent to avoid the consequences of an adverse costs order. The rule is not concerned with the claimant's motivation for the disposal of an asset (*Aoun v Bahri*, above). There does not have to be a subjective intention; all the defendant need do is show that the steps taken make enforcement more difficult (*Harris v Wallis* [2006] EWHC 630 (Ch)). In other words, the court is concerned with the effect of the steps and not the motivation for taking them (*Scott v Conwy County Borough Council (as Conwy Harbour Authority)* (16 February 2018, unreported), QBD (Admiralty) Teare J).

However, if intent to defeat any subsequent adverse costs order can also be shown then there is no doubt that this would influence the court's consideration of whether it is just to make an order.

In addition, there needs to be no temporal link between the arrangement of assets and the litigation. (See *Re Tonstate Group Ltd v Matayas* [2020] EWHC 328 (Ch).)

SECURITY FOR COSTS OF AN APPEAL

[19.12]

CPR 25.15 provides that an order for security for costs may be made against an appellant and a cross – appealing respondent on the same grounds as appear in CPR 25.13.

In *Antonelli v Allen* [2001] EWCA Civ 1563 the claimant paid £100,000 to her solicitor, who had subsequently been struck off the roll of solicitors, in dubious circumstances. She retrieved £70,000 of the money but lost her claim for the balance of £30,000 from the solicitor's partner. On the claimant obtaining permission to appeal, the defendant sought an order for security for costs under CPR 25.13(2)(a) and CPR 25.13(2)(g). The claimant had failed to respond to any questions about the fate of the £70,000 she had recovered, and there was an inference that she had dealt with that sum in such a way as to put it beyond the reach of any creditors. The respondent to the appeal was therefore entitled to security. The court fixed the amount of security at £10,000 with a provision that if payment was not made by a fixed date the appeal would be struck out automatically and that the appeal be stayed in the meantime.

In *Bell Electric Ltd v Aweco Appliance Systems GmbH & Co KG* [2002] EWCA Civ 1501, the defendant appealed against a judgment ordering it to pay to Bell within 14 days £100,000 by way of interim damages and £35,000 on account of costs. Aweco was in deliberate breach of the order to pay the judgment sum and its application for a stay had been refused. The failure or delay in making the payment was due not to any financial difficulty but was cynically based upon the practical difficulties for the respondent in seeking enforcement in a foreign jurisdiction. Accordingly, there was a compelling reason for the Court of Appeal to order that the appeal be stayed unless within 14 days Aweco paid into court £135,000 to abide its outcome.

A problem peculiar to appeals is that until permission to appeal has been granted there is no provision under CPR 25.15 to enable the court to order security. This is notwithstanding that sometimes the respondent to the appeal may incur not insubstantial costs during that period. A possible solution is under the court's powers under CPR 3.1 (see below).

Rule 36 of the Supreme Court Rules 2009 provides the Supreme Court with the power to order security for costs. The Supreme Court may, on the application of the respondent, order an appellant to give security for the costs of the appeal, and will set out the amount of the security and the manner in which it must be given. Security for costs will not generally be required for appellants who have been granted state funding, for Ministers or Government departments, or where the appeal is under the Child Abduction and Custody Act 1985. No security for costs is required in cross-appeals. Failure to provide security as required will result in the appeal being struck out by the Registrar although the appellant may apply to reinstate the appeal.

As with CPR 25.13 the court must still consider the justice of making an order for security for costs having regard to all the circumstances of the case.

Both CPR 52.6(2)(b) and CPR 52.18(1)(c) may operate to provide an order security for costs by the court imposing some form of payment in to court in respect of costs as a condition of granting permission to appeal or as a condition upon which an appeal may be brought. When considering the latter, the Supreme Court in *Goldtrail Travel Ltd v Aydin* [2017] UKSC 57 noted that the court should not impose a condition which has the effect of stifling a party's ability to participate in proceedings, but that the burden of proof in establishing that this will be the effect rests with the party advancing this argument.

SECURITY POST-JUDGMENT

[19.13]

In the case of *Republic of Dijibouti v Abdourahman Boreh* [2016] EWHC 1035 (Comm), the claimant had paid security during the proceedings. After judgment against it, including an order for costs on the indemnity basis, the defendant sought additional security for the costs already incurred. The claimant argued that whilst the court had jurisdiction to award security for the detailed assessment proceedings, it did not have jurisdiction to 'top-up' the earlier security. The court concluded that CPR 25.12 did convey such a jurisdiction and that it should be exercised (there being a change in circumstances since the previous order for security – namely the award of indemnity costs and the fact that a success fee had become payable as a result of the defendant's success).

IS IT JUST TO MAKE AN ORDER FOR SECURITY OF COSTS HAVING REGARD TO ALL THE CIRCUMSTANCES OF THE CASE?

[19.14]

Having considered the CPR 25.13(2) conditions, let us turn our attention to CPR 25.13(1)(a) and the second part of the twofold test. Even if the defendant has satisfied the court that one of the conditions under CPR 25.13(2) is met, the court retains a discretion and must be satisfied that it is just to order security. It is here that many of the authorities that emerged under s 726(1) of the Companies Act 1985 remain relevant and informative.

Discretion

[19.15]

In *Parkinson (Sir Lindsay) & Co Ltd v Triplan Ltd* [1973] QB 609, [1973] 2 All ER 273, CA, Lord Denning identified the following circumstances which the court might take into account in exercising its discretion:

(i) Whether the claimant's claim is bona fide and not a sham.
(ii) Whether the claimant has a reasonably good prospect of success.
(iii) Whether there is an admission by the defendant on the pleadings or elsewhere that the money is due.
(iv) Whether there is a substantial payment into court or an 'open offer' of a substantial amount.
(v) Whether the application for security is being used oppressively, eg so as to stifle a genuine claim.
(vi) Whether the claimant's want of means is being brought about by any conduct by the defendants, such as delay in payment or in doing their part of the work.
(vii) Whether the application for security is made at a late stage of the proceedings.

Prospects of success

[19.16]

If it can clearly be demonstrated that the claimant has a very high probability of success, that is a matter that can properly be weighed in the balance. Similarly, if it can be shown that there is a very high probability that the defendant will succeed that also is a matter that can be weighed. The court deplores attempts to go into the merits of the case, unless it can be clearly demonstrated one way or the other that there is a high degree of probability of success or failure (*Porzelack KG v Porzelack (UK) Ltd* [1987] 1 All ER 1074, [1987] 1 WLR 420 and re-affirmed by Leggatt J in *Dena Technology (Thailand) Ltd v Dena Technology Ltd* QBD (Comm) 14/02/2014). in *Al-Koronky v Time Life Entertainment Group Ltd* [2005] EWHC 1688 (QB), the court reminded itself of this in these terms:

> ' . . . the court should not, upon such an application, enter into the merits of the case in any detail, save in the exceptional case where one party or the other can demonstrate a high degree of probability of success'

which also held that a defendant should not be denied security merely because the claimant had succeeded in previous litigation.

Admission

[19.17]

If a defendant admits so much of the claim as would be equal to the amount for which security would have been ordered, the court may refuse security, for security can be provided by paying the admitted amount into court (*Hogan v Hogan (No 2)* [1924] 2 IR 14).

Negotiations

[19.18]

A defendant should not be adversely affected in seeking security merely because that party has attempted to reach a settlement. Evidence of negotiations conducted 'without prejudice', should not be admitted without the consent of the parties (*Simaan General Contracting Co v Pilkington Glass Ltd* [1987] 1 All ER 345, [1987] 1 WLR 516, CA).

No order if that would be oppressive

[19.19]

Where an order for security for costs against the claimant company might result in oppression in that the claimant company would be forced to abandon a claim which had a reasonable prospect of success, the court is entitled to refuse to make that order notwithstanding that the claimant company, if unsuccessful, will be unable to pay the defendant's costs (*Aquila Design (GRP Products) Ltd v Cornhill Insurance plc* [1988] BCLC 134, 3 BCC 364, CA). It is not necessary for the company to produce evidence of its inability to pursue the proceedings if an order for security is made for the application to be dismissed; it is sufficient if the company shows that there is a probability that it will be unable to pursue the proceedings. Unless it is clearly demonstrable one way or the other, it is not appropriate to go into the merits of the claim in such an application (*Trident International Freight Services Ltd v Manchester Ship Canal Co* [1990] BCLC 263, CA).

In *Absolute Living Developments Limited (In Liq) v DS7 Limited* [2018] EWHC 1432 (Ch), [2018] All ER (D) 104 (Jun), where it was conceded that the claimant would be unable to meet the defendant's costs and where the court concluded that there was no source of funding to raise money to meet any order for security for costs, the judge applied the balancing exercise described by Peter Gibson LJ in *Keary Developments Ltd v Tarmac Construction Ltd* [1995] 3 All ER 534, as:

> '... the injustice to the claimant if prevented from pursuing a proper claim by an order of security . . . Against . . . the injustice to the defendant if no security is ordered and at the trial the plaintiff's claim fails and the defendant finds himself unable to recover from the claimant the costs which have been incurred by him in defence of the claim.'

Having done so, he concluded that the interests of the creditors (as the company was in liquidation) outweighed those of the defendants and declined to order security.

On the other hand, in *Automotive Latch Systems Ltd v Honeywell International Inc* (above) the court observed that it was a common, if not inevitable, feature of any order for security that the paying party would expect to find a better use for the money if it did not have to pay it as security. However, there is a significant difference between finding a better use for money and not being able to find the money to fund the security.

In *Blue Sky One Ltd v Mahan Air* [2011] EWCA Civ 544, the appellant contended that any substantial order for security would stifle its appeal for which permission had been granted, which would be wrong as a matter of domestic law and would also infringe its rights under Article 6 of the Human Rights Act 1998. The court concluded that if such a submission were relied upon, the onus was upon the party alleging that its appeal would be stifled if a condition of security was imposed, to put before the Court full and frank evidence as to its means. The Court rejected the submission that the requirement for such evidence was incompatible with rights under Article 6, concluding that it is for the party seeking to establish its impecuniosity to prove its financial position. That a party alleging an order for security would stifle a claim is required to produce satisfactory evidence of a lack of funds and an absence of an alternate funding source was confirmed in *New Tasty Bakery Ltd v MA Enterprise (UK) Ltd* (13 April 2016, unreported), IPEC. In *PM v GL* [2018] EWHC 3502 (QB), the court, allowed an appeal, and not accepting that impecuniosity would operate as a bar to stifle the claim, ordered that unless the claimant paid sums due under an earlier costs order her claim would be struck out. In so doing, the judge found that the situation was analogous to that within a security for costs application and the onus was on a party alleging impecuniosity that would prevent compliance and so stifle a claim, to produce 'proper and sufficient' evidence in support of that allegation. This analogy of the considerations relevant to payment of interim costs and security for costs orders, in respect of the risk of stifling of claims, was affirmed by the court in *Siddiqi v Aidiniantz* [2020] EWHC 699 (QB).

In *Goldtrail Travel Ltd v Aydin* [2017] UKSC 57 (para **[19.12]** above) the Supreme Court summarised the position as follows:

- No order should be made if the effect would be to stifle the paying party's participation in the proceedings (para 16).
- The burden of proof is on the party alleging that its participation will be stifled (para 15).
- This extends to satisfying the court that there are not external sources of funding (para 23).
- Where security is sought against a company, the fact that it is a separate legal entity must be accepted. However, bold denials that an owner of a company would make sums available should be explored by reference to the realities of a company's financial position (para 24).

(See also 'Amount' below)

Co-claimant

[19.20]

Where the defendants obtained an order for security for costs against a claimant company which was not complied with, this did not entitle them to an order for security against an individual claimant as a condition of him being joined in the proceedings. (*Eurocross Sales Ltd v Cornhill Insurance plc* [1995] 4 All ER 950). Similarly, where a claimant company had failed to comply with an order to provide security but had executed a deed of assignment of its equitable interests in the claims to a shareholder justifying his joinder as a party under CPR 19.2, an order for security for costs could not be made against the shareholder under the guise of a condition imposed on joinder, except to the extent of security for any additional costs caused by or wasted as a result of his joinder: *Cie Noga D'Importation et D'Exportation SA v Abacha (as personal representatives of Sani Abacha (deceased))* (No 4) [2004] EWHC 2601 (Comm).

Confirming the approach set out in *Crabtree (B J) (Insulation) Ltd v GPT Communications Systems Ltd* (1990) 59 BLR 43, CA, in *Hello Quo The Movie Ltd v Duroc Media* [2014] EWHC 4622 (Ch), the Court declined to order security against one of two claimants as this would not have the desired effect as the other claimant could pursue the claim in any event. This would simply amount to a tactical advantage to the defendant.

Pre-action costs

[19.21]

In *Lobster Group Ltd v Heidelberg Graphic Equipment Ltd* [2008] EWHC 413 (TCC), lengthy pre-action mediation had failed and the first defendant sought security for the costs of the mediation from the claimant, which was now in administration. The court held that although as a matter of principle pre-action costs can be the subject of an application for security (*Re Gibson's Settlement Trusts, Mellors v Gibson* [1981] Ch 179, [1981] 1 All ER 233 and *McGlinn v Waltham Contractors Ltd* [2005] EWHC 1419 (TCC)) the court should be slow to exercise its discretion in favour of an applicant as there was a risk that if the pre-action period was lengthy the costs could be extensive and any subsequent attempt to obtain security might become penal in nature. The costs of the mediation were unlikely to be recoverable in any event and, even if they were, they should not form part of the security ordered. Costs of separate pre-action mediation were not 'costs of and incidental to the proceedings'. Both the course of the mediation and the reasons for its unsuccessful outcome were privileged matters and, as a matter of general principle, the costs incurred in respect of such procedure were not recoverable under the Senior Courts Act 1981, s 51. The claimant was ordered to provide security for costs from the commencement of proceedings up until the exchange of witness statements.

SECURITY FOR COSTS UNDER CPR 3.1

[19.22]

CPR 3.1 specifically permits the court to order a party to pay sums into court as a condition when making any order or if there has been a failure to comply with a rule, practice direction or any relevant pre-action protocol. Unlike Part 25, CPR 3.1 is not restricted to claimants: any party can be ordered to make a payment into court. The provision at CPR 3.1(3) is specifically referred to in CPR 13.3 as the court can impose conditions on setting aside a default judgment and CPR 24.6 when conditions can be imposed on the disposal of an application for summary judgment. Interestingly the wording of CPR 3.1(5) almost mirrors that of the amended overriding objective. It will be interesting to see whether, in this age of more robust case management enforcement, the court is more inclined to use the powers under CPR Part 3. We suspect that the answer will be no, for the reasons set out in the two cases considered below.

In *Olatawura v Abiloye* [2002] EWCA Civ 998, the court stated that before ordering security for costs in any case the court should be alert and sensitive to the risk that by making such an order it might be denying the party concerned the right to access to the court.

In *Huscroft v P&O Ferries Ltd* [2010] EWCA Civ 1483, the claimant lived in Portugal and the defendant applied for an order under CPR 3.1(3) and CPR 3.1(5) that he pay £20,000 into court as security for costs with conditions, on the grounds that the claim did not have a reasonable prospect of success, the claimant had failed to comply with court orders and did not have the financial resources to meet a judgment for costs against him. At a case management hearing, the district judge found that the claimant had not failed to comply with any rule, practice direction or pre-action protocol so he could not make an order under CPR 3.1(5), but instead he made an order under CPR 3.1(3)) that the claimant was to pay £5,000 into court as security for the costs and that in default of payment the claim was to be struck out. The district judge was overruled on appeal. The court stressed that litigants should not be encouraged to regard CPR 3.1(3) as providing a convenient means of circumventing the requirements of Part 25 and thereby of providing a less demanding route to obtaining security for costs. When a court was asked to consider making an order under CPR 3.1(3) or CPR 3.1(5) which was, or amounted to, an order for security for costs, or when it considered doing so of its own motion, it had to bear in mind the principles underlying CPR 25.12 and CPR 25.13. The order had enabled the defendant to obtain, on the back of case management directions, an order for security for costs which it could not have obtained under Part 25 and which was unrelated to the orders being made. It was inappropriate to make such an order. For an application of *Huscroft* see *R (on the application of Hersi & Co) v Legal Services Commission* (2 March 2016, unreported), QBD (Admin).

Huscroft was relied upon by the Court in *Carlton Advisors v Dorchester Holdings Ltd* [2014] EWHC 3341 (Comm), [2015] 1 Costs LR 1 as an explanation of the jurisdiction where it ordered a payment in by defendants when considering their application for a re-hearing under CPR 23.11 and where they had failed to comply with the overriding objective and had flouted previous orders. Indeed, the Court indicated that it would probably have dismissed the application if it had not had the ability to order the payment of some form of security 'as reassurance to the claimant that they are not going to have their money wasted in preparing fruitlessly for a trial'.

The difference between rule CPR 3.1 and CPR 25.15 was illustrated in *Great Future Ltd v Sealand Housing Corpn* [2003] EWCA Civ 682. The defendant, who had not complied with interim orders to pay £1 million on account of costs, sought permission to appeal against the judgment. The claimant sought orders that the interim orders be complied with and for security for its costs of the appeal before the application was heard. Although it could not rely on CPR 25.15 because there was no appeal until permission was granted, the Court of Appeal could exercise case management powers under CPR 3.1. There was no evidence that making the order sought would stifle the appeal and accordingly the orders were made. Accordingly, it is here that the lacuna in the CPR 25.15 provisions for security on appeals is filled.

THE AMOUNT OF SECURITY

[19.23]

The application must be supported by evidence (CPR 25.12(2)). Obviously, this should include details of the costs already incurred and an estimate of the future costs. As these applications will invariably arise in claims in the multi-track this process ought to be simplified and the expense reduced by making use of existing Precedents H and any costs budgets approved by the court (whilst the guidance it purports to give on the effect of 'incurred costs' in the costs management process has been clarified by rule change and the decision in *Harrison v University Hospitals Coventry and Warwickshire NHS Trust* [2017] EWCA Civ 792; *SARPD Oil International Ltd v Addax Energy SA* [2016] EWCA Civ 120, does serve as an illustration that budgets are of some assistance when determining the level of security).

Whilst the court's consideration of the costs will be far simpler as a result of any costs management orders, even then the court may discount the amount by the possibilities of either early settlement or the reduction of costs that are not within the approved budget on assessment. The court has power to order security in a sum less than the total potential order for costs. It may, for example, only be ordering security for the additional costs of enforcement (see for example *Sheikh Tahnoon Bin Saeed Bin Shakhboot Al Nehayan v John Kent* [2016] EWHC 613 (QB)). The entire process is a discretionary one. A balancing exercise is required (*Re Unisoft Group (No 2)* [1993] BCLC 532, ChD (Companies Ct)). As we have seen, the court will not make an order which would prevent a claimant from proceeding with a legitimate claim. An example of this was *Innovare Displays plc v Corporate Broking Services Ltd* [1991] BCC 174, CA, where the Court of Appeal held that 'sufficient security' for costs does not mean complete security, but security of a sufficiency in all the circumstances of the case as to be just. Accordingly, although the defendant sought to obtain an order for security of costs in the sum of £147,655, which it estimated would be its costs, the court held that a sum of £10,000 would be appropriate!

The fact that a claimant has either before (BTE) or after-the-event (ATE) insurance, is not in itself a sufficient reason for not making an order for security for costs. Nearly all BTE and ATE policies contain wide terms enabling an insurer to repudiate if a claim fails because of the insured's own conduct and concerns arise in the event of insolvency. Accordingly, there is no certainty that in the situation where the defendant would have an order for costs against the claimant (usually where the claim has been unsuccessful), the insurance will still be available as a source of meeting the defendant's costs. Both these concerns arose in *Catalyst Managerial Services v Libya Africa Investment Portfolio* [2017] EWHC 1236 (Comm) and the ATE insurance was found not to provide security. (See also *Al-Koronky v Time-Life Entertainment Group Ltd* [2006] EWCA Civ 1123 and Chapter 5 – Running Cases with Conditional Fee Agreements for further consideration of the link between funding and security.) In *Harlequin Property (SVG) Ltd v Wilkins Kennedy* [2015] EWHC 1122 (TCC), para 21, the court summarised recent authorities as follows:

> 'As a matter of principle, therefore, I conclude from this brief tour of the authorities that:

(a) adequate security for costs can be provided to a defendant by means other than a payment into court or a bank guarantee;
(b) depending on the terms of the insurance and the circumstances of the case, an ATE insurance policy may be capable of providing adequate security;
(c) there may be provisions within the ATE insurance policy which a defendant can point to and say that, on the happening of certain events, those provisions may reduce or obliterate the security otherwise provided;
(d) in that event, the court should approach such objections with care: in order to amount to a valid objection that an ATE policy does not provide appropriate security, the defendant's concern must be realistic, not theoretical or fanciful.'

In *Premier Motorauctions Ltd (in liq) v PriceWaterhouseCoopers LLP* [2017] EWCA Civ 1872, the court identified its role in this context as determining whether the particular ATE insurance in a given case does give the defendant sufficient protection, which would include consideration, amongst other matters, of the terms of the insurance, whether it contained anti-avoidance clauses and the likelihood of the insurer avoiding liability. Adopting this approach, Foskett J in *Bailey v Glaxosmithkline UK Ltd* [2017] EWHC 3195 (QB), reduced the security by 2/3 to take account of an ATE policy, where there was no anti-avoidance clause, but where the risk of avoidance was low.

Also of more interest in *Bailey v Glaxosmithkline UK Ltd* (above), was the decision to order more by way of security from the funders than the 'Arkin cap' (see Chapter 40 at [**40.7**]).

When considering the amount of security, the court can take account of the likelihood of costs ultimately being awarded on the indemnity basis. In *Danilina v Chernukhin* [2018] EWHC 2503 (Comm), the court acknowledged this and considered the different outcomes that would arise in these terms:

'Where there is no possibility of costs being assessed on the indemnity basis or where such possibility is no more than speculative the courts generally make orders for security for costs by reference to 60–70% of the incurred and expected costs . . . It appears to me that where there is a reasonable possibility of indemnity costs the order should be made (at any rate in this case where very substantial costs are involved) by reference to about 75% of the incurred and expected costs.'

These percentages were subsequently approved of, and adopted in *Re Ingenious Litigation* (see [**19.3**] above).

However, in *Phones 4U Ltd (in administration) v EE Ltd companies* [2020] EWHC 1943 (Ch), [2020] Costs LR 1065, the court concluded that if *Danilina* and *Re Ingenious Litigation* were setting the test for increased security as a consequence of there being a 'real possibility' or 'reasonable possibility' of an eventual order for indemnity costs (and the court was clear that there should be no attempt to read those cases as if they were a statutory test), this was contrary to the view of the Court of Appeal in *Stokors SA v IG Markets Ltd* [2012] EWCA Civ 1706. In that case, which was not cited in either *Danilina* or *Re Ingenious Litigation*, when addressing the same argument Tomlinson LJ stated:

'The only basis for seeking 80 per cent of the estimate to which the judge referred in his judgment was the suggestion that the defendant might recover indemnity costs. For what it is worth, I have never heard of security for costs being awarded on a more generous basis for that reason . . . ' (para 42)

In *Phones 4U Ltd*, the court concluded its consideration of an increased amount of security based on the prospect of an indemnity basis costs order in these terms:

> 'But in all the circumstances, I am wholly unable to reach a conclusion that this [an order for indemnity basis costs] is such a significant possibility or, to put it another way, that there is a real prospect of such an order so as to justify a requirement to provide security for costs on that basis.' (para 31)

VARIATION OF AN ORDER FOR SECURITY

[19.24]

In *Gordano Building Contractors Ltd v Burgess* [1988] 1 WLR 890, 132 Sol Jo 1091, CA, the claimant was ordered to give £20,000 security for the defendant's costs with 'liberty to both parties to apply'. Subsequently, the claimants obtained a letter from their bank stating that it would be willing to lend the claimants £20,000 to pay the costs if required. The claimants applied to have the order set aside but the judge held he had no jurisdiction to hear the application.

It was held on appeal that there were two questions: Can a claimant return to court in respect of the order if he can show a material change of circumstances? Can a claimant return if he produces fresh evidence as to the state of affairs extant at the date of the original order? The answer to the second question is simple: 'No'. If a claimant wishes to have an opportunity to produce further evidence he should, no doubt at some penalty as to costs, apply for an adjournment of the original security hearing. The answer to the first question must be that it is open to a claimant to apply to have an order for security set aside or varied in the light of changed circumstances by use of the provision at CPR 3.1(7) (the approach adopted in the unsuccessful application to vary in *Catalyst Management Services v Libya Africa Investment Portfolio* [2018] EWCA Civ 1676, [2018] 4 Costs LR 807, [2018] All ER (D) 48 (Aug)). In *Gordano* the judge had not considered whether there was a material change of circumstances and, if so, what, as a matter of discretion he would do about it. The appeal was allowed to the extent of remitting the matter to the judge for reconsideration.

In *Recovery Partners GB Ltd v Rukhadze* [2018] EWHC 95 (Comm) the court was considering variation in the context of release from an undertaking given in lieu of an order for security for costs. The case proceeded on the assumption by the parties that there had been a material change of circumstances. When considering the factors relevant to the release from an undertaking in this context the court highlighted the following as material:

- how long the old security has been in place and whether the costs which it secured have already been incurred;
- the extent of the difference (if any) between the quality of the old security and the quality of the new security;
- the strength of the explanation given for the claimant's change of position;
- in particular, whether or not, and if so to what extent, declining to permit the change would cause hardship or prejudice to the claimant or inhibit its ability to pursue its claim.

In *Harlequin Property (SVG) Ltd v Wilkins Kennedy (A firm)* [2015] EWHC 3050 (TCC), Coulson J (as he then was) concluded that it would be wrong in principle to reduce the security because the party giving it had spent more than envisaged on a phase of the litigation (and so had need of the money to fund its case). He concluded that variation should only take place if an exceptional event undermined the basis upon which the parties had originally approached the question of security.

In *Al-Baho v BGP Global Services Ltd* (4 July 2017, unreported), Ch, the court reiterated that the same threshold applied to setting aside as to variation of an order for security.

In an application for relief under the Arbitration Act 1996 where the parties had agreed £30,000 security for costs and had also agreed that it would not be increased even if there were a material change of circumstances, the court still retained a residual discretion to vary the agreement if there were wholly exceptional circumstances. In *Republic of Kazakhstan v Istil Group Inc* [2005] EWCA Civ 1468, there were such circumstances.

CROSS-UNDERTAKINGS IN DAMAGES WHEN SECURITY ORDERED

[19.25]

The Commercial Court Guide (Appendix 10, para 5) indicates that the court may require a cross-undertaking in damages from a party seeking security, in the event that subsequently it transpires that security should not have been ordered and the party giving it has suffered loss. In *Re the RBS (Rights Issue Litigation)* [2017] EWHC 1217 (Ch), the court stated that 'there is plainly jurisdiction in the court to stipulate such a condition in order to compensate in cases where no order for costs is ultimately made in favour of the applicant and against the respondent'. Such an order is unusual and in *TBD (Owen Holland) Ltd v Simons* [2020] EWCA Civ 1182, it was held that such cross-undertakings should only be required where there are special or unusual circumstances demanding such protection for the party giving security.

SECURITY FOR COSTS UNDER THE ARBITRATION ACT 1996

[19.26]

The Arbitration Act 1996, s 38(3) provides:

> 'The Tribunal may order a claimant to provide security for the costs of the arbitration. This power shall not be exercised on the ground that the claimant is:
>
> (a) An individual ordinarily resident outside the United Kingdom, or
>
> (b) A corporation or association incorporated or formed under the law of a country outside the United Kingdom, or whose central management and control is exercised outside the United Kingdom.'

This gives to the arbitrator a wide general discretion, which he must nevertheless exercise judicially – especially as the 'costs of the arbitration' include his own fees and expenses!

Another practical difference between security for costs in arbitration and in other litigation is the tradition in litigation that applications for security for costs are not heard by the trial judge, because privileged and prejudicial matters, such as offers for settlement, may have to be considered on the application. Parliament must have taken the view that arbitrators are made of sterner stuff and can more readily put such matters out of their minds, because arbitrators themselves deal with applications for security.

Where a party is challenging the enforcement of a foreign arbitration award, it is right for the court to treat that party as a defendant, with the consequence that the court has jurisdiction to grant security for costs against the holder of the award (*Dardana Ltd v Yukos Oil Co* [2002] EWCA Civ 543).

Section 70(6) of the Act empowers the court to order the applicant or appellant in an appeal against an award to provide security for the costs of the application or appeal (and that the application or appeal is dismissed if the order is not complied with), although such an order cannot be made on the grounds of residence outside the United Kingdom.

Section 75 empowers an arbitrator to make the same declarations and orders as the court charging property recovered with the payment of the solicitor's costs under s 73 of the Solicitors Act 1974.

Where an award is challenged under s 70(6) of the Arbitration Act 1996 the Court of Appeal in *Republic of Kazakhstan v Istil Group Inc* [2006] 1 WLR 596 made it clear that such applications engage the overriding objective and the correct approach is the same as that under CPR 25.12 and CPR 25.13.

In *Progas Energy Ltd v The Islamic Republic of Pakistan* [2018] EWHC 209 (Comm), the court decided, for a variety of reasons, that mere confirmation in a letter that a funder would meet any adverse costs order in a s 68 challenge to an award, was not a reason not to award security.

THE INTERESTS OF THE PARTIES IN SUMS PAID INTO COURT AS SECURITY FOR COSTS

[19.27]

The Court of Appeal considered the question of what interests the parties to a claim have in sums paid into court in *Crumpler v Candy Ltd* [2018] EWCA Civ 2256. This was in the context of determining whether the party paying the sum into court retained an interest in it as an existing asset which was capable of being charged. The court concluded that it did, but subject to an interest of the party whose costs the sum secured and subject to court order determining the ultimate destination of the sum. Giving the lead judgment Sir Colin Rimer concluded that:

> '... the payer of money into court by way of providing security . . . retains its property in the money, although of course (a) such interest is subject to the security interest that the payment gives to the defendants, and (b) the ultimate payment out of the money to one or other party (or both) is dependent on the making of a court order.'

CHAPTER 20

COSTS INDUCEMENTS TO SETTLE – PART 36 OFFERS AND OTHER ADMISSIBLE OFFERS

INTRODUCTION TO COSTS INDUCEMENTS TO SETTLE – PART 36 OFFERS AND OTHER ADMISSIBLE OFFERS

[20.1]

CPR 36 was completely rewritten with effect from 6 April 2015. Keen observers will have noted that only CPR 36.8 kept its previous number and its exact former wording. Despite this claim to fame it remains one of the least used CPR 36 provisions.

The explanation for the rewritten CPR 36 introduced by the 78th update to the CPR appearing on the Ministry of Justice website at the time identified the rationale as reflecting the large amount of case law in respect of the application of CPR 36 since the previous substantial amendment in 2007 and 'to simplify the rules as far as possible to make them more accessible to court users, particularly litigants in person'. Notwithstanding this the redrawn rule has already generated a further body of case law. This chapter addresses the current CPR 36. Commentary in the 2015 edition covers the previous provisions in respect of any issues still arising under them, although on some occasions authorities under the former regime inform the current one and are mentioned here.

CPR PD 36 was also altered (losing the APD tag at the same time), simply to reflect the revised rule numbers which it supplements. What was CPR PD 36B is no more.

A SELF-CONTAINED CODE

[20.2]

Where better to start than at the beginning? CPR 36.1 confirms that the rules are a self-contained procedural code (adopting the conclusion reached in *Gibbon v Manchester City Council* [2010] EWCA Civ 726, [2011] 2 All ER 258, [2010] 1 WLR 2081). In other words, as Moore-Bick LJ stated in that case:

> ' . . . it is to be read and understood according to its terms and without importing other rules derived from the general law . . . '

In making the point in *Webb (by her litigation friend) v Liverpool Women's NHS Foundation Trust* [2016] EWCA Civ 365, that the current version of CPR 44.2 expressly excludes consideration of offers to which the costs consequences of Part 36 apply, the court emphasised that Part 36 is a self-contained code (see **[20.22]** below for further consideration of this decision).

THE STRUCTURE OF PART 36

[20.3]

CPR 36 is split into two sections. Section I contains general rules and Section II contains specific provisions in relation to the Pre-Action Protocol for Low Value Personal Injury Claims where proceedings are started under CPR PD 8B. The latter will be considered separately at the end of the consideration of Part 36 at [**20.29**] under the heading Part 36 and CPR PD 8B. The remainder of the chapter is devoted to the general rules and other admissible offers, unless stated otherwise.

THE FORM AND CONTENT OF A PART 36 OFFER

[20.4]

CPR 36.5 provides that for an offer to be a valid one within CPR 36 the offer must:

- be in writing;
- make it clear that it is made under CPR 36;
- specify a period of not less than 21 days within which the defendant will be liable for the claimant's costs if the offer is accepted. This provision does not apply if the trial is less than 21 days after the offer. (This period is defined as the 'relevant period' under CPR 36.3(g) and for offers made less than 21 days before trial is up to the end of the trial);
- state whether it relates to the whole or part of the claim or to an issue (and if so which issue); and
- state whether it takes account of any counterclaim.

In certain circumstances the offer must contain more information – eg in a personal injury claim involving a claim for future pecuniary loss (CPR 36.18), where the claim involves a claim for provisional damages (CPR 36.19), and, more generally, in relation to the deduction of recoverable benefits (CPR 36.22). These are considered in more detail below.

CPR PD 36 still provides that a CPR 36 offer may be made using Form N242A, which has been updated as of June 2015. Given that the requirements of CPR 36.5 still open the door to inadvertent non-compliance it is difficult to understand why N242A is not used routinely as it acts as an aide memoire to ensure that the information above is included.

CPR 36.6 makes it plain that a defendant making an offer to pay a sum of money must make the offer as a single sum of money, and if the offer provides for payment of any part of the money after 14 days from acceptance then it cannot be a valid CPR 36 offer unless the claimant accepts the offer.

CPR 36.2 makes it clear that an offer not made under CPR 36.5 cannot be a CPR 36 offer (but may be an admissible offer relevant under CPR 44.2(4)(c)). This was a point made by the court in *James v James* [2018] EWHC 242 (Ch), where it had concluded that an offer was not one under CPR 36 when it stated the liability for costs of the offeree to be 'up to the end of the Relevant Period or, if later, the date of service of notice of acceptance of this Offer', as, contrary to CPR 36.13, this envisaged a liability to the end of the relevant period even if notice of acceptance was served before that date.

WHO MAY MAKE A PART 36 OFFER?

[20.5]

Whilst the wording of CPR 36.5(1)(c) refers to the offer providing the period during which the defendant will be liable to pay the claimant's costs if the offer is accepted, CPR 36.3 clearly refers to parties being the 'offeror' and the 'offeree'. CPR 36.6 makes it explicit that a defendant may make a Part 36 offer. This is confirmed by the references to Part 36 offers by both claimants and defendants in CPR 36.17. Whilst a counterclaiming defendant may make a Part 36 offer that is treated as a claimant's offer (see *AF v BG* [2009] EWCA Civ 757), it depends on the nature of the offer. In *Van Oord UK Ltd v Allseas UK Ltd* [2015] EWHC 3385 (TCC) the court decided that on a proper construction the offer made by the counterclaiming defendant had all the hallmarks of a defendant's offer and so CPR 36.17(4) did not apply.

WHEN MAY A PART 36 OFFER BE MADE?

[20.6]

A Part 36 offer may be made before proceedings (CPR 36.7(1)(a)). Indeed, in terms of a defendant seeking to maximise his costs protection and a claimant seeking to make the most of the possible sanctions if he receives an outcome at least as advantageous as his offer, the earlier that the offer is made the better. Where a Part 36 offer is accepted within the relevant period, the claimant will be entitled to recover pre-action costs as part of the costs entitlement under CPR 36.13(1). Cross application of CPR 44.9 suggests that, save in those cases subject to the fixed costs regime (see CPR 36.13(3), Section II of Part 36 and below), a deemed costs order is made on the standard basis. However, if acceptance is at a time before a claim form has been issued, this would be a deemed order in proceedings that do not exist. Concerns have been aired that both CPR 36.13 and CPR 36.14 setting out the consequences of acceptance are predicated on the basis that proceedings have been issued and as such it is unclear whether, where both offer and acceptance are pre-issue, there is, in fact, a defined entitlement to costs. This view is supported by the fact that CPR 44.9(2) specifically continues to exclude cases where a CPR 36 offer is accepted before the commencement of proceedings from the 'deemed costs order' regime. This seems to take a narrow view of 'proceedings' in CPR 36.13. As that provision immediately makes it clear that costs of the 'proceedings' includes pre-action costs we prefer a wider interpretation. Even on this interpretation the claimant cannot simply then commence detailed assessment proceedings if agreement of the amount of costs cannot be reached. This should create no practical difficulties because the claimant may then simply use the provisions of CPR 46.14 and issue costs only proceedings (see *Solomon v Cromwell Group plc* [2011] EWCA Civ 1584), but it adds both a tier of cost and some delay.

In *Calonne Construction Ltd v Dawnus Southern Ltd* [2019] EWCA Civ 754, the Court of Appeal confirmed that as CPR 20.3 provides for additional claims to be treated as claims (and CPR 36 is not disapplied as are some procedural provisions) and as CPR 36.7 provides that a Part 36 offer can be made at any time, including before the commencement of proceedings, there was nothing to prevent a defendant making a CPR 36 offer taking account of an anticipated counterclaim, even though it had yet to be stated formally.

WHEN IS A PART 36 OFFER ACTUALLY MADE?

[20.7]

CPR 36.7 provides, unsurprisingly, that an offer is made when it is served. Service is calculated by the application of CPR 6.

IN WHAT PROCEEDINGS MAY A PART 36 OFFER BE MADE?

[20.8]

Provided the offer is made in compliance with CPR 36.5 then it may be made in a claim, counterclaim, additional claim and appeal or cross appeal (CPR 36.2(3)). However, CPR 36.4 expressly requires a party wishing to rely upon an offer in appeal proceedings to make that offer in those proceedings. It is not sufficient to make an offer in the earlier proceedings. Even if the offer is effectively the same one it must expressly be made in the appeal proceedings. The N242A format assists in clarifying the specific proceedings in which the offer is made. CPR 36.4 also provides definition in tabular form to ensure that the wording of Section I of Part 36 is readily applicable to appeal proceedings. This provides that references to terms in the left hand column shall be treated as references to the corresponding term in the right hand column in appeals:

Term	*Corresponding term*
Claim	Appeal
Counterclaim	Cross-Appeal
Case	Appeal Proceedings
Claimant	Appellant
Defendant	Respondent
Trial	Appeal Hearing
Trial Judge	Appeal Judge

CLARIFICATION OF A PART 36 OFFER

[20.9]

As stated above, the only provision surviving the rewriting of CPR 36 intact and with its old number is that which enables a party to seek clarification of an offer (CPR 36.8). An offeree may seek clarification of the Part 36 offer provided that this is done within seven days of receipt of the offer. If the offeror fails to provide the clarification, then the offeree may apply to the court for an order that the offeror does so and, having determined the application, the court will set the date when the offer is then deemed to have been made. Where the court determines that clarification is required the logical outcome would be the relevant period after the date specified in the order for the provision of the clarification.

The decision in *Calonne Construction Ltd v Dawnus Southern Ltd* [2019] EWCA Civ 754 (see **[20.6]** above), suggests that greater use ought to be made of this provision. When deciding whether the defendant could make an offer in respect of a counterclaim that had yet to be stated formally, the Court of Appeal concluded that even had the nature and extent of it not already been known, any uncertainty could have been addressed by a request for clarification under CPR 36.8.

PART 36, ADMISSIONS AND PAYMENTS ON ACCOUNT

[20.10]

In *Littlestone v MacLeish* [2016] EWCA Civ 127, the Court of Appeal provided clarification of where there is both a Part 36 offer and a payment made under an admission of part of the claim for a lesser sum than the Part 36 offer. The court concluded that the combined effect was not to aggregate the two and increase the Part 36 offer by the amount of the sum paid pursuant to the admission: rather, the sum paid was to be treated as a payment on account of the Part 36 offer as much as it was a payment generally on account of the claim. In *Gamal v Synergy Lifestyle Ltd* [2018] EWCA Civ 210, the court confirmed that this is also the position where any payment on account of the claim is made, even where there is no admission, concluding that ' . . . where such a payment is made, there is a presumption of law that it is also on account of the earlier Part 36 offer'.

ACCEPTANCE, WITHDRAWAL AND CHANGE OF OFFER

General

[20.11]

CPR 36.11 provides some general rules. These are that an acceptance must be in writing and may be made at any time (provided the offer has not been withdrawn) even if subsequent offers have been made. This preserves the previous position that any number of CPR 36 offers may be available for acceptance at any given time, that a fresh offer does not automatically withdraw a previous offer and formal withdrawal of an offer is required.

However, this is subject to:

- formal court approval of any settlement on behalf of a child or protected party under CPR 21;
- the permission of the court where:

(i) the claim is against one or more defendants, not all of them are party to the offer, the liability of the defendants is not said to be several and the claimant does not discontinue against the non-offering defendant/s with the consent of the remaining defendants to the acceptance of the offer (CPR 36.15);

(ii) the relevant period has expired and there has been payment to the claimant of further deductible benefits since the date of the offer (CPR 36.11(3)(b));

(iii) an apportionment of the damages accepted is required under CPR 41.3A (relating to claims under the Fatal Accident Act 1976 and/or the Law Reform (Miscellaneous Provisions) Act 1934 (CPR 36.11(3)(c)); and

(iv) a trial is in progress (CPR 36.11(3)(d)).

Where the court gives permission it must deal with the award of costs, unless the parties have agreed this, and may order that the consequences follow those in CPR 36.13 (see below).

It is in respect of withdrawal of, and amendment to, offers that the revised Part 36 has introduced significant amendment (see **[20.16]** below).

The consequence of acceptance within the 'relevant period'

[20.12]

CPR 36.13 sets out the costs consequences of an acceptance of a CPR 36 offer.

The usual order at CPR 36.13(1) is that when a CPR 36 offer (whether made by the claimant or the defendant) is accepted within the 'relevant period', then the claimant is entitled to the costs up to the date of service of the notice of acceptance on the offeror (to allow for that being either the defendant or the claimant): see *James v James* (above at **[20.4]**) for the importance of expressing correctly the liability for costs.

Unless a fixed recoverable costs regime applies, the costs will be assessed on the standard basis (CPR 36.13(3)). In *Lahey v Pirelli Tyres Ltd* [2007] EWCA Civ 91, the claimant accepted a Part 36 payment by the defendant and thereby became entitled to the costs of the proceedings up to the date of serving notice of acceptance. However, at the outset of the detailed assessment, the defendant asked the district judge to order, before embarking on the detailed assessment, that the claimant should be only awarded 25% of the assessed costs. The defendant contended that in determining whether costs had been 'unreasonably incurred or are unreasonable in amount' (within the meaning of CPR 44.4(1) as was), the court was not constrained only to look at items of cost individually. It might conclude that a whole stage of the proceedings was unreasonable. It could look at the conduct of the parties in the round and not only by reference to specific items of costs. The district judge held there was no jurisdiction to order any such reduction. This decision was upheld on first appeal and again by the Court of Appeal. The effect of the CPR is that, upon acceptance of a Part 36 payment, 'a costs order is deemed to have been made on the standard basis'. This means the claimant is entitled to 100% of the assessed costs, this being the amount that the costs judge decides is payable at the conclusion of the detailed assessment. The costs judge has no power to vary that order. The power to vary or revoke an order given by CPR 3.1(7) is only exercisable in relation to an order that the court has previously made, and not to an order that is deemed to be made by operation of the rules.

In *Courtwell Properties Ltd v Greencore PF (UK) Ltd* [2014] EWHC 184 (TCC) Akenhead J cautioned parties entitled to an order for standard basis costs on acceptance of a CPR 36 offer to think 'long and hard' before seeking an indemnity costs order instead. He concluded that where the question of the correct basis for costs turned on material conflicts of evidence there would be few, if any, cases where it was proportionate to determine all or some of the settled issues in the case simply to be able to determine the costs issue. Indeed, it seems that it is only where the court is left with a costs discretion (eg late acceptance) and the deemed costs order does not apply, that such an application can be made. CPR 36.13(3) specifically provides that the costs order that flows from an acceptance of a CPR 36 offer is an order for costs on the standard basis. *Courtwell* supports this as the court was left with jurisdiction under CPR 36.10(4) (as was, now 36.13(4)) because the offer was made less than 21 days before trial. The court was clear that 'but for that Courtwell would have been limited by the rules to standard costs'.

This does not mean that where the court is left with a costs jurisdiction under CPR 36, an order for indemnity costs will never be made eg in *Rees v Oliver* [2019] EWHC 922 (Ch), where the offer was accepted outside the 'relevant period' and the costs liability could not be agreed, the court ordered indemnity basis costs where the facts took the case out of the 'norm'.

If there is a counterclaim and a CPR 36 offer made by a defendant makes it clear that the counterclaim has been taken into account in the offer, then if the offer is accepted the claimant's entitlements to costs include those incurred in dealing with the counterclaim (CPR 36.13(7)). In *James v James* (above), the court considered CPR 20 and CPR 36 in this context and concluded that an offer made by a counterclaiming defendant could be treated as a claimant's offer in relation to the counterclaim which took account of the claim as if that were the counterclaim.

Where the accepted offer is one made by the defendant, it deals with only part of the claim and at the time of accepting it the claimant abandons the balance of the claim, CPR 36.13(2) states that the claimant is only entitled to the costs of the part of the claim in respect of which the offer was made unless the court orders otherwise. The word 'only' is an important addition. Previously the claimant would have been entitled to the costs of the proceedings (not just the part to which the acceptance relates). This links to CPR 36.13(4), which provides, amongst other things, that where an offer is accepted at any time which does not relate to the whole of the claim, but where there is no abandonment of other elements of the claim, then unless the parties agree liability for costs, the court must determine this. This addition reflects, in part, concerns articulated in *Bellway Homes Ltd v Seymour (Civil Engineering Contractors) Ltd* [2013] EWHC 1890 (TCC) about the inability of a party to accept a Part 36 offer within the relevant period, but with the court to determine the issue of costs. However, the provision is limited to situations where the offer does not relate to the whole of the claim.

CPR 36.14 provides that acceptance of an offer will result in the claim being stayed as to the whole of the claim if the offer related to that (CPR 36.14(2)) and as to that part of the claim in respect of which the offer was made if the offer only related to part of the claim (CPR 36.14(3)). As set out above the provisions for determining costs on a part acceptance are set out in CPR 36.13. Any stay imposed under this rule does not prevent the court enforcing the terms of the offer or dealing with any question of costs (including interest)

(CPR 36.14(5)). Where the accepted offer is in respect of payment of a single sum of money, that must be made within 14 days of acceptance or the date of any subsequent order of the court if settlement involves a provisional award (CPR 41.2) or periodical payments (CPR 41.8), unless the parties agree otherwise. The acceptance is not binding where approval is required under CPR 21 until that approval has been given (CPR 36.14(4)) – in such circumstances the approval order will provide for payment.

CPR PD 36, para 3.1 is often overlooked. It is not sufficient simply to notify the court that a Part 36 offer has been accepted to conclude the claim. A copy of the notice of acceptance must be filed with the court. Until that is done, the claim continues.

If the agreed sum is not paid within 14 days of the acceptance, or within 14 days of the date fixed by the court under CPR 41.2 or CPR 41.8, then the claimant may enter judgment for the agreed sum. The court has no discretion to extend this 14 day period (see *Titmus v General Motors UK Ltd* (11 July 2016, unreported), QBD). If the offer accepted is not one that includes an offer to pay or accept a single sum of money and one party alleges that another has not honoured the terms of the settlement, then the party so alleging may apply to the court to enforce the terms without needing to issue fresh proceedings.

Acceptance where there is more than defendant

[20.13]

CPR 36.15 deals with the situation where the claimant wishes to accept a CPR 36 offer made by one but not all of the defendants. If the claimant pursues the defendants jointly or in the alternative then an offer may only be accepted if the claimant discontinues against those not making the offer and they consent to the acceptance of the offer. If the claim is against defendants severally, the claimant may accept the offer and continue against the remaining defendants. In any other situation the claimant must apply to the court for permission to accept the offer (CPR 36.15(4)).

The consequence of acceptance outside the relevant period

[20.14]

CPR 36.13(5) sets out the starting position upon acceptance of an offer outside the 'relevant period' where the parties cannot agree the incidence of costs. This provides that the claimant recovers the costs up to the expiry of the 'relevant period' and the offeree (depending upon whose offer it was) pays the offeror's costs from the expiry of the 'relevant period' to the date of acceptance. This general rule is qualified by the words 'unless it [the court] considers it unjust to do so'. This replaces the previous wording permitting the court to order otherwise and brings the wording in line with that used in CPR 36.17 which deals with costs consequences after judgment when dealing with the situations where either a claimant has not achieved a judgment more advantageous than a defendant's Part 36 offer or has achieved a judgment at least as advantageous as its own Part 36 offer. CPR 36.17(3) and 36.17(4) respectively set out orders that the court will make 'unless it considers it unjust to do so'.

This link between CPR 36.13 and CPR 36.17 is maintained in CPR 36.13(6) which requires the court, when considering if it is unjust to apply the general rule at CPR 36.13(5) to take account of all the circumstances and the factors at CPR 36.17(5), which are:

- the terms of any CPR 36 offer;
- the stage when any CPR 36 offer was made, including in particular how long before the trial started the offer was made;
- the information available to the parties at the time when the offer was made;
- the conduct of the parties with regard to giving of or refusal to give information for the purposes of enabling the offer to made or evaluated; and
- whether the offer was a genuine attempt to settle the proceedings.

The last of these did not appear in the previous incarnation of what is now CPR 36.17(5) and seems to be an attempt (and one well tucked away at that) to address 'tactical offers'. However, all offers are tactical and the reality is this provision (unlike the first two, which relate to any offer) is specific to the particular offer that the court is considering, which, whether a genuine attempt to settle proceedings, has certainly succeeded in so doing (see **[20.27]** below for consideration of 'genuine offers').

The cross application of the factors at CPR 36.17(5) removes the 'clean sheet' exercise of discretion referred to by Lang J in *Lumb v Hampsey* [2011] EWHC 2808 (QB). However, her conclusion illustrates the genesis of the new rule:

> 'In my view the test which I should adopt in deciding the issue under Rule 36.10(5) is similar to that set out in Rule 36.14. The test which I apply is whether the usual costs order set out in Rule 36.10(5) should be departed from because it would be unjust for the claimant to pay the defendant's costs after the expiry of the relevant period, in the particular circumstances of the case. Such a departure would be the exception rather than the rule (para 6).'

The Court of Appeal has provided a useful steer on the application of CPR 36.13(5) in personal injury claims in *Briggs v CEF Holdings Ltd* (13 July 2017, unreported). In this case the claimant accepted a CPR 36 offer 2¾ years after it was made and sought to avoid the usual consequences under CPR 36.13(5) on the basis that at the time of the offer, the offeree's recovery was incomplete and the prognosis was uncertain. Whilst acknowledging that decisions under the provision are fact specific, the judgment stressed that the court should not undermine the salutary purpose of CPR 36, the onus was on the offeree to show why the court should not make the 'usual order' and in this case, the risk of working out how the injuries may progress was simply a contingency of litigation. Accordingly, the decision to disapply CPR 36.13(5) was wrong as no injustice had been identified that warranted a departure from the rule. A similar argument over the difficulty of quantification of a personal injury claim failed in *Campbell v MOD* unreported 14 May 2019, in which Lambert J suggested that if quantification was so speculative at the time of the offer, then the claimant should apply to stay the proceedings until the claim was capable of quantification, as that would, at least, limit the costs which the defendant would incur before an informed decision could be taken on the offer.

In *Tuscon v Murphy* [2018] EWCA Civ 1461, where the claimant's conduct was described as misleading and dishonest in withholding information material to her arguments on inability to work and where the claimant accepted a Part 36 offer outside the relevant period, the Court of Appeal overturned the decision to depart from CPR 36.13(5)(a) and ordered the defendant to pay her costs up to the expiry of the relevant period. The court distinguished between the situation in this case, where the defendant had known of the information that the claimant had not disclosed at the time the offer was made, and those cases where the assessment of the level of the Part 36 offer is upset or undermined by subsequent events or subsequently discovered facts.

In *Briggs*, the court recognised that some cases would fall the other side of the line of justice. It referred to *SG (a minor by his mother and litigation friend) v Hewitt* [2012] EWCA Civ 1053 as one such case, where the court had departed from the usual order because the claimant had sustained facial scarring and a severe head injury and, at the time of the offer, was too young for final conclusions to be drawn, preventing advice being given. In giving her decision, Black LJ had been at pains to stress that the decision was fact specific:

> 'Some words of caution: as I have already said, costs decisions are particularly fact sensitive. The view I have formed of this case . . . is an amalgam of all of its features. It is unlikely to be replicated precisely in another case . . . so differences between the facts of this case and the facts of other cases may mean that the result in the other case should differ from the result in this one.'

Albeit a case on the previous provision, the decision of the Commercial Court in *Ted Baker plc v AXA Insurance UK plc* [2014] EWHC 4178 (Comm) gives a useful illustration of the link between the concepts of 'unjust' and 'proportionality' in a case specific context. In this case the claimants had succeeded on a preliminary liability trial, but subsequently failed to recover quantum in excess of the defendants' early Part 36 offer. The court declined to order the claimants to pay all of the defendant's costs as it would be unjust to do so as the defendants had adopted a wholly disproportionate approach to a central issue and could not 'hide' behind an effective Part 36 offer in taking any point and at any cost. In other words, the overriding objective of dealing with a case justly and at a proportionate cost applies also to Part 36 offers.

What of the position where there is a late acceptance of a claimant's offer? Can the claimant seek indemnity basis costs as would apply under CPR 36.17(4)(b) (see **[20.18]** below)? *Hislop v Perde* [2018] EWCA Civ 1726 provides the answers. The position varies depending upon whether the claim is one subject to fixed fees or not. For consideration of cases that fall within the fixed costs regime at CPR 45 Section IIIA, see **[20.31]**–**[20.32]** below. In those outside the fixed costs regime, the Court of Appeal confirmed that there is no presumption of an indemnity costs order because CPR 36.13 does not provide for this, but that such an order may be appropriate in cases where the facts justify it (in other words where the case is 'out of the norm' as per *Excelsior Commercial & Industrial Holdings Ltd v Salisbury Hamer Aspden & Johnston (Costs)* [2002] EWCA Civ 879: see Chapter 24 at **[24.8]**).

In *Houghton v PB Donoghue (Haulage and Plant Hire Ltd)* [2017] EWHC 1738 (Ch), the court considered an application under CPR 36.11(3)(d) to accept an unwithdrawn CPR 36 offer made almost six months previously, two days into a trial. In refusing permission Morgan J offered this general approach:

> 'I think that the philosophy exists that where a claimant decides to take his chances with the trial and then repents of his earlier decision to turn down the offer of settlement because the trial, he thinks, is going less well or more badly than predicted, that the court will often take the view that it is not right to give permission to impose a settlement on the reluctant defendant . . . Taking that approach does not mean that permission will never be given.'

This decision also reinforces that such an application must, obviously, be made to a judge who is not the trial judge.

The consequence of acceptance where the offer was made less than 21 days before the start of a trial

[20.15]

Where an offer is accepted which was made less than 21 days before the start of a trial, unless the parties agree the liability for costs, then the court must determine this. Note that CPR 36.13(5) and (6), considered above at **[20.14]** do not apply in this situation.

If a Part 36 offer is made less than 21 days before the start of the trial pursuant to CPR 36.17(7)(c) it does not carry the consequences of CPR 36.17(3) and (4) unless the court has abridged the 'relevant period' provision.

Withdrawal of, or a change to, a CPR 36 offer

[20.16]

CPR 36.9 specifies that a withdrawal or change:

- must be in writing;
- can only be effected if the offer has not already been accepted;
- only takes effect when it is served;
- may be effected without the permission of the court if the relevant period has expired; and
- may be withdrawn automatically within its terms (in other words a CPR 36 offer may now both set a relevant period and provide for automatic withdrawal).

It also provides that a change to make an improved proposal does not operate as a withdrawal of a previous offer (obviously unless that previous offer is expressly withdrawn), but is a new CPR 36 offer on improved terms with a fresh relevant period.

However, different provisions apply where the offeror wishes to withdraw an offer or change its terms to less advantageous ones to the offeree before the expiry of the relevant period and serves notice to that effect. CPR 36.10 provides that:

- if the offeree does not serve notice of acceptance within the relevant period, then the offeror's withdrawal/change has effect on the expiry of the relevant period (CPR 36.10(2a)); and
- if the offeree does accept the original offer before the end of the relevant period the acceptance takes effect unless the offeror applies to the court for permission to withdraw/change within seven days of the acceptance or, if earlier, before the first day of the trial. If the court permits withdrawal/change it must be satisfied that there has been a change of circumstances since the making of the offer and it is in the interests of justice (CPR 36.10(2)(b) and (3)).

This avoids the offeror being compelled to apply to court to withdraw during the relevant period, forcing the court to deal with an application which might be utterly irrelevant (in that the offeree might not be going to accept the offer anyway). Under CPR 36.10, the offeror waits until the expiry of the relevant period and then makes an informed decision, knowing whether an application is necessary. However, there is a downside. The offeree who accepts an offer cannot be sure until seven days have elapsed from acceptance that the offeror is not going to apply to withdraw/change the offer where notice has been given during the 'relevant period' of an intent to do so – creating a period of uncertainty.

If an offer is withdrawn then under CPR 36.17(7)(a) it does not carry the consequences of CPR 36.17(3) and (4). This mirrors the outcome in *Gulati v MGN Ltd* [2015] EWHC 1805 (Ch), where the court under the previous CPR 36 provisions concluded that where a claimant recovered more than had been offered in a withdrawn Part 36 offer, the consequences of CPR 36 could not apply to the withdrawn offer. In *Fox v Foundation Piling* [2011] EWCA Civ 790 (also under the old rules), Jackson LJ set out the consequence of withdrawal of a CPR 36 offer in these terms:

> 'A Part 36 offer which is subsequently withdrawn ceases to attract the consequences set out in rule 36.14 (now 36.17). Such an offer then constitutes an "admissible offer to settle" within rule 44.3 (4)(c) (now 44.2(4)(c).'

Whilst the court in *Ballard v Sussex Partnership NHS Foundation Trust* [2018] EWHC 370 (QB), referred to tension 'between the proposition that an offeror who withdraws a Part 36 offer cannot "reap the benefits" of what is now r.36.17 . . . and the proposition that such an offer is still "relevant" on the issue of costs', in fact the statement in *Fox* does no more than highlight the express wording of CPR 44.2(4)(c): that the court will have regard to, amongst other things, any admissible offer, and this is the key, to which the costs consequences under Part 36 do not apply. In other words, the offer may still be relevant in the overall exercise of the award of costs, but the weight attached to, and the consequences of, it are not prescribed in the rules. However, in *Thakkar v Patel* [2017] EWCA Civ 117, Jackson LJ concluded that 'the crucial question is whether the offeree acted reasonably or unreasonably in failing to accept the offer while it was on the table'. This conclusion received extensive consideration in *Blackpool Borough Council v Volkerfitzpatrick Ltd* [2020] EWHC 2120 (TCC), in which the court asked itself whether reasonable is determined by reference to the receiving party's perception of its own interests or simply when judged against the eventual outcome of the case. The defendant had made a Part 36 offer in respect of certain elements of the claim, but had later withdrawn the offer. The court answered its own question in these terms:

> ' . . . it does seem to me that: (a) the court must put itself into the position of the claimant at the time and not simply decide the case by reference to hindsight; but (b) the focus must be on the reasonableness of the refusal by reference to the facts and matters relevant to the merits of the claim as they ought reasonably to have appeared to the claimant at that time, not by reference to wider commercial factors.'

CPR PD 36, para 2.2 provides that any application for permission to withdraw an offer must be made on an application under CPR 23 and must not be dealt with by the trial judge (even if the application is made in the course of the trial).

However, whilst accepting that CPR 36 is a self-contained code, in *DB UK Bank Ltd (t/a DB Mortgages) v Jacobs Solicitors* [2016] EWHC 1614 (Ch) the court concluded that a Part 36 counter-offer operated so as to amount to a rejection of an offer made other than under Part 36. The reason for this was that common law principles apply to a situation not governed by Part 36, and here the offer in question was one made at common law and not under Part 36.

THE CONSEQUENCE OF NOT ACCEPTING A PART 36 OFFER

A defendant's offer not accepted by the claimant

[20.17]

Clearly if the claimant recovers more than the defendant's best Part 36 offer and less than any offer he has made, then Part 36 does not apply and the court determines costs under CPR 44.2 (see below).

If the claimant does not recover as much as the defendant's Part 36 offer then CPR 36.17(1)(a) is engaged and, under CPR 36.17(3), the defendant is entitled to costs from the date upon which the relevant period for acceptance expired and interest on those costs. This is subject to a financial limit on the enforcement of those costs if the claimant has 'QOCS' protection under CPR 44.14 – namely the aggregate of the damages and interest received by the claimant and any set off of costs under CPR 44.12 (see Chapter 22 at **[22.34]** on this point). The rule is silent about the costs prior to that date as those will fall to be determined within the analysis under CPR 44.2 (see Chapter 22 of the Costs Awards between the Parties). It is worth noting, as did the court in *Marathon Asset Management LLP v Seddon* [2017] EWHC 479 (Comm), that CPR 36.17(3)(b) does not contain any provision to match that under CPR 36.17(4) (see below) for an enhanced rate of interest on the defendant's costs.

A claimant's offer not accepted by the defendant

[20.18]

Obviously if the defendant does not accept a claimant's offer, but at trial the claimant is awarded less than the amount of the offer (ie does not receive a judgment at least as advantageous as the offer) and there is no relevant defendant's offer, then Part 36 does not apply and the court determines costs under CPR 44.2 (see Chapter 22 of the Costs Awards between the Parties).

However, CPR 36.17(1)(b) is engaged where a claimant obtains a judgment at least as advantageous as the offer and under CPR 36.17(4), the claimant is entitled to interest at a rate not exceeding 10% above base rate from expiry of the relevant period, costs on the indemnity basis and interest on the costs also at a rate not exceeding 10% above base rate. In respect of claimants' Part 36 offers made after 31 March 2013 where the judgment against the defendant is at least as advantageous to the claimant as the claimant's Part 36 offer then, in addition to the other benefits listed, the claimant will recover as an 'additional amount' an extra 10% of the amount awarded by the court on awards of up to £500,000 and on awards above this, 10% of the first £500,000 and an extra 5% of the amount awarded above £500,000, subject to an overall cap of £75,000. As stated above at **[20.14]** all these sanctions are 'unless the court considers it unjust' to impose them and, in the case of the entitlement to an 'additional amount', only when the case has been decided and only where there has not been a previous order for one. This qualification is curious. Is it designed to prevent awards in both parts of a split trial (certainly in *JMX v Norfolk and Norwich Hospitals NHS Foundation Trust* [2018] EWHC 675 (QB) the court concluded that until damages had been agreed or assessed following a liability only trial, the case had not been decided. However, it left open for argument whether the effective CPR 36 offer on liability would result in an additional amount calculated by reference to costs of the liability trial or the damages subsequently recovered), is it aimed at preventing an award on the substantive claim and on the costs claim under CPR 47.20(4) – notwithstanding CPR 47.20(7), which begs the question is a 'claim' to be equated to a 'case' (see the wording of CPR 36.17(4)(d) and CPR 47.20(7)) – is it aimed at preventing multiple awards where there have been a number of effective offers or at something else?

Whilst authorities are beginning to emerge giving a flavour of how the court is approaching arguments centred upon whether it is unjust to impose the CPR 36.17(4) consequences after an effective claimant's Part 36 offer, some useful general principles can be extracted from cases under the previous incarnation of CPR 36. However, those cases do not include consideration of the 'tactical offer' factor as it was not a part of that rule. Authorities on this point which do consider CPR 36.17(5) are considered separately at **[20.27]** below. What follows here is consideration of cases under the old regime and those under the current provision that do not include arguments on 'tactical offers'.

In *RXDA v Northampton Borough Council* (10 July 2015, unreported), QB, the court concluded that the court should look at each of the entitlements under CPR 37.17(4) separately when determining whether it was unjust to order them. Accordingly, it is possible for a court to order as many or as few of them as it considers appropriate in any particular case.

In *Elsevier Ltd v Munro* [2014] EWHC 2728 (QB), the court considered it unjust to award the additional amount where the claim had proceeded to trial at great speed, the offer expired only nine days before the start of the trial and the claimant's witness statements were only received on the last day of the 'relevant' period.

In *Novus Aviation Ltd v Alubaf Arab International Bank BSC (c)* [2016] EWHC 1937 (Comm), the court concluded that where the claimant had beaten its own offer because of a significant change in exchange rate (the offer was in sterling and the judgment in dollars), it would be unjust to make any of the orders that are now at CPR 36.17(4).

In contrast in *Cashman v Mid Essex Hospital Services NHS Trust* [2015] EWHC 1312 (QB), when overturning a decision reached in a detailed assessment of costs (cross applying CPR 47.20(4)) that the 'additional amount' should not be ordered, the court stressed that it was the terms of the offer that the court has to consider under CPR 36.17(4) and that the provisions are intended to reward claimants and penalise defendants. In passing, the court also confirmed that the 'additional amount' is an all or nothing sum, but that the court must not refuse to order it simply because it believes that some of the 'additional amount' is merited, but not all of it. The claimant is either entitled to the additional amount or not, and if the former, it has to be the full amount. The Senior Courts Costs Office decision in *White v Wincott Galliford Ltd* [2019] EWHC B6 (Costs) cast some doubt on whether the 'all or nothing' interpretation of CPR 36.17(4)(d) is correct. Although obiter, we prefer the view subsequently expressed by Stewart J in *JLE (by her mother and litigation friend, ELH) v Warrington & Halton Hospitals NHS Trust Foundation* [2019] EWHC 1582 (QB), in which the court pointed to the discretion in the wording of CPR 36.17(4)(a) and (c) and the lack of it in CPR 36.17(4)(d) and concluded:

> 'In short, if I had to, I would find that the 10% in subparagraph (d) is all or nothing. It must be awarded in full unless it is unjust to do so.' (para 78)

The same case briefly threatened to reintroduce the uncertainty of the 'near miss'. On a detailed assessment where the assessed costs came to almost £7,000 more than the claimant receiving party's CPR 47.20 offer of £425,000, the master declined to award the additional amount on the basis that, in the light of the small amount by which the claimant had exceeded the offer, the significant reduction in the bill and the relatively large additional amount compared to the amount by which the offer had been exceeded, the '"bonus" of 10% in this case would be a clearly disproportionate sum and it would be unjust to award it' *JLE (by her mother and litigation friend, ELH) v Warrington & Halton Hospitals NHS Trust Foundation* [2018] EWHC B18 (Costs). Fortunately, for those eager to keep CPR 36 as transparent as is possible and the consequences of offers readily measurable, Stewart J allowed the appeal, determining that:

> 'There was nothing unjust about the circumstances of this case. Indeed there was nothing unusual about the circumstances so that the high threshold of proving injustice could be properly regarded as met. That is important because if this case qualifies for withholding the additional award, that would be a green light to similar arguments in many, many other detailed assessments. It would also be a serious disincentive to encouraging good practice and incentivising parties to make and accept appropriate offers.'

What is the 'additional amount'? Is it damages or is it costs? The answer is important because the award of it may take a party over a damages (eg in the Intellectual Property Enterprise Court) or costs (in provisional assessments) cap. The answer, unsurprisingly, is that an 'additional amount' is precisely that: an 'additional amount'. In *OOO Abbott (A company incorporated in the Russian Federation) v Design Display Ltd* [2014] EWHC 3234 (IPEC), the court considered this in the context of the IPEC £500,000 damages cap and concluded that an 'additional amount' was not compensatory, but was solely an incentive to encourage resolution by use of CPR 36. Indeed, in *Thai Airways International Public Co Ltd v KI Holdings Co Ltd (formerly known as Koito Industries Ltd)* [2015] EWHC 1476 (Comm), the court confirmed that CPR 36.17(4) was a key ingredient of the purpose of CPR 36, which was to encourage parties to settle by sensible use of CPR 36.

In *Mohammed v The Home Office* [2018] EWHC 3051 (QB), the court considered the meaning of 'the amount awarded' in CPR 37.17(4)(d), specifically whether it includes interest awarded and, if so, whether that is interest before or after any enhancement under CPR 36.17(4)(a). The court identified three possible interpretations as follows:

- that it means the award of damages net of any interest (as per *Watchorn v Jupiter Industries Ltd* [2014] EWHC 3003 (Ch));

- that it means the award of damages together with interest awarded before any consideration of CPR 36 (as per *Bolt Burdon Solicitors v Tariq* [2016] EWHC 1507 (QB));
- that it means the award of damages together with all interest awarded, including any enhancement under CPR 36.17(4)(a).

Having considered competing authorities the court decided that:

> ' . . . the proper construction of r.36.17(4)(d)(i) is clear. In calculating the additional amount, the court should take into account the gross award that would have been made but for Part 36. That is the sum that the court was about to award when taken to the Part 36 offer. Such assessment therefore includes basic interest, whether awarded pursuant to contract . . . or to the court's discretionary power, but excludes any enhanced interest awarded under r.36.17(4)(a).'

The different consequences for claimants and defendants

[20.19]

CPR 36.17(3), considered above, makes no similar provisions for 'incentives' in favour of a defendant who has made an offer which is not beaten.

A defendant wishing to obtain costs on the indemnity basis must establish that there are circumstances which take the case out of the norm (*Excelsior Commercial and Industrial Holdings Ltd v Salisbury Hamer Aspden & Johnson (a firm)* [2002] EWCA Civ 879 and recently confirmed in *Shalaby v London North West Healthcare NHS Trust* [2018] EWCA Civ 1323, where the trial judge had erroneously understood the indemnity costs provision of CPR 36.17(4)(b) to apply to effective Part 36 offers made by defendants).

This discrepancy of sanction between claimants who fail to beat defendants' offers and defendants who fail to beat claimants' offers is further accentuated in those claims to which the qualified one-way costs shifting ('QOCS') provisions of CPR 44.13–CPR 44.16 apply (see **[20.17]** above and **[20.20]** below). This is all the more so, as the Court of Appeal in *Cartwright v Venduct* [2018] EWCA Civ 1654, unsurprisingly given that this is what it says, construed CPR 44.14(1), and the right to offset, as only applying to those cases where the court has awarded damages and interest. As a result, as there is no court order for damages where a Part 36 offer is accepted, then the claimant is protected from enforcement under CPR 44.14(1).

DEFENDANTS' PART 36 OFFERS AND QUALIFIED ONE WAY COSTS SHIFTING

[20.20]

In a case in which a claimant has the benefit of 'QOCS' (see Chapter 11 An Overview of the Key Costs Amendments to the Civil Procedure Rules), but fails to obtain a result more advantageous than a defendant's Part 36 offer, then the claimant will have to pay the defendant's costs from the date on which the relevant period for acceptance expired (under CPR 36.17(3)). However, the amount that may be enforced against the claimant under this costs order cannot, when added to any other interim costs orders against him which he has paid or has to pay, be more than the aggregate of orders for damages and interest (see **[20.17]** above) in the claimant's favour unless 1) one of the exceptions in CPR 44.16 applies and/or 2) a set-off of costs is ordered under CPR 44.12 (see Chapter 22 at [**22.34**]). In other words, the pendulum of sanctions under Part 36 has swung even further in favour of the claimant.

PART 36 CONSEQUENCES WHERE CPR 3.14 APPLIES

[20.21]

CPR 36.23 contains an important provision. CPR 3.14, in isolation, deems a party who has failed to comply with the requirement for filing a costs budget to have filed one containing court fees only. The effect of this is that unless the court orders otherwise (effectively that party obtains relief from sanctions) the party is precluded from recovering anything going forward save court fees where the court makes a costs management order and will struggle under CPR PD 44, para 3 where no costs management order is made. This creates the unwelcome position that the other party/ies in such cases know in advance that they have limited costs exposure when rejecting CPR 36 offers (removing the risk incentive to settle that CPR 36 was designed to produce). This flies in the face of the increased encouragement after 31 March 2013 for parties to resolve disputes.

CPR 36.23 is designed to address this in part. It provides that where the offeror is a party subject to the sanction of CPR 3.14 (or is otherwise limited in recovery of costs to the same fees), then, for the purpose of acceptance of an offer under CPR 36.13(5)(b) (acceptance after the expiry of the relevant period), CPR 36.17(3)(a) (costs in favour of the defendant under CPR 36 offer after judgment) and CPR 36.17(4)(b) (costs in favour of the claimant under CPR 36 offer after judgment), 'costs' in those rules, which would otherwise be limited by CPR 3.14, shall be 50% of the costs assessed without reference to the limitation, together with any other recoverable costs. In other words, a party subject to the restraints of CPR 3.14 retains an incentive to make CPR 36 offers (and as soon as possible to minimise the lack of budget) and the offeree still has some risk incentive to accept such offers. However, the inclusion of CPR 36.17(4)(b) is curious. If a claimant obtains an order for indemnity costs then the budgetary restriction of CPR 3.18 no longer applies (as it only applies to assessments on the standard basis) and therefore the provision either appears utterly superfluous as the provisions of CPR 3.14 have no effect or it is a well disguised sanction (ie that the failure to comply with CPR 3.13 still merits some penalty even if the costs order takes the defaulting receiving party outside CPR 3.18). We wonder whether the reference to CPR 36.17(4)(b) misunderstands the operation of CPR 3.14 and CPR 3.18. If not, it seems to lead to a sanction under CPR 3.14 where the specific costs management provisions do not impose one. It may be that the reference was aimed at those cases under CPR 36.17(4) where the court 'considers it unjust' to award indemnity costs, but this is not what the rule says and CPR 36.23 expressly refers to the situation where indemnity costs does apply. Perhaps the logic is to ensure that the failure to comply with CPR 3.13 results in the same CPR 36 consequence for both a claimant and a defendant offeror, even though, in the ordinary application of CPR 36.17, there is a difference in outcome for the offering claimant and defendant.

PART 36 AND SUCCESS IN PART

[20.22]

In *Walsh v Shanahan* [2013] EWCA Civ 675, the Court of Appeal held that where the claimant had succeeded on a claim for breach of fiduciary duty, had been unsuccessful on a claim for an account and had failed to recover more than the defendants' Part 36 offer it was entirely appropriate for the judge to have commenced the consideration of costs by asking what costs order would have been made if there had been no Part 36 offer.

Adopting this approach, the judge concluded that the appropriate order would have permitted the defendants to recover 90% of their costs. However, having then taken into account the Part 36 offer, the claimant was ordered to pay: (i) 90% of the defendants' costs until the expiry of the relevant period for acceptance of the Part 36 offer; and (ii) all of their costs thereafter.

The Court of Appeal considered this approach was both orthodox and rational. The costs after the expiry of the relevant period for acceptance were covered by the provisions of Part 36, but it was entirely logical for the judge to ignore the Part 36 offer when approaching overall success to determine the incidence of the pre-Part 36 costs. The defendants were the substantially successful parties, although their success was reduced by their unsuccessful resistance of the damages claim. This approach to the award of costs was entirely unexceptionable. The fact that the claimant would have been entitled to costs incurred in the relevant period had the Part 36 offer been accepted was irrelevant because it had not been accepted and the claimant had taken the risk of continuing the claim.

This case illustrates the enormous uncertainty and risk that rejecting a Part 36 offer can create. From a position where the claimant would have recovered damages and, under CPR 36.13, costs up to acceptance, the claimant went to a situation of no costs recovery and payment of virtually all those of the defendants.

In *Webb (by her litigation friend) v Liverpool Women's NHS Foundation Trust* [2016] EWCA Civ 365, the court had to determine the award of costs against a backdrop of the claimant having beaten her Part 36 offer at trial, but having failed in respect of one allegation of negligence. The trial judge awarded the claimant her costs, but with a 25% deduction to reflect that she had failed on the second allegation, with Part 36 consequences on the 75% costs awarded from the relevant date. In allowing the claimant's appeal against the percentage deduction and awarding her all her costs, the Court of Appeal restated the comments of Jackson LJ in *Fox v Foundation Piling* [2011] EWCA Civ 790 that 'in a personal injury action the fact that the claimant has won on some issues and lost on other issues along the way is not normally a reason for depriving the claimant of part of his costs'. It also decided that when determining the costs order under what is now CPR 36.17, the court does not first exercise its discretion under CPR 44.2. Whilst that approach does not prevent an issues-based order or percentage costs order, a successful claimant is to be deprived of all or part of the costs after the relevant date in respect of its Part 36 offer, only if the court considers that it would be unjust for an award of all or part of those costs in all the circumstances – in other words by application of CPR 36.17(5).

PART 36 OFFERS AND SPLIT TRIALS AND DISCLOSURE OF PART 36 OFFERS GENERALLY

[20.23]

CPR 36.12 now makes specific provision in the vexed area of split trials. It does so by reference to the definition of when 'a case is decided' in CPR 36.3. The definition is that a case is decided when all issues in the case have been determined, whether at one or more trials. This effectively codifies the view expressed by the court in the case of *Beasley (by his litigation friend) v Alexander* [2012] EWHC 2715 (QB), in which it construed 'until the case has been decided' as being a reference to final determination. However, as will become apparent from the comments below, some of the mischief that this then causes, and which was identified by Eder J in *Ted Baker plc v Axa Insurance UK plc* [2012] EWHC 1779 (Comm), when the court determines costs after a preliminary trial where the claim continues, is addressed by new provisions at CPR 36.16(3)(d) and (4).

Previously the court was not entitled to know whether any CPR 36 offers had been made. The effect of this was that the court could not fairly determine the incidence of costs in respect of the preliminary trial, as although it could identify the successful party it did not know whether there was any chance that the subsequent determination of outstanding issues (usually quantum) would engage any Part 36 offers which might displace the general rule under CPR 44.2. This resulted in many orders for costs reserved. In those cases where the court was able to make a costs award to one or other party it was usually because the parties had agreed on some form of disclosure relating to Part 36 offers. CPR 36.16 at least makes the process somewhat simpler, but, inevitably, cannot resolve the situation completely.

CPR 36.16(2) provides the general rule that the fact that an offer has been made and the terms of that offer must not be communicated to the trial judge until the case is decided. However, CPR 36.16(3) permits the court to be told of CPR 36 offers where:

- the defence of tender before claim has been raised;
- where a CPR 36 offer has been accepted and the claim is stayed;
- where the offeror and offeree agree in writing to disclosure; and
- where the case has not been decided but any part of it has been decided and the offer relates only to that part.

The last of these provisions goes some way to assist the court. However, where part of the case only has been decided, the trial judge may not be told the terms of any offers that do not relate to that part decided, but may be told that there are such offers (CPR 36.16(4)). The effect of this at the end of a preliminary trial is that the trial judge may consider CPR 36 offers that relate to that part decided and may know whether there are other CPR 36 offers in play. This makes the decision of whether an order for costs reserved is required or whether the court can proceed to make a costs order in respect of the preliminary part, far simpler. Where there is an offer that does not relate to the part decided (eg an overarching quantum offer where the preliminary point was breach of duty or limitation), an order reserving costs on the preliminary point remains likely. This is precisely what happened in *Interactive Technology Corpn Ltd v Ferster* [2017] EWHC 1510 (Ch) and in *Lifestyle Equities CV v Sportsdirect.com Retail Ltd* [2018] EWHC 962 (Ch) in which the court concluded that:

> 'Where there has been a Part 36 offer made and the parties have either been ordered to or agreed to split the trial between liability and quantum, the appropriate course is to wait until after the quantum issues have been resolved before attempting to address questions of costs.'

CPR 36.12 contains two further discrete provisions relating to Part 36 offers and determination of part only of a claim as follows:

- if the CPR 36 offer relates only to parts of the claim or issues that have been decided it can no longer be accepted; and
- if the CPR 36 offer is not one covered by the first provision it cannot be accepted earlier than seven days after judgment is given in the trial that does not decide all the issues (unless the parties agree otherwise) – no doubt to permit time for the parties to take stock and withdraw/change any earlier offers in the light of the outcome of that trial.

Accordingly, it seems that the Civil Procedure Rules Committee has reacted, so far as it is able to do so, to the concerns of Eder J in *Ted Baker plc*, ' . . . that there is a real problem here. In my view, there is an urgent need for CPR 36.13 (as was) to be reviewed and possibly reformulated in order to deal in particular with the question of split trials and the kind of difficulties which have arisen in the present case', while ensuring the necessary restriction on disclosure of any Part 36 offers that may still prove pertinent once the entire claim has been decided.

In *Sir Cliff Richard v BBC* (9 March 2018, unreported), Ch D, Mann J, one of the defendants had settled the claim with the claimant by way of Part 36, but maintained a contribution claim. It wished to prevent disclosure of the settlement sum relying on CPR 36.16, so that there was no risk this might influence the judge determining that claim. The court concluded that CPR 36.16 did not apply where an offer had been accepted, as it then ceased to be an offer, instead, being a binding settlement. However, the court retains a residual discretion to prevent disclosure if the settlement is relevant to outstanding claims, but there will be such serious prejudice that it outweighs this relevance.

The position in respect of disclosure within appeals is governed by CPR 52.22. The usual rule of non-disclosure until all issues other than costs have been determined applies, save where:

- the Part 36 offer is relevant to the substance of the appeal; or
- the disclosure of the fact that a Part 36 offer has been made is properly relevant to the matter to be decided.

PART 36 AND PERSONAL INJURY CLAIMS FOR FUTURE PECUNIARY LOSS

[20.24]

Under the Damages Act 1996 the court has the power to award losses for future pecuniary loss by way of periodical payments ('PPs'). Strictly, CPR 41.5 requires each party to state its case on PPs in the respective statements of case. In reality this is often overlooked and in anticipation CPR 41.5(2) and (3) provide that the court can order parties to make such statements and provide further information about them. One reason for this is that the court has to give an indication as soon as practicable as to whether a conventional lump sum award or PPs is likely to be the most appropriate form for the damages.

CPR 36.18 contains the first of five sequential provisions of the revised CPR 36 that come under the heading *'PERSONAL INJURY CLAIMS'*. It sets out detailed provisions for offers where future pecuniary losses arise. In reality the vast majority of claims are not suitable for PPs and settlement is on a lump sum basis with no application of these provisions. However, in those claims where PPs remain a live issue the following specific rules apply:

- An offer may be that all future pecuniary losses are dealt with by lump sum, all are dealt with by PPs or that part of the damages are dealt with by lump sum and part by PPs and that the whole or part of any other damages by lump sum.
- An offer must state the amount of the lump sum offered for all or part of any damages.
- An offer may state what part of the lump sum, if any, relates to future pecuniary loss and what part relates to other damages to be accepted in the form of a lump sum.
- An offer must state what part of the offer relates to damages for future pecuniary loss to be paid in the form of PPs and must specify the amount and duration of the PPs, the amount of any payments for substantial capital purchases and when those are to be made and whether each amount is to vary by reference to the retail prices index ('RPI'), some other index or not at all (remember when making such an offer that the court order under CPR 41.8 must specify variation annually by reference to the RPI unless the court orders otherwise).
- An offer must state that any part of the damages in the form of PPs will be funded to ensure continuity of payment is reasonably secure.
- If an offer is a mixture of lump sum and PPs, the acceptance can only be to the offer as a whole. In other words, the acceptance cannot be to part being funded in a specific way and leave alive an argument on the fashion of payment of the rest of the claim.
- Whoever makes the offer, if it includes payment of some part of the damages in the form of PPs and is accepted, it is for the claimant to apply to the court within seven days of acceptance for a formal court order under CPR 41.8.

PART 36 AND CLAIMS FOR PROVISIONAL DAMAGES

[20.25]

The second of the personal injury claims provisions is at CPR 36.19 and relates to claims for provisional damages.

Any party to a claim for provisional damages can make a Part 36 offer (CPR 36.19(1)). The offer must state:

- whether the proposed settlement includes an award of provisional damages;
- where it does, the offer must specify:

(i) that the sum offered is on the assumption that the claimant will not develop the disease or suffer the type of deterioration specified in the offer;

(ii) that the offer is subject to the condition that any application for further damages must be made within a particular time; and

(iii) what that time period is to be.

Regardless of who makes the offer, if it is accepted, the claimant must apply to the court within seven days of acceptance for an award of provisional damages under CPR 41.2.

The revised form N242A provides a clearer steer to consideration of this when making CPR 36 offers, specifically guiding to consideration of whether the claim is one for personal injury.

PART 36 AND RECOUPMENT OF STATE BENEFIT

[20.26]

Despite the change to CPR 36 the rule continues to say it all in respect of deduction of benefit. It is now found at CPR 36.22, which is set out in the Appendix.

PART 36 AND THE 'GENUINE OFFER'

[20.27]

As mentioned in **[20.14]**, CPR 36.17(5)(e) allows the court to determine that it is unjust to afford the claimant or defendant the benefits of CPR 36.17(3) or (4) respectively if the offer was not a genuine attempt to settle. This introduces formally the concept of the 'tactical offer' to which the court has referred in the past. Wisely the word chosen is 'genuine' and not 'tactical'. This recognises that all Part 36 offers are tactical. However, this does not make the determination of what is and is not a 'genuine' attempt to settle any easier.

In *Huck v Robson* [2002] EWCA Civ 398, the court was concerned with a road traffic accident in which it was likely the finding on liability would be either 50/50 or 100%. The claimant made a pre-action offer to accept a 95%–5% split on liability. The defendant rejected the offer and the trial judge refused to take it into account in the award of costs on the ground that the apportionment was 'illusory'. The Court of Appeal disagreed. It concluded that although a judge would be entitled to exercise discretion and refuse indemnity costs where an offer was purely tactical, for example to settle for 99.9% of the full value of the claim, that could not be said of the claimant's offer. The reduction of 5% provided the defendant with a real opportunity of settlement and did not represent the court's probable decision on liability. After applying the prescribed factors the court, by a majority, awarded the claimant the costs on the indemnity basis. The court identified the risk of a tactical offer as being that it was made solely to try to reap the benefit of CPR 36, rather than as a genuine attempt to settle. What is a genuine offer? Surely any offer that is designed to try to settle the case is a genuine one? In *Huck* the defendant had a clear choice – accept the offer and avoid the risk of a finding of 100% liability or take the chance. It was certainly genuine in the sense that the claimant must have recognised that if accepted there would be a deduction of 5% of the damages claimed.

As the April 2013 civil procedure reforms were, in part, to reduce costs by encouraging the parties to settle, it seems strange to penalise a party seeking to settle by making a concession from the stated best case. The provision also seems to open the door to uncertainty, which CPR 36 really could do without. In the *Huck* scenario, at what point might the court decide that the offer is not genuine – 96%, 97%, 98% or 99%?

Although, it seems strange to reintroduce uncertainty, and the opportunity for satellite argument, about when the provisions of CPR 36 will apply by reference to such a nebulous concept as a 'genuine offer', some themes are beginning to emerge.

The court rejected the argument that it might be prudent for a party making an offer that only allowed a small deduction to provide an accompanying explanation of why this was being offered in *JMX v Norfolk and Norwich Hospitals NHS Foundations Trust* [2018] EWHC 185 (QB). The court concluded that a 90% offer on liability in a clinical negligence case was a genuine offer. In so doing, the court declined to embark upon a mini-trial to determine how the risk should have looked to the offeror at the time of the offer, making the point that parties often have widely differing views in assessing the risk in the same case.

In contrast, when confronted by a decision with limited outcomes (a determination of whether the claimant was a minor), in *R (on the application of MVN) v London Borough of Greenwich* [2015] EWHC 663 (Admin) the court decided that it would be unjust to apply CPR 36.17(4) as the successful claimant's offer was to take 'nothing short of what was in issue in the proceedings' and was not a genuine offer. However, the binary decision required and the fact that the proceedings were of an inquisitorial nature restricts the relevance of the case. However, in another all or nothing case, *Jockey Club Racecourses Ltd v Willmott Dixon Construction Ltd* [2016] EWHC 167 (TCC), the court concluded that the claimant's offer to accept 95% of damages to be decided was a genuine one and although the date from which the indemnity costs order ran was deferred for other reasons, it was not unjust to apply the consequences of CPR 36.17(4). Notwithstanding that the offer was of an outcome that was not an option for the court and the discount offered was a modest one, it was still a valid one. Interestingly, counsel for the claimant conceded in argument that an offer of 98% might have been difficult to defend.

However, in *Rawbank SA v Travelex Banknotes Ltd* [2020] EWHC 1619 (Ch), the court, in determining that an offer that represented a discount of 0.3% of the total amount claimed was a genuine offer, concluded that:

> 'The critical question is not a mathematical one – the proportion of the discount – but whether it is possible to infer from the size of the discount that there is no genuine attempt to settle the proceedings.' Paragraph 29

Notwithstanding this, the court only imposed the sanctions under CPR 37.17(4)(a) and (b), reinforcing that the court must look at each sanction in CPR 37.17(4) separately, to determine if its imposition is unjust.

In *MGN Ltd v Yentob* [2015] EWCA Civ 1292, the court confirmed two fundamental (if rather obvious) points as follows:

> 'a) Whether an offer is more advantageous than the outcome achieved and whether it is unjust for the normal consequences of CPR 36.17 to apply, are separate inquiries.
> b) When determining the second inquiry, the court must make a finding as to whether or not it is unjust for the normal consequences of CPR 36.17(3) or (4), as appropriate, to apply.'

Of more assistance is the court's decision that, if, having dealt with the first inquiry, it becomes necessary to deal with second one, then there is no logical reason why the same material (the offer and the context of it) should not be relevant again. The court stated that this is an inevitable part of looking at 'all the circumstances' under CPR 36.17(5). The key is to avoid elision of the separate inquiries.

In *MR v Metropolitan Police Comr* [2019] EWHC 1970 (QB), the court determined that a CPR 36 offer to accept no damages, but an admission of liability, in a claim for false imprisonment and assault, where the claimant sought damages but also the vindication of a judgment that would clear his name, was a genuine offer to settle under CPR 36.17(5).

PART 36 AND THE SMALL CLAIMS TRACK

[20.28]

Although Part 36 does not apply to the small claims track (CPR 27.2) there is no reason why a party to a small claim should not make an offer which can be taken into account when considering unreasonable behaviour and awarding costs and disbursements (see CPR 27.14(3)). Bear in mind, of course, that the court will be applying the overriding objective to these claims and proportionality will still be the order of the day in any event and should limit the opportunity for unreasonable behaviour.

PART 36 AND CPR PD 8B

[20.29]

These provisions are set out in Section II of CPR 36 at CPR 36.24–CPR 36.30. They apply to claims where the relevant protocol has been followed and stage 3 proceedings have been started under CPR PD 8B. The provisions are exclusive, in that where they apply the rest of CPR 36 does not apply.

These rules provide that:

- while a party can make an offer in whatever way it wishes, it only has the consequences of CPR 36 if made in accordance with CPR 36 Section II (CPR 36.24(4));
- an offer to settle under the Protocol is a 'Protocol offer' (CPR 36.25(1));
- such an offer must be set out in the Court Proceedings Pack and contain the final total amount offered by each party (CPR 36.25(2));
- the Protocol offer is deemed made the first business day after the court proceedings pack is sent to the defendant;

- a Protocol offer is treated as being exclusive of interest and has costs consequences only in respect of stage 3 fixed costs and not in respect of any costs of an appeal from the stage 3 determination (CPR 36.27);
- Protocol offers must not be communicated to the court until after the determination of the claim and any other offer must never be communicated to the court (CPR 36.28);
- where the claimant obtains judgment for damages that are:
  - (i) less than or equal to the defendant's Protocol offer (net of deduction of CRU), the claimant must pay the defendant the relevant stage 3 fixed costs, interest on those costs from the first business day after date the offer is deemed made and any stage 3 disbursements allowed (CPR 36.29(2));
  - (ii) more than the defendant's offer, but less than the claimant's offer, the defendant pays the relevant stage 3 costs and any costs that remain outstanding under stages 1 and 2 (CPR 36.29(3));
  - (iii) equal to or more than the claimant's offer, the defendant must pay the claimant the fixed costs under (ii) above, interest on the entire damages at a rate not exceeding 10% above base rate starting with the date the protocol offer is deemed made (see above), interest on the fixed costs at a rate not exceeding 10% above base rate and the additional amount under CPR 36.17(4)(d) – 10% on damages up to £500,000, a further 5% on damages over £500,000 with an overall limit of £75,000.

PART 36 AND SETTLEMENT OF CLAIMS WITHOUT PROCEEDINGS BUT WHERE THERE HAS BEEN AN UNREASONABLE FAILURE TO FOLLOW A PERSONAL INJURY PRE-ACTION PROTOCOL THAT PROVIDES FOR FIXED COSTS

[20.30]

The Court of Appeal has considered the position where a claimant has unreasonably failed to follow a pre-action protocol that provides for fixed costs, but settled the claim by way of acceptance of a Part 36 offer within the relevant period, but before the issue of any proceedings. In *Williams v The Secretary of State for Business Energy and Industrial Strategy* [2018] EWCA Civ 852, the failure of the claimant to give full instructions to his solicitors that would have meant a claim was presented against only one defendant, rather than two, was unreasonable. As the claim ought only to have been brought against one defendant it should have been brought under the Pre-Action Protocol for Low Value Personal Injury (Employer's Liability and Public Liability) Claims. The Court of Appeal concluded that:

- CPR 45.24 does not apply as it expressly restricted to those cases where CPR 7 proceedings have been commenced and one of the scenarios set out at CPR 45.24(2), (2A) or (3) apples. In passing, and in accordance with *Cartwright v Venduct* [2018] EWCA Civ 1654 (see **[20.19]** above), the restriction in CPR 45.24(2) and (2A), to cases where judgment is given, suggests that this provision could never apply to cases resolved by acceptance of a CPR 36 offer (or, indeed, under a Tomlin order stay on terms).

- CPR 36.13 does apply.
- The provisions of CPR 44.4 and, in particular, CPR 44.11 relating to conduct, provide 'ample scope for a District Judge or a Costs Judge, when assessing the costs in a claim which was unreasonably made outside the EL/PL Protocol, to allow only the fixed costs set out in the EL/PL Protocol' (para 52) and so 'in a case not covered by r.45.24, . . . , a defendant can rely on the Part 44 conduct provisions to argue that only the EL/PL Protocol fixed costs should apply' (para 61). The usual result will be that the claimant is restricted to fixed costs and disbursements.
- A defendant settling such a claim by way of CPR 36 should raise any argument about restriction to fixed costs as soon as possible, and certainly in the acknowledgement of service to any CPR 46.14 costs-only proceedings (para 63).

PART 36 AND CLAIMS UNDER CPR 45 SECTION IIIA (CLAIMS WHICH NO LONGER CONTINUE UNDER THE PERSONAL INJURY PRE-ACTION PROTOCOLS)

[20.31]

The application of CPR 36 to these claims is governed by CPR 36.20 and CPR 36.21. This applies to cases where proceedings have started under the stage 3 procedure at CPR PD 8B.

The consequences of acceptance

[20.32]

CPR 36.20 applies specific provisions in these cases. In summary these are that:

- Where an offer is accepted within the relevant period the claimant recovers the fixed costs in Tables 6B, 6C or 6D of CPR 45 depending upon the stage reached in the claim at the time that the offer is accepted. This also applies if the offer relates to part only of the claim and at the time of acceptance the claimant abandons the remainder of the claim.
- Where a defendant's offer is accepted outside the 'relevant period' the claimant recovers the fixed costs under the appropriate table above (determined at the time that the 'relevant period' expired) and must pay the defendant's costs from the date of expiry of the 'relevant period' until acceptance of the offer (CPR 36.20(4)). This is qualified so that: i) where the claimant accepts the offer after the date on which the claim leaves the protocol, the claimant will be entitled to the stage 1 and 2 fixed costs in Table 6 or 6A in CPR 45 and must pay the defendant's costs from the date on which the protocol offer is deemed made (CPR 36.20(5)); ii) where the claim involves a soft tissue injury (as defined in the Road Traffic Accident Protocol) and the defendant makes the offer before receipt of the fixed cost medical report, the consequences set out in CPR 36.20(4) and (5) only take effect if the offer is accepted more than 21 days after receipt of the report by the defendant.

What, though, of the situation where the defendant accepts a claimant's offer outside the relevant period? In such cases the court concluded in *Hislop v Perde* [2018] EWCA Civ 1726 that CPR 36.13 does not apply, as CPR 36.20 does not preserve the applicability of that provision (contrast this to CPR 36.21, which expressly preserves CPR 36.17, see [20.33] below). As Coulson LJ highlighted:

> 'r.36.20 makes plain that it is the only rule which applies to the costs consequences of acceptance of a Part 36 offer in fixed costs cases.'

As a result, the correct interpretation of the rules results in late acceptance by a defendant of a CPR 36 offer in a fixed costs case falling within CPR 36.20, which is the specific rule. The court did point out that CPR 45.29J still offers the possibility of escape from the fixed costs restraints, but, as the issue was not before the court, declined to offer any conclusions about the scope and the extent of the provision.

In *Ho v Adelekun* [2020] EWCA Civ 1988, the Court of Appeal found that CPR 36.20 (fixed costs) applies in a case falling within CPR 45.29B, even if the Part 36 offer which has been accepted refers to payment of costs under CPR 36.13 (conventional costs of an amount to be assessed). A number of reasons were given for this conclusion, as follows:

- CPR 36.5(1) (form and content of a Part 36 offer) does not deal with the basis on which costs are to be determined;
- CPR 36.13(1) itself refers to the costs consequences under CPR 36.20 in appropriate cases;
- the offer was clearly intended to be a Part 36 offer, but it could not be, if it were treated as having departed from the provisions of Part 36 (and it would be so treated if the offer to pay costs under CPR 36.13 rather than 36.20 was binding);
- a reference to 'detailed assessment' in the offer was not wholly inapposite as the fixed costs regime 'does involve an assessment of some kind' (and of course the assessment provisions of CPR PD 47, para 5.7 might apply in respect of disbursement disputes in a fixed costs regime);
- it was inherently improbable, as should have been appreciated by a reasonable recipient of the offer, that the maker of the offer would have intended to offer more generous costs than prescribed by the rules; and
- the fact that both parties begin and end the proceedings with the expectation that fixed costs are all that will be recoverable, make it even more unlikely that an offer should be understood to be of anything other than those.

Whilst on the topic of 'an assessment of some kind', in *Ivanov v Lubbe* (17 January 2020, unreported) Central London County Court, the court concluded that there was no order for costs under CPR 36.20. Accordingly, if, as a result of any disagreement as to what is payable, a party requires an assessment by the court, then there is no automatic right to commence assessment proceedings. Instead, the correct approach is first to secure an order for costs by issuing an application for such an order under CPR Part 23.

Where the court makes an order for costs in favour of the defendant, the court must have regard to, and the costs must not exceed, the fixed costs applicable at the time of acceptance in Tables 6B, 6C or 6D in CPR 45, less the fixed costs to which the claimant is entitled. In addition, the parties are entitled to recover the disbursements allowed for any period in which they are entitled to costs.

Costs consequences following judgment

[20.33]

CPR 36.21 sets out the position. In essence the provisions of CPR 36.17 (considered above at **[20.17]**, **[20.18]** and **[20.19]**) apply, but with modifications. These are as follows:

- Where the claimant fails to obtain a judgment more advantageous than a defendant's CPR 36 offer, the claimant recovers the costs fixed for the stage applicable at the date at which the 'relevant period' expires on the defendant's offer and the claimant will be liable for the defendant's costs from that date until judgment. This is qualified so that if the defendant made the offer in a case involving a soft tissue injury before receipt of a fixed costs medical report under the Protocol, then these costs provisions only apply to costs incurred 21 days after the receipt of the report.
- Where the claimant fails to obtain a judgment more advantageous than the defendant's protocol offer the position is even worse for the claimant. In this situation the claimant will only be entitled to the Stage 1 and Stage 2 costs in Section III of CPR 45 and will be liable for the defendant's costs from the date upon which the protocol offer is deemed to be made until judgment. For the avoidance of doubt CPR 36.21(3)(c) clarifies that a judgment is less than the protocol offer after deductible amounts in the judgment award have been deducted (ie net of any CRU deductions – see CPR 36.22(1)(d) for the definition of 'deductible amount'). A Protocol offer is defined in CPR 36.25 and if the claim leaves the Protocol before the Court Proceedings Pack is sent to the defendant (as this is the trigger for when the offer is deemed made under CPR 36.26) the last offer made by the defendant before the claim leaves the Protocol is the Protocol offer and it is deemed made on the first business day after the claim leaves the Protocol. Again, this is qualified so that if the defendant made the offer in a case involving a soft tissue injury before receipt of a fixed costs medical report under the Protocol, then these costs provisions only apply to costs incurred 21 days after the receipt of the report.

When the court quantifies any award of costs made in favour of the defendant under the above provisions, the court must have regard to and the amount of costs shall not exceed the fixed costs under Tables B, C and D in CPR 45 less any residual amount of fixed costs to which the claimant remains entitled as set out above. The parties are also entitled to recover any disbursements allowed within the fixed costs regime that were incurred during a period when any costs order is in their favour.

What of the claimant who recovers judgment at least as advantageous as the proposals contained in his Part 36 offer? The Court of Appeal answered this question definitively in *Broadhurst v Tan* [2016] EWCA Civ 94. The court concluded that the resolution of any tension between CPR 36 and CPR 45 Section IIIA did not involve a decision of whether one was a specific and one a general rule, but that the position was one of a straightforward matter of interpretation. The interpretation of the court was that the combined effect of what are now CPR 36.17 and CPR 36.21 is that where a claimant makes a successful Part 36 offer, he is entitled to costs assessed on the indemnity basis (note that CPR 36.21 expressly preserves the effect of CPR 36.17). The court also decided that there was a distinction to be drawn between fixed costs and indemnity costs, stating that:

> 'Where a claimant makes a successful Part 36 offer in a section IIIA case, he will be awarded fixed costs to the last staging point provided by rule 45.29C and Table 6B. He will then be awarded costs to be assessed on the indemnity basis in addition from the date that the offer became effective. This does not require any apportionment. It will, however, lead to a generous outcome for the claimant. I do not regard this outcome as so surprising or so unfair to the defendant that it requires the court to equate fixed costs with costs assessed on the indemnity basis.'

PART 36 AND CPR 47.15(5)

[20.34]

What of the impact of an indemnity costs order made under CPR 36.17(4)(b) in a provisional assessment? How does that sit with the cap on costs? The answers are provided by the decision in the second appeal in *W Portsmouth and Co Ltd v Lowin* [2017] EWCA Civ 2172. The court decided that whilst an award of indemnity costs could be made in respect of the costs of provisional assessment, costs assessed under such an award could not exceed the cap in CPR 47.15(5). In reaching this conclusion the Court of Appeal determined that:

- Capped costs cannot be equated with fixed costs (this element of the first appeal decision was not subject to appeal).
- *Broadhurst v Tan* (above, see **[20.33]**) and the position in respect of fixed costs under CPR 36.21 is not directly applicable to the capped costs regime of provisional assessments.
- There is no tension between the provision of CPR 36.17(4)(b) that enables a party to have an assessment on the indemnity basis and CPR 47.15(5) that caps the costs, as the cap does not prevent an assessment on the indemnity basis, but simply restricts the amount that may be recovered.
- CPR 47.20(4), which applies CPR 36 to detailed assessments, does not disapply the provisions of CPR 47.15(5) and nor do the provisions of either CPR 47.15(5) itself or CPR 36.17(4)(b). The Court of Appeal concluded that 'there is nothing in any of those rules to suggest that rule 47.15(5) should be disapplied or modified'.
- The conclusion that the cap applies even where costs are awarded on the indemnity basis 'is also consistent with the policy behind both CPR rule 47.15 and Part 36. It does not undermine the intention to encourage the quick and cheap resolution of the assessment of costs in cases in which the costs claimed are £75,000 or below'.

Accordingly, an award of costs on the indemnity basis may be made in provisional assessments by application of CPR 36.17(4)(b) in the usual way (unless it is unjust to do so), but the costs assessed under such an award may not exceed the cap.

As the Court of Appeal was keen to stress, it is worth remembering that whilst a claimant making a valid CPR 36 offer in these circumstances may still be subject to the costs cap, the other consequences under CPR 36.17(4)(a), (c) and (d) apply without restriction.

DEEMED COSTS ORDER UNDER CPR 36.13 AND CPR 44.9 AND PAYMENTS ON ACCOUNT OF COSTS

[20.35]

The vexed question of whether it is possible to obtain a payment on account of costs (as opposed to a payment under an interim costs certificate) under a deemed order under CPR 44.9, following the acceptance of an offer within the relevant period under CPR 36.13, was finally answered in the affirmative by the Court of Appeal in *Global Assets Advisory Services Ltd v Grandlane Developments Ltd* [2019] EWCA Civ 1764. (See Chapter 25 for more detailed consideration of this.)

OTHER ADMISSIBLE OFFERS

Introduction

[20.36]

CPR Part 36 is not the full story of offers to settle. It is important to remember that CPR 36.2(2) provides that a party may make an offer to settle in whatever way that party may choose, but, and this is the important bit, if the offer is not made in accordance with CPR 36.5 it will not have the costs consequences specified in CPR 36. This emphasises that in deciding what order to make about costs under CPR 44.2(4) (see below) the court will have regard to any admissible offer which does not have the costs consequences of Part 36.

'Calderbank' letters

[20.37]

Since 1975 a frequently used alternative to a payment into court or Part 36 offer has been an offer contained in a Calderbank letter. It is called 'Calderbank' because it is a form of offer first approved by the Court of Appeal in *Calderbank v Calderbank* [1976] Fam 93, [1975] 3 All ER 333, [1975] 3 WLR 586, CA, and this is still a useful description. It is an offer made 'Without prejudice save as to costs'. The magic words are 'save as to costs' as was demonstrated in *Reed Executive plc v Reed Business Information Ltd* [2004] EWCA Civ 887. The defendant had made offers in privileged meetings and in 'without prejudice' correspondence on which it sought to rely on the question of costs. The court could not look at the correspondence. In its judgment the Court of Appeal said: 'Parties may negotiate in the faith and expectation that the negotiations cannot be used against them even on the question of costs unless the negotiations are expressly stated to be 'without prejudice save as to costs'. Magic words indeed.

In *Vestergaard Frandsen A/S (A company incorporated under the Laws of Denmark) v Bestnet* [2014] EWHC 4047 (Ch) the court concluded that the privilege afforded by without prejudice offers with no 'save as to costs' provision precluded the paying party raising them even if only to identify that the receiving party had failed to respond to them at all and even when conduct under CPR 44.2 had been raised as a costs issue by that party.

Even though offers no longer have to be accompanied by a payment into court there are still many circumstances in which a defendant may consider it advantageous to make a Calderbank offer rather than one which complies with Part 36. Some of these are:

- if the defendant cannot raise the money in a single sum or within the prescribed 14 days to enable him to make a Part 36 offer;
- to make a walk-away offer;
- to make an offer accompanied by an express denial of any admission;
- to make a package of proposals unsuitable for Part 36 offer;
- to offer to do remedial work;
- to make an apology;
- to offer to do further business;
- in a multi-party action; and
- to make a global offer (ie inclusive of costs as this cannot be a CPR 36 offer – see *Mitchell v James* [2002] EWCA Civ 997).

Those making Calderbank offers should take note of the decision in *MEF v St George's Healthcare NHS Trust* [2020] EWHC 1300 (QB), in which the court found that such an offer made before a detailed assessment hearing did not lapse at the start of the hearing (and so the receiving party's acceptance during the hearing, when it became apparent that things were not going well, was valid). In other words, a party does not even need the permission of the court as it would under CPR 36.11(3)(d), to accept an unwithdrawn Calderbank offer after a trial has begun.

The different consequences – to be a Part 36 offer or not to be a Part 36 offer

[20.38]

The key distinction is that an offer under CPR 44.2 cannot open the door for the imposition of the provisions of Part 36. As we have already seen Part 36 is its own self-contained procedural code. An offer is either within or without it.

Just before the April 2007 changes from payments into court to offers, the distinction between the two had blurred thanks to cases like *Trustees of Stokes Pension Fund v Western Power Distribution (South West) Plc* [2005] EWCA Civ 854, [2005] 3 All ER 775, [2005] 1 WLR 3595. *Stokes* determined that an offer 'should usually' be treated as having the consequences of the then Part 36 even in the absence of a payment into court if four conditions were satisfied:

- the offer had to be expressed in clear terms so that there could be no doubt what was being offered;
- the offer had to be open for acceptance for at least 21 days and otherwise accord with the substance of a Calderbank offer;
- the offer had to be genuine (not a sham or non-serious in some way); and

- the defendant should clearly have been good for the money when the offer was made.

Just when it seemed safe to transfer Stokes to history text books along came a timely reminder that it may yet live on. The case of *French v Groupama Insurance Co Ltd* [2011] EWCA Civ 1119, saw the Court of Appeal grappling with Calderbank letters and offers that failed to comply with CPR Part 36 as it was at the time that the offer was made.

In this case the claimant brought a claim based on breach of contract against her insurers in respect of subsidence at her home. At trial she was awarded £126,963.53. There had been pre-action offers on 22 December 2006 and 15 February 2007 of £115,000. The trial judge accepted that of the award about £20,000 was in respect of additional damages that the claimant suffered after the date of the offers and that, as such, the amount offered (which was inclusive of costs and interest) was more advantageous to her than what she subsequently recovered. The trial judge applied *Stokes* even though the defendant accepted that neither offer was within the CPR Part 36 provisions of the time, accorded the second offer letter the same status as a payment in (not the first letter because it did not satisfy all the requirements of *Stokes*) and ordered that the claimant should meet all the defendant's costs.

On appeal the Court of Appeal determined that the offer was not akin to a Part 36 offer because:

(a) an offer inclusive of costs could not be a Part 36 offer (*Mitchell v James* [2002] EWCA Civ 997); and

(b) the parties' agreement that when the offer was made it was privileged (and not qualified with the words 'save as to costs') meant it was not a Calderbank offer and,

therefore, the second condition of *Stokes* was not met.

Having concluded that *Stokes* and the transitional provisions of Part 36 did not apply and that the trial judge had erred, the Court of Appeal approached the issue of costs afresh under CPR 44.2, taking account of the offer as an admissible offer (but not one akin to a Part 36 offer) and concluded that there should be no order as to costs from 21 days after the February 2007 offer and that the defendant should pay the claimant's costs up to that date.

As an aside, if (a) above needed repeating, it received a more recent iteration in *Transocean Drilling UK Ltd v Providence Resources plc* [2016] EWHC 2611 (Comm).

The Court of Appeal returned to this topic in *F & C Alternative Investments (Holdings) Ltd v Barthelemy* [2012] EWCA Civ 843, where offers had been made 'without prejudice save as to costs' explicitly not as Part 36 offers but stating that the court would be invited to apply the same costs consequences as for Part 36 offers.

The trial judge referred to the 'infelicity in the wording' of Part 36 not making its use sensible in the present case where Part 7 proceedings meant the offeror would have to agree to pay the costs of those proceedings. The trial judge then made a costs order in the same terms as if Part 36 had applied. The decision was reversed by the Court of Appeal which held:

- this was not a Part 36 offer and consequently the judge had no jurisdiction to make a costs order under CPR 36;
- the judge's jurisdiction as to costs fell to be exercised under CPR 44.3 (now CPR 44.2);

- under Part 44 the costs regime of Part 36, whether indirectly or by analogy, cannot properly be invoked;
- there is no reason or justification, for indirectly extending Part 36 beyond its expressed ambit. To do so would tend to undermine the requirements of Part 36 and the repeated insistence of the courts that intended Part 36 offers should be very carefully drafted so as to comply with the requirements of Part 36.

The Court of Appeal had the opportunity to revisit the distinction between CPR 36 and CPR 44.2(4)(c) in *Coward v Phaestos* [2014] EWCA Civ 1256. The court stressed that CPR 36 and CPR 44 are entirely separate 'award of costs' regimes with different purposes and different outcomes. The former prescribes consequences whereas the latter involves consideration of offers as part of a generous exercise of discretion by the court.

An interesting departure from the rigid imposition of the CPR 36 strait jacket occurred in *Procter & Gamble Co v Svenska Cellulosa Aktiebolaget SCA* [2012] EWHC 2839 (Ch). The claimant sought to minimise its liability to make payment to Svenska and made a claimant's offer expressed to have the consequences of Part 36. The offer included an offer to pay the defendant's costs if it was accepted within 21 days. The effect of this offer was that the claimant was reversing the costs consequences under CPR 36.10 (now CPR 36.13) by giving up its entitlement to its costs and offering to pay the defendant's costs.

Having considered the decision in *F & C Alternative Investments (Holdings) Ltd v Barthelemy*, Hildyard J concluded as follows (with rule references to the previous version of CPR 36):

> 'In my view, the issue in the *F & C* case was really whether an offer accepted not to be within Part 36 could be given, by analogy, the same consequences as would have followed if it had been compliant and intended to be so. Here, the issue is whether CPR 36.2(2), and thus the gateway to CPR 36.10 and 36.14, is to be so strictly construed that it requires (by rule 36.2(2)(c)) the offer made to provide for the defendant to be liable for the claimant's costs even if the claimant expresses his offer to be a Part 36 offer, but as part of that offer, agrees to forsake that entitlement and instead pay the defendant his costs. Put another way, I do not accept that it is impossible for a claimant to comply with Part 36 unless he requires to be paid his costs and such payment to be made within a period of not less than 21 days.'

The decision of the Court of Appeal in *N J Rickard Ltd v Holloway* (3 November 2015, unreported), CA Civ Div confirms our view that the combination of CPR 36.1 and 36.5(c) actually prevents an offer such as this falling within CPR 36 as now codified. This was a landlord and tenant dispute, with a claim and counterclaim, in which the court concluded that the fact the landlord's offer was on the basis each party should bear its own costs, meant that the offer did not comply with the requirement for the offer to state that the defendant would be liable for the claimant's costs (CPR 36.5(c)). As such the trial judge was wrong to approach the costs award after trial under CPR 36, rather than under CPR 44.2.

Part 44 'near miss' offers

[20.39]

CPR 36.17(2) is clear that in monetary claims and in respect of monetary elements of claims 'more advantageous' means better in money terms by any amount, however small. In *Hammersmatch Properties (Welwyn) Ltd v Saint Gobain Ceramics & Plastics Ltd* [2013] EWHC 2227 (TCC) the claimant recovered £1,058,768, which exceeded the Part 36 offer by a mere £3,637.90, Ramsey J concluded that where a claimant had obtained a judgment more advantageous than the best Part 36 offer of the opposing party it would be wrong to revisit this 'near miss' when considering costs more generally under CPR 44.2(4)(c). He concluded that to determine otherwise would simply introduce by CPR Part 44 the very uncertainty that had been removed by what is now CPR 36.17(2). He doubted whether a 'near miss' offer added anything to broader conduct arguments that might flow based on an unreasonable refusal to negotiate.

Part 44 – the final words

[20.40]

In *Capita (Banstead) 2011 Ltd v RFIB Group Ltd* [2017] EWCA Civ 1032, the Court of Appeal, when upholding a decision to award the defendant its costs for a period based on a *Calderbank* offer, confirmed the position, making a clear distinction between treating an admissible offer under CPR 44.2 as a CPR 36 offer and treating it, as an exercise of discretion, as having the effect of a CPR 36 offer on the award of costs:

> 'It is well established that, in an appropriate case, the court may (our emphasis) treat a Calderbank offer as having the same effect as regards costs as a Part 36 offer. Whether or not the case is an appropriate one is quintessentially a matter for the discretion of the trial judge ...'

The final words on the subject should go to the Court of Appeal. Jackson LJ summarised the position in *Fox v Foundation Piling Ltd* [2011] EWCA Civ 790, [2011] 6 Costs LR 961, as follows:

> ' . . . parties are quite entitled to make Calderbank offers outside the framework of Part 36. Where a party makes such an offer and then achieves a more advantageous result, the court's discretion is wider. Nevertheless it may well be appropriate to order the party which has optimistically rejected the Calderbank offer to pay all costs since the date when that offer expired.'

CONCLUSION TO COSTS INDUCEMENTS TO SETTLE – PART 36 OFFERS AND OTHER ADMISSIBLE OFFERS

[20.41]

There can be little doubt that the additional benefit for the claimant under CPR 36.17 is intended:

- to make claimants think of a figure, deduct something from it and make an offer in the hope of recovering an additional percentage of the damages; and
- to make defendants think of a figure and add to it either in accepting claimants' offers or in making their own offers to buy off the risk of paying an additional amount of damages

This is to encourage settlement and avoid the situation that Jackson LJ described in *Fox v Foundation Piling Ltd* [2011] EWCA Civ 790, [2011] 6 Costs LR 961 in these terms:

> 'A not uncommon scenario is that both parties turn out to have been over-optimistic in their Part 36 offers. The claimant recovers more than the defendant has previously offered to pay, but less than the claimant has previously offered to accept . . . '

Whether the additional entitlement for the claimant at CPR 36.17(4)(d) has turned the intentions into reality is a moot point. One of Sir Rupert Jackson's recommendations as part of the 2013 reforms was that interested parties in the personal injury litigation field should try to devise a neutral computer program that valued general damages in smaller personal injury claims to avoid a costly process where the difference between the parties was only a small fraction of the costs incurred in having determination through the court. It was one of the few recommendations not to come to fruition (indeed not to get off the ground at all). His second attempt may result in an extended fixed fee regime with a prescribed percentage uplift to replace the strict CPR 36 consequences if the recommendations in his 2017 Fixed Recoverable Costs Review are implemented.

What does seem certain, though, is that the rewritten CPR 36 clarifies elements of the provision, so that less time is spent determining whether a particular offer is or is not a Part 36 offer. However, it introduces provisions that are likely to lead to satellite litigation eg:

- What is a genuine offer?
- Do the words 'provided that . . . there has not been a previous order under this sub-paragraph' in CPR 36.17(4)(d) mean that if an 'additional amount' is awarded as a result of a CPR 36 claimant's offer in the substantive claim, then the claimant cannot recover under this provision if he makes a relevant CPR 36 offer under CPR 47.20(4) in detailed assessment proceedings or is this aimed at the situation where a number of CPR 36 offers have been made and beaten? CPR 47.20(7) states that detailed assessment proceedings are to be regarded as an 'independent claim' for the purpose of CPR 36.17, suggesting another additional sum may be awarded. However, CPR 36.17(4)(d) does not talk of a 'claim', but of a 'case'.
- What is the significance of the inclusion of CPR 36.17(4)(b) in the 'escape' provision at 36.23, when an order for indemnity costs already provides the 'get out of gaol' card? Will paying parties in this situation seek to argue that as a specific rule it trumps the reference to 'standard basis' in CPR 3.18 and so the receiving party is limited to 50% of costs albeit on the indemnity basis rather than a complete release from CPR 3.14 that an indemnity costs order would otherwise provide?

However, CPR 36 would not be CPR 36 without some complications.

CHAPTER 21

COSTS INDUCEMENTS TO SETTLE – ADR

INTRODUCTION TO COSTS INDUCEMENTS TO SETTLE – ADR

[21.1]

In his '*Review of Civil Litigation Costs; Final Report*' Sir Rupert Jackson dwelt on the merits of Alternative Dispute Resolution ('ADR') at some length. He considered that:

> 'ADR is relevant to the present Costs Review in two ways. First, ADR (and in particular mediation) is a tool which can be used to reduce costs. At the present time disputing parties do not always make sufficient use of that tool. Secondly, an appropriately structured costs regime will encourage the use of ADR. It is a sad fact at the moment that many cases settle at a late stage, when substantial costs have been run up. Indeed some cases which ought to settle (because sufficient common ground exists between the parties) become incapable of settlement as a result of the high costs incurred. One important aim of the present Costs Review is to encourage parties to resolve such disputes at the earliest opportunity, whether by negotiation or by any available form of ADR.'

While his view was that the court has a greater role to play than it has done to date, there can be no doubt that the court has made attempts to steer parties, whether by stick, carrot or both, towards ADR. This is clear from the case law that has emerged. This is not surprising as CPR 1.4(1)(e) has always imposed upon the court, under its general duty to manage cases, the obligation to encourage and facilitate parties' use of ADR in appropriate cases. The greatest incentive provided by the court has been its willingness to consider costs sanctions where ADR has not been undertaken. However, the imposition of a costs sanction is not automatic.

THE *HALSEY* TEST

[21.2]

In *Halsey v Milton Keynes General NHS Trust; Steel v Joy* [2004] EWCA Civ 576, the Court of Appeal considered previous decisions to set out clear guidelines. In doing so, it held that there was no presumption that a party to a dispute should agree to mediation or other alternative dispute resolution processes. The general rule is that costs of litigation should follow the event. It concluded that refusal to agree to ADR does not justify departure from the general rule, unless it is shown that the successful party acted unreasonably in refusing to do so. To oblige truly unwilling parties to refer their disputes to mediation would be to impose an unacceptable obstruction on their right to access the court, and indeed a court order to mediate could itself be a violation of article 8 of the European Convention on Human Rights. The court set out the following factors that the court ought to consider when determining if a refusal to engage in ADR was reasonable or unreasonable:

- The nature of the dispute – although the court suggested a few categories of case that might be unsuitable for ADR it concluded that 'most cases are not by their very nature unsuitable for ADR'.
- The merits of the case – clearly the strength of a case is relevant to whether a refusal to engage in ADR is reasonable. The court acknowledged that if this were not accepted a party with a weak case could almost compel the other party to engage in ADR and make some concession by threat of an adverse costs order. However, as we know, a party's belief in the impregnability of his position is often as much self-righteous hope as it is reality. As the court summarised the position:

  > 'The fact that a party unreasonably believes that his case is watertight is no justification for refusing mediation. But the fact that a party reasonably believes that he has a watertight case may well be a sufficient justification for a refusal to mediate.'

- Whether other settlement methods have already been attempted – while the fact that previous offers have been made may illustrate that one party may be making efforts to settle and the other is blithely pressing on regardless and justifies the refusal of the offering party to enter into ADR, the court was keen to stress that ADR can prove successful even in cases where previous offers have not prompted counter-offers.
- Whether the costs of ADR would be disproportionately high – clearly this factor weighs heavier in justifying a refusal of ADR when the sums in dispute are smaller.
- Delay – the stage at which ADR is offered is relevant, as if it is suggested late in the day acceptance of it may have the effect of delaying the trial of the action.
- Whether the mediation has a reasonable prospect of success – objectively viewed does the ADR have any real prospect of success or would it simply have added an extra tier of costs to no avail?

FAILURE TO ENGAGE IN ADR LEADING TO A COSTS SANCTION (SOME EXAMPLES)

[21.3]

In *Dunnett v Railtrack plc (in railway administration)* [2002] EWCA Civ 303, on granting the claimant permission to appeal against the dismissal of his action for damages for negligence by Railtrack, the judge told both parties they should attempt alternative dispute resolution, but Railtrack refused to do so, on the grounds that it was not prepared to make any further payment to the claimant and was confident that it would succeed on the appeal. Railtrack did indeed succeed in having the appeal dismissed, but the Court of Appeal demonstrated its displeasure at Railtrack's outright refusal to consider ADR by depriving it of its costs, noting that parties and their lawyers should ensure that they are aware that it is one of their duties fully to consider ADR, especially when the court has specifically suggested it, and not merely flatly to turn it down. The court warned that to adopt that approach placed the party doing so at risk of adverse consequences in costs regardless of the outcome of the litigation.

The court maintained the same line in *Virani Ltd v Manuel Revert y CIA SA* [2003] EWCA Civ 1651, when it ordered an unsuccessful appellant to pay costs on the indemnity basis because of a refusal of the offer of the Court of Appeal's own mediation service on being granted permission to appeal, failed to negotiate or to enter into any form of ADR.

A party who agrees to mediation, but then causes the mediation to fail by reason of an unreasonable position in the mediation is in reality in the same position as a party who unreasonably refuses to mediate. In *Seventh Earl of Malmesbury v Strutt & Parker* [2007] EWHC 2199, the court determined that had the claimant made an offer which better reflected its true position, the mediation might have succeeded. The court said 'It would be wrong to say more', presumably because it could only say what it did because both parties waived privilege for the mediation. Taking account of unreasonable conduct in privileged mediation is not easy. The judge reduced the claimant's costs to 80% to reflect the unreasonable attitude in the mediation.

The Court of Appeal recently emphasised the importance of engaging properly in ADR, upholding a decision to order a defendant to pay 75% of the claimant's costs, notwithstanding that the claimant had not beaten an offer (albeit one that the defendants had withdrawn), in part because the defendants, whilst not refusing to mediate, dragged their feet and delayed the process until eventually the claimants lost confidence in ADR (*Thakkar v Patel* [2017] EWCA Civ 117).

The last two cases illustrate that the sanction that the court chooses to impose is a discretionary one. It is not an 'all or nothing' argument. Instead, it is a matter of judgment in the individual case. For example in *Wales (t/a Selective Investment Services) v CBRE Managed Services Ltd* [2020] EWHC 1050 (Comm), the court deprived the successful 1st defendant of 20% of its costs from the date upon which the other parties had suggested a mediation could actually take place.

FAILURE TO ENGAGE IN ADR – NO COSTS SANCTION (SOME EXAMPLES)

[21.4]

As a starting point, there will be cases where the court must first determine if certain actions amount to a refusal to engage in ADR (eg *Ali v Channel 5 Broadcast Ltd* [2018] EWHC 840 (Ch), [2018] 2 Costs LR 373).

Hurst v Leeming [2002] EWHC 1051 (Ch), was the first of a series of cases where the court refused to penalise a failure to mediate. Mr Leeming was held to have been justified in taking the view that mediation was not appropriate because it had no realistic prospect of success as, viewed objectively, the mediation had no real prospect of success. It was plain that Mr Hurst had been so seriously disturbed by the tragic course of events resulting from the dissolution of his partnership that he was incapable of a balanced evaluation of the facts, was determined to obtain a substantial sum in the mediation process and was not likely to accept any mediation which did not achieve that result, although his claim plainly entitled him to nothing (as he had conceded by the time of this decision).

Société Internationale de Telecommunications Aeronautiques SC v Wyatt Co (UK) Ltd (Maxwell Batley (a firm), Part 20 defendant) [2002] EWHC 2401 (Ch), was another case in which the court refused to impose a sanction for refusing to mediate. The judge refused to deprive Maxwell Batley of any of its costs because of its refusal to mediate on a number of grounds. The court found that the mediation was a device to persuade Maxwell Batley to make a large contribution to the sums due to the claimant, that Watson Wyatt would not be deterred from pursuing Maxwell Batley by a mediator, that Watson Wyatt had adopted bullying tactics to cajole Maxwell Batley to mediate, which the court found disagreeable and off-putting, even suggesting that Maxwell Batley's solicitor's reputation would suffer as a result of the way in which it was conducting the claim. Finally, Watson Wyatt told Maxwell Batley that the mediator was 'motoring' against Maxwell Batley and had told it that it could recover $10m from Maxwell Batley. The court concluded that the invitation, or rather demand, of Watson Wyatt to Maxwell Batley to participate in the mediation had been self-serving and it would be a grave injustice to Maxwell Batley to deprive it of any part of its costs because it had declined to mediate.

In *Northrop Grumman Mission Systems Europe Ltd v BAE Systems (Al Diriyah C4I) Ltd* [2014] EWHC 3148 (TCC) Ramsey J considered the refusal of the defendant to mediate on the basis that it had a strong claim was unreasonable, but balanced that against the fact that the claimant had rejected an offer to settle that was more advantageous than the eventual outcome. He concluded that the unreasonable failure to mediate should not impact on the costs order in that situation. The judgment also considers the 'positive impact' that an independent perspective offered by mediation can bring to a dispute, which can steer it to a resolution that recognises the strong case of one or other party – noting that a successful mediation does not have to result in the payment of money by one party to another. In other words, it qualifies, to an extent, the relevance of 'strength of case' as a reason to refuse ADR. It is right to note that the cost of mediation in *Northrop* would only have been about 1.3% of the amount in dispute.

In *Gore v Naheed* [2017] EWCA Civ 369, the Court of Appeal upheld the trial judge's unqualified award of costs to a successful party in a claim for damages and an injunction arising out of the obstruction of a right of way. This was despite the fact that the defendants sought some recognition in costs of the fact that the claimant had failed to engage in their suggestion that the matter should be referred to mediation. Whilst acknowledging that the claimant's solicitor had viewed mediation as having no prospect of success, which would simply add a tier of cost and that the trial judge had found the claim to raise complex questions of law rendering it unsuitable for mediation, Patten LJ appeared to take a rare judicial step back from encouragement for ADR, stating:

> 'Speaking for myself, I have some difficulty in accepting that the desire of a party to have his rights determined by a court of law in preference to mediation can be said to be unreasonable conduct particularly when, as here, those rights are ultimately vindicated.'

THE VOLUNTARY NATURE OF ADR

[21.5]

What remains clear, and was reinforced in Sir Rupert's final report, is that compulsory ADR continues to be a contradiction in terms. The pendulum of case law has swung from the assumption that it is unreasonable to refuse to mediate, to the assumption that such refusal is reasonable unless the other party can demonstrate otherwise. ADR is to be achieved by persuasion and encouragement from the court and not force. As stated the court's obligation to consider ADR as part of its case management duty has been an ever present in the CPR (CPR 1.4(2)(e)).

However, subject to the qualification in *Gore* (above), which the October 2017 Civil Justice Council interim report 'ADR and Civil Justice' noted had a discernible difference of emphasis from that of the Court of Appeal in *PGF II SA v OMFS CO 1 Ltd* [2013] EWCA Civ 1288 (see **[21.6]** below), the message is almost unambiguously clear that parties should consider routinely whether their disputes are suitable for ADR and appreciate that if the unsuccessful party can demonstrate that a refusal to mediate was unreasonable this could rebut the presumption that costs are paid to the successful party.

In *Burchell v Bullard* [2005] EWCA Civ 358, the Court of Appeal endorsed *Halsey* saying that the case made it plain there was a high rate of success achieved by mediation and also established its importance as a route to a just result running parallel with that of the court system. The court had given its stamp of approval for mediation and it was now the legal profession which had to become fully aware of and acknowledge its value. Interestingly, whilst the final report of the Civil Justice Council Working Group (see **[21.6]** below) 13 years on (November 2018) saw this as part of the three distinct challenges in relation to ADR, it also saw awareness of ADR on the bench and encouragement of ADR by the courts as components of the challenges.

Despite the warnings in *Halsey* and *Burchall* these cases were followed by another three cases in which a refusal to mediate was upheld: *Daniels v Metropolitan Police Comr* [2005] EWCA Civ 1312 (it was reasonable for a public body to contest what it reasonably considered to be an unfounded claim in order to deter similarly unfounded claims); *Wethered Estate Ltd v Davis* [2005] EWHC 1903 (Ch) (it was not unreasonable to refuse mediation until the true nature of the dispute had been defined) and *Hickman v Blake Lapthorn* [2006] EWHC 12 (QB) (a barrister who was not prepared to compromise a negligence claim against him had legitimately and reasonably refused to mediate). In *Hickman* the court gave the following guidance, reinforcing and refining the *Halsey* guidelines:

> '– A party cannot be ordered to submit to mediation as that would be contrary to article 6 of the European Convention on Human Rights.
> – The burden is on the unsuccessful party to show why the general rule of costs following the event should not apply, and it must be shown that the successful party acted unreasonably in refusing to agree to ADR.
> – A party's reasonable belief that he has a strong case is relevant to the reasonableness of his refusal otherwise the fear of costs sanctions may be used to extract unmerited settlements.
> – Where a case is evenly balanced a party's belief that he would win should be given little or no weight in considering whether a refusal was reasonable. The belief must be unreasonable.
> – The cost of mediation is a relevant factor.

> – Whether the mediation had a reasonable prospect of success is relevant to the reasonableness of a refusal to agree to mediation.
> – In considering whether the refusal to agree to mediation was unreasonable, it is for the unsuccessful party to show that there was a reasonable prospect that the mediation would have been successful.
> – Where a party refuses to take part in mediation despite encouragement from the court to do so, that is a factor to be taken into account.
> – Public bodies are not in a special position.'

In an interesting development on the question of enforced ADR, albeit in drawing a clear distinction between obliging parties to submit to mediation outside the court process and exercising a power as part of the court process, the Court of Appeal concluded in *Lomax v Lomax* [2019] EWCA Civ 1467 that the court's power under CPR 3.1(2)(m) to hear 'an Early Neutral Evaluation with the aim of helping the parties settle the case', is not dependent upon the consent of the parties to such a course of action:

> 'I see no reason to imply into subparagraph (m) any limitation on the court's power to order an ENE hearing to the effect that the agreement or consent of the parties is required. Indeed, in my view such an interpretation would be inconsistent with elements of the overriding objective, in particular the saving of expense and allotting to cases an appropriate share of the court's resources, and would, therefore, be contrary to rule 1.2(b).' Moylan LJ (para 32)

CONCLUSION TO COSTS INDUCEMENTS TO SETTLE – ADR

[21.6]

That ADR has a significant role in the control of costs is clear from the recommendations made by Sir Rupert at the end of his consideration of ADR. These are that:

- There should be a serious campaign:
  - (a) to ensure that all litigation lawyers and judges are properly informed about the benefits which ADR can bring; and
  - (b) to alert the public and small businesses to the benefits of ADR.
- An authoritative handbook should be prepared, explaining clearly and concisely what ADR is and giving details of all reputable providers of mediation. This should be the standard handbook for use at all Judicial College seminars and CPD training sessions concerning mediation

Unsurprisingly, within weeks of the April 2013 amendments to the CPR the handbook recommended by Sir Rupert was published, endorsed by, amongst others, the Judicial College. Copies were sent to all full-time judges. This coupled with a discrete phase in Precedent H for ADR/settlement could not make the position clearer – the judiciary expects parties to consider ADR at an early stage and a party not considering this as part of the assumptions within Precedent H and not providing a budget for this phase will have some explaining to do. This could lead to the curious situation where the court encourages an increase to a budget at the costs management stage to enable a party who has made no costs provision for ADR to have a pot of money to spend on it. At a time of great professional concern that the court's sole objective is to cut costs and slash budgets, this may prove to be the crunchiest carrot on offer.

The ADR Handbook received almost immediate endorsement by the Court of Appeal in *PGF II SA v OMFS CO 1Ltd* [2013] EWCA Civ 1288. In this case the Court of Appeal upheld the trial judge's decision not to award the defendant its costs for a period after a valid Part 36 offer in part because it had failed to respond to an offer to enter into ADR. Briggs LJ referred to the ADR Handbook and stated that silence in the face of an invitation to enter into ADR should, as a general rather than invariable rule, itself be treated as unreasonable conduct. It is right to say that recently, the Court of Appeal has been keen to stress both the general rule and the fact that it is not invariable. Patten LJ in *Gore* (above) was keen to stress the latter, namely 'that a failure to engage, even if unreasonable, does not automatically result in a costs penalty', whilst Jackson LJ in *Thakkar* (above), emphasised the former, stating that 'the message which this court sent out in PGF II was that to remain silent in the face of an offer to mediate is, absent exceptional circumstances, unreasonable conduct meriting a costs sanction, even in cases where mediation is unlikely to succeed'.

Ward LJ in *Wright v Michael Wright Supplies Ltd* [2013] EWCA Civ 234 even raised the spectre of revisiting *Halsey* and, in particular, the rule expressed by the Court of Appeal in that case that 'to oblige truly unwilling parties to refer their disputes to mediation would be to impose an unacceptable obstruction on their right to access to the court'. He expressed the concern that there are always cases that illustrate that parties determined to have their day in court cannot be compelled to try to resolve their dispute through ADR despite the most persuasive judicial cajoling. With customary eloquence he identified the problem in this way:

> 'You may be able to drag the horse (a mule offers a better metaphor) to water, but you cannot force the wretched animal to drink if it stubbornly resists. I suppose you can make it run around the litigation course so vigorously that in a muck sweat it will find the mediation trough more friendly and desirable. But none of that provides the real answer. Perhaps, therefore, it is time to review the rule in *Halsey* . . . .'

It seems that, despite this, *Halsey* still remains the cut-off point. In his Civil Court Structure Review: Interim Report, Briggs LJ hoped to 'make conciliation a culturally normal part of the civil court process'. However, he was equally clear, when considering an online court, that this should not be compulsory and that the court should respect the refusal of any party to engage in this form of ADR (see para 6.13 of the report). However, as mentioned above the Civil Justice Council ('CJC') has published both an interim report in October 2017 and a final report in November 2018 on 'ADR and Civil Justice'. Its conclusions were that there are three distinct challenges in relation to ADR as follows:

- the awareness of ADR, both in the general public and in the professions and on the bench;
- the availability, both in terms of funding and logistics and in terms of quality and regulation of the professionals involved;
- the encouragement of ADR by the Government and the Courts.

(para 2.2)

The ADR system to which the CJC report aspires is one in which:

- citizens are aware that when civil disputes arise there are alternatives to the present choice of capitulation or litigation;
- citizens are aware that those alternatives include approaches involving neutral third parties to assist settlement;
- those neutrals/the facilities are available in a practical and affordable form and operate with transparent standards of practice such that there is confidence in their training, their competence and their integrity;
- far from being a sign of weakness the use of and the offer of the use of such techniques is wise, culturally normal and indeed would be expected by the court; and
- the court would promote the use of ADR techniques to the extent that they would sanction those who did not agree to take reasonable steps toward settlement and reasonable steps towards the use of ADR. The parties would always be free to settle or not and the court would never sanction a failure to do so.

(para 2.3)

We shall see what happens. However, the moves in low value claims within the online court, to test making mediation an 'opt out' (CPR PD 51R, Section G) and the continuing clamour for a review of the *Halsey* guidelines, may signal a sea change.

CHAPTER 22

COSTS AWARDS BETWEEN THE PARTIES

INTRODUCTION TO COSTS AWARDS BETWEEN THE PARTIES

[22.1]

CPR 44.2(1) confers on the court a discretion as to whether costs are payable by one party to another, the amount of those costs and when they are to be paid. This power extends both to interim and final orders. In certain situations there is a deemed costs order, subject usually to a residual power for the court to order otherwise, and no court adjudication is required. Where there is no deemed order then the court must determine whether there is to be a costs order and, if there is, in whose favour it will be made. Finally there are some unusual situations where discrete rules apply. However, let us start with some of the easy bits.

NO ORDER AS TO COSTS

[22.2]

CPR PD 44, para 4.2 sets out, in tabular form, those costs orders that the court will commonly make. It links 'no order as to costs' and 'each party to pay own costs' together, and points out that such orders mean precisely what they say – the costs covered by the order are not to be recovered from the other party and each party has to pay its own costs.

CPR 44.10 takes this a step further and provides that where a court order makes no mention of costs at all, then the general rule is that no party is entitled to costs (including a pro bono award of costs). This was demonstrated in *Griffiths v Metropolitan Police Comr* [2003] EWCA Civ 313, when the court held not only that where an interim order was silent no party was entitled to their costs, but also that the trial judge had no jurisdiction to vary that order.

There are exceptions and these are at CPR 44.10(2) which states that where the court gives permission to appeal, permission to apply for judicial review or makes an order on a not on notice application, but is silent on costs, then an order for 'the applicant's costs in the case' is deemed included. A party may apply to vary the deemed order under CPR 44.10(3).

It would be wrong to leave CPR 44.10(2) without making reference to *Mackay and Busby v Ashwood Enterprises Ltd* [2013] EWCA Civ 959 in which the Court of Appeal stated that the deemed 'costs in the case' order provided for under CPR 44.10(2)(c) supported the contention that the court could in fact make an order for costs on a not on notice application against the party who had not had notice (founding the general jurisdiction under the broad provisions of s 51 of the Senior Courts Act 1981). This is, of course, subject to the right of a party not served to apply to vary or set aside the order under CPR 23.10.

Although FPR 28.2(1) expressly excludes CPR 44.10(2), the general rule at 44.10(1) does apply. The fact that it is a general rule rather than an absolute one was confirmed in *Timokhina v Timokhin* [2019] EWCA Civ 1284, in which the court concluded that this meant that the court was left with a residual discretion to award costs where an order had been silent about them.

THE MENU OF COSTS ORDERS AVAILABLE TO THE COURT

[22.3]

Reference has been made above to the table at CPR PD 44, para 4.2. This table is a useful point of reference in respect of costs orders following interim and appeal hearings and merits inclusion here:

Term	Effect
Costs Costs in any event	The party in whose favour the order is made is entitled to that party's costs in respect of the part of the proceedings to which the order relates, whatever other costs orders are made in the proceedings.
Costs in the case Costs in the application	The party in whose favour the court makes an order for costs at the end of the proceedings is entitled to that party's costs of the part of the proceedings to which the order relates.
Costs reserved	The decision about costs is deferred to a later occasion, but if no later order is made the costs will be costs in the case.
Claimant's/ Defendant's costs in case/ application	If the party in whose favour the costs order is made is awarded costs at the end the proceedings, that party is entitled to that party's costs of the part of the proceedings to which the order relates. If any other party is awarded costs at the end of the proceedings, the party in whose favour the final costs order is made is not liable to pay the costs of any other party in respect of the part of the proceedings to which the order relates.
Costs thrown away	Where, for example, a judgment or order is set aside, the party in whose favour the costs order is made is entitled to the costs which have been incurred as a consequence. This includes the costs of – preparing for and attending any hearing at which the judgment or order which has been set aside was made; preparing for and attending any hearing to set aside the judgment or order in question; preparing for and attending any hearing at which the court orders the proceedings or the part in question to be adjourned;

Term	Effect
	any steps taken to enforce a judgment or order which has subsequently been set aside.
Costs of and caused by	Where, for example, the court makes this order on an application to amend a statement of case, the party in whose favour the costs order is made is entitled to the costs of preparing for and attending the application and the costs of any consequential amendment to his own statement of case.
Costs here and below	The party in whose favour the costs order is made is entitled not only to that party's costs in respect of the proceedings in which the court makes the order but also to that party's costs of the proceedings in any lower court. In the case of an appeal from a Divisional Court the party is not entitled to any costs incurred in any court below the Divisional Court.
No order as to costs Each party to pay own costs	Each party is to bear that party's own costs of the part of the proceedings to which the order relates whatever costs order the court makes at the end of the proceedings.

It is worth pointing out that an order for 'costs reserved' becomes an order for 'costs in the case', if there is no later determination of where the responsibility for those costs lies.

In *Ontulmus v Collett* [2014] EWHC 4117 (QB) Warby J considered what happened to an interim order for 'costs in the case' when each party received an award of costs at the end of the claim. He concluded that the correct way to approach this was to determine which party's overall order for costs covered the period when the 'costs in the case' order was made and that party should benefit from the 'costs in the case' order.

Of course, this table is of no assistance when the court makes an order that a party's costs are to be paid by another, whether on an interim application or after a final hearing.

SOLICITOR'S DUTY TO NOTIFY THE CLIENT

[22.4]

CPR 44.8 provides that where a costs order is made against a represented party and that party is not present at the hearing at which the order is made the legal representative must inform the client of the order within 7 days of receipt by the legal representative of notice of the order. CPR PD 44 defines a party to include anyone who has instructed a legal representative to represent a party, eg a trade union, an insurer or the legal aid authority. In fact most professional instructors will make it a contractual term of instruction that notification takes place in these circumstances anyway. CPR PD 44, para 10.3 enables the court to require evidence of the steps taken by the legal representative to notify the client of the adverse costs order. This is a watered down version of original proposals for enforcement of this rule that provided for a legal representative who failed to comply to pay the costs. We have never seen an order that required a legal representative to provide proof of efforts to comply. The fact that there is no sanction for non-compliance may explain this, as the court is likely to be wary of making orders that it cannot enforce.

CPR PD 44, para 10.2 requires the legal representative to provide the client with an explanation of how the order came to be made when serving the notification.

THE TIME FOR COMPLIANCE WITH A COSTS ORDER

[22.5]

CPR 44.7 provides that unless the court specifies another date, a party must comply with an order for the payment of costs within 14 days of the date of the order specifying the amount of costs or, if the amount is quantified at a detailed assessment, in accordance with the final costs certificate (CPR 47.17(5)).

DEEMED COSTS ORDERS

Part 36

[22.6]

Part 36.13 provides for a deemed costs order in favour of the claimant on the acceptance of a Part 36 offer. This has been considered in more detail in Chapter 20 Costs Inducements to Settle – Part 36 Offers and other Admissible Offers, above. Just a reminder that this does not apply on acceptance of a pre-issue Part 36 offer and the costs only procedure should be used.

Discontinuance

[22.7]

CPR 38.6 provides that a claimant who discontinues is liable for the costs of the defendant against whom he discontinues for the costs up until the date of service of the notice of discontinuance, unless the court orders otherwise. If the discontinuance is of part of the proceedings only, then the liability is limited to the costs referable to that part and those cannot be assessed until the conclusion of the remainder of the proceedings. CPR 38.6(3) makes it clear that this general rule does not apply to claims allocated to the small claims track.

The Court of Appeal in *Brookes v HSBC Bank plc* [2016] EWCA Civ 354 set out the approach to be adopted when considering the default provision in CPR 38.6 in these terms:

> '(1) when a claimant discontinues the proceedings, there is a presumption by reason of CPR 38.6 that the defendant should recover his costs; the burden is on the claimant to show a good reason for departing from that position;
> (2) the fact that the claimant would or might well have succeeded at trial is not itself a sufficient reason for doing so;
> (3) however, if it is plain that the claim would have failed, that is an additional factor in favour of applying the presumption;

(4) the mere fact that the claimant's decision to discontinue may have been motivated by practical, pragmatic or financial reasons as opposed to a lack of confidence in the merits of the case will not suffice to displace the presumption;
(5) if the claimant is to succeed in displacing the presumption he will usually need to show a change of circumstances to which he has not himself contributed;
(6) however, no change in circumstances is likely to suffice unless it has been brought about by some form of unreasonable conduct on the part of the defendant which in all the circumstances provides a good reason for departing from the rule.'

The court concluded that a claimant trying to persuade the court to depart from the normal position 'must provide cogent reasons for doing so and is unlikely to satisfy that requirement save in unusual circumstances'. That the general rule is hard to dislodge is clear from the case law that has emerged.

In *Messih v McMillan Williams* [2010] EWCA Civ 844, the Court of Appeal held that if CPR 38.6 had been intended to create a general discretion as to costs on discontinuance it would have said so. The rule made it clear that the defendant started from the position of being entitled to costs and it was for the claimant to justify the making of some other order.

Where claimants deleted a claim by amendments to the particulars of claim this was in effect a discontinuance of that claim with the same costs consequences (*Isaac v Isaac* [2005] EWHC 435 (Ch)). Even changing circumstances are part and parcel of litigation and mere change alone will not suffice. In *Teasdale v HSBC Bank plc* [2010] EWHC 612 (QB), the court concluded that it would be difficult to see how any change in circumstances could amount to good reason unless connected with some conduct on the part of the defendant which merited a departure from the general rule. It was on this basis that the court did 'otherwise order' for a period of the claim in *Harrap v Brighton and Sussex University NHS Hospitals Trust* [2018] EWHC 1063 (QB), where new evidence emerged from a witness for the defendant at trial that was not in a witness statement and which was plainly relevant from the time of service of an expert's report by the claimant. The court concluded that the new evidence amounted to a change of circumstances that was due to the defendant's conduct. The court departed from the general rule for the period following service of the expert's report, making no order for costs.

It is clear from *Hoist UK Ltd v Reid Lifting Ltd* [2010] EWHC 1922 (Ch), that one of the factors the court will take into account on an application to depart from the general rule is the fact that such an application was made some time after discontinuance. The court also concluded that the fact that proceedings were discontinued before the application for a different costs order did not mean that there was no longer a claim in which to make the application (as the defendant ingeniously tried to argue). It mattered not: the application that there be no order for costs was nevertheless refused.

Interesting arguments are starting to arise where a claimant with 'qualified one-way costs shifting' protection discontinues, but the defendant seeks to set this aside under CPR 38.4 to enable it to pursue an application to strike out issued prior to discontinuance. The rationale is obvious, for if the claim is discontinued the claimant is protected against adverse costs unless the court gives permission to enforce under CPR 44.16, but if the claim is struck out that protection is automatically lost (CPR 44.15). CPR PD 44, para 12.4(c) permits the court to determine any issue of 'fundamental dishonesty' under CPR 44.16 after discontinuance without needing to set aside the discontinuance.

Strike out for non-payment of fees

[22.8]

If the claimant party fails to pay or obtain fee exemption from a fee payable for either the allocation of the claim or the trial, then pursuant to CPR 3.7(6)(b) and CPR 3.7A1(7) there is a deemed order that the claimant pays the defendant's costs unless the court orders otherwise (see also CPR 44.9(1)(a) below).

The basis of assessment under deemed orders

[22.9]

CPR 44.9(1) makes it clear that assessments under the deemed orders set out above are conducted on the standard basis. However, where the court has a residual discretion, that does extend to making an order for indemnity costs in place of standard basis costs on the application of the party against whom the claim has been discontinued, if it is appropriate to do so. It did just this in *Shahrokh Mireskandari v Law Society* [2009] EWHC 2224 (Ch), where the discontinued claim had always been utterly speculative. However, see Chapter 20 Costs Inducements to Settle – Part 36 Offers and other Admissible Offers *Courtwell Properties Ltd v Greencore PF (UK) Ltd* [2014] EWHC 184 (TCC), above at [**20.12**].

Interest on the costs assessed under a deemed order

[22.10]

CPR 44.9(4) is clear that any interest on costs runs from the date when the deemed costs order is made. It is interesting that in the 'deemed costs order' scenarios covered by CPR 44.9(4), where, by definition, the paying party is unlikely to know anything about the amount of the receiving party's costs, the rule makers provide for interest from the date of the deemed order, sharing none of the concerns of the court in *Involnert Management Inc v Aprilgrange Ltd* [2015] EWHC 2834 (Comm) (see Chapter 32 below at [**32.5**] for further consideration of this).

COSTS ORDERS BY CONSENT

[22.11]

The parties may agree where the liability for costs rests between themselves, whether in respect of interim or final orders. This can be done by way of consent order, consent judgment or Tomlin order. However, the court retains the discretion of whether to approve these orders and there a number of potential pitfalls to avoid.

Tomlin orders

[22.12]

A Tomlin order stays a claim on terms. The terms are usually contained in a schedule to the order. All too often parties still include the agreement in respect of costs in the schedule. This is acceptable if it is an agreement to pay a specified sum for costs. However, if the agreement is that the costs will be assessed if not agreed, then this must be recorded in the body of the order. If it is not, then there is no order giving a right to assessment proceedings and a failure to agree costs can present a major problem in recovering them.

Agreement in interim orders for costs to be assessed if not agreed

[22.13]

As we have considered earlier, an order for a detailed assessment is a case management decision. It must be made by the court in accordance with the overriding objective. This requires the court to consider proportionality. In most cases ordering a detailed assessment of the costs relating to an interim hearing is not proportionate. While this may have been included to avoid an argument at this stage on the amount of the costs, the likelihood is that the court will be reluctant to approve such an order, insisting that either the amount of costs is agreed or that there is a summary assessment of them there and then. Support for this approach is found at CPR PD 44, para 9.4.

Uncertain and unclear terms

[22.14]

It may sound obvious, but it is important that the parties consider carefully the costs order that is drafted before consenting to it. This is not only to ensure that it contains enforceable costs provisions, but also to be satisfied that the order states precisely what has been agreed after consideration of all potential consequences.

In *Richardson Roofing Co Ltd v Colman Partnership Ltd* [2009] EWCA Civ 839 under a consent order the claimant was to pay a fourth party's costs incurred and thrown away by the adjournment of the trial. Three years later, the fourth party served a draft bill of cost for its entire costs until the hearing ordering a preliminary issue. The fourth party issued proceedings seeking an order that the costs judge dealing with the assessment should be directed that the costs included the fourth party's preparation for trial because there was no prospect that the claim would be revived. The judge made an order directing the costs judge to carry out the assessment using the guidance set out in six specified paragraphs of his judgment.

The Court of Appeal thought it highly debatable whether the judge had had any jurisdiction to hear the application. The order in dispute was a consent order with no application to vary it. As the jurisdiction point had not been fully argued before the Court of Appeal, the point could not be decided and the court therefore assumed jurisdiction, despite its serious reservations. Even if the judge had jurisdiction, he should not have exercised it because the matter would ordinarily go before a costs judge for a detailed assessment. It was undesirable for judges to make this sort of order referring to guidance set out in their judgment, which was extremely diffuse. Judgments provide the reasons for the subsequent orders and any order made at the end of a judgment should stand on its own. The judge had failed to answer the issue in relation to the construction of the consent order and his consequent order was of no assistance to a costs judge. Accordingly, his order could not stand.

In *Newall v Lewis* [2008] EWHC 910 (Ch), the SCCO master decided that all that the parties had meant by 'incidental costs' in a consent order were the investigative costs pre-issue, which would be subject to detailed assessment and referral to a judge, and that all costs claimed post-issue, including incidental ones, were potentially recoverable and did not need to be referred to a judge. On appeal it was held, contrary to the master's conclusion, the order imposed the requirement on the costs judge of separating into distinct categories the costs of the Part 8 proceedings and the costs incidental to them. The correct approach was that if disputes on which costs had been expended pre-issue were relevant to the eventual proceedings and the other party's attitude had made it reasonable to expect them to be included in the litigation, those costs should be recoverable, *Re Gibson's Settlement Trusts, Mellors v Gibson* [1981] Ch 179, [1981] 1 All ER 233 applied. The matter was one of fact and legal analysis rather than discretion

Reserved costs

[22.15]

Again, do not expect the court to be too enamoured of the suggestion that costs are reserved to be dealt with later. If there is a good reason to do so then an explanation of this may be sensible.

CONTESTED AWARDS BETWEEN THE PARTIES

The starting point

[22.16]

CPR 44.2(2) contains the rebuttable presumption that the unsuccessful party pays the costs of the successful parties. However, like all 'general rules' in the CPR, CPR 44.2(2) is then followed by reasons why the court might depart from the starting point. However, it is only after the successful party has been identified that the court moves on to consider reasons to depart. To undertake the exercise as a combined one, while it may still lead to the same end result, does not accord with the rule. In *Straker v Tudor Rose (a firm)* [2007] EWCA Civ 368, Waller LJ gave this helpful guidance on the approach to 'between the parties' costs:

- First is it appropriate to make an order for costs?
- Second, if it is, the general rule is that the unsuccessful party will pay the costs of the successful party.
- Third, identify the successful party
- Fourth, consider whether there are any reasons for departing from the general rule in whole or in part. If so the court should make clear findings of the factors justifying the departure.

Who is the successful party?

[22.17]

In *A L Barnes Ltd v Time Talk (UK) Ltd* [2003] EWCA Civ 402, Longmore LJ set out at para 28 a formulation that the trial judge ought to adopt to determine the identity of the successful party:

> 'In deciding who is the successful party the most important thing is to identify the party who is to pay money to the other. That is the surest indicator of success and failure.'

He indicated that if the trial judge had asked himself this question:

> '... he would in my judgment have had to answer that it was the claimants who recovered more than the defendants had ever offered and thus it must be the claimants who were the successful party.'

This approach was endorsed by Ward LJ in *Day v Day* [2006] EWCA Civ 415. This was a case concerning the beneficial interest of parties in the proceeds of the sale of a property. The trial judge found that the shares were 2/5th and 3/5th respectively, but made only a time limited costs order declaring that after that time there was a 'no score draw'. In substituting an award for the claimant to recover her costs from the defendant Ward LJ stated at para 17:

> 'I would go further and say that in a case like this, the question of who is the unsuccessful party can easily be determined by deciding who has to write the cheque at the end of the case.'

The judgment of Lightman J in *Bank of Credit and Commerce International SA v Ali (No 3)* [1999] NLJ 1734 Vol 149 had been cited to the Court of Appeal in Day. Lightman J had formulated a definition of success as being 'For the purposes of the CPR success is not a technical term but a result in real life, and the question as to who has succeeded is a matter for the exercise of common sense.' Perhaps this simply puts into words what all practitioners know – that a look at the reactions of the parties in court when judgment is given is the surest indicator of success and failure. However, Ward LJ felt that this did not go far enough and adopted the simple approach set out above.

The logic of this simple formulation of success is patent. After all, it only answers the first question posed of who was the successful party and engages the general rule. The court then has the task of considering the factors at CPR 44.2(4) and CPR 44.2(5) to determine whether there is a reason to depart from that general rule. Many a cost order has been lost on that journey through the rules. There is adequate provision within them to ensure that a just outcome is received. Adopting a clear approach to identification of the successful party has the additional benefit of avoiding protracted and costly debate upon this point. Sadly that has not always proved to be the case

In *AL Barnes* Longmore LJ did qualify the position by stating that it should apply to what 'might generally be called commercial litigation' and this appears to be broadly what has transpired in the commercial arena. *F&C Alternative Investments (Holdings) Ltd v Barthelemy* [2011] EWHC 2807 (Ch), held that often it would be appropriate for the loser to pay the winner's costs, even where there had been issues on which the overall winner had lost. The court re- iterated that in commercial litigation, the starting point in working out who the winner is for the purposes of making costs orders would usually be to look at what money had been ordered to be paid as the payee would be the successful party.

Indeed, this approach seemed to be mirrored in non-commercial litigation, although much is often made of the decision in *Hullock v East Riding of Yorkshire County Council* [2009] EWCA Civ 1039, which, on first reading, seems to suggest that in a personal injury quantum only claim, things may be different. However, while the Court of Appeal judgment raises consideration of the identification of the 'real issue' and how that is determined as 'central . . . in determining who should pay the costs', in fact this consideration is limited to a period after an interim payment was made for a sum which ultimately proved to be the settlement sum. It is our view that this case helps little in the overall consideration of success.

However, the 'commercial' qualification led to a busy few days for the Court of Appeal in the summer of 2011 and it seems that the debate may still be raging.

In *Medway Primary Care Trust v Marcus* [2011] EWCA Civ 750, the claimant commenced proceedings alleging clinical negligence resulting in his left lower leg having to be amputated. The defendants admitted breach of duty but denied causation. Shortly before the trial as to liability, the appropriate quantum of the claim was agreed as being £525,000. At trial the issue of causation in respect of the amputation was decided against the claimant, but he was awarded damages of £2,000 for pain and suffering over a limited period of time relating to admitted breaches of duty in respect of the provision of pain killing medication. The trial judge decided that the claimant was the successful party, but then reduced the award of costs to 50% of his costs.

It was held on appeal by a majority that the £2,000 recovered did not constitute vindication for the claimant. The £2,000 was scant consolation for the claimant whose only real claim was for the amputation. The action was in reality all about the cause of the amputation and the costs were spent in advancing and defending that. The defendants were therefore the successful parties and so the starting point should be a costs order in their favour. There should then be a reduction for the fact that the claimant did succeed to a very small extent; the fact that the trust did not concede liability until a very late stage and because the trust's case as to breach of duty was not withdrawn until just before trial. The fact that there was no offer made under CPR Part 36 was not a ground for a reduction but it was relevant that the defendants had not written a 'Calderbank letter' offering, say, £3,000 plus costs proportionate to the recovery. However, the real claim failed and no rational person would have issued the proceedings and pursued these proceedings to recover only £2,000. The claimant was therefore ordered to pay 75% of the defendants' costs.

However, the dissenting judgment was given by Jackson LJ. It was on the basis that the defendants should have made a Part 36 offer, the claimant had a good claim for the £2,000 and the only way he could have recovered that sum was by pursing a claim through the court as the defendants had refused to pay anything. He was obviously attracted to the clarity of the 'who writes the cheque' evaluation of success and failure and keen to stress that it is the first stage in the CPR 44.2 (then CPR 44.3) test only, stating at paragraph 30

> 'In my view, in a personal injury case where (a) the claimant has pursued his claim in a reasonable manner, (b) the claimant recovers damages (other than nominal damages) and (c) there is no or no sufficient Part 36 offer, the starting point should

be that the claimant recovers his costs. That flows from rule 44.3(2)(a). The next question to consider is whether any adjustment should be made to reflect the issues on which the claimant has lost.'

Jackson LJ concluded that he regarded the claimant as the successful party, but that the trial judge's award to the claimant of 50% of his costs was 'on the generous side'.

Just eight days later he had the opportunity to revisit the topic in *Fox v Foundation Piling Ltd* [2011] EWCA Civ 790. The claimant had suffered personal injuries at work, having fallen carrying heavy equipment. He made a claim put at over £280,000. Only quantum was in issue. Surveillance evidence revealed him to have been less seriously affected than he alleged. On disclosure of the evidence he accepted a revised net offer of about £31,000 and the claim settled, but the parties were unable to agree on an appropriate costs order. The court was asked to determine the costs award. At first instance the court concluded that the claimant should pay the costs from the date of the first offer of about £23,000 made about 13 months before settlement. The court concluded that after that date the defendant was the successful party. It stated that even if it was wrong about the effect of the offer (and the claimant had subsequently accepted an offer that gave him a higher net receipt), the claimant's own conduct justified this order. Perhaps unsurprisingly, in the light of the pre-*Medway* authorities, by the time of the appeal the parties had agreed that the claimant was in fact the successful party for the purpose of CPR 44.2 (as is) and the argument was only about whether, and to what extent, the court should depart from that position.

Jackson LJ, giving the lead judgment of a unanimous Court of Appeal, which substituted an order that the defendant pay the claimant's costs on the standard basis, offered some timely reminders (both to practitioners and to the appellate judiciary).

- Where both parties are over optimistic with their Part 36 positions, the claimant should normally be regarded as the 'successful party', because s/he has been forced to bring proceedings in order to recover the sum awarded. (para 46)
- A defendant in possession of surveillance evidence should make a prompt and realistic Part 36 offer – see *Morgan v UPS* [2008] EWCA Civ 1476. Here the defendant had this evidence but delayed in making a realistic offer. Its remedy was to have made an early, modest Part 36 and its failure to do so prevented it seeking costs protection (paras 58–60).
- The fact that the successful party has won and lost some issues may be a good reason for modifying the usual order under CPR 44.2 AND this is commonly achieved by awarding the successful party a specified proportion of her/his costs (paras 47–49)
- The growing tendency of Courts at all levels (including the Court of Appeal) to depart from the starting point in CPR 44.2 too far and too often was an unwelcome trend which had itself increased costs by arguments at first instance and a 'swarm of appeals'. (para 62)

A definitive statement from an impeccable source appeared to have concluded the debate. There the matter seemed to lie. However, it would be wrong to leave the topic without reference to the decision of Briggs J in *Magical Marking Ltd & Phillis v Ware & Kay Ltd & 10 ors* [2013] EWHC 636 (Ch) which distinguished *Fox* on the basis that 'success' had been conceded by the time that the appeal was heard and was not a live issue before the Court of Appeal and that it did not, therefore, undermine the *Medway* line of authority on 'substantial success'. This reasoning was adopted in two recent cases, *Pepe's Piri Piri Ltd v Muhammad Ali Junaid* [2019] EWHC 2769 (QB) and *Brent London Borough Council v Davies* [2018] EWHC 3129 (Ch). Strictly it is undeniable that by the time of the appeal the defendant had conceded that the claimant was the successful party in *Fox*, but Jackson LJ's view could not have been expressed in clearer terms:

> 'In my view, there is no justification for departing from the usual starting point as set out in rule 44.3(2)(a) [now 44.2(2)(a)], namely that the unsuccessful party should pay the successful party's costs. The judge exercised his discretion on the wrong basis, namely the assumption that the defendant was the successful party. It therefore falls to this court to re-exercise that discretion.'

The Court of Appeal restated the proposition that generally success could be determined by which party had to pay money to the other in *Northampton Regional Livestock Centre Company Ltd v Cowling and Lawrence* [2015] EWCA Civ 651. In this case the claimant recovered money based on a breach of fiduciary duty, but failed in a claim in negligence. The court identified the claimant as the successful party under CPR 44.2(2)(a). The court also considered percentage costs order as opposed to issues based orders and preferred the former, awarding the claimant 50% of its costs. One reason for doing so is that approaching the award on an issue basis may detract from the determination of which party was the successful one (see **[22.22]** below on percentage and issue based orders generally).

For our part we prefer the *A L Barnes*, *Day* and *Fox* approach. At a time when the court has no desire or resource for further rounds of the 'costs wars' it has the virtue of clarity and simplicity. Concerns over conduct, partial success etc can be addressed in any event when looking at whether there are reasons to depart from this starting point as we shall see below with cases such as *Widlake v BAA Ltd* [2009] EWCA Civ 1256 illustrating how to achieve the desired outcome within the provisions of CPR 44.2. In that case Ward LJ reverted to the template of Longmore LJ in *Straker v Tudor Rose* (above at **[22.16]**) stating:

> 'Waller LJ was surely right to endorse Longmore LJ's views that the most important thing is to identify the party who is to pay money to the other even in a case of personal injury.' (Our emphasis)

However, as with a general rule, there is always an exception. In *Atlasjet Havacilik Sirketi v Ozlem Kupeli* [2018] EWCA Civ 1264, the Court of Appeal drew a distinction between a claim between individuals, where 'who pays whom may well be a straightforward and easily identified mark of who the unsuccessful party might be for the purposes of CPR rule 44.2(2)', and group actions, where 'looking at the litigation as a whole, there are other material factors' and 'where the concept of overall "success" may be a necessarily ambivalent concept.' Notwithstanding that it set aside the costs orders made below, which were based on the *A L Barnes*, *Day* and *Fox* basis, the court reassuringly reverted to the first consideration in *Straker v Tudor Rose* and determined that no order for costs was appropriate.

Reasons to depart from the general rule

(i) Conduct of the parties (CPR 44.2(4)(a) and 44.2(5))

[22.18]

CPR 44.2(5) makes it plain that the conduct concerned may be:

- both before and during proceedings;
- the unreasonable pursuit of, raising or contesting of a particular issue or allegation;
- the manner in which the case, an allegation or an issue has been pursued;
- the fact that a successful claimant has exaggerated the claim in whole or in part.

The starting point on conduct is the case of *Painting v University of Oxford* [2005] EWCA Civ 161. Judgment had been entered for the claimant in her personal injury claim and all that remained was the determination of quantum. The defendant paid £184,000 into court, but then secured video surveillance taken of the claimant. This showed she was able to walk normally without aid and was able to bend and straighten herself looking at display items in shops, all completely contrary to the level of disability she alleged. The University obtained permission to withdraw all the money in court save for £10,000 and contested quantum on the basis that the claimant had been exaggerating her claim. On the assessment of damages the judge found the claimant had indeed exaggerated her claim and awarded her only £22,000 but also her costs on the basis that she had beaten the payment into court. The Court of Appeal held that the judge should have taken into account all the provisions of CPR 44.2. The judge had only taken into account the inadequacy of the Part 36 payment. The court stated:

> 'Mrs Painting had been deliberately misleading in the course of the claim, and the fact that the exaggeration is intended and fraudulent is, to my mind, a very important element which needs to be addressed in any assessment of costs.'

The Court of Appeal was also singularly unimpressed that the claimant had not attempted to negotiate settlement. The upshot was that the claimant was ordered to pay the costs of the action from the date of the reduced payment into court, which was only about 3 weeks after the original sum had been offered. Accordingly, the claimant would have very little, if any money, left over from her damages.

We pause to note that Kay LJ made the point, subsequently re-iterated by Jackson LJ in *Fox v Foundation Piling Ltd* (which we have considered in the Chapter 20 Costs Inducements to Settle – Part 36 Offers and other Admissible Offers, above), about a defendant's salvation being by way of a realistic Part 36 offer, stating:

> 'What the University chose to do was to make a Part 36 payment which amounted to a rock-bottom figure even on the basis that it established exaggeration to the maximum extent. If it had chosen to do so, it could have pitched the payment higher without for a moment weakening its position on the central issue in the case.'

The following year the Court of Appeal had a further opportunity to consider conduct and exaggeration in *Jackson v Ministry of Defence* [2006] EWCA Civ 46, [2006]. The claimant had issued proceedings for personal injury against the MoD for injury suffered during a training exercise. He advanced substantial claims for damages for future loss of earnings and for specially adapted accommodation based on his account of his residual disability. The medical evidence did not support the claim of residual disability and those claims were eventually abandoned, reducing his claim from over £1 million to £240,000. The MoD made a Part 36 payment into court in the sum of £150,000. Damages of £155,000 were awarded and the Court of Appeal upheld the judge's reduction of the claimant's costs by 25% to reflect the fact that the award had only just beaten the payment into court and the fact the claimant had exaggerated his evidence. The reduction that the judge made in costs and the actual monetary reduction at the detailed assessment were likely to act as a disincentive to claimants who sought to make exaggerated claims. The order made was well within the judge's wide discretion.

What these cases go to show is that the ultimate outcome is fact specific, but there is a common theme that the starting point is that the successful party recovers costs and the court only then looks at departure from that position.

This point was never better illustrated than in *Widlake v BAA* (see above). The claimant brought an employers' liability claim. Her claim was put at around £34,000. The trial judge awarded £5,522.38 plus interest. More tellingly he found that the claimant had deliberately concealed her history of back pain 'in the hope of increasing the amount of compensation which she would recover'. He also noted that the claimant had not made any counter offers to the defendant's Part 36 offer and made no attempt to negotiate. However, the claimant still recovered more than the defendant's Part 36. The trial judge declared the defendant to be the real winner and ordered the claimant to pay the defendant's costs. The Court of Appeal disagreed and in so doing restated the correct approach to award costs is first to identify the successful party. Here that was the claimant. However, the court then considered the exaggeration and conduct and concluded:

> 'I start with the claimant getting her costs because she beat the payment in and was the successful party. That is the starting point. Those costs should not include costs related to Miss Porter's reporting and the costs judge must be directed to exclude those matters. Pursuing her claim in the exaggerated way she did had the result that this became heavily contested litigation whereas it might have settled. The defendant has been put to unnecessary expense. But an order for costs against the claimant is less justified where, as here, the defendant failed to alleviate its predicament by making a proper Part 36 offer and so lost the opportunity provided by the rules of recovering those costs from the claimant. The claimant's dishonesty must be penalised. The claimant's failure to negotiate a claim which was clearly capable of being settled must also be recognised. When I balance those factors, and attempt to do justice to both parties and to be fair to them, I conclude that the right order in this case is that there be no order for costs.' (para 44)

The Court of Appeal has been clear that there is no general rule that a finding of dishonest conduct will replace the general starting point under CPR 44(2)(a). An evaluation of the effect it has on the issues in the trial will be required. In *Neale v Hutchinson* [2012] EWCA Civ 345 the appellants, who had been successful at the trial of a boundary dispute, were found to have changed a measurement on a document and had sought to suggest that this had in fact been done by the respondents. The trial judge had been explicit in his condemnation of the appellants' dishonesty. The trial judge made a number of separate costs orders and in his reasoning made specific reference to the appellants' dishonesty. The Court of Appeal accepted and re-iterated the principle set out by Waller LJ in *Northstar Systems Ltd v Fielding* [2006] EWCA Civ 1660 that:

> 'There is no general rule that a losing party who can establish dishonesty must receive all his costs of establishing this dishonesty, however, disproportionate they may be.'

with Pitchford LJ concluding that:

> 'In my judgment, the judge erred in his unreserved acceptance of the sweeping proposition that the defendants (the appellants) should not expect to be able to fabricate documents and lie under oath in support of their case and still recover their costs if they succeed at trial.'

Instead the Court of Appeal stressed the importance of starting with the general rule at CPR 44.2(2) and then considering conduct as a reason to depart from that point, but, as repeated in *Soraya Safavi v Standview Ltd* [2018] EWCA Civ 539, with the court reminding itself that 'the full range of measures is available to ensure that the dishonest but successful party does not gain, and the honest but unsuccessful party does not lose, in consequence of the wrongdoing established'.

It is important to stress in this consideration of conduct and exaggeration that the fact that a claimant accepts a sum very much less than was originally claimed does not itself show there to have been exaggeration within CPR 44.2(5)(d). That paragraph could not have been intended to be satisfied merely because a genuine claim was overestimated. Exaggeration for the purposes of that rule must indicate conduct meriting criticism (*Morton v Portal Ltd* [2010] EWHC 1804 (QB)).

Remember, too, that pre-action conduct is also relevant. Gone are those pre-CPR days where parties could conduct themselves without concern prior to issue provided that they then were seen to be paragons of virtue once the claim had been issued.

> 'In my judgment it would be wrong to conclude, if there ever was a strict rule that pre-action conduct was relevant to costs only if causative of the bringing of an unsuccessful claim, or of increased expense in the subsequent litigation, that such a rule survives the introduction of the CPR. The language of Part 44 requires the court to have regard to the conduct of all the parties, both before as well as during the proceedings, and is otherwise wholly unqualified.' (*Bank of Tokyo-Mitsubishi UFJ Ltd v Baskan Gida Sanayi Ve Pazarlama As* [2009] EWHC 1696 (Ch))

The conduct of the proceedings themselves can also lead to a departure from the general rule. In *R (on the application of Scrinivasans Solicitors) v Croydon County Court* [2013] EWCA Civ 249 the claimant firm of solicitors was successful on a judicial review. However, the solicitors had abandoned and re-shaped points at the 11th hour and had pursued wrong criteria. The first instance judge indicated that the claimant had been successful but there was a considerable amount of failure to pursue the right submissions on the right point at the right time. Rather than make an issue based order the judge made no order for costs to reflect the poor conduct. The Court of Appeal concluded, rather damningly, that given how the litigation had been conducted the order in respect of costs was both justified and sensible!

In *Otkritie Capital International Ltd v Threadneedle Asset Management Ltd* [2017] EWCA Civ 274 the Court of Appeal concluded that having found that breach of guidelines meant that a party had conducted litigation below acceptable standards, the first instance court was within its discretion to make a costs order departing from the general rule of CPR 44.2(2)(a) based on that conduct. Once it had decided to depart from the general rule, then the only constraint on the order was the proper exercise of discretion.

(ii) Whether a party has succeeded on part of its case, even if that party has not been wholly successful (CPR 44.2(4)(b))

[22.19]

Mixing up partial success with the definition of the successful party can be easy. A party can win on a number of issues, but remain unsuccessful in the litigation. The pre-CPR days when the court did not look at the component parts of a claim, but simply the overall outcome, when determining where the costs liability lay, are long gone. However, even now there seems to be an acceptance that a successful party is likely to suffer reverses on certain issues along the way and that these do not necessarily sound in costs. As Jackson LJ said in *Fox*:

> 'In a personal injury action the fact that the claimant has won on some issues and lost on other issues along the way is not normally a reason for depriving the claimant of part of his costs.'

There is also a clear overlap between partial success and conduct in those cases that we have considered under the preceding ground for departure from the general rule.

However, there does not have to be. In *Dickinson, Simmonds, Verley and Moonsam v Tesco PLC, Stewart Alexander Group Ltd, O'Neil and Axa Corporate Solutions Assurances SA* (2013) [2013] EWCA Civ 226, the Court of Appeal was concerned with a dispute over whether to permit retrials in credit hire claims where fresh evidence had come to light. A car hire company had been joined for the purposes of costs determination. Axa contested every issue before the court. While it won on two issues relevant to the retrials these issues did not occupy much court time. The successful party was the car hire company. However, to reflect the partial success of *Axa* the court concluded that the car hire company should recover only 70% of its costs of the appeals.

In our view it is under this heading that the Court of Appeal could have recognised that the claimant in *Marcus v Medway* was the successful party (as he had recovered £2,000), but taken account of the fact that he had lost the substantial argument before the court on causation of the amputation. Whether, by doing so, it would have been sufficient to displace the general rule to the extent that justified an order for costs against the claimant is another matter.

(iii) Any admissible offer to settle made by a party which is drawn to the court's attention, and which is not an offer to which costs consequences under Part 36 apply (CPR 44.2(c))

[22.20]

See Chapter 20 on Part 36 and other admissible offers above. In particular, note the comments of Jackson LJ in *Fox v Foundation Piling Ltd (above)* making specific reference to the relevance of such offers:

> '. . . parties are quite entitled to make Calderbank offers outside the framework of Part 36. Where a party makes such an offer and then achieves a more advantageous result, the court's discretion is wider. Nevertheless it may well be appropriate to order that party which has optimistically rejected the Calderbank offer to pay all costs since the date when that offer expired.'

(iv) An illustration of departure from the general rule by use of the CPR 44.2(4) factors

[22.21]

NJ Rickard Ltd v Holloway (3 November 2015, unreported), CA (Civ Div) had a bit of everything for the connoisseur under CPR 44.2 – an identifiable successful party, a failed attempt at a CPR 36 offer, a failure to respond to requests to mediate, a counterclaim and success in part. The court concluded that whilst the landlord claimant was the successful party in that it recovered rent arrears, it had failed in a claim for substantial property damage over which much time had been spent, a counterclaim had succeeded by way of partial set off and the landlord had failed to respond to requests to mediate. Accordingly, the correct departure from the starting point was no order for costs.

THE MENU OF COSTS ORDERS AVAILABLE TO THE COURT TO GIVE EFFECT TO ITS CONCLUSIONS UNDER CPR 44.2–CPR 44.5

[22.22]

CPR 44.2(6) sets out a menu of the various orders, other than a simple order that one party pays all the costs to be assessed, which the court may make in favour of the party it has identified as the recipient of a costs order by consideration of CPR 44.2(2)–CPR 44.2(5). In order of practicality CPR 44.2(6)(a) to (f) are in descending order of desirability for the purposes of ease of any assessment of costs. Indeed CPR 44.2(7) states that (f) is to be avoided if it is possible to order either (a) or (c). Why is this? Well while it may seem clear to the trial judge that there have been obvious discrete issues in the case, the chances are that those will not be so transparent when costs have to be apportioned to the specific issues. This may not simply be an attempt to load the costs towards recovery. It is just as likely to be because the work done was of generic value to the claim as well as touching on the discrete issue in respect of which costs are recoverable. This was a problem highlighted in the case of *Dyson Technology Ltd v Strutt* [2007] EWHC 1756 (Ch), which confirmed that where the costs of the action are awarded to one party with the exception of costs relating to a particular matter or issue, the party in whose favour the costs of that issue were awarded is not entitled to recover anything except the extra costs generated by that issue and not to costs that were incurred and were equally attributable to other elements of the claim. Patten J expressed his concern with issue based orders as follows:

> 'The CPR make no special provision for dealing with costs of this type and some of the difficulties in the assessment of these costs arise directly from a common failure by judges to appreciate the complexities which can be created by orders which seek to split the responsibility for costs between the parties other than by an order for the payment of a simple percentage or proportion of the total costs bill.'

The difficulties envisaged by Patten J are obvious to those familiar with detailed assessments. The costs judge will have to master the issue in detail to determine what costs were properly incurred in dealing with it. Invariably the costs judge will probably be without the assistance of anyone who was present at the trial to clarify precisely how the trial judge expressed the formulation of the issue and without a transcript of the judgment – particularly as more detailed assessments will be dealt with under the provisional assessment procedure (CPR 47.15). All this adds to the cost of detailed assessment and to the amount of time absorbed in dealing with costs on this basis. The costs incurred on assessment may then not be proportionate to the benefit gained. In all the circumstances, contrary to what may seem at trial to be thought to be the case, a 'percentage' order under CPR 44.2(6)(a) made by the judge will often produce a fairer result than a 'distinct parts' order under CPR 44.2(6)(f). Moreover, such an order is consistent with the amended overriding objective of the CPR to deal with cases proportionately.

In *Verrecchia (t/a Freightmaster Commercials) v Metropolitan Police Comr* [2002] EWCA Civ 605, [2002], the court expressly emphasised that the CPR places an obligation on the court to make an issue based order which allows or disallows costs by reference to certain issues, only if other forms of order cannot be made which sufficiently reflect the justice of the case (CPR 44.2(7)).

The court will probably start with (a) and try *not* to work its way down the list. An illustration of this approach was that adopted by Mann J in *Sycamore Bidco Ltd v Breslin and Dawson* [2013] EWHC 583 (Ch). This was a claim concerning alleged misrepresentation and breach of warranty in a share purchase transaction. The claimant failed on misrepresentation, but was successful on breach of warranty. Mann J concluded that the claimant had lost on significant matters, those matters had led to a vast amount of evidence and it was appropriate to reflect this by a costs deduction. He was satisfied that this could be treated as a separate issue and reflected in an issue based costs order. However, in pursuit of a proportionate costs order the correct order was a percentage one and he awarded the claimant 60% of its costs.

This methodology was also endorsed in a personal injury context by Swift J in *Wilson v GP Haden (t/a Clyne Farm Centre)* [2013] EWHC 1211 (QB). Where the claimant had been successful overall, but had been unsuccessful on a causation issue, it was appropriate to order a percentage reduction in costs rather than to make an issue-based order. Swift J identified the pitfalls of an issue based costs order considered above, stating:

> 'It seems to me therefore, that in the circumstances of this case it would be right for me to depart to some extent from the usual rule that costs follow the event. Having said that, I must decide how that is to be done. I am not attracted by the defendant's submission that it should be done by way of requiring the costs judge to separate out all those costs relating to the issue of impact attenuation. It seems to me that such a course is likely to involve an element of complexity and undoubtedly would add to the costs.'

There is no reason why the route through CPR 44.2 may not result in the party defined as the successful one under CPR 44.2(2)(a), ultimately being the paying party under a percentage based order. This is precisely what happened in *Flanagan v Liontrust Investment Partners LLP* [2016] EWHC 446 (Ch). The claimant recovered money and was the successful party, but a combination of 'lost' issues, unfounded allegations and his evidence being insufficient to match his stated case, meant that the departure was sufficient to see him pay 60% of the defendant's costs (again the court preferring a percentage order, even though an issue based approach had been adopted to the various matters arising).

Accordingly, in most cases a 'distinct parts' order is not to be made. Wherever practicable, the judge should endeavour to form a view as to the percentage of costs to which the winning party should be entitled, or alternatively, whether justice would be sufficiently done by awarding costs from or until a particular date only, as suggested by CPR 44.2(6)(c). This must be done in a principled way. As Langstaff J cautioned in *Various Claimants v W M Morrison Supermarkets plc* [2018] EWHC 1123 (QB):

> ' . . . the percentage chosen should not simply be a figure plucked, as it were, from the air but one which attempts to balance the costs of the losing party in respect of the costs of the issues on which it succeeded'

An illustration of this exercise in practice was conducted by Yip J in *Welsh v Walsall NHS Healthcare Trust* [2018] EWHC 2491 (QB) when awarding the claimant 85% of her costs:

> 'In arriving at that percentage, I have looked at the approved costs budget for each party. I have considered how the costs break down and thought about the parties' conduct as it relates to the various costs stages . . . I do not pretend to have conducted any precise mathematical analysis. Rather, I have reached a judgment as to how best to do justice between the parties considering all the circumstances I have identified.'

Where the court is persuaded to make some form of issue-based order it is vital that this is done in a way that is clearly measurable (see for a recent example *Lloyds Bank plc v McBains Cooper* [2017] EWHC 30 (TCC), para 89).

Conclusion

[22.23]

If CPR 44.2 offers a clear template to the way in which the court will approach the award of costs between the parties, except in the specific situations considered below, then the comments of Jackson J in *Multiplex Constructions (UK) Ltd v Cleveland Bridge UK Ltd* [2008] EHWC 2280 (TCC) act as a useful step by step guide. There were eight steps. We have taken out one of the steps as it pre-dates the change to CPR 36.14A (now CPR 36.17) and the decision of Ramsey J in *Hammersmatch Properties Welwyn Ltd v Saint Gobain Ceramics & Plastics Ltd* (see Chapter 20 – Costs Inducements to Settle – Part 36 offers and Other Admissible Offers, above). Here are the remaining seven steps:

- The party which ends up receiving payment should generally be characterised as the overall successful party in respect of the entire action.
- The starting point is the general rule that the successful party is entitled to an order for costs.
- The judge must then consider what departures are required from that starting point, having regard to all the circumstances of the case.
- Where the circumstances of the case require an issue-based costs order that is what the judge should make. However, the judge should hesitate before doing so, because of the practical difficulties which this causes and because of the steer given by CPR 44.2(7).
- In many cases the judge can and should reflect the relative success of the parties on different issues by making a proportionate costs order.
- In considering the circumstances of the case the judge will have regard not only to any Part 36 offers made but also to each party's approach to negotiations (insofar as admissible) and general conduct of the litigation.
- In assessing a proportionate costs order the judge should consider what costs are referable to each issue and what costs are common to several issues. It will often be reasonable for the overall winner to recover not only the costs specific to the issues which he has won but also the common costs.

COSTS ISSUES FOR THE TRIAL JUDGE IN THE AWARD OF COSTS OR FOR THE COSTS JUDGE ON ASSESSMENT

[22.24]

Aaron v Shelton [2004] EWHC 1162 (QB) was a case much loved by those charged with assessing costs. This was because it could be relied upon to head off at the pass some challenging arguments relating to the receiving party's conduct (the sort we have already considered under 'Award of costs' above). The court held that where a losing party considers that he should not be liable to pay the whole of the costs of the claim by reason of the receiving party's conduct, he should make an application to the trial judge, raising this argument when the court is considering what orders as to costs should be made under CPR 44.2.

In fact there was also an authority suggesting quite the reverse, that of *Shirley v Caswell* [2000] Lloyd's Rep PN 955, (2000) Independent, 24 July, CA. In this case the claimant recovered about 1/12th of the value of the claim and had abandoned certain items of claim. The trial judge made a split costs order – 60% of the claimant's costs against the defendant and 40% of the defendant's costs against the claimant. The Court of Appeal concluded that:

> 'In the light of his findings the judge had been entitled to conclude in the instant case that a special order for costs in favour of the defendant was justified. However where, as here, the successful party had pursued issues which were later abandoned

> but had incurred costs in the process, such costs were not to be deducted by the trial judge from the costs recoverable by the successful party. The costs of abandoned issues were prima facie to be disallowed by a costs judge as costs unnecessarily incurred upon detailed assessment. To adopt the approach taken by the judge below would result in the successful party being penalised twice for pursuing unnecessary issues.'

In other words, make one costs order and let the assessing judge determine whether costs were reasonably incurred or not. Apart from seeking to deter the making of multiple costs order, the rationale seemed to be that the costs judge would be in a far better position to make a determination, given the additional information that would be available on a detailed assessment. The main reason that assessing judges disliked this decision was because the assumptions behind it were flawed. These assumptions were that the assessing judge would know what the trial judge had said and the reasons why that judge felt an inquiry was better held at assessment. However, invariably those who attend to conduct assessments have not attended the trial of the claim, the order of the trial judge is usually silent as to the specific concerns or particular findings on facts/issues that go to conduct, there is no transcript of the trial to enlighten the costs judge and those appearing before the assessing court have different notes of what the trial judge may have said! The overriding concern of the costs judge under *Shirley v Caswell* was that a mini re-trial on conduct would be necessary at the assessment.

To be fair the major concern of the Court of Appeal, as set out in the final sentence quoted above, was to avoid a party being doubly penalised.

The Court of Appeal clarified the position in *Ultraframe (UK) Ltd v Fielding* [2006] EWCA Civ 1660. It was held that the principle stated in *Aaron v Shelton* was too unqualified in application. Where the paying party had not sought an order from the judge reflecting the misconduct (in this case dishonesty) of the receiving party in the award of costs, that failure should not deprive the paying party from referring to it on the assessment of costs, or prevent the assessing judge from considering whether the costs incurred by the dishonest party were reasonable. Indeed, consideration of a party's conduct should normally take place both when the trial judge was considering what order for costs should be made, and then when the costs judge was assessing costs under that award. The court would want to ensure that dishonesty/misconduct was penalised, but that the dishonest party was not placed in double jeopardy. Ultimately, the key is one of the proper construction of the order for costs made by the trial judge.

In *Ultraframe* the court concluded that:

- the consideration of conduct should take place both under CPR 44.2 and CPR 44.4 (which is, after all, no more than these rules provide);
- the court must be astute to avoid double jeopardy;
- as a result the trial judge making the order should consider the effect of this order on the subsequent assessment of amount;
- the trial judge ought to help the assessing judge understand the residual task left when considering conduct under CPR 44.4;
- judges may wish to consider whether to make an order under CPR 44.11 before they make the costs order!

As is apparent it is not, therefore, in those cases where conduct is not taken before the trial judge that problems really emerge. *Ultraframe* is clear that the issue may still be raised before the trial judge. The more challenging position is where conduct is raised before the trial judge who either makes an order that discounts to reflect the conduct or decides that the conduct does not merit any departure from the general rule that the successful party recovers its costs (CPR 44.2). In both situations the assessing judge must ensure there is no double penalty – which is particularly hard where no deduction has been made and the costs judge may not even know that conduct was argued before the trial judge as the order will simply be for one party to pay the costs of another party.

Accordingly, it is important for the judge who is asked to take conduct into account at the end of the trial when considering the order as to costs, to consider what is likely to occur on the assessment. Where conduct is being reflected in an order made by the trial judge, it must be wise to make clear, ideally on the face of the order, whether the order is made on the basis that on the assessment the paying party would still be entitled to raise the conduct to argue that costs incurred in supporting the particular conduct were unreasonably incurred. Where the trial judge concludes that there is no conduct that justifies a departure from the general rule, it would be sensible for that to be recited in the order. However, the parties must also be vigilant to ensure that the intended effect of the trial judge's order is clear, rather than leaving the burden exclusively to the court. Otherwise the parties are storing up an argument for a later date and may well find, as anecdotally we know has happened, that the subsequent detailed assessment is adjourned for clarification to be sought from the trial judge or for a transcript of the costs judgment of the trial judge to be obtained. This cannot be proportionate.

In *Three Rivers District Council v Governor and Company of the Bank of England* [2006] EWHC 816 (Comm) the trial judge not only awarded indemnity costs to the defendants but offered to give the costs judge such assistance as he reasonably could, including answering his written questions and sitting with him on the assessment if necessary.

It is fair to say that following *Ultraframe*, there still seemed to be some confusion about how the issue of conduct might be addressed by both the trial judge and the costs judge. This was clarified in *Drew v Whitbread plc* [2010] EWCA Civ 53. This claim was allocated to the multi-track but the claimant only recovered damages well within the limits of the fast track. The judge awarded the claimant costs to be assessed on the standard basis. At the assessment, the district judge ruled that the claimant could never have recovered the damages being claimed, and that the claim should be treated as if it were a fast track one in order to ensure that costs were proportionate. The claimant appealed, contending that the district judge did not have the power to impose fast track costs, as in effect that rescinded the award of standard basis costs by the trial judge and was a retrospective re-allocation. The Court of Appeal held that the district judge had not been entitled simply to rule that she was going to assess the costs of trial as if the case were on the fast track. That would be to rescind the trial judge's order. The permissible approach was to assess the costs on the standard basis taking into account that the case ought to have been allocated to the fast track. A costs judge is entitled, as part of the process of assessment, to hold that a case should, if reasonably presented, have been allocated to the fast track, and to assess costs accordingly. The fact this point was not raised at trial did not preclude it. The approach in *Aaron v Shelton* was too narrow, and was disapproved. There might be some points which could not be raised at an assessment, because they would, in effect, require the costs judge to re-try the case. However, that did not mean there was a general rule that a failure to raise a matter at trial for the purposes of CPR 44.2 precluded the raising of the matter at assessment for CPR 44.4 purposes.

Waller LJ set out the link between the two procedural provisions as follows:

> 'In my view 44.3 and 44.5 [as were] are intended to work in harmony and it is intended that the parties' conduct (for example) may have to be considered under both. If what is sought is a special order as to costs which a costs judge should follow that obviously should be sought from the trial judge. If it is clear that a costs judge would be assisted in the assessment of costs by some indication from the trial judge about the way in which a trial has been conducted, a request for that indication should be sought.'

Earlier he had also set out how, in practice, the trial judge and costs judge might both consider conduct without that necessarily representing a risk of double penalty and scotched, once and for all, the *Aaron* argument that failure to raise conduct at trial precluded it being raised at assessment:

> 'On the face of the two provisions, in fulfilling their different functions, the trial judge under 44.3 and the costs judge under 44.5 are enjoined to take into account many similar factors. That may mean that if a factor has been raised before the trial judge and the trial judge has ruled on that factor, that will bind the costs judge but (and it is important to emphasise this) more often than not the costs judge has material which the trial judge did not have, and thus will not be bound. But the notion that if a party has not raised a matter under 44.3 he should be precluded from raising it under 44.5 does not sit easily with the express provisions.'

In other words, provided that the costs judge considers the factors at CPR 44.4 as part of the exercise of determining what costs have been reasonably incurred and are reasonable in amount (and now by final cross check against proportionality), that will not undermine the trial judge's costs order. An example arose in *O'Beirne v Hudson* [2010] EWCA Civ 52, where the consent order provided: 'The defendant do pay the claimant's reasonable costs and disbursements on the standard basis, to be subject to detailed assessment if not agreed.' The defendant argued that had the matter proceeded to allocation it would have been allocated to the small claims track and therefore it was liable for only fixed costs under CPR Part 27. The Court of Appeal held that although a costs judge cannot vary a costs order he could exercise his discretion in considering whether costs were reasonably incurred, and whether it was reasonable for the paying party to pay more than would have been recoverable in a case that would have been allocated to the small claims track. A costs judge cannot simply apply small claims track costs, but this would still be a highly material circumstance in considering what, by way of assessment, was reasonably incurred and reasonable in amount. Under CPR 44.4(1) the costs judge is required to take into account all of the circumstances of the case and that includes the fact that the case would almost certainly been allocated to the small claims track. Of course, this specific situation is now covered by CPR 46.13(3), which expressly permits the court to restrict costs to those that would have been allowed on the small claims track, if that was the track to which it would have been allocated if allocation had taken place (see [22.28] below).

Although it is surprising that it needs to be said, a court determining a hearing cannot defer the question of who pays the costs of that hearing to a costs judge as the exercise of awarding costs and assessing them under that award were two separate proceedings (*Old Street Homes Ltd v Chelsea Bridge Apartments Ltd* [2018] EWHC 1162 (Ch)).

PRE-ACTION COSTS, COSTS OF PRE-ACTION DISCLOSURE APPLICATIONS AND COSTS OF 'NORWICH PHARMACAL' APPLICATIONS

Pre-action costs and costs of pre-action disclosure applications

[22.25]

Section 51(1) of the Senior Courts Act 1981 provides that the costs 'of and incidental to all proceedings' shall be in the discretion of the court. *McGlinn v Waltham Contractors Ltd* [2005] EWHC 1419 (TCC), held that costs incurred in complying with any pre-action protocol are capable of being costs 'incidental to' any proceedings which are subsequently commenced. However, only in exceptional circumstances could costs incurred by a defendant at the stage of a pre-action protocol, in dealing with and responding to issues which were subsequently dropped from the action when the proceedings were commenced, be costs 'incidental to' those proceedings. It would be contrary to the whole purpose of the pre-action protocols if claiming parties were routinely penalised if they decided not to pursue claims in court which they had originally included in their protocol claim letters. The whole purpose of a pre-action protocol procedure is to narrow issues and to allow a prospective defendant, wherever possible, to demonstrate to a prospective claimant that a particular claim is doomed to failure. It would be wrong in principle to penalise a claimant for abandoning claims which the defendant has demonstrated are not going to succeed because to do so would be to penalise the claimant for doing the very thing which the protocol was designed to achieve. Even so, the defendant in *McGlinn* was £20,000 out of pocket as a result of complying with the protocol and responding to claims which did not subsequently form part of the proceedings.

Citation plc v Ellis Whittam Ltd [2012] EWHC 764 (QB), found it to be settled law that:

(1) if no claim form is issued, then there is no litigation and so there are no costs of litigation for a defendant, whatever costs might have been incurred in complying with a pre-action protocol; however
(2) if a claim form is issued, the costs incurred in complying with a pre-action protocol might be recoverable as costs incidental to any subsequent proceedings

By contrast pre-action disclosure is one area of a pre-proceedings skirmish between parties that comes with its own specific costs provisions. Notwithstanding this, anyone considering the rule and observing the standard orders that are routinely made up and down the country on a daily basis may ponder the relevance of the CPR provisions.

CPR 46.1 provides that the general rule is that the court will award the party against whom disclosure is sought his costs of:

(a) the application; and
(b) compliance with the order for disclosure.

We hazard a guess that the vast majority of pre-action disclosure orders made (virtually always by consent) contain a provision that the party giving disclosure pays the costs of the party applying for that disclosure and is utterly silent on the costs of compliance. This may be because the general rule is followed by an exception. This is that the court may make a different order having regard to all the circumstances, including the extent to which it was reasonable to oppose the application and whether the parties have complied with any pre-action protocol governing the claim. As the majority of these applications are made in personal injury claims where protocol disclosure has not been provided within the prescribed time limits, this may go some way to explaining the myriad departures from the general rule. However, even then case law suggests that these routine departures from the general rule may be a step too far.

In *SES Contracting Ltd v UK Coal plc* [2007] EWCA Civ 791, the claimant made a successful application for pre-action disclosure against the first named defendant under CPR 31.16. The application had been opposed and the judge ordered the first named defendant to pay the costs of the application. The Court of Appeal held the judge had failed to have sufficient regard to the general rule that the respondent to such an application was normally entitled to his costs. There was ample material to justify a departure from the general rule in this case, but not to the extent of ordering the first defendant to pay the whole of the claimant's costs. In the circumstances, the right order was no order as to costs. In the words of Moore-Bick LJ:

> 'If one is starting from the position set out in rule 48.1(2) [now 46.1] one would expect an order of this kind to be made only in a case where it was clearly unreasonable for the respondent to oppose the application or where the manner of his opposition was so unreasonable as to make it appropriate to require him to bear the whole of the parties' costs.'

This seems in keeping with the earlier decision of *Bermuda International Securities Ltd v KMPG (a Firm)* [2001] EWCA Civ 269, although the Court of Appeal in *SES Contracting* stated that it did not find this decision of much assistance. In this case KPMG had resisted disclosure 'root and branch', but the departure from the general rule was only to the extent that there should be no order as to costs.

Bermuda International Securities also contained the order that if subsequently substantive proceedings were issued between these parties then the costs of the pre-action disclosure would be costs in the case in those proceedings. The decision was cited with approval in *Jofa Ltd v Benherst Finance Ltd* [2019] EWCA Civ 899, in which the court was considering the appropriate costs order in Norwich Pharmacal applications (see below), but was considering the analogous situation under CPR 31.16:

> 'Where a successful application is made for pre-action disclosure under CPR 31.16 and the applicant has a prospective claim against the respondent for alleged wrongdoing, it seems to me that . . . it may often be appropriate to make the award of costs dependent on the outcome of any subsequent litigation.' (para 38)

Arnold J took this approach a step further in *Microsoft Corporation v Datel Design* [2011] EWHC 1986 (Ch). In that case the pre-action disclosure application had to be adjourned. By the time it returned to court it had been rendered otiose because, amongst other reasons, substantive proceedings had been issued. Arnold J reserved the costs of the pre-action disclosure proceedings to the trial judge in the substantive proceedings.

The Court of Appeal has determined that an application for pre-action disclosure in a claim falling within the CPR 45 Section IIIA fixed costs regime is an interim application in the overall case, being a claim for personal injury damages. Accordingly, in these cases, whilst determination of the award of costs still falls under CPR 46.1, CPR 45.29H applies to prescribe the amount of costs that can be recovered (see *Sharp v Leeds City Council* [2017] EWCA Civ 33). Notwithstanding this decision, somewhat perversely, the claimant making such an application is not protected from enforcement of an adverse costs order by qualified one-way costs shifting (CPR 44.13(1)).

The costs of 'Norwich Pharmacal' applications

[22.26]

A 'Norwich Pharmacal' application takes its name from the case of *Norwich Pharmacal v Customs and Excise Comrs* [1974] AC 133. Such an order is commonly made where a wrong has been done or arguably done and a third party who has become embroiled in the wrongdoing so as to facilitate it, albeit innocently, is ordered to provide information which is needed to enable the victim to sue the alleged wrongdoer. Such an application is made under CPR 31.18. CPR 46.1 does not apply to these applications, although, as stated above, analogies have been drawn between the two types of application. In 'Norwich Pharmacal' applications, the starting position is that the party seeking disclosure pays the costs of the person against whom such disclosure is sought, to include the costs of the application itself (see para 30; *Totalise plc v The Motley Fool Ltd* [2001] EWCA Civ 1897 as approved in *Cartier International AG v British Sky Broadcasting Ltd* [2018] UKSC 28).

SMALL CLAIMS TRACK COSTS

[22.27]

In the small claims track the court cannot order one party to pay any other anything towards that party's costs, fees and expenses except that which is prescribed in CPR 27.14(2) – save where there is a contractual right to costs (see *Chaplair Ltd v Kumari* [2015] EWCA Civ 798 where a lease provided for the payment of costs and Arden LJ concluded 'Because Chaplair had a right to all its costs, it was not restricted to the fixed costs which can be awarded under the CPR in a case on the Small Claims Track'). Note also that in *Alafco Irish Aircraft Leasing Sixteen Ltd v Hong Kong Airlines Ltd* [2019] EWHC 3668 (Comm), the court concluded that a reference to 'all reasonable' costs was no different from a reference to 'all costs' and did not prevent an order for indemnity costs (unsurprising as under CPR 44.4(1)(b) indemnity basis costs are those reasonably incurred and reasonable in amount).

The Court of Appeal has provided some general guidance as to the operation of CPR 27.14(2)(g) in respect of costs that the court may assess summarily where a party has behaved unreasonably. In *Dammermann v Lanyon Bowdler LLP* [2017] EWCA Civ 269 the court drew a parallel with the wasted costs jurisdiction test stating that:

> '. . . conduct cannot be described as unreasonable simply because it leads in the event to an unsuccessful result or because other more cautious legal representatives would have acted differently. The acid test is whether the conduct permits of a reasonable explanation. If so, the course adopted may be regarded as optimistic and as reflecting in a practitioner's judgment, but it is not unreasonable.'

The court has been clear in refusing to treat as unreasonable conduct the mere fact that a party has been unsuccessful as that would be to make a nonsense of the general 'no recoverable costs' rule in cases allocated to the small claims track (eg *Lastminute.com v Moskalevitvh* (2 April 2019, unreported), QBD Yip J).

Small claim fixed costs generally are considered further under the 'fixed costs' part of the next section for the detail. However, one important point to note is that the previous provisions at CPR 27.14(5) and CPR 27.14(6) are no more. They were deleted in the April 2013 amendments to the CPR and do NOT apply to any claim issued after that date. This coupled with the amendment to delete CPR 26.7(3), which had prevented the court from allocating a claim to a track with a lower limit than the value of the claim without the consent of the parties, means the court may now allocate a claim to the small claims track despite the value of the claim and if it does so the parties are subject to the small claim costs regime. Expect to see a number of claims, eg credit hire claims, in excess of £10,000 where the only issue is quantum and the only evidence is in the form of generic and ubiquitous basic rate reports allocated to the small claims track (with those same rate reports limited in length by specific order) as to do otherwise may not be a proportionate case management decision.

COSTS FOLLOWING ALLOCATION AND RE-ALLOCATION

[22.28]

Under CPR 46.11 the limitations on costs recovery in the small claims track (and indeed the fast track) apply to work done both before and after allocation to that track (save where the allocation is by way of re-allocation, in which case the provisions of CPR 46.13 apply – see below).

In *Lee v Birmingham City Council* [2008] EWCA Civ 891 the secure tenant's solicitors had sent to the defendant a letter of claim in respect of disrepair, invoking the Pre-action Protocol for Housing Disrepair Cases. In response most of the repairs were carried out and the council offered a global sum for damages and costs. It was agreed any action would have been allocated to the small claims track as it was for less than £5,000 and there was no claim for specific performance – it no longer being necessary. However, the Court of Appeal concluded that since the introduction of the protocol it was no longer the position that a claim only began on issue. The protocol included a warning that there was likely to be a costs penalty if a claim was not first pursued in accordance with its terms. This clearly evidenced that its object was to achieve settlement of disrepair claims without recourse to litigation. If the effect of making the claim was to compel the defendant to undertake the required work, then providing that the landlord was liable for the disrepair, the tenant should recover the reasonable costs of achieving that result. Under CPR 46.13 pre-allocation costs are unaffected by subsequent allocation anyway. Accordingly, the court's powers are unrestricted in respect of pre-allocation costs and it was perfectly proper to make an order in respect of them under CPR 46.11(2) if to do so was necessary to ensure that the protocol did not operate to prevent recovery of costs reasonably incurred in achieving the repair. We are somewhat surprised that there have not been more reported cases following this, as plainly the ruling affects all cases where there is a pre-action protocol and where partial settlement pre-issue reduces the value of the residual claim below the small claims threshold.

CPR 46.13 provides that where a party has obtained a costs order before allocation to any track, subsequent allocation will not affect the earlier award. This is true even if the subsequent allocation is to the small claims track. Accordingly, if, for example, either party makes an application for summary judgment before the case is allocated and defers allocation pending the outcome of that application, then either party may recover the costs of that application, depending upon the outcome.

However, CPR 46.13(3) gives clear guidance that when the court is assessing costs on a claim concluded without allocation, it may restrict the costs to those that would have been allowed on the track to which the claim would have been allocated. However, CPR 46.13(3) is limited to cases where the costs order is on the standard basis with CPR PD 46, para 8.2 containing an express reminder that the provision does not apply where costs are awarded on the indemnity basis.

If the court allocates a claim and subsequently re-allocates to a different track then the general rule is that any special costs rules that apply to the initial track will apply up to re-allocation and any special rules that apply to the subsequent track apply from the date of re-allocation. As noted before this is a general rule and so, inevitably, comes with an exception – that the court may order otherwise.

The case of *Francois v Barclays Bank plc* [2017] EWHC 3531 (QB) is a timely reminder that there can be no inference of re-allocation. Instead, there must be a formal court notification of re-allocation, given, amongst other things, the serious costs consequences that flow from allocation.

COSTS ONLY PROCEEDINGS

Procedure

[22.29]

From 3 July, 2000 the Civil Procedure (Amendment No 3) Rules 2000 introduced a useful procedure to be followed where parties to a dispute have reached an agreement on all issues, including which party is to pay the costs, but have failed to agree the amount of the costs where no proceedings have been started. Previously the only possible courses of action were to institute proceedings based upon the agreement seeking an order that the costs be assessed and paid pursuant to the agreement or the issue of substantive proceedings on the basis that in the absence of agreement about costs there was no concluded agreement and the entire dispute remained unresolved.

Under CPR 46.14 either party may start proceedings by issuing a claim form in accordance with Part 8. The claim form must contain details of the agreement and attach copies of documents that evidence it. Until April 2013 the court had either to make an order for costs or dismiss the claim. This is no longer the case and the court is not now so constrained. Under CPR 46.14(5) the court may make an order for costs. What it does if it does not make an order for costs appears now to be a matter of discretion – it is no longer obliged to dismiss the claim. CPR PD 46, para 9.10 refers a defendant opposing the claim to CPR Part 8 and the requirement to file a witness statement. The court will then give directions, including, if appropriate, the possibility of ordering the claim to continue, but as a Part 7 claim. The court may elect to resolve the dispute without allocation (CPR PD 46, para 9.11).

CPR PD 46, para 9.12 confirms that this rule does not prevent a party from issuing a claim form under Part 7 or Part 8 to sue on an agreement made in settlement of a dispute where that agreement makes provision for costs, nor from claiming in that case an order for costs or a specified sum in respect of costs. However, the Practice Direction has been altered with effect from 1 April 2013 so that if the sole issue in dispute is the amount of costs, then the CPR 46.14 procedure must be used. Part 7 or Part 8 proceedings may only be used whether there are other issues as well.

In cases where the assessment pursuant to the costs order under CPR 46.14 is by way of the provisional costs procedure, there have been arguments that the costs of this process are not costs of the substantive claim and so must be costs of the provisional assessment and so the costs incurred under those proceedings are included within the £1500 limit. This overlooks the fact that CPR 47.15 specifically states that it only applies to certain 'detailed assessment proceedings' and CPR 46.14 is titled 'Costs only proceedings'. It is clear that the latter are Part 8 proceedings – so the two are entirely separate creatures. In addition, 'detailed assessment' is defined in CPR 44.1 as a procedure for determining the amount of costs under Part 47. If there was still any doubt that has been dispelled by the Court of Appeal decision in *Tasleem v Beverley; Bartkauskaite v Bartkauskiene* [2013] EWCA Civ 1805, [2014] 4 Costs LO 551. However, this does emphasise the need to obtain an appropriate order for costs in the CPR 46.14 proceedings as an order that 'the costs of the costs only proceedings shall be costs in the assessment' opens the door for the argument. At the time the court makes the costs order in the CPR 46.14 proceedings there may already have been CPR 47.20 offers. Accordingly, it may be wrong for the court to determine the award of costs at that stage. An appropriate order may be that:

> 'The costs of the CPR 46.14 proceedings will be determined at the conclusion of the assessment proceedings (and in the event the assessment proceedings are settled there is liberty to restore for this purpose). Once the court has made the award of those costs it will proceed to carry out a summary assessment of the amount of costs payable under any award made.'

Summary or detailed assessment

[22.30]

In previous editions it was suggested that in no circumstances should a district judge or costs judge attempt to dispose of the application for an order for costs and then immediately embark upon a summary assessment of the costs in dispute. That is no longer the position. CPR PD 46, para 9.9, while retaining a general rule that the costs order under this procedure should be subject to detailed assessment, also states that if the order for assessment is made at a hearing and the court is then in a position to undertake a summary assessment it may do so. As these orders are invariably made as a paper work exercise without a hearing the proviso appears of limited effect. However, given the desire for proportionality we wondered whether parties would start asking the court to list these applications for hearing to enable the court to undertake a summary assessment. As CPR PD 46, para 9.6 gives the district judge or costs judge jurisdiction 'to hear and decide any issue which may arise in a claim issued under this rule . . . ' there seems no reason, in principle, why the court cannot accede to such a request. However, it seems that parties are not putting this to the test and the exercise remains a paper one with subsequent detailed assessment.

On the assumption that the general rule will apply more often than not (as after all it is the general rule) it is accepted that for bills of modest size or where there is a challenge to just one item then a detailed assessment may be an unnecessarily cumbersome and disproportionate method of resolution even under the provisional assessment scheme. However, it appears anecdotally, that this problem has often been resolved by the parties and the court creatively agreeing some short form of bill and Points of Dispute and Replies to the Points of Dispute dealing with the only issue in dispute. Of course, the CPR PD 47, para 5.7 procedure should be adopted anyway where the only dispute is as to disbursements.

CPR 46.14 and the fixed recoverable costs scheme

[22.31]

Solomon v Cromwell Group; Oliver v Doughty [2011] EWCA Civ 1584, were low value RTA claims which were settled pre-action by the acceptance of Part 36 offers. The claimants obtained orders for assessment under CPR 44.12A (now CPR 46.14) but then put in detailed bills for assessment on the ordinary standard basis. They contended that they were entitled to do so under CPR 36.10(1) (as was) and that they had the benefit of deemed costs orders. The defendants denied this, contending that the claimants' entitlement was confined to fixed recoverable costs by virtue of CPR 44.12A(4A). In *Solomon* the claimant succeeded before the district judge but lost on appeal to the circuit judge who held that CPR 36.10 simply had no application, as it only applied where there were 'proceedings'. In *Oliver* the defendant succeeded before the district judge, who held that fixed recoverable costs were a form of costs on the standard basis. The claimants appealed in each case and the *Oliver* appeal was leap-frogged to the Court of Appeal which held:

(1) The judge had been wrong in *Solomon* to decide that there were no 'proceedings' for the purpose of CPR 36.10. The terms of Part 36 as a whole made it clear that steps taken in contemplation of proceedings were to be regarded as 'proceedings' for the purpose of CPR 36.10(1).

(2) However, there could be no deemed costs order under CPR 44.12 (now CPR 44.9(2)) in the absence of actual court proceedings. An order for costs could not exist in a vacuum. The contrary view of the costs judge in *Alison Jones v Alcom UK Ltd* (24 February 2011) was not correct.

(3) An assessment in accordance with Part 45 Section II could not properly be regarded as an assessment on the standard basis. Therefore, there was a degree of conflict between CPR 36.10(1) and CPR 44.12A(4A).

(4) However, the Rule Committee would not have intended that a claimant in a low value RTA case who accepted a Part 36 offer pre-proceedings should recover costs on the standard basis, whereas such a claimant who accepted an offer other than under Part 36 should be limited to fixed recoverable costs. Accordingly, the rule that the general gave way to the particular applied, and CPR 44.12A(4A) and Part 45, Section II prevailed.

(5) Although a claimant had the right to start proceedings under either Part 7 or Part 8, it was doubtful that he could recover more than the fixed costs for which Section II of Part 45 provides. It was, though, not necessary to decide that as both claimants had issued under CPR 44.12A.

(6) It is possible to contract out of Part 45 Section II, at least in part, but on a construction of the correspondence in these cases that had not been done.

Both appeals were dismissed accordingly.

Basis of costs

[22.32]

CPR PD 46, para 9.4 states that 'unless the court orders otherwise or Section II of Part 45 applies the costs will be treated as being claimed on the standard basis.' This replaces the previous position which required the claimant to state in the claim form whether costs were claimed on the indemnity or standard basis with silence indicating the standard basis.

AGREEMENT IN ISSUED PROCEEDINGS IN RESPECT OF EVERYTHING EXCEPT COSTS

[22.33]

If the parties have agreed who will pay the costs but have not agreed the amount then, of course, they have reached agreement and there is no difficulty about the court ordering a detailed assessment of the costs. But what if the parties are agreed on everything but the incidence of costs: can they ask the court to resolve the issue? The simple answer is yes, but the court position when asked to do so and the ultimate outcome is far from straightforward.

The appropriate test is set out in *M v London Borough of Croydon* [2012] EWCA Civ 595. The Court of appeal held that where a claim has been settled, there is a sharp difference between (i) a case where a claimant has been wholly successful whether following a contested hearing or pursuant to a settlement, and (ii) a case where a claimant has only succeeded in part following a contested hearing, or pursuant to a settlement, and (iii) a case where there has been some compromise which does not actually reflect the claimant's claims. While in every case, the allocation of costs will depend on the specific facts, there are some points which can be made about these different types of case.

- In case (i), it is hard to see why claimants should not recover all their costs, unless there is some good reason to the contrary. Whether pursuant to judgment following a contested hearing, or by virtue of a settlement, claimants can, at least absent special circumstances, say that they have been vindicated, and, as the successful party, that they should recover their costs. In *R (on the application of Tesfay) v Secretary of State for the Home Department* [2016] EWCA Civ 415, the Court of Appeal highlighted the unique nature of judicial review proceedings stating that success in such proceedings has to be determined not only by reference to what was sought and the basis on which it was opposed, but also by reference to what is achievable (and in these proceedings the most that can be achieved is reconsideration of the decision under review).

  This 'success' approach was adopted by the court in non-judicial review proceedings in *Marcura Equities FZE v Nismar Ventures Ltd* [2018] EWHC 523 (QB), in which the court compared 'the parties' pleaded position with what was in fact obtained by the claimants under the eventual settlement to see whether the consent order involved the claimants receiving substantively all of the relief which they claimed and then considering whether there was any reason to depart from the general rule that the successful party should recover its costs under CPR 44.2.
- In case (ii), when deciding how to allocate liability for costs after a trial, the court will normally determine questions such as how reasonable claimants were in pursuing the unsuccessful claim, how important that was compared with the successful claim, and how much the costs were increased as a result of the claimants pursuing the unsuccessful claim.
- In case (iii), the court is often unable to gauge whether there is a successful party in any respect, and, if so, who it is. In such cases, therefore, there is an even more powerful argument that the default position should be no order for costs. However, in some such cases, it may well be sensible to look at the underlying claims and inquire whether it was tolerably clear who would have won if the matter had not settled. If it is, then that may well strongly support the contention that the party who would have won did better out of the settlement, and therefore did win.

This approach was confirmed in *Emezie v Secretary of State for the Home Department* [2013] EWCA Civ 733. The Court of Appeal was at pains to stress that the previous test distilled from *R (on the application of Boxall) v Waltham Forest London Borough Council* (2001) 4 CCL Rep 258 had been superseded by *M v London Borough of Croydon*. The correct starting point is to ask whether the claimant achieved by the settlement what was sought in the proceedings. The Court of Appeal concluded that in this case the answer to that question was yes and substituted an order for costs in the claimant's favour in place of no order for costs.

In *Md Ashif Khan v Secretary of State for the Home Department* [2018] EWCA Civ 1684, whilst confirming that 'the leading authority on this subject was and remains the decision of this Court in *R (on the application of M) v Croydon London Borough Council*', the court provided a reminder 'that costs applications must not be allowed to become in reality cases in which the underlying merits of a claim have to be determined. I would deprecate such satellite litigation ... inevitably, cases such as this turn on their own facts'. These warnings echo both the call for a proportionate approach to such applications and the conclusion that it is impossible to draw up an exhaustive list of factors to be considered, in *R (on the application of Baxter) v Lincolnshire County Council* [2015] EWCA Civ 1290.

However, in *R (on the application of Gudanaviciene) v Immigration and Asylum First Tier Tribunal* [2017] EWCA Civ 352, the Court of Appeal confirmed that *M v London Borough of Croydon* had not altered the position in respect of applications for judicial review of the decisions of tribunals or other inferior courts unless they either appeared as other than a neutral party or had been guilty of flagrant improper behaviour (as per *R (Davies) v Birmingham Deputy Coroner* [2004] EWCA Civ 207). If neither of those situations arose, there should be no order for costs. In *R (on the application of Paul Worthington) v HM Senior Coroner for Cumbria* [2018] EWHC 3386 (Admin), the court made clear that neutrality meant precisely that and the approach of a tribunal purportedly advancing a neutral position, but making submissions of a partisan nature, could not be condoned. In such a situation, the 'no order for costs' position would not apply and costs would be at large. Ironically, in this case, the coroner was the successful party and so secured a costs order pursuant to CPR 44.2. Similarly, in *D v Lord Chancellor* [2020] EWHC 736 (Admin), when filing an acknowledgement of service indicating that he was adopting a neutral position, the Lord Chancellor filed letters making it clear that the claims were disputed. The court found that the defendant's approach was not neutral, he had 'stepped into the ring' and should pay the costs.

Having answered the question in the first paragraph in the affirmative it is worth considering the full statement of the then Master of the Rolls, Lord Neuberger, confirming this to be the position in *M v London Borough of Croydon*, because it does contain the qualification that the court may decline so to do:

> 'It is open to parties in almost any civil proceedings to compromise all their differences save costs, and to invite the court to determine how the costs should be dealt with. The court has jurisdiction in such a case to determine who is to pay costs, but it is not obliged to resolve such a free-standing dispute about costs. Accordingly, by settling all issues save costs, the parties take the risk that the court will not be prepared to make any determination other than that there be no order for costs not only because that is the right result after analysing all the arguments, but also on the ground that such an exercise would be disproportionate.'

A final point of note on this topic is that when determining costs in this situation the court must be astute to the possibility that privilege may attach to discussions and documents that formed part of the substantive settlement and should not permit reliance in the absence of waiver of that privilege (see *Cammick v Ashby* (1 March 2016, unreported), CA (Civ Div)).

CLAIM AND COUNTERCLAIM AND SET OFF GENERALLY

[22.34]

For those worried that CPR 44.3(9) as was had not followed the rest of that part into CPR 44.2 do not panic. This rule is now accorded a subsection of its own and can be found at CPR 44.12 under the heading of 'Set-off'. In simplistic terms it allows the court to order that the costs assessed against a party who is also entitled to recover costs are to be set off against that entitlement. The alternative is that the court delays the issue of a final costs certificate for the costs to which that party is entitled until he has paid the costs assessed against him.

The rule covers, amongst other situations, the position where the claimant succeeds on the whole or on part of his claim and the defendant succeeds on the whole or on part of his counterclaim. However, as its heading suggests the rule extends to a far more general consideration of setting off respective costs orders.

In the context of cross claims it is infinitely preferable and proportionate for there to be only one order for costs adjusted appropriately by allowing a proportion or some other partial order as to costs in favour of one party rather than making cross-orders for costs in favour of the successful claimant and the successful defendant on his counterclaim.

If that is not possible and separate costs orders are made on the claim and the counterclaim, then it appears that the lengthy, tedious and often unfair investigation of the costs attributable to the claim and those attributable to the counterclaim prescribed in the case of *Medway Oil and Storage Co Ltd v Continental Contractors Ltd* [1929] AC 88, 98 LJKB 148, HL will still apply. Under this approach, if both claim and counterclaim are successful and separate costs orders are made, the counterclaim will have attributed to it only the increase in the costs which it had brought about, so that the result will be that the balance of the costs will almost certainly be in favour of the claimant and be unfair to the defendant. Of course, the reverse is true if the claim and counterclaim are both unsuccessful. There the defendant will recover all the costs save those that are attributable to the counterclaim only, for which he will be responsible. *Dyson Technology Ltd v Strutt* [2007] EWHC 1756 (Ch) demonstrated the importance of time records distinguishing between work done on the claim and work done on the counterclaim in cases where *Medway Oil* might apply.

In *Medway Oil*, the court also concluded that unless there was a specific order to this effect, costs could not be apportioned between claim and counterclaim. The case of *Hay v Szterbin* [2010] EWHC 1967 (Ch) concerned the difference between apportionment and division of costs. Under the terms of a Tomlin order settling the claim between the claimant and the third defendant, Green Wright Charlton (a firm) agreed to pay the costs of the claimant's action against it only. The costs judge, when asked to construe this agreement, determined that this meant the firm only had to pay those costs that related exclusively to the claim against it and nothing in respect of any costs common to the claim against all the defendants. The claimant had suggested that those costs could be apportioned between the defendants. On appeal the *Medway* distinction between division and apportionment of costs was confirmed. The third defendant would be liable by a process of division for those common costs that could be attributed exclusively to the claim against it. Items that did not relate solely to the claim against the third defendant were not susceptible to division and were irrecoverable under the order.

The potential for injustice created by *Medway Oil* is clear. Take the example of a road traffic accident in which both parties sustain injury and loss and both blame each other. If there is a claim and counterclaim and ultimately liability is apportioned between them, the defendant will not recover any liability costs (as those arose within the claim anyway) and will have to pay the claimant's costs of those because the claimant issued proceedings first. This creates a race to issue proceedings.

Fortunately, this approach is not always followed and the injustice is resolved by a different award of costs order.

The Court of Appeal in *Burchell v Bullard* [2005] EWCA Civ 358 found that the trial judge had been correct to dismiss the *Medway* approach because of the difficulty in the preparation of the bill of costs and the enormous complication of the process of detailed assessment in this building dispute. However, he had not found a better solution by resorting to an order that costs followed the event, ordering the defendants to pay the costs of the claim and the claimant to pay the defendant's costs of the counterclaim. In doing so he had fallen into the error of fettering his discretion and not considering what alternatives were available under CPR 44.2(6). The most obvious and frequently most desirable option should be that in CPR 44.2(6)(a) (considered above), namely that of ordering a proportion of the party's costs to be paid. An order for 'Costs following the event' was the general rule and in this kind of litigation, the event was determined by establishing who had written the cheque at the end of the case. In this case the defendants had done so and they therefore were the unsuccessful party. The starting point was that the claimant was entitled to the costs of the proceedings, claim and counterclaim taken together. The specific aspects of conduct identified in CPR 44.2(5) had then to be taken into account when considering a departure from the general rule. This approach resulted in the Court of Appeal ordering the defendants to pay 60% of the claimant's costs of the claim, counterclaim and the Part 20 proceedings and 60% of the claimant's liability to pay the Part 20 defendant's costs.

By departing from the *Medway Oil* approach and instead treating the exercise as one of set off the court is better able to recognise the justice of the situation. A helpful illustration of this was the case of *Square Mile Partnership Ltd v Fitzmaurice McCall Ltd* [2006] EWHC 236 (Ch). The court found that the claimant had to issue proceedings to compel the defendant to admit its claim and had to come to court in order to recover the money it obtained. However, most of the evidence and pre-trial work went to the main issue of the counterclaim upon which the defendant had been successful. Accordingly, both parties could be said to have succeeded on their respective claims in accordance with CPR 44.2. To award the claimant a significant proportion of its costs would not be just, as it would fail to reflect the defendant's successful counterclaim. To give the defendant its costs would be harsh, as the claimant had succeeded in recovering significant sums from the defendant despite losing on the counterclaim. Taking all the factors into account, the appropriate order was no order as to costs.

In *Villa Agencies SPF Ltd v Kestrel Travel Consultancy Ltd* [2012] EWCA Civ 219 the Court of Appeal stripped the vexed issue of costs on claim and counterclaim right back to the general rule at CPR 44.2(2). In this case the claimant sued for outstanding rent and the defendant counterclaimed for the same amount for repair work for which it had paid. The outcome was that there was a substantial deduction applied to the rent to take account of the repair work. The trial judge had decided that the case was 'all about the counterclaim' and made one costs order – namely that the claimant should pay 2/3rds of the defendant's costs. The Court of Appeal regarded the starting point as an error in principle. The claimant had ended up recovering a significant amount of its claim and was plainly the successful party. In reality the case was about whether the defendant owed anything to the claimant and the court had concluded that it did. The starting point was that the claimant was the successful party but there should be departures from the general rule to recognise that the counterclaim occupied most of the trial and the claimant had only succeeded in part. The Court of Appeal awarded the claimant 25% of its costs.

However, sometimes attempting to undertake the set off at the award of costs stage without knowing the respective costs of the parties would, itself, create an injustice. This was the conclusion reached by the court in *Amin v Amin and 17 others (costs)* [2007] EWHC 827 (Ch D), where it decided that where the costs on each side are very large it is not safe to carry out an exercise of setting-off by reference to percentages of one side's costs against the other. Instead, it is appropriate to ascertain a percentage of each side's costs which is payable to the other and leave the parties to turn those percentages into money amounts, whether by agreement or assessment, and to effect set-off at that level. The litigation concerned two actions concerning a partnership dispute and an unfair prejudice petition against a company in which the court decided that overall 35% of each side's total costs were to be attributed to the company action, and 65% to the partnership action. Although it was not appropriate to set off these figures against each other because of the disparity, the parties were of course free to agree to such a set-off should they wish to do so.

Set-off, although not under CPR 44.12, can take place in a broader sense, in the award of the trial judge under CPR 44.2 in connection with success on issues. We have included it here because this offers a contrast to the position in *Amin*. In *The Bank Of Tokyo-Mitsubishi UFJ, Ltd Baskan Gida Sanayi Ve Pazarlama AS* (see above) the parties were aware of their overall costs and the portion of these that was attributable to one very specific issue upon which the successful party had lost. Concessions were also made as to the likely percentage of those costs that would be recovered on an assessment – either under the standard or indemnity basis. Accordingly the trial judge was able to calculate the overall expenditure of the parties on this issue, work out what percentage that represented of the likely cost recovery of the successful party and make an order for costs in its favour but reduced by that percentage with a clear direction to the assessing costs judge to make no further deduction in respect of that issue. While this is a set-off, what the trial judge was in effect doing was a combination of the award of and quantification of the costs of that issue. He would not have been able to undertake the set off without the detailed costs information and concessions before him.

Previously we have referred to the unresolved conundrum under CPR 44.12, of whether it can be used to recover costs under a costs award where enforcement would otherwise not be possible as the paying party has protection under the QOCS regime. In other words, can a defendant in such a case offset costs against any costs due to the protected claimant? Is set off in this context a form of enforcement (as it certainly is not enforcement in a strict sense as defined by list of methods in CPR PD 70)? In *Howe v Motor Insurer Bureau* in an unreported judgment dealing with costs unreported 6 July 2017 (Court of Appeal) following the main decision at [2017] EWCA Civ 932, the Court of Appeal concluded that even in a case where the claimant is protected by QOCS, any costs due to the defendant may be offset against any costs due to the claimant. Subsequently, the Court of Appeal acknowledged the force in the argument that QOCS is a self-contained code and so set-off outside the regime should not be possible, but accepted that *Howe* is a binding authority to the contrary and so followed it (*Ho v Adelekun* [2020] EWCA Civ 517). This decision may be the subject of appeal to the Supreme Court. It also contained a suggestion that this was a topic that the Civil Procedure Rules Committee might wish to consider.

NO WINNER OR LOSER

[22.35]

We have seen above in *Square Mile Partnership Ltd* that the court can conclude that both parties have been successful on their respective claim and counterclaim and make no order for costs by way of a reasoned set-off. However, that is different from the court determining that neither party had been successful. This was precisely the situation in *Phonographic Performance Ltd v AEI Rediffusion Music Ltd* [1999] 2 All ER 299, CA, an appeal from an order for costs by the Copyright Tribunal, in which the Court of Appeal held that the Tribunal had erred in principle by seeking to find a winner and a loser and that in reality neither side had won. Accordingly, there should be no order for costs.

This was also the outcome in *Verrechia (t/a Freightmaster Commercials) v Metropolitan Police Comr* (above) where the claimant sought damages of £141,500 plus aggravated and exemplary damages under the Torts (Interference with Goods) Act 1977 in respect of 65 items which the police had failed to return to him. The claimant had offered to settle for £98,000 which was followed by a payment into court by the police of the sum of £5,500 in full settlement of the whole of the claimant's claim. The judge awarded damages in the sum of £37,300 plus interest with the result that neither party succeeded to the extent of their prior offers. The judge clearly thought the action had resulted in a 'draw'. Although when the case started there were some 65 items in issue, by the time of closing speeches, this had reduced to only 40. The appellant won in respect of half in number of these items. There were no criticisms relevant to costs in the conduct of either party. The appellant had won half of his case and lost on the rest. The police, as well as the appellant, had come to court to win that part of the case in which they succeeded. To this extent the judge was entitled to take the view that each side was the winner. Alternatively, it was open to the judge, in the light of the wide powers conferred by the CPR, to conclude that, in any event, the appellant should only have part of his costs as he had been successful in part only of his case, and that the police should have the cost of the part of the case on which they had been successful. On either basis the judge could properly conclude that the proportion of costs which each party should receive was 50% and that the net result was nil when these two percentages were set against each other.

In *Camertown Timber Merchants Ltd v Sidhu* [2011] EWCA Civ 1041, when deciding costs, the judge clearly took account of conduct. The defendant had tried to bolster his claim and the claimant had exaggerated his. Each party had won and lost on various points and both were unsatisfactory witnesses. The court's decision to make no order as to costs was one within its discretion. The order for costs following such a trial was a paradigm example of the exercise of discretion and the judge had not exceeded the ambit of discretion.

There are some cases where justice plainly requires the 'no order' approach. This is acceptable provided that this conclusion is reached by the court following an attempt to identify the successful party under CPR 44.2. In *Taylor v Burton* [2014] EWCA Civ 63, the Court of Appeal concluded that in a right of way dispute it was unrealistic to identify the successful party on the appeal and so made no costs order in relation to the appeal. It confirmed this view when the appeal in the same case resumed under [2015] EWCA Civ 188.

BULLOCK AND SANDERSON ORDERS

[22.36]

These orders arise where an action founded on either contract or tort against two separate defendants is successful against one and unsuccessful against the other. The court has a discretion (see *Mayer v Harte* [1960] 2 All ER 840, CA for the principles upon which such discretion is exercised) to order the unsuccessful defendant to pay the successful defendant's costs. This can be done in one of two ways:

(i) An order that the unsuccessful defendant pay directly to the successful defendant the latter's costs (known as a Sanderson order because it was first made in *Sanderson v Blyth Theatre Co* [1903] 2 KB 533, CA).

(ii) An order that the claimant pay the successful defendant's costs, permitting the claimant to add them to the costs ordered to be paid to him by the unsuccessful defendant (a Bullock order – *Bullock v London General Omnibus Co* [1907] 1 KB 264, CA).

Where the claimant has no means, then, subject to the court's discretion, the Sanderson order (ie (i) above) is the fairer way of dealing with the justice of the case. Neither order is appropriate in favour of a claimant who has sued both defendants because of a doubt as to the law as opposed to the facts, or where the causes of action against each are quite distinct, nor where the respective claims are not alternative or are based upon quite distinct sets of facts.

Irvine v Metropolitan Police Comr [2005] EWCA Civ 129 confirmed that the jurisdiction to make a Sanderson order survived the introduction of the CPR. The exercise of discretion in deciding whether to make such a costs order has to be guided by the overriding objective and CPR Part 44 and it has to be recognised that it is capable of working injustice against a successful defendant. The court had a wide discretion over costs. In determining whether to order an unsuccessful defendant to pay the costs of a successful defendant the relevant factors included whether the claim against the successful defendant had been made 'in the alternative', whether the causes of action had been connected with those on which the claimant had been successful and whether it had been reasonable for the claimant to join and pursue a claim against the successful defendant. Although a significant factor was likely to be whether one defendant blamed another, whether it had been reasonable to join that defendant and pursue the claim would depend on the facts of the case and whether the claimant could in fact sustain such a claim.

Moon v Garrett [2006] EWCA Civ 1121 confirmed the conclusion in *Irvine* (above) that there are no hard and fast rules as to when it is appropriate to make a *Bullock* or a *Sanderson* order. If claimants have acted reasonably in suing two defendants, it will be harsh if they end up paying the costs of suing the defendant against whom they have failed. Whether one defendant has blamed another will always be a factor. The fact that claims are not truly alternative does not mean that the court does not have the power to order one defendant to pay the costs of another.

Inevitably only in truly exceptional circumstances will a claimant who has lost against two separate defendants be able to recover the costs of pursuing one defendant from the other. Where claims made by the claimant against both the second and fourth defendants had failed, a *Bullock* order was not appropriate and the fourth defendants' costs were ordered to be borne by the claimant. It had been unreasonable for the claimant to pursue the fourth defendants but, even if it had been reasonable, it would be unjust to make the second defendant pay the costs of the unsuccessful pursuit of allegations against the fourth defendant where the second defendant had not blamed the fourth defendant or encouraged pursuit of the fourth defendant by the claimant (*McGlinn v Waltham Contractors Ltd* [2007] EWHC 698 (TCC)).

A final point, solely for aficionados, is that in *Sanderson* although the court approved of the jurisdiction to order an unsuccessful defendant to pay directly the costs of a successful defendant, the court actually made a *Bullock* type order.

STATE FUNDED PARTIES

[22.37]

This has been considered within the section on funding. However, by way of reminder:

- If an order for costs is made in favour of a legally aided party there must be a detailed assessment of those costs.
- If an order for costs is made against a legally aided party the amount of costs payable is also subject to a determination under s 26 of the Legal Aid, Sentencing and Punishment of Offenders Act 2012. This section provides that such costs:

> ' . . . must not exceed the amount (if any) which it is reasonable for the individual to pay having regard to all the circumstances including –

(a) the financial resources of all the parties to the proceedings; and
(b) their conduct in connection with the dispute to which the proceedings relate.'

Given the extremely limited availability of public funding after the cuts to civil legal aid availability, we suspect that s 26 determinations have become significantly less frequent.

APPEALS AGAINST COSTS AWARDS

[22.38]

2018 provided a reminder by the Court of Appeal that higher courts should be slow to entertain appeals on costs orders (*Notting Hill Housing Trust v Esan* (16 May 2018, unreported), CA (Civ Div))). If the CPR 44.2 template is followed, identifying first the successful party and then considering whether there is any reason to depart from the general rule that this party should recover its costs, any appeal can be based only on the argument that the court has exercised its discretion in a way that exceeded the generous ambit within which reasonable disagreement is possible.

CHAPTER 23

WASTED COSTS ORDERS

THE LAW ON WASTED COSTS ORDERS

[23.1]

From 1 October 1991, s 4 of the Courts and Legal Service Act 1990 inserted a new s 51 into the Senior Courts Act 1981 relating to both the High Court and the County Court introducing the concept of 'wasted costs', as follows:

> '(6) In any proceedings mentioned in sub-section (1) [in the Court of Appeal, High Court and County Court], the court may disallow or, (as the case may be) order the legal or other representative concerned to meet the whole of any wasted costs or such part of them as may be determined in accordance with Rules of Court.
> (7) In sub-section (6) "wasted costs" means any costs incurred by a party: (a) as a result of any improper, unreasonable or negligent act or omission on the part of any legal or other representative or any employee of such a representative; or (b) which in the light of any such act or omission occurring after they were incurred, the court considers it unreasonable to expect that party to pay.'

Recent authority suggests that 'legal or other representative' will be interpreted broadly. In *M A Lloyd & Son Ltd (in administration) v PPC International Ltd (t/a Professional Powercraft)* [2016] EWHC 2162 (QB), the court found that a solicitor employed by an organisation registered with the Solicitors Regulation Authority, but which was not authorised or licensed to carry out reserved activities, could still be subjected to a wasted costs order. Indeed, going even further, in *Ogiehor v Belinfantie* [2018] EWCA Civ 2423, when upholding an order that a litigant in person pay the costs thrown away by the adjournment of a trial on quantum after he had revealed the existence of an offer 'without prejudice save as to costs', the Court of Appeal considered that the three stage test for wasted costs (see **[23.5]** below) applied even though the court was dealing with a litigant in person. It concluded that the question was simply whether the three-stage test was met in light of the conduct of the appellant litigant in person. It determined that it was and that 'it appears . . . that the judge was correct to order that the Appellant should bear [the] costs'.

THE PROCEDURE FOR WASTED COSTS ORDERS

[23.2]

The relevant procedure is set out at CPR 46.8. Whenever the court is considering making such an order under s 51 it has to afford the legal representative against whom the order is being considered the opportunity to make written submissions or, if this is what the legal representative prefers, attend a court hearing where this will be considered, before any order is made. This may sound obvious, but the possibility of a wasted costs order may arise at a hearing where the relevant representative is not in attendance (for example counsel is in court and the solicitor is in the firing line) and/or where the representative is not in a position that day to explain his position.

The possibility of the legal representative responding by written submissions was introduced in April 2013. Another amendment at that time was to remove reference in the rules which suggested that the onus was on the legal representative to 'show cause' why the wasted costs order should not be made. The onus was always on the party seeking a wasted costs order (a good reason why the court should be shy of commencing such an inquiry). Under CPR 46.8 there is no such suggestion. Gone, too, are the provisions empowering the court to order an inquiry by and report from a costs judge or district judge and the option of referring the question of wasted costs to a costs judge or district judge, instead of making a wasted costs order (as opposed to referring to such a judge for assessment of amount, which is permissible – see below). In other words, the court considering the possibility of a wasted costs order should grasp the nettle and, having given the legal representative the opportunity to make submissions (whether written or oral), should decide whether or not to make an order. The intention is to make the procedure more efficient and proportionate.

An application for a wasted costs order may be made by any party or, pursuant to CPR PD 46, para 5.3, of the court's own initiative. We have referred above to one good reason that a court should be wary of commencing this process. Another is that if the court ultimately concludes that a wasted costs order is not justified then it will have put in chain a process that has caused the parties to incur costs for no purpose. Who then pays the costs incurred? If the court allows one party to take the initiative, then the award of the costs of the process falls to be considered between the parties under CPR 44.2 in the usual way.

CPR PD 46, para 5.2 indicates that an application for an order may be made at any stage up to and including detailed assessment proceedings, although in general, applications are best left until after the trial. Indeed, in *FilmLab Systems International Ltd v Pennington* [1994] 4 All ER 673 the court indicated that it 'would rarely be wise or right to seek to obtain such an order until after the trial'. In *Melchior v Vettivel* [2001] All ER (D) 351 the court made a wasted costs order after the conclusion of the trial and the sealing of the costs order. Even where the proceedings have been settled and stayed under a Tomlin order, there is no need to apply to lift the stay to make the application: see *Wagstaff v Colls* [2003] EWCA Civ 469. This only goes to emphasise that a wasted costs application is genuinely free standing.

It is important to note, as a result, that a party does not lose the right to apply for wasted costs by waiting until the trial or even the detailed assessment proceedings. The court is not being asked to overturn a previous costs order on such an application. The statutory power to make a wasted costs order is a discrete jurisdiction conveyed on the court.

Despite this clear indication that these applications are best left until trial, many are in respect of specific hearings (eg where one party's representative fails to attend and the hearing is adjourned, a costs order made against the party whose representative failed to attend and with wasted costs to be considered) and are relatively straightforward. These can be, and frequently are, dealt with at an interim stage. In practice what often happens is the court puts the representatives on notice that this will be considered at the next hearing, by which time no order is required because the representatives have accepted 'fault' and already discharged the other party's wasted costs. That this is an acceptable approach was endorsed by the Court of Appeal in *Ridehalgh v Horsefield* [1994] Ch 205 (see below).

Applications are either to be made under CPR Part 23 or by oral application at any hearing. If the application is made by Part 23 application then the notice and any evidence in support must identify what the legal representative is alleged to have done or failed to do and the costs that the legal representative may be ordered to pay or which are sought against him.

CPR PD 46, para 5.6 gives the court discretion as to how to case manage the procedure to be adopted. The two imperatives are that:

- the process is fair;
- the process is as simple and summary (and, therefore, proportionate) as possible.

The court should determine the procedure to be followed to meet the requirements of the individual case. In *Re a Barrister (wasted costs order)* [2001] EWCA Crim 1728 the court gave the following guidance:

- Elaborate pleadings should in general be avoided.
- No formal process of disclosure is appropriate.
- The court could not imagine any circumstances in which the applicant should be permitted to interrogate the respondent lawyer.
- On the other hand, the respondent must be entitled to present a full defence and must be informed of the conduct complained of, the amount claimed and the alleged causal link between the two.
- Hearings should be measured in hours, not days or weeks

If the court does decide to disallow some costs or order the representative to meet some costs the court must set the amount or direct a costs judge or district judge to set the amount (CPR 46.8(3)). The court may also direct that notice of any proceedings for wasted costs and/or any order made in those proceedings is given to the legal representative's client (CPR 46.8(4)).

WASTED COSTS AND CPR 44.11

[23.3]

The Court of Appeal concluded that whilst there might be certain specific situations where the guidance from the 'wasted costs' jurisprudence is equally applicable under CPR 44.11, it is much less so when considering conduct in connection with the assessment of costs. In *GSD Law Ltd v Wardman* [2017] EWCA Civ 2144, the Court of Appeal, when determining whether to uphold a decision under CPR 44.11 to disallow the entirety of costs sought, concluded that:

> 'On the face of it, the rule [CPR 44.11] could, for example, be relied on in support of an application for a party's legal representative to pay costs which the representative had caused another party to incur (pursuant to CPR 44.11(2)(b)) on the strength of unreasonable or improper conduct on the part of the representative "before or during the proceedings" and in a context unrelated to the assessment of costs (within CPR 44.11(1)(b)). An application of that kind would be indistinguishable from (or at least resemble closely) one under the wasted costs jurisdiction and

the guidance given in *Ridehalgh v Horsefield* and *Medcalf v Mardell* would seem to be just as applicable as it would be to a conventional wasted costs application.

However, where (as in the present case) it is suggested that costs "which are being assessed" should be disallowed (under CPR 44.11(2)(a)) because of "unreasonable or improper" conduct in connection with the assessment of costs, it appears to me that the guidance found in *Ridehalgh v Horsefield* and *Medcalf v Mardell* is much less relevant.'

SATELLITE LITIGATION

[23.4]

As stated above the court must look to resolve wasted costs applications in the simplest way possible. This includes ensuring that claims do not become side tracked by tangential litigation. The Court of Appeal addressed this in *Ridehalgh v Horsefield*, where, it set aside wasted costs orders against two solicitors and a barrister and in the lead case declined to make an order in a case referred to it by a different division of the Court of Appeal. In delivering the judgment of the court, the Master of the Rolls said that while judges must not reject the weapon which Parliament intended to be used for the protection of those injured by the unjustifiable conduct of the other side's lawyers, they must be astute to control what threatened to become a new and costly form of satellite litigation.

Of course, this definition of purpose is too restrictive. There is nothing to stop parties seeking wasted costs order against their own representatives, as well as another party's representative, as the House of Lords concluded in *Medcalf v Mardell (Weatherill)* [2002] UKHL 27. However, this may cause difficulties with privilege (see below). In this case, Lord Bingham reiterated the concerns of the Court of Appeal, that wasted costs orders should be confined to questions which are apt for summary disposal by the court, such as failures to appear; conduct which leads to an otherwise avoidable step in the proceedings; the prolongation of a hearing by gross repetition or extreme slowness in the presentation of evidence or argument. Such matters can be dealt with summarily on agreed facts or after a brief inquiry. Any hearing to investigate the conduct of a complex action is itself likely to be expensive and time-consuming. Compensating litigating parties who have been put to unnecessary expense was only one of the public interests to be considered. The robust case management demanded of judges ought to limit the circumstances in which wasted costs may arise as far worse a fate awaits those failing to comply with court prescribed steps in any case.

In summary, anyone considering applying for a wasted costs order should think twice.

The Practice Direction supplementing CPR 46.8 largely embodies the major findings of the Court of Appeal in *Ridehalgh*. As wasted costs orders are made under the statute and, therefore CPR 46.8 and CPR PD 46, para 5 govern merely the practice and procedure, not the principles, this is an area in which decisions made prior to the introduction of the CPR are still of relevance and assistance. The decisions of whether to embark upon an inquiry into wasted costs and, if so, whether to make such an order, involve separate exercises of discretion (the two stage test). The consideration of the latter involves a separate consideration (the three stage test). We shall consider those in turn.

TWO STAGE DISCRETION

[23.5]

Jurisdiction to make an order for wasted costs depends upon the exercise of the court's discretion at two stages. These stages are set out at CPR PD 46, para 5.7.

First, when the initial application is made. The court should not embark on the process automatically. The court must be satisfied that it has before it the evidence or other material which, if unanswered, would be likely to lead to a wasted costs order being made. It is at this stage, where the conduct complained of arises on an interim application that it may be justifiable not to defer application or, indeed, determination, as the judge at that hearing is likely to be in the best position to decide this. The Court of Appeal has stated that this discretion must be exercised judicially, but judges might, not infrequently, decide that further proceedings were not justified (*Re Freudiana Holdings Ltd* (1995) Times, 4 December, CA).

Second, even if the court is satisfied that legal representatives had acted improperly, unreasonably or negligently so as to waste costs, the court is not bound to make an order, but has to give sustainable reasons for the exercise of its discretion in that way. The Court of Appeal has emphasised that judges should approach their task with caution and where possible consider the applicability of other sanctions of a disciplinary nature.

In *Kagalovsky v Balmore Invest Ltd* [2015] EWHC 1337 (QB), [2015] 3 Costs LR 531, the court noted that CPR PD 46, para 5.7 sets out the two-stage procedure as a 'general rule' and concluded that in a case such as that with which it was concerned and which was not straightforward 'it would be both wrong and artificial' for the court to ignore detailed submissions from the respondent to an application at the first stage. The application failed as the basis for the application was 'demonstrably unsuitable for summary determination'.

THE APPROPRIATE THREE STAGE TEST

[23.6]

If the court embarks on an inquiry, how does it exercise its discretion as to whether to make an order for wasted costs? Section 51(7) of the Senior Courts Act 1981 defines wasted costs as 'any costs incurred by a party - (a) as a result of any improper, unreasonable or negligent act or omission on the part of any legal or other representative or any employee of such a representative . . . .' This is repeated in CPR PD 46, para 5.5 which sets out the limited situation in which the court may make such an order. However, in addition, CPR PD 46, para 5.5 also provides that the court may only make a wasted costs order:

- if the legal representatives conduct has caused a party to incur unnecessary costs, or has meant that costs incurred by a party prior to the unreasonable or negligent act or omission have been wasted;
- if it is just in all the circumstances to order the legal representative to compensate that party for the whole or part of these costs.

A striking illustration of the three stage test in action and the residual breadth of the court's discretion is the case of *R (on the application of Hide) v Staffordshire County Council* [2007] EWHC 2441 (Admin). The claimant's solicitor had engaged in behaviour which could rightly be regarded as improper, unreasonable and/or negligent. The proceedings were completely unnecessary. They were doomed to failure and a reasonably competent solicitor should have known as much. Inevitably the other party had incurred wholly unnecessary costs. Nevertheless, the judge reached the conclusion that he should not make an order against the solicitor. The reason for that conclusion related to the difficult financial circumstances in which the solicitor found herself. The third stage of the test was engaged. In this case, the evidence was that an order for wasted costs would carry a significant risk of causing the solicitor to become bankrupt. That would be a disproportionate consequence of her unreasonable and negligent conduct in the litigation. On that discrete basis, a wasted costs order was not made.

Having looked at a practical example of the three stage test from *Ridehalgh* let us look at the component parts in more detail.

Stage 1 Improper, unreasonable or negligent conduct

[23.7]

The definitions of improper, unreasonable and negligent are as follows:

> ' "Improper" covers, but is not confined to, conduct which would ordinarily be held to justify disbarment, striking off, suspension from practice or other serious professional penalty. It also covers conduct which according to the consensus of professional, including judicial, opinion could be fairly stigmatised as being improper whether it violated the letter of a professional code or not. (Lord Bingham)
>
> "Unreasonable" includes conduct which is vexatious, designed to harass the other side rather than advance the resolution of the case and it makes no difference that the conduct is the product of excessive zeal and not improper motive. Legal representatives cannot lend assistance to proceedings which are an abuse of process and they are not entitled to use litigious procedures for purposes for which they are not intended, as by issuing or pursuing proceedings for purposes unconnected with success in the litigation or pursuing a case known to be dishonest nor are they entitled to evade rules intended to safeguard the interests of justice, such as by knowingly failing to make full disclosure on an not on notice application or knowingly conniving with incomplete disclosure of documents. However, conduct is not unreasonable simply because it leads to an unsuccessful result or because other more cautious legal representatives would have acted differently. The acid test is whether the conduct permitted of a reasonable explanation. It is not unreasonable to be optimistic. (Lord Bingham)
>
> "Negligent" does not mean conduct which is actionable as a breach of the legal representative's duty to his own client. There is of course no duty of care to the other party. Negligence should be understood in an untechnical way to denote failure to act with the competence reasonably expected of ordinary members of the profession. However, the court firmly discountenanced any suggestion that an applicant for a

wasted costs order needed to prove under the negligence head anything less than he would have had to prove in an action for negligence (Lord Bingham).'

The court adopted the test in *Ali (Saif) v Sydney Mitchell & Co (a firm)* [1980] AC 198, [1978] 3 All ER 1033, HL: 'advice, acts or omissions in the course of their professional work which no member of the profession who is reasonably well-informed and competent would have given or done or omitted to do'; an error 'such as no reasonably well-informed and competent member of that profession could have made'. This approach was confirmed in *KOO Golden East Mongolia v Bank of Nova Scotia* [2008] EWHC 1120 (Admin), where the defendant bank claimed a wasted costs order against the solicitors who had acted for the unsuccessful claimant on the basis that the solicitors' conduct was persistently negligent and unreasonable in making and continuing to have the Central Bank of Mongolia as a party to the action because the solicitors should have appreciated that the bank was immune from suit because of the provisions of the State Immunity Act 1978. In dismissing the claim the court gave the following reasons:

- a bill of costs should have been served before making the application;
- the claimant should have been given a proper opportunity to pay the costs;
- the absence of an application to strike out the claim was hardly consistent with the submission that it was misconceived;
- the suggestion that 'no reasonable solicitor could have been optimistic' was well below the threshold for sufficient negligence or unreasonableness to justify a wasted costs order;
- even a binding authority fatal, or almost fatal, to the client's case might not justify a wasted costs order.

Stage 2 Causation

[23.8]

The causal link must be established by the applicant and failure to do so will result in no award being made. This rarely presents a problem. The misconduct required to satisfy the first stage is such that it almost inevitably has caused unnecessary costs. As most applications for wasted costs are made by the other party there is no difficulty with problems of privilege (to which we shall return below) that would prevent that party evidencing the loss alleged to have been caused. However, the court has been clear that the burden is on the party seeking a wasted costs order. The alleged conduct must, lead to identifiable wasted costs. In *Brown v Bennett (Wasted Costs) (No 1)* [2002] 1 WLR 713, the defendant contended that the court must be satisfied that there was a real prospect that the applicant would not have incurred all the costs that he did incur if the lawyers had not acted and advised as they did, and if the court were not so satisfied any uncertainty would have to be taken into account when assessing the level of costs or order against the lawyers. The court held that although there was a powerful argument in logic for awarding only a proportion of the total costs on the 'loss of chance' basis, this was not the appropriate approach to take. The court should ask itself whether, on the balance of probabilities, the applicant would have incurred the costs claimed from the lawyers if they had not acted or advised as they did.

It is clear that the party seeking a wasted costs order must identify to the court the specific loss caused. In *Nwoko v OYO State Government of Nigeria* [2014] EWHC 4538 (QB) the applicant produced a statement of costs which did not provide the detail necessary to identify the specific wasted costs in issue. Instead the applicant had assumed that the court would simply undertake a 'broad brush' approach. The court concluded that it was incumbent on the applicant to provide the court with evidence of the costs incurred as a result of the specific conduct relied upon to found the application.

Stage 3 It is just in all the circumstances to make an order

[23.9]

This is one of the two entirely discretionary elements of the process (the other being at the outset as to whether to embark on the wasted costs proceedings): see above 'two stage discretion'.

PROBLEMS WITH PRIVILEGE

[23.10]

As we have already noted in *Medcalf v Mardell (Weatherill)* [2002] UKHL 27, the House of Lords rejected the argument that s 51 conferred no right on a party to seek a wasted costs order against any legal representative other than his own. It did, however, hold that in these circumstances if the party for whom the legal representative was acting refused to waive legal privilege, thereby preventing the practitioner from telling the whole story, the court should not make a wasted costs order unless (a) satisfied there is nothing the practitioner could say, if unconstrained, to resist the order and (b) in all the circumstances it is fair to make the order. However, it was held in *Brown v Bennett* that it was permissible for the respondent barristers to be asked whether they saw or knew of non-privileged documents, provided that the purpose of the question was not to discover what was in the barristers' briefs or instructions, even though answering the question might reveal the contents of the instructions or brief. That distinction might appear to be a very narrow and technical one. However, it was self-evident that it would be quite impermissible for the barristers to answer the question if the purpose of putting the question was to find out if a particular document was in the instructions, even if the document was open. But, it was by no means self-evident that if the purpose of asking the question was solely to discover whether the document was seen by or known to counsel that the question should not be answered. The question was permissible even if it happened to reveal that open documents, as opposed to privileged documents, were included in counsels' briefs or instructions, provided that no prejudice was thereby caused to the client.

In *Dempsey v Johnstone* [2003] EWCA Civ 1134 (see below under 'Some unsuccessful cases – negligence'), the claimant was a publicly funded bankrupt whose claim was dismissed at trial on the ground that he had no arguable prospect of success. The defendant sought and obtained a wasted costs order against the claimant's solicitors on the ground that no reasonably competent legal representative would have continued with the action. The Court of Appeal held that the court had applied the right test but had come to the wrong conclusion because it took the view that the facts pleaded could not support the claim made as a matter of law. The Court of Appeal disagreed. The statement of claim settled by leading counsel was capable of supporting the claim: it was a matter for evidence. In determining that question, the court could only come to a conclusion adverse to the solicitors if it had the opportunity of seeing counsel's advice which was privileged. In the absence of waiver of privilege, it could not be inferred that the evaluation of the claim was negligent in the relevant sense within s 51 of the Senior Courts Act 1981.

THREATENING AN APPLICATION OR PUTTING THE OTHER SIDE ON NOTICE?

[23.11]

The threat of a wasted costs order should not be used as a means of intimidation. However, if one side considers that the conduct of the other has been improper, unreasonable or negligent and likely to cause a waste of costs it is not objectionable to notify the other side to that view. Whether the court views something as a threat or a notification will only become apparent if an application ensues.

WASTED COSTS AND PUBLIC FUNDING

[23.12]

It is incumbent on courts to bear in mind the peculiar vulnerability of legal representatives acting for assisted persons. It would subvert the benevolent purposes of state funding legislation if such representatives are subject to any unusual personal risk and their advice and conduct is not to be tempered by the knowledge that their client is not their paymaster and so not, in all probability, liable for the costs of the other side.

WASTED COSTS AND ADVOCACY

[23.13]

Although the legislation encroaches upon the traditional immunity of advocates by subjecting them to the wasted costs jurisdiction, full allowance must be made for the fact that an advocate in court often has to make decisions quickly and under pressure. Mistakes will, inevitably, be made and things done which the outcome may show with hindsight to have been unwise. Advocacy is more an art than a science: it cannot be conducted according to formulae. It is only when, with all allowances made, an advocate's conduct of court proceedings is quite plainly unjustifiable that it is appropriate to make a wasted costs order.

The question of an advocate's immunity from suit generally was re-visited by the House of Lords in *Arthur JS Hall & Co (a firm) v Simons* [2002] 1 AC 615, HL when it was decided that advocates no longer enjoy immunity from suit in respect of their conduct of civil and criminal proceedings.

WASTED COSTS WHERE THE SOLICITOR PLACES RELIANCE ON COUNSEL

[23.14]

To what extent is a solicitor able to avoid a wasted costs order by pointing to reliance on counsel? Case law seems clear. A solicitor plainly cannot delegate or abrogate professional responsibility simply by seeking the assistance of counsel. The solicitor must supply counsel with appropriate papers and consider the advice received. However, the more specialist the nature of the advice the more reasonable it is likely to be for the solicitor to accept it. In more specific instances the court has supplied a number of answers to the question, some more encouraging to solicitors than others.

The low watermark was *Davy-Chiesman v Davy-Chiesman* [1984] Fam 48, CA, Counsel had advised in writing that the husband should not seek a lump sum payment from his wife payable directly to him as otherwise it would be taken immediately by his trustee in bankruptcy. At a subsequent conference, counsel advised that the husband should seek a lump sum payable to him direct and abandon all his other claims. The court concluded that it ought to have been glaringly apparent to any reasonable solicitor that the only form of relief for which counsel was going to ask fell foul of the fundamental requirement that because of the bankruptcy any capital sum should not go direct to the husband. The duty the solicitor owed to inform the legal aid fund of any change of circumstances was not just to pass on any views expressed by counsel but to consider the effect of any change of circumstances. The solicitor was at that stage guilty of 'a serious dereliction of duty' or 'serious misconduct' and it was not sufficient absolution simply to act in accordance with the advice of counsel. The court acknowledged that in many circumstances a solicitor is protected from personal liability if acting on the advice of experienced counsel properly instructed. However, the protection to the solicitor is not automatically total. A solicitor is highly-trained and expected to be experienced in the particular area of law and accordingly did not and could not abdicate all responsibility by instructing counsel. In this case, the court concluded that the solicitor had entirely subordinated personal skill and ability to the dominant and forceful personality of counsel. As a result, The Law Society's application that the solicitor should pay both the husband's and wife's costs personally was allowed.

By way of contrast is the case of *R v Oxfordshire County Council, ex p Wallace* [1987] NLJ Rep 542, QBD. The applicant commenced judicial review proceedings against the local education authority and the local health authority. On the first day of the hearing, the applicant was given leave to discontinue the proceedings against the health authority who at the end of the hearing applied for an order for their costs to be paid personally by the applicant's solicitors.

Counsel for the health authority argued that counsel's advice that the health authority should be joined as a party was based quite clearly on an inaccurate statement of the statutory position and the advice that the decision of the health authority had been perverse was patently wrong, or ought to have been recognised as such by anyone with experience in this field, such as the applicant's solicitors. The solicitors should have realised that there was not an arguable case for judicial review against the health authority and so they should be personally liable for costs in spite of the advice of counsel. The solicitors argued that they had obtained counsel's specific advice and it was clear and unequivocal on the merits.

It was held that the case could be distinguished on its facts from *Davy-Chiesman*. In that case, counsel propounded a claim which on earlier advised was bound to fail, as the solicitors in the case knew, and it was not the one for which, on that advice, the client had been granted legal aid. In *R v Oxfordshire County Council*, counsel had been asked to advise specifically against whom the proceedings should begin and the form they should take. A mere mistake or error of judgment is insufficient to attract liability of a solicitor for the costs of the other parties, for which purpose it was necessary to establish gross or serious negligence. Accordingly, an order for costs on behalf of the health authority against the solicitors was refused.

In *Locke v Camberwell Health Authority* [1991] 2 Med LR 249, CA, it was held at first instance that the failure of a solicitor to ensure that pertinent information was before counsel advising on the merits in a negligence action constituted a gross dereliction of the solicitor's duty as an officer of the court and created a liability for the defendant's costs, thrown away. In advising on the merits, counsel did not have photocopies of the hospital notes, which there was a duty to request and which the solicitor had a duty to supply, and as a result the advice was short and inadequate. However, when it was established on appeal that the defendant had not in fact disclosed the relevant hospital notes, counsel and the solicitors were exonerated and the order set aside. The court concluded that, as a general rule, a solicitor should be entitled to rely upon the advice of counsel properly instructed, but must not do so blindly and must still exercise independent judgment.

However, the pendulum swung back again in *Count Tolstoy-Miloslavsky v Lord Aldington* [1996] 2 All ER 556, (CA) (after the decision in *Ridehalgh*), where the Court of Appeal, in upholding an order that Count Tolstoy should pay 60% of Lord Aldington's costs of an action brought by Count Tolstoy to set aside on the grounds of fraud the monumental libel damages awarded against him, said that:

> '. . . although the solicitors relied on fully instructed and very experienced, respected leading counsel who put his name to a statement of claim . . . counsel having extensive knowledge of the background of the case . . . this does not absolve the solicitors exercising their independent judgment nor allow them to close their eyes to the blindingly obvious . . .'.

This notwithstanding that the document the solicitors were expected to have prevented had been signed by both leading and junior counsel. It would seem that independent and courageous judgment is required.

WASTED COSTS AGAINST A BARRISTER IN RESPECT OF ADVICE GIVEN

[23.15]

In *Brown v Bennett* and *Medcalf v Mardell* (both above), it was submitted that a wasted costs order could only be made against barristers by virtue of their conduct when actually exercising a right of audience, in other words, when actually conducting a case in court. The basis for this argument was that a wasted costs order could only be made as a result of inappropriate conduct on the part of any 'legal or other representative' which s 51(13) limited to 'any person exercising a right of audience or right to conduct litigation'. As barristers, unlike solicitors, did not 'conduct litigation' they could only be liable when they were exercising a right of audience. Rejecting this argument, the court held that although it was true that the concept of conducting litigation would in many circumstances be understood to involve the traditional litigation activities of solicitors, 'a right to conduct litigation' was not defined in the Act and it was quite permissible to give that expression a meaning which was less technical and more vernacular. There was no reason why it should not extend to activities such as drafting or settling of documents and advising on prospects or procedure (in other words undertaking tasks that someone conducting litigation would ordinarily do). This carries a greater significance with the increasing use of 'direct access' to the Bar and the entitlement of suitably authorised barristers to conduct litigation.

SOME SUCCESSFUL APPLICATIONS

[23.16]

Successful examples we have already considered are the decisions in *Davy-Chiesman* and *Tolstoy-Miloslavsky v Aldington*. Here are a few others to give a flavour of how the court exercises its discretion.

Re a Company (006798 of 1995) [1996] 2 All ER 417, ChD

[23.17]

A solicitor swore an affidavit in support of a winding-up petition, asserting on oath a belief that a company was insolvent on the ground that a debt was owing and that the company was unable to pay its debts as they fell due. There were in fact no grounds upon which a competent solicitor could have reached that view on the material available to him and he was ordered to pay the costs of the company personally.

General Mediterranean Holdings SA v Patel [1999] 3 All ER 673, QBD (Comm Ct)

[23.18]

The defendants denied an allegation of fraud until shortly before the trial when they admitted it. The action was compromised on terms that there be no order for costs, but the claimant obtained a wasted costs order against the defendants' solicitor on the ground that the solicitor knew the defendants had admitted the existence of the fraud in other proceedings.

Thames Chambers Solicitors v Azad Miah [2013] EWHC 1245 (QB)

[23.19]

The solicitors against whom a wasted costs order was made had represented a client in debt recovery proceedings. They had known on receipt of instructions that their client was bankrupt and had been put on notice that they needed to obtain the trustee in bankruptcy's consent to continuation of the proceedings and failed to do so. The claim was struck out. The court was satisfied that the three stage test was satisfied.

A successful application in family proceedings

[23.20]

In *HU v SU* [2015] EWFC 535 the court concluded that the failure of one party's solicitors to seek permission of the court to extend the time for compliance with directions was both improper and unreasonable conduct and caused the other party to incur unnecessary costs and it was just to order them to pay the costs of an additional directions hearing. See Chapter 39 – Family Proceedings, generally for further consideration.

SOME UNSUCCESSFUL APPLICATIONS

[23.21]

To balance the consideration, a few examples of cases where the court declined to make a wasted costs order. There are more examples of these as they are more informative of the approach that the court takes.

(i) Problems with public funding

Trill v Sacher (No 2) [1992] 40 LS Gaz R 32, CA

[23.22]

Where a statement of claim was struck out for want of prosecution the defendants sought wasted costs orders against the solicitors for the legally – aided claimant. The solicitors' explanation for the delay related to the difficulties experienced in complicated cases such as the present, where the claimant had only a limited legal aid certificate. The solicitors' hands were tied in dealing with the Legal Aid authorities. The slow action by the authorities and by counsel in preparing written opinions had contributed to the delay. An order for wasted costs was set aside.

Re a Solicitor (wasted costs order) [1993] 2 FLR 959, CA

[23.23]

In this case a solicitor who was having difficulty resolving the position regarding the client's Legal Aid certificate had not sought an adjournment until the day before the fixed hearing date, causing expense to the other side and to its witnesses. The failure to warn the court or opponent in sufficient time was an error of judgment. However, the material now available showed that the Law Society accepted that the solicitor had found himself in an extremely difficult position. It would not be right to go further than to say the solicitor had been guilty of an error of judgment: it was not an instance of acting in dereliction of duty. A wasted costs order was not warranted.

The weight to be attached to these cases has been tempered only slightly by the decision in *Holden & Co LLP v Eastbourne Borough Council* 26th March 2014 (QBD), in which the Legal Aid Agency placed an embargo on work under the certificate pending further information. The embargo was lifted a few days before the appeal. The solicitors wrote to the court the day before the appeal stating that they had insufficient time to prepare, would not be attending and would agree to any adjournment. An adjournment was granted. However, a wasted costs order in respect of the other party's counsel's fee was made. This was on the basis that the solicitors should have written earlier (when the hearing might have been avoided) and that they still ought to have undertaken work at modest cost to themselves during the embargo. It is the latter, rather than the former, reason that qualifies the previous two cases somewhat.

(ii) Unrealistic time estimates

Re a Barrister (wasted costs order No 4 of 1993) (1995) Times, 21 April, CA

[23.24]

It is important for judges considering making a wasted costs order, which is a draconian order, to remember that they are removed from the daily demands of practice and to make allowance for difficulties with time estimates. The appellant had accepted a brief for a two-day trial listed at Derby Crown Court immediately prior to appearing in another trial at Nottingham Crown Court. The first trial was late starting and progressed more slowly than anticipated. In granting an adjournment of the second trial due to the unavailability of the barrister, the judge ordered the barrister to pay the consequential wasted costs. In quashing the order, the court said that although the barrister had been over-optimistic in failing to anticipate delays in the first trial, the conduct could not be described as unreasonable.

(iii) Cost benefit analysis

Turner Page Music v Torres Design Associates Ltd (1998) Times, 3 August, CA

[23.25]

The ability of the court to make a wasted costs order can have advantages, but it will be of no advantage if it is going to result in complex proceedings which involve detailed investigation of fact. If the situation involves detailed investigation of fact and indeed allegations of dishonesty then it may well be that the wasted costs procedure is largely inappropriate to cover the situation, save in what would be an exceptional case. If the situation involved breach of a solicitor's professional duty to a client that too might make it unsuited to a summary procedure. The claimant's application for a wasted costs order against the defendant's solicitors was dismissed.

(iv) Oral application or Part 23 application supported by evidence?

Regent Leisuretime Ltd v Skerrett [2006] EWCA Civ 1032

[23.26]

Although an oral application in the course of a hearing is possible pursuant to CPR PD 46, para 5.4(b), that is only likely to be sensible if the scope of the application in relation to the costs said to have been wasted is narrow and clear; for example, if an adjournment is necessary because of a solicitor's or counsel's conduct, as regards the costs thrown away by the adjournment. In this case the scope and nature of the costs claimed was wholly unclear at the time of the hearing before the judge and the Court of Appeal held that as a result the court should neither have allowed the application to be made orally nor even considered it at that stage. Instead it should have told the defendant litigants in person that if they wanted to apply for costs they should issue a Part 23 application notice supported by any evidence as required by CPR PD 46, para 5.9. There could have then have been either a first stage hearing or, if CPR PD 46, para 5.8 was satisfied, a hearing at which the first stage and, if relevant, the second stage were both considered.

(v) Negligence

Dempsey v Johnstone (above under 'Problems with privilege': [23.10]*)*

[23.27]

In this case the Court of Appeal reviewed authorities after *Ridehalgh* and concluded that the meaning of 'negligence' had not been modified as had been suggested in *Persaud v Persaud* [2003] EWCA Civ 394, where Peter Gibson LJ had suggested that something more than *'negligence'* was required: something akin to 'abuse of process'. Instead, the Court of Appeal concluded that where it is alleged that a legal representative has pursued a hopeless case, the question is whether no reasonably competent legal representative would have continued with the action. Latham LJ stated 'that negligence could be the appropriate word to describe a situation in which it is abundantly plain that the legal representative has failed to appreciate that there is a binding authority fatal to his client's case'. In this case in the absence of seeing counsel's advice, which was privileged, it could not be inferred that the evaluation of the claim was negligent in the relevant sense within s 51 of the Senior Courts Act 1981.

(vi) Causation of loss

Byrne v South Sefton (Merseyside) Health Authority [2001] EWCA Civ 1904

[23.28]

In *Byrne v South Sefton (Merseyside) Health Authority* [2001] EWCA Civ 1904, the solicitors had acted for the claimant in connection with allegations of clinical negligence by the defendant, but ceased to act for the claimant before he instructed other solicitors, who commenced proceedings. When the action was dismissed as out of time, the defendant applied for a wasted costs order against the previous solicitors on the grounds that its costs had been incurred as a result of the solicitors' failure to bring proceedings within the limitation period. Section 51(6) of the Senior Courts Act 1981 empowers costs to be awarded against 'a legal or other representative', while s 51(13) defines a legal or other representative as a person who has issued proceedings, exercised rights of audience or performed ancillary functions in relation to the conduct of litigation. The defendant's case against the solicitors rested on the very opposite, namely the fact that they had failed to do any of these things. Furthermore, there was no causative link between the conduct of these solicitors and the costs incurred by the defendant. The defendant's costs had not been incurred by the claimant's previous solicitors' failure to act, but by the claimant's current solicitors' decision to bring an action outside the limitation period.

The importance of a party seeking a wasted costs order, providing sufficient evidence in respect of the causation of loss was reiterated in *Re Bin Issa Al-Jaber Safiti* (19 December 2019, unreported) (Ch D).

(vii) Wasted costs and a legal representative's duty to the court

B v Pendlebury [2002] EWHC 1797

[23.29]

On an application for wasted costs in a case in which there has been no adjudication of the primary facts, the court should be reluctant to enquire into a state of affairs in which it has no solid foundation from which the process of analysis essential to the wasted costs procedure can proceed. The process and procedure envisaged in the Practice Direction is not readily to be equated with what was involved on a trial of issues. The phrases 'simple and summary as the circumstances will permit' (CPR PD 46, para 5.6) and 'after giving the legal representative an opportunity to give reasons' (now 'make representations') did not lend themselves as appropriate to a disputed trial involving consideration and resolution *of complex* and disputed evidence. The court found it to be axiomatic that a solicitor is bound by the instructions of the client. The solicitor is not obliged to act as a filter between the instructions provided by the client and the opposing party.

Quite simply, a solicitor owes no duty to the opposing party, but does, of course, owe such a duty to the court: *Orchard v South Eastern Electricity Board* [1987] QB 565, CA.

This duty to the court was confirmed in *Hallam-Peel & Co v Southwark London Borough Council* [2008] EWCA Civ 1120. A firm of solicitors had not acted unreasonably in raising a new point in possession proceedings, which led to further adjournments and its conduct did not involve a breach of duty to the court. Accordingly, a wasted cost order should not have been made against them and their appeal was allowed.

In *Persaud v Persaud* (above) the court explained that its jurisdiction to make a wasted costs order against a solicitor is founded on breach of the duty owed by the solicitor to the court to perform the duty as an officer of the court.

There is no doubt that the jurisdiction under s 51 of the Senior Courts Act 1981 to make a wasted costs order has now been extended to barristers, but before a wasted costs order can be made against a member of the Bar there must have been a breach of duty to the court by the barrister. It is not enough that the court considers the advocate has been arguing a hopeless case. The litigant is entitled to be heard; to penalise the advocate for presenting the client's case to the court would be contrary to constitutional principles. The position is different if the court concludes that there has been improper time-wasting by advocates or that advocates have knowingly lent themselves to an abuse of process. However, it is relevant to bear in mind that, if a party is raising issues or is taking steps which have no reasonable prospects of success or are scandalous or an abuse of process, both the aggrieved party and the court have powers to remedy the situation by invoking summary remedies – striking out, summary judgment, other peremptory orders etc. The making of a wasted costs order should not be a primary remedy; by definition, it only arises once the damage has been done. It is a procedure of last resort. There must be something more than negligence for the wasted costs jurisdiction to arise; there must be something akin to an abuse of process if the conduct of the legal representative is to create a liability under a wasted costs order. In the present case the conduct of counsel did not involve any breach of duty to the court, nor was there an abuse of process.

(viii) Disclosure

CMCS Common Market Commercial Services AVV v Taylor [2011] EWHC 324 (Ch)

[23.30]

There is no difference in principle between the ambit of a solicitor's duty in the conduct and supervision of disclosure and the conduct and supervision of redaction of disclosable documents before they are offered for inspection. The wasted costs jurisdiction is compensatory rather than punitive in nature and an applicant is required to establish that it would not have incurred the additional costs if the alleged breach of duty had not occurred. The reality in this case was that the redactions made had cried out for challenge, which was eventually successfully mounted. Had the solicitor made the more complete disclosure incumbent, it would have marginally increased the already strong prospects of a successful challenge but would not have led to a challenge being made earlier than it was. It was the client's decision not to comply with an 'unless order' that caused, or at least contributed to, the decision to abandon the defence and the client had been debarred by then from defending the claim. It had not been shown that the breach of duty had caused any wasted costs.

(ix) Earlier remedy

[23.31]

In *CMCS* and *Koo Golden East Mongolia (A Body Corporate) v (1) Bank Of Nova Scotia (2) Scotia Capital (Europe) Ltd (3) Central Bank Of Mongolia (t/a Mongolbank)* (both above) the court stressed that instead of waiting and applying retrospectively for a wasted costs order, the aggrieved party should make a prospective application – whether it be for an 'unless order' or to strike out – highlighting in CMCS that the particular abuse was one which was always within the ability of the other party to bring to an end by an appropriate application for a strike out or debarring order. Even if a solicitor's conduct did improperly enable the client to continue his claim unreasonably, it would still be a difficult and finely balanced question whether a wasted costs order was appropriate. Where there was an available remedy against the abusive party, the wasted costs jurisdiction was to be treated as a last resort.

(x) Wasted costs and family proceedings

[23.32]

See Chapter 39 – Family Proceedings, generally for further consideration.

(xi) Appeals

[23.33]

Appeals against wasted costs orders or the failure to make them are possible.

However, that does not mean that such appeals have been encouraged. There have been numerous cautionary statements warning against appeals from judges who have refused to make a wasted costs order. The Court of Appeal stressed in *Persaud* (above), that it will only be in a very rare case that it will interfere with the decision by the judge as to whether to make a wasted costs order. The rationale for this is that the judge who has conducted the trial will be fully aware of the conduct of legal representatives in the case.

Wall v Lefever [1998] FCR 605, CA

[23.34]

The wasted costs provisions of s 51 involve the tension between two important public interests. First, lawyers should not be deterred from pursing their clients' interests by fear of incurring a personal liability to their clients' opponents and second litigants should not be financially prejudiced by the unjustifiable conduct of litigation by their or their opponents' lawyers. Before launching an appeal against a refusal to make a wasted costs order by a judge at first instance who had heard the evidence, parties should exercise great care. If the judge concluded that the conduct complained of had not fallen within that prescribed by s 51, an appeal was only justified if some point of principle indicated that the judge's approach had been wholly wrong. Unsurprisingly, given the court used this case to reinforce this message, the Court of Appeal did not find that the judge had been 'wholly wrong'.

WASTED COSTS AND QUALIFIED ONE-WAY COSTS SHIFTING

[23.35]

As the qualified one-way costs shifting ('QOCS') provisions only serve to protect a claimant as defined by CPR 44.13(2) from enforcement of costs orders, it is clear that this regime has no relevance to either the making or the enforcement of an order for wasted costs against a claimant's representative.

WASTED COSTS AND UNREASONABLE BEHAVIOUR IN SMALL CLAIMS

[23.36]

In *Dammermann v Lanyon Bowdler* [2017] EWCA Civ 269, the Court of Appeal adopted the wasted costs jurisdiction when seeking to provide guidance on when a court might conclude that a costs award was justified in the small claims track pursuant to CPR 27.14(2)(g) – namely where there has been unreasonable behaviour. The court concluded that the test in *Ridehalgh* should be cross applied – whether the conduct permitted of a reasonable explanation.

In passing, we note that in his Fixed Recoverable Costs Review, Sir Rupert Jackson has suggested that the same test is applied to a determination of whether litigation conduct is such that it justifies a departure from the prescribed fixed fees.

CONCLUSION TO WASTED COSTS ORDERS

[23.37]

The best summary of the wasted costs jurisdiction is that set out in *Gray v Going Places Leisure Travel Ltd* [2005] EWCA Civ 189 where the Court of Appeal considered the link between the award of costs and the wasted costs process as follows:

- The making of an order as to who should bear the costs and on what basis, in respect of proceedings which go to trial, is, in principle, part of the overriding order made by the court at the conclusion of the trial.
- In the absence of at least a good reason to the contrary, the costs of proceedings should be dealt with by the tribunal which determines the issue which disposes of the case immediately after the judgment disposing of the case
- In principle there is no difference between a costs order against a party and a costs order against a non-party, they are all part of the judicial function involved in disposing of a case
- It is not mandatory that the application for wasted costs be made at the end of the trial. In many cases a party considering an application for a wasted costs order will ask the judge for time to consider whether to make such an application and, even if such an application is made, the normal course is for the court to give directions in relation to the disposal of the application rather than to deal with it straightaway.

- The application for a wasted costs order can be made after the order in relation to the proceedings has been drawn up, although, in the absence of good reason for the delay the court hearing the late application will not necessarily grant it.

CHAPTER 24

THE BASES OF COSTS

INTRODUCTION TO THE BASES OF COSTS

[24.1]

When the court is to assess the amount of costs it must do so on either the 'standard' or 'indemnity' basis (CPR 44.3(1)). CPR 44.3(4) provides that where an order for costs to be assessed is silent or, and sadly this does still happen, the court makes an order for assessment other than on the standard or indemnity basis, then the costs will be assessed on the standard basis. As a result of this most orders are actually silent on the basis, which means standard basis assessment.

The relevance of the different bases

[24.2]

Both bases will not allow costs unreasonably incurred and of an unreasonable amount. Prior to the CPR the only difference between the two bases was in respect of the burden of proof of reasonableness. On the standard basis any doubt as to reasonableness is to be resolved in favour of the paying party, while on the indemnity basis any doubt is to be resolved in favour of the receiving party. As former Chief Taxing Master Matthews succinctly put it: 'If there is no doubt, there is no difference'.

The CPR introduced a further distinction between the bases – the concept of proportionality. The effect of this distinction became more marked following the 2013 CPR amendments, and the elevated importance given to proportionality (see Chapter 14 – Prospective Costs Control – Proportionality). Remember that from April 2016 for any claims that involve consideration of both relevant proportionality tests, CPR PD 47, para 5.8(7) requires the bill for a detailed assessment to be divided into parts to distinguish between them. Given that we are almost eight years on from the changed approach to proportionality, we shall focus on the current regime. Detail on the distinction between the bases of costs prior to April 2013 can be found in the 2020 Edition of this text.

The effect of the distinction between an order for standard or indemnity basis on the assessment of costs

[24.3]

CPR 44.3(2)(a) contains this pithy provision:

> 'Where the amount of costs is to assessed on the standard basis, the court will –
>
> (a) only allow costs which are proportionate to the matters in issue. Costs which are disproportionate in amount may be disallowed or reduced even if they were reasonably or necessarily incurred . . . '

Pithy it may be, but of quite extraordinary potency. This means that on a standard basis assessment a costs judge/officer can undertake the assessment allowing what is reasonably incurred and reasonable in amount, add up the total allowed and then determine by reference to the new proportionality test at CPR 44.3(5) that this still leaves a figure that is disproportionate and reduce still further adopting the approach set out in *West v Stockport NHS Foundation Trust* [2019] EWCA Civ 1220 until satisfied that the figure is proportionate. (See Chapter 14 Prospective Costs Control – Proportionality, above)

In contrast there is no test of proportionality on the indemnity basis. As the new approach to proportionality is commonly accepted as seeing costs reduced on the standard basis to lower levels than under the previous provisions, then the benefit of an indemnity basis assessment increases.

Costs bases and budgets

[24.4]

In those cases in which a costs management order has been made by the court, then on a standard basis assessment in respect of budgeted costs, CPR 3.18 requires the court to have regard to the last approved or agreed budget and not to depart from it unless there is good reason to do so. There is no such constraint on an indemnity basis assessment. The costs management order does not impact on an indemnity basis assessment of the costs, confirmed most recently in *Lejonvarn v Burgess* [2020] EWCA CIV 114:

> 'In principle, the assessment of costs on an indemnity basis is not constrained by the approved cost budget . . . ' Coulson LJ, para 93

(See Chapter 15, para **[15.12]** above.)

Conclusion

[24.5]

For the reasons we have set out above, the difference between the amount assessed on a standard and indemnity basis assessment may now be sizeable. Proportionality lay at the heart of the 2013 reforms. An indemnity costs order bypasses the assessment of costs by reference to this and permits escape from any budget set (subject to the indemnity principle, of course). There may be more than a few percentage points difference in outcome. This provides a powerful incentive to pursue indemnity basis costs orders.

THE INDEMNITY BASIS – WHEN IS IT APPROPRIATE?

Introduction

[24.6]

With the exception of CPR Part 36, which specifically provides for an order for costs on the indemnity basis in a defined situation (CPR 36.17(4)(b) – see Chapter 20 above and **[24.23]** below) and costs under a contract where that contract specifically adopts wording equating to costs on an indemnity basis, indemnity costs can only be awarded by the court exercising its discretion under CPR 44.2. It does so by reference to the overriding objective and the factors that it is obliged to consider when deciding what order to make about costs (CPR 44.2(4) and CPR 44.2(5)). A useful reminder of this approach can be found in *Two Right Feet Ltd (in liq) v National Westminster Bank plc* [2017] EWHC 1745 (Ch).

Indemnity costs under a contract

[24.7]

In *Littlestone v Macleish* [2016] EWCA Civ 127, the court decided that a contractual provision that the lessee should pay 'all costs and expenses . . . which may be incurred' corresponded more closely with an order for costs on the indemnity, rather than the standard, basis, reminding itself that CPR 44.5(1) provides that where costs are paid under the terms of the contract, then unless the contract provides otherwise, those costs are presumed to be costs which have been reasonably incurred and are reasonable in amount.

Littlestone was considered and followed in *Alafco Irish Aircraft Leasing Sixteen Ltd v Hong Kong Airlines Ltd* [2019] EWHC 3668 (Comm). In this case, the court decided that a contractual term that the tenant should pay the landlord's 'reasonable costs and expenses' entitled the landlord to an order for indemnity costs.

How does the court exercise its discretion in cases where neither CPR 36.17(4)(b) nor a contractual entitlement to indemnity costs arises?

[24.8]

The discretion to make such an order is wide, indeed so wide that the Court of Appeal has shied away from setting a prescriptive list of circumstances where such an order would be appropriate. In *Excelsior Commercial & Industrial Holdings Ltd v Salisbury Hamer Aspden & Johnston (Costs)* [2002] EWCA Civ 879 Lord Woolf explained why guidance was of limited assistance:

> 'In my judgment it is dangerous for the court to try and add to the requirements of the CPR which are not spelt out in the relevant parts of the CPR. This court can do no more than draw attention to the width of the discretion of the trial judge and re-emphasise the point that has already been made that, before an indemnity order can be made, there must be some conduct or some circumstance which takes the case out of the norm.'

This approach has recently been affirmed by the Court of Appeal in *Blueco LTD v BWAT Retail Nominee* [2014] EWCA Civ 154, where the first instance decision that allegations of dishonesty took the case 'out of the ordinary', justified an award of indemnity costs. While the *Excelsior* comments were adopted by Coulson J in *Noorani v Calver* [2009] EWHC 592 (QB), he went a stage further extracting from the authorities to summarise the position as follows:

> 'Indemnity costs are no longer limited to cases where the court wishes to express disapproval of the way in which litigation has been conducted. An order for

> indemnity costs can be made even when the conduct could not properly be regarded as lacking in moral probity or deserving of moral condemnation. However, such conduct must be unreasonable "to a high degree". "Unreasonable" in this context does not mean merely wrong or misguided in hindsight.'

Coulson J then confirmed why specific guidance in this area is so difficult, saying:

> 'In any dispute about the appropriate basis for the assessment of costs, the court must consider each case on its own facts . . . '

The reference to unreasonableness is important. The Court of Appeal returned to this theme in *Whaleys (Bradford) Ltd v Bennett* [2017] EWCA Civ 2143. Whilst reaffirming the *Excelsior* approach and with Richards LJ cautioning against the use of 'exceptionality' as an articulation of the test (as it suggests a stricter test and is too reliant on context), the Court of Appeal stated that 'the norm' is not intended to be a question of the frequency with which something occurs, but, instead, is a reference to whether something is outside the ordinary and reasonable conduct of proceedings.

However, it should be remembered that in *Excelsior Commercial & Industrial Holdings Ltd v Salisbury Hamer Aspden & Johnson* (see above), Lord Woolf was at pains to stress that 'an indemnity costs order may be justified not only because of the conduct of the parties, but also because of other particular circumstances of the litigation'. This followed on the heels of the case of *Reid Minty (a firm) v Taylor* [2001] EWCA Civ 1723, in which the Court of Appeal determined that a party can be ordered to pay costs on the indemnity basis under CPR 44.2 even though there has been no moral lack of probity or conduct deserving of moral condemnation on its part. The provision specifically included a discretion to decide whether some or all of the costs awarded should be on the standard or indemnity basis. If costs were awarded on the indemnity basis, in many cases there would be some implicit expression of disapproval of the way in which the litigation had been conducted, but that would not necessarily be so in every case.

What does seem clear is that where the court has made an award of indemnity costs the cases in which it has done so can be divided between those where there has or has not been culpability and abuse of process.

(a) Culpability and abuse of process

[24.9]

Traditionally costs on the indemnity basis have only been awarded where there has been some culpability or abuse of process such as:

- deceit or underhandedness by a party;
- abuse of the court's procedure;
- failure to come to court with open hands;
- the making of tenuous and speculative claims;
- reliance on utterly unjustified defences;
- the introduction and reliance upon voluminous and unnecessary evidence;
- extraneous motives for the litigation (an example of which is the use of litigation for an ulterior commercial purpose – see *Amoco (UK) Exploration v British American Offshore Ltd* [2002] BLR 135 below); or

- discontinuance without explanation where allegations of serious dishonesty and fraud have been made.

What seems clear is the exercise of the discretion by the court is best considered by reference to specific examples of where the court has made indemnity costs orders. It is one of those instances where it is hard to pinpoint specific conduct, but one knows it when one sees it!

Unreasonableness

[24.10]

National Westminster Bank plc v Rabobank Nederland [2007] EWHC 1742 (Comm) found that the minimum nature of the conduct required to justify an order for costs on the indemnity basis was, except in very rare cases, that there had been a significant level of unreasonableness or otherwise inappropriate conduct in its widest sense. This could be pre-litigation conduct or in relation to the commencement or conduct of the litigation itself (mirroring the conduct provisions of CPR 44.2(5)(a)). The conduct must be looked at in the context of the entire litigation and a view taken as to whether the level of unreasonableness or inappropriateness is, in all the circumstances, high enough to engage such an order. In this case the entire underlying foundation of the defendant's core allegation was, from the very commencement of the counterclaim, deeply flawed and the allegation involved an assumption so improbable as to be far-fetched and the defendants had vigorously pursued claims of dishonesty despite the fact that such allegations were highly speculative, if not doomed from the start. The defendants had crossed the frontier by conducting litigation in a manner so unreasonable and/or so unsatisfactory as to justify an order for costs against it on the indemnity basis in respect of its counterclaim.

In *Denton v T H White* [2014] EWCA Civ 906, the then Master of the Rolls identified opportunistic technical challenges in respect of time limits and relief from sanction as unreasonable conduct that may merit an order for indemnity costs.

Unreasonable behaviour and underhandedness

[24.11]

In *Caliendo v Mischon De Reya* (14 March 2016, unreported), Ch Arnold J, following the substantive decision reported at [2016] EWHC 150 (Ch), the court concluded that the fact that the claim relied upon a false factual premise which the claimants knew to be false was sufficient to take the case 'out of the norm' and justify an indemnity costs order. Of further interest is that this was a budgeted case where the last budget was £1.2m and the costs incurred stood at £1.9m and so the indemnity costs order was clearly of significance.

Conduct of applications/stages of the case

[24.12]

In *Lifeline Gloves Ltd v Richardson* [2005] EWHC 1524 (Ch), the defendants successfully opposed the claimant's application for summary judgment with the costs being reserved. The defendants then withdrew their defence. The claimant was awarded its costs on the indemnity basis on the grounds that the defendants' conduct and the lack of merit in their defence amounted to unreasonable behaviour under CPR 44.2(4) justifying an award of indemnity costs. On the other side of CPR Part 24, in *Simmons & Simmons v Charles Hickox* [2013] EWHC 2141 (QB) a party who pursued summary judgment even though he knew, or ought to have known, that this was not justified was ordered to pay costs on the indemnity basis.

Whilst concluding that an indemnity basis costs order was not justified in respect of the defendant's approach to negotiations, the Court of Appeal upheld the award in *Manna v Central Manchester University Hospitals NHS Foundation Trust* [2017] EWCA Civ 12. It did so on the basis that the nature of the case took it out 'of the norm'. The defendant had advanced a case at trial that the claimant's carers had dishonestly set out to mislead professional advisers by exaggerating the difficulties providing care for the claimant.

Failure to come to court with open hands and misconduct

[24.13]

In *U & M Mining Zambia Ltd v Konkola Copper Mines plc* [2014] EWHC 3250 (Comm) the Court penalised a party which had applied for a not on notice freezing injunction, for failing to comply with its duty in such a situation to give full and frank disclosure when making the application. The applicant had failed to disclose contractual clauses that opened the possibility of exclusive jurisdiction for enforcement being in Zambia. The injunction was continued, but the applicant was penalised in an award of costs on the indemnity basis.

Unreasonable conduct and continued pursuit of a speculative claim

[24.14]

The risk of an indemnity costs order in such circumstances was succinctly stated up by Tomlinson J in *Three Rivers District Council v The Governor and Company of the Bank of England* [2006] EWHC 816 (Comm):

> '... where a claim is speculative, weak, opportunistic or thin, a claimant who chooses to pursue it is taking a high risk and can expect to pay indemnity costs'

In *Lejovarn* (above), the court made it clear that the use of the word 'hopeless' in *Elvanite Full Circle Ltd v AMEC Earth and Environmental (UK) Ltd* [2013] EWHC 1643 (TCC) was not intended to add some gloss to the description of claims falling within Tomlinson J's articulation, but was merely a factual statement of the strength of a particular case.

In *Two Right Feet Ltd (in liq) v National Westminster Bank plc* (above at [**24.7**]), the claimant discontinued, but the defendants successfully sought an order for indemnity costs under the 'unless the court orders otherwise' provision of CPR 38.6(1) relying upon a failure by the claimant to engage pre-action, the making of improper and unjust allegations, exaggeration of a claim which was speculative and not properly investigated, delay in discontinuing and various procedural failings. The court was satisfied that both the way in which the claim had been advanced and then conducted took it 'out of the norm'.

Abuse of court process and misconduct

[24.15]

A v B (No 2) [2007] EWHC 54 (Comm), concluded that provided that it can be established by a successful application for a stay, or an anti-suit injunction, as a remedy for breach of an arbitration or jurisdiction clause, that the breach had caused the innocent party reasonably to incur legal costs, then those costs should normally be recoverable on the indemnity basis. If costs were confined to the standard basis, there would necessarily be part of the successful applicant's costs of the application which had been properly incurred but could not be recovered by such an order because of the restricted process of assessment.

The unidentified portion of costs would then be a loss which could only be recoverable as damages for breach of the jurisdiction or arbitration agreement, if such a damages claim were permissible. Authority suggested it would not be permitted, which would lead to a fundamentally unjust outcome. The court found that there is no policy argument which precludes costs on the indemnity basis in this situation.

In *Clutterbuck & Paton v HSBC plc* [2016] 1 Costs LR 13, the court concluded that where a claimant raises allegations of serious dishonesty and fraud against a defendant and discontinues those claims without explanation, an order for indemnity costs should usually follow. This approach was adopted in *PJSC-Aeroflot Russian Airline v Leeds* [2018] EWHC 1735, which described it as 'sound', but declined to elevate it to a 'rule'.

It may not be a rule, but Hildyard J put it this way in *Hosking v Apax Partners LLP* [2018] EWHC 2732 (Ch), when ordering indemnity costs following an unexplained discontinuance four days into what had been expected to be a six-week hearing in a case described as 'high-risk litigation aggressively and very expensively pursued after failure of one sort or another in multiple jurisdictions, without demonstrable support in the contemporaneous documentary evidence', identifying the court's reluctance:

> ' . . . to permit parties which have invoked its jurisdiction and pursued proceedings for purposes or in a manner of which the Court disapproves to withdraw silently and deprive the other party of some proper recompense or vindication.' (para 53)

Unjustified defence

[24.16]

Cooper v P&O Stena Line Ltd [1999] 1 Lloyd's Rep 734, QBD (Admiralty Ct).

In an action for personal injuries, an allegation of malingering is a serious allegation of fraud and has to be pleaded. If the defendant had undertaken a proper investigation it was unlikely it would have defended on liability at all and in terms of quantum there never had been sufficient material on which to base the allegation of fraud. The unusual circumstances of the case justified the award of costs on the indemnity basis.

The introduction and reliance upon voluminous and unnecessary evidence

[24.17]

In *Digicel (St Lucia) Ltd (a company registered under the laws of St Lucia) v Cable & Wireless plc* [2010] EWHC 888, Ch D, the claimant had alleged bad faith and conspiracy, which were allegations of serious wrongdoing. The claims were very wide, which meant that the defendant had to respond to allegations that virtually everything it had done was unlawful. The claimant's witness statements had not been confined to evidence of facts within the witnesses own knowledge. The claimant had significantly overstated the quantum of its claim. On the basis of those findings, it was just that the successful defendant should recover its costs, provided those were reasonably incurred and reasonable in amount, without being subject to the possibility that some part of those costs should be disallowed on the grounds of proportionality, as would be the case under the standard basis. There was no injustice in denying the claimant the benefit of an assessment on a proportionate basis when it had showed no interest in proportionality by casting its claim disproportionately wide and requiring the defendant to meet such a claim. The claimant had also forfeited its right to the benefit of the doubt on reasonableness.

Extraneous motive for litigation

[24.18]

In *Amoco (UK) Exploration Co v British American Offshore Ltd* (see above), the claimant sought to avoid a contract which had become unprofitable by putting pressure on the defendant to renegotiate and, when this failed, by terminating the contract. The grounds of termination were different to those subsequently put forward at the trial. The claimant lost heavily and was ordered to pay costs on the indemnity basis because it had conducted itself throughout on the basis that its commercial interests took precedence over the rights and wrongs of the matter, and had then sought to justify its stance by reference to a constantly changing case.

Indemnity costs and causation of increased costs

[24.19]

Phoenix Finance Ltd v Federation International de l'Automobile [2002] EWHC 1028 (Ch), held that there is no need for a party when seeking an indemnity costs order to show that the conduct complained of has increased the costs. The question is the reasonableness or otherwise of the conduct and is not dependent upon whether the conduct, whether reasonable or unreasonable, has increased the costs payable.

Refusal of offers under CPR Part 44 and relevant CPR Part 36 offers by defendant

[24.20]

This does seem to be an area of some uncertainty requiring regular restatement of principle by the Court of Appeal. In both *Kiam v MGN Ltd (No 2)* [2002] EWCA Civ 66 and *Manna v Central Manchester University Hospitals NHS Foundation Trust* (above at **[24.12]**), the court was clear that a failure to beat an admissible offer under CPR Part 44 was unlikely, by itself, to be a reason to make an award of indemnity costs. Indeed, in *Manna*, Tomlinson LJ concluded that 'a judge should in my view be very slow to entertain a discussion as to whether parties to litigation have negotiated in a reasonable manner', making the point that CPR 36 was designed to provide an unambiguous route to an indemnity costs order that obviated the need for such arguments. In *Astex Therspeutics Ltd v Astrazeneca AB* [2018] EWCA Civ 2444, [2018] All ER (D) 164 (Nov), the Court of Appeal, in setting aside an order for indemnity costs made in part because of a refusal to accept an offer not made under CPR 36, stated that the judge should have asked 'what it was about the offer and its rejection that contributed to a conclusion that the conduct of the case [by the party who refused the offer] was outside the norm'. However, of course, there may be additional factors which, in combination with the offer, render such an order appropriate. In *Richmond Pharmacology Ltd v Chester Overseas Ltd* [2014] EWHC 3418 (Ch), the court concluded that whilst the rejection of reasonable attempts to settle will not normally, by itself, justify an award of indemnity costs, if coupled with other factors it may do so. As Simon Brown LJ concluded in *Kiam*, it will be:

> '... a rare case indeed where a refusal of a settlement offer will attract under Part 44 not merely an adverse order for costs but an order on an indemnity rather than standard basis.'

As we have seen when considering Part 44 offers in Chapter 20 Costs Inducements to Settle – Part 36 Offers and other Admissible Offers, above, the court has been at pains to stress that these offers should not be given the status of Part 36 offers and the sanctions imposed by Part 36.17 should not be applied to Part 44 offers. Interestingly in *Ontulmus v Collett* [2014] EWHC 4117 (QB) the Court imposed an order of indemnity costs upon claimants who accepted the defendants' CPR 36 offer out of time (for the period from the expiry of the 'relevant period' under CPR 36 to acceptance), even though CPR 36 does not contain any automatic sanction of indemnity costs in respect of defendant's offers. This was expressly on the basis that the claimants' conduct since the time of the defendants' offers took the case 'out of the norm'. A similar approach was taken in *Holmes v West London Mental Health Trust* (29 June 2018 unreported), QBD HHJ Gore QC, in which the acceptance of a CPR 36 offer one year after it was made was only one factor, amongst a plethora of procedural and substantive issues that took the case 'out of the norm', justifying indemnity costs from the relevant date.

The approach to CPR 44 offers seems to have informed the decision of the court in *MIOM 1 Ltd v Sea Echo ENE (No 2)* [2011] EWHC 2715 (Admlty). Here the court observed that CPR Part 61 (which deals with costs in admiralty claims) does not provide for costs on the indemnity basis where a CPR Part 61 offer is successful, whereas CPR Part 36 does provide for such costs when a

Part 36 offer was successful. That was a clear indication that the drafters of CPR Part 61 did not intend that indemnity costs should be awarded merely because a Part 61 offer had been successful. In those circumstances, it was not appropriate in a collision action in the Admiralty Division governed by CPR Part 61 to order costs on the indemnity basis merely because an offer had been successful.

More recently Akenhead J in *Igloo Regeneration (GP) Ltd v Powell Williams Partnership (Costs)* [2013] EWHC 1859 TCC made an award of costs against the claimants on the indemnity basis where they declined to accept an offer that was exactly in the terms that they had offered to accept a few days previously, but which had expired. This was against a backdrop where there had been no change of circumstances between the expiry of the claimants' offer and the making of the defendant's offer. It is clear that a specific factual context arose here and the order was not made simply on the back of a failure to accept a Part 44 offer.

Whilst CPR 36.17(4)(b) makes provision for an indemnity basis costs award in favour of a claimant (see **[24.23]** below), CPR 36.17(3) makes no such provision for a defendant. Instead, the costs the defendant is entitled to recover are, unless the court otherwise orders, on the standard basis. However, it is worth remembering that this is the starting point and, as Coulson LJ noted in *Lejonvarn*, that is not the end of the analysis. Referring to previous authorities he re-iterated that 'the fact that a defendant has beaten his of her own Part 36 offer is plainly a matter of importance in the exercise of the court's discretion under CPR Part 44'.

Indemnity costs and public funding

[24.21]

In *Brawley v Marczynski (No 2)* [2002] EWCA Civ 1453, costs were awarded on the indemnity basis to a publicly funded party in order to penalise the losing party's unreasonable conduct in the case. It is no impediment to an award of indemnity costs that the only beneficiaries of penalising the defendant's solicitors would be the claimant's lawyers.

(b) No culpability or abuse of process

[24.22]

In *Re Continental Assurance Co of London plc (in liq)* (13 June 2001, unreported) Park J was concerned with the situation where conduct had definitely increased the costs. He expressly disavowed his disapproval of some of the conduct of the liquidators as being the reason for his award of costs against them being on the indemnity basis. He did take into account what the consequences of the choice would be and where it would be appropriate for the benefit of any doubt to lie. He accepted that there is a clear steer in the CPR that in the normal case, costs should be awarded on the standard basis so that the benefit of any doubt should go to the paying party. However, this was not a normal, but a wholly exceptional case where it would be wrong and unacceptable for matters to be resolved against the respondents. The liquidators had pursued all issues at full length and right to the end, with the result that the amount of costs incurred must have been enormous. It was appropriate the costs of the successful respondents should be assessed on the indemnity basis so that they, and not the liquidators, received the benefit of any doubts. In other words, the order was made looking forwards to the assessment outcome and not back to the conduct.

Of course, proportionate case management should protect a receiving party whose costs have been budgeted from any costs effect of the conduct of the paying party. If it does not, then the receiving party on a standard basis assessment could still argue good reason to depart from the budget under CPR 3.18 relying on the subsequent conduct of the paying party as having altered the proportionality assessment under CPR 44.3(5) and CPR 44.4(1) that the court conducted at the costs management stage.

Whilst highlighting the fact that the decision whether to award indemnity costs depends on criteria which are not dependent upon the scale of the difference that the basis of costs would make to the costs assessment outcome, Coulson J in *Ocensa Pipeline Group Litigation (Arroyo v Equion Energia Ltd (formerly known as BP Exploration Company (Colombia) Ltd))* [2016] EWHC 3348 (TCC) when making an indemnity basis order in respect of part of the costs, accepted that consideration of those criteria included 'bearing in mind that removing the requirement of proportionality is always likely to be significant and that the effect of making an order for indemnity costs may be a matter of substantial financial significance'.

On the opposite side of this coin anyway is that proportionality represents a substantial check on costs and, as the court stressed in *Easyair Ltd (t/a Openair) v Opal Telecom Ltd* [2009] EWHC 779 (Ch), that is not something that should be removed from the consideration of amount of costs lightly.

Indemnity costs under Part 36

[24.23]

Costs on the indemnity basis may also be awarded as the result of a Part 36 offer (see Chapter 20 Costs Inducements to Settle – Part 36 Offers and other Admissible Offers, above).

Indemnity costs refused

[24.24]

Again a review of instances where the court has declined to make an order is informative.

In *John v Price Waterhouse (t/a PricewaterhouseCoopers)* [2002] 1 WLR 953, Ch D, [2001] 34 LS Gaz R 39 the defendant had successfully resisted the claimant's claim arising out of its conduct as auditor of the claimant companies. The defendant sought an order for costs on the indemnity basis on the ground that as auditor it was entitled to be indemnified out of the assets of the companies against all its costs. The court held that in its role of a litigant the defendant was entitled only to an order for costs on the standard basis. There was nothing to prevent the auditor from seeking to recover the difference between standard costs and indemnity costs in separate proceedings to enforce the relevant contractual terms.

In *Simms v Law Society* [2005] EWCA Civ 849, the judge fell into error. After making a 'between the parties' order for costs on the indemnity basis against the claimant, the judge rejected the claimant's attack on the proportionality of the Law Society's response to his application to the High Court, which he claimed had generated 'enormous costs', saying the matter could be dealt with on the detailed assessment. On appeal the order was varied to the standard basis.

In *Zissis v Lukomski* [2006] EWCA Civ 341, the district judge had awarded costs on the indemnity basis on the ground that if parties litigate only as to costs, then they must bear a greater risk that if they are unsuccessful they will be ordered to pay costs on the indemnity basis. In allowing an appeal against the order, the Court of Appeal held that there was no principle distinguishing litigation about costs from other litigation.

In *Balmoral Group Ltd v Borealis (UK) Ltd* [2006] EWHC 2531 (Comm), the successful defendant contended that the claimant's behaviour had been so unreasonable both before and during the proceedings, including the presentation of a grossly exaggerated claim, unreasonable failure to make efforts to settle and by the character of the technical evidence adduced, that costs should be awarded on the indemnity basis.

The judge held that justice does not demand that a resounding defeat should always carry with it an award of indemnity costs. The claimant's pre-action activity had not over-stepped the mark and although the claim for damages (loss of profits) was put very high and the explanation given by the claimant rested more on wishful thinking than evidential support, the court was not persuaded that continuing with the claim was so unreasonable that costs should be awarded on the indemnity basis. However, reinforcing that separate stages of a claim may be subject to costs orders on different bases, the deficient expert evidence adduced by the claimant had led to unnecessary costs incurred by the defendant and accordingly the costs incurred by the defendant in that respect were awarded on the indemnity basis.

In (*HLB Kidsons (a firm) v Lloyds Underwriters subscribing to Lloyd's Policy No 621/PKIDOO101* [2007] EWHC 2699 (Comm) the court concluded that a claimant's rejection of a defendant's Part 36 offer (which does not carry the same entitlement as a claimant's Part 36 offer does as to indemnity costs) does not, as of right, take the case out of the norm even though, in light of the outcome of the case, it may prove wrong to reject it. As Gloster J explained:

> 'In my judgment it is not appropriate, in the circumstances of this case, to make an order for indemnity costs. . . . there has been nothing in the conduct of the litigation of the claim by Kidsons that takes their rejection of the Part 36 offer out of the norm. In the light of my judgment, they were wrong to have done so, but no doubt they were advised by their legal advisors not to accept the offer. In a complex piece of commercial litigation of this nature, I cannot say they were unreasonable to have done so.'

CONCLUSION TO THE BASES OF COSTS

[24.25]

While it may seem a step too far to tread where the Court of Appeal has refused to and offer some guidelines (although Tomlinson J does so in *Three Rivers District Council v Bank of England* [2006] EWHC 816 (Comm)) there are certainly some clear themes that emerge from the case law considered. These are:

- the discretion of the court is broad and the exercise of it is entirely fact sensitive;
- the starting point is that costs on the standard basis is the usual order and therefore to justify an award of indemnity costs requires something out of 'the norm';
- the court must have regard to the factors set out at CPR 44.2(4) and CPR 44.2(5) when considering what costs order to make;
- this means that the court may take into account conduct before the issue of proceedings in reaching its decision (including compliance with pre-action protocols);
- it is not always necessary for there to have been deliberate misconduct, but there must be a substantial level of unreasonableness;
- the mere fact that parties may discontinue all or part of their claims, withdraw defences, be unsuccessful on a summary disposal or at trial does not represent something out of 'the norm' – something more is required;
- similarly a claimant's failure to accept a Part 36 offer or a party's failure to accept a Part 44 offer does not automatically result in an order for indemnity costs – something more is required and it depends on the context;
- a party taking opportunistic technical points and unreasonably refusing extensions of time or unreasonably opposing applications for relief from sanctions, may be exposed, amongst other costs sanctions, to indemnity costs.
- the intent behind an award of indemnity costs is to ensure that the receiving party does not have to surmount the test of proportionality and that the burden in respect of reasonableness is imposed on the paying party.

CHAPTER 25

PAYMENT ON ACCOUNT OF COSTS

PAYMENT ON ACCOUNT OF COSTS GENERALLY

[25.1]

The rule is found at CPR 44.2(8). The court will order the paying party to pay a reasonable sum on account unless there is good reason not to do so. It would appear that *Blackmore v Cummings* [2009] EWCA Civ 1276, which held, under the previous version of the rule, that there was no legal presumption that a party was entitled to have an interim payment on account can be consigned to the history books. What was not even to be elevated to a presumption is now mandatory in the absence of good reason.

This provision, when linked with the fact that in most multi-track claims the likelihood is that there will be a costs management order and so an approved or agreed budget, makes the entire process much simpler. Not only is a payment on account mandatory unless there is a good reason not to order one, but the assessment of the amount has become a far easier exercise because reference can be made to the budgeted figure. The fact that there may not be a statement of costs available in Form N260 or N260B to inform the judge as to the level of costs, does not preclude a payment on account being ordered (see *Astonleigh Residential v Goldfarb* [2014] EWHC 4100 (Ch)).

It is interesting to note that in a judgment that covered many of the issues that arise on award of costs and costs management (including whether there should be an order for indemnity basis costs, the relevance of a budget where there is an award of indemnity costs and good reason to depart from a budget) and which ran to 69 paragraphs, Coulson J in *Elvanite Full Circle Ltd v AMEC Earth and Environmental (UK) Ltd* [2013] EWHC 1643 (TCC) dealt with payment on account in just twelve lines. The main conclusion brooking no debate:

> 'The defendant is entitled to an interim payment on account of costs. Since, for the reasons that I have given, the costs management order is likely to be the benchmark for the costs to be recovered by the defendant, any interim award of costs should operate on the basis that the defendant's recoverable costs in this case are unlikely to be much less than the costs management order but unlikely to very much greater either.'

Changing the emphasis also has the effect of making a detailed assessment less attractive. One advantage of going to detailed assessment was to defer the date for payment of the costs. If the court orders something close to the budgeted amount as a payment on account any benefit of delay is lost.

Of course, as the court observed in *Cleveland Bridge UK Ltd v Sarens* [2018] EWHC 827 (TCC), unless a costs management order was made by agreement under CPR 3.15(2)(c), it will only be the budgeted costs that can fall within the 'benchmark' starting point referred to in the quoted passage and the court will have to consider payments on account of the non-costs managed 'incurred' costs separately and in addition to the payment set based on the budgeted costs. It will do so in the way that it deals with those cases under the pre-April 2013 regime which have not been subject to costs management, any multi track cases where no costs management order has been made (those cases that are currently, and were originally, exempted under CPR 3.12 and multi-track claims where the court decides not to make a costs management order) and fast track claims (not yet subject to any fixed cost regime) where no summary assessment is undertaken. Here the court may find it harder to determine the amount to be paid on account.

The benchmark case is still *Mars UK Ltd v Teknowledge Ltd* [1999] 2 Costs LR 44 Ch D. Albeit that this was a case governed by the discretionary power to order a payment on account, the court identified factors that might still be relevant as 'good reason' not to make an order eg an unsuccessful party's wish to appeal and the relative financial position of each party

Mars is cited to the court regularly on the quantification of the payment on account. Curiously if the submissions are to be believed it is, at different times, and depending on whether the paying party or the receiving party is advancing the submission, authority for a payment of a sum as low as 14.4% or as high as 66.66% of the costs claimed. In fact, Jacob J ordered the defendants to make an interim payment of £80,000. The total costs were in the order of £550,000. However, the costs award only provided for the receiving party to recover 60% of it costs. The judge assessed that only about 40% of the costs were in fact recoverable. The % awarded really depends on how one does the arithmetic. If one takes £80,000 as a percentage of £550,000 it does equal 14.4%. If one recognises that the costs order was for 60% only then the starting point is £330,000, which equals 24.2%. The way that Jacob J calculated the sum was to start by reducing the £550,000 by 60% (as that took account of his assessment that only about 40% of the costs would be recoverable). This left a figure of £220,000 (although oddly this was said to be about £200,000). The costs award was for 60% of costs and so the starting point was £120,000 of which £80,000 – 66.66% – was awarded. Actually, this arithmetical exercise is not particularly relevant because what it shows is the judge undertook his own approximate assessment of what he thought the likely recovery would be and awarded a significant proportion of that sum. Each case will be fact specific. Indeed, in *Mars* Jacob J took into account the claimant's pre-action heavy handedness and misconduct during the proceedings which informed his conclusion that he thought it unlikely that on a detailed assessment the claimant would recover more than 40% of the claimed costs.

One inevitability, given the primacy of proportionality, is that considerations of proportionality will inform payments on account. In *Rallison v North West London Hospitals NHS Trust* [2015] EWHC 3255 (QB), where a claim had settled for £450,000 (significantly less than had been claimed), the costs were said to be £1.1m, the claimant sought a payment on account of £570,000 and the defendant offered £250,000, the court determined that the first stage was to consider proportionality on a global basis. If, as it concluded here, the total sum was disproportionate, then the court should adopt a broad bush to individual items to determine what constituted a reasonable payment on account. In this case it concluded the global costs were disproportionate and ordered just over £306,000 on account.

Days Healthcare UK Ltd v Pihsiang Machinery Manufacturing Co Ltd [2006] EWHC 1444 (QB), raised the interesting issue of the effect on the detailed assessment proceedings where a defendant has failed to comply with an order to make an interim costs payment (in this case of £2 million plus interest). The receiving party claimant applied for an order that unless the payment was made, a final costs certificate should be issued in the full amount it had claimed. The court concluded that quite apart from any specific rule, the court has an inherent jurisdiction to control its own processes sufficiently enough to enable it to make the order sought. CPR 3.1(1) expressly preserves the inherent powers of the court, while CPR 3.1(3)(a) provides that where the court makes an order in the course of its general powers of management, it can do so subject to conditions, including a condition to pay a sum of money into court. However, as points of dispute had been properly served, the court decided that the appropriate order should provide for there still to be an assessment, but that the paying party defendants should not be permitted to participate further unless they made the interim payment.

The effect of non-payment on continued involvement in proceedings has received further consideration following the change that is CPR 44.2(8). In *Harb v HRH Prince Abdul Aziz Bin Fahd Bin Abdul Aziz* [2017] EWHC 258 (Ch), the court, having found the non-payment of a payment on account ordered by the Court of Appeal was because the claimant could not pay the sum from her own resources and had no sources of borrowing, concluded that any indefinite stay pending payment or strike out for non-payment would represent a disproportionate interference with the claimant's right of access to court under article 6(1) of the European Convention on Human Rights, as it would impair that right. In rejecting the defendant's submission that the claimant was in contempt for non-payment, Arnold J commented unequivocally:

> 'Non-payment of interim costs orders by litigants is, regrettably, a very common occurrence. If it amounted to a contempt of court which justified courts in not hearing the defaulting parties, many litigants would be shut out from pursuing or defending claims even in the absence of any substantive order to that effect. In my view that cannot be right.'

It seems that notwithstanding the directive in CPR 44.2(8), courts must be astute to the ability to pay and the effect of any order on any continuing proceedings. Further support for this proposition may be found in *Park Hotels and Resorts Ltd v Tarak Investments Ltd* (23 March 2016, unreported), Ch. Whilst making an 'unless order' in respect of the unpaid costs, the court felt it necessary to be satisfied that this order would not shut the paying party out of the litigation.

The CPR maintains a distinction between a payment on account (CPR 44.2(8)) and an interim costs certificate (CPR 47.16). The former, as we have seen, obliges the court where a costs award has been made to order a payment on account, unless there is good reason not so to do. The latter may only be requested after the receiving party has requested a detailed assessment. What of the situation where, between trial and the award of costs and filing N258 to request a detailed assessment hearing, the receiving party wishes to pursue further costs over and above those ordered by the trial judge on an interim basis? In *Dyson Ltd v Hoover Ltd* [2003] EWHC 624 (Ch) (a case decided under the previous and less stringent CPR provision), before the costs had been assessed under a costs order following acceptance of a CPR 36 order, the claimant applied to a different judge to the one who had made the costs order, for an amount to be paid on account of its costs. This was opposed on the grounds that as the court had not had the benefit of hearing the full trial or of conducting an enquiry into loss, the court was ill-placed to make any order for an interim payment. The court agreed, saying it had to exercise particular caution when invited to make an interim payment in these circumstances, because the judge was blind to the issues between the parties and the sums of money in dispute were considerable. The court stressed that it was important to bear in mind that the costs judge was empowered to issue an interim costs certificate at any time after the receiving party had filed a request for a detailed assessment hearing. This provision operated on the basis that the costs judge's power to order interim costs had been preceded by steps placing the court in the position to make an accurate assessment of the likely costs and to be able to decide whether an interim payment was appropriate and, if so, for how much it should be.

If anything, it appeared that this position had been strengthened by the wording of CPR 44.2(8). Under the previous provision, where the court had ordered a party to pay costs it had the power to order an amount on account before the costs were assessed. CPR 44.2(8) seemed less flexible, suggesting that the time for an order for payment on account is when the costs order between the parties is made. There had been conflicting first instance decisions on this point. However, the position has now been clarified by the Court of Appeal in *Global Assets Advisory Services Ltd v Grandlane Developments Ltd* [2019] EWCA Civ 1764. In this case the receiving party's entitlement to costs arose under a deemed costs order under CPR 44.9, following the acceptance of a CPR 36 offer within the relevant period. At 1st instance the court adopted the approach taken in *JP Finnegan v Frank Spiers T/A Frank Spiers Licensed Conveyancers* [2018] EWHC 3064 (Ch), in which the court had concluded that CPR 44.2(8) did not apply in respect of deemed orders consequential upon acceptance of a Part 36 offer within the relevant period, on the basis that Part 36 and not 44 spelled out the consequences of acceptance and those did not include a payment on account of costs. This conclusion was rejected by the Court of Appeal, with Asplin LJ observing:

> 'I can see no reason why the power to make an order under CPR r 44.2(8) should be restricted to circumstances in which the court has physically made the order as opposed to circumstances in which an order of the court is deemed to have been made. In both circumstances, it is the court which has ordered the party to pay the costs and accordingly, it seems to me that the circumstances fall within the wording of CPR r 44.2(8). A deemed order is no less an order of the court . . . Furthermore, the rationale for ordering a payment on account of costs is the same whether or not the order for costs is an order which is deemed to have been made.'

Indeed the court was clear that the provisions of CPR 36.13, relating to acceptance of an offer and CPR 44.2(8) sit together:

> '... there is no conflict or tension between CPR r 36.13(1) and CPR r 44.2(8) at all. It is not necessary to determine which provision must prevail. The former entitles a party to its costs of the proceedings on a particular basis and is complemented or supplemented by the latter which creates the jurisdiction to order a payment on account of those costs.'

Putting the final nail in the coffin of arguments that CPR 44.2(8) contains a temporal link, limiting the award of a payment on account to the time of the substantive decision, the court rejected the notion that only the trial judge could entertain applications for interim payments:

> 'It seems to me that the current wording [of 44.2(8)] cannot form the basis for a distinction between cases in which the application for an interim payment is heard by the trial judge and those in which it is not. It seems to me that it applies whether or not the trial judge hears the application for an interim payment. If the judge hearing the application considers that there is good reason not to make the order, the terms of CPR r 44.2(8) enable him to decline to do so.'

In general though, CPR 44.2(8) points to a reduction, if not cessation, of arguments about payments on account. The obligation on the court to make an order for payment on account unless there is good reason, shifts the burden to the paying party to satisfy the court why no such order should be made. The easier assessment of the amount in costs managed cases, by reference to a budget that has been set by phase expenditure that the court has already determined to be reasonable and proportionate means that a significant proportion of costs is likely to be ordered at this stage. This is amply demonstrated by the decision in *Thomas Pink Ltd v Victoria's Secret UK Ltd* [2014] EWHC 3258 (Ch). Birss J accepted that the position had been altered by the introduction of costs budgets when ordering a payment on account of 90% of the budgeted sum stating:

> 'It seems to me that the impact of costs budgeting on the determination of a sum for a payment on account of costs is very significant although I am not persuaded that it is so significant that I should simply award the budgeted sum.'

This was also the approach of Coulson J in *MacInnes v Gross* [2017] EWHC 127 (QB), when ordering a payment on account of 90% of an approved costs budget. He stated that he considered a 10% reduction was 'the maximum deduction that is appropriate in a case where there is an approved costs budget'.

ORDERS FOR COSTS UP TO A POINT IN PROCEEDINGS AND PAYMENTS ON ACCOUNT UNDER SUCH AN ORDER BEFORE THE CONCLUSION OF THOSE PROCEEDINGS

[25.2]

It seems counter-intuitive to be considering orders for costs of proceedings (albeit only up to the date reached) and payments on account of costs under such orders, where the proceedings remain unresolved and the ultimate outcome unknown. However, this is precisely the situation that confronted the court in *X v Hull & East Yorkshire Hospitals NHS Trust* [2019] 2 WLUK 723 (25 February 2019) (HHJ Robinson). In this case, there had been an order approving a liability settlement in 2012, which also included a provision for the defendant to pay the claimant's costs to that date. The claimant subsequently instructed other firms of solicitors. The current solicitors sought a payment on account of the costs of the quantum exercise, as the final prognosis remained unclear and it was agreed that final determination was unlikely to be possible until 2022. Two payments on account of costs under the 2012 order had been made, one of which included a sum to the current solicitors, albeit that their involvement post-dated the liability settlement.

HHJ Robinson QC identified the issues as follows:

- whether the court has power to make an interim order as to costs in the circumstance of a case such as this; and
- if the court does have such power, whether the court should exercise it.

Unsurprisingly, the defendant argued that there was no entitlement within the CPR and no jurisprudence to permit the court either to make an order in respect of the costs of proceedings that were extant or to order a sum to be paid on account of the costs for work in respect of which there had yet to be any costs order. The claimant pointed to the liability judgment, the absence of any relevant CPR 36 offers from the defendant and the significant sums paid on account of damages, submitting that the claimant would be virtually certain to recover the costs to date.

Making an order for costs up to the date of the application and awarding a payment on account under it, the judge concluded that:

- CPR 44.2(1) and (2) were drafted sufficiently broadly to permit an order for costs at this stage. Support for this can be found in CPR 44.2(6)(c), which permits an order for costs 'from or until a certain date only';
- the payments already made on account of damages, an estimation of the likely overall value of the claim and the absence of any CPR 36 offers made it virtually certain that the claimant would be entitled to the costs to date;
- the fact that £1.2 million had been paid by way of damages, interim payments evidenced 'success in part' under CPR 44.2(4)(b);
- there was no risk to the defendant as if overpayment took place, then this could be off-set against further damages awarded;
- in a case where there was likely to be such a delay between resolution of liability and quantification of the claim with significant sums being spent on the latter process in the meantime 'failure to ensure adequate cash flow during the period of inevitable delay may lead to the perverse and undesirable consequence that solicitors are unwilling to take on case such as this at an early stage'.

Clearly to make a payment on account in these circumstances the court must first be persuaded to make an order for costs (as that is a pre-requisite within CPR 44.2(8). This will mean that the party applying must satisfy the court under CPR 44.2(1), (2), (4) and (5) that such an order should be made in its favour. Assuming it is successful, it will then have to ensure that the court has sufficient evidence before it to justify ordering a payment on account and to enable quantification of the sum. In *RXK v Hampshire Hospitals NHS Foundation Trust* [2019] EWHC 2751 (QB), the court tentatively suggested that the following information should be provided:

> 'i) the type of funding agreement and details of any payments made under that agreement,
> ii) whether any Part 36 or other admissible offer has been made, and if so, full details of the offer,
> iii) details of any payments on account of damages made to date,
> iv) a realistic valuation of the likely damages to be awarded at trial,
> v) a realistic estimate of the quantum costs incurred to the date of the application,

vi) any other factor relevant to the final incidence of costs, such as the possibility of an issue-based costs order, arguments over rates or relevant conduct.
vii) the likely date of trial or trial window.'

SET-OFF AND PAYMENTS ON ACCOUNT

[25.3]

In *Benyatov v Credit Suisse Securities (Europe) Ltd* [2020] EWHC 682 (QB), [2020] 1 WLR 2913, [2020] Costs LR 379, the court had to consider what it described as a novel submission. The defendant had made three applications. As a result of one, parts of the claim were struck out. The claimant was ordered to pay the defendant's costs attributable to those parts. This was to be by detailed assessment at the end of the claim. The defendant made no application for a payment on account of those costs (rightly in the view of the judge as those costs would be difficult to identify until properly assessed by a costs judge in a fuller context of knowing the costs of pleading the defence and any calculation at this stage of the proceedings would necessarily be imprecise). The defendant was ordered to pay one-third of the claimant's costs of the unsuccessful applications. The claimant did seek a payment on account of those. The 'novel' submission was that no payment on account should be ordered because the defendant had a contingent entitlement to costs under an order made at the same hearing, and on the same application and it should not be prejudiced simply because of the greater difficulty of quantifying its costs as opposed to those of the claimant. The court concluded that:

- There could, and usually would, be a set-off of quantified costs (even when considering interim payments where both parties sought interim payments under respective orders for costs).
- However, where the party seeking a set-off could not properly make an application for an interim payment in respect of those costs, then the set-off should not be allowed.

In dealing with other grounds of opposition the court found that:

- the possibility of a paying party receiving future awards of costs against a receiving party is not a valid ground for opposing an interim payment. The effect of any future awards of costs should only be dealt with when those orders are made;
- in general, the possibility of an appeal against the order under which the payment on account is made is not a bar to ordering a payment on account (although in this case the judge deferred payment of the costs until determination of the application for permission to appeal).

Part IV

Quantification of costs

CHAPTER 26

FIXED COSTS

INTRODUCTION TO FIXED COSTS

[26.1]

Why is it that litigation solicitors always assume that fixed costs are the road to penury? Those dealing with non-contentious work have always worked on fixed or percentage figures, scale rates or some other easily definable and quotable figure from the outset. Before hourly billing became the dominant method, litigation in the county court was also based on scale figures. While they ultimately failed to keep pace with inflation the 'main preparation item' was a fixed sum as far back as the 1950s (when it was £40) to take a case to trial.

Perhaps it is the assumption that the case is bound to reach trial and will be bitterly fought along the way thereby exhausting the fixed fee. But that assumption can be disapproved by a quick look at any litigator's past cases. Most cases settle prior to litigation. Most that litigate settle well before trial. Those that get to a final hearing are a small, single figure percentage of the overall case load of most solicitors and of those many will only be fighting over quantum and not liability. For this reason the fixed fees are not based on the worst case scenario. To do so would be to overcompensate in most cases. But, the fact that the fee expects a settlement along the way should not give you the mindset that cases which do not settle early are simply to be seen as loss makers. They are the roundabouts to the early settlers' swings.

It is difficult to deal with fixed fees if you only have the odd civil litigation case. But if you have a basket, they should be capable of making a profit overall. If you cannot, then you have to look at the way your cases are run. The Portal (see **[26.15]** below) is challenging traditional providers of legal services with fees which are low by historic standards. They are the pinch point in the transition from hourly rates. But the rates coming into the fast track, as well as those applicable to the ever expanding small claims track, require you to consider your approach in such cases. It is generally a question of doing all, but only, the amount of work required to get the case 'home.' That may well entail revising your view of what actually needs to be done, compared with what has always been done and paid for by the opponent.

To the extent that the fixed fees do not cover your costs, including profit, you must remember that these are only the recoverable costs. There is nothing to stop you from claiming an additional sum from your client. This may be a further fixed figure. It may be a share of your client's damages via a DBA which is offset by the recoverable fee. It may be a CFA which also caters for a payment from the client. The 'direction of travel' in cases outside the multi-track is clearly towards one of fixing the recoverable element of fees. The Government has now consulted on Sir Rupert Jackson's last report, entitled 'Review of Civil Litigation Costs: Supplemental Report – Fixed Recoverable Costs' dated July 2017, and the proposals are discussed in detail at the end of this Chapter. In our view, it is better to work out a way for you to embrace such fees rather than adopt a Canute-like posture.

STRUCTURE OF THIS CHAPTER ON FIXED COSTS

[26.2]

The rearrangement of the sections of the CPR from April 2013 has brought all of the fixed costs provisions into Part 45 with the exception of those in the small claims track. There are now eight sections to Part 45 (including Section IIIA) and we deal with them in order before turning to the small claims track. As with the rest of this book, we have not set out the full rules in the Chapter but you will find them, including the tables, at the end of this book.

PART 45 SECTION I (CPR 45.1–CPR 45.8)

[26.3]

This section contains the traditional fixed costs regarding the commencement of the claim, entry of judgment and enforcement of judgments. It is the only section where VAT is not recoverable in addition to the fees set out. The amounts set out are those which will apply 'unless the court orders otherwise' (CPR 45.1 and CPR 45.3). It will be rare for a court to order otherwise but an example of a case where this happened is *Amber Construction Services Ltd v London Interspace HG Ltd* [2007] EWHC 3042 (TCC). Akenhead J took the view that the defendant had brought the proceedings on its own head by failing to pay an adjudication award in the context of a construction dispute. The claimant had followed the TCC Guide in such circumstances which required an application to be made in conjunction with the issue of proceedings. The application sought to abridge the time for acknowledging service and applying for summary judgment including a witness statement with contractual documents exhibited. It may well be this factor that particularly influenced the judge to allow considerably more than the £100 usually recovered (he awarded over £6,000). It seems debatable that some of the other reasons given, for example the fact that the defendant had argued in correspondence that it had a good defence, and indeed a counterclaim, should weigh heavily on whether fixed costs should be exceeded. If it were so, greater sums would be sought and paid with much greater regularity than does in fact take place.

Commencement costs

[26.4]

The fixed costs on commencement are the figures to be set out on the Claim Form. Relevant claims are those for specified damages over £25 or relate to claims for the recovery of goods or the possession of land (including under the accelerated procedure for assured shorthold tenancies). If a claim does not fall within these categories the words 'to be assessed' are to be entered on the claim form instead (CPR PD 45, para 1.3).

For damages claims the fixed costs are set out in Table 1 (CPR 45.2) and range between £50 and £100. Costs for possession or demotion claims are set out in Table 3 (other than under the accelerated procedure). They are £69.50 regardless of value.

In either case, there are additional costs for personal service of a defendant (£10) and £15 for personal service on any further defendants. It is not obvious why the figures are not the same for dealing with this documentation and its service. The sums involved hardly justify this differentiation.

Judgment costs

[26.5]

Table 2 (CPR 45.4) deals with costs on the entry of judgment in damages claims. There are various possibilities as to the route to judgment – in default of acknowledgment of service or defence; on admission; by summary judgment; or on delivery of goods – and so there is a range of costs recoverable. They also depend on whether the judgment figure exceeds £5,000. The range is between £22 and £85 other than for summary judgment where the figures are £175/£210.

There is no table in respect of possession claims because a standard amount of £57.25 applies to all possession or demotion claims save for the accelerated procedure cases (where a figure of £79.50 applies for both commencement and judgment upon an order for possession being made.)

For all other cases the judgment costs are added to the commencement costs.

Miscellaneous costs

[26.6]

Table 4 (CPR 45.7) sets out what are described as miscellaneous fixed costs but which are in fact costs of service. They cover the situations regarding personal service of a document at any point (£15); service by an alternative method or place approved by the court (£53.25); and service out of the jurisdiction (£68.25 if elsewhere in Great Britain or £77 otherwise).

No reference is made to the fixed costs recoverable in detailed assessment proceedings for a default costs certificate although this might have found a home here. Instead that is referred to in CPR PD 47, para 10.7 where £80 is allowed together with any court fee. Such sum is subject to the case not having been in the small claims track and to the court's power to order otherwise. These figure are specified in the Notice of Commencement.

Enforcement costs

[26.7]

Table 5 (CPR 45.8) sets out the fixed costs recoverable upon various methods of enforcement being used. Without exception they are very unlikely to cover the costs involved, not least where an attendance at court is required to achieve a final order. They are presumably intended to strike a balance between compensating the judgment creditor and not penalising too heavily a possibly already impecunious judgment debtor. Although, there is no 'unless the court otherwise orders' type saving, HHJ Kramer, sitting in the TCC, followed Akenhead J in *Amber Construction* in concluding that there was an inherent jurisdiction to award more than fixed costs where appropriate: *Blacknest Gate Ltd v Seymour Realty Ltd* (24 September 2020 QBD (TCC)).

Some of the nomenclature of the enforcement methods has changed – never for the shorter – but the methods have not changed. A third party debt order (previously a garnishee order) and a charging order have similar procedures but have different fixed costs (£98.50 and £110 respectively). The charging order allows for reasonable disbursements as well which reflects the need to register the charging order with HM Land Registry for it to have any effect.

Where the court does all of the work on receipt of the judgment creditor's application, the costs are particularly miserly. Attachment of earnings and warrants of execution are both under £10. There are no costs at all for a writ of execution (formerly a writ of fieri facias) in the High Court where the High Court Enforcement Officer (formerly the Sheriff) levies his own fees on the debtor.

For oral examinations under CPR 71.2, a half hourly rate of £15 is allowed. The questions will usually be posed by a court officer or, if complex by a district judge, but it is not unknown for the judgment creditor to ask questions of a debtor to see where any assets may lie.

Where an award is made elsewhere than in the High or County Court, fixed costs ranging between £30.75 and £75.50 are recoverable for an application to enforce such an award. There are no fewer than four bands here but as the top band is for £2,000 or more, that is presumably the most commonly used band in any event. If a judgment in one part of the United Kingdom is certified and registered in another part under the Civil Jurisdiction and Judgments Act 1982, the costs of that registration may also be claimed.

PART 45 SECTION II (CPR 45.9–CPR 45.15)

[26.8]

This section deals with the costs recoverable in personal injury cases arising out of road traffic accidents and has been known since its inception as the 'predictable (or predictive) costs regime'. It was the first of the sections in Part 45 which arose out of agreements hammered out by the personal injury industry under the auspices of the Civil Justice Council. It has to some extent been superseded by the implementation of the Portal (see Section III below). Originally any claim which settled pre-proceedings for under £10,000 would be subject to the provisions of this section. Now, many if not most of such claims are settled in the Portal and to which different provisions apply. Therefore in order for this section to apply a claim needs:

- To arise from an RTA occurring on after 6 October 2003
- To comprise a total value of agreed damages of £10,000 or less
- To have fallen out of the Portal
- To have settled pre-proceedings
- Not to involve a litigant in person
- Not to involve an untraced driver
- Not to be within the small claims limit

If a case comes within these criteria there is a self-contained code for calculating the fixed recoverable costs and disbursements as well as a mechanism for the claimant to apply for a higher sum in an appropriate case. Since the case must have settled pre-proceedings, 'costs only' proceedings under CPR 46.14 are required. (This provision used to be CPR 44.12A and some cases refer to CPR 44.12A proceedings as a result). Where a claimant was a child or protected party, an approval hearing would not take a case out of the criteria if the approval hearing was commenced under Part 8 in the usual way.

If the case started in the Portal and fell out after liability was admitted, there may be fees paid by the defendant to the claimant even though a settlement was not achieved whilst in the Portal. Where this has happened the interim payment needs to be deducted from the fixed costs calculated in accordance with this section (CPR 45.28).

Fixed costs

[26.9]

The solicitors' costs are calculated by reference to the damages received. Care has to be taken to calculate the correct level of damages. Interim payments need to be included. Any contributory negligence needs to be deducted and so too does any CRU deduction.

The formula set out in CPR 45.11 is:

- £800 as a base fee; plus
- 20% of the damages up to £5,000; plus
- 15% of any damages between £5,001 and £10,000
- 12.5% London weighting (see below)
- VAT on these sums

This formula, excluding London weighting, makes for a maximum recoverable sum of £2,550 (£800 + £1,000 + £750) plus VAT for damages of exactly £10,000.

London weighting

[26.10]

Where the claimant lives or works in London (as defined in CPR PD 45, para 2.6) and the legal representative also works in London, the additional 12.5% can be claimed. This was a hotly contested provision originally. Defendants thought that claimant lawyers would route work through London offices to benefit from the increase. Claimant lawyers thought that clients would find 'advice deserts' if they happened to live in London since solicitors would not deal with these cases without some reflection of the increased costs of practising in London.

Fixed disbursements

[26.11]

Unless a specific application is made to escape the fixed provisions, CPR 45.10 only allows the disbursements set out in CPR 45.11 to be recoverable. This provision was meant to simplify the issue of disbursements and therefore not prevent settlement being held up. However, a combination of factors has meant that often it was the disbursements which proved to be the sticking point. The defendants' fear that solicitors work would be repackaged as disbursements started the process. Some defendant negotiators have taken a very robust line with the aid of cases on medical report fees. Both sides have sometimes taken little notice of what is meant to be recoverable when putting claims forward or for challenging them. CPR PD 45, para 2.10 specifically provides for disbursement only proceedings under CPR 46.14 where the parties cannot agree the level of recoverable disbursements.

According to CPR 45.12 the court may allow any of the following disbursements but will not allow any other type. However, the final 'type' is described as 'any other disbursement that has arisen due to a particular feature of the dispute' (CPR 45.12(2)(c)) which leaves a large door open for the parties to disagree about a particular disbursement. The specific disbursements are the costs of obtaining:

- medical records;
- a medical report;
- a police report;
- an engineer's report;
- a DVLA search;
- counsel and court fees for an approval hearing if the claimant is a child or protected party (see **[26.13]**).

Medical fees

[26.12]

In *Stringer v Copley* [2012] Lexis Citation 68 HHJ (Michael) Cook considered the use of medical agencies in routine personal injury cases. He said that it had become common practice to instruct a medical agency to arrange a medical examination of the claimant; undertake the collation and obtaining of relevant medical reports; arrange the appointment with the medical expert and the claimant; deal with any cancellations or rearrangements and deliver the resultant medical report to the solicitors. Because of the specialisation, experience, expertise and contacts of the medical agency they were able to do this administrative work at least as efficiently, expeditiously and economically as most firms of solicitors using their own fee earners. There could be no objection in principle to the fees of the medical agency being recoverable between the parties, provided it could be demonstrated that their charges did not exceed the reasonable and proportionate costs of the work if it had been done by the solicitor. Where the invoice, or 'fee note', from the medical agency showed the medical consultant's fees and their own charges separately, it was possible for the costs officer to assess them both. But where a medical agency charged a composite fee, without differentiating between the amount of the medical consultant's fee and their own charges, the medical fees and the agency's charges were not sufficiently particularised. As such, the costs officer could not be satisfied that they did not exceed the reasonable and proportionate cost of a solicitor doing the work.

From a law of costs point of view this could not be faulted. Unfortunately, the practical implications of this (or perhaps simply the reluctance of medical reporting organisations to do as HHJ Cook stipulated) meant that the settlement of many cases was held up by a wait for further information. The same problem arose in relation to medical records which were often obtained by the medical agency for the benefit of the clinician. The decision of Master Hurst in *Woollard v Fowler* ([2005] EWHC 90051 (Costs)) did not resolve matters.

The temperature was reduced by an industry agreement reached between many of the liability insurers and the Association of Medical Reporting Organisations ('the AMRO agreement') which set standard figures for reports and which, with subsequent updates, have generally been adopted and allowed by the courts. The fixing of lower fees in the Portal for medical reports on soft tissue injuries may well have an impact on the AMRO agreement in due course (see **[26.19]**). A further challenge to medical agency fees relating to a seeming inconsistency in CPR 45.19 and CPR 45.29I was dismissed by HHJ Wood in *Beardmore v Lancashire County Council* (Liverpool CC 01/02/19) (see **[26.28]**).

Counsel's fees

[26.13]

The formal wording in respect of the approval hearing fees is 'where they are necessarily incurred by reason of one or more of the claimants being a child or protected party as defined in Part 21 – (i) fees payable for instructing counsel; or (ii) court fees payable on an application to the court.' You might think that the very fact that the claimant is a child would 'necessarily' incur the cost of counsel attending the approval hearing so that the judge could approve the settlement. After all, the court fee was necessarily incurred by the making of the application. However, a number of judges at first instance took the view that this was not so. A solicitor received a standard amount of costs for running the case. If he attended the approval hearing, no further costs would be incurred because there was no provision for any such costs to be paid. Therefore, the instruction of counsel was an additional cost and unless the case was a difficult one, it was an unreasonable one to incur. We always had some difficulty with the logic of such decisions. It appears that the decision of the Court of Appeal in *Aldred v Cham* [2019] EWCA Civ 1780 ought to have closed the door on this argument. The central reasoning – that counsel's advice had been incurred because the claimant was a child rather than because of a feature of the dispute – is unhelpful to claimants' solicitors in Section IIIA. But here paragraph 21 of the decision appears to take for granted that an advice is a necessity for an approval hearing.

Seeking to exceed the fixed recoverable costs

[26.14]

In *Solomon v Cromwell Group plc* [2011] EWCA Civ 1584 the Court of Appeal concluded that a claimant who beat his own Part 36 offer was still limited to fixed costs in a claim to which this section applies. In the light of *Broadhurst v Tan* (see **[20.33]**), there must be some doubt that the same conclusion would be reached based on the current incarnation of both Part 36 and Part 45. As such it may be possible to escape this section with a well-judged Part 36 offer.

CPR 45.13 contains the optimistic opening that the court 'will entertain a claim for an amount of costs . . . greater than the fixed recoverable costs' but then largely dashes hopes of escape by continuing that it will only do so 'if it considers there are exceptional circumstances' which would make it appropriate to do so. This has proved to be a high hurdle on the relatively rare occasions when an application has been made. The opponent's arguments tend to revolve around 'swings and roundabouts' and the extensive data that was available to the stakeholders and subsequently the Government when this section of Part 45 was brought in. Consequently, it will be a rare case whose facts are so extreme as to take it out of the data set originally used to calculate the figures. This 'high bar' was confirmed by Stewart J in *Ferri v Gill* [2019] EWHC 952 (QB) regarding the equivalent test in Section IIIA of Part 45 (see **[26.31]**). It is sometimes argued that in fact there are two high hurdles here. The first is the existence of exceptional circumstances. The second is that such circumstances make it appropriate to exercise the court's discretion. There may be some exceptional circumstances, perhaps relating to the claimant himself, which even if established do not make it appropriate for the defendant to pay on a standard basis.

In order to make sure parties think twice before a Part 8 claim is made, CPR 45.13 to CPR 45.15 spell out the costs consequences of such an application. There are two separate hurdles to overcome:

(1) The claimant must persuade the court that exceptional circumstances exist so that it is appropriate to exercise its discretion at all.
If the claimant fails to get past this hurdle, the court must make an order for fixed recoverable costs and disbursements only. The court may make an order for the claimant to pay the costs of the defendant in defending the proceedings.

(2) The claimant must persuade the court to allow increased costs at a figure at least 20% above the fixed figure (excluding VAT).

The assessment may be by summary or detailed assessment. If the claimant fails to achieve the 20% increase threshold, the court must order the defendant to pay the lesser of the fixed recoverable costs or the assessed costs. This provision (CPR 45.14(2)) makes it clear that assessed costs will not necessarily be higher than the fixed costs. As with hurdle 1, if the claimant does not overcome it, the court may make an order for the claimant to pay the defendant's costs of the Part 8 claim.

A little peculiarly, there is no specific provision for the claimant who surmounts both hurdles to be awarded costs. We do not think that is because the drafters assumed no one would ever manage this. It simply implies that costs will follow the event in the usual way and the claimant will receive his costs of the Part 8 claim to be assessed at the hearing.

PART 45 SECTION III (CPR 45.16–CPR 45.29)

[26.15]

The title of this section is 'The Pre-Action Protocols for low value personal injury claims in road traffic accidents and low value personal injury (employers' liability and public liability) claims'. The title gives away two things. The first is that the employers' liability ('EL') and public liability ('PL') claims have been grafted on to the original RTA Protocol making everything more awkwardly drafted than would probably have been the case if the protocol was drafted from scratch. But that could not happen because thousands of personal injury cases were already progressing through 'the Portal' as it is known. (The increase in the value of the scheme and its inclusion of EL and PL accident claims relates to all claims where the Claims Notification Form is sent on or after 31 July 2013. For EL disease claims the trigger point is whether a letter of claim has been sent by 31 July 2013). Perhaps fortunately, the pre-action protocol for Package Travel Claims has not produced a further graft onto the original wording of this Section. Instead it is attached to Section IIIA (see below) which contains the rules appropriate to cases which have not concluded in this Section.

The second is that the Protocols, together with the Part 8 procedure documentation run to an inordinate length given that the idea was meant to be a simple and cheap system to deal with low value cases where liability was not in dispute.

The length of the wording is a reflection of the drafters' intention to cover every eventuality. If you imagine for a moment, a cartoon where a wooden box contains two creatures who are experts at escaping from such boxes. Along comes the hero of the cartoon who is charged with keeping these creatures in the box. There then exists a scene where the hero is constantly nailing more and more pieces of wood on to the original box in order to plug gaps being created by the two creatures. Soon the box looks nothing like the original creation and is probably odds on to survive anything short of a nuclear explosion. That, in a way, is the situation here. Both claimant lawyers and defendant insurers have become experts at seeking to gain advantage on the pre-action playing field on which the vast majority of personal injury cases settle. Once the predictable costs regime came into play (see Part 45 Section II above), claimants' lawyers would escape its provisions and commence proceedings where they thought the defendant insurers were dragging their heels. The defendant insurers (or their lawyers) would then dispute the level of costs claimed as being caused by premature issuing of proceedings and so the allowed sums should be limited to those under the predictable costs regime. With this background, it is no surprise that the Protocol would need careful drafting to avoid manipulation by the parties.

In passing, it is worth noting that an appeal from a claim in Section III of Part 45 is by way of Part 52 rather than Part 45 (see *Wickes Building Supplies Ltd v Blair (No.2) (Costs)* [2020] EWCA Civ 17, [2020] 1 WLR 1246.

The three stages

[26.16]

For both protocols there are three stages. The first two occur prior to any court proceedings. The third stage requires a hearing by the court (but nothing else) and therefore is commenced by a Part 8 claim, hence the relevant Practice Direction is 8B.

Stage 1 is all about liability for the accident. The claimant puts forward his case via an online system known as the Portal. If the defendant denies liability (or does not respond) the case falls out of the Portal (see below). If the defendant admits liability, Stage 1 ends and the Stage 1 fee becomes payable.

It originally had to be paid within 10 days of the admission but this had the effect of a number of claims stopping at this point which was considered undesirable. Consequently, the Stage 1 fee is now only payable at the end of Stage 2.

Stage 2 is concerned with quantum and negotiation. The claimant obtains medical evidence to support the claim and sends this through to the defendant together with a Part 36 offer. If the defendant does not accept the claimant's valuation, he can put forward a counter offer and there is a short window for negotiation. If settlement is reached the claimant receives his damages. If not, the claimant has to initiate the Stage 3 procedure. In either event, his solicitor now receives the Stage 1 and Stage 2 costs. Even though the case has not concluded, the claimant is at no risk as to costs to this point and therefore the recoverable costs are to be paid over. The cost of the only significant disbursement, the medical report, is met directly by the defendant.

Stage 3 is about obtaining a court determination. There is nothing to prevent the parties negotiating formally after the window in Stage 2 has closed. (A good many cases settle in this way and are catered for within Section IIIA.) But in theory both parties have made their best offers by now. The claimant then completes a court proceedings pack and begins Part 8 proceedings. In addition to making their best offers, the parties are meant to have exchanged their evidence before the Part 8 proceedings are commenced. Any later served evidence should be disregarded by the court according to PD 8B and the party taking this point is not to be considered to oppose the claim to the extent that it should fall out of the Portal and require Part 7 proceedings to be commenced: *Wickes Building Supplies Ltd v Blair* [2019] EWCA Civ 1934, [2019] 4 WLR 148.

The court will either give a determination on paper as to the appropriate quantum or at a hearing if either party wants to take that latter step. Sealed offers are provided to the court as part of the court pack and so the judge is in a position to determine damages and costs on paper or at a hearing.

A word should be said here about claims needing approvals. More is said below because the options are varied. But for the moment, it is worth noting that an approval hearing could come at Stage 2 in order to approve a settlement between the parties or at Stage 3 where it is more akin to an assessment of damages hearing.

The fixed costs

[26.17]

In the Portal, the only recoverable costs allowed are the fixed costs and disbursements set out in this section. There is no opportunity to obtain assessed costs and therefore issues of seeking indemnity costs for the opponent's conduct do not arise. The same is true in relation to Part 36 offers in the Portal and which we deal with in Chapter 20 (see **[20.32]** in particular). The recoverable costs are contained in Tables 6 and 6A in the Practice Direction. There are rather more options than might be expected for a three stage procedure. The tables distinguish between RTA on the one hand and EL /PL on the other. They also break at £10,000, which was the original limit for the RTA protocol. These distinctions are predicated on the basis that EL/PL claims are perceived to be more difficult than RTA claims and that added value brings added complexity. There are further complications because the fees for stage 3 are broken down into the uninformative Type A, B and C costs. Type A fixed costs refer to the 'legal representative's costs' for running the third stage. Type B refers to the 'advocate's costs' where a hearing in person takes place and Type C refers to the written advice required for an approval hearing. The tables are set out at the end of the book but they are condensed as follows:

	Stage 1	**Stage 2**	**Stage 3**		
			A	**B**	**C**
RTA up to £10,000	£200	£300	£250	£250	£150
RTA above £10,000	£200	£600	£250	£250	£150
EL/PL up to £10,000	£300	£600	£250	£250	£150
EL/PL above £10,000	£300	£1300	£250	£250	£150

Where the parties reach agreement after the Part 8 proceedings have been sent to the court, but before they have been issued, the claimant will be entitled to a Type A payment so long as the agreed figure is more than the defendant's formal protocol offer.

'London weighting' applies here as it does in Section II. If the claimant lives or works in London and the legal representative also practises in London, the recoverable costs are increased by 12.5%. This provision does not apply to Type B or C costs in Stage 3. The definition of London is set out in Practice Direction 45.

'Counsel's' advice

[26.18]

Before the Portal was expanded vertically (by increasing the damages to £25,000) and horizontally (to include EL and PL claims), the only use of counsel which could be recovered was for the provision of a written advice and / or representation at an approval hearing or as an advocate at the Stage 3 hearing. The increased value of claims persuaded the rule makers that seeking advice on quantum was appropriate for the larger cases. Consequently CPR 45.23B allows for a Type C costs claim to be made where the damages are over £10,000. This provision looks fraught with difficulty. What happens if the solicitor thinks it is worth more than £10,000 but counsel disagrees? Which is the 'value' of the claim? It would seem fairly clear that the Advice would generally be taken as representing the correct figure, but what if a Stage 3 hearing decides damages are indeed more than £10,000? CPR 45.23B requires the advice to be 'reasonably required' and that will undoubtedly be viewed differently in different quarters. Finally, the advice can be obtained by 'a specialist solicitor or counsel.' Will defendants seek to argue that the solicitor was not a specialist and so the fee is not payable? (Why is it not specialist counsel anyway?) Will local arrangements between solicitors come to pass to earn further income by providing opinions on a reciprocal basis? This provision looks to be something of a sop to the junior Bar but it may simply lead to a lot of work being done and billed but never recovered.

The disbursements

[26.19]

The disbursements which may be recovered are set out at CPR 45.19. The prescribed items are in very similar terms to those in Section II ([**26.11**]). As with that Section, the rule says that the court may allow certain prescribed disbursements but will not allow any other type. It then finishes with the catch-all phrase that it may allow 'any other disbursement that has arisen due to a particular feature of the dispute' which appeared to us rather to destroy the strength of the earlier wording. However, the Court of Appeal in *Aldred v Cham* [2019] EWCA Civ 1780 has taken a more literal view of that phrase to exclude the costs of the written advice expected to be produced at approval hearings in Section IIIA (see [**26.28**] below). In respect of section III the cost of such advice is specifically provided for in Tables 6 and 6A as provided for in CPR 45.18(2).

The disbursements which are recoverable are the costs of obtaining medical records and a medical report. As mentioned above, in most cases the defendant has paid for the medical report and associated records directly. This is likely to change, at least for the time being, as EL and PL practitioners can be expected to take a less collaborative approach than some RTA lawyers whose clients have very largely needed standard medical evidence to support soft tissue claims.

Where the claim is for soft tissue 'whiplash' injuries arising out of an RTA, the claimant's choice of medical expert is effectively limited by restrictions made to the recoverable costs allowed for the report or reports required. A 'fixed cost medical report' is one which is produced by a doctor who is not treating the claimant (or recommends that he should do so.) These restrictions extend to associates of the doctor who have provided such treatment (or might do so). Only in exceptional circumstances will a fee for an expert who has treated the claimant (or might do so) be allowed.

The recoverable cost of a fixed cost medical report is £180 (slightly less than is allowed in the AMRO agreement) (see [**26.12**]). An addendum report fee by the same doctor is fixed at £50 (unless the doctor is a consultant orthopaedic surgeon) and a reply to Part 35 questions is £80.00. The cost of obtaining medical records is capped at £30.00 together with the record holder's own fee and which is limited to a maximum of £80.00 altogether. All of these figures are net of any VAT chargeable.

Further medical reports may be obtained in appropriate cases. There are prescribed fees for the most likely specialties. The claimant is not limited to those specialties nor to the sums claimed but will have to justify the use of the expert and the cost claimed in such circumstances. In practice, it is likely that those doctors who are accredited under the scheme and are willing to work for the prescribed fees will be instructed. These capped fees apply to all cases where the Claims Notification Form is dated on or after 1 October 2014.

Engineer's report fees and those for searching the DVLA and MID databases can be claimed. So too can court fees where an approval is needed, a Part 8 claim has to be issued for Stage 3 or where protective proceedings have been issued to avoid falling foul of limitation. This would be rare in RTA proceedings but may be more common in EL and PL cases. It is an area of potential disagreement, particularly where the defendant could agree to extend the limitation period rather than have proceedings issued to safeguard the claimant's position.

Offers

[26.20]

These are compulsory in the Portal in order to encourage settlement and have to be made before the Stage 3 procedure can be invoked. If they are not made, then the case falls out of the Portal. They are dealt with along with other Part 36 offers in Chapter 20.

Avoidance behaviour

[26.21]

If the defendant wishes the case to exit the Portal he has numerous ways of doing so, mostly simply by inaction on his part, and there are no specific sanctions if he decides to take this step. The expectation is that defendants, or more particularly their insurers, will always want to keep cases in the Portal and therefore will not act in this way.

There is and always has been a temptation for claimant lawyers to exit their client's case from the Portal in order to make the case more profitable. While that may sound pejorative, there is no obvious improvement in the evidence before a court to assess damages between a Stage 3 hearing and a disposal or other assessment of damages hearing so it does not appear to be a question of the client's damages as to why cases exited with alacrity. Consequently, CPR 45.24 spells out the costs consequences if a court considers that the claimant (or his lawyer) has not engaged properly with the Portal in one of the following ways:

- providing insufficient information in the Claim Notification Form;
- by unreasonably valuing the claim at more than £25,000 so that there is no need to comply with the Protocol;
- discontinuing the process set out in the Protocol unreasonably and starting Part 7 proceedings;
- commencing proceedings on the basis that an interim payment made is insufficient;
- acting unreasonably in any other way that causes the Protocol to be discontinued.

In any of these situations the court may demonstrate its displeasure by ordering the defendant to pay no more to a successful claimant than the appropriate Portal fixed costs and disbursements. In *Ryan v Hackett* [2020] EWHC 288 (QB), Stewart J allowed standard basis costs, notwithstanding an errant exit, where the case's value meant an exit would have occurred at a later point in any event. However, in *Williams v Secretary of State for Business, Energy and Industrial Strategy* [2018] EWCA Civ 852, the Court of Appeal reinforced the prospect of such cases being limited to fixed costs, albeit that the proceedings in that case had not actually been commenced in the Portal at all. The case was settled by acceptance of a Part 36 Offer (see **[20.30]** for a detailed consideration).

In *Bewicke-Copley v Ibeh* (1 May 2014, Oxford CC), DJ Vincent the court decided that the defendant was able to settle some aspects of the claim independently of others while the claim was in the Portal. The result was that the value of the remaining items meant the subsequent proceedings were allocated to the small claims track. There was no criticism of the claimant's view that the claim had to exit the Portal to deal with issues on which there was a complete dispute. But that did not mean that previously agreed items had not been settled and so should be taken into account in the allocation to track. Reference is made in the judgment to a number of first instance decisions regarding alleged 'avoidance behaviour' which were said to inform this decision.

Approval hearings

[26.22]

Where the claimant is a child and the parties have agreed liability and damages the claimant applies for an approval hearing using a Part 8 claim in the traditional way. If the court approves the settlement the claimant will be awarded a full house of Stage 1, Stage 2 and Type A, B and C costs from Stage 3 for the hearing (even though it is not a 'Stage 3 hearing' in the sense of a court assessing the damages) and disbursements.

However, if the court does not approve the settlement, it will only award Stage 1 and Stage 2 costs (and disbursements) at the time and the parties will be sent away to prepare for another hearing. This might be once a larger sum has been agreed or it might be an assessment of damages hearing because the parties cannot agree any larger figure. At the second hearing, the claimant will be awarded the Type A and C costs for the preparation work and the advice. The court will also award the Type B (advocacy) costs for one of the hearings. The court has the discretion to award an additional amount for the extra Type A and Type B fees incurred by having two hearings. The court can order either the claimant or defendant to pay such extra costs or it could decide to make no order in this respect.

Where the parties are apart at the end of Stage 2 but, having applied for a Stage 3 hearing the parties reach a settlement, the provisions of CPR 45.22 apply rather than CPR 45.21 (described in the previous paragraphs). The rules are identical in terms of what will be paid when and with what discretion. The only difference under this rule is that the Stage 3 hearing is used as the second hearing if the approval hearing is not originally successful. This rule is also built on the basis that the settlement is more than the defendant's protocol offer. If it were not, presumably the defendant would want to alter the incidence of costs.

In the unlikely event that the court considers that the claim is not suitable for approval to be determined by the court under the Stage 3 procedure, CPR 45.23 decrees that the court will order the defendant to pay the 'full house' costs of Stage 1, Stage 2 and Stage 3 A, B and C but there is no mention of disbursements being paid at this point.

Adjournment

[26.23]

Where the court adjourns a hearing – whether Stage 3 or approval – it may, in its discretion, order a party to pay an additional amount of Type B costs and any court fee for the adjournment.

Costs of the costs only proceedings

[26.24]

Should it be the case that a Part 8 claim is started for an approval hearing or for a Stage 3 hearing and then the case settles, it is to be hoped that the parties can agree the costs of these proceedings as well. But if the amount of costs is the sticking point (and not the principle of who should pay) either party may apply to the court for it to determine the costs by virtue of CPR 45.29. Where this happens the court will assess the costs in accordance with CPR 45.22 and CPR 45.25 and not CPR 44.5 which has no application here.

CPR 45.22 deals with costs based on the parties reaching agreement where the claimant is a child (see above). CPR 45.25 deals with two situations depending on the level of settlement agreed by the parties. If the settlement is more than the defendant's protocol offer, the claimant will be awarded any Stage 1 and 2 payments not already received. He will also receive Type A costs and his disbursement. But where the claimant has not beaten the offer the claimant will not get the Type A costs (but will get the other items) and the court may, in its discretion, order either party to pay the costs of the application.

PART 45 SECTION IIIA (CPR 45.29A–CPR 45.29L)

[26.25]

This section deals with the fixed recoverable costs for 'Claims which no longer continue under the RTA or EL/PL Pre-Action Protocols'. These changes apply to all cases where the CNF was sent on or after on 31 July 2013 and which is when this section came into the CPR. Although this section does not apply to disease claims, it does leave the great majority of personal injury claims in an entirely fixed costs world. Even claims for personal injuries abroad have started to come within the fixed costs regime. Since May 2018, many 'package travel claims' are also now dealt with via a pre-action protocol and, should they fall out of that scheme, will be bound by the costs allowed in Section IIIA. The claims have to be for gastric illness and there are other limitations but it would appear that the protocol will nip in the bud the rush by some claimant firms to move into new areas of personal injury work to avoid the fixed costs applicable to more traditional areas.

The Civil Justice Council report into Noise Induced Hearing Loss ('deafness') cases in September 2017 also proposed to continue the spread of fixed costs arrangements into disease claims.

It used to be the case that a claimant could escape any fixed costs structures if he could leave the Portal (which many cases did) and get to issue proceedings so as to leave the predictable costs regime (in Section II) behind as well.

Thereafter, with the exception of the trial costs (which were generally there simply to pay counsel's fees anyway) the solicitor was on to payment by hourly rate. Section IIIA means that this is no longer so for the great majority of cases. Allocation to the multi-track rather than the fast track is however sufficient: *Shahow Qader v Esure Services Ltd* [2016] EWCA Civ 1109. The Court of Appeal were obliged to read extra words into CPR 45.29B to achieve the intention of the rule makers as perceived by the Court. The Rule Committee promptly added the same words to the rule.

There is an escape clause (see [**26.31**]) but that is likely to be rarely successful based on similar applications made under Sections II and III. There is also the possibility of escaping by means of a successful Part 36 Offer. This is discussed in more detail in Chapter 20 following the Court of Appeal's decision in *Broadhurst & Taylor v Tan and Smith* [2016] EWCA Civ 94 where CPR 36.14A trumped CPR 45.29B. However, the general wind appears to be blowing against extending *Broadhurst* to other parts of Part 36; see for example Carr J's decision in *Parsa v DS Smith plc* (QBD (Birmingham) 25/03/2019).

This section borrows drafting from Sections II and III and so in the following paragraphs we have referred you to comments on those sections elsewhere in this chapter rather than repeating the comments here.

General points

[26.26]

(1) The 'London weighting' provision referred to in Section II [**26.10**] and Section III [**26.17**] appears here as well. So if the party and his solicitor work in London (as defined) or the claimant lives in London and the solicitor works there, a sum equivalent to 12.5% is added to the figures in the various tables. The only element which does not get a London weighting is the recoverable disbursements.

(2) VAT is payable in addition to the figures set out for costs.

(3) The only recoverable costs are the fixed costs and disbursements set out in this section. There are no outside costs or orders that can be brought in to these claims.

(4) The fixed costs are generally a combination of a base fee plus a figure equivalent to a percentage of the damages. While some parts of Tables 6C, 6D and 6E are internally consistent, the individual figures defy any summary and need to be viewed in full at the end of the book.

(5) Nevertheless the parameters of the tables are consistent amongst the three types of personal injury claim. In each case:
  - (a) There are five stages:
    - (i) pre-issue;
    - (ii) from issue but prior to allocation;
    - (iii) from allocation but prior to the date of listing;
    - (iv) from the date of listing but prior to the date of trial
    - (v) trial
  - (b) Where the case settles pre-issue the costs vary based on three value bands:
    - (i) £1,000 up to £5,000;
    - (ii) Over £5,000 up to £10,000
    - (iii) Over £10,000 up to £25,000.

(c) Once proceedings have been issued, the value of the case does not matter in terms of calculating the level of costs; it simply depends on the stage of settlement, if settled before trial.

(d) There is no increase in either the base fee or the percentage figure between stages (iv) and (v) set out above. Therefore there is no incentive to run a case to a hearing as any form of costs building exercise. The only increase to the recoverable costs is the addition of the trial advocacy fee. In *Bruno Manuel Dos Santos Mendes v Hochtief (UK) Construction Ltd* [2016] EWHC 976 (QB), Coulson J concluded that the advocate's fee is payable where a case settles on the day of the trial but before the trial begins. (As such he distinguished the line of cases regarding success fees under the old rule 45.16 (see **[6.43]**).)

(e) The trial advocacy fees are the same whether it is an RTA, EL or PL claim. They are contained in four bands which does not fit with the rest of these costs but does tie in with the fixed costs in Section VI. With the exception of the top band, the figures appear to have been increased by roughly 3% since their equivalent figures in Section VI were last up-rated in October 2007. The fees are:

Value of the claim	Trial advocacy fee
No more than £3,000	£500
£3,001 – £10,000	£710
£10,001 – £15,000	£1,070
£15,001 – £25,000	£1,705

The description of stages at general point 5 above indicates that there is a linear progression of a case. That is clearly how the tables were intended to be used. However, it overlooked the point that many cases would not be defended as such and so they would go to a disposal hearing rather than be allocated to track. The case could be described as having settled after issue but before allocation. Equally it could be said to have settled only after the case has been listed for hearing but before the disposal hearing actually takes place. The difference in recoverable fees can be considerable. In a public liability case, the fees are £2,450 plus 17.5% of the damages payable or £3,790 plus 27.5% respectively.

The Court of Appeal considered this point in *Bird v Acorn Group Ltd* [2016] EWCA Civ 1096. The Court described it as a short point, notwithstanding the breadth of counsels' submissions. Briggs LJ determined that listing a case for a disposal hearing following judgment is the same as listing for trial for the purposes of considering Table 6D and therefore the claimant received the higher amount in column three. The same would be true for Tables 6B (RTA) and 6C (EL).

Interim Applications

[26.27]

Where an interim application is made, the recoverable costs are one-half of the applicable Type A and Type B costs in Table 6 and 6A: in other words, £125 each. London Weighting, disbursements and VAT are all potentially payable in addition.

An application by a claimant for pre-action disclosure from the defendant, a so-called PAD application, is an example of an interim application under CPR 45.29H. The claimant in *Sharp v Leeds City Council* [2017] EWCA Civ 33 was unsuccessful in arguing that PAD applications were free-standing and the costs of them should be outside Part IIIA. The sums now allowed suggest that such applications will be much rarer in personal injury claims in the future, despite the Court of Appeal's suggestion that recalcitrant defendants might have to pay costs via the 'exceptional circumstances' route (see **[26.31]**). The Court said that claimants might still succeed on such applications, notwithstanding the possibility that many defendants do not comply with their protocol obligations and so such conduct may not appear to found exceptional conduct at first sight.

Disbursements

[26.28]

These are set out in CPR 45.29I. The wording follows Sections II and III in that some disbursements may be allowed; any others must not be; but case specific disbursements can in theory at least be made an exception. The categories that may be allowed are:

- Medical records and reports (see **[26.19]** in Section III for more detail)
- Non-medical expert reports
- Advice from a specialist solicitor or counsel (see **[26.18]** in Section III)
- Court fees
- Expert's trial attendance fees where the court has given the expert permission to attend
- Travelling and subsistence expenses for a party or their witness attending the hearing
- Loss of earnings or leave for a party or their witness attending the hearing (see Practice Direction 45 for the limits on this)
- In an RTA case, an engineer's report (on the condition of the car and any repairs rather than as contemplated in the second bullet point above) and DVLA or MID searches

In *Beardmore v Lancashire County Council* (Liverpool CC 01/02/19), HHJ Wood examined the provisions of CPR 45.29I. In particular, the discrepancy between subparagraphs 45.29I(2)(a) and 45.29I(2A)(c) regarding the cost of obtaining medical records. In the first of these subparagraphs, 'the cost' is not defined. In the second (regarding soft tissue injury cases), it specifically makes reference to a maximum of £30 plus the direct cost of the record provider. The defendant argued that the absence of any reference to the £30 (for example) meant that no cost of the medical agency (or presumably solicitor) could be claimed in addition to the record provider's own fee in a public liability case. However, Judge Wood took the view that such an approach would mean that in RTA cases, generally, this would forbid such fees and that would make no sense given that they were specifically allowed in soft tissue injury RTA cases. Any such prohibition could easily have been set out by the rule makers. The amount to be allowed was the reasonable and proportionate costs of obtaining the records and that sum was not limited to the £30 maximum allowed for soft tissue injury RTA cases.

Since the relevant parts of CPR 45.19 are written in the same terms as CPR 45.29I, this decision would appear to apply to cases in Section II as well as Section IIIA.

By contrast, the limitation on counsel's fees to £150 plus VAT (a Type C fee) in Section III does not apply to Section IIIA where the case has left the Portal. So held Lambert J in *Finsbury Food Group plc v Dover* [2020] EWHC 3276 (QB) and which makes sense given that cases fall out of the Portal for various reasons, some of which would need little recourse to counsel but others may need a good deal.

Taking variations further, the route by which counsel's advice in approval hearings is dealt with differently in each of Sections II, III and IIIA. In Section II specific reference to a claim as a disbursement can be found in CPR 45.18 (see **[26.13]**). In Section III the fee can be found as 'Type C fixed costs' in Tables 6 and 6A (see **[26.19]**). But there is no specific provision in IIIA and so you are left using the phrase that the court may allow 'any other disbursement that has arisen due to a particular feature of the dispute'. We had taken the view that this was a broad catch-all description which appeared rather to destroy the strength of the earlier wording. However, the Court of Appeal in *Aldred v Cham* [2019] EWCA Civ 1780 has taken a more literal view of that phrase to exclude the costs of the written advice expected to be produced at approval hearings in Section IIIA. The Court concluded that the need for the advice emanated from the fact the claimant was a child rather than any particular feature of the dispute. As such the cost was to be found within the sums in Table 6B.

In the judgment reference is made avoiding busy district judges having to compare the various rules in Part 45 to consider the variations. At first blush, this decision may give rise to district judges being busy in having to determine whether the evidence is sufficiently clear that the settlement ought to be approved without a written advice at all (CPR PD 21, para 5.2). Some judges will no doubt require advice in all cases, but others will be more sympathetic to the idea of avoiding a cost which may have to be met by the protected party or child from their damages.

Defendant's costs

[26.29]

It appeared for a long time as if the defendant's costs were not going to be subject to fixed costs which would have been a surprising outcome. While defendants do not win many personal injury claims and QOCS make enforcement of any costs order impossible in most cases, there are defendants with counterclaims as well as defendants who successfully uphold Part 36 offers. There are also defendants who are successful in interim applications. CPR 45.29F deals with defendant's costs. As with claimants, defendants are entitled to London weighting, VAT and disbursements where appropriate.

The general rule is that, unlike claimants, the defendant will not necessarily be awarded the fixed recoverable costs set out in Tables 6C, 6D and 6E. The court is required to have regard to those Tables and is not to make an award that exceeds them. But that does not prevent the court from allowing less than the fixed figures.

In order to use the Tables the court has to decide what the value of the claim is. This will usually be the amount specified on the claim form but excluding any contributory negligence; amounts not in dispute; interest or costs; or vehicle damage (if an RTA claim). If the claim form does not state the value, the court will look at the statement of value required by CPR 16.3. If the claimant has stated he cannot reasonably say how much is likely to be recovered the value will be taken to be the maximum ie £25,000.

Part 36, and in particular CPR 36.20, applies rather than this section where the claimant accepts the defendant's offer or fails to beat the defendant's offer at trial. If the claimant is struck out or found to be fundamentally dishonest under CPR 44.15 and CPR 44.16, the court will assess the defendant's costs without reference to CPR 45.29F and therefore the fixed recoverable costs in this section.

Counterclaims

[26.30]

Where a defendant successfully brings a counterclaim which includes a claim for personal injury to which the RTA Protocol applies, the order for costs will be assessed in the same way as if the defendant were the claimant bringing a claim.

However, where there is no claim for personal injuries within the counterclaim, the defendant will only be entitled to costs amounting to one half of the applicable Type A and Type B costs (ie £125) in Table 6 together with London Weighting, VAT and disbursements where appropriate.

Escaping the fixed fees

[26.31]

Unlike CPR 45.13 in Section II, the court does not ask to be entertained in this section. Nevertheless the two (or three) hurdles that need to be jumped – exceptionality and a 20% increase on the fixed figures – are the same as in CPR 45.13 to CPR 45.15 (see [**26.14**]).

An application may be made by the claimant or the defendant. If the court is not persuaded of the exceptional nature of the case, or that it is not appropriate to exercise the court's discretion in any event, the claimant will be limited to the fixed recoverable costs set out in this section. The defendant may also get those figures but will not necessarily get that much. CPR 45.29J says the court will allow an amount that 'has regard to' the fixed recoverable costs. It makes it clear that the assessed figure will not exceed the fixed figure.

If the court agrees that there are exceptional circumstances but, having assessed the costs, does not award a sum that is 20% or more above the fixed figures, the court will allow the lower of the assessed figure or the fixed figure. As with the rules in Section II, it is clear that the court may allow a lower figure than the fixed costs in an appropriate case.

In either of these failed eventualities, the court may decide not to award the costs of the proceedings to the receiving party. Indeed the court may make the receiving party pay the costs of the paying party in respect of the proceedings and/or assessment.

In *Ferri v Gill* [2019] EWHC 952 (QB), Stewart J overturned the deputy costs judge's conclusion that exceptionality was only a 'low bar' to surmount. In accordance with numerous judicial pronouncements in the Senior Courts, it was in fact a high bar. In our experience, it is one that is seldom overcome.

PART 45 SECTION IV (CPR 45.30–CPR 45.32)

[26.32]

The Patents County Court underwent a package of reforms in October 2010 in relation to procedure, transfers and costs dealt with by Parts 63, 30 and 45 of the CPR respectively. From 1 October 2013 it also underwent a change of name so that it became the Intellectual Property Enterprise Court ('IPEC'). The reforms (other than the change of name) might seem to be esoteric to many but in our view, they hold the seeds of future rules and practice, particularly in the fast track and bear some scrutiny as a result. We have said this for some years now and as such are interested to see the outcome of the costs capping pilot which appears to be based on the IPEC arrangements (see **[26.54]**).

HHJ Birss QC (now Birss J) was in part responsible for implementing the new rules and has been responsible for decisions tackling a number of issues arising from the fixed, or scale, fee structure imposed. Some of those decisions can easily be transferred into costs budgeting issues already and if the Jackson Review proposals for fast track costs come into play these decisions can certainly be 'read across' there as well.

The most complicated cases involving intellectual property are still run in the Intellectual Property list in the Patents Court in the High Court. Cases which fit within certain parameters can be transferred to IPEC at the first Case Management Conference (see, for example, Arnold J's consideration of the relevant factors in *IOT IP GmbH v Haandle Ltd* [2019] EWHC 534 (Pat)). For cases that are transferred, there are then two tracks in the IPEC. The great majority of the rules, the cases that follow them and all of the costs provisions referred to in the following paragraphs relate to the multi-track cases. Nevertheless there is also a small claims track for cases up to £10,000 involving most but not all of the claims that can be brought in the IPEC multi-track. There is a simplified procedure and costs are limited to those set out in Part 27 for small claims track cases generally: CPR 63.27(4). In *Twentieth Century Fox Film Corpn v Cyclone Events Ltd* [2019] EWHC 1758 (IPEC), HHJ Hacon gave a short judgment on matters to be considered when a court is asked to transfer an IPEC case to the small claims version.

Scale management

[26.33]

The guiding principle of HHJ Birss QC in a series of judgments is to allow the court to 'facilitate access to justice for smaller litigants in intellectual property cases.' The key to doing this is to ensure that there is certainty that the cost capping figures will not be exceeded except in the most unusual case. Every early judgment makes this comment. In *Westwood v Knight* [2011] EWPCC 11, he puts it this way

> 'The correct approach must be to apply the limits if they can possibly be applied, recognizing however that in the end the court always has a discretion as to costs and that includes the amount of costs. It is a discretion which in my judgment will very rarely (if ever) be exercised to exceed the limits set by Section [IV]. For one thing specific exceptions are provided for [r. 45.30]. Furthermore to exercise discretion on a wider basis in all but the most rare and exceptional case would undermine the very object of the scale in the first place. For the scale to give a measure of certainty to litigants it has to be possible to be sure that the limits will apply well before any costs are incurred and most likely before any action has even commenced.'

The exceptions to which the judge refers relate to a finding that one party's conduct amounts to an abuse of process or where there is a certificate of contested validity relating to a patent or registered design. The extent of the conduct required was highlighted by Judge Hacon in *F H Brundle v Perry* [2014] EWHC 979 (IPEC). He considered that CPR 45.31 required a case to be 'truly exceptional' and the case before him 'was not truly exceptional on the scale of unsatisfactory behaviour.' As such it could be taken into account in awarding the amount of costs but only insofar as the costs remained within the overall caps set by the scales (see next heading). HHJ Melissa Clarke decided that the defendant's conduct was an abuse in *Link Up Mitaka Ltd (t/a The Big Word) v Language Empire Ltd* [2018] EWHC 2728 (IPEC) and consequently disapplied the caps. She recognised the policy issues referred to by HHJ Birss QC but, having found an abuse, considered herself to be under a duty to reflect that following dicta of Lord Diplock in *Hunter v Chief Constable of the West Midlands Police* [1982] AC 529.

In *Skyscape Cloud Services Ltd v Sky plc* [2016] EWHC 1340 (IPEC), HHJ Hacon decided that the lack of clarity in the claimant's case was not close to an abuse and was not truly exceptional. As such he refused to lift the overall cap but did decide to raise one of the individual caps from £3,000 to £8,000 which still left the overall costs being with the overarching cap. His description of the claimant's conduct as being 'not ideal' was presumably something of an understatement.

The scale figures do not apply where costs are awarded on the indemnity basis: *Phonographic Performance Ltd v Hagan* [2016] EWHC 3076 (IPEC). Following the approach of the Court of Appeal in *Broadhurst v Tan* [2016] EWCA Civ 94, HHJ Hacon allowed the ceiling imposed by fixed costs set out in the CPR to be ignored where a claimant had beaten his own Part 36 offer and so (what is now) CPR 36.17 applied. HHJ Hacon revisited this point in *Martin v Kogan* [2017] EWHC 3266 (IPEC) and concluded that the approach in *Hagan* was unlikely to be justified in most cases where indemnity basis costs orders were made following a Part 36 offer. It was more likely that the Jackson Supplementary Report approach would be followed. That was to allow a further 25% to the capped figures, always subject to the discretion of the court.

Other than these exceptions the scale costs apply to all cases in the IPEC although where a case has transferred from the High Court, the provisions do not relate to the pre-transfer costs incurred.

The scales

[26.34]

There are two tables set out in the Practice Direction. Table A relates to activities undertaken when dealing with the question of liability. Table B relates to quantum activities and which will take the form either of an inquiry as to damages or an account of profits. Against each activity is a scale figure which is in fact a cap since it is the maximum amount of costs allowed for that stage unless the court exercises its discretion.

Overarching these individual stages and caps are global caps set out in CPR 45.31. In relation to liability, the cap is £50,000. For quantum it is £25,000. These sums are inclusive of VAT where recoverable (*Response Clothing Ltd v Edinburgh Woollen Mill* [2020] EWHC 721 (IPEC)). They are also the maximum claimed even if there is more than one opponent. In *Gimex International Groupe Import Export v The Chill Bag Company Ltd* [2012] EWPCC 34 the successful claimant sought to claim £45,000 from each of two defendants. HHJ Birss QC was clear that if Gimex had lost the case it would not have been required to pay more than £50,000 even though there were two defendants. On that basis it would be wrong to allow it to 'share out its single costs bill as between two sets of defendants and thereby recover more than £50,000 in costs in these proceedings.'

The caps are inclusive of any additional liabilities claimed (*Henderson v All Around the World Recordings Ltd* [2013] EWPCC 19) where the case was commenced in IPEC. Judge Birss QC indicated in *Henderson* that the non-recovery of success fees might be a reason to refuse a transfer from the High Court. That comment was picked up by Mann J in the case of *Crocker Enterprises v Giordano Poultry* [2013] EWHC 2491 (Ch) when refusing a transfer. The effective capping of the claimant's costs was one of the two 'weighty' matters which militated against a transfer notwithstanding the modest sums in issue. The non-recovery of the success fee would, absent a 'fancy clause', fall on the claimant. If such a clause were present, the effect would fall on the claimant's lawyers.

The scale figures were varied on 1 October 2013 to coincide with the coming into being of the IPEC in place of the Patents county court. If a case was already proceeding in the Patents county court, it was the original (lower) figures which apply to the case (Birss J in *Phonographic Performance Ltd v Hamilton Entertainment Ltd* [2013] EWHC 3801 (IPEC)).

Assessment

[26.35]

The default method of assessment of costs in the IPEC is by summary assessment. This is so even if the trial lasted more than a day (unlike the fast track). Consequently, the rules as to interim payments and detailed assessment proceedings are specifically disapplied by CPR 45.30(3).

Where there are costs from High Court proceedings pre-transfer, these are assessed summarily in the normal way (see Chapter 27). Otherwise, the assessment of costs is something of a hybrid between the usual summary assessment and the application of costs capping. In order to carry this out the receiving party needs to break down its costs claimed into the stages in Tables

A and B. Where this was not done, the court did its best to carry out a summary assessment but disallowed costs relating to disclosure entirely for a period. Recorder Campbell, in *Lumos Skincare Ltd v Sweet Squared Ltd* [2012] EWPCC 28 said, having found that he had no clear information on the defendant's disclosure, 'I am not prepared either to make assumptions in the defendant's favour about matters which the defendant could have proved, or to award some arbitrary sum, since to do so would be unfair to the claimant. I therefore make no award for the defendant's costs relating to disclosure over this period.'

In *Westwood* the receiving party did provide a breakdown of costs by stages and furthermore a summary schedule setting out totals for each stage. HHJ Birss QC thought the schedule was a useful document and commended it to other litigants in the future. It is easy to see a similarity with the Precedent H used for costs budgeting.

Once the judge has looked at each stage's breakdown and established a summarily assessed figure, he then compares that figure with the scale maximum and will allow the lower of the two. HHJ Birss QC's description of this procedure in *Westwood* is careful to say that if this procedure is followed correctly the lower of the two figures is 'very likely' to be the right figure, rather than definitely will be that figure. However, the robustness of his decisions to date leave little room for doubt that they will be the final figure, subject to the overall cap. If the assessed figure is above the scale maximum the parties and the court can be confident that there is more than sufficient work to justify the maximum recoverable sum. If the figure is lower, the paying party has had his liability specifically assessed on that case's own circumstances.

The final stage is to compare the total of the figures allowed for each stage, whether the scale maximum or a lower assessed figure, with the global caps of £50,000 or £25,000 as the case may be. The approach is very similar to the comparison of assessed and scale figures for each stage. The lower of the totalled figures and the global maximum will be allowed. This limit does not apply to any High Court costs summarily assessed and which are payable in addition (see *Westwood* as an example of this.)

Costs outside the scales?

[26.36]

Again, there is a similarity to the costs management approach on display here. There is no scale figure for pre-action costs which would militate against parties using the pre-action protocol. However, where the costs can properly be claimed against a post proceedings stage, for example the drafting of witness statements or considering disclosure, such costs should be claimed under that stage rather than as pre-action costs. As such, the only irrecoverable costs ought to be those dealing specifically with the protocol itself.

As with costs management, there is no 'general costs of the action,' or similar stage, into which costs can be placed. As such the approach according to HHJ Birss QC in *Westwood* was not to take 'too narrow a view of the scope of the stages in Table A. I say that because even if a broad view of the scope of those stages is taken, this would not undermine the system.'

Even a broad view of the stages was not sufficient to bring certain costs claimed in *Technetix BV (a company incorporated under the laws of the Netherlands) v Teleste Ltd* [2018] EWHC 1941 (IPEC) within them. The claimant patentee applied to adjourn the trial on the first day in order to pursue an argument only raised in its pre-trial skeleton argument. Having decided to adjourn the trial, HHJ Hacon disapplied the costs caps to the costs involved in the adjournment which would be assessed after the trial.

In *National Guild of Removers & Storers Ltd v Central Moves Ltd* [2017] EWHC 3175 (IPEC) the proceedings began in the multi-track of the IPEC before being transferred by consent to the IPEC small claims track. The claimant subsequently sought its costs prior to the allocation but HHJ Hacon took the view that the approach in CPR Part 46 generally on allocation and re-allocation should apply. The usual course would be for a case allocated to the small claims track to be limited to fixed costs throughout, albeit that the court could always order otherwise. That approach had been correctly applied by the district judge here.

The order for costs

[26.37]

The awarding of costs between the parties is carried out in the same way as in any other court, ie in accordance with Part 44 with costs following the event as the starting point.

If the court decides to reflect the parties' success and failure with a percentage order or issues based order, how does that fit in with the scale figures? HHJ Birss QC considered this in *BOS GmbH & Co KG v Cobra UK Automotive Products Division Ltd* [2012] EWPCC 44. He came to the view that 25% of the claimant's costs should be deducted as a result of a failure on certain issues. He thought that a further 10% should be deducted to reflect the issues on which the defendant should have his costs. On the basis that the parties' costs were of similar amounts, the better way to reflect this was to reduce the percentage of the claimant's costs rather than allow the claimant their costs of the particular issue. (No doubt he had CPR 44 in his mind although this is not specifically stated.) So, he ended up with deducting the 25% and the 10% from the starting point of a 100% order and awarded the claimant 65% of its costs.

The key issue then was the order in which the summary assessment should be carried out. Should the assessed figure for each stage be reduced to 65% and then compared with the scale maximum as the claimant contended, or should the assessed figure be compared with the scale maximum and then 65% of whichever was the lower figure allowed (as the defendant said)? HHJ Birss QC referred to CPR 45.31(2) which states that the global caps apply 'after the court has applied the provision on set off in accordance with rule [44.12(a)].' In his view, the correct approach was therefore to reduce the assessed figure to reflect the percentage order and then compared that figure with the scale maximum for the relevant stage. He accepted that if the originally assessed figure is considerably higher than the maximum there may be little effect in the percentage order because the party would only receive the scale maximum whether that was lower than the 100% or 65% figure. But this was more in accord with CPR 45.31(2) in its operation. He also considered that the other approach would have a disproportionate effect since it would never allow more than 65% of the scale maximum which was too low in this particular case.

The *BOS GmbH* decision was followed by HHJ Hacon in *Global Flood Defence Systems Ltd & UK Flood Barriers Ltd v Johann Van Den Noort Beheer BV and Johann Heinrich Reindart Vanden Noort and Flood Control International Ltd* [2016] EWHC 189 (IPEC). Only some of the issues had been resolved at the time costs were being assessed. In order to take appropriate account of set offs and the maximum sums allowable under the IPEC scheme, the assessment had to be postponed until all issues had been resolved. In essence the various claims and counterclaims of the parties within a single set of proceedings amounted to a single 'claim' in the rules.

Unreasonable conduct

[26.38]

To the extent that a party has behaved unreasonably, the court may make an award of costs against him in accordance with CPR 63.26(2). Such costs will be assessed summarily at the end of the hearing and such sums will, in accordance with CPR 45.32, be payable in addition to the total costs payable for the proceedings generally. These may still be limited by the overall caps, hence why HHJ Hacon decided not to find unreasonable conduct in *Technetix* (see **[26.36]**).

PART 45 SECTION V (CPR 45.33–CPR 45.36)

[26.39]

It just goes to show how many Part 7 claims HM Revenue and Customs issue that it has its own section in Part 45. This section closely follows Section I in its format. There is a table (Table 7) of commencement costs ranging from £33 to £180 based on bands which run from £25 to £500 near the bottom to £300,000 and above at the top. There is also a table (Table 8) of judgment costs but that barely justifies being a table since the fixed costs are either £15 or £20 depending upon whether the judgment sum is under or over the £5,000 threshold.

Other provisions in this section, such as 45.36, mimic provisions in Section I (CPR 45.3 in this example), to confirm that if payment of the damages and fixed costs is made within 14 days of service of the proceedings, there are no further costs payable.

PART 45 SECTION VI (CPR 45.37–CPR 45.40)

[26.40]

This section was a free transfer from Part 46 as part of the reorganisation of the costs section in the CPR in April 2013. The trial costs in the fast track were fixed when the Woolf Reforms were brought into play on 26 April 1999. They have continued to be the only fixed fees on the Fast Track notwithstanding the view of Lord Woolf that this was an important remedy for the evil of costs that he identified in his report. They have only been changed on two occasions since then. The first, in October 2007, was an uplifting of the original figures. Since this took a good eight years to come through (and have not changed for a further 14 years), the delay remains an example of what often happens when the Government decides to fix costs. The second occasion was to tie in with the increase in the scope of the fast track from £15,000 to £25,000 in April 2009. The original three bands were supplemented with a fourth to cater for proceedings between £15,000 and £25,000 where the proceedings were issued on 6 April 2009 or later.

Scope of 'fast track trial costs'

[26.41]

The costs awarded under this section are for the preparation and appearance at a fast track trial. They do not include any other disbursements and nor do they include VAT. As such, if the party cannot recover VAT, it can be charged to the client in addition to the relevant figure for costs.

The word 'trial' includes an assessment of damages hearing where liability has already been admitted. It does not include summary judgment hearings or approval hearings.

If the case has not been allocated to the fast track then the fees do not apply. This does not prevent a judge assessing costs on a case allocated to the multi-track from taking note of what would have been allowed on the fast track in an appropriate case (*Drew v Whitbread* [2010] EWCA Civ 53).

Amount of costs

[26.42]

The figures are set out in Table 9 in PD 45. They are as follows

Value of the claim	Costs
No more than £3,000	£485
£3,001 – £10,000	£690
£10,001 – £15,000	£1,035
£15,001 – £25,000	£1,690

The only circumstances in which the court can award any other sum instead of one of these figures are if:

(a) the court decides:
  (i) not to award any costs at all;
  (ii) to apportion the costs to reflect the respective degrees of success of the parties;
  (iii) to set off the costs of the parties' claims and make an award of the difference to one party;

(b) one or more of the parties have behaved improperly during the trial:
  (i) if it is a winning party, the trial costs may be reduced as the court considers appropriate (and this may be if the behaviour is 'only' unreasonable rather than improper);
  (ii) if it is a losing party, the trial costs may be supplemented by such additional amount as the court considers appropriate;

(c) a party has a legal representative present in addition to the advocate and the court considers it was 'necessary' for the legal representative to attend. If so the allowable amount is £345;

(d) a successful party is a litigant in person in which case he can claim costs in accordance with CPR 46.5. Where the litigant in person can show financial loss, the two-thirds figure is based on the appropriate trial costs for the value of the case;

(e) it is necessary to have a separate trial of an issue in which case the court must award at least £485 but will otherwise not award more than two thirds of the standard costs (of any of the higher bands).

Calculating the value of the claim

[26.43]

For the purposes of calculating into which band a claim should fall, the value of the claim for a successful claimant is the total amount of the judgment excluding any interest, costs or reduction for contributory negligence. For the defendant it is the amount specified in the claim form (excluding interest and costs). If there is no specification in the claim form of the level of damages, the statement of value on the claim form required by r 16.3 will be used unless the claimant states that he cannot reasonably say how much the claim is worth and in which case the value will be treated as being more than £15,000. This means that the defendant will receive the highest level of costs if he is successful.

If both parties have claims and the defendant's counterclaim is the more valuable, the calculation of value for either party will be based on the defendant's counterclaim.

If the claim is for a remedy other than money, the case will be treated as having a value between £3,000 and £10,000 unless the court otherwise orders. If there is a non-monetary claim and a money claim, this provision will apply unless the money claim is for more than £10,000 and in which case the relevant higher bracket applies.

If the same advocate acts for more than one claimant, and each one has a separate claim against the defendant, the value of the claims is based on the aggregate amount of the damages; whether it is the claimants or the defendant who is successful.

Multiple parties

[26.44]

Where the same advocate acts for more than one party, the court will only make one award in his favour and the parties instructing him are only jointly entitled to such costs. Similarly, where there is a single defendant against multiple opponents, the court may only make one order in favour of the defendant.

PART 45 SECTION VII (CPR 45.41–CPR 45.44)

[26.45]

The fixed costs in this section of Part 45 are a hybrid of a fixed costs provision – which is why the section is covered here – and a protection to parties with limited resources who are involved in environmental claims. These provisions are dealt with in detail at **[18.13]** from the costs protection angle, including the judicial review of these provisions as a whole and the decision of Dove J on considering the level of the caps imposed in *R v Secretary of State for Justice, ex p RSPB* [2017] EWHC 2309 (Admin).

What is the Aarhus Convention you might say? CPR 45.41(2) defines a claim arising from the Convention as being:

> ' . . . a claim brought by one or more members of the public by judicial review or review under statute which challenges the legality of any decision, act or omission of a body exercising public functions, and which is within the scope of Article 9(1), 9(2) or 9(3) of the UNECE Convention on Access to Information, Public Participation in Decision-Making and Access to Justice in Environmental Matters done at Aarhus, Denmark on 25 June 1998.'

Part of the Convention requires proceedings to be capable of being brought in the Convention countries without ruinous risk. As such there are special provisions in this section to limit the claimant's exposure to costs. The general rule (CPR 45.43(1)) is that a claimant cannot be ordered to pay a greater amount in costs to a defendant than is the amount prescribed in that rule. The amount payable depends upon the nature of the claimant. If the claimant is an individual and is not acting on behalf of a business or other legal entity, the sum is £5,000. In any other case it is £10,000 (CPR 45.43(2)). Where there is more than one claimant, the cap for each claimant's liability is aggregated (see *R (on the application of Botley Parish Action Group) v Eastleigh Borough Council* [2014] EWHC 4388 (Admin)).

However, the sums set out in CPR 45.43 can be varied following an application by the opponent. This variation ought to occur as early in proceedings as possible so that the parties know where they stand. That is not always possible, for example where the parties fail to provide the requisite information. In *CPRE Surrey v Waverley Borough Council* [2018] EWHC 2969 (Admin), the assessment did not occur until the final judgment had been given. By that time, one of the assessments was not required (because the relevant party had lost). The judge made the other assessment and concluded that an overall cap of £30,000 was appropriate. By then the opponent's costs had been set out in sufficient detail for the judge to award it £30,000 since the relevant costs would undoubtedly have exceeded this figure on assessment.

The definition at CPR 45.41(2) set out above came into being on 1 October 2019. Prior to that date, the provision only applied to judicial review proceedings. Statutory reviews, such as those under s 288 of the Town and Country Planning Act 1990, were not covered. Consequently, a judge at first instance who sought to use the court's inherent jurisdiction to make a protective costs order was overturned by the Court of Appeal (*Venn v Secretary of State for Communities and Local Government* [2014] EWCA Civ 1539).

Where the claimant has not stated that the Convention applies, or has specifically stated that it does not apply, the costs protection provisions of this section do not apply either.

The defendant's potential liability in costs in a Convention claim is limited to £35,000 (CPR 45.43(3)). However, where the defendant states that the Convention does not apply in the acknowledgment of service and defence, he risks increasing his potential liability. The court will decide whether the Convention applies at the earliest opportunity so that the parties know where they stand. If the court accepts the defendant's position that the proceedings are not a Convention claim, it will usually make no order as to costs (CPR 45.44(3)(a)). But if the court decides against the defendant and holds that it is a Convention claim, it will normally order the defendant to pay the claimant's costs on the indemnity basis. This may well cause the recoverable costs to be more than the prescribed fixed costs of £35,000 but that is no bar to their recovery (CPR 45.44(3)(b)). The same fate may befall an interested party who opposes the claimant's categorisation of the case as a Convention claim (and where the defendant's neutrality meant it did not lose its limitation on liability (*R (on the application of Kent) v Teesside Magistrates Court & HJ Banks & Co Ltd* [2020] EWHC 304 (Admin)).

THE SMALL CLAIMS TRACK

[26.46]

The intention of the small claims track is made clear in CPR 27.1 where it talks of providing a special procedure for dealing with claims and limiting the costs that can be recovered by that procedure. This is done by stripping out many of the procedural requirements of civil litigation as far as possible and enabling a party to 'act as his own lawyer' as Lord Diplock put it in *Hobbs v Marlowe* [1978] AC 16 when discussing a predecessor system for small claims.

Unlike all of the other fixed costs provisions, the costs in relation to small claims track cases are set out in CPR 27.14 and Practice Direction 27, sub-para 7. There are also one or two relevant references to Part 44 in relation to allocation as discussed below.

Recoverable fixed costs

[26.47]

By removing the procedural requirements so that a party can represent himself, the court rules justify there being no recoverability of the costs of legal representation. This includes any fee or reward charged by a party's lay representative.

There are five exceptions to this general point:

(1) The fixed costs on commencement of a claim under Part 45 Section I can be claimed, whether or not the case actually comes within the relevant definition in that section for the type of case involved.
(2) If advice is taken in respect of an injunction or specific performance then legal fees can be claimed. Such costs are limited to £260.

(3) If a party has behaved unreasonably, the court can order such further costs as it thinks fit and will summarily assess these (CPR 27.14(2)(g)). Rejecting an offer will not of itself amount to unreasonable behaviour but it may be taken into account by the court.
(4) Where a personal injury case started in the Portal and the defendant admitted liability for the accident but it then transpired that the level of damages were below £1,000 and so the case fell out of the Portal. In such circumstances, and so long as the claimant reasonably believed the value was more than £1,000, the Stage 1 and, if appropriate Stage 2, costs are payable by the defendant.
(5) Where there is a contractual claim for costs, they will be recoverable in accordance with CPR 44.5 regardless of any allocation to the small claims track (see **[36.7]**).

In *Dammermann v Lanyon Bowdler LLP* [2017] EWCA Civ 269, the Court of Appeal considered the third exception above. It was reluctant to give general guidance but made reference to the guidance in *Ridehalgh v Horsfield* [1994] Ch 205 which is considered further at **[22.27]**.

Recoverable disbursements

[26.48]

There are various disbursements that can be claimed:
(1) any court fees paid;
(2) travelling, accommodation and subsistence expenses incurred by a party or witness in attending the hearing limited to a maximum of £95;
(3) loss of earnings or leave incurred by a party or witness in attending the hearing limited to a maximum of £95;
(4) Experts' fees limited to £750 per expert;
(5) In an appeal, the cost of any reasonably incurred approved transcript.

Allocation and re-allocation to track

[26.49]

As with all tracks, the allocation procedure will consider the small claims track to be the 'normal' track where certain criteria are met, particularly relating to the value of the claim. In such cases the costs restrictions set out above automatically apply to all costs incurred before and after allocation.

There are two qualifications to this point.
(1) Any costs orders made prior to allocation will continue to be effective and entitle the party to assessed costs (CPR 46.13(1) overriding CPR 46.11(2))
(2) Where a case is allocated to one track and then re-allocated to another, any 'special rules' about costs in either track will apply up to/after the re-allocation as the case may be. This is always subject to the court ordering otherwise (CPR 46.13(2)).

Qualification No 2 obviously depends upon the reallocation being notified to the parties. In *Francois v Barclays Bank plc* (Slade J 28/11/17), a claim for £500 was allocated to the small claims track. But before the hearing could take place the trial centre informed the parties that it had been listed for a fast track trial. After several further ineffective hearings the case was listed for a two-day hearing. Slade J described allocation (and therefore reallocation) to a track as being significant for both procedural and costs reasons. The parties therefore had to receive formal notice of any reallocation so that they could challenge it if they so wished. No order for reallocation was identifiable notwithstanding the many later orders made. Costs were limited to the small claims track limits.

Prior to 1 April 2013, the court could allocate a case to the small claims track even if its value was above the limits which would have made it the normal track. In those circumstances, the costs restrictions would also apply unless the parties agreed that the fast track costs provisions should apply instead. Where that happened, the fixed trial costs (see [**26.42**] above) would not apply but they would not be exceeded when the court came to assess the costs overall. This provision (CPR 27.14(5) and (6)) was removed on 1 April 2013 and so if the court now allocates a larger value case to the small claims track, the costs restrictions will apply regardless of the parties' wishes.

Appeals and allocation and re-allocation

[26.50]

It is by no means certain that an appeal to the Court of Appeal will be sufficient to break the case free from the costs shackles imposed by CPR 27.14. You should therefore consider appeals very carefully from a costs perspective if the case is in the small claims track when the decision being appealed was made.

In *Akhtar v Boland* [2014] EWCA Civ 943 the Court of Appeal confirmed that the limitations imposed by CPR 27.14 applies to second appeals (ie to the Court of Appeal). In *Conlon v Royal Sun Alliance Insurance plc* [2015] EWCA Civ 92, the Court of Appeal refused to re-allocate a case before it from the small claims track to the multi-track when that application had only been made four months after the notice of appeal had been filed. The defendant had behaved reasonably in relation to the original proceedings and the various proceedings and so should not be required to meet the costs of the appellant.

The Jackson Review: Supplementary Report

[26.51]

It was obviously one of Sir Rupert Jackson's biggest bugbears that fixed costs recovered by the winner from the loser in all fast track claims had not come to fruition four years after the implementation of most of the other recommendations in his Review. He made a number of speeches regarding fixed recoverable costs and in November 2016, he was asked by the Lord Chief Justice and the Master of the Rolls to carry out a further review in respect of extending the use of such costs. His report was delivered by the end of July 2017 and the Government produced a consultation paper in March 2019 whose consultation period ended in June 2019. Despite the time that has now passed since then, at the time of writing, the Government's conclusions based on the consultation are not known for certain. But there can be little doubt that many, if not all, of the recommendations Sir Rupert made will find their way into the CPR in due course based on the questions and comments made in the consultation paper.

Intermediate track

[26.52]

The most innovative aspect of the Supplementary Report was the proposal to create a track between the existing fast and multi-tracks. It was intended to deal with cases whose value was above the fast track limit of £25,000 but would be expected to be more streamlined procedurally than multi-track cases. The proposed upper limit for the intermediate track was £100,000. Complex cases between £25,000 and £100,000 would still be allocated to the multi-track.

The Government, however, has not accepted that a further track is required. Instead, it has suggested extending the fast track to cover 'intermediate cases'. It does not explain how matters such as the fast track limit of one day hearings will cater for cases whose criteria include up to a three-day trial, but it may be that this is less difficult than it might first appear. The uninspiring term 'intermediate' seems likely to be suitably transient.

Grids

[26.53]

The Report contained tables of the proposed levels of the fixed recoverable costs in both the fast and intermediate tracks. These tables were called grids and follow essentially the same format. A number of sequential stages were set out from before the commencement of proceedings until trial. Four bands of complexity were matched to those stages providing fees which increased as the case progressed. The simplest complexity band in the fast track set out specific figures. The sums allowed in all of the other complexity bands in the fast-track and all of the bands in the intermediate track were comprised of two elements. The first was a specific, base figure. The second was a sum equal to a percentage of the damages. This approach followed the figures set out in Section IIIA of Part 45 and indeed could be traced to Section II of that Part which first established the two part calculation and, by including a figure which is based on a percentage of the damages, established what might be described as a proportionate relationship to the damages.

The increase in the figures as the case progressed was entirely to be expected. Perhaps more surprising was the description of the figures as being cumulative. But before you add the boxes together to get a maximum of £17,150 and 135% of the damages, it is not cumulative in that manner. The figure in each box in the grid is simply higher than the previous figure (at least for the specific sums) and so is increasing in quantity by successive additions, which can also be said to be cumulative. The idea of Sir Rupert allowing your client's costs to exceed the damages was never a very likely prospect.

In the fast track table, specific trial advocacy fees were set out, again as was similar to other sections of Part 45. The intermediate track grid also included several 'stages' where fees for advocacy, drafting statements of case and/or advising, whether in writing or in conference could be claimed. The phrase 'counsel/specialist lawyer' was used for such stages on the basis that the rules could not insist on counsel providing advocacy or indeed the advice etc.

As with CPR 45.23B (see [**26.18**]) solicitors who consider themselves to be specialist in running their cases may feel their hackles rising at the difference between (any) counsel and only specialist (other) lawyers receiving fees in these stages.

The Government accepted that the figures in the grids had been contemplated by Sir Rupert and his assessors based on figures compiled by the economist assessor who had received data from lawyers involved in such cases. As such, the Government proposed that the figures in the grids should be implemented as set out. Presumably the two grids will simply be used for fast track cases depending upon value given the Government's rejection of an intermediate track.

Fixed or capped?

[26.54]

The fast track grid relates to cases other than personal injury (and for which Section IIIA will generally be used). The intermediate track grid relates to both personal injury and non-personal injury cases. For personal injury cases, the figures in the intermediate track grid are fixed at the sums/percentages set out. For non-personal injury cases however, the figures are a cap and so the recoverable costs may be less than the figures set out in the grid.

The rationale for this is that there is a minimum amount of work required in any personal injury case in order to get it to a position where the parties can settle it. There will always be a number of cases which run to trial and which will be rather more expensive to run as a result. On the 'swings and roundabouts' approach, the fixed recoverable costs are considered by Sir Rupert to be reasonable overall. The same is not true in relation to non-personal injury cases. Such claims may be settled by little more than a letter before action or may require a large amount of investigation. Using the costs set out in the grid as capped figures allow for a smaller amount of costs to be recovered in the former cases and a larger amount in the latter.

Sir Rupert also recommended that there be a pilot of business and property cases with a value up to £250,000 using capped figures and streamlined procedures. Such a pilot was approved and began on 14 January 2019 for two years. The figures and indeed approach clearly have been inspired by the IPEC arrangements in Section IV of Part 45 (see [**26.32**]).

Proposals for clinical negligence and NIHL cases

[26.55]

Sir Rupert's further recommendations included industry discussions for fixed recoverable costs in clinical negligence cases. Such discussions would require agreement as to streamlining the process in order to make progress on agreeable fixed figures. The extent of work done in many clinical negligence cases prior to any proceedings means that an agreement between claimant practitioners and the defendant insurers ought to be much more effective in controlling costs. At the time of writing, a Civil Justice Council report on discussions is awaited.

Noise Induced Hearing Loss (NIHL) claims, according to the consultation paper have increased significantly in recent years. A Civil Justice Council working party produced a report in September 2017 recommending a more transparent pre-action process and fixed costs both pre and post-commencement of proceedings. The consultation follows the working party's recommendations.

Aarhus and other judicial review claims

[26.56]

Sir Rupert's further recommendations included extending the costs restrictions in Aarhus convention claims to other, statutory, reviews and to bring case management into 'heavy' judicial review cases. These proposals are covered at **[26.45]** and **[18.13]** respectively.

For the future

[26.57]

Sir Rupert recommended that the figures should be reviewed every three years. The history of reviews of fixed costs is not a glorious one. However, the momentum in this area is now such that the scope of cases which attract fixed recoverable costs is likely to be reviewed one way or another within the next three years in any event.

Once the recommended reforms have bedded in, Sir Rupert suggested that consideration should be given to looking to extend the scope of the intermediate track and the range of fixed costs. He also suggested a grid for incurred costs in different categories of case and a pre-action procedure for seeking leave to exceed such fixed figures. If achievable, this might square the circle of fixed costs and costs management. It is impracticable based on current procedures for a court to budget a case prior to commencement of court proceedings. Unless or until that was possible, the best method of seeking to influence parties' behaviours regarding costs prospectively is to have fixed or capped recoverable costs pre-issue. This has been achieved in the IPEC arrangements, but not otherwise.

CHAPTER 27

SUMMARY ASSESSMENT

INTRODUCTION TO SUMMARY ASSESSMENT

[27.1]

Since 26 April 1999 whenever the court makes an order that one party is to pay costs to another party, then unless the costs are fixed costs, the court must either make a summary assessment of those costs or order a detailed assessment. This remains the position and the rule is found at CPR 44.6.

In his preliminary report Sir Rupert Jackson put forward 3 options in respect of the summary assessment procedure as follows:

- Option 1: make no change to the present rules governing summary assessment.
- Option 2: abolish the summary assessment procedure and instead encourage judges to order interim payments on account of costs, alternatively provisional assessments.
- Option 3: restructure the summary assessment procedure

His conclusion was that:

> 'I am quite satisfied that option 3 is the proper way forward. Summary assessment is a valuable tool which has made a substantial contribution to civil procedure, not least by deterring frivolous applications and reducing the need for detailed assessment proceedings. The summary assessment procedure should be retained and improvements should be made in order to meet the criticisms which have been expressed . . . '

The summary assessment procedure remained. But how summary is summary? In *Morgan v Spirit Group Ltd* [2011] EWCA Civ 68, when overturning the decision of the recorder, the Court of Appeal made the obvious point that the court must undertake either a summary or detailed assessment of the costs. The recorder had not done so. Instead, in a paragraph, the recorder had simply determined a proportionate figure and added something to that to allow for the existence of what he had, erroneously, described as 'a contingent fee agreement'. Summary though the assessment is intended to be, the court concluded that what had taken place here was not a summary assessment. So, summary though the procedure may be, it must still recognisably be an assessment. This is particularly important if, after determining the reasonable costs, the court then steps back to consider the proportionality of the costs under CPR 44.3(2)(a), as, clearly, this must be a discernibly different discrete process.

WHO CONDUCTS A SUMMARY ASSESSMENT?

[27.2]

We have confidently and consistently stated that a summary assessment of the costs of a hearing or a trial must be carried out by the judge who conducted that hearing. CPR PD 44, para 9.7 precludes the court that awards costs from ordering a summary assessment before a costs officer. If a summary assessment is not undertaken at the hearing at which costs are awarded then the court may give directions for its later hearing before the same judge unless a detailed assessment is ordered. To us that means that unless a detailed assessment is ordered, then either the judge conducting the hearing undertakes the summary assessment at that hearing or he has the option of giving directions for its later determination before him. Coulson J in *Transformers and Rectifiers Ltd v Needs Ltd* [2015] EWHC 1667 (TCC) was asked to consider a slightly different scenario – namely where the application had been dealt with on paper without a hearing. However, in his judgment he commented more widely and noted the change in CPR PD 44, para 9.7 from the use of the word 'must' to the use of the word 'may' and concluded that this meant that:

> 'The provision at paragraph 9.7 of the PD is permissive: if time does not permit the summary assessment then and there, it may be heard later by the same judge. Equally, therefore, it may be heard by another judge.' (para 9)

We confess that we find this interpretation challenging. If it is correct, then what purpose do the words 'by the same judge' serve in the PD? Our view is that the word 'may' means that if the judge does not undertake a summary assessment then and there, but wishes to undertake a summary, as opposed to detailed, assessment, he may give directions for that hearing. In other words, the provision is permissive in the sense that directions for a further summary assessment hearing may be given, BUT only before the same judge.

In the context of applications and cases that are heard, the judge's comments that 'It seems to me that, not only is there nothing in the rules or the PD which prevents a different judge from summarily assessing the costs of a hearing conducted (or an order made) by a different judge, but such a blanket prohibition would make no practical sense' and 'I consider that, in appropriate circumstances, another judge may be able summarily to assess the costs arising out of a hearing conducted . . . by another judge' overlook the definition of summary assessment found in CPR 44.1(1). Even if there is ambiguity in CPR PD 44, para 9.7, which we do not accept, a rule takes precedence over a practice direction. The definition is clear that a summary assessment must be before the judge who heard the case or application. The definition is:

> ' "Summary assessment" means the procedure whereby costs are assessed by the judge who has heard the case or application.'

While we accept that there is an argument that a case dealt with without a hearing may not fall within CPR 44.1 (leaving aside the interesting question of whether a case/application can be heard, even if it is dealt with without a hearing, and we revert to our comments above about the PD in respect of these instances), it seems clear that the rules are more prescriptive than the court acknowledged where a case/application has been dealt with at a hearing.

THE BENEFITS OF A SUMMARY ASSESSMENT

[27.3]

There are benefits to both the parties and to the court in conducting a summary, as opposed to a detailed, assessment. These are as follows:

- A summary assessment is more proportionate than a detailed assessment – both in terms of the costs of the parties and the court time involved. This is true even with the fixed cost of the provisional costs regime introduced in CPR 47.15.
- The judge who has awarded the costs has a better understanding of the issues/case than the assessing judge will ever have. Indeed, with the greater continuity that comes with continuity in some courts, the judge may well have been involved throughout the court proceedings. In *Mahmood v Penrose* [2002] EWCA Civ 457, the Court explained the reasoning behind summary assessment was that the person who has actually heard the case and knows about it is in a position to make a summary assessment.
- In cases that have been costs managed the assessment process should be much simplified as the court is likely to be dealing with the pre-budget costs only. Accordingly, the uncertainty of the outcome of a summary assessment is much reduced.
- There is no delay. The receiving party will receive the costs far earlier than waiting for a detailed assessment. The paying party's liability is crystallised earlier, avoiding a prolonged period when interest on costs at 8% falls due.
- The court is spared dealing with the usual standard objections that fill the first few pages of Points of Dispute and which invariably occupy court time to little or no avail. The assessment is focused on the key issues.

WHEN IS A SUMMARY ASSESSMENT APPROPRIATE?

[27.4]

The simple answer, following on from the benefits listed above, is that summary assessment should be carried out in preference to detailed assessment as often as possible. CPR PD 44, para 9.2 sets out a general rule that the court should conduct a summary assessment unless there is good reason not to do so:

- at the conclusion of a trial within the fast track: and
- at the conclusion of any other hearing that has lasted no more than a day.

The general rule applies to all hearings that have lasted – the word is 'lasted', not 'listed', so the test is hindsight not foresight – not more than one day

There was some debate about whether the apparent distinction between 'a trial' and 'a hearing' precludes a summary assessment after a multi-track trial. The debate was short lived. The court may and, whenever possible, should, conduct summary assessments after multi-track trials. Indeed CPR PD 29, para 10.5 specifically refers to summary assessments at multi-track trials in appropriate cases. This ought to be appropriate more often now that most multi-track claims will have been costs managed (see, for example, the decision in *Sony Communications AB v SSH Communications Security Corpn* [2016] EWHC 2985 (Pat)) and now that the judiciary is astute to the key concept of proportionality when making case management decisions (of which a decision whether to have a summary or detailed assessment is certainly one). Indeed 'other hearings' includes not only multi-track trials, but also appeals in the Court of Appeal which do not last more than a day. This expectation is notwithstanding one of the conclusions of the 'Review of Civil Litigation Costs: Final Report', that recognised that in larger cases and with judges less familiar with costs an increase in referral to detailed assessment would be appropriate in these terms:

> 'If any judge at the end of a hearing within Costs PD paragraph 13.2 (now PD 44, para 9) considers that he or she lacks the time or the expertise to assess costs summarily (either at that hearing or on paper afterwards), then the judge should order a substantial payment on account of costs and direct detailed assessment.'

Although the general rule applies to cases that last no more than one day it was held in *Q v Q (Family Division: costs: summary assessment)* [2002] 2 FLR 668 (Fam) that there is no presumption against summary assessment in relation to costs where hearings last more than one day. Indeed, CPR PD 44, para 9.1 requires summary assessment to be considered in every case where a costs award is made and fixed costs do not apply. Frequently the insurmountable difficulty for the court in undertaking a summary assessment in a case that lasts in excess of one day is that the parties have not prepared costs statements, because they do not anticipate that there will be a summary assessment and they are not obliged by the rules to file and serve them in such cases. However, there is nothing in the rules to prevent a party preparing, filing and serving such a statement voluntarily. Nor is there any reason why the court, as a case management decision, either at the pre-trial review or on the first day of the trial, should not order the parties to file and serve a costs statement. Again, we would expect efficient parties and courts to adopt these practices.

WHEN IS A SUMMARY ASSESSMENT INAPPROPRIATE?

[27.5]

CPR PD 44 sets out a number of situations where the court may decide not to undertake a summary assessment or must not do so. Other situations where the court/parties may wish to defer assessment also arise.

When the court decides not to undertake a summary assessment

(a) Exception to the general rule

[27.6]

The general rule at CPR PD 44, para 9.2 provides the court with the option of not undertaking a summary assessment where there is 'good reason' not to do so. It gives as an example where the paying party shows substantial grounds for disputing the sum claimed for costs that cannot be dealt with summarily. The most obvious example of this might be a challenge to the overall retainer. However, do not expect that the court will simply rubber stamp 'good reason' and order a detailed assessment. For the reasons already specified the court should be reluctant to defer the assessment. Accordingly, it is likely to delve behind a bold assertion of substantive issue to ascertain whether there is genuinely an issue that requires more detailed investigation or whether the paying party is speculating in the hope that on detailed assessment it may stumble upon something.

Decisions on whether costs orders are suitable for summary assessment will be contextual. The 'good reason' exception to the general rule is a matter for discretion (eg in *Broseley London Ltd v Prime Asset Management Ltd (Trustee of the Mashel Family Trust)* [2020] EWHC 1057 (TCC), the court concluded that although the hearing did not exceed one day, the fact that the costs sought were over £100,000 made a summary assessment unsuitable. It is interesting to note in passing, and it may be coincidence rather than an emerging theme, that in *Les Ambassadeurs Club Ltd v Albluewi* [2020] EWHC 1368 (QB), albeit as one of many reasons given when declining to undertake a summary assessment, the court also referred to a £100,000 threshold, deciding that as the costs exceeded that level they were too substantial to be dealt with summarily). In contrast, albeit in the Shorter Trials Scheme under CPR PD 57AB in which summary assessment is prescribed save in exceptional circumstances, in *Eli Lilly and Co v Genetch, Inc* [2020] EWHC 564 (Pat), the court undertook a summary assessment where the costs claimed for a two-day hearing were £855,000 and £675,000 respectively. It rejected the submission that the level of costs equated to exceptional circumstances.

Another obvious reason, is the situation where the receiving party is a litigant in person alleging financial loss. In *Neil v Stephenson* (2000) CLW, 8 December, QBD although the claimant, acting in person, had his action struck out, he had been awarded his costs of an interim hearing. When the claim was struck out, the judge acceded to the claimant's request for a detailed assessment to give him an opportunity to demonstrate that he should be entitled to recover the value of a contract which his business had allegedly lost as a result of his attendance at the interim hearing.

(b) Commercial Courts

[27.7]

Paragraph F14.2 of the Commercial Courts Guide provides 'active consideration will generally be given by the court to adopting the summary assessment procedure in all cases where the schedule of costs of the successful party is no more than £100,000, but the parties should always be prepared for the court to assess costs summarily even where the costs exceed this amount'. There is further guidance in the ensuing paragraphs:

> 'In carrying out a summary assessment of costs, the court may have regard amongst other matters to:
>
> (i) advice from the Chief Costs Judge on costs of specialist solicitors and counsel;
> (ii) any information published by, or provided to the court at its request by, one or more of the specialist associations (referred to at section A4.2) on average charges by specialist solicitors and counsel.'

The figure is an interesting one. Under the Regional Costs Judge scheme, which was introduced in 2005/6, one of the criteria for reference to a regional costs judge by a district judge was that the costs claimed exceeded £50,000. This has been increased to £100,000. So, notwithstanding that assessment of costs is part and parcel of their daily diet of cases, district judges have, until recently, been referring cases to a specialist where the costs exceed £50,000 and continue to do so where the costs exceed £100,000, while there is an expectation that commercial judges will undertake summary assessments of all cases where the costs are up to the same level!

(c) Costs in the case

[27.8]

Originally, the costs practice direction provided that generally there would be no summary assessment of costs if an order has been made for costs in the case. However, this restriction was removed. There was a time when it was thought that the court would summarily assess the costs of all parties where an order for 'costs in the case' was made, to obviate the need for a detailed assessment of these later when it became known in whose favour the ultimate costs order had fallen. We have never known this done. Neither the parties nor the court seem to have the will to undertake what will largely prove to be a fruitless exercise.

(d) Where there is a deferred payment retainer in place

[27.9]

Since 31 March 2013, the court is not concerned with any success fee, and it need make no provision in respect of it, as that falls to be dealt with exclusively between the solicitor and the client. However, where the receiving party's liability to his solicitor has not arisen (for example where success under the CFA is defined as obtaining an award of damages, rather than success at an interim hearing along the way) then plainly under the indemnity principle the paying party cannot be ordered to make any payment unless and until a liability does arise. What does the court do?

Our preferred form of order in this situation is:

> '1(a) The (claimant/defendant) shall pay the (defendant's/claimant's) costs of and incidental to the application dated the (insert). The costs are summarily assessed as follows:
>
> | | |
> |---|---|
> | profit costs | V |
> | disbursements (non-counsel) | W |
> | disbursements (counsel) | X |
> | VAT | Y |
> | Total | Z |
>
> These costs shall be paid by the (defendant/claimant) to the (claimant/defendant) within 14 days of the (defendant/claimant) receiving written notice from the

(claimant/defendant) or his solicitors confirming that the (claimant/defendant) has a liability under the terms of his fee arrangement with his solicitors to pay these costs. Liberty to apply

The order has the benefit of there being an uncomplicated and proportionate procedure to obtain the assessed costs once the client has a liability to his solicitor, without the application having to return to the court.

Many solicitors have sought to avoid the restriction on immediate payment under a CFA, by excluding pre-action and interim applications from the substantive CFA that covers the claim and which defines success in overall terms. On each occasion of a pre-action or interim application a separate CFA is written with success defined as a variant on obtaining the order sought, including an order for costs from the other party/parties. Others have sought to draft the substantive CFA so that immediate payment of costs is due on each and every successful pre-action or interim application. Our experience is that this is a much more difficult exercise as there is a danger of triggering the client's liability at an earlier stage than that which has been sold to the client under the 'no win, no fee' sales pitch.

Interestingly, for CFAs entered into after 31 March 2013 and for DBAs, there is no longer any need to serve and file a notice of funding (Form N251). The rationale is obvious – additional liabilities are no longer recoverable between the parties and so notice that they may exist is only of relevance to the client. However, this does mean that the only check on whether an immediate entitlement to costs has arisen is by the receiving party's solicitor's accurate completion of the certificate on the FORM N260 (see below). We wonder how many orders for costs to be paid within 14 days are made on interim applications with the court accepting the accuracy of the signed certificate, when in fact the funding mechanism agreed does not, at that stage, create any liability for the client to pay the solicitor.

(e) Qualified One Way Costs Shifting ('QOCS')

[27.10]

There may be arguments that in cases to which the QOCS provisions apply (see CPR 44.13), that there is no purpose in the summary assessment of costs pursuant to a costs order against the claimant. Of course, the QOCS protection is only from the enforcement of any adverse costs order. As such this means that the court must still make an award of costs in the usual way (see Chapter 22) and should then decide whether to order a detailed assessment or undertake a summary assessment.

Our view is that the court should still undertake a summary assessment of costs in respect of costs awards on interim hearings whenever it is able to do so. This is because it makes any subsequent off-setting exercise under CPR 44.14 much simpler at the end of the case and also quantifies a discrete part of the costs if another exception to the QOCS regime subsequently arises under CPR 44.15 and/or CPR 44.16. This is also our view where the claimant successfully recovers damages at trial that exceed any adverse interim costs awards, but there is an adverse costs order at trial (whether for all or part of the costs) – again because off setting under CPR 44.14 arises.

Clearly the court should also undertake a summary assessment, if it is able to do so, where a QOCS protected claim is struck out as under CPR 44.15 the protection is automatically lost.

However, where the claimant is unsuccessful at trial and recovers nothing or where the claimant successfully recovers some damages and interest at trial, but the adverse interim costs awards already exceed these sums, then there seems little purpose in undertaking the assessment as nothing assessed at the trial can be off set under CPR 44.14. In these situations it may be that the defendant will not pursue an order for costs. If it does the court should still make an order, but may decide it is not proportionate to expend time then summarily assessing the costs and it is certainly not proportionate to order a detailed assessment. In this situation the court may think it appropriate to adjourn the summary assessment generally with liberty to restore and order that the costs are assessed at nil if no request to restore is received within say 28 days. This gives the defendant an opportunity to consider whether anything that emerged in the trial/judgment opens the door to subsequent enforcement under CPR 44.16.

If there is an argument under CPR 44.16 then plainly an assessment of the amount of costs becomes pertinent.

When the court must not undertake a summary assessment

(a) Mortgagee's costs

[27.11]

CPR PD 44, para 9.3 disapplies the general rule to the mortgagee's costs of mortgage possession proceedings or other proceedings relating to a mortgage unless the mortgagee waives this exclusion and asks for an award of costs against another party. The rationale for this provision is that usually a mortgagee does not seek an award of costs because it is entitled to recover the costs under the terms of the mortgage deed. CPR PD 44, paras 7.2 and 7.3 set out more detailed provisions in respect of costs under a mortgage, ultimately directing that where there is a dispute as to the amount the court may direct an assessment under CPR 44.5 (costs under a contract).

(b) A public funded party

[27.12]

CPR PD 44, para 9.8 provides that where one of the parties is in receipt of state funding there cannot be a summary assessment of any costs ordered to be paid to that party by the other party. This is because the Legal Aid Act 1988 and Legal Service Commission regulations require those costs to be the subject of a detailed assessment. There is nothing to prevent a summary assessment against a state funded party, although there will need to be a determination of the assisted person's liability to pay those costs for the purposes of the Legal Aid, Sentencing and Punishment of Offenders Act 2012, s 26 and the exercise may prove to be an academic one only (see Chapter 10 – State Funded Parties).

(c) Children or protected parties

[27.13]

CPR PD 44, para 9.9(1) prevents a summary assessment of the costs due to a child or a protected party, unless their solicitor agrees not to make any further charge to the client beyond that recovered from the other party. However, CPR PD 44, para 9.9(2) permits the court to make a summary assessment of any costs due from a child or protected party. At first blush this seems at odds with CPR 46.4(2) which provides that 'the general rule is that (a) the court must order a detailed assessment of the costs payable by, or out of money belonging to, any party who is a child or protected party . . . '. However, CPR PD 44, para 9.9(2) makes sense when it is recognised that CPR 46.2 only states a general rule and that both 46.4(5) and CPR PD 46, para 2.1 permit exceptions to the general rule.

CPR 46.4(5) was introduced recognising particular issues arising with the use after 31 March 2013 of CFAs with success fees that come from the client's damages and of DBAs where the payment due to the solicitors may exceed the recoverable costs and the shortfall may also be sought from the client's damages. So far as children are concerned, the procedural difficulties were partially resolved by amendments to CPR 21.12 and CPR 46.4(5) in April 2015, which combined to permit a summary assessment of any liability for any element of the success fee or DBA payment in respect of personal injury claims where the damages do not exceed £25,000. In the well-intentioned haste to introduce those changes, the amendments actually created considerable problems in respect of protected parties. Although those were identified in the 2016 edition of this text, it was not until Turner J had to consider the amendments in *Leddington v Kabul* [2017] EWHC 3262 (QB) and referred with approval to the rule change proposed by us, that the Civil Procedure Rules Committee revisited the problematic provision. A further amendment, adopting our revision of CPR 21.12(1A), made in April 2019 has finally resolved the issue.

This topic and other amendments made to CPR 21.12 and its PD are considered in Chapter 34 at [**34.4**] and [**34.5**].

(d) Agreed costs

[27.14]

CPR PD 44, para 9.10 provides that the court will not endorse disproportionate and/or unreasonable costs. Accordingly, the Practice Direction states that when the amount of the costs to be paid has been agreed, the order should make it clear that it was made by consent.

(e) Agreement 'save as to costs'

[27.15]

Where the parties have agreed the outcome of an application and wish to avoid a court hearing they should seek to agree a figure for costs or agree that there is to be no order for costs. It is not for the court to assess costs summarily in their absence (see CPR PD 44, para 9.4).

THE EXTENT OF THE COSTS TO BE ASSESSED

[27.16]

The summary assessment at the end of a multi-track or fast track trial will deal with the costs of the whole of the claim, remembering that the advocacy costs of the fast track trial are fixed. Of course, from 31 July 2013 all fast track road traffic accident, employers' and public liability claims where the claim notification form was sent after that date are subject to fixed costs provisions. From 7 May 2018, all fast track claims to which the Pre-Action Protocol for Resolution of Package Travel Claims applies are similarly fixed. No assessment will be necessary in those cases if the award of costs is in the claimant's favour (CPR 44.6(1) excludes fixed costs orders). If it is in the defendant's favour then an assessment will be required but given that the court cannot exceed what the claimant would have recovered under the fixed costs provisions, this is likely to be far simpler than prior to this (see CPR 45.29F(2)–(7)).

A summary assessment at the end of an interim application will deal with the costs of the application or matter to which it related. Again, no assessment will be necessary in cases subject to the fixed costs regime in CPR 45 Section IIIA as CPR 45.29H provides the mechanism to calculate the recoverable costs permitted. An interesting situation arises where the court disposes of an interim application without a hearing. As the fixed costs under CPR 45.29H provide a calculation that is, in part, based on an advocacy fee, should the fee be reduced in this situation? Our view is that it should not because:

- The fee is fixed and there is no discretion to reduce it. The wording is not, in any way, qualified as it could have been if it was intended that half the advocate's fee would only be included if advocacy is required.
- The reference to Type B costs in tables 6 and 6A is not an indication that there must be advocacy, but instead is just a reference to a sum of money to enable calculation of the fixed fee. In other words, CPR 45.29H simply sets out a formula to arrive at an amount.
- CPR 45.29H refers to the costs of an interim application (and not to the costs of an interim hearing).

THE STATEMENT OF COSTS

N260

[27.17]

CPR PD 44, para 9.5(1) makes it the duty of the parties and their legal representatives to assist the judge in undertaking a summary assessment. As such the parties must provide a written statement of costs that should follow as closely as possible Form N260. This must particularise the information specified in the Practice Direction and be signed by the party or his legal representative and include the certificate contained on that form (save in certain public funding situations and where the party is represented by someone in his employment).

The Form N260 was altered at the time of the April 2013 amendments to the CPR and has been altered subsequently in June 2015. An oddity is the reference to 'interim application/fast track trial' in the preamble rather than application/trial/appeal as previously for, as set out above [**27.4**], a summary assessment is not limited to interim applications and fast track trials. Experience shows that some solicitors adapt the N260 to produce their own form which fails to provide the requisite information. In the light of the robust judicial insistence upon procedural compliance, those who use an out of date form or their own form that does not follow the format of the N260 as closely as possible, should expect sanctions of some sort. Here is a suggestion – simply use the current Form N260.

The post-March 2013 form was introduced as a result of the almost universal criticism of the lack of information on the old form (endorsed by Sir Rupert Jackson) and the potential that this created 'broad brush' injustice. The new form now has an additional sheet that provides for a breakdown of the time claimed for documents so that the judge has a far clearer idea of what work the receiving party has done. However, do not expect the assessment to become a quasi-detailed assessment with the court going through each individual item listed in the document breakdown. The assessment remains a summary one and the breakdown is only informative of how time has been spent. Indeed, the very reason that one of us dislikes the new form is that the breakdown smacks of, and encourages, something more than a summary process!

N260A and N260B

[27.18]

One area where Form N260 is deficient in respect of assessments of the costs of the entire claim is in its link to costs management orders. As we have seen earlier under CPR 3.15(8), the court sets the budgeted costs by total sum per phase and under CPR 3.18 on a standard basis assessment (and this includes a summary assessment) has regard to the amount of the budgeted costs for each phase of the proceedings and only departs from the last approved or agreed budget when satisfied that there is 'good reason' to do so. From April 2016, a bill for detailed assessment has had to facilitate the comparison between budget and costs claimed (CPR PD 47, para 5.8(8)) and between budgeted and non-budgeted costs within a phase. However, at that time, Form N260 remained unaltered. This divide between information in a bill for assessment and a statement of costs for summary assessment became even wider with the introduction of the electronic bill. Once again, Form N260 remained resolutely unaltered. As such, direct comparison with the budgeted sums for the phases of the claim was impossible. All that Form N260 reveals is whether the overall claim for costs is within or without the overall sum for the budgeted costs and the costs incurred at the time of the costs management order. This creates a very real risk that the court will be more reluctant to undertake summary assessments on the basis that more information to enable budget comparison will be available on detailed assessment. This is unfortunate because:

- The 'broad brush' of summary assessment makes determination of the issues far easier and, therefore, more proportionate for the court.

- Where the case has been costs managed the summary assessment procedure has the attraction of being a much simpler one than it was for those judges less familiar with costs – see *Sony Communications International Ab v SSH Communications Security Corpn* [2016] EWHC 2985 (Pat).

However, salvation may be at hand. The 'Programme of Works' set out in the minutes of the Civil Procedure Rules Committee meeting in October 2017 identified that Form N260 was scheduled for further consideration. This consideration has led to the voluntary pilot introduced in April 2019 by CPR PD 51X. In summary, the pilot:

- runs from 1 April 2019 to 31 March 2021;
- introduces Forms N260A (for interim applications) and N260B (final hearings) which may be used during the currency of the pilot;
- permits the use of the appropriate Form N260A or N260B in all cases in which costs are to be summarily assessed, regardless of when the claim commenced;
- provides that parties or their legal representatives who use Form N260A or N260B instead of Form N260, must treat any reference in the rest of the CPR to Form N260 as a reference to Form N260A or N260B as appropriate. Similarly, any reference to a statement of costs is to be treated as including a reference to a statement of cost in Form N260A or N260B as appropriate;
- requires parties who are filing Form N260B in a case that has been costs managed, to file Precedent Q simultaneously; and
- gives parties the option of using the forms in paper or electronic form, but if the latter is used, then they must file and serve the paper/pdf form and at the same time provide the electronic spreadsheet form to the paying party and to the court, by e-mail or other electronic means.

There is a danger that whilst Form N260B will facilitate budget comparison for CPR 3.18 purposes, the provision of significantly more information will take the 'summary' out of 'summary assessments'. Courts and parties will have to be astute to control and contain this risk. The new forms are a work in progress. In response to user feedback, the Civil Procedure Rules Committee has already made revisions, redrafting the guidance notes (in Tab 6 'Guidance Tab' of the forms) and ensuring the same information is being obtained in the forms, and using the same language as Precedent S (where possible), for the purposes of consistency.

THE SUMMARY ASSESSMENT PROCEDURE

[27.19]

The statement must be filed at court and copies served on any party against whom an order for payment is intended to be sought not less than 24 hours before the time fixed for the hearing or 2 days before a fast track trial. The beauty of this procedure is that when the solicitor is filling in his statement of costs he does not know whether his client is going to be the receiving or the paying party, which should assist him to take a balanced view of the exercise. CPR PD 44, para 9.6 says that failure to comply will be taken into account in the decision about what order to make in respect of costs (so it is relevant to the award as well as the amount of assessed costs) and the defaulter will be at the risk of an order for costs if his failure necessitates an adjournment or a detailed assessment – see *Wheeler v The Chief Constable of Gloucestershire Constabulary* [2013] EWCA Civ 1791 where the outcome was an order for detailed assessment, but with the receiving party to pay the costs of those proceedings. Even worse, at first blush that party might not recover any costs at all because the Practice Direction makes the preparation, lodging and serving of a statement of costs a condition precedent to applying for costs (CPR PD 44, para 9.5(2) refers to the fact that a party intending to seek costs must prepare a written statement and CPR PD 44, para 9.5(4) states that this must be filed and served the prescribed time before the hearing).

However, in *MacDonald v Taree Holdings Ltd* [2001] 1 Costs LR 147 it was held that, despite the use of the word 'must', the provision is not mandatory and a deputy district judge had been wrong to refuse the successful party's application for summary assessment of his costs on the grounds that he had not served a statement of costs upon the respondent 24 hours in advance. The court held that it has a wide discretion when deciding whether to award costs under Part 44 and in applications for award of costs and summary assessments of those costs, the failure to serve a statement of costs was often being used for grounds for depriving a party of his costs or for curtailing a party's costs. Where, however, the only factor against awarding costs was merely a failure to serve a statement without aggravating factors, a party should not be deprived of all his costs. The court should take the matter into account but its reaction should be proportionate. The question the court should ask itself was what, if any, prejudice there had been to the paying party and how should that prejudice be reflected. The court should consider: first, whether it would be appropriate to have a brief adjournment for the paying party to consider the statement and then proceed to a summary assessment of the costs. In that event, the judge should err in favour of awarding a lighter figure; secondly, whether the matter should be stood over for a detailed assessment; thirdly, whether the matter should be stood over for a summary assessment at a later date or for summary assessment to be dealt with in writing.

Given the cross application of the new robustness in ensuring compliance we wonder whether the Macdonald line will hold. It did in the case of *Kingsley v Orban* [2014] EWHC 2991 (Ch) where the court looked at whether there were aggravating factors, determined there were not and, the first instance court not having adjourned for a short period to allow the paying party time to consider the statement before proceeding to assess, allowed the paying party to raise further points on appeal (all of which failed). However, no mention is made in the judgment in that case of Wheeler. While the Court of Appeal in Wheeler did not go the whole way and either make no order for costs or assess the costs at nil, it is worth bearing in mind that in Wheeler the paying party had also failed to file and serve Form N260. CPR PD 44, para 9.5(4) uses mandatory language 'must be filed' and 'must be served'.

A different approach was adopted by Akenhead J in *Group M UK Ltd v Cabinet Office* [2014] EWHC 3863 (TCC) where a statement of costs was served only three hours before the handing down of a judgment when costs were to be considered. The Form N260 did not contain the breakdown of time spent on documents. Akenhead J applied the *Denton v T H White* [2014] EWCA Civ 906 three-stage test to the breaches, concluding that the breaches were serious, that there was no good reason for them but that it would be wholly disproportionate to allow no costs and, instead, imposed a 'delay discount' of £2,240 as a sanction for what he determined to be a breach 'at the lower end of serious'. A similar sanction was imposed in *Simpson v MGN Ltd* [2015] EWHC 126 (QB), where the claimant had filed, but not served a statement of costs. The court made a reduction from the assessed costs reflecting the additional costs that this failure had caused.

Interestingly, in *R (on the application of Kuznetsov) v London Borough of Camden* [2019] EWHC 3910 (Admin), the court declined to make an award of costs in favour of a party that had failed to file a statement of costs. Of course, CPR PD 44, para 9.6 makes it clear that a failure to comply with para 9.5, without reasonable excuse, will be taken into account by the court in deciding what order to make about costs. This case illustrates that the decision may be not to award costs at all.

The conclusion, it seems, is that the result of a failure to serve within the time specified will be case specific, but that the court may well impose some form of sanction to mark the breach of the requirements of the rules.

A trap for the unwary arises on detailed assessments. The costs of these proceedings will, where a costs order of those proceedings is made in favour of one party, be summarily assessed at the end of the hearing. Until 1 April 2013 there was a provision, at what was then CPR PD 47, para 45.3, that no party had to file a costs statement of the costs of the detailed assessment unless specifically required to do so by the court. This provision did not make it into the new rules. Accordingly, a party seeking costs of the detailed assessment proceedings must comply with CPR PD 44, para 9.5(4)(b) and file and serve a statement of costs 24 hours before the assessment hearing.

THE SUMMARY ASSESSMENT HEARING

[27.20]

While *Morgan v Spirit Group Ltd* (above) is clear that the court must conduct a summary assessment process, what that is will vary from judge to judge. Some will take longer than others. Some will prefer to deal with the challenges one by one and make a ruling before moving on to the next area of dispute. Others will hear all the challenges and then produce one judgment dealing with them all. Neither approach is wrong. This permissible variation is not surprising when one considers the actual definition of summary assessment, which is less than enlightening. It appears at CPR 44.1(1) and states that a summary assessment 'means the procedure whereby costs are assessed by the judge who has heard the case or application.'

In essence the court must consider the costs in the same way that it would within a detailed assessment, but does so within a much reduced time span – for example the White Book carries a specimen timetable for a fast track trial that allows 30 minutes for costs (both the award and assessment of these). Advocates will raise the same points routinely seen within Points of Dispute, such as challenges to:

- The indemnity principle
- The hourly rate/grade of fee earner
- The amount of time spent

- The sums spent on disbursements
- The amount of counsel's fees (where not fixed)
- The overall proportionality of the costs

The court must determine these challenges by reference to CPR 44.3(2) on a standard basis assessment and CPR 44.3(3) on an indemnity basis (see Chapter 24 Bases of Costs, above). The court will also have regard to the factors at CPR 44.4 (the seven pillars of wisdom as were – now eight with the introduction of reference to the last agreed or approved budget). A reminder of the importance of so doing was given in *Bush v King* (7 November 2017, unreported), QBD. These factors are examined fully in Chapter 31 Detailed Assessment at **[31.14]**.

HOURLY RATES

[27.21]

While hourly rates will be considered in far more detail in Chapter 31, the Senior Courts Costs Office ('SCCO') guideline hourly rates included within its *Guide to the Summary Assessment of Costs* is, if not peculiar to summary assessments, certainly more particularly directed at these than at detailed assessments. In summary assessments it is rare to see arguments about the guideline rates, other than as to the appropriate grade of fee earner suitable to conduct the work carried out and whether the location of the solicitor (rather than the client and the court) determines the appropriate rate. Having said this, because the rates remain those introduced in 2010 (for reasons discussed below), some arguments are being advanced at assessments that these figures should be the subject of some inflationary increase and, anecdotally, some courts are accepting this and others are not. In the context of the Court of Protection, the decision of Master Whalan in *PLK (Court of Protection: Costs)* [2020] EWHC B28, in which he increased the 2010 rates by 20% has been widely reported.

The guidelines set out the hourly rate for different levels of fee earner in different regions of the country. The title of the document gives a number of clues – namely that the rates are guideline only and are for use in summary assessments. However, the broader application of the rates is a topic for discussion elsewhere as already noted.

After their first introduction the guidelines were updated regularly. Most procedural text books will show the relevant rates back to 2003 and most courts have their own tables of the rates to assist judges when dealing with older cases. Until 2005 rates were set for each court. After that the country was divided in to 4 bands (one being London, although that is in turn divided into 'City of London', 'Centre' and 'Outer London') and different rates were set for each band. From 2009 onwards, the minimal differential between Band 2 and 3 led to them being merged with the same rates and to the then remaining outside London bands being re-titled National 1 and National 2. (What also seemed to happen that year and has previously gone unremarked upon, except by us, was that East Sussex became lost in the relocation and, having been in band 1, has escaped the clutches of the guideline rates ever since.)

However, the rates have not been updated since January 2010, when they were broadly increased in line with inflation. This was originally for good reason. The combination of implementation of the recommendations from the final report of Sir Rupert Jackson and the 'will they be, won't they be' approach of the government to the introduction of fixed fees in the fast track, meant that the future of guideline hourly rates became uncertain. Although subsequently the Civil Justice Council reported on guideline hourly rates in 2014 and further consequential consultation took place with the Law Society and the Ministry of Justice, the Master of the Rolls concluded in April 2015 that the rates at 2010 levels would 'remain in force for the foreseeable future'. Accordingly, the 2010 guideline rates remain 'an integral part of the process of judges making summary assessments of costs in proceedings . . . and form a part . . . in the preparation of detailed assessments' with two amendments of substance from 1 October 2014. These are that:

- Grade A includes Fellows of the Chartered Institute of Legal Executives with at least eight years post qualification experience; and
- Suitably qualified Costs Lawyers are eligible for Grade B or C rates, depending upon the complexity of the work that has been undertaken.

In addition, the Master of the Rolls felt able to accept recommendations that:

- there should not be a Grade A* category of fee earner;
- there should not be different rates for specialist fields of litigation;
- there should not be different rates for detailed assessments of costs (but that there should be more flexibility for the assessing judge on detailed assessments).

and reject the suggestion that there should be a Grade E category for paralegals.

So, with the two amendments, the current rates remain divided between four categories of fee earner:

- Solicitors and Fellows of the Chartered Institute of Legal Executives with over eight years' post qualification experience including at least eight years' litigation experience.
- Solicitors and legal executives with over four years' post qualification experience including at least four years' litigation experience and suitably qualified Costs Lawyers (where the complexity of work justifies it).
- Other solicitors and legal executives and fee earners of equivalent experience and suitably qualified Costs Lawyers (where the complexity of work justifies it).
- Trainee solicitors, paralegals and fee earners of equivalent experience.

Note that the word 'partner' does not appear – the rates are set by experience and not status. Members of the Institute of Legal Executives who are not qualified as legal executives either come within the lowest category or must argue a case based on equivalent experience. It is surprising how often arguments emerge on assessment as to whether a particular fee earner meets what appear to be clearly defined criteria – and not just in terms of equivalent experience, but as to whether they have the period of post qualification experience necessary to come within a particular category. The level of offended indignation can be high.

It appears that the dissatisfaction expressed by the court in *Ohpen Operations UK Ltd v Invesco Fund Managers Ltd* [2019] EWHC 2504 (TCC) that the 2010 rates 'are not helpful in determining reasonable rates in 2019' and that 'further updated guidelines would be very welcome' has led to a further review. A working group of the Civil Justice Council has been established to look afresh at Guideline Hourly Rates. It was due to report towards the end of 2020. Although the project was suspended almost immediately upon the outbreak of the Covid-19 pandemic, it still appears to be on schedule as, at the time of writing, the suspension has been lifted. A consultation period is anticipated early in 2021.

COUNSEL'S FEES

[27.22]

Counsel's fees are prescribed in fast track trials under CPR 45.38. Beyond this there are no set rates for counsel (other than those for advocates under the fixed costs regimes at CPR 45 Sections III and IIIA). The multiplicity of scenario under which the court is assessing counsel's fees militates against this. However, the SCCO Guide to the Summary Assessment of Costs does set out some figures based on the SCCO's statistics for what it describes as 'run of the mill proceedings'. The commentary stresses that these are not recommended rates, but reference points for judges looking for starting points upon which to assess counsel's fees. However, it is pertinent to note that the Guide is the 2005 edition and the figures are derived from significantly dated data.

PROPORTIONALITY

[27.23]

Remember that whether using Form N260, N260A or N260B, once the reasonably incurred and reasonable in amount costs have been assessed, the court must, on standard basis assessments, apply CPR 44.3(2)(a), stepping back (whether or not the parties request it to do so) to determine whether the sum so assessed is proportionate. If it is not, it will then reduce the costs further by reference to the definition in CPR 44.3(5) and any wider circumstances to such sum as it deems to be proportionate (subject, in budgeted cases to a minimum of the budgeted sum per phase, unless that has been reduced for 'good reason' under CPR 3.18). Increasingly, therefore, an in-depth consideration of hourly rate and other challenges on reasonableness may not determine the ultimate outcome of the summary assessment.

APPEALS FROM SUMMARY ASSESSMENT

[27.24]

See Chapter 33 Appeals against Assessments (below)

CONCLUSION TO SUMMARY ASSESSMENT

[27.25]

It is clear from the final report of Sir Rupert Jackson that summary assessments are here to stay (albeit affecting a more restricted range of claims if his proposals for extension to the existing fixed recoverable costs regimes made in his July 2017 Supplemental Report are implemented). However, even if they are, with the introduction of costs budgets and the increased emphasis on proportionality, we believe that there should be an increased incidence of these assessments after final hearings. Parties should be prepared for this. Failure to comply with the procedural requirements for filing and serving the statement of costs and departures from the Form N260 format are likely to result in increasingly less lenient treatment. Compliance is likely to result in far earlier recoupment of costs from the paying party.

There is still more work to be done to encourage and facilitate summary assessment at the end of costs managed cases. Whilst there has been significant progress with work linking the format for bills for detailed assessments to the budget phases, by the requirement to divide bills as per costs management phases under CPR PD 47, para 5.8(8) and by the introduction of the new bill, these do not directly assist on summary assessment. It will be interesting to see how the pilot at CPR PD 51X works in practice and whether it results in an increase in the use of summary assessments in costs managed cases.

Finally, the increasing incidence of costs management means, inevitably, that the judiciary across the board is developing a level of understanding of costs never previously required. The experience acquired will be brought to bear at a summary assessment and the number of judges feeling uncomfortable with the process, and so the occasions of deferring costs to a detailed assessment, should reduce.

CHAPTER 28

DETAILED ASSESSMENT – PROCEDURE

INTRODUCTION TO THE PROCEDURE FOR DETAILED ASSESSMENT

[28.1]

Detailed assessment proceedings in many ways look like the baby brother of the proceedings in which an order for costs was originally created. The parties exchange Statements of Case (see Chapter 29) and then have a hearing (sometimes now on paper) if they cannot resolve their differences. In larger cases, there may also be the need for witness statements and even expert evidence. One area in which detailed assessment proceedings are unique is that of disclosure. It is usually only the documents held by the party whose bill is being assessed – the receiving party – that are of interest. Some documents, such as the inter-party correspondence and exchanged witness statements, are obviously in the hands of both parties. Some documents, such as receipts to vouch for the larger disbursements claimed, need to be disclosed to the opponent, the paying party. Most others, however, are protected by privilege and so do not have to be disclosed to the opponent. Nevertheless, the court will have seen them and the receiving party will seek money in relation to the work done that is revealed by them. This looks completely contrary to all notions of natural justice. The judge takes on the role of protecting the paying party by raising matters of concern, eg on the retainer terms or as part of assessing whether the time claimed for an activity in the bill is reasonable as evidenced by, for example, an attendance note. It is a position which gives rise to certain issues and these are discussed at **[28.49]** below.

The structure of this Chapter, as with previous editions, is to deal with some specific considerations first, then to deal with the procedure in detail and finally to look at assessments in some discrete areas. But, before dealing with these things, we first need to say something about the advance of technology in this process since the last edition.

[28.2]

We have been moving into a digital age for some time now with the common use of email rather than letter and the change from a paper bill to an electronic bill utilising spreadsheet software (see Chapter 29). Things come in threes, or so we are told generally, and this has resulted in three fundamental changes in the way detailed assessment proceedings are carried out and their common theme is that they rely on electronic or virtual factors.

The first change only affects the High Court and so, in the costs world, this largely means the SCCO, but does apply to District Registries around the country as well. The SCCO has returned to its pre-1999 position of having no paper files created for the cases brought before it. As from 20 January 2020, it has been mandatory for parties to begin detailed assessment proceedings, or to bring applications within proceedings, by filing the relevant documents electronically rather than on paper. The only exceptions to this are where the party is a litigant in person or the case has been transferred from the County Court. (For the avoidance of doubt, the detailed assessment of bills arising from orders made in 'London' County Court hearing centres (see **[28.10]**) does not count as a transfer). Applications in older cases which retain the old seven-digit reference number should also be e-filed rather than be sent in on paper.

The change to an electronic case management system by the SCCO – known as CE File – is part of a High Court wide roll-out. There does not appear to be any proposal to replace the County Court's own system with CE File and consequently we are in a position where there are two distinct systems between the High Court and the County Court, as indeed occurred before the CPR came into being in 1999. In order to cater for this, we have highlighted the difference in procedure at various points between the SCCO and the County Court in respect of detailed assessment proceedings. The question of communicating with the court, particularly e-filing, is specifically dealt with at **[28.28]**.

The second change arises from the pandemic and the need for social distancing etc. From March 2020, hearings have been undertaken almost exclusively with the judge being 'remote' ie somewhere else from the parties. This has either been by telephone or by video hearing. The practical effects are discussed at **[28.57]** and are linked to the third change. But it is already clear that lengthier and more complicated hearings can be dealt with by telephone than had previously been considered and that video hearings are very likely to replace many appearances in person where the hearing is short and/or the travelling involved is problematic.

The third change concerns the use of documents at hearings. The use of electronic bundles is mandated by PD 51O where the court uses CE File. They have proved useful to all courts, particularly during the 'lockdown' period. In detailed assessment hearings, the extent of the documentation that needs to be available can be enormous. The logistics of this are discussed at **[28.51]** but the judicial experience has generally been that finding the relevant document to look at is often quicker on screen than the receiving party's advocate disappearing into a forest of boxes with the air of someone searching for their errant drive from the fifth tee. As with all bundles lodged with the court, the quality of the organising is key. The word 'bookmark' is destined to become commonplace in hearings: it is already in PD 51O.

METHOD OF ASSESSMENT

[28.3]

CPR Rule 44.6 provides that:

> 'The amount of any costs ordered to be paid by one party is ascertained either by
>
> (a) A summary assessment by the judge at the end of a hearing [see Chapter 27]; or
>
> (b) A detailed assessment by a costs officer. The provisions for detailed assessment are contained in CPR Part 47.'

A 'costs officer' encompasses costs judges, district judges and authorised court officers (CPR 44.1).

A provisional assessment may take place if the bill is valued at £75,000 or less in accordance with CPR 47.15. It is essentially a detailed assessment carried out by the judge without the parties attending. As the name implies, it is not necessarily the final word and the parties can seek what amounts to a detailed assessment of some or all of the bill if they wish to challenge a provisional assessment (see Chapter 30).

So, in fact there are really only two forms of assessment, summary or in detail. A provisional assessment is a subsidiary form of detailed assessment for smaller bills.

PRELIMINARY ISSUES

[28.4]

This part of the chapter looks at the following questions. Can I start the detailed assessment proceedings yet? If so, where should that be? How do I stop the procedure if I reach agreement with my opponent?

ENTITLEMENT TO START DETAILED ASSESSMENT PROCEEDINGS

[28.5]

There are two points to consider, and the first one will not take very long in the great majority of cases.

Stayed by appeal?

[28.6]

If your client has an order for costs at the end of proceedings, he is entitled to have those costs assessed regardless of whether the opponent seeks to appeal that order as part of an appeal against the judgment (or even if it is the only thing he is seeking to appeal). CPR 47.2 is admirably brief and clear on this point. If the opponent wants a stay of the detailed assessment proceedings, he needs to apply to the court for an order. Do not be seduced by arguments that the assessment will be a 'sterile exercise' and therefore pointless. Most appeals fail so the chances are the assessment will stand and your client will be able to recover his money more quickly than if he had waited.

Of course, what can be done is not necessarily what should be done. If you consider the judgment may well be overturned on appeal you may wish to ponder the advisability of having your client's bill drawn in the meantime. If your fears are realised, the only person paying the costs of having the bill drawn will be your client.

If you contemplate waiting until the opponent's appeal has been heard, make sure you protect yourself against subsequent arguments about the delay in commencing detailed assessment proceedings. It is remarkable how often a paying party is prepared to argue that CPR 47.2 is clear and his opponent should have got on with the detailed assessment proceedings because the appeal proceedings were 'obviously hopeless' from the outset. At the very least, you should offer to delay the proceedings only upon condition that no arguments regarding delay can be brought for the period that the appeal proceedings are on foot.

The same position applies in the rare situation in personal injury cases where provisional damages have been ordered. The proceedings are at an end when that order is made and the costs can be assessed (CPR PD 47, para 1.1).

'Forthwith' orders

[28.7]

The general rule is that costs of proceedings will be assessed at the end of the proceedings, rather than part way through (CPR 47.1). This obviously does not apply in relation to the costs of interim applications which are dealt with summarily at the end of the application.

It does mean that for this general rule to be usurped, the court has to make an order that the costs are to be assessed 'forthwith' or 'immediately' or a similar term. The usual order that costs are 'to be assessed on the standard basis' will not do. Detailed assessment proceedings brought under such an order whilst the substantive case is still going can be challenged immediately by the paying party and the notice of commencement may be set aside (CPR PD 47, para 1.3).

What happens if your client has an order for the costs regarding liability (or similar) at the end of a split trial? Do you have to wait until the loss has been quantified? The answer is no. Rule 47.1 talks of the costs of 'proceedings, or any part of the proceedings' being concluded. While the provision can be read either way, it is generally assumed to mean that a costs order in respect of a discrete part of the proceedings can be assessed while the remainder continues. There is, in any event, nothing to prevent the parties agreeing to treat the proceedings as concluded even though they are continuing (CPR PD 47, para 1.2). Appeal proceedings are treated as separate proceedings. Nevertheless, where the order for costs arises from an interim appeal, rather than a final appeal, the order needs to be termed as a 'forthwith' order if it is to be assessed before the underlying proceedings are concluded: *Khaira v Shergill* [2017] EWCA Civ 1687. There is no issue of course if the appeal costs have been summarily assessed. The decision in *Khaira* also confirmed that there is no difficulty in having Supreme Court costs assessed straightaway because the Supreme Court has its own costs rules (not the CPR) (see **[28.82]**).

You may wonder why this rule exists. Its purpose is to ensure that all costs are assessed by the same person at the same time and this continues notwithstanding the introduction of summary assessments at the end of interim hearings. The assessing judge may have bills from both parties for different periods of the case. There may be several different parties who have bills to be assessed and some of whom were released from the proceedings before the end. Considering whether bills are disproportionate, whether at the beginning of the assessment or at the end, is much more difficult where the costs involved are only for part of the case.

There is little case law on this issue. The general rule is clear and the rationale is perfectly understandable. An additional argument in support of limiting the use of forthwith orders arises where the unsuccessful party to date is, or may be, insolvent. It may not be able to meet the assessed costs prior to the end of the case and it may be entitled to a set off subsequently. This argument was persuasive to Morgan J in *Rawlinson & Hunter Trustees SA v ITG Ltd* [2015] EWHC 1924 (Ch) which followed *Hicks v Russell Jones & Walker* [2001] CP Rep 25.

Practice Direction 47, para 1.4 contains the useful provision that where there has been an order for a detailed assessment of interim costs and there is no prospect of the claim continuing, the court may authorise the commencement of detailed assessment proceedings.

VENUE OF DETAILED ASSESSMENT

[28.8]

The rule regarding where to commence detailed assessment proceedings (CPR 47.4) is, at first sight, a triumph of opaque drafting. You may not be surprised to learn that proceedings should be commenced at 'the appropriate office.' This may be the SCCO or a County Court hearing centre which is different from the one in which the case was proceeding. This is so, even if a formal transfer of the case is not actually made.

In fact the provision for the correct venue is quite detailed and so the definition of 'the appropriate office' is better left to the practice direction (CPR PD 47, para 4) than trying to draft an unwieldy rule in Part 47. The arrangements are as follows:

- High Court and Court of Appeal cases – the SCCO;
- District Registries or County Court cases:
  - The Registry/hearing centre in which the case proceeded when the order for costs was made; or to which it has subsequently been transferred; unless it is a
  - 'London' hearing centre – who refer cases to the SCCO (see below)
- Tribunal, body or other person – the County Court (unless in 'London').

In *The Public Service Ombudsman for Wales v Heesom* [2015] EWHC 3306 (QB) the court considered the correct venue for detailed assessment proceedings where proceedings had been brought in the Administrative Court in London but were transferred to Cardiff so that the case could ultimately be heard in Wales. The receiving party's costs lawyer sought to issue an application in Cardiff for an interim payment and a direction to transfer the proceedings to the SCCO. The court returned the papers with a note that the application should be made directly to the SCCO. When the case came before Master Haworth, he refused the claimant's application to transfer the proceedings to Cardiff. Hickinbottom J reviewed the High Court structure and the CPR in order to conclude that the proceedings should have been treated as having been transferred to the Cardiff District Registry in the original proceedings and the detailed assessment procedure should be undertaken there.

[28.9]

The rather narrower question of whether the 'venue' of the hearing is in-person at court or remotely in some fashion is dealt with at [28.54].

'London' cases

[28.10]

The following County Court hearing centres do not deal with detailed assessment hearings (PD 47, para 4(2)). As such, when a request for a detailed assessment hearing is made (see below) the request needs to be sent to the SCCO. If it is sent to the original Court, it will be returned with a brief message to that effect. The original Court will deal with any interlocutory stages before the request, for example, setting aside a default costs certificate. It will also deal with enforcement proceedings arising from the sum assessed by the SCCO. In some ways, the SCCO acts as a trial centre for detailed assessment proceedings. The hearing centres affected are set out in the Practice Direction as follows:

Barnet	Croydon	Romford
Brentford	Edmonton	Uxbridge
Bromley	Ilford	Wandsworth*
Central London	Kingston	Willesden
Clerkenwell and Shoreditch	Mayors and City of London	

* The Government announced the planned closure of Wandsworth County Court in July 2018 but, at least at the time of going to print, reports of its closure had been greatly exaggerated. Based on the paragraph above you should be requesting a detailed assessment from the SCCO rather than Wandsworth in any event.

'Difficult' cases

[28.11]

In addition to taking on London cases, the SCCO regularly has files referred to it by a court that would otherwise be 'the appropriate office.' The criteria according to the practice direction (para 4.3(2)) are:

- the size of the bill;
- the difficulty of the issues involved;
- the likely length of the hearing;
- the cost to the parties;
- any other relevant matter.

A case is only meant to be referred if it is appropriate to do so based on these criteria. In practice, most hearing centres will take little persuading to transfer a case which might require several days of court time to be dealt with, particularly if both parties are agreed that this should happen.

Regional Costs Judges

[28.12]

In order to limit the need to refer cases physically to the SCCO, an alternative was introduced of 'regional costs judges' who comprise district judges with a particular interest or expertise in costs and who could deal with the case more locally. Such judges can have cases transferred to them if they (the cases) contain complex arguments on points of law or an issue affecting a group of similar cases are identified in the points of dispute or reply, or indeed are referred to in argument at a detailed assessment hearing itself. Alternatively, cases may by referred if they are of sufficient value or will take a long time to deal with. The current criteria thresholds are £100,000 and at least two days respectively. The most recent list of regional costs judges can be found online in the SCCO Guide.

Cases concerning costs involved in Court of Appeal proceedings can only be dealt with by the SCCO even if the case originated in the county court.

REACHING AGREEMENT

Prior to requesting a hearing

[28.13]

Most cases issued in the courts settle before they reach a final hearing. So too do most detailed assessment proceedings. Where agreement is reached during the exchange of the statements of case (see Chapter 29), there is no court involvement – documents are only served, not filed – and so there is no need to do anything formally to bring the detailed assessment proceedings to an end. It is, in effect, a settlement pre-proceedings.

Formalising the agreement

[28.14]

The court is engaged once the receiving party seeks a detailed assessment hearing. The case will be given a hearing date, albeit that in larger cases, it may only be a directions hearing. Rule 47.10 enables either party to seek a costs certificate to confirm the agreed sums for the bill and the costs of the detailed assessment proceedings themselves. Such a certificate may be an interim or final certificate. The benefits of the certificate are (a) to protect either party from any subsequent suggestion that the agreement reached was on different terms and (b) to enable the receiving party to enforce the agreement if payment is not forthcoming. (If the paying party had paid more on account than was agreed in settlement, the protection would be for the paying party but that would be a very rare occurrence indeed.)

A receiving party may discontinue the detailed assessment proceedings in accordance with Part 38. Once a request for a hearing date has been made the receiving party needs the court's permission to do so. This provision in the practice direction (CPR PD 47, para 9.4) aims to protect the paying party from being left without a mechanism to seek any costs he has incurred in the detailed assessment proceedings. However, given that the receiving party has already been awarded costs in the substantive proceedings, it will be a rare case where he decides to discontinue the detailed assessment proceedings and thereby not receive any costs at all.

Informal agreement

[28.15]

In practice, most parties reach agreement on the quantum payable to the receiving party and are content to deal with payment without the benefit (and cost) of obtaining a formal certificate. An exchange of letters will suffice for the parties. A letter from the receiving party to the court confirming settlement will usually be sufficient for a hearing to be vacated, regardless of whether the paying party also writes to the court.

THE DETAILED ASSESSMENT PROCEDURE

[28.16]

This section, as the title suggests, deals with the procedure of detailed assessment proceedings. The issues regarding the drafting of the bill of costs and subsequent documents – what we have called the 'statements of case' – are dealt with in Chapter 29. For the purposes of this Chapter, the documents are assumed to be compliant with the requirements of the CPR and case law.

COMMENCING DETAILED ASSESSMENT

[28.17]

Detailed assessment proceedings are commenced by the service of a notice of commencement in form N252 together with a bill of costs. These documents obviously need to be served on the paying party. They also need to be served on any other 'relevant person' as specified in CPR PD 47, para 5.5. Any such relevant person becomes a party to the detailed assessment proceedings in addition to the receiving party(ies) and paying party(ies). Who might be a relevant person? The practice direction describes three broad categories:

> '(a) Any person who has already taken part in the proceedings and who is directly liable under a court order for costs. (This would normally describe the paying party.)
> (b) Any person who tells the receiving party that he has a financial interest in the outcome of the assessment and wishes to be a party.
> (c) Any other person whom the court orders to be treated as such.'

If a receiving party is in doubt about the relevance of a person, he can ask the court for directions (CPR PD 47, para 5.5(2)), or simply serve on that person anyway and leave them to decide whether to take any part. The court is unlikely to make that person a party to the proceedings unless he applies to do so in accordance with Part 19.

Notice of Commencement

[28.18]

The notice of commencement contains the bare bones of information. The order for assessment (or equivalent) and its date needs to be set out. So too does the total claimed in the bill of costs and, separately, a further sum which will be added to the total of the bill if a default costs certificate is obtained in the absence of the paying party's points of dispute. This sum comprises the court fee and fixed costs (currently amounting to £146 – see [**28.30**]).

The time by which points of dispute need to be served also has to be inserted into the form. The general rule is 21 clear days and is looked at in more detail at [**28.25**]. If the notice is to be served outside England and Wales you will need to consult the rules in Section IV of Part 6 to make sure that sufficient time is allowed. The notice is treated as if it were a claim form and the points of dispute as if they were a defence.

Additional documents

[28.19]

In addition to the notice of commencement and bill of costs, the receiving party needs to serve any or all of the following documents, where appropriate:

- copies of the fee notes of counsel and any expert whose fees are claimed in the bill;
- written evidence as to any other disbursements which are claimed and which exceed £500;
- where recoverable success fees or ATE premiums are concerned, the further documents and information required by Section 32 of the (old) Costs Practice Direction;
- a statement of parties on whom the notice of commencement etc is being served. (Although CPR PD 47, para 5.2 suggests this needs to be done in all cases, this is often ignored where the paying party or parties are clear and there is no other relevant person.)

Whilst the bill may have been served by email if it is an electronic bill, the remainder of the documents will still need to be served upon the paying party in paper form (including the summary paper version of the e-bill (PD 47, para 5.1A)).

Delay in commencing proceedings

[28.20]

The period for commencing detailed assessment proceedings is three months after the event giving rise to the right of assessment (CPR 47.7). The most common event is a court order for costs but it could also be, for example, an acceptance of a Part 36 offer or a notice of discontinuance. (If a Part 36 offer is accepted before the commencement of proceedings, the receiving party will need to commence Part 8 proceedings in accordance with CPR 46.14 (see [**20.6**]) before being able to begin the detailed assessment proceedings.)

If the receiving party does not commence detailed assessment proceedings within the time prescribed by the rules (or by any direction of the court), the paying party's remedy is to make an application under Part 23 for an 'unless' order. CPR 47.8 empowers the court to order that unless the receiving party commences proceedings within a specified period all or part of the costs will be disallowed. Such applications are in fact rarely made, perhaps because the paying party does not wish to bring forward the day when he will have to hand over money to the receiving party. But where the application is made, the receiving party invariably ends up serving a notice of commencement and bill of costs to begin the detailed assessment proceedings before the application is heard so the application has a galvanising effect. Furthermore, the receiving party almost always ends up paying the costs of the application since there are few cases where the receiving party could not feasibly have a bill drawn and served a notice within three months of the right to do so having arisen. Moreover, the application is the gateway to seeking any sanction greater than interest being disallowed (see next heading).

Where the paying party has not made an application under CPR 47.8, there is nothing to prevent the receiving party from commencing the assessment proceedings at any time, the only sanction being the court's power to disallow interest for the delayed period (CPR 47.8(3)(b)). While the court's power is entirely discretionary as to the period of interest to be disallowed, conventionally it is for the period from three months after the order for assessment until the notice of commencement is served, which can be several years later. The conventional approach was not followed by Legatt J in *Involnert Management Inc v Apilgrange Ltd* [2015] EWHC 2834 (Comm). This decision is discussed in detail in Chapter 32.

Delay in the commencement of proceedings was not a bar to an application for a payment on account of costs according to Freedman J in *Argus Media Ltd v Halim* [2020] EWHC 1062 (QB), albeit that it did have an impact on the size of the payment ordered.

'Misconduct' in the form of delay

[28.21]

Where a paying party makes an application under CPR 47.8, it is sometimes accompanied by an application under CPR 44.11 which empowers the court to disallow all or part of the costs where there has been misconduct. If the application is only made as part of the points of dispute to be heard at the final detailed assessment hearing, rather than at the beginning of the proceedings, the case law does not hold out much hope for applications under CPR 44.11 based on costs delays.

In *Botham v Khan* and *Lamb v Khan* [2004] EWHC 2602 (QB) the court held that disallowance of costs pursuant to CPR 44.11 (then CPR 44.14) on the ground of misconduct would be a disproportionate sanction. Although there was culpable delay by the defendant, the claimants had not availed themselves of the right to apply under CPR 47.8(1) for an order requiring the defendant to commence detailed assessment within a specified period. The delay had not prevented a fair assessment of the defendant's costs although the process would be more difficult than if it had been carried out on a timely basis.

The paying party was equally unsuccessful under CPR 44.11 in *Haji-Ioannou v Frangos* [2006] EWCA Civ 1663, even though the delay was for more than five years. The court decided that CPR 47.8 and CPR 44.14 (now CPR 44.11) were not inconsistent and there was no case for imposing upon the defendants the further sanction of disallowing any part of their costs under CPR 44.14 in addition to loss of interest under CPR 47.8. The delay was not deliberate or wilful and the claimant had not himself been a model of expedition. Where the relevant rule not only gave the paying party the option of preventing further delay by himself taking the initiative but also spelled out the normal sanction for such delay, the court should be hesitant to impose further penalties by way of reducing otherwise allowable costs.

Delay no breach of Article 6

[28.22]

The fact that the remedy for delay is in the hands of the paying party was clearly demonstrated in *Less v Benedict* [2005] EWHC 1643 (Ch). The claimants had been ordered to pay the defendant's costs and the defendant served notices of commencement within the time limit specified in CPR 47.7. But, as a result of confusion and oversight it was not until three and half years later that the defendant re-served the notices on the claimants at their last known addresses. The claimants submitted their right to a hearing within a reasonable time under Article 6 of the European Convention on Human Rights would be breached if the costs assessment was allowed to continue; the excessive and unreasonable delay without explanation was an abuse of process; the claimants could not have a fair hearing as they no longer had access to the relevant files. The court held there had been no violation of the claimant's rights under Article 6 because CPR 47.8 provided a mechanism for the claimants to bring the matter to the attention of the court to obtain a hearing within a reasonable time. If a party failed to take advantage of that mechanism it could not be said that he had thereby been deprived of his rights under Article 6. The court would not, by proceeding to a hearing, be sanctioning a continuance of a breach of any rights, but would be taking remedial action to correct the consequences of such a breach.

STATEMENTS OF CASE

[28.23]

You will find all of the drafting requirements of the bill of costs (whether paper or electronic), points of dispute and replies in Chapter 29.

E-bills are required in multi-track cases for work done after 1 April 2018. The only exceptions are if there are relevant fixed or scale costs (eg the IPEC), the receiving party is unrepresented or the court otherwise orders. E-bills are required for between the parties' costs, not for solicitor and client (though there is no reason why they could not be used if both parties wished).

Initially, courts were concerned that if the work done post-April 2018 was extremely modest, there would be an attempt to avoid the drafting of an e-bill and instead simply have a paper bill for all work done. Whilst applications have been made to this end, they have not been as prevalent as feared. The take up of e-bills during various pilot periods had been woeful and the prospect of avoiding preparation of bills in spreadsheet form appeared to be very likely.

Adding to this prospect was the general reluctance to record time contemporaneously in phases, tasks and activities to enable the benefits of an e-bill to be realised.

Time has moved on and now the period since 1 April 2018 is sufficient for work to be set out electronically. This does not mean that everyone has embraced the change. Regularly, the court's request for the e-bill is met with the comment that the case was not in the multi-track because it had not been allocated before it concluded. As such, a paper bill had been produced. The fact that such cases would not be subject to a CMO – and so there would be no need to split the bill into phases – is another incentive for some to continue to use paper rather than a spreadsheet.

Serving bills of costs

[28.24]

As we have seen, the bill of costs is served with the notice of commencement. Sometimes, it is informally served upon the paying party as part of a negotiation of costs. While that is sometimes seen as an aggressive form of negotiation, particularly if no schedule of costs has been previously provided, it certainly concentrates the mind of the paying party. Where the bill is for a substantial sum, it will take some time to draft and there is plenty to be said for going straight for a bill rather than producing a schedule. The cost of preparing the bill is conventionally the last item of the bill itself and so is recoverable in negotiation. The cost of producing a schedule is sometimes disputed by the paying party and there appears to be no direct authority on the point.

If the paying party asks for an electronic copy of a paper bill at any time prior to the detailed assessment hearing, the receiving party must provide it free of charge within 7 days of the request, always assuming that it can be copied electronically.

If the bill is an e-bill, a pdf (or similar) summary version needs to be served with the Notice of Commencement. The expectation is that the pdf version of Costs Precedent S will generally be used. The xlsx (or similar) detailed version will have to be served by email or portable media.

Serving points of dispute

[28.25]

The points of dispute need to be served within the time period set out on the notice of commencement. This is a minimum of 21 days after the date of service of the notice. (While the rules provide for the parties to agree to shorten this period, in practice a paying party who wants to get on with proceedings will simply serve his points of dispute as soon as possible). In order to deal with the vagaries of the post, some receiving parties add a day or two to the minimum period. Others will allow for a longer period, especially on larger bills, rather than have to deal with a request for further time.

The points of dispute need to be served on every other party in the detailed assessment proceedings. This is the purpose of the statement of parties referred to above. It is surprisingly common that paying parties overlook serving points of dispute on any other paying parties.

According to CPR 47.9(3) a party who serves his points of dispute outside the 21 day period may not be heard further in the detailed assessment proceedings unless the court gives him permission to do so. This is very much a backstop provision aimed at enabling a court to deal with one of several paying parties who serves his points of dispute late and takes little or no part until much later in proceedings. It would be a very rare case indeed that a court would decline to give permission for a party liable to pay the costs assessed by the court to be heard on that assessment. In the post-*Mitchell* era, Akenhead J considered this provision to amount to a sanction in *Baker v Hallam Estate Ltd* [2013] EWHC 1046 (QB) and so an application for relief from sanctions was required. However that position was swiftly reversed on appeal ([2014] EWCA Civ 661) and the position as described above was effectively reinstated.

The real risk in not serving the points of dispute promptly is the issuing of a default costs certificate (see **[28.30]** below). If the points of dispute are served out of time but still arrive before the court has issued a default costs certificate, the court must not do so (CPR 47.9(5)) and if it has done so in ignorance of that service, the receiving party should inform the court that he is not entitled to the certificate and the court will set it aside without an application (CPR 47.12(1)) (see **[28.35]**).

Offer with Points of Dispute

[28.26]

Prior to April 2013, a paying party needed to make an offer (then called a Part 47 offer) within 14 days of being served with the bill of costs for that offer to have maximum costs protection when the court came to consider the costs of the detailed assessment proceedings.

When the rules and practice directions were recast, this provision was removed. Instead, CPR PD 47, para 8.3 brought in a new requirement. To date, the open offers required by this rule have not excited much interest at detailed assessment hearings. For the reasons given below, it is not clear that it has had much effect on settlement negotiations either.

The rule requires the paying party to state in an open letter accompanying the points of dispute 'what sum, if any, that party offers to pay in settlement of the total costs claimed'. Such offer appears to be separate from any Part 36 offer since the practice direction specifically states that a paying party may also make a Part 36 offer.

What is the purpose of requiring a paying party to make an open offer? Presumably, it will generally be for a lesser sum than any Part 36 offer since otherwise there would be no purpose in Part 36 offers. But if it is lower, the paying party will generally wish to rely on any separate Part 36 offer anyway. Since the provision qualifies the requirement with 'if any' it suggests that there may not have to be any offer made anyway. It is easy to see that the Rule Committee was likely to have a few qualms at obliging a paying party to make an obligatory offer. As we have seen elsewhere in this book, it is not impossible for the entire bill to be disallowed, particularly where a CFA or DBA is used. If the paying party is putting forward indemnity principle arguments, it may well not want to make any offer at all.

With the recasting of CPR 3.9 regarding relief from sanctions and the general increase in robust case management, a failure by a paying party to make an offer with the points of dispute, afforded the receiving party with an apparent opportunity to compel an offer to be made, or a sanction to be applied. However, it would seem to be a disproportionate sanction to allow a default costs certificate on the basis that no points have been served if no offer had accompanied them (as some receiving parties sought to persuade the courts). To avoid being placed in this position, paying parties often simply make a nil offer.

Optional Replies

[28.27]

CPR 47.13 entitles the receiving party to serve replies within 21 days of service of the points of dispute. The heading in the rules is 'Optional Reply' and there is no compulsion on the receiving party to serve any such document. Anecdotally, some courts have upheld any point of dispute to which there has been no reply. That is simply wrong and runs counter to the aim of limiting replies to aspects which are helpful. It has meant that the requirement for any replies served to be limited to points of principle and concessions has not been observed in many cases. It is difficult to criticise the parties if the judiciary takes an inconsistent line on what is required.

If the receiving party decides to serve a reply, he should do so within 21 days of receipt of the points of dispute according to CPR 47.13. But there is no sanction in the rules if they are not served within this period and they are often served later, sometimes in the run up to the hearing itself. There is no obvious need to seek the court's permission to rely upon them if they are served late. The court's permission is never expressly required in CPR PD 47, para 13.10 although it can refuse to allow variations that have been made to the reply (or other statements of case.) If the reply is the original version, but simply served late, it is almost always bound to be allowed in before the court. This is especially so since the purpose of the reply is either to explain any confusing parts of the bill raised in the points of dispute or it is to narrow the issues and therefore is concessionary in nature which is always a good thing.

The assessing judge will generally expect to see a reply to any general points of dispute, particularly where a provisional assessment is being conducted. If, for example, a retainer issue is raised in the points of dispute, the reply is the perfect place in which to dispel any doubts raised by the paying party. The judge will not thank a receiving party for failing to provide such an answer if it would have been simple to do so and instead he has had to spend time trawling through the receiving party's papers (should he have them) to find the answer.

COMMUNICATING WITH THE COURT

Communicating with the County Court

[28.28]

It is well worth noting that the detailed assessment procedure up to this point has been entirely a matter between the parties. There is no involvement of the court and if, as often happens, agreement is reached between the parties, the court will not have been troubled by the detailed assessment proceedings at all.

But if you need to apply to the court, then you need to be aware of the two different procedures depending upon whether you are dealing with the SCCO or the County Court. (If you have a case in the District Registry – essentially a branch office of the High Court – then follow the SCCO route.)

For County Court proceedings, letters sent by email, post or DX (but not by more than one method ideally), as well as telephone calls, remain the methods of communication in addition to personal attendances.

Communicating with the SCCO

[28.29]

As from 20 January 2020, the main communication method is meant to be by electronically filing ('e-filing') documents via a website into the CE File system which contains, amongst other things, the court file. This is so whether the filing concerns an application, a request for a hearing date or simply routine correspondence.

CE File was first brought to the Chancery Division, before being rolled out to the Queen's Bench Division, the SCCO and other parts of the High Court, including the District Registries around the country. Whilst there is essentially the same numbering convention between the various divisions, there is very limited, if any, scope for the costs judge to look at the court file from the original proceedings. This may come with time, but for the moment at least, you would be well advised to assume that the judge can only see the documents that have been e-filed for the purpose of the proceedings in the SCCO.

Use of the new system will no doubt evolve as familiarity of both the court and its users occurs. You should note three early matters on e-filing documents. The first is that each person needs to register in order to be able to use the system. There is no firm-wide username and password. This is terrific for 'tracking and tracing' problems or glitches in the system since it can pinpoint exactly who caused the problem and when. But it might persuade you to delegate the use of CE File to a limited number of people who are, or become, proficient in dealing with the website. That might mean you not being able to file that last minute document so easily (otherwise documents can be e-filed at any time) but will avoid time being wasted by a number of occasional users. This leads into the second point.

The second is that, unlike paper documents filed through the post (or in person), the court, and therefore in practice the judge, is not automatically seized of e-filed documents. The filing first has to be accepted or rejected by a member of the court staff. Rejection may occur for various reasons eg the wrong fee has been paid. The existence of an acceptance procedure inevitably builds in some delay into the system. If you try to file something at the last moment, it is likely to find its way no further than the acceptance queue. The costs judge can only see the unilluminating phrase 'unprocessed filings' are on the file. The aim must be to get documents on to the court file rather earlier than has been the situation to date. Perhaps pretend that you are using second class post rather than Amazon Prime.

The third point regarding e-filing concerns the naming of the documents filed. For reasons that are not obvious, the programming of CE File means that the choice of how to describe a document varies depending upon the route chosen to upload it. You should use 'add an associated document' rather than simply 'add a document' to get the best range. You may not think it makes any difference but the costs judge faced with a dozen documents all simply marked as 'exhibit' is not going to think kindly of you and indeed the documents may be rejected so that they have to be re-filed with proper descriptions.

OBTAINING A DEFAULT COSTS CERTIFICATE

[28.30]

The ability to obtain a default costs certificate is a continuation of the philosophy of not involving the court until it is clear that there is a dispute for the court to resolve. Where points of dispute are not served within 21 days of service of the notice of commencement, the receiving party is entitled to apply to the court for a default costs certificate under CPR 47.9(4).

(i) Default costs certificate in the County Court

[28.31]

In the County Court, the request for a default costs certificate is made by using forms N254 and N255 which are a request for a default costs certificate and the certificate itself respectively. The request provides sufficient information regarding the service of the notice of commencement and the amount in the bill to enable the court to process the request in a stand-alone fashion. Consequently, the introduction of electronic bills makes no difference to this procedure.

(ii) Default costs certificate in the SCCO

[28.32]

Unlike the pre-CE File arrangements, in the SCCO, a file has to be created and there is a specific option for default costs certificates when e-filing. It remains the case that there is no template Certificate, so when requesting a default costs certificate you should also file a draft certificate (N255) for sealing by the court.

In the same manner as a request for default judgment on a specified damages claim, the only costs recoverable for seeking judgment are fixed by the court rules. The fixed costs are set out in CPR PD 47, para 10.7 at £80; a sum which has not altered since the CPR came into force in 1999. The court fee is currently £66 (Fee 5.3 in the Civil Proceedings Fees Order 2008 (as amended)).

The default costs certificate requires payment within 14 days as with other court orders. The paying party's time from the moment he is served with the notice of commencement to being required to pay a default costs certificate may therefore be less than six weeks.

A paying party faced with a default costs certificate therefore either has to seek to set that certificate aside, if he wants to challenge the sums claimed, or to deal with payment. If he cannot pay, he can make an application to the court to stay enforcement proceedings. Such applications will be heard by either the court which issued the certificate or one which has general jurisdiction to enforce the certificate (if different).

Enforcement proceedings based on the certificate will similarly be brought by the receiving party in such courts, save that no enforcement proceedings can be brought in the SCCO. They should be brought in the court in which the original proceedings took place. If there were no such proceedings, then enforcement proceedings need to be brought in the Queen's Bench Division.

Pro Bono Representation

[28.33]

Where the receiving party is represented by a legal team acting under s 194 of the Legal Services Act 2007, a copy of the default costs certificate (or interim or final costs certificate) needs to be sent to the nominated charity.

Pro bono representation under the Act is distinct from a solicitor or counsel agreeing to act without fee for a party. The pro bono lawyer needs to nominate one of the prescribed charities who will receive the benefit of the costs that would otherwise be payable by the client to that lawyer. In effect, the costs are received from the opponent in a successful case, rather than the client, and the indemnity principle issue that arises is suspended by the provisions of the Act.

Once the pro bono agreement is set up, the charity is clearly entitled to know when an order in its favour is made. Similarly, if a certificate is set aside for any reason, it is entitled to know about that as well. The relevant rules dealing with this notification are:

- default costs certificates – CPR 47.11(4) and CPR 47.12(3);
- interim costs certificates – CPR 47.16(4);
- final costs certificates – CPR 47.17(6).

A word of caution if you are considering acting pro bono in a Tribunal case rather than court proceedings. Section 194 defines the term 'civil court' and it does not include Tribunals such as the Tax Chamber of the Upper Tribunal: *Raftopoulou v Revenue & Customs Comrs* [2015] UKUT 630 (TCC).

SETTING ASIDE A DEFAULT COSTS CERTIFICATE

Procedure

[28.34]

The need for speed and the documents that are required to support the application are set out below.

County Court – The application in triplicate with the court fee or PBA number need to be filed with the court in the usual way. So too will any evidence in response. A hearing bundle may be required depending upon the complexity of the matter but is always likely to be appreciated if it is filed in good time.

SCCO – The application needs to be e-filed and, since it is likely to be the first interaction with the court, will involve creating a new case. Any evidence in response will also need to be e-filed under the SCCO reference (not any earlier reference from another part of the High Court). In accordance with PD 51O, a hearing bundle – both electronic and on paper – needs to be filed with the court. Unless the bundle is particularly large, it can be e-filed (see **[28.53]** for more on this).

Mandatory setting aside

[28.35]

The court must set aside a default costs certificate if the receiving party was not entitled to it according to CPR 47.12(1). That is not a surprising situation you might think. But it helps to set it out directly so that receiving parties do not seek to oppose a set aside application on grounds similar to those set out below. It would be all too simple for a receiving party to argue that the court should not set aside an invalidly obtained certificate unless the paying party had demonstrated some 'good' reason to do so. Arguments that the same result was inevitable and that the court's resources should not be used to set aside something that was ultimately going to be achieved anyway can be envisaged. You might think it a rare case that all of the costs in a bill are allowed on an assessment, but it is not unheard of. Moreover, if the paying party did not provide points of dispute with the application, it could well lead to the receiving party arguing that this demonstrated the paying party had no real arguments anyway.

The rules prior to April 2013 placed an obligation on the receiving party to set aside an invalidly obtained default certificate. This would usually be where the paying party had not been given the minimum period of time to serve points of dispute, or there had been a problem with service of the notice of commencement, or a combination of both. That provision has gone and so it would appear possible for the paying party to apply to the court for a mandatory setting aside as well as for the normal discretionary setting aside. Only a receiving party's request can be dealt with by a court officer (CPR PD 47, para 11.1) but a paying party's request could be dealt with by a judge without a hearing if the circumstances were sufficiently clear cut. In practice, such applications are likely to be listed in the expectation that the receiving party will agree to the application if the circumstances are as the paying party alleges.

Discretionary setting aside

[28.36]

In order to set aside a validly obtained certificate, a paying party must demonstrate to the court that there is 'some good reason' why the certificate should be set aside so the proceedings can continue (CPR 47.12(2)).

Reason for the default

[28.37]

There is a need to make the application swiftly because one of the factors the court will take into account is whether the application has been made 'promptly' (CPR PD 47, para 11.2(2)). But, it is equally important that the application is made with evidence to support it (CPR PD 47, para 11.2(1)). Parties often concentrate on the reasons why they had failed to serve the points of dispute in time, even though such 'reasons' are no more than over-work, lack of organisation etc which, it ought to be clear objectively, are not reasons but simply a description of the occasional lapse in a busy professional's life. While each party must decide for themselves as to how much detail they need to put in to describe the oversights, he should realise that the judge will have heard such comments many times before and have his own view about how acceptable such conduct is. It might be thought better simply to take the blame on the chin and move on to the 'good reason' part of the application as quickly as possible. Obviously if there is an issue about any service of the document at all (or simply delay so the paying party has not been given the requisite time), full detail is required because, if proved, the certificate would have to be set aside regardless of any other merit as discussed under the previous heading.

With the increase in litigants in person in costs proceedings, the reason for default is often health related. Parties have to be virtually incapacitated for health reasons to weigh heavily. Although its own facts are peculiar, the case of *Alexander Mikhaylovich Omatov v Macaria Investment Ltd* (29 November 2011, Newey J) illustrates how easily alleged medical issues can appear inadequate to support an argument that really bears on the application overall.

Good reason to continue

[28.38]

In addition to the application notice form N244, the application should exhibit a copy of the bill and default costs certificate (which the court will not otherwise have). Furthermore, there should be a copy of the points of dispute which the paying party proposes to serve if the certificate is set aside. CPR PD 47, para 11.2(3), which sets out these requirements, says that certificates will only be set aside 'as a general rule' if these documents are filed and served with the application. Preparing points of dispute costs money and if the application is not granted, that money will have been wasted. But do not let that deter you from having them drafted for they are fundamental to the application. They show that the paying party is serious about wanting to take part in the detailed assessment proceedings notwithstanding the default certificate. They also provide the court with a clear explanation of why the case should continue. If they do not do this, it can only be because there is little that is worth challenging in the bill. At that point, overriding objective considerations come into play regarding allocating further court resources to the case.

Points of dispute also take time to prepare. In order to make your application promptly, we would suggest that, where necessary, the application is issued while the points are being drafted, so that they can be filed and served prior to the application being heard. There may be some comment from your opponent about being unable to consider your application until those points are received, but unless your opponent is prepared to confirm that no point will be taken about how promptly the application was made, the safer course of action is to issue pending the points of dispute being prepared.

Setting aside on terms

[28.39]

As with setting aside default judgments in substantive proceedings, the court can attach conditions to the terms on which the certificate is set aside. This power comes from the court's case management powers in Part 3 and as such its scope is wide. In particular, a court which has some doubts about the merits of setting aside the certificate may decide to require the defaulting party to make an interim payment of costs to the receiving party. CPR PD 47, para 11.3 refers to the expectation in CPR 44.2(8) for a court to make an interim payment of costs when it makes a relevant order. The fact that the judge hearing the application did not make the original order for costs does not detract from this power.

The order for an interim payment is usually made in 'unless' terms so that the default costs certificate is not set aside absent the payment. This form of wording generally ensures that the payment is made promptly but that was not the case in *Khandanpour v Chambers* [2019] EWCA Civ 570. Although the full payment was received before 9am on the day following the last day for payment, both the district and circuit judges refused an application for relief from sanctions. It took the Court of Appeal to grant relief and that effort (and cost) should be a salutary lesson to anyone else in this position.

REQUESTING A HEARING DATE

Procedure

[28.40]

County Court – The request is made by filing the paper N258 and relevant documents together with the court fee or PBA number.

SCCO – The N258 request needs to be e-filed together with the associated documents and details of your firm's PBA number.

Time for requesting a hearing date

[28.41]

CPR 47.14(1) requires the receiving party to request a detailed assessment hearing date within three months of the last date on which a notice of commencement could be served based on CPR 47.7 or any court order. Therefore, in theory at least, the interlocutory phases of the detailed assessment proceedings should take no longer than six months from the order of costs (etc) being made before the court is asked to fix a hearing.

In practice, CPR 47.14(1) is treated in much the same way as CPR 47.7 regarding the commencement of proceedings (see **[28.11]**). The rule is expressed in mandatory fashion ('must') but there is no need to seek relief from any sanction if the request is made outside the stipulated three months. The court will still provide a hearing date whenever the request in form N258 is made. Unless the paying party makes an application under CPR 47.14(2) to compel the receiving party to file a request (on pain of disallowing some or all of the bill), the only sanction which the court can impose for a breach of CPR 47.14(1) is the disallowance of interest.

For some reason, paying parties tend to take this point rather less often than in respect of delay in actually commencing detailed assessment proceedings. Perhaps it reflects the fact that any delay is usually related to the parties negotiating with a view to avoiding a court hearing.

Documents to accompany the request

[28.42]

CPR PD 47, para 13.2 sets out items (a) to (l(v)) which, depending upon the circumstances, may be required to accompany the form N258 request. In order to assist the receiving party, form N258 provides a checklist of the documents required.

One of the documents is the 'document giving the right to detailed assessment'. This is usually the order from the court at the end of a contested hearing showing the order for costs; a notice of acceptance of a Part 36 offer, or a notice of discontinuance. Less often it may be an arbitration award or an order or award from a statutory tribunal or other body.

Notwithstanding the introduction of the new Precedent G in the costs precedents which combines the points of dispute and replies, the practice direction continues to talk of annotated points of dispute. The purpose of annotation is to show the judge which items have been agreed and their value and which items remain in dispute. Such annotation is rarely done, unless it is part of the reply that the receiving party is serving anyway.

The final document to go with the request is the fee which is payable by reference to the Civil Proceedings Fees Order 2008 (as amended). The current fees begin at £369 for a bill that does not exceed £15,000 and increase to a maximum of £6,160 for bills of more than £500,000. The most that can be charged for a bill going to provisional assessment is £1,106.

Filing an electronic bill of costs

[28.43]

The e-bill cannot sensibly be fully printed out on paper. A summary version only will have been served in hard copy on the paying party. The full version will have been served electronically.

County Court – When requesting a hearing date, the summary paper version will need to be lodged with the N258 in the usual way together with the various other accompanying documents as described above. The bill will need to be emailed separately to the court. There appears to be a certain amount of autonomy being given to individual groups of courts as to email arrangements and so you should contact the relevant part of the County Court to establish email addresses and anything which might resemble a local practice direction.

SCCO – The e-bill can be e-filed in the same way as any other document which accompanies the request for the detailed assessment hearing. (The same is true of the electronic N260s.) Currently, at least, a PDF of the summary version of the e-bill also needs to be e-filed. It is beyond our ken as to why that is a helpful document for the court to have. It could always be recreated by looking at/printing the relevant tab on the e-bill itself if there was ever any reason to need it.

There is no longer any need to send a copy of the e-bill to the email address sccoebills@justice.gov.uk unless there is some reason why the e-bill could not be e-filed.

What the court does

[28.44]

Having safely banked your money, the court office will consider whether the documents have been received in accordance with CPR PD 47, para 13.2. If they have not, a request for the missing documentation will be made or the papers will be returned depending upon how lacking the papers are initially.

The court will then look to see if the case should be dealt with by provisional assessment. The key document is the notice of commencement. If the bill is said to be for no more than £75,000, it will usually be referred for provisional assessment. If there is a clear need for evidence to be given it will not be listed for a provisional assessment. (See Chapter 30 for more details.)

If the case is outside the terms of the provisional assessment criteria, it will be listed for a detailed assessment hearing, unless the court decides to give some directions or fix a preliminary appointment. Practices vary between courts. At the SCCO the costs judge or costs officer will review the file before giving directions (which may simply be to list the case for hearing.) In some other courts the parties are required to discuss the case to make sure that the issues have been narrowed as far as possible.

The court will give the parties (and anyone else who is relevant) at least 14 days' notice of the hearing unless they have agreed to short notice.

For electronic bills, the court will need to marry up the electronic version with the paper documents so that the judge can give directions.

Disbursement only assessment

[28.45]

If the dispute only concerns disbursements, the court will ordinarily deal with the case on the papers, ie without the need for a hearing. (There remains of course the party's entitlement to ask the court to order 'otherwise.') In such circumstances, the judge will give written reasons to the parties as to his decision (CPR PD 47, para 13.5).

INTERIM COSTS CERTIFICATE

[28.46]

Once a hearing date has been requested, a party may seek an interim costs certificate. In order to do so, an application notice is required in accordance with Part 23 (CPR PD 47, para 15).

The court has wide powers to issue a certificate for such sum as it considers appropriate. It may require the money to be paid into court rather than to the receiving party. Where there is pro bono representation (see **[28.33]**), a copy of the certificate needs to be sent to the nominated charity. Similarly, if an existing certificate is varied or cancelled, the charity needs to be notified of the change.

Provisional assessments

[28.47]

Some courts will issue interim costs certificates without a hearing but practice varies. Where the case will be heard by provisional assessment, the interim certificate application is unlikely to be heard before the assessment takes place. If there is no challenge to the provisional assessment, there will be a final certificate shortly after the hearing and the need for an interim certificate will be rendered otiose. However, if a post-provisional hearing is required, particularly if the paying party is the challenger, an interim certificate is likely to be issued at the point when the notice of challenge is received if an application has previously been filed with the court.

PROVISIONAL ASSESSMENT

[28.48]

Once a request for a detailed assessment hearing has been filed with the court, cases which fit within the requirements of CPR 47.15 and CPR PD 47, para 14 will be assessed provisionally. This procedure is dealt with fully at Chapter 30. If the provisional assessment is challenged, a hearing will be convened to deal with the item or items challenged. There are specific costs provisions in relation to such a hearing, but otherwise it will take place in a manner akin to a detailed assessment hearing.

The costs judges and costs officers at the SCCO routinely requested papers in support of bills to be provisionally assessed, notwithstanding that the original pilot scheme and the drafting of the rules did not expect this to occur. One of the effects of the lockdown period has been to show that, at least as far as the court is concerned, lodging documents electronically rather than sending in boxes of papers is the preferred approach. In any event, 'papers' are now only being requested if they are necessary to determine a point raised on the particular case, rather than as a matter of course.

THE DETAILED ASSESSMENT HEARING

[28.49]

One of the reasons that practitioners read textbooks and commentaries is, of course, to familiarise themselves with the procedure in a particular court and not simply to understand the applicable law. It is perhaps strange therefore, that such books do not normally describe how a hearing actually takes place. Sometimes, the practitioner has the benefit of seeing the process for themselves as part of their training or attending someone else's case, but that is not always so. There are certain peculiarities in the detailed assessment hearing which are likely to catch out even seasoned practitioners from other spheres. In that spirit, we offer the following description of a detailed assessment hearing, accepting that each judge will deal with things in his own way.

The previous paragraph has been present in recent editions. We would suggest the need to be familiar with the actualities of the procedure is all the more pressing where there is a prospect that the hearing will be remote.

Preparing for the hearing

[28.50]

The judge, at least in an ideal world, will have read the receiving party's papers that have been lodged with the court. In practice, this is more likely to have occurred at the SCCO, or where a regional costs judge (see **[28.12]**) is hearing the case. Practices vary between judges, but any time will have been used to consider specific points raised by the paying party, eg in respect of the retainer, or to get a flavour of how the receiving party's solicitor has conducted the file. For example, has there been a lot of time spent on activities that do not justify that time? Or has there been an economy of effort shown that more than justifies the time spent? Does the correspondence suggest endless letters to the client or others simply copying them into others' correspondence to keep them 'updated' or has the paying party's correspondence increased the time and effort required to deal with things than should have been the case?

The paying party will be expected to have reviewed the points of dispute in the light of any replies to see if explanations or concessions have narrowed the dispute between the parties. While this should have been done when the replies were served, the paying party may not have made any firm decisions on whether to accept any concessionary figures offered by the receiving party for example. The judge at the hearing is going to expect the paying party to set out his position clearly in respect of such matters.

The theory is that the paying party is limited to raising the issues set out in the points of dispute. As a result, the receiving party can prepare for the arguments it has to meet. That theory is subject to the three following points:

(1) If the explanation for one issue at the hearing leads to another point being legitimately taken by the paying party, the court will invariably allow that further point to be dealt with at the hearing.

(2) As discussed in Chapter 29 on statements of case, any of the major documents can be amended without permission prior to the hearing. It is a matter for the court to decide whether to allow those variations at the hearing itself. Sometimes the amended documents are served late in the day entitling the opponent to an adjournment but that is not always the case.

(3) In a long running case, a finding of disproportionality under the *Lownds* test (see below) might render each and every item being considered regardless of whether the item was challenged in the points of dispute.

Lodging documents for the hearing

[28.51]

For the purposes of the following comments, we have assumed that you would be lodging paper files in the County Court and electronic bundles in the SCCO. The complete opposite is entirely possible and in which case you would need to read the commentary regarding the 'wrong' court.

(i) Lodging documents in the County Court

[28.52]

If you are planning to lodge your original papers with the court, you need to remember to prepare for the hearing before doing so. Even if you have lived with the case for years, you are unlikely to remember the detail sufficiently to deal with the court's questions unless you have refreshed your memory. If, however, you decide to copy your files to send to the court, early preparation is less important since you will have retained a copy from which to prepare.

CPR PD 47, para 13.11 requires the papers to be lodged between 7 and 14 days before the hearing. (It is worth checking with the court due to hear the case as they vary in the enthusiasm with which they wish to receive papers beforehand. Cases before regional costs judges will always require the lodgement of papers.) CPR PD 47, para 13.12 expects the papers to be lodged in the following order:

(i) instructions and briefs to counsel arranged in chronological order together with all advices, opinions and drafts received and response to such instructions;
(ii) reports and opinions of medical and other experts;
(iii) any other relevant papers;
(iv) a full set of any relevant statements of case;
(v) correspondence, file notes and attendance notes.

Where there are points of principle, skeleton arguments are sometimes filed and served shortly before the hearing. Regrettably, they are often not a series of propositions backed by authorities but simply a speaking note for the advocate and/or a chronology or rehash of events to suit the point being argued.

(ii) Lodging documents in the SCCO

[28.53]

In the SCCO, both a paper and an electronic bundle have to be lodged for a 'trial' according to PD 51O. Translating that requirement into a detailed assessment environment is not entirely straightforward. It may always be beneficial to check what the court is expecting to receive, but an electronic bundle of the core documents (eg those relevant to the points of principle) is likely to be required, even if the receiving party wishes to lodge boxes of paper generally.

The electronic bundle and any other documents such as skeleton arguments or witness statements should be e-filed in good time for the hearing. Following the 7- to 14-day period required by the Practice Direction is a good starting point and the SCCO's general requirements can be found in the Senior Costs Judge's Practice Note dated July 2020 (which can be found at the end of the Appendix).

What about the documents to support the time claimed in the bill? They will not be in the core bundle. Furthermore, what about the documents numerous firms now only store on a case management system and so have no paper version? Do they have to be printed out?

Unlike the core bundle, which has to be produced electronically, it is a matter for the receiving party as to whether they wish to produce the supporting documents electronically or on paper. If it is the latter, then the comments above for the County Court apply.

If, however, a party wishes to rely on documents electronically – there is a general encouragement in the Practice Note to do so – then considerable advancements have occurred since the last edition of this book. Pre-pandemic, the use of electronic bundles generally required the receiving party to provide the court with a laptop loaded with (usually) emails and documents. Other options such as memory sticks and links to third-party file-sharing platforms were seen with considerable suspicion.

However, from March 2020, the ability to provide the court with a file that can be viewed wherever the judge may be has proved to be a considerable success. The need for portable media has evaporated by the ability of receiving parties to upload supporting documents either to CE File or to the 'Document Upload Centre' (DUC), which has been created by HMCTS. The third option is for the use of what the practice note describes as a 'safe third party online file-sharing platform'.

For either of the first two methods, your papers need to be turned into pdf format with appropriate bookmarking. Using CE File is possibly the simplest of the three options but it has a limit of 50MB for a single document. Up to ten documents can be filed together which are each less than 50MB so the limit can be exceeded, but at the expense of the simplicity of a single document to use. If you use this option, make sure you label the document or documents clearly so that they can be used easily. There are several situations where the judge will only be able to see that label and will be assisted if they clearly denote what is in the pdf without it having to be opened.

The DUC has no limit to the size of the document that can be uploaded. The document is placed in a location where only the receiving party and the judge can access it so there is no problem regarding any loss of privilege. The practice note refers to requiring the permission of the court. That permission is bound to be forthcoming but you will need assistance from a court clerk to access the DUC and so, one way or another, you will need to discuss this with the court.

Many solicitors have an extranet so that their clients can see the progress of their case or matter or have access to documentation. Some firms have essentially offered the court the same access as a method of providing supporting documents. An evolution of this approach may well ultimately prove to be the norm since it avoids anything having to be recreated. But for the moment it raises some practical issues and is forbidden to be used by costs officers as employees of the Ministry of Justice.

Skeleton arguments need to be e-filed with sufficient time for them to be approved and so become available to the judge. Whilst PD 51O deprecates using email as well as e-filing, there are many barristers' clerks who err cautiously by emailing skeletons to the judge or their clerk as well as e-filing them.

During the hearing

[28.54]

Not very long ago, a hearing could only mean an attendance in a court room before the judge. A 'telephone hearing' would always be identified by using the full description to distinguish itself from a hearing. Stewart J in *PME v Scout Association* (see **[30.13]**) criticised the description of a provisional assessment on paper as being a hearing.

We now need to become used to an array of adjectives to describe hearings. There are three obvious possibilities:

(1) The judge and the parties are assembled in one room (ie a traditional hearing) which is now called an 'in person' hearing.

(2) The judge is in the court room but the parties, or at least one of the parties, is elsewhere and appears by video or telephone, which may be described as a 'hybrid' hearing (or a 'partly remote' hearing).

(3) The judge and all of the parties are in different locations, the hearing is conducted by video or by telephone and is known as a 'remote' hearing.

In-person hearing

[28.55]

The only differences between an old hearing and a new in-person hearing arise from the needs of social distancing etc. The need to keep some distance apart limits the number of attendees who can fit into any given court room. The handing up of documents – if paper files are used – is problematic. If papers have been lodged an appropriate time before the hearing, then the judge can look at them but the traditional toing and froing of papers and files clearly cannot occur for the time being. This is one reason why the practice note encourages the use of electronic bundles even at an in-person hearing.

Hybrid hearing

[28.56]

The idea of one party being present with the judge whilst the other is, literally, out of the room, cuts across conventional practice where either the judge or the other party step out of the room if one side has to leave the court room. The same point was also a major concern when telephone hearings were first introduced. However, flexibility has won the day and there will be situations where one party simply cannot attend and the other wishes to do so, where such hearings will be held. The ability to do so will not stop the anxiety of the non-attending party as to what is going on out of the video eyeline (or particularly if a telephone is used). So, where one party has difficulty attending, it is more likely that the other will not do so either on most occasions.

Remote hearing

[28.57]

Whether by telephone or video, remote hearings have proved to be much more robust than previously suspected. Cases lasting several days have been successfully dealt with and the number of adjournments was much lower than might have been anticipated. The use of electronic bundles has been embraced, out of necessity, and familiarity has caused a preference for such documents, rather than leafing through endless folders.

Preparation for the hearing has always been important but remote hearings have appeared to heighten its importance. Readily being able to guide the judge to the relevant document helps to create the impression of a well-run case. Similarly, a well-ordered authorities bundle allows the judge to concentrate on the argument rather than locating the document or passage that the advocate is discussing. When everyone is in different places, it can be hard to see what difficulty the judge is having.

Preparation also relates to gathering all the documents into a single pdf if at all possible. Numerous emails on the morning of the hearing with attachments containing attendance notes or letters that apparently have been missed are not ideal. The late pdfs tend to be more difficult to identify, even if they are all opened so that they are in theory ready to be looked at. Offering to email missing documents when the point of dispute is actually being dealt with is even less impressive. Unless the item is of considerable value, you should steel yourself to be told that it is too late for emailing such things.

It is not obvious why remote hearings should take longer than in-person hearings, but in our experience, they do, even where it appears that the advocates are moving along through the points. It is well recognised that they are also more tiring than in-person hearings. So do not be surprised if the judge declines to deal with final issues at a late hour at such hearings.

Justice being seen to be done

[28.58]

Whilst detailed assessment hearings are no longer held 'in chambers' but are in public, the only people able to attend the hearing and take part are the receiving party, the paying party and any other party who has served points of dispute in accordance with rule 47.9. Of course, in an appropriate case, the court can decide to allow others to take part but that is only likely to be so where it assists the resolution of the case and not simply because they may be affected by its result in an indirect fashion.

Where there is an in person or hybrid hearing, a member of the public is perfectly entitled to sit in the court room unless it has been marked as being in private (or similar). The same is true in principle for remote hearings but there is obviously a practical issue of connecting with a Skype or Teams call, for example. It is an issue to which the HMCTS staff are alive.

As mentioned at the very beginning of this chapter, certain notions of natural justice are apparently offended by the conduct of a detailed assessment hearing. There has never been the concept of an agreed bundle for the advocates to work from and even the advent of the electronic core bundle only contains documents the receiving party is prepared to produce. The other papers lodged by the receiving party are protected by privilege so they cannot be seen by the paying party unless privilege is waived. Nevertheless, they have been (or at least could be) seen by the judge and may conclusively determine points in issue between the parties. There are times when the privileged documents are of such importance to an issue which itself is important in the context of the assessment that the judge considers the document needs to be disclosed if it is to be relied upon by the receiving party. The judge cannot compel disclosure of a privileged document. He can, however, require that party to choose whether to disclose it or whether to rely on other evidence to support his position. This is discussed in more detail below under the heading '*Elections*'.

Points of principle

[28.59]

Usually, any points of principle or points generally applicable to the bill are dealt with first at the assessment. It is sometimes the case that counsel, or other advocate, appear solely to deal with such matters before stepping aside for another person to deal with the detail of the bill. For larger bills, the court will sometimes list a hearing solely to deal with these preliminary issues. This may help the parties with questions of representation. More importantly, it minimises the extent of the preparation that needs to be undertaken by the court and in particular the parties, thereby minimising the cost of the hearing all round. The change to considering proportionality after the costs have been assessed for reasonableness means that this is becoming a posterior issue rather than a preliminary one.

One challenge that is regularly made, particularly by litigants in person, is to the order which gives rise to the detailed assessment itself. This is not usually a challenge made following acceptance of a Part 36 Offer or service of a Notice of Discontinuance. It usually follows an order of the court. Such a challenge is always dealt with (and dismissed) as a preliminary issue. The case of *Cope v United Dairies (London) Ltd* [1963] 2 QB 33 is the authority to confirm that the judge carrying out the detailed assessment has no jurisdiction to revise the order for costs that has been made. A party wishing to challenge that order has to appeal it. The assessing judge may well have to interpret the effect and sometimes the scope of the order but that is the extent of it.

In *Maiden London Ltd v Ruddick* [2018] EWHC 3684 (QB), the deputy costs judge sought to interpret the order for costs in a way which, it seems to us, was very likely the intention of the original judge. Before him had been three appeals on which he made partial costs orders in favour of the

Respondents. He awarded costs for a period less any costs commonly incurred. The costs judge treated that as meaning that common costs could only be claimed once, rather than twice or even three times. But, the order was clear in itself and the costs judge was overturned by Yip J for exceeding her powers of interpretation on assessment.

Challenging individual items

[28.60]

The following description assumes that both parties are represented. Please see **[28.67]** below where one of the parties does not appear. Where there are preliminary points, the court will decide as to which party it wishes to hear first depending upon the issue raised, although generally it will be for the paying party to go first. Such points are dealt with in a very similar fashion to an application before any other court. At the end of the parties' submissions the court will give its ruling. If there is a lot of material put before the court, including case law, the decision may be reserved.

When the detail of the bill comes to be considered, it is invariably for the paying party to make his submission first. Often there is little more to be said than is encapsulated by the particular point of dispute. The nature of a detailed assessment is to some extent explanatory. The paying party challenges an aspect as being irrecoverable for one of a number of reasons; the receiving party explains the context in which the item has been incurred and the judge rules on whether the item is allowed, disallowed or allowed in part. This process is repeated for each of the items in dispute. If any items are no longer pursued by the paying party, or have been conceded by the receiving party, the relevant item is marked as being allowed or disallowed as the case may be on the bill.

The final item on the bill is conventionally the cost of preparing the bill itself and any time claimed for the solicitor who signs the bill checking its accuracy and completing the certificates on the bill. These costs are claimed as being within the scope of the original order for costs. However, the costs involving in any costs negotiations, serving the notice of commencement and dealing with the statements of case etc are the costs of the detailed assessment proceedings and the receiving party needs to obtain a further order of the court to receive these (see **[28.50]**). Consequently, once the challenged items have all been determined, the parties need to be in a position to address the court on the costs of the detailed assessment proceedings.

Quantifying the assessment

[28.61]

One of the requirements of the e-bill used is that it will automatically recalculate the totals as the data is changed. Consequently, the sum assessed for the bill is available at all times to the court and the parties. Where, however, the bill is wholly or partly on paper, calculations are required. Those experienced in attending such detailed assessment proceedings tend to be able to keep a running score so that they know how much the assessed costs are as soon as the final item has been ruled upon. Unless this is the case, the parties need to 'make up' the bill either precisely or at least sufficiently to be able to ascertain whether any offers are relevant to the question of the costs of the detailed assessment proceedings. If there has been an in-person hearing, the parties can put their heads together, so to speak, and either make their calculations in the courtroom or by 'stepping outside' so that they can clarify any figures without the pressure of the judge watching. If the hearing is remote, even in part, the video or telephone link will usually be ended and reconvened when the parties are ready to resume.

Costs of the assessment

[28.62]

The parties then make any submissions about the costs of the detailed assessment proceedings. These may be on the principle of who should meet the costs (see **[28.71]** for more detail). They may be only on the amount. Invariably the costs are summarily assessed rather than in detail (which would require a further hearing).

After the hearing

Paper bills

[28.63]

Traditionally, the original bill would be returned to the receiving party at the end of the hearing for it to be completed. It would then accompany a request for a final costs certificate (previously called the allocatur). This reflected the pre-CPR High Court practice of there being no court file (of any kind). Now that all courts have their own files, the practice of returning the original to the receiving party has decreased and the parties usually complete their own copies of the bill with the original remaining with the court. We think this is true even where the paper bill is located on an electronic file, as in CE File, though it is too soon to be definitive. (An annotated copy of the paper bill can be scanned onto the court file.)

E-bills

[28.64]

The theory is that the judge and the advocates will all be working from their own copy of the bill and so will save their copy with the agreed figure at the end of the assessment. The need for the court's copy becomes redundant and so too does any suggestion of having to complete the summary for the purposes of a final costs certificate since the court will know exactly what sum ought to be set out there.

In the 'real world', the figures do not always seem to tally and retracing steps is a time consuming and potentially difficult task. Whilst it is easy to make alterations to the bill, the key task is to ensure you keep a good record of what has been decided and how that decision has been reflected in the bill. You will then be able to go back to the scene of the crime and recreate as necessary (no-one ever wants to return if they have had a good result).

Other matters

[28.65]

A request for a final costs certificate is dealt with below; so too are provisions regarding appeals. (It is worth noting that the rule on the time limit for appeals has been altered so that time does not start to run until the last day of the detailed assessment where that assessment takes place on more than one day (CPR 47.14(7)).

The receiving party needs to make arrangements to remove any paper files from the court if he is not able to carry them away at the end of the hearing.

Elections

[28.66]

In addition to making submissions as to the context in which the item claimed in the bill came about, the receiving party may wish to refer the judge to a document such as a file note or attendance note to support, for example, the time claimed. Alternatively, the judge may require the receiving party to make the document available to him. In either event, the receiving party does not waive his privilege to the document simply by producing it to the court. In many cases, the judge will allow or disallow the item having considered the proffered document. If the item is disallowed the paying party is unlikely to be too concerned about what the document said in most cases. If the amount is allowed, however, it is incumbent upon the judge to confirm that he is satisfied that the item is necessary or reasonable as the case may be and preferably give some reason, however brief, as to why that is so. Otherwise, the paying party has little idea why his challenge has failed.

In some situations, a judge is not prepared to deal with the item on this basis. An obvious example is the use of a CFA. At the height of the 'costs wars' extremely technical challenges were raised as to the construction of CFAs and their compliance with both primary and secondary legislation. The paying party clearly needed to be afforded an opportunity to look at the CFA in order to raise any points he wished about its compliance. Equally, receiving parties understandably wished to avoid disclosing their CFAs because any minor non-compliance would have fatal consequences to the recoverability of their costs.

If the judge is not prepared to deal with an item as set out above, he invokes a procedure sometimes called the rule in *Goldman v Hesper* [1988] 1 WLR 1238 or the 'Pamplin procedure' (*Pamplin v Express Newspapers Ltd* [1985] 1 WLR 689) and which was enshrined in the court rules when the CPR came into being. Its current incarnation can be found at CPR PD 47, para 13.13 which says:

> 'The court may direct the receiving party to produce any document which in the opinion of the court is necessary to enable it to reach its decision. These documents will in the first instance be produced to the court, but the court may ask the receiving party to elect whether to disclose the particular document to the paying party in order to rely on the contents of the document, or whether to decline disclosure and instead rely on other evidence.'

The workings of this rule are helpfully discussed in *Hollins v Russell* [2003] EWCA Civ 718. The case concerned, amongst other things, the disclosure of the CFAs in *Hollins* and the various conjoined cases. The Court took the view that the CFA was of such fundamental importance that a receiving party would have to be put to its election if the case reached a hearing. The delicacy of balancing the receiving party's right to legal professional privilege and the paying party's right to natural justice can be seen in the wording of this judgment. In our view, the judgment clearly says that a receiving party has to make an election if the case gets to a hearing but not before. Some paying parties argue that it should be disclosed earlier: some receiving parties say that it is not authority for an election at all.

Many of the cases in this area relate to the disclosure of the solicitors' retainer. In the cases of *Dickinson v Rushmer* [2002] Costs LR 128, Rimer J required the receiving party to disclose retainer documents if he intended to rely upon them. He considered it to be 'almost self-evident' that the most basic aspects of fairness required the paying party to be able to see documents in order to make submissions upon them. In *South Coast Shipping v Havant Borough Council* [2002] 3 All ER 779, Pumfrey J concluded that the rule, as set out in the Practice Direction, was compatible with the requirements of the European Convention on Human Rights.

All of the cases we have referred to are at pains to point out that putting a party to his election is only going to be required in rare cases. Most of the time, the parties should be content with the judge looking at the documents himself and making his assessment accordingly. This was described as 'an informal, sensible, pragmatic and time and cost saving procedure' by Davis J in *Gower Chemicals* (see below). In *Goldman*, Taylor LJ said that the 'contents of documents will almost always be irrelevant to considerations of taxation which are more concerned with time taken, the length of documents, the frequency of correspondence and other aspects reflecting on costs.' So, only 'where it is necessary and proportionate should the receiving party be put to his election. The redaction and production of privileged documents, or the adducing of further evidence, will lead to additional delay and increase costs' (Pumfrey J in *South Coast Shipping*.)

One area where disclosure is likely to be required is in respect of unused expert evidence. If the receiving party contends that, notwithstanding that it had not been disclosed, it was reasonable for him to have incurred the cost of such evidence, he may well be put to his election. If the case had not advanced sufficiently for that evidence to be disclosed in accordance with a court timetable, for example, there may be no issue. But if the case concluded at or near trial and it is clear the evidence was not going to be relied upon, then an issue is raised that means the judge may well put the party to his election. In the *Gower Chemicals* litigation (*Various claimants in the Gower Chemicals Group Litigation v Gower Chemicals* [2008] EWHC 735 (QB)) the defendant paying party took issue with a claim for the cost of a number of expert reports which had not been disclosed. The costs judge refused to look at the report before putting the claimants to their election. The claimants appealed this decision although did not explain to Davis J specifically why they did not wish to disclose the evidence to support its cost. The appeal was dismissed with the judge following the rationale of the other cases set out above.

He did cause one issue by supporting the costs judge's decision not to look at the evidence at all before putting the receiving party to their election. This is not how the Practice Direction describes the procedure but understandably Davis J thought it easier for the costs judge not to consider something and then have to put it out of his mind. Practically speaking, it does make for a potential problem with the judge's pre hearing preparation if he is not clear on which documents he can see and which he cannot. If it were simply a matter of undisclosed reports, it would be relatively easy to avoid any pre-reading assuming that the point was raised in the points of dispute. However, there is nothing to suggest that there is any such limitation and it is inevitable that on some occasions a judge will already have seen the document before considering whether to put the receiving party to his election.

Non-attendance by one of the parties

[28.67]

If the receiving party does not attend a hearing, it is invariably because either there has been an issue with receiving notification or the case has in fact settled but the court has not been informed. An adjournment will almost inevitably follow in respect of the first scenario.

Where the paying party does not attend, the court is usually faced with an application to allow the bill of costs 'as drawn'. Such an approach ignores the points of dispute before the court and as such is usually refused and the points of dispute read out one at a time and then answered by the receiving party. Such hearings are sometimes referred to as 'Days Healthcare' hearings although the circumstances are rather different.

In *Days Healthcare UK Ltd v Pihsiang Machinery Manufacturing Co Ltd* [2006] EWHC 1444 (QB), the defendant paying parties were ordered to make an interim payment of costs in the sum of £2,000,000 but did not do so. There was no doubt that this was a matter of wouldn't pay rather than couldn't pay. The claimant made an application to debar the defendants from the detailed assessment hearing and that application was granted. But the judge agreed with the costs judge that this order did not affect the points of dispute already served and so the court, as above, required the costs judge to go through each point of dispute, inviting a response from the receiving party and making a decision as necessary. In effect, the court deals with the hearing as a cross between a paper assessment and an oral hearing.

The willingness of the court to debar a party from taking part in proceedings for breaches of costs orders was confirmed in *Tonstate Group Ltd v Wojakowski* [2020] EWHC 1004 (Ch). But the judge drew the line at the use of non-payment of orders relating to other proceedings to found the application.

In *Michael Wilson & Partners Ltd v Sinclair* [2017] EWHC 2424 (Comm), the defendants had not paid an interim costs order of more than £1,000,000. The court gave guidance on how to approach applications to debar the opponent from continued participation. It would be a rare case where an immediate debarring order would be made. Generally, an unless order should be made to give the paying party time to remedy his default so as to continue to participate in the proceedings. Where the paying party alleged impecuniosity, the court would need to see cogent evidence in support.

Misconduct under CPR 44.11

[28.68]

At **[28.21]**, we have already considered 'misconduct' in respect of a delay in commencing detailed assessment proceedings or in requesting a detailed assessment hearing. Such applications have traditionally been by far the most common under this rule. Applications may be based either on a failure by the other party to comply with a rule, practice direction or order: or they may relate to that party's conduct before or during the substantive proceedings or in the detailed assessment proceedings. The conduct has to be shown to be either (or both) unreasonable or improper and those terms, according to the Court of Appeal in *Lahey v Pirelli Tyres Ltd* [2007] EWCA Civ 91, are defined as per the *Ridehalgh* definitions in wasted costs applications (see [23.5]).

A party who can show non-compliance or inappropriate conduct may then seek to persuade the court that it should disallow all or part of the costs being assessed or to make the defaulting party pay another party's costs as a result of the default. Applications generally under this heading appear to be on the rise in an attempt to obtain a wholesale percentage reduction of the bill, regardless of the merits of any of the individual points of dispute.

Such applications in our experience are time consuming, usually require evidence including sometimes cross examination of witnesses on the alleged failures or wrongdoing. A stark example of this is the case of *GSD Law Ltd v Craig Wardman of St Gobain Building Distribution* [2017] EWCA Civ 2144 where the district judge had spent three days hearing evidence on two sample cases from the 14 clients for whom the claimant had acted. The paying party managed to persuade the district judge to disallow all of the costs of the sample files and the Court of Appeal upheld the district judge's decision. The court concluded that the summary nature of a wasted costs application (see Chapter 23) was not so relevant where misconduct was alleged, as here. It was important for the allegations to be clearly set out and for the receiving party and/or his solicitor to have the opportunity to respond.

The conduct may be the party's or his solicitors'. If it is the latter (and it often is), the conduct may include that of a third party. In *Gempride v Bamrah & Lawlords of London Ltd* [2018] EWCA Civ 1367, the fault partly lay with the independent costs draftsman who drafted a bill claiming a higher hourly rate than agreed by the solicitor with herself (as client). She certified the bill as being correct and then also gave misleading responses to the points of dispute regarding the availability of BTE insurance. The costs judge disallowed all costs above a litigant in person's rate in the unusual circumstances of the case under CPR 44.11. The Court of Appeal endorsed the costs judge's decision regarding misconduct but considered the sanction too harsh and halved it.

Proportionality

[28.69]

We have discussed proportionality extensively in Part 3 of this book, particularly in Chapter 14. The conclusion of the Jackson Review Final Report was clear in advocating a reversal of the *Lownds* test (see below) for work incurred after 1 April 2013. The wording of CPR 44.3 clearly underpins this conclusion but does not prescribe a specific procedure. No particular procedure was prescribed previously in the CPR, hence the need for the Court of Appeal to describe the *Lownds* test. In the conjoined cases of *West* and *Demouilpied v Stockport NHS Foundation Trust* [2019] EWCA Civ 1220, the Court of Appeal has similarly provided guidance on how to consider proportionality for post-April 2013 work.

The guidance provided in *West* and indeed in other decisions such as *Malmsten v Bohinc* [2019] EWHC 1386 (Ch) suggest that the proportionality of specific items may be considered during the detailed assessment hearing and not simply once the reasonable costs have been established. It may be in a rare case that this is so but in our view, it will generally be necessary, in order to ensure that costs on the standard basis are both reasonable and proportionate, for the reasonable sums to be assessed before the court considers whether such sums are also proportionate.

This means that the 'making up' of the bill – ie the adding up – has to be done before the parties can address the court on proportionality. One advantage of e-bills is that the figure will be available immediately and so the hearing can continue seamlessly from reasonableness challenges to the consideration of proportionality.

The Court of Appeal in *West* gave judges direction on how to deal with reductions to costs considered to be disproportionate. In essence, this involves looking at the solicitors and counsels' fees to locate the reductions. This approach is considered in detail at [**14.5**] and [**14.6**].

Proportionality – The *Lownds* Test

[28.70]

For cases where work was done before 1 April 2013, the question of proportionality is to be considered by reference to the test in *Lownds v Home Office* [2002] EWCA Civ 365. It requires a global assessment of proportionality which was inevitably a difficult process where only some of the work was subject to that test (and the remainder was subject to the test in CPR 44.3). Realistically, there are no longer any cases where all of the costs have been incurred before April 2013 and so any long-standing cases have, at most, an element of costs which require the application of the *Lownds* test.

The test therefore is heading for obsolescence, but for the sake of completeness, we record that the Court of Appeal set out a two-stage test. First the judge was to look at the costs claimed in the bill on a 'global' basis. Did he consider the overall costs to be disproportionate, or at least have the appearance of being so? If the judge answered this in the negative, he would assess the costs to see whether they had been reasonably incurred and were reasonable in amount. But if the judge answered his question positively, he was to allow only those costs which were 'necessarily' incurred (and reasonable in amount.).

It is clear that the test of necessity was intended to be a higher hurdle than simply one of reasonableness. But the *Lownds* judgment itself cautioned against too high a hurdle being erected by the court. Often, the result was that it was difficult to spot the difference between assessments conducted on the basis of necessity and those simply on the basis of reasonableness.

The alternative approach by many judges was to consider the bill to be globally proportionate but certain items to be disproportionate, for example the documents item. This enabled the court to concentrate solely on the items that appeared to be problematic. This approach was supported by the decision of Morland J in *Giambrone v JMC Holidays Ltd (formerly Sunworld Holidays Ltd)* [2002] EWHC 2932 (QB). It is a decision that was still being referred to regarding the test in CPR 44.3 but has effectively been superseded by the comments made in *West*.

Assessments where there are CMOs

[28.71]

CPR 3.18 is clear that costs which have been budgeted can only be disturbed for a 'good reason'. The way this fits into the costs budgeting arrangements overall is discussed at **[15.13]**. In particular, we look there at the decision of HHJ Dight in *Barts Health NHS Trust v Salmon* [2019] Lexis Citation 27 which looks at the question of what is a good reason? In this Chapter, we look at the practicalities of dealing with CMOs in relation to detailed assessment.

The case law, including *Salmon*, appears to assume that once a decision has been made regarding the presence or absence of a good reason, the issues raised by the new provisions have been overcome. That is optimistic in our view.

One of the problems with costs budgeting, as identified by Sir Rupert Jackson in his Supplementary Report, is the stage at which it takes place. By that time, a significant percentage of costs have already been incurred (and which cannot therefore be budgeted) even where cases get to trial. Cases which settle early into proceedings may be almost entirely comprised of 'incurred' costs. Sir Rupert has suggested certain solutions to this issue, but for the moment, bills for detailed assessment with CMOs often involve more costs that still have to be assessed in the conventional or 'classic' manner, than those which have been budgeted. Consequently, it can be a long way into the detailed assessment before the benefits of the budgeted costs come into play.

When the assessment does reach the budgeted parts of the bill, the hearing reaches a crossroad. Where no good reason to depart from the budget is alleged (or is alleged but is unsuccessful) the assessment reaches the concluding elements very quickly. The costs of the bill preparation, if challenged, need to be assessed (they are not part of the 1% or 2%) and then all that remains is the question of proportionality. This has already been considered in respect of the budgeted parts and so it is only a live issue regarding the incurred costs. This is considered in more detail at **[15.11]**.

If, on the other hand, a good reason to depart from the budget is established, the hearing moves into relatively uncharted water. Points of dispute and replies are rarely drafted on the basis that a good reason will be established. This is perhaps understandable because it may not be clear on what basis the good reason will be found by the judge. Even if it is clear, there is no definitive method by which a judge will allow departure from the budgeted sum. Options include assessing the entirety of the relevant part; dealing only with challenges that are in the points of dispute; taking a broad brush to the figure in excess of the budget etc. The approach will depend very much on the individual circumstances of the case and may well require a certain latitude to the contents of the points of disputes and replies.

The difference in the time taken to conduct the detailed assessment depending upon the decision regarding good reason is very stark. It may well become the norm for the parties to confirm their positions on the question of any 'good reason' arguments prior to listing the detailed assessment hearing in order to use court time efficiently. (It is, perhaps surprisingly, often not clear from the points of dispute and replies.)

COSTS OF THE DETAILED ASSESSMENT PROCEEDINGS

Award of costs

[28.72]

The detailed assessment procedure is a quantification exercise of the costs awarded to a (receiving) party in previous proceedings. If the paying party puts the receiving party to the task of justifying the costs claimed before a court, the presumption in CPR 47.20 is that the receiving party will receive the costs of having to do so. The only exceptions are where the provisions of any Act, or a rule or practice direction provide otherwise or the court decides to make a different order. The court will only make a different order if:

- the conduct of the parties warrants it;
- the bill has been reduced by an amount which justifies it; or
- a party has unreasonably claimed the costs of a particular item (or occasionally unreasonably disputed it) (CPR 47.20(3)).

Where the court decides to reflect such circumstances in its order, it may reduce the costs of assessment by a percentage or specific sum, it may decide to make no order as to costs or award them to the paying party.

As discussed in Chapter 21, ADR in the form of mediation and early neutral evaluation is entering the world of costs. The paying party does not always agree to invitations to go to ADR. There have been first instance decisions where the court has been prepared to alter the receiving party's order for costs to an assessment on the indemnity basis in such circumstances. Whilst we would not wish to discourage attempts to settle short of the court door, we do think there is something qualitatively different about penalising the losing party when compared with *Halsey* etc discussed in Chapter 21.

Offers

[28.73]

Until April 2013, a paying party was able to make an offer under CPR 47.19 which, if not beaten, would afford protection against the receiving party seeking the costs of the detailed assessment proceedings. It was an echo of Part 36 but did not have the same rigidity and it left open the question of whether a Part 36 offer on costs could be made in any event.

The recasting of the costs rules clarified this situation by making clear (CPR 47.20(4)) that Part 36 offers by both parties can be made. The terminology of Part 36 is adapted so that, for example, the claimant in Part 36 is the receiving party in Part 47. The scope for making complicated offers on costs which will afford any protection is probably limited and the occasions when offers will be withdrawn is also likely to be rare in practice.

One of the problems with CPR 47.19 offers was whether such offers included the costs of the detailed assessment proceedings themselves, or whether they simply related to the costs in the bill. Where offers did include such costs they would wrap everything up if accepted, but were difficult to disentangle if they were relied upon at an assessment. The opposite occurred if the detailed assessment costs were left outside the offer. Parties may still take either option under the new rules. It would seem to be unlikely that an all-inclusive offer can properly be made under Part 36 given the decision of the Court of Appeal in *Mitchell v James* [2002] EWCA Civ 997.

What about an offer that complies with PD 47, para 19 in that it says it does not include interest but does not comply with Part 36 because it needs to include interest until the end of the expiry of the 21-day period for automatic acceptance? In *King v City of London Corpn* [2019] EWCA Civ 2266, the Court of Appeal took the firm line that such offers do not comply with Part 36 and as such were ineffective when seeking to claim the additional items set out in CPR 36.17(4).

CPR PD 47, para 19 confirms that any offer, whether under Part 36 or not, ought to specify exactly what it contains, in particular whether it includes the costs of the preparation of the bill, VAT or interest. If the offer is silent on these aspects, it will be taken to include all of them.

The encouragement to claimants (here receiving parties) to make Part 36 offers has led to additional amounts and essentially punitive levels of interest being awarded under CPR 36.17(4). Some judges were reluctant to allow these additional sums in detailed assessment proceedings. But Proudman J confirmed that there was no difference between detailed assessment proceedings and the underlying proceedings in *Cashman v Mid Essex Hospital Services NHS Trust* [2015] EWHC 1312 (QB). Rather oddly, the decision of *Cashman* was not referred to the deputy costs judge in *JLE (A Child by her Mother and Litigation Friend, ELH) v Warrington & Halton Hospitals NHS Trust Foundation Trust*, which would have resolved the issue regarding the additional amount (as Stewart J confirmed ([2019] EWHC (QB))).

Without prejudice (save as to costs)

[28.74]

Negotiations on a 'without prejudice save as to costs' basis are, as the description suggests, admissible on the question of the costs of the relevant proceedings. However, negotiations on a completely 'without prejudice' basis are not. The parties may negotiate in the faith and expectation that purely without prejudice negotiations could not be used against them even on the question of costs. Although there were some exceptions to that rule, costs was not one of them (*Reed Executive Plc v Reed Business Information Ltd* [2004] EWCA Civ 887).

Where the paying party is concerned about the level of costs, he will sometimes make a 'Calderbank' offer rather than a Part 36 offer so as to allow him to make an offer of something other than standard basis costs up. These offers are discussed at **[20.37]**. The differences between Part 36 offers and Calderbank offers made under Part 44 are more extensive than might first appear. For example, a Part 36 offer will automatically require permission of the court if the offeree wishes to accept it once a trial (for which read detailed assessment) has begun. In *MEF v St George's Healthcare NHS Trust* [2020] EWHC 1300 (QB), the defendant had reiterated a previously made offer in the run-up to the detailed assessment hearing but had not limited it to, for example, the beginning of the hearing. Consequently, part way through the second day of a three-day hearing, the receiving party's advocate handed over a letter accepting the Calderbank offer including agreeing to pay the defendant's costs from the expiry of the offer. The costs judge held that to be a valid common law offer and acceptance and that the different rules concerning Part 36 offers shone no light on that acceptance. On appeal, Morris J agreed.

FINAL COSTS CERTIFICATE

[28.75]

Following the detailed assessment hearing of a paper bill, the parties calculate the costs allowed on assessment by completing or 'making up' the bill. With an e-bill, the allowed sum can be seen immediately. In many cases, once the figure has been agreed between the parties it is paid by one to the other and no further step is required. For this reason, no post-assessment order or certificate is produced unless requested.

If the receiving party wishes to be in a position to enforce the costs as assessed, he needs a final costs certificate which is the quantified order for costs. CPR 47.17 expects the completion of the bill and a request for a final certificate to be made within 14 days of the assessment. There is no effective penalty if it is done later. The practice direction also enables the paying party to make an application to compel the certificate to be produced but such an application must be the rarest of beasts. It takes a good deal of conjecture to think of any situation in which the paying party wishes to be able to demonstrate his indebtedness with a formal certificate; unless he is contemplating insolvency (and in which case there will be problems with enforcement anyway).

Final costs certificate in the County Court

[28.76]

Unlike a default costs certificate there is no request form: CPR 47.17 is written on the basis that the completed bill acts as the request. The key part of the bill is the summary which needs to show the figures that are claimed so that they can be transposed onto the final certificate. CPR PD 47, para 16 contains a number of requirements to be satisfied before a certificate will be issued. For example, receipted fee notes from counsel and receipted fee notes for any other disbursement over £500 (and so not covered by Certificate (5) on the bill). Given that these disbursements will have been allowed by the assessing judge – and quite possibly disputed in detail – these provisions are rather cautious. They are also perhaps a little anachronistic. In many cases counsel will be paid from the fees recovered from the opponent. If that recovery cannot take place in the absence of a final certificate, there is little purpose in requiring a receipted fee note. These restrictions may also help to explain why most receiving parties do not obtain a final costs certificate after a detailed assessment.

While the practice direction hints that the court will draw the final costs certificate, we would recommend that you send in copies for sealing rather than rely on the court's resources. Your certificate is likely to be processed much more quickly as a result.

Final costs certificate in the SCCO

[28.77]

The draft certificate needs to be e-filed. Although the PD 47 requirements regarding vouchers etc equally apply in the SCCO, the fact that the same officer or judge who assessed the bill will approve the certificate tends to mean that it is rare for the court to require the vouchers. Indeed, given that the figures for the certificate are often provided to the court before the end of the assessment, it is not uncommon for draft certificates to be sent in for sealing without a completed bill, let alone the vouchers.

Setting aside a final costs certificate

[28.78]

Since this certificate is only produced after a detailed assessment hearing, the circumstances in which a setting aside (other than for mathematical error) takes place will be few and far between. However, in *Mainwaring v Goldtech Investments Ltd (No 2)* [1999] 1 All ER 456, CA a receiving party delayed for about six years in serving a bill of costs on one of two paying parties. The first paying party's assessment had been completed and a certificate issued. When the second party successfully applied to set aside the certificate and had the costs against them disallowed in their entirety because of the delay, the first paying party succeeded in having the costs award against her also set aside in its entirety, because there could not be two certificates in different amounts arising from a single costs order imposing joint and several liability.

APPEAL FROM A DETAILED ASSESSMENT HEARING

[28.79]

There is a completely different approach to appeals from an authorised court officer than from a costs judge or district judge. It was considered by Stewart J in *PME v Scout Association* and we deal with it in Chapter 33 as part of appeals from detailed assessments generally.

OTHER DETAILED ASSESSMENT PROCEEDINGS

Court of Protection

[28.80]

Deputies are entitled by virtue of the Mental Capacity Act 2005 and the Court of Protection Rules 2017 to payment of their charges, whether as a professional deputy or not. There is a clear regard for keeping the cost of assessment to a minimum since payment of the fees is likely to come out of the protected person's property. Consequently, there are provisions for the payment of fixed costs where the work is limited and the option of a short form bill where the fees are below £3,000. Furthermore, most Court of Protection bills are assessed provisionally to avoid the need for attendance and further detail can be found in Chapter 30 on such assessments. As with all essentially solicitor and client costs, electronic bills are not required for work done after 6 April 2018.

The costs of the application for the appointment of the deputy include all work up to the date of the appointment. All costs thereafter are treated as general management charges and are assessed if an order for such charges has been made. That order needs to be included with the N258 requesting an assessment (along with the other papers usually lodged in accordance with CPR PD 47, para 13.2) for the first year's management charges. Thereafter it is not required because the SCCO keeps a record of such orders and the costs allowed.

Legal Aid

[28.81]

A legally aided party who has an order for costs to be assessed against a non-legally aided party will use the same procedure as for any other between the parties' bill. The party's solicitors may decide to waive its entitlement to any costs from the Legal Aid Agency (perhaps because they would form a statutory charge on their client's property) and in which case the assessment will be dealt with in exactly the same way as any other assessment. If costs unrecovered from the opponent are going to be sought from the Legal Aid Agency, there are two differences from the usual procedure. The bill will be drawn in a six column format (see **[29.3]**) so that unrecovered items can potentially be transferred to the legal aid columns. At the end of the detailed assessment, the receiving party's advocate will either stay behind to seek assessment of any purely legal aid items or they will be assessed by the judge on paper.

Supreme Court proceedings

[28.82]

Part 7 of the Supreme Court Rules 2009 deals with costs in the Supreme Court accompanied by Practice Direction No 13. Costs may be awarded on either the standard or the indemnity basis with the same definitions as in the CPR. There is provision for the paying party to file and serve points of dispute and for the receiving party to respond.

Rule 47 provides that submissions as to costs are to be made *before* judgment unless before the close of oral argument a party applies to defer making submissions until after judgment. The court could direct oral submissions immediately after judgment, or the simultaneous or sequential filing of written submissions or written submissions followed by oral submissions.

Under rule 49 either party may request a provisional assessment of costs by the Registrar. There are no similar provisions to those set out in Chapter 30 regarding the costs consequences of an 'appeal' of a provisional assessment. If either or both parties are dissatisfied with that assessment the registrar will try to resolve it in correspondence. If that fails he will appoint an oral hearing before two costs officers, one of whom will be a costs judge and the other an appointee of the President – in practice, this is usually the Registrar.

The function of Supreme Court costs officers is to carry out the detailed assessment (rule 49(1) and SCPD No 13, para 16.1). That is the limit of their jurisdiction. Decisions as to whether the receiving party is to receive less than 100% of the assessed costs are reserved to the court in the exercise of the discretion given to it by rule 46(1). Costs officers must confine their attention to the basis of assessment prescribed by rule 50, subject to any directions that might be given to them by the court: *R (on the application of Edwards) v Environment Agency (Cemex UK Cement Ltd, intervening)* [2010] UKSC 57.

There is no appeal from a decision of the costs officers on the quantum of any sums allowed. An appeal on a point of principle lies to a single Supreme Court Justice. He may affirm the costs officers' decision or he may refer the issue to a panel of Justices to decide it and who may or may not require an oral hearing to do so.

Tribunal (Employment (Appeal) Tribunal)

[28.83]

Costs may be recoverable in the First-tier Employment Tribunal or the Employment Appeal Tribunal (part of the Upper Tribunal) where there has been unreasonable conduct. In *Monfared v Spire Healthcare Ltd UKEAT/0131/18/RN*, Laing J, sitting as an EAT Judge reviewed an assessment of costs by the ET Judge where unreasonable conduct had been found. Amongst other things, (see [**29.32**]), she concluded that the costs of the detailed assessment proceedings (ie the cost of preparing the bill) were included in the order for costs made by the Tribunal. There is a 28-day time limit for making an application for such costs.

An order for costs is made under rule 78(1) of the Employment Tribunal Rules of Procedure 2013. The Tribunal can make an order specifying a sum up to £20,000. Alternatively, it can order a detailed assessment by either a County Court judge or an Employment judge and that may involve an amount above £20,000. Rule 84 requires the Tribunal to take into account the payee's ability to pay. In *Kuwait Oil Co v Al-Tarkait* UKEATPA/0210/19/00 (4 December 2019), Kerr J upheld an order made which limited the respondent's recoverability of non-fixed costs to the aggregate of the claimant's damages and the costs which the claimant himself was entitled to claim from the respondent. 'Capping' could apply to either specific or assessed sums under the Tribunal's rules in order to take account of the ability to pay.

Where the Appeal Tribunal varies the first instance decision, the 28 days only begins to run from the date of the EAT judgment. For example, see *Soll (Vale) (A Firm) v M Jaggers* ((6 October 2017, unreported), Judge Eady QC). The EAT returned the case to the Tribunal to consider the reasonableness of Mr Jaggers' pursuit of his original claim for the purposes of a costs award by the Tribunal. The EAT did not consider the defence of the appeal to be unreasonable in the main and the one element that might have been unreasonable had not obviously resulted in any additional costs. As such the EAT made no order for costs against Mr Jaggers in respect of the appeal proceedings.

Tribunal (Property Chamber)

[28.84]

The Land Registration Act 2002 empowered the Adjudicator to award costs in respect of cases referred to him by the Land Registry in relation to disputes over land. The procedure for dealing with costs was originally set out in the Adjudicator to Her Majesty's Land Registry (Practice and Procedure) Rules 2003. The position was simplified as part of the reorganisation of the Tribunals structure so that the Adjudicator (now President) and her deputies have become part of the property chamber. The Tribunal Procedure (First-tier Tribunal) (Property Chamber) Rules 2013 came into force on 1 July 2013 and so replaced the Adjudicator Regulations.

The rules import the provisions of the CPR (reg 13(8)) regarding a detailed assessment and so replace the CPR lite arrangements set out previously and to which most people appearing before it had little or no knowledge. The amount of costs may be determined by a summary assessment, in which case the Tribunal judge will deal with the costs. They may be agreed by the parties or they may be dealt with by a detailed assessment. If it is the last of these options, the hearing may well be conducted by a Master from the SCCO sitting as a Deputy Tribunal judge.

Civil Recovery Orders

[28.85]

The Director of the Assets Recovery Agency may apply to the High Court for a property freezing order or an interim receiving order in an appropriate case under Part 5 of the Proceeds of Crime Act 2002. The property is then vested in a trustee for civil recovery. Any person who has incurred legal expenses in the proceedings – and the court has ordered their costs to be paid from the property – is meant to try to agree them initially with the Director. If agreement is reached, the Director will authorise the trustee to pay those costs from the property in trust. If they cannot be agreed, the costs will have to be assessed in accordance with the Proceeds of Crime Act 2002 (Legal Expenses in Civil Recovery Proceedings) Regulations 2005 (and 2008).

The regulations specify that CPR Part 47 applies save that the three month time limits for commencing detailed assessment (CPR 47.7) and for requesting a hearing (CPR 47.14) are both reduced to two months.

Costs are assessed on the standard basis but the hourly rates allowable are subject to restrictions set out in regulation 17. There are two columns of figures which are based on seniority in respect of both solicitors and counsel. In order to get into the second, higher column the case need to involve 'substantial novel or complex issues of law or fact'. All of the rates set out in the table can be enhanced if the legal representatives are based in London as defined by postcodes. An increase of 20% is allowed for 'Central London' (postcodes EC1-4, SW1, W1 and WC1-2). An increase of 10% is allowed for 'Outer London' (BR, CR, DA, E, N, NW, SE, SW, UB and W.) The rates are not particularly high and so it may not matter that there appears to be no discretion for the court to award a lower hourly rate if to do otherwise would offend the indemnity principle.

High Court Enforcement Officers

[28.86]

The High Court Enforcement Officers Regulations 2004 set out fees which may be charged by HCEOs (formerly Sheriffs) in respect of the executions against goods which they carry out on behalf of judgment creditors. Not all of the items listed in Schedule 3 are fixed and so it is open for the party liable to pay the HCEO's fees to challenge them in accordance with the Regulations.

An application needs to be made to the SCCO which will be listed for a directions hearing. The costs judge will firstly consider whether to make an order for detailed assessment of the costs in dispute. If he does, then he will also give directions regarding the need for documents to expand upon the parties' positions, if they have not already been set out sufficiently, together with directions for the hearing. The provisions of the CPR will apply to such proceedings.

CHAPTER 29

DETAILED ASSESSMENT – STATEMENTS OF CASE

INTRODUCTION TO STATEMENTS OF CASE IN DETAILED ASSESSMENT

[29.1]

You will not find the description 'Statements of Case' used in the CPR to describe the documents in a detailed assessment but we have used the description which normally refers to Particulars of Claim, Defence and so forth for two reasons. The first is aesthetic. It is ungainly and unnecessarily lengthy to refer regularly to 'bill of costs, points of dispute and reply' and so where we talk about these documents together we have used the phrase statements of case and have headed this chapter appropriately.

Second, and more importantly, it is no bad thing to echo the ethos as well as the terminology of the underlying case's pleadings. In detailed assessment proceedings the bill of costs is intended to set out detailed information upon which the receiving party relies and the solicitor has to sign several certificates at the end of the bill to confirm the accuracy of the document. Doing so is 'no empty formality'. Similarly the points of dispute are intended, concisely, to set out the objections to the bill in a way that the receiving party (and the court) can understand. Replies are meant to answer questions raised by the points of dispute to narrow the issues. The fact that all three documents came in for criticism during the Jackson Review suggests that, historically, parties have not necessarily taken the care that parties take when drafting the statements of case in the original proceedings.

At the end of this chapter you will find a section on the tricky subject of how costs 'common' to more than one party are dealt with. This section could have been placed in Chapter 28 regarding how detailed assessments work. But we have placed it in this chapter because an understanding of the law in this area underpins consideration of what items are to be included or excluded in the bill: similarly, what items might be challenged in the points of dispute. Equally this section could have been placed, at least in part, in Chapter 1 in respect of a solicitor's retainer. But we think it is easier to understand the varying aspects of common costs if they are grouped together.

THE PAPER BILL OF COSTS: FORM AND CONTENT

[29.2]

If you have never seen a bill of costs, you may find it helpful to look at the model bills annexed to Practice Direction 47 (precedents A to E) before going further. This comment holds good even if you are contemplating an electronic bill of costs because it is meant to replicate the essence of a paper bill in spreadsheet form. It may well give you a clue about seemingly inexplicable aspects of the bill. Even if you have seen a bill of costs, the model bills are a useful resource and highlight, for example, the difference between bills drafted for costs solely between the parties, and those where a claim is to be made against the Legal Aid fund, or both an opponent and the Legal Aid fund.

Moves have been afoot for some time to bring the format of a bill into the computer age so that it is easier to get the time recorded as the case progresses to populate the bill created at the end of the proceedings without a costs draftsman having to start from scratch. These moves are described at **[29.24]** onwards. Computer print outs have often been treated with some scepticism by the courts in terms of demonstrating the time that has been spent. But that has changed over time (see for example Ward LJ's comment in *Ralph Hume Garry* at **[2.9]**). It is likely to continue changing as computerised time recording is used more directly. Nevertheless, although the format of the bill may change in the way aspects are grouped together, it will not alter the building blocks on which a bill is drafted and ultimately the assessment takes place. The format of the bill can be broken down into the following sections – the title page; the narrative; the heads of costs and their detail; the summary; and the certificates. The next part of this chapter follows these sections after some preliminary words about the very format of a paper bill.

3 and 6 column bills

[29.3]

Sometimes reference is made to '3 column bills' or '6 column bills.' Model bills A, B and E demonstrate the 3 column version with columns for profit costs, disbursements and VAT. Model bill C demonstrates the 6 column version. Where some costs are claimed against an opponent and some claimed against the Legal Aid Fund, two sets of 3 columns are set out, hence the 6 column format. Between the parties' items are set out on one set of the 3 columns while items such as the costs of reporting to the Legal Aid Agency, are set out on the other set. Where, on assessment, the court decides that an item is not recoverable from the opponent, it may transfer it over to the Legal Aid columns if it thinks that the item should be paid by the Legal Aid Fund. The Fund is essentially in the place of the client and as a client is liable for his solicitor's reasonably incurred costs, so too will the Legal Aid Fund, even if they are not recoverable from the opponent. (Some items may be considered unreasonably incurred and not be allowed against either the opponent or the Fund.)

4 column bills

[29.4]

The format of a bill takes a while to master. It has evolved over time and the various Reviews and reforms have never altered the basic format hugely. It is still, as was said in the interim Jackson report, modelled on a 'Victorian account book.' Model Bill D is drawn in a different way in respect of the columns and was an attempt to update the standard 3 column approach. It is a 4 column bill with two sets of two columns. The first set is headed, 'amount claimed' and the second set, 'amount allowed.' When the bill is drafted, figures for profit costs and disbursements share one column with VAT having a separate column. The costs claimed would all be set out in the first set of the two columns. If the bill reached an assessment, the amount allowed for each item would then be recorded in the other two columns.

However, this did not accord with most courts' approach of striking through disallowed items and writing in the revised figure (if any). Moreover it made it very difficult to separate the disbursements from the profit costs. As such it is rarely used but there could be no formal objection to it should you decide that it is the one for you.

THE TITLE PAGE

[29.5]

As with all court pleadings the bill starts by setting out the full title of the proceedings. There are three further items that need to be included on this page. The first applies in all circumstances; the second and third only apply where relevant.

(1) The order for assessment – The front page needs to set out, usually in 'the tramlines', the order or provision which entitles the party to have the bill assessed. This will usually be a court order but could be the acceptance of a Part 36 offer or on the discontinuance of a claim where the provisions in Part 36 and Part 38 respectively provide for a party's entitlement to costs. The various options for this are set out in CPR PD 47, para 13.3. The order for assessment was formerly known as the reference to tax.

(2) VAT registration number – this is the solicitor's registration number rather than the client's. It is only required if VAT is to be claimed from the paying party. Where the receiving party can recover the VAT he has paid to his legal representatives as input tax, that VAT cannot be recovered from the opponent. See **[2.13]** for more detail on this point.

(3) Legal Aid information – where the party has been legally aided, certain information as to the certificates provided by the LSC/LAA needs to be set out.

THE NARRATIVE

[29.6]

The practice direction (CPR PD 47, para 5.11) describes this section as being 'background information' but it is universally known as the narrative because most of what is put down is a retelling of the subject matter of the proceedings and then the course of the proceedings. As the practice direction puts it, the information that should be set out covers three areas.

(1) A brief description of the proceedings up to the date of the Notice of Commencement – note the word 'brief.' The best narratives are ones which describe the subject matter and then the proceedings in a concise fashion. But many drafters are tempted to throw in endless detail which tests the resolve of the judge as to whether to get to the end of the

narrative or not. In literary terms, it should be a pacy page turner, not some turgid and dense prose. Just as importantly, it should show some sense of objectivity in describing events. All too often the description of what happened and why tends to descend into partisan mud throwing. Why is this? The belief must be that setting out, for example, all the terms of the shareholders' agreement or all of the injuries sustained in a severe accident of themselves demonstrate how important and complex the litigation was. Similarly, describing the endless delay and obfuscation of the opponent (in the receiving party's eyes) in every interlocutory skirmish clarifies why the time spent was spent and guards against allegations of disproportionate cost. But such things will become clear to the judge in his pre-reading (if he has chance) or during the detailed assessment (if he hasn't). Filling pages of the bill with inordinate detail sets the receiving party off on the wrong foot because it does the opposite of what it intended.

Although it is said that the narrative should continue up to the date of the notice of commencement (see [**28.17**] but essentially up to the date of the bill itself), in practice the narrative rarely goes this far. It usually ends either with the event that created the order for assessment, eg accepting the Part 36 offer or carries on while the conclusion is put into effect, eg perfecting the order of the court based on a judgment given at trial.

(2) A statement of the status of the fee earners involved and the hourly rates claimed – the introduction of the Guideline Hourly Rates (see [**31.22**]) has led to some misconceptions in this requirement. The description of the fee earners may be along traditional lines – partner, solicitor, trainee solicitor – in accordance with the client care letter and any agreement such as a contentious business agreement. There is no requirement for such descriptions to tie in with the four bands that the Guideline uses: just as there is no requirement for the rates claimed to tie in with the Guideline rates. The hourly rates are allowed at whatever the court considers to be the reasonable rate for the fee earner concerned.

Some firms have specialised in niche areas and have taken the view that they should describe some of their employees by reference to similarly niche, specialist titles. There is nothing wrong with doing this and as the traditional retainer becomes more flexible in work being done by outsourced companies as well as solicitor's firms, such titles are likely to proliferate.

What is important is that the bill gives some information about the experience and expertise of such fee earners so that the paying party can form his own view of the reasonableness of the rate claimed. Where the fee earner has a professional qualification such as a solicitor, chartered legal executive or barrister, the number of years of Post Qualification Experience is usually sufficient.

The wording of the practice direction points out that hourly rates do not need to be given if the solicitor is not claiming via hourly rates. This will only apply to a solicitor and client assessment. On any between the parties' assessment, even where a Damages-Based Agreement is used, the work done will be claimed using hourly rates.

(3) A brief explanation of any agreement or arrangement between the receiving party and his legal representatives which affects the costs claimed in the bill – the effect of any agreement on the costs claimed is a manifestation of the indemnity principle, meaning that the receiving party cannot claim any more costs from his opponent than he is liable to pay his own legal representatives. If we carry on the DBA example mentioned above, the limit of costs payable by the receiving party to his lawyers will be a percentage of the damages recovered (see Chapter 7 for more detail.) If the costs set out in a bill calculated by the amount of time spent exceed that percentage sum the bill must confirm that the amount sought from the paying party is an amount equal to the percentage sum and not the arithmetical total of the figures in the bill.

HEADS OF COSTS

[29.7]

Up to the end of the narrative, a novice viewer of a bill would be feeling relatively comfortable with the format used. It is at the point that the detail of the bill arrives, and to some extent its order, that many people start to become flummoxed. The bill is meant to be split into the following headings and if there is more than one part to the bill (see below) then these headings, or at least the relevant ones, will be repeated in each part. We discuss the issues raised by each one in turn.

(1) Attendances at court and upon counsel

[29.8]

This heading essentially produces a chronology of the action. Pre-proceedings, there may be advice received from counsel in writing, at the telephone or in person. The date of such advice will fix the chronology which is useful to all parties and the judge in getting a flavour of the case. Once proceedings have started, the dates of the pleadings, case management conferences and interim applications will continue the chronology until the trial, or earlier settlement.

The time spent at hearings and attending conferences with counsel will be included here and so too will be counsel's fees for advocacy at court or advice in conference or in writing. One of the peculiarities about the arrangement of the headings is that the letters and telephone calls between the solicitor and counsel to arrange these attendances at court and conferences are invariably only captured under heading (6). It makes sense in that it is neater to place the number of letters, etc in one place rather than a smaller number against each activity under this heading. But if the costs of an attendance at court or counsel are disallowed, it would be simpler to strike out the communications relevant to that activity at the same time.

The Practice Direction (at para 5.16) requires the bill to aid the chronology by including orders which do not assist the receiving party. This may be an application where there was no order for costs or the costs might have been payable by the receiving party to the paying party in any event. It might simply be a relevant event from which no specific charge is made. These entries assist the court to get an overall picture but regularly upset paying parties, particularly litigants in person, who think that costs are being claimed in relation to such hearings etc even if phrases such as 'no fees claimed' are prominently displayed.

(2) Attendances on and communications with the client

[29.9]

This heading generally comes second only to work done on documents in terms of being the largest item. The nature of the attendances and communication is changing over time. The traditional model of the client visiting the solicitor in his offices to provide instructions periodically and with the occasional letter in between to keep the client abreast of developments is disappearing. The traditional arrangement required the solicitor to be located near to the client but that is no longer the case in many situations. In such circumstances the number of personal attendances now tends to be much lower but in their place will be more letters, telephone calls or increasingly emails, or a combination of all three. Electronic communications are discussed at **[29.18]** below. The relative informality of emails and the ease with which they can be sent does mean that they can mount up when dealing with the client.

Should the solicitor attend upon the client or the client upon the solicitor? Where personal attendances do take place, it has been the position for a long time that the client is to visit the solicitor. This was on the basis that the client could be expected to put himself out in the cause of his action sufficiently to call on the solicitor. To do otherwise, would be seen as a 'luxury' which the paying party, certainly on a standard basis assessment, ought not to meet. With ever increasing client care and competition for some clients, solicitors are regularly visiting their clients rather than vice versa. Such travelling time is likely to continue to be seen as a luxury, particularly when electronic communication, including video conferencing, is often a perfectly good substitute. The cost of travelling to see the client may be recoverable where the client could not realistically attend upon the solicitor. Seriously injured claimants or those suffering from terminal diseases are often visited at home or in hospital to take instructions and such travelling is usually allowed on assessment.

(3) Attendances on and communications with witnesses including any expert witnesses

[29.10]

In contrast with the client, travelling time to visit a witness is often recoverable, particularly if the witness has no connection with the party. The cost of drafting and finalising witness statements falls into the documents item (heading (7)) but the letters or emails forwarding drafts etc will be seen here.

At one time correspondence with expert witnesses would be little different from lay witnesses. But the rise of medical reporting organisations in the medical field has changed the approach quite considerably. A pro-forma is often all that is required to obtain a report. The agency will organise the examination and the medical records and deliver the report in time scales that used to appear to be wildly optimistic. The agency's cost has proved a contentious issue at certain times (see **[26.12]**) but if the cost of the report is in line with the AMRO agreement, it is paid more often than not without issue.

The more esoteric medical experts are often still instructed directly in a similar way to non-medical experts. As with lay witnesses, the time spent reviewing draft reports and suggesting amendments and additions falls into the work done on documents heading (and so too does the letter of instruction). It is the more routine communication regarding matters such as the willingness to accept instructions in the first place, dates of availability for trial and payment of fees that are set out here.

(4) Attendances to inspect any property or place for the purposes of the proceedings

[29.11]

This heading speaks for itself and is not one that is present in most bills.

(5) Attendances on and communications with other persons including offices of public records

[29.12]

The obvious 'other person' is the paying party and any other parties to the proceedings. Given that the paying party was obviously present during telephone calls with the paying party and received the receiving party's letters it is surprising how often the amount of time on attendances or the number of routine letters or emails are challenged. If there is one item that ought to pass without argument it ought to be this one. The only exception is where there are regularly several letters written each day where there was no particular urgency and could seemingly have been rolled up into one letter rather than the several claimed for.

Unlike the other items in the bill, the paying party has as much information as the receiving party here. Accordingly, any challenge to the reasonableness of the items claimed ought to be set out with precision rather than a general 'some of the correspondence appears to be non-progressive.' Anything less may be given short shrift from the court.

Where the attendances or communications have resulted in a fee being paid, for example for a search, the fee will be set out under this heading as a disbursement as well.

(6) Communications with counsel

[29.13]

As mentioned in (1) above the rest of the engagement with counsel is set out separately. This means that a telephone advice might be set out under heading (1) but a routine telephone call with counsel falls under this heading. If it was not advice that was being proffered it is often argued that the time was not reasonably spent. It is often difficult to distinguish between attendances or correspondence upon counsel and the same activities with his clerk. Both are recoverable in principle but can lead to a higher level of communications than might otherwise be the case.

The traditional use of counsel at specific points of the case with discrete instructions appears to be on the wane. With counsel becoming more of a team player in many areas of litigation and also having a keener interest in progress where his fees depend upon the outcome, he often wishes to have more regular contact. It is now often the case that counsel is sent documents to keep him updated as to developments regardless of whether he is expected to do anything with them at the time. This can lead to significant numbers of communications being claimed under this heading. It also renders the receiving party's solicitor vulnerable to the argument that he is being over reliant on counsel and as such should not be entitled to the hourly rate being claimed.

(7) Work done on documents

[29.14]

This is the largest and in some ways most unsatisfactory item in the bill. The Practice Direction (para 5.18) requires any of the headings from (2) to (10) to use a schedule where any item has 20 or more entries for attendances or non-routine communications. In practice it is the documents item which invariably requires a schedule. Attendance upon the client (heading 2) is the only other heading where schedules are regularly seen.

The work done on documents, whether set out in the bill or in a schedule, is listed chronologically. At a busy period in a case, the solicitor may well be dealing with several different aspects at the same time. This can mean that a discrete area of work, for example dealing with disclosure, may have entries spread over several different pages of the documents schedule which can lead to some difficulty in taking an overall view of the reasonableness of the time spent. The revision of the bill format mentioned at the beginning of this chapter and discussed further at the end is aimed at altering the documents item in particular. The idea is to group items together so an overall view on say disclosure can be taken. There is no easy answer, however, because the costs often have to be split into time periods, and a gathering of all the work by area (or phase to use the costs budgeting terminology) may fall foul of this. If there is a change in the legal representation from one firm to another and the work done straddles the two firms' involvement some assessment is going to have to be employed to determine how much of an overall figure is payable to each firm. Even a simple change in the VAT rate would cause complications.

In addition to the problems caused by the chronological approach to the documents item is the effect of an item by item approach to each item claimed in the schedule. Where a bill was considered to be disproportionate under the *Lownds* test (see **[28.5]**) the theory was that every item in the bill would then have to be considered. That would often mean, ironically enough, a disproportionate amount of court time being used to consider each and every item. Even on an ordinary standard basis assessment, some paying parties seek to challenge virtually every entry in the documents item. If the paying party wants to have each item considered in detail, or, less often, the receiving party wants that approach, the court has little option but to oblige the parties once they have been reminded of the overriding objective and in particular the need to allocate an appropriate amount of the court's resources to a particular case.

Many parties wish the court to exercise a broad brush approach to the documents item. Others will want part of the documents item to be considered in detail and then will extrapolate the judge's findings to the whole documents item, or those in later parts, without going through them in the same detail. Whichever approach is adopted, the paying party is relying on the judge having had the chance to look through the receiving party's papers to some extent to get a feeling for the amount of time claimed for the work done.

The introduction of costs management phases has caused bills of costs to be subdivided into numerous parts. Consequently, the documents item has been split into many, shorter document items. An unintended consequence of this is that, to date, it has made detailed assessments much longer than previously was the case. A single documents item of several hundreds of hours would inevitably be assessed in a broad and relatively speedy manner. Where there are numerous documents items however, paying parties appear to feel obliged to challenge items in much more detail on assessment.

(8) Work done in connection with negotiations with a view to settlement if not already covered in the previous headings

[29.15]

Cases regularly settle at a Joint Settlement (aka Round Table) Meeting and such time is clearly recoverable in principle. If a third party were added to assist the parties to reach a settlement, then as a general principle, such costs would also amount to work done in negotiations with a view to settlement. The third party would be a mediator and you need to be careful about the terms of a mediation if you expect to be recovering the costs of the mediation from your opponent in the proceedings.

All formal mediations have paperwork to deal with the costs of the mediation as well as many other factors such as confidentiality. In the optimistic air of a potential settlement, it is usually the case that each party agrees to share the costs of the mediator, the venue and the catering (etc) equally. Some agreements also stipulate that the party's own costs of attending the mediation will be borne by the party. It is not unusual for one or more parties to be reticent about attending a mediation at all and so agreements as to the costs of it sometimes have to be adjusted as a result.

What happens if a party agrees to bear his own costs of the mediation, does not reach a settlement and then subsequently wins the litigation? In *NatWest Bank v Feeney* [2006] EWHC 90066 (Costs) Master Campbell considered an agreement in these terms and decided that the Tomlin Order which concluded the case did not overturn that agreement. The case was appealed to Eady J who, in an unreported decision, dismissed the appeal. The mediation agreement had a specific provision enabling the parties to amend the standard wording and the issue was raised in the guidance notes but the parties had made no amendment. Consequently the successful defendants could not claim their modest attendance costs nor the more significant fees of their counsel.

At the hearing Master Campbell also disallowed the defendants' share of the mediators' fee. When providing a written judgment on this point he took a different view but had already given his judgment and so the fee continued to be disallowed. Despite the explanation of why he had come to different conclusion in the written judgment it appears that Eady J preferred the original approach and dismissed the appeal on this aspect as well. As such, it seems that the mediator's fee is recoverable if either the agreement allows for it to be subsequently recoverable or is silent on the issue. It is only if the agreement says that each party will pay a proportion of the fee will it be irrecoverable. Even then this could be overturned by the final order expressly incorporating such costs.

In *Lobster Group Ltd v Heidelberg Graphic Equipment Ltd* [2008] EWHC 413 (TCC), Coulson J confirmed the approach in NatWest Bank. However he drew a distinction between mediations which take place after proceedings have commenced (as in NatWest Bank) and those which occur pre-proceedings. In respect of the latter he said:

> 'First, unlike the costs incurred in a pre-action protocol, I do not believe that the costs of a separate pre-action mediation can ordinarily be described as 'costs of and incidental to the proceedings.' On the contrary, it seems to me to be clear that they are not. They are the costs incurred in pursuing a valid method of alternative dispute resolution . . . As a matter of general principle, therefore, I do not believe that the costs incurred in respect of such a procedure are recoverable under s 51 [Senior Courts Act 1981].'

The question of costs of and incidental to proceedings is considered in detail under heading (10) below.

(9) Attendances on and communications with London and other agents and work done by them

[29.16]

The idea of a 'country' solicitor instructing a London solicitor to act as his agent has something of John Major's warm beer and cricket on the village green quotation about it. It is easy to forget that prior to the CPR coming into existence in 1999 the High Court had no files and so the original application notice had to be produced before the Master for the hearing date and the eventual order to be endorsed upon it (by way of example). In that sort of environment, last minute faxes and emails for the court file could not take place and a local physical presence was required. Some solicitors still use London agents as a cost effective alternative to them travelling to a hearing in the High Court and such costs are added to the bill as if the work was done by the solicitor on the record (CPR PD 47, para 5.22(6)).

If some commentators are correct and the legal process unravels so that work we would currently call solicitors' work is done by a variety of entities, it may be under this heading that such work would be placed.

In *Crane v Canons Leisure* [2007] EWCA Civ 1352, the Court of Appeal wrestled with this problem. The receiving party's solicitors had been instructed via a Collective Conditional Fee Agreement with a success fee. For the detailed assessment, the solicitors instructed a firm of costs consultants. They claimed the work, under the agency principle as their own work and so sought a success fee on the base costs. The paying party argued that, based on the definition in the CCFA, the work was properly described as a disbursement because the work was carried out by external costs draftsmen rather than employees of the solicitors and as such no success fee should be payable. By a majority decision, the Court of Appeal took the view that the work carried out by the costs consultants was the type of work that the solicitors were retained to do. The solicitors may have chosen to delegate the work, but they never relinquished control of and responsibility for it. The classification of the work carried out could not sensibly depend on whether the solicitors did the work themselves or whether they delegated it to another solicitor or whether they delegated it to costs draftsmen who were not solicitors. Accordingly, the costs consultant's work was properly described as 'solicitors' work' done on behalf of the solicitors and so the consultant's fees were properly described as base costs within the terms of the CCFA thereby attracting a success fee.

(10) Other work which was of or incidental to the proceedings

[29.17]

Section 51 of the Senior Courts Act 1981 is the foundation stone of the court's power to award costs. It is usually mentioned in the context of the court awarding costs against non-parties (see Chapter 40) but its terms are also prayed in aid where the costs of peripheral work to the case are sought to be claimed by the winner of proceedings. This is because the terms of s 51 talk of costs 'of and incidental' to the proceedings.

In *Contractreal Ltd v Davies* [2001] EWCA Civ 928, Arden LJ reviewed various authorities and considered that the phrase 'of and incidental to' is a 'time-hallowed phrase in the context of costs' and that it had received a limited meaning so that it denoted 'some subordinate costs to the costs of the action.'

In *Re Gibson's Settlement Trusts, Mellors v Gibson* [1981] Ch 179, [1981] 1 All ER 233, Sir Robert Megarry considered that there were three features of work which the court should consider which rendered it 'of and incidental to' an action. These strands were that:

(1) The work involved was 'of use and service' to the action.
Later cases confirmed that this was not an absolute test in the sense that the receiving party had to show that it was actually used at the hearing. Otherwise any case that settled short of a hearing could not possibly meet that test. The work needs to be 'likely' to be of use and service.

(2) It was relevant to the action.

(3) It could fairly be attributed to the conduct of the defendant.

The case was concerned with, amongst other things, whether pre-proceedings work could be considered to be of and incidental to the costs of the proceedings. Based on the three strands of reasoning above, Sir Robert Megarry confirmed that it could.

Costs incurred in one set of proceedings cannot, as a general rule, be recovered in another. For example, see *Wright v Bennett* [1948] 1 KB 601, [1948] 1 All ER 410, CA where papers prepared for counsel were used at first instance and then used again before the appeal court. The court in the second proceedings is entitled to make its own order as to costs and the recoverable costs for one party will flow from the terms of that order and not as a result of the order in the first set of proceedings.

But what happens where the costs are incurred in the context of proceedings where no costs can be awarded? In a line of cases starting with *Ross v Bowbelle (Owners)* [1997] 1 WLR 1159, [1997] 2 Lloyd's Rep 196 courts have decided that work done in respect of inquests can be recovered in a civil claim for damages as long as they come within the three strand test set out in *Re Gibson's Settlement Trusts*. Davis J in *Roach v Home Office* [2009] EWHC 312 (QB) considered a number of costs judge decisions following *Re Gibson* and has been the leading case in this area ever since. In *Fullick v Metropolitan Police Comr* [2019] EWHC 1941 (QB), Slade J followed the reasoning in *Roach* whilst determining the approach to proportionality to be adopted post-April 2013.

The logic of these decisions is that inquests are evidence gathering opportunities and as the work could be claimed if the evidence was obtained by separate interviews of witnesses, why should that evidence not be obtained by attending and cross examining witnesses at the inquest? The inquest costs are not automatically recoverable and are case specific. You should consider what issues are still live if you are going to attend at an inquest and expect the costs to be recoverable in a civil claim. If the deceased died immediately there can be no evidence as to quantum (unlike in the *Bowbelle* case). So, if the intended defendant admits liability for civil damages prior to the inquest taking place, it is difficult to see what 'use and service' attending will be, even if the family understandably wishes to be represented. To what extent is attendance at preliminary hearings an evidence gathering opportunity? Is the attendance at the inquest to make submissions to the coroner as to the verdict (in the hope of getting a more favourable verdict with which to pursue a civil claim) recoverable? The case law is clear that the existence of a potential civil claim will not necessarily enable the funding of attending an inquest to be achieved by a roundabout method. Given the dicta in *Contractreal* above, inquest costs will regularly be challenged by paying parties as they are often significantly greater than the costs of the rest of the claim which does not sit comfortably with the concept of being subordinate to the costs of the action itself.

THE DETAIL IN STATEMENTS OF CASE

The building blocks

[29.18]

(1) *Consecutive numbering* – each item in the bill needs to be consecutively numbered (para 5.15). Practices vary to some extent on this but the guiding principle ought to be that it is difficult to break the time claimed into too many different items. The precedent bills set out the sort of method to be adopted. They can be found in the Schedule of Costs Precedents annexed to Practice Direction 47. They are not mandatory in their format but it is desirable that they should be followed where possible.

The use of consecutive numbers enables the paying party to identify the items which he seeks to challenge in the points of dispute (see below).

(2) *Dividing the bill into parts* – the bill is essentially a chronological document running from the first instruction by the client to the conclusion of the case. There may be circumstances during the life of the case which mean that it would be appropriate to divide the bill into the work done prior to the circumstance occurring and the work done thereafter. The possibilities are almost endless (see para 5.8 for further examples) but traditionally the four most common reasons are:

(i) The client has had the benefit of Legal Aid for some of the case but not all of it; or has been a litigant in person for some of the case but not all of it.

(ii) The case has transferred from one firm of solicitors to another. As a result there is a new retainer, new fee earners (unless the transfer has taken place because the person dealing with the case has moved), new hourly rates etc to take into account.

(iii) The VAT rate has changed. If there is no division of the bill into two (or more) parts, the allocation of VAT to work done during different periods is extremely difficult.

(iv) The solicitor has rendered interim statute bills during the life of the case (see Chapter 2 in respect of interim bills). The rendering of these bills creates a limit to the costs that can be recovered between the parties. In order for the paying party and the court to understand whether the indemnity principle is in danger of being breached the between the parties' costs claimed need to be set out in respect of the same periods as are covered by the interim statute bill(s). For reasons explained in Chapter 2, requests for payments on account do not have the same effect.

From 1 October 2015 further reasons for dividing the bill have been set out in PD 47 para 5.8. The requirements of costs budgeting mean that bills need to be drafted in parts to mirror the phases in the budgets so that it can be seen whether the budgets for the individual phases have been exceeded or not. Additional parts to show the costs of the costs budgeting are required. A split between pre and post-April 2013 work is also required to assist with considerations of proportionality (see [28.70]). It might have been thought that this division would have been obvious but, based on bills produced before the courts, it was not sufficiently obvious and so has had to be spelled out in the Practice Direction.

There are issues in preparing bills to reflect the phases in Precedent H and the terms of any Costs Management Order. For example, the guidance for completing the Precedent H does not sit happily with the requirements for drafting a bill in respect of work done on budgets. According to the Precedent H Guidance, some work should be recorded in the CMC phase and the remainder in the 'non-phase' 1% or 2% parts regarding costs management. That leaves work in the bill in different places and makes it hard to consider the 2% cap.

(3) *Six minute units* – not everyone records their time in six minute units (indeed not everyone records their time at all). Often attendance notes will show time claimed in 5 minute units, particularly multiples of 5 such as 15 minutes and 30 minutes. Some people record their time to the minute and will regularly have 11 minute telephone calls or a meeting timed at 2 hours and 14 minutes. There is nothing inherently wrong with charging in any of these methods as long as the client knows the basis on which you calculate your time.

The court expects to allow the time for routine letters and emails out and telephone calls (in or out) to be allowed on a unit basis of 6 minutes each. The relevant hourly rate for the fee earner involved will enable the value to be charged in the bill. There is always at least one person in a firm (and often many more) who cavil at the idea of this rounding up of time. But such arguments are only valid in relation to the time claimed as a charge to the client. The court sets out the method in which costs are to be recoverable from the opponent and the party's bill needs to comply with the Practice Direction (para 5.22). In any event, the requirement regarding 6 minute units only applies to routine communications and client care documentation invariably explains this charging method to clients nowadays anyway. But if you feel particularly strongly about this, you can always point to the fact that the court will allow 6 minute units 'in general' and so you could have your bill drawn in a different manner. You should not expect a court to entertain your arguments in respect of the opponent's bill with any enthusiasm however.

The six minute unit charge for letters and emails out 'will include perusing and considering the routine letters or emails in.' This reflects the fact that routine correspondence can often be dealt with very quickly, for example a letter sending a cheque in respect of a fee note received. To be able to claim 6 minutes for considering the letter (fee note) received and a further 6 minutes for sending a two line letter in response would encourage the time claimed to mount up very quickly on very routine matters. Hence, the inclusion of the consideration of the letter in. Sometimes a separate 6 minute item is claimed for considering a routine communication on the basis that there was no need for any response and as such the time considering the incoming document is otherwise lost. Such arguments do not generally succeed on a between the parties' assessment but if the client agreed to pay the costs of letters in then there is no reason in principle why the cost should not be sought. Traditionally letters in were claimed at half the rate of letters out, presumably on the basis that they would often not require any specific action.

We all know that an email may not take very long to create and send. Should such brief emails count as a 6 minute unit? The original draft of the Costs Practice Direction in 1999 set the rate at 3 minutes. That suggested that no email took very long to write and experience has shown that longer and longer emails are now sent and fewer formal letters are sent, particularly to clients. The amount of fee earner input, even in a short email, is often comparable with standard letters produced by case management systems or by the fee earner asking their secretary or assistant to send 'the usual letter' which is then charged at the fee earner's rate.

Text messages and other 'electronic communications' can be claimed if they can be demonstrated to have occurred and their contents are available for the court to scrutinise. The Practice Direction (para 5.22(2)) is a little wary of such new-fangled things. These electronic communications – other than emails – are allowed at the court's discretion, which is how emails used to be allowed before they became the equivalent of letters.

(4) *Attendances* – these are sometimes called personal attendances. They may be face to face but also may be by telephone or video conference. If they are by telephone they need to be for longer than six minutes since otherwise they would fall into the 'routine communications' item instead.

(5) *Communications* – these are defined at para 5.13. They include 'letters out', ie ones that you send elsewhere, emails out and telephone calls. The Practice Direction says that non-routine communications (ie ones that are of substance (see routine communications by contrast below) 'must be set out in chronological order.' In practice, the time taken to write longer letters or emails tends to be included in the documents item rather than under the heading of, for example, the client. Longer telephone calls however, do appear under the heading of the person to whom the call was made (eg the client) and as such are really treated as an attendance (see previous heading).

(6) *Routine communications* – these are defined at para 5.14. They comprise the same activities as longer communications but, 'because of their simplicity should not be regarded as letters or emails of substance or telephone calls which properly amount to an attendance.' They are simply counted up and set out as two figures, one for telephone calls and one for letters or emails out.

(7) *Travelling (and waiting) costs* – where these costs are claimed, for example in attending court, they should be charged at the rate agreed with the client, always assuming that such rate is no higher than the rate agreed in respect of the other work done. Traditionally, this rate would be half or two-thirds of the hourly rate generally claimed because of the absence of any 'B' factor for care and conduct (see Chapter 31) and this is still the case in some agreements with clients. In default of any specific agreement however, the time will be charged at the hourly rate claimed for other activities in the bill.

(8) *Local travelling expenses* – the expenses incurred by legal representatives in attending the local court (or indeed anywhere else locally) are not allowed. The rule of thumb set out in the Practice Direction (para 5.22(3)) as to what is local is 10 miles from the court dealing with the case at the time. That rule is becoming increasingly anachronistic where proceedings are issued centrally and then transferred to a court which may be many miles away from the solicitor.

(9) *The cost of postage, etc* – whether documents are sent by post, courier, DX; messages are sent by fax or telex; or outgoing telephone calls are made, the costs associated with the use of these methods is not generally recoverable. Where the cost is unusually heavy or the circumstances unusual, the court may exceptionally allow sums in respect of these items. The use of couriers because of urgency, eg the imminent expiry of a limitation period will only be allowed if the urgency does not appear to have been created by delay on the part of either the client or his legal representatives. The use of couriers because of a lack of trust in the postal system, etc will not be recoverable between the parties.

This provision of the Practice Direction (para 5.22(4)) is sometimes used by paying parties to challenge the cost of conference calls arranged by commercial organisations so that the calls can be recorded. If such a call is required for a telephone hearing, the cost is usually recoverable since it is a requirement of PD 23, para 6.10. If it is for the purpose of a conference between the client and his legal representatives, then it is less likely to be recoverable.

(10) *The cost of making copies* – as with postage, etc, the cost of copying is not usually recoverable because it is seen to be included in the overheads of running a firm of solicitors. The test is whether the copying is unusually numerous for the nature of the case or the copying is carried out in unusual circumstances. Claims tend to be made following a trial where numerous copies of the trial bundles have had to be produced externally and there is an invoice to be met. It is difficult to suggest that a trial can be considered to be an unusual circumstance in litigation. Consequently the cost of copying trial bundles is unlikely to be recoverable in most circumstances.

If a claim is to be made, the number of copies, their purpose and the costs claimed for them must be set out in the bill. There is no going rate for the cost of copying and the rate chosen will have to be justified on the assessment if challenged. Equally the paying party will have to justify any contrary figure put forward. The cost should not include the time spent in the sum put forward. To the extent that the creation of trial bundles is a fee earner task, the time claimed should be included in the documents item and not here.

(11) *The cost of preparing the bill* – this is usually the last item in the bill. It is incurred before the Notice of Commencement is served and, in accordance with the Practice Direction (para 5.19), is an item taken to fall under the order for costs giving rise to the existence of the bill. In *Monfared v Spire Healthcare Ltd* UKEAT/0131/18/RN Laing J confirmed that, at least in EAT proceedings, the cost of preparing the bill for detailed assessment comes within the original costs order. Costs incurred thereafter however are costs of the detailed assessment proceedings and a further order is needed to recover these (unless they are agreed between the parties). Therefore entries included for considering the points of dispute, preparing replies, making up (completing) the bill after the detailed assessment hearing are not recoverable in the bill itself, nor is a provisional sum for such matters.

At one time, this item would be a disbursement and often calculated by reference to a percentage of the costs 'as drawn'. That practice has largely died out and the cost is usually calculated as with other work by reference to an hourly rate and the time spent. The hourly rate is often claimed by reference to the Guideline rates for either a Grade C or Grade D fee earner.

THE SUMMARY IN STATEMENTS OF CASE

[29.19]

As you would expect, this is the shortest section of the bill. It is one which can often be the most useful section. It gives the reader an overview of the extent of the profit costs, disbursements and VAT which have been claimed (para 5. 20). Where there is more than one part to the bill, a summary for each part needs to be provided. If there are totals at the foot of each page, these also need to be included in the summary. Most summaries fit on a single page as a table, but in larger bills, or ones that have a lot of parts (such as bills for group actions) the summary can run for several pages. The summary can also be the simplest way of locating certain items, particularly large disbursements, which might have been placed in several different areas of the bill.

The main purpose of the summary however is to enable the receiving party, and then the court, to be clear as to the amount allowed on assessment and which figure will then be transferred to a final costs certificate if the receiving party requests it (see **[28.63]**). Since it is not completed until decisions at the assessment have been made, it cannot be confidently completed at any earlier point. Traditionally it would be filled in using pencil so that it could be rubbed out and completed in ink. With computerisation, including self-totalling software, it is more common for the summary to be completed at the outset and a reprinted bill produced after the assessment. Why complete the summary in any manner prior to the assessment? It gives all the parties, and the court, an overview of the size of the bill from the outset. It therefore gives the figure for the notice of commencement. It is often helpful when the parties are negotiating and it helps the court consider the time estimate for listing when a hearing is requested.

CERTIFICATES IN STATEMENTS OF CASE

[29.20]

The practice direction perhaps plays down the importance of the certificates in simply saying that the bill must contain such certificates set out in Precedent F of the Schedule of Costs Precedents as are appropriate. As mentioned at the outset of this chapter, the signing of the certificates is 'no empty formality' according to the Court of Appeal in *Bailey v IBC Vehicles Ltd* [1998] 3 All ER 570, 142 Sol Jo LB 126, CA. To reinforce the strength of that comment, the Court of Appeal in *Hollins v Russell* [2003] EWCA Civ 718 felt the need to spell out no fewer than five reasons why the solicitor's signature should not be taken as sacrosanct in relation to CFAs. The effect of *Bailey* is that, unless a paying party can point to a case specific reason as to why there should be some doubt over the veracity of the certificates signed by the receiving party's solicitor, the court need not enquire into the matters certified. By way of example, the court does not need to see receipts or other documents to vouch for the payment of disbursements under £500. The trade-off for this position, therefore, is that if the certificates have been wrongly signed, it is a serious matter indeed and can lead to professional conduct sanctions which traditionally would have meant the court referring the solicitor to the Law Society.

It was for this reason that the Court of Appeal in *Hollins* was concerned about the effect CFAs were having on the certificate signing process. Numerous cases had come before the courts where the indemnity principle certificate had been signed (as must happen on all bills) to say that the claimant was not seeking more from the defendant than he was liable to pay to his solicitor. However, those courts had then concluded that the CFA had not complied with the legislative requirements (see Chapter 6) and as a result the CFA had become unenforceable against the client. Since the client was no longer liable for his solicitor's costs, neither was the defendant and the certificate signed by the solicitor was false as a result. What should the court do in circumstances where the solicitor thought that his CFA was compliant and so signed the bill certificate, but was found to be wrong as a result of the court's decision? Reporting the solicitor to the Law Society seemed a draconian step but the need for the parties and the courts to be able to rely on the certificates was not to be underestimated.

The Court concluded that, in relation to CFAs, the position in *Bailey* could not stand. This did not mean that a different certificate (or even no certificate) should be signed. Instead, the paying party would be able to see the CFA and decide whether it wanted to take any points which might render the CFA unenforceable. Interestingly, it was not for the court to be the watchdog on this issue. The court could rely on the paying party to raise a point if there was one. The Court did not go so far as to say that the receiving party had to disclose his CFA to the opponent since that was a privileged document. But it did require the court to put the receiving party 'to his election' about either disclosing it or relying on something else to prove his retainer (see **[28.66]** for more detail on this procedure.)

All certificates must be signed by the receiving party or by his solicitor (apart from certificate (6) see below). Where the bill claims costs in respect of work done by more than one firm of solicitors, certificate (1), appropriately completed, should be signed on behalf of each firm. The remaining certificates only need to be completed by the firm on record. There can be practical difficulties in getting solicitors who have ceased trading or fallen out with the client to co-operate in the production of the bill with the later firm of solicitors. Where the conducting solicitor has moved from one firm to another he may be able to sign all the certificates on behalf of both firms by amending the certificates appropriately.

Bear in mind that the client could always sign the certificate which would be a lot easier logistically in many cases. Where the earlier solicitor's fees are based on an agreement contingent on the outcome (CFA or DBA) it would be wise to think twice before taking this approach. If there is anything wrong with the enforceability of the agreement, the client would not want to have affirmed anything in the bill which would prevent him otherwise being the beneficiary of an unenforceable agreement. But, in this situation, any solicitor who does not co-operate in the recovery of fees from the opponent is risking leaving himself without any payment whatsoever.

The risk is not all on the earlier solicitor's side however. Parties who, having instructed two firms of solicitors, commenced detailed assessment proceedings with the bill of one firm alone, were given a bitter pill to swallow by the court in *Harris v Moat Housing Group South Ltd* [2007] EWHC 3092 (QB). The appellants ('either oblivious or heedless of the provisions of the practice direction,' said Christopher Clarke J) failed to include the costs of their previous solicitors in their bill of costs, and the costs of their second solicitors were compromised by agreement with the paying party. If the appellants had, either in their notice of commencement or in the bills or otherwise, made clear that the amount claimed was only part of their claim to costs and that they would be claiming later in respect of the work of their first solicitors; and the agreement was that the respondents would pay a sum in respect of the costs claimed, recognising that the costs in respect of the first solicitors were still to be dealt with, the appellants would not have been prevented from making a claim in respect of those costs. There would have been a failure to comply with the Practice Direction, but subject to any sanction that the court thought fit to impose there would be no reason in principle why the court should not assess the remaining costs in dispute. However, the position here was different, because what had been settled was the amount of the receiving party's costs pursuant to particular orders. If they had left out of their bill part of what they should have claimed and there had been a settlement of the bill, they could not recover more than the amount agreed. The omission was their misfortune.

If, as sometimes occurs, the bill certificates are not signed prior to a detailed assessment hearing taking place, the court will at the very least, not allow a final costs certificate to be produced until the certificates have been signed. This will prevent any enforcement of the sums allowed on assessment.

The Certificates cover the following issues:

A. Mandatory Certificates

[29.21]

(1) *Accuracy*: This certificate starts with the overarching confirmation that 'this bill is both accurate and complete'. It then confirms that the indemnity principle has not been breached. In other words that 'the costs claimed herein do not exceed the costs which the receiving party is required to pay me/my firm'.

Additionally, this certificate confirms that any employed legal representative who carried out work for which costs are claimed is employed by the receiving party. This certificate supported the rule that an employed solicitor could not carry out litigation for anyone other than his employer. That restriction, to the extent that it still applies, is likely to be removed with the arrival of Alternative Business Structures etc.

Finally this certificate confirms that any work done for a legally aided client was carried out pursuant to a certificate from the Legal Aid Agency (or earlier equivalent.)

(2) *Interest and interim payments*: This certificate deals with activities that have happened during the case and since the case has ended but before it has come back to court to be assessed.

Both certificates are written in the alternative. Either there has been a ruling affecting the receiving party (or his solicitor)'s entitlement to interest (and in which case details need to be given of the date and text of the ruling together with the identity of the judge); or there has been no such ruling.

Similarly, there has either been one or more interim payments (and in which case the date, amount and the identity of the person making the payment are needed for each payment); or there have been no such payments.

The presumption in the rules at CPR 44.2(8) that an interim payment will be awarded will mean that this certificate will be answered more often in the positive than has previously been the case.

B. Legal Aid cases

[29.22]

(3) *Position of a Legally Aided client*: This certificate is made pursuant to reg 119 of the Civil Legal Aid (General) Regulations 1989. It deals with the issue of whether the client has an interest in the detailed assessment proceedings. For example, if the client may have to meet any shortfall in costs received from the opponent through the operation of the statutory charge.

Where the client does have an interest, the certificate confirms that a copy of the bill has been sent to the client with an explanation of the nature of his interest and the steps that can be taken to safeguard his interest in the assessment. Furthermore, the client has not requested that the costs officer be informed of his interest and has not requested a copy of the notice of hearing to be sent to him. If the client has no interest, then the certificate will record this and of course there is no need to send the bill to the client with the explanation.

The purpose of this certificate therefore is to deal in a simple way with clients who do not need or wish to attend the hearing being left in peace. Otherwise, they would need to be sent a Notice of Hearing on the basis that they might have an interest and would turn up at the hearing, more often than not, for little or no purpose. Where a client has an interest and does wish to receive notice of the hearing, this certificate cannot be fully completed and the client's details should appear on the statement of parties lodged with the Request for a Detailed Assessment Hearing.

(4) *Notification re counsel's fees and consent to FCC*: This certificate is made pursuant to regs 112 and 121 of the Civil Legal Aid (General) Regulations 1989. It gives consent to the signing of the final costs certificate within 21 days of detailed assessment.

As part of this, the certificate confirms that either counsel has been notified in writing of any fees reduced or disallowed on the detailed assessment (and if so, when) or that there were no such reductions rendering notice to counsel to be unnecessary.

C. Disbursements and VAT

[29.23]

(5) *Lower value disbursements paid*: This certificate saves a considerable amount of effort on the part of the receiving party's solicitor and the court. If it cannot be completed, the receiving party will have to produce vouchers for every single disbursement in the bill, no matter how small. The only reason for not signing this certificate is where the smaller disbursements have not been paid and that might raise alarm bells as to how the case has been financed and / or the state of the receiving party's file if the solicitor cannot properly certify that everything has been paid. Why counsel does not have to be paid is something of a peculiarity. It may stem from the honorarium approach to his fees discussed in Chapter 2.

(6) *VAT position*: The VAT certificate is a forest of square brackets and opportunities to cross out the various options envisaged by the drafters of the certificate. In short, the solicitors or auditors certify, supposedly with the benefit of the client's last completed VAT return, that the receiving party is entitled to claim all / a percentage / none of the VAT charged on costs and disbursements as input tax in accordance with Section 24 of the Value Added Tax Act 1994.

If the client can recover all the VAT he has paid (or will pay) as input tax then he will not be able to recover it from the opponent. If he can recover a percentage, then he can only claim the remaining percentage. If he cannot recover any VAT then of course he can seek his VAT from the opponent.

This certificate is different from the others in two respects. The first is that the client's auditors can sign it. Every other certificate can only be signed by the party or the solicitor. Second, if the dispute as to VAT recoverability arises after service of the bill, this certificate may be filed and served as a supplementary document and is treated as amending the bill under paragraph 13.10 of Practice Direction 47.

Transitional arrangements

[29.24]

Where a CMO has been made, paper bills of costs need to take into account the amendments to both CPR 47.6 and its accompanying practice direction which took effect from 1 October 2015.

(a) Further parts to the bill: Practice Direction 47, para 5.8 already referred to the need to split a bill into two or more parts depending upon the circumstances (see **[29.18]**). The list was extended to require separate parts for work done before and after 1 April 2013 (para 5.8(7)) as well as by phase together with additional parts for the costs of completing the Precedent H originally and other budgeting costs thereafter (para 5.8(8)).

The purpose behind the amendments to CPR PD 47, para 5.8 is clear. Paragraph 5.8(7) allows the court to consider proportionality under the *Lownds* test for the pre-April 2013 work and in accordance with CPR 44.3(2) for the later work (see **[28.66]**). Paragraph 5.8(8) enables the court to consider the sums claimed as against the last approved budget. This will clarify the need for any arguments there may be as to whether a good reason to depart from that budget needs to be shown. The parts concerning the cost of producing the Precedent H etc are required to allow a calculation under CPR PD 3E, para 7.2 (see **[15.10]**).

(b) New schedules: CPR 47.6 requires a 'breakdown of the costs claimed for each phase of the proceedings' where a CMO has been made to be served along with the Notice of Commencement and bill of costs.

The splitting of the bill into a separate part for each phase is not sufficient in itself to consider it against the approved budget. The costs incurred prior to the CMO in that phase and those post-dating the CMO and which have been budgeted need to be distinguishable. The pre-CMO costs will always need to be assessed. Time will tell as to the extent to which the budgeted costs need to be assessed. Practice Direction 47 could have required two or more parts for each phase but there was obviously a concern that the bill would become unwieldy if every bill needed to be split into a minimum of 15–20 parts. This would be unlikely to aid the parties or the court in getting to grips with the overall costs, even if none of the other matters set out in PD 47, para 5.8 occurred regarding representation or funding. Instead, para 5.8(8) merely requires the costs incurred to be distinguishable from the estimated, budgeted costs within each part.

CPR 47.6 also requires a schedule to be produced to assist in considering the CMO and the costs actually claimed. There is a model for you to follow – Precedent Q. Depending upon the ease with which your time recording can be interrogated, it might take a while to produce the schedule but it is not a mini-bill for each part. Instead, it takes a high level view to allow the parties and the court to see whether, on the face of it, there is any issue with the costs claimed in the bill and the amounts agreed or approved in the budget. On some occasions, the court may decide that the information contained in Precedent Q is not sufficient to deal with questions raised under CPR 3.18 and in which case, specific directions will be given. But in most instances, the schedule should be enough to allow parties and courts to compare the information in the bill and the last approved budget.

ELECTRONIC BILLS OF COSTS

A brief history

[29.25]

One of Sir Rupert Jackson's recommendations was for a redesign of the format of bills of costs. In September 2010, a working group was formed by the Association of Costs Lawyers with a core remit to design a model bill of costs which satisfied Sir Rupert's aims. In October 2011, the working group produced an interim report which recommended a change of format based on the Uniform Task-Based Management System (UTBMS) already well-established in the USA. The group saw no point in trying to reinvent the wheel when there was a tested system which could be tailored to the jurisdiction of England and Wales and the requirements of the Civil Procedure Rules. The group was then chaired by Jeremy Morgan QC who passed the reins on retirement to Alexander Hutton QC.

The UTBMS codes provide for bills to be prepared by reference to phases, tasks and activities (see below). One of the benefits of using these codes is the facility to import data directly from solicitors' practice management software if the time spent is recorded correctly originally. This would enable bills to be produced at the push of a button as Sir Rupert sought to make possible. This would not just be for formal bills of costs for detailed assessment. Summary assessment schedules, costs budgets and any number of other documents could be produced at different levels of generality from the same data entries.

In order to assess the ramifications of moving two centuries forward in the format of the bill of costs, it seemed sensible to Sir Rupert and subsequently to the Civil Procedure Rule Committee to test out that format by way of a pilot. The obvious choice of court was the SCCO and a voluntary pilot began there on 1 October 2015. Where the Notice of Commencement was served after 1 October 2015, any bill lodged at the SCCO in the electronic format would automatically be considered to be part of the voluntary pilot. The pilot was originally meant to last for six months until 1 April 2016 but was extended twice up to 30 September 2017. The voluntary pilot applied to any case where the bill was lodged at the SCCO and therefore this included cases in the County Court heard in the London Hearing Centres (see CPR PD 47, para 4.2(1)) as well as High Court and Court of Appeal bills. The take up in the pilot period was modest to say the least.

Format of the Electronic Bill

[29.26]

It has always been a characteristic of this book that model bills have been included within its pages to assist an understanding of their content. We had to admit defeat in the 2016 edition in respect of the format of precedent AA that was to be used in the pilot. The same was true of the revised pilot bill, precedent AB, and this remains the position now that the pilot phase has ended and precedent S has entered the costs precedents.

All of the electronic bills are essentially in the form of an Excel spreadsheet. Other proprietary software is of course available and the designers of the bills have made great efforts to ensure that they can be produced by case management software as well as by those with much more limited access to technology. In theory at least, it could be produced on paper without any time-recording software. But in reality, even for those who do not record their time electronically, it is likely that their recourse will be to use costs lawyers to draft the bill on their own software in the same way that almost all bills in the recent past have been produced via computer programs.

The amount of the information which populates the bills is considerable and not all of it is required by the court as such. For example, although there are 17 worksheets in precedent S, the last three contain what is described as reference data which will not be required on the detailed assessment. Such columns can then be hidden from view. The first 14 worksheets essentially follow the order of a paper bill, beginning with a front sheet, a narrative (or synopsis) and the legal team involved. Thereafter, worksheets enable calculations and comparisons to be made between actual and budgeted costs and any other division of the bill to cope with changed VAT rates, change in representation etc. The detail of the bill is set out at worksheets 12 (communications) and 14 (all items). Between them is a worksheet containing a reduced version of worksheet 14 which is suitable for printing for service as the paper copy.

As those familiar with spreadsheets will appreciate, they have the power to make many calculations simultaneously. So, when one figure is altered on a spreadsheet, the consequent alterations to figures elsewhere will happen at the same time. On a detailed assessment, the judge might decide to vary some of the fee earners' hourly rates. That decision will be written on the bill and manual calculations will have to be made when completing the bill of each element of time recorded at the reduced hourly rate. Using the electronic bill, those consequent calculations will be made immediately and automatically. The process of completing the bill will be carried out by software rather than human endeavour.

Such calculations are one benefit of the new format. But, in our view, its power is really to be found in its ability to isolate the particular information required to be considered on a particular point in issue. To do that, the relevant data has to be sorted so that all the relevant information is to hand (but only that data). In order to sort the information efficiently, a lot of data has to be captured to assist with the winnowing out of the irrelevant. This is a long way from traditional costs drafting of individual items based on paper attendance notes, or even by the number of pages of a document such as a pleading. But it is not that far from the common use of spreadsheets by many people in practice and describing it in writing is not the way that learning how to use spreadsheets is generally taught. It is a brave new world, but not necessarily as Aldous Huxley suggested.

Problems with time recording

[29.27]

Our enthusiasm for the capturing and then isolating of the relevant information has clearly not been reciprocated by the profession. There has been a considerable reluctance to record time via the UTBMS codes endorsed by the Hutton Committee, let alone to produce bills based on them. The UTBMS codes anglicised by the Hutton Committee were known, somewhat inaccurately, as J codes. After the lack of take up in the pilot of electronic bills, Sir Rupert Jackson suggested that J codes, which were seen as being unduly prescriptive, should be made optional and that less formal time recording would suffice. But such time recording still required the holy trinity of task, phase and activity to be recorded which was at least one element greater than computerised time recording traditionally captured. As such, it was always going to be difficult to see that this relaxation would be any more attractive to a reluctant profession and so it has proved.

Consequently, the Rule Committee set the date of 6 April 2018 as being the time from which an electronic bill needed to be used and, effectively, time recording which captured task, phase and activity needed to be in place. Only a firm which was content to pay a costs draftsman to recode work retrospectively could afford to ignore the April 2018 deadline. The cost of such work would not be recoverable from the opponent and would appear to be prohibitively time consuming and therefore expensive. The coding suggested to be used with Precedent S is set out in Schedule 2 to PD 47. It is the same schedule as was previously attached to the pilot practice direction.

Phases, tasks and activities

[29.28]

In order to understand the codes in Schedule 2 to PD 47, it is first necessary to be clear about the difference between a phase, a task and an activity.

A *phase* is largely in line with the phases used for producing a costs budget. There are additional phases for other matters such as interim applications, funding and costs management time spent.

A *task* is 'what' work is being done. It breaks down the areas of work within a phase. So, for example, the tasks under the phase of issue/statements of case are: (i) Issue and Serve Proceedings and Preparation of Statement(s) of Case; (ii) Review of Other Party(s)' Statements of Case; (iii) Requests for Further Information; and (iv) Amendment of Statements of Case.

An *activity* is 'how' the work is done. The codes break down the work in a way that is familiar to all who have recorded their time. Activities such as drafting or reviewing documents; or communicating with the client, experts, opponents all have separate codes.

Let us take an example of drafting your client's witness statement. The Phase Code in this example is 5. The task code is 13 and the activity code is 10. These three pieces of information are required for each piece of work to be recorded.

Pilot error?

[29.29]

The reluctance of solicitors to put bills into the pilot may well come to haunt the profession during the next few years. To move from a 19th century format to a 21st century version in one leap is a significant achievement, but is bound to have any number of teething problems. They are likely to be of the sort that do not readily admit of an appealable issue and will only resolve when enough courts have had sufficient experience of using the new bills for 'best practice' to emerge. Uncertainty and inconsistency are bound to stalk the courts in the interim.

Perhaps more importantly, there are longer term problems that will arise in our view and which will mean that the new bill will fall short of the aims of Sir Rupert in two main respects. Let us illustrate the issue by taking the example above for recording the drafting of the client's witness statement. Let us suppose that the statement is in response to the opponent's statement. The time for drafting the statement should be recorded as 5/13/10 as set out above. The time for reviewing the opponent's statement in the first place should be recorded as 5/14/10. The model fee earner will diligently separate out the work into the two different codes, providing an explanatory narrative to each entry. If using proprietary software, it may well be that some of the coding will be done behind the scenes for the fee earner. If you and your colleagues are such model fee earners then a bill as Sir Rupert envisaged could be produced at the push of a handful of buttons.

Unfortunately, most solicitors do not live up to such requirements, or at least not consistently. Questions are raised on assessment about information being wrongly attributed even though they may not always matter depending upon how some of the information is grouped. More fundamentally, the requirement for a narrative to complete a time posting appears to have resulted in many straightforward items being recorded with a very brief, standardised narrative entry. Whilst providing some information, this approach destroys any really case-specific narrative which would be helpful to the recipient of the bill and who may be the client or the opponent as well as, ultimately, the assessing judge. The absence of any meaningful narrative – which is the part that takes the time and is more usually seen as a chore – may prevent the effective grouping of work in a single place and being dealt with as one item. In the absence of anything case-specific; clients, opponents and judges find themselves with a comparative lack of (explanatory) information when attempting to assess the reasonableness of the time set out.

In addition to these practical issues, there are also issues of confidentiality and relevance. The data entered into time-recording software is privileged and confidential; it cannot simply be made available to the court and litigation opponents without some process of vetting to preserve confidentiality. Work which is not recoverable under the particular terms of an order for costs has to be filtered out. More prosaically, so too should any client items. In each case, human intervention and judgment is required.

POINTS OF DISPUTE

[29.30]

In comparison with the bill of costs, points of dispute have to provide very little information and as such they have few procedural requirements. More time is spent in the CPR in dealing with the consequences of a party not serving his points of dispute than in what should be in them in the first place.

The introduction of electronic bills has not, at least in the short term, caused any alteration in the requirements for points of dispute. They will still be prepared in accordance with Precedent G. No doubt some paying parties will seek to annotate the electronic bill to show how much lower the costs claimed ought to be in the paying party's opinion. Indeed there are some who advocate incorporating the points of dispute (and any replies) into the bill so that all of the statements of case are in one document. Whilst that has a pleasing aspect to it as a concept, the reality would presumably be a separate page or pages in the spreadsheet for the parties and the court to navigate between. Whether that is in practice any better than paper points of dispute on the desk and the bill on the screen remains to be seen.

Structure

[29.31]

There is one model points of dispute and that can be found at Precedent G of the Schedule of Costs forms annexed to PD 47. It was revised in April 2013 but it was very largely, and almost literally, a matter of form over substance. Points of dispute would tend to be on landscape oriented paper but now they are on portrait. Instead of the points made by the paying party being side by side with the receiving party's replies, they are placed one above the other. This change of orientation has allowed for a space to be included after each reply to a point and before the next point with the anticipatory heading of 'costs officer's decision.' But as there are no requirements as to how large the box is for that decision, the boxes tend to be sized to fit comfortably on the paper. As such, there is often insufficient room for the judge to write anything resembling a reasoned decision and just occasionally there is far too much. The drafter of the points should at least consider whether it is a general point of principle which might require considerable space or an individual item where enough space to write a figure is, more or less, all that is required.

In the rules regarding Provisional Assessments (see Chapter 30), there appears to be an expectation that the Precedent G document is the one that contains the costs officer's decisions. In practice that does not always seem to occur but it is one more reason to consider allowing more space for the judge if you are usually cheese-paring in this respect.

Format

[29.32]

Other than stating that the points of dispute may challenge any item of the bill, CPR 47.9 says nothing on how the points should be written. Such guidance as there is, is contained in CPR PD 47, para 8 and the model document in the Precedents.

According to para 8.2, 'Points of dispute must be short and to the point'. They must follow Precedent G so far as practicable. In particular they must:

(a) identify any general points or matters of principle which require decision before the individual items in the bill are addressed; and
(b) identify specific points, stating concisely the nature and grounds of dispute.

Sub-section 8.2 concludes that 'once a point has been made it should not be repeated but the numbers where the point arises should be inserted in the left hand box as shown in Precedent G'.

So to recap: the points should be short and to the point, stated concisely and not repeated. Anyone would think that they had previously been verbose. In his final report Sir Rupert Jackson observed:

> 'Points of dispute are said to be overlong, therefore expensive to read and expensive to reply to. Points of reply are similarly prolix. Both of these pleadings are in large measure formulaic and are built up from standard paragraphs held by solicitors on their databases. In addition, there are lengthy passages in the points of dispute and the points of reply dealing with time spent on documents.'

There should be no need to plead to every individual item in a bill of costs, but this practice stems to some extent from the wording of CPR 47.14(6): 'Only items specified in the points of dispute may be raised at the hearing, unless the court gives permission.' The alternative would be to allow the paying party to bring points in at the hearing without warning but such trial by ambush tactics went out when the Woolf Reforms brought in the cards on the table approach.

In fact, some paying parties have used the reforms as an opportunity to keep points of dispute brief and not deal with the objections in detail. While this means the end of long repetitive comments about the documents item in particular, it does take the parties back towards a trial by ambush.

The introduction of provisional assessments militates against brevity and selectivity. The points of dispute are the only opportunity the paying party is going to have to influence a judge carrying out a provisional assessment. On that basis, the kitchen sink is almost bound to be pleaded along with everything else.

The introduction of electronic bills has often had the same effect. The opportunity to challenge each and every line in the detail of the bill has been taken up by many paying parties. We had hoped that this was a 'bedding in' process for drafters of points of dispute to electronic bills, but our experience is that this is becoming more common and not less.

In addition to deciding what ought to be challenged to their client's advantage, drafters are (or at least should be) giving consideration to how the court is likely to want to see points raised. This depends upon the ease with which any particular judge is going to be able to manipulate the electronic bill detail. But, for all judges, a challenge to items which can easily be sorted by phase, activity, fee earner etc is preferable to one where the line or item numbers are set out en masse. The latter approach can be very cumbersome in isolating the relevant entries. You will endear yourself to the court if you indicate in the challenge how you have sorted the data so that the judge can do the same thing.

The extremes of verbosity and brevity in points of dispute were illustrated in the case of *Mount Eden Land Ltd v Speechly Bircham LLP* [2014] EWHC 169 (QB). The claimant was challenging its former solicitors' fees which consisted of £105,000 over 50 invoices. Master Campbell was faced with two versions of the points of dispute. The first was long winded and the second (having been ordered to set out the points as briefly as possible) consisted of tick boxes saying items were excessive and/or that there was no supporting evidence. The first version was entirely non-specific regarding the items challenged: the second provided no detail whatsoever as to why any particular item was 'excessive' etc. Master Campbell accepted the solicitors' argument that the revised schedule did not comply with the direction he had given to the claimant. He considered that a detailed assessment could not take place using either the original or the revised points of dispute without an entirely disproportionate amount of court time being required. He was not prepared to give the claimant a third opportunity to produce something of utility to the court. When appealed on these decisions, Teare J agreed with him on all aspects. The unusual nature of this case is that the court was able to bring the case to an end simply by staying the proceedings. The solicitors had already been paid and so the only party to lose out by the stay was the claimant who had brought this procedural position onto its own head.

Similarly, in *Ainsworth v Stewarts Law* [2019] EWCA Civ 897, the senior costs judge was faced with poorly drafted points of dispute in a solicitor and client assessment. He took almost as draconian approach in disallowing the challenges to the documents items in their entirety. The points of dispute did not challenge any specific entries to those items notwithstanding that the solicitors' file had been inspected by the former client's costs lawyer. The replies indicated that the solicitors could not prepare to deal with such a challenge. The robust case management decision, as it was described by the appeal judge, was made to further the overriding objective (particularly the avoidance of going part heard) and was upheld on appeal by the High Court (not the Court of Appeal as the reference would suggest). The attempt by the former client to describe everything as being excessive and consequently unusual – thereby seeking to reverse the burden of proof onto the solicitors – backfired completely.

Where the paying party is a litigant in person, the succinct and particularised intention of points of dispute is often lost. Broad points are made, often regarding the merits of the litigation rather than the costs actually claimed. The *Mount Eden* approach of staying proceedings is not available between the parties because the costs will not have been paid before the case comes to a hearing. Judges therefore will usually seek to discern the challenges and deal with them as best as they can. For example, in *Monfared v Spire Healthcare Ltd*, Laing J upheld the Employment Tribunal's decisions where the assessing judge had been given no help by the paying party's points of dispute.

Calculating offers

[29.33]

The exercise of setting out the challenges to the bill of costs should, amongst other things, enable the paying party to come to a view as to by how much he can realistically expect to reduce the receiving party's bill on assessment. That figure should inform the offers made to settle the case short of a hearing. The more realistic the figure is, the more helpful it will be. It is unusual to succeed (or fail) on every argument put before a judge and there are bound to be grey areas where some experience is going to be beneficial. Offers made should logically exceed the best case scenario set out in the points of dispute. The need for open offers with the points of dispute and the effect of such offers, as well as Part 36 offers is considered elsewhere (see **[28.26]**).

REPLY TO POINTS OF DISPUTE

[29.34]

The heading above CPR 47.13 is 'Optional Reply' and, as that suggests, the receiving party does not have to put in a reply to the points of dispute (although it appears that some courts take a dim view of parties who do not reply to points of dispute (see **[28.27]**)). It may be very clear without a further document as to what the argument is between the parties.

Sub-section 12 of PD 47 contains three stipulations, the first of which is that the reply must follow Precedent G whenever practicable (see points of dispute above for the overall look of Precedent G). The second and third requirements are:

- it must be limited to responses on the points of principle or to concessions on the individual items; and
- it must not contain general denials, specific denials or standard form responses.

The quotation regarding the prolixity of points of dispute above applies as much to replies as to points of dispute. The purpose of a document which simply 'maintains' the claimed figure or 'rejects' all offers made without any counter proposal was always a waste of time. If there was no reply, the receiving party would be taken to be defending the challenge in the points of dispute anyway. That is why they are described as being optional.

The point made above regarding drafting points of dispute on bills which will be provisionally assessed also applies to replies. The receiving party gets two goes at providing information to the costs officer with the bill and the replies. There is something to be said for keeping the bill narrative relatively brief and saving all the ammunition for the reply but the key thing is to make sure the information is in front of the provisional assessor in some shape or form. Having said this, the practice of serving replies only when a receiving party knows the bill will be provisionally assessed (and thereby adding extra detail that would have been given orally at a detailed assessment hearing) is more likely to result in them not being allowed in at all. They should be served in accordance with the rule so that they are included within the documents enclosed with the request for a detailed assessment hearing.

In the example Precedent G annexed to PD 47 there is a challenge to the receiving party's retainer which is described as a 'point of principle' and a challenge to the hourly rates claimed which is described as a 'general point.' It has been argued by paying parties that there is a difference between points of principle and general points because the wording of CPR 47.13 expressly requires replies only to address points of principle. Based on that argument, the receiving party cannot respond to the paying party's submissions on matters such as hourly rates. That is not an attractive proposition in our view and the better approach is to consider all such general items to be preliminary issues on which it is appropriate for the receiving party to reply. Indeed it can be positively helpful on provisional assessments in reducing the amount of time taken (see [**28.27**]). Replies to specific items however need to be limited to those which make a concession or partial concession (usually a counter proposal on the number of items or time spent).

PART 18 REQUESTS

[29.35]

The frequency and extent of Part 18 requests in detailed assessment proceedings increased whilst paying parties sought to challenge additional liabilities, ie recoverable CFA success fees and ATE premiums. Such challenges, if successful, might bring a considerable windfall (see the 'Golden Rule' at the beginning of Chapter 4). Consequently, bills which would otherwise have settled were taken to a court hearing to see if a knockout blow could be delivered. In order to try to reduce the cost of having to pay for the assessment hearing where no such blow was landed, paying parties would try to obtain further information than would usually be received from the bill in order to weigh up the prospects of running such an argument. In *Hutchings v British Transport Police Authority* [2006] EWHC 90064 (Costs), the senior costs judge, sitting as a recorder, gave guidance on requests for further information under para 35.7 of the Costs Practice Direction. The starting point was the overriding objective, and in particular the requirement of proportionality. The court should not willingly do anything which is likely to promote further satellite litigation. The defendant's Part 18 request originally ran to 13 questions all of which the deputy district judge had refused on the grounds it was a fishing expedition. On appeal the senior costs judge described the application as a brash and ill-considered attempt to uncover information which would enable the defendant to challenge the claimant's bill on a technical point but he allowed three of the requests as being reasonable and proportionate. The other questions could be raised as part of the points of dispute and argued on the assessment.

The genie is out of the bottle in relation to Part 18 requests and so they remain an option even though the era of recoverability has come to an end. While there is no equivalent of para 35.7 in the new CPR PD 47, there is no suggestion that a Part 18 request, as a matter of principle, could only be made in respect of additional liabilities. The nature of points of dispute is that they are often a request for information where the wording of the bill is not understood or seems to contradict itself or does not appear to be consistent with other things about which the paying party is aware. The main reason for converting such requests into something more formal under Part 18 was the receiving party's refusal to answer the questions posed. If, or when, another situation arises where requests for information are routinely rebuffed, the use of Part 18 may rise again.

In *XYZ v Various sub nom Re PIP Breast Implant Litigation* [2013] EWHC 3643 (QB), Thirlwall J refused to order the defendants to answer enquiries in respect of their ability to meet any award for damages or costs in group litigation proceedings. Nevertheless, she was persuaded to require the defendants to provide information about their ability to fund their participation in the litigation as part of the court's case management powers under CPR 3.1(2)(m).

COSTS COMMON TO THE PARTIES

Solicitor and Client

[29.36]

The concept of a retainer between the solicitor and his client is discussed at the very beginning of this book. It is a contract and so contractual obligations follow. The indemnity principle means that any limitation on the extent of the costs payable under the retainer is effective in limiting the costs that can subsequently be claimed from an opponent. So far, so good. Complications start to occur when more than one client instructs the same solicitor. Is each client liable for all of the solicitor's fees so that the solicitor does not lose out if, for example, one or more becomes insolvent? Or is that liability entirely several?

In *Baylis v Kelly* [1997] 2 Costs LR 212, Chadwick J went through the authorities stretching back to *Burridge v Bellew* (1875) 32 IT 807. That decision was referred to in the central paragraph of *Ellingsen v Det Scandinaviske Compani* [1919] 2 KB 567 as follows:

> 'If there has been a joint contract between the solicitor and his clients, each client is liable for the whole costs; and if there were separate contracts, each will be liable for his own portion of them; and as pointed out by Amphlett B. in *Burridge v Bellew*, the fact that after separate retainers the defence is conducted jointly does not make the liability joint.'

Consequently, where there are separate retainers, the solicitor will lose out if one of the clients becomes unable to pay their share. The old cases consider that result to be an 'injustice' or a 'curious' outcome, but nevertheless it was considered to be the right result. More recently, the fundamental challenges to CFAs resulted in a number of cases where the claimant's retainer became unenforceable and the solicitor therefore lost out. Where solicitors act in multi-party litigation using CFAs it is almost inevitable that the defendants will scrutinise the circumstances in which those CFAs were made – often with the use of the cancellable agreements legislation. If some of the CFAs can be found unenforceable, the general costs will be reduced by the number of those unenforceable agreements unless a joint liability is founded by the other CFAs or by a separate costs sharing agreement.

Chadwick J helpfully stated that the following propositions could be established from the case law:

- Where a solicitor acts for a number of clients in the same action on separate retainers, each client is entitled to a separate bill.
- That solicitor and client bill would be assessed with regard to the principle that the client would only be charged with the costs properly attributable to his case.
- Any costs solely relating to the case of one client should be charged to him to the exclusion of the other clients.
- The court must have regard to the nature of each client's case in order to determine whether there were distinct issues in relation to particular clients – if so the costs relating to those issues (so far as can be identified) should be attributed to the particular clients.
- The general costs of the action must be apportioned pro-rata between the clients.
- It is irrelevant that the effect of an apportionment is that a solicitor cannot recover some part of the apportioned costs.

In so far as the general costs are concerned, the pro-rata arrangement applies where each client has a separate retainer. Where there is a joint retainer between clients, the pro-rata 'rule of thumb' can be displaced. In *Walker v Burton* [2013] EWHC 811 (Ch), the general costs were able to be split between three of the six clients since they were each responsible for all the costs.

The leading cases, such as *Baylis* have tended to concentrate on the costs payable by individual defendants rather than claimants. That there is no difference in principle between claimants and defendants was confirmed by HHJ Cooke in *Walker*.

Between the Parties

[29.37]

In the infinite complexity of litigation with which bills of costs have to contend, it is inevitable that sometimes work done by a solicitor needs to be claimed over more than one bill. Similarly a party is not always awarded all of its costs in the proceedings. In either situation, some work is likely to be carried out which has to be split between more than one bill or reduced to take account of the terms of the Order. It is not hard to imagine a meeting with your clients which discussed matters wider than the proceedings which gave rise to the Order under assessment and/or on which only some of the clients were successful. Part of that attendance can be claimed in the bill but not all of it. How should this be done?

Apportionment and Division

[29.38]

'The distinction between division and apportionment may in certain circumstances be a thin one', said Viscount Haldane but the distinction was 'fundamental'. The distinction was described in these terms:

> 'When the court gives "part of" the costs of the action, it may do so in two ways; the one will involve an apportionment of the whole of the general charges, the other will extend only to the excess of expense incurred in consequence of the particular matter to be "excepted".'

At the time this definition was written in a legal commentary, the distinction described the difference between the Chancery masters who apportioned the common costs and the Common law masters who divided the extra expense from the relevant costs. The *Medway Oil* decision (below) decisively favoured the common law approach and so the distinction between apportionment and division should now be seen in a different light. It is the court which makes the original costs order that may apportion the costs between the parties. The court which assesses those costs may divide the items which can be claimed from those which cannot.

Issues based orders are the genesis for most of the problems. They can generate very lengthy and difficult detailed assessments and the need to divide costs between issues is the main reason for this. In Chapter 22 we discuss the orders that the court should make in preference to an issues based order ([**22.22**]).

It is very common to hear the word 'apportion' being used in all circumstances and generally where the word division would be more apt. This is not helped by the need to apportion costs that are common between clients of the same solicitor, whether pro-rata or otherwise (see solicitor and client above).

The example often given of a common cost item which would need to be divided is counsel's brief fee on a hearing where his client is successful on one issue but not on another. For example, the client succeeds on liability but fails to achieve an award of quantum that is higher than a Part 36 offer made by the opponent. Depending upon whether it was liability or quantum that took up most of counsel's preparation and hearing time, the amount recoverable by the client for the brief fee might be divided to a greater or lesser extent.

An example often given of a common cost that could not be divided, or is 'unitary' in nature, is the issue fee. It is said that such fee needs to be paid regardless of whether all the claimants are successful (and so can recover their costs). That may have been so when a single fee was payable to start proceedings. But these days the fee is based on a value bracket and it is not difficult to imagine a situation where the fee payable by the successful claimant would have been less if he had brought proceedings on his own than the fee paid to cover the claims of his unsuccessful co-claimant as well. It is this sort of point which demonstrates that an assessment requiring division by the assessing judge can become very time consuming. It is no wonder that many decisions in this area begin by the judge commenting that a simpler order would have made everyone's life much easier.

Where one party is awarded the costs of the action

[29.39]

As mentioned above, in *Medway Oil & Storage Co v Continental Contractors Ltd* [1929] AC 88 the House of Lords considered the divergent procedures left over from the difference between Chancery practice and the Common law courts prior to their coming together in the 1870s. Viscount Haldane's lead judgment sets out the numerous cases which had grappled with the problem of sharing costs between claim and counterclaim where both parties had succeeded – or as in *Medway Oil* itself, both parties had lost. The House of Lords followed the Common law approach. While it might, in some cases, produce a harsh result, Viscount Haldane explained the policy of the courts was to find a principle which would 'extricate the law of taxation in cases like the present one from the hopeless confusion' which the previous case law revealed. The 'true rule' is that the claim should be treated as if it stood alone and the counterclaim should bear only the amount by which the costs of the proceedings have been increased by it. The effect of this is that almost all of the costs are attributed to the main action rather than the counterclaim.

The rule in *Medway Oil* was extended by the Court of Appeal in *Cinema Press Ltd v Pictures & Pleasures Ltd* [1945] KB 356. The Court confirmed that a party who was awarded the costs of the action, save for the costs of a particular issue, was in the same position as the party who has the costs of the claim rather than the counterclaim. In other words, only those costs of the issue which increased the overall costs are recoverable by the party with the issues based order: all of the other costs are the party's who won overall.

This approach was confirmed in the CPR world by the decision of Patten J in *Dyson Technology Ltd v Strutt* [2007] EWHC 1756. He overturned the costs judge's decision which sought to implement a Chancery style apportionment to some of the common costs citing the case of *Fourie* (see below) in support. Patten J upheld the approach taken in *Medway Oil* and *Cinema Press*.

The court may make a direction as to apportionment

[29.40]

The House of Lords in *Medway Oil* appreciated that the approach it prescribed might lead to harsh consequences. Consequently, it stated that the general rule of not apportioning costs common to the claim and counterclaim could be varied by the court making a 'special direction.' In *Fourie v Le Roux* [2006] EWHC 1840 (Ch) the Court of Appeal had decided that the *Medway Oil* approach would be unjust on the complicated set of facts arising from a number of injunction hearings. The Vice Chancellor said that 'justice would be done by a direction to the costs judge to apportion between the parties . . . the total costs of the application for and discharge of the First Order and the costs of the further application . . . '. At the detailed assessment, the costs judge essentially took a *Medway Oil* approach and considered that all of the costs had been incurred by the first order and so allowed all of the costs. On appeal, Warren J found himself having to try to put the Court of Appeal's wishes into practice. He concluded that the costs judge's approach was wrong but that was just the start. How the apportionment was to occur was 'difficult to know.' In the end he gave an indication that a 50/50 split might be appropriate.

Specific and non-specific common costs

[29.41]

Costs may be incurred that are relevant to the claim and counterclaim or to discrete issues as well as the costs of the general action. The *Medway Oil* approach defines how such costs should be looked at as a starting point. But that is not the end of the matter. These 'common costs' come in two varieties which are usually described as being (a) 'specific' common costs or (b) 'non-specific' or 'general' common costs.

Where common costs are considered to be 'specific', they need to be divided between the claim and counterclaim or between the issues. The example given above regarding counsel's brief fee is a good example of a common cost which would need to be divided if only some of the matters on which counsel was instructed were successful.

Where common costs are considered to be 'non-specific' they are not divided and go to the party who has the costs of the claim or the general costs of the action. An example of a non-specific common cost would be an interim application fee of £255 for an application brought by two claimants but only one of whom was successful. The fee would still be the same if only the successful claimant had made the application and it is not divided in two simply because the other claimant was unsuccessful.

In *Cinema Press* the taxing master applied the *Medway Oil* principle initially but failed to go on to divide the specific common costs so as to isolate the time spent and the proportion of the disbursements incurred on the issue on which the defendant had succeeded. As a result, the Court of Appeal overturned the taxing master's decision.

Claims successful against only some defendants

[29.42]

In *Hay v Szterbin* [2010] EWHC 1967 (Ch) the claimant pursued her former solicitors (the third defendant) as well as Mr and Mrs Szterbin in relation to the purchase of a vineyard. The claim was compromised by sums paid by the solicitors to all of the other parties. There was no order as to costs in respect of the claim against the first and second defendants. The third defendant agreed to pay the claimant's costs which 'relate exclusively' to the professional negligence claim against it and which 'do not encompass any costs' relating to the claim against the first and second defendants. The parties were agreed that any costs that were specifically against the solicitor were recoverable and those specifically against Mr and Mrs Szterbin were not. They disagreed on what was to happen to the costs which were common to both claims. Master

Haworth accepted the defendant's contention that the order agreed by the parties could only be construed as disallowing any costs which were also incurred in part against the Szterbins. On appeal, Newey J took the view that the costs judge's decision only related to non-specific common costs. They would have been incurred anyway in order to pursue the other defendants. In accordance with the agreed order, they could not be considered to relate exclusively to the third defendant and so were not recoverable. Where there were specific common costs however, the amount which related to the third defendant could be divided from the amount relating to the first and second defendants and that amount would be recoverable.

In *Jean Mary Doris Haynes (Personal Representative of the Estate of Brian Haynes Deceased) v Department for Business Innovation and Skills* [2014] EWHC 643 (QB), Jay J was required to consider whether the costs claimed against the eighth defendant of ten should be 'disaggregated, apportioned or divided' as he described it. The Government department was one of five defendants who had been made a Part 36 offer by the claimant. It was the only one to accept the offer and the claims against all the other defendants were discontinued before service of any proceedings. The sum accepted was roughly a tenth of the stated value of the claim overall. The (eighth) defendant argued that, in addition to the costs specifically incurred against it, it should only be liable for one tenth of the common costs incurred against all of the defendants. That proposition was accepted by both the costs officer and costs judge on appeal. Jay J, however, came to the conclusion that the non-specific common costs were recoverable in their entirety following the reasoning in *Dyson*. They would have been incurred in any event and division would not be appropriate.

The specific common costs however, on general principles, ought to be assessed on an item by item approach to see what would be the correct sum to be divided in each instance. The imposition of a broad brush approach using fractions was not appropriate. However, the case specific answer here was to leave that approach undisturbed. The claimant's solicitors had not lodged any papers with the court before the costs judge and so he had had little option but to take the approach that he had. Jay J was mindful of the cost of the item by item approach and so, on the facts before him, decided the costs judge's refusal to adjourn so that papers could be put before him, was reasonable. The case would be remitted to the costs judge to assess the additional non-specific common costs to be allowed.

Only some claimants successful

[29.43]

Where some claimants are successful in their claims against a defendant, but others are not, the individual costs are obviously recoverable for the successful ones and irrecoverable for the others. But what about the common costs? Can they be absorbed by the successful claimants so that 100% of the common costs can be claimed notwithstanding the lack of success by some of the claimants? For the reasons given at the beginning of this section, the answer is no unless there is a joint retainer.

In *Walker*, HHJ David Cooke, sitting as a High Court judge, considered the arrangements made between six claimants and their solicitor. 'The villagers' as the six were called, were of varying means. While they paid fees privately, three of the six met the bills. Once CFAs were required, the solicitor entered into CFAs with the three who had been paying the bills but did not do so with the others. The solicitor had previously written to all six referring to them being jointly and severally liable for his fees and the court found that there was a joint retainer between the villagers and the solicitor. Accordingly, when it came to recovering those fees, Judge Cooke was in no doubt that they were all recoverable in principle. The fact that three of the six who 'retained' the solicitor in the professional conduct sense had no liability to pay the fees did not matter. The three who had signed CFAs were each responsible for all the fees anyway.

No claimants successful

[29.44]

You might not think that there would be anything too difficult regarding a case where all the claimants have been unsuccessful: the defendant will be entitled to his costs against all of the claimants. To the extent that the claimants were acting in concert, they will be jointly and severally liable for those costs. Where the costs have been incurred in respect of defending a part of the claim only by some of the claimants, it is only those claimants who will be liable for those discrete costs. This much is consistent with the foregoing paragraphs and was confirmed by Warby J in *Ontulmus v Collett* [2014] EWHC 4117 (QB).

But it is not always the case that claimants acting in concert do so until the bitter end. Quite often, some will settle during the proceedings leaving only some to continue to trial. Those who settle usually do so on terms regarding their liability for costs as against the defendant. What happens if the remaining claimants argue that the settling claimants should make a contribution to the costs ordered to be paid by the remainder who went to trial?

In *Dufoo v Tolaini* [2014] EWCA Civ 1536 the appellant had been one of the claimants in a claim brought against Mr Tolaini. The appellant was the only one of those claimants to pursue the case to trial and he had been ordered to pay 80% of the defendant's costs on the indemnity basis. The appellant appealed that decision and sought a contribution from his erstwhile co-claimants and who were respondents to the appeal. They defended the appeal on the basis that they had settled their differences with the defendant on terms that there was to be no order as to costs against them. Both the trial judge and Jackson LJ giving the lead judgment in the Court of Appeal said they found this to be a difficult issue. On the one hand, parties are encouraged to settle where possible and awarding a contribution to another party would reduce that encouragement. On the other hand, the appellant was not a party to the settlement agreement and had only been one of several claimants who had pursued the defendant in the same manner for most of the case. Jackson LJ said:

> 'When different parties advance the same unsuccessful case against their common adversary, the normal starting point for a court considering costs is that they should all contribute to the recoverable costs of the successful party.'

He decided that the existence of the settlement agreement was not in the end sufficient to overturn that starting point and concluded, at paragraph 69 that:

> 'In a multi-party action the court has power under CPR 44.2 to order that party A should contribute to the costs payable by party B to their mutual adversary. In the unusual facts of this case it is appropriate to exercise that power.'

The respondents also argued that the indemnity basis order was made because the appellant had been guilty of altering the evidence to support his case. In a ruling which may have suited the justice of the occasion but was not likely to assist the assessment of the costs, the difference of the costs to be awarded on assessment between a standard and an indemnity basis was not to be recoverable by the appellant from the respondents. Jackson LJ appeared to have in mind the practical difficulties of this when suggesting that a percentage of the indemnity basis costs ought to be allowed. Ultimately, the Court of Appeal decided that it was not in a position to assess the level of the contribution costs and so remitted the case to the trial judge to exercise his discretion afresh with the benefit of the guidance given.

Separate representation

[29.45]

The commentary above relates to a number of parties instructing a single solicitor. But what happens where parties whose interests are aligned choose to instruct separate legal teams? Regularly parties in this position jointly instruct counsel even if they retain their own solicitors but this is not always so. The costs involved are inevitably multiplied and the proceedings (and hearings) slow to a crawl as each party's legal team (and advocate) often feel the need to justify their involvement. Ideally, the case managing judge will highlight the issue to the parties prospectively but if not, the trial judge may give directions to the costs judge as to the unreasonableness of the costs involved eg see *Ong v Ping* [2015] EWHC 3258 (Ch).

CHAPTER 30

DETAILED ASSESSMENT – PROVISIONAL ASSESSMENT

INTRODUCTION TO DETAILED ASSESSMENT – PROVISIONAL ASSESSMENT

[30.1]

Litigators of a certain age may recall having bills of costs provisionally assessed by the court in days gone by. In some areas, such as Court of Protection work, this method has continued. As from April 2013, the use of provisional assessment for a large swathe of bills in civil cases, changed the nature of detailed assessment of costs in a fundamental way.

In this Chapter we look at the scheme together with some comments on the provisional assessments in Legal Aid only and Court of Protection bills. Like CPR 45.17 and its accompanying practice direction, this Chapter is comparatively short. The idea of a paper based assessment is a simple idea and ought to be set out as such. But those who have come across the workings of the Portal (see Chapter 26) will know how a simple idea can generate the most unwieldy 'clarification' through protocols and practice direction. We do not advocate a similarly detailed approach to provisional assessments but it is clear that the existing rule and practice direction leave considerable room for local practice. That in turn leads to doubt as to how any particular court will deal with both practical and legal matters and that is not helpful given the scope of assessments which fall within these arrangements. It is worth making the point (also made in Chapter 28) that provisional assessment is essentially just a stage in the detailed assessment procedure. It is not a third form of assessment to go with summary and detailed assessment. If a case is not suitable for a provisional assessment, it will go straight to a detailed assessment. If a party does not like the outcome of the provisional assessment, he can require there to be a detailed assessment, albeit the rules as to who pays the costs of that hearing are altered from the normal rules. The method by which the bill is assessed is essentially the same as if the parties are there. The purpose of the provisional assessment scheme is to make the detailed assessment process quicker and cheaper; not to create a new form of assessment.

THE PILOT SCHEME

[30.2]

Provisional assessments were piloted as part of the Jackson Review which ran from 1 October 2010 until 31 March 2013 in the Leeds, York and Scarborough County Courts. Under the pilot scheme the provisional assessment of parties' costs took place without an oral hearing where the base costs were under £25,000. Practice Direction 51E (now revoked) set out the details.

Leeds County Court dealt with 119 cases entering the pilot during the first year, most of which were personal injury claims. Of the 100 cases which proceeded to provisional assessment, 17 led to requests for subsequent oral hearings (9 by paying parties and 8 by receiving parties). Only two cases went as far as the oral hearing. In a report based on the Leeds data, Sir Rupert Jackson recommended that the provisional assessment procedure should be incorporated into the Civil Procedure Rules.

THE PROVISIONAL ASSESSMENT PROCEDURE

Requesting a provisional assessment

[30.3]

All of the procedural requirements for provisional assessments can be found at CPR 47.15 and CPR PD 47, para 14.

The journey towards a provisional assessment starts from the same place as any other detailed assessment, namely a notice of commencement and bill of costs. The parties serve points of dispute and any replies and if the case has not settled, the receiving party will request a hearing date by filing an N258 and supporting documents. The N258 was changed in April 2013 to cater for provisional assessments. The receiving party has to request a provisional assessment if the value in the Notice of Commencement is £75,000 or less. If it is more, he requests a detailed assessment hearing and gives a time estimate in the usual way.

As we have pointed out in Part 3 of this book (eg **[11.16]**), the effect of the Court of Appeal's decision in *BNM v MGN* [2017] EWCA Civ 1767 is to remove additional liabilities from the definition of costs in the post-April 2013 CPR. On that basis, the Notice of Commencement and/or a covering letter to the court requesting a detailed assessment of costs ought to distinguish between the base costs and the additional liabilities in considering whether the £75,000 threshold has actually been exceeded. In practice we suspect that courts will simply continue to go by the figure on the Notice of Commencement and that this point will only be raised by losing parties seeking to reduce the costs of the detailed assessment hearing.

Suitability for a provisional assessment

[30.4]

Upon receipt of the N258, the court will consider the suitability of the case for the provisional assessment procedure. Practices will vary from court to court. In the SCCO a costs officer or Master will look at the file.

What makes a case suitable? That is the wrong question. All cases will be considered suitable unless they have a case specific reason for not being so. Having said this, the procedure does not apply to Solicitors Act 1974 assessments between solicitors and clients.

When considering why a provisional assessment might not be suitable, two things need to be borne in mind. The first is that matters such as the importance of the case to the client or the complexity of the facts or issues in the proceedings giving rise to the detailed assessment are not going to be good reasons for an oral hearing. The assessor is going to be able to get to grips with the issues etc just as well by reading the papers at a provisional assessment as he would be if he had read some papers before the detailed assessment hearing.

The second issue is whether evidence is going to be required. Most detailed assessments are successfully completed without any formal evidence being given. Advocates often tread a thin line between submissions and evidence in detailed assessment hearings although that is inevitable where explanations are being requested on a variety of matters. But where there is an evidential dispute over the facts, for example regarding the terms or formation of the retainer, there will be little option but to have a hearing so that such evidence as may be required can be given and tested.

Such issues may not be apparent on an initial sift of the case for non-suitability. If the case gets to the point of being provisionally assessed, there is no reason why the judge cannot halt that assessment and list the case for a hearing instead (CPR 47.15(6)).

Supporting papers

[30.5]

The court will not undertake a provisional assessment until it is in receipt of 'the relevant supporting documents' specified in CPR PD 47, para 14. These documents should in fact have been lodged with the N258 in the first place. But this provision (CPR 47.15(3)) enables the court to decline to carry out any assessment until the minimum amount of paperwork has been filed. The practice direction stipulates the following documents in addition to the N258.

- The notice of commencement, bill of costs, annotated points of dispute from each paying party, any replies, the order for assessment and the other relevant documents that should be filed with the N258 for any detailed assessment (CPR PD 47, para 13.2)
- An additional copy of the bill, including a statement of the costs claimed in respect of the detailed assessment drawn on the assumption that there will not be an oral hearing following the provisional assessment
- All Part 36 and similar offers which must be placed in a sealed envelope and marked 'Part 36 or similar offers' but making sure that there is no indication as to which party made the offer(s). This should include the paying party's open letter served with the points of dispute in accordance with CPR PD 47, para 8.3.
- A completed Precedent G (combining the points of dispute and any reply)

In the pilot scheme, these were all the papers that were filed with the court and there was no provision for any further documents to be lodged to try to influence the assessor. It is perhaps surprising in those circumstances that there were no reports of the points of dispute or replies becoming longer as a result. (The cynic would suggest it was perhaps difficult for that to happen.) Furthermore, the fact that the limit was £25,000 might well have meant that there was less need to provide any further documentation.

CPR 45.17(4) states clearly that the provisional assessment will be based on the information contained in the bill and supporting papers and the contentions set out in Precedent G. Nevertheless, in the SCCO, which used to have a separate provision in the old costs rules regarding the lodging of papers, when other courts did not, additional documents may be requested where they appear to be necessary to decide a particular issue.

Some parties only appreciate the prospect of a provisional assessment rather than a detailed assessment hearing when they get notice of the date of the provisional assessment. That notice spurs them on to file and serve replies that would not otherwise be prepared (if they are the receiving party) or simply to write to the court to expand upon their client's position. Such correspondence is always prefaced with a suggestion that it is written to assist the court but it is debatable that this will ever be the case. If the judge finds himself unable to reach a decision on a particular issue he is perfectly entitled to end the provisional assessment process and list the case for a detailed assessment hearing. If he makes a decision which is wrong in some way, the party can always seek a post-provisional hearing. Attempting to deal with arguments in numerous letters and other documents as well as those raised in the points of dispute and replies is generally going to be unhelpful rather than helpful. It also leads to a position where each party feels compelled to respond to whatever is written by their opponent.

The six week limit

[30.6]

According to CPR PD 47, para 14.4(1) the court will use its best endeavours to carry out the assessment within six weeks of receipt of the N258 and supporting papers. This is a very unusual use of a 'best endeavours' clause. Its purpose appears to be to focus judicial and court manager minds on the need to get on with these assessments rather than to put them at the end of the box work. There is not the slightest hint of what would happen if the six week time period cannot be met. Early surveys of the turnaround time for provisional assessments around the country indicated a variation between a few weeks and the best part of a year.

Practices vary as to the best way to get through this work. For example, in the pilot, the cases were listed for a 'hearing' even though the parties were not able to attend, whereas the costs officers and judges at the SCCO have taken the opposite approach, ie not listing the cases. As long as they can be dealt with expeditiously this may well result in a speedier turn around for parties.

Carrying out the provisional assessment

[30.7]

The rule and practice direction are silent on exactly how the bill should be assessed. They merely deal with how the results of the assessment are recorded. The reason for the silence is two-fold. First, the method of assessing the bill is essentially the same for a provisional assessment as it is for a detailed assessment (see **[28.50]**). The points of dispute and any replies stand in the place of any oral submissions but as long as the point is raised, the court is seized of the issue and will consider the relevant documents and information before coming to a decision on that point.

The second reason can be highlighted by asking what does the CPR have to say about the conduct of a detailed assessment hearing or indeed any application or trial? In fact there is nothing in the rules regarding how a hearing is run. That is left to the judge and will be entirely case specific. However, since the provisional assessment is carried out without the parties being present, there is an understandable wish to know how it is done.

One of the main differences is the need for the assessor to make an intelligible note of his decision on each point so that the parties can understand the reasoning for that decision when they receive the result. During a detailed assessment hearing, the judge may, for example decide to reduce the hourly rate claimed and will record this by simply striking out the hourly rate set out in the narrative, or at the beginning of a subsequent part of the bill, and substitute the allowed rate in pen. Where the parties are not present to hear the assessor's reasoning, they are left with the decision (eg the reduced hourly rate) but no explanation. That is not a satisfactory exercise of judicial involvement because part of justice being done is to have reasons for the decisions reached. The following options are open to the judge to explain the decisions reached:

(a) he can set out reasons on the bill;
(b) he can set out reasons on the Precedent G;
(c) he can set out reasons on a separate schedule to go in or with a covering letter;
(d) he can decide to let the amendments speak for themselves on the minor aspects and give reasons as per (a) to (c) above for the points of principle.

The attraction of (c) over (a) or (b) is that there is no issue of space. As described in Chapter 29, the size of the box in which to give reasons in Precedent G seems to depend on how well the box fits on to the page rather than necessarily leaving an adequate amount of room for the decision to be set out. Similar considerations apply on the bill itself in certain areas. Nevertheless, annotating the bill is likely to be the most common option, particularly as it does not require the judge or member of the court staff to type out the reasons.

Option (d) does not really deal with the justice point raised above but will probably be seen on smaller items. At most there will be a very terse comment about it such as 'not recoverable' which arguably is no better than there being no comment at all.

We have been careful to avoid describing the provisional assessment as a hearing, or even a hearing on paper. Such terminology was deprecated by Stewart J in *PME v The Scout Association* [2019] EWHC 3421 (QB), [2020] 1 WLR 1217, [2019] Costs LR 2003 as discussed below.

Provisional assessments and proportionality

[30.8]

The issue of proportionality is dealt with in detail in Chapter 14. Its application is also considered separately on detailed assessment (**[28.70]**). In short, the *Lownds* test will still be applied to work done before 1 April 2013 but for work thereafter proportionality will be considered by reference to CPR 44.3(2). (The *Lownds* test will apply to all of the costs if the underlying proceedings were commenced prior to 1 April 2013). Under the *Lownds* test, the question of proportionality is dealt with at the beginning of the assessment and this causes no difficulty on a provisional assessment. But the test in CPR

44.3(2) requires the court first to assess reasonable sums based on the challenges made. The court is then required to consider the overall figure for those reasonably allowed items and decide whether the overall figure is also proportionate.

This causes a practical problem in many courts because the assessing judge does not have the time (or often the inclination) to add up the bill to see what the sum of the reasonable items is. Assuming he does not add up the bill, what should the judge do? He can send the bill back to the receiving party, request that the bill is 'made up' and then consider proportionality when the bill is returned. But that is cumbersome and requires two distinct judicial efforts, even if the judge has made notes on his views as to proportionality originally to assist when the bill returns. Involving the judge twice invites the process taking considerably longer than was the intention. The alternative is to record on the bill or Precedent G something along the lines that 'any figure over £x will be considered disproportionate' which will generally mean that the bill does not come back to the court. But this requires either a good sense of what the reasonable sums will add up to or risking something akin to a de facto summary assessment. While not perfect, we prefer the first approach as being the least awful option.

Notifying the parties of the assessment

[30.9]

The change in the scope of provisional assessments means that the rule and practice direction have essentially been drafted in a vacuum, notwithstanding the running of the pilot scheme. This is evident in the provisions regarding annotation.

CPR 47.15(7) explains that a copy of the bill, as provisionally assessed, will be sent to each party. CPR PD 47, para 14.2(2) envisages that the court will return a copy of the Precedent G with the court's decisions noted upon it. This suggests that the only markings on the bill will be the reduced figures where that is appropriate together with whatever sum is allowed for the costs of the provisional assessment (see below). The reasons will be set out separately on the Precedent G. For the reasons given above, this may not be a viable option in some cases. In any event it does seem odd that the rule refers to one document being returned and the practice direction refers to another. It seems probable that many assessors will put all the information on the bill and it will only be that document that is sent to the parties together with the notice regarding what to do next. Those judges who wish to limit the number of challenges to the detailed assessment may consider it worthwhile to have a schedule of reasons to use to explain why some items are not recoverable and which could be rather longer than manuscript reasons given on the bill or Precedent G.

Costs of the provisional assessment

[30.10]

CPR 47.15(5) originally stated simply that the court would not award more than £1,500 to any party in respect of the provisional assessment. This was subsequently clarified to confirm that the £1,500 figure does not include either VAT, where appropriate, nor the court fee. It is worth considering how much the court is likely to award by way of provisional assessment costs since CPR 47.15(5) confirms that it is to be done on the basis that there will be no subsequent, oral hearing. The receiving party will have to:

- consider the points of dispute;
- draft any replies;
- give consideration to the open offer and any Part 36 offers made.
- draft the N258 and collate the papers to be sent to the court.

However, the cost of preparation of the bill is already catered for on the bill itself and, compared with a detailed assessment, there is no time to be claimed for:

- preparing the papers for lodging with the court (or at least not as much);
- preparing the advocate for the hearing;
- attending the hearing and travelling to and from it.

The schedules which are lodged with the court which exceed the recoverable limit generally have considerable time claimed for (unsuccessful) negotiations. Absent such time, these activities set out above will, in the general run of things, not be sufficient to reach the capped limit.

One way of avoiding the cap in CPR 47.15(5) was thought to be to obtain an indemnity basis order for the costs of the provisional assessment. In the absence of any real opportunity for poor conduct to justify such an order, the answer for the receiving party would be to make a Part 36 offer and then to beat it on the provisional assessment. The claimant in *Lowin v Portsmouth & Co Ltd* did just that but the costs judge considered the cap to override an indemnity basis order flowing from rule 36.17(4)(b). The claimant was successful on appeal to Laing J but the Court of Appeal reinstated the costs judge's decision. Whilst the costs could be awarded on the indemnity basis rather than the standard basis, they were still capped at £1,500 plus VAT and the court fee. The case of *Broadhurst v Tan* (see **[20.33]**) was not directly applicable ([2017] EWCA Civ 2172).

Considering Part 36 offers

[30.11]

Contrary to the implications raised by the filing of sealed envelopes, the court is not necessarily going to look at any Part 36 or similar offers at this stage. For example, a sum will be allowed on the bill on the assumption that the receiving party is entitled to the costs of the provisional assessment.

If a party is content with the provisional assessment, other than the costs of the assessment itself which have been awarded to the receiving party, there is a specific procedure set out at CPR PD 47, para 14.6. While a post-provisional oral hearing has to be requested, the court will invariably invite the parties to make written submissions and the issue will be finally determined (ie not provisionally determined) without a hearing. The precise procedure may vary depending upon the circumstances of the case.

When would this circumstance occur?:

- It will generally be because the paying party has made an offer which has not been beaten and wishes to have an order for the costs of the provisional assessment.
- It may simply be that the paying party considers that the award has been too generous and so the amount should be made more reasonable.

- It may also be because the receiving party has beaten his own offer and seeks an order for additional costs and interest in accordance with CPR 36.17.

Concluding the provisional assessment

[30.12]

Upon receipt of the notice of provisional assessment and annotated bill and/or Precedent G, the parties must agree the total sum due to the receiving party based on the court's decisions. If the parties cannot agree the arithmetic they must refer the disputed sums to the court and a decision will be made upon the written submissions of the parties (CPR PD 47, para 14.4(2)).

Unless one of the parties challenges the provisional assessment (see next heading), the provisional assessment will be binding on the parties save in exceptional circumstances (CPR 47.15(7)). There is no requirement to obtain a final costs certificate to complete the process but the procedure is available if a certificate is required for enforcement proceedings, for example.

Challenging the provisional assessment

[30.13]

The parties will receive a notice with the provisionally assessed bill telling them what they may do next. Their options are:

(a) to accept the provisional assessment (see previous section);
(b) to challenge all of the items assessed;
(c) to challenge some of the items assessed;
(d) to challenge the costs of the assessment (see section headed 'considering Part 36 offers').

Where a party decides to challenge some or all of the items assessed in the bill, he must file and serve a written request for an oral hearing. This has to be done within 21 days of receipt of the notice otherwise the provisional assessment will be binding in all but exceptional circumstances.

The request needs to identify the item or items which the challenger wishes to be reviewed at the hearing. It must also provide a time estimate for the hearing. Upon receipt of the request, the court will fix a date and time for the hearing and will give the parties at least 14 days' notice of the time and place of that hearing.

Some thought needs to be given to the strategy regarding the oral hearing. Stewart J in *PME* made it clear that only items which were challenged at an oral hearing could subsequently be appealed (whether that was to a costs judge from a costs officer in the SCCO or from a costs judge or district judge to an appellate judge). The reasoning was that an appeal has to be from a hearing and a provisional assessment was not a hearing. So, if you receive notice of the provisional assessment and are contemplating an appeal, not just an oral hearing, then you need to make sure you have challenged everything which will form part of that appeal.

The post-provisional hearing

[30.14]

At the hearing the court will consider afresh the issues raised. While there is nothing to prevent one judge from hearing a case which another had provisionally assessed, this is unlikely to occur in practice. Human nature will dictate that a judge essentially hearing an appeal from himself will generally only move from his original decision if there are factors of which he was unaware originally.

The would be challenger needs to consider very carefully the costs provisions in respect of a post-provisional hearing set out at CPR 47.15(10). The rule is written so that the challenger will pay the costs of and incidental to the post-provisional hearing unless he 'achieves an adjustment' in his favour of 20% or more of the sum provisionally assessed. This means that if the bill is assessed at 80% of the bill as originally drawn, the receiving party would need to get the total up to at least 96% or the paying party down to at most 64% to avoid paying the costs of the oral hearing. So, unless the assessment is particularly harsh or particularly generous, it will be very difficult to challenge the bill without having to pay the costs of doing so. For a bill at the top end of the provisional assessment limit it may be worthwhile to do so in any event but that would be rare.

One of the options above was to challenge some of the items but not all of them. The costs hurdle is the same however many items are challenged so if only one item is challenged it will have to be very significant for it not to be inevitable that the challenger will have to pay the costs even if successful.

There is a saving provision of the court ordering otherwise and the practice direction (CPR PD 47, para 14.5) specifically refers to the conduct of the parties and the existence of any offers made. It may be that a Part 36 offer made prior to the detailed assessment proceedings by the paying party could alter the incidence of costs completely. However, a Part 36 offer made after the provisional assessment simply to reduce the hurdle that would otherwise have to be overcome at the post-provisional hearing is unlikely to be received favourably by the court.

COURT OF PROTECTION

[30.15]

Requests for detailed assessment of the costs of proceedings in the Court of Protection should be directed to the Senior Courts Costs Office using form N258 (or N258B if, as is likely, the costs are being paid out of a fund.) The SCCO will normally deal with Court of Protection assessments on a provisional basis by post. If the solicitor is not satisfied with the assessment, the costs officer must be informed within 14 days of receipt of the provisional assessment. The costs officer will usually carry out an informal review of any items with which the deputy is dissatisfied. If any informal review does not remedy the dissatisfaction, the SCCO will then fix a date for an oral hearing. In practice the costs officer will deal with any enquiries by telephone or letter.

Authorised court officers (see [**33.10**]) generally deal with any bills below £100,000 and a Master will deal with any larger bills. The documents to be lodged in support of the bill are those set out in CPR PD 47, para 13.12.

LEGAL AID

[30.16]

In days gone by, the courts would regularly assess 'legal aid only' bills where the solicitor would be paid from the Legal Aid fund (in its various incarnations.) That practice has dwindled as assessment of such costs has gradually been subsumed by the Legal Aid Agency itself.

Where a legally aided party settles the between the parties' element of his costs without a detailed assessment hearing, it is still possible for the court to assess the legal aid only elements as if the detailed assessment hearing had been reached.

TRUSTS AND OTHER FUNDS

[30.17]

CPR 47.19 is described, in a rather wordy fashion, as setting out the 'detailed assessment procedure where costs are payable out of a fund other than the community legal service fund' (or LASPO). It is accompanied by CPR PD 47, para 18.

The procedure is that the receiving party needs to request an assessment within three months of the event giving rise to the entitlement to assessed costs. The request is in form N258B. The court may require the bill to be served on other parties if it considers they have a financial interest in the outcome. This would usually be a beneficiary of the trust but may be the trustee in some cases.

The court will provisionally assess the bill and return it to the receiving party who has 14 days to request an oral hearing should he wish to do so. If a hearing is requested, notice will be given to any person with a financial interest as well as the receiving party. If no request is made (or the oral hearing has taken place) the receiving party will be expected to complete the bill so that the final certificate can be produced, always assuming the receiving party is legally represented.

CHAPTER 31

TIME AND VALUE

INTRODUCTION TO TIME AND VALUE

[31.1]

The use of time as the yardstick by which the size of a solicitor's bill is measured is embedded within both contentious and non-contentious work. The time taken on a matter is part of assessing the reasonableness of the fee charged even where it is not based on an hourly rate. Even Damages-Based Agreements, whose rationale is an agreement of a fee based on the damages, have to be able to be viewed from an hourly rate basis in order to recover the client's costs.

Not only is time one of the prescribed factors for both contentious and non-contentious business, and in routine matters it is the most important, it also runs like a thread through the other factors. The importance and complexity of the matter, the difficulty or novelty of questions raised can all affect the amount of time spent. An hourly cost rate applied to recorded time, in the words of Donaldson J:

> ' . . . if calculated accurately, informs a solicitor of the minimum figure which he must charge, if he is not to make an actual loss on the transaction. Second, it gives him an idea of the relationship between the overheads attributable to the transaction and the profit accruing to him. This latter point is plainly relevant in the broad sense that the nature of some transactions will justify much larger profits than others of a more routine type. But we must stress that it is only one of a number of cross-checks on the fairness and reasonableness of the final figure. The final figure will result from an exercise in judgment, not arithmetic, whatever arithmetical cross-checks may be employed.'
>
> (*Treasury Solicitor v Regester* [1978] 2 All ER 920, QBD.)

This chapter looks at time from all angles since it should be used as a management tool as well as for charging. As you would expect, there have been many cases which have considered the issues raised. At the beginning of Chapter 26 on fixed costs we queried the legal fraternity's desire to use hours rather than fixed fees as the basis of charging. There are other alternatives, particularly value which we also look at here. But we cannot get away from the point that paying for a reasonable amount of time, and no more, for a particular piece of work is in our psyche. As Lord Denning said in the 1980s when deciding the case of *Chamberlain v Boodle and King (a firm)* [1982] 3 All ER 188, [1982] 1 WLR 1443, CA:

> 'These rates per hour are over a pound a minute. It would seem there must be a very good system of timing – almost by stopwatch – if that is to be the rate of payment.'

TIME AS A MANAGEMENT TOOL

[31.2]

Time is a solicitor's raw material, his stock in trade. In the same way that businesses keep control over materials and stock, a solicitor should keep control over his own and his employees' time. The first relevance of time is therefore to the good running and management of a solicitor's practice. Could the time be put to better use?

Time recording and time costing were introduced to solicitors' firms in the days when it was slowly dawning on them that they were no longer certain to make a profit simply by working all hours that God sent and charging as much as the matter or client would stand. It was for that reason that the profession introduced time costing – to see whether work was being run at a profit or at a loss. It had nothing to do with charging – indeed conveyancing was still on a fixed scale but conveyancers were exhorted to cost their time to see what profit, if any, they were making. The object, therefore, was to check whether work which was being charged on a scale or some other basis was in fact being done at a profit. As a result many Central London firms stopped doing domestic conveyancing. In the present climate of competitive charging in both non-contentious and contentious work, with costs for the latter being increasingly restricted by being fixed, capped or subject to a predictable matrix (see Chapter 26), it is more important than ever for a solicitor to know what each area of work is costing and whether it can be charged for at a profit.

The Expense of Time

[31.3]

For the system to work you have to know how much each job costs and to do this you have to calculate the cost to the firm of each fee earner in reasonable units of time. There have been a variety of different methods of costing work but the method suggested by the Law Society in its booklet *The Expense of Time* has seemed to most firms using it simple and satisfactory. It has also been extolled in previous editions of this book as including a simplified back-of-an-envelope approach upon which it is difficult to improve. Regrettably, it is now out of print and very difficult to get hold of, even online. Fortunately, the 2014 Civil Justice Council Costs Committee's report on Guideline Hourly Rates (see **[31.22]**) used the same approach and so you can find a modern version in that report. The Expense of Time calculation basically divides the firm into fee earners and non-fee earners and then divides the projected overheads of the firm, including the salaries of the non-fee earners, between the fee earners, after building in various adjustments such as notional salaries for partners, deduction of interest on the client account and applying the retail price index and the estimated rate of inflation.

Recording non-chargeable time

[31.4]

If fee earners record their non-chargeable time under various categories as well as their chargeable time, the firm's management will have an overall picture of each fee earner's day and can identify how he spent his time. This 'big brother' aspect of time recording does not commend itself to everyone, and it is often not very effective since non-chargeable time is often nebulous and so can lead to 'time-dumping' on difficult to measure activities such as marketing.

TIME AS A CHARGING TOOL

[31.5]

We have seen that the recording and costing of time was introduced for the purpose of knowing whether work was being done at a profit or a loss and that it had the additional advantage of affording management information for those who desired it. It was not intended as a basis of charging. What then happened was that costs judges applying the rules for the assessment of costs; those responsible for devising those rules; and indeed the profession itself, all realised that the cost of doing the work was a useful method of quantifying both contentious and non-contentious work, particularly in routine matters.

Nevertheless, this was using time costing for a purpose for which it was never intended, so it was not really surprising when complaints began to ring out that the formula was too unreliable and too unsophisticated to bear the burden that had been imposed on it. As an aid to business efficiency, the costing of time was a matter of only domestic concern to each firm costing its work. If the formula they used, or their arithmetic, was wrong, it was only they who were misled into thinking they were making a bigger or smaller profit than they really were.

The painful plodder's charter

[31.6]

Another objection to time charging is the same as the objection to the historical quantitative methods of assessment. We now laugh at the thought of payment calculated in relation to the height of the file or the weight of papers, but payment by the metre, the kilo or the hour are all equally flawed: they all relate to quantity not quality. Payment based on time means that the longer a solicitor takes to do the work, the more he is paid. The greater his skill and expertise, the greater his expedition, the less time he will record and the less will be his reward. Where a solicitor brings to bear years of experience, or has a flash of inspiration, it happens so quickly that the time recording clock has barely moved. High quality work which should be encouraged is in fact severely penalised in any system of charges based solely on time. Charges based on the time spent reward the painful plodder for his slowness and inefficiency while penalising the speed and efficiency of others. In contending that this basis of charging is against the client's interests an American commentator referred to the 'misaligned interests of the hourly rate'.

CALCULATING THE HOURLY CHARGING RATE

A solicitor's hourly rate

[31.7]

For those who have only practised since the Civil Procedure Rules came into being in 1999, the 'hourly rate' which they charge tends to be a single figure which is either based on the guideline hourly rates (see [**31.22**]) or is a figure provided by the firm's management as the rate to be charged. In some firms, there may be different rates for different fee earners to charge depending upon the type of work undertaken but that is relatively rare. Even rarer, is the concept of charging a bespoke hourly rate for an individual piece of work. Where this happens, it tends now to be a reduction from a solicitor's published or 'rack' rate depending upon the negotiating power of the client, rather than a rate designed to reflect the complexity, urgency or other material factor of the work in question.

Many solicitors simply understand that they have a single hourly rate that they charge on all matters and which is increased annually or upon achieving some further qualification or status and notified to clients. But this is a blunt approach to achieving an appropriate hourly rate and the courts have long been uncomfortable with the simplicity of the CPR's approach. Consequently, cases are periodically reported which show that the pre-CPR approach is alive and well such as *KMT v Kent County Council* [2012] EWHC 2088 (QB). We shall now look at the pre-CPR approach which can safely be said is also a post CPR approach.

A and B factors

[31.8]

This approach to assessment was explained by Brightman J in *Re Eastwood, Lloyds Bank Ltd v Eastwood* [1975] Ch 112, [1973] 3 All ER 1079, CA, in the following extract from his judgment:

> 'During the hearing of the argument I was given certain advice by the assessors as to the manner in which a taxation proceeds at the present day . . . The advice given to me is this:
>
>> "At the present day, on the taxation of a bill of costs of a firm of solicitors in private practice which has been engaged in litigation on behalf of a client . . . the taxation invariably proceeds on the following basis. The firm informs the taxing master of the period of time that has been spent by any partner or employee of the firm on any 'relevant' aspect of the case: the word 'relevant' is intended to exclude time spent on a part of the case for which there is a fixed charge prescribed by statute or rule. The firm submits (a) what is the proper cost per hour of the time so spent, having regard to a reasonable estimate of the overhead expenses of the solicitors' firm including (if the time spent is that of an employee) the reasonable salary of the employee or (if the time spent is that of a partner) a notional salary. The firm will also submit (b) what is a proper additional sum to be allowed over and above (a) by way of further profit costs."
>
> '

This philosophy was further expounded in *Lazarus (Leopold) Ltd v Secretary of State for Trade and Industry* (1976) 120 Sol Jo 268, [1976] Costs Law Rep 62 in which Kerr J promoted '(a)' and '(b)' to 'A' and 'B' and ever since they have been known as the A factor and the B factor. This was also the first time that the expression 'direct cost' was used:

> 'In his Answer the master helpfully summarised the practice concerning the computation of Item 26 in cases such as this. Having considered the weight of the proceedings and the responsibility and skill involved, the practice is then to arrive at a total figure consisting of two elements which are referred to as A and B in the judgment of the Court of Appeal in *Eastwood*'s case.
>
> The computation of the A figure involves an assessment of the reasonable direct cost, that is to say the grade of person (senior solicitor, assistant solicitor, legal executive, etc) whom it was reasonable to employ at each stage; an approximation of the cost of employment of each individual by considering the number of hours for each of them to be reasonably engaged; and assessing a rate per hour sufficient to cover the salary and the appropriate share of the general overheads of each such person. The assessment of the appropriate rate per hour would be based on the taxing master's knowledge and experience of the average solicitor or executive employed by the average firm in the area concerned. The total hours of each person multiplied by an approximate cost per hour, together with an allowance for letters, telephone calls and telex messages, then produces what the Court of Appeal referred to as the A figure. The B figure is then conventionally assessed by adding a percentage to the A figure which is appropriate in all the circumstances to cover matters which cannot be calculated on an hourly basis, that is to say supervision and other indirect expenses, together with what the master referred to in his Answer as "imponderables", which reflect the degree of skill, responsibility and the other factors set out in [what is now CPR Rule 44.4]. As mentioned above, the increase for the B figure claimed in the present case was just under 50 per cent, which would be perfectly normal and certainly not excessive in cases of this type. This is the figure which, in the case of an independent firm of solicitors, is expected to make a contribution to the profits of the firm. The appropriateness of the total of A and B, arrived at in this way, is then considered against the background of the proceedings as a whole and rounded off to a convenient sum which appears right in all the circumstances.'

The A factor was therefore identified as the hourly expense rate, and the B factor as the profit, A and B together giving the hourly charging rate. The A factor is arrived at by ascertaining the amount and cost of the time spent, while the B factor is arrived at by the application of the factors prescribed in the Solicitors' (Non-Contentious Business) Remuneration Order 2009, art 3 or in CPR 44.4.

Ascertaining the Direct Cost ('A' Factor)

[31.9]

Basing your rates on what other firms are charging or by adopting the going rates being allowed on between the parties' assessments of costs will not tell you whether you are making a profit or loss on a particular kind of work. There is no satisfactory substitute for each firm of solicitors undertaking an *Expense of Time* type calculation at least annually. On an assessment of costs between a solicitor and his client in both contentious and non-contentious costs, the costs officer starts with the retainer. In days gone by, the letter of retainer (if any) might be silent as to the hourly expense rates charged and in which case the costs officer would consider the actual cost to the firm of doing the work and whether that cost was reasonable in the context of the nature of the work. Now that virtually all retainer letters and agreements make express provision for hourly rates, the costs officer starts from the position of knowing the composite hourly charging rate and, where appropriate, working backwards to establish the direct cost. As between the solicitor and his client, the hourly rate set out in the retainer letter or agreement, particularly where that document is signed, is going to be very persuasive, if not conclusive, evidence of the reasonable hourly rate.

However, it does not follow that this amount will be allowed between the parties, regardless of how meticulously you may have calculated your hourly expense rate. If you choose to be a prestigious firm with luxurious offices and expensive cars – as you are perfectly entitled to do – and your client chooses you and your firm – as he is perfectly entitled to do – it is not reasonable that the loser in litigation should have to pay your above-average expense rates because of your sybaritic lifestyle. Between the parties' costs assessed on the standard basis must be both reasonable and proportionate.

How are judges to decide what the hourly cost rate should be? By sitting day in and day out, hearing solicitors disputing or accepting the rates of others and forming a view as to market rates. The judges do not lay down the rates. They adjudicate on the opposing contentions of the parties. Guidance on hourly cost rates was given in two cases:

Hirst J in *Stubbs v Board of Governors of the Royal National Orthopaedic Hospital* [1997] Costs Law Rep 117:

> 'Stress is placed on the average cost of the average solicitor or legal executive – in the particular area concerned . . . In arriving at a figure, the essence of the exercise was an appropriate apportionment of the estimated overhead expenses of the solicitors' firm having regard to the position, status, and likely rate of remuneration of the persons who were employed on the case under consideration. This is of its very nature suitable for assessment by the taxing master in the light of his very wide experience; it is also a matter which is properly approached by reference to averages since it is unlikely that there will be a very wide divergence between comparable firms of solicitors operating in similar fields of work in similar geographical areas.'

In *Finley v Glaxo Laboratories Ltd* [1997] Costs Law Rep 106, Hobhouse J said:

> ' . . . The next point – and it is the one which formed the main part of the argument before me – is the rate per hour which should be allowed. It is clear that the rate which should be allowed is the actual cost, assessed on an objective basis. In other words, it is not answered merely by reference to what has been the cost to the solicitor in question of doing the relevant work on an hourly basis. It has to be assessed on an objective basis having regard to what is reasonable. Therefore, one must consider the position of other solicitors in question. One has to consider whether it is the appropriate level of fee earner that is claimed for. In the present matter it has been accepted, and I accept, that the appropriate level of fee earner for a case of this character was a senior litigation partner; and the solicitor concerned matched that description.'

The introduction of composite hourly rates seems to have meant that solicitors very rarely are in a position to provide the court with the sort of information that these two cases describe. Why that is so is open to conjecture since a knowledge of the cost to the firm of running a piece of litigation ought to be a prized piece of management information. It is notable that the 2014 report on the Guideline Hourly Rates (see **[31.22]**) used an Expense of Time calculation as the bedrock of its attempt to produce evidence-based justification for new guideline rates. The report concluded that more guideline rates should fall than be increased, albeit that it also proposed a change in the bandings which inevitably distorts this conclusion to a degree. To date the guideline rates have been seen as the floor below which a suitably qualified fee earner's rates could not fall. But the terms of the report are careful to say that figures above or below the guideline rates might be appropriate in a particular case. These words may pave the way for paying parties to argue that a rate below the relevant guideline rate should be allowed in the absence of any individual calculation, particularly on a standard basis assessment where the paying party gets the benefit of any doubt. Once in a while, an expense of time type calculation is contained within a witness statement from the receiving party's solicitor but it is far from common. The absence of any firm-specific information also leaves the field open to the paying parties' advocates to use the guideline rates as indicative of the direct cost and which (for reasons discussed below) can mean a ceiling on the recoverable hourly rates which is below the rates actually agreed with the client.

An expense of time calculation is feasible in private practice but what if you are an employed solicitor in an organisation? The Court of Appeal in *Re Eastwood* came to the entirely sensible conclusion that employed solicitors' rates should be treated as if they were in private practice so that convoluted evidence about overheads etc did not need to be produced on assessment. In *Sidewalk Properties Ltd v Twinn* [2015] UKUT 0122 (LC) the Upper Tribunal criticised the first-tier tribunal's decision to require evidence as to overheads to be produced on the basis that the 'old cases' were no longer good law. The first-tier tribunal should have relied on the long standing presumptions as to hourly rates in *Re Eastwood*.

Unrecordable time

[31.10]

Time not capable of being recorded and not included in the A factor, was described by Walton J in *Maltby v D J Freeman & Co (a firm)* [1978] 2 All ER 913, Ch D:

> 'No professional man, or senior employee of a professional man, stops thinking about the day's problems the minute he lifts his coat and umbrella from the stand and sets out on the journey home. Ideas, often very valuable ideas, occur in the train or car home, or in the bath, or even while watching television. Yet nothing is ever put down on a time sheet, or can be put down on a time sheet adequately to reflect this out of hours devotion of time.'

Supervision

[31.11]

We will see in *Re Frascati (in chambers)* (2 December 1981, unreported, QBD) (**[31.28]**) that time which should have been recorded but wasn't, should be taken into account in the A factor. What sort of time are we dealing with here? Supervision is one example.

R v Sandhu (29 November 1984, reported in the Lord Chancellor's Department's *Taxing Compendium*) identified three categories of supervision:

(i) The ordinary day-to-day supervision which is part of the overheads of the firm reflected in the basic mark-up – or indeed in the partners' non-chargeable time.

(ii) Supervision where a senior fee earner takes a direct hand in the case, in which event he should record his time and charge for it in the direct costs in the A factor.

(iii) Where a junior fee earner competently conducts the case with the assistance of regular but unquantified supervision from a senior fee earner whose time is not charged in the direct cost. This supervision is covered by the B factor.

A kissing cousin of supervision is the question of inter-fee earner discussions. Based on old, unreported cases, the submission is often made that such discussions are never recoverable between the parties and are tantamount to supervision. If they are not supervision, they are a manifestation of too many people being involved in the running of the case. That, we would suggest, is something of an old fashioned approach and that teamwork is often required in larger cases. Where there are members of a team, they need to be kept informed in some manner. The issue is really one of degree. As Laing J said in *TUI UK Ltd v Tickell* [2016] EWHC 2741 (QB):

> 'I agree with the Master that, in principle, if, as here, much of the work on files was being done by paralegals under the supervision of legal executives, it was necessary, from time to time, to have discussions between fee earners, specifically supervising solicitors, including partners.'

Consequently, the 144 hours of inter-fee earner discussion allowed by the costs judge were upheld.

Ascertaining the Profit Element ('B' Factor)

[31.12]

So far we have been concerned only with the cost of doing the work (the A factor), to which must, of course, be added the solicitor's reasonable profit (the B factor) to ascertain the hourly charging rate. This is an exercise in evaluating the prescribed factors other than time in CPR 44.4 or art 3. It is not an approach that is unique to solicitors. Businesses of all shapes and sizes regularly price work on the basis of cost plus profit.

The profit percentage in routine matters is generally accepted as 50%, in other words, one-third of the composite charging rate. In pre-CPR assessments travelling and waiting would not justify any B factor and attendance upon counsel in conference or trial would generally be allowed at 35%. Solicitor advocacy would often justify more than 50%. All of these percentages were based on the theory that the solicitor was taking more or less responsibility for the conduct of the case during the particular activity than the standard 50%. In a non-routine case the receiving party could seek an increased charging rate because of the B factor, and indeed the paying party could seek a reduction of the profit element. This is discussed below.

The use of a composite rate in the CPR has risked removing all of the controls, checks and balances built into between the parties' costs over the years. A combined rate in no way reduces the amount of costs, it merely makes the calculation less transparent. Whether or not the A and B factors are identified or concealed in a charging rate, they are still there in terms of costs plus profit. It should also be remembered that the B factor is not solely concerned with profit, it also covers such matters as unrecordable time, supervision and other indirect expenses which would otherwise be unremunerated.

Starting point for assessing the B factor

[31.13]

In *Property and Reversionary Investment Corpn Ltd v Secretary of State for the Environment* [1975] 2 All ER 436, [1975] 1 WLR 1504, 119 Sol Jo 274, Donaldson J said that when looking at the B factor:

> '. . . it is wrong always to start by assessing the direct and indirect expense to the solicitor, represented by the time spent on the business. This must always be taken into account, but it is not necessarily, or even usually, a basic factor to which all others are related. Thus, although the labour involved will usually be directly related to, and reflected by, the time spent, the skill and specialised knowledge involved may vary greatly for different parts of that time. Again not all time spent on a transaction necessarily lends itself to being recorded, although the fullest possible records should be kept.
>
> This error is compounded if, as an invariable rule, the figure representing the expense of recorded time spent on the transaction is multiplied by another figure to reflect the other factors. The present case provides an illustration of this error. The responsibility and value of the property involved were linked factors, but neither was affected by whether the recorded time spent was 30 hours or 60 hours. Yet the application of a multiplier would double the responsibility/value factor, if the recorded time spent had happened to be 60 rather than 30 hours.
>
> In my judgment the proper approach is to start by taking a broad look at "all the circumstances of the case" and in particular the general nature of the business. This should be followed by a systematic consideration of the factors specified in the paragraphs of [art 3] of the order.'

All the circumstances of the case are intended to be covered by the factors represented by the Seven Pillars of Wisdom.

THE SEVEN PILLARS OF WISDOM

[31.14]

In *Cox v MGN* [2006] EWHC 1235 (QB), the court explained that it is:

> '. . . required to take into account all the circumstances including, in particular, the factors listed at what is now CPR 44.4(3), which are sometimes referred to as the "Seven Pillars of Wisdom". It is necessary to have regard to the solicitor's particular skill, effort, specialised knowledge and responsibility. Obviously, also, the case in hand must be assessed for importance, complexity, difficulty or novelty. All the while the court will apply the test of proportionality.'

The phrase 'seven pillars of wisdom' comes originally from the Book of Proverbs and there is something almost biblical about the way it has stood firm against attempts to bring those pillars down over time. The seven pillars contained in Order 62 of the Rules of the Supreme Court were revised by the CPR to include the issue of conduct which lay centrally in the Woolf Reforms that led to the CPR. Consequently conduct became the first pillar and the issues of complexity and novelty had to share a bed in a later pillar. The Jackson reforms have added a further pillar by making reference to the receiving party's last approved or agreed budget. Whether the phrase 'the eight pillars of wisdom' will take hold is a matter for conjecture. These pillars were, until the recasting of the rules in April 2013, also used for considering the issue of proportionality by the *Lownds v Home Office* test ([**28.66**]).

But the new pillars – conduct of the parties and the level of a budget set during proceedings – do not assist with considering the factors in the case which establish the appropriate B factor to include in the hourly charging rate. So for our purposes, the seven pillars that need to be considered are the longer standing ones, namely:

(1) the amount or value of any money or property involved;
(2) the importance of the matter to all the parties;
(3) the complexity of the matter;
(4) the difficulty or novelty of the questions raised;
(5) the skill, labour, specialised knowledge and responsibility involved;
(6) the place where and the circumstance in which the work was done;
(7) the time spent on the case.

Together with the value of the case, the time spent is one of the only two factors that are quantifiable. The remaining factors are ones which the judge weighs in the balance, but cannot ascribe any particular figure to them. Let us look at some of them in more detail. The relevant case law comes largely from decisions on non-contentious business where the other factors have tended to weigh more heavily in bills which often have been fixed fee (gross sum) bills. When challenged by the client, the courts have been faced with deciding whether the fees charged are "fair and reasonable" without always having the crutch of hourly rates to fall back on.

But these cases are of value when trying to justify (or challenge) an hourly rate on detailed assessment and so they should not be dismissed as only relevant in non-contentious work, even if the value bands discussed immediately below do not appear to be relevant. They may, if nothing else, also give food for thought for 'hybrid' DBA arrangements where the mix of hourly rates and value relates to the successful outcome and does not run into the difficulty that the description 'hybrid DBA' usually connotes (see Chapter 7).

A word of warning. The invariable use of a rate which aggregates the A and B factors often leads to some artificiality in detailed assessment proceedings when advocates argue for a particular hourly rate based on an A plus B type calculation using the Seven Pillars of Wisdom. The importance to the client, the complexity of the case, the novelty etc are regularly referred to by the parties. But at no point is any suggestion made that the hourly rate claimed has been set with any such factors in mind. As is said in the introduction to this chapter, most solicitors use the same hourly rate for everything they do. It is at least arguable that the correct method of establishing the reasonable hourly rate cannot be for the court to consider a list of factors which the solicitor himself did not consider.

AMOUNT OR VALUE

[31.15]

The use of value to determine the charge to the client is discussed in detail at [**31.36**]. For the moment, it is enough to appreciate that the size of the subject matter in dispute can lead to greater responsibility for the solicitor. With such responsibility comes the possibility of justifying a higher charging rate.

In non-contentious work, one element of a solicitor's fees has been a sum based on the value of the property or estate involved. The current 'scale' is set out at [**31.36**] based on the case of *Jemma Trust v Liptrott* [2003] EWCA Civ 1476. As part of the Court's guidance, it said:

> 'There should be no hard and fast rule that charges cannot be made separately by reference to the value of the estate; value can, by contrast, be taken into account as part of the hourly rate; value can also be taken into account partly in one way and partly in the other. What is important is that (a) it should be transparent on the face of the bill how value is being taken into account; and (b) in no case should it be taken into account more than once.'

For contentious work, the value element has to be included within the hourly rate, at least insofar as the fees reflecting value are sought ultimately to be recovered from another party. In non-contentious work, the client will be paying and so the value element can be set out separately. This, at least in high value matters, is usually done by reference to a scale or yardstick of percentages which reduce as the value becomes higher. This is described as being 'regressive'. In *Treasury Solicitor v Regester* Donaldson J said:

> 'Turning now to value, we remind ourselves that scale fees have been abolished. Nevertheless, it is reasonable and fair to the client that the remuneration should not be disproportionate to the value of the property involved. It was therefore useful to employ a yardstick to assess that relationship. Various yardsticks, with a regressive basis, can be suggested . . . The fact is that there is no right yardstick, although some may be wrong.'

Donaldson J continued:

> 'Remuneration has to be assessed for all the circumstances taken together, and the purpose of a regressing yardstick is, as we have said, to check that the provisional figure bears a reasonable relationship to the value of the property. This is not only reasonable but also fair to both parties and in particular to the client.'

Even in 1978, proportionality had its place in the consideration of solicitors' fees.

SKILL ETC

[31.16]

Where a solicitor brings to bear great skill and experience far in excess of that of the average solicitor, or where one of the other factors such as complexity, documents, place, title or importance to the client may result in the amount of time spent being an irrelevance.

Although the *Property and Reversionary* and *Treasury Solicitor v Regester* cases dealt with non-contentious commercial matters, there is no reason why there should not be an identical approach in non-routine contentious matters, where the value, the adrenalin or another factor overwhelms the time involved. A gross sum bill to the client can be calculated on these principles. Should the client request a detailed bill or details be ordered on a Solicitors Act assessment the solicitor will be expected to produce a breakdown in terms of hourly rates. Even if the rates appear to be ludicrously high, the overall total may be justified on the approach of *Property and Reversionary* and *Treasury Solicitor v Regester*.

The display of skill by the solicitor in getting to the nub of the case or by bringing it home with the minimum effort ought to be rewarded and not penalised. This point is made under the heading 'Painful Plodder's Charter' at [**31.6**] above.

PLACE/CIRCUMSTANCES

[31.17]

In *Treasury Solicitor v Regester*, Donaldson J identified an additional factor, 'the adrenalin factor'. It is the increased responsibility when time becomes important in a different sense to the rest of this chapter – there is little time to play with and the solicitor has to get things right first time. It seems to us that this conveniently falls within the factor of 'the circumstances in which work or any part of it was done'. In any event, the judge described it in this way:

> 'We then looked at the eight factors and asked ourselves, what was the factor or factors, if any, which distinguished this transaction from the general run of such transactions? The answer was clearly "the adrenalin factor". By this, we mean that the solicitor had not only to work fast but had absolutely no margin for error. The transaction had to be completed by 31 July come what might, or their client had lost not only this deal but all possibility of avoiding the effects of the development land tax. In a different case we might have found that there was plenty of time and that the transaction was very similar to one with which the solicitors had previously been concerned for the same client. This would have caused us to look in the reverse direction . . . recorded time does not provide an arithmetical basis for a charge in cases such as this. Its relevance is to check whether the provisional figures for remuneration bear a reasonable relationship to the overheads attributable to the transaction. In this case, the figures which we had in mind did not seem to bear an unusual relationship to the overheads in a transaction of this type, and we therefore obtained no positive assistance from considering this factor.'

WHAT LEVEL OF B FACTOR TO CLAIM?

Starting point

[31.18]

In practice the starting point is to expect to claim 50% for the B factor as being appropriate for the run of the mill case. Most people will readily appreciate that if there is something that is out of the ordinary, it may increase the percentage towards, and sometimes over, 100%. But the beauty of the A and B approach is that the percentage allowed for the B factor could go down as well as up to bring the overall costs to an appropriate figure. So, where someone has made a meal or a mess of a case, the percentage increase for care and conduct for that work could be nothing.

In other cases, it could be much higher than average. For example, where a junior fee earner has done work which could justifiably have been done by a senior partner he may be rewarded with a 200% mark-up for care and conduct on his hourly expense rate. Similarly, if someone has been brilliant, or had extraordinary responsibility, or has been very expeditious, this is the place to take it into account – otherwise the fee earner will be penalised by his own expedition.

In these examples the paying party is not penalised by the A and B approach. The fee earner who made a meal of the case would find the extra work, if allowed, would do no more than make up for the lack of any B factor on the work that should have been required. The junior fee earner with a £125 an hour expense rate who is given a 200% mark-up receives no more than would a solicitor with a £250 an hour expense rate and a 50% mark-up. Similarly, a solicitor who did all the work himself quickly and without using counsel, even with a 200% mark-up, would be unlikely to cost the paying party any more than if the average solicitor had taken an average length of time and incurred average counsel's fees. A solicitor who is expeditious and efficient is entitled to benefit from, and not be penalised by, the lack of time he has spent on the matter. The result is reward for merit – and that is the difference between time-costing and time-charging.

Just one caveat to that. The higher the level of fee earner, the more he is expected to know. Therefore the higher the expense rate the lower the mark-up – you cannot expect to be rewarded twice.

Case law examples

[31.19]

There was consideration of the B factor mark-up in *Finley v Glaxo Laboratories Ltd* where Hobhouse J said:

> 'The solicitor claimed 125%. The Registrar allowed 85% so as to give a composite figure of £65 per hour in conjunction with the £35 per hour rate. The solicitor was, at the material times, effectively a sole practitioner. He had another solicitor with him for part of the time but that is not material to the present case. He had a special experience and knowledge of vaccine and similar matters. He brought to the consideration of the plaintiff's case a familiarity with the subject matter and a measure of expertise appropriate to a lawyer dealing with that class of case. It must also be borne in mind that he had acted for the plaintiff previously in the tribunal matter, so that he was aware of the background through that source. He is a practitioner in Newcastle . . . That takes me to the second half of the calculation, which is the question of uplift and the "B" factor.
>
> The district registrar is quite right that at the end of any assessment of this kind he should stand back for a moment and consider the implications and the overall picture presented by his decision on the detail. That is what he is doing there. But it also shows that there is a relationship between the percentage that he chose to allow and the hourly rate. There are many other passages in his reasons where he allows the overall profit assessment to colour his views about the hourly rate. I

> consider – and counsel has not sought to argue to the contrary – that, having substantially altered the hourly rate, it is appropriate and proper for me to reconsider the uplift that has been allowed.
>
> . . .
>
> I have to consider what is the appropriate uplift for a senior partner in the conduct of a case of this character at the stage which it had reached. The starting point for this exercise is 50%; that is the advice I received, and it is also the practice in the North East. If one is concerned with a High Court or potential High Court action, that is the appropriate starting point for the uplift. Likewise I am satisfied that 125% was far too high for a case of this kind. One of the reasons, I suspect, why 125% was even being considered by the solicitor is the too low figure that he might have feared he was going to be allowed as an hourly rate. As I have already made clear, I would not lend support to the adoption of an unduly low hourly rate and then seeking to put it right by applying a higher uplift percentage. The right approach is that which I have emphasised, namely to adopt a realistic approach to the hourly rate to reflect the actual cost of the fee earner involved, and then to apply an appropriate but not excessive uplift.
>
> The advice that I have had from my assessors in this matter is that no more than 75% is the maximum justifiable uplift in a case of this character, at the stage that it was at, and involving the work which it did involve at that stage. I am advised, and I have also formed the view, that 85% is too high and cannot be supported.'

Evans J also dealt with mark-up in *Johnson v Reed Corrugated* [1992] 1 All ER 169, QBD as follows:

> ' . . . the range for normal, ie non-exceptional cases, starts at 50% . . . an appropriate figure for "run-of-the-mill" cases. The figure increases above 50% so as to reflect a number of possible factors — including the complexity of the case, any particular need for special attention to be paid to it, and any additional responsibilities which the solicitor may have undertaken towards the client, and others, depending upon the circumstances—but only a small percentage of accident cases results in an allowance of over 70%. To justify a figure of 100% or even one closely approaching 100% there must be some combination of factors which mean that the case approaches the exceptional.'

He too allowed 75%.

The major test case of *Loveday v Renton (No 2)* [1992] 3 All ER 184, QBD relating to the whooping cough vaccine was adjudged to merit a 125% B factor. The action ran between 1982 and 1988 and culminated in a 300-page judgment which took two days to read. The trial itself lasted for 65 working days. The documentation ran to some 100 lever arch files and The Wellcome Foundation had prepared a 'library' of some 50 files containing literature on the subject. The case was truly exceptional in terms of weight, complexity and responsibility. In delivering his judgment Hobhouse J emphasised that the court deplored any artificially depressed rates being compensated for by artificially inflated mark-up figures. He continued:

> 'To justify an uplift in excess of 100% it is necessary, as has recently been re-stated by Evans J in Johnson v Reed Corrugated Cases Ltd to demonstrate that the case is exceptional. There has been a tendency among some firms of solicitors to put forward grossly inflated percentages by way of uplift and a failure to appreciate that to justify an uplift even as high as 100% requires the demonstration that the case is exceptional. In the present case, having regard to the features to which I have referred, I am satisfied (not without some hesitation) that the taxing master was

wrong to alter his own original assessment on bill A of an uplift of 125%. I consider that 125% is at the top end of the bracket of uplift which would be proper for this case overall and I would not have interfered with a figure which lay somewhere between 125% and 100%. But I do accept the solicitors' submission before me that 100% was too low for bill A and I therefore shall reinstate the original allowance of 125%.'

Self-imposed ceiling?

[31.20]

Based on the case law, solicitors cannot expect to obtain mark-ups in excess of 75% except in the heaviest and most complex cases and probably only those which involve a contested hearing. Unless the receiving party has some form of Expense of Time calculation, the only way the receiving party can demonstrate to the court its A factor direct cost is by dividing the guideline hourly rate into a notional A and B (invariably by deducting a third to represent a 50% uplift). Let's take the National Regional 2 Band A fee earner rate of £201 as our example. The notional A factor will be two thirds of this figure – £134 – and the B factor will be £67. If the B factor is increased to 75% the figure will be £100.50 which when added to the A factor achieves an hourly rate of £234.50. This is the rate that may be the maximum achievable for almost any case run by a solicitor in National Region 2. Whichever band is appropriate, receiving parties regularly find themselves in difficulty in justifying hourly rates on detailed assessment. This is because the A and B calculation requires them to justify 100% or more for the B factor on what cannot be described as exceptional cases of the *Loveday v Renton* type.

The issue is particularly acute where CFAs have meant that the client has had little interest in the hourly rates sought because he has been given an indication by his solicitor that the hourly rates are payable by the opponent and if the court reduces them on assessment the solicitor will live with that reduction. In such circumstances there is little incentive to put anything but an aspirational hourly rate in the client care and/or CFA documentation. If the rates you are seeking in your agreements with clients exceed the guideline rates in the table at **[31.25]**, you should consider making sure you have an Expense of Time type calculation discussed at the beginning of this chapter to justify your charging rates rather than having to rely on the guideline rates. If, as the report proposed, the guideline rates may come down in certain areas, action on this issue ought to be all the more pressing.

THE A AND B TEST

[31.21]

The first case following the introduction of the CPR to confirm that the A and B factors were alive and well was *Higgs v Camden and Islington Health Authority* [2003] EWHC 15 (QB). The nine-year-old claimant was awarded £3.5 million damages for inadequate care during the first 35 minutes of his life, resulting in catastrophic injuries. It was held that the guideline hourly rates had only limited significance in cases such as this, given in particular that brain damage at birth is a particularly sensitive subject matter for litigation and that the specific demands placed upon solicitors by clients and litigation friends will vary widely from case to case). The guidelines expressly state that costs and fees exceeding the guidelines 'may well be justified' in an appropriate case at the discretion of the court. Further, the guideline figures were not supposed to replace the experience and knowledge of those familiar with the local area and the field generally. Accordingly, the guideline figures were not of great value in this instance. The paying party on appeal criticised the costs judge for carrying out an old 'A plus B' calculation in order to test the reasonableness of the rate charged by the partner. However, the bill of costs did in fact claim an inclusive rate of £300 per hour and the court found that the costs judge did no more than use the A plus B method as one of the measures and indicators to ensure that he was able to gauge the propriety or otherwise of a figure of £300 per hour. He used the A plus B type analysis to inform his consideration of the reasonableness of the inclusive rate sought; he had in mind the solicitor's expense rate and he took the seven pillars of wisdom into account in reaching the final figure. The court upheld the award of £300 an hour which represented £150 an hour with a 100% mark-up. (It could, of course, have been £200 an hour with a 50% mark-up.)

In *KMT v Kent County Council* [2012] EWHC 2088 (QB), the claimant, together with her sisters were the subject of sexual, physical and emotional abuse while in the care of the defendant and brought claims via the Official Solicitor who instructed Irwin Mitchell. The costs judge decided that it was reasonable to instruct a Central London (now London 2) firm and allowed £335, £255, £180 and £120 for fee earners corresponding to guideline bands A to D respectively. The costs judge applied a 'cross-check' by taking the relevant guideline figure (£263 for the Grade A, by way of example) and reducing it by a third to deduct the notional 50% B factor said to be included in the guideline rates. That left him with £175 and to which he added a 75% B factor given the complexities of the case. This gives £307 in round terms and was sufficient to confirm to the costs judge that his assessment of a reasonable figure was supported by the cross check. Eady J on appeal described the approach adopted as 'one that falls very much within the remit of a costs judge'.

GUIDELINE HOURLY RATES

History

[31.22]

The Supreme Courts Costs Office (as it was then) originally issued Guideline Hourly Rates ('GHR') as part of its Guide to the Summary Assessment of Costs. That document was produced at the time of the introduction of the CPR at the behest of the then Vice Chancellor, Sir Richard Scott. The wording of the Guide has not altered but revised Rates were regularly issued by the SCCO until 2006. The 2007 and subsequent revisions were issued by the Master of the Rolls following reports from the Advisory Committee on Civil Costs ('ACCC'). During this latter period the revisions were essentially based on inflation rate rises. The last revision occurred in 2010 because the Master of the Rolls at the time required any further revisions to be evidence based and not simply an inflation increase on the existing figures. The ACCC was relieved of this responsibility by the Government and the baton was passed to the Costs Committee of the Civil Justice Council.

The terms of reference to the Costs Committee were 'to conduct a comprehensive, evidence-based review of the nature of the Guideline Hourly Rates and to make recommendations to the Master of the Rolls.' The deadline for this report was January 2014 but it was put back to March 2014 and was not in fact delivered until 29 May 2014. That slippage reflected the difficulties faced by the Committee in conducting a review that could properly be described as both comprehensive and evidence based. The participation in the Costs Committee's widely publicised survey was modest, albeit in line with response rates to Law Society surveys. Other survey data was also available to the Committee and in particular to its economist members. Nevertheless, in the absence of any budget to carry out dedicated research, the data gathered proved insufficient to give the Committee a great deal of confidence in some of its recommendations. Furthermore, the Master of the Rolls decided that he was obliged to reject the proposed GHR which he appreciated made the present position deeply unsatisfactory. He said that 'the evidence on which its recommendations are based is not a sufficiently strong foundation on which to adopt the rates proposed.' As such no changes would be made in the rates 'at the present time.' Far more comprehensive evidence would be required and that would require resources not available to the Committee so far. 'It is imperative that sound and reliable evidence is obtained.' You may consider that there is a certain irony in this laudable requirement for evidence to be needed to revise the rates. The original figures produced for the SCCO came from local law societies and court user groups convening to agree on the going rates in their locality. There was little evidence produced for these figures originally and they have been revised by reference to further town hall type meetings before increasing the rates for inflation. The Costs Committee's figures do have some evidence to support their figures even if it is not comprehensive.

Use of the Guideline Hourly Rates

[31.23]

As is implicit in the title of the document in which the GHR are included ('Guide to the Summary Assessment of Costs), they have been intended for use in summary assessments rather than detailed assessments. The Guide refers to their use at the end of Fast Track trials or interim hearings lasting less than a day. The genesis of the Guide, including the GHR, was for the benefit of judges who were suddenly required to carry out summary assessments as a result of the advent of the CPR.

Accordingly, whenever hourly rates are challenged at a detailed assessment, one party (invariably the receiving party) decries the use of the GHR because they are only relevant to summary assessment. It is said by such parties, often quoting first instance case law, that the GHR can be no more than a starting point, or possibly a cross check, for the rate allowed by the judge. The calculation of the hourly rate should be carried out by a consideration of the Pillars of Wisdom discussed earlier in this Chapter. Such consideration allows for a deeper understanding of the factors of the case which give rise to an appropriate hourly rate – a luxury not afforded to a judge at the end of a fast track trial or application.

In practice, many courts have taken the view that the GHR is, or should be, the going rate to be allowed and rarely, if ever, deviate from the published figures. Where practitioners have courts with such views, the GHR does become the going rate since few solicitors wish to appeal their local district judges repeatedly on such matters. The tension between those who use the GHR as a starting point and those who use it rigidly is clearly set out in the Costs Committee's report. The Committee's general view seems to us to set out the correct position at paragraph 6.7.5:

> '. . . while summary and detailed assessments are distinct processes, it is unrealistic for them to be completely disaggregated and was mindful of the fact that the evidence considered by the Committee was not focused on seeking to distinguish between the expense of time and various mark ups associated with hourly rates for the kind of case which would result in a summary assessment compared with one that would be the subject of a detailed assessment. The GHR are themselves guidelines and a benchmark for summary assessments. As such, they may provide a helpful starting point in the detailed assessment process, but no more than that. The court's discretion and exercise of judgment in the application of the eight pillars of wisdom will be of significance in both forms of assessment, more obviously so in detailed assessments.'

The GHR are set out in a table which is made up of grades of fee earner and geographical bands. The terminology has suffered from unnecessary meddling. The different categories of fee earners have been referred to as 'grades' of fee earner, apart from the 2010 GHR which, for no obvious reason, decided to call them 'bands'. That change in terminology has not seemingly registered with practitioners or the judiciary. The word 'band' has continued to be use to distinguish the locality of solicitors. When fee earners were banded rather than graded, geographical bands became regions. That change in appellation has not stuck either. The Costs Committee's report uses grades for fee earners and bands for location and we unapologetically do the same, notwithstanding the rejection of the revised GHR which arguably leaves the 2010 GHR intact in relation to such matters.

Revision of the Guideline Hourly Rates

[31.24]

It will not have escaped your attention that it is a decade since the last revision of the GHR. Complaints by receiving parties about the geriatric nature of the rates were, for a long time, couched in diplomatic terms at detailed assessment hearings. However, the dam of frustration burst as soon as O'Farrell J, in *Ohpen Operations UK Ltd v Invesco Fund Managers Ltd* [2019] EWHC 2504 (TCC), criticised the GHR's vintage when assessing a City firm's costs summarily. With some understatement she said:

> '. . . the hourly rates of the defendant's solicitors are much higher than the SCCO guideline rates. It is unsatisfactory that the guidelines are based on rates fixed in 2010 and reviewed in 2014, as they are not helpful in determining reasonable rates in 2019. The guideline rates are significantly lower than the current hourly rates in many London City solicitors, as used by both parties in this case. Further, updated guidelines would be very welcome.'

Almost overnight, advocates appeared to be pitying the court's task of assessing hourly rates when having to rely on figures that were so obviously out of date. O'Farrell J's views are not alone. HHJ Davis-White QC, sitting as a High Court Judge in *Crumpler v Candey Ltd* [2019] EWHC 3558 (Ch), had no difficulty in accepting the rates claimed by the solicitor were similar to those of other firms involved in related proceedings. Rates of £500–£700 for Grade A and £300–£400 were well above even City of London rates (see below) but, as it was a dispute between a solicitor and its former client, the judge preferred to work from these rates since they had been agreed at the start of the retainer. The use of GHR rates and an extrapolation of A and B Factor calculations were roundly rejected.

There is certainly a wind blowing towards some form of revision of the mature GHR figures. This leads immediately to the problem of evidence (see previous heading). If we are to assume that solicitors would be no better at providing the necessary information than they have been previously, what can any committee do? It appears that data is being collected for the purpose of potential recommendations. In the meantime, news of any first instance decisions touching upon the GHR figures is eagerly seized upon eg, Master Whalan's decision on Court of Protection cases in the matters of *PLK and others* [2020] EWHC B28 (Costs) even if they are clearly seeking to limit their applicability to a discrete area or set of facts.

Grades of Fee Earner

[31.25]

Originally there were only two grades of fee earner but that swiftly increased to four and which have not altered thereafter. The Costs Committee recommended, and the Master of the Rolls accepted, that the category of qualification needed to come within a particular grade, ought to be updated. Consequently, they have been revised to reflect the advance of Chartered Legal Executives and costs lawyers. However, Lord Dyson did not accept the proposal that there should be a fifth category to reflect more junior fee earners – usually described as 'paralegals' – as category (E).

Neither the Costs Committee nor the Master of the Rolls considered that there should be a further category (dubbed A*) to cater for fee earners with much more than eight years' litigation experience. Also, there was no recommendation for GHR for specific types of work even though personal injury, clinical negligence and commercial work were considered. Accordingly, the categories are now as follows:

(A) Solicitors and Chartered Legal Executives with 8 years' or more post qualification experience.*

(B) Solicitors and Chartered Legal Executives with four years' or more post qualification experience. Costs lawyers undertaking advocacy or litigation.

(C) Solicitors and Chartered Legal Executives with less than four years' post qualification experience. Costs lawyers with more than 1 years' experience.

(D) Trainee solicitors, paralegals and other fee earners. Costs lawyers with less than 1 years' experience.

*Post-qualification civil litigation experience.

The advancement of Chartered Legal Executives and costs lawyers is built upon the increased recognition and regulation caused by the Legal Services Act 2007. The Costs Committee and the Master of the Rolls accepted that Legal Executives were now partners in law firms as well as being appointed to the bench. Costs lawyers have passed examinations and are subject to individual regulation by the Costs Lawyers Standards Board. Consequently, there is a distinction to be drawn between both of these categories of legal professional and unqualified and unregulated paralegals, managing clerks and costs draftsmen. The Guide to Summary Assessment made this point in respect of Fellows of the Institute of Legal Executives (as they were then) but the point will no doubt be bolstered whenever new guidance is eventually published.

Where a fee earner is very experienced, but unqualified, it is possible to seek a grade higher than D. But, as with almost all things, he who asserts must prove. So if you have such a fee earner you should think about producing a witness statement to set out the experience rather than rely on assertions made by your advocate. In *Paturel v Marble Arch Services Ltd* [2005] EWHC 1055 (QB), Cox J, with the benefit of her assessors' advice, allowed an unqualified legal executive to receive a Grade B rate (which had also been allowed at the original assessment), where he could also point to 15 years of prior litigation experience.

The Guide states that:

> '. . . many High Court cases justify fee earners at a senior level. However the same may not be true of attendance at pre-trial hearings with counsel. The task of sitting behind counsel should be delegated to a more junior fee earner in all but the most important pre-trial hearings. As with hourly rates the costs estimate supplied by the paying party may be of assistance. What grade of fee earner did they use?
>
> In some proceedings solicitors appear as advocates more frequently than they used to. It must be borne in mind that, especially in substantial hearings, it may be more economical if the advocacy is conducted by counsel rather than a solicitor. In all cases the court should consider whether the decision to instruct counsel has led to an increase in costs and whether that increase is justifiable.'

The Guide also points out that an hourly rate in excess of the guideline figures may be appropriate for Band A fee earners in substantial and complex litigation where other factors, including the value of the litigation, the level of complexity, the urgency or importance of the matter as well as any international element would justify a significantly higher rate to reflect higher average costs.

For example, in *Global Marine Drillships Ltd v La Bella* [2010] EWHC 2498 (Ch D), Smith J on a summary assessment held that although the guideline figure for a Grade A fee earner was £317, given the nature of the application and the urgency, a figure higher than the guideline figure was justified and he allowed £400. It was an application for committal and the defendant faced being sent to prison.

Locality of Fee Earners

[31.26]

We have already mentioned the unnecessary substitution of the word 'region' for 'band' in earlier versions of the GHR. There has also been a change in the three London bands which were described as City, Central and Outer London but are now known by the more utilitarian London 1, 2 and 3. The then Senior Costs Judge's dictum of 'City rates for City work' does not have the same ring if 'London 1' is used instead. The Costs Committee recommended a change to two London bands, ie Inner and Outer London. The latter would be based on the London boroughs, a sensible idea compared with the current arrangement set out at PD 47, para 4 which includes Gravesend but not Wembley or Romford for example which would appear to be more obviously London. However, this recommendation has fallen foul of the general rejection of the proposed hourly rates so we remain with three London bands set out in the tables below.

For work done outside London, there has been a relentless consolidation. Initially, there were GHR for each court. They were then swept up into three bands seemingly based loosely on court groupings. More recently the bands have effectively reduced to two bands since bands 2 and 3 have the same rates. The Costs Committee recommended a single National band. However the recommendation is described as being that 'the Committee feels left with no alternative but to recommend a single National rate outside London' with the proviso of good grounds being shown to a court in a claim for a local variation. The terms of the recommendation show clearly that the Committee did not think that it had the evidence it needed on this subject so there is no surprise that it was not accepted.

In some ways, one of the main uses for the regional bands has been to be a tool for paying parties to use to argue about the use of solicitors from a more expensive region by the receiving party (see 'Distant solicitor' [**31.32**]).

The Guideline Hourly Rates

[31.27]

The Guideline Hourly Rates are set out below.

Year	Guideline Hourly Rates 2010				Costs Committee's Recommendations			
Bands	A	B	C	D	A	B	C	D
London 1	409	296	226	138	375	265	194	147
London 2	317	242	196	126	375	265	194	147
London 3	229–267	172–229	165	121	261	173	140	112
National 1	217	192	161	118	237	157	127	102
National 2	201	177	146	111	237	157	127	102

As set out above, the GHR are often used as a starting point in detailed assessments as well as in summary assessments. It must be arguable that the figures proposed by the Costs Committee are also a useful, if different, starting point. After all, they are based on information obtained more recently: the

2010 GHR are based on little evidence originally with subsequent increases for inflation. The Costs Committee recommendations are based on Inner and Outer London together with one National band as discussed above.

Any case less than ten years' old only needs to have the 2010 GHR figures, rather than the earlier versions. For these reasons we have set out the 2010 GHR together with the Costs Committee's figures in the table above. The following is a separate table going back to 2003 for cases that have taken rather longer to reach their conclusion.

Year	2003				2005			
Bands	A	B	C	D	A	B	C	D
London 1	342	247	189	116	359	259	198	122
London 2	263	200	163	105	276	210	171	110
London 3	189–221	142–189	137	100	198–232	149–198	144	105
National 1	175	155	130	95	184	163	137	100
National 2	165	145	120	90	173	152	126	95
National 3	150	135	115	85	158	142	121	90
Year	2007				2008			
Bands	A	B	C	D	A	B	C	D
London 1	380	274	210	129	396	285	219	134
London 2	292	222	181	116	304	231	189	121
London 3	210–246	158–210	152	111	219–256	165–219	158	116
National 1	195	173	145	106	203	180	151	110
National 2	183	161	133	101	191	168	139	105
National 3	167	150	128	95	174	156	133	99
Year	2009							
Bands	A	B	C	D				
London 1	402	291	222	136				

London 2	312	238	193	124	
London 3	225–263	169–225	168	124	
National 1	213	189	158	116	
National 2/3	198	174	144	109	

Finally, the following table sets out the current geographical bands.

London 1	EC1, EC2, EC3, EC4
London 2	W1, WC1, WC2, SW1
London 3	All other London postcodes (W, NW, N, E, SE, SW) and Bromley, Croydon, Dartford, Gravesend and Uxbridge
National 1	Aldershot, Basingstoke, Birkenhead, Birmingham Inner, Bournemouth (including Poole), Cambridge City, Canterbury, Cardiff (Inner) Chelmsford South, Dorset, Epsom, Essex and East Suffolk, Fareham, Farnham, Guildford, Hampshire, Harlow, Isle of Wight, Kingston, Leeds Inner (within 2 kilometres radius of the City Art Gallery), Lewes, Liverpool, Maidstone, Medway, Manchester Central, Newcastle City Centre (within a 2-mile radius of St Nicholas Cathedral), Norwich (City), Nottingham (City), Oxford, Portsmouth, Southampton, Swindon, Thames Valley, Watford, Winchester, Wiltshire
National 2/3	Altrincham, Bath, Birmingham (Outer), Bradford, Bury St Edmunds, Cambridge County, Cardiff (Outer), Chelmsford North, Cheltenham, Chester, Cornwall, Coventry, Cumbria, Derbyshire, Devon, Dewsbury, Doncaster, Dudley, Evesham, Exeter, Gloucester, Grimsby, Halifax, Harrogate, Hereford, Hertford, Hitchin, Huddersfield, Hull (City), Hull (Outer), Keighley, Kidderminster, Leeds (Outer), Leicester, Leigh, Lincoln, Lowestoft, Ludlow, Luton, Manchester (Outer), Newcastle (other than City Centre), Newport, Norfolk, Northampton, Nottingham, Nuneaton, Oswestry, Peterborough, Plymouth, Pontefract, Redditch, Ripon, Rugby, Scarborough, Sheffield, Shrewsbury, Skegness, Skipton, South Yorkshire, Stafford, Stourbridge, Stratford, St Helens, Stoke, Tamworth, Taunton, Teesside, Telford, Salford, Southport, Stockport, Swansea, Wakefield, Wales (North, South & West), Walsall, Warwick, Wigan, Wolverhampton, Worcester, Yeovil, York

ASSESSING THE TIME SPENT

Proving the time was spent

[31.28]

The costs officer must be satisfied that the amount of time claimed was actually spent. Properly kept and detailed time records are helpful in support of a bill provided they explain the nature of the work as well as recording the time involved. In *Jemma Trust Co Ltd v Liptrott* [2003] EWCA Civ 1476, the court held that there was no obligation on a solicitor to keep attendance notes in respect of either contentious or non-contentious work. The true position is that in both kinds of work the burden is on the solicitor not only to show that the time claimed has been spent, but that it had been reasonable to spend that time. The keeping of an attendance note is one way, but not the only way, in which this can be demonstrated. The failure to keep such notes exposes the solicitor to the risk of being unable to prove the reasonableness of the time spent. In the *Jemma Trust* case the costs judge, after examining all the files, was satisfied that the time recorded had been reasonably spent.

While the absence of records could result in the disallowance or diminution of the charges claimed, the records themselves will not be accepted as conclusive evidence that the time recorded either has been spent, or if spent, is 'reasonably' or 'proportionately' chargeable. Always keep in mind the words of Payne J in *Re Kingsley* (1978) 122 Sol Jo 457:

> 'I ought to add that this case illustrates the dangers which are present if reliance is placed on a modern system of recording, without at the same time retaining the old and well tried practice of keeping attendance notes showing briefly the time taken and the purport of the work done day by day. It may be that this case will invite attention to the importance of appreciating the limits to which the computer system can be used in cases where taxation of costs must follow litigation and to the necessity of preserving as well the use of the traditional systems.'

Whilst there has been a reluctance in general to accept computer print-outs as incontrovertible evidence of the number of hours spent since then, the general 'electrification' of the detailed assessment process recently (see Chapter 28), has led to much less of the 'garbage in, garbage out' mentality.

Letters received and copies of letters sent, instructions to counsel, statements of case, witness statements and all other documents are tangible records and evidence of the work involved. All other work, such as attendances on the client, counsel, court and witnesses, telephone conversations, perusals, considering the facts and law, does not automatically create records of itself and a solicitor must be able to prove that he has done work of this nature. The best way is to create and keep records of it. Inferences can be drawn and oral evidence given but it is in the solicitor's interests to have available on assessment the best possible evidence of work done, and this can most easily be provided by making contemporaneous records. However, here are some words of comfort from Parker J in *Re Frascati (in chambers)* (2 December 1981, unreported, QBD):

> 'The right to charge cannot depend upon the question whether discussions are recorded or unrecorded. It must depend, initially, upon whether they in fact took place and occupied the time claimed. If they are recorded in attendance notes this will no doubt ordinarily be accepted as sufficient evidence of those facts. If they are

not so recorded it may well be that the claimant is unable to satisfy the taxing (costs) officer or master (costs judge) as to the facts. But neither the presence nor the absence of an attendance note is conclusive. It may well be for example that it is wholly impractical in some instances to keep such notes. In an exceptionally complex case, such as this which is occupying two fee earners there may be short but important discussions in respect of which it would be wholly unreasonable to expect attendance notes to be kept. In such cases an estimate of the time involved is inevitable. The question which then arises for decision is whether the estimate given is reasonable. This is a matter wholly for the taxing authorities. In general, however, all such discussions involving any substantial period of time should be recorded and an estimated addition should only be allowed for short discussions which it would be impracticable to record.'

A number of points arise:

(1) We are dealing here with time which could have been recorded but for some reason was not, and not with unrecordable time, such as supervision, which is covered, depending upon its nature, by either the 'A' or the 'B' factor (see [**31.11**]).

(2) How the time was recorded does not, for these purposes, matter. It can be on the most sophisticated computer system or on the back of old envelopes. If the latter contains greater detail of the work which was done it is preferable to the former. The problem with most computer systems is that they do not require, and the fee earner regularly fails to provide, a sufficient narrative. A separate file note is essential. With a mark-up for care and control on all contentious work it is not only the time but also the quality of the work that needs to be recorded. A standard form of memorandum with a panel in which to indicate the relevant CPR Rule 44.4 factors for mark-up could be invaluable.

(3) Experience shows that many solicitors have now trained themselves adequately to record the time spent on attendances but they are not so well disciplined in respect of time spent on the preparation and perusal of documents such as pleadings, instructions to counsel and, particularly in long actions, refreshing their memory from the statements of case, affidavits, attendance notes, correspondence and opinions. These are the danger areas.

(4) Time spent considering the law and procedure is usually non-chargeable – and the higher the expense rate, the more law and procedure the fee earner is expected to know. In a review of criminal costs it was held that leading and junior counsel can be assumed to be fully up-to-date with the law in the field in which they hold themselves out as practising in and they will not be paid for researching the law unless the case is unusual or infrequent (*Perry v Lord Chancellor* (1994) Times, 26 May, QBD). The same principle of course applies to civil work and to solicitors.

(5) Where there has been an omission to record time, the costs draftsman – and the costs officer – must rely on their own experience to assess from the documents in the file what time a competent solicitor would have spent on their preparation and perusal. The documents prove the work has been done but someone has to put a time and value on that work.

In *Johnson v Reed Corrugated Cases Ltd* [1992] 1 All ER 169, QBD Evans J was less enthusiastic about giving credit for unrecorded time, saying:

'In my judgment, the submission that there were unrecorded occasions when chargeable time was spent on these cases must be rejected. This leaves the registrar's decision that in practice not all time will be fully recorded, even for those items of work in respect of which a claim is made. The claims invariably are for global figures, mostly to the nearest five minutes. No doubt there were some occasions when the periods spent were slightly more, others when it was slightly less. There is no evidence that any substantial items were not recorded at all. In my judgment, therefore, this item must be disallowed.'

Was the time reasonably spent?

[31.29]

This is an objective test between the parties. Was it reasonable to do all the work that was done and was it done within a reasonable time? If on the standard basis, was it proportionate to the matters in issue? If it was excessive or irrelevant it will be unreasonable or disallowed. In contentious costs on the standard basis any doubt as to reasonableness will be resolved in favour of the paying party. Between a solicitor and his client the same objective tests apply, together with the express and implied subjective assumptions prescribed by CPR 46.9(3). Since solicitor and client costs are assessed on the indemnity basis, any doubt will be resolved in favour of the solicitors.

The level of fee earner

[31.30]

Has a senior partner done work which should have been done by a junior solicitor? If so, only the expense rate of a junior solicitor can be allowed. Has a junior solicitor done the work of a senior partner? Again only the expense rate of a junior solicitor can be allowed. However, in both examples, the hourly rate can be appropriately adjusted by the application of the other prescribed factors – perhaps to award the partner for his expertise and expedition and the junior solicitor for punching above his weight.

Is the hourly rate too high?

[31.31]

As already mentioned, rates above the going rate can be claimed on the basis of the prescribed factors other than time, but there are other circumstances in which the going rate for a particular court may be exceeded on a detailed assessment.

In *Jones v Secretary of State for Wales* [1997] 2 All ER 507, QBD, a provincial firm of solicitors' costs were allowed at a higher figure than the local rate because it demonstrated that it was more specialised than the norm for the area. Pitmans of Reading were in effect a London firm who had moved to Reading and were doing work that only a London firm could do. The judge was of the view that it would be odd and undesirable if the higher London rate could be recovered by a London firm, but not the somewhat lower rate claimed by Pitmans for doing a case which otherwise would probably have to be handled by a London firm.

A note of caution about this approach was sounded in *Cox v MGN*:

'If you wish to take yourself out of the norm you have to provide the court with evidence to enable you to do so. You may have a niche practice, and you may be able

> to persuade celebrities that you are the solicitor to go to at whatever rate you choose to charge them, but without evidence that your overheads are out of the ordinary there is no basis for holding that a Jones [*Jones v Secretary of State for Wales* [1997] 2 All ER 507] increase should apply.'

In *Jones* there was evidence that the salary costs were similar to a London firm rather than a Reading firm thereby enabling Pitmans to explain the increased overheads in the manner referred to in *Cox*.

Distant solicitor

[31.32]

In *Truscott v Truscott, Wraith v Sheffield Forgemasters Ltd* [1998] 1 All ER 82, CA and *Sullivan v Co-operative Insurance Society Ltd* ([1999] 2 Costs LR 158, CA, the Court of Appeal addressed the question of whether the liability of an unsuccessful party ordered to pay costs should be restricted to what a reasonably competent solicitor practising in the area of the court (or in the area where the successful party lived) might have been expected to charge, or whether the successful party should be entitled to recover the sums claimed by the solicitor who was in fact instructed to act on his behalf. The court held that a costs judge had to consider whether, having regard to all the relevant considerations, the successful party had acted reasonably in instructing the particular solicitors.

In *Truscott* the claimant had been ill-served by local solicitors in the Brighton County Court and had instructed London solicitors who rectified the matter and obtained a wasted costs order against the original solicitors. The court held that it was reasonable for a London firm to have been instructed in these circumstances and that as their charges were reasonable by London standards they were allowed. The same principles applied in *Wraith* but in that case the only reason why the work went to London solicitors was that the claimant's trade union had adopted the practice of sending all their work to these solicitors. The action was proceeding in the Sheffield District Registry and the court was satisfied there were firms of solicitors in Sheffield or Leeds well qualified to do the work. The trade union knew, or ought to have known, what sort of legal fees it would have to expend to obtain competent services and their connection with one firm of solicitors in London was of limited relevance. *Sullivan* applied the same test over the Pennines, holding there were in Manchester, and in many other centres outside London, legal practitioners who conducted cases of substantially greater weight and complexity than the present case, every day of their working lives. Although the fact that a trade union or other organisation habitually used a particular firm of solicitors was a relevant factor, it was of limited relevance in an individual case. There were no weighty factors in the context of costs justifying the trade union in employing London solicitors to conduct litigation in Manchester. Subjectively the choice may have been entirely reasonable, but between the parties the various circumstances had to be balanced objectively.

The following cases provide examples of how the Court of Appeal guidance has been applied to specific cases by the High Court.

Wraith was followed in *A v Chief Constable of South Yorkshire Police* [2008] EWHC 1658 (QB) where in proceedings in Sheffield the court disallowed the costs of specialist London solicitors on the grounds that a reasonable person in the position of the claimant would have enquired about solicitors in Sheffield with experience of bringing claims against the police. Such enquiries would have brought to his attention a law firm in Sheffield that undertook police misconduct cases. He would have appreciated that there was a substantial difference in rates and would have instructed the Sheffield firm.

In *Ryan v Tretol Group Ltd* [2002] EWHC 1956 (QB), the claimant in an asbestosis claim instructed local solicitors, but after the legal executive dealing with the matter left the firm, the claimant was dissatisfied with the service he was receiving. The claim was legally and factually complex and in the circumstances it was reasonable for the claimant to change his legal representatives to a London firm with considerable asbestosis experience in the absence of other firms with similar experience in the claimant's locality.

Subjective factors also applied in *Higgins v Ministry of Defence* [2010] EWHC 654 (QB). At the age of 82 the claimant, who lived in Broadstairs in Kent, was diagnosed with asbestosis by a local consultant who told Mr Higgins that his condition was advanced and there was no treatment. By this time Mr Higgins was able to walk very little, and his daughter had moved in to care for him. The consultant mentioned a firm of solicitors in Central London, fieldfisher, who had experience in these matters and whom the claimant consulted.

The claimant had been exposed to asbestos during the course of his work for the Ministry of Defence in Davenport and the solicitors were able to reach a settlement, but could not agree the costs. The solicitors claimed an hourly rate of £345 while the defendants argued that according to the guidelines for summary assessment the recoverable hourly rate would have been up to £200 for Kent and up to £250 for outer London firms. The judge could find no point of principle saying: 'It is not in dispute that a reasonable litigant would normally be expected to investigate the hourly rates of solicitors whom he might instruct, and that he will normally be expected to consider a number of other factors, including the time and costs associated with geographical location, before choosing whom to instruct and to take advice on these and other matters before he does so'. It would not be objectively reasonable to expect an 82 year old man who had just been informed that he was incurably ill, to undertake a trawl of local solicitors, in circumstances where an experienced consultant had given him the name of fieldfisher as solicitors who specialised in this field. None of the alternative firms whose names were put forward were markedly more accessible from Broadstairs than is London. The costs judge had considered all the relevant factors including the claimant's age and the urgency of the case before deciding it reasonable for Mr Higgins to have instructed fieldfisher and it would not be appropriate for the court to interfere with his decision on appeal.

Gazeley v Wade [2004] EWHC 2675 (QBD) went the other way. The appellant appealed against a decision that he should recover costs from the respondents on the basis of rates applicable to solicitors in the Norwich area although his solicitors were London libel specialists. The costs judge was not wrong to find it unreasonable for the appellant to instruct London libel specialists rather than a local firm in Norwich in respect of his defamation claim against a national newspaper even though he erred in deciding that the case 'was obviously a Norfolk case'. The fact that the claimant was from Norfolk did not make it a Norfolk case. At the relevant time the likelihood was that the hearing would have been in London. Moreover, it was a grave libel published nationwide by defendants based in London. However, it was important to recognise that in order to have the necessary or proportionate expertise available, it was not always necessary to instruct London specialist solicitors. An important factor was that any competent litigation solicitor in the country could call upon specialist members of the Bar at very short notice. The costs judge's conclusion of the unreasonableness of instructing London solicitors was based on the particular facts of the case, in the light of his very wide experience of litigation generally, including the role of specialist practitioners.

That the nature of the work is relevant to the level of fees was demonstrated by the senior costs judge in *King v Telegraph Group Ltd* [2004] EWCA Civ 613. City rates for City solicitors are recoverable only where the City solicitor is undertaking City work, which is normally heavy commercial or corporate work. Defamation is not in that category, and, particularly given the reduction in damages awards for libel, is never likely to be. A City firm which undertakes work, which could be competently handled by a number of Central London solicitors, is acting unreasonably and disproportionately if it seeks to charge City rates.

COUNSEL'S FEES

Guideline application fees

[31.33]

Prior to their latest incarnation, there used to be, at the end of the SCCO Guide to Summary Assessment, benchmark rates for counsel's attendance at short hearings. Unlike the solicitors' rates, the benchmark rates for counsel were very rarely relied upon in detailed assessments. That probably explains why they are no longer incorporated in the guidance and we have followed suit by omitting the text here. The figures can be found in previous editions or in older SCCO Guide to Summary Assessments.

The starting point

[31.34]

The test for counsel's fees is usually said to come from *Simpsons Motor Sales (London) Ltd v Hendon Corporation* [1964] 3 All ER 833, [1965] 1 WLR 112. The fee is based on a reasonably competent counsel being instructed rather than someone pre-eminent in the field.

The test for the reasonableness of using leading counsel is generally taken from the case of *Juby v London Fire and Civil Defence Authority* [1990] Lexis Citation 2078. In fact it discusses and gives guidance on the relevant factors for using two counsel; leading counsel alone or junior counsel alone. The guidance is useful notwithstanding an overall view from the judge that all decisions are case specific. Much more recently, Moulder J in *Bush v King* (07/11/2017) considered the question of when it is reasonable to instruct leading counsel when concluding that the costs judge had applied the wrong test. It was not a question of whether or not the trial was within the capability of the existing junior counsel but it was the separate question of whether it was reasonable to instruct leading counsel based on the seven pillars of wisdom in CPR 44.4.

Brief fees

[31.35]

The traditional approach is that the time spent is a relevant factor in assessing a brief fee but it is not appropriate to determine a brief fee simply by having regard to an hourly rate. In *XYZ v Schering Health Care* SCCO Costs Appeal No 9 of 2004 leading counsel had been required to prepare large amounts of material, and to undertake complex cross-examinations which required highly specialised skills. It could not be said that his brief fee was unreasonable.

There is a trend towards brief fees becoming more regularly the product of hours multiplied by hourly rate. Large corporations such as insurance companies as well as Government departments appear to be wedded to the idea that hourly rates provide certainty and transparency. How they could be any more certain or transparent than a previously agreed fixed fee is not immediately obvious. Nevertheless, the arithmetical approach has achieved a sufficient hold that the Bar Council's advisory note entitled 'Counsel's Fee Notes and Records' exhorts counsel to keep records of the complexity, urgency etc wherever the brief fee agreed exceeds the number of hours spent multiplied by counsel's hourly rate.

Historically, brief fees were payable in full once the brief had been delivered even if the case settled prior to the hearing. That 'old, very old, rule' according to Jack J in *Miller v Hales* [2006] EWHC 1717 (QB) meant that counsel's clerk was keen to 'deem' a brief as being delivered even when the papers had not physically arrived. More recently, it has been accepted that the brief should 'abate' to a sum which reflected the work actually done by the time of settlement and, possibly, the hole in counsel's diary that such settlement created.

VALUE BILLING IN NON-CONTENTIOUS BUSINESS

[31.36]

The assessment of fair and reasonable remuneration is an art not a science. It is arrived at by a commonsense feel of the matter – not by the application of a rigid formula by a computer. The charging options available in non-contentious matters are hourly rate only; hourly rate plus value; fixed fee; contingency fee agreement; or non-contentious business agreement. The last three categories are dealt with elsewhere in Part 2 of this book. Hourly rates have been dealt with earlier in this chapter so the following comments concentrate on the idea of charging the client an hourly rate based fee with a value charge in addition.

Hourly rate plus value

[31.37]

In certain areas of work, such as probate, it may be appropriate to include a value element in the method of charging. However, the question of whether a value element is charged is a matter of judgement for the solicitor and for agreement between the solicitor and the client. It is certainly not mandatory.

Where a value element is used, the overall consideration must always be that the charges are fair and reasonable, having regard to all the circumstances of the matter, in accordance with Article 3 of the Solicitors' (Non-Contentious Business) Remuneration Order 2009, as amended.

The leading case in this area is *Jemma Trust Co Ltd v Liptrott* [2003] EWCA Civ 1476. The Court of Appeal held that a value charge can either be made in addition to an hourly rate, or it can be included in the hourly rate, but the value element must not be reflected in both charges. Where appropriate, charges may consist of two elements:

(1) *Hourly rate*. This should be an inclusive figure incorporating the fee earner's expense rate and any appropriate care and conduct uplift. [So if the second (value) element is not charged, the solicitor is remunerated in the normal way.]

(2) *Value element*. Account may be taken of the value of the assets in the estate. In calculating the value element of the charge, the following approach may be helpful:

First, consider the value, nature and number of assets. It is usual to divide the estate (ie total value of the assets left after death) into two parts:

(a) *The deceased's residence*. The value of the deceased's home, or as much of it as he or she owned, if it was shared with another person. For example, where the property is jointly owned by two people, the value is reduced by half.

(b) The value of the rest of the estate.

Second, apply an appropriate percentage. An appropriate percentage should be considered in the light of the circumstances of the matter but the following may be helpful:

(a) Solicitor not acting as an executor – Value of gross estate less residence 1%; Value of residence 0.5%;

(b) Solicitor acting as sole executor or joint executor with another person – Value of gross estate less residence 1.5%; Value of residence 0.75%.

The final figure should always be reviewed to ensure that the charges are fair and reasonable having regard to all the circumstances.

High value estates

[31.38]

When dealing with high value estates, consideration should be given to reducing the value element percentage charged in order to ensure that the overall level of charge is fair and reasonable.

In *Jemma Trust*, the costs judge had held that a solicitor's charges for administering a large estate should no longer be based on both hourly rates and an additional element in respect of value. The estate in question was worth nearly £10 million for the administration of which the solicitor had elected to charge on the basis of an hourly rate for work carried out and in addition he charged 1.5% of the gross value of the estate (save for the house, which was charged at 0.5%) as a value element. This resulted in a value element of £227,000 in addition to the hourly rate charges of £386,000, totalling some £613,000 plus VAT. The master concluded that now hourly rates are calculated invariably on the basis of sophisticated time recording material, it is anachronistic and wrong to include an additional element in respect of value.

The Court of Appeal held that he was wrong on two counts. First, it is still appropriate for solicitors administering an estate and charging the time spent on administration to charge a separate fee based on the value of the estate, provided of course it is fair and reasonable remuneration in the light of all the circumstances. Second, by disallowing a charge based on the value element and only allowing a miserly hourly rate, the costs judge had in effect failed to have any regard to the value element. The Law Society's advice in its 1995 publication 'An Approach to Non-Contentious costs', and its subsequent 1999 booklet, was that in high value estates 'consideration should be given to reducing the value element percentage' was insufficiently firm. The regressive scale adopted in *Maltby v D J Freeman & Co* [1978] 2 All ER 913, [1978] 1 WLR 431 should be used, resulting, when updated for inflation, in the following figures for work done in 2003:

(1)	Up to £1 million	1.5%
(2)	Over £1 million up to £4 million	½%
(3)	Over £4 million up to £8 million	1/6%
(4)	Over £8 million up to £12 million	1/12%

The Court of Appeal gave this guidance:

'(1) Much the best practice is for a solicitor to obtain prior agreement as to the basis of his charges not only from the executors but also, where appropriate, from any residuary beneficiary who is an entitled third party under the 1994 Order [*now the 2009 Order*]. This is encouraged in the 1994 booklet and letter 8 of Appendix 2 to the 1999 booklet provides a good working draft of such agreement. We support that encouragement;

(2) in any complicated administration, it will be prudent for solicitors to provide in their terms of retainer for interim bills to be rendered for payment on account; this is, of course, subject to the solicitor's obligation to review the matter as a whole at the end of the business so as to ensure that he has claimed no more than is fair and reasonable, taking into account the factors set out in the 1994 Order;

(3) there should be no hard and fast rule that charges cannot be made separately by reference to the value of the estate; value can, by contrast, be taken into account as part of the hourly rate; value can also be taken into account partly in one way and partly in the other. What is important is that:

(a) it should be transparent on the face of the bill how value is being taken into account; and

(b) in no case should it be taken into account more than once;

(4) in many cases, if a charge is separately made by reference to the value of the estate, it should usually be on a regressive scale. The bands and percentages will be for the costs judge in each case; the suggestions to the costs judge set out in paragraph 30 may be thought by him to be appropriate for this case but different bands and percentages will be appropriate for other cases and figures set out in paragraph 30 cannot be any more than a guideline;

(5) it may be helpful at the end of the business for the solicitor or, if there is an assessment, for the costs judge, when a separate element of the bill is based on the value of the estate, to calculate the number of hours that would notionally be taken to achieve the amount of the separate charge. That may help to determine whether overall the remuneration claimed or assessed is fair and reasonable within the terms of the 1994 Order;
(6) it may also be helpful to consider the Law Society's Guidance in cases where there is no relevant and ascertainable value factor which is given in the 1994 booklet at paragraph 13.4. If the time spent on the matter is costed out at the solicitor's expense rate (which should be readily ascertainable from the Solicitor's Expense of Time calculations) the difference between that sum (the cost to the solicitor of the time spent on the matter) and the final figure claimed will represent the mark-up. The mark-up (which should take into account the factors specified in the 1994 Order including value) when added to the cost of the time spent must then be judged by reference to the requirement that this total figure must represent "such sum as may be fair and reasonable to both solicitor and entitled person".'

Routine non-contentious work

[31.39]

In all other routine non-contentious matters, where there is an ascertainable value element, consider whether the non-value factors are subsumed by value. It used to be only in exceptional circumstances that there would be a mark-up expressed as a percentage of time in addition to the value factor. However, the fall in the value of money since the value yardsticks were set means that there are now probably fewer cases where a value factor in itself is sufficient. If there is a value factor the usual mark-up on time might be less, perhaps between 25% and 33% in matters other than routine domestic conveyancing, or none at all following *Jemma Trust Co Ltd v Liptrott*, above.

ALTERNATIVES TO TIME AS A MANAGEMENT TOOL

Budgeting

[31.40]

You can prepare a budget of expenses for the next year. You can divide that by 12. You now know that if in each month you do not bill at least that amount you are running at a loss. You can take it a stage further by adding to your budgeted expenses for the forthcoming year the profit you hope to make during that period and dividing that total by 12. This gives you a total target figure for bills delivered. Having calculated the figure for bills to deliver during the year, it can be apportioned among the fee earners so that the total targets of the fee earners equal your overall target. If each fee earner accepts his target as realistic, you know you should reach your overall target for the year. As a result of monthly checks you will have an early warning if any fee earner is falling behind his target. Each month you will know whether you are on, ahead of or behind your target.

Fee earner targets

[31.41]

There is no point in one solicitor (the principal) employing another solicitor or legal executive (the assistant), paying him a salary, supplying him free of charge with accommodation, secretarial services and all the other tools of his profession, unless that assistant either makes a profit for his principal or relieves the principal of routine work, thereby enabling the principal to undertake more profitable work. A rough formula which has stood the test of time is that a fee earner's share of the overheads is not less than one-and-a-half times his salary. An assistant with a salary of £40,000 a year will have a share of the overheads of £60,000 a year, meaning that he must bill £100,000, or two-and-a-half times his salary, to break even. If to this is added a modest profit of half his salary, this produces a target of £120,000, or three times his salary. A survey of surveyors identified what they called a factor of 2.7–3.0; they had reached the same conclusion – that unless an assistant earns at least three times his salary, his employment must be justified by some means other than the profit he is making for the firm.

These two aspects of management control depend solely upon the calculation of expenses and projected profit. They do not of themselves require any recording or costing of time.

ALTERNATIVES TO TIME AS A CHARGING TOOL

[31.42]

There are various ways in which solicitors' charges could be calculated, other than on the basis of time. Examples are according to value, scale, commission, salary, fixed fees, a contingency basis, and a quantum meruit.

Not only does time not enter into any of these bases, the less time a solicitor takes to do the work where time is not the basis of calculation, the bigger the profit he makes because he has more time to spend on other work.

In an article in *The Lawyer*, Anne Gallagher considered various methods of charging in the United States. She identified four basic billing methods: hourly, fixed-fee and contingency, all of which determine in advance the billing method that will be used, and 'value billing', where the lawyer retrospectively determines what the fee will be, based upon either subjective or agreed-upon criteria. Some or all of these may be of interest to your clients as an alternative to simply paying by the hour. Variations of billing methods included:

(i)	Blended hourly rate	All services are charged at a common hourly rate whether for a senior partner, junior partner or associate.
(ii)	Fixed fee plus hourly rate	Certain defined services are charged on a fixed-fee basis, while the remainder of the time expended is billed on an hourly basis.
(iii)	Hourly rate plus premium	The established hourly rate is standard or lower than standard with a bonus paid if certain results are achieved.

(iv)	Percentage fees	The actual amount of the fee depends on the value of the total transaction.
(v)	Unit charges	For a defined segment of service, a unit charge is established, usually in combination with hourly billing.
(vi)	Relative value fees	A fee is established based on the relative value of the activity. For example, time spent answering correspondence may be assigned a lower value than time spent in research or negotiation.
(vii)	Availability only retainer	No services are included in this arrangement, which is established to ensure that legal counsel will be available when needed and not available to represent an adverse party. Fees are then paid as rendered.

CHAPTER 32

INTEREST ON COSTS

INTRODUCTION TO INTEREST ON COSTS

[32.1]

The entitlement to interest arises under statute as follows:

- Section 35A of the Senior Courts Act, sub-s (1), provides:

> ' . . . subject to rules of court, in proceedings (whenever instituted) before the High Court for the recovery of a debt or damages there may be included in any sum for which judgment is given simple interest, at such rate as the court thinks fit or as rules of court may provide, on all or any part of the debt or damages in respect of which judgment is given, or payment is made before judgment, for all or any part of the period between the date when the cause of action arose . . . '

- Section 74(1) of the County Courts Act 1984 is similar:

> ' . . . the Lord Chancellor may by order made with the concurrence of the Treasury provide any sums to which this subsection applies shall carry interest at such rate in between such time as may be prescribed by the order.'

- Section 17(1) of the Judgments Act 1838 continues the provision:

> ' . . . every judgment debt shall carry interest at the rate of . . . from such time as shall be prescribed by rules of court until the same shall be satisfied, and such interest may be levied under a writ of execution on such judgment.'

The Judgments Act 1838, s 17 provides for the recovery of interest on costs in the High Court, while the County Court (Interest on Judgment Debts) Order 1991, made under the County Courts Act 1984, s 74, provides for interest to be paid on 'relevant judgments'. A relevant judgment is one for not less than £5,000 or in respect of a 'qualifying debt' as defined by the Late Payment of Commercial Debts (Interest) Act 1998, into which we need not and shall not delve.

THE INCIPITUR RULE (AS OPPOSED TO THE ALLOCATUR RULE)

[32.2]

The dispute as to the date from which interest on costs runs went all the way up to the House of Lords where, in *Hunt v R M Douglas (Roofing) Ltd* [1990] 1 AC 398, it was held that interest on costs is a judgment debt for the purpose of s 17 above and that it runs from the date on which judgment is pronounced and not from the date of the costs officer's certificate. The former is known as the *incipitur rule* and the latter as the *allocatur rule*. Neither rule is entirely satisfactory but it was held that the balance of justice favoured the incipitur rule because the unsuccessful party had unnecessarily caused the costs to be incurred and that as neither rule covered costs incurred before the judgment, the application of the allocatur rule, generally speaking, does greater injustice than the operation of the incipitur rule, even though this means the successful party may recovers interest on disbursements before they are paid and costs after judgment before they are incurred. This has now been enshrined in CPR 40.8(1) as follows:

> '(1) Where interest is payable on a judgment pursuant to section 17 of the Judgments Act 1838 or section 74 of the County Courts Act 1984, the interest shall begin to run from the date that judgment is given unless—
>
> (a) a rule in another Part or a Practice Direction makes different provision; or
>
> (b) the court orders otherwise.
>
> (2) The court may order that interest shall begin to run from a date before the date that judgment is given.'

In *Simcoe v Jacuzzi UK Group plc* [2012] EWCA Civ 137, the claimant appealed against a judgment that interest of 8% should be added to damages only from the allocatur date. It was held on appeal that the fact the claimant's solicitors were acting under a conditional fee arrangement did not justify departing from the general rule that interest on the costs runs from the incipitur date. The court concluded that the solicitors will have done the work which was reflected in the costs awarded to the claimant and will have incurred overheads on which those costs were based.

The effect of a claimant not paying anything to the solicitors until after the costs have been recovered from the defendant is that those solicitors finance the client's litigation, and should not be expected to continue to do so until the costs awarded are agreed or assessed.

The same case raised the possibility that CPR 40.8(1) might be ultra vires in the county court. The coming in to force of the County Courts (Interest on Judgment Debts) (Amendment) Order 2019 resolves that difficulty. The explanatory memorandum to the order expressly provides that 'the amendments will ensure that the County Court has the more flexible powers envisaged by CPR rule 40.8'.

ORDERS DEEMED TO HAVE BEEN MADE

[32.3]

CPR 44.9(4) provides that interest payable pursuant to of the Judgments Act 1838, s 17 or the County Courts Act 1984, s 74 on costs deemed to have been ordered (namely where a claim has been struck out for non-payment of fees under CPR 3.7, CPR 3.7A1 and CPR 3.7B, where a CPR 36 offer is accepted or where a claimant discontinues under CPR 38) shall begin to run from the date on which the event which gives rise to the entitlement to costs occurred.

ENHANCED INTEREST

[32.4]

CPR 36.17(4) provides that, where at trial the judgment against a defendant is more advantageous to a claimant than the proposals contained in a claimant's Part 36 offer, the court must, unless it considers it unjust to do so, order that the claimant is entitled to his costs on the indemnity basis and interest on those costs at a rate not exceeding 10% above base rate. It is worth noting, as did the court in *Marathon Asset Management LLP v Seddon* [2017] EWHC 479 (Comm), that there is no similar provision in CPR 36.17(3)(b).

BACKDATING AND POST-DATING OF INTEREST – THE COURT'S DISCRETION

[32.5]

In *Nykredit Mortgage Bank plc v Edward Erdman Group Ltd (No 2)* [1998] 1 All ER 305, HL the House of Lords said that the Court of Appeal had been 'lured into error' when in *Kuwait Airways Corpn v Iraqi Airways Co (No 2)* [1995] 1 All ER 790, CA it had held that the Rules of the Supreme Court empowered it to backdate its order for costs to enable interest to run from the original judgment. Statute apart, courts have no power to award interest on costs, however desirable it might be for the court to have power to order the payment of interest on costs from a date earlier than the date on which the court gave judgment. However, although the court had no general inherent power to order the payment of interest, the result of the appeal had been that orders in the courts below should not have been made and that some of the money previously paid by the defendants to the plaintiffs as damages and costs pursuant to orders of the trial judge and the Court of Appeal had fallen to be repaid to them. This could have been an idle exercise unless the court was able to make consequential orders that achieved, as near as reasonably practicable, the necessary restitution which included interest on the money to be repaid. The power to do so was derived from the inherent jurisdiction of the House of Lords, which was also possessed by the Court of Appeal.

To enable lower courts to do the same, the Civil Procedure (Modification of Enactments) Order 1998 amended the Judgments Act 1838, s 17(1) to provide that interest will run from such time as is prescribed by rules of court. The resultant rule is CPR 44.2(6)(g) which empowers any court to award 'interest on costs from or until a certain date, including a date before judgment'. (See [32.2] above for consideration of the amendment to the 'County Courts (Interest on Judgment Debts) Order 1991 so as to align the provisions with rule 40.8 of the Civil Procedure Rules 1998 as that rule applies to the County Court'.)

Powell v Herefordshire Health Authority [2002] EWCA Civ 1786, was a clinical negligence claim on behalf of a child who suffered severe brain damage soon after birth. Liability was admitted and judgment entered by consent in April 1994. The damages were not assessed until June 2001, when there was an award of £2,175,000. The claim for interest on the costs almost exceeded the amount of the bill itself, being dated back to April 1994. The delay had arisen from uncertainly about the medical prognosis rather than any sloth on the part of the claimant or the lawyers. The defendant contended that interest should run from June 2001, the date of the actual assessment of the quantum of damages. On the assumption that these were the only two dates available, the costs judge ordered interest from the date of the judgment rather than the date of the quantification of damages. In overturning the costs judge the Court of Appeal noted that neither party had referred the costs judge to the power conferred on the court by CPR 44.2(6)(g) which gave discretion to select any date which fitted the justice of the case. By the time of the case the parties had settled the interest point and so we shall never know what would have been the outcome of a decision under CPR 44.2(6)(g).

In *Amoco (UK) Exploration Co v British American Offshore Ltd (No 2)* [2002] BLR 135, QBD (Comm Ct) the court exercised this power to order interest to run from a date prior to judgment to recognise the reality of when the costs expenditure actually occurred, with the judge stating:

> 'For my part, I think it may well be appropriate for at least in substantial proceedings involving commercial interests of significant importance both in balance sheet and reputational terms, that the court should award interest on costs under CPR Part 44.3(6)(g) [now 44.2(6)(g)] where substantial sums have inevitably been expended perhaps a year or more before the award of costs is made and interest begins to run on it under the general rule.'

By contrast In *Colour Quest Ltd v Total Downstream UK plc* [2009] EWHC 823 (Comm), the unusual nature of the case and the substantial costs involved justified an order that interest should only run from six months after the judgment. At a hearing which Steel J noted was said to cost £250 per minute, he concluded:

> ' . . . justice requires a postponement of the liability for the interest until a later date. This was indeed a case very much out of the norm where the costs are very large indeed. Indeed the claimants themselves wish to double the time allowed for the presentation of a detailed account for assessment. The disparity between the claimants' costs and those assessed as due may, it is contended, run to millions. It follows that payments on account are exposed to an enormous margin of error. In my judgement the starting date should be extended to 6 months from today.'

As Clarke J held in *Fattal v Walbrook Trustees (Jersey) Ltd* [2009] EWHC 1674 (Ch):

> 'The ability of the High Court to depart from the incipitur rule was conferred in order that the court could take account of the fact that money would often be expended before any judgment, Conversely, where money has not been expended, for example where the bulk of the costs have been paid at a date long after the relevant judgment, justice requires that the date of commencement of the interest is postponed beyond the date of that judgment.'

More recently the Court of Appeal in *Secretary of State for Energy and Climate Change v Jones* [2014] EWCA Civ 363 upheld a decision by Swift J that the claimants were entitled to interest on disbursements for a pre-judgment period at the rate agreed in a disbursement funding agreement under which their solicitors agreed to provide the claimants with sums to discharge the disbursements as they arose. The Court of Appeal concluded that the judge had been correct in looking at the clients' means and not those of their solicitors.

Conversely, in *Involnert Management Inc v Aprilgrange Ltd* [2015] EWHC 2834 (Comm) the Court concluded that while *Hunt* (above at **[32.2]**) set out the 'default date' from which Judgments Act rate interest runs, CPR 40.8(1)(b) conferred a discretion to be exercised by reference to what is just in the circumstances and that a reasonable objective benchmark was the expiry of the three month period under CPR 47.7 for the commencement of detailed assessment proceedings as by then the paying party would have the bill and be able to make an informed assessment of the likely liability. Even though the court provided for interest to run at the Bank of England Base Rate plus 2% from the dates when the costs were incurred until a date three months after the orders for costs were made, the suggested benchmark seems odd because:

(i) in most multi-track cases the paying party will have a clear idea of the receiving party's costs from the last agreed or approved budget;

(ii) in many other cases a schedule of costs is produced for the purpose of negotiation prior to a formal bill;

(iii) in those cases where CPR 44.3(2)(a) applies, there is nothing to stop the paying party making its own realistic assessment of what is a proportionate sum by reference to the factors at CPR 44.3(5) and any wider circumstances and paying that sum on account;

(iv) CPR 44.2(8) encourages the court to award sums on account of costs (as, indeed, happened in this case) and, as seen in Chapter 25 at **[25.1]**, there is nothing to prevent a court making such an order even in the absence of a statement of costs *(Astonleigh Residential v Goldfarb* [2014] EWHC 4100 (Ch)). It might be thought that what is sauce for the court is also sauce for the paying party;

(v) in deemed costs order cases under CPR 44.9, interest runs from the date of the event giving rise to the entitlement to costs (eg under Part 36 from the date of acceptance).

What these authorities show is that the court has a broad discretion. While the incipitur rule may be appropriate in the majority of cases there is nothing that requires the court to find any exceptional circumstances to depart from this when exercising its discretion under CPR 44.2(6)(g). As Clarke J stated in *Fattal* (above) 'The most important criterion is that any order should reflect what justice requires' and it is the pursuit of that goal which should inform the exercise of discretion.

THE RATE OF INTEREST

[32.6]

Since April 1993 the rate of interest on judgment debts has been 8%, as prescribed by the Judgment Debts (Rate of Interest) Order 1993. This is despite the reduction of interest rates on funds invested in court. The impact of Covid-19 has seen the special account rate reduced to 0.1% (from 1 June 2020). The basic court funds rate is an even less appealing 0.05% (from 1 June 2020). Even prior to this, the rates were only at 0.5% and 0.3% respectively. Judgment rate interest therefore remains a good investment – provided the judgment and costs are eventually paid. Indeed, where there is a paying party good for the money and there are no cash flow problems for the receiving party we can understand why there may have been a reluctance to seek payments on account of costs before the detailed assessment as this is a rate of return on funds to be envied.

In respect of county court judgments where the judgment creditor applies to enforce payment of the judgment by execution or some other means, interest will not accrue if the enforcement process is wholly or partly successful. This is set out in the County Court (Interest on Judgment Debts) Order 1991, SI 1991/1184, at art 4. Presumably, this provision was made because, if the enforcement process is wholly successful the judgment will have been satisfied, while if it is only partly successful it will be too complicated to calculate the interest on the various amounts outstanding from time to time.

The County Courts (Interest on Judgment Debts) (Amendment) Order 2019, SI 2019/903 provides an amendment to art 2 of the 1991 Order so that the court may award interest on judgment debts from a date prior to the judgment. This amendment will ensure that the County Court can now exercise the power so to do provided by CPR 40.8(2).

Where the court is considering whether to award an enhanced interest rate under CPR 36.17(4)(c), the Court of Appeal tendered advice in *OMV Petrom SA v Glencore International AG* [2017] EWCA Civ 195 to the effect that provided it is proportionate in the context of the case (see para 38 of the judgment), interest under this provision may include a non-compensatory amount to encourage good practice. This is by way of both encouraging parties to enter into reasonable settlement discussions and marking the court's disapproval of unreasonable conduct.

CHAPTER 33

APPEALS AGAINST ASSESSMENTS

INTRODUCTION TO APPEALS AGAINST ASSESSMENTS

[33.1]

One of the least illuminating ways to spend a few hours is to read the transcript of an assessment hearing (particularly a detailed assessment). However, this is the task that falls to an appellate court on an appeal from an assessment. In the course of an assessment, where the court is dealing with myriad disputes (often challenges to six minute units), judgments come thick and fast. The key is that the court gives adequate reasons for its decision on each challenge (even if it is simply to justify the decision whether the six-minute unit is allowed or is assessed off the bill). However, it is the failure to give such reasons that often leads to an appeal.

THE IMPORTANCE OF REASONS

[33.2]

In *English v Emery Reimbold & Strick Ltd* [2002] EWCA Civ 605 the Court of Appeal provided some clear guidance on reasons and appeals. For these purposes references to substantive decisions may just as easily be to decisions made within an assessment. The court held (amongst other matters):

(1) Where an application for permission to appeal on the ground of lack of reasons is made to judges at first instance, they should consider whether the judgment is defective for lack of reasons, adjourning for that purpose if necessary. If they conclude that it was, then they should remedy the defect by providing additional reasons, and then refuse permission to appeal. If they conclude that the reasons were adequate, then permission to appeal should be refused.

(2) Where an application for permission to appeal on the ground of lack of reasons is made to an appellate court, and it appears to that court that the application is well – founded, it should consider adjourning the application and remitting to the trial judge with an invitation to provide reasons, or additional reasons. Where the appellate court is in doubt as to the adequacy of reasons it may be appropriate to adjourn the application to an oral hearing on notice to the respondent.

(3) Where permission to appeal is granted on the ground of inadequate reasons, the appellate court should review the judgment in the light of the evidence and submissions at trial in order to determine whether it was apparent why the court reached the decision it did. If the reasons are apparent and valid, the appeal should be dismissed. If the reasons are still not apparent the appeal court will have to consider whether to proceed to a rehearing or direct a new trial.

(4) If the reasons for a judge's order as to costs are plain, as where costs followed the event, there is no need for the judge to give reasons for a costs order. However, the CPR sometimes require a more complex approach to costs, and judgments dealing with costs will more often need to identify the provisions of the rules which have been in play and why those have led to the order made. Where no express reason for a costs order is given the appeal court will approach the material facts on the assumption that the judge has a good reason for the order made, and where there is a perfectly rational explanation for the order, the appeal court is likely to draw the inference that this is what motivated the judge in making the order. Accordingly it is only in cases where an order for costs is made with neither reasons nor any obvious explanation for the order that it is likely to be appropriate to give permission to appeal on the ground of lack of reasons.

A SIMPLE FORMULATION OF REASONING WHEN ASSESSING ITEMS AND OVERALL PROPORTIONALITY

[33.3]

In practice when dealing with actual sums in the bill, as opposed to substantive preliminary points, the judge at first instance ought to be able to make decisions virtually immune from appeal by the adoption of a simple formulation of words, eg 'the item is/is not reasonably incurred' and if reasonably incurred 'is/is not reasonable in amount' and if not reasonable in amount 'the reasonable amount is £x' and by way of proportionality cross check at the end 'Having reached the sum that is reasonably incurred and reasonable in amount it is necessary under CPR 44.3(2)(a) to view that sum against the factors at CPR 44.3(5) and any wider circumstances to ensure that the sum is proportionate. The relevant considerations under CPR 44.3(5) and any wider relevant circumstances are (insert as relevant). In the light of these factors in my judgment the sum is/is not proportionate' and if not proportionate to look at the component parts (eg phases or discrete headline items such as counsel's fee or expert fees) 'and I assess the proportionate sum by reference to the factors identified and in respect of (those phases or discrete headline items that are disproportionate) as £y'. Similarly, parties wishing to challenge/defend a particular item or the amount of time spent on it ought to be focussing on the same wording, which is no more than an expression of the tests that the court must adopt under the rules (CPR 44.3 and CPR 44.4).

PERMISSION TO APPEAL

[33.4]

In all costs appeals (save those from an authorised costs officer – see below), the appellant will require permission to appeal (CPR 52.3(1)). As with other appeals, the appellant may seek permission from the judge conducting the assessment and, if the first instance judge refuses permission, or if no application is made to the first instance judge, from the appeal court. CPR 52.6

provides that permission to appeal in respect of first appeals will only be granted where the court considers that the appeal would have a real prospect of success or there is some other compelling reason why the appeal should be heard. On second appeals, there is a qualification to the former of the two requirements for first appeals and that is that the appeal must, in addition, raise an important point of principle or practice (CPR 52.7(2)(a)(ii)).

The Court of Appeal has no jurisdiction to entertain an appeal against the refusal of the judge to grant permission to appeal against the decision of the costs judge (Access to Justice Act 1999, s 54(4)). It also has no jurisdiction to review the judge's decision (see *Riniker v University College London* [2001] 1 WLR 13, CA).

An appeal does not act as a stay and a separate application for a stay of enforcement must be made. It is likely that a court granting a stay will make it dependent upon some form of payment (if only to ensure that the appellate process is not being used simply as a device to defer payment).

GROUNDS FOR APPEAL

[33.5]

The only grounds of appeal are those prescribed in CPR 52.21(3), namely that the decision was wrong or unjust because of a serious procedural or other irregularity in the proceedings.

'Wrong' may be an error of i) law, ii) fact or iii) the exercise of discretion. While the appellate court will readily entertain an appeal on a question of law, it will need considerable persuasion to interfere with a finding of fact or the exercise of discretion.

The meaning of 'wrong' was considered in *Griffiths v Solutia UK Ltd (formerly Monsanto Chemicals Ltd)* [2001] EWCA Civ 736, the relevant part of the judgment being:

> 'The question before us is whether the deputy judge was entitled to conclude that the decision of the costs judge was wrong. The test which the deputy judge had to apply, in determining whether or not the costs judge's decision was wrong, was explained by this court in *Tanfern v Cameron-McDonald* [2000] 1 WLR 1311, para 32, where Brooke LJ says as follows:
>
> > "The first ground for interference speaks for itself. The epithet 'wrong' is to be applied to the substance of the decision made by the lower court. If the appeal is against the exercise of a discretion by the lower court, the decision of the House of Lords in *G v G (minors: custody appeal* [1985] 1 WLR 647 warrants attention. In that case Lord Fraser of Tullybelton said, at page 652
> >
> > 'Certainly it would not be useful to inquire whether different shades of meaning are intended to be conveyed by words such as "blatant error" used by the President in the present case, and words such as "clearly wrong", "plainly wrong" or "simply wrong" used by other judges in other cases. All these various expressions were used in order to emphasise the point that the appellate court should only interfere when they consider that the judge of first instance has not merely preferred an imperfect solution, which is different from an alternative imperfect solution which the Court of Appeal might or would have adopted, but has exceeded the generous ambit within which a reasonable disagreement is possible.'

> The task that faces us is to apply that same test. Essentially the test requires the appellate court to consider whether or not, in a case involving the exercise of discretion, the judge has approached the matter applying the correct principles, has taken into account all relevant considerations and has not taken into account irrelevant considerations, and has reached a decision which is one which can properly be described as a decision which is within the ambit of reasonable decisions open to the judge on the facts of the case." '

In *Johnsey Estates (1990) Ltd v Secretary of State for the Environment, Transport and the Regions* [2001] EWCA Civ 535, the Court of Appeal held that an appellate court should not interfere with the judge's exercise of discretion merely because it takes the view that it would have exercised that discretion differently. This requires an appellate court to exercise a degree of self – restraint. It must recognise the advantage which the trial judge enjoys as a result of 'feel' for the case which that judge has tried. Indeed, it is not for an appellate court even to consider whether it would have exercised the discretion differently unless it has first reached the conclusion that the judge's exercise of discretion is flawed. That is to say, that the judge has erred in principle, taken into account matters which should have been left out of account, left out of account matters which should have been taken into account or reached a conclusion which is so plainly wrong that it can be described as perverse.

The case of *Tabidi v British Broadcasting Corpn* [2020] EWCA Civ 733 is a clear illustration of a costs appeal being allowed because the court (tribunal), when exercising its discretion, took into account an impermissible consideration, taking the decision outside the ambit of reasonable decisions.

The Court of Appeal noted in *Dixon v Blindley Heath Investments Ltd* [2015] EWCA Civ 1023 that 'appeals in relation to costs are discouraged', citing with approval *SCT Finance v Bolton* [2002] EWCA Civ 56 and in particular this passage:

> 'This is an appeal in relation to costs. As such, it is overcast from start to finish by the heavy burden faced by the appellant in establishing that the judge's decision falls outside the discretion in relation to costs . . . this court discourages such appeals by interpreting such discretion widely.'

However, in this case the Court of Appeal granted permission to appeal, recognising that despite the starting point set out above, the court must remain astute to correct plain injustice.

THE TIME FOR APPEALING

[33.6]

As appeals are governed by CPR Part 52, the time period for an appeal is prescribed within that rule at CPR 52.12(2). This provides that an appellant must file notice of the appeal within 21 days of the date of the decision of the lower court against which an appeal is pursued or such other period, being either longer or shorter, that the lower court may have directed.

What does this mean in the context of a detailed assessment where the court is making many decisions that together lead to an overall conclusion? In *Kasir v Darlington & Simpson Rolling Mills Ltd* [2001] 2 Costs LR 228, QBD, at the end of a four day detailed assessment it was left to the respective costs draftsmen to agree the calculations arising out of the costs judge's findings and to submit the resultant assessed bill to him. Unfortunately, they were unable to agree the result, which necessitated another hearing, which in turn led to further correspondence so that the final figure was not agreed until 5 months after the original assessment. The claimant submitted notice of appeal within 14 days of the final agreement. The court held that this was out of time, as the time period ran from the decisions on the items under appeal. This means that in lengthy assessments the final date for applications for appeal will vary depending upon which day of the assessment the decision being appealed was made. This might result in the parties having to file several appellant's notices. It also results in parties having to make decisions on interim items before the overall outcome of the assessment is known. The practical solution offered by the judge in this case was that the parties could agree and/or the costs judge could order at the start of an assessment that the time for any appeals is extended to a date, either 21 days or some other agreed and ordered period, after the last day of the assessment.

CPR 47.14(7) was introduced in the April 2013 reforms and resolves part of the difficulty. It specifies that where a detailed assessment is carried out at more than one hearing then the time for appealing does not run until the conclusion of the final hearing unless the court orders otherwise. It is important to ensure that preliminary hearings on specific points of dispute are defined as part of the detailed assessment hearing. However, the position remains the same as before if there is one hearing over a number of consecutive days. In other words, the time provisions are more generous where there are a number of discrete hearings than one hearing with many decisions extending over a number of days. Consequently, parties should seek confirmation that time only runs on any decision (regardless of the day on which it was reached) from the end of the hearing.

The decision of Turner J in *Webb Resolutions Ltd v E-Surv Ltd* [2014] EWHC 49 is essential reading on this topic. In that case he applied the approach taken by the Court of Appeal when considering CPR 3.9 (see Chapter 15) to the wording of CPR 52.3(5) [as was, now 52.4(6)] that requires that any request for an oral reconsideration of a refusal of permission to appeal on paper 'must' be filed within seven days of service of the notice that permission has been refused. He concluded that must equates to mandatory in this context.

ROUTE OF APPEALS

[33.7]

The revised CPR PD 52A at Section III – Destinations of Appeal, sets out the new routes. Table 1 sets out the route for civil appeals as follows:

Table 1 – Proceedings other than family or insolvency proceedings

Court	Deciding judge	Decision under appeal	Destination
County	DJ	Any, other than a decision in non-insolvency proceedings brought pursuant to the Companies Acts	CJ(CC)
		A decision in non-insolvency proceedings brought pursuant to the Companies Acts	HCJ or Registrar
	CJ	Any	HCJ
High	Master, Registrar or DJ	Any	HCJ
	HCJ	Any	CA
Intellectual Property Enterprise Court	DJ	Any	Enterprise Judge
	Enterprise Judge	Any	CA

In summary, the revised rules remove the distinction between 'final' and 'interim' decisions and generally provide that a first appeal lies to the next tier of judiciary.

A footnote to CPR PD 52A, para 3.5 also confirms that:

> 'For a second appeal (an appeal from a decision of the County Court or the High Court which was itself made on appeal), the destination is the Court of Appeal (save where the original decision was a decision of an officer authorised to assess costs by the Lord Chancellor: see article 6 of the Access to Justice Act 1999 (Destination of Appeals) Order 2016).'

REVIEW NOT RE-HEARING

[33.8]

Appeals against assessment decisions are not full re-hearings, unless the appellate court so orders. Instead they are limited to a review of the decision under appeal (CPR 52.21(1)).

THE ROLE OF ASSESSORS

[33.9]

The costs rules used to provide for the appointment of assessors to sit with the judge on a review of a decision at a taxation of costs. These were usually a costs officer and a practising lawyer (generally a solicitor unless the appeal was in connection with counsel's fees when a barrister would be used). There is no longer such a specific provision. However, courts may, and regularly still do, avail themselves of the assistance of assessors under their powers deriving from the Senior Courts Act 1981, s 70 or the County Court Act 1984, s 63 as provided for in CPR 35.15. Regularly at county court level the appellate court will involve the local Regional Costs Judge. In the High Court the use of masters from the Senior Court Costs Office is customary. In the High Court, the judge may well wish to sit with more than one assessor, the other one still, traditionally, being drawn from the professions.

CPR 35.15(3) prescribes that it is a matter for the court to determine the extent to which the assessor is involved. This may simply be to prepare a report or to attend the entire hearing and advise the court. However, it is important to stress that:

- if the assessor prepares a report for the court that must be sent to the parties before the hearing and the parties may use it at the hearing;
- the assessor will not give oral evidence and cannot be cross examined or questioned (CPR PD 35, para 10.4);
- the final decision remains that of the court (and the court may disagree with its assessor/s);
- the court must give at least 21 days' notice to the parties that it proposes to sit with an assessor (naming that assessor). Any party may object to the appointment provided that notice of the objection is made to the court in writing within 7 days of receiving the notice and the court will take the objection into account when determining whether to sit with the assessor (CPR PD 35, paras 10.1–10.3).

Save where the assessor is a salaried member of the judiciary (eg a costs judge or regional costs judge) the assessor's remuneration shall be determined by the court and shall form part of the costs of the proceedings. The court may order any party to deposit in the court office a specified sum in respect of the assessor's fees and may defer the involvement of the assessor until this has been done.

APPEALS FROM THE DECISIONS MADE ON DETAILED ASSESSMENT BY AUTHORISED COURT OFFICERS

[33.10]

An authorised costs officer is 'any officer of the county court, district registry, family court, the high court or costs office whom the Lord Chancellor has authorised to assess costs (CPR 44.1(1)). CPR PD 47, para 3.1 sets out the financial limits on their jurisdiction (base costs excluding VAT do not exceed £35,000, save in respect of principal officers where the limit is £110,000.)

CPR 47.3 sets out the powers of authorised costs officers stating that they have the same powers as the court on detailed assessment proceedings save that they cannot make 'wasted costs orders', orders in relation to misconduct, orders imposing sanctions for delay in commencing detailed assessment and cannot undertake assessments of the amount that a client should pay his solicitor save in respect of assessments where the money is payable by a child or protected party under CPR 46.4. The parties do have the right to object to a detailed assessment by an authorised costs officer and the court may then order the assessment to be conducted by a costs judge or district judge.

As already stated the appellate route prescribed by CPR Part 52 does not apply to appeals from authorised court officers. Instead the relevant rules relating to appeals from costs officers are set out at CPR 47.21-CPR 47.24. These provide that:

- any party to detailed assessment proceedings may apply to appeal without needing permission;
- the appeal lies to a costs judge or a district judge of the High Court;
- the appeal notice must be filed within 21 days after the date of the decision being appealed against;
- the court will serve the notice and give notice of the appeal hearing date;
- the court will re-hear the detailed assessment proceedings giving rise to the appeal and in so doing may give such directions and make such order as it sees fit. In other words, the jurisdiction on appeal extends beyond the customary review of the decision being appealed. However, on this point, it is worth noting the decision in *PME v The Scout Association* [2019] EWHC 3421 (QB) in the context of the extent of an appeal in a provisional assessment and subsequent oral hearing before an authorised court officer, in which the court concluded that:

> 'i) At the stage of provisional assessment the parties can accept the provisional assessment or challenge it – with risk as to costs.
>
> ii) If they challenge it they have to set out the items which are challenged. These are then determined at the oral hearing.
>
> iii) Parties may challenge all the decisions in the provisional assessment. There is no limit.
>
> iv) However, if they do not then they are entitled to (a) an oral determination of the issues they have identified and (b) an appeal by way of re-hearing of the decision in relation to those issues.'

The relevant procedural requirements are set out at CPR PD 47, paras 20.1–20.6 and include:

- prescription of the relevant appeal notice (Form N161);
- provisions for filing a suitable record of the judgment appealed against, whether by transcript, the bill annotated with reasons or agreed advocates notes of the reasons as approved by the authorised court officer. Specific obligations are imposed on the respondent to the appeal where the appellant was unrepresented before the authorised court officer and there is no official record;
- provision for amending the notice of appeal where there is no record of the judgment or reasons for it available by the time the notice has to be filed. In this situation the notice must be completed as best as is possible. Any later application to amend will require the permission of the judge hearing the appeal,

CONCLUSION TO APPEALS AGAINST ASSESSMENTS

[33.11]

Appeals from assessments tend to be on substantive issues as opposed to challenges to individual amounts of time. The provisional detailed assessment process (see Chapter 30 – Detailed Assessment – Provisional Assessment, above) under CPR 47.15, with its own 'oral hearing' review process, may reduce the number of appeals with the parties being satisfied by the opportunity to challenge the court's initial decision.

Where better to end a chapter on appeals than with a warning on the question of costs of appeals. Remember that on any appeal, whether on costs or not, where the appeal will last a day or less a party must file and serve a statement of costs for summary assessment. In *Wheeler v Chief Constable of Gloucestershire Constabulary* [2013] EWCA Civ 1791 (see Chapter 27) the successful respondent to the appeal had failed to file and serve a statement of costs (as indeed had the appellant). The court was unable to conduct a summary assessment. It ordered a detailed assessment, but with the receiving party to pay the costs of those proceedings.

Part V

Special cases

CHAPTER 34

CHILDREN AND PROTECTED PARTIES

INTRODUCTION TO CHILDREN AND PROTECTED PARTIES

[34.1]

Phrases to describe a party who lacks the capacity to litigate have come and gone with some rapidity. A 'party under a disability' and a 'patient' have given way to a 'protected party', which CPR 21.1(2) defines as a party, or an intended party, who lacks capacity to conduct the proceedings. Similarly, a 'minor' or an 'infant' has been replaced by 'child' even though that word is not age restricted in common parlance. According to the CPR however, it means a person under 18 (CPR 21.1(2)(b)).

LITIGATION FRIEND

[34.2]

A protected party must have a litigation friend to conduct proceedings on his behalf (CPR 21.2(1)) and a child must have one unless the court permits the child to conduct his own proceedings (CPR 21.2(3)).

Where the child or protected party is a claimant, the litigation friend must give an undertaking to pay any costs which the child or protected party may be ordered to pay in relation to the proceedings, subject to any right to be repaid from the assets of the child or protected party (CPR 21.4(3)) whether the litigation friend has become one without a court order (CPR 21.5) or has been appointed under a court order (CPR 21.6). The litigation friend's liability for costs continues until the child or protected party serves notice that the litigation friend's appointment has ceased (giving the party's new address for service and stating whether they intend to carry on the proceedings) or the litigation friend serves notice on the parties that their appointment to act has ceased (CPR 21.9(6)). This is notwithstanding that the litigation friend's appointment ceases when the child reaches the age of 18 (CPR 21.9(1)).

COSTS PAYABLE BY AND TO LITIGATION FRIENDS

[34.3]

In the previous edition we reported, and commented upon, the case of *Barker v Confiance* [2019] EWHC 1401 (Ch), which raised issues of principle as to the circumstances in which a litigation friend can be ordered to pay costs and considered whether orders for costs should be made against children themselves. The former included analysis of whether there is a distinction to be drawn between litigation friends for claimants and those for defendants. Morgan J undertook an extensive review of (1) jurisprudence pre-dating s 51 of the Senior Courts Act 1981; (2) Halsbury's Laws, s 51(3) of the Senior Courts Act 1981 ('SCA 1981'); and (3) CPR 21. This decision was appealed. In *Glover v Barker* [2020] EWCA Civ 1112, the Court of Appeal undertook a similarly extensive review of procedure, s 51 of the SCA 1981 and jurisprudence. The court reached the following conclusions of general application:

> 'Drawing the threads together, it seems to me that the position in relation to costs orders against litigation friends in civil litigation can be summarised as follows:
>
> i) At any rate where a litigation friend has not previously given an undertaking to pay the costs at issue, the power to make an order for costs against a litigation friend derives exclusively from section 51 of the 1981 Act;
> ii) When deciding whether an order should be made against a litigation friend under section 51, the "ultimate question" is "whether in all the circumstances it is just to make the order";
> iii) It will typically be just to order a claimant's litigation friend to pay costs if such an order would have been made against the claimant himself had he not been a child or protected party, but it remains the case that the Court is exercising a discretion and entitled have regard to the particular circumstances;
> iv) There is no presumption that a defendant's litigation friend should bear costs which the defendant would have been ordered to pay if not a child or protected party. That the litigation friend controlled the defence of a claim which succeeded will not of itself generally make it just to make an adverse costs order against the litigation friend. Factors that might, depending on the specific facts, be thought to justify such an order include bad faith, improper or unreasonable behaviour and prospect of personal benefit. If a director causes his company to litigate "solely or substantially for his own benefit" (to quote Lord Brown in *Dymocks*), that may point towards a costs order against him. The fact that a litigation friend stands to gain a substantial personal benefit must also, I think, be capable of weighing in favour of a costs order against him.'

EXPENSES INCURRED BY A LITIGATION FRIEND

[34.4]

Under CPR 21.12 and CPR PD 21, para 11.1 a litigation friend who incurs expenses on behalf of a child or protected party in any proceedings is entitled to recover the amount paid or payable out of any money recovered or paid into court to the extent that it has been reasonably incurred and is reasonable in amount.

Under a combination of CPR 21.12(8) and CPR PD 21, para 11 determination of the amount may take place:

- at the approval hearing if the expenses are not of a type recoverable as costs between the parties;
- in a claim for damages for personal injury, at the hearing awarding damages or at the hearing to approve a settlement or at any time thereafter if the claimant is a child, the damages awarded or approved are £25,000 or less and the court undertakes a summary assessment of the costs claimed by the child's solicitor as the success fee under a conditional fee agreement or the balance of a payment under a

'damages based agreement' under CPR 46.4(5)(b). It is not clear why CPR PD 21, para 11(1A) restricts this application to children as CPR 46.4(5)(b) permits summary assessment in respect of both children and protected parties, albeit with some differences considered below at **[34.5]**;

- on application where costs are fixed under CPR 45 Sections II, III and IIIA, where no claim is made under CPR 45.13 or CPR 45.29J for an amount exceeding the fixed recoverable costs; and
- at a detailed assessment.

Although CPR PD 21, para 11.1 seems to suggest that expenses and costs are to be treated the same for these purposes, that is not the case. As items which have been disallowed on an assessment cannot be claimed from the child or protected party (CPR 21.12(3)), in reality, the first provision above means that those expenses may always be sought at the approval hearing as they are not costs (see below on the confusing definitions suggesting some expenses may be costs).

CPR 21.12(6) provides that where the court awards, or the claim settles for, £5,000 or less, the litigation friend's costs and expenses can only exceed 25% of the settlement with the court's permission. They cannot be more than 50% in any event. However, CPR 21.12(7) limits the costs deduction to 25% of general damages and past pecuniary loss in all claims covered by CPR 21.12(1), regardless of value. Accordingly, whilst the court may permit the deduction of up to 50% of all damages under £5,000 pursuant to CPR 21.12(6), the costs element of this cannot exceed the 25% of general damages and past pecuniary loss limited by CPR 21.12(7). This means the rules permit the possibility of greater deductions for expenses than for costs.

The use of the word expenses is a confusing one – made all the more so by the words in brackets at the end of CPR 21.12(3) suggesting that some expenses might also be costs. As set out above and considered in more detail below, that might involve a different procedure (either a summary or detailed assessment) and result in a lower cap on deductions. The definition of 'costs' found at CPR 44.1 adds to the confusion by including, amongst other things, 'expenses'. There is no definition in the CPR of 'expenses' for these purposes. This is unfortunate because:

- If an expense is also costs it may determine whether a formal summary or detailed assessment is required.
- If an expense is also costs, it may affect the monetary implementation of the deduction cap.
- There is an argument that the elision of treatment of 'success fee' and 'sum payable under a damages based agreement' is incorrect. The argument is that the former plainly falls as 'costs' as it is calculated by reference to costs, whereas the latter is a payment (there is no use of the word 'costs' in regulation 2 of the Damages Based Agreements Regulations) and is simply an indivisible sum calculated by reference to damages. The argument is probably specious as it is challenging to see a payment under a 'damages based agreement' as anything other than 'fees', 'charges' or 'remuneration' under CPR 44.1, which is not an exhaustive definition anyway. However, a simple amendment to CPR 44.1 to include overt reference to payments under a 'damages based agreement' would end the debate.

- In *Herbert v HH Law Ltd* [2019] EWCA Civ 527, although not a child or protected party case, the Court of Appeal considered the question of whether an 'after the event' ('ATE') insurance premium, other than the one under CPR 21.12(2)(a), is a disbursement. It concluded that, on the evidence before it, the premium met neither of the tests that identify disbursements (in that the solicitors were neither obliged to pay the premium, nor was it a custom that they do so) and so was not to be treated as a disbursement. This may create further ambiguity in respect of payment of the premium because in *BNM v MGN* [2017] EWCA Civ 1767, the Master of the Rolls concluded that:

  > ' . . . I do not consider that ATE insurance premiums fall within the natural meaning of "expenses" of litigation. They have nothing to do with the cost of issuing and progressing the litigation, any more than the premiums on a householder's or car owner's insurance which contains litigation cover. Both before the event insurance and after the event insurance offset the risk of a person's financial exposure as a result of litigation but they are not expenses of the litigation itself.' (para 73)

  While this comment was in the context of consideration of recoverable premiums under the transitional provisions of CPR 48.1, para 73, does begin with the words 'In any event' and 'expenses' are no more defined in the pre-1 April 2013 rules than they are now.

DEDUCTIONS FROM THE FUNDS OF CHILDREN AND PROTECTED PARTIES FOR COSTS INCURRED BY A LITIGATION FRIEND

[34.5]

As the Supreme Court recently restated in *Dunhill v Burgin* [2014] UKSC 18, when setting aside a previously approved settlement, the purpose of the protection afforded to children and protected parties is to protect them from themselves and their legal advisers by imposing external (court) checks on the propriety of any settlement. Recent rule changes to allow summary assessment of certain proposed deductions in respect of children do not undermine this intent. Instead they simply afford a more proportionate approach, which, if anything, reduces the costs exposure of a child.

Deductions from the damages of children and protected parties have taken on a different complexion following the abolition of recoverable 'additional liabilities' after 31 March 2013. Inevitably, there has been increased use of CFAs with success fees that come from the client's damages and of DBAs where the payment due to the solicitors may exceed the recoverable costs and the shortfall may also be sought from the client's damages. So far as children are concerned, the procedural difficulties of a proportionate determination of deductions in lower value personal injury cases were partially resolved by amendments to CPR 21.12 and CPR 46.4(5) in April 2015. These combine to permit a summary assessment of any liability for any element of the success fee or DBA payment in respect of personal injury claims where the damages do not exceed £25,000. What they do not do, in respect of CFA cases, is allow the party's solicitors to use this route to recover any solicitor client costs that represent any shortfall between their base costs and the recoverable costs (see

CPR 46.4(5) wording, which defines 'costs payable as 'only the success fee'). However, in the well-intentioned haste to introduce even these changes, the amendments actually created considerable problems in respect of protected parties, which were identified in the 2016 edition of this text. It was not until Turner J had to consider the amendments in *Leddington v Kabul* [2017] EWHC 3262 (QB) and referred with approval the change of wording to CPR 21.12(1A) proposed by us, that the Civil Procedure Rules Committee revisited the problematic provision. A further amendment, adopting the suggested revision of CPR 21.12(1A), made in April 2019, has finally resolved the main issue and removed the unintended apparent absolute bar to deduction from the damages of protected parties. However, CPR PD 21, para 11.1(1A) has not been amended and still seems to conflict with CPR 46.4(5)(b) as it does not provide an opportunity under CPR 21.12(1) for the litigation friend of a protected party to seek a deduction by way of a summary assessment in the limited circumstances permitted under CPR 46.4(5). Whilst CPR 21.12 is the specific rule in respect of protected parties, it is its PD which contains the restriction and we would expect CPR 46.4(5) to prevail as that does not conflict with the provision at CPR 21.12(1).

However, there remains a distinction between deductions from the damages of children and from those of protected parties. The restriction in CPR 21.12(1A)(2), limits the CPR 46.4(5) jurisdiction, in respect of children, to personal injury claims where the damages which have been agreed or ordered to be paid do not exceed £25,000. There is neither a restriction on the type of proceedings, nor on the level of damages on the scope of CPR 46.4(5) in respect of protected parties. Actually this makes only limited practical differences, for CPR PD 44, para 9.9(1) precludes a summary assessment of the recoverable 'between the parties' costs of a child or a protected party, unless their representative waives the right to further costs (which, in the specific context of seeking a deduction, they are expressly not doing). In non-fixed and non-agreed recoverable costs cases therefore, this will prevent the determination of the solicitor client costs, which in turn will prevent the calculation of the success fee in monetary, rather than percentage, terms in CFA cases and will prevent calculation of the shortfall between recovered costs and the payment in DBA cases. Accordingly it is only likely to be in non-fixed, but agreed costs cases, where the lack of the CPR 21.12(1A)(2) limitations, offers those seeking a deduction from the damages of a protected party the possibility of an easier and quicker route to resolution.

Other procedural changes in April 2019:

- added the requirement at CPR PD 21, para 11.4A, for solicitors seeking a deduction from the damages of children under CPR 21.12(1A), to include in the supporting witness statement or to accompany it, with a copy bill or informal breakdown in the form of a schedule of the solicitor and own client base costs incurred. This is so that the CFA success fee or DBA shortfall can be calculated. This highlights another distinction between the position in respect of children and protected parties. CPR PD 21, para 11.3 does not apply at all to protected parties. Instead, the only witness statement requirement for the litigation friend of a protected party is that at para 11.2, which provides the court with far less information. It may be that the court will interpret the requirement to set out the reason the costs or expenses were incurred in a broad sense and prudent litigation friends may choose to provide such of the information and documentation required under para 11.3 as is relevant in any event (see [**34.6**] below);

- made provision in CPR 21.12(8) to permit deductions from damages in fixed costs cases under CPR 45 Sections II, III and IIIA (save where a claim for costs exceeding fixed recoverable costs is made under either CPR 45.13 or 45.29J – as until such an application is resolved the amount recovered 'between the parties' remains uncertain and so too, therefore, does the amount of any shortfall between those and solicitor client costs) despite there being no agreement in respect of non-fixed disbursements.

Even in cases where a summary assessment of the solicitor client costs liability is permitted under CPR 46.4(5), this is not prescriptive, given the use of the word 'may' in this provision. However, where it is able to conduct a summary assessment, it is difficult to imagine why the court would not do so as this will inevitably be a more proportionate approach than to order even a reduced form of detailed assessment and avoids the draconian costs implications of such an assessment.

Whenever it determines the extent to which a deduction will be permitted, the court must have regard to CPR 21.12(4) and (5). These in turn refer to the provisions of CPR 44.4(3), the usual considerations of determination of amount of costs, and CPR 46.9, the basis of an assessment between solicitor and client (with CPR 46.9(4) of particular relevance in 'success fee' cases). It will be interesting to see what, if any, relevance the court places on the fixed success fees that applied between the parties to cases under pre-1 April 2013 conditional fee agreements. However, strictly the court is back to an unfettered discretion. This is more challenging in 'damages based agreement' cases, as the payment is simply that – a contractual agreement between the solicitor and the litigation friend for the latter to make a payment to the former. There is no requirement in the regulations that this is set by reference to risk (and this is accepted by CPR PD 21, para 11.3 which refers only to a risk assessment in success fee cases – see [**34.6**] below).

On a more general point about deductions, the Court of Appeal concluded in *Aldred v Cham* [2019] EWCA Civ 1780 that the cost of counsel's opinion advising on the appropriateness of a proposed settlement within the fixed costs regime at Section IIIA of CPR 45, is not a disbursement 'reasonably incurred due to a particular feature of the dispute', but rather it is as a result of a characteristic of the claimant. As such it falls outside recoverable disbursements under CPR 45.29I(2)(h). In any event, the court concluded that this item of work fell within the fixed costs set out in Table 6B (which could not be expected to list every item of work contained within it. This was a routine item of work arising in thousands of claims under Section IIIA, it was not separately provided for in the rule and so must be deemed to be included within the fixed costs). Cross application of this conclusion has created a difficulty with courts undertaking approval hearings by telephone during the Covid-19 restriction on 'face-to-face' hearings. The requirement for approval is due to a characteristic of the claimant and not the dispute and the fact that there is a need to conduct this remotely is certainly not due to a particular feature of the dispute. Accordingly, if the court requires the claimant to arrange a telephone attendance, then the costs of the call provider are irrecoverable. CPR 45.29J does not assist, as disbursements are excluded from the court's jurisdiction to consider additional costs due to exceptional circumstances. It follows that if the approval hearing is to be remote (and it may be that this becomes more routine even when 'face-to-face' hearings are possible), then claimants should request a remote format that does not incur any charge, otherwise they will be absorbing this within the existing fixed fee. Unlike in *Aldred*, this potential problem extends beyond CPR 45 Section IIIA and also arises in CPR 45 Section II and III cases (see the restrictive wording in CPR 45.12(2)(c), CPR 45.13(1) and CPR 45.19(2)(e)).

THE PROCEDURE FOR DETERMINATION OF EXPENSES AND/OR COSTS

[34.6]

Amendments to CPR PD 21 set out the procedure for a litigation friend seeking deductions from damages, whether in respect of expenses or costs and whether in respect of a child or a protected party. In other words these requirements apply at an approval hearing summary assessment, or a separate summary assessment if later, and at a detailed assessment.

The litigation friend must file a witness statement setting out:

- the nature and amount of the costs or expense; and
- the reason the costs or expense were incurred.

(See CPR PD 21, para 11.2.)

In addition, specific requirements apply under CPR PD 21, para 11.3 where the application is made under CPR 21.12(1A). These requirements are that the witness statement must include (or be accompanied by):

- a copy of the agreement;
- the risk assessment by reference to which the success fee was set (note that there is no requirement for 'risk' documentation in respect of a 'damages based agreement' for reasons already considered under [**34.5**] above). While the Conditional Fee Agreements Order 2013 (SI 2013/689) does not specify a requirement for a risk assessment, it seems that the prudent solicitor should prepare one in children cases recognising the requirements of this PD. That risk in the individual case being considered is fundamental to the determination of the appropriate success fee deduction is clear from the decision in *Herbert v HH Law Ltd* [2019] EWCA Civ 527, in which the court, in rejecting a 100% success fee set as part of a business model, concluded that the 'amount of a success fee is traditionally related to litigation risk, as reasonably perceived by the solicitor or counsel at the time the agreement was made'. It is important to note that the presumptions under CPR 46.9(3)(a) and/or (b) did not apply. It should also be remembered that *Herbert* was not a child or protected party case, in which the court will be scrutinising the success fee set and suggestions of 'informed consent' with an eagle-eye;
- the reasons for selecting a particular form of funding;
- the advice given in relation to funding arrangements;
- details of costs agreed, recovered or fixed; and

- confirmation of the sum agreed or awarded in respect of pain, suffering and loss of amenity ('PSLA') and damages for pecuniary loss other than future pecuniary loss net of any DWP sums (as the maximum deduction for costs of 25% is set by reference to PSLA and past pecuniary loss).

The last requirement suggests that where the court is determining the damages, rather than approving them, the application for payment out must be made at a later date as the applicant will know neither the award nor the breakdown of damages to enable the statement to be filed in advance of the hearing/trial.

Obviously, to calculate either the amount of a success fee or the payment due under a damages based agreement under CPR 21.12(1A)(b) at an approval hearing, the court will first need to undertake:

- A solicitor client assessment in respect of a success fee case, as the success fee is determined by reference to these costs (albeit that the sum recoverable from the damages under that percentage, may then be limited by reg 5 of the Conditional Fees Agreement Order 2013, SI 2013/689 and by CPR 21.12(6) and/or (7)), and not, as appears to be the approach routinely taken in court, by reference to that percentage being applied to the recoverable costs (unless the retainer is linked to any applicable recoverable fixed costs).
- In DBA cases, a calculation of the fixed costs applicable (or an assessment of the costs in those cases where fixed recoverable costs do not apply), so that it can determine whether there is any shortfall under the DBA payment after deduction of the recoverable costs (the Damages Based Agreement Regulations 2013, SI 2013/609, reg 4).

APPEAL

[34.7]

An obvious problem arises if the court does not permit the recovery of the damages based payment over and above the recoverable costs, the success fee or other costs/expenses from the damages (whether at approval, a summary or a detailed assessment hearing). How can that decision be challenged? The child/protected party may have no interest in an appeal (indeed quite the reverse). Does this mean that there is nothing the solicitor can do? One possibility may be for the solicitor to apply to be joined for the purpose of launching an appeal. It is far from clear whether this is permissible, but the judgment in *Khans solicitor (a firm) v Chifuntwe* [2013] EWCA Civ 481 may be seen as an authority, albeit arising in an entirely different context, for the proposition that solicitors may apply to be joined where their interest in costs and, by extension, expenses departs from those of the client.

CONCLUSION TO CHILDREN AND PROTECTED PARTIES

[34.8]

Whilst procedural progress has been made, it seems evident that difficulties with deductions from damages remain. In particular:

- there are still procedural conundrums (eg can there be summary assessments of deductions in protected party cases – and if so why is the scope for these greater than in those involving children?);
- the treatment of residual sums payable by children and protected parties after recovery under damages based agreements. Specifically, on what basis can the court interfere with the contractual payment, if it does not exceed the caps imposed by reg 4 of the DBA Regulations 2013 (SI 2013/609) and CPR 21.12;
- can after-the-event insurance premiums be recovered? If they are neither disbursements nor an 'expense of litigation', can they be treated as some other form of recoverable expense?
- how can decisions be appealed in those cases where the child and the legal representatives have divergent financial interests?
- should CPR 46.4(2)(b)(ii) not refer to Section IIIA of Part 45 as well as Sections II and III?

Amendments to the CPR may have been introduced, but there is still scope, and a need, for greater clarification.

CHAPTER 35

LITIGANTS IN PERSON

INTRODUCTION TO LITIGANTS IN PERSON

[35.1]

The Litigants in Person (Costs and Expenses) Act 1975 provides that where any costs of a litigant in person ('LIP') are ordered to be paid by any other party to proceedings there may be allowed (subject to any rule of the court) on assessment or determination of the costs, sums in respect of any work done and any expenses and losses incurred by the LIP in connection with the proceedings. In simple terms the court has the power to award an LIP his costs quantified by either summary or detailed assessment. The provisions of the Act apply to all civil proceedings in the Supreme Court, the Senior Courts, the Family Court, the County Court, the First-tier Tribunal and the Upper Tribunal, in which any order is made that the costs of a LIP are to be paid by any other party to those proceedings or in any other way.

Prior to the coming into force of the Act in April 1976, LIPs (other than those who were practising solicitors) whose costs were ordered to be paid were entitled to recover from the paying party no more than such out-of-pocket expenses as had been properly incurred. The Act enabled LIPs to recover the same category of costs as would have been allowed if the work had been done by a solicitor on the litigant's behalf, limited in amount to such sum as was required to compensate the litigant for the time reasonably spent on preparing and conducting the case, subject to any rules of court.

The term 'self-represented party' briefly gathered attraction from those who considered the term litigant in person to be unwieldy. But, as the rules of court stem from the 1975 Act, the terminology employed by that enactment has prevailed. The Master of the Rolls issued a statement confirming this to be the case. Notwithstanding this and its heading, CPR PD 46, para 3 refers to a 'self-represented litigant' throughout!

WHO IS A LITIGANT IN PERSON?

[35.2]

CPR 46.5(6) provides that a litigant in person includes a company or other corporation which is acting without a legal representative, a barrister, solicitor, solicitor's employee or other authorised litigator who is acting for himself. The decision in *London Scottish Benefit Society v Chorley* (1884) 13 QBD 872, CA and the exception within CPR 46.5(6)(b) for individuals who are represented by a firm in which they are a partner was considered in *Malkinson v Trim* [2002] EWCA Civ 1273; *R (on the application of the Bar Standards Board) v Disciplinary Tribunal of the Council of the Inns & Sivanandan* [2014] EWHC (Admin) 1570, [2016] EWCA Civ 478; and *Halborg v EMW Law LLP* [2017]

EWCA Civ 793. The conclusion reached was that there is a clear distinction between the solicitor/barrister litigant in person and the solicitor who instead of acting in person is represented by his or her firm.

In *Halborg*, Etherton MR summed up the common law position from *Chorley* as follows:

> 'The common law principle established by the Chorley case ("the Chorley principle") may be summarised as being that: (1) a solicitor who acts for himself as a party to litigation can recover not only his out of pocket expenses but also his profit costs, but he cannot recover for anything which his acting in person has made unnecessary; (2) the reason is not because of some special privilege but on the purely pragmatic grounds that (a) there has actually been an expenditure of professional skill and labour by the solicitor party, (b) that expenditure is measurable, (c) the solicitor party would otherwise employ another solicitor and, if successful, would be entitled to recover the costs of that other solicitor, and (d) since he cannot recover for anything which his acting in person has made unnecessary, the unsuccessful party will have the benefit of that disallowance and so would pay less than if the solicitor party had instructed another solicitor.'

The court confirmed that CPR 46.5 was codifying the principles derived from *Chorley* as refined in *Malkinson* (by the express exclusion from the litigant in person provisions of those mentioned in brackets in CPR 46.5(6)(b)) and decided that:

- In CPR 46.5(6)(b), the word 'firm' includes a solicitor in sole practice and 'partner' includes the situation where there is only one principal in a firm.
- An LLP is a corporation and so is governed exclusively by CPR 46.5(6)(a), as CPR 46.5(6)(b) applies only to individuals.
- Where an LLP is a solicitors LLP which acts by its members or employees, it should be treated no differently from in-house legal representatives in possession of practising certificates or equivalent authorisations. As such it is not a litigant in person under CPR 46.5(6)(a) as it is acting with a legal representative.
- A solicitors LLP falls outside CPR 46.5(6)(b) even though it is an authorised person in relation to an activity which constitutes the conduct of litigation (within the meaning of the Legal Services Act 2007 ('the 2007 Act')) and so, on the face of it, falls within CPR 46. 5(6)(b)(v). This is because CPR 46.5(6)(b) is to be interpreted as applying only to individuals.

It is therefore important for solicitor litigants, especially if sole practitioners, to make it clear that they are acting through their firm and not in person, for example by using the firm's, and not private, notepaper.

In *Robinson v EMW Law LLP* [2018] EWHC 1757 (Ch), the court applied the *Chorley* principles to a case where a solicitor retained on a consultancy agreement with a firm representing him, sought to recover costs of his own work which were neither within his retainer liability to that firm nor part of the consultancy work for which he was engaged. It was argued on his behalf that although he was not acting as a litigant in person, he was entitled to recover his costs as a practising solicitor doing work in his own case, even though he was not a partner or member of the firm for whom he consulted. The court agreed confirming that:

> '. . . the rationale of the principle should apply equally where a solicitor in practice instructs another firm to act for him, but relieves that firm from part of the work required in his case by doing it himself . . . (para 32)
>
> . . . it is a claim for expenditure in terms of measurable skill and labour, which the solicitor is entitled to recover on the basis that it avoided his having to pay another solicitor to do the work.' (para 39)

In *R (on the application of the Bar Standards Board) v Disciplinary Tribunal of the Council of the Inns & Sivanandan* (above) the court concluded that cross application of the CPR, and in particular CPR 46.5, had no place in the tribunal, but that had that not been the case, CPR 46.5(4)(a) did not permit a barrister to recover the cost incurred of the provision of 'professional skill'. This is because a barrister self-representing cannot come within the 'firm' exception that applies to solicitors in CPR 46.5(6)(b). However, the Court of Appeal, constrained by statute so to do, remitted the matter to the Bar Standards Board to fix the costs under its own disciplinary tribunal rules.

PROFESSIONAL LITIGANTS IN PERSON

[35.3]

In *Re Nossen's Patent* ([1969] 1 WLR 638) it was held that when it was appropriate a corporate litigant should recover, on a 'between the parties' basis, a sum in respect of expert services performed by its own staff, the amount must be restricted to a reasonable sum for the actual and direct costs of the work undertaken, and not a proportion of the corporation's overheads, no part of such expenditure being occasioned by the litigation. An accountant LIP could at most recover for work done themselves, what the cost of obtaining the expert advice of an independent professional would have been, but is not entitled to recover the costs of general assistance to the expert in the conduct of the litigation (*Sisu Capital Fund Ltd v Tucker* [2005] EWHC 2170 (Ch)). See **[35.2]** above in respect of the distinction between legal professional acting for themselves and acting as formal legal representatives.

FINANCIAL LOSS

[35.4]

The recoverable costs of LIPs depend upon whether they can show that they have suffered any financial loss in dealing with the proceedings. If they can prove a loss, they may claim a sum which does not exceed the amount of the actual financial loss (CPR 46.5(4)(a)). If no loss can be shown, a claim may still be made for the amount of time reasonably spent at the prescribed rate (CPR 46.5(4)(b)). This rate is set out in CPR PD 46, para 3.4. It is currently £19 per hour. In either case, the amount is subject to the cap at CPR 46.5(2) (see **[35.5]** below). The hourly rate compares unfavourably with that allowed under the Employment Appeal Tribunal (Amendment) Rules 2004, which also contains an inbuilt annual increase and which currently stands at £40 per hour. Whilst on the topic of LIP rates, the maximum sum for loss of earnings of a party or a witness at a small claim final hearing is £95 per day (CPR PD 27, para 7.3). The increase to both this and the LIP hourly rate in 2015 were to reflect the increase in the average weekly earnings index since the previous amendment to rate in 2011. By way of aside, this £95 is more than a party or witness may recover in claims falling within Section IIIA that do not exceed £10,000. Those parties and witnesses are limited to £90 per day.

The Two Thirds Rule – CPR 46.5(2)

[35.5]

Rules of court have always limited the costs recoverable by a LIP to two-thirds of the amount which would have been allowed to a legal representative. The reasoning behind this figure is that a solicitor's charges traditionally included a 50% profit mark-up on the expense rate, but as a LIP may not make a profit out of the costs of litigation, the 50% is deducted, leaving two-thirds.

Since there is no profit mark up on disbursements, the two thirds rule does not apply to them.

The provision that a LIP may only recover two-thirds of what a notional solicitor would have charged limits the amount the LIP may claim for any particular item. The correct approach for the assessment of a LIP claiming at the specified rate is to ascertain what the total is for an item and then compare that with two-thirds of the notional solicitor's rate and allow the lower of the two items. This means that the bill of costs drawn by the LIP must be gone through in some detail, item by item (*Morris v Wiltshire & Woodspring District Council* (16 January 1998, unreported, QBD).

In *R (on the application of Wulfsohn) v Legal Services Commission* [2002] EWCA Civ 250, a successful LIP produced a rough costs schedule purporting to show that he had been engaged for over 1,200 hours on research and he also gave oral evidence confirming this, which the court had no reason to disbelieve. In these circumstances the right course was to start with the cap imposed by CPR 46.5(2) which provides that the costs of a litigant in person shall not exceed two-thirds of the amount which would have been allowed if the litigant in person had been represented by a legal representative. The litigant in person produced a letter to him from a firm of solicitors saying: 'On the limited information that we have been provided by yourself and the Citizens Advice Bureau in the Royal Courts of Justice and having seen at a very preliminary stage the documentation with regards the matter we would estimate that the legal costs would be in the region of £15,000 to £20,000 plus VAT'. Doing the best it could on the information in front of it, the court, 'being extremely rough-and-ready' about it, took the figure of £15,000 which resulted in a cap of £10,000. In addition to that, the court allowed photocopying, postage and travelling totalling £460, resulting in a total award of costs of £10,460, instead of the £120 awarded by the trial judge.

Under the proportionality cross check in CPR 44.3(2)(a), the court must determine what is the proportionate figure that a notional solicitor would have been allowed overall and then ensure that the total figure at the end of any assessment of the LIP's costs does not exceed two thirds of this sum.

Legal Costs

[35.6]

Although litigants may have acted in person without a solicitor on the record, they are nevertheless entitled to recover payments reasonably made for legal services in two respects:

(1) Legal services relating to the conduct of the proceedings (CPR 46. 5(3)(b)).
(2) The costs of obtaining expert assistance in connection with assessing the claim for costs, including representation on a detailed assessment (CPR 46.5(3)(c)).

There is no guidance given in respect of (1). It will usually be a solicitor but with the relaxation of the Bar's prohibition on effectively conducting proceedings, it may be a barrister via the direct access scheme.

By contrast, there is a list of no fewer than seven categories of expert set out in CPR PD 46, para 3.1 including two different kinds of 'costs draftsmen' and costs lawyers.

The price of a LIP not using a solicitor was dramatically illustrated in *Agassi v Robinson (Inspector of Taxes)* [2005] EWCA Civ 1507. Former Wimbledon champion, Andre Agassi, in his battle with the taxman retained a tax expert who was a member of the Chartered Institute of Taxation licensed to instruct counsel directly. No solicitors were involved. Mr Agassi was awarded his costs as a LIP. Although Mr Agassi could recover counsel's fee as a disbursement he was not entitled to recover as a LIP costs in respect of work done by the tax expert which would normally have been done by a solicitor.

Agassi was followed in the SCCO in *Cuthbert v Gair (t/a Bowes Manor Equestrian Centre)* (2008) 152 Sol Jo (no 38) 29. The claimant issued proceedings for damages for personal injuries suffered while attending an equestrian event, but served notice of discontinuance. On the detailed assessment of the defendants' costs, the defendants sought to recover payments made to a loss adjuster by the defendants' insurers, both before and after solicitors were instructed. The work of the loss adjuster under the first invoice included corresponding with the claimant's solicitor, investigating the accident, obtaining witness statements and dealing with documentation. That work was work that would normally be carried out by a solicitor and the defendants were not entitled to recover costs in respect of it.

In respect of a second invoice, for work done by the loss adjuster after solicitors had been instructed, it was necessary to assess the relationship between the defendant's solicitors and the loss adjuster. If the defendant's solicitors had sought assistance from the loss adjuster on an agency basis, then they would have been entitled to recover their costs, not as a disbursement, but as a profit cost, following *Crane v Canons Leisure Centre* [2007] EWCA Civ 1352. However no true agency agreement existed between the solicitors and the loss adjuster: there was no letter of instruction and no terms of engagement. On that basis, it was not possible for the defendants to recover the loss adjuster's fees after the solicitors had been instructed.

Furthermore, the work undertaken by the loss adjuster did not fall within the category of 'expert assistance' that otherwise might have rendered the costs recoverable (*Re Nossen's Letter Patent* [1969] 1 WLR 638). The case was a simple one of an insurer contracting out part of its work in order to investigate claims made against the insured. It was routine work, which many insurers would have undertaken in-house. The mere fact that the defendants' insurer chose to contract out that work did not render the costs recoverable.

The meaning of 'legal services relating to the conduct of the proceedings' received further consideration in the case of *Campbell v Campbell* [2018] EWCA Civ 80, in which the claimant endeavoured to recover the costs of a firm of Jersey advocates. The advocate who had provided assistance to the claimant was not entitled to practise as a solicitor in England and Wales at the time. The court determined that legal services must be 'provided by or under the supervision of a lawyer' and that lawyer must be 'someone who can be competent to supply services "relating to the conduct of the proceedings", which will be proceedings in this jurisdiction'. The court concluded that a foreign lawyer could not meet this requirement, and could not be regarded as a lawyer or as providing legal services. What matters, for the purposes of CPR 46.5(3)(b), is expertise in the law and procedure governing the relevant proceedings, namely that of England and Wales.

Fast Track Trial Costs

[35.7]

Where a LIP appears at a Fast Track trial, CPR 45.39(5) makes express provision for how costs are to be awarded. It maintains the distinction between LIPs who can demonstrate a financial loss and those that cannot:

- LIPs who can prove financial loss will receive two thirds of the amount that would have been award as advocates' fees;
- LIPs who cannot prove financial loss will receive an amount in respect of the time spent reasonably doing the work at the rate of £19 per hour (still subject to the two thirds cap under CPR 46.5(2)).

The amount of the advocate's fees is set in 4 bands as discussed in Chapter 26. Those figures are only varied if there has been unreasonable or improper behaviour by one or more of the parties during the hearing.

PROCEDURE TO QUANTIFY LOSS

[35.8]

The procedural requirements for LIPs who wish to pursue financial loss are set out at CPR PD 46, paras 3.2 and 3.3. These require the LIP who wishes to prove financial loss to produce written evidence relied upon in support to the court and the party against whom these costs are sought at least 24 hours before the hearing at which the issue may be decided. This evidence must also be served with the notice of commencement in respect of any detailed assessment proceedings.

THE FUTURE OF LITIGANTS IN PERSON

[35.9]

The suggestion that there may be a new type of representative – the professional McKenzie Friend with some rights to conduct litigation – raises potentially interesting issues. The long-awaited outcome of the Judicial Consultation '*Reforming the courts' approach to McKenzie Friends*' was revealed in 2017. The original proposal for discussion included a provision at draft CPR 3.22(12) that saw a prohibition on the recovery as a disbursement by a LIP of the fees of any Court Supporter (McKenzie Friend). However, the large volume of responses resulted in a decision to consider the proposals further through the establishment of a working group. The working group subsequently reported back to the Lord Chief Justice and the Judicial Executive Board ('JEB'). The result was the February 2019 Consultation Response 'Reforming the courts approach to McKenzie Friends'. The upshot was that whilst the JEB remains deeply concerned about the proliferation of unregulated remunerated McKenzie Friends 'it is for the government to consider appropriate steps to be taken to enable LiPs to secure effective access to legal assistance, legal advice and, where necessary, representation'. The Response paper has been referred for consideration by the Lord Chancellor. Whatever the eventual outcome, the rise in the number of LIPs in the court system, leading inevitably to an increase in assessments involving consideration of financial loss, is likely to give CPR 46.5 an increased prominence.

CHAPTER 36

COSTS PAYABLE UNDER A CONTRACT

INTRODUCTION TO COSTS PAYABLE UNDER A CONTRACT

[36.1]

CPR 44.5 and CPR PD 44, para 7 deal with the amount of costs recoverable where they are payable pursuant to a contract. The most obvious example of this situation relates to mortgage agreements but it is possible for general contractual arrangements to come within these provisions, notwithstanding the old maxim that the law does not protect a party from a bad bargain (including provisions as to payment of costs).

MORTGAGES

[36.2]

Many contracts, particularly mortgages, contain provisions to the effect that one or other party will be liable for the costs incurred pursuant to the contract. Under the terms of a mortgage deed, the mortgagee is usually entitled to add to his security his usual and proper costs of proceedings between himself and the mortgagor or any surety. He does not require an order from the court to do so. For an example of this, see *AIB Group plc v Turner* [2016] EWHC 219 (Ch). However, the court has an equitable jurisdiction to disallow all or part of a mortgagee's costs as being unreasonably incurred or of an unreasonable amount, in fixing the terms of redemption. In addition to his costs of proceedings between himself and the mortgagor, a mortgagee may recover the reasonable and proper costs of proceedings between himself and a third party where what is impugned is the title to the estate. But where a third party impugns the title to a mortgage or the enforcement or exercise of some right or power accruing to the mortgagee under it, the mortgagee's costs of the proceedings, even though reasonable and proper, are not recoverable from the mortgagor (*Parker-Tweedale v Dunbar Bank plc (No 2)* [1991] Ch 26, CA).

There is a presumption that costs payable under a mortgage or any other contract are reasonably and properly incurred and such costs are to be paid on the indemnity basis (*Gomba Holdings (UK) Ltd v Minories Finance Ltd (No 2)* [1993] Ch 171, [1992] 4 All ER 588, CA).

CPR 44.5 is a summary of the law as explained above, supplemented by the provisions of CPR PD 44, para 7. To reflect the advantageous position of a mortgagee with such a contractual entitlement, CPR PD 44, para 9.3 varies the general rule otherwise usually applying for the timing of summary assessment. Paragraph 9.3 states:

> 'The general rule in paragraph 9.2 does not apply to a mortgagee's costs incurred in mortgage possession proceedings or other proceedings relating to a mortgage unless

the mortgagee asks the court to make an order for the mortgagee's costs to be paid by another party.'

In other words, the costs will not be summarily assessed by the court unless the mortgagee wishes this to take place.

A mortgagor who wishes to challenge the level of fees paid by the mortgagee to its solicitor (and claimed from the mortgagor) could bring proceedings under s 71 of the Solicitors Act 1974 as the 'party chargeable'. But the issues outlined in *Tim Martin Interiors Ltd v Akin Gump LLP* [2011] EWCA Civ 1574 need to be considered before doing so (see [**3.24**]). An inquiry as to the level of costs incurred via the Chancery Division initially may be the better approach.

LANDLORD AND TENANT

[36.3]

The Court of Appeal in *Church Comrs v Ibrahim* [1997] 1 EGLR 13, [1997] 03 EG 136, CA, confirmed that the principles in *Gomba Holdings* are not confined to mortgage cases. It held that in general the landlord is not to be deprived of a contractual right to indemnity costs. Although the court always retains a discretion on costs, that discretion should be used to reflect the contractual agreement between the landlord and the tenant unless the landlord's conduct is improper or unreasonable. This decision clarified the landlord's position on costs and made it easier either to negotiate or obtain from the court adequate compensation for the costs of litigation against defaulting tenants. However, the wording of the indemnity clause must be clear and a claim to costs should be fully pleaded in the particulars of claim (or in the defence: *Renewable Power & Light Ltd v McCarthy Tetrault* [2014] EWHC 3848 (Ch)).

In *Forcelux Ltd v Binnie* [2009] EWCA Civ 1077 the tenant had fallen into arrears with payment of ground rent and charges and the landlord obtained a default judgment against him. The landlord obtained an order for possession which a district judge set aside in the exercise of his discretion under CPR 39.3 and granted relief from forfeiture on terms as to payment of outstanding monies. The Court of Appeal confirmed the setting aside of the possession order. The landlord claimed to be entitled to its costs of the entirety of the proceedings on the basis that the tenant had covenanted in the lease to pay 'all costs charges and expenses (including legal costs . . .) which may be incurred by the lessor in or in contemplation . . . of any steps or proceedings under Section 146 of the Landlord and Tenant Act 1925'.

The Court of Appeal held that possession proceedings brought to enforce a right of re-entry following a notice under s 146(1) of the Act were proceedings 'under' that section. The possession action was within the scope of the words 'any statutory proceedings' within the scope of the covenant. It followed that the application to set aside the possession order was as much an application as the application for relief and forfeiture coupled with it, and was also within the scope of those words. However, the tenant had been the substantial winner of the appeal. Even assuming that the contractual provisions in the lease covered the costs of the appeal, which was a matter of construction, the contractual right was not an absolute one and did not oust the jurisdiction of the court to make another order if there were good reasons for doing so. In the circumstances, the tenant was entitled to a costs order which departed from the contract in the exercise of the court's discretion. Similarly, in *Fairbairn v Etal Court Maintenance Ltd* [2015] UKUT 639 (LC) the landlord could not rely on the contractual provisions to allow it to recoup money paid to its solicitors for an unsuccessful defence of proceedings brought against it by the tenant.

The tenant fared less well in *Christoforou v Diogenis* [2013] UKUT 586 (LC) where the Upper Tribunal dismissed his appeal against a decision of the Leasehold Valuation Tribunal. The tenant had withheld his service charge payment and his landlord had commenced proceedings in the LVT for recovery of the sums owing. That had ultimately required proceedings in the County Court as well and involved incurring £21,000 in costs altogether. They were claimed as administration charges as part of the rent. When the tenant resisted the claim for costs, the landlord proceeded to a second LVT under the Commonhold and Leasehold Reform Act 2002 for a determination of whether the covenant in the lease regarding legal costs could be used to pay these costs. The tribunal decided that the clause was sufficiently wide and that the costs were properly to be regarded as administration charges under the Act. The Upper Tribunal upheld those decisions as well as the conclusion that the costs incurred had not been disproportionately incurred. While it was true that costs were not recoverable in the LVT as such, they were recoverable in any event under the covenant in the lease.

Legal costs in three separate actions brought against the leaseholders by the landlord were largely recoverable in *Eshraghi v 7/9 Avenue Road (London House) Ltd* [2020] UKUT 208 (LC). Proceedings concerning repairs – even though originally disputed by the landlord – and unpaid service charges were both matters of good estate management which could be claimed under the lease's provisions. The third claim had involved litigation regarding who were the directors of the leasehold company. Whilst the landlord's costs were initially incurred for the benefit of the building and its tenants as a whole, since they concerned interference with the management (a view which was shared by the court) by the claimants wrongly holding themselves out to be directors. However, that changed when the claimants gave undertakings that they would not hold themselves out in this way any longer. Thereafter, the dispute was about control of the landlord company. Such arguments about corporate governance did not come within the terms of the lease regarding good estate management etc.

Service charge claims

[36.4]

There are three potential routes for a landlord to recover costs from his tenant. A court order may be possible if formal court proceedings are available. A provision in the lease itself may deal with this if it is sufficiently precise although this seems to be relatively rare. The third option is via the service charge. There are numerous decisions in the Upper Tribunal on appeal from the First-tier Tribunal on the landlord relying upon the terms of the service charge, eg, *Cannon and Cannon v 38 Lambs Conduit LLP* [2016] UKUT 371 (LC).

The decisions are at pains to point out that the particular service charge provision needs to be examined given the difference in the drafting of them from lease to lease. Thereafter, ordinary contractual construction principles apply in the context of the lease. The leading decision is *Arnold v Britton* [2015] UKSC 36 and at para 15 Neuberger L summarised this approach as being ascertaining the intention of the parties by:

> '. . . focussing on the meaning of the relevant words . . . in their documentary, factual and commercial context. That meaning has to be assessed in the light of (i) the natural and ordinary meaning of the clause, (ii) any other relevant provisions of the lease, (iii) the overall purpose of the clause and the lease, (iv) the facts and circumstances known or assumed by the parties at the time that the document was executed, and (v) commercial common sense, but (vi) disregarding subjective evidence of any party's intentions.'

There is no need to construe the terms of the service charge restrictively and general wording has been held to be sufficient in the context of a particular case. But, rather obviously, the clearer the natural meaning of the clause is, the more difficult it will be for a party to persuade a court to depart from it.

Where a tenant exercises his right under the Leasehold Reform Housing and Urban Development Act 1993 to extend his lease, the tenant is required to pay the landlord's costs in accordance with s 60 of that Act. The sums involved are generally modest but if you are dealing with a dispute of such costs, the decision of HHJ Huskinson in *Sinclair Gardens Investments (Kensington) Ltd v Wisbey* [2016] UKUT 203 (LC) contains an examination of what is and is not recoverable by the landlord within s 60.

Costs in the First-tier Tribunals

[36.5]

Where proceedings are brought in the First-tier Tribunal (Property Chamber) – formerly the Land Valuation Tribunal – costs are only recoverable between the parties where the behaviour can be criticised (see rule 13 of the Tribunal Procedure (First-tier Tribunal) (Property Chamber) Rules 2013). This limited ability to recover costs demonstrates the importance of a contractual provision to recover costs between landlords and tenants.

For example, in *Marcus J Staples v Danute Liuba Cranfield* [2018] UKUT 341 (LC), four of the five tenants of a leasehold property took the freeholder (who was also the other tenant) to court to appoint a manager of the property in place of the freeholder. An order was duly made under s 24 of the Landlord and Tenant Act 1987. The freeholder failed to comply with that order and so the appellant, as the new manager, applied for further directions from the court. The First-tier Tribunal Property Chamber (Residential Property) ('FTT') concluded that Rule 13 of its procedural rules only allowed it to make an order for costs where there had been unreasonable conduct in this sort of case. The non-compliance with the earlier order occurred prior to the application before the Tribunal and so could not be taken into account (based on earlier authority). There was no power to award costs under s 24 of the Act when seeking directions and so the appellant could not have an order for costs. His fees would have to be paid out of the service charge. HHJ Huskisson, sitting in the Upper Tribunal, agreed with the FTT's conclusion about the absence of any free-standing power under s 24. But he concluded that the earlier non-compliance amounted to unreasonable conduct in the 'bringing defending or conducting proceedings' under Rule 13 and so the freeholder could be ordered to pay costs if the FTT ultimately concluded that the conduct complained of did in fact amount to unreasonable conduct.

CONTRACTUAL COSTS

[36.6]

The *Gomba Holdings* approach was followed in spirit, if not expressly stated, in *Alafco Irish Aircraft Leasing Sixteen Ltd v Hong Kong Airlines Ltd* [2019] EWHC 3668 (Comm). Moulder J was requested by the successful claimant to award indemnity basis costs on either a conduct basis or via a term in the contract. She was not persuaded that the defendant's conduct had been 'out of the norm' and so declined to make the order based on conduct. However, she did construe the contractual term of paying 'on demand all reasonable costs and expenses (including reasonable legal expenses)' as being appropriate to found an indemnity basis costs order. In this, she said she was following the Court of Appeal in *Littlestone v Macleish* [2016] EWCA Civ 127, (2016) Times, 15 April notwithstanding that Briggs LJ was considering a clause which did not contain the word 'reasonable'. As she pointed out, even an indemnity basis order requires the receiving party to demonstrate that the costs claimed are reasonable.

In *Venture Finance plc v Mead* [2005] EWCA Civ 325, the claimant had obtained judgment by consent for less than one-third of the amount claimed but there was nothing that enabled the judge to decide why it had been willing to settle for that sum. It was impossible to say that one party had obviously won and the other had obviously lost. The judge had erred in principle. He had wrongly thought that the only order for costs that gave effect to the parties' contractual rights was that each defendant should be liable for only 50% of the whole costs of the proceedings. The contractual obligation on each defendant was to pay all costs and expenses arising out of the recovery of monies from that defendant under the guarantee. The right course for the judge was to consider, in relation to each defendant, the extent to which the whole costs of the proceedings could be said to arise out of the claim to recover under the guarantee obligations of that defendant. That approach might have led to a conclusion that a proper proportion of the whole costs of proceedings to be awarded against each defendant was 100%, or some lower proportion. It was difficult to see how the appropriate proportion could be as low as 50%. If the claimant could not recover 100% of its costs from the second defendant, it would be left with a shortfall as the first defendant was bankrupt.

The judge had also erred in thinking that he was required to apply what is now CPR 44.5 (Amount of costs where costs are payable under a contract) when making the costs order. That rule applied only at the stage when the court was assessing costs and not when it was deciding by whom costs should be paid. The judge should have been exercising his discretion under what is now CPR rule 44.2 and the Senior Courts Act 1981, s 51(3).

The case of *Astrazeneca UK Ltd v International Business Machines Corpn* [2011] EWHC 3373 (TCC), confirmed that while, in principle, there might be two alternative bases for obtaining costs, namely under the terms of an express contractual indemnity or by the exercise of the court's discretion pursuant to s 51 of the Senior Courts Act 1981 and the CPR, the fact that the court made an order pursuant to s 51 did not detract from any contractual right to claim indemnity costs. It is clear that in exercising its discretion under CPR 44.2, the court should ordinarily exercise that discretion so as to reflect the contractual right.

Equally, if the court were giving effect to a contractual right to costs, then the provisions of CPR 44.5 and CPR PD 44, para 7 would provide, first, that the costs recoverable were those which had been reasonably incurred and reasonable in amount, and, second, that the costs payable should be disallowed if the court was satisfied by the paying party that costs had been unreasonably incurred or were unreasonable in amount. The fact that there was a contractual obligation to pay costs meant that the court ought to exercise its discretion so as to reflect those contractual rights and also be consistent with the requirements of CPR 44.5.

In *Renewable Power & Light Ltd* the court decided that the defendant was entitled to its contractual indemnity. Morgan J then considered the best way of dealing with assessing that indemnity. He said:

> 'The next question is: how procedurally is the amount of the indemnity in relation to costs to be quantified? Should I enter judgment for an indemnity to be assessed and then direct an account or an inquiry, perhaps before a costs judge? It seems to me that the most convenient course is simply to make a declaration of Grant Thornton's entitlement to an indemnity and then to make an order for costs which reflects that entitlement, and then to direct a detailed assessment of the relevant costs on the indemnity basis. It seems to me that procedural course is supported by the approach in *Gomba Holdings*.'

Contractual versus fixed costs

[36.7]

In *Chaplair Ltd v Kumari* [2015] EWCA Civ 798, the landlord defendant brought proceedings in the County Court for unpaid rent and service charges. There were related proceedings brought in the Leasehold Valuation Tribunal. The Court of Appeal found that the costs incurred in the LVT proceedings could be claimed under the terms of the lease. The Court then went on to consider the basis on which those costs should be quantified. In the County Court proceedings the parties agreed to them being allocated to the small claims track because the sums involved did not exceed £10,000. The appellant defendant argued that the small claims track limits as to recoverable costs must apply to the LVT proceedings. The respondent argued that the costs were payable based on the contract between the parties and these did not contemplate limitations based on court tracks. The Court of Appeal preferred the landlord's position and upheld HHJ Wulwik's judgment. The Court was allowing the contractual claim for costs to take effect through CPR 44.5. CPR 27.14 had to be read subject to that provision in order to give statutory effect to the decision in *Gomba Holdings* (see [**26.47**]).

CHAPTER 37

MULTI-PARTY LITIGATION

INTRODUCTION TO MULTI-PARTY LITIGATION

[37.1]

Many cases are brought by more than one claimant or are defended by more than one defendant. The CPR is drafted to cope with such multiplicity at the outset and for the bringing or removing of parties during the proceedings. Indeed, entities such as litigation funders are sometimes made parties only during the detailed assessment proceedings.

Such cases are a world away from claims which are brought by a mass of claimants against large, insured defendants or financial institutions. Such proceedings bring case management issues for the court: these are usually dealt with by seeking to define common issues which can be determined so that resolution of all of the claims can then be achieved.

Prior to the CPR's introduction, the case management wheel was reinvented for each set of proceedings by a practice direction being created for the purposes of the litigation and being signed off by the Lord Chief Justice or Lord Chancellor. The advent of the CPR afforded an opportunity to bring a more consistent and structured approach, hence Section III of CPR Part 19 which contains the rules concerning Group Litigation Orders ('GLOs') which are discussed below.

For cases which cannot show sufficient homogeneity to merit a GLO, the courts tend to adopt similar strategies of test or lead claimants who can produce factual examples on which the parties can argue their points of principle.

It is not always possible to ascertain whether a GLO was made in an individual case, even when reading the judgments of the court. Unless we think that there is a specific difference between the approach in GLOs and other cases, we have not sought to distinguish between the two in this chapter. Nor do we seek to deal with the pros and cons of group litigation nor its procedural niceties (unless they impact on costs) as such, the focus is very much on the costs issues arising from litigation between multiple parties.

You may find the answer to specific questions regarding multiple parties in Part 29 concerning how common costs are apportioned and divided between parties and in respect of solicitors and their clients (see **[29.36]**).

ORDERS FOR COSTS

Between the parties

[37.2]

The starting point to note is that there is no difference between multi-party actions, including GLOs, and any other proceedings. Consequently, you are referred to Chapter 22 in respect of the considerations of the court when making an award for costs: in a nutshell whether costs should follow the event or not.

The multiplicity of parties can bring additional complexity to deciding who won. At **[22.17]** we refer to the case of *BCCI v Ali (No 3)* [1999] NLJ 1734 Vol 149 in which Lightman J concluded that there had been a draw and so there should be no order for costs. Also, in *Atlasjet Havacilik Anonim Sirketi v Kupeli* [2018] EWCA Civ 1264, the Court of Appeal considered this issue upon an appeal where the trial judge had awarded the claimants 33% of their costs. The court decided that the 'who wrote the cheque' test was too simplistic in group litigation where only 14 of 792 received a cheque. Having undertaken a fact-specific analysis, the court decided that the appropriate course was to make no order as to costs given the extent of the success of the original defendant on the preliminary issues such that two of the three categories of claimant failed completely. Neither side had come anywhere near achieving a complete success.

In *Jones v Secretary of State for Energy and Climate Change* [2012] EWHC 3647 (QB) (the phurnacite litigation), Swift J had to consider the appropriate costs order to make where the lead claimants had lost at trial on some of the issues; namely causation of skin and bladder cancer. The parties were in full agreement on one point, namely that whatever she did, the judge should not make an issue-based order for costs as such would present 'extremely complex problems for the judge carrying out the detailed assessment of costs and would in all probability add significantly to the costs of the assessment process'. The judge noted how the general rule was that the successful party will usually get their costs and that there was no reason to treat GLO cases any differently. The defendants' arguments as to what percentage reduction should be made to reflect the issues upon which the claimants had lost concentrated too much, in the judge's eyes, on what time had been spent on such issues at trial. She felt, no doubt correctly, that she must consider work done on the litigation as a whole. She accepted that the interests of justice demanded that there must be some reduction in the claimants' entitlement to costs to reflect the issues on which they had lost, this being more than simply a case of the inevitable loss of one or two issues on the way to ultimate success at trial, and in adopting an admittedly 'broad brush approach', awarded the claimants 80% of their common costs.

Fraser J allowed the claimants 90% of their costs of the common issues following a trial on the 23 identified issues in *Bates v Post Office Ltd* [2019] EWHC 1373 (QB). The defendant argued that the hearing was akin to a preliminary issues hearing between parties when seeking to persuade the judge to reserve the costs until causation and quantum had been dealt with. Fraser J was clear in his view that there were considerable differences between a GLO case considering common issues and preliminary issues in an ordinary case. For example, according to CPR 46.6(5) he was required to decide how much of the hearing related to the common GLO issues as opposed to other individual matters. The order for costs was very much dependent on not only the facts and issues but also the bespoke procedure chosen to deal with the particular group litigation.

Between the claimants

[37.3]

Owing to the fact that a few claims are selected out of a large number as test cases, issues can crop up regarding how the costs of those cases are to be apportioned among all of the claimants in a variety of circumstances. For example, when a between the parties' costs award in their favour is obtained is for much less than the solicitor and client costs, or where there is an adverse costs order. Such problems can be headed off by an appropriately worded costs sharing agreement and many pieces of group litigation are dealt with in this way. There is no mention of such agreements in the CPR and it takes experience to know of the need for essentially a second agreement with each client. Where that has not been done, arguments of the following sort can ensue.

In *Ochwat v Watson Burton (a firm)* [1999] All ER (D) 1407, the test case claimants won on the general issues of duty of care and breach of that duty, but failed on causation. The judge awarded the defendants 75% of their costs of which he ordered the test case claimants to pay 75% and the remaining claimants 25%. On appeal it was held that this was unfair to the test case claimants and that the costs awarded to the defendants should be paid by all the claimants.

In a further decision in the *BCCI v Ali* proceedings ((13 April 2000, unreported), Ch D) of some 300 claimants, five were chosen as test cases. They were not awarded any between the parties' costs, (although as seen above, they were not ordered to pay any either) but the non-test case claimants argued that the solicitor and client costs should be paid solely by the test case claimants, on the grounds that they had lost because of their own dishonesty. The court found that when the test cases were chosen it was the common expectation of all the claimants that the test case costs would be shared equally, and it so ordered.

GROUP LITIGATION ORDERS

[37.4]

A GLO will be made where the claims can demonstrate sufficient 'common or related issues of fact or law' (CPR 19.10) to justify the formalities and effects of a GLO. Where the parties can demonstrate such issues, a register of claims will be created and all claimants on the register (and those who join later) will be bound by decisions in the proceedings, unless they persuade the court otherwise. The GLO will identify the court dealing with the case and give case management directions, often on a fixed, regular basis to ensure that progress is being made. The making of a GLO represents a commitment on the part of the court (as well as the parties) to provide additional resources to manage the litigation. Two potentially leading firms were reminded of the need for co-operation between firms in *Lungowe v Vedanta Resources plc company* [2020] EWHC 749 (TCC), [2020] BLR 410. Fraser J's concise judgment contains any number of critical comments regarding the two firms appearing to safeguard their own interests rather than acting in the spirit of a GLO. Perhaps the most trenchant observation, at paragraph 25, is that the 'hybrid' order suggested by the solicitors (so that there were two strands of cases run by the different firms) was not an accurate description of the order sought and that it 'had more similarities to Frankenstein's monster'.

The claimants were also limited to one counsel team, a proposition which Fraser J considered to be so obvious that it had not been stated expressly anywhere else before. The GLO issues were bound to involve a 'co-existence of interest' amongst all the claimants and so could be represented by one team, at least until any non-GLO issues fell to be considered.

Consequently, the court needs to be in a position to consider fully whether to make such an order. Applications made prematurely may therefore be penalised in costs: *Re VW NOX Emissions Group Litigation* [2018] EWHC 2308 (QB).

There is no mention of how costs are to be dealt with in either Section III of Part 19 or its accompanying practice direction (CPR PD 19B). The rules regarding costs are to be found in CPR 46.6 (there is nothing additional in CPR PD 46).

Definitions

[37.5]

CPR 46.6, when first introduced in the CPR in 2000 (as CPR 48.6), sought to codify previous case law regarding multi-party proceedings. In particular, the distinction between costs incurred for the good of all (or at least most) of the parties on one side of the proceedings and those costs incurred solely for the individual party. Such costs were known as either common costs or individual costs. The latter really need no definition in CPR 46.6 and are discussed at **[37.6]** below.

The definition of common costs is more detailed. First, they relate to costs incurred upon the matters which have been identified as the GLO issues. These are the issues that justify case managing the claims together under a GLO. This is not necessarily the same as the issues with which the court ultimately needs to grapple at the end of the case to determine the claims.

Second, they concern costs incurred by the lead legal representative in administering the matter. Neither of these categories is a surprise. The third, and more awkward, category is for individual costs incurred whilst that individual's case was identified as a test case. It is obvious that such costs ought to be dealt with in common between the claimants rather than left to the individual who happens to be one of the test cases. Even so, there is still scope for skirmishes along the boundaries of the individual costs of test case claimants, for example as to whether a piece of work actually fell within the issues being tested.

Individual, joint or several liability?

[37.6]

A group litigant is a litigant on the GLO register. The starting point in respect of liability for costs is that the group litigant will be liable to his solicitor for a several share of the common costs and all of his individual costs. If the claim is successful he will obviously seek to get such costs back from his opponent. If the case is unsuccessful, then, in addition to being liable for his own solicitor's costs, he will also be liable for a several share of his opponent's costs.

There are several nuances to be considered to this starting point. The first is that the rules allow for the court to make some other order in respect of any of these costs. The second is that many group litigants use CFAs and may use DBAs in the future. The extent of the liability to the group litigant's own solicitor will be less than the full costs where unsuccessful and there may in fact be no liability at all.

What about litigants who arrive late at the party or who leave early? Their liability for their individual costs is not affected and they remain liable for them. In relation to common costs, the court is expressly given the power to order that a late arriving litigant is to be liable for a proportion of the common costs already incurred (CPR 46.6(6)) and similarly may require a litigant whose claim is removed from the register to be liable for a proportion of costs up to the date of departure (CPR 46.6(7)).

The toing and froing of claimants on a GLO register is presumably why the successful defendants in *Sharp v Blank* [2020] EWHC 1870 (Ch), [2020] Costs LR 835 sought to base their order for costs as being against those claimants on the register at a particular point ('at the conclusion of the hearing'). This was contrary to the terms of the GLO which required a quarterly calculation based on the number of claimants on the register at the beginning of that quarter. Sir Alistair Norris said that, unless the burdensome provision could not be completed (eg because of inadequate records), then the costs order that he made could not disturb the liability amongst the claimants as set out in the GLO.

CPR 46.6 does not expressly permit the court to award costs after a party's date of departure but, given the Court of Appeal's decision in *Dufoo v Tolaini* [2014] EWCA Civ 1536 (see **[29.44]**), removal from the register may not be the end of the matter.

COMMON COSTS

[37.7]

The position outside GLO cases largely mirrors the codified position in CPR 46.6. Where a client is a member of a group involved in litigation which is awarded costs against the other party he is entitled to recover the costs for which he would have been liable to his solicitor. He is liable to his solicitor for all costs properly incurred whether they were incurred solely on his behalf or whether they were incurred for the benefit of the group and he has only to pay an appropriate proportion.

In *Rowe v Ingenious Media Holdings plc* [2020] EWHC 235 (Ch), Nugee J considered an application by the claimants for an order that they would only be severally liable if any adverse costs orders were made against them. The judge accepted that the default position in GLO cases of several liability could not be automatically applied to this case since it was not subject to a GLO. But he considered it to be the common approach, essentially because of the views of the Court of Appeal in *Ward v Guinness Mahon plc* [1996] 1 WLR 894. In that case, the court considered who should bear the risk of a shortfall in recovery where the defendant was successful and some of the claimants were unable to pay their share. Should it be the defendant or the remainder of the claimants? The Court of Appeal in *Ward* was firmly of the view that it should be the defendant and so several liability only should be required of the claimants. In a nutshell, the defendant was in no worse position under such an order than it would have been if each claimant had sued it individually and some of them were unable to meet the costs of the defendant's successful defence.

Furthermore, Nugee J said that the several liability shares should be calculated pro rata rather than per capita. In other words, those claimants with smaller claims would only meet a smaller share of the defendant's costs than claimants who were seeking much larger sums.

It would be good practice for a solicitor to mention in a client care letter that some of the work to be done would be for the benefit of a group of clients and that individuals would be liable only for their share. It would be sensible for a firm to keep records of the number of clients for whom it was acting at any time. Such records would help to demonstrate, if need be, that the proportion claimed for any individual client was justified. Where solicitors intend to claim a share of costs incurred by other solicitors, it would be wise for them to ensure that the terms of the agreement between the solicitors is clearly defined, to demonstrate more easily that the bill under scrutiny is reasonable and proportionate. In short, such records are desirable because they would be an aid to proving the reasonableness of a bill; they are not required as a pre-requisite to the recovery of a share of common costs.

Where the litigation has been funded under CFAs entered into by each client, it would only be necessary for the individual client to demonstrate that there is an agreement between him and his solicitor collateral to the CFA specifically relating to generic costs if generic costs were in some way different from costs incurred solely for the individual client. There is therefore no requirement for any additional or collateral agreement relating to generic costs in a CFA for a successful claimant to recover such costs in an action where no group litigation order has been made (*Brown v Russell Young & Co* [2007] EWCA Civ 43).

There is nothing fundamentally different or special about common costs; they are simply costs that have been shared for the sensible purpose of keeping the costs of each claim down. However, there is often everything fundamentally different about assessing common costs in practice (see **[29.36]**).

INDIVIDUAL COSTS

[37.8]

Individual costs do not generally cause any particular problem in group litigation. For a start, in many cases the sums involved are very modest when compared to the generic costs that have been incurred. The individual costs are usually limited to taking initial evidence regarding the claim, matters which are specific to each claimant on causation and quantum as well as offers etc. Especially where there are a lot of low value cases run together, these individual costs are minimal. Moreover, they are by definition costs incurred by a single claimant using his solicitor and they are assessed in exactly the same way as if the claimant had simply brought his own action.

In *Owen v Ministry of Defence* [2006] EWHC 990 (QB), the claimant in group litigation was awarded personal damages for clinical negligence. The claimants as a whole were unsuccessful at the trial of the generic issues and the MoD sought to set off Mr Owen's proportionate share of the costs of the trial against either his costs of his individual action or against his damages. The court decided that, although the claimant might have benefited had the generic issues been resolved differently, the fact remained that the claimant had proved that he sustained injury and consequential loss and damage, as a consequence of negligent treatment. He would have succeeded in that action whether or not the generic issues had been litigated. The formation of the group litigation and his involvement in it, as to which he had no real choice, inevitably resulted in a very substantial delay in the resolution of his claim. The justice of the case required that neither the claimant's own order for costs nor his damages should be subject to a set-off of his share of the generic costs.

COSTS MANAGEMENT

[37.9]

Budgets in group litigation potentially need to cater for both the generic and the individual costs. Each case is different and it may be that the parties would prefer simply to budget the generic costs until liability has been established. Thereafter, individual budgets for each claimant can be fixed. The important point is to remember that all of the costs need to be budgeted, unless the court and/or the parties agree otherwise. Where cases are commenced individually or in small groups before coalescing in conjoined proceedings, it is surprisingly easy to overlook the generic component when preparing budgets for the claimant(s). How to demonstrate which costs are generic in a single budget, or the reasonableness and proportionality of generic costs in a budget split between several sets of proceedings are only two of the many potential complications.

The case management of GLO cases is dealt with by a High Court Judge. It is often the case that a costs judge sits with the judge when dealing with costs issues such as costs management. Sometimes the litigation is divided into phases or 'waves'. The budgeting then tends to follow the scope of such phases. For a hands on decision regarding a GLO budget, including an application to vary for significant development, please see Turner J's decision in the *British Steel Coke Oven Workers Litigation* [2020] EWHC 771 (QB).

COSTS CAPPING

[37.10]

In *Various Claimants v Corby Borough Council* [2008] EWHC 619 (TCC), the claimants were children born to mothers who had lived in or close to Corby during the 1980s and 1990s. They alleged that as a result of negligent work, toxins had escaped and had affected pregnant women so as to cause birth defects in their offspring.

The parties accepted that an overall costs cap should be fixed. In fixing such a cap, the court had to have regard to the constituent elements making up each party's submitted costs estimates. It was impossible to predict with absolute precision or accuracy how much individual heads of costs would ultimately cost and an overall costs cap allowed an element of flexibility. Each party had agreed a CFA with their solicitors and the claimants had taken out ATE insurance. It was accepted that the costs capping should not be on the basis of what their CFA would allow the successful party. Nor was the claimants' insurance taken into account. It was necessary to take an informed but broad-brush approach to the amount of the costs cap to be fixed upon each of the parties.

The parties agreed that a contingency was a fair and sensible allowance to make given the nature of the litigation and the likely encountering of expenditure or increase in levels of expenditure which was probably inevitable even if it could not be specifically foreseen which the judge fixed at 5%. The parties had liberty to apply to the court for adjustment of the costs caps if, unforeseeably and beyond the reasonable control of the party in question, circumstances so changed or new circumstances arose such that there was a genuine need to adjust the figures.

In *Barr v Biffa Waste Services Ltd* [2009] EWHC 2444 (TCC), the judge was asked to impose a costs-capping order on the claimants' costs equivalent to the £1m limit of their ATE insurance. The judge declined to do so, saying that it was entirely random to try to link the amount of any appropriate costs capping order to the amount of available ATE cover when such was beyond the scope of any control by either the defendant or the court. The judge further refused to make a costs capping order, holding that he was not satisfied that it would be impossible to control the claimants' costs through a combination of case management and detailed assessment. However, the judge did recognise the potential unfairness of the defendant's wider commercial position when faced with a group of claimants whose costs liability, if the claim failed, was likely to exceed the value of the ATE cover and made an order noting that the claimants' recently provided estimate of future costs 'was to be taken as a reasonable estimate of such costs and therefore their likely maximum recovery at the end of trial', albeit with leave to apply to modify that estimate if later events showed such would be appropriate.

DISCONTINUANCE

[37.11]

In *Sayers v Merck SmithKline Beecham plc* [2001] EWCA Civ 2017, appeals arose in relation to the details of costs sharing in three separate multi-party actions. However likely it might be that, if common issues were directed at trial, the costs of those issues would be ordered to follow the determination of those issues rather than await the individual fate of each claimant's action, it would be wrong to say that that should always be the presumption. Parties who settle their cases did not usually need any presumptive order as to the incidence of costs since costs would be part of the discussion leading to a settlement in any event. Discontinuers, however, gave rise to a more difficult problem. The order usually made in these circumstances was too blunt an instrument and was unnecessarily favourable to defendants, at a stage of the proceedings when it was as yet unknown whether the claimants as a whole were to be successful in the common issues which were to be tried. The orders would be amended to read:

> 'If in any quarter a claimant discontinued his claim against any one or more of the defendants or it is dismissed by an order of the court whereby the claimant is ordered to pay such defendant's costs, then he will be liable for his individual costs incurred by such defendants up to the last day of that quarter; liability for common costs and disbursement to be determined following the trial of common issues, with permission to apply if such trial does take place.'

OPT-OUT GROUP LITIGATION

[37.12]

Whilst group litigation, in the sense of a number of legal entities bringing proceedings together, has always been possible, the Consumer Rights Act 2015 ('CRA 2015') has brought a further option into being. This consists of proceedings which involve individuals unless they specifically opt out of the proceedings.

The CRA 2015 amended the Competition Act 1998 to bring in claims under ss 47A and 47B. Both sections relate to the bringing of collective proceedings in the Competition Appeals Tribunal (CAT) to enforce private rights. Group litigation may be opt-in or opt-out if the relevant threshold tests are met so that a Collective Proceedings Order ('CPO') is made. In essence, it is similar to a GLO in that it relates to case management rather than the substantive issues.

According to s 47B, a Tribunal can only make a CPO if two conditions are satisfied. First, the person who brought the proceedings should be authorised to act as the class representative, and second, the claims must be eligible for inclusion in collective proceedings (because they raise the same, similar or related issues of fact or law and are suitable to be brought in collective proceedings). So far, proceedings brought under these provisions have not persuaded the CAT that a CPO should be made but it is fair to say that there is currently a considerable amount of judicial scrutiny of whether arrangements satisfy the requirements.

In respect of the first condition, namely being a class representative, see *UK Trucks Claim Ltd v Fiat Chrysler Autos* [2019] CAT 26 where the Tribunal considered matters at great length. These ruminations included the nature of the litigation funding agreements between the bodies seeking to be the class representatives and their commercial backers (see **[10.20]**) and whether the specific arrangements with the funders and ATE insurers were sufficient to cover the claimants' and defendants' costs. The *UK Trucks* case did not consider the second condition, regarding eligibility for inclusion, because the *Merricks v Mastercard Incorporated* litigation (see eg [2017] CAT 16 and [2019] EWCA Civ 674) is currently before the Supreme Court on this question. It was heard in May 2020 but, at the time of writing, no decision had been handed down.

Another case which has been delayed in deciding whether a CPO should be made is *Michael O'Higgins FX Class Representative Ltd* [2020] CAT 9. Given the delay, the potential claimants proposing Mr O'Higgins as class representative and further potential claimants represented by a Mr Evans, asked the CAT to determine who should be the class representative as a preliminary issue. Using the old terminology of 'carriage of the action' this decision was described as a 'carriage dispute'. Notwithstanding the apparent attraction of establishing who should represent the claimants in an opt-out dispute as a preliminary issue, the Tribunal, in a cautious judgment, decided that the carriage dispute should be dealt with at the same time as deciding whether a certificate for a CPO should be given at all. The potential infighting highlighted by the O'Higgins and Evans camps has unfortunate echoes of the *Lungowe* case in GLO litigation (see [**37.4**]).

Given that the damages sought are potentially significant because of the theoretical number of claimants used to calculate the monies at stake in these cases, it is well worth continuing to watch this space.

FUNDING

[37.13]

Time will tell as to whether the introduction from 1 April 2013 of Damages-Based Agreements will lead to much of a change in the attractiveness, or otherwise, to legal representatives and clients of seeking to consolidate multiple claims into one piece of group litigation. Until the regulations are revised this would seem to be unlikely: see Chapter 7.

Many of the problems in funding group litigation have stemmed from setting up CFA agreements at the outset. The ending of the recoverability of success fees and ATE premiums may limit the challenges brought by defendants. But for the time being, group litigation is routinely a hotbed of challenges to the proper formation of retainers: see eg *Kupeli v Cyprus Turkish Airlines* [2017] EWCA Civ 1037.

How deep are the defendants' (funder's) pockets?

[37.14]

Courts have been asked to consider whether a party's ability to participate in the litigation up to trial and any appeal ought to be known by other parties in this expensive form of litigation. In *XYZ v Various sub nom Re PIP Breast Implant Litigation* [2013] EWHC 3643 (QB) Thirlwall J was persuaded to require the defendants to provide information about their ability to fund their participation in the litigation as part of the court's case management powers under CPR 3.1(2)(m). However enquiries in respect of the defendants' ability to meet any award for damages or costs were not required for this purpose and could not be ordered as a Part 18 request. Approximately one year later Thirlwall J heard a further application in the same proceedings regarding ostensibly the addition of a further insurer as a sixth defendant. She categorised the application as in fact an attempt to 'establish in advance the depths of another insurer's pockets' contrary to years of jurisprudence that a claimant must take the defendant as he finds him. As such it was in effect a variation on the same application she had heard the year before ([2014] EWHC 4056 (QB)).

The third instalment of the *XYZ* litigation [2017] EWHC 287 (QB) saw Thirlwall LJ, as she had become by this time, considering whether one of the defendant's insurers should pay the claimants' costs rather than the defendant. The claimants' argument ran that the insurer was controlling the litigation and as such should pay the costs in line with the Court of Appeal's decision in *TGA Chapman Ltd v Christopher and Sun Alliance* [1998] 2 All ER 873 (see **[40.9]**). As can be seen from the earlier judicial instalments, the financial pockets of the defendants in *XYZ* were always a concern to the claimants. The judge concluded that if the defendant had informed the claimants that it could not meet any judgments in respect of the 426 claimants whose cases fell in an uninsured period, the claimants would not have brought their claims. The insurer would then have faced the 197 insured claims and would have had to meet the full extent of the costs of those claimants. By ensuring that the defendant did not reveal the true position regarding the uninsured claimants, so that those claimants also ran their cases to a conclusion, the insurers found themselves only liable for 197/623 of the claimants' costs and had saved themselves costs as a result. At least that was the position until Thirlwall LJ decided that the insurers should pay the costs of all of the claimants, a decision which was subsequently upheld by the Court of Appeal ([2018] EWCA Civ 1099). The final chapter in this saga is the Supreme Court overturning the Court of Appeal and Thirlwall LJ's decision. The Supreme Court determined that there had been too rigid a separation of the insured and uninsured claims in the original judgment and that rather more was required to place the insurer in a *TGA Chapman* situation of meddling rather than simply funding litigation which included insured risks (see [2019] UKSC 48).

In *Various Claimants v Giambrone & Law (a Firm) and AIG (Europe) Ltd* [2019] EWHC 34 (QB), Foskett J found that AIG, as the defendants' funders, were exercising control in a *TGA Chapman* fashion in not settling claims against the defendants' LLP. Yet, at the same time, they were exercising too little control in simply bankrolling the case against the original partnership who were allowed to defend a hopeless claim. The net result was an unnecessary 18 day trial and the costs of which AIG were required to pay in part over and above their indemnity to their insured. In concluding that too little control might be a dangerous thing, Foskett J summarised the principle in the following paragraph:

> '78. In my view, where an indemnity insurer substantially relinquishes control of the conduct of the litigation to the insured (or fails to take steps to control it when there are grounds for intervening), and does so in the expectation that it will be immune from a costs liability towards the opposing party if the opposing party is successful, that expectation is open to be falsified by the court in a section 51 application, particularly if the prospects of success for the insured are assessed as poor.'

Given the Supreme Court's subsequent ruling in *XYZ*, it must be doubtful that an insurer relinquishing control in the manner described by Foskett J will find itself on the wrong end of a s 51 order.

How deep are the claimants' (funder's) pockets?

[37.15]

Similar applications have been made by the Royal Bank of Scotland Plc in group actions brought against it. In *Wall v The Royal Bank of Scotland plc* [2016] EWHC 2460 (Comm), the judge ordered the identification of any third party funders notwithstanding the distinct possibility that the claimant had sufficient ATE insurance to satisfy an application for security for costs. The trial was a year away and the judge concluded there was plenty of time for an application for security to be made if the defendant decided to do so having been informed of the identity of the claimant's backers.

In *Re RBS Rights Issue Litigation* [2017] EWHC 1217 (Ch), a different High Court judge decided that the claimants did not need to identify their ATE insurer(s). Whilst the existence of adequate ATE insurance might be sufficient to knock out any application for security, it is clear that the judge took the view, similarly to Thirlwall J in *XYZ* that the application was really aimed at enforcement post proceedings rather than case management during the proceedings. The judge (Hildyard J) did accede to the application to identify the third party funders, however. He drew a distinction between the claimants providing financial information themselves and them providing information as to their backers. He specifically indicated that he gave no encouragement to a subsequent application for security for costs once the identity of the third party funders was identified, not least because the trial was not far away. The judge accepted that there appeared to have been a delay in the bringing of the application and that such delay was a material factor to be considered. But, it was outweighed by the 'watershed' of many of the claimants' cases having settled and the potential liability for significant costs subsequently falling on many fewer shoulders. Despite the lack of encouragement, Hildyard J nevertheless granted a subsequent application for security for costs against the funders. It is clear that he was mindful of the revelation in the intervening period that the ATE insurance was limited and was in fact no longer covering work done at the time of the application (or presumably up to trial). As such, the third party backers must have appeared to be the only potential source of recovery if the defendant was successful.

In the *Ingenious Litigation* (also discussed at [**37.7**]), the defendants successfully sought security for costs. But they were unsuccessful in arguing that the litigation funder was potentially liable for the costs of self-funded claimants as well as the funded claimants. Given the Supreme Court's guidance in *XYZ* (see [**37.14**]) the funder would have to be shown to be the 'real claimant', in other words, controlling the running of the case. Given that the self-funded claimants had no relationship with the funder, that was not a likely prospect in respect of their cases.

And finally . . .

[37.16]

No discussion of the assessment of costs in group litigation could fail to make some mention of *Motto (1) Trafigura Ltd (2) Trafigura Beheer BV* [2011] EWHC 90201 (Costs) where the Senior Costs Judge dealt with preliminary issues raised on assessment of the £104m bill of costs incurred. These issues largely concerned the usual arguments on detailed assessment such as proportionality and reasonableness rather than GLO specific arguments. But, as well as being the largest bill ever to be seen in the SCCO it was also noteworthy for the bravura argument of the paying party regarding hourly rates before the Senior Costs Judge. 30,000 French speaking Ivorian clients using CFAs was apparently still a 'run of the mill' case.

CHAPTER 38

TRUSTEES AND PERSONAL REPRESENTATIVES

ENTITLEMENT TO COSTS OUT OF THE TRUST OR ESTATE

[38.1]

Trustees and personal representatives have a duty to protect the trust fund or the estate. If, in so doing, they are able to recover any costs from another party or source, then they will claim them in the ordinary way. But if this is not possible, they are entitled to their costs of any proceedings undertaken in their capacity of trustee or personal representative out of the trust fund or estate. HHJ Matthews discusses this approach and the distinction between 'litigation costs orders' between the parties on the one hand and the indemnity from the estate on the other in *Mussell v Patience* [2019] EWHC 1231 (Ch).

Such costs will be assessed on the indemnity basis to the extent that they have been properly incurred. Whether that has happened depends upon all the circumstances, but in particular whether they have acted in the interests of the trust or estate rather than for some other benefit (including their own.) The fact that the trustee has defended a claim which includes a claim against the trustee personally is not necessarily determinative that the trustee has not acted in the interest of the trust. The reasonableness of bringing or defending proceedings (and the conduct of them) will be considered and so too will the question of whether the trustee obtained directions from the court before bringing or defending those proceedings (CPR 46.3 and CPR PD 46, para 1). For recent examples of the court's consideration of the reasonableness of an executor's actions, see *Price v Saundry* [2020] EWCA Civ 2261 and *Gibbons v Smith* [2020] EWHC 1727 (Ch).

Similarly, in the large scale administration of Lehman Brothers, the administrators brought matters before the court for determination. Hildyard J considered that the questions had required judicial determination once the administrators and various creditors' arguments had been set out. As such it was appropriate for the costs of the proceedings to be paid out of the surplus available to creditors. Related proceedings however were considered to be essentially commercial litigation and the usual rule of costs following the event would apply with the unsuccessful party paying the other parties' costs: *Re Lehman Brothers International (Europe) (in administration) sub nom (1) Anthony Victor Lomas (2) Steven Anthony Pearson (3) Paul David Copley (4) Russell Downs (5) Julian Guy Parr (the Joint Administrators of Lehman Brothers International (Europe) (in administration) v Burlington Loan Management Ltd* [2018] EWHC 924 (Ch).

Also, in the context of an insolvent business, Chief ICC Judge Briggs reviewed the authorities regarding the making of a costs order against an office holder in the case of *Nimat Halal Food Ltd company v Patel (in his capacity as administrator of Tariq Halal Meat (Ilford) Ltd)* [2020] EWHC 734 (Ch), [2020] BPIR 976. His conclusion following that review was that:

> 'An order should not ordinarily be made against an office holder personally. Something more is required. Something more relates to the conduct of the office holder. The degree of conduct deserving of a personal costs order will depend on the circumstances of each case. A mere mistake is unlikely to be sufficient. Acting in a neutral manner, on an appeal from a rejection of proof, is unlikely to be sufficient. Acting for a personal advantage in resisting an appeal is very likely to lead to a personal costs order. Such conduct would present a "special case" and a "good reason" and may be characterised as "irrational conduct", or "unreasonable conduct".'

In the present case, the administrator's conduct did not warrant a personal costs order.

COSTS AGAINST TRUSTEES

[38.2]

A trustee or personal representative who has acted outside his duty or has acted in his own interests or otherwise unreasonably not only will be unable to recover his costs out of the fund or estate, but he may be ordered to pay the costs of another party personally. Similarly, although trustees and personal representatives will generally be justified in making an application to obtain the opinion of the court on a matter of construction or difficulty, if they appeal against the court's decision unsuccessfully, they may expect to be ordered to pay the costs of the appeal personally (*Re Earl of Radnor's Will Trusts* (1890) 45 Ch D 402, CA). Only in exceptional circumstances, say, for example, where large interests are at stake or where the interests of unborn persons are affected, will the costs be ordered to be paid out of the estate.

Where the trustee is the respondent to an appeal, there should be no difficulty in the trustee being paid out of the estate. The costs of the beneficiaries may be paid out of the estate or may be paid between the opposing parties in the case. In *Anne-Marie Helene Harrison-Mills v The Public Trustee* [2019] EWCA Civ 966, one of the beneficiaries appealed the construction of a settlement deed by the High Court where the judge had also awarded costs to be paid by the appellant beneficiary, who was a litigant in person. Although her substantive appeal failed, the construction she put on the deed had been considered by the trustee's counsel before proceedings and who had considered the point to be arguable. The Court of Appeal agreed and concluded that all parties' costs should be paid out of the estate in line with the usual procedure where the trustee had brought the matter before the court originally.

PRE-EMPTIVE ORDERS

[38.3]

Trustees or personal representatives may apply to the court before commencing or defending proceedings for an order that, win or lose, they will be entitled to their costs out of the property in dispute, before the facts have been fully investigated and before the law has been fully argued. This may be appropriate if there is a risk of a suggestion that the trustee has acted unreasonably or in his own interest. This is known as a 'Beddoe application' (*Re Beddoe, Downes v Cottam* [1893] 1 Ch 547, 62 LJ Ch 233, CA) (see [**18.14**]). A recent example of a court considering whether to grant such an application can be found in *Lines (as administrator of the Estate of Mrs NE Brock, deceased) v Maureen Wilcox* [2019] EWHC 1451 (Ch).

Such a pre-emptive costs order affords the trustees the comfort of knowing that they will be indemnified against the costs of the claim. In addition to asking for an indemnity in respect of the costs, a *Beddoe* application usually asks the court for directions as to whether the claim should be continued or defended. This may, exceptionally, extend to whether an appeal should be pursued: see *Airways Pension Scheme Trustee Ltd v Fielder* [2019] EWHC 29 (Ch) and then to settling the appeal ([2019] EWHC 3032 (Ch)).

PROSPECTIVE COSTS ORDERS

[38.4]

CPR 64.2(a) and CPR PD 64A, para 6 apply to claims for the court to determine any question arising in the administration of a deceased person's estate or the execution of a trust. This includes a direction that the beneficiaries' costs should be paid in advance out of the trust fund – 'a prospective costs order'. The procedure for such costs applications is found within the Practice Direction to Part 64 Estates, Trusts and Charities.

Where a trustee has the power to enter into a contract, no prospective order is required as the trustee is entitled to recover any monies from the trust that he has paid out. But if the trustee does not have this power, or simply decides not to exercise it, he may apply to the court for a prospective costs order.

To the extent that the order relates to the trustee's own costs, the court can simply authorise those costs to be paid from the fund. If there are any other party's costs, the court can direct that the agreed (or assessed) costs be paid either on the standard or indemnity basis. Interim payments may be made on account of such costs. A model form of order is annexed to the practice direction.

Applications will be dealt with by the court on paper where possible. If the trustee considers that an oral hearing is required, he needs to cover this in the evidence supporting his application. If the court is minded to refuse the application on paper, it will inform the trustee so that he can ask for a hearing if he wishes to do so.

DETAILED ASSESSMENT OF COSTS FROM THE TRUST OR ESTATE

[38.5]

The procedure for this is set out at CPR 47.19 and CPR PD 47, para 18. Since most assessments are carried out provisionally, it is discussed in Chapter 30 at [**30.16**].

[38.6]

Executors are entitled to all 'just allowances', according to PD 40A, para 4, on the taking of an account of the executor's costs. As long as the costs have been incurred in the 'fair execution' of the trust they will be allowed. The executor does not have to show that all of the costs of the instructed solicitor are reasonable in the manner of a detailed assessment if they are challenged by beneficiaries. The production of receipted invoices to show that the money has been spent on matters connected with the administration is sufficient to vouch the legal expenses in the estate accounts. Beneficiaries are not entitled to receive sufficient information in respect of the legal costs to decide whether to bring proceedings under s 71 of the Solicitors Act 1974: *Mussell & Williams v Patience & Patience* [2018] EWHC 430 (Ch).

SUMMARY ASSESSMENT OF COSTS FROM THE TRUST OR ESTATE

[38.7]

Where a bankruptcy order is annulled because it should never have been made, the petitioning creditor will usually pay the trustee in bankruptcy's costs for work done whilst the order was in place. If the annulment application is unsuccessful, the trustee is entitled to his costs from the bankrupt's estate. The bankrupt's usual route for challenging the costs of the trustee is via rule 18.35 of the Insolvency Rules 1986, but where the costs are legal costs incurred as a result of an application before the court, Roth J concluded there was no reason why the costs could not be summarily assessed by the judge who heard the application rather than them being sent off for a detailed assessment. He decided to do precisely that in *Ardawa v Uppal* [2019] EWHC 1663 (Ch) and reduced the 'wholly unreasonable and disproportionate' costs from £15,980 plus VAT to £6,000 plus VAT.

CHAPTER 39

FAMILY PROCEEDINGS

FAMILY PROCEDURE RULES 2010

[39.1]

Since the introduction of the CPR there have been successive attempts to unify the treatment of costs in civil and family proceedings, most recently by the Family Procedure Rules 2010 ('FPR'). These rules came into force on 5 April 2011. The costs of all family proceedings are now governed by the FPR Part 28 and the Practice Direction 28A which supplements it. While FPR 28 had been updated to take account of the amendments to the costs provisions in the CPR as a result of the April 2013 reforms, FPR PD 28A, curiously, had not, but in the main now has – save that para 3.1 still refers to the Costs PD in the singular. However, as paragraph 2.5 of PD 28A now states that 'all subsequent editions of the CPR PDs 44, 46 and 47 as and when they are published and come into effect shall in the same way extend to all family proceedings', it matters not. There remains one continuity error in the updated FPR at 28.3(3) where, having correctly identified the new CPR 44.2(6)–(8) and CPR 44.12, the FPR mistakenly refers back to CPR 44.3 and not CPR 44.2.

In general terms FPR 28 provides that the court has discretion to make any costs order at any time (FPR 28.1). However, this discretion is subject to the application of almost all of CPR 44, CPR 46 and CPR 47 to the decision making process and by the qualification in FPR 28.3(5), that 'the general rule in financial remedy proceedings is that the court will not make an order requiring one party to pay the costs of another party'. This general rule is itself subject to an exception in FPR 28.3(6), that the court may make an order for one party to financial remedy proceedings to pay costs to another party at any stage where the conduct of that party in relation to the proceedings justifies this. That conduct is 'in relation' to the proceedings, but may be either/both before or during them.

As a result of the adoption of large parts of the CPR, FPR 28 is not entirely self-contained. The costs provisions of the CPR must be referred to separately, with appropriate modifications as provided in the rules.

ONE IMPORTANT DEPARTURE FROM THE CPR – THE STARTING POINT WHERE COSTS ARE TO BE AWARDED

[39.2]

From the outset, the general rule in civil cases that the unsuccessful party pays the costs of the successful party that is enshrined in CPR 44.2(2) was disapplied in family proceedings by the Family Proceedings (Miscellaneous Amendment) Rules 1999. So what guidance is there on the starting point for any award of costs? The Court of Appeal in both *Judge v Judge* [2008] EWCA

Civ 1458 (a case about setting aside a financial remedy order) and *Baker v Rowe* [2009] EWCA Civ 1162 (a case where interveners in a financial remedy claim sought to assert a beneficial interest in a property), having decided that both scenarios fell outside the 'no costs' provision, made it clear that, effectively, the judge starts with a 'clean sheet'. In the former case Wilson LJ said this:

> 'He (the judge) had before him a clean sheet: but by reference to the facts of the case, and in particular, the wife's responsibility for the generation of the costs of a failed application, he remained perfectly entitled to record upon it, as he did, that he would start from the position that the husband was entitled to his costs.'

Indeed, in the case of *Solomon v Solomon* [2013] EWCA Civ 1095, where the court of appeal was considering, amongst other matters, a costs order made against an unsuccessful applicant for relief under s 37 of the Matrimonial Causes Act 1973, Ryder LJ, in upholding the costs order, referred back to the starting point for 'clean sheet' cases set out by Butler Sloss LJ in *Gojkovic v Gojkovic* [1991] 2 FLR 233 (CA) where she said as follows:

> ' . . . there still remains the necessity for some starting point. That starting point, in my judgment, is that costs prima facie follow the event . . . but may be displaced much more easily than, and in circumstances which would not apply, in other Divisions of the High Court.'

Some may see the distinction between the 'general rule' in CPR 44.2 and a starting point of 'costs follow the event' as a subtle one.

WHAT ARE FINANCIAL REMEDY PROCEEDINGS FOR THE PURPOSE OF FPR 28.3?

[39.3]

Judge v Judge (above) and *Baker v Rowe* (above) also raised the issue of whether they were 'financial remedy proceedings'. Inevitably, before turning to consider costs in the different types of matter that come before the Family Court, we need to be clear about what types of case are, subject to the exception at FPR 28.3(6) above, financial remedy cases and so cases in which the 'no order for costs' regime applies. Financial remedy proceedings are those that involve applications for the following remedies:

- periodical payments;
- lump sum;
- property adjustment;
- variation;
- pension sharing;
- under s 10(2) of the Matrimonial Causes Act 1973/s 48(2) of the Civil Partnership Act 2004.

However, it is important to note that, for the purposes of FPR 28.3, the following remedies, some of which may arise during applications for one of the 'no costs order' remedies above, are excluded from that regime, and fall to be dealt with under the costs provisions that apply in all other cases under FPR 28.2:

- maintenance pending suit;

- avoidance of transactions intended to prevent or reduce financial relief (s 37 of the Matrimonial Causes Act 1973) – but see qualification at **[39.16]** below;
- legal services order;
- maintenance pending outcome of the proceedings;
- interim periodical payments;
- any other form of application for an interim order apart from an interim variation order;
- appeals;
- preliminary issue applications;
- setting aside an order made in financial remedy proceedings;
- enforcement (note that CPR 45.8 'Fixed Enforcement Costs' does apply under FPR 28.2(1)).

In addition to that list of exceptions, FPR PD 28A, para 4.2(b) also excludes the following applications for a financial remedy from those to which the 'no costs' rule at FPR 28.3 applies:

- Children Act 1989, Sch 1;
- Matrimonial Causes Act 1973, s 27;
- Civil Partnership Act 2004, Sch 5, Part 9;
- Matrimonial Causes Act 1973, s 35;
- Civil Partnership Act 2004, Sch 5, para 69;
- Domestic Proceedings and Magistrates' Courts Act 1978, Part 1;
- Civil Partnership Act 2004, Sch 6.

To this list must be added appeals in financial remedy proceedings (see *WD v HD* [2015] EWHC 1547 (Fam) considered below at **[39.18]**) and applications to set aside consent orders (see *AB v CD* [2016] EWHC 2482 (Fam)).

Having identified those proceedings that fall in the 'no costs' provision, to which we shall return, let us start with FPR 28.2 and consider how costs are dealt with in the different types of case where they are 'live' before the court.

A. APPLICATIONS OTHER THAN IN FINANCIAL REMEDY PROCEEDINGS

General

[39.4]

The whole of Part 44 (except CPR 44.2(2), (3) and CPR 44.10(2), (3)), CPR 46 and CPR 47 and CPR 45.8 apply. As stated the most significant of the exceptions to Part 44 is CPR 44.2(2)) with the effect that the starting point in family proceedings is the clean slate referred to above. However, this is not quite so broad a discretion as it appears. The remainder of CPR 44.2 applies (see above under Chapter 22 – Costs awards between the parties). In other words, the court retains a discretion to determine whether costs are payable by one party to another, if so the amount of those costs and when they are to be paid. In making any decision about whether costs are payable the court still must consider the CPR 44.2(4) and (5) factors, not as to whether they represent reasons to depart from a starting assumption, but to determine the outcome.

Accordingly, in family proceedings that are not financial remedy proceedings, to which FPR 28.3 applies, the court is neither bound by the presumption that there will be no order for costs as it is where the rule applies, nor is it bound by the 'general' civil rule that the unsuccessful party pays the costs of the successful party. The court therefore has a wide discretion.

Applications other than in 'No Costs' Financial Remedy Proceedings – Children Act 1989 Applications

(a) Children Act 1989 Schedule 1 applications

[39.5]

Schedule 1 of the Children Act 1989 provides three forms of financial relief for a child: (1) a maintenance order, settlement and transfer of property order to be made in favour of a child against either or both of its parents; (2) a periodical payments order and lump sum order to be made in favour of a child who has reached 18; and (3) the court may vary a maintenance agreement containing financial arrangements for the child either during the lifetime of the parent or after the death of one of them. The application may be made by a parent or guardian or the child itself if over 18.

These are essentially family proceedings, but not financial remedy proceedings. Any issue as to costs therefore falls to be dealt with under the relevant provisions of the CPR, as provided for by FPR 28.2 Even without litigation misconduct the parties are at risk of a 'between the parties' costs order but they are able to protect their costs position by making a 'Calderbank' offer – see below and Chapter 20 – Costs inducements to settle-Part 36 offers and other admissible offers.

(b) Private law Children Act 1989 applications

[39.6]

Although the court has the power to make such order for costs as it thinks fit in family proceedings, it is unusual in a case involving children for an order for costs against a party to be made.

The decision in *Re T (Children)* [2012] UKSC 36 restated the principle set out by Cazalet J in *Re M (Local Authority's Costs)* [1995] 1 FLR 533 that the general practice of not awarding costs in the absence of reprehensible behaviour or an unreasonable stance accorded with the interests of justice.

In private law Children Act 1989 applications too, orders for costs against a party will be rare. If parties are to be encouraged to put aside personal differences for the welfare of their children, making one party pay a costs order to another is not seen as the greatest way to foster this co-operation. However, where the court is satisfied that a party's conduct of the proceedings has been unreasonable, then that party will be at risk of an adverse costs order.

[39.7]

An illustration of the conduct of a party leading to a costs order is the case of *Re E-R (Child Arrangements)* [2016] EWHC 805. In this case the child's mother had died and the child lived with friends with whom she and the child lived before her death. The father applied for the child to live with him.

Although he was unsuccessful in this application (he was originally successful, but that decision was successfully appealed), Cobb J concluded that this application was not unreasonable. However, making an order that the father should contribute £10,000 towards the friends' costs, the court concluded that in certain aspects of his conduct of the proceedings the father had acted both reprehensibly and unreasonably. The contribution was to reflect those instances of that conduct. The court expressly reminded itself that CPR 44.2(2) had no application, but directed itself to the conduct provisions at CPR 44.2(4) and (5), which do apply.

[39.8]

In *Re G (costs: child case)* [1999] 3 FCR 463, CA, [1999] 2 FLR 250 the Court of Appeal held that 'it was unusual to order costs in a family case, although it would be appropriate to order costs where a parent, even a litigant in person, went beyond the limit of what was reasonable to pursue the application before the court'. Even though the judge had found the father's case to be hopeless, the court held that hopelessness and unreasonableness were not necessarily the same thing. Furthermore, a greater degree of generosity might be appropriate in ruling that pursuing an application had become unreasonable where the litigant was acting in person rather than where there was receipt of legal advice. It seems that this distinction between 'hopelessness' and 'unreasonableness' has survived under the Child Arrangements Programme, even where the court repeatedly gives indications at both the First Hearing and Dispute Resolution Appointment and at the subsequent freestanding Dispute Resolution Appointment, but a party persists notwithstanding these and is ultimately unsuccessful for the reasons previously articulated by the court at the earlier appointments. This appears to be in recognition of the greater number of litigants in person conducting these applications.

Some assistance may be gleaned from the case of *HH v BLW (Appeal: Costs: Proportionality)* [2013] 1 FLR 420. The court at first instance made an order for costs in the sum of £2,468 against the applicant father who withdrew his application for contact to his 15 year old daughter. The decision not to proceed was made after the father had heard from the Cafcass officer that the child was firmly expressing an unwillingness to have contact. The father appealed against the decision to award costs to the mother. In considering the application for permission to appeal, Holman J disagreed with the view of the district judge that the father's application had been misconceived and the outcome a foregone conclusion. His view was that the father had been entitled to await the recommendation of the Cafcass officer before deciding what course to take and it was entirely reasonable of him to do so. Had he decided to pursue the application in the face of the Cafcass report he would have been foolish and a costs order would have been justified. Nonetheless, Holman J was unable to say that the high hurdle in order to succeed on an application for permission to appeal had been cleared. Coupled with that, the application of the overriding objective, in particular proportionality, determined that the application should fail.

Re D (Children) [2016] EWCA Civ 89 is a reminder that for the court to consider awarding costs in private law proceedings it must first identify its jurisdiction so to do. In this case the court entertained a dispute between the father and an independent social worker in respect of the latter's fees for supervising the father's contact, without explaining the basis upon which it did so. The Court of Appeal was clear that if the dispute was between the father and the independent social worker (and there was insufficient information to conclude this issue) then it fell to be determined as a contractual dispute which, absent settlement, should be determined in the county court. The case was remitted only on the basis that the jurisdiction that the recorder had purported to exercise was unclear and that a determination upon that issue was required to ascertain whether there was any basis upon which the family court could intervene.

Re A (A Child) (13 March 2018, unreported), CA (Civ Div) provides reminders both that the provisions of CPR PD 44, para 9 apply (and a party seeking costs must file and serve a statement of them) and that in the absence of reprehensible behaviour there should be no order for costs in children cases.

(c) Public law Children Act 1989 applications

[39.9]

See the comments in Chapter 23 – Wasted Costs Orders at [**23.20**] and the cases of *Re M (A child)* 5 July 2012 (CA); *HU v SU* [2015] EWFC 535; and *Re A (wasted costs orders)* [2013] EWCA Civ 43.

In *E S Children* [2014] EWCA Civ 135 the father appealed successfully against a placement order and the case was remitted for further consideration under an interim care order. The father sought his costs of the appeal which he had funded privately. He did not argue that the local authority had engaged in reprehensible behaviour or that there should be any liability for the first instance proceedings, accepting precedent that public policy considerations militated against possible financial deterrents to local authorities pursuing proceedings as part of their responsibility for the protection of children. However, he argued that a parent should not be deterred from challenging decisions on appeal which impacted on the crucial parent/child relationship. Here he argued that the local authority had recognised the deficiencies of the first instance judgment but had still resisted the appeal. The father was successful. However, the Supreme Court allowed the appeal of the Local Authority under *Re S (Children) (Care proceedings: Proper evidence for placement order)* [2015] UKSC 20, stating that the general rule that a Local Authority should not pay costs in care proceedings extended to appeals and there were no exceptional circumstances justifying departure from this position. The court also confirmed that in children cases CPR 44.2(4)(b) does not apply and CPR 44.2(4)(c) has only limited impact.

Redbridge London Borough Council v A [2016] EWHC 2627 (Fam) is a reminder that certain conduct still requires judicial scrutiny of the cost consequences. The court ordered the local authority 'to show cause' why it should not pay the costs of a hearing at short notice to address its repeated and continued non-compliance with case management directions and any costs of the final hearing that had to be vacated due to the 'sorry and depressing set of circumstances outlined during the course of this short judgment'.

However, *Re S* confirms that notwithstanding the limited examples set out above, costs orders in public law cases are rare indeed. This is not surprising given the decision of the Supreme Court in *Re T (Children)* (above at [**39.6**]). The Supreme Court was concerned with the position of interveners joined to care proceedings for the determination of allegations against them. All bar one of the interveners were exonerated. Two of those exonerated had spent £52,000, which they had been obliged to borrow and which, it was said, would take 15 years to pay off. They sought costs orders against the Local Authority. The trial judge had refused the application. The Court of Appeal reversed that decision and although the case came before the Supreme Court on condition that its decision would not be relied upon by that Local Authority to deprive these interveners of the benefit of the decision of the Court of Appeal, the Supreme Court restored the trial judge's decision. The Supreme Court concluded that 'the general practice of not awarding costs against a party, including a local authority, in the absence of reprehensible behaviour or an unreasonable stance, is one that accords with the ends of justice…'.

However, it seems that the door remains open for interveners to recover costs. In *Re F Children* (3 February 2016, unreported), CA the Court of Appeal upheld a decision by the trial judge to order a mother to pay an intervener's costs, notwithstanding that the court had joined the intervener to determine allegations that the mother had stated she did not wish to pursue. The allegations had been serious, required determination and the mother had been the source of them. The court found the allegations to be false, the children to have been coached, the mother's approach to be an attempt to sabotage the proceedings and to deflect attention away from her. The Court of Appeal upheld the judge's award of costs against the mother reiterating that a costs order could be made where it was just and appropriate to do so to reflect reprehensible or unreasonable conduct.

In *LR v A Local Authority* [2019] EWCA Civ 680, in declining to make costs orders against the local authority and Cafcass, after overturning a care order, the court drew a clear distinction between conduct falling short of the standard expected in care proceedings and reprehensible conduct and adoption of an unreasonable stance.

In *W (A Child), Re* [2020] EWCA Civ 77, [2020] Costs LR 303, the Court of Appeal reiterated that costs should only be awarded in children cases where the conduct of the paying party had been either reprehensible or its stance had been unreasonable. In this case, the local authority had failed to be even-handed in its presentation of the case at first instance and had failed to concede (save to a limited extent) that the order made was unsustainable and the appeal was bound to succeed. As a result, it was ordered to pay a contribution to the appellant's costs.

The case of *A Local Authority v A Mother* [2018] EWHC 1841 (Fam), [2018] All ER (D) 136 (Jul) provides a useful summary of the relevant procedure and case law and a practical illustration of the application of CPR 44 in public law children cases, as well as providing some guidance to enable a summary assessment of the amount, if an award of costs is made.

Appeal

[39.10]

Consideration of the cases referred to suggests that costs in Children Act cases are much more likely to be awarded on an appeal than at first instance in private children cases. Perhaps the reason is that at first instance nobody knows what the judge is going to find. On an appeal in private children cases both parties have the chance to take stock and make an offer. Accordingly, it is easier to identify conduct meriting an adverse costs order.

In *Re M* [2009] EWCA Civ 311, referred to in *Re S (Children) (Care proceedings: Proper evidence for placement order)* [2015] UKSC 20, the Court of Appeal refused permission to appeal from the High Court judge's order that the husband should pay the wife's costs of her successful appeal from the district judge. The husband through his counsel had opposed the appeal 'root and branch' and announced that he intended to apply for costs if the appeal were successfully opposed. Such litigants, if the losing party, could not complain when the judge took the view that they should contribute to or pay the costs.

In *Gibbs v Gibbs* (31 August 2017, unreported), CA, the court made an order for indemnity costs against a mother applying for permission to appeal a committal order against her out of time, made for her breaches of a prohibited steps order. There was no prospect of any appeal succeeding and it was totally without merit. Her insistence on attendance in person rather than by video link had resulted in an adjournment. She was ordered to pay costs on the indemnity basis.

Applications other than in 'No Costs' Financial Remedy Proceedings – Interim Orders, Interventions, Family Law Act 1996 Orders and other Common 'Family' Remedies

[39.11]

There are a number of applications/claims dealt with in the family court, and, as we shall see at (d) below, the civil court, that fall outside the 'no costs' regime.

(a) Maintenance pending suit ('MPS')

[39.12]

Prior to the introduction of the FPR 2010 MPS applications had come within the previous 'no costs' regime. This is no longer the position and the protection afforded by FPR 28.3 is not extended to MPS applications. Instead these applications are 'clean sheet' cases – **[39.2]** above. Since the removal of this protection it seems that the number of MPS applications has dropped off. It is not clear whether this is because parties are not bringing speculative applications, are agreeing well founded applications rather than running the risk of an adverse court order or whether, simply, the worry of an adverse costs order is acting as an unfortunate deterrent.

(b) Interventions

[39.13]

See *Baker v Rowe* above. As costs are 'live' in intervener proceedings, parties should think carefully about whether they do need to invite others to intervene or whether the issues raised can simply be dealt with between the parties. Of course, this is likely to depend upon whether, whatever the findings in respect of any property related to the potential intervener, there are sufficient other assets to give effect to the outcome under s 25 of the Matrimonial Causes act

1973 without actual recourse to that property. As interveners are usually other extended family members or companies linked to the parties, the costs issues that arise can be significant, both emotionally as well as financially.

(c) *Family Law Act 1996 orders*

[39.14]

These types of application (non-molestation injunction, occupation orders and transfer of tenancy applications) fall within FPR 28.2. The starting point is the 'clean sheet' – see **[39.2]** above. In the vast majority of cases that are unopposed no costs order is sought 'between the parties'. However, where the proceedings are contested costs orders are more common and the *Gojkovic* starting point is of assistance.

(d) *Trusts of Land and Appointment of Trustees Act ('TLATA') 1996*

[39.15]

While strictly TLATA applications are not family proceedings, they often involve family type disputes eg between former cohabitants. For the family practitioner the fact that TLATA disputes are governed by the CPR can present challenges. TLATA claims are usually CPR Part 8 claims. Although the April 2014 amendments to the costs management rules removed CPR Part 8 claims from standard inclusion in that regime (see Chapter 15 Prospective costs control – Costs and case management), CPR PD 3E, para 2 makes it clear that TLATA applications are one of the types of claim where the court may consider it particularly appropriate to exercise its discretion to costs manage (CPR PD 3E, para 2(c)).

It is worth noting that in *Baker v Rowe* (above) where the interveners asserted a beneficial interest in a property within existing financial remedy proceedings, the Court of Appeal took the view that these assertions were not made as a claim under s 14 of TLATA, but instead were claims made by parties to an existing application for financial remedy in family proceedings. The distinction being important because as such neither the costs management regime, nor the general rule in CPR 44.2 applies (although as we have set out above the latter may be a distinction without a difference in outcome).

(e) *Avoidance of transactions intended to prevent or reduce financial relief*

[39.16]

There appears to be some confusion as to whether applications under s 37 of the Matrimonial Causes Act 1973 are or are not excluded from the 'no costs regime'. Certainly, avoidance of disposition orders are defined as 'financial orders' and therefore financial 'remedy orders' for the purpose of FPR 2.3. There is a view that orders restraining disposal under s 37(2)(a) are not avoidance orders and should be treated differently to setting aside disposition orders under s 37(2)(b) and (c). However, all three subsections may have the effect of avoiding a disposition. Perhaps the simpler approach is to accept that applications under s 37(2)(a) and (b) are made within the financial relief proceedings (in the case of (a) because the subsection refers to the existing proceedings and in the case of subsection (b) because that is what s 37(2) states) and as such are interim orders and so excluded from the 'no costs' regime by operation of FPR 28.3 (4)(b)(i) and by application FPR 9.7(1)(e). This was certainly the approach adopted by Mostyn J and approved of by the Court of Appeal in *Solomon v Solomon* [2013] EWCA Civ 1095.

Applications other than in 'No Costs' Financial Remedy Proceedings – Divorce Petitions

[39.17]

Costs in divorce petitions are governed by FPR 28.2.

In the case of undefended petitions the District Judge will determine, when granting a certificate that a party is entitled to a decree nisi or decree of judicial separation in matrimonial proceedings or a conditional order or a separation order in civil partnership proceedings, whether its intention is to make a costs order. The starting point is a 'clean sheet'. In practice, most courts appear to order costs against the respondent when one is sought, where the ground relied upon in the matrimonial proceedings is one of those traditionally described as a 'fault' one – adultery, unreasonable behaviour and desertion. In civil partnership proceedings this approach is mirrored with the 'fault' grounds being those at s 44(5) (a) and (d) – unreasonable behaviour and desertion.

FPR 7.21 sets out the procedure by which a party receiving the certificate from the court may be heard on the question of costs – whether to argue that the court should make a costs order where it has not indicated an intention to do so or that it should not where it has indicated an intention to do so. Amendments to the FPR in July 2015 have removed the difficulty of the court not knowing in advance whether there will be a costs dispute on pronouncement of decree nisi. Now under FPR 7.21(2) any party wishing to be heard on costs will not be heard unless that party has, not less than 14 before the hearing listed in the certificate, given written notice to the court of an intention to attend and apply for, or oppose, an order for costs. By the same time the party wishing to be heard must serve the notice on all other parties. As the certificate will usually have listed the case amongst many others for pronouncement with little or no time formally allocated for this, if a party has given notice FPR 7.21(3) permits the court to make any further directions in respect of the hearing – which may be to seek a response from the other parties and/or list the costs dispute separately from the pronouncement of decree nisi when there will be sufficient time to deal with the matter.

Calderbank offers

[39.18]

There is no equivalent of CPR Part 36 in family proceedings (although that provision will apply to 'TLATA' claims). As a consequence, parties may resort to making what is known as a 'Calderbank offer' in an attempt to protect their position on costs. A 'Calderbank' offer is so-called because it is a form of offer first approved by the Court of Appeal in *Calderbank v Calderbank* [1976] Fam 93, [1975] 3 All ER 333, [1975] 3 WLR 586 CA, and this is still a useful description. It is an offer made 'Without prejudice save as to costs'. In other words, it is not an open offer but, by dint of the magic words 'save as to costs' is admissible on the question of costs. As such it may not be seen by the court except in the context of costs between the parties once the substantive issues have been determined. If the magic words are omitted then the offer is a privileged one and is only admissible if all parties to it waive that privilege – something to which a party likely to be prejudiced by so doing is unlikely to agree.

Wherever there is a risk that costs may be ordered between the parties it is sensible to make offers to settle, if necessary using Calderbank terms, 'without prejudice save as to costs'.

Calderbank offers are not admissible before the court in financial remedy proceedings to which Rule 28.3 applies, except at the Financial Dispute Resolution appointment. However, they are in all other family proceedings. CPR 44.2(4)(c) specifically requires the court to consider any admissible offers made as one of the circumstances of the case to be taken into account in the exercise of its discretion in determining the award of costs – see Chapter 20 Costs inducements to settle-Part 36 offers and other admissible offers. Note that in *WD v HD* [2015] EWHC 1547 (Fam) Moor J concluded that Rule 28.3 applied only to the initial proceedings and not to appeals. The court indicated that Calderbank offers had a place in appeals because they have 'the added advantage that litigants [were] able to protect themselves in appeals where the costs of the appeal [could] be totally disproportionate to the amount at stake'.

The Ministry of Justice and Family Rules Committee 'Consultation in relation to the treatment of Calderbank offers when determining issues relating to costs' closed in October 2019. The outcome is awaited.

B. FINANCIAL REMEDY PROCEEDINGS WHERE FPR 28.3 APPLIES

[39.19]

In financial remedy proceedings, to which FPR 28.3 applies, the court's costs discretion is limited. The general rule for such applications is that the court will not make an order requiring one party to pay the costs of another party. This is subject to FPR 28.3(6):

> 'The court may make an order requiring one party to pay the costs of another party at any stage of the proceedings where it considers it appropriate to do so because of the conduct of a party in relation to the proceedings (whether before or during them).'

Therefore, the court may depart from the general rule if there is litigation conduct which justifies the making of an order for costs.

The matters relevant to deciding whether there has been any such conduct are set out at FPR 28.3(7) and the court is required to have regard to them:

(a) any failure by a party to comply with these rules, any order of the court or any practice directions which the court considers relevant;
(b) any open offer to settle made by a party;
(c) whether it was reasonable for a party to raise, pursue or contest a particular allegation or issue;
(d) the manner in which a party has pursued or responded to the application or a particular allegation or issue;

(e) any other aspect of a party's conduct in relation to proceedings which the court considers relevant; and although not an aspect of conduct the court must also weigh in the balance;

(f) the financial effect on the parties of any costs order.

It is important to stress that while (b) above allows the court to consider any open offers that have been made, FPR PD 28, para 4.3 specifically excludes 'without prejudice' or 'without prejudice save as to costs' offers from consideration when deciding what, if any, costs orders to make – see **[39.23]** below.

[39.20]

Further assistance in the application of FPR 28.3(6) and (7) is set out in Practice Direction 28A at para 4.4, which was amended in May 2019 and now provides as follows:

> '4.4 In considering the conduct of the parties for the purposes of rule 28.3(6) and (7) (including any open offers to settle), the court will have regard to the obligation of the parties to help the court to further the overriding objective (see [FPR 2010] rules 1.1 and 1.3) and will take into account the nature, importance and complexity of the issues in the case. This may be of particular significance in applications for variation orders and interim variation orders or other cases where there is a risk of the costs becoming disproportionate to the amounts in dispute. The court will take a broad view of conduct for the purposes of this rule and will generally conclude that to refuse openly to negotiate reasonably and responsibly will amount to conduct in respect of which the court will consider making an order for costs. This includes in a "needs" case where the applicant litigates unreasonably resulting in the costs incurred by each party becoming disproportionate to the award made by the court. Where an order for costs is made at an interim stage the court will not usually allow any resulting liability to be reckoned as a debt in the computation of the assets.'

Accordingly, although the list in FPR 28.3(7) is an exhaustive list, and the court cannot avail itself of its broad brush and sweep up all the circumstances of the case, there are additional factors set out in the Practice Direction to which the court must also have regard.

This results in the following principles:

(a) Paragraph 4.4 of the Practice Direction is clearly aimed at proportionality. This provision highlights the position that is frequently encountered in applications to vary a periodical payments order, where costs often outweigh any financial benefit that may be obtained even from a successful application. This clear indication that the court will be looking particularly at cases of that sort should encourage both parties to such an application to take a pragmatic view before disproportionate costs are incurred. The corollary is the exclusion of maintenance pending suit applications from FPR 28.3 thus disapplying the 'no order' presumption.

(b) The amendment to para 4.4 to include a refusal to negotiate reasonably and responsibly places an increased importance on offers, the effect of which had largely been neutralised by the 'no costs' provision. That this is so was confirmed by the Family Procedure Rules Committee Costs Working Group leading up to this amendment, when it stated:

> 'The FPRC is concerned that insufficient emphasis is given to encouraging parties to engage reasonably and responsibly in negotiations. In particular,

there is a concern that little positive guidance was given in PD.28A to assist the parties to understand the likely costs consequences of failing to litigate sensibly and failing to engage in sensible negotiations and/or of making an open proposal which is significantly higher or lower than the award ultimately made by the court' Paragraph 5.4 (Consultation in relation to the treatment of Calderbank offers when determining issues relating to costs)

To illustrate the importance of the amendment to the Practice Direction, in *MB v EB (No 2)* [2019] EWHC 3676 (Fam), whilst ordering the wife to pay some of the husband's costs, the court declined to order her to pay those which the judge had found to have been incurred by the unreasonable conduct of the husband for failing to engage in negotiations.

(c) The court must consider the financial effect on the parties of any costs order under FPR 28.3(7)(f). This is unrelated to conduct and involves an assessment of where any costs order would leave the parties financially. It is a necessary exercise in applications for a financial remedy since it may be the case that if an adverse costs order were to be made it may have the effect of undermining the basis upon which the court's substantive order was made.

The overriding objective

[39.21]

In *GS v L (No 2) (Costs)* [2013] 1 FLR 407, King J suggested that the starting point for an assessment of conduct must be the overriding objective contained in FPR 2010, Part 1.

Part 1 of FPR 2010 sets out the overriding objective that the court is expected to further, with the help of the parties. The overriding objective to deal with a case justly must be applied by the court whenever it exercises any power given to it by the rules. This includes the power to make orders for costs, whether that power is exercised under FPR 28.2 or FPR 28.3.

Accordingly, a party's conduct in the litigation must be viewed in the context of what is expected from the parties by way of assistance in the furthering of the overriding objective to deal with a case justly. This in turn includes, so far as is practicable:

(a) ensuring that it is dealt with expeditiously and fairly;
(b) dealing with the case in ways which are proportionate to the nature, importance and complexity of the issues;
(c) ensuring that the parties are on an equal footing;
(d) saving expense; and
(e) allotting to it an appropriate share of the court's resources, while taking into account the need to allot resources to other cases.

In *GS v L*, King J made an issues-based costs order against the husband who doggedly pursued his erroneous contention that the proceedings raised issues of Spanish law and should therefore be heard in Spain. As a result, a case that could have been dealt with in two days instead became protracted and unduly complicated, all this incurring disproportionate costs. The judge ordered the husband to pay a fixed sum towards the wife's costs, roughly equating to one third.

The matrimonial pot

[39.22]

A fundamental difference between civil and matrimonial litigation, is that in civil litigation no order for costs means each party must pay its own costs out of its own resources, but in matrimonial litigation there are no outside resources and the costs of both parties must come out of the family assets. Abolishing 'between the parties' costs orders does not alter the basic fact that all the costs must come out of the matrimonial pot, nor does it answer the basic question of how the costs are to be allocated fairly between the parties. An inevitable consequence of the abolition of costs orders is that many aspects of costs which were previously dealt with on a detailed assessment by a costs judge, now need to be considered by the judge conducting the final hearing before he or she can make an order, in quantum of costs and any penalties for litigation misconduct.

Quantification

[39.23]

If litigation conduct is established, one approach is for the court to quantify the costs of both parties arising out of the misconduct, and then order that the total of those costs be paid out of the share of the offending party, otherwise the sanction has no teeth.

The judge must also decide whether a costs order should be on the standard or the indemnity basis. There are different kinds and levels of what may be called litigation misconduct in family matters, not all of them necessarily justify the award of indemnity costs. Indeed, is the sanction for the misconduct not the disapplication of the 'no costs' general rule? It might be said that then ordering indemnity costs represents a double sanction.

'Calderbank' offers in 'no costs' financial remedy proceedings

[39.24]

FPR 28.3(8) specifically excludes the reliance upon Calderbank offers in financial remedy proceedings, save for the purposes of Financial Dispute Resolution ('FDR') hearings under the provisions in FPR 9.17 which require the applicant to file with the court all offers, proposals and responses to them, including any admissible without prejudice offers no less than 7 days before the FDR (FPR 9.17(3) and (4)).

Calderbank offers therefore have a very limited role in financial remedy proceedings. They carry no costs sanction and therefore if privilege is sought the mere heading 'Without Prejudice' will suffice. The district judge is able to comment on the offers, or, indeed, lack of them, and to observe, perhaps, that a lack of any genuine attempts to settle may amount to litigation conduct. At this stage, and indeed during any subsequent proceedings, there may be two separate strands of negotiation with more generous proposals contained in correspondence which will be admissible before the district judge at the FDR hearing but not before any other judge. Parties may therefore continue to make 'Calderbank' offers in negotiations more favourable than those known to the court but if settlement is not reached, the offers will have no costs consequences.

It is the open offers of the parties that will be relevant when considering costs consequences. Before considering how the court will view the open offers, it is important to understand what costs information and what 'open offers' the court will have before it throughout the financial remedy proceedings.

Rules relating to the provision of costs information and the importance of 'open offers' in financial remedy proceedings

[39.25]

The Family Procedure Rules were amended in June 2020 to ensure that far more specific costs information is provided to the court as an application for financial remedy proceeds. This will enable the court and the parties, amongst other consequences, to look at specific periods of costs, and consider the direct consequences over those periods of an adverse costs order made on the basis of conduct. These amendments provide:

- the parties must file and serve estimates of costs they have incurred up to the date of any hearing by one day before that hearing (FPR 9.27);
- the parties must file and serve an estimate of costs they expect to incur up to Financial Dispute Resolution appointment ('FDR') by one day before the First Directions Appointment ('FDA');
- the parties must file and serve an estimate of costs they expect to incur up to the final hearing by one day before the FDR;
- the parties must file and serve a full costs statement of all costs incurred and those expected to be incurred up to and including the end of the final hearing by 14 days before the final hearing;
- any costs estimate/statement must confirm service on the other party and that it has been discussed with the client;
- a copy of the estimate/statement must be brought to the hearing;
- the amount of costs in the estimate/statement must be recorded in a recital to the order made at the hearing;
- failure to comply must be recorded in a recital to the order and must be rectified within three days of the hearing;
- the parties are under an obligation to make open proposals 21 days after the FDR (unless the court specifies another time by which these should be made) (FPR 9.27A). This is in addition to FPR 9.28, which is re-titled 'Duty to make open proposals before a final hearing'.

Of course, the parties are free to make open proposals for settlement at any stage.

Open proposals in 'no costs' financial remedy proceedings

[39.26]

Accordingly, at the final hearing, the parties' total liability for costs and their open proposals are known to the judge before deciding what financial orders to make. It is the open offers that will influence the costs debate – hence the amendment to FPR PD 28, para 4.4 stressing the need to negotiate openly in a reasonable and responsible way.

Needs and adverse costs orders (FPR 28.3(6), (7) and PD 28 para 4.4)

[39.27]

What if the court concludes that a party has not litigated reasonably and this has resulted in the incurrence of costs by each party becoming disproportionate to the substantive made in their favour on a needs basis by the court? A fee shifting order in a big money case where the family assets exceed the aggregate needs of the family creates no problem, but what about the great majority of cases where there is simply not enough money to go around to start with? Take the example of a case where needs have been assessed so that one party requires £300,000 to enable re-housing (for the party and for children under 18) and the court awards this, but then is asked to make a costs order against that party. The effect of a costs order would be to reduce the sum awarded after deduction of those costs to less than that which enables the party. FPR PD 28, para 4.4 clearly envisages that the fact the case is a 'needs' one does not preclude the court making an adverse costs order.

The dilemma arises whenever a 'between the parties' costs order for litigation misconduct would result in the needs of one of the parties not being met. A fee-shifting order upsets the delicate balance between meeting the needs of both parties and meeting the needs of only one of them. When those needs are, as is so often the case, inextricably intertwined with the needs of the children, then, as the example illustrates, the problem becomes even more acute. Perhaps in a deferred sale situation, payment of the costs can be postponed until the sale and payment is made out of the resultant share of the party who was responsible for misconduct. However, even then, the longer-term needs of that party may militate against this.

Which is to take priority – the needs of a party or punishing a party for litigation misconduct? FPR 28.3(7)(f) requires the court to have regard to the financial effect on the parties of making a costs order. It is difficult to see how, in the example given, the court can undermine the needs basis of its order when first consideration under s 25 of the Matrimonial Causes Act 1973 is to the welfare of the children (which so often equates to their housing needs). If a party's and the children's needs are in any event going to override the making of a 'between the parties' costs order then surely the rule is purposeless in many 'needs' cases. If that is not the case and the amendment to FPR PD 28, para 4.4 was intended to signal that even in needs cases, unreasonable conduct of litigation will lead to adverse costs orders, how does that sit with the first consideration being to children in a needs case? We suspect that there will be an increased incidence of reliance on open offers evidencing litigation misconduct, requiring the court to undertake a balancing act between the 'financial effect on the parties of any costs order' (FPR 28.3(7)(f)) and the other factors at FPR 28.3(7) and PD 28, para 4.4.

Needs and cases where there is no costs order between the parties

[39.28]

If there is no litigation misconduct the general rule that there will be no order for costs will apply. However, this is too simplistic a statement. The court will have the costs statement at the final hearing and will know what costs each party has incurred and how much of that liability each has paid – indeed there may well be arguments that family assets have been eroded by one or both parties to pay all or some of their costs liability. How should the court treat the costs liability (whether discharged or to be discharged)?

[39.29]

The consultation paper on Costs in Ancillary Relief Proceedings and Appeals in Family Proceedings' which preceded the introduction of the 'no costs' rule in the previous version of the FPR, at paragraph 27 is unambiguous:

> 'The purpose of applying a "no order for costs" principle in ancillary relief proceedings is to stress to the parties, and to their legal advisers, that running up costs in litigation will serve only to reduce the resources that the parties will have left to support them in their new lives apart. The proposed amendments to the costs rules are designed to establish the principle that, in the absence of litigation misconduct, the normal approach of the court to costs in ancillary relief proceedings should be to treat them as part of the parties' reasonable financial needs and liabilities. Costs will have to be paid from the matrimonial "pot" and the court will then divide the remainder between the parties.'

On this approach there are problems:

- There is no control over the costs a party could claim out of the matrimonial pot. Solicitor and client costs are on the indemnity basis to which the test of proportionality does not apply and if the client accepts the solicitor's costs, those costs cannot be challenged on the grounds of being unreasonable. The client is contractually bound to pay them. So how could they be reduced even if either the court or the other party objects to the amount claimed coming out of the pot?
- Where is the incentive for a party to control the legal costs if half are in effect to be paid by the other spouse?
- What if one party is economical and the other is not? Should the economical party have to subsidise the other?
- Is there any incentive for a party to act in person to reduce costs if the other party has legal representation paid out of the pot?

Each of these factors gives rise to what has been described as 'back-door adverse costs orders' Only if you adopt what has been called the Leadbeater technique – used by Balcombe J in *Leadbeater v Leadbeater* [1985] FLR 789, [1985] Fam Law 280 – and deal with the gross assets – notionally writing back any costs already paid – do you arrive at the position of each party paying their own costs out of their share of the assets. However, this raises some of the issues under [**39.30**] below.

Recent decisions have discouraged the *Leadbeater* approach. In *R v R (financial remedies: needs and practicalities)* [2011] EWHC 3093 (Fam), the wife's costs were approximately double those of her husband. Although the judge, Coleridge J, was sympathetic to the wife he was 'driven to say that he would discourage the pursuit of this add-back principle or approach, which inevitably leads to a quasi-assessment of costs during the hearing, but without the court having all the material which would be available to, for instance, a costs judge. It also rather flies in the face of the non-order starting point and leads to debates about costs by the back door, which the 'no costs' rule was designed to try to reduce or prevent.'

[39.30]

An alternative approach is that referred to in *Judge v Judge* (above) by Wilson LJ when considering FPR 1991, r 2.71 (the predecessor to FPR 28.3). He stated that:

> 'The general rule . . . is only a concomitant of the modern approach in applications for ancillary relief that the sum owed by each party in respect of his own costs will be treated as his liability for the purposes of calculating the substantive award.' (para 51)

However, this approach, too, has its difficulties:

- If a party's liability for costs is to be taken out of the equation altogether and treated as a personal debt to be paid out of their share of the assets, this can drive a coach and horses through a needs-based order. What of the position where, for example, one party who is the primary carer of the children of the marriage, needs £150,000 to re-house, but has a costs liability of £20,000. Does that party then receive £170,000? If so, it is another back-door order for costs in the guise of a needs-based asset division.

  In *WG v HG* [2018] EWFC 84, the court declined to add the entire costs liability of the wife to the Duxbury fund that was based on need, leaving her to pay about one quarter of that fund in costs. In so doing, Francis J commented:

  > 'The wife will, therefore, have to find some £500,000 in order to fund that part of the costs which I am not ordering the husband to pay. I recognise that this will deplete her Duxbury fund. I have very carefully considered whether this is fair. It might be said that I have assessed her needs at a given figure. If I have done that, then how can I leave her with a lower sum which, by definition, does not meet her needs? This conundrum happens in so many cases. People who engage in litigation need to know that it has a cost . . . The consequences of the above will be that the wife will have a Duxbury fund not of the £2 million that I intended but of about £1.5 million. This will generate for her less than £75,000 a year net, for life. This is a small fortune for most people. Parties cannot spend £1 million on their representation without being prepared to face the consequences of their decision to incur that level of expenditure.'

- If liability for costs is to be taken into account as a debt in sharing the assets what if one party has incurred twice the costs of the other? Should the court look behind the solicitor and client screen and hold a mini Solicitors Act assessment and, for the purposes of s 25 of the Matrimonial Causes Act 1973, ignore any costs above the amount it regards as reasonable?
- If one party has paid more of the costs liability than the other as the proceedings progress, does that party lose out as only the outstanding costs are taken into account as a debt?

Wasted costs

[39.31]

There is one way for an order for costs based on litigation misconduct not to be met out of the matrimonial pot – that is if, in fact, the litigation misconduct arises in the way the leads to an enquiry into whether there should be a wasted costs order against that party's solicitors. CPR 46.8, which enables the court to order the legal representative of one party to pay the costs of the other for misconduct, has not been disapplied from financial remedy proceedings nor have the wasted costs provisions of s 51(7) of the Senior Courts Act 1981. However, as is clear from Chapter 23 – Wasted Costs Orders, the court should be wary of embarking upon the wasted costs process.

In *Fisher Meredith v JH and PH (financial remedy: appeal: wasted costs)* [2012] EWHC 408 (Fam) the wife's solicitors applied to adjourn to allow third parties to be joined to the proceedings where the husband alleged that family members were in fact the beneficial owners of shares in a company held in his name.

The district judge allowed the adjournment but ordered the wife to pay wasted costs and her solicitors to 'show cause' why they should not be personally liable for these.

At the wasted costs hearing the district judge ordered the wife's solicitors to pay the costs, stating that insufficient thought had been given as to the enforceability of any orders against third parties.

On appeal the judge distinguished between a case where a party states that property or shares in the name of the third party belong to the other party and where (as here) it was alleged that shares in which the other party clearly had legal title, belonged to a third party.

In the former case the obligation to join the third party would be on the party so alleging. In the latter case, the duty to clarify the position for the court, by joining a third party, was not clear cut at all. Indeed, there might be good reasons why the party with legal title might wish to join the third parties in order to reinforce the position of ownership. For those reasons the wasted costs order was set aside.

However, in *HU v SU* [2015] EWFC 535 (see **[23.20]**) the court did make a wasted costs order against solicitors in respect of a directions hearing where their delay in applying to vary directions necessitated that hearing.

In *In the matter of C (A child) (Wasted Costs)* [2015] EWHC 3259 (Fam), whilst finding that both parties had been partially responsible for the failure to manage the case effectively, the court found that the father's solicitors conduct satisfied the *Ridehalgh v Horsefield* [1994] Ch 205 criteria (see Chapter 23) and made a limited wasted costs order.

However, parties should be as cautious about invoking the wasted costs procedure in family proceedings as in civil proceedings for, as we have seen in Chapter 23, it can prove an expensive one and may simply make an already unhappy costs position far worse.

PROVISION OF COSTS INFORMATION

[39.32]

See **[39.25]** above for detail as to the procedural requirements for provision of costs information in financial remedy proceedings that are governed by FPR 28.3.

In addition, FPR PD 28A, para 4.5 provides that where it is intended to ask the court to exercise its discretion to make an order for costs because of the litigation conduct of the other party, this should ordinarily be made plain either in open correspondence or a skeleton argument before the hearing.

In any case in which it is appropriate that the court should make a summary assessment of costs in the event of a successful application, a statement of costs in the format of CPR Form N260 must be filed.

LEGAL SERVICES ORDERS IN APPLICATIONS IN MATRIMONIAL AND CIVIL PARTNERSHIP PROCEEDINGS

[39.33]

While the Legal Aid, Sentencing and Punishment of Offenders Act 2012 will, most likely, be remembered by family practitioners as the death knell for public funding in the vast majority of cases, ss 49 and 50 inserted provisions designed to address difficulties of funding certain family proceedings. The sections seek to address the position where there is such an imbalance of financial position between the parties that it results in an inequality of arms to the extent that one party cannot secure representation. These sections inserted ss 22ZA and 22ZB into the Matrimonial Causes Act 1973, and they permit the court to make 'orders for the payment of legal services' – already known colloquially as 'legal services orders'.

What is a legal services order?

[39.34]

A legal services order is one that requires one party to the marriage/civil partnership to pay to the other an amount for the purpose of enabling the other party to secure legal services for the relevant proceedings (s 22ZA(1)). An order can be either by way of a 'one – off' lump sum, may be by instalments (secured or unsecured) and may even be deferred in part or in full (ss 22ZA(6) and (7)). Any order made may also be varied at any stage by the court if there has been a 'material change of circumstances (s 22ZA(8)).

What proceedings are covered by these provisions?

[39.35]

The new provisions apply only to proceedings for decrees (of divorce, nullity and judicial separation) under the Matrimonial Causes Act 1973. However, there are mirror provisions in the Civil Partnership Act 2004 in respect of dissolution. In addition, the provisions apply to proceedings for financial relief under both statutes. However, there are no equivalent statutory provisions in respect of, for example, applications under Schedule 1 of the Children Act 1989 – see below at **[39.38]**. Assuming that the provisions apply, the types of 'legal service' which an order may cover are set out in s 22ZA(10) and are:

- advice as to how the law applies in particular circumstances;
- advice and assistance in relation to the proceedings;
- advice and assistance in relation to settlement or other resolution of the dispute that is the subject of the proceedings;

- advice and assistance in relation to enforcement of decisions made or settlements reached in the proceedings.

The subsection stresses that 'legal services' includes representation and also applies at any form of dispute resolution, including mediation.

The requirements for an application

[39.36]

There are two stages to an application for a legal services order.

The first stage is that, pursuant to s 22ZA(3), the court may not make a legal services order unless it is satisfied that without the amount ordered the applicant for the order would not reasonably be able to obtain appropriate legal services. This consideration includes the court being satisfied that the applicant cannot secure a loan to obtain funding and is unlikely to secure funding by offering a charge over any assets that might be recovered. In an era of creative litigation funding the general view was that it was hard to imagine many cases where an applicant would be able to meet these criteria. However, the judgment of Mostyn J in *Rubin v Rubin* [2014] EWHC 611 (Fam) suggests this view was unduly pessimistic (see [**39.37**]) below.

The second stage is that even if the applicant does satisfy the court under the first stage, then the court is still obliged to consider the factors in s 22ZB when it is asked to make or vary a legal services order. These are:

- the income, earning capacity, property and other financial resources which each of the applicant and the paying party has or is likely to have in the foreseeable future;
- the financial needs, obligations and responsibilities which each of the applicant and the paying party has or is likely to have in the foreseeable future;
- the subject matter of the proceedings, including the matters in issue in them;
- whether the paying party is legally represented in the proceedings;
- any steps taken by the applicant to avoid all or part of the proceedings, whether by proposing or considering mediation or otherwise;
- the applicant's conduct in relation to the proceedings;
- any amount owed by the applicant to the paying party in respect of costs in the proceedings or other proceedings to which both the applicant and the paying party are or were party; and
- the effect of the order or variation on the paying party.

Section 22ZB(3) specifically charges the court, when considering the last of the factors listed above, to have regard to any undue hardship that the order or variation may cause to the paying party and whether the effect of it would prevent the paying party from obtaining legal services.

Application of the provisions

[39.37]

To a large extent the new provisions broadly codify, in statutory form, the approach taken by judges since Holman J started the ball rolling in *A v A (maintenance pending suit: provision for legal fees)* [2001] 1 FLR 377. In *Currey v Currey (No 2)* [2006] EWCA Civ 1338 Wilson LJ regarded the criteria that are now s 22ZA(4) as central to the exercise of the court's discretion whether to make a costs allowance. Indeed, Mostyn J in *MET v HAT* [2013] EWHC 4247 (Fam) said as much at paragraph 36:

> 'The statutory provision, in my judgment, does no more than to codify the principles to be collected in this regard in the authorities, most recently in *Currey v Currey* [2007] 1 FLR 946. Under s. 22ZA(3) the court cannot make a costs allowance unless it is satisfied that without the amount of the allowance, the applicant would not reasonably be able to obtain appropriate legal services for the purposes of the proceedings or any part of the proceedings, and for the purposes of this provision the court must be satisfied in particular that the applicant is not reasonably able to secure a loan to pay for the services (see s. 22ZA(4)(b)).'

In *Rubin v Rubin* (see above) Mostyn J analysed the new provisions in more detail and set out 14 principles as follows:

> '13. I have recently had to deal with a flurry of such applications and there is no reason to suppose that courts up and down the country are not doing likewise. Therefore it may be helpful and convenient if I were to set out my attempt to summarise the applicable principles both substantive and procedural.
> (i) When considering the overall merits of the application for a LSPO the court is required to have regard to all the matters mentioned in s 22ZB(1)–(3).
> (ii) Without derogating from that requirement, the ability of the respondent to pay should be judged by reference to the principles summarised in *TL v ML* [2005] EWHC 2860 (Fam) at para 124 (iv) and (v), where it was stated:
>
> > "Where the affidavit or Form E disclosure by the payer is obviously deficient the court should not hesitate to make robust assumptions about his ability to pay. The court is not confined to the mere say-so of the payer as to the extent of his income or resources. In such a situation the court should err in favour of the payee.
> >
> > Where the paying party has historically been supported through the bounty of an outsider, and where the payer is asserting that the bounty had been curtailed but where the position of the outsider is ambiguous or unclear, then the court is justified in assuming that the third party will continue to supply the bounty, at least until final trial."
>
> (iii) Where the claim for substantive relief appears doubtful, whether by virtue of a challenge to the jurisdiction, or otherwise having regard to its subject matter, the court should judge the application with caution. The more doubtful it is, the more cautious it should be.
> (iv) The court cannot make an order unless it is satisfied that without the payment the applicant would not reasonably be able to obtain appropriate legal services for the proceedings. Therefore, the exercise essentially looks to the future. It is important that the jurisdiction is not used to outflank or supplant the powers and principles governing an award of costs in CPR Part 44. It is not a surrogate inter partes costs jurisdiction. Thus a LSPO should only be awarded to cover historic unpaid costs where the court is satisfied that without such a payment the applicant will not reasonably be able to obtain in the future appropriate legal services for the proceedings.
> (v) In determining whether the applicant can reasonably obtain funding from another source the court would be unlikely to expect her to sell or charge her home or to deplete a modest fund of savings. This aspect is however highly fact-specific. If the home is of such a value that it appears likely that it will be sold at the conclusion of the proceedings then it may well be reasonable to expect the applicant to charge her interest in it.

(vi) Evidence of refusals by two commercial lenders of repute will normally dispose of any issue under s 22ZA(4)(a) whether a litigation loan is or is not available.
(vii) In determining under s 22ZA(4)(b) whether a Sears Tooth arrangement can be entered into a statement of refusal by the applicant's solicitors should normally answer the question.
(viii) If a litigation loan is offered at a very high rate of interest it would be unlikely to be reasonable to expect the applicant to take it unless the respondent offered an undertaking to meet that interest, if the court later considered it just so to order.
(ix) The order should normally contain an undertaking by the applicant that she will repay to the respondent such part of the amount ordered if, and to the extent that, the court is of the opinion, when considering costs at the conclusion of the proceedings, that she ought to do so. If such an undertaking is refused the court will want to think twice before making the order.
(x) The court should make clear in its ruling or judgment which of the legal services mentioned in s 22ZA(10) the payment is for; it is not however necessary to spell this out in the order. A LSPO may be made for the purposes, in particular, of advice and assistance in the form of representation and any form of dispute resolution, including mediation. Thus the power may be exercised before any financial remedy proceedings have been commenced in order to finance any form of alternative dispute resolution, which plainly would include arbitration proceedings.
(xi) Generally speaking, the court should not fund the applicant beyond the FDR, but the court should readily grant a hearing date for further funding to be fixed shortly after the FDR. This is a better course than ordering a sum for the whole proceedings of which part is deferred under s 22ZA(7). The court will be better placed to assess accurately the true costs of taking the matter to trial after a failed FDR when the final hearing is relatively imminent, and the issues to be tried are more clearly defined.
(xii) When ordering costs funding for a specified period, monthly instalments are to be preferred to a single lump sum payment. It is true that a single payment avoids anxiety on the part of the applicant as to whether the monthly sums will actually be paid as well as the annoyance inflicted on the respondent in having to make monthly payments. However, monthly payments more accurately reflect what would happen if the applicant were paying her lawyers from her own resources, and very likely will mirror the position of the respondent. If both sets of lawyers are having their fees met monthly this puts them on an equal footing both in the conduct of the case and in any dialogue about settlement. Further, monthly payments are more readily susceptible to variation under s 22ZA(8) should circumstances change.
(xiii) If the application for a LSPO seeks an award including the costs of that very application the court should bear in mind s 22ZA(9) whereby a party's bill of costs in assessment proceedings is treated as reduced by the amount of any LSPO made in his or her favour. Thus, if an LSPO is made in an amount which includes the anticipated costs of that very application for the LSPO, then an order for the costs of that application will not bite save to the extent that the actual costs of the application may exceed such part of the LSPO as is referable thereto.
(xiv) A LSPO is designated as an interim order and is to be made under the Part 18 procedure (see FPR rule 9.7(1)(da) and (2)). 14 days' notice must be given (see FPR rule 18.8(b)(i) and PD9A para 12.1). The application must be supported by written evidence (see FPR rule 18.8(2) and PD9A para 12.2). That evidence must not only address the matters in s 22ZB(1)-(3) but must include a detailed estimate of the costs both incurred and to be incurred. If the application seeks a hearing sooner than 14 days from the date of issue of the application pursuant to FPR rule 18.8(4) then the written evidence in support must explain why it is fair and just that the time should be abridged.'

The (only) good news for the paying party is that any sums paid to the applicant under a legal services order will stand to his or her credit against any costs that are assessed to be paid to the applicant in the proceedings (s 22ZA(9)).

LEGAL SERVICES ORDERS AND APPLICATIONS UNDER SCHEDULE 1 TO THE CHILDREN ACT 1989, THE INHERITANCE (PROVISION FOR FAMILY AND DEPENDANTS) ACT 1975, PART III OF THE MATRIMONIAL AND FAMILY PROCEEDINGS ACT 1984 AND SECTION 8 OF THE CHILDREN ACT 1989

[39.38]

As has already been stated the provisions in respect of legal services orders do not extend to proceedings under Schedule 1 of the Children Act 1989. They do not apply to the Inheritance (Provision for Family and Dependants) Act 1975 or Part III of the Matrimonial and Family Proceedings Act 1984 either. This is a curiosity that Mostyn J felt worthy of mention in *Rubin v Rubin*. However, he referred to the continuation of the practice established by Charles J in *M-T v T* [2006] EWHC 2494 (Fam). In that case the court made an allowance for legal costs in an application for interim periodical payments. Mostyn J made it clear that the 14 principles he had set out in *Rubin* would apply to equivalent applications made under the above statutes but with:

- some modification to principle (x) as the first sentence would be redundant;
- no determination of the position as to whether an order could extend to funding ADR;
- payments likely to be monthly and not by lump sum (noting that this was mandatory in applications under the Matrimonial and Family Proceedings Act).

In Children Act applications, when exercising its discretion, the court must be clear that the pursuit of the substantive claim for which funding is sought is for the benefit of the child. In *G v G* [2009] EWHC 2080 Moylan J made an award of interim periodical payments of £40,000 as a contribution to the costs of the applicant mother. The court held that there was jurisdiction to make such an order under Schedule 1 if it was considered appropriate to do so for the benefit of the children. In that case Moylan J took the view that it would be of benefit to the children if the mother were properly represented. It was relevant to his decision that there was a significant financial imbalance between the parents, the applicant was conducting the litigation in an entirely responsible way, and the respondent could well afford to pay.

Whilst declining to make a legal services order in *MG v FG (Schedule 1: Application to strike out: Estoppel: Legal Costs Funding)* [2016] EWHC 1964 (Fam), Cobb J confirmed that there was jurisdiction to make a legal services order in Schedule 1 claims.

Mostyn J returned to the question of funding orders in *MG v JF* [2015] EWHC 564 (Fam) in the context of Children Act 1989, s 8 proceedings and the removal of Legal Aid as a funding source. He ordered the father of the child to make significant contributions to the costs of the respondents saying this:

> 'Even though MG and JG are certainly not entitled to an order for costs they are entitled to seek an order for costs funding. To J that may seem (with reason) to be a specious distinction without a difference, but that is where we find ourselves, now that the fourth pillar of the welfare state has been largely demolished.'

In *HB v A Local Authority (Local Government Association intervening)* [2017] EWHC 524 (Fam), the High Court rejected the submission that it had an inherent jurisdiction to make a costs funding order against a local authority, where there was a lawful refusal of legal aid in accordance with the statutory scheme for legal aid. In this case, the local authority had pursued wardship, rather than care proceedings under which the applicant would have been entitled to non-means tested legal aid. An element of the argument advanced was to suggest an equivalency between the order sought and a legal services order under s 22 or Schedule 1. The court rejected this saying:

> 'I cannot accept the submission that there is a simple equivalency between the position of parties who are amenable to costs funding orders in private law proceedings and a local authority in public law proceedings.'

SOLICITOR AND CLIENT

[39.39]

Under s 58A(1) of the Courts and Legal Services Act 1990 it is not permissible for solicitors to enter into a conditional fee agreement ('CFA') in family proceedings (see Chapter 4 Creating CFAs). However, this does not preclude creative retainers deferring payment of fees until a later date.

In *Denton v Denton* [2004] EWHC 1308 (Fam) a SCCO costs judge was in error when he found that a client care letter in matrimonial proceedings sent to the wife by her solicitor containing the clause 'we have agreed that a claim for costs will not be made until money is received at the end of the case' was a conditional fee agreement which did not comply with the regulations, and was therefore unenforceable. The Court, on appeal, was satisfied that the letter, taken as a whole, showed that the wife was to be liable for her own costs and the phrase meant that the solicitor agreed not to claim his costs until the conclusion of the case, a position wholly in line with the manner in which family proceedings were often undertaken.

Similarly, an agreement by a wife to pay her solicitor's fees in divorce proceedings out of such sums as the court might award her in the proceedings was not champertous and invalid (*Sears Tooth (a firm) v Payne Hicks Beach (a firm)* [1997] 2 FLR 116). Indeed, as we have seen above at [**39.37**], one of the pre-conditions for a legal services order is that a Sears Tooth agreement is not available.

ASSESSMENT OF COSTS

(a) No presumption of detailed assessment

[39.40]

The general rule in CPR PD 44, para 9.1 is that whenever the court makes an order about costs it should consider whether to undertake a summary as opposed to a detailed assessment. Even if the hearing has lasted over one day, and CPR PD 44, para 9.2(b) might imply that a detailed assessment is the usual order, the power to make a summary assessment must be considered in every case. In family cases in particular, in addition to the extra costs involved, the perpetuation of the matter by detailed assessment runs counter to the satisfactory resolution of disputes (*Q v Q (Family Division costs: summary assessment)* [2002] 2 FLR 668 (Fam)).

(b) Discrete issues

[39.41]

As so many aspects of family matters, such as the divorce, children and financial relief, are dealt with by solicitors at the same time, often in the same attendance, telephone call or letter, it is particularly important to be able to distinguish between them for the purposes of the summary assessment of the costs of a specific application. Otherwise, there is the risk that the statement of costs may include either more or less than the work done for that particular application. This is a particular issue where part of the application is subject to the 'no costs' regime', but a specific application falls outside that eg applications for maintenance pending suit within financial order proceedings. At the very least those letters, attendance notes etc relating to that particular application should be clearly identifiable to facilitate both quantification and justification of those discrete costs, if appropriate.

ENFORCEMENT OF COSTS AWARDS

(a) Statutory demand

[39.42]

Rule 12.3 of the Insolvency Rules 1986 provided:

> '(1) Subject as follows, in bankruptcy . . . all claims by creditors are provable as debts against . . . the bankrupt . . . The following are not provable – (a) in bankruptcy, any fine imposed for an offence and any obligation arising under an order made in family proceedings or under a maintenance assessment made under the Child Support Act 1991 . . . '

On this basis, Mr Levy, who was a bankrupt, applied to set aside a statutory demand served by the Legal Aid Board, now the Legal Aid Agency, claiming £62,732 costs incurred by his former wife in her family proceedings. Although there was jurisdiction to make a bankruptcy order on a petition based upon a non-provable debt, the jurisdiction was discretionary and would not be exercised except in special circumstances. It was puzzling that s 382(1) contemplated that a non-provable debt might be regarded as a bankruptcy debt, but it was difficult to conceive of any circumstances where that would occur (*Levy v Legal Services Commission* [2001] 1 All ER 895, CA, [2001] 1 FCR 178).

(b) Bankruptcy

[39.43]

The Insolvency (Amendment) Rules 2005 which came into force on 1 April 2005 provided that lump sum orders and costs orders made in family proceedings are now provable in bankruptcy in respect of bankruptcy orders made on or after that date. This provision now appears at Rule 14.2 of the Insolvency (England and Wales) Rules 2016. Arrears of periodical payments and under child support assessments are still not provable.

(c) Judgment summons

[39.44]

Schedule 8 to the Administration of Justice Act 1990, which prescribes the matrimonial orders enforceable by judgment summons, does not specifically mention orders for costs, but FPR 33.16(1)(a) contemplates enforcement of costs orders by judgment summons by providing that on the hearing of a judgment summons the judge may make a new order for payment of the amount due where the original order is for a lump sum provision or costs.

In *Mubarak v Mubarak* [2001] 1 FLR 673, [2000] All ER (D) 1797, CA, the Court of Appeal held that the existing judgment summons procedure under s 5 of the Debtors Act 1869 was not human rights compliant. Judgment summons proceedings for contempt are classified as criminal proceedings and the requirement that the debtor shall attend before the court to 'show cause' why he should not be sent to prison amounts to an unacceptable reversal of the burden of proof and removes the protection against self-incrimination. Accordingly, FPR 33.14(4) is clear that a debtor may not be compelled to give evidence.

The procedure to be adopted by a party issuing a judgment summons is set out at FPR 33.10 and includes the requirement for the application to be accompanied by all the evidence upon which the applicant relies.

LEGAL AID AND THE FADING OF THE LIGHT

[39.45]

2014 saw the real effect in family proceedings of the withdrawal in availability of most legal aid and this has been reinforced over subsequent years. The difficulties of the withdrawal of legal aid were considered in *OA Children* (CA Civ Div) 4 April 2014. When confronted by confusion over the progress of proceedings, the Court of Appeal remitted the case for rehearing and commented that the case demonstrated the difficulties where no parties were represented, where legal aid to the family court had been curtailed and where many litigants were struggling to represent themselves. The Government's post-implementation review of the effects of the Legal Aid, Sentencing and Punishment of Offenders Act 2012 published in February 2019 brought no relief (indeed the executive summary reveals, and also seems to revel in, the fact that as a result of taking some matters 'out of scope' for legal aid, spending fell by approximately £160 million in 2017–18).

However, in the meantime, there have been a few flickers of hope as judges have been creative, and necessarily so, to try to ensure that lack of funding does not introduce unfairness to the Family Court.

(a) Sharing the cost of expert evidence where only one party legally aided

[39.46]

In *JG v Lord Chancellor and the Law Society (interested party)* [2014] EWCA Civ 656, the Court of Appeal allowed an appeal against a dismissal of an application for judicial review of a decision by the Legal Aid Agency not to fund in full the cost of a psychological assessment ordered by the court. The proceedings were private children proceedings and the child had been made a party. A joint expert's report was ordered, but with the child, who had public funding, bearing the entire cost (the parents not being in a position to fund any proportion of the fee). The Court of Appeal allowed the appeal and made a declaration that the refusal to fund the report was unlawful. However, the decision is not quite so far reaching as appears at first blush. The factual position was that the idea for the report was always that of the guardian representing the child and although a joint instruction was ordered this was simply completion of the process initiated by the guardian. The mere fact others might have input into the instructions did not make them liable for the costs. In other words these decisions are fact sensitive. Certainly the case does not permit the loading of costs in such circumstances to the party/parties who have legal aid as legitimate if this is a pure device to circumvent the inability of another party/other parties who is/are not legally aided to contribute.

(b) Adjourning for legal assistance

[39.47]

The enormous problems that can confront the court when dealing with family proceedings when parties are unrepresented was highlighted by the decision of the President of the Family Division in *Q v Q* [2014] EWFC 7, when he adjourned a private children case for a wider consideration of how representation and the funding of expert evidence might be achieved where public funding had been withdrawn and the need to deal with a case justly seemed to demand assistance. He posed the problem facing family courts in such situations in these terms:

> 'Assuming that public funding in the form of legal aid is not going to be available to the father, because his public funding has been withdrawn and an appeal against that withdrawal has been dismissed, and on the footing that, although the father has recently gained employment, his income is not such as to enable him to fund the litigation, there is a pressing need to explore whether there is any other way in which the two problems I have identified can be overcome, the first problem being the funding of the attendance of the experts, the second being the funding of the father's representation . . .

> . . . As I have said, the domestic obligation on the court is to act justly and fairly and, to the extent that it is practicable, ensure that the parties are on an equal footing . . .
>
> . . . I mention those cases merely as illustrative of the kind of issues which arise in this kind of situation. I emphasise I do so without expressing any view at all as to whether, in the circumstances I am faced with, unless there is some resolution of the present financial impasse, there would be a breach of either Article 6 or Article 8.
>
> There may be a need in this kind of situation to explore whether there is some other pocket to which the court can have resort to avoid the problem, if it is necessary in the particular case – I emphasise the word "necessary" – in order to ensure a just and fair hearing . . . . It is arguable that, failing all else, and bearing in mind that the court is itself a public authority subject to the duty to act in a Convention compliant way, if there is no other way of achieving a just and fair hearing, then the court must itself assume the financial burden, as for example the court does in certain circumstances in funding the cost of interpreters.'

The Ministry of Justice declined to intervene and on further consideration, with two other cases that included serious allegations raising issues of the advice needed to the father and the way in which the mother would be tested as to her evidence, the President concluded that, while a last resort, to enable the court to deal justly under the overriding objective there would be cases where HM Courts and Tribunals Service would have to fund particular steps or representation. He concluded with this plea:

> 'The Ministry of Justice, the LAA and HMCTS may wish to consider the implications' (*Q v Q: Re B: Re C* [2014] EWFC 31).'

This approach was adopted at first instance in *Re K and H (Children: unrepresented father: cross examination of child)* [2015] EWFC 1 where the judge in a fact-finding case ordered HMCTS to fund representation for the father to conduct cross examination of the mother. However, allowing the appeal (*Re K and H (Children)* EWCA Civ 543), the Court of Appeal concluded that there was no power to require the Lord Chancellor to provide funding for representation outside the mechanism provided in the Legal Aid, Sentencing and Punishment of Offenders Act 2012. The Court of Appeal did acknowledge that difficulties might arise in more complicated cases and recommended that:

> 'In order to avoid the risk of a breach of the Convention, consideration should be given to the enactment of a statutory provision for (i) the appointment of a legal representative to conduct the cross-examination and (ii) the payment out of central funds of such sums as appear to be reasonably necessary to cover the cost of the legal representative.'

(c) Delay in funding provision, human rights and intermediaries

[39.48]

In *Re D A child (No 2)* [2015] EWFC 2 the President of the Family Division expressed concerns where he believed that the complexities of securing legal aid had been beyond the capacities of the parents, that it was unthinkable that legal aid should not be available and the delays that had ensued had been unconscionable. He concluded that this raised both Art 6 and Art 8 issues within the ECHR and that the court might increasingly have to fund intermediaries to assist in such situations. Intermediaries were to assist unrepresented litigants communicate effectively and so were not a form of representation for which other funding could be secured (a distinction accepted by the Court of Appeal in *Re H and K* (above)). The President's comments about the funding issues make uncomfortable reading:

> 'This is a case about three human beings. It is a case which raises the most profound issues for each of these three people . . . Yet for much of the time since their son was taken from them *(the parents)* – far too much time – the focus of the proceedings has had to be on the issue of funding, which has indeed been the primary focus of the last three hearings. The parents can be forgiven for thinking that they are trapped in a system which is neither compassionate nor even humane.'

(d) Lay advocates

[39.49]

In *Re C (Lay Advocates) (No 2) sub nom Secretary of State for Justice v A Local Authority* [2020] EWHC 1762 (Fam), the court revisited an earlier decision and clarified that the funding of lay advocates where essential to ensure that there is no breach of a party's right under art 6 of the Convention for the Protection of Human Rights and Essential Freedoms should be dealt with as follows:

- HMCTS would fund the provision of lay advocates, in appropriate circumstances, for parties at court hearings;
- the Legal Aid Agency would fund the provision of lay advocates, if satisfied that it was a justifiable and reasonable disbursement, to support and assist parties in communicating with their legal representatives outside court.

CHAPTER 40

COSTS AGAINST NON-PARTIES

INTRODUCTION TO COSTS AGAINST NON-PARTIES

[40.1]

The position in respect of costs orders against non-parties is set out at CPR 46.2. It is a rule without an accompanying practice direction. It sets out a reminder that the relevant jurisdiction under which the court can make such an order is s 51 of the Senior Courts Act 1981 and prescribes the procedure that must be adopted. In essence, this is a two-stage procedure. Whenever the court is considering making such an order it must join the person against whom such an order is contemplated as a party (stage 1) and provide an opportunity to that person to attend court when the position will be considered (stage 2). The rule does not provide any guidance on how the court might interpret the statutory provision which is itself broad – the court has the power to determine by whom and to whom costs are to be paid and to what degree. Further guidance has come from the case law that has emerged on the subject, albeit that the court has long been clear that the exercise of the jurisdiction should not become 'overcomplicated by authority' (*Turvill v Bird* [2016] EWCA Civ 703) and that s 51 confers a discretion not confined by specific limitations (*Petromec Inc v Petroleo Brasileiro SA Petrobras* [2006] EWCA Civ 1038 – see below at **[40.5]**).

It is worth noting that the title of this provision is 'Costs orders in favour of or against non-parties'. This wording is repeated in CPR 46.2(1). In other words, the rule permits costs orders both against and for non-parties.

THE GENERAL APPROACH TO COSTS AGAINST NON-PARTIES

[40.2]

Symphony Group plc v Hodgson [1993] 4 All ER 143, CA has been regarded as the seminal case on non-party costs. The claimant obtained injunctive relief against the defendant who had left its employment to join Halvanto, a competitor, in breach of restrictive covenants in his contract of employment. The claimant neither added Halvanto as a defendant nor initiated proceedings against it nor told it that it might seek to make it liable for costs. Halvanto's managing director gave evidence for the defendant. The defendant was protected against a cost liability to the claimant by a legal aid certificate. As a result the aggrieved claimant sought and successfully obtained an order that Halvanto should pay its costs of the action. In allowing Halvanto's appeal the court said that since *Aiden Shipping Co Ltd v Interbulk, The Vimeira (No 2)* [1986] AC 965, [1986] 2 All ER 409, HL the courts had entertained claims for costs against non-parties where a person who was not a party:

- had some management of or financed an action;

- had caused the action;
- was a party to a closely related action which had been heard at the same time but not consolidated; or
- was involved in group litigation.

The court identified the following material considerations to be taken into account, which remain the guiding principles when considering costs orders against non-parties:

(a) An order for the payment of costs by a non-party will always be exceptional. The judge should treat any application for such an order with considerable caution.

(b) It will be even more exceptional for such an order to be made where the applicant has a cause of action against the non-party and could have joined that party to the substantive claim. Joinder as a party gives the person concerned all the protection conferred by the rules, eg the framing of issues, involvement in the disclosure process and the knowledge of what the issues are before giving evidence.

(c) Even if the applicant can provide a good reason for not joining the non-party against whom there is a valid cause of action, warning should be given to the non-party that the applicant might apply for costs against that non-party at the earliest opportunity.

(d) An application should normally be determined by the trial judge.

(e) The fact that the trial judge might have expressed views on the conduct of the non-party neither constitutes bias nor the appearance of bias (and is not, therefore, a basis for recusal of that judge).

(f) The procedure for the determination of costs is a summary procedure, not necessarily subject to all the rules that would apply in an action. Accordingly, subject to any statutory exceptions, judicial findings are inadmissible as evidence of the facts on which they are based in proceedings between one of the parties to the original proceedings and a stranger. However, in the summary procedure for solicitors to pay the costs of an action to which they were not a party, the judge's findings of fact might be admissible. This departure from basic principles could only be justified if the connection of the non-party with the original proceedings was so close that there would be no injustice by allowing the exception to the general rule.

(g) The normal rule is that witnesses in either civil or criminal proceedings enjoy immunity from any form of civil action in respect of evidence given during the proceedings. Insofar as the evidence of a witness in proceedings might lead to an application for non-party costs against them or their company, this introduces an exception to a valuable general principle.

(h) The fact that an employee or even a director or managing director of a company gives evidence in an action does not normally mean that the company is taking part in that action.

(i) The judge should be alert to the possibility that an application for costs against a non-party is motivated by resentment or an inability to obtain an effective order for costs against a state-funded litigant (and now, presumably, a party protected by qualified one-way costs shifting (see **[40.24]** below).

However, in *Deutsche Bank AG v Sebastian Holdings Incorporated* [2016] EWCA Civ 23, the Court of Appeal, in a postscript, stressed, that the above are guidelines only and not rules and that the case of *Dymocks Franchise Systems (NSW) Pty Ltd v Todd* [2004] UKPC 39 (see **[40.7]** below) 'explains and interprets the Symphony guidelines in a way which reflects the variety of circumstances in which the court is likely to be called upon to exercise the discretion'. The court in Deutsche concluded:

> 'We think it important to emphasise that the only immutable principle is that the discretion must be exercised justly. It should also be recognised that, since the decision involves an exercise of discretion, limited assistance is likely to be gained from the citation of other decisions at first instance in which judges have or have not granted an order of this kind.'

Notwithstanding this, some clear and helpful patterns of both procedure and approach emerge from previous decisions that assist in determining whether or not an application for non-party costs should be made.

It should be noted that this was not the end of the case, as in *Deutsche Bank AG v Sebastian Holdings Inc* [2017] EWHC 917 (Comm), the court rejected an application to set aside the non-party costs order or to stay the assessment of costs pending an application to the ECHR on the basis that the making of an order against the non-party breached article 6 rights (see **[40.4]** below).

THE APPLICATION PROCEDURE

[40.3]

An application for a non-party costs order should be made to the trial judge, even if that judge has expressed a view about the conduct of the non-party. It is not wrong for a judge to mention the possibility of an application for a non-party costs order at the outset of the trial (*Equitas Ltd v Horace Holman & Co Ltd* [2008] EWHC 2287 (Comm)).

An application for an order to join a party for the purpose of seeking an order for costs should normally explain the nature of the claim against the intended party and the purpose to be served by joining that party. If it is clear that a joinder of an intended party is an abuse of process, then the court will dismiss the application. In *PR Records Ltd v Vinyl 2000 Ltd* [2007] EWHC 1721 (Ch), it was held that a Master had been wrong to refuse to join the second defendant as a party to the proceedings and not to permit the matter to proceed to the second stage hearing envisaged under CPR 46.2(1)(b). The application had not involved an abuse of process of the court. At the stage of considering joinder, it is not appropriate to attempt a preliminary assessment of the merits in order to see whether an application for a non-party cost order has a real prospect of success.

REQUIREMENTS FOR NOTICE OF AN APPLICATION

[40.4]

A relevant consideration in the exercise of the court's discretion whether to make an order for costs against a non-party is whether the non-party has received notice, before or during the litigation, that they may be made subject to an order for costs. Although CPR 46.2 contains no requirement for notice to be given, the court has repeatedly taken account of whether notice has been given and when. In *Weatherford Global Products Ltd v Hydropath Holdings Ltd* [2014] EWHC 3243 (TCC) Akenhead J reviewed the case law. He dismissed contentions that the failure to give notice either precluded an order or automatically represented a factor that would reduce the percentage of any costs made. Instead lack of notice is a material factor, but the weight attached to it is case sensitive. That this is the correct approach was confirmed by the Court of Appeal in *Deutsche Bank AG* (see **[40.2]** above). The court stated that a failure to give notice was not fatal to an application for non-party costs. Instead, notice was a relevant factor, the weight of which would vary from case to case:

> 'As was made clear in *Dymocks*, however, that is to read too much into the Symphony guidelines. The importance of a warning will vary from case to case and may depend on the extent to which it would have affected the course of the proceedings: see per Lord Brown at paragraph 31. If the third party against whom an order for costs is sought is the real party to the litigation, the absence of a warning may be of little consequence.' (para 32)

Excellent practical illustrations of the contextual determination of the weight to be given to a failure to give notice can be found in the recent decisions of *Sony/ATV Music Publishing LLC v WPMC Ltd (in liq)* [2018] EWCA Civ 2005 and *Kazakhstan Kagazy PLC v Zhunus* [2019] EWHC 2630 (Comm). In the former, the court set aside a costs order when notice was not given to the non-party until a year after judgment. The delay in giving notice was, in the circumstances, the decisive factor, where other matters were 'fairly evenly balanced'. In the latter, the court made a non-party costs order in the absence of a warning, as contextually, 'in the hard-fought nature of the litigation' it would have been improbable that the claimants could have obtained sufficient information from the second defendant to enable them to give warning to the fourth and fifth defendants that they would be pursued to pay costs ordered against the second defendant and, even if warning had been given, it was fanciful to think that would have made any difference to the funding being provided to the second defendant.

THE APPROACH OF THE COURT TO MANAGING AN APPLICATION

[40.5]

Whether the jurisdiction should be exercised at all is, of course, another matter entirely and the extent to which a respondent has, in fact, funded any proceedings may be very relevant to the exercise of discretion. In addition to the risk that the exercise of the jurisdiction to order a non-party to proceedings to pay the cost of those proceedings becomes over-complicated by reference to authority, the parties must be astute to the proportionality issues that such an application raises (see *Petromec v Petrobras* [2006] EWCA Civ 1038 and **[40.1]** above).

In *Robertson Research International Ltd v ABG Exploration BV* (1999) Times, 3 November, QBD (Pat Ct), after directions for trial had been given in a robustly defended action, the defendant company gave notice that it was ceasing to trade, its solicitors came off the record and it consented to judgment for the entire sum claimed. By then it was an empty shell. The claimant joined as parties a director and the financial controller of the defendant company alleging that they had known there was no defence, seeking an order for costs against them. The defendants argued that in view of the strictures in wasted costs matters that such applications will not be heard unless they can be dealt with summarily, the applications should be dismissed. The master accepted these submissions, but on appeal, Laddie J held that although such orders would always be exceptional, it was not necessary that the applications had to be capable of being dealt with summarily. The matter could be dealt with appropriately by, for example, limiting it to principle issues, limiting or dispensing with cross examination and limiting the length of the hearing.

However, what does seem clear is that the procedure should not be adopted where the sums involved are relatively small (see the postscript on disproportionate costs in *Sims v Hawkins* [2007] EWCA Civ 1175). This consideration has become even more important following the CPR amendments of April 2013. The decision to join a party and embark upon a non-party costs application is a case management one to which the amended overriding objective applies. If the preliminary determination is that the exercise is disproportionate by reference to the definition at CPR 44.3(5) and the wider circumstances of the case, then the court is unlikely to permit joinder and move to the second stage of CPR 46.2.

Re Land and Property Trust Co plc (No 4) [1994] 1 BCLC 232, CA illustrates that once an application has been made the court must ensure that the process for determination is a fair one. The judge had refused the directors' application for an adjournment to enable them to have a proper opportunity of putting in evidence and the failure to do so was an error in principle. On the fresh evidence that was available before the Court of Appeal, the order for costs ought not to have been made.

IS IT A PREREQUISITE THAT THE NON-PARTY HAS PROVIDED FUNDING FOR THE CLAIM?

[40.6]

Although the non-party has provided funding in most of the reported cases, it is not essential, in the sense of being a jurisdictional pre-requisite to the exercise of the court's discretion. If the evidence is that a respondent to the application has effectively controlled the proceedings and has sought to derive potential benefit from them, that will be enough to establish the jurisdiction.

While the absence of provision of funding is not a bar to an application, the mere fact that the non-party has provided funding also does not, itself, automatically justify an order. In *Petromec Inc v Petroleo Brasileiro SA Petrobas* (above) the Court of Appeal stated that in a situation where non-party directors can be described as the 'real party', seeking their own benefit, controlling and/or funding the litigation and even where they have acted in good faith or without any impropriety, justice may well demand that they be liable in costs on a fact sensitive and objective assessment of the circumstances. This last point confirms the comments of Rix LJ in *Goodwood Recoveries Ltd v Breen* [2005] EWCA Civ 414 that:

> 'Where a non-party director can be described as the "real party", seeking his own benefit, controlling and/or funding the litigation, then even where he has acted in good faith or without any impropriety, justice may well demand that he be liable in costs on a fact-sensitive and objective assessment of the circumstances.'

In *Lingfield Properties (Darlington) Ltd v Padgett Lavender Associates* [2008] EWHC 2795 (QB), the court refused to join a company secretary personally as a party to the proceedings for the purposes of a non-party costs order. Although he was no longer a director he had been the principal person involved in managing the company's claims and this particular claim had depended on his evidence. He was the only person through whom the company had acted. He had also arranged the funding of the claim, although he had not funded it personally. Nevertheless, it was clear he was not the real party to the claim. The board properly applied its mind independently to the matters to be decided in the litigation. The company risked its own assets and made arrangements for funding the litigation that did not materially depend upon the financial contribution of the company secretary. The company remained the real party to the litigation.

CAUSATION OF COSTS AND THE 'ARKIN CAP'

Causation of costs

[40.7]

In *Dymocks Franchise Systems (NSW) Pty Ltd v Todd* (see **[40.2]** above), the Privy Council held that costs would be awarded against a non-party who had not merely funded the proceedings but had substantially controlled them, or was to benefit from them or who promoted and funded proceedings by an insolvent company solely or substantially for their own financial benefit. The Privy Council also took the opportunity to review the relevant case law and, amongst other matters, defined 'exceptional' in the context of non-party costs orders as conveying nothing more than something outside the 'norm' where a party funds a claim or defence for their own benefit at their own expense. It also confirmed that once a court has determined that a case is 'exceptional' what it must do is determine whether, in all the circumstances, it is just to make a non-party costs order.

Arkin v Borchard Lines Ltd [2005] EWCA Civ 655, picking up on *Dymocks Frachise Systems*, is seen as the first really clear illustration that causation of costs is not strictly required. In this case MPC, a professional funding company, entered into a funding agreement with the claimant, whereby it funded the employment of expert witnesses, the preparation of their evidence and the organisation of the enormous quantities of documents which it became necessary to investigate before the trial. The defendant sought a non-party costs order arguing that, in principle, professional funders, as distinct from pure funders, who are maintaining litigation for their profit, should be liable for the costs of the defendants if the claim fails, which in this case it did.

MPC resisted the claim, submitting that conditional fee agreements with professional funders which have the purpose of enabling impecunious claimants to pursue claims of real substance which, but for such funding, they could not have done, should not be visited with costs orders against the funders if the claim fails.

At first instance the court held that in these circumstances the public policy objectives of the deterrence of weak claims and of the protection of the due administration of justice from interference by those who fund litigation must yield to the objective of making access to the courts available to impecunious claimants with claims of sufficient substance. An order for costs against MPC would, undoubtedly, operate as a strong deterrent to professional funders to provide support for impecunious claimants with large and complex claims.

On appeal the Court of Appeal, relying on the summary of the jurisdiction set out in *Dymocks Franchise Systems* (above), held that a professional funder, who finances part of a claimant's costs of litigation, ought potentially to be liable for the costs of the opposing party *to the extent of the funding provided*. The likelihood that the decision would result in professional funders taking a larger cut of any award to reflect this heightened risk was deemed preferable in the pursuit of 'overall justice' to leaving a successful defendant in such a claim without the ability to recover costs. Interestingly, as a harbinger of the April 2013 reforms, the court felt that this would act as a natural check on costs, as the non-party funder would want to keep costs proportionate to limit its potential exposure and this exposure risk would also act as a deterrent against speculative claims.

The approach adopted in *Arkin* was followed in *Excalibur Ventures LLC v Texas Keystone Inc* [2014] EWHC 3436 (Comm), 164 NLJ 7631 (and upheld on appeal [2016] EWCA Civ 1144), in which the court capped the liability of the non-party funder to the contribution it had made to the losing party's costs plus the amount that had already been ordered to be paid by way of security for costs. Longmore LJ, giving the lead judgment in the Court of Appeal explained the rationale in these terms:

> 'I can discern no principle whether of fairness, justice or otherwise pursuant to which the Platinum funders' investments earmarked for the provision of security should be treated any differently from their or Psari's and Mr Lemos' investment earmarked for the payment of Excalibur's own costs.'

In *Total Spares & Supplies Ltd v Antares SRL* [2006] EWHC 1537 (Ch), highlighting qualifications in both *Dymocks* and *Arkin* on the imperative of causation of costs, the court concluded that:

> ' . . . it cannot in my judgment any longer be said that causation is a necessary pre-condition to an order for costs against non-party. Causation will often be a vital factor but there may be cases where, in accordance with principle, it is just to make an order for costs against a non-party who cannot be said to have caused the costs in question.' (para 54)

In this case, the court decided that there could be cases where, in accordance with principle, it was just to make an order for costs against a non-party who could not be said to have caused the costs in question. In the circumstances, of the case it was just to make an order.

In fact, detailed consideration of causation is usually of academic interest only in practical terms, for it is difficult to imagine how either the funding provided or the control of litigation by a non-party will not inevitably cause the non-funded party to incur further costs (save perhaps in group litigation, where the funding is provided to some, but not all, of the claimants or defendants). This was the point made by the court in *Adris v Royal Bank of Scotland (Cartel Client Review Ltd, additional parties)* [2010] EWHC 941 (QB). Here the allegations before the court were the more usual ones of control and a consideration of who was the 'real party'. However, the court also concluded that it was hard to see how a party could 'control' litigation without it following that such conduct had a bearing on the incurrence of costs by the other side. The same was true of funding – funding was necessary and it followed that in its absence the litigation may not have started or continued – with the inevitable consequence that some or all of the costs would not have been incurred.

The Arkin cap

[40.8]

The 'Arkin cap', set out above, has been the subject of increasing criticism. In his 'Review of Civil Litigation Costs: The Final Report' in December 2009, Sir Rupert Jackson commented:

> 'In my view, it is wrong in principle that a litigation funder, which stands to recover a share of damages in the event of success, should be able to escape part of the liability for costs in the event of defeat. This is unjust not only to the opposing party (who may be left with unrecovered costs) but also to the client (who may be exposed to costs liabilities which it cannot meet)
>
> I recommend that either by rule change or by legislation third party funders should be exposed to liability for adverse costs in respect of litigation which they fund. The extent of the funder's liability should be a matter for the discretion of the judge in the individual case. The funder's potential liability should not be limited by the extent of its investment in the case.' (paras 4.6 and 4.7)

Although there has been neither rule change nor legislation, the days of the 'Arkin cap' as an inviolable limit are gone, although it remains relevant, depending on context.

While a decision on the issue of security for costs, the rot set in *Bailey v Glaxosmithkline UK Ltd* [2017] EWHC 3195 (QB), [2018] 4 WLR 7, [2017] 6 Costs LR 1209. Foskett J ordered a payment of security from the funders that exceeded the 'Arkin cap' (see Chapter 19 at [**19.5**]). However, he did so expressly separating considerations at an interim stage when security is ordered and those at the end of the case, making the point that the 'Arkin cap' is not relevant until the conclusion of the claim. At that stage, the cap might be disapplied, but that if not, that part of the sum paid into court that exceeds the cap can then be repaid. In reaching this decision, the court made the following three points about the 'Arkin cap':

- to apply the cap at an interim stage in an unquestioning way, fetters the broad discretion that the court has on costs under s 51 of the Senior Courts Act 1981;
- the Court of Appeal in *Arkin* was concerned with a case where the funder had funded a discrete part of the proceedings only, not one where the costs were underwritten in their entirety; and
- in any case there may be an argument that funding has been provided in an objectionable way, taking it outside the protection afforded by *Arkin*.

This was taken even further than what was effectively an interim decision in *Bailey*, when in *Davey v Money* [2019] EWHC 997 (Ch), the court analysed the 'Arkin' cap and concluded that in *Arkin*:

> '... the Court of Appeal should not be taken to have been intending to prescribe a rule to be followed in every subsequent case involving commercial funders [and] there is no subsequent authority in which the *Arkin* cap has been treated as a principle to be applied automatically in any case involving a commercial funder.'

The upshot was that the court ordered the non-party to pay all the costs due under the costs order (which was one for indemnity costs), without any cap being applied. The court was at pains to stress that each decision will turn on its own facts.

Finally, the Court of Appeal had cause to reconsider the 'Arkin cap' in *Chapelgate Credit Opportunity Master Fund Ltd v Money* [2020] EWCA Civ 246 concluding that:

- 'The only immutable principle is that the discretion (whether to make a non-party costs order) must be exercised justly'.
- The decision in *Arkin* was from a time when non-party funding was 'nascent' and CFA and ATE funding was relatively new.
- Whilst the 'Arkin cap' had not become redundant (indeed there might be cases similar to *Arkin*, where it was likely to remain of particular relevance, other factors should be considered, eg the potential return for the funder).

Newey LJ set out the conclusions in this fashion:

> 'I do not consider that the *Arkin* approach represents a binding rule. Judges, as it seems to me, retain a discretion and, depending on the facts, may consider it appropriate to take into account matters other than the extent of the funder's funding and not to limit the funder's liability to the amount of that funding. In the case of a funder who funded only a distinct part of a claimant's costs, a judge might well decide that it should pay no larger sum towards the defendant's costs. A judge could also, however, consider the funder's potential return significant. The more a funder had stood to gain, the closer he might be thought to be to the "real party" ordinarily ordered to pay the successful party's costs in accordance with the guidance given in paragraph 25(3) of the *Dymocks* judgment (for which, see paragraph 22 above). In the case of a funder who had funded the lion's share of a claimant's costs in return for the lion's share of the potential fruits of litigation against multiple parties, it would not be surprising if the judge ordered the funder to bear at least the lion's share of the winners' costs, regardless of whether the funder's outlay on the claimant's costs had been a lesser figure.'

An illustration of a case where the cap may still be relevant is *Burnden Holdings (UK) Ltd v Fielding* [2019] EWHC 2995 (Ch), striking a balance between deterring funders and recognition of the successful party's entitlement to recover costs. This was cited as an example in *Chapelgate*.

Conclusions

[40.9]

The conclusions that we draw from this review of the case law are:

- while it was once stated to be a pre-condition of a non-party costs order that additional costs had been incurred (see *Hamilton v Al Fayed* [2002] EWCA Civ 665 per Simon Brown LJ at para 54, considered at [**40.18**] below), that is no longer the case;
- the fact that the non-party has caused additional costs to be incurred is an additional factor supporting an order against the non-party;
- in most cases (certainly those where the non-party has provided funding to an otherwise impecunious party) causation is, in any event, easy to establish – but for the funding provided the claim or defence could not have been maintained and the other party, inevitably, would have avoided incurring the costs of a contested claim;
- the liability of non-party funders is no longer necessarily limited by the '*Arkin* cap'. Instead, the extent of any liability is a matter of judicial discretion, with a steer that 'the more a funder stood to gain, the closer he might be thought to be to the "real party" ordinarily ordered to pay the successful party's costs . . . '. The greater the investment and potential return of the funder, the greater the potential liability to have to pay in excess of the '*Arkin* cap' (para 38, *Chapelgate Credit Opportunity Master Fund Ltd* (above)).

SPECIFIC CATEGORIES OF NON-PARTIES TRADITIONALLY IN THE FIRING LINE

[40.10]

As set out above, the court identified in *Symphony Group plc v Hodgson* the type of conduct on behalf of a non-party that might lead to an order for costs. A review of the case law readily reveals categories of non-party with a specific risk of exposure to a non-party costs order. We shall look at them in turn, then consider separately the position of funders and solicitors, where very specific considerations arise, and finally look briefly at non-party costs orders in the family jurisdiction where normally a 'no costs' regime applies. However, as the Court of Appeal has reminded us in *Deutsche Bank AG* (see [**40.2**] above), it is important to understand that each case will turn on its own facts and that case law can do no more than offer guidance as to what has and has not been sufficient in the past to merit the visitation of a costs order against a non-party.

Insurers

[40.11]

Inevitably the position of insurers has come under scrutiny given their interest in the outcome of claims where they are providing an indemnity to an insured. Certain themes have emerged.

Insurers who take over the defence of an action and conduct it for their own benefit may properly be said to be the real defendants. In such a situation in *Pendennis Shipyard Ltd v Magrathea (Pendennis) Ltd (in liq)* [1998] 1

Lloyd's Rep 315 (QB) they were ordered to pay the costs although they were not a party to the action. This approach was adopted in *Legg v Stert Garage Ltd* [2016] EWCA Civ 97 in which the Court of Appeal upheld a costs order against the defendant's insurer on the basis that the insurer's approach was exclusively or predominantly in its own interest, but for the funding the defendant would not have defended the claim and the insurer's conduct was causative of the claimants' costs. *Legg* cited with approval *Palmer v Palmer* [2008] EWCA Civ 46, in which the Court of Appeal considered the authorities in respect of orders against non-party insurers and concluded that 'a critical issue was whether the insurers were motivated either exclusively or at least predominantly, by a consideration of its own interest in the manner in which it conducted the defence of the litigation'.

In *TGA Chapman Ltd v Christopher* and *Sun Alliance* [1998] 2 All ER 873, CA (also cited in *Legg*), the Court of Appeal held that the defendant's liability insurers were liable for the full amount of a judgment of £1,100,000 plus costs even though their liability under the insurance policy was limited to £1,000,000 inclusive of opponents' costs. The insurers were in a different position from those in *Murphy* (below) because, as in *Pendennis* above, the litigation was funded, controlled and directed by the insurance company motivated entirely by its own interest. The same reasoning was adopted in *Plymouth and South West Co-operative Society Ltd v Architecture, Structure and Management Ltd* [2006] EWHC 3252 (TCC), where the insured had virtually no assets and had ceased trading, but the insurers had fought the claim to protect their own liability to the defendant of £2 million under the policy.

In contrast in *Murphy v Young & Co's Brewery plc and Sun Alliance and London Insurance plc* [1997] 1 All ER 518, [1997] 1 WLR 1591, CA legal expenses insurers were not liable to pay more than the limit of their cover merely on the grounds that they had funded the litigation under a commercial agreement.

In *XYZ v Travelers Insurance Company Ltd* [2017] EWHC 287 (QB), the court made a non-party costs order against an insurer in respect of the costs of the successful claimants in respect of claims that were uninsured, where it was the insurer in respect of other claims. This was on the basis that the insurer was both involved in and influenced the conduct of the litigation of the uninsured claims. The court found that but for the insurer's interest, the defendant would have confirmed that it was not insured and the claimants would not have pursued the claims. The decision was upheld on appeal on the bases that the insurer's interests were in play in the uninsured claims, that it stood to benefit from the outcome of the proceedings and that, had a costs order been made against the claimants, it would have received a contribution to its costs from the sums paid by the uninsured claimants to the defendant (*Travelers Insurance Co Ltd v XYZ* [2018] EWCA Civ 1099. However, the Supreme Court, in allowing the appeal, in *Travelers Insurance Co Ltd v XYZ* [2019] UKSC 48, rejected key elements of the analysis in the courts below and set out some concluding propositions, as follows:

> 'First, the underlying question, whether the non-party has either become the real defendant in relation to an insured claim, or intermeddled in an uninsured claim, is fundamental to the exercise of the section 51 jurisdiction, in insurance cases. It is the conduct of the non-party which matters, rather than the mere rarity of the case.

Secondly, the Chapman principles are useful guidelines for establishing whether the liability insurer has become the real defendant in all but name, in a case where some part of the claim (including the claim for costs) is or may lie outside the limits of cover, so that the insured has at least a prima facie joint interest with the insurer in the outcome of the litigation.

Thirdly , the Chapman principles are not likely to be of assistance where the question is (as here) whether the liability insurers crossed the line in becoming involved in the funding it and conduct of the defence of wholly uninsured claims, as opposed to claims where there is limited cover. In such cases the insurer may cross the line by conduct falling well short of total control, and without becoming the real defendant, if the insurer intermeddles in the uninsured claim in a manner which it cannot justify.

But, fourthly, where there is a connection between uninsured claims and claims for which the insurer has provided cover, it may well be that the legitimate interests of the insurer will justify some involvement by the insurer in decision-making and even funding of the defence of the uninsured claims without exposing the insurer to liability to pay the successful claimant's costs. This is just such a case because of the very close connection between insured and uninsured claims, raising common issues to be tried together in test cases in group litigation, and the limited nature of Travelers' involvement in the uninsured claims.

Fifthly, causation remains an important element in what an applicant under section 51 has to prove, namely a causative link between the particular conduct of the non-party relied upon and the incurring by the claimant of the costs sought to be recovered under section 51. If all those costs would have been incurred in any event, it is unlikely that a section 51 order ought to be made.

Sixthly, the non-disclosure of limits of cover by the defendant at the request of the insurer is unlikely to amount to relevant conduct, for as long as the law continues to make that non-disclosure legitimate.

Seventhly, asymmetry or lack of reciprocity in costs risk, as between the uninsured claimant and the defendant's insurer, is unlikely on its potential costs exposure. own to be a reason for the making of a non-party costs order against the insurer where, as here, the asymmetry arises because a claimant sues an uninsured and insolvent defendant and incurs several-only costs liability in group litigation.' (paras 76–82)

Company Directors

[40.12]

As with insurers there has been a plethora of cases that concern the liability of the officers of limited companies for costs of claims involving those companies where the specific company subject to a potential liability is impecunious. A review of cases where orders have not and have been made gives a flavour of the approach which the court has adopted in such a situation. This review again comes with the inevitable reminder that the discretion is a broad one and that the exercise of it will be fact specific.

(a) Orders not made

[40.13]

In *Taylor v Pace Developments Ltd* [1991] BCC 406, CA, the Court of Appeal held that the controlling director of a one-man company should not be liable personally for the costs of defending an action even though he knew the company would not be able to meet the claimant's costs should the company's defence prove unsuccessful. The court found that to impose a liability in such a situation would be far too great an inroad into the principle of limited liability. However, a sole director might still be made liable if the company's defence transpired not to be bona fide (eg where a company had been advised that there was no defence).

Gardiner v FX Music Ltd [2000] All ER (D) 144, ChD confirmed that in the case of a sole or guiding director of an insolvent company, a non-party costs order is not normally made unless it can be shown that the director caused the company to bring or defend proceedings improperly.

In *Spartafield Ltd v Penten Group Ltd* [2017] EWHC 1121 (TCC) no order was made, even though the director had funded 25% of the company's costs and some of his evidence had not been accepted at trial. The court accepted that the litigation was in respect of sums due to creditors of the company and not in respect of repayment of loans made by him. The fact that not all his evidence was accepted was not unusual in litigation.

(b) Orders made

[40.14]

In *North West Holdings plc, Re, Secretary of State for Trade and Industry v Backhouse* [2001] EWCA Civ 67, two companies were ordered to be wound up, the judge having found that no proper books of account had been kept, that the businesses of the companies were intertwined with the defendant personally, who treated the companies' funds as his own, and that a savings scheme marketed through the companies lacked intrinsic merit. After judgment, the Secretary of State warned the defendant for the first time that he intended to apply for a costs order against him personally. The judge ordered the defendant to pay the costs personally because he had defended the proceedings solely to protect his own reputation and position without seriously considering the interests of the companies or their creditors. The crucial question was whether the relevant director held a bona fide belief that the companies had arguable defences and that it was in the companies' interests to advance those defences. If he did so believe, to make a non-party pay the costs would constitute an unlawful inroad into the principle of limited liability. However, on the facts, the defendant had not considered the companies' interests but only his own; there was ample evidence to justify the costs order despite the absence of an early warning concerning costs.

In *Goodwood Recoveries Ltd v Breen: Breen v Slater* (see **[40.6]** above), a Michael Slater controlled the claimant debt recovery company and was also a consultant solicitor in a firm which funded proceedings brought by the company under a conditional fee agreement. The costs of the litigation brought by the claimant company would not have been incurred without Mr Slater's involvement. He formulated the claim and brought it, albeit in the name of the company. He was the real party for whose benefit the litigation was brought. He did not fund it, but only because it was funded under a CFA by the firm of solicitors for whom he acted as a consultant and in whose name he undertook the conduct of the litigation. A lack of *bona fides* is not necessarily a condition of claiming against a non-party, if that non-party was really the party for whose benefit the case was conducted. In any event the whole of the costs of the litigation were caused by Mr Slater's dishonesty or impropriety, irrespective of whether he had any *bona fide* belief in the claim. Therefore, it was not necessary to decide whether there had to be a causal link between all the costs and the alleged impropriety: it was appropriate to order Mr Slater to pay the whole of the costs and not merely the additional costs which could be attributed directly to improper conduct on his part.

In *Deutsche Bank AG v Sebastian Holdings Inc* (above) the Court of Appeal upheld a costs order against a director whom the court at first instance had determined was the 'real party' on the basis that he was the sole shareholder and director of a company, had directed the litigation on its behalf, had funded or made funds available for the company to pursue the litigation, was the principal witness of fact and stood to benefit from the litigation. The fact that he had also given false evidence was 'no more than one aspect of his efforts to influence the outcome of the proceedings to his own advantage'. The court reiterated that an order for non-party costs against a director had nothing to do with 'piercing the corporate veil', citing Lewison LJ in *Threlfall v ECD Insight Ltd* [2013] EWCA Civ 1444 who stated:

> 'If a non-party costs order is made against a company director, it is quite wrong to characterise it as piercing or lifting the corporate veil; or to say that the company and the director are one and the same.'

Liquidators and receivers

[40.15]

Although the court has jurisdiction to order a liquidator, as a non-party to proceedings brought by an insolvent company, to pay costs personally, it will only exercise that jurisdiction in exceptional circumstances where there has been impropriety on the part of the liquidator, particularly in view of the fact that the prospective remedy of obtaining an order for security for costs is available to the defendant (see Chapter 19 – Prospective Costs Control – Security for Costs, above). The caution necessary in all cases when an attempt is made to render a non-party liable for costs is all the greater in the case of a liquidator having regard to public policy considerations (*Metalloy Supplies Ltd (in liq) v MA (UK) Ltd* [1997] 1 All ER 418, CA). Once again, an examination of relevant case law offers pointers to the key components necessary to establish a personal liability on the part of the receivers or liquidators.

The court has been clear that the decision in *Aiden Shipping Co Ltd v Interbulk Ltd, The Vimeira (No 2)* (1986) AC 965, H, [1986] 2 All ER 409, HL does not justify the judicial creation of a substantive rule that receivers should be personally responsible for the costs of a successful party: quite the contrary. Repeating a theme recurrent in the non-party costs jurisdiction, the court confirmed that each case will be determined on its own facts.

In *Dolphin Quays Developments Ltd (In Administrative and Fixed Charge Receivership) v Mills* [2007] EWHC 1180 (Ch), the court set out the importance of drawing a distinction between the inevitable functions of receivers and liquidators and the type of conduct necessary to trigger a non-party costs order. The application was refused as this was an entirely normal case of receivers seeking to enforce a contractual right forming part of the security. The fact that the claim failed might be unusual, but that did not mean it was exceptional. This claim could hardly be classified as 'exceptional'. If an order were made in this case then it would have to be made in all such cases. Neither the receivers nor the bank could be viewed as the real parties to the litigation. Again, the court made the point that the applicant could have applied for security for costs from the company when the litigation was first instigated.

However, an order is possible. In *Burnden Holdings (UK) Ltd (in liq) v Fielding* [2019] EWHC 2995 (Ch) (see **[40.8]** above), the court made a non-party costs order against the firm in which the liquidator was a partner, but on the basis of its funding of unsuccessful litigation brought by the liquidator.

It is clear that the court regards a failure to obtain security for costs in appropriate cases as an important factor in the exercise of its discretion. However, even then this must be viewed in context and is merely a factor to which the court will have regard.

Accordingly, there is still scope for a non-party costs order against a receiver or against a creditor in appropriate cases, especially where it can be shown that the non-party was the 'real party'. Costs orders against receivers will more readily be made where a company is in liquidation and the receiver's agency has terminated, or where the successful party has not been able to obtain security for costs.

Tribunals

[40.16]

The court has power to order costs against a tribunal whose decision was overturned on appeal, but only if the tribunal effectively makes itself a party by appearing on the appeal or taking steps to defend its determination (*Providence Capitol Trustees Ltd v Ayres* [1996] 4 All ER 760, ChD). Where, in a successful appeal against a decision of the Pensions Ombudsman, the ombudsman had appeared at the appeal and made representations in support of his determination, it was held that the costs recoverable from him were not limited to the amount by which they had been increased by his appearance but could, in principle, extend to the whole of the successful party's costs in making the appeal (an early in road into the 'causation' argument). This approach was followed in *Moore's (Wallisdown) Ltd v Pensions Ombudsman* [2002] 1 All ER 737, ChD.

Witnesses

[40.17]

In *Phillips v Symes* [2004] EWHC 2330 (Ch), the court had to consider the extent to which witnesses could incur a liability for costs. The case concerned an expert evaluation of the capacity of one party. A cost order was made against the expert witness, who by his evidence had caused significant expense to be incurred in a flagrant reckless disregard of his duties to the court. The court was clear that it would be wrong to exclude a power for it to award costs against witnesses in appropriate circumstances. However, the court should be astute to prevent any unfair questioning of witnesses designed solely to set up the possibility of a later application for non-party costs. This case revisited the issue of notice in the context of possible orders against witnesses, stating that a party contemplating applying for a non-party costs order against a lay witness would inevitably have to give early notice to that person, in contrast to the position of legal representatives who would need no reminding of the possibility of wasted costs orders.

Rare though non-party orders are against experts, they are made. In *Thimmaya v Lancashire NHS Foundation Trust* [2020] 1 WLUK 437 HHJ Evans, the court made a non-party costs order of sizeable proportions against a medical expert in a clinical negligence case. Amongst other failings, the expert had been unable to articulate the breach of duty test, and subsequently accepted that he had not been well enough to give expert evidence at trial.

In *Saxton v Bayliss* [2013] EWHC 3136 (Ch) the court set aside a non-party costs order made at first instance against a witness (the wife of the first appellant) in boundary dispute proceedings. Although she was a defendant, she was not a party to that part of the proceedings that was being resolved by preliminary trial. The court, drawing assistance from the non-party costs regime, including in respect of witnesses, reminded itself that such an order was always exceptional, that the jurisdiction should be exercised with caution and that notice of an impending application should be given to the non-party. The court also took account of the fact that the additional costs incurred as a result of this particular evidence were minimal in the context of the overall costs.

In *Deutsche Bank AG* (above), the court concluded that it was important to respect the principles underlying witness immunity, but that the possibility that there may be cases where an order against a witness for part or all of the costs should not be excluded.

On the other side of the coin is the position where a witness incurs costs in compliance with court procedure and seeks to recover those costs. It is worth remembering, as stated in the introduction, that CPR 46.2 is headed *'Costs orders in favour of or against non-parties'*. In *Individual Homes Ltd v Macbream Investments Ltd* (2002) Times, 14 November the claimant had issued and served a witness summons under CPR 34 on an employee of the Halifax Bank of Scotland plc requiring his attendance at the hearing of the claim and the production by him of the bank's documentation. The court held that it was an anomaly that if the application had been made under s 34 of the Senior Courts Act 1981 (non-party disclosure of documents), the rules would have provided that the person against whom the order had been made could recover the costs of compliance with the order (pursuant to what is now CPR 46.1), but that there was no equivalent provision in Part 34 to enable a witness to recover the costs of complying with a witness summons. The conclusion reached was that the courts of first instance have jurisdiction to resolve this anomaly under CPR 46.2 to award costs where it is just and reasonable. However, the court also held it was inappropriate to order that the bank be joined to the proceedings for the purpose of pursuing these costs. The claimant was ordered to pay the costs incurred by the bank in complying with the summons.

Funders

[40.18]

While it is glaringly obvious, as a starting point to an application based on the non-party having provided funding, the applicant must be able to establish that the respondent to the application actually funded the litigation. In *Shah v Karanjia* [1993] 4 All ER 792, ChD, an application against a non-party failed both because he had been given no adequate warning of the application and because of lack of evidence that he had actually funded the proceedings.

The case of *Hamilton v Al Fayed (No 2)* [2002] EWCA Civ 665, sought to define the type of funding that would be needed as part of the requirement for a non-party costs order. The court distinguished between 'pure' funders, who made donations in support of a litigant as an act of charity, and 'professional' funders, such as insurers, who were almost always contractually bound to fund the litigation. It concluded that:

- An order for costs would rarely be made against a charitable, philanthropic, altruistic or merely sympathetic donor who, on the information before him, had reasonable grounds for believing that the litigant had reasonable grounds for asserting his right or a defence to the claim, and who wished to ensure that a genuine dispute was not lost or inadequately contested by default due to financial constraint.
- If pure funders were regularly exposed to liability under s 51, such funds would dry up and access to justice would thereby on occasions be lost. They should not, therefore, ordinarily be held liable.
- So long as the law continued to allow impoverished parties to litigate without having to provide security for their opponents' costs, those sympathetic to their plight should not be discouraged from assisting them to secure representation. In the light of the recent further reductions in the availability of public funding never has this sentiment had greater resonance.

In *Gulf Azov Shipping Co Ltd v Chief Humphrey Irikefe Idisi* [2004] EWCA Civ 292, the court allowed an appeal by a Nigerian lawyer against a costs order made against him for personally intervening on behalf of one of the defendants against whom damages had been awarded for the wrongful detention of the claimant's vessel. That defendant's assets were subject to a worldwide freezing order in an attempt to enforce the award. The lawyer could not be criticised for assisting the defendant financially in instructing solicitors of high standing and for assisting the defendant in attempting to discharge his costs liabilities. There was no suggestion that the lawyer had been personally interested in the outcome of the litigation.

The benefit derived by the funder does not have to be a direct financial one and funding motivated by personal animosity may also justify a non-party costs order (*Vaughan v Jones and Fowler* [2006] EWHC 2123 (Ch)). This raises some potentially interesting arguments in relation to the growth of 'crowd funding'. Do those who are prepared to contribute by way of 'crowd funding' to the cost, for example, of disputes over parking charges and new bridges over the Thames stand to benefit other than in a direct financial way from the litigation (perhaps because they hope to see the removal of a type of parking charge/penalty that they may have to pay in the future as motorists or because of a general animosity towards those charging for parking)? Are they aware of the risk?

In *Re Hellas (Luxembourg)* (20 July 2017, unreported), Ch D, the court concluded that, in appropriate cases, there is an inherent or implied jurisdiction to order a party to give disclosure of the identity of any funders and the terms of any such funding. Snowden J found that this had to follow from the provisions of CPR 25.14, if the power to order security from someone other than the claimant under CPR 25.14(2)(b) is to be purposeful.

Orders made

[40.19]

In *Locabail (UK) Ltd v Bayfield Properties Ltd (No 3)* [2000] 2 Costs LR 169, ChD, the first husband of one of the defendants had given evidence on her behalf at the trial when he had been found to be an unsatisfactory witness, prone to exaggeration. He admitted to funding his former wife's action and recommending a solicitor to her. The claimants sought costs against him and he was joined in the action solely in relation to the claim for costs. It was not appropriate to punish the former husband by awarding costs solely on the basis of his funding the litigation of another and behaving unsatisfactorily as a witness. However he was ordered to pay the claimants' costs on the following bases:

(a) he had funded proceedings knowing that his former wife would be unable to satisfy a costs order if unsuccessful;
(b) his intense identification with his former wife's position in his own evidence;
(c) his indifference to the legal and factual issues in the case; and
(d) the court's rejection of the factual basis of his former wife's case.

In *Thomson v Berkhamsted Collegiate School* [2009] EWHC 2374 (QB), the claimant was a 25-year-old unemployed university graduate who sued the private school he had attended between 1994 and 2002 for injury, loss and damages of nearly £1 million for failing to prevent him being bullied. He discontinued the proceedings two weeks into the trial. He was unable to meet any costs order and the defendant wished to seek a non-party costs order against his parents. Pursuant to that application the school sought orders requiring the parents to file and serve disclosure statements setting out correspondence between them and their son's solicitors, experts and counsel, and orders against the son with respect to disclosure and his claim of legal professional privilege.

The parents were not merely funders but were directly concerned with the facts of the claim and played an active role in the litigation. It was doubtful that it would have been funded if the parents had not made funds available themselves. Accordingly, an application for non-party costs had a reasonable prospect of success. The only doubt was over whether the parents gained a benefit from the litigation and sought to control its course. The defendant could only demonstrate the element of control if it knew what communications the parents had had with the solicitors, counsel and experts in the case. Accordingly the school was entitled to disclosure.

In *Automotive Latch Systems Ltd v Honeywell International, Inc* [2010] EWHC 1031 (Comm), the claimant was ordered to pay the defendant's costs, some of them on the indemnity basis, and the defendant applied under the Senior Courts Act 1981, s 51(3) for a non-party to pay those costs. The non-party was in control of both the claimant and the litigation; the claimant had only continued in existence in order to pursue the litigation; the non-party had lent money to the claimant and in doing so was funding the litigation. The non-party had also sought and procured funding for the litigation from external investors, in addition to his own funding contribution. He was the principal witness for the claimant without whose evidence the claim would not have been sustainable. The non-party had a 74% holding in the claimant and stood to benefit personally to a very considerable extent if the claim succeeded. Applying the relevant principles, the case was a clear one for the imposition of a non-party costs order.

Solicitors

As funders

[40.20]

In a previous edition Michael Cook warned that *Arkin v Borchard* (above [40.7]) opened the door for the argument that in certain situations a solicitor who invests time, and perhaps funds disbursements, becomes a 'commercial funder'. His particular concern was where lawyers agree substantial success fees under conditional fee agreements when acting for impecunious clients without insurance cover for the defendant's costs if the claim fails. As he put it:

> 'Quite simply, the financing of litigation by a solicitor is maintenance and because he seeks to profit out of it, it is champertous maintenance. Success fees are the solicitor's share of the proceeds of litigation. Champerty is unlawful and therefore a champertous retainer is unenforceable: that is why it was necessary in s 58(3) of the Courts and Legal Services Act 1990 to provide that a CFA should not be unenforceable for that reason alone. Section 58(3) did not purport to abolish a solicitor's liability to a third party as the maintainer of litigation.'

Lawful, or justifiable, maintenance is no longer against public policy. In the words of Lord Scarman in *Wallersteiner v Moir (No 2)* [1975] 1 All ER 849. 'The maintenance of other people's litigation is no longer regarded as a mischief: trade unions, trade protection societies, insurance companies and the State do it regularly and frequently'. However, as was said by Lord Denning in *Hill v Archbold* [1968] 1 QB 686, and confirmed in case after case thereafter: 'It is perfectly justifiable and is accepted by everyone as lawful, provided always that the one who supports the litigation, if it fails, pays the costs of the other side'

Hodgson v Imperial Tobacco Ltd [1998] 2 All ER 673 is often quoted as authority to the contrary. It is not. The court in *Hodgson* simply held that the existence of a CFA did not alter the circumstances in which a legal adviser could be personally liable for the costs of a party. The position was not any different than other retainer arrangements. The court did not say that a CFA put a solicitor in a better position than any other maintainer of litigation, and why should it? Why should a successful defendant be in a worse position against a maintainer of litigation because that person is a member of the legal profession who, like other professional maintainers, is making a profit out of it?

The consequences of the abolition of recovery of additional liabilities, but preservation of conditional fee agreements with success fees (but being a matter of solicitor client costs) and the introduction of Damages Based Agreements ('DBAs'), which are, in effect, no more than a form of contingency fee agreement, demand further examination of the position of the legal representative.

In *Myatt v National Coal Board* [2007] EWCA Civ 307 the Court of Appeal had dismissed the claimants' appeals against the finding of the costs judge that the conditional fee agreements they had entered into with their solicitors were unenforceable and therefore although the four claimants had each succeeded in their claim for damages for personal injuries, the indemnity principle precluded them from recovering costs from the defendants.

The claimants had no insurance against any liability for costs because it was a condition precedent to the liability of the insurers under the claimants' after the event policies that enforceable conditional fee agreements were in place. Accordingly, the claimants had contested the appeal without any valid funding mechanism in place to meet the appeal costs of the successful defendant. In those circumstances the defendant sought an order for the costs of the appeals against the solicitors under s 51 of the Senior Courts Act 1981.

There were 60 other cases where clients had entered into CFAs with the solicitors in similar circumstances, who had a total a sum in the region of £200,000 at stake.

These four claimants did have a financial interest in the appeals because they were liable for their own disbursements which, including the now irrecoverable insurance premium, averaged £2,500 to be paid out of their modest damages of £3,000–£4,000.

The court referred extensively to the judgment in *Tolstoy-Miloslavsky v Aldington* [1996] 1 WLR 736 quoting Rose LJ at page 743:

> 'Sections 51(1) and (3) of the Supreme Court Act 1981 do not confer jurisdiction to make an order for costs against legal representatives when acting as legal representatives . . . '

but highlighting that he had in the same case qualified this statement respectively as follows:

> 'There are only three categories of conduct which can give rise to an order for costs against a solicitor:
>
> 1. It is within the wasted costs jurisdiction of section 51(6) and (7);
> 2. It is otherwise a breach of duty to the court . . . eg if he acts even unwittingly without authority or in breach of an undertaking;
> 3. If he acts outside the role of solicitor eg in a private capacity or as a true third party funder for someone else.' (per Rose LJ)

In *Myatt* the court found that the third category described by Rose LJ included a solicitor who is 'a real party . . . in very important and critical respects' and who 'not merely funds the proceedings but substantially also contributes, or at any rate, is to benefit from them'. The mere fact that the same solicitor is formally on the court record advancing or defending proceedings for the client does not, itself, act as a bar to an application by the successful opposing party under s 51(1) and (3) of the Senior Courts Act 1981, that the solicitor should pay some or all of the costs.

Were it not for the relatively minor financial interest of the claimants in the disbursements (minor in the context of the solicitors' overall exposure to costs that were potentially irrecoverable), only the claimants' solicitors would have had an interest in the appeal, which the Court of Appeal concluded took them outside the role of solicitors. Indeed Dyson LJ thought it unlikely that the individual claimants would have pursued an appeal solely for the minimal disbursements. In these circumstances the court held that it would be very surprising if the fact that the claimants had a modest financial interest meant that the solicitor's financial interest counted for nothing when deciding what order for costs it was just to make.

The court reiterated that the non-party need not be the <u>only</u> real party to the litigation. It is enough that the non-party is '<u>a real party</u> . . . in very important and critical respects'.

The Court of Appeal held that there was no good reason why those observations should not apply with equal force to solicitors as to non-solicitors and was in no doubt that there is jurisdiction to make an order under s 51(3) against a solicitor where litigation is pursued by the client for the benefit, or to a substantial degree for the benefit, of the solicitor.

The Court of Appeal held that the fair and just order to make in this case was to order the solicitors to pay 50% of the defendant's costs of the appeal. In arriving at this percentage the court took into account the fact that the claimants had a residual real financial interest in the success of the appeals; their disbursements represented approximately one third of the total costs incurred by them before their claims were settled. It also took into account the fact that the solicitors were not given a warning until the appeals had been dismissed that an application for costs might be made against them.

In *Myatt* the court accepted that the authorities did not set out in definitive terms where the line in the sand is drawn between the case where solicitors acts purely as the legal representatives in the ordinary way on behalf of a client and are therefore immune from the jurisdiction of the court under s 51(1) and (3), and, on the other hand, a case where the solicitors' acts are such that they become 'a real party' to the claim. However, Lloyd LJ also chose to refer to a passage from the judgment of Roch LJ in *Tolstoy-Miloslavsky v Aldington* which rather neatly sets out the line that the court will be looking for on the facts of each individual case where arguments as to the extent of the solicitors' role arise:

> 'The legal representative who acts as a legal representative does not make himself a quasi party and no jurisdiction to make an order for costs against him under s.51(1) and (3) arises. However, a legal representative who goes beyond conducting proceedings as a legal representative and behaves as a quasi party will not be immune from a costs order under s 51(1) and (3) merely because he is a barrister or a solicitor'.

The court was clear, though, that there is a distinction to be made between privately paying clients who retain a costs liability to the solicitors – even if it is notional – and those represented under conditional fee agreements where the clients do not have and have not had any personal liability to pay the solicitors' costs.

The court concluded in *Myatt* that it was correct to regard the solicitors in relation to the conduct of the appeal as having acted in part for the sake of their own benefit in a respect which was of no interest or concern to their clients, and as having acted as a matter of business to seek to establish their right to be paid, other than by their own clients, the profit costs on these four cases and all the others of which these were representative. In those circumstances, which could be common in relation to cases where the enforceability of a CFA is at stake, but would be most unusual in any other situation, it was proper to regard the solicitors as having acted in respect of the appeal in a dual capacity; acting for their clients, certainly and with a real interest of those clients to protect, but primarily acting for their own sake. In other words they had crossed the line drawn by Roch LJ.

The introduction of damages based agreements where the client may, in some circumstances, have no liability to solicitors other than in respect of non-advocate disbursements (where the claim is unsuccessful) again creates the potential for solicitors to become quasi parties. If a claim is unsuccessful the solicitors will not be paid. While it may indeed be in the client's interest to appeal, there can be no doubt that a successful appeal would also be in the interests of the solicitors, who would then be paid. The advice and the decision making process will need to be clear to protect solicitors in such a situation.

However, no doubt, of enormous relief to solicitors at a time when they are having to be more creative in terms of the funding arrangements into which they are prepared to enter, are the decisions in the cases of *Heron v TNT (UK) Ltd* [2013] EWCA Civ 469 and *Flatman v Germany* [2013] EWCA Civ 278 (see Chapter 12 – The Indemnity Principle, above). In the former case the Court of Appeal upheld the judge's decision to refuse an order under s 51 on the basis that a solicitor retained under a conditional fee agreement without any backing 'after the event insurance', had not become 'a real party' to the claim. In the latter case the Court of Appeal again concluded that a solicitor in the same situation who also funded the disbursements was, similarly, not the 'real party' or even 'a real party' to the litigation.

Solicitors should also be astute to the power of the court to order disclosure of information to a party in receipt of an order for costs who is trying to ascertain who had funded the paying party. This is on the basis that to make the court's power to order costs against a non-party effective there has to be an inherent power to discover the identity of the non-party (*SC DG Petrol SRL v Vitol Banking Ltd* (24 October 2014, unreported), Comm, Walker J).

Lack of authority

[40.21]

In *Skylight Maritime SA v Ascot Underwriting* [2005] EWHC 15 (Comm), proceedings were brought against solicitors on the grounds of breach of warranty of authority in commencing proceedings on behalf of a one-yacht Panamanian company against insurance brokers without authority from the client to begin proceedings. In such circumstances the general rule is that the court has jurisdiction to make a summary order against the solicitor for the costs incurred by the opposite party caused by the solicitor's unauthorised conduct (*Yonge v Toynbee* [1910] 1 KB 215). However, in this case there were substantial issues of fact that could not be resolved in the course of the usual summary procedure and therefore the application for a summary determination was refused.

In *(1) David Warner (2) SMP Trustees Ltd v Merriman White (A Firm)* [2008] EWHC 1129 (Ch) a firm of solicitors issued a petition purporting to act on behalf of the two petitioners, when it had, in fact, only obtained instructions from one of them and the other had no knowledge of the proceedings until it was ordered to give security for costs. In striking the other party from the petition and ordering the solicitors to pay the costs of the other parties the court drew attention to the Guide to the Professional Conduct of Solicitors, which was explicit about a solicitor's duty to ensure that there were clear instructions from a client where instructions are given by a third party.

In *Zoya Ltd v Sheik Nasir Ahmed (t/a Property Mart)* [2016] EWHC 2249 (Ch) the court made it clear that that there must be both reliance and a causal link between the breach of the warranty of authority to represent and the loss which is claimed from the solicitor who gives the warranty in the first place.

Negligent solicitors

[40.22]

In *Marley v Rawlings* [2014] UKSC 51 the Supreme Court had to grapple with costs where the parties were, respectively, the residuary beneficiary if the validity of the will was upheld (which it was by the Supreme Court overturning the decision of the Court of Appeal and the first instance judge) and those who would have inherited under the intestacy provisions if the will was not valid. It may be unfair to include this case under a separate heading as it also involves insurers of the negligent solicitor, who had prepared the will and that of the testator's spouse at the same time and inadvertently had them sign the will of the other and not their own, funding the costs of one party. The Supreme Court concluded that the unsuccessful respondents' decision to fight the litigation was not unreasonable, but that an order for costs out of the estate would leave nothing (the estate being about £70,000). Rather than leave the successful party to claim against the negligent solicitor who in turn would be indemnified by the insurers, it was appropriate to order the costs of all parties to be paid by the 'non- party' insurers (having given them a chance to make representations).

McKenzie friends

[40.23]

At a time when the increased use of McKenzie friends and the increased incidence of paid McKenzie friends has already resulted in a Judicial Executive Board consultation, the case of *R (on the application of Laird) v Secretary of State for the Home Department* (25 February 2016, unreported), QB (Admin) merits consideration. An order for costs was sought against the claimant's two McKenzie friends. The court concluded that:

- There was no reason why McKenzie friends should be treated any differently from other non-parties and so were not excluded from the non-party costs regime.
- McKenzie friends should not be deterred from assisting unrepresented litigants by concern that they might be subjected to a costs order.
- However, a McKenzie friend who overstepped the remit of the role (and in this case acted outside the claimant's express authority) could be subject to a non-party costs order.

In fact, the original order of a contribution to the claimant's costs by the McKenzie friends was set aside on the basis that they had received no notice of the possibility that an order would be sought against them and because of the impact the order would have on them.

NON-PARTY COSTS AND QUALIFIED ONE-WAY COSTS SHIFTING ('QOCS')

[40.24]

On the face of it this topic has no relevance to non-party costs orders as the QOCS regime only provides the claimant in the proceedings set out in CPR 44.13(1) with protection from enforcement of costs. However, a combination of CPR 44.16(2)(a) and CPR 44.16(3) permits the court to make an order against a specific category of non-party – namely a person, other than the claimant, for whose financial benefit the whole or part of the claim was brought. The accompanying Practice Direction at CPR PD 44, para 12.2 gives examples of claims for the financial benefit of others as subrogated claims and credit hire claims. CPR PD 44, para 12.5, commenting on orders against non-parties in this context, refers to s 51(3) of the Senior Courts Act and CPR 46.2 and CPR 44.16(3) expressly makes the provision subject to CPR 46.2.

Previously, we queried whether the jurisdiction under CPR 44.16(3) adds anything to the existing provisions for costs against non-parties analysing the competing arguments as follows:

- The fact that the rule makers had chosen to include this separate provision, suggested that the answer was yes, otherwise why include anything at all.
- However, the express references to CPR 46.2 in CPR 44.16(3) itself and to s 51(3) and CPR 46.2 in the PD, the overarching statutory jurisdiction in respect of costs in s 51(3) and the absence of any other defined criteria by which the court may determine applications under CPR 44.16(3), resulted in the conclusion that the rule was superfluous, other than a) by way of identifying specific categories of non-party in the firing line and b) as a reminder to parties and the court of the availability of a non-party costs order.

We anticipated that authority might be forthcoming. So it proved. In *Select Car Rentals (North West) Ltd v Esure Services Ltd* [2017] EWHC 1434 (QB), Turner J agreed with the proposition advanced in the second bullet point above, concluding, amongst other matters:

> 'In summary, I find as follows:
>
> i) CPR Part 44.16 does not introduce a bespoke and distinct type of discretion to be exercised in cases falling within the QOCS regime as it applies to non-parties.
> ii) The wording of CPR Part 44.16 is entirely consistent with the way in which the proper approach to the discretion to order costs against a non-party has developed in recent case law.'

NON-PARTY COSTS ON THE INDEMNITY BASIS

[40.25]

In *Excalibur Ventures LLC v Texas Keystone Inc* [2016] EWCA Civ 1144 (above at [**40.7**]), the court considered the position of a commercial funder liable for non-party costs where the order made against the party it had funded was one on the indemnity basis. The court was clear that the decision of whether to make a non-party costs order is entirely separate from the decision, if an order is made, as to the costs basis upon which those costs should be paid. On the latter point, in dismissing the appeal, Tomlinson LJ stated:

> '. . . I particularly agree with and wish to associate myself with the judge's general approach, which is to emphasise that the derivative nature of a commercial funder's involvement should ordinarily lead to his being required to contribute to the costs on the basis upon which they have been assessed against those whom he chose to fund. That is not to say that there is an irrebuttable presumption that that will be the outcome, but rather that that is the outcome which will ordinarily, in the nature of things, be just and equitable.'

In reaching his decision, he rejected the argument that if funders have not been guilty of discreditable conduct or conduct which can be criticised, they should not be visited by an indemnity costs order. This was, essentially, for three reasons:

- That argument overlooks that conduct is just one factor in the court's overall determination.
- It is not sufficient to look at the question solely from the perspective of the funder as this 'ignores the character of the action which the funder has funded' and its effects on the other party.
- This makes an assumption that the funder is only responsible for its own conduct. Tomlinson LJ could see 'no principled basis upon which the funder can disassociate itself from the conduct of those whom it has enabled to conduct the litigation and upon whom it relies to make a return on its investment'.

NON-PARTY COSTS AND INTEREST

[40.26]

In *Sony/ATV Music Publishing LLC v WPMC Ltd (in liq)* [2017] EWHC 456 (Ch), the court had ordered a defendant caught by the provisions of CPR 36.17(4)(c) to pay interest on the claimant's costs at 8% above base rate. The court subsequently made a non-party costs order in respect of the costs. The court concluded that in making the decision to order non-party costs it is exercising a statutory discretion. As such that discretion extends both to whether to make an order and, if it does, to the amount it orders. The court determined that the onus was on the non-party to show why it would not be just for it to pay interest for the same period and at the same rate. Although the substantive order for non-party costs in this case was set aside (see **[40.4]** above), and so the interest awarded became irrelevant, the decision on the principle remains.

FAMILY CASES

[40.27]

While FPR 28.1 affords the court a wide discretion to make such order for costs as it thinks just, the prevailing position in the family courts is that the starting point is 'no order for costs' between the parties. However, it is important to note that the family court also has the jurisdiction to make non-party costs awards. In *HB (mother) v (1) PB (father) (2) OB (a child by his guardian) & Croydon London Borough Council (respondent on issues of costs only)* [2013] EWHC 1956 (Fam) Cobb J concluded that there was limited authority on these awards in the family court. However, he found that the clear failure of the local authority to consider guidance that existed on fabricated illness when compiling its report under s 37 of the Children Act 1989 had led to fruitless hearings at which the father had incurred wasted costs. He referred to the 'exceptionality test' in non-family cases, concluded that a local authority charged with preparing a report was sufficiently closely connected with the court proceedings, that its failures in the case were exceptional and had caused costs to be incurred that would not otherwise have arisen and ordered the local authority to pay the father's costs of the abortive hearings.

The President of the Family Division applied this decision in *Re Capital Translation and Interpreting Ltd* [2015] EWFC 5 when acceding to the application by a local authority for a non-party costs order against the named company for the costs of an adoption hearing that could not proceed when interpreters failed to attend the hearing. This was against the backdrop of similar failures earlier in the same proceedings.

CHAPTER 41

ARBITRATION

INTRODUCTION TO ARBITRATION

[41.1]

The law relating to arbitration is contained in the Arbitration Act 1996, which was greeted with universal acclaim as a model statute in both form and content when it came into force on 1 January 1997. Sections 59–65 set out the key costs provisions, but these are supplemented by specific provisions elsewhere in the statute.

COSTS OF THE ARBITRATION DEFINED

[41.2]

Section 59 provides that the costs of the arbitration include the arbitrator's fees and expenses, the fees and expenses of any arbitral institution involved and the legal and other costs of the parties to the arbitration. Section 63 makes it clear that costs include those of and incidental to any proceedings to determine the amount of the recoverable costs

Section 28 of the Act makes the parties jointly and severally liable for such of the arbitrator's reasonable fees and expenses as are appropriate in the circumstances. It also makes provision for parties to agree with arbitrators their fees and expenses, including capping and restrictions, or to apply to the court for them to be considered and adjusted.

Section 37(2) provides that the arbitrator's expenses include the fees and expenses of any expert, legal adviser or assessor appointed by the arbitrator.

In *Essar Oilfield Services Ltd v Norscot Rig Management PVT Ltd* [2016] EWHC 2361 (Comm) the court concluded that 'other costs' in s 59(1)(c) did include the cost of third party funding as this provision should neither be construed narrowly nor as equating to legal costs.

AGREEMENT AS TO PAYMENT OF COSTS

[41.3]

Section 60 provides that any agreement between the parties that a party is to meet the whole or part of the costs of the arbitration whatever the outcome of it may be, is only valid if that agreement was made after the dispute being arbitrated arises. In other words s 60 of the Act preserves the unusual prohibition in respect of arbitrations that the parties may not in the arbitration agreement provide that each party shall pay its own costs in any event, and extends the prohibition to agreements that one party shall pay the other party's costs whatever the outcome of the arbitration. The purpose is to try to create a level playing field between large and small contractors, and not deter a party from commencing arbitration proceedings because it will be liable for its own costs in any event. This consideration does not apply to any post-dispute agreement into which the parties may wish to enter.

Section 62 provides that any agreement between the parties as to liability for the costs of the arbitration extends only to those costs that are recoverable, unless the parties agree otherwise.

Where there was a dispute as to whether or not the parties had reached an agreement in respect of the amount of costs and the arbitrator had dealt with this, the court confirmed that this was something that may be dealt with by the arbitrator (see *Sun United Maritime Ltd v Kasteli Marine Inc, The Imme* [2014] EWHC 1476 (Comm)).

THE AWARD OF COSTS

[41.4]

The general rules that apply to the award of costs in arbitrations are to be found in s 61. This empowers the arbitrator to award the whole or part of the costs of the arbitration to either party, subject to (i) a valid agreement between the parties as to the liability for costs and (ii) the general principle that costs follow the event except where it appears to the tribunal that in the circumstances this is not appropriate in relation to the whole or part of the costs. Matters such as exaggeration, conduct, failure on particular issues, reasonableness, proportionality and sealed offers were relevant to the award of arbitration costs long before these concepts were introduced into civil litigation by the CPR. CPR 44.1 applies CPR Parts 44–47 to the costs of arbitration proceedings and to this extent the practice has been codified in the CPR both in respect of the principles on which costs are both awarded and quantified, but also in respect of offers to settle. CPR Part 62, and its supplementary practice direction, apply to arbitration proceedings but do not specifically mention costs.

Offers

[41.5]

If a sealed offer is made in arbitration, being the arbitral equivalent of a CPR Part 36 offer, a respondent is normally entitled to payment of costs from the date of the offer if the award in respect of the claim and interest is less than the offer. The arbitrator is not entitled to take into account whether an award of costs would be made in favour of the claimant, because that would require the claimant to assess not only the likelihood of achieving an award on the claim and interest exceeding the offer, but also, if there was a risk of an order that the claimant pay the respondent's costs, the chance of obtaining an award greater than the offer and the respondent's costs. Such a result would hinder settlement and introduce complications inconsistent with the principle that the costs should follow the event (*Everglade Maritime Inc v Schiffahrtsgesellschaft Detlef von Appen mbH* [1993] QB 780, CA).

As it is customary for an award to deal at one and the same time both with the parties' claims and with the question of costs, the existence of a sealed offer has to be brought to the attention of the arbitrator before the decision has been reached. Otherwise, the arbitrator may have to revise that decision on costs in the light of the terms of the sealed offer when seen. However, obviously, if adopting the former approach the offer should remain sealed and the content unknown until the substantive decision has been reached as it would be wholly improper for the arbitrator to look at it before reaching a final decision on the matters in dispute other than as to costs.

There are arbitrators and umpires who feel that the former procedure is not satisfactory. They take the view that respondents will feel that their defence is weakened if the arbitrator knows that they have made a sealed offer, even if the figure is concealed. If this is so, respondents may be deterred from making a sealed offer. The solutions are either to adopt a procedure where the award of costs is not dealt with at the same time as the award or for an arbitrator to require the respondents to provide a sealed envelope at the end of the hearing, which is to contain either a statement that no sealed offer has been made or the sealed offer itself. If this procedure is adopted, the existence or otherwise of an offer is concealed from the tribunal until the moment at which it has to consider that part of the award which relates to costs, the delivery of a sealed envelope of itself becomes devoid of all significance (*Tramountana Armadora SA v Atlantic Shipping Co SA* [1978] 2 All ER 870, [1978] 1 Lloyd's Rep 391).

Fairness and serious irregularity

[41.6]

An arbitrator's power to award costs under s 61 of the Act or under the applicable procedural rules is subject to the general duty under s 33(1)(a) of the Act to act fairly and impartially as between the parties. Accordingly, if the arbitrator has been troubled by matters not raised by the parties, but upon which reliance is to be placed in making the order as to costs, the arbitrator must bring them to the attention of the parties before so doing so that the parties have an opportunity to address these issues. It was held in *Ghangbola v Smith & Sherriff Ltd* [1998] 3 All ER 730 that failure to do so constituted a serious irregularity within the meaning of s 68(2)(a) of the Act.

In *Maurice J Bushell & Co v Graham Irvine Born* (22 February 2017, unreported), Ch D, Murray Rosen QC, the court remitted a decision on costs, despite the concerns of the appellant that it had lost faith in the arbitrator to undertake a fair hearing. It did so on the basis that the original decision was flawed because the arbitrator had erred in law and not because there was any reason to doubt his impartiality. Accordingly, fairness did not require the court to take over the exercise of determination of costs from the arbitrator.

In *Oldham v QBE Insurance (Europe) Ltd* [2017] EWHC 3045 (Comm), the court considered the link between fairness under s 33 and the court's intervention under s 68(2)(a), identifying that the applicant must show a failure to act fairly, amounting to a serious irregularity giving rise to substantial injustice. The court stressed that this was a high threshold, deliberately so to limit the intervention of courts in arbitral process and to sustain the need for finality of awards. However, in this case, where the applicant had not been afforded a fair opportunity to advance an argument as to why he should not pay the costs of the arbitration, the court concluded that there was a breach of s 33 and a serious irregularity and remitted the matter to the arbitrator for reconsideration.

COSTS AGAINST THE ARBITRATOR

[41.7]

Section 29 provides the arbitrator with immunity unless the act or omission to act complained off is shown to have been in bad faith. However, this does not prevent an order for costs being made against an arbitrator, although such orders are extremely rare (*Cofely Ltd v Bingham* [2016] EWHC 240 (Comm) and *C Ltd v D* [2020] EWHC 1283 (Comm), which referred to *Cofley* as an 'exceptional case').

RECOVERABLE COSTS

The basis of costs and proportionality

[41.8]

Prior to the introduction of the CPR arbitrators were empowered and encouraged to assess costs themselves where possible and otherwise to refer them to the court, subject always to the right of the parties to agree what costs were recoverable. Costs were, in effect, on the standard basis as it was defined before 26 April 1999, unless the arbitrator ordered otherwise. However, the application of the CPR now incorporates the specific additional test of proportionality.

Section 63(3) of the Act permits the arbitrator to award costs on such basis 'as he thinks fit'. Where costs awarded between the parties are to be determined by the court, the effect of sections 63(4) and (5) is that they are assessed on the standard basis as it was defined before the introduction of the CPR, unless the arbitrator or the court orders otherwise, namely costs of a reasonable amount in respect of those costs reasonably incurred. However, CPR 44.1(2) requires the court to apply CPR Parts 44–47 to arbitration proceedings and these include the principle of proportionality at CPR 44.3(2) and (5). We therefore appear to have the unsatisfactory, and no doubt unintentional, position that arbitrators may, if they think fit, ignore the test of proportionality, but the court must apply it (and as we have seen the new CPR 44.3(2)(a) heightens the implications of a proportionality cross check on costs). Plainly, the court may 'order otherwise' and award costs on the indemnity basis. The approach is the same as in non-arbitration proceedings, namely that there is some conduct or circumstance that takes the case 'out of the norm' (see **Chapter 24**). Such a finding was made where the claimants discontinued two applications under s 68 which were weak and where an application by the respondent for security for costs of the applications was imminent (*Koshigi Ltd v Donna Union Foundation* [2019] EWHC 122 (Comm)).

Non-solicitors

[41.9]

Where a party is represented in an arbitration by a person who is not qualified as a barrister or solicitor, but who provides similar services, and an award is made providing for payment of that party's costs by the other party or for such costs to be assessed in the High Court if not agreed, the court has power to allow the costs of the unqualified person in relation to the conduct of the arbitration. The prohibition in s 25(1) of the Solicitors Act 1974 against the recovery of costs in respect of anything done by any unqualified person 'acting as a solicitor' does not apply to an unqualified person representing a party in an arbitration since an unqualified person does not 'act as a solicitor' within the meaning of s 25(1) merely by doing acts of a kind commonly done by solicitors. Acts prohibited by s 25(1) are limited to acts which are lawful only for a qualified solicitor to do and which only a solicitor may perform, or acts purportedly done in that capacity. They do not include acts commonly done by a solicitor but which do not involve a representation that the person so acting is acting as a solicitor. A person acting as an advocate for a party in arbitration proceedings who is not qualified as a barrister or solicitor and does not hold themselves out as such is not acting as a barrister or solicitor and accordingly the party employing him is not precluded from entitlement to payment of his costs (*Piper Double Glazing Ltd v DC Contracts (1992) Ltd* [1994] 1 All ER 177 – in which Potter J found that no part of the arbitral process involved acts which could be said to be 'acting as a solicitor').

Recoverability

[41.10]

Section 63 provides three methods of resolving the question of costs recoverability, namely by:

- agreement;
- determination by the arbitrator. In which case the arbitrator must specify the basis on which he has acted, the items of recoverable costs and the amount allowed for each item;
- application to the court in the absence of either of the above. Either party may apply to the court.

Does an award of costs 'to be agreed or assessed in default of agreement' permit the arbitrator to determine the costs, or does it amount either to a reference to the court or to a failure by the arbitrator to determine the costs, enabling the receiving party to apply to the court? In *M/S Alghanim Industries Inc v Skandia International Insurance Corpn* [2001] 2 All ER (Comm) 30 it was held that the phrase is not to be construed as a determination of the proceedings with a reference of assessment to the court in the event that the parties could not agree. The arbitrator had not expressly declined to assess and settle the costs, requiring the matter to go to the court. An award of costs to be agreed or assessed in default of an agreement is not a refusal to assess but is neutral in its language: it leaves open the possibility of an application by either party to the arbitrator. This was consistent with the spirit of the Act that as far as possible matters should be resolved by arbitration rather than application to the court.

The arbitrator's fees and expenses

[41.11]

Section 64 permits the recovery within the recoverable costs of the arbitration of such reasonable fees and expenses of the arbitrator as are appropriate in the circumstances – again with the proviso that the parties can agree otherwise. Section 64(1) is also subject to any order of the court made under ss 24 and 25 of the Act on the removal or resignation of an arbitrator.

As already noted s 28 of the Act makes the parties jointly and severally liable for such appropriate reasonable fees and expenses. It also makes provision for the parties to apply to the court for them to be considered and adjusted.

In addition to the provisions of s 64, s 37(2) provides that 'expenses' may include the fees and expenses of experts, legal advisers and assessors appointed by the arbitrator. Of course, for these to be recoverable, they too must be reasonable.

Any dispute about the reasonableness of an arbitrator's fees and expenses may be resolved by the court under s 64(2). However, this is subject to the right of the parties and the arbitrator set out in s 64(4) to agree the amount of his fees and expenses at the outset, creating a contract with which the court cannot later interfere. If the agreement relates only to hourly or daily rates, the court can investigate the reasonableness of the time spent, but not the agreed amounts.

If an application is made to the court to determine the fees and expenses, s 28(2) makes provision for the court to order that the amount of an arbitrator's fees and expenses shall be considered and adjusted by such means and upon such terms as it may direct. This course was successfully adopted by the paying party in *Agrimex Ltd v Tradigrain SA* [2003] EWHC 1656 (Comm), in respect of the fees of a legal draftsman employed by the arbitrators to assist them in drafting the award. The draftsman was a solicitor of only three years' post-qualification experience, but charged £9,300 out of total costs of under £20,000. After deprecating the use of legal draftsmen except in very special circumstances, the court held that the charges were disproportionate and that no competent lawyer could have spent the amount of time upon which the claim was based. The solicitor's fee was allowed at £5,000 – which would have been even lower had not this been the amount proposed by the paying party!

It is not improper for a party appointing an arbitrator to agree the fees before appointment since the appointing party and the proposed arbitrator are respectively free to appoint someone else or not to accept the appointment, if the terms are not mutually acceptable. However, once an appointment has been made it is contrary to the arbitrator's quasi-judicial status to bargain unilaterally with only one party in respect of the fees and any agreement made between the appointing party and the arbitrator after appointment has been accepted, for the payment of fees, without the consent of the other party, probably constitutes misconduct, and is, in any event, liable to render the arbitrator vulnerable to the imputation of bias. Although it is not improper for an arbitrator to stipulate at the time of appointment for a commitment fee to be made payable in any event even if the arbitration does not take place, once appointed an arbitrator is not entitled unilaterally to change the terms of the contract by demanding a commitment fee unless there is a significant and substantial change in the commitment required which justifies the payment of a further fee (*Norjarl K/S A/S v Hyundai Heavy Industries Co Ltd* [1992] 1 QB 863).

Section 56 empowers the arbitrator to refuse to deliver the award unless the fees and expenses are paid in full. This is no doubt designed to prevent the situation where the arbitrator fears that all parties are likely to be so dissatisfied with the decision that obtaining payment from either will prove difficult.

Limits on the recoverable costs

[41.12]

Adopting a philosophy which the Civil Procedure Rules are only now embracing, s 65 of the Arbitration Act 1996 empowers the arbitrator, unless the parties have agreed otherwise, to limit the costs recoverable in the arbitration either as a whole or in respect of a specified part. This enables arbitrators either on their own initiative or, more likely, on the application of one of the parties to specify prospectively the maximum liability for costs of the arbitration. Section 65(2) provides that any such direction may be made at any stage but this must be done sufficiently far in advance of the costs to which the limit relates being incurred for the limit to be of effect. A clear harbinger of the prospective costs management orders introduced in CPR 3.12–CPR 3.18 seventeen years later.

However, as proportionality does not feature in costs dealt with by the arbitrator (and as a consequence in the relevant procedures adopted in the arbitration), this will not necessarily act as a brake to prevent either party spending a disproportionate amount on costs (as it might under the overriding objective and costs management within the CPR), but it will put a cap on the amount they can recover from the other party.

Any cap imposed may be varied at any time under s 65(2), but again subject to the qualifications that the variation cannot be retrospective and must be made sufficiently in advance of the costs under the exiting cap being incurred for the lower limit sought to be taken into account. In other words, if the costs have already been spent or the attempt to vary is late in the process when the parties are committed to a course from which it is not possible to deviate, there should be no variation.

Under s 57(3)(a) of the 1996 Act, an arbitrator has the default power to 'correct an award so as to remove any clerical mistake or error arising from an accidental slip or omission'. In *Gannet Shipping Ltd v Eastrade Commodities Inc* [2002] 1 All ER (Comm) 297, the court held that the arbitrator also had jurisdiction to vary the costs order at the same time. The costs error was an error 'arising from' the 'accidental slip' in the amount awarded, and accordingly it could be corrected. Furthermore, the court found that the costs award could also have been amended under the jurisdiction to intervene conferred by both s 68(2)(a) (failure by the tribunal to comply with the natural justice principle in s 33 of the 1996 Act) and s 68(2)(i) (irregularity in the conduct of the proceedings or in the award which is admitted by the tribunal). The only limiting factor on the intervention is the need to show substantial injustice.

Section 57(3)(b) permits the arbitrator to make an additional award, including one of costs, if such a claim was made, but was not dealt with in the original award.

FAILURE TO GIVE REASONS

[41.13]

Under s 52(4) of the Act, an award 'shall contain reasons for the award'. In the light of this statutory requirement it is odd that there is no sanction in s 52(4) for a failure to include reasons. A failure to include reasons for a costs award does not render the award void but simply allows a party to seek reasons by means of an application to the court under s 68 of the 1996 Act on the basis that the arbitrator has failed to comply with the requirements as to the form of the award (s 68(2)(h); *Ridler v Walter* [2001] TASSC 98, Supreme Court of Tasmania).

APPLICATIONS TO THE COURT

[41.14]

There are a number of provisions in the Act under which costs issues arising from an arbitration may be put before the court. We have considered some of them but by way of summary these are:

- s 28(2) to have the amount of the arbitrator's fees and expenses considered and adjusted;
- s 56(2) where the arbitrator refuses to deliver the award except upon full payment of fees and expenses;
- s 63(4) to determine the recoverable costs of the arbitration;
- s 64(2) to determine the reasonable fees and expenses of the arbitrator;
- s 68 on grounds of serious irregularity;
- s 69 by appeal on the grounds of a serious error of law in the award of costs;
- s 70(4) for an order that the arbitrator provides proper reasons for his award of costs (this is either by an application or on an appeal).

THE COSTS OF ENFORCEMENT

[41.15]

Enforcement of an award involves an application under CPR 62.18 for permission to enforce the award as a judgment with the option of entering judgment in the terms of the award (see s 66 of the Act). The application should be for costs to be included in the order giving permission and if judgment is to be obtained 'for the costs of any judgment to be entered'.

SECURITY FOR COSTS

[41.16]

(See Chapter 19 – Prospective Costs Control Security for Costs, above).

CONCLUSION TO ARBITRATION

[41.17]

While any decision about costs relating to an arbitration remains with the arbitrator, the Arbitration Act 1996 provides a statutory code for determination of any issues arising. Once matters have been put before the court, then the provisions of either CPR Part 62 or, if the matter relates to costs, CPR Parts 44–47 apply.

Appendix

Civil Procedure Rules and Practice Directions

Part 3	The court's case and costs management powers
Part 36	Offers to settle and payments into court
Part 44	General rules about costs
Part 45	Fixed costs
Part 46	Costs Payable by or to Particular Persons
Part 47	Procedure for detailed assessment of costs and default provisions
Part 48	Part 2 of the Legal Aid, Sentencing and Punishment of Offenders Act 2012 relating to civil litigation funding and costs: transitional provision in relation to pre-commencement funding arrangements

Solicitors Act 1974

Part III	Remuneration of solicitors

Criminal Justice and Courts Act 2015

s 88	Capping of costs
s 89	Capping of costs: orders and their terms

Practice Notice by the Senior Costs Judge – Hearings and Detailed Assessments in the Senior Courts Costs Office

PART 3 THE COURT'S CASE AND COSTS MANAGEMENT POWERS

I CASE MANAGEMENT

[CPR 3.1]

3.1 The court's general powers of management

(1) The list of powers in this rule is in addition to any powers given to the court by any other rule or practice direction or by any other enactment or any powers it may otherwise have.

(2) Except where these Rules provide otherwise, the court may—

- (a) extend or shorten the time for compliance with any rule, practice direction or court order (even if an application for extension is made after the time for compliance has expired);
- (b) adjourn or bring forward a hearing;
- (bb) require that any proceedings in the High Court be heard by a Divisional Court of the High Court;
- (c) require a party or a party's legal representative to attend the court;
- (d) hold a hearing and receive evidence by telephone or by using any other method of direct oral communication;
- (e) direct that part of any proceedings (such as a **counterclaim**) be dealt with as separate proceedings;
- (f) **stay** (GL) the whole or part of any proceedings or judgment either generally or until a specified date or event;
- (g) consolidate proceedings;
- (h) try two or more claims on the same occasion;
- (i) direct a separate trial of any issue;
- (j) decide the order in which issues are to be tried;
- (k) exclude an issue from consideration;
- (l) dismiss or give judgment on a claim after a decision on a preliminary issue;
- (ll) order any party to file and exchange a costs budget;

(m) take any other step or make any other order for the purpose of managing the case and furthering the overriding objective, including hearing an Early Neutral Evaluation with the aim of helping the parties settle the case.

(3) When the court makes an order, it may—

(a) make it subject to conditions, including a condition to pay a sum of money into court; and

(b) specify the consequence of failure to comply with the order or a condition.

(3A) Where the court has made a direction in accordance with paragraph (2)(bb) the proceedings shall be heard by a Divisional Court of the High Court and not by a single judge.

(4) Where the court gives directions it will take into account whether or not a party has complied with the Practice Direction (Pre-Action Conduct) and any relevant **pre-action protocol** (GL).

(5) The court may order a party to pay a sum of money into court if that party has, without good reason, failed to comply with a rule, practice direction or a relevant pre-action protocol.

(6) When exercising its power under paragraph (5) the court must have regard to—

(a) the amount in dispute; and

(b) the costs which the parties have incurred or which they may incur.

(6A) Where a party pays money into court following an order under paragraph (3) or (5), the money shall be security for any sum payable by that party to any other party in the proceedings.

(7) A power of the court under these Rules to make an order includes a power to vary or revoke the order.

(8) The court may contact the parties from time to time in order to monitor compliance with directions. The parties must respond promptly to any such enquiries from the court.

[CPR 3.8]

3.8 Sanctions have effect unless defaulting party obtains relief

(1) Where a party has failed to comply with a rule, practice direction or court order, any sanction for failure to comply imposed by the rule, practice direction or court order has effect unless the party in default applies for and obtains relief from the sanction.

(Rule 3.9 sets out the circumstances which the court will consider on an application to grant relief from a sanction)

(2) Where the sanction is the payment of costs, the party in default may only obtain relief by appealing against the order for costs.

(3) Where a rule, practice direction or court order—

(a) requires a party to do something within a specified time, and

(b) specifies the consequence of failure to comply,

the time for doing the act in question may not be extended by agreement between the parties except as provided in paragraph (4).

(4) In the circumstances referred to in paragraph (3) and unless the court orders otherwise, the time for doing the act in question may be extended by prior written agreement of the parties for up to a maximum of 28 days, provided always that any such extension does not put at risk any hearing date.

[CPR 3.9]

3.9 **Relief from sanctions**

(1) On an application for relief from any sanction imposed for a failure to comply with any rule, practice direction or court order, the court will consider all the circumstances of the case, so as to enable it to deal justly with the application, including the need—

(a) for litigation to be conducted efficiently and at proportionate cost; and

(b) to enforce compliance with rules, practice directions and orders.

(2) An application for relief must be supported by evidence.

II COSTS MANAGEMENT

[CPR 3.12]

3.12 **Application of this Section and the purpose of costs management**

(1) This Section and Practice Direction 3E apply to all Part 7 multi-track cases except—

(a) where the claim is commenced on or after 22 April 2014 and the amount of money claimed as stated on the claim form is £10 million or more; or

(b) where the claim is commenced on or after 22 April 2014 and is for a monetary claim which is not quantified or not fully quantified or is for a non-monetary claim and in any such case the claim form contains a statement that the claim is valued at £10 million or more; or

(c) where in proceedings commenced on or after 6th April 2016 a claim is made by or on behalf of a person under the age of 18; or

(d) where the proceedings are the subject of fixed costs or scale costs; or

(e) where the court otherwise orders.

(1A) This Section and Practice Direction 3E will apply to any other proceedings (including applications) where the court so orders.

(2) The purpose of costs management is that the court should manage both the steps to be taken and the costs to be incurred by the parties to any proceedings (or variation costs as provided in rule 3.15A) so as to further the overriding objective.

[CPR 3.13]

3.13 **Filing and exchanging budgets and budget discussion reports**

(1) Unless the court otherwise orders, all parties except litigants in person must file and exchange budgets—

(a) where the stated value of the claim on the claim form is less than £50,000, with their directions questionnaires; or

(b) in any other case, not later than 21 days before the first case management conference.

(2) In the event that a party files and exchanges a budget under paragraph (1), all other parties, not being litigants in person, must file an agreed budget discussion report no later than 7 days before the first case management conference.

(3) The court—

(a) may, on its own initiative or on application, order the parties to file and exchange costs budgets in a case where the parties are not otherwise required by this Section to do so;

(b) shall (other than in an exceptional case) make an order to file and exchange costs budgets if all parties consent to an application for such an order.

(4) The court may, in a substantial case, direct that budgets are to be limited in the first instance to part only of the proceedings and extended later to cover the whole proceedings.
(5) Every budget must be dated and verified by a statement of truth signed by a senior legal representative of the party.
(6) Even though a litigant in person is not required to prepare a budget, each other party (other than a litigant in person) must provide the litigant in person with a copy of that party's budget.

[CPR 3.14]

3.14 **Failure to file a budget**

Unless the court otherwise orders, any party which fails to file a budget despite being required to do so will be treated as having filed a budget comprising only the applicable court fees.

[CPR 3.15]

3.15 **Costs management orders**

(1) In addition to exercising its other powers, the court may manage the costs to be incurred (the budgeted costs) by any party in any proceedings.
(2) The court may at any time make a "costs management order". Where costs budgets have been filed and exchanged the court will make a costs management order unless it is satisfied that the litigation can be conducted justly and at proportionate cost in accordance with the overriding objective without such an order being made. By a costs management order the court will—

- (a) record the extent to which the budgeted costs are agreed between the parties;
- (b) in respect of the budgeted costs which are not agreed, record the court's approval after making appropriate revisions;
- (c) record the extent (if any) to which incurred costs are agreed.

(3) If a costs management order has been made, the court will thereafter control the parties' budgets in respect of recoverable costs.
(4) Whether or not the court makes a costs management order, it may record on the face of any case management order any comments it has about the incurred costs which are to be taken into account in any subsequent assessment proceedings.
(5) Save in exceptional circumstances—

- (a) the recoverable costs of initially completing Precedent H (the form to be used for a costs budget) shall not exceed the higher of—
  - (i) £1,000; or
  - (ii) 1% of the total of the incurred costs (as agreed or allowed on assessment) and the budgeted costs (agreed or approved); and
- (b) all other recoverable costs of the budgeting and costs management process shall not exceed 2% of the total of the incurred costs (as agreed or allowed on assessment) and the budgeted (agreed or approved) costs.

(Precedent H is annexed to Practice Direction 3E.)
(6) The court may set a timetable or give other directions for future reviews of budgets.
(7) After a party's budgeted costs have been approved or agreed, the party must re-file and re-serve the budget—

- (a) in the form approved or agreed with re-cast figures; and

(b) annexed to the order approving the budgeted costs or recording the parties' agreement.

(8) A costs management order concerns the totals allowed for each phase of the budget, and while the underlying detail in the budget for each phase used by the party to calculate the totals claimed is provided for reference purposes to assist the court in fixing a budget, it is not the role of the court in the costs management hearing to fix or approve the hourly rates claimed in the budget.

[CPR 3.15A]

3.15A **Revision and variation of costs budgets on account of significant developments ('variation costs')**

(1) A party ('the revising party') must revise its budgeted costs upwards or downwards if significant developments in the litigation warrant such revisions.

(2) Any budgets revised in accordance with paragraph (1) must be submitted promptly by the revising party to the other parties for agreement, and subsequently to the court, in accordance with paragraphs (3) to (5).

(3) The revising party must—

(a) serve particulars of the variation proposed on every other party, using the form prescribed by Practice Direction 3E;

(b) confine the particulars to the additional costs occasioned by the significant development; and

(c) certify, in the form prescribed by Practice Direction 3E, that the additional costs are not included in any previous budgeted costs or variation.

(4) The revising party must submit the particulars of variation promptly to the court, together with the last approved or agreed budget, and with an explanation of the points of difference if they have not been agreed.

(5) The court may approve, vary or disallow the proposed variations, having regard to any significant developments which have occurred since the date when the previous budget was approved or agreed, or may list a further costs management hearing.

(6) Where the court makes an order for variation, it may vary the budget for costs related to that variation which have been incurred prior to the order for variation but after the costs management order.

[CPR 3.16]

3.16 **Costs management conferences**

(1) Any hearing which is convened solely for the purpose of costs management (for example, to approve a revised budget) is referred to as a "costs management conference".

(2) Where practicable, costs management conferences should be conducted by telephone or in writing.

[CPR 3.17]

3.17 **Court to have regard to budgets and to take account of costs**

(1) When making any case management decision, the court will have regard to any available budgets of the parties and will take into account the costs involved in each procedural step.

(2) Paragraph (1) applies whether or not the court has made a costs management order.

(3) Subject to rule 3.15A, the court—

(a) may not approve costs incurred before the date of any costs management hearing; but

(b) may record its comments on those costs and take those costs into account when considering the reasonableness and proportionality of all budgeted costs.

(4) If an interim application is made but is not included in a budget, the court may, if it considers it reasonable not to have included the application in the budget, treat the costs of such interim application as additional to the approved budgets.

[CPR 3.18]

3.18 Assessing costs on the standard basis where a costs management order has been made

In any case where a costs management order has been made, when assessing costs on the standard basis, the court will—

(a) have regard to the receiving party's last approved or agreed budgeted costs for each phase of the proceedings;

(b) not depart from such approved or agreed budgeted costs unless satisfied that there is good reason to do so;

(c) take into account any comments made pursuant to rule 3.15(4) or paragraph 7.4 of Practice Direction 3E and recorded on the face of the order.

(Attention is drawn to rules 44.3(2)(a) and 44.3(5), which concern proportionality of costs.)

III COSTS CAPPING

[CPR 3.19]

3.19 Costs capping orders – General

(1) For the purposes of this Section—

(a) "costs capping order" means an order limiting the amount of future costs (including disbursements) which a party may recover pursuant to an order for costs subsequently made; and

(b) "future costs" means costs incurred in respect of work done after the date of the costs capping order but excluding the amount of any additional liability.

(2) This Section does not apply to judicial review costs capping orders under Part 4 of the Criminal Justice and Courts Act 2015 or to protective costs orders.

(Rules 46.16 to 46.19 make provision for judicial review costs capping orders under Part 4 of the Criminal Justice and Courts Act 2015.)

(3) *Omitted.*

(4) A costs capping order may be in respect of –

(a) the whole litigation; or

(b) any issues which are ordered to be tried separately.

(5) The court may at any stage of proceedings make a costs capping order against all or any of the parties, if—

(a) it is in the interests of justice to do so;

(b) there is a substantial risk that without such an order costs will be disproportionately incurred; and

(c) it is not satisfied that the risk in subparagraph (b) can be adequately controlled by–

(i) case management directions or orders made under this Part; and

(ii) detailed assessment of costs.

(6) In considering whether to exercise its discretion under this rule, the court will consider all the circumstances of the case, including—

(a) whether there is a substantial imbalance between the financial position of the parties;

(b) whether the costs of determining the amount of the cap are likely to be proportionate to the overall costs of the litigation;

(c) the stage which the proceedings have reached; and

(d) the costs which have been incurred to date and the future costs.

(7) A costs capping order, once made, will limit the costs recoverable by the party subject to the order unless a party successfully applies to vary the order. No such variation will be made unless—

(a) there has been a material and substantial change of circumstances since the date when the order was made; or

(b) there is some other compelling reason why a variation should be made.

PRACTICE DIRECTION 3E—COSTS MANAGEMENT

THIS PRACTICE DIRECTION SUPPLEMENTS PART 3

A. Production of Costs Budgets

[CPR PD 3E.1]

1. In cases where the Claimant has a limited or severely impaired life expectation (5 years or less remaining) the court will ordinarily disapply cost management under Section II of Part 3.

[CPR PD 3E.2]

2. An order for the provision of costs budgets with a view to a costs management order being made may be particularly appropriate in the following cases—
(a) unfair prejudice petitions under section 994 of the Companies Act 2006;
(b) disqualification proceedings pursuant to the Company Directors Disqualification Act 1986;
(c) applications under the Trusts of Land and Appointment of Trustees Act 1996;
(d) claims pursuant to the Inheritance (Provision for Family and Dependants) Act 1975;
(e) any Part 8 claims or other applications involving a substantial dispute of fact and/or likely to require oral evidence and/or extensive disclosure; and
(f) personal injury and clinical negligence cases where the value of the claim is £10 million or more.

B. Documents to be lodged for costs budgeting purposes

[CPR PD 3E.3]

3. (a) Save in exceptional circumstances or where the court orders otherwise, the parties are not expected to lodge any documents other than Precedent H and the budget discussion report. Both are annexed, to this practice direction. If the Excel format precedent on the MOJ website is used, the calculation on page one will calculate the totals automatically and the phase totals are linked to this page also.
(b) Precedent T, also annexed to this practice direction, is to be used in the event of variation of a budget pursuant to rule 3.15A.

C. Budget format

[CPR PD 3E.4]

4. (a) Unless the court otherwise orders, a budget must be in the form of Precedent H annexed to this Practice Direction. It must be in landscape format with an easily legible typeface.
(b) In cases where a party's budgeted costs do not exceed £25,000 or the value of the claim as stated on the claim form is less than £50,000, the parties must only use the first page of Precedent H.
(The wording for a statement of truth verifying a budget is set out in Practice Direction 22.)

[CPR PD 3E.5]

5. In deciding the reasonable and proportionate costs of each phase of the budget the court will have regard to the factors set out at Civil Procedure Rules 44.3(5) and 44.4(3) including a consideration of where and the circumstances in which the work was done as opposed to where the case is heard.

[CPR PD 3E.6]

6. The table below identifies where within the budget form the various items of work, in so far as they are required by the circumstances of your case, should be included. The time estimated may have to be justified on the budget hearing along with the grade of fee earner doing the work.

[CPR PD 3E.7]

7. Allowance must be made in each phase for advising the client, taking instructions and corresponding with the other party/parties and the court in respect of matters falling within that phase.

[CPR PD 3E.8]

8. The time spent in preparing the budget and associated material must not be claimed in the draft budget under any phase. The maximum figures permitted under rule 3.15(5) should be inserted once the costs budget has been approved by the court.

[CPR PD 3E.9]

9. The 'contingent cost' sections of this form should be used for anticipated costs which do not fall within the main categories set out in this form. Examples might be the trial of preliminary issues, applications to amend, applications for disclosure against third parties or (in libel cases) applications re meaning. Costs which are disputed (such as the need for a particular 17 expert) should be set out in the appropriate phase of the budget and if necessary marked as disputed. Only costs which are more likely than not to be incurred should be included.
(Variation of an approved or agreed budget is dealt with in rule 3.15A.)

D. Assumptions

[CPR PD 3E.10]

10. (a) The assumptions that are reflected in the table below are not to be repeated. Include only those assumptions that significantly impact on the level of costs claimed such as the duration of the proceedings, the number of experts and witnesses or the number of interlocutory applications envisaged. Brief details only are required in the box beneath each phase. Additional documents should only be prepared in exceptional circumstance and, where they are disregarded by the court, the cost of preparation may be disallowed.
(b) Written assumptions are not normally required by the Court in cases where the parties are only required to lodge the first page.

Phase	Includes	Does NOT include
Pre-action	• Pre-Action Protocol correspondence • Investigating the merits of the claim and advising client • Settlement discussions, advising on settlement and Part 36 offers • All other steps taken and advice given pre action	• Any work already incurred in relation to any other phase of the budget
Issue/statements of case	• Preparation of Claim Form • Issue and service of proceedings	

	• Preparation of Particulars of Claim, Defence, Reply, including taking instructions, instructing counsel and any necessary investigation • Considering opposing statements of case and advising client • Part 18 requests (request and answer) • Any conferences with counsel primarily relating to statements of case • Updating schedules and counter schedules of loss • Amendments to statements of case	
CMC	• Completion of DQs • Arranging a CMC • Reviewing opponent's budget • Correspondence with opponent to agree directions and budgets, where possible • Preparation for, and attendance at, the CMC • Finalising the order • Any further CMC that is built into the proposed directions order	• Preparation of costs budget for first CMC
Disclosure	• Obtaining documents from client and advising on disclosure obligations • Reviewing documents for disclosure, preparing disclosure report or questionnaire response and list • Inspection • Reviewing opponent's list and documents, undertaking any appropriate investigations • Correspondence between parties about the scope of disclosure and queries arising • Consulting counsel, so far as appropriate, in relation to disclosure	• Applications for specific disclosure • Applications and requests for third party disclosure
Witness Statements	• Identifying witnesses • Obtaining statements	• Arranging for witnesses to attend trial (include in trial preparation)

	• Preparing witness summaries • Consulting counsel, so far as appropriate, about witness statements • Reviewing opponent's statements and undertaking any appropriate investigations • Applications for witness summaries	
Expert Reports	• Identifying and engaging suitable expert(s) • Reviewing draft and approving report(s) • Dealing with follow-up questions of experts • Considering opposing experts' reports • Any conferences with counsel primarily relating to expert evidence • Meetings of experts (preparing agenda etc.)	• Obtaining permission to adduce expert evidence (include in CMC or a separate application) • Arranging for experts to attend trial (include in trial preparation)
PTR	• Bundle • Preparing and agreeing chronology, case summary and dramatis personae (if ordered and not already prepared earlier in case) • Completing and filing pre-trial checklists • Correspondence with opponent to agree directions • Preparation for and attendance at the PTR	• Assembling and/or copying the bundle (this is not fee earners' work)
Trial Preparation	• Trial bundles • Witness summonses, and arranging for witnesses to attend trial • Any final factual investigations • Supplemental disclosure and statements(if required) • Counsel's brief fee • Agreeing brief fee	• Assembling and/or copying the trial bundle (this is not fee earners' work) • Counsel's refreshers

	• Any pre-trial conferences and advice from counsel • Pre-trial liaison with witnesses	
Trial	• Solicitors' attendance at trial • All conferences and other activity outside court hours during the trial • Attendance on witnesses during the trial • Counsel's trial refreshers • Dealing with draft judgment and related applications	• Preparation for trial • Counsel's brief fee for trial (include in trial preparation)
ADR/Settlement	• Any conferences and advice from counsel in relation to settlement • Work directed to settlement negotiations and meetings between the parties and any other ADR (including mediation), to include Part 36 and other offers and advising the client • Approval of settlement if needed • Drafting settlement agreement or Tomlin order • Advice to the client on settlement (excluding advice included in the pre-action phase)	

E. Budget discussion reports

[CPR PD 3E.11]

11. The budget discussion report required by rule 3.13(2) must set out—

(a) those figures which are agreed for each phase;

(b) those figures which are not agreed for each phase; and

(c) a brief summary of the grounds of dispute.

The parties are encouraged to use the Precedent R Budget Discussion Report annexed to this practice direction.

F. Costs management orders

[CPR PD 3E.12]

12. When reviewing budgeted costs, the court will not undertake a detailed assessment in advance, but rather will consider whether the budgeted costs fall within the range of reasonable and proportionate costs.

G. Oppressive behaviour

[CPR PD 3E.13]

13. Any party may apply to the court if it considers that another party is behaving oppressively in seeking to cause the applicant to spend money disproportionately on costs and the court will grant such relief as may be appropriate.

Annexes

Annex A: Precedent H

In the: [to be completed]
Parties: [to be completed]
Claim number: [to be completed]

Costs budget of [Claimant / Defendant] dated [ ]

PRECEDENT H

Work done / to be done	Incurred		Estimated		Total (£)
	Disbursements (£)	Time costs (£)	Disbursements (£)	Time costs (£)	
Pre-action costs					
Issue / statements of case					
CMC					
Disclosure					
Witness statements					
Expert reports					
PTR					
Trial preparation					
Trial					
ADR / Settlement discussions					
GRAND TOTAL (including both incurred costs and estimated costs)					

This estimate excludes VAT (if applicable), success fees and ATE insurance premiums (if applicable), costs of detailed assessment, costs of any appeals, costs of enforcing any judgment and [complete as appropriate]

Approved budget		£
Budget drafting	1% of approved budget or £1,000	£
Budget process	2%	£

Statement of truth
This budget is a fair and accurate statement of incurred and estimated costs which it would be reasonable and proportionate for my client to incur in this litigation.

Signed

Position   Date

Precedent H (04.17) Page 1 of 6

In the: [to be completed]
Parties: [to be completed]
Claim number: [to be completed]

		RATE (per hour)	PRE-ACTION COSTS				ISSUE / STATEMENTS OF CASE				CMC			
			Incurred costs	Estimated costs		TOTAL	Incurred costs	Estimated costs		TOTAL	Incurred costs	Estimated costs		TOTAL
			£	Hours	£		£	Hours	£		£	Hours	£	
	Fee earners' time													
1														
2														
3														
4														
Add line														
5	Time Value (1 to 4)													
	Expert's costs													
6	Fees													
7	Disbursements													
	Counsel's fees													
8	Leading counsel													
9	Junior counsel													
Add line														
10	Court fees													
11	Other Disbursements													
12	**Total Disbursements (6 to 11)**													
13	**Total (5 + 13)**													
							Assumptions: Issue / statements of case:				Assumptions: CMC:			

Page 2 of 6

In the: [to be completed]
Parties: [to be completed]
Claim number: [to be completed]

		RATE (per hour)	DISCLOSURE				WITNESS STATEMENTS			
			Incurred costs	Estimated costs		TOTAL	Incurred costs	Estimated costs		TOTAL
			£	Hours	£		£	Hours	£	
	Fee earners' time									
1										
2										
3										
4										
Add line										
5	Time Value (1 to 4)									
	Expert's costs									
6	Fees									
7	Disbursements									
	Counsel's fees									
8	Leading counsel									
9	Junior counsel									
Add line										
10	Court fees									
11	Other Disbursements									
12	**Total Disbursements (6 to 11)**									
13	**Total (5 + 13)**									
			Assumptions: disclosure.				Assumptions: witness evidence.			

Page 3 of 6

In the: [to be completed]
Parties: [to be completed]
Claim number: [to be completed]

		RATE (per hour)	EXPERT REPORTS (see separate breakdown for expert fees)			
			Incurred costs	Estimated costs		TOTAL
			£	Hours	£	
	Fee earners' time					
1						
2						
3						
4						
Add line						
5	Time Value (1 to 4)					
	Expert's costs					
6	Fees					
7	Disbursements					
	Counsel's fees					
8	Leading counsel					
9	Junior counsel					
Add line						
10	Court fees					
11	Other Disbursements					
12	**Total Disbursements (6 to 11)**					
13	**Total (5 + 13)**					

Assumptions: expert evidence.

EXPERT FEE SUMMARY Drafting note: Completing this summary will populate totals for fees in table on left					
	incurred	estimated	estimated	estimated	Total estimated
Type		report	conference	joint stms	
Add line					
Sub total					
Total expert fees (incurred and estimated)					

Page 4 of 6

In the: [to be completed]
Parties: [to be completed]
Claim number: [to be completed]

		RATE (per hour)	PTR				TRIAL PREPARATION				TRIAL			
			Incurred costs	Estimated costs		TOTAL	Incurred costs	Estimated costs		TOTAL	Incurred costs	Estimated costs		TOTAL
			£	Hours	£		£	Hours	£		£	Hours	£	
	Fee earners' time													
1														
2														
3														
4														
Add line														
5	Time Value (1 to 4)													
	Expert's costs													
6	Fees													
7	Disbursements													
	Counsel's fees													
8	Leading counsel													
9	Junior counsel													
Add line														
10	Court fees													
11	Other Disbursements													
12	**Total Disbursements (6 to 11)**													
13	**Total (5 + 13)**													
			Assumptions:PTR.				Assumptions:Trial prep.				Assumptions:Trial.			

In the: [to be completed]
Parties: [to be completed]
Claim number: [to be completed]

			SETTLEMENT / ADR				Contingent cost A: [explain in assumptions box below]				Contingent cost B: [explain in assumptions box below]			
		RATE (per hour)	Incurred costs	Estimated costs		TOTAL	Incurred costs	Estimated costs		TOTAL	Incurred costs	Estimated costs		TOTAL
	Fees		£	Hours	£		£	Hours	£		£	Hours	£	
	Fee earners' time													
1														
2														
3														
4														
Add line														
5	Time Value (1 to 4)													
	Expert's costs													
6	Fees													
7	Disbursements													
	Counsel's fees													
8	Leading counsel													
9	Junior counsel													
Add line														
10	Court fees													
11	Other Disbursements													
12	**Total Disbursements (6 to 11)**													
13	**Total (5 + 13)**													
			Assumptions:Settlement / ADR.				Assumptions : CONTINGENT COST A.				Assumptions : CONTINGENT COST B.			

Add Contingencies

Page 6 of 6

Annex B: Precedent R

PRECEDENT R

Precedent R : Budget discussion report.						Budgeted costs for :		C/D/etc			
Party:	C/D etc			X				CCMC Date			
Court:	Name			Y							
Case Number	Number			Z							
	Incurred costs	Budgeted costs : claimed			Budgeted costs : offered			*Paying party comments on offers made*	Order	Judge's comments / sums alllowed	
Phase		Claimed	Time £	Disbs £	Offered	Time £	Disbs £		Budgeted costs	Judge	Judge
Pre action costs		na	na	na	na	na	na	na		Time (hours)	Disbs
Issue / stm of case		£0.00			£0.00						
CMC		£0.00			£0.00						
Disclosure		£0.00			£0.00						
Witness stms		£0.00			£0.00						
Experts reports		£0.00			£0.00						
PTR	na	£0.00			£0.00						
Trial preparation	na	£0.00			£0.00						
Trial	na	£0.00			£0.00						
ADR		£0.00			£0.00						
Contingent cost A:	na	£0.00			£0.00						
Contingent cost B:	na	£0.00			£0.00						
Total budgeted costs	Incurred	Claimed	Time £	Disbs £	Offered	Time £	Disbs £		Budgeted costs		
	£0.00	£0.00	£0.00	£0.00	£0.00	£0.00	£0.00		£0.00		
		Claimed	Total of budgeted and incurred costs		Offered			Post CCMC costs summary			
Incurred		£0.00			£0.00			Incurred	£0.00		
Budgeted costs claimed		£0.00			£0.00			Budgeted sum ordered	£0.00		
GT		£0.00			£0.00			GT	£0.00		

Annex C: Precedent T

Precedent T Summary Sheet

Court:	Name		**Current Budget date:**		
Parties:	Parties		**Date Precedent T served:**		
Claim number:	Number		**Cost budget for:**	Party	
Work done / to be done	**Current Budget Costs (prior to variation)**		**Variations (+ or -)**	**Total estimated costs after variation (£)**	**Completion by the Court :** ***Estimated costs allowed or agreed after variation***
	Incurred (£)	**Estimated (£)**	**Variation in estimate (see explanation sheet for details)**		
Pre-action costs					
Issue /statements of case			*£0.00*	**£0.00**	
CMC			*£0.00*	**£0.00**	
Disclosure			*£0.00*	**£0.00**	
Witness statements			*£0.00*	**£0.00**	
Expert reports			*£0.00*	**£0.00**	
PTR			*£0.00*	**£0.00**	
Trial preparation			*£0.00*	**£0.00**	
Trial			*£0.00*	**£0.00**	
ADR / Settlement discussions			*£0.00*	**£0.00**	
Contingent cost A:			*£0.00*	**£0.00**	
Contingent cost B:			*£0.00*	**£0.00**	
	Total incurred	Total estimated	Variation	**Total estimated costs after variation (£)**	
Sub Totals	£0.00	£0.00	***£0.00***	**£0.00**	
Grand Total (including both incurred costs and estimated costs)		**£0.00**		**£0.00**	

This estimate excludes VAT (if applicable), success fees and ATE insurance premiums (if applicable), costs of detailed assessment, costs of any appeals, costs of enforcing any judgment and [complete as appropriate]

Approved budget after variation *(Incurred and estimated)*	

Variation certification pursuant to Part 3.15 (A) 3(c)

I certify that the costs and disbursements included in this variation are not included in any previous budgeted costs or variation (including any contingency), whether agreed or approved by the court.

Signed	
Name (printed)	
Position	
Dated	

Precedent T Particulars

Court:	Name					
Parties:	Parties					
Claim number:	Number					
Cost budget for:	Party					
	VARIATION			Significant Development		Opposing party comments
	Variation *(+ or -)*			*[General Explanation for Variation: significant development]*	Paying party's offer	*Comment if not agreed*
Phase	**Time £ (A)**	**Disbs £ (B)**	**TOTAL (A+B)**	Explanation for particular phase *(where variation in any phase exceeds £10k complete xx)*		Brief explanation if not agreed by the opposing party
Issue /statements of case			£0.00	xx		
CMC			£0.00	xx		
Disclosure			£0.00	xx		
Witness statements			£0.00	xx		
Expert fees (see table below for disbs summary and total)		£0.00	£0.00	xx		
PTR			£0.00	xx		
Trial preparation			£0.00	xx		
Trial			£0.00	xx		
ADR / Settlement discussions			£0.00	xx		
Contingent cost A:			£0.00	xx		
Contingent cost B:			£0.00	xx		
		Total	£0.00	Total	£0.00	

Expert fee summary : variation +/- disbursements only

	estimated	estimated	estimated		Previous
Type	report	conference	joint stms	Total	budgeted total figure
xx				£0.00	
Total expert fees : estimated	£0.00	£0.00	£0.00	£0.00	£0.00

PRACTICE DIRECTION 3F—COSTS CAPPING

THIS PRACTICE DIRECTION SUPPLEMENTS SECTION III OF CPR PART 3

Section I of this Practice Direction – General Rules about Costs Capping

When to make an application

[CPR PD 3F.1]

1.1 The court will make a costs capping order only in exceptional circumstances.
1.2 An application for a costs capping order must be made as soon as possible, preferably before or at the first case management hearing or shortly afterwards. The stage which the proceedings have reached at the time of the application will be one of the factors the court will consider when deciding whether to make a costs capping order.

Costs budget

[CPR PD 3F.2]

2 The budget required by rule 3.20 must be in the form of Precedent H annexed to Practice Direction 3E–Costs Management.

Schedule of costs

[CPR PD 3F.3]

3 The schedule of costs referred to in rule 3.20(3)—
(a) must set out –
- (i) each sub-heading as it appears in the applicant's budget (column 1);
- (ii) alongside each sub-heading, the amount claimed by the applicant in the applicant's budget (column 2); and
- (iii) alongside the figures referred to in subparagraph (ii) the amount that the respondent proposes should be allowed under each sub-heading (column 3); and

(b) must be supported by a statement of truth.

Assessing the quantum of the costs cap

[CPR PD 3F.4]

4.1 When assessing the quantum of a costs cap, the court will take into account the factors detailed in rule 44.5 and the relevant provisions supporting that rule in the Practice Direction supplementing Part 44. When considering a party's budget of the costs they are likely to incur in the future conduct of the proceedings, the court may also take into account a reasonable allowance on costs for contingencies.

Section II of this Practice Direction – Costs Capping in Relation to Trust Funds

Costs capping orders in relation to trust funds

[CPR PD 3F.5]

5.1 In this Section, "trust fund" means property which is the subject of a trust, and includes the estate of a deceased person.
5.2 This Section contains additional provisions to enable –
(a) the parties to consider whether to apply for; and
(b) the court to consider whether to make of its own initiative,
a costs capping order in proceedings relating to trust funds.
5.3 This Section supplements rules 3.19 to 3.21 and Section I of this Practice Direction.
5.4 Any party to such proceedings who intends to apply for an order for the payment of costs out of the trust fund must file and serve on all other parties written notice of that intention together with a budget of the costs likely to be incurred by that party.
5.5 The documents mentioned in paragraph 5.4 must be filed and served –
(a) in a Part 7 claim, with the first statement of case; and
(b) in a Part 8 claim, with the evidence (or, if a defendant does not intend to serve and file evidence, with the acknowledgement of service).
5.6 When proceedings first come before the court for directions the court may make a costs capping order of its own initiative whether or not any party has applied for such an order.

PART 36 OFFERS TO SETTLE

[CPR 36.1]

36.1 **Scope of this Part**

(1) This Part contains a self-contained procedural code about offers to settle made pursuant to the procedure set out in this Part ("Part 36 offers").

(2) Section I of this Part contains general rules about Part 36 offers.

(3) Section II of this Part contains rules about offers to settle where the parties have followed the Pre-Action Protocol for Low Value Personal Injury Claims in Road Traffic Accidents ("the RTA Protocol") or the Pre-Action Protocol for Low Value Personal Injury (Employers' Liability and Public Liability) Claims ("the EL/PL Protocol") and have started proceedings under Part 8 in accordance with Practice Direction 8B.

SECTION I PART 36 OFFERS TO SETTLE

General

[CPR 36.2]

36.2 Scope of this Section

(1) This Section does not apply to an offer to settle to which Section II of this Part applies.

(2) Nothing in this Section prevents a party making an offer to settle in whatever way that party chooses, but if the offer is not made in accordance with rule 36.5, it will not have the consequences specified in this Section.

(Rule 44.2 requires the court to consider an offer to settle that does not have the costs consequences set out in this Section in deciding what order to make about costs.)

(3) A Part 36 offer may be made in respect of the whole, or part of, or any issue that arises in—

(a) a claim, counterclaim or other additional claim; or

(b) an appeal or cross-appeal from a decision made at a trial.

(Rules 20.2 and 20.3 provide that counterclaims and other additional claims are treated as claims and that references to a claimant or a defendant include a party bringing or defending an additional claim.)

[CPR 36.3]

36.3 Definitions

In this Section—

(a) the party who makes an offer is the "offeror";

(b) the party to whom an offer is made is the "offeree";

(c) a "trial" means any trial in a case whether it is a trial of all issues or a trial of liability, quantum or some other issue in the case;

(d) a trial is "in progress" from the time when it starts until the time when judgment is given or handed down;

(e) a case is "decided" when all issues in the case have been determined, whether at one or more trials;

(f) "trial judge" includes the judge (if any) allocated in advance to conduct a trial; and

(g) "the relevant period" means—

(i) in the case of an offer made not less than 21 days before a trial, the period specified under rule 36.5(1)(c) or such longer period as the parties agree;

(ii) otherwise, the period up to the end of such trial.

[CPR 36.4]

36.4 Application of Part 36 to appeals

(1) Except where a Part 36 offer is made in appeal proceedings, it shall have the consequences set out in this Section only in relation to the costs of the proceedings in respect of which it is made, and not in relation to the costs of any appeal from a decision in those proceedings.

(2) Where a Part 36 offer is made in appeal proceedings, references in this Section to a term in the first column below shall be treated, unless the context requires otherwise, as references to the corresponding term in the second column—

Terms	*Corresponding term*
Claim	Appeal
Counterclaim	Cross-appeal
Case	Appeal proceedings
Claimant	Appellant
Defendant	Respondent
Trial	Appeal hearing
Trial judge	Appeal judge

Making offers

[CPR 36.5]

36.5 **Form and content of a Part 36 offer**

(1) A Part 36 offer must—

(a) be in writing;

(b) make clear that it is made pursuant to Part 36;

(c) specify a period of not less than 21 days within which the defendant will be liable for the claimant's costs in accordance with rule 36.13 or 36.20 if the offer is accepted;

(d) state whether it relates to the whole of the claim or to part of it or to an issue that arises in it and if so to which part or issue; and

(e) state whether it takes into account any counterclaim.

(Rule 36.7 makes provision for when a Part 36 offer is made.)

(2) Paragraph (1)(c) does not apply if the offer is made less than 21 days before the start of a trial.

(3) In appropriate cases, a Part 36 offer must contain such further information as is required by rule 36.18 (personal injury claims for future pecuniary loss), rule 36.19 (offer to settle a claim for provisional damages), and rule 36.22 (deduction of benefits).

(4) A Part 36 offer which offers to pay or offers to accept a sum of money will be treated as inclusive of all interest until—

(a) the date on which the period specified under rule 36.5(1)(c) expires; or

(b) if rule 36.5(2) applies, a date 21 days after the date the offer was made.

[CPR 36.6]

36.6 **Part 36 offers – defendant's offer**

(1) Subject to rules 36.18(3) and 36.19(1), a Part 36 offer by a defendant to pay a sum of money in settlement of a claim must be an offer to pay a single sum of money.

(2) A defendant's offer that includes an offer to pay all or part of the sum at a date later than 14 days following the date of acceptance will not be treated as a Part 36 offer unless the offeree accepts the offer.

[CPR 36.7]

36.7 **Time when a Part 36 offer is made**

(1) A Part 36 offer may be made at any time, including before the commencement of proceedings.

(2) A Part 36 offer is made when it is served on the offeree.
(Part 6 provides detailed rules about service of documents.)

Clarifying, withdrawing and changing the terms of offers

[CPR 36.8]

36.8 **Clarification of a Part 36 offer**

(1) The offeree may, within 7 days of a Part 36 offer being made, request the offeror to clarify the offer.

(2) If the offeror does not give the clarification requested under paragraph (1) within 7 days of receiving the request, the offeree may, unless the trial has started, apply for an order that the offeror do so.

(Part 23 contains provisions about making an application to the court.)

(3) If the court makes an order under paragraph (2), it must specify the date when the Part 36 offer is to be treated as having been made.

[CPR 36.9]

36.9 **Withdrawing or changing the terms of a Part 36 offer generally**

(1) A Part 36 offer can only be withdrawn, or its terms changed, if the offeree has not previously served notice of acceptance.

(2) The offeror withdraws the offer or changes its terms by serving written notice of the withdrawal or change of terms on the offeree.

(Rule 36.17(7) deals with the costs consequences following judgment of an offer which is withdrawn.)

(3) Subject to rule 36.10, such notice of withdrawal or change of terms takes effect when it is served on the offeree.

(Rule 36.10 makes provision about when permission is required to withdraw or change the terms of an offer before the expiry of the relevant period.)

(4) Subject to paragraph (1), after expiry of the relevant period—
- (a) the offeror may withdraw the offer or change its terms without the permission of the court; or
- (b) the offer may be automatically withdrawn in accordance with its terms.

(5) Where the offeror changes the terms of a Part 36 offer to make it more advantageous to the offeree—
- (a) such improved offer shall be treated, not as the withdrawal of the original offer; but as the making of a new Part 36 offer on the improved terms; and
- (b) subject to rule 36.5(2), the period specified under rule 36.5(1)(c) shall be 21 days or such longer period (if any) identified in the written notice referred to in paragraph (2).

[CPR 36.10]

36.10 **Withdrawing or changing the terms of a Part 36 offer before the expiry of the relevant period**

(1) Subject to rule 36.9(1), this rule applies where the offeror serves notice before expiry of the relevant period of withdrawal of the offer or change of its terms to be less advantageous to the offeree.

(2) Where this rule applies—

(a) if the offeree has not served notice of acceptance of the original offer by the expiry of the relevant period, the offeror's notice has effect on the expiry of that period; and

(b) if the offeree serves notice of acceptance of the original offer before the expiry of the relevant period, that acceptance has effect unless the offeror applies to the court for permission to withdraw the offer or to change its terms—

(i) within 7 days of the offeree's notice of acceptance; or

(ii) if earlier, before the first day of trial.

(3) On an application under paragraph (2)(b), the court may give permission for the original offer to be withdrawn or its terms changed if satisfied that there has been a change of circumstances since the making of the original offer and that it is in the interests of justice to give permission.

Accepting offers

[CPR 36.11]

36.11 Acceptance of a Part 36 offer

(1) A Part 36 offer is accepted by serving written notice of acceptance on the offeror.

(2) Subject to paragraphs (3) and (4) and to rule 36.12, a Part 36 offer may be accepted at any time (whether or not the offeree has subsequently made a different offer), unless it has already been withdrawn.

(Rule 21.10 deals with compromise, etc. by or on behalf of a child or protected party.)

(Rules 36.9 and 36.10 deal with withdrawal of Part 36 offers.)

(3) The court's permission is required to accept a Part 36 offer where—

(a) rule 36.15(4) applies;

(b) rule 36.22(3)(b) applies, the relevant period has expired and further deductible amounts have been paid to the claimant since the date of the offer;

(c) an apportionment is required under rule 41.3A; or

(d) a trial is in progress.

(Rule 36.15 deals with offers by some but not all of multiple defendants.)

(Rule 36.22 defines "deductible amounts".)

(Rule 41.3A requires an apportionment in proceedings under the Fatal Accidents Act 1976 and Law Reform (Miscellaneous Provisions) Act 1934.)

(4) Where the court gives permission under paragraph (3), unless all the parties have agreed costs, the court must make an order dealing with costs, and may order that the costs consequences set out in rule 36.13 apply.

[CPR 36.12]

36.12 Acceptance of a Part 36 offer in a split-trial case

(1) This rule applies in any case where there has been a trial but the case has not been decided within the meaning of rule 36.3.

(2) Any Part 36 offer which relates only to parts of the claim or issues that have already been decided can no longer be accepted.

(3) Subject to paragraph (2) and unless the parties agree, any other Part 36 offer cannot be accepted earlier than 7 clear days after judgment is given or handed down in such trial.

[CPR 36.13]

36.13 **Costs consequences of acceptance of a Part 36 offer**

(1) Subject to paragraphs (2) and (4) and to rule 36.20, where a Part 36 offer is accepted within the relevant period the claimant will be entitled to the costs of the proceedings (including their recoverable pre-action costs) up to the date on which notice of acceptance was served on the offeror.

(Rule 36.20 makes provision for the costs consequences of accepting a Part 36 offer in certain personal injury claims where the claim no longer proceeds under the RTA or EL/PL Protocol.)

(2) Where—

(a) a defendant's Part 36 offer relates to part only of the claim; and

(b) at the time of serving notice of acceptance within the relevant period the claimant abandons the balance of the claim,

the claimant will only be entitled to the costs of such part of the claim unless the court orders otherwise.

(3) Except where the recoverable costs are fixed by these Rules, costs under paragraphs (1) and (2) are to be assessed on the standard basis if the amount of costs is not agreed.

(Rule 44.3(2) explains the standard basis for the assessment of costs.)

(Rule 44.9 contains provisions about when a costs order is deemed to have been made and applying for an order under section 194(3) of the Legal Services Act 2007.)

(Part 45 provides for fixed costs in certain classes of case.)

(4) Where—

(a) a Part 36 offer which was made less than 21 days before the start of a trial is accepted; or

(b) a Part 36 offer which relates to the whole of the claim is accepted after expiry of the relevant period; or

(c) subject to paragraph (2), a Part 36 offer which does not relate to the whole of the claim is accepted at any time,

the liability for costs must be determined by the court unless the parties have agreed the costs.

(5) Where paragraph (4)(b) applies but the parties cannot agree the liability for costs, the court must, unless it considers it unjust to do so, order that—

(a) the claimant be awarded costs up to the date on which the relevant period expired; and

(b) the offeree do pay the offeror's costs for the period from the date of expiry of the relevant period to the date of acceptance.

(6) In considering whether it would be unjust to make the orders specified in paragraph (5), the court must take into account all the circumstances of the case including the matters listed in rule 36.17(5).

(7) The claimant's costs include any costs incurred in dealing with the defendant's counterclaim if the Part 36 offer states that it takes it into account.

[CPR 36.14]

36.14 **Other effects of acceptance of a Part 36 offer**

(1) If a Part 36 offer is accepted, the claim will be stayed.

(2) In the case of acceptance of a Part 36 offer which relates to the whole claim, the stay will be upon the terms of the offer.

(3) If a Part 36 offer which relates to part only of the claim is accepted, the claim will be stayed as to that part upon the terms of the offer.

(4) If the approval of the court is required before a settlement can be binding, any stay which would otherwise arise on the acceptance of a Part 36 offer will take effect only when that approval has been given.

(5) Any stay arising under this rule will not affect the power of the court—

(a) to enforce the terms of a Part 36 offer; or

(b) to deal with any question of costs (including interest on costs) relating to the proceedings.

(6) Unless the parties agree otherwise in writing, where a Part 36 offer that is or includes an offer to pay or accept a single sum of money is accepted, that sum must be paid to the claimant within 14 days of the date of—

(a) acceptance; or

(b) the order when the court makes an order under rule 41.2 (order for an award of provisional damages) or rule 41.8 (order for an award of periodical payments), unless the court orders otherwise.

(7) If such sum is not paid within 14 days of acceptance of the offer, or such other period as has been agreed, the claimant may enter judgment for the unpaid sum.

(8) Where—

(a) a Part 36 offer (or part of a Part 36 offer) which is not an offer to which paragraph (6) applies is accepted; and

(b) a party alleges that the other party has not honoured the terms of the offer,

that party may apply to enforce the terms of the offer without the need for a new claim.

[CPR 36.15]

36.15 **Acceptance of a Part 36 offer made by one or more, but not all, defendants**

(1) This rule applies where the claimant wishes to accept a Part 36 offer made by one or more, but not all, of a number of defendants.

(2) If the defendants are sued jointly or in the alternative, the claimant may accept the offer if—

(a) the claimant discontinues the claim against those defendants who have not made the offer; and

(b) those defendants give written consent to the acceptance of the offer.

(3) If the claimant alleges that the defendants have a several liability(GL) to the claimant, the claimant may—

(a) accept the offer; and

(b) continue with the claims against the other defendants if entitled to do so.

(4) In all other cases the claimant must apply to the court for permission to accept the Part 36 offer.

Unaccepted offers

[CPR 36.16]

36.16 **Restriction on disclosure of a Part 36 offer**

(1) A Part 36 offer will be treated as "without prejudice except as to costs".

(2) The fact that a Part 36 offer has been made and the terms of such offer must not be communicated to the trial judge until the case has been decided.

(3) Paragraph (2) does not apply—

(a) where the defence of tender before claim has been raised;

(b) where the proceedings have been stayed under rule 36.14 following acceptance of a Part 36 offer;
(c) where the offeror and the offeree agree in writing that it should not apply; or
(d) where, although the case has not been decided—
(i) any part of, or issue in, the case has been decided; and
(ii) the Part 36 offer relates only to parts or issues that have been decided.

(4) In a case to which paragraph (3)(d)(i) applies, the trial judge—
(a) may be told whether or not there are Part 36 offers other than those referred to in paragraph (3)(d)(ii); but
(b) must not be told the terms of any such other offers unless any of paragraphs (3)(a) to (c) applies.

[CPR 36.17]

36.17 Costs consequences following judgment

(1) Subject to rule 36.21, this rule applies where upon judgment being entered—
(a) a claimant fails to obtain a judgment more advantageous than a defendant's Part 36 offer; or
(b) judgment against the defendant is at least as advantageous to the claimant as the proposals contained in a claimant's Part 36 offer.

(Rule 36.21 makes provision for the costs consequences following judgment in certain personal injury claims where the claim no longer proceeds under the RTA or EL/PL Protocol.)

(2) For the purposes of paragraph (1), in relation to any money claim or money element of a claim, "more advantageous" means better in money terms by any amount, however small, and "at least as advantageous" shall be construed accordingly.

(3) Subject to paragraphs (7) and (8), where paragraph (1)(a) applies, the court must, unless it considers it unjust to do so, order that the defendant is entitled to—
(a) costs (including any recoverable pre-action costs) from the date on which the relevant period expired; and
(b) interest on those costs.

(4) Subject to paragraph (7), where paragraph (1)(b) applies, the court must, unless it considers it unjust to do so, order that the claimant is entitled to—
(a) interest on the whole or part of any sum of money (excluding interest) awarded, at a rate not exceeding 10% above base rate for some or all of the period starting with the date on which the relevant period expired;
(b) costs (including any recoverable pre-action costs) on the indemnity basis from the date on which the relevant period expired;
(c) interest on those costs at a rate not exceeding 10% above base rate; and
(d) provided that the case has been decided and there has not been a previous order under this sub-paragraph, an additional amount, which shall not exceed £75,000, calculated by applying the prescribed percentage set out below to an amount which is—
(i) the sum awarded to the claimant by the court; or
(ii) where there is no monetary award, the sum awarded to the claimant by the court in respect of costs—

Amount awarded by the court	*Prescribed percentage*
Up to £500,000	10% of the amount awarded
Above £500,000	10% of the first £500,000 and (subject to the limit of £75,000) 5% of any amount above that figure.

(5) In considering whether it would be unjust to make the orders referred to in paragraphs (3) and (4), the court must take into account all the circumstances of the case including—

(a) the terms of any Part 36 offer;

(b) the stage in the proceedings when any Part 36 offer was made, including in particular how long before the trial started the offer was made;

(c) the information available to the parties at the time when the Part 36 offer was made;

(d) the conduct of the parties with regard to the giving of or refusal to give information for the purposes of enabling the offer to be made or evaluated; and

(e) whether the offer was a genuine attempt to settle the proceedings.

(6) Where the court awards interest under this rule and also awards interest on the same sum and for the same period under any other power, the total rate of interest must not exceed 10% above base rate.

(7) Paragraphs (3) and (4) do not apply to a Part 36 offer—

(a) which has been withdrawn;

(b) which has been changed so that its terms are less advantageous to the offeree where the offeree has beaten the less advantageous offer;

(c) made less than 21 days before trial, unless the court has abridged the relevant period.

(8) Paragraph (3) does not apply to a soft tissue injury claim to which rule 36.21 applies.

(Rule 44.2 requires the court to consider an offer to settle that does not have the costs consequences set out in this Section in deciding what order to make about costs.)

Personal injury cases

[CPR 36.18]

36.18 **Personal injury claims for future pecuniary loss**

(1) This rule applies to a claim for damages for personal injury which is or includes a claim for future pecuniary loss.

(2) An offer to settle such a claim will not have the consequences set out in this Section unless it is made by way of a Part 36 offer under this rule.

(3) A Part 36 offer to which this rule applies may contain an offer to pay, or an offer to accept—

(a) the whole or part of the damages for future pecuniary loss in the form of—

(i) a lump sum;

(ii) periodical payments; or

(iii) both a lump sum and periodical payments;

(b) the whole or part of any other damages in the form of a lump sum.

(4) A Part 36 offer to which this rule applies—

(a) must state the amount of any offer to pay or to accept the whole or part of any damages in the form of a lump sum;

(b) may state—

(i) what part of the lump sum, if any, relates to damages for future pecuniary loss; and

(ii) what part relates to other damages to be paid or accepted in the form of a lump sum;

(c) must state what part of the offer relates to damages for future pecuniary loss to be paid or accepted in the form of periodical payments and must specify—

(i) the amount and duration of the periodical payments;

(ii) the amount of any payments for substantial capital purchases and when they are to be made; and

(iii) that each amount is to vary by reference to the retail prices index (or to some other named index, or that it is not to vary by reference to any index); and

(d) must state either that any damages which take the form of periodical payments will be funded in a way which ensures that the continuity of payments is reasonably secure in accordance with section 2(4) of the Damages Act 1996 or how such damages are to be paid and how the continuity of their payment is to be secured.

(5) Rule 36.6 applies to the extent that a Part 36 offer by a defendant under this rule includes an offer to pay all or part of any damages in the form of a lump sum.

(6) Where the offeror makes a Part 36 offer to which this rule applies and which offers to pay or to accept damages in the form of both a lump sum and periodical payments, the offeree may only give notice of acceptance of the offer as a whole.

(7) If the offeree accepts a Part 36 offer which includes payment of any part of the damages in the form of periodical payments, the claimant must, within 7 days of the date of acceptance, apply to the court for an order for an award of damages in the form of periodical payments under rule 41.8.

(Practice Direction 41B contains information about periodical payments under the Damages Act 1996.)

[CPR 36.19]

36.19 **Offer to settle a claim for provisional damages**

(1) An offeror may make a Part 36 offer in respect of a claim which includes a claim for provisional damages.

(2) Where the offeror does so, the Part 36 offer must specify whether or not the offeror is proposing that the settlement shall include an award of provisional damages.

(3) Where the offeror is offering to agree to the making of an award of provisional damages, the Part 36 offer must also state—

(a) that the sum offered is in satisfaction of the claim for damages on the assumption that the injured person will not develop the disease or suffer the type of deterioration specified in the offer;

(b) that the offer is subject to the condition that the claimant must make any claim for further damages within a limited period; and

(c) what that period is.

(4) Rule 36.6 applies to the extent that a Part 36 offer by a defendant includes an offer to agree to the making of an award of provisional damages.

(5) If the offeree accepts the Part 36 offer, the claimant must, within 7 days of the date of acceptance, apply to the court for an award of provisional damages under rule 41.2.

[CPR 36.20]

36.20 **Costs consequences of acceptance of a Part 36 offer where Section IIIA of Part 45 applies**

(1) This rule applies where—

(a) a claim no longer continues under the RTA or EL/PL Protocol pursuant to rule 45.29A(1); or

(b) the claim is one to which the Pre-Action Protocol for Resolution of Package Travel Claims applies.

(2) Where a Part 36 offer is accepted within the relevant period, the claimant is entitled to the fixed costs in Table 6B, Table 6C or Table 6D in Section IIIA of Part 45 for the stage applicable at the date on which notice of acceptance was served on the offeror.

(3) Where—

(a) a defendant's Part 36 offer relates to part only of the claim; and

(b) at the time of serving notice of acceptance within the relevant period the claimant abandons the balance of the claim,

the claimant will be entitled to the fixed costs in paragraph (2).

(4) Subject to paragraphs (5), (6) and (7), where a defendant's Part 36 offer is accepted after the relevant period—

(a) the claimant will be entitled to the fixed costs in Table 6B, Table 6C or Table 6D in Section IIIA of Part 45 for the stage applicable at the date on which the relevant period expired; and

(b) the claimant will be liable for the defendant's costs for the period from the date of expiry of the relevant period to the date of acceptance.

(5) Subject to paragraphs (6) and (7), where the claimant accepts the defendant's Protocol offer after the date on which the claim leaves the Protocol—

(a) the claimant will be entitled to the applicable Stage 1 and Stage 2 fixed costs in Table 6 or Table 6A in Section III of Part 45; and

(b) the claimant will be liable for the defendant's costs from the date on which the Protocol offer is deemed to have been made to the date of acceptance.

(6) In a soft tissue injury claim, if the defendant makes a Part 36 offer before the defendant receives a fixed cost medical report, paragraphs (4) and (5) will only have effect if the claimant accepts the offer more than 21 days after the defendant received the report.

(7) In this rule, "fixed cost medical report" and "soft tissue injury claim" have the same meaning as in paragraph 1.1(10A) and (16A) respectively of the RTA Protocol.

(8) For the purposes of this rule a defendant's Protocol offer is either—

(a) defined in accordance with rules 36.25 and 36.26; or

(b) if the claim leaves the Protocol before the Court Proceedings Pack Form is sent to the defendant—

(i) the last offer made by the defendant before the claim leaves the Protocol; and

(ii) deemed to be made on the first business day after the claim leaves the Protocol.

(9) A reference to—

(a) the "Court Proceedings Pack Form" is a reference to the form used in the Protocol; and

(b) "business day" is a reference to a business day as defined in rule 6.2.

(10) Fixed costs shall be calculated by reference to the amount of the offer which is accepted.

(11) Where the parties do not agree the liability for costs, the court must make an order as to costs.

(12) Where the court makes an order for costs in favour of the defendant—

(a) the court must have regard to; and

(b) the amount of costs ordered must not exceed,

the fixed costs in Table 6B, Table 6C or Table 6D in Section IIIA of Part 45 applicable at the date of acceptance, less the fixed costs to which the claimant is entitled under paragraph (4) or (5).

(13) The parties are entitled to disbursements allowed in accordance with rule 45.29I incurred in any period for which costs are payable to them.

[CPR 36.21]

36.21 **Costs consequences following judgment where section IIIA of Part 45 applies**

(1) Where—

(a) a claim no longer continues under the RTA or EL/PL protocol pursuant to rule 45.29A(1); or

(b) the claim is one to which the Pre-Action Protocol for Resolution of Package Travel Claims applies,

rule 36.17 applies with the following modifications.

(2) Subject to paragraphs (3), (4) and (5), where an order for costs is made pursuant to rule 36.17(3)—

(a) the claimant will be entitled to the fixed costs in Table 6B, 6C or 6D in Section IIIA of Part 45 for the stage applicable at the date on which the relevant period expired; and

(b) the claimant will be liable for the defendant's costs from the date on which the relevant period expired to the date of judgment.

(3) Subject to paragraphs (4) and (5), where in a claim to which paragraph (1)(a) applies, the claimant fails to obtain a judgment more advantageous than the defendant's Protocol offer—

(a) the claimant will be entitled to the applicable Stage 1 and Stage 2 fixed costs in Table 6 or 6A in Section III of Part 45; and

(b) the claimant will be liable for the defendant's costs from the date on which the Protocol offer is deemed to be made to the date of judgment; and

(c) in this rule, the amount of the judgment is less than the Protocol offer where the judgment is less than the offer once deductible amounts identified in the judgment are deducted.

("Deductible amount" is defined in rule 36.22(1)(d).)

(4) In a soft tissue injury claim, if the defendant makes a Part 36 offer or Protocol offer before the defendant receives a fixed cost medical report, paragraphs (2) and (3) will only have effect in respect of costs incurred by either party more than 21 days after the defendant received the report.

(5) In this rule "fixed cost medical report" and "soft tissue injury claim" have the same meaning as in paragraph 1.1(10A) and (16A) respectively of the RTA Protocol.

(6) For the purposes of this rule a defendant's Protocol offer is either—

(a) defined in accordance with rules 36.25 and 36.26; or

(b) if the claim leaves the Protocol before the Court Proceedings Pack Form is sent to the defendant—

(i) the last offer made by the defendant before the claim leaves the Protocol; and

(ii) deemed to be made on the first business day after the claim leaves the Protocol.

(7) A reference to—

(a) the "Court Proceedings Pack Form" is a reference to the form used in the Protocol; and

(b) "business day" is a reference to a business day as defined in rule 6.2.

(8) Fixed costs must be calculated by reference to the amount which is awarded.

(9) Where the court makes an order for costs in favour of the defendant—

(a) the court must have regard to; and

(b) the amount of costs ordered shall not exceed,

the fixed costs in Table 6B, 6C or 6D in Section IIIA of Part 45 applicable at the date of judgment, less the fixed costs to which the claimant is entitled under paragraph (2) or (3).

(10) The parties are entitled to disbursements allowed in accordance with rule 45.29I incurred in any period for which costs are payable to them.

[CPR 36.22]

36.22 Deduction of benefits and lump sum payments

(1) In this rule and rule 36.11—

(a) "the 1997 Act" means the Social Security (Recovery of Benefits) Act 1997;

(b) "the 2008 Regulations" means the Social Security (Recovery of Benefits)(Lump Sum Payments) Regulations 2008;

(c) "recoverable amount" means—

(i) "recoverable benefits" as defined in section 1(4)(c) of the 1997 Act; and

(ii) "recoverable lump sum payments" as defined in regulation 1 of the 2008 Regulations;

(d) "deductible amount" means—

(i) any benefits by the amount of which damages are to be reduced in accordance with section 8 of, and Schedule 2 to the 1997 Act ("deductible benefits"); and

(ii) any lump sum payment by the amount of which damages are to be reduced in accordance with regulation 12 of the 2008 Regulations ("deductible lump sum payments"); and

(e) "certificate"—

(i) in relation to recoverable benefits, is construed in accordance with the provisions of the 1997 Act; and

(ii) in relation to recoverable lump sum payments, has the meaning given in section 29 of the 1997 Act, as applied by regulation 2 of, and modified by Schedule 1 to, the 2008 Regulations.

(2) This rule applies where a payment to a claimant following acceptance of a Part 36 offer would be a compensation payment as defined in section 1(4)(b) or 1A(5)(b) of the 1997 Act.

(3) A defendant who makes a Part 36 offer must, where relevant, state either—

(a) that the offer is made without regard to any liability for recoverable amounts; or

(b) that it is intended to include any deductible amounts.

(4) Where paragraph (3)(b) applies, paragraphs (5) to (9) will apply to the Part 36 offer.

(5) Before making the Part 36 offer, the offeror must apply for a certificate.

(6) Subject to paragraph (7), the Part 36 offer must state—

(a) the gross amount of compensation;
(b) the name and amount of any deductible amounts by which the gross amount is reduced; and
(c) the net amount of compensation.

(7) If at the time the offeror makes the Part 36 offer, the offeror has applied for, but has not received, a certificate, the offeror must clarify the offer by stating the matters referred to in paragraph (6)(b) and (c) not more than 7 days after receipt of the certificate.

(8) For the purposes of rule 36.17(1)(a), a claimant fails to recover more than any sum offered (including a lump sum offered under rule 36.6) if the claimant fails upon judgment being entered to recover a sum, once deductible amounts identified in the judgment have been deducted, greater than the net amount stated under paragraph (6)(c).

(Section 15(2) of the 1997 Act provides that the court must specify the compensation payment attributable to each head of damage. Schedule 1 to the 2008 Regulations modifies section 15 of the 1997 Act in relation to lump sum payments and provides that the court must specify the compensation payment attributable to each or any dependant who has received a lump sum payment.)

(9) Where—
(a) further deductible amounts have accrued since the Part 36 offer was made; and
(b) the court gives permission to accept the Part 36 offer,

the court may direct that the amount of the offer payable to the offeree shall be reduced by a sum equivalent to the deductible amounts paid to the claimant since the date of the offer.

(Rule 36.11(3)(b) states that permission is required to accept an offer where the relevant period has expired and further deductible amounts have been paid to the claimant.)

Miscellaneous

[CPR 36.23]

36.23 Cases in which the offeror's costs have been limited to court fees

(1) This rule applies in any case where the offeror is treated as having filed a costs budget limited to applicable court fees, or is otherwise limited in their recovery of costs to such fees.

(Rule 3.14 provides that a litigant may be treated as having filed a budget limited to court fees for failure to file a budget.)

(2) "Costs" in rules 36.13(5)(b), 36.17(3)(a) and 36.17(4)(b) shall mean—
(a) in respect of those costs subject to any such limitation, 50% of the costs assessed without reference to the limitation; together with
(b) any other recoverable costs.

SECTION II RTA PROTOCOL AND EL/PL PROTOCOL OFFERS TO SETTLE

[CPR 36.24]

36.24 Scope of this Section

(1) Where this Section applies, Section I does not apply.

(2) This Section applies to an offer to settle where the parties have followed the RTA Protocol or the EL/PL Protocol and started proceedings under Part 8 in accordance with Practice Direction 8B ("the Stage 3 Procedure").

(3) A reference to the Court Proceedings Pack Form is a reference to the form used in the relevant Protocol.

(4) Nothing in this Section prevents a party making an offer to settle in whatever way that party chooses, but if the offer is not made in accordance with this Section, it will not have any costs consequences.

[CPR 36.25]

36.25 **Form and content of a Protocol offer**

(1) An offer to settle which is made in accordance with this rule is called a Protocol offer.

(2) A Protocol offer must—

(a) be set out in the Court Proceedings Pack (Part B) Form; and

(b) contain the final total amount of the offers from both parties.

[CPR 36.26]

36.26 **Time when a Protocol offer is made**

(1) The Protocol offer is deemed to be made on the first business day after the Court Proceedings Pack (Part A and Part B) Form is sent to the defendant.

(2) In this Section "business day" has the same meaning as in rule 6.2.

[CPR 36.27]

36.27 **General provisions**

A Protocol offer—

(a) is treated as exclusive of all interest; and

(b) has the consequences set out in this Section only in relation to the fixed costs of the Stage 3 Procedure as provided for in rule 45.18, and not in relation to the costs of any appeal from the final decision of those proceedings.

[CPR 36.28]

36.28 **Restrictions on the disclosure of a Protocol offer**

(1) The amount of the Protocol offer must not be communicated to the court until the claim is determined.

(2) Any other offer to settle must not be communicated to the court at all.

[CPR 36.29]

36.29 **Costs consequences following judgment**

(1) This rule applies where, on any determination by the court, the claimant obtains judgment against the defendant for an amount of damages that is—

(a) less than or equal to the amount of the defendant's Protocol offer;

(b) more than the defendant's Protocol offer but less than the claimant's Protocol offer; or

(c) equal to or more than the claimant's Protocol offer.

(2) Where paragraph (1)(a) applies, the court must order the claimant to pay—

(a) the fixed costs in rule 45.26; and

(b) interest on those fixed costs from the first business day after the deemed date of the Protocol offer under rule 36.26.

(3) Where paragraph (1)(b) applies, the court must order the defendant to pay the fixed costs in rule 45.20.

(4) Where paragraph (1)(c) applies, the court must order the defendant to pay—
  (a) interest on the whole of the damages awarded at a rate not exceeding 10% above base rate for some or all of the period starting with the date specified in rule 36.26;
  (b) the fixed costs in rule 45.20;
  (c) interest on those fixed costs at a rate not exceeding 10% above base rate; and
  (d) an additional amount calculated in accordance with rule 36.17(4)(d).

[CPR 36.30]

36.30 **Deduction of benefits**

For the purposes of rule 36.29(1)(a) the amount of the judgment is less than the Protocol offer where the judgment is less than that offer once deductible amounts identified in the judgment are deducted.

("Deductible amount" is defined in rule 36.22(1)(d).)

PRACTICE DIRECTION 36A—OFFERS TO SETTLE

THIS PRACTICE DIRECTION SUPPLEMENTS CPR PART 36

Formalities of Part 36 offers and other notices under this Part

[CPR PD 36A.1]

1.1 A Part 36 offer may be made and accepted using Form N242A.

1.2 Where a Part 36 offer, notice of acceptance or notice of withdrawal or change of terms is to be served on a party who is legally represented, the document to be served must be served on the legal representative.

Application for permission to withdraw or change the terms of a Part 36 offer

[CPR PD 36A.2]

2.1 Rule 36.10 makes provision as to the circumstances in which the offeror must seek the permission of the court in order to withdraw a Part 36 offer or change its terms to be less advantageous to the offeree before expiry of the relevant period.

2.2 The permission of the court must, unless the parties agree otherwise, be sought—

(1) by making an application under Part 23, which must be dealt with by a judge other than the trial judge;

(2) at a trial or other hearing, provided that it is not to the trial judge.

(Rule 36.3 defines "the trial judge".)

Acceptance of a Part 36 offer

[CPR PD 36A.3]

3.1 Where a Part 36 offer is accepted in accordance with rule 36.11(1), the notice of acceptance must be served on the offeror and filed with the court where the case is proceeding.

3.2 Where the court's permission is required to accept a Part 36 offer, the permission of the court must, unless the parties agree otherwise, be sought—

(1) by making an application under Part 23, which must be dealt with by a judge other than the trial judge;

(2) at a trial or other hearing, provided that it is not to the trial judge.

(Rule 36.3 defines "the trial judge".)

3.3 Where rule 36.11(3)(b) applies, the application for permission to accept the offer must—

(1) state—

(a) the net amount offered in the Part 36 offer;

(b) the deductible amounts that had accrued at the date the offer was made;

(c) the deductible amounts that have subsequently accrued; and

(2) be accompanied by a copy of the current certificate.

PART 44 GENERAL RULES ABOUT COSTS

SECTION I GENERAL

[CPR 44.1]

44.1 Interpretation and application

(1) In Parts 44 to 47, unless the context otherwise requires—

"authorised court officer" means any officer of—

(i) the County Court;
(ii) a district registry;
(iii) the Family Court;
(iiia) the High Court; or
(iv) the Costs Office,

whom the Lord Chancellor has authorised to assess costs;

"conditional fee agreement" means an agreement enforceable under section 58 of the Courts and Legal Services Act 1990;

"costs" includes fees, charges, disbursements, expenses, remuneration, reimbursement allowed to a litigant in person under rule 46.5 and any fee or reward charged by a lay representative for acting on behalf of a party in proceedings allocated to the small claims track;

"costs judge" means a taxing master of the Senior Courts;

"Costs Office" means the Senior Courts Costs Office;

"costs officer" means—

(i) a costs judge;
(ii) a District Judge; or

(iii) an authorised court officer;

"detailed assessment" means the procedure by which the amount of costs is decided by a costs officer in accordance with Part 47;

"the Director (legal aid)" means the person designated as the Director of Legal Aid Casework pursuant to section 4 of the Legal Aid, Sentencing and Punishment of Offenders Act 2012, or a person entitled to exercise the functions of the Director;

"fixed costs" means costs the amounts of which are fixed by these rules whether or not the court has a discretion to allow some other or no amount, and include—

(i) the amounts which are to be allowed in respect of legal representatives' charges in the circumstances set out in Section I of Part 45;

(ii) fixed recoverable costs calculated in accordance with rule 45.11;

(iii) the additional costs allowed by rule 45.18;

(iv) fixed costs determined under rule 45.21;

(v) costs fixed by rules 45.37 and 45.38;

"free of charge" has the same meaning as in section 194(10) of the 2007 Act;

"fund" includes any estate or property held for the benefit of any person or class of person and any fund to which a trustee or personal representative is entitled in that capacity;

"HMRC" means HM Revenue and Customs;

"legal aid" means civil legal services made available under arrangements made for the purposes of Part 1of the Legal Aid, Sentencing and Punishment of Offenders Act 2012;

"paying party" means a party liable to pay costs;

"the prescribed charity" has the same meaning as in section 194(8) of the 2007 Act;

"pro bono representation" means legal representation provided free of charge;

"receiving party" means a party entitled to be paid costs;

"summary assessment" means the procedure whereby costs are assessed by the judge who has heard the case or application;

"VAT" means Value Added Tax;

"the 2007 Act" means the Legal Services Act 2007.

("Legal representative" has the meaning given in rule 2.3).

(2) The costs to which Parts 44 to 47 apply include—

(a) the following costs where those costs may be assessed by the court—

(i) costs of proceedings before an arbitrator or umpire;

(ii) costs of proceedings before a tribunal or other statutory body; and

(iii) costs payable by a client to their legal representative; and

(b) costs which are payable by one party to another party under the terms of a contract, where the court makes an order for an assessment of those costs.

(3) Where advocacy or litigation services are provided to a client under a conditional fee agreement, costs are recoverable under Parts 44 to 47 notwithstanding that the client is liable to pay the legal representative's fees and expenses only to the extent that sums are recovered in respect of the proceedings, whether by way of costs or otherwise.

[CPR 44.2]

44.2 **Court's discretion as to costs**

(1) The court has discretion as to—
- (a) whether costs are payable by one party to another;
- (b) the amount of those costs; and
- (c) when they are to be paid.

(2) If the court decides to make an order about costs—
- (a) the general rule is that the unsuccessful party will be ordered to pay the costs of the successful party; but
- (b) the court may make a different order.

(3) The general rule does not apply to the following proceedings—
- (a) proceedings in the Court of Appeal on an application or appeal made in connection with proceedings in the Family Division; or
- (b) proceedings in the Court of Appeal from a judgment, direction, decision or order given or made in probate proceedings or family proceedings.

(4) In deciding what order (if any) to make about costs, the court will have regard to all the circumstances, including—
- (a) the conduct of all the parties;
- (b) whether a party has succeeded on part of its case, even if that party has not been wholly successful; and
- (c) any admissible offer to settle made by a party which is drawn to the court's attention, and which is not an offer to which costs consequences under Part 36 apply.

(5) The conduct of the parties includes—
- (a) conduct before, as well as during, the proceedings and in particular the extent to which the parties followed the Practice Direction – Pre-Action Conduct or any relevant pre-action protocol;
- (b) whether it was reasonable for a party to raise, pursue or contest a particular allegation or issue;
- (c) the manner in which a party has pursued or defended its case or a particular allegation or issue; and
- (d) whether a claimant who has succeeded in the claim, in whole or in part, exaggerated its claim.

(6) The orders which the court may make under this rule include an order that a party must pay—
- (a) a proportion of another party's costs;
- (b) a stated amount in respect of another party's costs;
- (c) costs from or until a certain date only;
- (d) costs incurred before proceedings have begun;
- (e) costs relating to particular steps taken in the proceedings;
- (f) costs relating only to a distinct part of the proceedings; and
- (g) interest on costs from or until a certain date, including a date before judgment.

(7) Before the court considers making an order under paragraph (6)(f), it will consider whether it is practicable to make an order under paragraph (6)(a) or (c) instead.

(8) Where the court orders a party to pay costs subject to detailed assessment, it will order that party to pay a reasonable sum on account of costs, unless there is good reason not to do so.

[CPR 44.3]

44.3 **Basis of assessment**

(1) Where the court is to assess the amount of costs (whether by summary or detailed assessment) it will assess those costs—

(a) on the standard basis; or

(b) on the indemnity basis,

but the court will not in either case allow costs which have been unreasonably incurred or are unreasonable in amount.

(Rule 44.5 sets out how the court decides the amount of costs payable under a contract.)

(2) Where the amount of costs is to be assessed on the standard basis, the court will—

(a) only allow costs which are proportionate to the matters in issue. Costs which are disproportionate in amount may be disallowed or reduced even if they were reasonably or necessarily incurred; and

(b) resolve any doubt which it may have as to whether costs were reasonably and proportionately incurred or were reasonable and proportionate in amount in favour of the paying party.

(Factors which the court may take into account are set out in rule 44.4.)

(3) Where the amount of costs is to be assessed on the indemnity basis, the court will resolve any doubt which it may have as to whether costs were reasonably incurred or were reasonable in amount in favour of the receiving party.

(4) Where—

(a) the court makes an order about costs without indicating the basis on which the costs are to be assessed; or

(b) the court makes an order for costs to be assessed on a basis other than the standard basis or the indemnity basis,

the costs will be assessed on the standard basis.

(5) Costs incurred are proportionate if they bear a reasonable relationship to—

(a) the sums in issue in the proceedings;

(b) the value of any non-monetary relief in issue in the proceedings;

(c) the complexity of the litigation;

(d) any additional work generated by the conduct of the paying party; and

(e) any wider factors involved in the proceedings, such as reputation or public importance.

(6) Where the amount of a solicitor's remuneration in respect of non-contentious business is regulated by any general orders made under the Solicitors Act 1974, the amount of the costs to be allowed in respect of any such business which falls to be assessed by the court will be decided in accordance with those general orders rather than this rule and rule 44.4.

(7) Paragraphs (2)(a) and (5) do not apply in relation to—

(a) to cases commenced before 1st April 2013; or

(a) costs incurred in respect of work done before 1st April 2013,

and in relation to such cases or costs, rule 44.4(2)(a) as it was in force immediately before 1st April 2013 will apply instead.

[CPR 44.4]

44.4 **Factors to be taken into account in deciding the amount of costs**

(1) The court will have regard to all the circumstances in deciding whether costs were—

(a) if it is assessing costs on the standard basis—

(i) proportionately and reasonably incurred; or
(ii) proportionate and reasonable in amount, or
(b) if it is assessing costs on the indemnity basis—
(i) unreasonably incurred; or
(ii) unreasonable in amount.

(2) In particular, the court will give effect to any orders which have already been made.

(3) The court will also have regard to—
(a) the conduct of all the parties, including in particular—
(i) conduct before, as well as during, the proceedings; and
(ii) the efforts made, if any, before and during the proceedings in order to try to resolve the dispute;
(b) the amount or value of any money or property involved;
(c) the importance of the matter to all the parties;
(d) the particular complexity of the matter or the difficulty or novelty of the questions raised;
(e) the skill, effort, specialised knowledge and responsibility involved;
(f) the time spent on the case;
(g) the place where and the circumstances in which work or any part of it was done; and
(h) the receiving party's last approved or agreed budget.

(Rule 35.4(4) gives the court power to limit the amount that a party may recover with regard to the fees and expenses of an expert.)

[CPR 44.5]

44.5 **Amount of costs where costs are payable under a contract**

(1) Subject to paragraphs (2) and (3), where the court assesses (whether by summary or detailed assessment) costs which are payable by the paying party to the receiving party under the terms of a contract, the costs payable under those terms are, unless the contract expressly provides otherwise, to be presumed to be costs which—
(a) have been reasonably incurred; and
(b) are reasonable in amount,
and the court will assess them accordingly.

(2) The presumptions in paragraph (1) are rebuttable. Practice Direction 44 – General rules about costs sets out circumstances where the court may order otherwise.

(3) Paragraph (1) does not apply where the contract is between a solicitor and client.

[CPR 44.6]

44.6 **Procedure for assessing costs**

(1) Where the court orders a party to pay costs to another party (other than fixed costs) it may either—
(a) make a summary assessment of the costs; or
(b) order detailed assessment of the costs by a costs officer,
unless any rule, practice direction or other enactment provides otherwise.

(Practice Direction 44 – General rules about costs sets out the factors which will affect the court's decision under paragraph (1).)

(2) A party may recover the fixed costs specified in Part 45 in accordance with that Part.

[CPR 44.7]

44.7 Time for complying with an order for costs

(1) A party must comply with an order for the payment of costs within 14 days of—

(a) the date of the judgment or order if it states the amount of those costs;

(b) if the amount of those costs (or part of them) is decided later in accordance with Part 47, the date of the certificate which states the amount; or

(c) in either case, such other date as the court may specify.

(Part 47 sets out the procedure for detailed assessment of costs.)

[CPR 44.8]

44.8 Legal representative's duty to notify the party

Where—

(a) the court makes a costs order against a legally represented party; and

(b) the party is not present when the order is made,

the party's legal representative must notify that party in writing of the costs order no later than 7 days after the legal representative receives notice of the order.

(Paragraph 10.1 of Practice Direction 44 defines "party" for the purposes of this rule.)

[CPR 44.9]

44.9 Cases where costs orders deemed to have been made

(1) Subject to paragraph (2), where a right to costs arises under—

(a) rule 3.7 or 3.7A1 (defendant's right to costs where claim is struck out for non-payment of fees);

(a1) rule 3.7B (sanctions for dishonouring cheque);

(b) rule 36.13(1) or (2) (claimant's entitlement to costs where a Part 36 offer is accepted); or

(c) rule 38.6 (defendant's right to costs where claimant discontinues),

a costs order will be deemed to have been made on the standard basis.

(2) Paragraph 1(b) does not apply where a Part 36 offer is accepted before the commencement of proceedings.

(3) Where such an order is deemed to be made in favour of a party with *pro bono* representation, that party may apply for an order under section 194(3) of the 2007 Act.

(4) Interest payable under section 17 of the Judgments Act 1838 or section 74 of the County Courts Act 1984 on the costs deemed to have been ordered under paragraph (1) will begin to run from the date on which the event which gave rise to the entitlement to costs occurred.

[CPR 44.10]

44.10 Where the court makes no order for costs

(1) Where the court makes an order which does not mention costs—

(a) subject to paragraphs (2) and (3), the general rule is that no party is entitled—

(i) to costs; or

(ii) to seek an order under section 194(3) of the 2007 Act,

in relation to that order; but

(b) this does not affect any entitlement of a party to recover costs out of a fund held by that party as trustee or personal representative, or under any lease, mortgage or other security.

(2) Where the court makes—

(a) an order granting permission to appeal;

(b) an order granting permission to apply for judicial review; or

(c) any other order or direction sought by a party on an application without notice,

and its order does not mention costs, it will be deemed to include an order for applicant's costs in the case.

(3) Any party affected by a deemed order for costs under paragraph (2) may apply at any time to vary the order.

(4) The court hearing an appeal may, unless it dismisses the appeal, make orders about the costs of the proceedings giving rise to the appeal as well as the costs of the appeal.

(5) Subject to any order made by the transferring court, where proceedings are transferred from one court to another, the court to which they are transferred may deal with all the costs, including the costs before the transfer.

[CPR 44.11]

44.11 **Court's powers in relation to misconduct**

(1) The court may make an order under this rule where—

(a) a party or that party's legal representative, in connection with a summary or detailed assessment, fails to comply with a rule, practice direction or court order; or

(b) it appears to the court that the conduct of a party or that party's legal representative, before or during the proceedings or in the assessment proceedings, was unreasonable or improper.

(2) Where paragraph (1) applies, the court may—

(a) disallow all or part of the costs which are being assessed; or

(b) order the party at fault or that party's legal representative to pay costs which that party or legal representative has caused any other party to incur.

(3) Where—

(a) the court makes an order under paragraph (2) against a legally represented party; and

(b) the party is not present when the order is made,

the party's legal representative must notify that party in writing of the order no later than 7 days after the legal representative receives notice of the order.

[CPR 44.12]

44.12 **Set Off**

(1) Where a party entitled to costs is also liable to pay costs, the court may assess the costs which that party is liable to pay and either—

(a) set off the amount assessed against the amount the party is entitled to be paid and direct that party to pay any balance; or

(b) delay the issue of a certificate for the costs to which the party is entitled until the party has paid the amount which that party is liable to pay.

SECTION II QUALIFIED ONE-WAY COSTS SHIFTING

[CPR 44.13]

44.13 Qualified one-way costs shifting: scope and interpretation

(1) This Section applies to proceedings which include a claim for damages—

(a) for personal injuries;

(b) under the Fatal Accidents Act 1976; or

(c) which arises out of death or personal injury and survives for the benefit of an estate by virtue of section 1(1) of the Law Reform (Miscellaneous Provisions) Act 1934,

but does not apply to applications pursuant to section 33 of the Senior Courts Act 1981 or section 52 of the County Courts Act 1984 (applications for pre-action disclosure), or where rule 44.17 applies.

(2) In this Section, "claimant" means a person bringing a claim to which this Section applies or an estate on behalf of which such a claim is brought, and includes a person making a counterclaim or an additional claim.

[CPR 44.14]

44.14 Effect of qualified one-way costs shifting

(1) Subject to rules 44.15 and 44.16, orders for costs made against a claimant may be enforced without the permission of the court but only to the extent that the aggregate amount in money terms of such orders does not exceed the aggregate amount in money terms of any orders for damages and interest made in favour of the claimant.

(2) Orders for costs made against a claimant may only be enforced after the proceedings have been concluded and the costs have been assessed or agreed.

(3) An order for costs which is enforced only to the extent permitted by paragraph (1) shall not be treated as an unsatisfied or outstanding judgment for the purposes of any court record.

[CPR 44.15]

44.15 Exceptions to qualified one-way costs shifting where permission not required

Orders for costs made against the claimant may be enforced to the full extent of such orders without the permission of the court where the proceedings have been struck out on the grounds that—

(a) the claimant has disclosed no reasonable grounds for bringing the proceedings;

(b) the proceedings are an abuse of the court's process; or

(c) the conduct of—

(i) the claimant; or

(ii) a person acting on the claimant's behalf and with the claimant's knowledge of such conduct,

is likely to obstruct the just disposal of the proceedings.

[CPR 44.16]

44.16 Exceptions to qualified one-way costs shifting where permission required

(1) Orders for costs made against the claimant may be enforced to the full extent of such orders with the permission of the court where the claim is found on the balance of probabilities to be fundamentally dishonest.

(2) Orders for costs made against the claimant may be enforced up to the full extent of such orders with the permission of the court, and to the extent that it considers just, where—

- (a) the proceedings include a claim which is made for the financial benefit of a person other than the claimant or a dependant within the meaning of section 1(3) of the Fatal Accidents Act 1976 (other than a claim in respect of the gratuitous provision of care, earnings paid by an employer or medical expenses); or
- (b) a claim is made for the benefit of the claimant other than a claim to which this Section applies.

(3) Where paragraph (2)(a) applies, the court may, subject to rule 46.2, make an order for costs against a person, other than the claimant, for whose financial benefit the whole or part of the claim was made.

[CPR 44.17]

44.17 **Transitional provision**

This Section does not apply to proceedings where the claimant has entered into a pre-commencement funding arrangement (as defined in rule 48.2).

SECTION III DAMAGES-BASED AGREEMENTS

[CPR 44.18]

44.18 **Award of costs where there is a damages-based agreement**

(1) The fact that a party has entered into a damages-based agreement will not affect the making of any order for costs which otherwise would be made in favour of that party.

(2) Where costs are to be assessed in favour of a party who has entered into a damages-based agreement—

- (a) the party's recoverable costs will be assessed in accordance with rule 44.3; and
- (b) the party may not recover by way of costs more than the total amount payable by that party under the damages-based agreement for legal services provided under that agreement.

PRACTICE DIRECTION 44—GENERAL RULES ABOUT COSTS

THIS PRACTICE DIRECTION SUPPLEMENTS PART 44 OF THE CIVIL PROCEDURE RULES

Section I — General

Subsection 1 of this Practice Direction

Documents and forms

[CPR PD 44.1]

1.1 In respect of any document which is required by Practice Directions 44 to 47 to be signed by a party or that party's legal representative, the provisions of Practice Direction 22 relating to who may sign apply as if the document in question was a statement of truth. Statements of truth are not required in assessment proceedings unless a rule or Practice Direction so requires or the court so orders.

(Practice Direction 22 makes provision for cases in which a party is a child, a protected party or a company or other corporation and cases in which a document is signed on behalf of a partnership.)

1.2 Form N260 is a model form of Statement of Costs to be used for summary assessments.

(Further details about Statements of Costs are given in paragraph 9.5 below.)

Precedents A, B and C in the Schedule of Costs Precedents annexed to this Practice Direction are model forms of bills of costs to be used for detailed assessments. A party wishing to rely upon a bill which departs from the model forms should include in the background information of the bill an explanation for that departure.

(Further details about bills of costs are given in Practice Direction 47.)

Subsection 2 of this Practice Direction — Special provisions relating to VAT

Scope of this subsection

[CPR PD 44.2]

2.1 This subsection deals with claims for VAT) which are made in respect of costs being dealt with by way of summary assessment or detailed assessment.

VAT Registration Number

2.2 The number allocated by HMRC to every person registered under the Value Added Tax Act 1994 (except a Government Department) must appear in a prominent place at the head of every statement, bill of costs, fee sheet, account or voucher on which VAT is being included as part of a claim for costs.

Entitlement to VAT on Costs

2.3 VAT should not be included in a claim for costs if the receiving party is able to recover the VAT as input tax. Where the receiving party is able to obtain credit from HMRC for a proportion of the VAT as input tax, only that proportion which is not eligible for credit should be included in the claim for costs.

2.4 The receiving party has responsibility for ensuring that VAT is claimed only when the receiving party is unable to recover the VAT or a proportion thereof as input tax.

2.5 Where there is a dispute as to whether VAT is properly claimed the receiving party must provide a certificate signed by the legal representatives or the auditors of the receiving party substantially in the form illustrated in Precedent F in the Schedule of Costs Precedents annexed to Practice Direction 47. Where the receiving party is a litigant in person who is claiming VAT, evidence to support the claim (such as a letter from HMRC) must be produced at the hearing at which the costs are assessed.

2.6 Where there is a dispute as to whether any service in respect of which a charge is proposed to be made in the bill is zero rated or exempt from VAT, reference should be made to HMRC and its view obtained and made known at the hearing at which the costs are assessed. Such enquiry should be made by the receiving party. In the case of a bill from a solicitor to the solicitor's legal representative's own client, such enquiry should be made by the client.

Form of bill of costs where VAT rate changes

2.7 Where there is a change in the rate of VAT, suppliers of goods and services are entitled by sections 88 (1) and 88(2) of the Value Added Tax Act 1994 in most circumstances to elect whether the new or the old rate of VAT should apply to a supply where the basic and actual tax points span a period during which the rate changed.

2.8 It will be assumed, unless a contrary indication is given in writing, that an election to take advantage of the provisions mentioned in paragraph 2.7 and to charge VAT at the lower rate has been made. In any case in which an election to charge at the lower rate is not made, such a decision must be justified to the court assessing the costs.

Apportionment

2.9 Subject to 2.7 and 2.8, all bills of costs, fees and disbursements on which VAT is included must be divided into separate parts so as to show work done before, on and after the date or dates from which any change in the rate of VAT takes effect. Where, however, a lump sum charge is made for work which spans a period during which there has been a change in VAT rates, and paragraphs 2.7 and 2.8 above do not apply, reference should be made to paragraphs 30.7 or 30.8 of the VAT Guide (Notice 700) (or any revised edition of that notice) published by HMRC. If necessary, the lump sum should be apportioned. The totals of profit costs and disbursements in each part must be carried separately to the summary.

Change in VAT rate between the conclusion of a detailed settlement and the issue of a final certificate

2.10 Should there be a change in the rate between the conclusion of a detailed assessment and the issue of the final costs certificate, any interested party may apply for the detailed assessment to be varied so as to take account of any increase or reduction in the amount of tax payable. Once the final costs certificate has been issued, no variation under this paragraph will be permitted.

Disbursements not classified as such for VAT purposes

2.11

(1) Legal representatives often make payments to third parties for the supply of goods or services where no VAT was chargeable on the supply by the third party: for example, the cost of meals taken and travel costs. The question whether legal representatives should include VAT in respect of these payments when invoicing their clients or in claims for costs between litigants should be decided in accordance with this Practice Direction and with the criteria set out in the VAT Guide (Notice 700).

(2) Payments to third parties which are normally treated as part of the legal representative's overheads (for example, postage costs and telephone costs) will not be treated as disbursements. The third party supply should be included as part of the costs of the legal representatives' legal services and VAT must be added to the total bill charged to the client.

(3) Disputes may arise in respect of payments made to a third party which the legal representative shows as disbursements in the invoice delivered to the receiving party. Some payments, although correctly described as disbursements for some purposes, are not classified as disbursements for VAT purposes. Items not classified as disbursements for VAT purposes must be shown as part of the services provided by the legal representative and, therefore, VAT must be added in respect of them whether or not VAT was chargeable on the supply by the third party.

(4) Guidance as to the circumstances in which disbursements may or may not be classified as disbursements for VAT purposes is given in the VAT Guide (Notice 700, paragraph 25.1). One of the key issues is whether the third party supply—

- (a) was made to the legal representative (and therefore subsumed in the onward supply of legal services); or
- (b) was made direct to the receiving party (the third party having no right to demand payment from the legal representative, who makes the payment only as agent for the receiving party).

(5) Examples of payments under subparagraph (4)(a) are: travelling expenses, such as an airline ticket, and subsistence expenses, such as the cost of meals, where the person travelling and receiving the meals is the legal representative. The supplies by the airline and the restaurant are supplies to the legal representative, not to the client.

(6) Payments under subparagraph (4)(b) are classified as disbursements for VAT purposes and, therefore, the legal representative need not add VAT in respect of them. Simple examples are payments by a legal representative of court fees and payment of fees to an expert witness.

Litigants in person

2.12 Where a litigant acts in person, that litigant is not treated for the purposes of VAT as having supplied services and therefore no VAT is chargeable in respect of work done by that litigant (even where, for example, that litigant is a solicitor or other legal representative). Consequently in such circumstances a bill of costs should not claim any VAT.

Government Departments

2.13 On an assessment between parties, where costs are being paid to a Government Department in respect of services rendered by its legal staff, VAT should not be added.

Payment pursuant to an order under section 194(3) of the 2007 Act

2.14 Where an order is made under section 194(3) of the 2007 Act, any bill presented for agreement or assessment pursuant to that order must not include a claim for VAT.

Subsection 3 of this Practice Direction – Costs budgets

Costs budgets

[CPR PD 44.3]

3.1 In any case where the parties have filed budgets in accordance with Practice Direction 3E but the court has not made a costs management order under rule 3.15, the provisions of this subsection shall apply.

3.2 If there is a difference of 20% or more between the costs claimed by a receiving party on detailed assessment and the costs shown in a budget filed by that party, the receiving party must provide a statement of the reasons for the difference with the bill of costs.

3.3 If a paying party—

(a) claims to have reasonably relied on a budget filed by a receiving party; or

(b) wishes to rely upon the costs shown in the budget in order to dispute the reasonableness or proportionality of the costs claimed,

the paying party must serve a statement setting out the case in this regard in that party's points of dispute.

3.4 On an assessment of the costs of a party, the court will have regard to the last approved or agreed budget, and may have regard to any other budget previously filed by that party, or by any other party in the same proceedings. Such other budgets may be taken into account when assessing the reasonableness and proportionality of any costs claimed.

3.5 Subject to paragraph 3.4, paragraphs 3.6 and 3.7 apply where there is a difference of 20% or more between the costs claimed by a receiving party and the costs shown in a budget filed by that party.

3.6 Where it appears to the court that the paying party reasonably relied on the budget, the court may restrict the recoverable costs to such sum as is reasonable for the paying party to pay in the light of that reliance, notwithstanding that such sum is less than the amount of costs reasonably and proportionately incurred by the receiving party.

3.7 Where it appears to the court that the receiving party has not provided a satisfactory explanation for that difference, the court may regard the difference between the costs claimed and the costs shown in the budget as evidence that the costs claimed are unreasonable or disproportionate.

Subsection 4 of this Practice Direction — Court's discretion as to costs: Rule 44.2

Court's discretion as to costs: rule 44.2

[CPR PD 44.4]

4.1 The court may make an order about costs at any stage in a case.

4.2 There are certain costs orders which the court will commonly make in proceedings before trial. The following table sets out the general effect of these orders. The table is not an exhaustive list of the orders which the court may make.

Term	Effect
Costs Costs in any event	The party in whose favour the order is made is entitled to that party's costs in respect of the part of the proceedings to which the order relates, whatever other costs orders are made in the proceedings.
Costs in the case Costs in the application	The party in whose favour the court makes an order for costs at the end of the proceedings is entitled to that party's costs of the part of the proceedings to which the order relates.
Costs reserved	The decision about costs is deferred to a later occasion, but if no later order is made the costs will be costs in the case.
Claimant's/ Defendant's costs in case/application	If the party in whose favour the costs order is made is awarded costs at the end the proceedings, that party is entitled to that party's costs of the part of the proceedings to which the order relates. If any other party is awarded costs at the end of the proceedings, the party in whose favour the final costs order is made is not liable to pay the costs of any other party in respect of the part of the proceedings to which the order relates.
Costs thrown away	Where, for example, a judgment or order is set aside, the party in whose favour the costs order is made is entitled to the costs which have been incurred as a consequence. This includes the costs of – preparing for and attending any hearing at which the judgment or order which has been set aside was made; preparing for and attending any hearing to set aside the judgment or order in question; preparing for and attending any hearing at which the court orders the proceedings or the part in question to be adjourned; any steps taken to enforce a judgment or order which has subsequently been set aside.
Costs of and caused by	Where, for example, the court makes this order on an application to amend a statement of case, the party in whose favour the costs order is made is entitled to the costs of preparing for and attending the application and the costs of any consequential amendment to his own statement of case.

Term	Effect
Costs here and below	The party in whose favour the costs order is made is entitled not only to that party's costs in respect of the proceedings in which the court makes the order but also to that party's costs of the proceedings in any lower court. In the case of an appeal from a Divisional Court the party is not entitled to any costs incurred in any court below the Divisional Court.
No order as to costs Each party to pay own costs	Each party is to bear that party's own costs of the part of the proceedings to which the order relates whatever costs order the court makes at the end of the proceedings.

Subsection 5 of this Practice Direction — Fees of Counsel

Fees of Counsel

[CPR PD 44.5]

5.1

(1) When making an order for costs the court may state an opinion as to whether or not the hearing was fit for the attendance of one or more counsel, and, if it does so, the court conducting a detailed assessment of those costs will have regard to the opinion stated.

(2) The court will generally express an opinion only where—

(a) the paying party asks it to do so;

(b) more than one counsel appeared for a party; or

(c) the court wishes to record its opinion that the case was not fit for the attendance of counsel.

5.2

(1) Where the court refers any matter to the conveyancing counsel of the court the fees payable to counsel in respect of the work done or to be done will be assessed by the court in accordance with rule 44.2.

(2) An appeal from a decision of the court in respect of the fees of such counsel will be dealt with under the general rules as to appeals set out in Part 52. If the appeal is against the decision of an authorised court officer, it will be dealt with in accordance with rules 47.22 to 47.24.

Subsection 6 of this Practice Direction – Basis of assessment: Rule 44.3

Costs on the indemnity basis

[CPR PD 44.6]

6.1 If costs are awarded on the indemnity basis, the court assessing costs will disallow any costs—

(a) which it finds to have been unreasonably incurred; or

(b) which it considers to be unreasonable in amount.

Costs on the standard basis

6.2 If costs are awarded on the standard basis, the court assessing costs will disallow any costs—

(a) which it finds to have been unreasonably incurred;

(b) which it considers to be unreasonable in amount;

(c) which it considers to have been disproportionately incurred or to be disproportionate in amount; or

(d) about which it has doubts as to whether they were reasonably or proportionately incurred, or whether they are reasonable and proportionate in amount.

Subsection 7 of this Practice Direction — Amount of costs where costs are payable pursuant to a contract: Rule 44.5

Application of rule 44.5

[CPR PD 44.7]

7.1 Rule 44.5 only applies if the court is assessing costs payable under a contract. It does not—

(a) require the court to make an assessment of such costs; or

(b) require a mortgagee to apply for an order for those costs where there is a contractual right to recover out of the mortgage funds.

Costs relating to a mortgage

7.2

(1) The following principles apply to costs relating to a mortgage.

(2) An order for the payment of costs of proceedings by one party to another is always a discretionary order: section 51 of the Senior Courts Act 1981 ("the section 51 discretion").

(3) Where there is a contractual right to the costs, the discretion should ordinarily be exercised so as to reflect that contractual right.

(4) The power of the court to disallow a mortgagee's costs sought to be added to the mortgage security is a power that does not derive from section 51, but from the power of the courts of equity to fix the terms on which redemption will be allowed.

(5) A decision by a court to refuse costs in whole or in part to a mortgagee may be—

- (a) a decision in the exercise of the section 51 discretion;
- (b) a decision in the exercise of the power to fix the terms on which redemption will be allowed;
- (c) a decision as to the extent of a mortgagee's contractual right to add the mortgagee's costs to the security; or
- (d) a combination of two or more of these things.

(6) A mortgagee is not to be deprived of a contractual or equitable right to add costs to the security merely by reason of an order for payment of costs made without reference to the mortgagee's contractual or equitable rights, and without any adjudication as to whether or not the mortgagee should be deprived of those costs.

7.3

(1) Where the contract entitles a mortgagee to—

- (a) add the costs of litigation relating to the mortgage to the sum secured by it; or
- (b) require a mortgagor to pay those costs,

the mortgagor may make an application for the court to direct that an account of the mortgagee's costs be taken.

(Rule 25.1(1)(n) provides that the court may direct that a party file an account.)

(2) The mortgagor may then dispute an amount in the mortgagee's account on the basis that it has been unreasonably incurred or is unreasonable in amount.

(3) Where a mortgagor disputes an amount, the court may make an order that the disputed costs are assessed under rule 44.5.

Subsection 8 of this Practice Direction — Procedure for assessing costs: Rule 44.6

Procedure for assessing costs: rule 44.6

[CPR PD 44.8]

8.1 Subject to paragraph 8.3, where the court does not order fixed costs (or no fixed costs are provided for) the amount of costs payable will be assessed by the court. Rule 44.6 allows the court making an order about costs either—

(a) to make a summary assessment of the amount of the costs; or

(b) to order the amount to be decided in accordance with Part 47 (a detailed assessment).

8.2 An order for costs will be treated as an order for the amount of costs to be decided by a detailed assessment unless the order otherwise provides.

8.3 Where a party is entitled to costs some of which are fixed costs and some of which are not, the court will assess those costs which are not fixed. For example, the court will assess the disbursements payable in accordance with rules 45.12 or 45.19. The decision whether such assessment should be summary or detailed will be made in accordance with paragraphs 9.1 to 9.10 of this Practice Direction.

Subsection 9 of this Practice Direction — Summary assessment: General provisions

When the court should consider whether to make a summary assessment

[CPR PD 44.9]

9.1 Whenever a court makes an order about costs which does not provide only for fixed costs to be paid the court should consider whether to make a summary assessment of costs.

Timing of summary assessment

9.2 The general rule is that the court should make a summary assessment of the costs—

(a) at the conclusion of the trial of a case which has been dealt with on the fast track, in which case the order will deal with the costs of the whole claim; and

(b) at the conclusion of any other hearing, which has lasted not more than one day, in which case the order will deal with the costs of the application or matter to which the hearing related. If this hearing disposes of the claim, the order may deal with the costs of the whole claim,

unless there is good reason not to do so, for example where the paying party shows substantial grounds for disputing the sum claimed for costs that cannot be dealt with summarily.

Summary assessment of mortgagee's costs

9.3 The general rule in paragraph 9.2 does not apply to a mortgagee's costs incurred in mortgage possession proceedings or other proceedings relating to a mortgage unless the mortgagee asks the court to make an order for the mortgagee's costs to be paid by another party.

(Paragraphs 7.2 and 7.3 deal in more detail with costs relating to mortgages.)

Consent orders

9.4 Where an application has been made and the parties to the application agree an order by consent without any party attending, the parties should seek to agree a figure for costs to be inserted in the consent order or agree that there should be no order for costs.

Duty of parties and legal representatives

9.5

(1) It is the duty of the parties and their legal representatives to assist the judge in making a summary assessment of costs in any case to which paragraph 9.2 above applies, in accordance with the following subparagraphs.

(2) Each party who intends to claim costs must prepare a written statement of those costs showing separately in the form of a schedule—

(a) the number of hours to be claimed;
(b) the hourly rate to be claimed;
(c) the grade of fee earner;
(d) the amount and nature of any disbursement to be claimed, other than counsel's fee for appearing at the hearing;
(e) the amount of legal representative's costs to be claimed for attending or appearing at the hearing;
(f) counsel's fees; and
(g) any VAT to be claimed on these amounts.

(3) The statement of costs should follow as closely as possible Form N260 and must be signed by the party or the party's legal representative. Where a party is—
(a) an assisted person;
(b) a LSC funded client;
(c) a person for whom civil legal services (within the meaning of Part 1 of the Legal Aid, Sentencing and Punishment of Offenders Act 2012) are provided under arrangements made for the purposes of that Part of that Act; or
(d) represented by a person in the party's employment,
the statement of costs need not include the certificate appended at the end of Form N260.

(4) The statement of costs must be filed at court and copies of it must be served on any party against whom an order for payment of those costs is intended to be sought as soon as possible and in any event—
(a) for a fast track trial, not less than 2 days before the trial; and
(b) for all other hearings, not less than 24 hours before the time fixed for the hearing.

9.6 The failure by a party, without reasonable excuse, to comply with paragraph 9.5 will be taken into account by the court in deciding what order to make about the costs of the claim, hearing or application, and about the costs of any further hearing or detailed assessment hearing that may be necessary as a result of that failure.

No summary assessment by a costs officer

9.7 The court awarding costs cannot make an order for a summary assessment of costs by a costs officer. If a summary assessment of costs is appropriate but the court awarding costs is unable to do so on the day, the court may give directions as to a further hearing before the same judge.

Assisted persons etc

9.8 The court will not make a summary assessment of the costs of a receiving party who is an assisted person or LSC funded client or who is a person for whom civil legal services (within the meaning of Part 1 of the Legal Aid, Sentencing and Punishment of Offenders Act 2012) are provided under arrangements made for the purposes of that Part of that Act.

Children or protected parties

9.9

(1) The court will not make a summary assessment of the costs of a receiving party who is a child or protected party within the meaning of Part 21 unless the legal representative acting for the child or protected party has waived the right to further costs (see Practice Direction 46 paragraph 2.1).

(2) The court may make a summary assessment of costs payable by a child or protected party.

Disproportionate or unreasonable costs

9.10 The court will not give its approval to disproportionate or unreasonable costs. When the amount of the costs to be paid has been agreed between the parties the order for costs must state that the order is by consent.

Subsection 10 of this Practice Direction — Legal representative's duty to notify party: Rule 44.8

Legal representative's duty to notify party: rule 44.8

[CPR PD 44.10]

10.1 For the purposes of rule 44.8 and paragraph 10.2, "party" includes any person (for example, an insurer, a trade union or the LSC or Lord Chancellor) who has instructed the legal representative to act for the party or who is liable to pay the legal representative's fees.

10.2 A legal representative who notifies a party of an order under rule 44.8 must also explain why the order came to be made.

10.3 Although rule 44.8 does not specify any sanction for breach of the rule the court may, either in the order for costs itself or in a subsequent order, require the legal representative to produce to the court evidence showing that the legal representative took reasonable steps to comply with the rule.

Subsection 11 of this Practice Direction — Court's powers in relation to misconduct: Rule 44.11

Court's powers in relation to misconduct: rule 44.11

[CPR PD 44.11]

11.1 Before making an order under rule 44.11, the court must give the party or legal representative in question a reasonable opportunity to make written submissions or, if the legal representative so desires, to attend a hearing.

11.2 Conduct which is unreasonable or improper includes steps which are calculated to prevent or inhibit the court from furthering the overriding objective.

11.3 Although rule 44.11(3) does not specify any sanction for breach of the obligation imposed by the rule the court may, either in the order under rule 44.11(2) or in a subsequent order, require the legal representative to produce to the court evidence that the legal representative took reasonable steps to comply with the obligation.

Section II – Qualified one-way costs shifting

Subsection 12 of this Practice Direction – Qualified one-way costs shifting

Qualified one-way costs shifting

[CPR PD 44.12]

12.1 This subsection applies to proceedings to which Section II of Part 44 applies.

12.2 Examples of claims made for the financial benefit of a person other than the claimant or a dependant within the meaning of section 1(3) of the Fatal Accidents Act 1976 within the meaning of rule 44.16(2) are subrogated claims and claims for credit hire.

12.3 "Gratuitous provision of care" within the meaning of rule 44.16(2)(a) includes the provision of personal services rendered gratuitously by persons such as relatives and friends for things such as personal care, domestic assistance, childminding, home maintenance and decorating, gardening and chauffeuring.

12.4 In a case to which rule 44.16(1) applies (fundamentally dishonest claims)—

(a) the court will normally direct that issues arising out of an allegation that the claim is fundamentally dishonest be determined at the trial;

(b) where the proceedings have been settled, the court will not, save in exceptional circumstances, order that issues arising out of an allegation that the claim was fundamentally dishonest be determined in those proceedings;

(c) where the claimant has served a notice of discontinuance, the court may direct that issues arising out of an allegation that the claim was fundamentally dishonest be determined notwithstanding that the notice has not been set aside pursuant to rule 38.4;

(d) the court may, as it thinks fair and just, determine the costs attributable to the claim having been found to be fundamentally dishonest.

12.5 The court has power to make an order for costs against a person other than the claimant under section 51(3) of the Senior Courts Act 1981 and rule 46.2. In a case to which rule 44.16(2)(a) applies (claims for the benefit of others)—

(a) the court will usually order any person other than the claimant for whose financial benefit such a claim was made to pay all the costs of the proceedings or the costs attributable to the issues to which rule 44.16(2)(a) applies, or may exceptionally make such an order permitting the enforcement of such an order for costs against the claimant.

(b) the court may, as it thinks fair and just, determine the costs attributable to claims for the financial benefit of persons other than the claimant.

12.6 In proceedings to which rule 44.16 applies, the court will normally order the claimant or, as the case may be, the person for whose benefit a claim was made to pay costs notwithstanding that the aggregate amount in money terms of such orders exceeds the aggregate amount in money terms of any orders for damages, interest and costs made in favour of the claimant.

12.7 Assessments of costs may be on a standard or indemnity basis and may be subject to a summary or detailed assessment.

PART 45 FIXED COSTS

I

FIXED COSTS

II

ROAD TRAFFIC ACCIDENTS—FIXED RECOVERABLE COSTS

III

THE PRE-ACTION PROTOCOLS FOR LOW VALUE PERSONAL INJURY CLAIMS IN ROAD TRAFFIC ACCIDENTS AND LOW VALUE PERSONAL INJURY (EMPLOYERS' LIABILITY AND PUBLIC LIABILITY) CLAIMS

IIIA

CLAIMS WHICH NO LONGER CONTINUE UNDER THE RTA AND EL/PL PRE-ACTION PROTOCOLS AND CLAIMS TO WHICH THE PRE-ACTION PROTOCOL FOR RESOLUTION OF PACKAGE TRAVEL CLAIMS APPLIES – FIXED RECOVERABLE COSTS

SECTION I FIXED COSTS

[CPR 45.1]

45.1 **Scope of this Section**

(1) This Section sets out the amounts which, unless the court orders otherwise, are to be allowed in respect of legal representatives' charges.

(2) This Section applies where—

- (a) the only claim is a claim for a specified sum of money where the value of the claim exceeds £25 and—
  - (i) judgment in default is obtained under rule 12.4(1);
  - (ii) judgment on admission is obtained under rule 14.4(3);
  - (iii) judgment on admission on part of the claim is obtained under rule 14.5(6);
  - (iv) summary judgment is given under Part 24;
  - (v) the court has made an order to strike out a defence under rule 3.4(2)(a) as disclosing no reasonable grounds for defending the claim; or
  - (vi) rule 45.4 applies;

(b) the only claim is a claim where the court gave a fixed date for the hearing when it issued the claim and judgment is given for the delivery of goods, and the value of the claim exceeds £25;

(c) the claim is for the recovery of land, including a possession claim under Part 55, whether or not the claim includes a claim for a sum of money and the defendant gives up possession, pays the amount claimed, if any, and the fixed commencement costs stated in the claim form;

(d) the claim is for the recovery of land, including a possession claim under Part 55, where one of the grounds for possession is arrears of rent, for which the court gave a fixed date for the hearing when it issued the claim and judgment is given for the possession of land (whether or not the order for possession is suspended on terms) and the defendant—

(i) has neither delivered a defence, or counterclaim, nor otherwise denied liability; or

(ii) has delivered a defence which is limited to specifying his proposals for the payment of arrears of rent;

(e) the claim is a possession claim under Section II of Part 55 (accelerated possession claims of land let on an assured shorthold tenancy) and a possession order is made where the defendant has neither delivered a defence, or counterclaim, nor otherwise denied liability;

(f) the claim is a demotion claim under Section III of Part 65 or a demotion claim is made in the same claim form in which a claim for possession is made under Part 55 and that demotion claim is successful; or

(g) a judgment creditor has taken steps under Parts 70 to 73 to enforce a judgment or order.

(Practice Direction 7B sets out the types of case where a court will give a fixed date for a hearing when it issues a claim.)

(3) No sum in respect of legal representatives' charges will be allowed where the only claim is for a sum of money or goods not exceeding £25.

(4) Any appropriate court fee will be allowed in addition to the costs set out in this Section.

(5) The claim form may include a claim for fixed commencement costs.

[CPR 45.2]

45.2 Amount of fixed commencement costs in a claim for the recovery of money or goods

(1) The amount of fixed commencement costs in a claim to which rule 45.1(2)(a) or (b) applies—

(a) will be calculated by reference to Table 1; and

(b) the amount claimed, or the value of the goods claimed if specified, in the claim form is to be used for determining the band in Table 1 that applies to the claim.

(2) The amounts shown in Table 4 are to be allowed in addition, if applicable.

Table 1
Fixed costs on commencement of a claim for the recovery of money or goods

Relevant Band	Where the claim form is served by the court or by any method other than personal service by the claimant	Where – the claim form is served personally by the claimant; – there is only one defendant	Where there is more than one defendant, for each additional defendant personally served at separate addresses by the claimant
Where— — The value of the claim exceeds £25 but does not exceed £500	£50	£60	£15
Where— — The value of the claim exceeds £500 but does not exceed £1,000	£70	£80	£15
Where— — The value of the claim exceeds £1,000 but does not exceed £5,000; or — the only claim is for delivery of goods and no value is specified or stated on the claim form	£80	£90	£15
Where— — the value of the claim exceeds £5,000	£100	£110	£15

[CPR 45.3]

45.3 When defendant only liable for fixed commencement costs

Where—

(a) the only claim is for a specified sum of money; and

(b) the defendant pays the money claimed within 14 days after being served with the particulars of claim, together with the fixed commencement costs stated in the claim form,

the defendant is not liable for any further costs unless the court orders otherwise.

[CPR 45.4]

45.4 Costs on entry of judgment in a claim for the recovery of money or goods

Where—

(a) the claimant has claimed fixed commencement costs under rule 45.2; and

(b) judgment is entered in a claim to which rule 45.1(2)(a) or (b) applies in the circumstances specified in Table 2, the amount to be included in the judgment for the claimant's legal representative's charges is the total of—

(i) the fixed commencement costs; and

(ii) the relevant amount shown in Table 2.

Table 2
Fixed costs on entry of judgment in a claim for the recovery of money or goods

	Where the amount of the judgment exceeds £25 but does not exceed £5,000	Where the amount of the judgment exceeds £5,000
Where judgment in default of an acknowledgment of service is entered under rule 12.4 (1) (entry of judgment by request on claim for money only)	£22	£30
Where judgment in default of a defence is entered under rule 12.4 (1) (entry of judgment by request on claim for money only)	£25	£35
Where judgment is entered under rule 14.4 (judgment on admission), or rule 14.5 (judgment on admission of part of claim) and claimant accepts the defendant's proposal as to the manner of payment.	£40	£55
Where judgment is entered under rule 14.4 (judgment on admission), or rule 14.5 (judgment on admission on part of claim) and court decides the date or times of payment	£55	£70
Where summary judgment is given under Part 24 or the court strikes out a defence under rule 3.4 (2)(a), in either case, on application by a party	£175	£210
Where judgment is given on a claim for delivery of goods under a regulated agreement within the meaning of the Consumer Credit Act 1974 and no other entry in this table applies	£60	£85

[CPR 45.5]

45.5 **Amount of fixed commencement costs in a claim for the recovery of land or a demotion claim**

(1) The amount of fixed commencement costs in a claim to which rule 45.1(2)(c), (d) or (f) applies will be calculated by reference to Table 3.

(2) The amounts shown in Table 4 are to be allowed in addition, if applicable.

Table 3
Fixed costs on commencement of a claim for the recovery of land or a demotion claim

Where the claim form is served by the court or by any method other than personal service by the claimant	Where – the claim form is served personally by the claimant; – there is only one defendant	Where there is more than one defendant, for each additional defendant personally served at separate addresses by the claimant
£69.50	£77	£15

[CPR 45.6]

45.6 **Costs on entry of judgment in a claim for the recovery of land or a demotion claim**

(1) Where—

(a) the claimant has claimed fixed commencement costs under rule 45.5; and

(b) judgment is entered in a claim to which rule 45.1(2)(d) or (f) applies, the amount to be included in the judgment for the claimant's legal representative's charges is the total of—

(i) the fixed commencement costs; and

(ii) the sum of £57.25.

(2) Where an order for possession is made in a claim to which rule 45.1(2)(e) applies, the amount allowed for the claimant's legal representative's charges for preparing and filing—

(a) the claim form;

(b) the documents that accompany the claim form; and

(c) the request for possession,

is £79.50.

[CPR 45.7]

45.7 **Miscellaneous fixed costs**

Table 4 shows the amount to be allowed in respect of legal representative's charges in the circumstances mentioned.

Table 4
Miscellaneous fixed costs

For service by a party of any document required to be served personally including preparing and copying a certificate of service for each individual served	£15
Where service by an alternative method or at an alternative place is permitted by an order under rule 6.15 for each individual served	£53.25
Where a document is served out of the jurisdiction—	
(a) in Scotland, Northern Ireland, the Isle of Man or the Channel Islands	£68.25

(b)	in any other place	£77

[CPR 45.8]

45.8 **Fixed enforcement costs**

Table 5 shows the amount to be allowed in respect of legal representatives' costs in the circumstances mentioned. The amounts shown in Table 4 are to be allowed in addition, if applicable.

Table 5
Fixed enforcement costs

For an application under rule 70.5(4) that an award may be enforced as if payable under a court order, where the amount outstanding under the award:	
exceeds £25 but does not exceed £250	£30.75
exceeds £250 but does not exceed £600	£41.00
exceeds £600 but does not exceed £2,000	£69.50
exceeds £2,000	£75.50
On attendance to question a judgment debtor (or officer of a company or other corporation) who has been ordered to attend court under rule 71.2 where the questioning takes place before a court officer, including attendance by a responsible representative of the solicitor:	
	for each half-hour or part, £15.00
	(When the questioning takes place before a judge, he may summarily assess any costs allowed.)
On the making of a final third party debt order under rule 72.8(6)(a) or an order for the payment to the judgment creditor of money in court under rule 72.10(1)(b):	
if the amount recovered is less than £150	one-half of the amount recovered
Otherwise	£98.50
On the making of a final charging order under rule 73.10(7)(a) or 73. 10A(3)(a):	£110.00
	The court may also allow reasonable disbursements in respect of search fees and the registration of the order.
Where a certificate is issued and registered under Schedule 6 to the Civil Jurisdiction and Judgments Act 1982, the costs of registration	£39

Where permission is given under rule 83.13 to enforce a judgment or order giving possession of land and costs are allowed on the judgment or order, the amount to be added to the judgment or order for costs—		
(a)	basic costs	£42.50
(b)	where notice of the proceedings is to be to more than one person, for each additional person	£2.75
Where a writ of control as defined in rule 83.1(2)(k) is issued against any party		£51.75
Where a writ of execution as defined in rule 83.1(2)(l), is issued against any party		£51.75
Where a request is filed for the issue of a warrant of control under rule 83.15, for a sum exceeding £25		£2.25
Where a request is filed for the issue of a warrant of delivery under rule 83.15 for a sum exceeding £25		£2.25
Where an application for an attachment of earnings order is made and costs are allowed under rule 89.10 or CCR Order 28, rule 10, for each attendance on the hearing of the application		£8.50

SECTION II ROAD TRAFFIC ACCIDENTS – FIXED RECOVERABLE COSTS

[CPR 45.9]

45.9 **Scope and interpretation**

(1) Subject to paragraph (3), this Section sets out the costs which are to be allowed in—

- (a) proceedings to which rule 46.14(1) applies (costs-only proceedings); or
- (b) proceedings for approval of a settlement or compromise under rule 21.10(2),

in cases to which this Section applies.

(2) This Section applies where—

- (a) the dispute arises from a road traffic accident occurring on or after 6 October 2003;
- (b) the agreed damages include damages in respect of personal injury, damage to property, or both;
- (c) the total value of the agreed damages does not exceed £10,000; and
- (d) if a claim had been issued for the amount of the agreed damages, the small claims track would not have been the normal track for that claim.

(3) This Section does not apply where—

- (a) the claimant is a litigant in person; or
- (b) Section III or Section IIIA of this Part applies.

(4) In this Section—

"road traffic accident" means an accident resulting in bodily injury to any person or damage to property caused by, or arising out of, the use of a motor vehicle on a road or other public place in England and Wales;
"motor vehicle" means a mechanically propelled vehicle intended for use on roads; and
"road" means any highway and any other road to which the public has access and includes bridges over which a road passes.

[CPR 45.10]

45.10 **Application of fixed recoverable costs**

Subject to rule 45.13, the only costs which are to be allowed are—

(a) fixed recoverable costs calculated in accordance with rule 45.11; and
(b) disbursements allowed in accordance with rule 45.12.

(Rule 45.13 provides for where a party issues a claim for more than the fixed recoverable costs.)

[CPR 45.11]

45.11 **Amount of fixed recoverable costs**

(1) Subject to paragraphs (2) and (3), the amount of fixed recoverable costs is the total of—

(a) £800;
(b) 20% of the damages agreed up to £5,000; and
(c) 15% of the damages agreed between £5,000 and £10,000.

(2) Where the claimant—

(a) lives or works in an area set out in Practice Direction 45; and
(b) instructs a legal representative who practises in that area,

the fixed recoverable costs will include, in addition to the costs specified in paragraph (1), an amount equal to 12.5% of the costs allowable under that paragraph.

(3) Where appropriate, VAT may be recovered in addition to the amount of fixed recoverable costs and any reference in this Section to fixed recoverable costs is a reference to those costs net of any such VAT.

[CPR 45.12]

45.12 **Disbursements**

(1) The court—

(a) may allow a claim for a disbursement of a type mentioned in paragraph (2); but
(b) will not allow a claim for any other type of disbursement.

(2) The disbursements referred to in paragraph (1) are—

(a) the cost of obtaining—
  (i) medical records;
  (ii) a medical report;
  (iii) a police report;
  (iv) an engineer's report; or
  (v) a search of the records of the Driver Vehicle Licensing Authority;
(b) where they are necessarily incurred by reason of one or more of the claimants being a child or protected party as defined in Part 21—
  (i) fees payable for instructing counsel; or
  (ii) court fees payable on an application to the court; or

(c) any other disbursement that has arisen due to a particular feature of the dispute.

[CPR 45.13]

45.13 **Claims for an amount of costs exceeding fixed recoverable costs**

(1) The court will entertain a claim for an amount of costs (excluding any success fee or disbursements) greater than the fixed recoverable costs but only if it considers that there are exceptional circumstances making it appropriate to do so.

(2) If the court considers such a claim appropriate, it may—

(a) summarily assess the costs; or

(b) make an order for the costs to be subject to detailed assessment.

(3) If the court does not consider the claim appropriate, it will make an order for fixed recoverable costs (and any permitted disbursements) only.

[CPR 45.14]

45.14 **Failure to achieve costs greater than fixed recoverable costs**

(1) This rule applies where—

(a) costs are assessed in accordance with rule 45.13(2); and

(b) the court assesses the costs (excluding any VAT) as being an amount which is less than 20% greater than the amount of the fixed recoverable costs.

(2) The court must order the defendant to pay to the claimant the lesser of—

(a) the fixed recoverable costs; and

(b) the assessed costs.

[CPR 45.15]

45.15 **Costs of the costs-only proceedings or the detailed assessment**

Where—

(a) the court makes an order for fixed recoverable costs in accordance with rule 45.13(3); or

(b) rule 45.14 applies, the court may—

(i) decide not to make an award of the payment of the claimant's costs in bringing the proceedings under rule 46.14; and

(ii) make orders in relation to costs that may include an order that the claimant pay the defendant's costs of defending those proceedings.

SECTION III THE PRE-ACTION PROTOCOLS FOR LOW VALUE PERSONAL INJURY CLAIMS IN ROAD TRAFFIC ACCIDENTS AND LOW VALUE PERSONAL INJURY (EMPLOYERS' LIABILITY AND PUBLIC LIABILITY) CLAIMS

[CPR 45.16]

45.16 **Scope and interpretation**

(1) This Section applies to claims that have been or should have been started under Part 8 in accordance with Practice Direction 8B ("the Stage 3 Procedure").

(2) Where a party has not complied with the relevant Protocol rule 45.24 will apply.

The "relevant Protocol" means—

(a) the Pre-Action Protocol for Personal Injury Claims in Road Traffic Accidents ("the RTA Protocol"); or

(b) the Pre-action Protocol for Low Value Personal Injury Claims (Employers' Liability and Public Liability) Claims ("the EL/PL Protocol").

(3) A reference to "Claim Notification Form" or Court Proceedings Pack is a reference to the form used in the relevant Protocol.

[CPR 45.17]

45.17 **Application of fixed costs, and disbursements**

The only costs allowed are—

(a) fixed costs in rule 45.18;

(b) disbursements in accordance with rule 45.19; and

(c) where applicable, fixed costs in accordance with rule 45.23A or 45.23B.

[CPR 45.18]

45.18 **Amount of fixed costs**

(1) Subject to paragraph (4), the amount of fixed costs is set out in Tables 6 and 6A.

(2) In Tables 6 and 6A —

"Type A fixed costs" means the legal representative's costs;

"Type B fixed costs" means the advocate's costs; and

"Type C fixed costs" means the costs for the advice on the amount of damages where the claimant is a child.

(3) "Advocate" has the same meaning as in rule 45.37(2)(a).

(4) Subject to rule 45.24(2) the court will not award more or less than the amounts shown in Tables 6 and 6A.

(5) Where the claimant—

(a) lives or works in an area set out in Practice Direction 45; and

(b) instructs a legal representative who practises in that area,

the fixed costs will include, in addition to the costs set out in Tables 6 and 6A, an amount equal to 12.5% of the Stage 1 and 2 and Stage 3 Type A fixed costs.

(6) Where appropriate, VAT may be recovered in addition to the amount of fixed costs and any reference in this Section to fixed costs is a reference to those costs net of any such VAT.

Table 6 – Fixed costs in relation to the RTA Protocol

Where the value of the claim for damages is not more than £10,000		Where the value of the claim for damages is more than £10,000	
Stage 1 fixed costs	£200	Stage 1 fixed costs	£200
Stage 2 fixed costs	£300	Stage 2 fixed costs	£600
Stage 3—		Stage 3—	
Type A fixed costs	£250	Type A fixed costs	£250
Type B fixed costs	£250	Type B fixed costs	£250
Type C fixed costs	£150	Type C fixed costs	£150

Table 6A – Fixed costs in relation to the EL/PL Protocol

Where the value of the claim for damages is not more than £10,000		Where the value of the claim for damages is more than £10,000	
Stage 1 fixed costs	£300	Stage 1 fixed costs	£300
Stage 2 fixed costs	£600	Stage 2 fixed costs	£1300
Stage 3—		Stage 3—	
Type A fixed costs	£250	Type A fixed costs	£250
Type B fixed costs	£250	Type B fixed costs	£250
Type C fixed costs	£150	Type C fixed costs	£150

[CPR 45.19]

45.19 Disbursements

(1) Subject to paragraphs (2A) to (2E), the court—

(a) may allow a claim for a disbursement of a type mentioned in paragraphs (2) or (3); but

(b) will not allow a claim for any other type of disbursement.

(2) In a claim to which either the RTA Protocol or EL/PL Protocol applies, the disbursements referred to in paragraph (1) are—

(a) the cost of obtaining—

(i) medical records;

(ii) a medical report or reports or non-medical expert reports as provided for in the relevant Protocol;

(iii) . . .

(iv) . . .

(b) court fees as a result of Part 21 being applicable;

(c) court fees payable where proceedings are started as a result of a limitation period that is about to expire;

(d) court fees in respect of the Stage 3 Procedure; and

(e) any other disbursement that has arisen due to a particular feature of the dispute.

(2A) In a soft tissue injury claim to which the RTA Protocol applies, the only sums (exclusive of VAT) that are recoverable in respect of the cost of obtaining a fixed cost medical report or medical records are as follows—

(a) obtaining the first report from an accredited medical expert selected via the MedCo Portal: £180;

(b) obtaining a further report where justified from [an expert from] one of the following disciplines—

(i) Consultant Orthopaedic Surgeon (inclusive of a review of medical records where applicable): £420;

(ii) Consultant in Accident and Emergency Medicine: £360;

(iii) General Practitioner registered with the General Medical Council: £180; or

(iv) Physiotherapist registered with the Health and Care Professions Council: £180;

(c) obtaining medical records: no more than £30 plus the direct cost from the holder of the records, and limited to £80 in total for each set of records required. Where relevant records are required from more than one holder of records, the fixed fee applies to each set of records required;

(d) addendum report on medical records (except by Consultant Orthopaedic Surgeon): £50; and

(e) answer to questions under Part 35: £80.

(2B) Save in exceptional circumstances, no fee may be allowed for the cost of obtaining a report to which paragraph (2A) applies where the medical expert—

(a) has provided treatment to the claimant;

(b) is associated with any person who has provided treatment; or

(c) proposes or recommends that treatment that they or an associate then provide.

(2C) The cost of obtaining a further report from an expert not listed in paragraph (2A)(b) is not fixed, but the use of that expert and the cost must be justified.

(2D) Where appropriate, VAT may be recovered in addition to the cost of obtaining a fixed cost medical report or medical records.

(2E) In this rule, 'accredited medical expert', 'associate', 'associated with', 'fixed cost medical report' 'MedCo' and 'soft tissue injury claim' have the same meaning as in paragraph 1.1(A1), (1A), (10A), (12A), and (16A), respectively, of the RTA Protocol.

(3) In a claim to which the RTA Protocol applies, the disbursements referred to in paragraph (1) are also the cost of—

(a) an engineer's report; and

(b) a search of the records of the—

(i) Driver Vehicle Licensing Authority; and

(ii) Motor Insurance Database.

[CPR 45.20]

45.20 **Where the claimant obtains judgment for an amount more than the defendant's relevant Protocol offer**

Where rule 36.29(1)(b) or (c) applies, the court will order the defendant to pay—

(a) where not already paid by the defendant, the Stage 1 and 2 fixed costs;

(b) where the claim is determined—

(i) on the papers, Stage 3 Type A fixed costs;

(ii) at a Stage 3 hearing, Stage 3 Type A and B fixed costs; or

(iii) at a Stage 3 hearing and the claimant is a child, Type A, B and C fixed costs; and

(c) disbursements allowed in accordance with rule 45.19.

[CPR 45.21]

45.21 **Settlement at Stage 2 where the claimant is a child**

(1) This rule applies where—

(a) the claimant is a child;

(b) there is a settlement at Stage 2 of the relevant Protocol; and

(c) an application is made to the court to approve the settlement.

(2) Where the court approves the settlement at a settlement hearing it will order the defendant to pay—

(a) the Stage 1 and 2 fixed costs;

(b) the Stage 3 Type A, B and C fixed costs; and

(c) disbursements allowed in accordance with rule 45.19.

(3) Where the court does not approve the settlement at a settlement hearing it will order the defendant to pay the Stage 1 and 2 fixed costs.

(4) Paragraphs (5) and (6) apply where the court does not approve the settlement at the first settlement hearing but does approve the settlement at a second settlement hearing.

(5) At the second settlement hearing the court will order the defendant to pay—

- (a) the Stage 3 Type A and C fixed costs for the first settlement hearing;
- (b) disbursements allowed in accordance with rule 45.19; and
- (c) the Stage 3 Type B fixed costs for one of the hearings.

(6) The court in its discretion may also order—

- (a) the defendant to pay an additional amount of either or both the Stage 3—
  - (i) Type A fixed costs;
  - (ii) Type B fixed costs; or
- (b) the claimant to pay an amount equivalent to either or both the Stage 3—
  - (i) Type A fixed costs;
  - (ii) Type B fixed costs.

[CPR 45.22]

45.22 **Settlement at Stage 3 where the claimant is a child**

(1) This rule applies where—

- (a) the claimant is a child;
- (b) there is a settlement after proceedings are started under the Stage 3 Procedure;
- (c) the settlement is more than the defendant's relevant Protocol offer; and
- (d) an application is made to the court to approve the settlement.

(2) Where the court approves the settlement at the settlement hearing it will order the defendant to pay—

- (a) the Stage 1 and 2 fixed costs;
- (b) the Stage 3 Type A, B and C fixed costs; and
- (c) disbursements allowed in accordance with rule 45.19.

(3) Where the court does not approve the settlement at the settlement hearing it will order the defendant to pay the Stage 1 and 2 fixed costs.

(4) Paragraphs (5) and (6) apply where the court does not approve the settlement at the first settlement hearing but does approve the settlement at the Stage 3 hearing.

(5) At the Stage 3 hearing the court will order the defendant to pay—

- (a) the Stage 3 Type A and C fixed costs for the settlement hearing;
- (b) disbursements allowed in accordance with rule 45.19; and
- (c) the Stage 3 Type B fixed costs for one of the hearings.

(6) The court in its discretion may also order—

- (a) he defendant to pay an additional amount of either or both the Stage 3—
  - (i) Type A fixed costs;
  - (ii) Type B fixed costs; or
- (b) the claimant to pay an amount equivalent to either or both of the Stage 3—
  - (i) Type A fixed costs;
  - (ii) Type B fixed costs.

(7) Where the settlement is not approved at the Stage 3 hearing the court will order the defendant to pay the Stage 3 Type A fixed costs.

[CPR 45.23]

45.23 **Where the court orders that the claim is not suitable to be determined under the Stage 3 Procedure and the claimant is a child**

Where—

(a) the claimant is a child; and

(b) at a settlement hearing or the Stage 3 hearing the court orders that the claim is not suitable to be determined under the Stage 3 Procedure,

the court will order the defendant to pay—

(i) the Stage 1 and 2 fixed costs; and

(ii) the Stage 3 Type A, B and C fixed costs.

[CPR 45.23A]

45.23A **Settlement before proceedings are issued under Stage 3**

Where—

(a) there is a settlement after the Court Proceedings Pack has been sent to the defendant but before proceedings are issued under Stage 3; and

(b) the settlement is more than the defendant's relevant Protocol offer,

the fixed costs will include an additional amount equivalent to the Stage 3 Type A fixed costs.

[CPR 45.23B]

45.23B **Additional advice on the value of the claim**

Where—

(a) the value of the claim for damages is more than £10,000;

(b) an additional advice has been obtained from a specialist solicitor or from counsel;

(c) that advice is reasonably required to value the claim,

the court will order the defendant to pay—

the fixed costs may include an additional amount equivalent to the Stage 3 Type C fixed costs.

[CPR 45.24]

45.24 **Failure to comply or electing not to continue with the relevant Protocol – costs consequences**

(1) This rule applies where the claimant—

(a) does not comply with the process set out in the relevant Protocol; or

(b) elects not to continue with that process,

and starts proceedings under Part 7.

(2) Subject to paragraph (2A), where a judgment is given in favour of the claimant but—

(a) the court determines that the defendant did not proceed with the process set out in the relevant Protocol because the claimant provided insufficient information on the Claim Notification Form;

(b) the court considers that the claimant acted unreasonably—

(i) by discontinuing the process set out in the relevant Protocol and starting proceedings under Part 7;

(ii) by valuing the claim at more than £25,000, so that the claimant did not need to comply with the relevant Protocol; or

(iii) except for paragraph (2)(a), in any other way that caused the process in the relevant Protocol to be discontinued; or

(c) the claimant did not comply with the relevant Protocol at all despite the claim falling within the scope of the relevant Protocol,

the court may order the defendant to pay no more than the fixed costs in rule 45.18 together with the disbursements allowed in accordance with rule 45.19.

(2A) Where a judgment is given in favour of the claimant but the claimant did not comply with the process in paragraph 6.3A(2) of the RTA Protocol, the court may not order the defendant to pay the claimant's costs and disbursements save in exceptional circumstances.

(3) Where the claimant starts proceedings under paragraph 7.28 of the RTA Protocol or paragraph 7.26 of the EL/PL Protocol and the court orders the defendant to make an interim payment of no more than the interim payment made under paragraph 7.14(2) or (3) of the RTA Protocol or paragraph 7.17(2) or (3) of the EL/PL Protocol the court will, on the final determination of the proceedings, order the defendant to pay no more than–

(a) the Stage 1 and 2 fixed costs; and

(b) the disbursements allowed in accordance with rule 45.19.

[CPR 45.25]

45.25 **Where the parties have settled after proceedings have started**

(1) This rule applies where an application is made under rule 45.29 (costs-only application after a claim is started under Part 8 in accordance with Practice Direction 8B).

(2) Where the settlement is more than the defendant's relevant Protocol offer the court will order the defendant to pay—

(a) the Stage 1 and 2 fixed costs where not already paid by the defendant;

(b) the Stage 3 Type A fixed costs; and

(c) disbursements allowed in accordance with rule 45.19.

(3) Where the settlement is less than or equal to the defendant's relevant Protocol offer the court will order the defendant to pay—

(a) the Stage 1 and 2 fixed costs where not already paid by the defendant; and

(b) disbursements allowed in accordance with rule 45.19.

(4) The court may, in its discretion, order either party to pay the costs of the application.

[CPR 45.26]

45.26 **Where the claimant obtains judgment for an amount equal to or less than the defendant's relevant Protocol offer**

Where rule 36.29(1)(a) applies, the court will order the claimant to pay—

(a) where the claim is determined—

(i) on the papers, Stage 3 Type A fixed costs; or

(ii) at a hearing, Stage 3 Type A and B fixed costs;

(b) any Stage 3 disbursements allowed in accordance with rule 45.19.

[CPR 45.27]

45.27 **Adjournment**

Where the court adjourns a settlement hearing or a Stage 3 hearing it may, in its discretion, order a party to pay—

(a) an additional amount of the Stage 3 Type B fixed costs; and

(b) any court fee for that adjournment.

[CPR 45.28]

45.28 **Account of payment of Stage 1 and Stage 2 fixed costs**

Where a claim no longer continues under the relevant Protocol the court will, when making any order as to costs including an order for fixed recoverable costs under Section II or Section IIIA of this Part, take into account the Stage 1 and Stage 2 fixed costs that have been paid by the defendant.

[CPR 45.29]

45.29 **Costs-only application after a claim is started under Part 8 in accordance with Practice Direction 8B**

(1) This rule sets out the procedure where—

(a) the parties to a dispute have reached an agreement on all issues (including which party is to pay the costs) which is made or confirmed in writing; but

(b) they have failed to agree the amount of those costs; and

(c) proceedings have been started under Part 8 in accordance with Practice Direction 8B.

(2) Either party may make an application for the court to determine the costs.

(3) Where an application is made under this rule the court will assess the costs in accordance with rule 45.22 or rule 45.25.

(4) Rule 44.5 (amount of costs where costs are payable pursuant to a contract) does not apply to an application under this rule.

SECTION IIIA CLAIMS WHICH NO LONGER CONTINUE UNDER THE RTA AND EL/PL PRE-ACTION PROTOCOLS AND CLAIMS TO WHICH THE PRE-ACTION PROTOCOL FOR RESOLUTION OF PACKAGE TRAVEL CLAIMS APPLIES – FIXED RECOVERABLE COSTS

[CPR 45.29A]

45.29A **Scope and interpretation**

(1) Subject to paragraph (3), this section applies—

(a) to a claim started under—

(i) the Pre-Action Protocol for Low Value Personal Injury Claims in Road Traffic Accidents ("the RTA Protocol"); or

(ii) the Pre-Action Protocol for Low Value Personal Injury (Employers' Liability and Public Liability) Claims ("the EL/PL Protocol"),

where such a claim no longer continues under the relevant Protocol or the Stage 3 Procedure in Practice Direction 8B; and

(b) to a claim to which the Pre-Action Protocol for Resolution of Package Travel Claims applies.

(2) This section does not apply to a disease claim which is started under the EL/PL Protocol.

(3) Nothing in this section shall prevent the court making an order under rule 45.24.

[CPR 45.29B]

45.29B **Application of fixed costs and disbursements – RTA Protocol**

Subject to rules 45.29F, 45.29G, 45.29H and 45.29J, and for as long as the case is not allocated to the multi-track, if, in a claim started under the RTA Protocol, the Claim Notification Form is submitted on or after 31st July 2013, the only costs allowed are—

(a) the fixed costs in rule 45.29C;

(b) disbursements in accordance with rule 45.29I.

[CPR 45.29C]

45.29C **Amount of fixed costs – RTA Protocol**

(1) Subject to paragraph (2), the amount of fixed costs is set out in Table 6B.

(2) Where the claimant—

(a) lives or works in an area set out in Practice Direction 45; and

(b) instructs a legal representative who practises in that area,

the fixed costs will include, in addition to the costs set out in Table 6B, an amount equal to 12.5% of the costs allowable under paragraph (1) and set out in Table 6B.

(3) Where appropriate, VAT may be recovered in addition to the amount of fixed recoverable costs and any reference in this Section to fixed costs is a reference to those costs net of VAT.

(4) In Table 6B—

(a) in Part B, "on or after" means the period beginning on the date on which the court respectively—

(i) issues the claim;

(ii) allocates the claim under Part 26; or

(iii) lists the claim for trial; and

(b) unless stated otherwise, a reference to "damages" means agreed damages; and

(c) a reference to "trial" is a reference to the final contested hearing.

Table 6B – Fixed costs where a claim no longer continues under the RTA Protocol

A. If Parties reach a settlement prior to the claimant issuing proceedings under Part 7			
Agreed damages	At least £1,000, but not more than £5,000	More than £5,000, but not more than £10,000	More than £10,000
Fixed costs	The greater of— (a) £550; or (b) the total of— (i) £100; and (ii) 20% of the damages	The total of— (a) £1,100; and (b) 15% of damages over £5,000	The total of— (a) £1,930; and (b) 10% of damages over £10,000

B. If proceedings are issued under Part 7, but the case settles before trial			
Stage at which case is settled	On or after the date of issue, but prior to the date of allocation under Part 26	On or after the date of allocation under Part 26, but prior to the date of listing	On or after the date of listing but prior to the date of trial
Fixed costs	The total of— (a) £1,160; and (b) 20% of the damages	The total of— (a) £1,880; and (b) 20% of the damages	The total of— (a) £2,655; and (b) 20% of the damages

C. If the claim is disposed of at trial	
Fixed costs	The total of— (a) £2,655; and (b) 20% of the damages agreed or awarded; and (c) the relevant trial advocacy fee

D. Trial advocacy fees				
Damages agreed or awarded	Not more than £3,000	More than £3,000, but not more than £10,000	More than £10,000, but not more than £15,000	More than £15,000
Trial advocacy fee	£500	£710	£1,070	£1,705

[CPR 45.29D]

45.29D **Application of fixed costs and disbursements – EL/PL Protocol and Pre-Action Protocol for Resolution of Package Travel Claims**

Subject to rules 45.29F, 45.29H and 45.29J, and for as long as the case is not allocated to the multi-track, in a claim started under the EL/PL Protocol or in a claim to which the Pre-Action Protocol for Resolution of Package Travel Claims applies, the only costs allowed are—

(a) fixed costs in rule 45.29E; and

(b) disbursements in accordance with rule 45.29I.

[CPR 45.29E]

45.29E **Amount of fixed costs – EL/PL Protocol and Pre-Action Protocol for Resolution of Package Travel Claims**

(1) Subject to paragraph (2), the amount of fixed costs is set out—

(a) in respect of employers' liability claims, in Table 6C; and

(b) in respect of public liability claims and claims to which the Pre-Action Protocol for Resolution of Package Travel Claims applies, in Table 6D.

(2) Where the claimant—

(a) lives or works in an area set out in Practice Direction 45; and

(b) instructs a legal representative who practises in that area,

the fixed costs will include, in addition to the costs set out in Tables 6C and 6D, an amount equal to 12.5% of the costs allowable under paragraph (1) and set out in Table 6C and 6D.

(3) Where appropriate, VAT may be recovered in addition to the amount of fixed recoverable costs and any reference in this Section to fixed costs is a reference to those costs net of VAT.

(4) In Tables 6C and 6D—

(a) in Part B, "on or after" means the period beginning on the date on which the court respectively—

(i) issues the claim;

(ii) allocates the claim under Part 26; or

(iii) lists the claim for trial; and

(b) unless stated otherwise, a reference to "damages" means agreed damages; and

(c) a reference to "trial" is a reference to the final contested hearing.

Table 6C – Fixed costs where a claim no longer continues under the EL/PL Protocol – employers' liability claims

A. If Parties reach a settlement prior to the claimant issuing proceedings under Part 7			
Agreed damages	At least £1,000, but not more than £5,000	More than £5,000, but not more than £10,000	More than £10,000
Fixed costs	The total of— (a) £950; and (b) 17.5% of the damages	The total of— (a) £1,855; and (b) 12.5% of damages over £5,000	The total of— (a) £2,500; and (b) 10% of damages over £10,000

B. If proceedings are issued under Part 7, but the case settles before trial			
Stage at which case is settled	On or after the date of issue, but prior to the date of allocation under Part 26	On or after the date of allocation under Part 26, but prior to the date of listing	On or after the date of listing but prior to the date of trial
Fixed costs	The total of— (a) £2,630; and (b) 20% of the damages	The total of— (a) £3,350; and (b) 25% of the damages	The total of— (a) £4,280; and (b) 30% of the damages

C. If the claim is disposed of at trial	
Fixed costs	The total of— (a) £4,280; and (b) 30% of the damages agreed or awarded; and (c) the relevant trial advocacy fee

D. Trial advocacy fees				
Damages agreed or awarded	Not more than £3,000	More than £3,000, but not more than £10,000	More than £10,000, but not more than £15,000	More than £15,000
Trial advocacy fee	£500	£710	£1,070	£1,705

Table 6D – Fixed costs where a claim no longer continues under the EL/PL Protocol – public liability claims

A. If Parties reach a settlement prior to the claimant issuing proceedings under Part 7			
Agreed damages	At least £1,000, but not more than £5,000	More than £5,000, but not more than £10,000	More than £10,000
Fixed costs	The total of— (a) £950; and (b) 17.5% of the damages	The total of— (a) £1,855; and (b) 10% of damages over £5,000	The total of— (a) £2,370; and (b) 10% of damages over £10,000

B. If proceedings are issued under Part 7, but the case settles before trial			
Stage at which case is settled	On or after the date of issue, but prior to the date of allocation under Part 26	On or after the date of allocation under Part 26, but prior to the date of listing	On or after the date of listing but prior to the date of trial
Fixed costs	The total of— (a) £2,450; and (b) 17.5% of the damages	The total of— (a) £3,065; and (b) 22.5% of the damages	The total of— (a) £3,790; and (b) 27.5% of the damages

C. If the claim is disposed of at trial	
Fixed costs	The total of— (a) £3,790; and (b) 27.5% of the damages agreed or awarded; and (c) the relevant trial advocacy fee

D. Trial advocacy fees				
Damages agreed or awarded	Not more than £3,000	More than £3,000, but not more than £10,000	More than £10,000, but not more than £15,000	More than £15,000
Trial advocacy fee	£500	£710	£1,070	£1,705

[CPR 45.29F]

45.29F Defendants' costs

(1) In this rule—

(a) paragraphs (8) and (9) apply to assessments of defendants' costs under Part 36;

(b) paragraph (10) applies to assessments to which the exclusions from qualified one way costs shifting in rules 44.15 and 44.16 apply; and

(c) paragraphs (2) to (7) apply to all other cases under this Section in which a defendant's costs are assessed.

(2) If, in any case to which this Section applies, the court makes an order for costs in favour of the defendant—

(a) the court will have regard to; and

(b) the amount of costs order to be paid shall not exceed,

the amount which would have been payable by the defendant if an order for costs had been made in favour of the claimant at the same stage of the proceedings.

(3) For the purpose of assessing the costs payable to the defendant by reference to the fixed costs in Table 6, Table 6A, Table 6B, Table 6C and Table 6D, "value of the claim for damages" and "damages" shall be treated as references to the value of the claim.

(4) For the purposes of paragraph (3), "the value of the claim" is—

(a) the amount specified in the claim form, excluding—

(i) any amount not in dispute;

(ii) in a claim started under the RTA Protocol, any claim for vehicle related damages;

(iii) interest;

(iv) costs; and

(v) any contributory negligence;

(b) if no amount is specified in the claim form, the maximum amount which the claimant reasonably expected to recover according to the statement of value included in the claim form under rule 16.3; or

(c) £25,000, if the claim form states that the claimant cannot reasonably say how much is likely to be recovered.

(5) Where the defendant—

(a) lives, works or carries on business in an area set out in Practice Direction 45; and

(b) instructs a legal representative who practises in that area,

the costs will include, in addition to the costs allowable under paragraph (2), an amount equal to 12.5% of those costs.

(6) Where an order for costs is made pursuant to this rule, the defendant is entitled to disbursements in accordance with rule 45.29I.

(7) Where appropriate, VAT may be recovered in addition to the amount of any costs allowable under this rule.

(8) Where, in a case to which this Section applies, a Part 36 offer is accepted, rule 36.20 will apply instead of this rule.

(9) Where, in a case to which this Section applies, upon judgment being entered, the claimant fails to obtain a judgment more advantageous than the defendant's Part 36 offer, rule 36.21 will apply instead of this rule.

(10) Where, in a case to which this Section applies, any of the exceptions to qualified one way costs shifting in rules 44.15 and 44.16 is established, the court will assess the defendant's costs without reference to this rule.

[CPR 45.29G]

45.29G **Counterclaims under the RTA Protocol**

(1) If in any case to which this Section applies—

(a) the defendant brings a counterclaim which includes a claim for personal injuries to which the RTA Protocol applies;

(b) the counterclaim succeeds; and

(c) the court makes an order for the costs of the counterclaim,

rules 45.29B, 45.29C, 45.29I, 45.29J, 45.29K and 45.29L shall apply.

(2) Where a successful counterclaim does not include a claim for personal injuries—

(a) the order for costs of the counterclaim shall be for a sum equivalent to one half of the applicable Type A and Type B costs in Table 6;

(b) where the defendant—

(i) lives, works, or carries on business in an area set out in Practice Direction 45; and

(ii) instructs a legal representative who practises in that area,

the costs will include, in addition to the costs allowable under paragraph (a), an amount equal to 12.5% of those costs;

(c) if an order for costs is made pursuant to this rule, the defendant is entitled to disbursements in accordance with rule 45.29I; and

(d) where appropriate, VAT may be recovered in addition to the amount of any costs allowable under this rule.

[CPR 45.29H]

45.29H **Interim applications**

(1) Where the court makes an order for costs of an interim application to be paid by one party in a case to which this Section applies, the order shall be for a sum equivalent to one half of the applicable Type A and Type B costs in Table 6 or 6A.

(1A) Where the order for costs is made in a claim to which the Pre-Action Protocol for Resolution of Package Travel Claims applies, the order shall be for a sum equivalent to one half of the applicable Type A and Type B costs in Table 6A.

(2) Where the party in whose favour the order for costs is made—

(a) lives, works or carries on business in an area set out in Practice Direction 45; and

(b) instructs a legal representative who practises in that area,

the costs will include, in addition to the costs allowable under paragraph (1), an amount equal to 12.5% of those costs.

(3) If an order for costs is made pursuant to this rule, the party in whose favour the order is made is entitled to disbursements in accordance with rule 45.29I.

(4) Where appropriate, VAT may be recovered in addition to the amount of any costs allowable under this rule.

[CPR 45.29I]

45.29I Disbursements

(1) Subject to paragraphs (2A) to (2E), the court—

(a) may allow a claim for a disbursement of a type mentioned in paragraphs (2) or (3); but

(b) will not allow a claim for any other type of disbursement.

(2) In a claim started under the RTA Protocol, the EL/PL Protocol or the Pre-Action Protocol for Resolution of Package Travel Claims, the disbursements referred to in paragraph (1) are—

(a) the cost of obtaining medical records and expert medical reports as provided for in the relevant Protocol;

(b) the cost of any non-medical expert reports as provided for in the relevant Protocol;

(c) the cost of any advice from a specialist solicitor or counsel as provided for in the relevant Protocol;

(d) court fees;

(e) any expert's fee for attending the trial where the court has given permission for the expert to attend;

(f) expenses which a party or witness has reasonably incurred in travelling to and from a hearing or in staying away from home for the purposes of attending a hearing;

(g) a sum not exceeding the amount specified in Practice Direction 45 for any loss of earnings or loss of leave by a party or witness due to attending a hearing or to staying away from home for the purpose of attending a hearing; and

(h) any other disbursement reasonably incurred due to a particular feature of the dispute.

(2A) In a soft tissue injury claim started under the RTA Protocol, the only sums (exclusive of VAT) that are recoverable in respect of the cost of obtaining a fixed cost medical report or medical records are as follows—

(a) obtaining the first report from an accredited medical expert selected via the MedCo Portal: £180;

(b) obtaining a further report where justified from [an expert from] one of the following disciplines—

(i) Consultant Orthopaedic Surgeon (inclusive of a review of medical records where applicable): £420;

(ii) Consultant in Accident and Emergency Medicine: £360;

(iii) General Practitioner registered with the General Medical Council: £180; or

(iv) Physiotherapist registered with the Health and Care Professions Council: £180;

(c) obtaining medical records: no more than £30 plus the direct cost from the holder of the records, and limited to £80 in total for each set of records required. Where relevant records are required from more than one holder of records, the fixed fee applies to each set of records required;

(d) addendum report on medical records (except by Consultant Orthopaedic Surgeon): £50; and

(e) answer to questions under Part 35: £80.

(2B) Save in exceptional circumstances, no fee may be allowed for the cost of obtaining a report to which paragraph (2A) applies where the medical expert—

(a) has provided treatment to the claimant;

(b) is associated with any person who has provided treatment; or

(c) proposes or recommends treatment that they or an associate then provide.

(2C) The cost of obtaining a further report from an expert not listed in paragraph (2A)(b) is not fixed, but the use of that expert and the cost must be justified.

(2D) Where appropriate, VAT may be recovered in addition to the cost of obtaining a fixed cost medical report or medical records.

(2E) In this rule, 'accredited medical expert', 'associate', 'associated with', 'fixed cost medical report' 'MedCo' and 'soft tissue injury claim' have the same meaning as in paragraph 1.1(A1), (1A), (10A), (12A), and (16A), respectively, of the RTA Protocol.

(3) In a claim started under the RTA Protocol only, the disbursements referred to in paragraph (1) are also the cost of—

(a) an engineer's report; and

(b) a search of the records of the—

(i) Driver Vehicle Licensing Authority; and

(ii) Motor Insurance Database.

[CPR 45.29J]

45.29J Claims for an amount of costs exceeding fixed recoverable costs

(1) If it considers that there are exceptional circumstances making it appropriate to do so, the court will consider a claim for an amount of costs (excluding disbursements) which is greater than the fixed recoverable costs referred to in rules 45.29B to 45.29H.

(2) If the court considers such a claim to be appropriate, it may—

(a) summarily assess the costs; or

(b) make an order for the costs to be subject to detailed assessment.

(3) If the court does not consider the claim to be appropriate, it will make an order—

(a) if the claim is made by the claimant, for the fixed recoverable costs; or

(b) if the claim is made by the defendant, for a sum which has regard to, but which does not exceed the fixed recoverable costs,

and any permitted disbursements only.

[CPR 45.29K]

45.29K Failure to achieve costs greater than fixed recoverable costs

(1) This rule applies where—

(a) costs are assessed in accordance with rule 45.29J(2); and

(b) the court assesses the costs (excluding any VAT) as being an amount which is in a sum less than 20% greater than the amount of the fixed recoverable costs.

(2) The court will make an order for the party who made the claim to be paid the lesser of—

(a) the fixed recoverable costs; and

(b) the assessed costs.

[CPR 45.29L]

45.29L **Costs of the costs-only proceedings or the detailed assessment**

(1) Where—

(a) the court makes an order for costs in accordance with rule 45.29J(3); or

(b) rule 45.29K applies,

the court may—

(i) decide not to award the party making the claim the costs of the costs only proceedings or detailed assessment; and

(ii) make orders in relation to costs that may include an order that the party making the claim pay the costs of the party defending those proceedings or that assessment.

SECTION IV SCALE COSTS FOR CLAIMS IN THE INTELLECTUAL PROPERTY ENTERPRISE COURT

[CPR 45.30]

45.30 **Scope and interpretation**

(1) Subject to paragraph (2), this Section applies to proceedings in the Intellectual Property Enterprise court.

(2) This Section does not apply where—

(a) the court considers that a party has behaved in a manner which amounts to an abuse of the court's process; or

(b) the claim concerns the infringement or revocation of a patent or registered design or registered trade mark the validity of which has been certified by a court or by the Comptroller-General of Patents, Designs and Trade Marks in earlier proceedings.

(3) The court will make a summary assessment of the costs of the party in whose favour any order for costs is made. Rules 44.2(8), 44.7(b) and Part 47 do not apply to this Section.

(4) "Scale costs" means the costs set out in Table A and Table B of the Practice Direction supplementing this Part.

[CPR 45.31]

45.31 **Amount of scale costs**

(1) Subject to rule 45.32, the court will not order a party to pay total costs of more than—

(a) £50,000 on the final determination of a claim in relation to liability; and

(b) £25,000 on an inquiry as to damages or account of profits.

(2) The amounts in paragraph (1) apply after the court has applied the provision on set off in accordance with rule 44.12(a).

(3) The maximum amount of scale costs that the court will award for each stage of the claim is set out in Practice Direction 45.

(4) The amount of the scale costs awarded by the court in accordance with paragraph (3) will depend on the nature and complexity of the claim.

(4A) Subject to assessment where appropriate, the following may be recovered in addition to the amount of the scale costs set out in Practice Direction 45 – Fixed Costs—

- (a) court fees;
- (b) costs relating to the enforcement of any court order; and
- (c) wasted costs.

(5) Where appropriate, VAT may be recovered in addition to the amount of the scale costs and any reference in this Section to scale costs is a reference to those costs net of any such VAT.

[CPR 45.32]

45.32 **Summary assessment of the costs of an application where a party has behaved unreasonably**

Costs awarded to a party under rule 63.26(2) are in addition to the total costs that may be awarded to that party under rule 45.31.

SECTION V FIXED COSTS: HM REVENUE AND CUSTOMS

[CPR 45.33]

45.33 **Scope, interpretation and application**

(1) This Section sets out the amounts which, unless the court orders otherwise, are to be allowed in respect of HM Revenue and Customs charges in the cases to which this Section applies.

(2) For the purpose of this Section—

- (a) "HMRC Officer" means a person appointed by the Commissioners under section 2 of the Commissioners for Revenue and Customs Act 2005 and authorised to conduct County Court proceedings for recovery of debt under section 25(1A) of that Act;
- (b) "Commissioners" means commissioners for HMRC appointed under section 1 of the Commissioners for Revenue and Customs Act 2005;
- (c) "debt" means any sum payable to the Commissioners under or by virtue of an enactment or under a contract settlement; and
- (d) "HMRC charges" means the fixed costs set out in Tables 7 and 8 in this Section.

(3) HMRC charges must, for the purpose of this Section, be claimed as "legal representative's costs" on relevant court forms.

(4) This Section applies where the only claim is a claim conducted by an HMRC Officer in the County Court for recovery of a debt and the Commissioners obtain judgment on the claim.

(5) Any appropriate court fee will be allowed in addition to the costs set out in this Section.

(6) The claim form may include a claim for fixed commencement costs.

[CPR 45.34]

45.34 **Amount of fixed commencement costs in a County Court claim for the recovery of money**

The amount of fixed commencement costs in a claim to which rule 45.33 applies—

- (a) will be calculated by reference to Table 7; and

(b) the amount claimed in the claim form is to be used for determining which claim band in Table 7 applies.

Table 7 – Fixed Costs on Commencement of a County Court Claim Conducted by an HMRC Officer

Where the value of the claim does not exceed £25	**Nil**
Where the value of the claim exceeds £25 but does not exceed £500	£33
Where the value of the claim exceeds £500 but does not exceed £1,000	£47
Where the value of the claim exceeds £1,000 but does not exceed £5,000	£53
Where the value of the claim exceeds £5,000 but does not exceed £15,000	£67
Where the value of the claim exceeds £15,000 but does not exceed £50,000	£90
Where the value of the claim exceeds £50,000 but does not exceed £100,000	£113
Where the value of the claim exceeds £100,000 but does not exceed £150,000	£127
Where the value of the claim exceeds £150,000 but does not exceed £200,000	£140
Where the value of the claim exceeds £200,000 but does not exceed £250,000	£153
Where the value of the claim exceeds £250,000 but does not exceed £300,000	£167
Where the value of the claim exceeds £300,000	£180

[CPR 45.35]

45.35 **Costs on entry of judgment in a County Court claim for recovery of money**

Where—

(a) an HMRC Officer has claimed fixed commencement costs under Rule 45.34; and

(b) judgment is entered in a claim to which rule 45.33 applies,

the amount to be included in the judgment for HMRC charges is the total of—

(i) the fixed commencement costs; and

(ii) the amount in Table 8 relevant to the value of the claim.

Table 8 – Fixed Costs on Entry of Judgment of a County Court Claim Conducted by an HMRC Officer

Where the value of the claim does not exceed £5,000	£15
Where the value of the claim exceeds £5,000	£20

[CPR 45.36]

45.36 **When the defendant is only liable for fixed commencement costs**

Where—

(a) the only claim is for a specified sum of money; and

(b) the defendant pays the money claimed within 14 days after service of the particulars of claim, together with the fixed commencement costs stated in the claim form,

the defendant is not liable for any further costs unless the court orders otherwise.

SECTION VI FAST TRACK TRIAL COSTS

[CPR 45.37]

45.37 **Scope of this Section**

(1) This Section deals with the amount of costs which the court may award as the costs of an advocate for preparing for and appearing at the trial of a claim in the fast track (referred to in this rule as "fast track trial costs").

(2) For the purposes of this Section—

"advocate" means a person exercising a right of audience as a representative of, or on behalf of, a party;

"fast track trial costs" means the costs of a party's advocate for preparing for and appearing at the trial, but does not include—

(i) any other disbursements; or

(ii) any value added tax payable on the fees of a party's advocate; and

"trial" includes a hearing where the court decides an amount of money or the value of goods following a judgment under Part 12 (default judgment) or Part 14 (admissions) but does not include –

(i) the hearing of an application for summary judgment under Part 24; or

(ii) the court's approval of a settlement or other compromise under rule 21.10.

[CPR 45.38]

45.38 **Amount of fast track trial costs**

(1) Table 9 shows the amount of fast track trial costs which the court may award (whether by summary or detailed assessment).

Table 9

Value of the claim	Amount of fast track trial costs which the court may award
No more than £3,000	£485
More than £3,000 but not more than £10,000	£690
More than £10,000 but not more than £15,000	£1,035
For proceedings issued on or after 6th April 2009, more than £15,000	£1,650

(2) The court may not award more or less than the amount shown in the table except where—

(a) it decides not to award any fast track trial costs; or

(b) rule 45.39 applies,

but the court may apportion the amount awarded between the parties to reflect their respective degrees of success on the issues at trial.

(3) Where the only claim is for the payment of money—

(a) for the purpose of quantifying fast track trial costs awarded to a claimant, the value of the claim is the total amount of the judgment excluding—
  (i) interest and costs; and
  (ii) any reduction made for contributory negligence; and
(b) for the purpose of quantifying fast track trial costs awarded to a defendant, the value of the claim is—
  (i) the amount specified in the claim form (excluding interest and costs);
  (ii) if no amount is specified, the maximum amount which the claimant reasonably expected to recover according to the statement of value included in the claim form under rule 16.3; or
  (iii) more than £15,000, if the claim form states that the claimant cannot reasonably say how much is likely to be recovered.

(4) Where the claim is only for a remedy other than the payment of money, the value of the claim is deemed to be more than £3,000 but not more than £10,000, unless the court orders otherwise.

(5) Where the claim includes both a claim for the payment of money and for a remedy other than the payment of money, the value of the claim is deemed to be the higher of—
(a) the value of the money claim decided in accordance with paragraph (3); or
(b) the deemed value of the other remedy decided in accordance with paragraph (4),

unless the court orders otherwise.

(6) Where—
(a) a defendant has made a counterclaim against the claimant;
(b) the counterclaim has a higher value than the claim; and
(c) the claimant succeeds at trial both on the claim and the counterclaim,

for the purpose of quantifying fast track trial costs awarded to the claimant, the value of the claim is the value of the defendant's counterclaim calculated in accordance with this rule.

[CPR 45.39]

45.39 Power to award more or less than the amount of fast track trial costs

(1) This rule sets out when a court may award—
(a) an additional amount to the amount of fast track trial costs shown in Table 9 in rule 45.38(1); or
(b) less than those amounts.

(2) If—
(a) in addition to the advocate, a party's legal representative attends the trial;
(b) the court considers that it was necessary for a legal representative to attend to assist the advocate; and
(c) the court awards fast track trial costs to that party,

the court may award an additional £345 in respect of the legal representative's attendance at the trial.

(3) If the court considers that it is necessary to direct a separate trial of an issue then the court may award an additional amount in respect of the separate trial but that amount is limited in accordance with paragraph (4) of this rule.

(4) The additional amount the court may award under paragraph (3) will not exceed two-thirds of the amount payable for that claim, subject to a minimum award of £485.

(5) Where the party to whom fast track trial costs are to be awarded is a litigant in person, the court will award—

- (a) if the litigant in person can prove financial loss, two-thirds of the amount that would otherwise be awarded; or
- (b) if the litigant in person fails to prove financial loss, an amount in respect of the time spent reasonably doing the work at the rate specified in Practice Direction 46.

(6) Where a defendant has made a counterclaim against the claimant, and—

- (a) the claimant has succeeded on his claim; and
- (b) the defendant has succeeded on his counterclaim,

the court will quantify the amount of the award of fast track trial costs to which—

- (i) but for the counterclaim, the claimant would be entitled for succeeding on his claim; and
- (ii) but for the claim, the defendant would be entitled for succeeding on his counterclaim,

and make one award of the difference, if any, to the party entitled to the higher award of costs.

(7) Where the court considers that the party to whom fast track trial costs are to be awarded has behaved unreasonably or improperly during the trial, it may award that party an amount less than would otherwise be payable for that claim, as it considers appropriate.

(8) Where the court considers that the party who is to pay the fast track trial costs has behaved improperly during the trial the court may award such additional amount to the other party as it considers appropriate.

[CPR 45.40]

45.40 **Fast track trial costs where there is more than one claimant or defendant**

(1) Where the same advocate is acting for more than one party—

- (a) the court may make only one award in respect of fast track trial costs payable to that advocate; and
- (b) the parties for whom the advocate is acting are jointly entitled to any fast track trial costs awarded by the court.

(2) Where—

- (a) the same advocate is acting for more than one claimant; and
- (b) each claimant has a separate claim against the defendant,

the value of the claim, for the purpose of quantifying the award in respect of fast track trial costs is to be ascertained in accordance with paragraph (3).

(3) The value of the claim in the circumstances mentioned in paragraph (2) or (5) is—

- (a) where the only claim of each claimant is for the payment of money—
  - (i) if the award of fast track trial costs is in favour of the claimants, the total amount of the judgment made in favour of all the claimants jointly represented; or
  - (ii) if the award is in favour of the defendant, the total amount claimed by the claimants,

  and in either case, quantified in accordance with rule 45.38(3);
- (b) where the only claim of each claimant is for a remedy other than the payment of money, deemed to be more than £3,000 but not more than £10,000; and

(c) where claims of the claimants include both a claim for the payment of money and for a remedy other than the payment of money, deemed to be—
   (i) more than £3,000 but not more than £10,000; or
   (ii) if greater, the value of the money claims calculated in accordance with subparagraph (a) above.

(4) Where—
   (a) there is more than one defendant; and
   (b) any or all of the defendants are separately represented,

the court may award fast track trial costs to each party who is separately represented.

(5) Where—
   (a) there is more than one claimant; and
   (b) a single defendant,

the court may make only one award to the defendant of fast track trial costs, for which the claimants are jointly and severally liable.

(6) For the purpose of quantifying the fast track trial costs awarded to the single defendant under paragraph (5), the value of the claim is to be calculated in accordance with paragraph (3) of this rule.

SECTION VII COSTS LIMITS IN AARHUS CONVENTION CLAIMS

[CPR 45.41]

45.41 **Scope and interpretation**

(1) This Section provides for the costs which are to be recoverable between the parties in Aarhus Convention claims.

(2) In this Section—
   (a) "Aarhus Convention claim" means a claim brought by one or more members of the public—
      (i) by judicial review or review under statute which challenges the legality of any decision, act or omission of a body exercising public functions, and which is within the scope of Article 9(1) or 9(2) of the UNECE Convention on Access to Information, Public Participation in Decision-Making and Access to Justice in Environmental Matters done at Aarhus, Denmark on 25 June 1998 ("the Aarhus Convention"); or
      (ii) by judicial review which challenges the legality of any such decision, act or omission and which is within the scope of Article 9(3) of the Aarhus Convention;
   (b) references to a member or members of the public are to be construed in accordance with the Aarhus Convention.

(3) This Section does not apply to appeals other than appeals brought under section 289(1) of the Town and Country Planning Act 1990 or section 65(1) of the Planning (Listed Buildings and Conservation Areas) Act 1990, which are for the purposes of this Section to be treated as reviews under statute.

(Rule 52.19A makes provision in relation to costs of an appeal.)

The Aarhus Convention is available on the UNECE website at www.unece.org/env/pp/welcome.html.)

[CPR 45.42]

45.42 **Opting out, and other cases where rules 45.43 to 45.45 do not apply to a claimant**

(1) Subject to paragraph (2), rules 45.43 to 45.45 apply where a claimant who is a member of the public has—

(a) stated in the claim form that the claim is an Aarhus Convention claim; and

(b) filed and served with the claim form a schedule of the claimant's financial resources, which is verified by a statement of truth and provides details of—

(i) the claimant's significant assets, liabilities, income and expenditure; and

(ii) in relation to any financial support which any person has provided or is likely to provide to the claimant, the aggregate amount which has been provided and which is likely to be provided.

(2) Subject to paragraph (3), rules 45.43 to 45.45 do not apply where the claimant has stated in the claim form that although the claim is an Aarhus Convention claim, the claimant does not wish those rules to apply.

(3) If there is more than one claimant, rules 45.43 to 45.45 do not apply in relation to the costs payable by or to any claimant who has not acted as set out in paragraph (1), or who has acted as set out in paragraph (2), or who is not a member of the public.

[CPR 45.43]

45.43 **Limit on costs recoverable from a party in an Aarhus Convention claim**

(1) Subject to rules 45.42 and 45.45, a claimant or defendant in an Aarhus Convention claim may not be ordered to pay costs exceeding the amounts in paragraph (2) or (3) or as varied in accordance with rule 45.44.

(2) For a claimant the amount is—

(a) £5,000 where the claimant is claiming only as an individual and not as, or on behalf of, a business or other legal person;

(b) £10,000 in all other cases.

(3) For a defendant the amount is £35,000.

(4) In an Aarhus Convention claim with multiple claimants or multiple defendants, the amounts in paragraphs (2) and (3) (subject to any direction of the court under rule 45.44) apply in relation to each such claimant or defendant individually and may not be exceeded, irrespective of the number of receiving parties.

[CPR 45.44]

45.44 **Varying the limit on costs recoverable from a party in an Aarhus Convention claim**

(1) The court may vary the amounts in rule 45.43 or may remove altogether the limits on the maximum costs liability of any party in an Aarhus Convention claim.

(2) The court may vary such an amount or remove such a limit only on an application made in accordance with paragraphs (5) to (7) ("an application to vary") and if satisfied that—

(a) to do so would not make the costs of the proceedings prohibitively expensive for the claimant; and

(b) in the case of a variation which would reduce a claimant's maximum costs liability or increase that of a defendant, without the variation the costs of the proceedings would be prohibitively expensive for the claimant.

(3) Proceedings are to be considered prohibitively expensive for the purpose of this rule if their likely costs (including any court fees which are payable by the claimant) either—

(a) exceed the financial resources of the claimant; or

(b) are objectively unreasonable having regard to—

(i) the situation of the parties;

(ii) whether the claimant has a reasonable prospect of success;

(iii) the importance of what is at stake for the claimant;

(iv) the importance of what is at stake for the environment;

(v) the complexity of the relevant law and procedure; and

(vi) whether the claim is frivolous.

(4) When the court considers the financial resources of the claimant for the purposes of this rule, it must have regard to any financial support which any person has provided or is likely to provide to the claimant.

(5) Subject to paragraph (6), an application to vary must—

(a) if made by the claimant, be made in the claim form and provide the claimant's reasons why, if the variation were not made, the costs of the proceedings would be prohibitively expensive for the claimant;

(b) if made by the defendant, be made in the acknowledgment of service and provide the defendant's reasons why, if the variation were made, the costs of the proceedings would not be prohibitively expensive for the claimant; and

(c) be determined by the court at the earliest opportunity.

(6) An application to vary may be made at a later stage if there has been a significant change in circumstances (including evidence that the schedule of the claimant's financial resources contained false or misleading information) which means that the proceedings would now—

(a) be prohibitively expensive for the claimant if the variation were not made; or

(b) not be prohibitively expensive for the claimant if the variation were made.

(7) An application under paragraph (6) must—

(a) if made by the claimant—

(i) be accompanied by a revised schedule of the claimant's financial resources or confirmation that the claimant's financial resources have not changed; and

(ii) provide reasons why the proceedings would now be prohibitively expensive for the claimant if the variation were not made; and

(b) if made by the defendant, provide reasons why the proceedings would now not be prohibitively expensive for the claimant if the variation were made.

(Rule 39.2(3)(c) makes provision for a hearing (or any part of it) to be in private if it involves confidential information (including information relating to personal financial matters) and publicity would damage that confidentiality.)

[CPR 45.45]

45.45 **Challenging whether the claim is an Aarhus Convention claim**

(1) Where a claimant has complied with rule 45.42(1), and subject to rule 45.42(2) and (3), rule 45.43 will apply unless—

(a) the defendant has in the acknowledgment of service—

(i) denied that the claim is an Aarhus Convention claim; and

(ii) set out the defendant's grounds for such denial; and

(b) the court has determined that the claim is not an Aarhus Convention claim.

(2) Where the defendant denies that the claim is an Aarhus Convention claim, the court must determine that issue at the earliest opportunity.

(3) In any proceedings to determine whether the claim is an Aarhus Convention claim—

(a) if the court holds that the claim is not an Aarhus Convention claim, it will normally make no order for costs in relation to those proceedings;

(b) if the court holds that the claim is an Aarhus Convention claim, it will normally order the defendant to pay the claimant's costs of those proceedings to be assessed on the standard basis, and that order may be enforced even if this would increase the costs payable by the defendant beyond the amount stated in rule 45.43(3) or any variation of that amount.

PRACTICE DIRECTION 45—FIXED COSTS

THIS PRACTICE DIRECTION SUPPLEMENTS PART 45

Section I of Part 45 – Fixed costs

Fixed costs in small claims

[CPR PD 45.1]

1.1 Under Rule 27.14 the costs which can be awarded to a claimant in a small claim include the fixed costs payable under Part 45 attributable to issuing the claim.

1.2 Those fixed costs are the sum of—

(a) the fixed commencement costs calculated in accordance with Table 1 of Rule 45.2;

(b) the appropriate court fee or fees paid by the claimant.

Claims to which Part 45 does not apply

1.3 In a claim to which Part 45 does not apply, no amount shall be entered on the claim form for the charges of the claimant's legal representative, but the words "to be assessed" shall be inserted.

Section II of Part 45 – Road traffic accidents: Fixed recoverable costs in costs-only proceedings

Scope

[CPR PD 45.2]

2.1 Section II of Part 45 ('the Section') provides for certain fixed costs to be recoverable between parties in respect of costs incurred in disputes which are settled prior to proceedings being issued. The Section applies to road traffic accident disputes as defined in rule 45.9(4)(a), where the accident which gave rise to the dispute occurred on or after 6th October 2003.

2.2 The Section does not apply to disputes where the total agreed value of the damages is within the small claims limit or exceeds £10,000. Rule 26.8(2) sets out how the financial value of a claim is assessed for the purposes of allocation to track.

2.3 Fixed recoverable costs are to be calculated by reference to the amount of agreed damages which are payable to the receiving party. In calculating the amount of these damages—

(a) account must be taken of both general and special damages and interest;

(b) any interim payments made must be included;

(c) where the parties have agreed an element of contributory negligence, the amount of damages attributed to that negligence must be deducted;

(d) any amount required by statute to be paid by the compensating party directly to a third party (such as sums paid by way of compensation recovery payments and National Health Service expenses) must not be included.

2.4 The Section applies to cases which fall within the scope of the Uninsured Drivers Agreement dated 13 August 1999. The section does not apply to cases which fall within the scope of the Untraced Drivers Agreement dated 14 February 2003.

Fixed recoverable costs formula

2.5 The amount of fixed costs recoverable is the sum of –

(a) £800;

(b) 20% of the agreed damages up to £5,000; and

(c) 15% of the agreed damages between £5,000 and £10,000.

For example, agreed damages of £7,523 would result in recoverable costs of £2,178.45 i.e.

£800 + (20% of £5,000) + (15% of £2,523).

Additional costs for work in specified areas

2.6 The area referred to in rules 45.11(2), 45.18(5), 45.29C(2), 45.29E(2), 45.25F(5), 45.29G(2) and 45.29H consists of (within London) area served by the County Court hearing centres at Barnet, Brentford, Central London, Clerkenwell and Shoreditch, Edmonton, Ilford, Mayors and City of London, Romford, Wandsworth and Willesden and (outside London) the County Court hearing centres at of Bromley, Croydon, Dartford, Gravesend and Uxbridge.

Multiple claimants

2.7 Where two or more potential claimants instruct the same legal representative, the provisions of the section apply in respect of each claimant.

Information to be included in the claim form

2.8 Costs only proceedings are commenced using the procedure set out in rule 46.14. A claim form should be issued in accordance with Part 8. Where the claimant is claiming an amount of costs which exceed the amount of the fixed recoverable costs the claim form must give details of the exceptional circumstances to justify the additional costs.

2.9 The claimant must also include on the claim form details of any disbursements. The disbursements that may be claimed are set out in rule 45.12(1). If the disbursement falls within 45.12(2)(c) (disbursements that have arisen due to a particular feature of the dispute) the claimant must give details of the particular feature of the dispute that made the disbursement necessary.

Disbursements

2.10 If the parties agree the amount of the fixed recoverable costs and the only dispute is as to the payment of, or amount of, a disbursement, then proceedings should be issued under rule 46.14.

Section IIIA — Claims Which No Longer Continue Under The RTA Or EL/PL Protocols – Disbursements

Claims for loss of earnings: Rule 45.29I(2)(g)

[CPR PD 45.2A]

2A.1 Where, under rule 45.29I(2)(g) (loss of earnings), the court allows a claim for any loss of earnings or leave by a party or witness due to attending a hearing or staying away from home for the purpose of attending a hearing, the specified sums, per day, for each person are—

(a) £90, where the value of the claim for damages is not more than £10,000; and

(b) £135, where the value of the claim for damages is more than £10,000.

Section IV of Part 45 – Scale costs for proceedings in the Intellectual Property Enterprise Court

Tables A and B

[CPR PD 45.3]

3.1 Tables A and B set out the maximum amount of scale costs which the court will award for each stage of a claim in the Intellectual Property Enterprise Court.
3.2 Table A sets out the scale costs for each stage of a claim up to determination of liability.
3.3 Table B sets out the scale costs for each stage of an inquiry as to damages or account of profits.

Table A

Stage of a claim	Maximum amount of costs
Particulars of claim	£7,000
Defence and counterclaim	£7,000
Reply and defence to counterclaim	£7,000
Reply to defence to counterclaim	£3,500
Attendance at a case management conference	£3,000
Making or responding to an application	£3,000
Providing or inspecting disclosure or product/process description	£6,000
Performing or inspecting experiments	£3,000
Preparing witness statements	£6,000
Preparing experts' report	£8,000
Preparing for and attending trial and judgment	£16,000
Preparing for determination on the papers	£5,500

Table B

Stage of a claim	Maximum amount of costs
Points of claim	£3,000

Stage of a claim	Maximum amount of costs
Points of defence	£3,000
Attendance at a case management conference	£3,000
Making or responding to an application	£3,000
Providing or inspecting disclosure	£3,000
Preparing witness statements	£6,000
Preparing experts' report	£6,000
Preparing for and attending trial and judgment	£8,000
Preparing for determination on the papers	£3,000

Section VI of Part 45 – Fast track trial costs

Scope

[CPR PD 45.4]

4.1 Section VI of Part 45 applies to the costs of an advocate for preparing for and appearing at the trial of a claim in the fast track.
4.2 It applies only where, at the date of the trial, the claim is allocated to the fast track. It does not apply in any other case, irrespective of the final value of the claim.
4.3 In particular it does not apply to a disposal hearing at which the amount to be paid under a judgment or order is decided by the court (see paragraph 12.4 of Practice Direction 26)).

PART 46 COSTS — SPECIAL CASES

SECTION I
COSTS PAYABLE BY OR TO PARTICULAR PERSONS

SECTION II
COSTS RELATING TO LEGAL REPRESENTATIVES

SECTION III
COSTS ON ALLOCATION AND RE-ALLOCATION

SECTION IV
COSTS-ONLY PROCEEDINGS

SECTION V
COSTS IN CLAIMS FOR JUDICIAL REVIEW

SECTION VI
JUDICIAL REVIEW COSTS CAPPING ORDERS UNDER PART 4 OF THE CRIMINAL JUSTICE AND COURTS ACT 2015

SECTION I COSTS PAYABLE BY OR TO PARTICULAR PERSONS

[CPR 46.1]

46.1 **Pre-commencement disclosure and orders for disclosure against a person who is not a party**

(1) This paragraph applies where a person applies—

(a) for an order under—

(i) section 33 of the Senior Courts Act 1981; or

(ii) section 52 of the County Courts Act 1984,

(which give the court powers exercisable before commencement of proceedings); or

(b) for an order under—

(i) section 34 of the Senior Courts Act 1981; or

(ii) section 53 of the County Courts Act 1984,

(which give the court power to make an order against a non-party for disclosure of documents, inspection of property etc.).

(2) The general rule is that the court will award the person against whom the order is sought that person's costs—

(a) of the application; and

(b) of complying with any order made on the application.

(3) The court may however make a different order, having regard to all the circumstances, including—

(a) the extent to which it was reasonable for the person against whom the order was sought to oppose the application; and

(b) whether the parties to the application have complied with any relevant pre-action protocol.

[CPR 46.2]

46.2 Costs orders in favour of or against non-parties

(1) Where the court is considering whether to exercise its power under section 51 of the Senior Courts Act 1981 (costs are in the discretion of the court) to make a costs order in favour of or against a person who is not a party to proceedings, that person must—

(a) be added as a party to the proceedings for the purposes of costs only; and

(b) be given a reasonable opportunity to attend a hearing at which the court will consider the matter further.

(2) This rule does not apply—

(a) where the court is considering whether to—

(i) make an order against the Lord Chancellor in proceedings in which the Lord Chancellor has provided legal aid to a party to the proceedings;

(ii) make a wasted costs order (as defined in rule 46.8); and

(b) in proceedings to which rule 46.1 applies (pre-commencement disclosure and orders for disclosure against a person who is not a party).

[CPR 46.3]

46.3 Limitations on court's power to award costs in favour of trustee or personal representative

(1) This rule applies where—

(a) a person is or has been a party to any proceedings in the capacity of trustee or personal representative; and

(b) rule 44.5 does not apply.

(2) The general rule is that that person is entitled to be paid the costs of those proceedings, insofar as they are not recovered from or paid by any other person, out of the relevant trust fund or estate.

(3) Where that person is entitled to be paid any of those costs out of the fund or estate, those costs will be assessed on the indemnity basis.

[CPR 46.4]

46.4 Costs where money is payable by or to a child or protected party

(1) This rule applies to any proceedings where a party is a child or protected party and—

(a) money is ordered or agreed to be paid to, or for the benefit of, that party; or

(b) money is ordered to be paid by that party or on that party's behalf.

("Child" and "protected party" have the same meaning as in rule 21.1(2).)

(2) The general rule is that—

(a) the court must order a detailed assessment of the costs payable by, or out of money belonging to, any party who is a child or protected party; and

(b) on an assessment under paragraph (a), the court must also assess any costs payable to that party in the proceedings, unless—

(i) the court has issued a default costs certificate in relation to those costs under rule 47.11; or

(ii) the costs are payable in proceedings to which Section II or Section III of Part 45 applies.

(3) The court need not order detailed assessment of costs in the circumstances set out in paragraph (5) or in Practice Direction 46.

(4) Where—

(a) a claimant is a child or protected party; and

(b) a detailed assessment has taken place under paragraph (2)(a),

the only amount payable by the child or protected party is the amount which the court certifies as payable.

(This rule applies to a counterclaim by or on behalf of a child or protected party by virtue of rule 20.3.)

(5) Where the costs payable comprise only the success fee claimed by the child's or protected party's legal representative under a conditional fee agreement or the balance of any payment under a damages based agreement, the court may direct that—

(a) the assessment procedure referred to in rule 46.10 and paragraph 6 of Practice Direction 46 shall not apply; and

(b) such costs be assessed summarily.

[CPR 46.5]

46.5 Litigants in person

(1) This rule applies where the court orders (whether by summary assessment or detailed assessment) that the costs of a litigant in person are to be paid by any other person.

(2) The costs allowed under this rule will not exceed, except in the case of a disbursement, two-thirds of the amount which would have been allowed if the litigant in person had been represented by a legal representative.

(3) The litigant in person shall be allowed—

(a) costs for the same categories of—

(i) work; and

(ii) disbursements,

which would have been allowed if the work had been done or the disbursements had been made by a legal representative on the litigant in person's behalf;

(b) the payments reasonably made by the litigant in person for legal services relating to the conduct of the proceedings; and

(c) the costs of obtaining expert assistance in assessing the costs claim.

(4) The amount of costs to be allowed to the litigant in person for any item of work claimed will be—

(a) where the litigant can prove financial loss, the amount that the litigant can prove to have been lost for time reasonably spent on doing the work; or

(b) where the litigant cannot prove financial loss, an amount for the time reasonably spent on doing the work at the rate set out in Practice Direction 46.

(5) A litigant who is allowed costs for attending at court to conduct the case is not entitled to a witness allowance in respect of such attendance in addition to those costs.

(6) For the purposes of this rule, a litigant in person includes—

(a) a company or other corporation which is acting without a legal representative; and

(b) any of the following who acts in person (except where any such person is represented by a firm in which that person is a partner)—

(i) a barrister;

(ii) a solicitor;

(iii) a solicitor's employee;

(iv) a manager of a body recognised under section 9 of the Administration of Justice Act 1985; or

(v) a person who, for the purposes of the 2007 Act, is an authorised person in relation to an activity which constitutes the conduct of litigation (within the meaning of that Act).

[CPR 46.6]

46.6 Costs where the court has made a group litigation order

(1) This rule applies where the court has made a Group Litigation Order ("GLO").

(2) In this rule—

"individual costs" means costs incurred in relation to an individual claim on the group register;

"common costs" means—

(i) costs incurred in relation to the GLO issues;

(ii) individual costs incurred in a claim while it is proceeding as a test claim, and

(iii) costs incurred by the lead legal representative in administering the group litigation; and

'group litigant' means a claimant or defendant, as the case may be, whose claim is entered on the group register.

(3) Unless the court orders otherwise, any order for common costs against group litigants imposes on each group litigant several liability for an equal proportion of those common costs.

(4) The general rule is that a group litigant who is the paying party will, in addition to any liability to pay the receiving party, be liable for—

(a) the individual costs of that group litigant's claim; and

(b) an equal proportion, together with all the other group litigants, of the common costs.

(5) Where the court makes an order about costs in relation to any application or hearing which involved—

(a) one or more GLO issues; and

(b) issues relevant only to individual claims,

the court will direct the proportion of the costs that is to relate to common costs and the proportion that is to relate to individual costs.

(6) Where common costs have been incurred before a claim is entered on the group register, the court may order the group litigant to be liable for a proportion of those costs.

(7) Where a claim is removed from the group register, the court may make an order for costs in that claim which includes a proportion of the common costs incurred up to the date on which the claim is removed from the group register.

(Part 19 sets out rules about group litigation.)

[CPR 46.7]

46.7 **Orders in respect of pro bono representation**

(1) Where the court makes an order under section 194(3) of the 2007 Act—

- (a) the court may order the payment to the prescribed charity of a sum no greater than the costs specified in Part 45 to which the party with pro bono representation would have been entitled in accordance with that Part and in respect of that representation had it not been provided free of charge; or
- (b) where Part 45 does not apply, the court may determine the amount of the payment (other than a sum equivalent to fixed costs) to be made by the paying party to the prescribed charity by—
  - (i) making a summary assessment; or
  - (ii) making an order for detailed assessment,

of a sum equivalent to all or part of the costs the paying party would have been ordered to pay to the party with pro bono representation in respect of that representation had it not been provided free of charge.

(2) Where the court makes an order under section 194(3) of the 2007 Act, the order must direct that the payment by the paying party be made to the prescribed charity.

(3) The receiving party must send a copy of the order to the prescribed charity within 7 days of receipt of the order.

(4) Where the court considers making or makes an order under section 194(3) of the 2007 Act, Parts 44 to 47 apply, where appropriate, with the following modifications—

- (a) references to "costs orders", "orders about costs" or "orders for the payment of costs" are to be read, unless otherwise stated, as if they refer to an order under section 194(3);
- (b) references to "costs" are to be read as if they referred to a sum equivalent to the costs that would have been claimed by, incurred by or awarded to the party with pro bono representation in respect of that representation had it not been provided free of charge; and
- (c) references to "receiving party" are to be read, as meaning a party who has pro bono representation and who would have been entitled to be paid costs in respect of that representation had it not been provided free of charge.

SECTION II COSTS RELATING TO LEGAL REPRESENTATIVES

[CPR 46.8]

46.8 **Personal liability of legal representative for costs – wasted costs orders**

(1) This rule applies where the court is considering whether to make an order under section 51(6) of the Senior Courts Act 1981 (court's power to disallow or (as the case may be) order a legal representative to meet, "wasted costs").

(2) The court will give the legal representative a reasonable opportunity to make written submissions or, if the legal representative prefers, to attend a hearing before it makes such an order.

(3) When the court makes a wasted costs order, it will—
- (a) specify the amount to be disallowed or paid; or
- (b) direct a costs judge or a District Judge to decide the amount of costs to be disallowed or paid.

(4) The court may direct that notice must be given to the legal representative's client, in such manner as the court may direct—
- (a) of any proceedings under this rule; or
- (b) of any order made under it against his legal representative.

[CPR 46.9]

46.9 **Basis of detailed assessment of solicitor and client costs**

(1) This rule applies to every assessment of a solicitor's bill to a client except a bill which is to be paid out of the Community Legal Service Fund under the Legal Aid Act 1988 or the Access to Justice Act 1999.

(2) Section 74(3) of the Solicitors Act 1974 applies unless the solicitor and client have entered into a written agreement which expressly permits payment to the solicitor of an amount of costs greater than that which the client could have recovered from another party to the proceedings.

(3) Subject to paragraph (2), costs are to be assessed on the indemnity basis but are to be presumed—
- (a) to have been reasonably incurred if they were incurred with the express or implied approval of the client;
- (b) to be reasonable in amount if their amount was expressly or impliedly approved by the client;
- (c) to have been unreasonably incurred if—
  - (i) they are of an unusual nature or amount; and
  - (ii) the solicitor did not tell the client that as a result the costs might not be recovered from the other party.

(4) Where the court is considering a percentage increase on the application of the client, the court will have regard to all the relevant factors as they reasonably appeared to the solicitor or counsel when the conditional fee agreement was entered into or varied.

[CPR 46.10]

46.10 **Assessment procedure**

(1) This rule sets out the procedure to be followed where the court has made an order under Part III of the Solicitors Act 1974 for the assessment of costs payable to a solicitor by the solicitor's client.

(2) The solicitor must serve a breakdown of costs within 28 days of the order for costs to be assessed.

(3) The client must serve points of dispute within 14 days after service on the client of the breakdown of costs.

(4) The solicitor must serve any reply within 14 days of service on the solicitor of the points of dispute.

(5) Either party may file a request for a hearing date—
- (a) after points of dispute have been served; but
- (b) no later than 3 months after the date of the order for the costs to be assessed.

(6) This procedure applies subject to any contrary order made by the court.

SECTION III COSTS ON ALLOCATION AND RE-ALLOCATION

[CPR 46.11]

46.11 Costs on the small claims track and fast track

(1) Part 27 (small claims) and Part 45 Section VI (fast track trial costs) contain special rules about—

(a) liability for costs;

(b) the amount of costs which the court may award; and

(c) the procedure for assessing costs.

(2) Once a claim is allocated to a particular track, those special rules shall apply to the period before, as well as after, allocation except where the court or a practice direction provides otherwise.

[CPR 46.12]

46.12 Limitation on amount court may allow where a claim allocated to the fast track settles before trial

(1) Where the court—

(a) assesses costs in relation to a claim which—

(i) has been allocated to the fast track; and

(ii) settles before the start of the trial; and

(b) is considering the amount of costs to be allowed in respect of a party's advocate for preparing for the trial,

it may not allow, in respect of those advocate's costs, an amount that exceeds the amount of fast track trial costs which would have been payable in relation to the claim had the trial taken place.

(2) When deciding the amount to be allowed in respect of the advocate's costs, the court will have regard to—

(a) when the claim was settled; and

(b) when the court was notified that the claim had settled.

(3) In this rule, "advocate" and "fast track trial costs" have the meanings given to them by Part 45 Section VI.

[CPR 46.13]

46.13 Costs following allocation, re-allocation and non-allocation

(1) Any costs orders made before a claim is allocated will not be affected by allocation.

(2) Where—

(a) claim is allocated to a track; and

(b) the court subsequently re-allocates that claim to a different track,

then unless the court orders otherwise, any special rules about costs applying—

(i) to the first track, will apply to the claim up to the date of re-allocation; and

(ii) to the second track, will apply from the date of re-allocation.

(3) Where the court is assessing costs on the standard basis of a claim which concluded without being allocated to a track, it may restrict those costs to costs that would have been allowed on the track to which the claim would have been allocated if allocation had taken place.

SECTION IV COSTS-ONLY PROCEEDINGS

[CPR 46.14]

46.14 Costs-only proceedings

(1) This rule applies where—

(a) the parties to a dispute have reached an agreement on all issues (including which party is to pay the costs) which is made or confirmed in writing; but

(b) they have failed to agree the amount of those costs; and

(c) no proceedings have been started.

(2) Where this rule applies, the procedure set out in this rule must be followed.

(3) Proceedings under this rule are commenced by issuing a claim form in accordance with Part 8.

(4) The claim form must contain or be accompanied by the agreement or confirmation.

(5) In proceedings to which this rule applies the court may make an order for the payment of costs the amount of which is to be determined by assessment and/or, where appropriate, for the payment of fixed costs.

(6) Where this rule applies but the procedure set out in this rule has not been followed by a party—

(a) that party will not be allowed costs greater than those that would have been allowed to that party had the procedure been followed; and

(b) the court may award the other party the costs of the proceedings up to the point where an order for the payment of costs is made.

(7) Rule 44.5 (amount of costs where costs are payable pursuant to a contract) does not apply to claims started under the procedure in this rule.

SECTION V COSTS IN CLAIMS FOR JUDICIAL REVIEW

[CPR 46.15]

46.15 Claims for judicial review: costs against interveners

(1) In this rule the terms "intervener" and "relevant party" have the same meaning as in section 87 of the Criminal Justice and Courts Act 2015 ("the 2015 Act").

(2) A relevant party may apply to the court for an order for an intervener to pay costs in accordance with section 87 of the 2015 Act.

(Section 87 of the 2015 Act applies to judicial review proceedings in the High Court and Court of Appeal.)

(Rule 54.17 makes provision for any person to be able to apply for permission to file evidence or make representations at the hearing of a judicial review.)

SECTION VI COSTS IN CLAIMS FOR JUDICIAL REVIEW

[CPR 46.16]

46.16 Judicial review costs capping orders – general

(1) For the purposes of this Section—

(a) "judicial review costs capping order" means a costs capping order made by the High Court or the Court of Appeal in accordance with sections 88, 89 and 90 of the 2015 Act; and

(b) "the 2015 Act" means the Criminal Justice and Courts Act 2015.

(2) This Section does not apply to a costs capping order under rule 3.19.

(Rule 3.19 makes provision for orders limiting the amount of future costs (including disbursements) which a party may recover pursuant to an order for costs subsequently made.)

[CPR 46.17]

46.17 **Applications for judicial review costs capping orders**

(1) An application for a judicial review costs capping order must—

(a) be made on notice and, subject to paragraphs (2) and (3), in accordance with Part 23; and

(b) be supported by evidence setting out—

(i) why a judicial review costs capping order should be made, having regard, in particular, to the matters at sub-sections (6) to (8) of section 88 of the 2015 Act and sub-section (1) of section 89 of that Act;

(ii) a summary of the applicant's financial resources;

(iii) the costs (and disbursements) which the applicant considers the parties are likely to incur in the future conduct of the proceedings; and

(iv) if the applicant is a body corporate, whether it is able to demonstrate that it is likely to have financial resources available to meet liabilities arising in connection with the proceedings.

(2) Subject to paragraph (3), the applicant must serve a copy of the application notice and copies of the supporting documents on every other party.

(3) On application by the applicant, the court may dispense with the need for the applicant to serve the evidence setting out a summary of the applicant's financial resources on one or more of the parties.

(4) The court may direct the applicant to provide additional information or evidence to support its application.

[CPR 46.18]

46.18 **Court to consider making directions**

If the applicant is a body corporate, and the evidence supporting its application in accordance with rule 46.17(1)(b)(iv) sets out that it is unable to demonstrate that it is likely to have financial resources available to meet liabilities arising in connection with the proceedings, the court must consider giving directions for the provision of information about the applicant's members and their ability to provide financial support for the purposes of the proceedings.

[CPR 46.19]

46.19 **Applications to vary judicial review costs capping orders**

(1) An application to vary a judicial review costs capping order must be made on notice and, subject to paragraphs (2) and (3), in accordance with Part 23.

(2) Subject to paragraph (3), the applicant must serve a copy of the application notice and copies of any supporting documents on every other party.

(3) If the application is supported by evidence setting out a summary of the applicant's financial resources, the court may, on application by the applicant, dispense with the need for the applicant to serve such evidence on one or more of the parties.

PRACTICE DIRECTION 46—COSTS SPECIAL CASES

THIS PRACTICE DIRECTION SUPPLEMENTS PART 46

Awards of costs in favour of a trustee or personal representative: Rule 46.3

[CPR PD 46.1]

1.1 A trustee or personal representative is entitled to an indemnity out of the relevant trust fund or estate for costs properly incurred. Whether costs were properly incurred depends on all the circumstances of the case including whether the trustee or personal representative ("the trustee")—

(a) obtained directions from the court before bringing or defending the proceedings;

(b) acted in the interests of the fund or estate or in substance for a benefit other than that of the estate, including the trustee's own; and

(c) acted in some way unreasonably in bringing or defending, or in the conduct of, the proceedings.

1.2 The trustee is not to be taken to have acted for a benefit other than that of the fund by reason only that the trustee has defended a claim in which relief is sought against the trustee personally.

Costs where money is payable by or to a child or protected party: Rule 46.4

[CPR PD 46.2]

2.1 The circumstances in which the court need not order the [detailed] assessment of costs under rule 46.4(2) are as follows—

(a) where there is no need to do so to protect the interests of the child or protected party or their estate;

(b) where another party has agreed to pay a specified sum in respect of the costs of the child or protected party and the legal representative acting for the child or protected party has waived the right to claim further costs;

(c) where the court has decided the costs payable to the child or protected party by way of summary assessment and the legal representative acting for the child or protected party has waived the right to claim further costs;

(d) where an insurer or other person is liable to discharge the costs which the child or protected party would otherwise be liable to pay to the legal representative and the court is satisfied that the insurer or other person is financially able to discharge those costs ; and

(e) where the court has given a direction for summary assessment pursuant to rule 46.4(5).

Litigants in person: Rule 46.5

[CPR PD 46.3]

3.1 In order to qualify as an expert for the purpose of rule 46.5(3)(c) (expert assistance in connection with assessing the claim for costs), the person in question must be a—

(a) barrister;

(b) solicitor;

(c) Fellow of the Institute of Legal Executives;

(d) Fellow of the Association of Costs Lawyers;

(e) law costs draftsman who is a member of the Academy of Experts;

(f) law costs draftsman who is a member of the Expert Witness Institute.

3.2 Where a self represented litigant wishes to prove that the litigant has suffered financial loss, the litigant should produce to the court any written evidence relied on to support that claim, and serve a copy of that evidence on any party against whom the litigant seeks costs at least 24 hours before the hearing at which the question may be decided.

3.3 A self represented litigant who commences detailed assessment proceedings under rule 47.5 should serve copies of that written evidence with the notice of commencement.

3.4 The amount, which may be allowed to a self represented litigant under rule 45.39(5)(b) and rule 46.5(4)(b), is £19 per hour.

Orders in respect of pro bono representation: Rule 46.7

[CPR PD 46.4]

4.1 Where an order is sought under section 194(3) of the Legal Services Act 2007 the party who has pro bono representation must prepare, file and serve a written statement of the sum equivalent to the costs that party would have claimed for that legal representation had it not been provided free of charge.

Personal liability of legal representative for costs – wasted costs orders: Rule 46.8

[CPR PD 46.5]

5.1 A wasted costs order is an order—

(a) that the legal representative pay a sum (either specified or to be assessed) in respect of costs to a party; or

(b) for costs relating to a specified sum or items of work to be disallowed.

5.2 Rule 46.8 deals with wasted costs orders against legal representatives. Such orders can be made at any stage in the proceedings up to and including the detailed assessment proceedings. In general, applications for wasted costs are best left until after the end of the trial.

5.3 The court may make a wasted costs order against a legal representative on its own initiative.

5.4 A party may apply for a wasted costs order—

(a) by filing an application notice in accordance with Part 23; or

(b) by making an application orally in the course of any hearing.

5.5 It is appropriate for the court to make a wasted costs order against a legal representative, only if—

(a) the legal representative has acted improperly, unreasonably or negligently;

(b) the legal representative's conduct has caused a party to incur unnecessary costs, or has meant that costs incurred by a party prior to the improper, unreasonable or negligent act or omission have been wasted;

(c) it is just in all the circumstances to order the legal representative to compensate that party for the whole or part of those costs.

5.6 The court will give directions about the procedure to be followed in each case in order to ensure that the issues are dealt with in a way which is fair and as simple and summary as the circumstances permit.

5.7 As a general rule the court will consider whether to make a wasted costs order in two stages—

(a) at the first stage the court must be satisfied—

  (i) that it has before it evidence or other material which, if unanswered, would be likely to lead to a wasted costs order being made; and

  (ii) the wasted costs proceedings are justified notwithstanding the likely costs involved;

(b) at the second stage, the court will consider, after giving the legal representative an opportunity to make representations in writing or at a hearing, whether it is appropriate to make a wasted costs order in accordance with paragraph 5.5 above.

5.8 The court may proceed to the second stage described in paragraph 5.7 without first adjourning the hearing if it is satisfied that the legal representative has already had a reasonable opportunity to make representations.

5.9 On an application for a wasted costs order under Part 23 the application notice and any evidence in support must identify—

(a) what the legal representative is alleged to have done or failed to do; and

(b) the costs that the legal representative may be ordered to pay or which are sought against the legal representative.

Assessment of solicitor and client costs: Rules 46.9 and 46.10

[CPR PD 46.6]

6.1 A client and solicitor may agree whatever terms they consider appropriate about the payment of the solicitor's charges. If however, the costs are of an unusual nature, either in amount or the type of costs incurred, those costs will be presumed to have been unreasonably incurred unless the solicitor satisfies the court that the client was informed that they were unusual and that they might not be allowed on an assessment of costs between the parties. That information must have been given to the client before the costs were incurred.

6.2 Costs as between a solicitor and client are assessed on the indemnity basis. The presumptions in rule 46.9(3) are rebuttable.

6.3 If a party fails to comply with the requirements of rule 46.10 concerning the service of a breakdown of costs or points of dispute, any other party may apply to the court in which the detailed assessment hearing should take place for an order requiring compliance. If the court makes such an order, it may—

(a) make it subject to conditions including a condition to pay a sum of money into court; and

(b) specify the consequence of failure to comply with the order or a condition.

6.4 The procedure for obtaining an order under Part III of the Solicitors Act 1974 is by a Part 8 claim, as modified by rule 67.3 and Practice Direction 67. Precedent J of the Schedule of Costs Precedents is a model form of claim form. The application must be accompanied by the bill or bills in respect of which assessment is sought, and, if the claim concerns a conditional fee agreement, a copy of that agreement. If the original bill is not available a copy will suffice.

6.5 Model forms of order, which the court may make, are set out in Precedents K, L and M of the Schedule of Costs Precedents.

6.6 The breakdown of costs referred to in rule 46.10 is a document which contains the following information—

(a) details of the work done under each of the bills sent for assessment; and

(b) in applications under Section 70 of the Solicitors Act 1974, a cash account showing money received by the solicitor to the credit of the client and sums paid out of that money on behalf of the client but not payments out which were made in satisfaction of the bill or of any items which are claimed in the bill.

6.7 Precedent P of the Schedule of Costs Precedents is a model form of breakdown of costs. A party who is required to serve a breakdown of costs must also serve–

(a) copies of the fee notes of counsel and of any expert in respect of fees claimed in the breakdown, and

(b) written evidence as to any other disbursement which is claimed in the breakdown and which exceeds £250.

6.8 The provisions relating to default costs certificates (rule 47.11) do not apply to cases to which rule 46.10 applies.

6.9 The time for requesting a detailed assessment hearing is within 3 months after the date of the order for the costs to be assessed.

6.10 The form of request for a hearing date must be in Form N258C. The request must be accompanied by copies of—

(a) the order sending the bill or bills for assessment;

(b) the bill or bills sent for assessment;

(c) the solicitor's breakdown of costs and any invoices or accounts served with that breakdown;
(d) a copy of the points of dispute;
(e) a copy of any replies served;
(f) a statement signed by the party filing the request or that party's legal representative giving the names and addresses for service of all parties to the proceedings.

6.11 The request must include the estimated length of hearing.

6.12 On receipt of the request the court will fix a date for the hearing, or will give directions.

6.13 The court will give at least 14 days notice of the time and place of the detailed assessment hearing.

6.14 Unless the court gives permission, only the solicitor whose bill it is and parties who have served points of dispute may be heard and only items specified in the points of dispute may be raised.

6.15 If a party wishes to vary that party's breakdown of costs, points of dispute or reply, an amended or supplementary document must be filed with the court and copies of it must be served on all other relevant parties. Permission is not required to vary a breakdown of costs, points of dispute or a reply but the court may disallow the variation or permit it only upon conditions, including conditions as to the payment of any costs caused or wasted by the variation.

6.16 Unless the court directs otherwise the solicitor must file with the court the papers in support of the bill not less than 7 days before the date for the detailed assessment hearing and not more than 14 days before that date.

6.17 Once the detailed assessment hearing has ended it is the responsibility of the legal representative appearing for the solicitor or, as the case may be, the solicitor in person to remove the papers filed in support of the bill.

6.18 If, in the course of a detailed assessment hearing of a solicitor's bill to that solicitor's client, it appears to the court that in any event the solicitor will be liable in connection with that bill to pay money to the client, it may issue an interim certificate specifying an amount which in its opinion is payable by the solicitor to the client.

6.19 After the detailed assessment hearing is concluded the court will –
(a) complete the court copy of the bill so as to show the amount allowed;
(b) determine the result of the cash account;
(c) award the costs of the detailed assessment hearing in accordance with Section 70(8) of the Solicitors Act 1974; and
(d) issue a final costs certificate.

Costs on the small claims and fast tracks: Rule 46.11

[CPR PD 46.7]

7.1
(1) Before a claim is allocated to either the small claims track or the fast track the court is not restricted by any of the special rules that apply to that track but see paragraph 8.2 below.
(2) Where a claim has been so allocated, the special rules which relate to that track will apply to work done before as well as after allocation save to the extent (if any) that an order for costs in respect of that work was made before allocation.
(3) Where a claim, issued for a sum in excess of the normal financial scope of the small claims track, is allocated to that track only because an admission of part of the claim by the defendant reduces the amount in dispute to a sum within the normal scope of that track; on entering judgment for the admitted part before allocation of the balance of the claim the court may allow costs in respect of the proceedings down to that date.

Costs following allocation, re-allocation and non-allocation: Rule 46.13

[CPR PD 46.8]

8.1 Before reallocating a claim from the small claims track to another track, the court must decide whether any party is to pay costs to the date of the order to re-allocate in accordance with the rules about costs contained in Part 27 If it decides to make such an order the court will make a summary assessment of those costs in accordance with that Part.

8.2 Where a settlement is reached or a Part 36 offer accepted in a case which has not been allocated but would, if allocated, have been suitable for allocation to the small claims track, rule 46.13 enables the court to allow only small claims track costs in accordance with rule 27.14. This power is not exercisable if the costs are to be paid on the indemnity basis.

Costs-only proceedings: Rule 46.14

[CPR PD 46.9]

9.1 A claim form under rule 46.14 should not be issued in the High Court unless the dispute to which the agreement relates was of such a value or type that proceedings would have been commenced in the High Court.

9.2 A claim form which is to be issued in the High Court at the Royal Courts of Justice will be issued in the Costs Office.

9.3 Attention is drawn to rule 8.2 (in particular to paragraph (b)(ii)) and to rule 46.14(3). The claim form must—

(a) identify the claim or dispute to which the agreement relates;
(b) state the date and terms of the agreement on which the claimant relies;
(c) set out or attach a draft of the order which the claimant seeks;
(d) state the amount of the costs claimed.

9.4 Unless the court orders otherwise or Section II of Part 45 applies the costs will be treated as being claimed on the standard basis.

9.5 The evidence required under rule 8.5 includes copies of the documents on which the claimant relies to prove the defendant's agreement to pay costs.

9.6 A costs judge or a District Judge has jurisdiction to hear and decide any issue which may arise in a claim issued under this rule irrespective of the amount of the costs claimed or of the value of the claim to which the agreement to pay costs relates. The court may make an order by consent under paragraph 9.8, or an order dismissing a claim under paragraph 9.10 below.

9.7 When the time for filing the defendant's acknowledgement of service has expired, the claimant may request in writing that the court make an order in the terms of the claim, unless the defendant has filed an acknowledgement of service stating the intention to contest the claim or to seek a different order.

9.8 Rule 40.6 applies where an order is to be made by consent. An order may be made by consent in terms which differ from those set out in the claim form.

9.9 Where costs are ordered to be assessed, the general rule is that this should be by detailed assessment. However when an order is made under this rule following a hearing and the court is in a position to summarily assess costs it should generally do so.

9.10 If the defendant opposes the claim the defendant must file a witness statement in accordance with rule 8.5(3). The court will then give directions including, if appropriate, a direction that the claim shall continue as if it were a Part 7 claim. A claim is not treated as opposed merely because the defendant disputes the amount of the claim for costs.

9.11 A claim issued under this rule may be dealt with without being allocated to a track. Rule 8.9 does not apply to claims issued under this rule.

9.12 Where there are other issues nothing in rule 46.14 prevents a person from issuing a claim form under Part 7 or Part 8 to sue on an agreement made in settlement of a dispute where that agreement makes provision for costs, nor from claiming in that case an order for costs or a specified sum in respect of costs but the "costs only" procedure in rule 46.14 must be used where the sole issue is the amount of costs.

Judicial review costs capping orders under Part 4 of the Criminal Justice and Courts Act 2015: rules 46.16 to 46.19

[CPR PD 46.10]

10.1 Unless the court directs otherwise, a summary of an applicant's financial resources under rule 46.17(1)(b)(ii) must provide details of—
(a) the applicant's significant assets, liabilities, income and expenditure; and
(b) in relation to any financial support which any person has provided or is likely to provide to the applicant, the aggregate amount—
(i) which has been provided; and
(ii) which is likely to be provided.

10.2 An application to the High Court for a judicial review costs capping order must normally be contained in, or accompany, the claim form.

PART 47 PROCEDURE FOR DETAILED ASSESSMENT OF COSTS AND DEFAULT PROVISIONS

SECTION I GENERAL RULES ABOUT DETAILED ASSESSMENT

[CPR 47.1]

47.1 **Time when detailed assessment may be carried out**

The general rule is that the costs of any proceedings or any part of the proceedings are not to be assessed by the detailed procedure until the conclusion of the proceedings, but the court may order them to be assessed immediately.

(Practice Direction 47 gives further guidance about when proceedings are concluded for the purpose of this rule.)

[CPR 47.2]

47.2 **No stay of detailed assessment where there is an appeal**

Detailed assessment is not stayed pending an appeal unless the court so orders.

[CPR 47.3]

47.3 **Powers of an authorised court officer**

(1) An authorised court officer has all the powers of the court when making a detailed assessment, except—

- (a) power to make a wasted costs order as defined in rule 46.8;
- (b) power to make an order under—
  - (i) rule 44.11 (powers in relation to misconduct);
  - (ii) rule 47.8 (sanction for delay in commencing detailed assessment proceedings);
  - (iii) paragraph (2) (objection to detailed assessment by authorised court officer); and
- (c) power to make a detailed assessment of costs payable to a solicitor by that solicitor's client, unless the costs are being assessed under rule 46.4 (costs where money is payable to a child or protected party).

(2) Where a party objects to the detailed assessment of costs being made by an authorised court officer, the court may order it to be made by a costs judge or a District Judge.

(Practice Direction 47 sets out the relevant procedure.)

[CPR 47.4]

47.4 **Venue for detailed assessment proceedings**

(1) All applications and requests in detailed assessment proceedings must be made to or filed at the appropriate office.

(Practice Direction 47 sets out the meaning of "appropriate office" in any particular case)

(2) The court may direct that the appropriate office is to be the Costs Office.

(3) In the County Court, a court may direct that another County Court hearing centre is to be the appropriate office.

(4) A direction under paragraph (3) may be made without proceedings being transferred to that court.

(Rule 30.2 makes provision for the transfer within the County Court of proceedings for detailed assessment of costs.)

SECTION II COSTS PAYABLE BY ONE PARTY TO ANOTHER – COMMENCEMENT OF DETAILED ASSESSMENT PROCEEDINGS

[CPR 47.5]

47.5 **Application of this Section**

This Section of Part 47 applies where a cost officer is to make a detailed assessment of—

(a) costs which are payable by one party to another; or

(b) the sum which is payable by one party to the prescribed charity pursuant to an order under section 194(3) of the 2007 Act.

[CPR 47.6]

47.6 **Commencement of detailed assessment proceedings**

(1) Detailed assessment proceedings are commenced by the receiving party serving on the paying party—

(a) notice of commencement in the relevant practice form;

(b) a copy or copies of the bill of costs, as required by Practice Direction 47; and

(c) if required by Practice Direction 47, a breakdown of the costs claimed for each phase of the proceedings.

(Rule 47.7 sets out the period for commencing detailed assessment proceedings.)

(2) The receiving party must also serve a copy of the notice of commencement, the bill and, if required by Practice Direction 47, the breakdown on any other relevant persons specified in Practice Direction 47.

(3) A person on whom a copy of the notice of commencement is served under paragraph (2) is a party to the detailed assessment proceedings (in addition to the paying party and the receiving party).

(Practice Direction 47 deals with—

other documents which the party must file when requesting detailed assessment;

the court's powers where it considers that a hearing may be necessary;

the form of a bill; and

the length of notice which will be given if a hearing date is fixed.)

(Paragraphs 7B.2 to 7B.7 of the Practice Direction – Civil Recovery Proceedings contain provisions about detailed assessment of costs in relation to civil recovery orders.)

[CPR 47.7]

47.7 **Period for commencing detailed assessment proceedings**

The following table shows the period for commencing detailed assessment proceedings.

Source of right to detailed assessment	**Time by which detailed assessment proceedings must be commenced**
Judgment, direction, order, award or other determination	3 months after the date of the judgment etc
	Where detailed assessment is stayed pending an appeal, 3 months after the date of the order lifting the stay.
Discontinuance under Part 38	3 months after the date of service of notice of discontinuance under rule 38.3; or

Source of right to detailed assessment	Time by which detailed assessment proceedings must be commenced
	3 months after the date of the dismissal of application to set the notice of discontinuance aside under rule 38.4
Acceptance of an offer to settle	3 months after the date when the right to costs arose.

[CPR 47.8]

47.8 **Sanction for delay in commencing detailed assessment proceedings**

(1) Where the receiving party fails to commence detailed assessment proceedings within the period specified—

(a) in rule 47.7; or

(b) by any direction of the court,

the paying party may apply for an order requiring the receiving party to commence detailed assessment proceedings within such time as the court may specify.

(2) On an application under paragraph (1), the court may direct that, unless the receiving party commences detailed assessment proceedings within the time specified by the court, all or part of the costs to which the receiving party would otherwise be entitled will be disallowed.

(3) If—

(a) the paying party has not made an application in accordance with paragraph (1); and

(b) the receiving party commences the proceedings later than the period specified in rule 47.7,

the court may disallow all or part of the interest otherwise payable to the receiving party under—

(i) section 17 of the Judgments Act 1838; or

(ii) section 74 of the County Courts Act 1984,

but will not impose any other sanction except in accordance with rule 44.11 (powers in relation to misconduct).

(4) Where the costs to be assessed in a detailed assessment are payable out of the Community Legal Service Fund, this rule applies as if the receiving party were the solicitor to whom the costs are payable and the paying party were the Legal Services Commission.

[CPR 47.9]

47.9 **Points of dispute and consequence of not serving**

(1) The paying party and any other party to the detailed assessment proceedings may dispute any item in the bill of costs by serving points of dispute on—

(a) the receiving party; and

(b) every other party to the detailed assessment proceedings.

(2) The period for serving points of dispute is 21 days after the date of service of the notice of commencement.

(3) If a party serves points of dispute after the period set out in paragraph (2), that party may not be heard further in the detailed assessment proceedings unless the court gives permission.

(Practice Direction 47 sets out requirements about the form of points of dispute.)

(4) The receiving party may file a request for a default costs certificate if—

(a) the period set out in paragraph (2) for serving points of dispute has expired; and

(b) the receiving party has not been served with any points of dispute.

(5) If any party (including the paying party) serves points of dispute before the issue of a default costs certificate the court may not issue the default costs certificate.

(Section IV of this Part sets out the procedure to be followed after points of dispute have been served.)

[CPR 47.10]

47.10 **Procedure where costs are agreed**

(1) If the paying party and the receiving party agree the amount of costs, either party may apply for a costs certificate (either interim or final) in the amount agreed.

(Rule 47.16 and rule 47.17 contain further provisions about interim and final costs certificates respectively)

(2) An application for a certificate under paragraph (1) must be made to the court which would be the venue for detailed assessment proceedings under rule 47.4.

SECTION III COSTS PAYABLE BY ONE PARTY TO ANOTHER – DEFAULT PROVISIONS

[CPR 47.11]

47.11 **Default costs certificate**

(1) Where the receiving party is permitted by rule 47.9 to obtain a default costs certificate, that party does so by filing a request in the relevant practice form.

(Practice Direction 47 deals with the procedure by which the receiving party may obtain a default costs certificate.)

(2) A default costs certificate will include an order to pay the costs to which it relates.

(3) Where a receiving party obtains a default costs certificate, the costs payable to that party for the commencement of detailed assessment proceedings will be the sum set out in Practice Direction 47.

(4) A receiving party who obtains a default costs certificate in detailed assessment proceedings pursuant to an order under section 194(3) of the 2007 Act must send a copy of the default costs certificate to the prescribed charity.

[CPR 47.12]

47.12 **Setting aside a default costs certificate**

(1) The court will set aside a default costs certificate if the receiving party was not entitled to it.

(2) In any other case, the court may set aside or vary a default costs certificate if it appears to the court that there is some good reason why the detailed assessment proceedings should continue.

(Practice Direction 47 contains further details about the procedure for setting aside a default costs certificate and the matters which the court must take into account)

(3) Where the court sets aside or varies a default costs certificate in detailed assessment proceedings pursuant to an order under section 194(3) of the Legal Services Act 2007, the receiving party must send a copy of the order setting aside or varying the default costs certificate to the prescribed charity.

SECTION IV COSTS PAYABLE BY ONE PARTY TO ANOTHER – PROCEDURE WHERE POINTS OF DISPUTE ARE SERVED

[CPR 47.13]

47.13 **Optional Reply**

(1) Where any party to the detailed assessment proceedings serves points of dispute, the receiving party may serve a reply on the other parties to the assessment proceedings.

(2) The receiving party may do so within 21 days after being served with the points of dispute to which the reply relates.

(Practice Direction 47 sets out the meaning of "reply".)

[CPR 47.14]

47.14 **Detailed assessment hearing**

(1) Where points of dispute are served in accordance with this Part, the receiving party must file a request for a detailed assessment hearing within 3 months of the expiry of the period for commencing detailed assessment proceedings as specified—

(a) in rule 47.7; or

(b) by any direction of the court.

(2) Where the receiving party fails to file a request in accordance with paragraph (1), the paying party may apply for an order requiring the receiving party to file the request within such time as the court may specify.

(3) On an application under paragraph (2), the court may direct that, unless the receiving party requests a detailed assessment hearing within the time specified by the court, all or part of the costs to which the receiving party would otherwise be entitled will be disallowed.

(4) If—

(a) the paying party has not made an application in accordance with paragraph (2); and

(b) the receiving party files a request for a detailed assessment hearing later than the period specified in paragraph (1),

the court may disallow all or part of the interest otherwise payable to the receiving party under—

(i) section 17 of the Judgments Act 1838; or

(ii) section 74 of the County Courts Act 1984,

but will not impose any other sanction except in accordance with rule 44.11 (powers in relation to misconduct).

(5) No party other than—

(a) the receiving party;

(b) the paying party; and

(c) any party who has served points of dispute under rule 47.9,

may be heard at the detailed assessment hearing unless the court gives permission.

(6) Only items specified in the points of dispute may be raised at the hearing, unless the court gives permission.

(7) If an assessment is carried out at more than one hearing, then for the purposes of rule 52.12 time for appealing shall not start to run until the conclusion of the final hearing, unless the court orders otherwise.

(Practice Direction 47 specifies other documents which must be filed with the request for hearing and the length of notice which the court will give when it fixes a hearing date.)

[CPR 47.15]

47.15 Provisional Assessment

(1) This rule applies to any detailed assessment proceedings commenced in the High Court or the County Court on or after 1 April 2013 in which the costs claimed are the amount set out in paragraph 14.1 of the practice direction supplementing this Part, or less.

(2) In proceedings to which this rule applies, the parties must comply with the procedure set out in Part 47 as modified by paragraph 14 Practice Direction 47.

(3) The court will undertake a provisional assessment of the receiving party's costs on receipt of Form N258 and the relevant supporting documents specified in Practice Direction 47.

(4) The provisional assessment will be based on the information contained in the bill and supporting papers and the contentions set out in Precedent G (the points of dispute and any reply).

(5) In proceedings which do not go beyond provisional assessment, the maximum amount the court will award to any party as costs of the assessment (other than the costs of drafting the bill of costs) is £1,500 together with any VAT thereon and any court fees paid by that party.

(6) The court may at any time decide that the matter is unsuitable for a provisional assessment and may give directions for the matter to be listed for hearing. The matter will then proceed under rule 47.14 without modification.

(7) When a provisional assessment has been carried out, the court will send a copy of the bill, as provisionally assessed, to each party with a notice stating that any party who wishes to challenge any aspect of the provisional assessment must, within 21 days of the receipt of the notice, file and serve on all other parties a written request for an oral hearing. If no such request is filed and served within that period, the provisional assessment shall be binding upon the parties, save in exceptional circumstances.

(8) The written request referred to in paragraph (7) must—

- (a) identify the item or items in the court's provisional assessment which are sought to be reviewed at the hearing; and
- (b) provide a time estimate for the hearing.

(9) The court then will fix a date for the hearing and give at least 14 days' notice of the time and place of the hearing to all parties.

(10) Any party which has requested an oral hearing, will pay the costs of and incidental to that hearing unless—

- (a) it achieves an adjustment in its own favour by 20% or more of the sum provisionally assessed; or
- (b) the court otherwise orders.

SECTION V INTERIM COSTS CERTIFICATE AND FINAL COSTS CERTIFICATE

[CPR 47.16]

47.16 Power to issue an interim certificate

(1) The court may at any time after the receiving party has filed a request for a detailed assessment hearing –

- (a) issue an interim costs certificate for such sum as it considers appropriate; or
- (b) amend or cancel an interim certificate.

(2) An interim certificate will include an order to pay the costs to which it relates, unless the court orders otherwise.

(3) The court may order the costs certified in an interim certificate to be paid into court.

(4) Where the court –

(a) issues an interim costs certificate; or

(b) amends or cancels an interim certificate,

in detailed assessment proceedings pursuant to an order under section 194(3) of the 2007 Act, the receiving party must send a copy of the interim costs certificate or the order amending or cancelling the interim costs certificate to the prescribed charity.

[CPR 47.17]

47.17 **Final costs certificate**

(1) In this rule a "completed bill" means a bill calculated to show the amount due following the detailed assessment of the costs.

(2) The period for filing the completed bill is 14 days after the end of the detailed assessment hearing.

(3) When a completed bill is filed the court will issue a final costs certificate and serve it on the parties to the detailed assessment proceedings.

(4) Paragraph (3) is subject to any order made by the court that a certificate is not to be issued until other costs have been paid.

(5) A final costs certificate will include an order to pay the costs to which it relates, unless the court orders otherwise.

(Practice Direction 47 deals with the form of a final costs certificate.)

(6) Where the court issues a final costs certificate in detailed assessment proceedings pursuant to an order under section 194(3) of the 2007 Act, the receiving party must send a copy of the final costs certificate to the prescribed charity.

SECTION VI DETAILED ASSESSMENT PROCEDURE FOR COSTS OF A LSC FUNDED CLIENT OR AN ASSISTED PERSON WHERE COSTS ARE PAYABLE OUT OF THE COMMUNITY LEGAL SERVICE FUND

[CPR 47.18]

47.18 **Detailed assessment procedure where costs are payable out of the Community Legal Services Fund**

(1) Where the court is to assess costs of a LSC funded client or an assisted person which are payable out of the Community Legal Services Fund, that person's solicitor may commence detailed assessment proceedings by filing a request in the relevant practice form.

(2) A request under paragraph (1) must be filed within 3 months after the date when the right to detailed assessment arose.

(3) The solicitor must also serve a copy of the request for detailed assessment on the LSC funded client or the assisted person, if notice of that person's interest has been given to the court in accordance with community legal service or legal aid regulations.

(4) Where the solicitor has certified that the LSC funded client or that person wishes to attend an assessment hearing, the court will, on receipt of the request for assessment, fix a date for the assessment hearing.

(5) Where paragraph (3) does not apply, the court will, on receipt of the request for assessment provisionally assess the costs without the attendance of the solicitor, unless it considers that a hearing is necessary.

(6) After the court has provisionally assessed the bill, it will return the bill to the solicitor.

(7) The court will fix a date for an assessment hearing if the solicitor informs the court, within 14 days after receiving the provisionally assessed bill, that the solicitor wants the court to hold such a hearing.

[CPR 47.19]

47.19 **Detailed assessment procedure where costs are payable out of a fund other than the community legal service fund**

(1) Where the court is to assess costs which are payable out of a fund other than the Community Legal Service Fund, the receiving party may commence detailed assessment proceedings by filing a request in the relevant practice form.

(2) A request under paragraph (1) must be filed within 3 months after the date when the right to detailed assessment arose.

(3) The court may direct that the party seeking assessment serve a copy of the request on any person who has a financial interest in the outcome of the assessment.

(4) The court will, on receipt of the request for assessment, provisionally assess the costs without the attendance of the receiving party, unless the court considers that a hearing is necessary.

(5) After the court has provisionally assessed the bill, it will return the bill to the receiving party.

(6) The court will fix a date for an assessment hearing if the receiving party informs the court, within 14 days after receiving the provisionally assessed bill, that the receiving party wants the court to hold such a hearing.

SECTION VII COSTS OF DETAILED ASSESSMENT PROCEEDINGS

[CPR 47.20]

47.20 **Liability for costs of detailed assessment proceedings**

(1) The receiving party is entitled to the costs of the detailed assessment proceedings except where—

(a) the provisions of any Act, any of these Rules or any relevant practice direction provide otherwise; or

(b) the court makes some other order in relation to all or part of the costs of the detailed assessment proceedings.

(2) Paragraph (1) does not apply where the receiving party has pro bono representation in the detailed assessment proceedings but that party may apply for an order in respect of that representation under section 194(3) of the 2007 Act.

(3) In deciding whether to make some other order, the court must have regard to all the circumstances, including—

(a) the conduct of all the parties;

(b) the amount, if any, by which the bill of costs has been reduced; and

(c) whether it was reasonable for a party to claim the costs of a particular item or to dispute that item.

(4) The provisions of Part 36 apply to the costs of detailed assessment proceedings with the following modifications—

(a) "claimant" refers to "receiving party" and "defendant" refers to "paying party";

(b) "trial" refers to "detailed assessment hearing";

(c) a detailed assessment hearing is "in progress" from the time when it starts until the bill of costs has been assessed or agreed;

(d) for rule 36.14(7) substitute "If such sum is not paid within 14 days of acceptance of the offer, or such other period as has been agreed, the receiving party may apply for a final costs certificate for the unpaid sum."

(e) a reference to "judgment being entered" is to the completion of the detailed assessment, and references to a "judgment" being advantageous or otherwise are to the outcome of the detailed assessment.

(5) The court will usually summarily assess the costs of detailed assessment proceedings at the conclusion of those proceedings.

(6) Unless the court otherwise orders, interest on the costs of detailed assessment proceedings will run from the date of default, interim or final costs certificate, as the case may be.

(7) For the purposes of rule 36.14, detailed assessment proceedings are to be regarded as an independent claim.

SECTION VIII APPEALS FROM AUTHORISED COURT OFFICERS IN DETAILED ASSESSMENT PROCEEDINGS

[CPR 47.21]

47.21 **Right to appeal**

Any party to detailed assessment proceedings may appeal against a decision of an authorised court officer in those proceedings.

[CPR 47.22]

47.22 **Court to hear appeal**

An appeal against a decision of an authorised court officer lies to a costs judge or a District Judge of the High Court.

[CPR 47.23]

47.23 **Appeal procedure**

(1) The appellant must file an appeal notice within 21 days after the date of the decision against which it is sought to appeal.

(2) On receipt of the appeal notice, the court will—

(a) serve a copy of the notice on the parties to the detailed assessment proceedings; and

(b) give notice of the appeal hearing to those parties.

[CPR 47.24]

47.24 **Powers of the court on appeal**

On an appeal from an authorised court officer the court will—

(a) re-hear the proceedings which gave rise to the decision appealed against; and

(b) make any order and give any directions as it considers appropriate.

PRACTICE DIRECTION 47—PROCEDURE FOR DETAILED ASSESSMENT OF COSTS AND DEFAULT PROVISIONS

THIS PRACTICE DIRECTION SUPPLEMENTS PART 47

Time when assessment may be carried out: Rule 47.1

[CPR PD 47.1]

1.1 For the purposes of rule 47.1, proceedings are concluded when the court has finally determined the matters in issue in the claim, whether or not there is an appeal, or made an award of provisional damages under Part 41.

1.2 The court may order or the parties may agree in writing that, although the proceedings are continuing, they will nevertheless be treated as concluded.

1.3 A party who is served with a notice of commencement (see paragraph 5.2 below) may apply to a costs judge or a District Judge to determine whether the party who served it is entitled to commence detailed assessment proceedings. On hearing such an application the orders which the court may make include: an order allowing the detailed assessment proceedings to continue, or an order setting aside the notice of commencement.

1.4 A costs judge or a District Judge may make an order allowing detailed assessment proceedings to be commenced where there is no realistic prospect of the claim continuing.

No stay of detailed assessment where there is an appeal: Rule 47.2

[CPR PD 47.2]

2. An application to stay the detailed assessment of costs pending an appeal may be made to the court whose order is being appealed or to the court which will hear the appeal.

Powers of an authorised court officer: Rule 47.3

[CPR PD 47.3]

3.1 The court officers authorised by the Lord Chancellor to assess costs in the Costs Office and the Principal Registry of the Family Division are authorised to deal with claims where the base costs excluding VAT do not exceed £35,000 in the case of senior executive officers, or their equivalent, and £110,000 in the case of principal officers.

3.2 Where the receiving party, paying party and any other party to the detailed assessment proceedings who has served points of dispute are agreed that the assessment should not be made by an authorised court officer, the receiving party should so inform the court when requesting a hearing date. The court will then list the hearing before a costs judge or a District Judge.

3.3 In any other case a party who objects to the assessment being made by an authorised court officer must make an application to the costs judge or District Judge under Part 23 setting out the reasons for the objection.

Venue for detailed assessment proceedings: Rule 47.4

[CPR PD 47.4]

4.1 For the purposes of rule 47.4(1) the 'appropriate office' means—

(a) the district registry or the County Court hearing centre in which the case was being dealt with when the judgment or order was made or the event occurred which gave rise to the right to assessment, or to which it has subsequently been transferred;
(b) where a tribunal, person or other body makes an order for the detailed assessment of costs, a County Court hearing centre (subject to paragraph 4. 2); or
(c) in all other cases, including Court of Appeal cases, the Costs Office.

4.2
(1) This paragraph applies where the appropriate office is any of the following County Court hearing centres: Barnet, Brentford, Bromley, Central London, Clerkenwell and Shoreditch, Croydon, Edmonton, Ilford, Kingston, Mayors and City of London, Romford, Uxbridge, Wandsworth and Willesden.
(2) Where this paragraph applies—
(a) the receiving party must file any request for a detailed assessment hearing in the Costs Office and, for all purposes relating to that detailed assessment (other than the issue of default costs certificates and applications to set aside default costs certificates), the Costs Office will be treated as the appropriate office in that case;
(b) default costs certificates should be issued and applications to set aside default costs certificates should be issued and heard in the relevant County Court hearing centre; and
(c) unless an order is made under rule 47.4(2) directing that the Costs Office as part of the High Court shall be the appropriate office, an appeal from any decision made by a costs judge shall lie to the Designated Civil Judge for the London Group of County Court hearing centres or such judge as the Designated Civil Judge shall nominate. The appeal notice and any other relevant papers should be lodged at the Central London Civil Justice Centre.

4.3
(1) A direction under rule 47.4(2) or (3) specifying a particular court, registry or office as the appropriate office may be given on application or on the court's own initiative.
(2) Unless the Costs Office is the appropriate office for the purposes of rule 47.4(1) an order directing that an assessment is to take place at the Costs Office will be made only if it is appropriate to do so having regard to the size of the bill of costs, the difficulty of the issues involved, the likely length of the hearing, the cost to the parties and any other relevant matter.

Commencement of detailed assessment proceedings: Rule 47.6

[CPR PD 47.5]

5.1 In the circumstances provided for in this paragraph, bills of costs for detailed assessment must be in electronic spreadsheet format and compliant with paragraphs 5.A1 to 5.A4 ("electronic bills") while in all other circumstances bills of costs may be electronic bills or may be on paper ("paper bills") and compliant with paragraphs 5.7 to 5.21. Precedents A, B, C and D in the Schedule of Costs Precedents annexed to this Practice Direction are model forms of paper bills of costs for detailed 4 assessment. The circumstances in which bills of costs must be electronic bills are that—
(a) the case is a Part 7 multi-track claim, except—
(i) for cases in which the proceedings are subject to fixed costs or scale costs;
(ii) cases in which the receiving party is unrepresented; or
(iii) where the court has otherwise ordered; and
(b) the bills of costs relate to costs recoverable between the parties for work undertaken after 6 April 2018 ("the Transition Date").

5.A1 A model electronic bill is annexed to this version of this Practice Direction as Precedent S. The online version of this Practice Direction at www.justice.gov.uk/cou

rts/procedure-rules/civil/rules/part-47-procedure-for-detailed-assessment/practice-direction-46-costs-special-cases2 annexes Precedent S in spreadsheet and pdf formats.

5.A2 Electronic bills may be in either Precedent S spreadsheet format or any other spreadsheet format which—

(a) reports and aggregates costs based on the phases, tasks, activities and expenses defined in Schedule 2 to this Practice Direction;
(b) reports summary totals in a form comparable to Precedent S;
(c) allows the user to identify, in chronological order, the detail of all the work undertaken in each phase;
(d) automatically recalculates intermediate and overall summary totals if input data is changed;
(e) contains all calculations and reference formulae in a transparent manner so as to make its full functionality available to the court and all other parties.

5.A3 The provisions of paragraphs 5.7 to 5.21 of this Practice Direction shall apply to electronic bills insofar as they are not inconsistent with the form and content of Precedent S. Where those paragraphs require or recommend division of the bill into parts, electronic bills (unless the format of the bill already provides the requisite information, for example in identifying the costs within each phase) should incorporate a summary in a form comparable to the "Funding and Parts Table" in Precedent S to provide the information that would otherwise be provided by its division into parts.

5.A4 Where a bill of costs otherwise falls within paragraph 5.1(a) but work was done both before and after the Transition Date, a party may serve and file either a paper bill or an electronic bill in respect of work done before that date and must serve and file an electronic bill in respect of work done after that date.

5.1A Subject to paragraph 5.1B, whenever electronic bills are served or filed at the court—

(a) they must be served or filed in hard copy, in a manageable paper format as shown in the pdf version of Precedent S; and
(b) a copy of the full electronic spreadsheet version must at the same time be provided to the paying party, or as appropriate filed at court, by e-mail or other electronic means.

5.1B Whenever an electronic bill is filed at the Costs Office using Electronic Working (see Practice Direction 510)—

(a) a copy of the full electronic spreadsheet version and a pdf version must be uploaded; and
(b) the electronic bill must not be filed at court by any other means.

5.2 On commencing detailed assessment proceedings, the receiving party must] serve on the paying party and all the other relevant persons the following documents—

(a) a notice of commencement in Form N252;
(b) a copy (or, where paragraph 5.A4 applies, copies) of the bill of costs;
(c) copies of the fee notes of counsel and of any expert in respect of fees claimed in the bill;
(d) written evidence as to any other disbursement which is claimed and which exceeds £500;
(e) a statement giving the name and address for service of any person upon whom the receiving party intends to serve the notice of commencement;
(f) if a costs management order has been made (and if the same information is not already fully provided in an electronic bill), a breakdown of the costs claimed for each phase of the proceedings. Precedent Q in the Schedule of Costs Precedents annexed to this Practice Direction is a model form of breakdown of the costs claimed for each phase of the proceedings.

5.3 The notice of commencement must be completed to show as separate items—

(a) the total amount of the costs claimed in the bill;
(b) the extra sum which will be payable by way of fixed costs and court fees if a default costs certificate is obtained.

5.4 Where the notice of commencement is to be served outside England and Wales the date to be inserted in the notice of commencement for the paying party to send points of dispute is a date (not less than 21 days from the date of service of the notice) which must be calculated by reference to Section IV of Part 6 as if the notice were a claim form and as if the date to be inserted was the date for the filing of a defence.

5.5

(1) For the purposes of rule 47.6(2) a "relevant person" means—
  (a) any person who has taken part in the proceedings which gave rise to the assessment and who is directly liable under an order for costs made against that person;
  (b) any person who has given to the receiving party notice in writing that that person has a financial interest in the outcome of the assessment and wishes to be a party accordingly;
  (c) any other person whom the court orders to be treated as such.

(2) Where a party is unsure whether a person is or is not a relevant person, that party may apply to the appropriate office for directions.

(3) The court will generally not make an order that the person in respect of whom the application is made will be treated as a relevant person, unless within a specified time that person applies to the court to be joined as a party to the assessment proceedings in accordance with Part 19 (Parties and Group Litigation).

5.6 Where—

(a) a paper bill is capable of being copied electronically; and

(b) before the detailed assessment hearing,

a paying party requests an electronic copy of the bill, the receiving party must supply the paying party with a copy in its native format (for example, in Excel or an equivalent) free of charge not more than 7 days after receipt of the request.

Form and contents of bills of costs — general

5.7 A bill of costs may consist of such of the following sections as may be appropriate—

(1) title page;

(2) background information;

(3) items of costs claimed under the headings specified in paragraph 5.12;

(4) summary showing the total costs claimed on each page of the bill;

(5) schedules of time spent on non-routine attendances; and

(6) the certificates referred to in paragraph 5.21.

If the only dispute between the parties concerns disbursements, the bill of costs shall be limited to items (1) and (2) above, a list of the disbursements in issue and brief written submissions in respect of those disbursements.

5.8 Where it is necessary or convenient to do so, a bill of costs may be divided into two or more parts, each part containing sections (2), (3) and (4) above. Circumstances in which it will be necessary or convenient to divide a bill into parts include the following—

(1) Where the receiving party acted in person during the course of the proceedings (whether or not that party also had a legal representative at that time) the bill must be divided into different parts so as to distinguish between;
  (a) the costs claimed for work done by the legal representative; and
  (b) the costs claimed for work done by the receiving party in person.

(2) Where the receiving party had pro bono representation for part of the proceedings and an order under section 194(3) of the Legal Services Act 2007 has been made, the bill must be divided into different parts so as to distinguish between—
  (a) the sum equivalent to the costs claimed for work done by the legal representative acting free of charge; and
  (b) the costs claimed for work not done by the legal representative acting free of charge.

(3) Where the receiving party was represented by different legal representatives during the course of the proceedings, the bill must be divided into different parts so as to distinguish between the costs payable in respect of each legal representative.

(4) Where the receiving party obtained legal aid or LSC funding or is a person for whom civil legal services (within the meaning of Part 1 of the Legal Aid,

Sentencing and Punishment of Offenders Act 2012) were provided under arrangements made for the purposes of that Part of that Act in respect of all or part of the proceedings, the bill must be divided into separate parts so as to distinguish between—

(a) costs claimed before legal aid or LSC funding was granted or before civil legal services were provided;

(b) costs claimed after legal aid or LSC funding was granted or after civil legal services were provided; and

(c) any costs claimed after legal aid or LSC funding ceased or after civil legal services ceased to be provided.

(5) Where the bill covers costs payable under an order or orders under which there are different paying parties the bill must be divided into parts so as to deal separately with the costs payable by each paying party.

(6) Where the bill covers costs payable under an order or orders, in respect of which the receiving party wishes to claim interest from different dates, the bill must be divided to enable such interest to be calculated.

(7) Where the case commenced on or after 1 April 2013, the bill covers costs for work done both before and after that date and the costs are to be assessed on the standard basis, the bill must be divided into parts so as to distinguish between costs shown as incurred for work done before 1 April 2013 and costs shown as incurred for work done on or after 1 April 2013.

(8) Where a costs management order has been made, the costs are to be assessed on the standard basis and the receiving party's budget has been agreed by the paying party or approved by the court, the bill must be divided into separate parts so as to distinguish between the costs claimed for each phase of the last approved or agreed budget, and within each such part the bill must distinguish between the costs shown as incurred in the last agreed or approved budget and the costs shown as estimated.

(9) Where a costs management order has been made and the receiving party's budget has been agreed by the paying party or approved by the court, (a) the costs of initially completing Precedent H and (b) the other costs of the budgeting and costs management process must be set out in separate parts.

5.9 Where a party claims costs against another party and also claims costs against the LSC or Lord Chancellor only for work done in the same period, the costs claimed against the LSC or Lord Chancellor only can be claimed either in a separate part of the bill or in additional columns in the same part of the bill. Precedents B and C in the Schedule of Costs Precedents annexed to this Practice Direction show how bills should be drafted when costs are claimed against the LSC only.

Form and content of bills of costs: Title page

5.10 The title page of the bill of costs must set out—

(1) the full title of the proceedings;

(2) the name of the party whose bill it is and a description of the document showing the right to assessment (as to which see paragraph 13.3 of this Practice Direction);

(3) if VAT is included as part of the claim for costs, the VAT number of the legal representative or other person in respect of whom VAT is claimed;

(4) details of all legal aid certificates, LSC certificates, certificates recording the determinations of the Director of Legal Aid Casework and relevant amendment certificates in respect of which claims for costs are included in the bill.

Form and content of bills of costs: Background information

5.11 The background information included in the bill of costs should set out—

(1) a brief description of the proceedings up to the date of the notice of commencement;

(2) a statement of the status of the legal representatives' employee in respect of whom costs are claimed and (if those costs are calculated on the basis of hourly rates) the hourly rates claimed for each such person.

(3) a brief explanation of any agreement or arrangement between the receiving party and his legal representatives, which affects the costs claimed in the bill.

Form and content of bills of costs: Heads of costs

5.12 The bill of costs may consist of items under such of the following heads as may be appropriate—

(1) attendances at court and upon counsel up to the date of the notice of commencement;
(2) attendances on and communications with the receiving party;
(3) attendances on and communications with witnesses including any expert witness;
(4) attendances to inspect any property or place for the purposes of the proceedings;
(5) attendances on and communications with other persons, including offices of public records;
(6) communications with the court and with counsel;
(7) work done on documents:
(8) work done in connection with negotiations with a view to settlement if not already covered in the heads listed above;
(9) attendances on and communications with London and other agents and work done by them;
(10) other work done which was of or incidental to the proceedings and which is not already covered in the heads listed above.

5.13 In respect of each of the heads of costs—

(1) 'communications' means letters out e-mails out and telephone calls;
(2) communications, which are not routine communications, must be set out in chronological order;
(3) routine communications must be set out as a single item at the end of each head;

5.14 Routine communications are letters out, e-mails out and telephone calls which because of their simplicity should not be regarded as letters or e-mails of substance or telephone calls which properly amount to an attendance.

5.15 Each item claimed in the bill of costs must be consecutively numbered.

5.16 In each part of the bill of costs which claims items under head (1) in paragraph 5.12 (attendances at court and upon counsel) a note should be made of—

(1) all relevant events, including events which do not constitute chargeable items;
(2) any orders for costs which the court made (whether or not a claim is made in respect of those costs in this bill of costs).

5.17 The numbered items of costs may be set out on paper divided into columns. Precedents A, B and C in the Schedule of Costs Precedents annexed to this Practice Direction illustrate various model forms of bills of costs.

5.18 In respect of heads (2) to (10) in paragraph 5.12 above, if the number of attendances and communications other than routine communications is twenty or more, the claim for the costs of those items in that section of the bill of costs should be for the total only and should refer to a schedule in which the full record of dates and details is set out. If the bill of costs contains more than one schedule each schedule should be numbered consecutively.

5.19 The bill of costs must not contain any claims in respect of costs or court fees which relate solely to the detailed assessment proceedings other than costs claimed for preparing and checking the bill.

5.20 The summary must show the total profit costs and disbursements claimed separately from the total VAT claimed. Where the bill of costs is divided into parts the summary must also give totals for each part. If each page of the bill gives a page total the summary must also set out the page totals for each page.

5.21 The bill of costs must contain such of the certificates, the texts of which are set out in Precedent F of the Schedule of Costs Precedents annexed to this Practice Direction, as are appropriate.

5.22 The following provisions relate to work done by legal representatives—

(1) Routine letters out, routine e-mails out and routine telephone calls will in general be allowed on a unit basis of 6 minutes each, the charge being calculated by reference to the appropriate hourly rate. The unit charge for letters out and e-mails out will include perusing and considering the routine letters in or e-mails in.

(2) The court may, in its discretion, allow an actual time charge for preparation of electronic communications sent by legal representatives, which properly amount to attendances provided that the time taken has been recorded.

(3) Local travelling expenses incurred by legal representatives will not be allowed. The definition of 'local' is a matter for the discretion of the court. As a matter of guidance, 'local' will, in general, be taken to mean within a radius of 10 miles from the court dealing with the case at the relevant time. Where travelling and waiting time is claimed, this should be allowed at the rate agreed with the client unless this is more than the hourly rate on the assessment.

(4) The cost of postage, couriers, out-going telephone calls, fax and telex messages will in general not be allowed but the court may exceptionally in its discretion allow such expenses in unusual circumstances or where the cost is unusually heavy.

(5) The cost of making copies of documents will not in general be allowed but the court may exceptionally in its discretion make an allowance for copying in unusual circumstances or where the documents copied are unusually numerous in relation to the nature of the case. Where this discretion is invoked the number of copies made, their purpose and the costs claimed for them must be set out in the bill.

(6) Agency charges as between principal legal representatives and their agents will be dealt with on the principle that such charges, where appropriate, form part of the principal legal representative's charges. Where these charges relate to head (1) in paragraph 5.12 (attendances at court and on counsel) they must be included in their chronological order in that head. In other cases they must be included in head (9) (attendances on London and other agents).

Period for commencing detailed assessment proceedings: Rule 47.7

[CPR PD 47.6]

6.1 The time for commencing the detailed assessment proceedings may be extended or shortened either by agreement (rule 2.11) or by the court (rule 3.1(2)(a)). Any application is to the appropriate office.

6.2 The detailed assessment proceedings are commenced by service of the documents referred to. Permission to commence assessment proceedings out of time is not required.

Sanction for delay in commencing detailed assessment proceedings: Rule 47.8

[CPR PD 47.7]

7 An application for an order under rule 47.8 must be made in writing and be issued in the appropriate office. The application notice must be served at least 7 days before the hearing.

Points of dispute and consequences of not serving: Rule 47.9

[CPR PD 47.8]

8.1 Time for service of points of dispute may be extended or shortened either by agreement (rule 2.11) or by the court (rule 3.1(2)(a)). Any application is to the appropriate office.

8.2 Points of dispute must be short and to the point. They must follow Precedent G in the Schedule of Costs Precedents annexed to this Practice Direction, so far as practicable. They must:

(a) identify any general points or matters of principle which require decision before the individual items in the bill are addressed; and
(b) identify specific points, stating concisely the nature and grounds of dispute. Once a point has been made it should not be repeated but the item numbers where the point arises should be inserted in the left hand box as shown in Precedent G.
8.3 The paying party must state in an open letter accompanying the points of dispute what sum, if any, that party offers to pay in settlement of the total costs claimed. The paying party may also make an offer under Part 36.

Procedure where costs are agreed and on discontinuance: Rule 47.10

[CPR PD 47.9]

9.1 Where the parties have agreed terms as to the issue of a costs certificate (either interim or final) they should apply under rule 40.6 (Consent judgments and orders) for an order that a certificate be issued in the terms set out in the application. Such an application may be dealt with by a court officer, who may issue the certificate.
9.2 Where in the course of proceedings the receiving party claims that the paying party has agreed to pay costs but that the paying party will neither pay those costs nor join in a consent application under paragraph 9.1, the receiving party may apply under Part 23 for a certificate either interim or final to be issued.
9.3 Nothing in rule 47.10 prevents parties who seek a judgment or order by consent from including in the draft a term that a party shall pay to another party a specified sum in respect of costs.
9.4
(1) The receiving party may discontinue the detailed assessment proceedings in accordance with Part 38 (Discontinuance).
(2) Where the receiving party discontinues the detailed assessment proceedings before a detailed assessment hearing has been requested, the paying party may apply to the appropriate office for an order about the costs of the detailed assessment proceedings.
(3) Where a detailed assessment hearing has been requested the receiving party may not discontinue unless the court gives permission.
(4) A bill of costs may be withdrawn by consent whether or not a detailed assessment hearing has been requested.

Default costs certificate: Rule 47.11

[CPR PD 47.10]

10.1
(1) A request for the issue of a default costs certificate must be made in Form N254 and must be signed by the receiving party or his legal representative.
(2) The request must be accompanied by a copy of the document giving the right to detailed assessment and must be filed at the appropriate office. (Paragraph 13.3 below identifies the appropriate documents).
10.2 A default costs certificate will be in Form N255.
10.3 Attention is drawn to Rules 40.3 (Drawing up and Filing of Judgments and Orders) and 40.4 (Service of Judgments and Orders) which apply to the preparation and service of a default costs certificate. The receiving party will be treated as having permission to draw up a default costs certificate by virtue of this Practice Direction.
10.4 The issue of a default costs certificate does not prohibit, govern or affect any detailed assessment of the same costs which are payable out of the Community Legal Service Fund or by the Lord Chancellor under Part 1 of the Legal Aid, Sentencing and Punishment of Offenders Act 2012.
10.5 An application for an order staying enforcement of a default costs certificate may be made either–
(a) to a costs judge or District Judge of the court office which issued the certificate; or

(b) to the court (if different) which has general jurisdiction to enforce the certificate.

10.6 Proceedings for enforcement of default costs certificates may not be issued in the Costs Office.

Default costs certificate: Fixed costs on the issue of a default costs certificate

10.7 Unless paragraph 1.2 of Practice Direction 45 (Fixed Costs in Small Claims) applies or unless the court orders otherwise, the fixed costs to be included in a default costs certificate are £80 plus a sum equal to any appropriate court fee payable on the issue of the certificate.

10.8 The fixed costs included in a certificate must not exceed the maximum sum specified for costs and court fee in the notice of commencement.

Setting aside default costs certificate: Rule 47.12

[CPR PD 47.11]

11.1 A court officer may set aside a default costs certificate at the request of the receiving party under rule 47.12. A costs judge or a District Judge will make any other order or give any directions under this rule.

11.2

(1) An application for an order under rule 47.12(2) to set aside or vary a default costs certificate must be supported by evidence.

(2) In deciding whether to set aside or vary a certificate under rule 47.12(2) the matters to which the court must have regard include whether the party seeking the order made the application promptly.

(3) As a general rule a default costs certificate will be set aside under rule 47.12 only if the applicant shows a good reason for the court to do so and if the applicant files with the application a copy of the bill, a copy of the default costs certificate and a draft of the points of dispute the applicant proposes to serve if the application is granted.

11.3 Attention is drawn to rule 3.1(3) (which enables the court when making an order to make it subject to conditions) and to rule 44.2(8) (which enables the court to order a party whom it has ordered to pay costs to pay an amount on account before the costs are assessed). A costs judge or a District Judge may exercise the power of the court to make an order under rule 44.2(8) although he did not make the order about costs which led to the issue of the default costs certificate.

Optional reply: Rule 47.13

[CPR PD 47.12]

12.1 A reply served by the receiving party under Rule 47.13 must be limited to points of principle and concessions only. It must not contain general denials, specific denials or standard form responses.

12.2 Whenever practicable, the reply must be set out in the form of Precedent G.

Detailed assessment hearing: Rule 47.14

[CPR PD 47.13]

13.1 The time for requesting a detailed assessment hearing is within 3 months of the expiry of the period for commencing detailed assessment proceedings.

13.2 The request for a detailed assessment hearing must be in Form N258. The request must be accompanied by—

(a) a copy of the notice of commencement of detailed assessment proceedings;

(b) a copy of the bill of costs,

(c) the document giving the right to detailed assessment (see paragraph 13.3 below);

(d) a copy of the points of dispute, annotated as necessary in order to show which items have been agreed and their value and to show which items remain in dispute and their value;

(e) as many copies of the points of dispute so annotated as there are persons who have served points of dispute;

(f) a copy of any replies served;

(g) copies of all orders made by the court relating to the costs which are to be assessed;

(h) copies of the fee notes and other written evidence as served on the paying party in accordance with paragraph 5.2 above;

(i) where there is a dispute as to the receiving party's liability to pay costs to the legal representatives who acted for the receiving party, any agreement, letter or other written information provided by the legal representative to the client explaining how the legal representative's charges are to be calculated;

(j) a statement signed by the receiving party or the legal representative giving the name, e-mail address, address for service, reference and telephone number and fax number, if any, of—

  (i) the receiving party;

  (ii) the paying party;

  (iii) any other person who has served points of dispute or who has given notice to the receiving party under paragraph 5.5(1)(b) above;

and giving an estimate of the length of time the detailed assessment hearing will take;

(k) where the application for a detailed assessment hearing is made by a party other than the receiving party, such of the documents set out in this paragraph as are in the possession of that party;

(l) where the court is to assess the costs of an assisted person or LAA funded client or person to whom civil legal services (within the meaning of Part 1 of the Legal Aid, Sentencing and Punishment of Offenders Act 2012) are provided under arrangement made for the purposes of that Part of that Act—

  (i) the legal aid certificate, LAA certificate, the certificate recording the determination of the Director of Legal Aid Casework and relevant amendment certificates, any authorities and any certificates of discharge or revocation or withdrawal;

  (ii) a certificate, in Precedent F(3) of the Schedule of Costs Precedents;

  (iii) if that person has a financial interest in the detailed assessment hearing and wishes to attend, the postal address of that person to which the court will send notice of any hearing;

  (iv) if the rates payable out of the LAA fund or by the Lord Chancellor under Part 1 of the Legal Aid, Sentencing and Punishment of Offenders Act 2012 are prescribed rates, a schedule to the bill of costs setting out all the items in the bill which are claimed against other parties calculated at the legal aid prescribed rates with or without any claim for enhancement: (further information as to this schedule is set out in paragraph 17 of this Practice Direction);

  (v) a copy of any default costs certificate in respect of costs claimed in the bill of costs;

(m) if a costs management order has been made, a breakdown of the costs claimed for each phase of the proceedings.

13.3 "The document giving the right to detailed assessment" means such one or more of the following documents as are appropriate to the detailed assessment proceedings—

(a) a copy of the judgment or order of the court or tribunal giving the right to detailed assessment;

(b) a copy of the notice sent by the court under Practice Direction 3B paragraph 1, being notification that a claim has been struck out under rule 3.7 or rule 3.7A1 for non-payment of a fee;

(c) a copy of the notice of acceptance where an offer to settle is accepted under Part 36 (Offers to settle);

(d) a copy of the notice of discontinuance in a case which is discontinued under Part 38 (Discontinuance);

(e) a copy of the award made on an arbitration under any Act or pursuant to an agreement, where no court has made an order for the enforcement of the award;

(f) a copy of the order, award or determination of a statutorily constituted tribunal or body.

13.4 On receipt of the request for a detailed assessment hearing the court will fix a date for the hearing, or, if the costs officer so decides, will give directions or fix a date for a preliminary appointment.

13.5 Unless the court otherwise orders, if the only dispute between the parties concerns disbursements, the hearing shall take place in the absence of the parties on the basis of the documents and the court will issue its decision in writing.

13.6 The court will give at least 14 days' notice of the time and place of the detailed assessment hearing to every person named in the statement referred to in paragraph 13.2(j) above.

13.7 If either party wishes to make an application in the detailed assessment proceedings the provisions of Part 23 apply.

13.8

(1) This paragraph deals with the procedure to be adopted where a date has been given by the court for a detailed assessment hearing and—
 (a) the detailed assessment proceedings are settled; or
 (b) a party to the detailed assessment proceedings wishes to apply to vary the date which the court has fixed; or
 (c) the parties to the detailed assessment proceedings agree about changes they wish to make to any direction given for the management of the detailed assessment proceedings.

(2) If detailed assessment proceedings are settled, the receiving party must give notice of that fact to the court immediately, preferably by fax.

(3) A party who wishes to apply to vary a direction must do so in accordance with Part 23.

(4) If the parties agree about changes they wish to make to any direction given for the management of the detailed assessment proceedings—
 (a) they must apply to the court for an order by consent; and
 (b) they must file a draft of the directions sought and an agreed statement of the reasons why the variation is sought; and
 (c) the court may make an order in the agreed terms or in other terms without a hearing, but it may direct that a hearing is to be listed.

13.10

(1) If a party wishes to vary that party's bill of costs, points of dispute or a reply, an amended or supplementary document must be filed with the court and copies of it must be served on all other relevant parties.

(2) Permission is not required to vary a bill of costs, points of dispute or a reply but the court may disallow the variation or permit it only upon conditions, including conditions as to the payment of any costs caused or wasted by the variation.

13.11 Unless the court directs otherwise the receiving party must file with the court the papers in support of the bill not less than 7 days before the date for the detailed assessment hearing and not more than 14 days before that date.

13.12 The papers to be filed in support of the bill and the order in which they are to be arranged are as follows—

(i) instructions and briefs to counsel arranged in chronological order together with all advices, opinions and drafts received and response to such instructions;

(ii) reports and opinions of medical and other experts;

(iii) any other relevant papers;

(iv) a full set of any relevant statements of case

(v) correspondence, file notes and attendance notes;

13.13 The court may direct the receiving party to produce any document which in the opinion of the court is necessary to enable it to reach its decision. These documents will in the first instance be produced to the court, but the court may ask the receiving party to elect whether to disclose the particular document to the paying party in order to rely on the contents of the document, or whether to decline disclosure and instead rely on other evidence.

13.14 Once the detailed assessment hearing has ended it is the responsibility of the receiving party to remove the papers filed in support of the bill.

Provisional assessment: Rule 47.15

[CPR PD 47.14]

14.1 The amount of costs referred to in rule 47.15(1) is £75,000.

14.2 The following provisions of Part 47 and this Practice Direction will apply to cases falling within rule 47.15—

(1) rules 47.1, 47.2, 47.4 to 47.13, 47.14 (except paragraphs (6) and (7)), 47.16, 47.17, 47.20 and 47.21; and

(2) paragraphs 1, 2, 4 to 12, 13 (with the exception of paragraphs 13.4 to 13.7, 13.9, 13.11 and 13.14), 15, and 16, of this Practice Direction.

14.3 In cases falling within rule 47.15, when the receiving party files a request for a detailed assessment hearing, that party must file—

(a) the request in Form N258;

(b) the documents set out at paragraphs 8.3 and 13.2 of this Practice Direction;

(c) an additional copy of any paper bill and a statement of the costs claimed in respect of the detailed assessment drawn on the assumption that there will not be an oral hearing following the provisional assessment;

(d) the offers made (those marked "without prejudice save as to costs" or made under Part 36 must be contained in a sealed envelope, marked "Part 36 or similar offers", but not indicating which party or parties have made them);

(e) completed Precedent G (points of dispute and any reply).

14.4

(1) On receipt of the request for detailed assessment and the supporting papers, the court will use its best endeavours to undertake a provisional assessment within 6 weeks. No party will be permitted to attend the provisional assessment.

(2) Once the provisional assessment has been carried out the court will return Precedent G (the points of dispute and any reply) with the court's decisions noted upon it. Within 14 days of receipt of Precedent G the parties must agree the total sum due to the receiving party on the basis of the court's decisions. If the parties are unable to agree the arithmetic, they must refer the dispute back to the court for a decision on the basis of written submissions.

14.5 When considering whether to depart from the order indicated by rule 47. 15(10) the court will take into account the conduct of the parties and any offers made.

14.6 If a party wishes to be heard only as to the order made in respect of the costs of the initial provisional assessment, the court will invite each side to make written submissions and the matter will be finally determined without a hearing. The court will decide what if any order for costs to make in respect of this procedure.

Power to issue an interim certificate: Rule 47.16

[CPR PD 47.15]

15. A party wishing to apply for an interim certificate may do so by making an application in accordance with Part 23.

Final costs certificate: Rule 47.17

[CPR PD 47.16]

16.1 At the detailed assessment hearing the court will indicate any disallowance or reduction in the sums claimed in the bill of costs by making an appropriate note on the bill.

16.2 The receiving party must, in order to complete the bill after the detailed assessment hearing make clear the correct figures agreed or allowed in respect of each item and must re-calculate the summary of the bill appropriately.

16.3 The completed bill of costs must be filed with the court no later than 14 days after the detailed assessment hearing.

16.4 At the same time as filing the completed bill of costs, the party whose bill it is must also produce receipted fee notes and receipted accounts in respect of all disbursements except those covered by a certificate in Precedent F(5) in the Schedule of Costs Precedents annexed to this Practice Direction.

16.5 No final costs certificate will be issued until all relevant court fees payable on the assessment of costs have been paid.

16.6 If the receiving party fails to file a completed bill in accordance with rule 47.17 the paying party may make an application under Part 23 seeking an appropriate order under rule 3.1.

16.7 A final costs certificate will show—

(a) the amount of any costs which have been agreed between the parties or which have been allowed on detailed assessment;

(b) where applicable the amount agreed or allowed in respect of VAT on such costs.

This provision is subject to any contrary statutory provision relating to costs payable out of the Community Legal Service Fund or by the Lord Chancellor under Part 1 of the Legal Aid, Sentencing and Punishment of Offenders Act 2012.

16.8 A final costs certificate will include disbursements in respect of the fees of counsel only if receipted fee notes or accounts in respect of those disbursements have been produced to the court and only to the extent indicated by those receipts.

16.9 Where the certificate relates to costs payable between parties a separate certificate will be issued for each party entitled to costs.

16.10 Form N257 is a model form of interim costs certificate and Form N256 is a model form of final costs certificate.

16.11 An application for an order staying enforcement of an interim costs certificate or final costs certificate may be made either—

(a) to a costs judge or District Judge of the court office which issued the certificate; or

(b) to the court (if different) which has general jurisdiction to enforce the certificate.

16.12 An interim or final costs certificate may be enforced as if it were a judgment for the payment of an amount of money. However, proceedings for the enforcement of interim costs certificates or final costs certificates may not be issued in the Costs Office.

Detailed assessment procedure where costs are payable out of the Community Legal Service Fund or by the Lord Chancellor under Part 1 of the Legal Aid, Sentencing and Punishment of Offenders Act 2012: Rule 47.18

[CPR PD 47.17]

17.1 The time for requesting a detailed assessment under rule 47.18 is within 3 months after the date when the right to detailed assessment arose.

17.2

(1) The request for a detailed assessment of costs must be in Form N258A. The request must be accompanied by—

- (a) a copy of the bill of costs;
- (b) the document giving the right to detailed assessment (see paragraph 13.3 above);
- (c) copies of all orders made by the court relating to the costs which are to be assessed;
- (d) copies of any fee notes of counsel and any expert in respect of fees claimed in the bill;

(e) written evidence as to any other disbursement which is claimed and which exceeds £500;

(f) the legal aid certificates, LAA certificates, certificates recording the determinations of the Director of Legal Aid Casework, any relevant amendment certificates, any authorities and any certificates of discharge, revocation or withdrawal; and

(g) a statement signed by the legal representative giving the representative's name, address for service, reference, telephone number, e-mail address and, if the assisted person has a financial interest in the detailed assessment and wishes to attend, giving the postal address of that person, to which the court will send notice of any hearing.

(2) The relevant papers in support of the bill as described in paragraph 13. 12 must only be lodged if requested by the costs officer.

17.3 Where the court has provisionally assessed a bill of costs it will send to the legal representative a notice, in Form N253 annexed to this practice direction, of the amount of costs which the court proposes to allow together with the bill itself. The legal representative should, if the provisional assessment is to be accepted, then complete the bill.

17.4 If the solicitor whose bill it is, or any other party wishes to make an application in the detailed assessment proceedings, the provisions of Part 23 applies.

17.5 It is the responsibility of the legal representative to complete the bill by entering in the bill the correct figures allowed in respect of each item, recalculating the summary of the bill appropriately and completing the Community Legal Service assessment certificate (Form EX80A).

Costs payable by the Legal Services Commission or Lord Chancellor at prescribed rates

17.6 Where the costs of an assisted person or LAA funded client or person to whom civil legal services (within the meaning of Part 1 of the Legal Aid, Sentencing and Punishment of Offenders Act 2012) are provided under arrangements made for the purposes of that Part of that Act are payable by another person but costs can be claimed against the LAA or Lord Chancellor at prescribed rates (with or without enhancement), the solicitor of the assisted person or LAA funded client or person to whom civil legal services are provided must file a legal aid/ LAA schedule in accordance with paragraph 13.2(l) above. If on paper (a "paper schedule") the schedule should follow as closely as possible Precedent E of the Schedule of Costs Precedents annexed to this Practice Direction. If an electronic bill of costs is served on the other person an electronic schedule may, subject to paragraphs 17.7 and 17.8 below, be prepared and filed as if it were an electronic bill.

17.7 The schedule must set out by reference to the item numbers in the bill of costs, all the costs claimed as payable by another person, but the arithmetic in the schedule should claim those items at prescribed rates only (with or without any claim for enhancement).

17.8 Where there has been a change in the prescribed rates during the period covered by the bill of costs, a paper schedule (as opposed to the bill) should be divided into separate parts, so as to deal separately with each change of rate. The paper schedule must also be divided so as to correspond with any divisions in the bill of costs. If the schedule is an electronic schedule, unless the format of the schedule already provides the requisite information it should incorporate a summary in a form comparable to the "Funding and Parts Table" in Precedent S to provide the information that would otherwise be provided by its division into parts.

17.9 If the bill of costs sets out costs claimed against the LAA or Lord Chancellor only, the schedule may be set out in a separate document or, alternatively, may be included in the bill, shown separately from the costs claimed against other parties.

17.10 The detailed assessment of the legal aid/LAA schedule will take place immediately after the detailed assessment of the bill of costs but on occasions, the court may decide to conduct the detailed assessment of the legal aid/LAA schedule separately from any detailed assessment of the bill of costs. This will occur, for example, where a default costs certificate is obtained as between the parties but that certificate is not set aside at the time of the detailed assessment of the legal aid costs.

17.11 Where costs have been assessed at prescribed rates it is the responsibility of the legal representative to enter the correct figures allowed in respect of each item and to recalculate the summary of the legal aid/LAA schedule.

Detailed assessment procedure where costs are payable out of a fund other than the Community Legal Service Fund or by the Lord Chancellor under Part 1 of the Legal Aid, Sentencing and Punishment of Offenders Act 2012: Rule 47.19

[CPR PD 47.18]

18.1 Rule 47.19 enables the court to direct under rule 47.19(3) that the receiving party must serve a copy of the request for assessment and copies of the documents which accompany it, on any person who has a financial interest in the outcome of the assessment.

18.2 A person has a financial interest in the outcome of the assessment if the assessment will or may affect the amount of money or property to which that person is or may become entitled out of the fund. Where an interest in the fund is itself held by a trustee for the benefit of some other person, that trustee will be treated as the person having such a financial interest unless it is not appropriate to do so. 'Trustee' includes a personal representative, receiver or any other person acting in a fiduciary capacity.

18.3 The request for a detailed assessment of costs out of the fund should be in Form N258B, be accompanied by the documents set out at paragraph 17.2(1)(a) to (e) and the following—

(a) a statement signed by the receiving party giving his name, e-mail address, address for service, reference and telephone number,

(b) a statement of the postal address of any person who has a financial interest in the outcome of the assessment; and

(c) if a person having a financial interest is a child or protected party, a statement to that effect.

18.4 The court will decide, having regard to the amount of the bill, the size of the fund and the number of persons who have a financial interest, which of those persons should be served and may give directions about service and about the hearing. The court may dispense with service on all or some of those persons.

18.5 Where the court makes an order dispensing with service on all such persons it may proceed at once to make a provisional assessment, or, if it decides that a hearing is necessary, give appropriate directions. Before deciding whether a hearing is necessary, the court may require the receiving party to provide further information relating to the bill.

18.6

(1) The court will send the provisionally assessed bill to the receiving party with a notice in Form N253. If the receiving party is legally represented the legal representative should, if the provisional assessment is to be accepted, then complete the bill.

(2) The court will fix a date for a detailed assessment hearing, if the receiving party informs the court within 14 days after receiving the notice in Form N253, that the receiving party wants the court to hold such a hearing.

18.7 The court will give at least 14 days notice of the time and place of the hearing to the receiving party and to any person who has a financial interest and who has been served with a copy of the request for assessment.

18.8 If any party or any person who has a financial interest wishes to make an application in the detailed assessment proceedings, the provisions of Part 23 (General Rules about Applications for Court Orders) apply.

18.9 If the receiving party is legally represented the legal representative must complete the bill by inserting the correct figures in respect of each item and must recalculate the summary of the bill.

Costs of detailed assessment proceedings – rule 47.20: Offers to settle under part 36 or otherwise

[CPR PD 47.19]

19. Where an offer to settle is made, whether under Part 36 or otherwise, it should specify whether or not it is intended to be inclusive of the cost of preparation of the bill, interest and VAT. Unless the offer states otherwise it will be treated as being inclusive of these.

Appeals from authorised court officers in detailed assessment proceedings: Rules 47.22 to 47.25

[CPR PD 47.20]

20.1 This Section relates only to appeals from authorised court officers in detailed assessment proceedings. All other appeals arising out of detailed assessment proceedings (and arising out of summary assessments) are dealt with in accordance with Part 52 and Practice Directions 52A to 52E. The destination of appeals is dealt with in accordance with the Access to Justice Act 1999 (Destination of Appeals) Order 2016.

20.2 In respect of appeals from authorised court officers, there is no requirement to obtain permission, or to seek written reasons.

20.3 The appellant must file a notice which should be in Form N161 (an appellant's notice).

20.4 The appeal will be heard by a costs judge or a District Judge of the High Court, and is a re-hearing.

20.5 The appellant's notice should, if possible, be accompanied by a suitable record of the judgment appealed against. Where reasons given for the decision have been officially recorded by the court an approved transcript of that record should accompany the notice. Where there is no official record the following documents will be acceptable—

(a) the officer's comments written on the bill;

(b) advocates' notes of the reasons agreed by the respondent if possible and approved by the authorised court officer.

When the appellant was unrepresented before the authorised court officer, it is the duty of any advocate for the respondent to make a note of the reasons promptly available, free of charge to the appellant where there is no official record or if the court so directs. Where the appellant was represented before the authorised court officer, it is the duty of the appellant's own former advocate to make a note available. The appellant should submit the note of the reasons to the costs judge or District Judge hearing the appeal.

20.6 Where the appellant is not able to obtain a suitable record of the authorised court officer's decision within the time in which the appellant's notice must be filed, the appellant's notice must still be completed to the best of the appellant's ability. It may however be amended subsequently with the permission of the costs judge or District Judge hearing the appeal.

Schedule of costs precedents

A: Model form of bill of costs (receiving party's solicitor and counsel on conditional fee agreement terms)

B: Model form of bill of costs (detailed assessment of additional liability only)

C: Model form of bill of costs (payable by Defendant and the LSC)

D: Model form of bill of costs (alternative form, single column for amounts claimed, separate parts for costs payable by the LSC only)

E: Legal Aid/ LSC Schedule of Costs

F: Certificates for inclusion in bill of costs

G. Points of Dispute and Reply

H: Costs Budget

J: Solicitors Act 1974: Part 8 claim form under Part III of the Act

K: Solicitors Act 1974: order for delivery of bill

L: Solicitors Act 1974: order for detailed assessment (client)

M: Solicitors Act 1974: order for detailed assessment (solicitors)

P: Solicitors Act 1974: breakdown of costs

Q: Model for of breakdown of the costs claimed for each phase of the proceedings

S: Precedent S

T: Precedent T

Schedule of costs precedents
Precedent A

IN THE HIGH COURT OF JUSTICE		2011-B-9999
QUEEN'S BENCH DIVISION		
BRIGHTON DISTRICT REGISTRY		
	BETWEEN	
	AB	Claimant
	- and -	
	CD	Defendant

Claimant's bill of costs to be assessed pursuant to the order dated 2nd April 2013

V.A.T. No 33 4404 90

In these proceedings the claimant sought compensation for personal injuries and other losses suffered in a road accident which occurred on 1st January 2011 near the junction between Bolingbroke Lane and Regency Road, Brighton, East Sussex. The claimant had been travelling as a front seat passenger in a car driven by the defendant. The claimant suffered severe injuries when, because of the defendant's negligence, the car left the road and collided with a brick wall.

The defendant was later convicted of various offences arising out of the accident including careless driving and driving under the influence of drink or drugs.

In the civil action the defendant alleged that immediately before the car journey began the claimant had known that the defendant was under the influence of alcohol and therefore consented to the risk of injury or was contributorily negligent as to it. It was also alleged that, immediately before the accident occurred, the claimant wrongfully took control of the steering wheel so causing the accident to occur.

The claimant first instructed solicitors, E F & Co, in this matter in July 2011. The claim form was issued in October 2011 and in February 2012 the proceedings were listed for a two day trial commencing 25th July 2012. At the trial the defendant was found liable but the compensation was reduced by 25% to take account of contributory negligence by the claimant. The claimant was awarded a total of £78,256.83 plus £1,207.16 interest plus costs.

The claimant instructed E F & Co under a retainer which specifies the following hourly rates.

Partner — £217 per hour plus VAT

Assistant Solicitor — £192 per hour plus VAT

Other fee earners — £118 per hour plus VAT

Success fees exclusive of disbursement funding costs: 40%

Success fee in respect of disbursement funding costs: 7.5% (not claimed in this bill)

Except where the contrary is stated the proceedings were conducted on behalf of the claimant by an assistant solicitor, admitted November 2008.

E F & Co instructed Counsel (Miss GH, called 1992) under a conditional fee agreement dated 5th June 2001 which specifies a success fee of 75% and base fees, payable in various circumstances, of which the following are relevant

Fees for interim hearing whose estimated duration is up to 2 hours: £600

Brief for trial whose estimated duration is 2 days: £2,000

Fee for second and subsequent days: £650 per day

Item No	Description of work done	V.A.T.	Disbursements	Profit Costs
	8th July 2011 – EF & Co instructed			
1	7th October 2011 – Claim issued			
2	Issue fee	—	£685.00	
	21st October 2011 – Particulars of claim served			
	25th November 2011 – Time for service of defence extended by agreement to 14th January 2012			
3	Fee on allocation	—	£220.00	
	20th January 2012 – case allocated to multi-track			
	9th February 2012 – Case management conference at which costs were awarded to the claimant and the base costs were summarily assessed at £400 (paid on 24th February 2012)			
	23rd February 2012 – Claimant's list of documents			
	12th April 2012 – Payment into court of £25,126.33			
	13th April 2012 – Filing pre-trial check list			
4	Paid listing fee	—	£110.00	
5	Paid hearing fee		£1,090.00	
	25th July 2012 – Attending first day of trial: adjourned part heard			
	Engaged in Court 5.00 hours £960.00			

Item No	Description of work done		V.A.T.	Disbursements	Profit Costs
	Engaged in conference 0.75 hours	£144.00			
	Travel and waiting 1.5 hours	£288.00			
6	Total solicitor's fee for attending				£1,392.00
7	Counsel's base fee for trial (Miss GH)		£400.00	£2,000.00	
8	Fee of expert witness (Dr. IJ)		—	£850.00	
9	Expenses of witnesses of fact		—	£84.00	
	26th July 2012 – Attending second day of trial when judgment was given for the claimant in the sum of £78,256.53 plus £1207.16 interest plus costs				
	To Summary		£ 400	£5,039.00	£1,392.00
	Engaged in Court 3.00 hours	£576.00			
	Engaged in conference 1.5 hours	£288.00			
	Travel and waiting 1.5 hours	£288.00			
10	Total solicitor's fee for attending				£1,152.00
11	Counsel's fee for second day (Miss GH)		£190.00	£950.00	
	Claimant				
12	8th July 2011 – First instructions: 0.75 hours by Partner				£162.75
	Other timed attendances in person and by telephone – See Schedule 1				
13	Total base fee for Schedule 1 – 7.5 hours				£1,440.00

Item No	Description of work done	V.A.T.	Disbursements	Profit Costs
14	Routine letters out and telephone calls – 29 (17 + 12) total fee			£556.80
	Witnesses of Fact			
	Timed attendances in person, by letter out and by telephone – See Schedule 2			
15	Total base fee for Schedule 2 – 5.2 hours			£998.40
16	Routine letters out, e mails and telephone calls – 8 (4 + 2 + 2)total base fee			£153.60
17	Paid travelling on 10th October 2011	£4.59	£22.96	
	Medical expert (Dr. IJ)			
18	11th September 2011 – long letter out 0.33 hours: fee			£63.36
19	31st January 2012 – long letter out 0.25 hours: fee			£48.00
20	23rd May 2012 – telephone call 0.2 hours fee			£38.40
21	Routine letters out and telephone calls – 10 (6 + 4) total fee			£192.00
22	Dr. IJ's fee for report	—	£500.00	
	Defendant and his solicitor			
23	8th July 2011 – timed letter sent 0.5 hours: fee			£96.00
24	19th February 2012 – telephone call 0.25 hours: fee			£48.00
25	Routine letters out and telephone calls – 24 (18 + 6) total fee			£460.80

Item No	Description of work done		V.A.T.	Disbursements	Profit Costs
	Communications with the court				
26	Routine letters out and telephone calls – 9 (8 + 1) total fee				£172.80
	To Summary		£194.59	£1,472.96	£5,582.91
	Communications with Counsel				
27	Routine letters out, e mails and telephone calls – 19 (4 + 7 + 8) tota fee				£364.80
	Work done on documents				
	Timed attendances – See Schedule 3				
28	Total fees for Schedule 3 – 0.75 hours at £217, 44.5 hours at £192, 12 hours at £118				£10,122.75
	Work done on negotiations				
	23rd March 2012 – meeting at offices of Solicitors for the Defendant				
	Engaged – 1.5 hours	£288.00			
	Travel and waiting – 1.25 hours	£240.00			
29	Total fee for meeting				£528.00
	Other work done				
	Preparing and checking bill				
	Engaged: Solicitor – 1 hour	£192.00			
	Engaged: Costs Draftsman – 4 hours	£480.00			
30	Total fee on other work done				£672.00
31	VAT on solicitor's fees (20% of £18,662.46)		£3,731.49		

Item No	Description of work done	V.A.T.	Disbursements	Profit Costs
32	VAT on Counsel's base fees (20% of £3,950)"	£790.00		
	To Summary	£4,521.49		£11,687.55
	SUMMARY			
	Page 2	£400.00	£5,039.00	£1,392.00
	Page 3	£194.59	£1,472.96	£5,582.91
	Page 4	£4,521.49		£11,687.55
	Totals:	£5,116.08	£6,511.96	£18,662.46
	Grand total:			£30,290.50

Schedule of costs precedents
Precedent B

IN THE HIGH COURT OF JUSTICE 2000 - B - 9999
QUEEN'S BENCH DIVISION
BRIGHTON DISTRICT REGISTRY
BETWEEN

AB Claimant
- and -
CD Defendant

Claimant's bill of costs to be assessed pursuant to the order dated 26th July 2001

V.A.T. NO 33 4404 90

In these proceedings the claimant sought compensation for personal injuries and other losses suffered in a road accident which occurred on Friday 1st January 1999 near the junction between Bolingbroke Lane and Regency Road, Brighton, East Sussex. The claimant had been travelling as a front seat passenger in a car driven by the defendant. The claimant suffered severe injuries when, because of the defendant's negligence, the car left the road and collided with a brick wall.

The defendant was later convicted of various offences arising out of the accident including careless driving and driving under the influence of drink or drugs.

In the civil action the defendant alleged that immediately before the car journey began the claimant had known that the defendant was under the influence of alcohol and therefore consented to the risk of injury or was contributorily negligent as to it. It was also alleged that, immediately before the accident occurred, the claimant wrongfully took control of the steering wheel so causing the accident to occur.

The claimant first instructed solicitors, E F & Co, in this matter in July 2000. The claim form was issued in October 1999 and in February 2000 the proceedings were listed for a two day trial commencing 25th July 2001. At the trial the defendant was found liable but the compensation was reduced by 25% to take account of contributory negligence by the claimant. The claimant was awarded a total of £78,256.83 plus £1,207.16 interest plus costs, and the base costs were summarily assessed

The claimant instructed E F & Co under a conditional fee agreement dated 8th July 2000 which specifies the following base fees and success fees.

Partner – £180 per hour plus VAT

Assistant Solicitor – £140 per hour plus VAT

Other fee earners – £85 per hour plus VAT

Success fees exclusive of disbursement funding costs: 40%

Success fee in respect of disbursement funding costs: 7.5% (not claimed in this bill)

Except where the contrary is stated the proceedings were conducted on behalf of the claimant by an assistant solicitor, admitted November 1999.

E F & Co instructed Counsel (Miss GH, called 1992) under a conditional fee agreement dated 5th June 2001 which specifies a success fee of 75% and base fees, payable in various circumstances, of which the following are relevant.

Fees for interim hearing whose estimated duration is up to 2 hours: £600

Brief for trial whose estimated duration is 2 days: £2,000

Fee for second and subsequent days: £650 per day

Item No	Description of work done	V.A.T.	Disbursements	Profit Costs
	8th July 2000 – EF & Co instructed			
	22nd July 2000 – AEI with Eastbird Legal Protection Ltd			
1	Premium for policy	—	£120.00	
	9th February 2001 – Case management conference at which costs were awarded to the Claimant and the base costs were summarily assessed at £400			—
2	Success fee on costs of case management conference (40% of £400) plus VAT	£28.00		£160.00
	28th June 2001 – Pre trial review: costs in the case (base costs included base costs at trial)			
	25th July 2001 – First day of trial			
	26th July 2001 – Second day of trial at which judgment was given for the claimant as follows:			
	Compensation: £78,256.83			
	Interest thereon: £1,207.16			
	Base costs to trial			
	Solicitor's fees: £12,500.00 plus £2187.50 VAT thereon			
	Counsel's fees: £3,200.00 plus £560.00 VAT thereon			
	Other disbursements: £2,300.00 plus £4.02 VAT thereon			—
3	Success fee on solicitor's base costs awarded at trial (40% of £12,500) plus VAT	£875.00		£5,000.00

Item No	Description of work done		V.A.T.	Disbursements	Profit Costs
4	Success fee on Counsel's base costs awarded at trial (75% of £3,200) plus VAT		£420.00	£2,400.00	
	Other work done				
	Preparing and checking bill				
	Engaged: Solicitor – 0.25 hours	£ 35.00			
	Engaged: Costs draftsman – 1.75 hours	£ 148.75			
5	Total base fee for other work done plus VAT		£32.16		£183.75
6	Success fee for other work done (40% of £183.75) plus VAT		£12.87		£73.50
		Totals:	£1,368.03	£2,520.00	£5,417.25
		Profit Costs			£5,417.25
		Disburse-ments			£2,520.00
		VAT			£1,368.03
		Grand total:			£9,305.28

Schedule of costs precedents
Precedent C

IN THE HIGH COURT OF JUSTICE		1999 - B - 9999
QUEEN'S BENCH DIVISION		
BRIGHTON DISTRICT REGISTRY		
BETWEEN		
	AB	Claimant
	- and -	
	CD	Defendant

Claimant's bill of costs to be assessed pursuant to the order dated 26th July 2000 and in accordance with Regulation 107A of the Civil Legal Aid (General) Regulations 1989

Legal Aid Certificate No 01. 01. 99. 32552X issued on 9th September 1999.

V.A.T. No 33 4404 90

In these proceedings the claimant sought compensation for personal injuries and other losses suffered in a road accident which occurred on Friday 1st January 1999 near the junction between Bolingbroke Lane and Regency Road, Brighton, East Sussex. The claimant had been travelling as a front seat passenger in a car driven by the defendant. The claimant suffered severe injuries when, because of the defendant's negligence, the car left the road and collided with a brick wall.

The defendant was later convicted of various offences arising out of the accident including careless driving and driving under the influence of drink or drugs.

In the civil action the defendant alleged that immediately before the car journey began the claimant had known that the defendant was under the influence of alcohol and therefore consented to the risk of injury or was contributorily negligent as to it. It was also alleged that, immediately before the accident occurred, the claimant wrongfully took control of the steering wheel so causing the accident to occur.

The claimant first instructed solicitors, E F & Co, in this matter in July 1999. The claim form was issued in October 1999 and in February 2000 the proceedings were listed for a two day trial commencing 25th July 2000. At the trial the defendant was found liable but the compensation was reduced by 25% to take account of contributory negligence by the claimant. The claimant was awarded a total of £78,256.83 plus £1,207.16 interest plus costs.

The proceedings were conducted on behalf of the claimant by an assistant solicitor, admitted November 1998. The bill is divided into two parts.

Part 1
Costs payable by the defendant to the date of grant of legal aid

This covers the period from 8th July 1999 to 8th September 1999. In this part the solicitor's time is charged at £140 per hour (including travel and waiting time) and letters out and telephone calls at £14.00 each.

Part 2
Costs payable by the defendant and L.S.C. from the date of grant of legal aid

This part covers the period from 9th September 1999 to the present time, the client having the benefit of a legal aid certificate covering these proceedings. In this part, solicitor's time in respect of costs payable by the defendant has been charged as in Part 1 plus costs draftsman's and trainee's time charged at £85 per hour. Solicitor's time in respect of costs payable by the LSC only are charged at the prescribed hourly rates plus enhancement of 50%.

Preparation: £74

Attending counsel in conference or at court: £36.40

Travelling and waiting: £32.70

Routine letters out: £7.40

Routine telephone calls: £4.10

	Description of work done	Payable by L.S.C. only			Payable by Defendant			
Item No	Part 1: COSTS TO DATE OF GRANT OF LEGAL AID.	V.A.T.	Disbursements	Profit Costs	V.A.T.	Disburse-ments		Profit Costs
	Claimant							
1	8th July 1999 – First Instructions – 0.75 hours							£105.00
2	Routine Letters out – 3							£42.00
	Witnesses of Fact							
3	Routine Letters out – 2							£28.00
	The Defendant							
4	8th July 1999 – Timed letter sent – 0.5 hours							£70.00
5	VAT on total profit costs							
	(17.5% of £245)				£42.88			
	To Summary				£42.88	£ -		£245.00
	Part 2: COSTS FROM DATE OF GRANT OF LEGAL AID							
	7th October 1999 – Claim issued							
6	Issue fee				—	£400.00		
	21st October 1999 – Particulars of claim served							
	25th November 1999 – Time for service of defence extended by agreement to 14th January 2000							
	17th January 2000 – Filing allocation questionnaire							

	Description of work done		Payable by L.S.C. only	Payable by Defendant			
7	Fee on allocation			—	£80.00		
	20th January 2000 – Case allocated to multi-track						
	9th February 2000 – Case management conference						
	Engaged 0.75 hours	£105.00					
	Travel and waiting 2.00 hours	£280.00					
		————					
8	Total solicitor's fee for attending						£385.00
	23rd February 2000 – Claimant's list of documents						
	12th April 2000 – Payment into court of £25,126.33						
	13th April 2000 – Filing pre-trial check list						
9	Fee on listing			—			
	28th June 2000 – Pre-trial review				£400.00		
	Engaged 1.5 hours	£210.00					
	Travel and waiting 2.00 hours	£280.00					
10	Total solicitor's fee for attending						£490.00
11	Counsel's brief fee for attending pre-trial review (Miss GH)		£105.00	£600.00			

	Description of work done		**Payable by L.S.C. only**		**Payable by Defendant**				
	To Summary		£ —	£ —	£ —	£105.00	£1,480.00		£875.00
	25th July 2000 – Attending first day of trial: adjourned part heard								
	Engaged in court 5.00 hours	£700.00							
	Engaged in conference 0.75 hours	£105.00							
	Travel and waiting 1.5 hours	£210.00							
		———							
12	Total solicitor's fee for attending								£1,015.00
13	Counsel's brief fee for trial (Miss GH)					£350.00	£2,000.00		
14	Fee of expert witness (Dr IJ)					—	£850.00		
15	Expenses of witnesses of fact					—	£84.00		
	26th July 2000 – Attending second day of trial when judgment was given for the claimant in the sum of £78,256.83 plus £1,207.16 interest plus costs								
	Engaged in court 3.00 hours	£420.00							

	Description of work done		Payable by L.S.C. only	Payable by Defendant			
	Engaged in conference						
	1.5 hours	£210.00					
	Travel and waiting 1.5 hours	£210.00					
16	Total solicitor's fee for attending						£840.00
17	Counsel's fee for second day (Miss GH)			£113.75	£650.00		
	Claimant ˜ (1) Payable by Defendant						
	Timed attendances in person and by telephone – see Schedule 1						
18	Total fees for Schedule 1 – 7.50 hours						£1,050.00
19	Routine letters out and telephone calls – 26 (14 + 12)						£364.00
	Claimant ˜ (2) Payable by LSC only						
	11th September 1999 – telephone call						
	Engaged 0.25 hours	£18.50					
	Enhancement 50%	£9.25					
20	Total solicitor's fee		£27.75				
	10th April 2000 – telephone call						

	Description of work done		Payable by L.S.C. only		Payable by Defendant			
	Engaged 0.1 hours	£4.10						
	Enhancement 50%	£2.05						
21	Total solicitor's fee			£6.15				
	Witnesses of fact							
	Timed attendances in person, by letter out and by telephone – see Schedule 2							
22	Total fees for Schedule 2 – 5.2 hours							£728.00
23	Routine letters out (including e mails) and telephone calls – 6 (4 + 2)							£84.00
24	Paid travelling on 9th October 1999					£4.02	£22.96	
	To Summary		£ —	£ —	£33.90	£467.77	£3,606.96	£4,081.00
	Medical expert (Dr IJ)							
25	11th September 1999 – long letter out 0.33 hours							£46.20
26	30th January 2000 – long letter out 0.25 hours							£35.00
27	23rd May 2000 – telephone call 0.2 hrs						£28.00	

	Description of work done		Payable by L.S.C. only	Payable by Defendant			
28	Routine letters out and telephone calls – 10 (6 + 4)						£140.00
29	Dr IJ's fee for report			—	£350.00		
	Solicitors for the defendant						
30	19th February 2000 – telephone call 0.25 hours						£35.00
31	Routine letters out and telephone calls – 24 (18 + 6)						£336.00
	Communications with the court						
32	Routine letters out and telephone calls – 9 (8 + 1)						£126.00
	Communications with Counsel						
33	Routine letters out (including e mails) and telephone calls – 19 (11 + 8)						£266.00
	Legal Aid Board and LSC ~ Payable by LSC only						
	2nd August 2000 – Report on case						
	Engaged 0.5 hours	£37.00					
	Enhancement 50%	£18.50					
34	Total solicitor's fee		£55.50				
	Routine letters out and telephone calls						

	Description of work done		Payable by L.S.C. only	Payable by Defendant		
	Letters out – 2	£14.80				
	Telephones call – 4	£16.40				
35	Total solicitor's fee		£31.20			
	Work done on documents					
	Timed attendances – see Schedule 3					
36	Total fees for Schedule 3 – 45.25 hours at £140 + 12 hours at £85					£7,355.00
	Work done on negotiations					
	23rd March 2000 – meeting at offices of solicitors for the Defendant					
	Engaged – 1.5 hours	£210.00				
	Travel and waiting 1.25 hours	£175.00				
37	Total solicitor's fee for meeting					£385.00
	Other work done ˜ (1) Payable by Defendant					
	Preparing and checking bill					
	Engaged: Solicitor – 1 hour	£140.00				
	Engaged: Costs Draftsman -					
	4 hours	£340.00				

	Description of work done		Payable by L.S.C. only		Payable by Defendant			
38	Total on other work done (1)							£480.00
	To Summary		£ —	£ —	£86.70	£ —	£350.00	£9,232.20
	Other work done ˜ (2) Payable by LSC only							
	Preparing and checking bill							
	Engaged: Solicitor – no claim							
	Engaged: Costs Draftsman – 1 hour	£74.00						
39	Total on other work done (2)			£74.00				
40	VAT on total profit costs payable by Defendant (17.5% of £14,176.20)			£2,480.84				
41	VAT on total profit costs payable by LSC only (17.5% of £205.60)		£35.98					
	To summary		£35.98	£ —	£74.00	£2,480.84	£ —	£ —
	SUMMARY							
	Part 1 – Pre Legal Aid		£ —	£ —	£ —	£42.88	£ —	£245.00
	Page 3							
	Part 2 – Costs since grant of legal aid							

Description of work done	Payable by L.S.C. only			Payable by Defendant			
Page 3	£ —	£ —	£ —	£105.00	£1,480.00		£875.00
Page 4	£ —	£ —	£33.90	£467.77	£3,606.96		£4,081.00
Page 5	£ —	£ —	£86.70	£ —	£350.00		£9,232.20
Page 6	£35.98	£ —	£74.00	£2,480.84	£ —		£ —
Totals	£35.98	£ —	£194.60	£3,096.49	£5,436.96		£14,433.20
Grand totals							
Costs payable by Defendant							£22,966.65
Costs payable by LSC only							£230.58
Grand total:							£23,197.23

Schedule of costs precedents
Precedent D

IN THE HIGH COURT OF JUSTICE		1999 – B – 9999
QUEEN'S BENCH DIVISION		
BRIGHTON DISTRICT REGISTRY		
BETWEEN		
	AB	Claimant
	- and -	
	CD	Defendant

Claimant's bill of costs to be assessed pursuant to the order dated 26th July 2000 and in accordance with Regulation 107A of the Civil Legal Aid (General) Regulations 1989

Legal Aid Certificate No 01. 01. 99. 32552X issued on 9th September 1999.

V.A.T. No 33 4404 90

In these proceedings the claimant sought compensation for personal injuries and other losses suffered in a road accident which occurred on Friday 1st January 1999 near the junction between Bolingbroke Lane and Regency Road, Brighton, East Sussex. The claimant had been travelling as a front seat passenger in a car driven by the defendant. The claimant suffered severe injuries when, because of the defendant's negligence, the car left the road and collided with a brick wall.

The defendant was later convicted of various offences arising out of the accident including careless driving and driving under the influence of drink or drugs.

In the civil action the defendant alleged that immediately before the car journey began the claimant had known that the defendant was under the influence of alcohol and therefore consented to the risk of injury or was contributorily negligent as to it. It was also alleged that, immediately before the accident occurred, the claimant wrongfully took control of the steering wheel so causing the accident to occur.

The claimant first instructed solicitors, E F & Co, in this matter in July 1999. The claim form was issued in October 1999 and in February 2000 the proceedings were listed for a two day trial commencing 25th July 2000. At the trial the defendant was found liable but the compensation was reduced by 25% to take account of contributory negligence by the claimant. The claimant was awarded a total of £78,256.83 plus £1,207.16 interest plus costs.

The proceedings were conducted on behalf of the claimant by an assistant solicitor, admitted November 1998. The bill is divided into three parts.

Part 1
Costs payable by the defendant to the date of grant of legal aid

This covers the period from 8th July 1999 to 8th September 1999. In this part the solicitor's time is charged at £140 per hour (including travel and waiting time) and letters out and telephone calls at £14.00 each.

Part 2
Costs payable by the defendant from the date of grant of legal aid

This part covers the period from 9th September 1999 to the present time, the client having the benefit of a legal aid certificate covering these proceedings. In this part, solicitor's time in respect of costs payable by the defendant has been charged as in Part 1 plus costs draftsman's and trainee's time charged at £85 per hour.

Part 3
Costs payable by the LSC only

This part covers the same period as Part 2. In this part solicitor's time in respect of costs payable by the LSC only are charged at the prescribed hourly rates plus enhancement of 50%.

Preparation: £74

Attending counsel in conference or at court: £36.40

Travelling and waiting: £32.70

Routine letters out: £7.40

Routine telephone calls: £4.10

Item No	Item	Amount claimed	VAT	Amount allowed	VAT
	Part 1: COSTS PAYABLE BY THE DEFENDANT				
	Claimant				
1	8th July 1999 – First Instructions – 0.75 hours	£105.00	£18.38		
2	Routine Letters out – 3	£42.00	£7.35		
	Witnesses of Fact				
3	Routine Letters out – 2	£28.00	£4.90		
	The Defendant				
4	8th July 1999 – Timed letter sent – 0.5 hours	£70.00	£12.25		
	To Summary	£245.00	£42.88		
	Part 2: COSTS PAYABLE BY THE DEFENDANT				
	7th October 1999 – Claim issued				
5	Issue fee	£400.00	—		
	21st October 1999 – Particulars of claim served				
	25th November 1999 – Time for service of defence extended by agreement to 14th January 2000				
	17th January 2000 – Filing allocation questionnaire				
6	Fee on allocation	£80.00	—		

Item No	Item		Amount claimed	VAT	Amount allowed	VAT
	20th January 2000 – Case allocated to multi-track					
	9th February 2000 – Case management conference					
	Engaged 0.75 hours	£105.00				
	Travel and waiting 2.00 hours	£280.00				
7	Total solicitor's fee for attending		£385.00	£67.38		
	23rd February 2000 – Claimant's list of documents					
	12th April 2000 – Payment into court of £25,126.33					
	13th April 2000 – Filing pre-trial check list					
8	Fee on listing		£400.00	—		
	28th June 2000 – Pre-trial review					
	Engaged 1.5 hours	£210.00				
	Travel and waiting 2.00 hours	£280.00				
9	Total solicitor's fee for attending		£490.00	£85.75		
10	Counsel's brief fee for attending pre-trial review (Miss GH)		£600.00	£105.00		

Item No	Item		Amount claimed	VAT	Amount allowed	VAT
	25th July 2000 – Attending first day of trial: adjourned part heard					
	Engaged in court 5.00 hours	£700.00				
	Engaged in conference 0.75 hours	£105.00				
	Travel and waiting 1.5 hours	£210.00				
11	Total solicitor's fee for attending		£1,015.00	£177.63		
12	Counsel's brief fee for trial (Miss GH)		£2,000.00	£350.00		
13	Fee of expert witness (Dr IJ)		£850.00			
14	Expenses of witnesses of fact		£84.00			
	26th July 2000 – Attending second day of trial when judgment "was given for the claimant in the sum of £78,256.83 plus"					
	"£1,207.16 interest plus costs"					
	Engaged in court 3.00 hours	£420.00				
	Engaged in conference 1.5 hours	£210.00				
	Travel and waiting 1.5 hours	£210.00				

Item No	Item	Amount claimed	VAT	Amount allowed	VAT
15	Total solicitor's fee for attending	£840.00	£147.00		
16	Counsel's fee for second day (Miss GH)	£650.00	£113.75		
	Claimant				
	Timed attendances in person and by telephone – see Schedule 1				
17	Total fees for Schedule 1 – 7.50 hours	£1,050.00	£183.75		
18	Routine letters out and telephone calls – 26 (14 + 12)	£364.00	£63.70		
	Witnesses of fact				
	"Timed attendances in person, by letter out and by"				
	telephone – see Schedule 2				
19	Total fees for Schedule 2 – 5.2 hours	£728.00	£127.40		
20	Routine letters out (including e mails) and telephone calls – 6 (4 + 2)	£84.00	£14.70		
21	Paid travelling on 9th October 1999	£22.96	£4.02		
	Medical expert (Dr IJ)				
22	11th September 1999 – long letter out 0.33 hours	£46.20	£8.09		

Item No	Item	Amount claimed	VAT	Amount allowed	VAT
23	30th January 2000 – long letter out 0.25 hours	£35.00	£6.13		
24	23rd May 2000 – telephone call 0.2 hours	£28.00	£4.90		
25	Routine letters out and telephone calls – 10 (6 + 4)	£140.00	£24.50		
26	Dr IJ's fee for report	£350.00	—		
	Solicitors for the defendant				
27	19th February 2000 – telephone call 0.25 hours	£35.00	£6.13		
28	Routine letters out and telephone calls – 24 (18 + 6)	£336.00	£58.80		
	Communications with the court				
29	Routine letters out and telephone calls – 9 (8 + 1)	£126.00	£22.05		
	Communications with Counsel				
30	Routine letters out (including e mails) and telephone calls – 19 (11 + 8)	£266.00	£46.55		
	Work done on documents				
	Timed attendances – see Schedule 3				
31	Total fees for Schedule 3 – 45.25 hours at £140 + 12 hours at £85	£7,355.00	£1,287.13		

Item No	Item		Amount claimed	VAT	Amount allowed	VAT
	Work done on negotiations					
	23rd March 2000 – meeting at offices of solicitors for the Defendant					
	Engaged – 1.5 hours	£210.00				
	Travel and waiting – 1.25 hours	£175.00				
32	Total solicitor's fee for meeting		£385.00	£67.38		
33	**Other work done**					
	Preparing and checking bill					
	Engaged: Solicitor – 1 hour	£140.00				
	Engaged: Costs Draftsman 4 hours	£340.00				
	Total on other work done		£480.00	£84.00		
	To summary		£19,625.16	£3,055.70		
	Part 3: COSTS PAYABLE BY LSC ONLY					
	Claimant					
	11th September 1999 – telephone call					
	Engaged 0.25 hours	£18.50				
	Enhancement 50%	£9.25				
34	Total solicitor's fee		£27.75	£4.86		
	10th April 2000 – telephone call					

Item No	Item		Amount claimed	VAT	Amount allowed	VAT
	Engaged 0.1 hours	£4.10				
	Enhancement 50%	£2.05				
35	Total solicitor's fee		£6.15	£1.08		
	Legal Aid Board and LSC					
	2nd August 2000 – Report on case					
	Engaged 0.5 hours	£37.00				
	Enhancement 50%	£18.50				
36	Total solicitor's fee		£55.50	£9.71		
	Routine letters out and telephone calls					
	Letters out – 2	£14.80				
	Telephone calls – 4	£16.40				
37	Total solicitor's fee		£31.20	£5.46		
	Other work done					
	Preparing and checking bill					
	Engaged: Solicitor – no claim					
	Engaged: Costs Draftsman – 1 hours	£74.00				
38	Total on other work done		£74.00	£12.95		
	To summary		194.60	34.06		
	SUMMARY					
	Costs payable by the Defendant					
		Part 1	£245.00	£42.88		
		Part 2	£19,625.16	£3,055.70		

Item No	Item	Amount claimed	VAT	Amount allowed VAT
	Total costs payable by the Defendant	£19,870.16	£3,098.58	
	Costs payable by LSC only			
	Part 3	£194.60	£34.06	
	Grand Totals			
	Costs payable by the Defendant	£19,870.16	£3,098.58	
	Costs payable by LSC only	£194.60	£34.06	
	Grand total	£20,064.76	£3,132.63	

Schedule of costs precedents
Precedent E

Legal Aid/LSC Schedule of Costs

IN THE HIGH COURT OF JUSTICE	1999 - B - 9999
QUEEN'S BENCH DIVISION	
BRIGHTON DISTRICT REGISTRY	
BETWEEN	

AB	Claimant
- and -	
CD	Defendant

Claimant's bill of costs: Legal Aid/LSC Schedule

Item No	Description of work done		V.A.T.	Disbursements	Profit Costs
6	Issue fee		—	£400.00	
7	Allocation fee		—	£80.00	
8	Solicitor's fee for hearing				
	Engaged 0.75 hours	£55.50			
	Enhancement thereon at 50%	£27.75			
	Travel and waiting 2.00 hours	£65.40			
	Total solicitor's fee for attending				£148.65
9	Fee on listing		—	£400.00	
10	Solicitor's fee for hearing				
	Engaged 1.5 hours	£111.00			
	Enhancement thereon at 50%	£55.50			
	Travel and waiting 2.00 hours	£65.40			
	Total solicitor's fee for attending				£231.90
11	Counsel's fee		£105.00	£600.00	
12	Solicitor's fee for trial				
	Engaged in court 5.00 hours	£182.00			
	Engaged in conference 0.75 hours	£27.30			
	Enhancement thereon at 50%	£104.65			
	Travel and waiting 1.50 hours	£49.05			
	Total solicitor's fee for attending				£363.00
13	Counsel's brief fee for trial		£350.00	£2,000.00	
14	Expert's fee for trial		—	£850.00	

Item No	Description of work done		V.A.T.	Disbursements	Profit Costs
15	Witnesses' expenses		—	£84.00	
	To summary		£455.00	£4,414.00	£743.55
16	Solicitor's fee for trial (second day)				
	Engaged in court 3.00 hours	£109.20			
	Engaged in conference 1.50 hours	£54.60			
	Enhancement thereon at 50%	£81.90			
	Travel and waiting 1.50 hours	£49.05			
	Total solicitor's fee for attending				£294.75
17	Counsel's fee for second day of trial		£113.75	£650.00	
18	Timed attendances on Claimant (1)				
	7.5 hours	£555.00			
	Enhancement thereon at 50%	£277.50			£832.50
19	Routine communications with Claimant (1)				
	Letters out – 14	£103.60			
	Telephone calls – 12	£49.20			£152.80
22	Timed attendances on and communications with witnesses of fact				
	5.2 hours	£384.80			
	Enhancement thereon at 50%	£192.40			£577.20
23	Routine communications with witnesses of fact				
	Letters out – 4	£29.60			

Item No	Description of work done		V.A.T.	Disbursements	Profit Costs
	Telephone calls – 2	£8.20			£37.80
24	Paid travelling		£4.02	£22.96	
25	Timed attendance on medical expert				
	0.33 hours	£24.42			
	Enhancement thereon at 50%	£12.21			£36.63
26	Timed communications with medical expert				
	0.25 hours	£18.50			
	Enhancement thereon at 50%	£9.25			£27.75
27	Timed communications with medical expert				
	0.2 hours	£14.80			
	Enhancement thereon at 50%	£7.40			£22.20
28	Routine communications with medical expert				
	Letters out – 6	£44.40			
	Telephone calls – 4	£16.40			£60.80
29	Expert's fee for report		—	£350.00	
30	Timed communications with solicitors for Defendant				
	0.25 hours	£18.50			
	Enhancement thereon at 50%	£9.25			£27.75
31	Routine communications with solicitors for Defendant				
	Letters out – 18	£133.20			
	Telephone calls – 6	£24.60			£157.80

Item No	Description of work done		V.A.T.	Disbursements	Profit Costs
32	Routine communications with the court				
	Letters out – 8	£59.20			
	Telephone calls – 1	£4.10			£63.30
	To summary		£117.77	£1,022.96	£2,291.28
33	Routine communications with Counsel				
	Letters out – 11	£81.40			
	Telephone calls – 8	£32.80			£114.20
36	Work done on documents				
	57.25 hours	£4,236.50			
	Enhancement thereon at 50%	£2,118.25			£6,354.75
37	Work done on negotiations				
	Engaged – 1.5 hours	£111.00			
	Enhancement thereon at 50%	£55.50			
	Travel and waiting – 1.25 hours	£40.88			£207.38
38	Other work done (1)				
	Preparing and checking bill				£370.00
40	VAT on total profit costs set out above (17.5% of £10,216.86)		£1,787.95		
	To summary		£1,787.95	£ —	£7,046.33
	SUMMARY				
	Page 1		£455.00	£4,414.00	£743.55
	Page 2		£117.77	£1,022.96	£2,291.28
	Page 3		£1,787.95	£ —	£7,046.33
	Totals:		£2,360.72	£5,436.96	£10,081.16
	Grand total:				£17,878.84

Schedule of costs precedents
Precedent F: Certificates for inclusion in bill of costs

- Appropriate certificates under headings (1) and (2) are required in all cases. The appropriate certificate under (3) is required in all cases in which the receiving party is an assisted person or a LSC funded client. Certificates (4), (5) and (6) are optional. Certificate (6) may be included in the bill, or, if the dispute as to VAT recoverability arises after service of the bill, may be filed and served as a supplementary document amending the bill under paragraph 39.10 of Practice Direction 47.
- All certificates must be signed by the receiving party or by his solicitor. Where the bill claims costs in respect of work done by more than one firm of solicitors, certificate (1), appropriately completed, should be signed on behalf of each firm.

(1) Certificate as to accuracy

I certify that this bill is both accurate and complete [and]

☐ *(where the receiving party was funded by legal aid)*

[in respect of Part(s) . . . . of the bill] all the work claimed was done pursuant to a certificate/contract issued by the Legal Services Board/ LSC granted to the assisted person.

☐ *(where costs are claimed for work done by an employed solicitor)*

[in respect of Part(s) . . . . of the bill] the case was conducted by a legal representative who is an employee of the receiving party.

☐ *(other cases where costs are claimed for work done by a solicitor)*

[in respect of Part(s) . . . . of the bill] the costs claimed herein do not exceed the costs which the receiving party is required to pay me/my firm.

(2) Certificate as to interest and payments

I certify that:

☐ No rulings have been made in this case which affects my/the receiving party's entitlement (if any) to interest on costs.

or

☐ The only rulings made in this case as to interest are as follows:

[give brief details as to the date of each ruling, the name of the Judge who made it and the text of the ruling]

and

☐ No payments have been made by any paying party on account of costs included in this bill of costs.

or

☐ The following payments have been made on account of costs included in this bill of costs:

[give brief details of the amounts, the dates of payment and the name of the person by or on whose behalf they were paid]

(3) Certificate as to interest of assisted person/ LSC funded client pursuant to Regulation 119 of the Civil Legal Aid (General) Regulations 1989

I certify that the Legally Aided person/LSC funded client has no financial interest in the detailed assessment.

or

I certify that a copy of this bill has been sent to the Legally Aided person/LSC funded client pursuant to Regulation 119 of the Civil Legal Aid General Regulations 1989 with an explanation of his/her interest in the detailed assessment and the steps which can be taken to safeguard that interest in the assessment. He/she has/has not requested that the costs officer be informed of his/her interest and has/has not requested that notice of the detailed assessment hearing be sent to him/her.

(4) Consent to the signing of the certificate within 21 days of detailed assessment pursuant to Regulation 112 and 121 of the Civil Legal Aid (General) Regulations 1989

I certify that notice of the fees reduced or disallowed on detailed assessment has been given in writing to counsel on [date].

or

I certify that: there having been no reduction or disallowance of counsel's fees it is not necessary to give notice to counsel.

I/we consent to the final costs certificate being issued immediately.

(5) Certificate in respect of disbursements not exceeding £500

I hereby certify that all disbursements listed in this bill which individually do not exceed £500 (other than those relating to counsel's fees) have been duly discharged.

(6) Certificate as to recovery of VAT

With reference to the pending assessment of the [claimant's/defendant's] costs and disbursements herein which are payable by the [claimant/defendant] we the undersigned [legal representative of] [auditors of] the [claimant/defendant] hereby certify that the [claimant/defendant] on the basis of its last completed VAT return [would/would not be entitled to recover would/be entitled to recover only percent of the] Value Added Tax on such costs and disbursements, as input tax pursuant to section 24 of the Value Added Tax Act 1994.

Schedule of costs precedents
Precedent G

IN THE HIGH COURT OF JUSTICE — 2000 – B – 9999
QUEEN'S BENCH DIVISION
OXBRIDGE DISTRICT REGISTRY
BETWEEN

WX — Claimant
- and -
YZ — Defendant

Points of dispute served by the defendant

Point 1 General point	Rates claimed for the assistant solicitor and other fee earners are excessive. Reduce to £158 and £116 respectively plus VAT.
	Receiving Party's Reply:
	Costs Officer's decision:
Point 2 Point of principle	The claimant was at the time a child/protected person/insolvent and did not have the capacity to authorise the solicitors to bring these proceedings.
	Receiving Party's Reply:
	Costs Officer's decision:
Point 3 (6), (12), (17), (23), (29), (32)	(i) The number of conferences with counsel is excessive and should be reduced to 3 in total (9 hours). (ii) There is no need for two fee earners to attend each conference. Limit to one assistant solicitor in each case.
	Receiving Party's Reply:
	Costs Officer's decision:
Point 4 (42)	The claim for timed attendances on claimant (schedule 1) is excessive. Reduce to 4 hours.
	Receiving Party's Reply:
	Costs Officer's decision:
Point 5 (47)	The total claim for work done on documents by the assistant solicitor is excessive. A reasonable allowance in respect of documents concerning court and counsel is 8 hours, for documents concerning witnesses and the expert witness 6.5 hours, for work done on arithmetic 2.25 hours and for other documents 5.5 hours. Reduce to 22.25 hours.

	Receiving Party's Reply:
	Costs Officer's decision:
Point 6 (50)	The time claimed for preparing and checking the bill is excessive. Reduce solicitor's time to 0.5 hours and reduce the costs draftsman's time to three hours.
	Receiving Party's Reply:
	Costs Officer's decision:

Served on . . . . [date] by. . . . . [name] [legal representative of] the Defendant.

Schedule of costs precedents
Precedent H

See Practice Direction 3E.

Schedule of costs precedents
Precedent J

IN THE HIGH COURT OF JUSTICE Claim No
SUPREME COURT COSTS OFFICE
IN THE MATTER OF [name of solicitor or solicitors' firm]
Claimant
Defendant(s)

Claim form (CPR Part 8)

Details of claim (see also overleaf)

The following orders are applied for:

() An order in standard form for the delivery of a bill of costs in [all cases and matters] [the following causes and matters. . . . .] in which
the Defendant has acted for the Claimant(s).

() An order in standard form for the detailed assessment of the bill(s) dated . . . . [and] [bearing the invoice numbers . . . .
delivered by the [claimant/Defendant] to the [Defendant/Claimant/person named . . . .]

() An order dealing with the costs of this application

Defendant's name and address £

Court fee
Solicitor's costs
Issue date

Claim No	

Details of claim (continued)

Statement of Truth

*(I believe) (The Claimant believes) that the facts stated in these particulars of claim are true. *I am duly authorised by the Claimant to sign this statement.

Full name . . . . Name of Claimant's solicitor's firm

Signed . . . . position or office held . . . . *(Claimant) (Litigation friend) (Claimant's solicitor) (if signing on behalf of firm or company)

*delete as appropriate

Claimant's or claimant's solicitor's address to which documents should be sent if different from overleaf. If you are prepared to accept service by DX, fax or e-mail, please add details.

Schedule of costs precedents
Precedent K: Order for delivery of a Bill

Solicitor's Act: order for delivery of bill

DATED the [DATE]

IN THE HIGH COURT OF JUSTICE **[Claim No]**

[DIVISION]

[JUDGE TYPE] [JUDGE NAME]

[CLAIMANT]

BETWEEN:

Claimant

- and -

[DEFENDANT]

Defendant

UPON THE APPLICATION OF THE [PARTY]

[the parties and their representatives who attended]

AND UPON HEARING

AND UPON READING the documents on the Court File

IT IS ORDERED THAT

(1) The [PARTY] must within [NUMBER OF DAYS] deliver to the [PARTY] or to his solicitor, a bill of costs in all causes and matters in which he has been concerned for the [PARTY]

(2) The [PARTY] must give credit in that bill for all money received by him from or on account of the [PARTY]

Schedule of costs precedents
Precedent L: Order for Detailed Assessment (Client)

Order on Client's Application for Detailed Assessment of Solicitor's Bill

DATED the

IN THE HIGH COURT OF JUSTICE

BETWEEN:

Claimant

- and -

Defendant

UPON THE APPLICATION OF THE [PARTY]

[the parties and their representatives who attended]

AND UPON HEARING

AND UPON READING the documents on the Court File

IT IS ORDERED THAT

(1) A detailed assessment must be made of the bill dated [ ] delivered to the claimant by the defendant.

(2) On making the detailed assessment, the court must also assess the costs of these proceedings and certify what is due to or from either party in respect of the bill and the costs of these proceedings.

(3) Until these proceedings are concluded the defendant must not commence or continue any proceedings against the claimant in respect of the bill mentioned above.

(4) Upon payment by the claimant of any sum certified as due to the defendant in these proceedings the defendant must deliver to the claimant all the documentation in the defendant's possession or control which belong to the claimant.

Schedule of costs precedents
Precedent M: Order for Detailed Assessment (Solicitor)

SCHEDULE OF COSTS PRECEDENTS
PRECEDENT M
Order on Solicitor's Application for Assessment Under the Solicitor's Act 1974 Part III

Upon hearing ... upon reading ...

IT IS ORDERED THAT

(1) A detailed assessment must be made of the bill dated [ ] delivered to the defendant by the claimant.

(2) If the defendant attends the detailed assessment the court making that assessment must also assess the costs of these proceedings and certify what is due to or from either party in respect of the bill and the costs of these proceedings.

(3) Until these proceedings are concluded the claimant must not commence or continue any proceedings against the defendant in respect of the bill mentioned above.

(4) Upon payment by the defendant of any sum certified as due to the claimant in these proceedings the claimant must deliver to the defendant all the documentation in the claimant's possession or control which belong to the defendant.

Schedule of costs precedents
Precedent P: Solicitors Act: Breakdown of Costs

IN THE HIGH COURT OF JUSTICE		Claim Number
QUEEN'S BENCH DIVISION		
SUPREME COURT COSTS OFFICE		
BETWEEN		
	EF	Claimant
	- and -	
	GH & Co	Defendants

Breakdown of defendant's bill of costs dated 27th February 2012 to be assessed pursuant to the order dated 27th April 2012

The claimant instructed the defendants in connection with a summons for careless or inconsiderate driving which had been served upon him. By letter dated 21st October 2011 the defendants wrote to the claimant setting out their terms of business including the hourly rates of the fee earners who would act on his instructions. On 23rd October 2011 the claimant dated and signed a copy of that letter and returned it to the defendants so indicating his acceptance of the terms set out.

The proceedings were of the highest importance to the claimant who feared losing his licence and who wished to defend any civil proceedings that might be taken against him as a result of the prosecution. The defendants entered into correspondence with the CPS and eventually obtained their witness statements and invited them to consent to an adjournment because of the absence overseas of an important witness for the claimant (Mr LM). Eventually the defendants successfully applied to the court for an adjournment, and also applied for and obtained a witness summons. At the trial the claimant was found guilty and was fined £300 and 4 points were endorsed on his driving licence.

Proceedings were conducted by an assistant solicitor admitted in 2000 whose time is charged at an agreed rate of £192.00 per hour with routine letters out and telephone calls at an agreed rate of £19.20 each. At the trial a trainee attended with counsel. The trainee's time is charged at an agreed rate of £118. per hour.

Cash account for client: EF

Received		**Paid**	
From client on account generally:		Refund to client:	
24th October 2011	1,500.00	27th February 2012	385.00
From client on account generally:			
19th February 2012	1,000.00	Balancing Item	2,115.00
	2,500.00		2,500.00
Balance due to client EF:	£2,115.00		

Item no	Item		V.A.T. £	Disbursements £	Profit Costs £
	Attendances on Court and Counsel				
	5th November 2011 — application made for an adjournment for the convenience of a witness				
	13th November 2011 — contested hearing of the application				
	Engaged 10 minutes	£ 32.00			
	Travel and waiting 30 minutes	£ 96.00			
1	Total solicitor's fee for hearing		£25.60		£128.00
	17th November convenience of a witness — conference with counsel				
	Engaged 45 minutes	£ 144.00			
	Travel and waiting 1 hour	£ 192.00			
2	Total solicitor's fee for conference		£67.20		£336.00
3	Counsel's fee for conference paid (Miss JK)				
	15th February 2012 — Brief to counsel — 4 pages A4		£30.00	£150.00	
	23rd February 2012 — attending the trial				
	Trainee engaged in court 1 hour	£ 118.00			
	Engaged in conference 30 minutes	£ 59.00			
	Travel and waiting (apportioned) 45 minutes	£ 88.50			
4	Total trainee solicitor's fee for trial		£53.10		£265.50
5	Counsel's brief fee (paid: Miss JK)		£60.00	£300.00	

Item no	Item	V.A.T. £	Disbursements £	Profit Costs £
	Claimant			
6	21st October 2011 — first instructions 1 hour	£38.40		£192.00
7	16th November 2011 — finalising proof of evidence 45 minutes	£28.80		£144.00
8	Routine letters out and telephone calls — 12 (9 + 3)	£46.08		£230.40
	Witness (Mr LM)			
	Personal attendance by trainee solicitor			
	Engaged 45 minutes £ 88.50			
	Travel and waiting 1 hour £118.00			
9	Total trainee solicitor's fee for attendance	£41.30		£206.50
10	Routine letters out — 6	£35.04		£175.20
	Other persons			
11	Routine letters out and telephone calls to the CPS — 8 (6 + 2)	£30.72		£153.60
	Communications with the court			
12	Routine letters out — 6	£23.04		£115.20
	Communications with Counsel			
13	Routine letters out and telephone calls — 8 (4 + 4)	£30.72		£153.60

Item no	Item	V.A.T. £	Disbursements £	Profit Costs £
	Work done on documents			
14	Instructions to counsel — 30 minutes	£19.20		£96.00
15	Attendance note of conference — 15 minutes	£9.60		£48.00
16	Brief to counsel — 30 minutes	£19.20		£96.00
17	Attendance note of trial (trainee) — 45 minutes	£17.70		£88.50
		£575.70	£450.00	£2428.50
	Summary			
	Total costs claimed in breakdown £2,878.50 + £575.70 VAT.			
	(Total costs billed £2,500.00 + £500.00 VAT)			

Schedule of costs precedents
Precedent Q

Model form of breakdown of the costs claimed for each phase of the proceedings

SUMMARY OF COSTS AS CLAIMED VS AMOUNTS IN LAST APPROVED / AGREED BUDGET							
Precedent H Budget Phase	**Phase Name**	**Pre Budget £**	**Budgeted £**			**Last Approved/ Agreed Budget £**	**Departure from Last Approved/ Agreed Budget £**
Pre-action	Initial and Pre-Action Protocol Work	3,440.23	0.00			0.00	0.00
ADR/ Settlement	ADR/ Settlement	0.00	4,972.50			500.00	4,472.50
Issue/ Pleadings	Issue/ Statements of Case	2,208.50	0.00			2,750.00	–2,750.00
Disclosure	Disclosure	0.00	3,738.46			5,000.00	–1,261.54
Witness Statements	Witness Statements	0.00	3,646.50			6,000.00	–2,353.50
Expert Reports	Expert Reports	0.00	4,835.00			1,500.00	3,335.00
PTR	Case and Costs Management Hearings	0.00	2,159.00			4,500.00	–2,341.00
CMC	Interim Applications and Hearings (Interlocutory Applications)	960.54	0.00			2,500.00	–2,500.00
Trial Preparation	Trial Preparation	0.00	17,635.00			15,000.00	2,635.00
Trial	Trial	0.00	23,187.50			35,000.00	–11,812.50

Schedule of costs precedents
Precedent S

IN THE

DIVISION **Claim No.**

BETWEEN:

Claimant

- and -

Defendant

BILL OF COSTS to be assessed on the basis and paid by the pursuant to orders dated

CERTIFICATES PAGE

I certify that this bill is both accurate and complete and

in respect of the bill the costs claimed herein do not exceed the costs which the receiving party is required to pay my firm.

CERTIFICATE AS TO INTEREST AND PAYMENTS

I certify that

No rulings have been made in this case which affects my/the receiving party's entitlement to interest on costs.

and

CERTIFICATE IN RESPECT OF DISBURSEMENTS NOT EXCEEDING £500

I hereby certify that all disbursements listed in this bill which individually do not exceed £500 (other than those relating to counsel's fees) have been duly discharged.

CERTIFICATE IN RESPECT OF VAT

With reference to the pending assessment of the [claimant's/defendant's] costs and disbursements herein which are payable by the [claimant/defendant] we the undersigned [solicitors to] [auditors of] the [claimant/defendant] hereby certify that the [claimant/ defendant] on the basis of its last completed VAT return [would/would not be entitled to recover would/be entitled to recover only percent of the] Value Added Tax on such costs and disbursements, as input tax pursuant to the Value Added Tax Act 1994.

Signed...

ABC Firm
VAT NO:

Page 2 of 24

MASTER CHRONOLOGY

Date	Details

Page 4 of 24

LEGAL TEAM, HOURLY RATES AND COUNSEL'S SUCCESS FEES

LTM	LTM Name	LTM Status	LTM Grade	Further Relevant Information	LTM Rate	LTM Rate Effective From	Counsel SF %

FUNDING & PARTS TABLE

Part ID	Description	Solicitors' Success Fee	VAT Rate	Profit Costs incurred	Indemnity Principle Limit	Recoverable % of incurred profit costs	Profit Costs as Claimed
				-		100.00%	-

Page 6 of 24

TABLE OF COSTS AS SUMMARILY ASSESSED

Part ID	Date	Hearing Description	Counsel	Profit Costs Allowed	Counsel Fees Allowed	Disbursements Allowed	Solicitor's Success Fee %	Counsel Success Fee %	Solicitor's Success Fee	Counsel's Success Fee	VAT %	VAT on Solicitor's Success Fee	VAT on Counsel's Success Fee	Total Success Fees inc VAT
							#NA	#NA	#NA	#NA	#NA	#NA	#NA	#NA
Total Base Costs Summarily Assessed				£0.00	£0.00	£0.00								£0.00
Total Success Fees including VAT									#NA	#NA		#NA	#NA	#NA

MAIN SUMMARY BY PHASE

Total Bill **0.00**

Success Fees on Summarily Assessed Costs 0.00

Phase Sort Order Number	Phase Name	Counsel's Base Fees	Other Disbursements	Base Profit Costs	Total Base Costs	Solicitor's Success Fees	Counsel's Success Fees	Total VAT	ATEI Premium	Total Costs
	-	0.00	0.00	0.00	0.00	0.00	0.00	0.00	0.00	0.00
Grand Total		**0.00**	**0.00**	**0.00**	**0.00**	**0.00**	**0.00**	**0.00**	**0.00**	**0.00**

Page 8 of 24

SUMMARY BY TASK, ACTIVITY AND EXPENSES

Total Bill **0.00**

Success Fees on Summarily Assessed Costs 0.00

Task Sort Order Number	Task Name	Activity Name	Expense Name	LTM Grade	Time	Base Profit Costs	Counsel's Base Fees	Other Disbursements	Total Base Costs	Solicitor's Success Fees	Counsel's Success Fees	Total VAT	ATEI Premium	Total Costs
-					0.00	0.00	0.00	0.00	0.00	0.00	0.00	0.00	0.00	0.00
Grand Total					0.00	0.00	0.00	0.00	0.00	0.00	0.00	0.00	0.00	0.00

SUMMARY OF COSTS AS CLAIMED VS AMOUNTS IN LAST APPROVED / AGREED / SUBMITTED BUDGET

Precedent H Phase	Incurred Pre-Budget	Last Approved Budget / Agreed Budget Figure	Incurred Post-Budget	Departure from Last Approved / Agreed Budget
Pre-action	-		-	0.00
Issue/Pleadings	-		-	0.00
CMC	-		-	0.00
Disclosure	-		-	0.00
Witness Statements	-		-	0.00
Expert Reports	-		-	0.00
PTR	-		-	0.00
Trial Preparation	-		-	0.00
Trial	-		-	0.00
ADR/Settlement	-		-	0.00
Contingent Cost A	-		-	0.00
Contingent Cost B	-		-	0.00
Contingent Cost C	-		-	0.00
	-	-	-	-

MAIN SUMMARY - BY PART

Total Bill **0.00**

Success Fees on Summarily Assessed Costs 0.00

Part Name	Part ID	Counsel's Fees	Other Disbursements	Base Profit Costs	Total Base Costs	Solicitor's Success Fees	Counsel's Success Fees	Total VAT	Sum of ATEI Premium	Total Costs
-		-	-	-	0.00	-	-	-	-	0.00
Grand Total		0.00	0.00	0.00	0.00	0.00	0.00	0.00	0.00	0.00

Page 11 of 24

SUMMARY OF COMMUNICATIONS

Task Sort Order Number	Task Name	External Party Name	Communication Method	Time	Base Profit Costs
	Total			0.00	0.00
Grand Total				0.00	0.00

Page 12 of 24

DETAILED BILL - (PRINT VERSION)

Item No	Date	Phase Name	Task Name	Activity Name	Expense Name	Pre, Post or Non Budget	Description of work	External Party Name	LTM Grade	Time	Base Profit Costs	Disbursements
1		-	-	-	-				-		0.00	

Page 13 of 24

BILL DETAIL

DATA ENTRY SECTIONS															
Item No	Entry No	Part ID	Date	Description of work	LTM	Time	Estima ted ("E")	Counsel's Base Fees	Other Disbursements	VAT On Other Disbursements	ATEI Premium	Pre, Post or Non Budget	Phase Code	Task Code	Activity Code
1															

Page 14 of 24

BILL DETAIL (Continuation)

DATA ENTRY SECTIONS (Continuation)										
Expense Code	Precedent H Phase	Entry Alloc %	External Party Name	Communication Method	Base Profit Costs (copy)	Disbursements Total (copy)	Part Name	Phase Name	Task Name	Activity Name
					0.00		-	-	-	-

BILL DETAIL (Continuation)

DATA ENTRY SECTIONS (Continuation)								PROFIT COSTS SECTION					COUNSEL'S FEE SECTION			
Expense Name	LTM Status	LTM Grade	LTM Rate	Funding Percent Allowed	Success Fee %	VAT Rate	Profit Costs Incurred (not including any indemnity cap)	Base Profit Costs (including any indemnity cap)	VAT on Base Profit Costs	Success Fee on Base Profit costs	VAT on Success Fee on Base Profit Costs	Total Profit Costs (inc SF and VAT)	VAT on Base Counsel Fees	Counsel's Success Fee	VAT on Counsel's Success Fee	Total Counsel Fees (inc Success Fee and VAT)
-	-	-	0.00	0.00%	0.00%	0.00%	0.00	0.00	0.00	0.00	0.00	0.00	0.00	0.00	0.00	0.00

Page 16 of 24

BILL DETAIL (Continuation)

DISBURSEMENTS SECTION		TOTALS					SORT ORDERS			
Total Other Disbursements (inc VAT)	Disbursements Total (without success fees)	Total Base Costs	Total Profit Costs	Total Disbursements (including success fees)	Total VAT	Total Costs	Phase Sort Order Number	Task Sort Order Number	Activity Sort Order Number	Expense Sort Order Number
0.00	0.00	0.00	0.00	0.00	0.00	0.00	-	-	-	-

Page 17 of 24

REFERENCE AND LOOKUP TABLE - PHASES AND TASKS

Phase Code	Task Code	Phase in Bill of Costs	Phase in Precedent H	Task Name	Task Description	Phase Sort Order	Task Sort Order Number
P1		Initial and Pre-Action Protocol Work	Pre-Action Costs		Work relating to the obtaining of instructions, identification of witnesses, dealing with locus and evidential issues, dealing with and identifying legal issues arising from the case and strategy, and dealing with any protocol related matters, if not covered elsewhere.	1	
	T1	Initial and Pre-Action Protocol Work	Pre-Action Costs	Factual investigation	Work required to understand the facts of the case including instructions from the client and the identification of potential witnesses		1
	T2	Initial and Pre-Action Protocol Work	Pre-Action Costs	Legal investigation	Includes identification of the legal issues raised by the case facts and developing the strategy for the case.		2
	T3	Initial and Pre-Action Protocol Work	Pre-Action Costs	Pre-action protocol (or similar) work	Communications at an initial stage in compliance with pre-action protocol including letters before action and responses.		3
P2		Issue / Statements of Case	Issue / Statements of Case		Covers issue and acknowledgment of proceedings, Statements of Case and Further Information requests/responses. Includes taking instructions, making inquiries and searches, researching, drafting, editing, filing and all meetings and communications for the purpose of such documents.	2	
	T4	Issue / Statements of Case	Issue / Statements of Case	Issue and Serve Proceedings and Preparation of Statement(s) of Case	Work related to effecting service, including dealing with process servers or the foreign process office. Work in preparation of claims, petitions and any other originating process, Statements of Case, Part 20 proceedings, including reviewing those of other parties whether or not a responsive document is served. Includes all work with counsel thereon and all dealings with client and others in connection therewith. In appeals includes Appellants' and Respondents' Notices and supporting skeleton arguments.		4
	T5	Issue / Statements of Case	Issue / Statements of Case	Review of Other Party(s)' Statements of Case	Considering Other Party(s)' Claim Form and Statements of Case.		5
	T6	Issue / Statements of Case	Issue / Statements of Case	Requests for Further Information	Preparing and considering requests for Further Information and responses thereto.		6
	T7	Issue / Statements of Case	Issue / Statements of Case	Amendment of Statements of Case	Preparing and considering amendments to originating process, Statements of Case, Part 20 proceedings. In appeals refers to amendments to Appellants' and Respondents' Notices and supporting skeleton arguments.		7
P3	T8	Case Management Conference	CMC	Case Management Conference	Work relating to such hearings and the preparation for them, including PTR and CMC's. This does not include interim applications heard at the same time (excludes costs management).	3	8
P4		Disclosure	Disclosure		Work relating to gathering and reviewing documents for potential disclosure, preparing disclosure lists and practical steps of disclosure.	4	

Page 18 of 24

REFERENCE AND LOOKUP TABLE - PHASES AND TASKS

Phase Code	Task Code	Phase in Bill of Costs	Phase in Precedent H	Task Name	Task Description	Phase Sort Order	Task Sort Order Number
	T9	Disclosure	Disclosure	Preparation of the disclosure report and the disclosure proposal	Preparation of the disclosure report and the disclosure proposal to comply with obligations that came in on 1-April-2013 (applicable to both manual and e-disclosure). All Disclosure related work required for the CMC. Additionally, this task encompasses work such as determining the location of documents, letters to client re disclosure obligations and setting up client based disclosure teams.		9
	T10	Disclosure	Disclosure	Obtaining and reviewing documents	Obtaining and reviewing documents to determine relevance (applicable to both manual and e-disclosure).	T10	10
	T11	Disclosure	Disclosure	Preparing and serving disclosure lists	Preparing and serving disclosure lists (applicable to both manual and e-disclosure).		11
	T12	Disclosure	Disclosure	Inspection and review of the other side's disclosure for work undertaken after exchange of disclosure lists.	Inspection and review of the other side's disclosure for work undertaken after exchange of disclosure lists (applicable to both manual and e-disclosure).		12
P5		Witness statements	Witness statements		Work that relates to the identification of potential witnesses and preparing their evidence for trial (excludes witness evidence in relation to interim applications).	5	
	T13	Witness statements	Witness statements	Taking, preparing and finalising witness statement(s)	Work involved in identifying appropriate witnesses, tracing and communicating with same, taking instructions for, preparing and serving witness statements or affidavits, preparing and serving witness summaries, preparing and serving any notices under Civil Evidence or similar Acts, preparing and serving witness summonses, including reviewing other materials for these purposes and all dealings with client, witnesses, inquiry agents, counsel, Other Party(s) and others in relation to own side witness statements.		13
	T14	Witness statements	Witness statements	Reviewing Other Party(s)' witness statement(s)	Considering Other Party(s)' witness statements, affidavits, witness summaries, Civil Evidence Act or similar notices, reviewing same in context of other evidence and material, considering strategy to deal with issues raised.		14
P6		Expert reports	Expert reports		Work that relates to the identification of potential experts and preparing their evidence for trial (excludes expert evidence in relation to interim applications).	6	
	T15	Expert reports	Expert reports	Own expert evidence	Identifying and interviewing experts and consultants (testifying or non-testifying), working with them, and developing expert reports. Reviewing case in the light of such evidence. Considering questions asked by Other Party(s) of own experts and experts' responses. Arranging experts' discussions. Considering reports of experts' discussions. Includes all communications or other work with counsel, and all communications with Other Party.		15

REFERENCE AND LOOKUP TABLE - PHASES AND TASKS

Phase Code	Task Code	Phase in Bill of Costs	Phase in Precedent H	Task Name	Task Description	Phase Sort Order	Task Sort Order Number
	T16	Expert reports	Expert reports	Other Party(s)' expert evidence	Considering Other Party(s)' expert evidence, preparing and asking questions of their experts, considering replies, reviewing case in light of such evidence.		16
	T17	Expert reports	Expert reports	Joint expert evidence	As [JH10] (own expert evidence) with appropriate modifications.		17
P7	T18	Pre-Trial Review	PTR	Pre Trial Review	Work in preparing for and attending any Pre Trial Review (excluding Costs Management).	7	18
P8		Trial preparation	Trial preparation		Work for the preparation of the trial not included in the other phases.	8	
	T19	Trial preparation	Trial preparation	Preparation of trial bundles	Time spent identifying documents for inclusion in the trial bundles, working with the other parties to agree the trial bundles, preparing and updating the trial bundles.		19
	T20	Trial preparation	Trial preparation	General work regarding preparation for trial	All other time spent in preparing for and supporting a trial, including developing overall trial strategy, preparing own witnesses for trial, working on cross-examination, preparing opening and closing arguments, , identifying documents for use at trial, preparing demonstrative materials, making any physical arrangements for trial etc		20
P9		Trial	Trial		Covers preparation for advocacy including written trial submissions and all other work from the first day on which a trial or appeal begins or, if settled, was due to begin.	9	
	T21	Trial	Trial	Advocacy	Preparation by advocates of written and oral openings, closings or skeleton arguments; preparation for examination of witnesses; preparation of and for all applications made during trial; considering all submissions of other parties; attendance of advocates during trial. Includes all dealings by advocates with others (e.g. solicitors, clients, witnesses) for these purposes.		21
	T22	Trial	Trial	Support of advocates	Work by lawyers other than advocates relating to the above matters and all attendances at court on trial days including conferences or meetings before or after court and travel and waiting. Where there is a substantial gap between trial days, work should be allocated to whichever is the more appropriate of the Trial Preparation and Trial phases.		22
	T23	Trial	Trial	Judgment and post-trial activity	Considering draft judgments, preparing and considering any written responses to the court, submissions or skeleton arguments in relation to judgment or consequential orders, preparation for and attendance at hearings when reserved judgments handed down or consequential orders considered, all dealings relating to form of judgment or order. Includes all meetings and communications relating thereto.		23
P10		ADR / Settlement	ADR / Settlement		Work that is directed to settlement including ADR	10	
	T24	ADR / Settlement	ADR / Settlement	Mediation	Work related to proposals for mediation, preparation and attendance at the mediation and any follow-up work.		24

Page 20 of 24

REFERENCE AND LOOKUP TABLE - PHASES AND TASKS

Phase Code	Task Code	Phase in Bill of Costs	Phase in Precedent H	Task Name	Task Description	Phase Sort Order	Task Sort Order Number
	T25	ADR / Settlement	ADR / Settlement	Other Settlement Matters	Work that is directed to settlement including Part 36 and other offers and consequent negotiations (includes all forms of ADR other than mediation).		25
P11		Interim Applications and Hearings (Interlocutory Applications)	Contingencies		Work covering all proposed and actual interim applications and hearings. Includes taking instructions, making inquiries, research, preparing and filing applications, supporting evidence and skeleton arguments including reviewing those of other parties whether or not a responsive document is served, preparing for and attending hearings and all meetings and communications for the purpose of such applications or hearings.	11	
	T26	Interim Applications and Hearings (Interlocutory Applications)	Contingencies	Applications relating to originating process or Statement of Case or for default or summary judgment	Includes applications as to service or jurisdiction, to strike out or amend all or part of a claim or Statement of Case, or for the variation of parties.		26
	T27	Interim Applications and Hearings (Interlocutory Applications)	Contingencies	Applications for an injunction or committal	Work performed related to applications for an injunction or committal.		27
	T28	Interim Applications and Hearings (Interlocutory Applications)	Contingencies	Applications for disclosure or Further Information	Work performed related to applications for disclosure or Further Information		28
	T29	Interim Applications and Hearings (Interlocutory Applications)	Contingencies	Applications concerning evidence	Work performed related to applications concerning evidence		29
	T30	Interim Applications and Hearings (Interlocutory Applications)	Contingencies	Applications relating to Costs alone	Includes applications for security for costs, costs capping and protective costs orders. Does not include budgeting or costs management orders which are dealt with at [JB40]. Does not include applications proceeding as to costs alone where a substantive application for some other relief has settled.		30
	T31	Interim Applications and Hearings (Interlocutory Applications)	Contingencies	Permission applications	All permission applications where permission to proceed is required, such as in judicial review proceedings or on appeal.		31
	T32	Interim Applications and Hearings (Interlocutory Applications)	Contingencies	Other applications	All other types of application not covered by the categories above		32
P12	T33	Funding	N/A	Funding	All work relating to reviewing funding options, securing funding and reports to funders during the life of the case.	12	33
P13		Budgeting incl. costs estimates	N/A		All work throughout the life of the case relating to budgeting and costs management, excluding the 'costs assessment' and 'funding' related work and preparation for and attendance at any costs management hearing, all of which have discrete phases.	13	

REFERENCE AND LOOKUP TABLE - PHASES AND TASKS

Phase Code	Task Code	Phase in Bill of Costs	Phase in Precedent H	Task Name	Task Description	Phase Sort Order	Task Sort Order Number
	T34	Budgeting incl. costs estimates	N/A	Budgeting - own side's costs	Preparing budgets solely for the client and monitoring costs incurred for the purposes of any required variations. Performing budgetary work related to obtaining third party funding/ATE insurance.		34
	T35	Budgeting incl. costs estimates	N/A	Budgeting - Precedent H	Initially completing Precedent H - This task is confined to preparing and compiling the first budget required by the court in the form of Precedent H.		35
	T36	Budgeting incl. costs estimates	N/A	Budgeting - between the parties	Work on budgeting between the parties following initial completion of the first budget, including the monitoring of costs incurred against the budget and any applications for variation of a budget.		36
P14	T37	Costs Management Conference	N/A	Costs Management Conference	Work in preparing for and attending any Costs Management Conference / Hearing including the hearing of any applications to vary a budget.	14	37
P15		Costs Assessment	N/A		Work related to the assessment or agreement of costs following trial or settlement of the underlying action	15	
	T38	Costs Assessment	N/A	Preparing costs claim	Includes the reconciliation of the costs claimed to any approved budget in and the preparation of the bill of costs for detailed assessment		38
	T39	Costs Assessment	N/A	Points of dispute, Replies and Negotiations	Work on the formal procedural steps under CPR 47 following service of a bill of costs together with Part 36 and other offers to settle costs and consequent negotiations		39
	T40	Costs Assessment	N/A	Hearings	Includes preparation for and attendance at hearings for directions and interim certificate applications as well as the detailed assessment itself		40
	T41	Costs Assessment	N/A	Post Assessment Work (excluding Hearings)	Includes post-hearing calculations and all other work required to finalise the amounts due for principal, interest and the costs of the assessment		41

REFERENCE AND LOOKUP TABLE FOR ACTIVITIES

Activity Code	Activity Name	Activity Description	Activity Sort Order Number
A1	Appear For/Attend	Any appearance for or attendance at a scheduled event related to the matter	1
A2	Communicate (with Counsel)	Any communication by letter, fax, email, telephone, meetings and conferences with own-side Counsel	2
A3	Communicate (with client)	Any communication by letter, fax, email, telephone, meetings and conferences with client	3
A4	Communicate (witnesses)	Any communication by letter, fax, email, telephone, meetings and conferences with witnesses	4
A5	Communicate (experts)	Any communication by letter, fax, email, telephone, meetings and conferences with experts	5
A6	Communicate (Other Party(s)/other outside lawyers)	Any communication by letter, fax, email, telephone, meetings and conferences with opposing lawyers or other outside lawyers not representing the client	6
A7	Communicate (other external)	Any communication by letter, fax, email, telephone, meetings and conferences with other external parties not already categorised within these activity codes	7
A8	Communicate (internally within legal team)	Any internal communications within firm.	8
A9	Billable Travel Time	Includes time spent waiting associated with the matter when other billable services are not performed for the client.	9
A10	Plan, Prepare, Draft, Review	Any planning or preparation associated with a matter; Any drafting or revision or other preparation of documents or other material; Any review or analysis of documents or other material; Any handling of documents, files or data.	10

REFERENCE AND LOOKUP TABLE FOR EXPENSES

Expense Code	Expense Name	Expense Sort Number
X1	Counsel's Fees	1
X2	Experts' Fees	2
X3	Court Fees	3
X4	Arbitrators' or Mediators' Fees	4
X5	Witness Expenses	5
X6	Transcripts	6
X7	Litigation Support Suppliers (incl eDisclosure)	7
X8	Consultants, Other Professionals or Foreign Lawyers	8
X9	Travel Expenses	9
X10	Copying/Imaging	10
X11	ATEI Premiums	11
X12	Medical Records	12
X13	Translation Costs	13
X14	Bank Fees	14
X15	Process Server Fees	15

Schedule of costs precedents
Precedent T

Precedent T Summary Sheet

Court:	Name		Current Budget date:		
Parties:	Parties		Date Precedent T served:		
Claim number:	Number		Cost budget for:	Party	
Work done / to be done	**Current Budget Costs (prior to variation)**		**Variations (+ or -)**	**Total estimated costs after variation (£)**	**Completion by the Court :** ***Estimated costs allowed or agreed after variation***
	Incurred (£)	**Estimated (£)**	**Variation in estimate (see explanation sheet for details)**		
Pre-action costs					
Issue /statements of case			£0.00	**£0.00**	
CMC			£0.00	**£0.00**	
Disclosure			£0.00	**£0.00**	
Witness statements			£0.00	**£0.00**	
Expert reports			£0.00	**£0.00**	
PTR			£0.00	**£0.00**	
Trial preparation			£0.00	**£0.00**	
Trial			£0.00	**£0.00**	
ADR / Settlement discussions			£0.00	**£0.00**	
Contingent cost A:			£0.00	**£0.00**	
Contingent cost B:			£0.00	**£0.00**	
	Total incurred	Total estimated	Variation	**Total estimated costs after variation (£)**	
Sub Totals	£0.00	£0.00	***£0.00***	**£0.00**	
Grand Total (including both incurred costs and estimated costs)		**£0.00**		**£0.00**	

This estimate excludes VAT (if applicable), success fees and ATE insurance premiums (if applicable), costs of detailed assessment, costs of any appeals, costs of enforcing any judgment and [complete as appropriate]

Approved budget after variation *(Incurred and estimated)*	

Variation certification pursuant to Part 3.15 (A) 3(c)

I certify that the costs and disbursements included in this variation are not included in any previous budgeted costs or variation (including any contingency), whether agreed or approved by the court.

Signed	
Name (printed)	
Position	
Dated	

Precedent T Particulars

Court:	Name					
Parties:	Parties					
Claim number:	Number					
Cost budget for:	Party					
	VARIATION			Significant Development		Opposing party comments
	Variation ***(+ or -)***			*[General Explanation for Variation: significant development]*	Paying party's offer	*Comment if not agreed*
Phase	**Time £ (A)**	**Disbs £ (B)**	**TOTAL (A+B)**	Explanation for particular phase *(where variation in any phase exceeds £10k complete xx)*		Brief explanation if not agreed by the opposing party
Issue /statements of case			£0.00	xx		
CMC			£0.00	xx		
Disclosure			£0.00	xx		
Witness statements			£0.00	xx		
Expert fees (see table below for disbs summary and total)		£0.00	£0.00	xx		
PTR			£0.00	xx		
Trial preparation			£0.00	xx		
Trial			£0.00	xx		
ADR / Settlement discussions			£0.00	xx		
Contingent cost A:			£0.00	xx		
Contingent cost B:			£0.00	xx		
		Total	£0.00	Total	£0.00	

Expert fee summary : variation +/- disbursements only

	estimated	estimated	estimated		Previous
Type	report	conference	joint stms	Total	budgeted total figure
xx				£0.00	
Total expert fees : estimated	£0.00	£0.00	£0.00	£0.00	£0.00

Schedule 2: phases, tasks, activities and expenses

1. The phases are:

	Phase in Bill of Costs	Phase in Precedent H
1.	Initial and Pre-Action Protocol Work	Pre-Action Costs
2.	Issue / Statements of Case	Issue / Statements of Case
3.	Case Management Conference	CMC
4.	Disclosure	Disclosure
5.	Witness statements	Witness statements
6.	Expert reports	Expert reports
7.	Pre-Trial Review	PTR
8.	Trial preparation	Trial preparation
9.	Trial	Trial
10.	ADR / Settlement	ADR / Settlement discussions
11.	Interim Applications and Hearings (Interlocutory Applications)	Contingencies
12.	Funding	N/A
13.	Budgeting incl. costs estimates	N/A
14.	Costs Management Conference	N/A
15.	Costs Assessment	N/A

2. The tasks are:

	Phase		Task
1.	Initial and Pre-Action Protocol Work		
		1.	Factual investigation
		2.	Legal investigation
		3.	Pre-action protocol (or similar) work
2.	Issue / Statements of Case		
		4.	Issue and Serve Proceedings and Preparation of Statement(s) of Case
		5.	Review of Other Party(s)' Statements of Case
		6.	Requests for Further Information
		7.	Amendment of Statements of Case
3.	Case Management Conference		
		8.	Case Management Conference
4.	Disclosure		
		9.	Preparation of the disclosure report and the disclosure proposal

	Phase		Task
		10.	Obtaining and reviewing documents
		11.	Preparing and serving disclosure lists
		12.	Inspection and review of the other side's disclosure for work undertaken after exchange of disclosure lists.
5.	Witness statements		
		13.	Taking, preparing and finalising witness statement(s)
		14.	Reviewing Other Party(s)' witness statement(s)
6.	Expert reports		
		15.	Own expert evidence
		16.	Other Party(s)' expert evidence
		17.	Joint expert evidence
7.	Pre-Trial Review		
		18.	Pre-Trial Review
8.	Trial preparation		
		19.	Preparation of trial bundles
		20.	General work regarding preparation for trial
9.	Trial		
		21.	Advocacy
		22.	Support of advocates
		23.	Judgment and post-trial activity
10.	ADR / Settlement		
		24.	Mediation
		25.	Other Settlement Matters
11.	Interim Applications and Hearings (Interlocutory Applications)		
		26.	Applications relating to originating process or Statement of Case or for default or summary judgment
		27.	Applications for an injunction or committal
		28.	Applications for disclosure or Further Information
		29.	Applications concerning evidence

	Phase		Task
		30.	Applications relating to Costs alone
		31.	Permission applications
		32.	Other applications
12.	Funding		
		33.	Funding
13.	Budgeting incl. costs estimates		
		34.	Budgeting - own side's costs
		35.	Budgeting - Precedent H
		36.	Budgeting - between the parties
14.	Costs Management Hearing		
		37.	Costs Management Hearing
15.	Costs Assessment		
		38.	Preparing costs claim
		39.	Points of dispute, Replies and Negotiations
		40.	Hearings
		41.	Post Assessment Work (excluding Hearings)

3. The activities are:

	Activity
1.	Appear For/Attend
2.	Communicate (with Outside Counsel)
3.	Communicate (with client)
4.	Communicate (witnesses)
5.	Communicate (experts)
6.	Communicate (Other Party(s)/other outside lawyers)
7.	Communicate (other external)
8.	Communicate (internally within legal team)
9.	Billable Travel Time
10.	Plan, Prepare, Draft, Review

4. The expense categories include but are not limited to:

	Expense
1.	Counsel's Fees
2.	Experts' Fees
3.	Court Fees
4.	Arbitrators' or Mediators' Fees
5.	Witness Expenses

6.	Transcripts
7.	Litigation Support Suppliers (incl. eDisclosure)
8.	Consultants, Other Professionals or Foreign Lawyers
9.	Travel Expenses
10.	Copying/Imaging
11.	ATEI Premiums
12.	Medical Records
13.	Translation Costs
14.	Bank Fees
15.	Process Server

5. Descriptions of the tasks and activities are set out in Precedent S.

PART 48 PART 2 OF THE LEGAL AID, SENTENCING AND PUNISHMENT OF OFFENDERS ACT 2012 RELATING TO CIVIL LITIGATION FUNDING AND COSTS: TRANSITIONAL PROVISION IN RELATION TO PRE-COMMENCEMENT FUNDING ARRANGEMENTS

[CPR 48.1]

48.1.

(1) The provisions of CPR Parts 43 to 48 relating to funding arrangements, and the attendant provisions of the Costs Practice Direction, will apply in relation to a pre-commencement funding arrangement as they were in force immediately before 1 April 2013, with such modifications (if any) as may be made by a practice direction on or after that date.

(2) A reference in rule 48.2 to a rule is to that rule as it was in force immediately before 1 April 2013.

[CPR 48.2]

48.2.

(1) A pre-commencement funding arrangement is—

(a) in relation to proceedings other than insolvency-related proceedings, publication and privacy proceedings or a mesothelioma claim—

(i) a funding arrangement as defined by rule 43.2(1)(k)(i) where—

(aa) the agreement was entered into before 1 April 2013 specifically for the purposes of the provision to the person by whom the success fee is payable of advocacy or litigation services in relation to the matter that is the subject of the proceedings in which the costs order is to be made; or

(bb) the agreement was entered into before 1 April 2013 and advocacy or litigation services were provided to that person under the agreement in connection with that matter before 1 April 2013;

(ii) a funding arrangement as defined by rule 43.2(1)(k)(ii) where the party seeking to recover the insurance premium took out the insurance policy in relation to the proceedings before 1 April 2013;

(iii) a funding arrangement as defined by rule 43.2(1)(k)(iii) where the agreement with the membership organisation to meet the costs was made before 1 April 2013 specifically in respect of the costs of other parties to proceedings relating to the matter which is the subject of the proceedings in which the costs order is to be made;

(b) in relation to insolvency-related proceedings, publication and privacy proceedings or a mesothelioma claim—

(i) a funding arrangement as defined by rule 43.2(1)(k)(i) where—

(aa) the agreement was entered into before the relevant date specifically for the purposes of the provision to the person by whom the success fee is payable of advocacy or litigation services in relation to the matter that is the subject of the proceedings in which the costs order is to be made; or

(bb) the agreement was entered into before the relevant date and advocacy or litigation services were provided to that person under the agreement in connection with that matter before the relevant date;

(ii) a funding arrangement as defined by rule 43.2(1)(k)(ii) where the party seeking to recover the insurance premium took out the insurance policy in relation to the proceedings before the relevant date.

(2) In paragraph (1)—

(a) "insolvency-related proceedings" means any proceedings—

(i) in England and Wales brought by a person acting in the capacity of—

(aa) a liquidator of a company which is being wound up in England and Wales or Scotland under Parts IV or V of the Insolvency Act 1986; or

(bb) a trustee of a bankrupt's estate under Part IX of the Insolvency Act 1986;

(ii) brought by a person acting in the capacity of an administrator appointed pursuant to the provisions of Part II of the Insolvency Act 1986;

(iii) in England and Wales brought by a company which is being wound up in England and Wales or Scotland under Parts IV or V of the Insolvency Act 1986; or

(iv) brought by a company which has entered administration under Part II of the Insolvency Act 1986;

(b) "news publisher" means a person who publishes a newspaper, magazine or website containing news or information about or comment on current affairs;

(c) "publication and privacy proceedings" means proceedings for—

(i) defamation;

(ii) malicious falsehood;

(iii) breach of confidence involving publication to the general public;

(iv) misuse of private information; or

(v) harassment, where the defendant is a news publisher.

(d) "a mesothelioma claim" is a claim for damages in respect of diffuse mesothelioma (within the meaning of the Pneumoconiosis etc. (Workers' Compensation) Act 1979; and

(e) "the relevant date" is the date on which sections 44 and 46 of the Legal Aid, Sentencing and Punishment of Offenders Act 2012 came into force in relation to proceedings of the sort in question.

PRACTICE DIRECTION 48—PART 2 OF THE LEGAL AID, SENTENCING AND PUNISHMENT OF OFFENDERS ACT 2012 RELATING TO CIVIL LITIGATION FUNDING AND COSTS: TRANSITIONAL PROVISION AND EXCEPTIONS

THIS PRACTICE DIRECTION SUPPLEMENTS PART 48

Transitional Provisions: General

[CPR PD 48.1]

1.1 Sections 44 and 46 of the Legal Aid, Sentencing and Punishment of Offenders Act 2012 ("the 2012 Act") make changes to the effect that a costs order may not include, respectively, provision requiring the payment by one party of all or part of a success fee payable by another party under a conditional fee agreement or of an amount in respect of all or part of the premium of a costs insurance policy taken out by another party. These changes come into force on 1 April 2013.

1.2 Sections 44(6) and 46(3) of the 2012 Act make saving provisions to the effect, respectively, that these changes do not apply so as to prevent a costs order including such provision where the conditional fee agreement in relation to the proceedings was entered into (or, in relation to a collective conditional fee agreement, services were provided to the party under the agreement), or the costs insurance policy in relation to the proceedings taken out, before the date on which the changes come into force.

1.3 The provisions in the CPR relating to funding arrangements have accordingly been revoked (either in whole or in part as they relate to funding arrangements) with effect from 1 April 2013; but they will remain relevant, and will continue to have effect notwithstanding the revocations, after that date for those cases covered by the saving provisions.

1.4 The provisions in the CPR in force prior to 1 April 2012 relating to funding arrangements include—

(a) CPR 43.2(1)(a), (k), (l), (m), (n), (o), 43.2(3) and 43.2(4);
(b) CPR 44.3A, 44.3B, 44.12B, 44.15 and 44.16;
(c) CPR 45.8, 45.10, 45.12, 45.13, Sections III to V (45.15 to 45.19, 45.20 to 22 and 45.23 to 26), 45.28 and 45.31 to 45.40;
(d) CPR 46.3;
(e) CPR 48.8.

Mesothelioma claims

[CPR PD 48.2]

2.1 By virtue of section 48 of the 2012 Act, the changes relating to recoverable success fees and insurance premiums which are made by sections 44 and 46 of the Act may not be commenced, and accordingly will not apply, in relation to mesothelioma claims (defined by section 48(2) of the Act as having the same meaning as in the Pneumoconiosis etc. (Workers' Compensation) Act 1979) until such time as a review has been carried out and the conclusions of that review published. It will accordingly remain possible for a costs order in favour of a party to such proceedings to include provision requiring the payment of success fees and premiums under after the event costs insurance policies, and so the provisions of the CPR relating to funding arrangements as in force immediately prior to 1 April 2013 will continue to apply in relation to such proceedings, whether commenced before or after 1 April 2013. This will include the provision for fixed recoverable success fees in respect of employers' liability disease claims in Section V of Part 45

(CPR 45.23 to 45.26), which will otherwise cease to apply other than to claims in which a CFA was entered into or a costs insurance policy taken out before 1 April 2013).

2.2 On the later date when sections 44 and 46 are brought into force in relation to mesothelioma claims, the saving provisions of sections 44(6) and 44(3) will have effect in relation to funding arrangements in such claims as they do more generally, save that the operative date for the saving provisions will not be 1 April 2013 but the later date.

Insolvency-related proceedings and publication and privacy proceedings

[CPR PD 48.3]

3.1 Sections 44 and 46 of the 2012 Act are not being commenced immediately in relation to certain proceedings related to insolvency. Until such time as those sections are commenced in relation to those proceedings, therefore, they are in a similar position as regards funding arrangements to mesothelioma claims.

3.2 Similarly, sections 44 and 46 of the 2012 Act are not being commenced immediately in respect of publication and privacy proceedings, which will accordingly be in a similar position as regards funding arrangements to mesothelioma claims and insolvency-related proceedings until such time as those sections are commenced in relation to them.

New provision in relation to clinical negligence claims

[CPR PD 48.4]

4.1 Section 46 of the 2012 Act enables the Lord Chancellor by regulations to provide that a costs order may include provision requiring the payment of an amount in respect of all or part of the premium of a costs insurance policy, where—

(a) the order is made in favour of a party to clinical negligence proceedings of a prescribed description;

(b) the party has taken out a costs insurance policy insuring against the risk of incurring a liability to pay for one or more expert reports in respect of clinical negligence in connection with the proceedings (or against that risk and other risks);

(c) the policy is of a prescribed description;

(d) the policy states how much of the premium relates to the liability to pay for such an expert report or reports, and the amount to be paid is in respect of that part of the premium.

4.2 The regulations made under the power are the Recovery of Costs Insurance Premiums in Clinical Negligence Proceedings Regulations 2013 (S.I. 2013/92). The regulations relate only to clinical negligence cases where a costs insurance policy is taken out on or after 1 April 2013, so the provisions in force in the CPR prior to 1 April 2013 relating to funding arrangements will not apply.

SOLICITORS ACT 1974

(c 47)

[SOL 56]

56. Orders as to remuneration for non-contentious business

(1) For the purposes of this section there shall be a committee consisting of the following persons—

(a) the Lord Chancellor;

(b) the Lord Chief Justice;

(c) the Master of the Rolls;

(d) the President of the Society;

(da) a member of the Legal Services Board nominated by that Board;

(e) a solicitor, being the president of a local law society, nominated by the Lord Chancellor to serve on the committee during his tenure of office as president; and

(f) for the purpose only of prescribing and regulating the remuneration of solicitors in respect of business done under the Land Registration Act 2002, the Chief Land Registrar appointed under that Act.

(2) The committee, or any three members of the committee (the Lord Chancellor being one), may make general orders prescribing the general principles to be applied when determining the remuneration of solicitors in respect of non-contentious business.

(3) The Lord Chancellor, before any order under this section is made, shall cause a draft of the order to be sent to the Society; and the committee shall consider any observations of the Society submitted to them in writing within one month of the sending of the draft, and may then make the order, either in the form of the draft or with such alterations or additions as they may think fit.

(4) The principles prescribed by an order under this section may provide that solicitors should be remunerated—

(b) by a gross sum; or

(c) by a fixed sum for each document prepared or perused, without regard to length; or

(d) in any other mode; or

(e) partly in one mode and partly in another.

(5) The general principles prescribed by an order under this section may provide that the amount of such remuneration is to be determined by having regard to all or any of the following, among other, considerations, that is to say—

(a) the position of the party for whom the solicitor is concerned in the business, that is, whether he is vendor or purchaser, lessor or lessee, mortgagor or mortgagee, or the like;

(b) the place where, and the circumstances in which, the business or any part of it is transacted;

(c) the amount of the capital money or rent to which the business relates;

(d) the skill, labour and responsibility on the part of the solicitor, or any employee of his who is an authorised person, which the business involves;

(e) the number and importance of the documents prepared or perused, without regard to length.

(5A) In subsection (5) "authorised person" means a person who is an authorised person in relation to an activity which is a reserved legal activity, within the meaning of the Legal Services Act 2007 (see section 18 of that Act).

(6) An order under this section may authorise and regulate—

(a) the taking by a solicitor from his client of security for payment of any remuneration, to be ascertained by assessment or otherwise, which may become due to him under any such order; and

(b) the allowance of interest.

(7) So long as an order made under this section is in operation the assessment of bills of costs of solicitors in respect of non-contentious business shall, subject to the provisions of section 57, be subject to that order.

(8) Any order made under this section may be varied or revoked by a subsequent order so made.

(9) The power to make orders under this section shall be exercisable by statutory instrument which shall be subject to annulment in pursuance of a resolution of either House of Parliament; and the Statutory Instruments Act 1946 shall apply to a statutory instrument containing such an order in like manner as if the order had been made by a Minister of the Crown.

[SOL 57]

57. **Non-contentious business agreements**

(1) Whether or not any order is in force under section 56, a solicitor and his client may, before or after or in the course of the transaction of any non-contentious business by the solicitor, make an agreement as to his remuneration in respect of that business.

(2) The agreement may provide for the remuneration of the solicitor by a gross sum or by reference to an hourly rate, or by a commission or percentage, or by a salary, or otherwise, and it may be made on the terms that the amount of the remuneration stipulated for shall or shall not include all or any disbursements made by the solicitor in respect of searches, plans, travelling, taxes, fees or other matters.

(3) The agreement shall be in writing and signed by the person to be bound by it or his agent in that behalf.

(4) Subject to subsections (5) and (7), the agreement may be sued and recovered on or set aside in the like manner and on the like grounds as an agreement not relating to the remuneration of a solicitor.

(5) If on any assessment of costs the agreement is relied on by the solicitor and objected to by the client as unfair or unreasonable, the costs officer may enquire

into the facts and certify them to the court, and if from that certificate it appears just to the court that the agreement should be set aside, or the amount payable under it reduced, the court may so order and may give such consequential directions as it thinks fit.

(6) Subsection (7) applies where the agreement provides for the remuneration of the solicitor to be by reference to an hourly rate.

(7) If, on the assessment of any costs, the agreement is relied on by the solicitor and the client objects to the amount of the costs (but is not alleging that the agreement is unfair or unreasonable), the costs officer may enquire into—

(a) the number of hours worked by the solicitor; and

(b) whether the number of hours worked by him was excessive.

[SOL 58]

58. Remuneration of a solicitor who is a mortgagee

(1) Where a mortgage is made to a solicitor, either alone or jointly with any other person, he or the firm of which he is a member shall be entitled to recover from the mortgagor in respect of all business transacted and acts done by him or them in negotiating the loan, deducing and investigating the title to the property, and preparing and completing the mortgage, such usual costs as he or they would have been entitled to receive if the mortgage had been made to a person who was not a solicitor and that person had retained and employed him or them to transact that business and do those acts.

(2) Where a mortgage has been made to, or has become vested by transfer or transmission in, a solicitor, either alone or jointly with any other person, and any business is transacted or acts are done by that solicitor or by the firm of which he is a member in relation to that mortgage or the security thereby created or the property thereby charged, he or they shall be entitled to recover from the person on whose behalf the business was transacted or the acts were done, and to charge against the security, such usual costs as he or they would have been entitled to receive if the mortgage had been made to and had remained vested in a person who was not a solicitor and that person had retained and employed him or them to transact that business and do those acts.

(3) In this section "mortgage" includes any charge on any property for securing money or money's worth.

[SOL 59]

59. Contentious business agreements

(1) Subject to subsection (2), a solicitor may make an agreement in writing with his client as to his remuneration in respect of any contentious business done, or to be done, by him (in this Act referred to as a "contentious business agreement") providing that he shall be remunerated by a gross sum or by reference to an hourly rate, or by a salary, or otherwise, and whether at a higher or lower rate than that at which he would otherwise have been entitled to be remunerated.

(2) Nothing in this section or in sections 60 to 63 shall give validity to—

(a) any purchase by a solicitor of the interest, or any part of the interest, of his client in any action, suit or other contentious proceeding; or

(b) any agreement by which a solicitor retained or employed to prosecute any action, suit or other contentious proceeding, stipulates for payment only in the event of success in that action, suit or proceeding; or

(c) any disposition, contract, settlement, conveyance, delivery, dealing or transfer which under the law relating to bankruptcy is invalid against a trustee or creditor in any bankruptcy or composition.

[SOL 60]

60. Effect of contentious business agreement

(1) Subject to the provisions of this section and to sections 61 to 63, the costs of a solicitor in any case where a contentious business agreement has been made shall not be subject to assessment or (except in the case of an agreement which provides for the solicitor to be remunerated by reference to an hourly rate) to the provisions of section 69.

(2) Subject to subsection (3), a contentious business agreement shall not affect the amount of, or any rights or remedies for the recovery of, any costs payable by the client to, or to the client by, any person other than the solicitor, and that person may, unless he has otherwise agreed, require any such costs to be assessed according to the rules for their assessment for the time being in force.

(3) A client shall not be entitled to recover from any other person under an order for the payment of any costs to which a contentious business agreement relates more than the amount payable by him to his solicitor in respect of those costs under the agreement.

(4) A contentious business agreement shall be deemed to exclude any claim by the solicitor in respect of the business to which it relates other than—

(a) a claim for the agreed costs; or

(b) a claim for such costs as are expressly excepted from the agreement.

(5) A provision in a contentious business agreement that the solicitor shall not be liable for his negligence, or that of any employee of his, shall be void if the client is a natural person who, in entering that agreement, is acting for purposes which are outside his trade, business or profession.

(6) A provision in a contentious business agreement that the solicitor shall be relieved from any responsibility to which he would otherwise be subject as a solicitor shall be void.

[SOL 61]

61. Enforcement of contentious business agreement

(1) No action shall be brought on any contentious business agreement, but on the application of any person who—

(a) is a party to the agreement or the representative of such a party; or

(b) is or is alleged to be liable to pay, or is or claims to be entitled to be paid, the costs due or alleged to be due in respect of the business to which the agreement relates,

the court may enforce or set aside the agreement and determine every question as to its validity or effect.

(2) On any application under subsection (1), the court—

(a) if it is of the opinion that the agreement is in all respects fair and reasonable, may enforce it;

(b) if it is of the opinion that the agreement is in any respect unfair or unreasonable, may set it aside and order the costs covered by it to be assessed as if it had never been made;

(c) in any case, may make such order as to the costs of the application as it thinks fit.

(3) If the business covered by a contentious business agreement (not being an agreement to which section 62 applies) is business done, or to be done, in any action, a client who is a party to the agreement may make application to a costs officer of the court for the agreement to be examined.

(4) A costs officer before whom an agreement is laid under subsection (3) shall examine it and may either allow it, or, if he is of the opinion that the agreement is

unfair or unreasonable, require the opinion of the court to be taken on it, and the court may allow the agreement or reduce the amount payable under it, or set it aside and order the costs covered by it to be assessed as if it had never been made.

(4A) Subsection (4B) applies where a contentious business agreement provides for the remuneration of the solicitor to be by reference to an hourly rate.

(4B) If on the assessment of any costs the agreement is relied on by the solicitor and the client objects to the amount of the costs (but is not alleging that the agreement is unfair or unreasonable), the costs officer may enquire into—

- (a) the number of hours worked by the solicitor; and
- (b) whether the number of hours worked by him was excessive.

(5) Where the amount agreed under any contentious business agreement is paid by or on behalf of the client or by any person entitled to do so, the person making the payment may at any time within twelve months from the date of payment, or within such further time as appears to the court to be reasonable, apply to the court, and, if it appears to the court that the special circumstances of the case require it to be re-opened, the court may, on such terms as may be just, re-open it and order the costs covered by the agreement to be assessed and the whole or any part of the amount received by the solicitor to be repaid by him.

(6) In this section and in sections 62 and 63 "the court" means—

- (a) in relation to an agreement under which any business has been done in any court having jurisdiction to enforce and set aside agreements, any such court in which any of that business has been done;
- (b) in relation to an agreement under which no business has been done in any such court, and under which more than £50 is payable, the High Court;
- (c) in relation to an agreement under which no business has been done in any such court and under which not more than £50 is payable, the county court which would, but for the provisions of subsection (1) prohibiting the bringing of an action on the agreement, have had jurisdiction in any action on it;

and for the avoidance of doubt it is hereby declared that in paragraph (*a*) "court having jurisdiction to enforce and set aside agreements" includes the county court.

[SOL 62]

62. Contentious business agreements by certain representatives

(1) Where the client who makes a contentious business agreement makes it as a representative of a person whose property will be chargeable with the whole or part of the amount payable under the agreement, the agreement shall be laid before a costs officer of the court before payment.

(2) A costs officer before whom an agreement is laid under subsection (1) shall examine it and may either allow it, or, if he is of the opinion that it is unfair or unreasonable, require the opinion of the court to be taken on it, and the court may allow the agreement or reduce the amount payable under it, or set it aside and order the costs covered by it to be assessed as if it had never been made.

(3) A client who makes a contentious business agreement as mentioned in subsection (1) and pays the whole or any part of the amount payable under the agreement without it being allowed by the officer or by the court shall be liable at any time to account to the person whose property is charged with the whole or any part of the amount so paid for the sum so charged, and the solicitor who accepts the payment may be ordered by the court to refund the amount received by him.

(4) A client makes a contentious business agreement as the representative of another person if he makes it—

- (a) as his guardian,

(b) as a trustee for him under a deed or will,

(c) as a deputy for him appointed by the Court of Protection with powers in relation to his property and affairs, or

(d) as another person authorised under that Act to act on his behalf.

[SOL 63]

63. **Effect on contentious business agreement of death, incapability or change of solicitor**

(1) If, after some business has been done under a contentious business agreement but before the solicitor has wholly performed it—

(a) the solicitor dies, or becomes incapable of acting; or

(b) the client changes his solicitor (as, notwithstanding the agreement, he shall be entitled to do),

any party to, or the representative of any party to, the agreement may apply to the court, and the court shall have the same jurisdiction as to enforcing the agreement so far as it has been performed, or setting it aside, as the court would have had if the solicitor had not died or become incapable of acting, or the client had not changed his solicitor.

(2) The court, notwithstanding that it is of the opinion that the agreement is in all respects fair and reasonable, may order the amount due in respect of business under the agreement to be ascertained by assessment, and in that case—

(a) the costs officer, in ascertaining that amount, shall have regard so far as may be to the terms of the agreement; and

(b) payment of the amount found by him to be due may be enforced in the same manner as if the agreement had been completely performed.

(3) If in such a case as is mentioned in subsection (1)(b) an order is made for the assessment of the amount due to the solicitor in respect of the business done under the agreement, the court shall direct the costs officer to have regard to the circumstances under which the change of solicitor has taken place, and the costs officer, unless he is of the opinion that there has been no default, negligence, improper delay or other conduct on the part of the solicitor, or any of his employees, affording the client reasonable ground for changing his solicitor, shall not allow to the solicitor the full amount of the remuneration agreed to be paid to him.

[SOL 64]

64. **Form of bill of costs for contentious business**

(1) Where the remuneration of a solicitor in respect of contentious business done by him is not the subject of a contentious business agreement, then, subject to subsections (2) to (4), the solicitor's bill of costs may at the option of the solicitor be either a bill containing detailed items or a gross sum bill.

(2) The party chargeable with a gross sum bill may at any time—

(a) before he is served with a writ or other originating process for the recovery of costs included in the bill, and

(b) before the expiration of three months from the date on which the bill was delivered to him,

require the solicitor to deliver, in lieu of that bill, a bill containing detailed items; and on such a requirement being made the gross sum bill shall be of no effect.

(3) Where an action is commenced on a gross sum bill, the court shall, if so requested by the party chargeable with the bill before the expiration of one month from the service on that party of the writ or other originating process, order that the bill be assessed.

(4) If a gross sum bill is assessed, whether under this section or otherwise, nothing in this section shall prejudice any rules of court with respect to assessment, and the solicitor shall furnish the costs officer with such details of any of the costs covered by the bill as the costs officer may require.

[SOL 65]

65. Security for costs and termination of retainer

(1) A solicitor may take security from his client for his costs, to be ascertained by assessment or otherwise, in respect of any contentious business to be done by him.

(2) If a solicitor who has been retained by a client to conduct contentious business requests the client to make a payment of a sum of money, being a reasonable sum on account of the costs incurred or to be incurred in the conduct of that business and the client refuses or fails within a reasonable time to make that payment, the refusal or failure shall be deemed to be a good cause whereby the solicitor may, upon giving reasonable notice to the client, withdraw from the retainer.

[SOL 66]

66. Assessments with regard to contentious business

Subject to the provisions of any rules of court, on every assessment of costs in respect of any contentious business, the costs officer may—

(a) allow interest at such rate and from such time as he thinks just on money disbursed by the solicitor for the client, and on money of the client in the hands of, and improperly retained by, the solicitor or an employee of the solicitor; and

(b) in determining the remuneration of the solicitor, have regard to the skill, labour and responsibility involved in the business done by him or by any employee of his who is an authorised person (within the meaning of section 56(5A)).

[SOL 67]

67. Inclusion of disbursements in bill of costs

A solicitor's bill of costs may include costs payable in discharge of a liability properly incurred by him on behalf of the party to be charged with the bill (including counsel's fees) notwithstanding that those costs have not been paid before the delivery of the bill to that party; but those costs—

(a) shall be described in the bill as not then paid; and

(b) if the bill is assessed, shall not be allowed by the costs officer unless they are paid before the assessment is completed.

[SOL 68]

68. Power of court to order solicitor to deliver bill etc

(1) The jurisdiction of the High Court to make orders for the delivery by a solicitor of a bill of costs, and for the delivery up of, or otherwise in relation to, any documents in his possession, custody or power, is hereby declared to extend to cases in which no business has been done by him in the High Court.

(2) The county court and the family court each have the same jurisdiction as the High Court to make orders making such provision as is mentioned in subsection (1) in cases where the bill of costs or the documents relate wholly or partly to

contentious business done by the solicitor in the county court or (as the case may be) the family court.

(3) In this section and in sections 69 to 71 "solicitor" includes the executors, administrators and assignees of a solicitor.

[SOL 69]

69. Action to recover solicitor's costs

(1) Subject to the provisions of this Act, no action shall be brought to recover any costs due to a solicitor before the expiration of one month from the date on which a bill of those costs is delivered in accordance with the requirements mentioned in subsection (2); but if there is probable cause for believing that the party chargeable with the costs—

(a) is about to quit England and Wales, to become bankrupt or to compound with his creditors, or

(b) is about to do any other act which would tend to prevent or delay the solicitor obtaining payment,

the High Court may, notwithstanding that one month has not expired from the delivery of the bill, order that the solicitor be at liberty to commence an action to recover his costs and may order that those costs be assessed.

(2) The requirements referred to in subsection (1) are that the bill must be—

(a) signed in accordance with subsection (2A), and

(b) delivered in accordance with subsection (2C).

(2A) A bill is signed in accordance with this subsection if it is—

(a) signed by the solicitor or on his behalf by an employee of the solicitor authorised by him to sign, or

(b) enclosed in, or accompanied by, a letter which is signed as mentioned in paragraph (a) and refers to the bill.

(2B) For the purposes of subsection (2A) the signature may be an electronic signature.

(2C) A bill is delivered in accordance with this subsection if—

(a) it is delivered to the party to be charged with the bill personally,

(b) it is delivered to that party by being sent to him by post to, or left for him at, his place of business, dwelling-house or last known place of abode, or

(c) it is delivered to that party—

(i) by means of an electronic communications network, or

(ii) by other means but in a form that nevertheless requires the use of apparatus by the recipient to render it intelligible,

and that party has indicated to the person making the delivery his willingness to accept delivery of a bill sent in the form and manner used.

(2D) An indication to any person for the purposes of subsection (2C)(c)—

(a) must state the address to be used and must be accompanied by such other information as that person requires for the making of the delivery;

(b) may be modified or withdrawn at any time by a notice given to that person.

(2E) Where a bill is proved to have been delivered in compliance with the requirements of subsections (2A) and (2C), it is not necessary in the first instance for the solicitor to prove the contents of the bill and it is to be presumed, until the contrary is shown, to be a bill bona fide complying with this Act.

(2F) A bill which is delivered as mentioned in subsection (2C)(c) is to be treated as having been delivered on the first working day after the day on which it was sent (unless the contrary is proved).

(3) Where a bill of costs relates wholly or partly to contentious business done in the county court and the amount of the bill does not exceed £5,000, the powers and duties of the High Court under this section and sections 70 and 71 in relation to that bill may be exercised and performed by the county court.

(4) . . .

(5) In this section references to an electronic signature are to be read in accordance with section 7(2) of the Electronic Communications Act 2000 (c 7).

(6) In this section—

"electronic communications network" has the same meaning as in the Communications Act 2003 (c 21);

"working day" means a day other than a Saturday, a Sunday, Christmas Day, Good Friday or a bank holiday in England and Wales under the Banking and Financial Dealings Act 1971 (c 80).

[SOL 70]

70. **Assessment on application of party chargeable or solicitor**

(1) Where before the expiration of one month from the delivery of a solicitor's bill an application is made by the party chargeable with the bill, the High Court shall, without requiring any sum to be paid into court, order that the bill be assessed and that no action be commenced on the bill until the assessment is completed.

(2) Where no such application is made before the expiration of the period mentioned in subsection (1), then, on an application being made by the solicitor or, subject to subsections (3) and (4), by the party chargeable with the bill, the court may on such terms, if any, as it thinks fit (not being terms as to the costs of the assessment), order—

- (a) that the bill be assessed; and
- (b) that no action be commenced on the bill, and that any action already commenced be stayed, until the assessment is completed.

(3) Where an application under subsection (2) is made by the party chargeable with the bill—

- (a) after the expiration of 12 months from the delivery of the bill, or
- (b) after a judgment has been obtained for the recovery of the costs covered by the bill, or
- (c) after the bill has been paid, but before the expiration of 12 months from the payment of the bill,

no order shall be made except in special circumstances and, if an order is made, it may contain such terms as regards the costs of the assessment as the court may think fit.

(4) The power to order assessment conferred by subsection (2) shall not be exercisable on an application made by the party chargeable with the bill after the expiration of 12 months from the payment of the bill.

(5) An order for the assessment of a bill made on an application under this section by the party chargeable with the bill shall, if he so requests, be an order for the assessment of the profit costs covered by the bill.

(6) Subject to subsection (5), the court may under this section order the assessment of all the costs, or of the profit costs, or of the costs other than profit costs and, where part of the costs is not to be assessed, may allow an action to be commenced or to be continued for that part of the costs.

(7) Every order for the assessment of a bill shall require the costs officer to assess not only the bill but also the costs of the assessment and to certify what is

due to or by the solicitor in respect of the bill and in respect of the costs of the assessment.

(8) If after due notice of any assessment either party to it fails to attend, the officer may proceed with the assessment ex parte.

(9) Unless—

(a) the order for assessment was made on the application of the solicitor and the party chargeable does not attend the assessment, or

(b) the order for assessment or an order under subsection (10) otherwise provides,

the costs of an assessment shall be paid according to the event of the assessment, that is to say, if the amount of the bill is reduced by one fifth, the solicitor shall pay the costs, but otherwise the party chargeable shall pay the costs.

(10) The costs officer may certify to the court any special circumstances relating to a bill or to the assessment of a bill, and the court may make such order as respects the costs of the assessment as it may think fit.

(11) . . .

(12) In this section "profit costs" means costs other than counsel's fees or costs paid or payable in the discharge of a liability incurred by the solicitor on behalf of the party chargeable, and the reference in subsection (9) to the fraction of the amount of the reduction in the bill shall be taken, where the assessment concerns only part of the costs covered by the bill, as a reference to that fraction of the amount of those costs which is being assessed.

[SOL 71]

71. **Assessment on application of third parties etc**

(1) Where a person other than the party chargeable with the bill for the purposes of section 70 has paid, or is or was liable to pay, a bill either to the solicitor or to the party chargeable with the bill, that person, or his executors, administrators or assignees may apply to the High Court for an order for the assessment of the bill as if he were the party chargeable with it, and the court may make the same order (if any) as it might have made if the application had been made by the party chargeable with the bill.

(2) Where the court has no power to make an order by virtue of subsection (1) except in special circumstances it may, in considering whether there are special circumstances sufficient to justify the making of an order, take into account circumstances which affect the applicant but do not affect the party chargeable with the bill.

(3) Where a trustee, executor or administrator has become liable to pay a bill of a solicitor, then, on the application of any person interested in any property out of which the trustee, executor or administrator has paid, or is entitled to pay, the bill, the court may order—

(a) that the bill be assessed on such terms, if any, as it thinks fit; and

(b) that such payments, in respect of the amount found to be due to or by the solicitor and in respect of the costs of the assessment, be made to or by the applicant, to or by the solicitor, or to or by the executor, administrator or trustee, as it thinks fit.

(4) In considering any application under subsection (3) the court shall have regard—

(a) to the provisions of section 70 as to applications by the party chargeable for the assessment of a solicitor's bill so far as they are capable of being applied to an application made under that subsection;

(b) to the extent and nature of the interest of the applicant.

(5) If an applicant under subsection (3) pays any money to the solicitor, he shall have the same right to be paid that money by the trustee, executor or administrator chargeable with the bill as the solicitor had.

(6) Except in special circumstances, no order shall be made on an application under this section for the assessment of a bill which has already been assessed.

(7) If the court on an application under this section orders a bill to be assessed, it may order the solicitor to deliver to the applicant a copy of the bill on payment of the costs of that copy.

[SOL 72]

72. **Supplementary provisions as to assessments**

(1) Every application for an order for the assessment of a solicitor's bill or for the delivery of a solicitor's bill and for the delivery up by a solicitor of any documents in his possession, custody or power shall be made in the matter of that solicitor.

(2) Where a costs officer is in the course of assessing a bill of costs, he may request the costs officer of any other court to assist him in assessing any part of the bill, and the costs officer so requested shall assess that part of the bill and shall return the bill with his opinion on it to the costs officer making the request.

(3) Where a request is made as mentioned in subsection (2), the costs officer who is requested to assess part of a bill shall have such powers, and may take such fees, in respect of that part of the bill, as he would have or be entitled to take if he were assessing that part of the bill in pursuance of an order of the court of which he is an officer; and the costs officer who made the request shall not take any fee in respect of that part of the bill.

(4) The certificate of the costs officer by whom any bill has been assessed shall, unless it is set aside or altered by the court, be final as to the amount of the costs covered by it, and the court may make such order in relation to the certificate as it thinks fit, including, in a case where the retainer is not disputed, an order that judgment be entered for the sum certified to be due with costs.

[SOL 73]

73. **Charging orders**

(1) Subject to subsection (2), any court in which a solicitor has been employed to prosecute or defend any suit, matter or proceedings may at any time—

(a) declare the solicitor entitled to a charge on any property recovered or preserved through his instrumentality for his assessed costs in relation to that suit, matter or proceeding; and

(b) make such orders for the assessment of those costs and for raising money to pay or for paying them out of the property recovered or preserved as the court thinks fit;

and all conveyances and acts done to defeat, or operating to defeat, that charge shall, except in the case of a conveyance to a bona fide purchaser for value without notice, be void as against the solicitor.

(2) No order shall be made under subsection (1) if the right to recover the costs is barred by any statute of limitations.

[SOL 74]

74. **Special provisions as to contentious business done in county courts**

(1) The remuneration of a solicitor in respect of contentious business done by him in the county court shall be regulated in accordance with sections 59 to 73, and for that purpose those sections shall have effect subject to the following provisions of this section.

(2) . . .

(3) The amount which may be allowed on the assessment of any costs or bill of costs in respect of any item relating to proceedings in the county court shall not, except in so far as rules of court may otherwise provide, exceed the amount which could have been allowed in respect of that item as between party and party in those proceedings, having regard to the nature of the proceedings and the amount of the claim and of any counterclaim.

[SOL 75]

75. **Saving for certain enactments**

Nothing in this Part of this Act shall affect the following enactments, that is to say—

(a) . . .

(b) . . .

(c) any of the provisions of the Costs in Criminal Cases Act 1973;

(d) . . .

(e) any other enactment not expressly repealed by this Act which authorises the making of rules or orders or the giving of directions with respect to costs, or which provides that any such rule, order or direction made or given under a previous enactment shall continue in force.

CRIMINAL JUSTICE AND COURTS ACT 2015

(c 2)

[CJC 88]

88. **Capping of costs**

(1) A costs capping order may not be made by the High Court or the Court of Appeal in connection with judicial review proceedings except in accordance with this section and sections 89 and 90.

(2) A "costs capping order" is an order limiting or removing the liability of a party to judicial review proceedings to pay another party's costs in connection with any stage of the proceedings.

(3) The court may make a costs capping order only if leave to apply for judicial review has been granted.

(4) The court may make a costs capping order only on an application for such an order made by the applicant for judicial review in accordance with rules of court.

(5) Rules of court may, in particular, specify information that must be contained in the application, including—

(a) information about the source, nature and extent of financial resources available, or likely to be available, to the applicant to meet liabilities arising in connection with the application, and

(b) if the applicant is a body corporate that is unable to demonstrate that it is likely to have financial resources available to meet such liabilities, information about its members and about their ability to provide financial support for the purposes of the application.

(6) The court may make a costs capping order only if it is satisfied that—

(a) the proceedings are public interest proceedings,

(b) in the absence of the order, the applicant for judicial review would withdraw the application for judicial review or cease to participate in the proceedings, and

(c) it would be reasonable for the applicant for judicial review to do so.

(7) The proceedings are "public interest proceedings" only if—

(a) an issue that is the subject of the proceedings is of general public importance,

(b) the public interest requires the issue to be resolved, and

(c) the proceedings are likely to provide an appropriate means of resolving it.

(8) The matters to which the court must have regard when determining whether proceedings are public interest proceedings include—

(a) the number of people likely to be directly affected if relief is granted to the applicant for judicial review,

(b) how significant the effect on those people is likely to be, and

(c) whether the proceedings involve consideration of a point of law of general public importance.

(9) The Lord Chancellor may by regulations amend this section by adding, omitting or amending matters to which the court must have regard when determining whether proceedings are public interest proceedings.

(10) Regulations under this section are to be made by statutory instrument.

(11) A statutory instrument containing regulations under this section may not be made unless a draft of the instrument has been laid before, and approved by a resolution of, each House of Parliament.

(12) In this section and sections 89 and 90—

"costs capping order" has the meaning given in subsection (2);

"the court" means the High Court or the Court of Appeal;

"judicial review proceedings" means—

(a) proceedings on an application for leave to apply for judicial review,

(b) proceedings on an application for judicial review,

(c) any proceedings on an application for leave to appeal from a decision in proceedings described in paragraph (a) or (b), and

(d) proceedings on an appeal from such a decision,

and the proceedings described in paragraphs (a) to (d) are "stages" of judicial review proceedings.

(13) For the purposes of this section and section 89, in relation to judicial review proceedings—

(a) the applicant for judicial review is the person who is or was the applicant in the proceedings on the application for judicial review, and

(b) references to relief being granted to the applicant for judicial review include the upholding on appeal of a decision to grant such relief at an earlier stage of the proceedings.

[CJC 89]

89. Capping of costs: orders and their terms

(1) The matters to which the court must have regard when considering whether to make a costs capping order in connection with judicial review proceedings, and what the terms of such an order should be, include—

(a) the financial resources of the parties to the proceedings, including the financial resources of any person who provides, or may provide, financial support to the parties;

(b) the extent to which the applicant for the order is likely to benefit if relief is granted to the applicant for judicial review;

(c) the extent to which any person who has provided, or may provide, the applicant with financial support is likely to benefit if relief is granted to the applicant for judicial review;

(d) whether legal representatives for the applicant for the order are acting free of charge;

(e) whether the applicant for the order is an appropriate person to represent the interests of other persons or the public interest generally.

(2) A costs capping order that limits or removes the liability of the applicant for judicial review to pay the costs of another party to the proceedings if relief is not granted to the applicant for judicial review must also limit or remove the liability of the other party to pay the applicant's costs if it is.

(3) The Lord Chancellor may by regulations amend this section by adding to, omitting or amending the matters listed in subsection (1).

(4) Regulations under this section are to be made by statutory instrument.

(5) A statutory instrument containing regulations under this section may not be made unless a draft of the instrument has been laid before, and approved by a resolution of, each House of Parliament.

(6) In this section—

"free of charge" means otherwise than for or in expectation of fee, gain or reward;

"legal representative", in relation to a party to proceedings, means a person exercising a right of audience or conducting litigation on the party's behalf.

PRACTICE NOTICE BY THE SENIOR COSTS JUDGE – HEARINGS AND DETAILED ASSESSMENTS IN THE SENIOR COURTS COSTS OFFICE

31 July 2020

Introduction

1. As a result of the hard work and determination of the court staff and the willingness to adapt shown by most practitioners we have managed to hear almost all cases listed since March 2020. Very few hearings have been adjourned.

2. Based on our experience over the last few months we can now say how hearings will need to be conducted for the foreseeable future. This practice note applies only to hearings in the SCCO and applies from 1 August 2020.

Detailed assessment hearings

3. It is for the costs judge or costs officer to decide the format of the hearing. Hearings will fall into one of 3 formats:

(1) Remote hearings with the judge and all parties appearing by telephone or video.

(2) Partly remote hearings with the judge and one or more parties in court and one or more parties appearing by telephone or video.

(3) Hearings with the judge and all parties in court.

4. The notice of hearing sent by the court to the parties will state the format of the hearing. Parties may apply in writing for a different format within 14 days of receipt of the notice of hearing. The court will make the arrangements for video hearings and invitations will be sent to the representatives nominated by the parties. If the hearing is to be held by telephone, the receiving party should arrange the conference call in accordance with paragraph 6.10 of PD 23A, unless the court has directed otherwise.

Filing papers in support of the bill electronically

5. A party who wishes to lodge its papers in support of the bill electronically should discuss how it should do so with the clerk to the relevant costs judge or with the costs officer well in advance of the deadline for lodging the papers. There are 3 ways in which papers may be filed electronically:

(a) Via CE File. The size limit on CE File is 50MB although parties can in one filing file up to 10 documents with each not exceeding 50MB: PD510 paragraph 5. 2(2).

(b) With the permission of the court, via the HMCTS document upload centre. This enables the court staff to invite professional court users to upload documents required for hearings, which may be too large to be submitted via CE File. Documents uploaded are then accessible by the costs judge or costs officer.

(c) With the permission of the court, via a safe third party online file-sharing platform. (However, please note that Ministry of Justice rules prevent costs officers from accessing third party systems).

6. Documents filed electronically, whether by CE File or by the document upload centre, must comply with paragraph 10 of PD 510 and also with the guidance on PDF bundles published online.

They must be formatted as one PDF document with bookmarks as appropriate for each constituent document and must be the subject of optical character recognition.

They must be filed not less than 7 days before the start of the hearing, as required by PD 47 paragraph 13.11.

Filing papers in advance of detailed assessment hearings other than electronically

7. Experience has shown that hearings work much more efficiently where the receiving party has filed its papers electronically. Parties are encouraged therefore to file their papers in support of the bill electronically whether or not they have been working paperlessly. Where the receiving party's solicitors have been working paperlessly, it is unlikely that the cost of printing their files will be recoverable.

8. If the receiving party files its papers in support of the bill other than electronically:

(a) The receiving party will nevertheless be expected to file an electronic bundle of key documents (that is, the documents relevant to the issues raised in the points of dispute, but not including the documents already filed by CE File) rather than "core bundles" or the like on paper. The bundle should comply with paragraph 10 of PD 51O and the guidance referred to at paragraph 6 above.

(b) The papers must be physically received at the SCCO not less than 7 days before the start of the hearing (as required by PD 47 paragraph 13.11). If papers are filed late the hearing may be adjourned.

9. Parties should file electronically any documents to which they will wish to refer at a hearing, because handing up papers or files in hearings may not now be permitted. That will be a matter for the costs judge or costs officer conducting the hearing.

10. Skeleton arguments and the like must be filed electronically (by CE File or email) at least 2 days before the hearing. Statements of costs for summary assessment must be filed using CE File not less than 24 hours before the time fixed for the hearing.

Applications and criminal costs appeals

11. While applications and criminal costs appeals can be heard in court with the parties present, greater use will be made of remote hearings (by video or telephone) in appropriate cases. The application notice or notice of hearing will identify the format of the hearing.

12. PD 51O paragraph 10.1 requires the applicant to file by CE File an electronic bundle at least 3 days before the hearing in the format required by paragraph 10.3.

Provisional assessments and Court of Protection bills

13. Between the parties bills under £75,000 will continue to be provisionally assessed, however the receiving party will not be required to file papers in support of the bill unless expressly requested by the court. The court may request all of the papers in support of the bill or only those relating to a particular issue or issues. Where papers in support of the bill are requested, they should where possible be filed electronically.

14. The provisions relating to detailed assessment hearings (above) will apply to oral hearings of provisional assessments and appeals from costs officers.

15. On the provisional assessment of the bill of a deputy appointed by the Court of Protection, the deputy's solicitor must still file the papers in support of the bill with the bill, but is encouraged to do so electronically via either CE File or the HMCTS document upload centre (see paragraphs 5 and 6 above).

Andrew Gordon-Saker
Senior Costs Judge
July 2020

Index

[all references are to paragraph number]

B

G

H

L

R

S

T